From Paul to Mark

FROM *Paul* TO *Mark*
PALEOCHRISTIANITY

Laura Knight-Jadczyk

Red Pill Press
2021

ISBN 978-1-7349074-1-4

Published by Red Pill Press (www.redpillpress.com)
295 Scratch Branch Rd.
Otto, NC 28763
USA

First edition.

Contents

To my husband. This is my UFT, now it is your turn.

Acknowledgements

Juliana Barembuem, Niall Bradley, Lucien Koch, Harrison Koehli, Joseph Quinn, all of whom made this unwieldy text better, especially Harrison my "Bible Buddy" and the main editor of this text. His contributions have been invaluable even when we sometimes disagree. Sergey Kopeyko brought the efforts of all the rest of us together in book form.

I owe a huge debt to many biblical scholars whose brilliance and insight made it possible for me to piece together the picture that emerged from studying their works. I must also acknowledge quite a few classical scholars whose historical analyses have acted on me in such a way as to benefit my methodology. I believe I have acknowledged all individually throughout the text and in footnotes. I apologize if I missed anyone. I will not apologize for lengthy quotes; sometimes, the words of the original author simply cannot be improved upon and any attempts to do so only mangle the message.

Special gratitude to Richard Pervo, Philip R. Davies, Russell Gmirkin, and Robert M. Price for reading the text and offering many helpful suggestions.

Foreword

This book began as a close study of the history of the time during which Christianity arose. I was focused on searching for any clue that anybody anywhere during that time might have known or alluded to a historical Jesus of Nazareth, even obliquely. Yes, others have done this before me, and I surely stand on the shoulders of giants of biblical research, but I think I have been able to bring some fresh views to the table. Like many researchers, such as Michael Goulder and Fr. Thomas Brodie, I have just followed the texts where they lead and have been forced to realize that many ideas – whether old or new, consensus or fringe – had to be discarded when a major flaw in the argument was exposed by a cold, hard fact. The process has taken most of my adult life – more intensely in the last dozen years or so. And though I am still an amateur by the standards of the trained Old Testament, New Testament and Classical scholars, I have relied on so many of them for ideas and data that I would only hope one or two might take the time to read what I have assembled from their much appreciated labors.

This book covers many topics, some of which may seem tangential to its main subject. Doing the research, it became obvious that only by looking at the problem from different angles might sufficient light be shone on the solution so as to make it clear. The state of the evidence is far from ideal, and requires a wide net. Two thousand years of what amounts to a cover-up isn't easily cleared away to reveal the few barest facts that have managed to slip through the net of deception. But in the end, I think I have elucidated some things about the times, the actors, and the events. It's not perfect, and I'm sure there may be things I've missed; I've noted several unanswered questions here and there in the text, as well as problems that would be better dealt with by an expert in one or another field.

During the years I was working on this book, I had the great privilege to correspond with a number of brilliant scholars, several of whom stand out as having been extraordinarily kind and helpful to me, an amateur. Two of them died while I was still laboring and the loss was devastating to me. This was so even though I did not know them personally other than by correspondence, and because I was very much attached to their way of thinking and working, their books and articles; knowing that there would be no more from either of them left me feeling utterly bereft. Professors Philip R. Davies (1945–2018)[1] and Richard Pervo (1942–2017)[2] read the early, shorter version, knew what I thought at the end, and considered it to be more than

---

[1] Short list of works of Philip R. Davies: *1QM: The War Scroll from Qumran: Its Structure and History* (1977); *The Damascus Document* (1982); *Cities of the Biblical World: Qumran* (Lutterworth, 1982); *Daniel* (1985); *Scribes and Schools* (1998); *In Search of "Ancient Israel"* (1992); *The Complete World of the Dead Sea Scrolls*, written with George J. Brooke, Phillip R. Callaway (2002); *Whose Bible Is It Anyway?* (2004).

[2] Short list of works of Richard I. Pervo: *Profit with Delight: The Literary Genre of the Acts of the Apostles* (1987); *Luke's Story of Paul* (1990); *Rethinking the Unity of Luke and Acts* (with Mikael C. Parsons) (1993); *Dating Acts: Between the Evangelists and the Apologists* (2006); *Acts: A Commentary* (2008); *The Mystery of Acts: Unravelling Its Story* (2008); *The Making of Paul: Constructions of the Apostle in Early Christianity* (2010); *The Acts of Paul: A New Translation with Introduction and Commentary* (2014); *The Gospel of Luke* (2014); *The Acts of John* (2015); *The Pastorals and Polycarp* (2016).

an interesting solution. They both suggested that I should develop the arguments which were cursory at best at the time they read it. I don't know if I have been able to do that to their satisfaction. Barring some shocking discovery of ancient texts buried in the sands of Egypt or something equally unlikely that would reveal what really happened in the first century, I don't think we will ever see the smoking gun, let alone hear the shot. But the smell of gunpowder in the room may be enough to lead us to the answers. Bible scholar Adam Winn has pointed out that the inherent uncertainty of historical analysis should not prevent us from attempting such analysis and seeking plausible interpretations and reconstructions utilizing the available historical data. Obviously, some historical reconstructions are better than others and the best are those that seek to ground a text in a historically verifiable setting that can be supported by dense historical data.[3] In the end, it is simply a matter of historical reconstruction and what is most likely to have happened based on the usual historical methodology, setting aside all confessional beliefs.

However, confessional beliefs are not the only dogmas that can block one's vision of the past. Any theory that is taken as a priori truth, whether consciously acknowledged or not, can seriously limit our understanding of history, so we must strive towards as *true* an understanding of the world we live in as possible. This then will allow us to practice what English philosopher R. G. Collingwood called 're-enacting history' – putting ourselves in the shoes of historical actors, so to speak.[4] For this to work, we need both sides of the equation: meticulous historical research and as much knowledge about the workings of our world and our role in it as possible. So, to give you a better understanding of where I'm coming from, let me give you some background on how I view our present condition and how in many ways, it echoes the conflicts that were going on at the time of the Apostle Paul and early Christianity, and how this might help us make sense of the historical data we have.

First let me note that several of the authors I quote in this book are Christian. Others, including many of the 'Jesus mythicists,' are secular atheists. I agree with the atheists that the Christian scholars' religious beliefs hamper their objectivity. But when it comes to the atheists, I think they are fundamentally wrong about the nature of reality, and this hampers their own work in other ways. So count yourself warned. I'm not a member of either camp and some of my remarks below and throughout the text are sure to offend not just the fundamentalists, but the atheists too. But rest assured: these views do not have a bearing on my actual historical conclusions. The sensitive reader is free to skip over such sections and continue on where the historical argument resumes.

As many of my readers know, my husband is a mathematical physicist and an expert in hyperdimensional physics.[5] He has spent his life in pursuit of GUFT – Grand Unified Field Theory – the Holy Grail of physics, while I have pursued a similar goal in history and religion. In a sense, this book is my religio-historical UFT. As such, it doesn't just contain my historical

[3]Adam Winn, *Reading Mark's Christology Under Caesar: Jesus the Messiah and Roman Imperial Ideology* (Downers Grove, Illinois: IVPAcademic, 2018). pp. 24–25.

[4]R. G. Collingwood, *The Idea of History* (Oxford University Press, 1994 [1946]).

[5]Arkadiusz Jadczyk & Robert Coquereaux, *Riemannian Geometry, Fibre Bundles, Kaluza-Klein Theories and All That* (World Scientific Publishing Company, 1988). Also: Arkadiusz Jadczyk, *Quantum Fractals: From Heisenberg's Uncertainty To Barnsley's Fractality* (World Scientific Publishing Company, 2014).

arguments and conclusions. It is informed by my own worldview, and contains some of my thoughts about the nature of reality and how humanity interfaces with that reality: religion.

"Religion is a cultural sign language which promises a gain in life by corresponding to an ultimate reality." So writes Gerd Theissen in his book *A Theory of Primitive Christian Religion*.[6]

> The definition leaves open whether and in what sense there is an ultimate reality. In religion, a gain in life is often to be understood in a very tangible way, above all as health and help ... But often religions promise something more sublime in addition: a life in truth and love, a gain of identity in the crises and changes of life – even the promise of eternal life.[7]

He expands on this by explaining:

> Cognitively, religions have always offered a comprehensive interpretation of the world: they assign human beings their place in the universe of things ... Religion maintains belief in a hidden order of things – and it functions where our knowledge fails in cognitive crises (for example in the question of what lies beyond this world in which we live and what removes us from ourselves at death).[8]

Theissen notes that a religious sign system consists of: 1) myths that explain in narrative form what fundamentally determines the world and life; 2) rites, which people perform to depict the other reality indicated in myths; and 3) ethics, where behavior acquires a symbolic meaning by being related to the reality described in the myths. Believing the myths, performing the rites that bring one into contact with the ultimate reality, and conforming one's behavior to the demands of that reality constitute religion.

Of utmost importance is the implication that *knowing or inferring something about ultimate reality can help an individual to live a better life*, in harmony with the way things actually are. Christianity most certainly promised this 'gain in life' at its inception. But somehow, today, what was once seen to be a path to a better life has changed into a way of life that, to outsiders, seems delusional. In our day, scientific materialism reigns supreme. Secular humanist atheism and its totally materialist view of reality is at war with the idea that consciousness is something real and that non-material realities exist. Even religious groups haven't escaped the effects.

While scientific materialism is a modern phenomenon, I think the seeds of this conflict of worldviews were present even at the origins of Christianity. Very early in Christianity's history, Christians began to misunderstand its original message and distort it. The main reason for the distortion of that message was the very thing that the message was intended to defeat: an earthly, 'materialistic' interpretation of the gospel.

In many ways, scientific materialism is a modern incarnation of the old conflict between the flesh and the Spirit, to use Paul's terms, only taken to new extremes. Often not explicitly formulated or even acknowledged, this belief system is based on the idea that the material world is all there is, and everything else – consciousness in particular – is derived from it, a mere side effect. What's more, it is often assumed that the physical world is causally closed, which implies that our free will is just an illusion and no communication with the divine is possible. But for this belief system to make any sense, if only superficially, its proponents need their own creation myth to explain the complexity of human life, experience and consciousness: enter Darwinism.

---

[6]Gerd Theissen, *A Theory of Primitive Christian Religion* (London: SCM Press, 1999).
[7]Theissen (1999), p. 7.
[8]Theissen (1999), p. 7.

A random material universe, so the story goes, is somehow capable to produce life by chance; the complexity of our experience, including our so-called illusion of having free will, so the story continues, is just a product of selecting 'advantageous' traits over long timespans. Never mind that if the physical universe is causally closed and we have no free will, then our consciousness is entirely useless and certainly not advantageous for survival.[9] But if we have free will, that is, if our minds can somehow break the causal chains of the strictly physical world, then there must be something seriously wrong with materialist doctrine.[10]

But the materialists are determined to hold the line against any single acknowledgment of any process that is not totally random, accidental, and material. Evolution is their gospel, Darwin their savior. Their story is that the Big Bang was the explosion of a primal atom, and all matter in the Universe was in this incredibly dense atom. Everything that has happened since is just the result of random jostling of particles that, over billions of years, may form affinities by accident, and different forms of matter arise. Eventually, some of this matter jostles against some other bit of matter, some sort of electrical (or other) interaction takes place, and that is 'life.'

But make no mistake about it! The Big Bang theory is creationism, just without the creator. Materialists believe that matter sprang suddenly into existence with nothing prior. That primal atom was there, and they make no attempt to explain it. That's exactly the same as saying 'God was just there' and decided to create the universe. In fact, many Christian scientists like Big Bang theory, because it is compatible with their belief that God created the universe out of nothing. Archeologist Steven Mithen writes:

> Creationists believe that the mind sprang suddenly into existence fully formed. In their view it is a product of divine creation. They are wrong: the mind has a long evolutionary history and can be explained without recourse to supernatural powers.[11]

As you can see, Mithen is arguing from as false a premise as the 'God-did-it-in-six-days' gang. He has already made a big leap of assumption that when anyone speaks about 'mind' they are speaking exclusively about a mind that is tied to a physical body. It apparently never occurs to him that pure consciousness is what is meant by 'mind' and not masses of neurons talking to each other with chemical and electrical signal systems. The very idea that consciousness might exist prior to matter is anathema to the materialists, yet that very idea in its most basic form is being discussed in recent years as the foundation of all existence in the form of pure information. At the same time, a close study of the matter reveals that many scientists involved in biochemical research have actually gutted classical Darwinism and some of them are coming forward and saying so plainly.[12]

---

[9] Karl Popper argues this point in some depth; see Karl Popper and John C. Eccles, *The Self and Its Brain: An Argument for Interactionism* (Routledge, 1984).

[10] For a thorough philosophical refutation of materialism in general, see for example Thomas Nagel, *Mind & Cosmos: Why the Materialist Neo-Darwinian Conception of Nature Is Almost Certainly False* (Oxford University Press, 2012); David Ray Griffin, *God Exists But Gawd Does Not: From Evil to New Atheism to Fine-Tuning* (Process Century Press, 2016); Bernardo Kastrup, *The Idea of the World: A Multi-Disciplinary Argument for the Mental Nature of Reality* (Iff Books, 2019); Rupert Sheldrake, *Science Set Free: 10 Paths to New Discovery* (Deepak Chopra, 2013).

[11] Steven Mithen, *The Prehistory of the Mind* (Thames & Hudson, 1999).

[12] See, for example, Michael J. Behe, *Darwin's Black Box: The Biochemical Challenge to Evolution* (2nd ed., Free Press, 2006), *The Edge of Evolution: The Search for the Limits of Darwinism* (Free Press, 2008) and *Darwin*

Proponents of Darwinism or neo-Darwinism insist that there are clear distinctions between science and religion. Indeed, there are obvious differences in the style and content of a laboratory experiment and a claim to divinely revealed knowledge. Materialists say that science is concerned with knowledge of the proven and visible, while religion is concerned with *mindless* faith in the unprovable and invisible. And yet, when the facts are known, one must ask: is natural selection really a proven system based on demonstrated knowledge, or is it an unproven hypothesis in which there are so many contraindications that belief in it is also, in the final analysis, only a matter of faith? Natural selection is no more visible than a Deity and, frankly, less likely to do what is claimed than supernatural intervention!

Just as Christians tend to believe there is more evidence for the historical Jesus than actually exists, most people (scientists included) tend to believe there is more evidence for 'natural selection' than there actually is. For example, there is plenty of lab evidence that natural selection breaks existing genes; there is so far no evidence of it creating new ones, or substantially 'improving' existing ones via additional information. For those readers shocked by such statements, I can only recommend you read the works listed in the previous footnote, starting with those of Michael Behe. If you read even just those with an open mind, I believe you will change your mind about the power of 'natural selection.'[13]

Evolutionists are often found taunting those who think that something higher is involved in our existence – that their miracles of special creation can, by definition, be neither proved nor disproved. Yet the evolutionists arrive at similar propositions, especially when they exclude any possibility of something that guides and propels evolutionary processes. The main difference between the believers in miracles of special creation and believers in accidental variations is that the former has God Almighty pulling the strings and the latter has only impossible probabilities of jostling atoms and molecules as its ultimate reality. Not much difference, eh? Both are an affront to reason.

Devolves: The New Science About DNA That Challenges Evolution (HarperOne, 2019); David Berlinski, *The Deniable Darwin* (Discovery Institute, 2010); Stephen C. Meyer, *Signature in the Cell: DNA and the Evidence for Intelligent Design* (HarperOne, 2009) and *Darwin's Doubt: The Explosive Origin of Animal Life and the Case for Intelligent Design* (HarperOne, 2013); Matti Leisola and Jonathan Witt, *Heretic: One Scientist's Journey from Darwin to Design* (Discovery Institute, 2018); and the references in footnote 10 above.

[13]Frank Ryan, *Virolution* (Collins, 2009); John C. Sanford, *Genetic Entropy* (FMS Publications, 2014). Just because I ascribe a high probability to consciousness/information existing outside of, and even prior to, matter/material universe, does not mean that I am in the 'creationist' camp. For me, the most stunning evidence of intelligent design is the study of living systems. All the evidence from so-called paranormal phenomena is only suggestive, and can be explained (whether adequately or not is another question) by resorting to physical systems and their outputs and inputs. But the *systems* analyses are something else. Does that mean one must fall back on the 'God did it' routine? I don't think so. I think that it is something that needs to be studied and considered by truly open-minded experts. Information systems can be studied and inferences made; it's already being done to some extent. It is just simply that a larger-scale application needs to be made. We may only ever be able to infer things about a level of reality just above – or around – our own, but that is already something. There may be levels beyond that; we just don't know. What I do know is that an awful lot of what is called 'paranormal' is very much like quantum phenomena and cannot be subjected to the purely material demands for 'proof' that repeating experiments imply. Therefore, physics needs to be extended to study such things rationally even if results appear, on their face, to be irrational. I mean, how crazy is it that the cat might be dead or alive or even dead/alive at once?

And here we come to an interesting idea: the difficulty for both believers in purely mechanistic evolution and the creationists is that *any cosmology that is sufficiently explanatory of the phenomena we observe in our universe has deeper dynamics and implications.* The evolutionists and creationists both seem incapable of the truly abstract, subtle thinking required to parse these implications. It is as though both types are confined within a set of cognitive restrictions that drive their perceptions, experiences and priorities. And this is, I believe, exactly what happened to the work of the Apostle Paul. His visions of other realities inspired ideas that were abstract and subtle, and he presented them in the terms and understandings available at the time, but most of the people around him simply could not grasp what he was about. And so, the gospel that Paul taught was 'materialized' and what we have had since that process began is a shadow on a cave wall of what Paul really intended to convey. But we will come to all of this much further on.

Looking back at the history – more particularly, the archaeology – we notice how much like the Roman Empire our present civilization actually is. The Romans were certainly rational and scientific in many respects. They had factories which produced tableware that has been found at the farthest reaches of the Empire, even in peasant homes. They had factories that manufactured roof tiles that covered the heads of even the poorest workers and their livestock. A cache of letters was found in northern Britain where soldiers wrote home to have socks sent to them, which were, apparently, mass produced. The Roman army was superior because it had standardized equipment, produced in mass quantities at factories located in hubs of the Empire. Grain, olives, oil, foodstuffs of all kinds, luxury goods, were mass-produced and distributed throughout the Roman world. Literacy was obviously very widespread, even to the working classes. There were roads, sanitation systems, *haute cuisine*; in short, everything that we take for granted as essential to civilization. The only difference seems to be that we have harnessed sources of power that the Romans did not have, which enables our civilization to aspire to globalization. But in almost every other way, we are exactly like them. It is only science that has made us bigger and badder, so to say. And, as the saying goes, the bigger they are, the harder they fall. That fall may be the extinction of the human race.

> The end of the Roman Empire witnessed horrors and dislocation of a kind I sincerely hope never to have to live through; and it destroyed a complex civilization, throwing the inhabitants of the West back to a standard of living typical of prehistoric times. Romans before the fall were as certain as we are today that their world would continue forever, substantially unchanged. They were wrong. We would be wise not to repeat their complacency.[14]

In my view, science took a serious wrong turn in the middle of the nineteenth century, about the time Darwin published his *Origin of Species*, and we live in a spiritual Dark Age as a consequence. If a true, free, intelligent science, supported and encouraged by all of society, had actually been the norm since its inception, not the exception, we might live in a world where our very existence was not a shame to the planet that gave us birth. Humankind might know how to live in harmony not only with each other, but with the world in which we are born. As it is, our technological progress has no moral compass, and our scientific worldview is founded on irrational ideas like

---

[14]Bryan Ward-Perkins, *The Fall of Rome and the End of Civilization* (Oxford University Press, 2005), p. 183.

Darwinism. When you add in authoritarian ideologues with various personality disorders,[15] you can see why I take Ward-Perkins's warning above so seriously.

It seems to me that the Apostle Paul, living in the Roman Empire described above, indeed had visions of other realities that parallel the realities described by some of the most advanced physics. I have written about all of these things at great length elsewhere so I won't belabor the topic now.[16] Suffice it to say that the evidence collected over my 50 years of research suggests very, very strongly, that our reality is only one of many, and it is embedded in, or extruded from, a higher and different reality where consciousness and information play the guiding roles. And even that higher reality is only part of a cosmic informational structure that bears some anecdotal resemblance to scenes and experiences described throughout the ages by mystics and seers.

The Apostle Paul was a mystic and seer, and he was the true bringer of the gospel of Christ, as I will argue in this book. However, what we know of this gospel today is distorted and hidden by two thousand years of materialism, the very thing that Paul's gospel was intended to refute. Apparently, little has changed since Paul experienced his visions, began his mission, and wrote his letters. The atheists reject the truth of his experiences and visions; the fundamentalists misinterpret it.

It will be helpful for the reader of this book to have at least some knowledge of the basic history of Christianity, to have read the New Testament at least once, especially Paul's letters contained therein. I will try, as often as it seems needed, to include the actual text under discussion to save the reader from frantic flipping of pages.[17] At the same time, for the serious reader, it would help to have a good copy of the New Revised Standard Version (NRSV) Bible on hand, or even the Amplified Translation by Zondervan. You can get by with your standard King James Version (KJV), but please understand, a lot of advances have been made in text studies and translation that you might be missing. On the other hand, you can probably read this book without referring to the New Testament (NT) and get plenty out of it.

Setting aside beliefs and assumptions is often the most difficult thing to do. But if you can do that, if you can follow the texts wherever they lead and draw correct inferences, then the reward is getting as close to the truth of the gospel as is possible. After two thousand years of the Lie of materialism against which Paul fought with his whole being, that is certainly no small thing.

---

[15]Robert Altemeyer, *The Authoritarians* (Cherry Hill Publishing, 2008); Andrew Lobaczewski, *Political Ponerology* (Red Pill Press, 2006).

[16]Some of my books, all published by Red Pill Press, include: *The Wave or Adventures with Cassiopaea* (8 volumes, 2007–2012), *The Secret History of the World* (3 volumes, 2006–2014), *High Strangeness: Hyperdimensions and the Process of Alien Abduction* (2008).

[17]Unless otherwise noted, all italics or bolding in quotations, whether from the Bible or other sources, are my own.

Introduction

John Knox's Methodological principle: In cases of conflict, priority must be given to Paul's letters against Acts.

~~~

Scholarly opinion has long agreed that the writings of Paul are the earliest Christian documents. This presents certain problems. Paul never mentions John the Baptist; never says anything about a betrayal by Judas or Peter's denial of Jesus. This latter item is surprising since Paul was – according to his own account – in direct conflict with Peter and the Jerusalem church. There are numerous occasions when citing a saying of Jesus would have settled an issue, but Paul never does that. More than once, Paul contradicts what the later Gospels[18] say, but more often, the Gospels appear to be putting Paul's words into Jesus' mouth. In other cases, when Paul says he is giving 'a commandment of the Lord,' we note that, according to the Gospels, 'the Lord' never said any such thing, and Paul is explicit that he got his instructions via revelation, not from any teachings transmitted by men.

Paul also doesn't write anything about the 'twelve apostles' *as described in the Gospels and Acts*. The single mention of them in the epistles lacks any specific detail, and what it does say *contradicts* the Gospels.[19] Paul only knows Cephas, James and John, the so-called pillars, *with whom he is in direct conflict*, and a 'Peter' who was an apostle like himself. Paul taught that all who believed in Jesus would be saved and that the Jewish Law was null and void to those 'in Christ.' James appears to have been the one insisting that the Law – becoming a full-fledged Jew – was the only way to salvation. Paul speaks of Jewish plots and conspiracies against his converts, and he mentions "another gospel" of circumcision, rivals who proclaim "another Jesus" and implies that the leaders of the Jerusalem church were "enemies of the Cross of Christ." One line of force that can be drawn from Paul's writings is that Paul's Jesus does not appear to be the Jesus of the Jerusalem church of Cephas, James and John. This is, of course, a serious problem and the feats of theological legerdemain that have been performed to paper over this issue are astonishing!

Paul also never mentions or alludes to the idea that any of the apostles had ever been companions of an earthly Jesus. When he refers to James as "the Lord's Brother," he may mean a member of an order of devotees since he also refers to "the brethren of the Lord"[20] repeatedly

---

[18]In this work, gospel with a lowercase *g* is used to refer to the message preached by Paul or others; Gospel with a capital *G* is used to refer to the written Gospels included in the New Testament. The word gospel comes from the Greek *euangelion*, meaning 'good news.'

[19]1 Cor. 15:5, where Paul says that Jesus appeared first to Cephas, "then to the twelve." In the Gospels, Judas has already betrayed Jesus, so he appears only to "the eleven." Also, the Qumran community had a system of twelve elders and three priests (pillars?), so it was possibly a common organizational practice.

[20]1 Cor. 9:5. See Richard Carrier, *On the Historicity of Jesus* (Sheffield Phoenix Press, 2014), pp. 582–92, where he argues that Paul simply called James "the Lord's brother" in Gal. 1:19 in order to distinguish him from any

throughout all his letters. Nowhere does he suggest or hint that Cephas, James and John were taught anything by Jesus; they are simply leaders of a sect in Jerusalem with which Paul is trying to establish some sort of cooperation for reasons that aren't entirely clear, considering the dynamics he reveals.

But, despite this *prima facie* evidence that something is terribly wrong with the picture, many scholars are still insisting that there was a 'Jesus of Nazareth' *as depicted in the Gospels* somewhere behind it all, and that the Gospels relied on oral traditions and/or 'sayings Gospels' to construct their stories (obviously, Paul never heard of them). David Oliver Smith's study of the Gospels: *Matthew, Mark, Luke and Paul* – taken with the earlier works of Michael Goulder, Thomas Brodie, D. R. MacDonald, Mary Ann Tolbert, and other notable scholars – on the literary allusions, mimesis and rhetorical structures found in the first Gospel, Mark, puts a period to that hope for a 'historical Jesus as depicted in the Gospels.'

Smith demonstrated the use of Paul's letters and the Letter to the Hebrews in the construction of the Gospel of Mark. Additionally, the authors of Matthew and Luke also went back to Paul's letters and expanded on Mark's text in several places. The conclusion is that, where they agree, the writers of the synoptic Gospels got their teachings of Jesus *from Paul's epistles.* That doesn't mean that there wasn't a historical individual who inspired the literary character, Jesus of Mark. It just means that the stories told about him are unlikely to be true. All of this amounts to compelling evidence that the Gospels are not independent accounts of the same historical events since almost nothing in the Gospels is historical, but rather derived from other sources.

Thus, it seems obvious that in order to get a full grip on who Paul was and what he was thinking and doing with such passionate conviction and intensity, methodologically, we need to first dispense with any reference to the later invention of Jesus of Nazareth in the Gospels. We need to concentrate on the fact that *something* moved Paul powerfully, and in order to determine what it was we need to situate Paul in an accurate historical context.

In addition to preventing the later Gospels from coloring our interpretation of Paul's view of Christ with possible later fabrications, we must also reject the use of the Acts of the Apostles and its later depiction of Paul. Acts presents itself as a history of Christianity after Jesus, following the careers of Peter and Paul, Christianity's two most famous apostles. As Richard Pervo has made abundantly clear in his detailed studies, it is no such thing.[21] Rather, it is something like a second-century 'historical novel' with an agenda, just like the Gospels.

To put it simply, the author of Acts picked out some authentic names and events from texts extant in his time, used Paul's letters as inspiration, though never referring to them, and wrote his novel around them, with the purpose of presenting the image that everyone got along in the early church and there was a smooth transition from the originally Jewish Jesus to the pontifical establishment in Rome. Paul's letters – even heavily edited as they surely are – paint a very different and contradictory picture. In methodological terms, Acts is not a historical document, while the letters of Paul *are* – but only if we approach them without prejudices.

---

other apostles with that name, implying that James wasn't an apostle. Paul wrote, "I saw none of the other apostles [besides Cephas], only the Lord's brother [i.e. the Christ-follower] James." This comes out in 1 Cor. 15, too, where he says Christ appeared "to James, then to all the apostles."

[21]Richard I. Pervo, *Dating Acts: Between the Evangelists and the Apologists* (Polebridge Press, 2006).

What documents might the author of Acts have used to create a plausible setting for his narrative? And to which contemporary sources can we turn for the historical context we need in order to place Paul's life and work?

The only historian whose works have survived to give us a detailed picture of the times and places in which Paul lived and worked is Joseph bar Matthias, AKA Titus Flavius Josephus, who lived ca. 37–100 AD.[22] This places his work about one generation after Paul, who is said to have been active in the late 30s through to the 50s or 60s AD.[23] (More about Josephus below.) As Pervo argues, the author of Acts likely used Josephus' works; they weren't simply drawing on the same historical sources. Several studies have demonstrated that the author of Acts also used Paul's letters as sources, though deliberately pretending to be unaware of them because the history being constructed was contradictory to what the letters depicted.

However, we encounter a similar problem with Josephus that we encounter with the Gospels and Acts: even though Josephus claims to be writing history, we cannot necessarily rely on using his works as an accurate historical source. As modern Josephus scholars point out, researchers must be careful before accepting what he wrote at face value.[24] And this means we must also account for this when analyzing how *ancient* authors used his works, like the authors of the Gospels and Acts. They too could not have known that much of what Josephus wrote was embellished, confused, or even, in some cases, falsified.

Later Christian writings cannot be relied upon for real history. And even the contemporary sources with the most relevant context are of often-dubious reliability. So we are surrounded by problems. We are left with the fact that Paul's letters are arguably the earliest Christian historical documents, the only firsthand source we have for many events and ideas. So it should go without saying that we need to utilize them conscientiously and effectively. But even reading *them* with the genuine history of the time firmly in mind can be problematical, as the work of Baur, Knox, Lüdemann, Trobisch, Price, Tyson, BeDuhn, Campbell, and others reveal.[25] In

---

[22]The fact that the works of Josephus were used (along with other texts and stories) in the construction of the Gospels may be signaled by 'coded messages' included in the texts. For example, in his autobiography, Josephus Bar Mathias asked permission of Titus to bring down three crucified men (friends of his) and one survives. In the four Gospels, Joseph of Arimathea (pun on Joseph bar Mathias?) asks permission to bring Jesus' body down. There was no city named Arimathea during this time. Mark 15:46: "Then Joseph bought a linen cloth, and taking down the body, wrapped it in the linen cloth, and laid it in a tomb that had been hewn out of the rock. He then rolled a stone against the door of the tomb." Luke 23:50-52: "Now there was a good and righteous man named Joseph, who, though a member of the council, had not agreed to their plan and action. He came from the Jewish town of Arimathea, and he was waiting expectantly for the kingdom of God. This man went to Pilate and asked for the body of Jesus." Matthew 27:57: "When it was evening, there came a rich man from Arimathea, named Joseph, who was also a disciple of Jesus." John 19:38-40: "After these things, Joseph of Arimathea, who was a disciple of Jesus, though a secret one because of his fear of the Jews, asked Pilate to let him take away the body of Jesus. Pilate gave him permission; so he came and removed his body. Nicodemus, who had at first come to Jesus by night, also came, bringing a mixture of myrrh and aloes, weighing about a hundred pounds. They took the body of Jesus and wrapped it with the spices in linen cloths, according to the burial custom of the Jews."

[23]Tacitus (ca. 56–117), as well as later historians such as Plutarch, Suetonius and Cassius Dio, also related events during this time, but only Josephus devotes so much detail to Judea/Syria and the surrounding regions.

[24]For example, Steve Mason, Shaye Cohen, Étienne Nodet.

[25]F. C. Baur, *Paul the Apostle of Jesus Christ. His Life and Works, His Epistles and Teachings* (2 vols; Hendrickson, 2003 [1845]); Jason D. BeDuhn, *The First New Testament: Marcion's Scriptural Canon* (Polebridge Press, 2013); Campbell, *Framing Paul* (Eerdmans, 2014); John Knox, *Chapters in a Life of Paul* (Mercer University Press,

general, we have to keep in mind that conflicts between pagans and Christians often led to wars of words, particularly the written word. And if we are considering a war between different types of Christians, things can get very confusing very fast. Additionally, the history of the destruction and redaction of texts is appalling.

Interpolations in Paul's Letters

William O. Walker, in his book *Interpolations in the Pauline Letters*,[26] addresses this problem head on. He demonstrates that many interpolations can be identified with some confidence, so it is surprising that many more scholars are not acknowledging the problem. He points out that he is certainly not the first: scholars J. C. O'Neill and Winsome Munro argued for extensive interpolations throughout the letters of Paul. Walker cites many other eminent scholars who have noted the problem:

> The text of the Pauline letters that lies behind all the extant manuscripts bears signs of harmonization with the pastorals. That is, all extant manuscripts of the corpus contain interpolations from a scribe who knew the pastorals and who altered the text of Paul's own letters to conform with them.[27]

I would suggest that the author of the largely fictional book of Acts not only used Paul's letters for inspiration, but may very well have been the one who edited them to conform to his fictional scenarios when he thought he could get away with it.

> Despite repeated suggestions that particular passages in the Pauline letters are to be regarded as later additions, however, 'there has been no scholarly agreement on the probability, or even the plausibility of any of these hypotheses about glosses and interpolations'.[28] ... Doughty observes that interpolation theories are 'not generally presupposed by Pauline scholarship; further, they actually encounter fierce resistance in some quarters'. According to Winsome Munro, scholars are more inclined to view entire epistles as pseudonymous than to agree that 'short packets of material' are non-Pauline additions. ... Lamar Cope observes ... Once it has been established that particular letters are either Pauline or non-Pauline, 'they have been treated as wholes', with little attention to the possibility of non-Pauline passages within otherwise authentically Pauline letters or, for that matter, of authentically Pauline passages within otherwise non-Pauline writings.[29]

Walker says the major problem is that no one is paying attention to the most important preliminary issues, which are:

1. the a priori probability of interpolations in the Pauline letters;

1987 [1950]); Gerd Lüdemann, *Paul, Apostle to the Gentiles: Studies in Chronology* (Fortress Press, 1984); David Trobisch, *Paul's Letter Collection: Tracing the Origins* (Quiet Waters Publications, 2001) and *The First New Testament* (Oxford University Press, 2011 [2000]); Joseph B. Tyson, *Marcion and Luke-Acts: A Defining Struggle* (University of South Carolina Press, 2006).

[26]Sheffield Academic Press, 2002.

[27]Dennis R. MacDonald, *The Legend and the Apostle* (Westminster John Knox Press, 1983), p. 86

[28]Furnish, *Pauline Studies*, p. 325.

[29]Walker (2002), pp. 20–21.

2. whether direct text-critical evidence is an essential prerequisite for the recognition of individual interpolations;

3. the burden-of-proof question as it relates to the identification of interpolations;

4. what types of data would count as evidence for interpolation.[30]

Regarding item 1, the *a priori* probability of interpolations in the Pauline corpus, Walker cites numerous examples from more ancient authors up to the evidence within the varied text traditions of the NT that we actually have.

> Richard I. Pervo has suggested that the type of Christianity reflected in the distinctive readings of the Western text[31] 'has many affinities to right-wing Deutero-Paulinism of second century Asia Minor.' ... Moreover, in his view, these readings demonstrate that one technique used by representatives of this type of Christianity was 'the revision of texts through addition and deletion'; indeed, they 'show that there were people quite willing to attempt such modifications' of early Christian writings.[32]

Winsome Munro cited the curse at Rev. 22:18–19 as evidence that both redactional expansion and editorial deletion were widely practiced at the time, before, and since.

Obviously, it is highly unlikely, considering the stakes that will be described further on, that Paul's writings would be exempt from minor to extensive modification. Defenders of the miscreants argue that Paul's letters "represent a distinctively different genre." True enough. J. C. O'Neill points out:

> 'they are odd as letters anyway' ... 'no ancient letters, except letters modelled on Paul's, are so long and so like treatises in parts' ... 'the oddness in Paul's letters' may be due to the fact that they 'have been treated in exactly the same way as the rest of the sacred books contained within the Old and New Testament canons' ... 'they are odd as letters' precisely because they have 'been glossed and interpolated'.[33]

Not only have they been glossed and interpolated, in some cases it's arguable that entire letters have been 'reconstructed' using pieces of varied letters that were never intended to be juxtaposed and combined as the editors have done.

> Most scholars agree that at least some of the Pauline letters were in fact subject to various forms of editorial activity; thus, for example, 2 Corinthians is widely regarded as a 'composite' letter, composed of parts of at least two originally separate letters.[34]

---

[30] Walker (2002), p. 21.

[31] "The Western text-type is one of several text-types used in textual criticism to describe and group the textual character of Greek New Testament manuscripts. It is the predominant form of the New Testament text witnessed in the Old Latin and Syriac Peshitta translations from the Greek, and also in quotations from certain 2nd and 3rd century Christian writers, including Cyprian, Tertullian and Irenaeus. ... Although the Western text-type survives in relatively few witnesses, some of these are as early as the earliest witnesses to the Alexandrian text-type. Nevertheless, the majority of text critics consider the Western text in the Gospels to be characterised by periphrasis and expansion; and accordingly tend to prefer the Alexandrian readings. On the other hand, in the letters of St Paul, the counterpart Western text is more restrained, and a number of text critics regard it as the most reliable witness to the original." (Wikipedia.org, 'Western text-type.')

[32] Pervo, 'Social and Religious aspects of the Western Text,' in *The Living Text* (1985), pp. 229–41, cited in Walker (2001), p. 33.

[33] Walker (2001), p. 34.

[34] Walker (2001), p. 35.

Walker concludes that interpolations *are to be assumed simply on a priori grounds*, that *direct text-critical evidence is not essential for their recognition*, that the burden of proof in their identification is *lighter* than the assumption that there are no – or few – interpolations; specific evidence for interpolation is often obvious.[35] Further complicating the issue is to know who made the edits and when. For example, Trobisch argues that the first editor may have been Paul himself, preparing a collection of letters for extended distribution.[36] Further edits may have been made by direct followers of Paul, or by his ideological opponents and later orthodox writers far removed from Paul's time and original intent.

I would like to say here that what Walker et al. have said about the Pauline letters applies to *all ancient texts* that have survived down to our own day, and more particularly texts that survive from known tendentious times and circumstances such as New Testament texts and all texts about the history of the time when Christianity was emerging. Editing, amending, interpolating, miming and falsifying texts was a significant industry in certain times and places, and we need to always keep that in mind; and also that many ancient texts are contentious for one reason or another and need to be *interrogated* intelligently, not taken at face value.

Now we turn to the history of Paul's letters, as far as we can know it.

Marcion and Paul

The first we know about Paul's letters, they are already a collection. The early second-century 'heretic' Marcion (85–160 AD) published a collection of ten letters before any other early Christian figure makes reference to them. But we only know about this collection via polemics against Marcion written by the early church fathers: Justin (100-165? AD),[37] Tertullian (155–240? AD), Irenaeus (130–202 AD), etc. The actual oldest manuscript we possess is known as P[46] and originally included ten letters in the following order: Romans, Hebrews, 1 and 2 Corinthians,

---

[35]Walker argues that 1 Cor. 11:3–16, 1 Cor. 2:6–16, 1 Cor. 12:31b–14:1a, and Rom. 1:18–2:29 are in fact non-Pauline interpolations, and goes on to summarize arguments for the same conclusion regarding five additional passages. However, if the text of Marcion's Pauline letter collection (see below for a fuller discussion) is taken as earlier than the canonical version, many of these passages are present, and therefore cannot be argued as late interpolations, demonstrating that arguments for interpolation may be plausible, but can probably only rarely be definitive. If Walker's particular hypotheses are correct, however, these interpolations must have been made prior to the appearance of Marcion's collection. For a list of interpolation hypotheses supported by the Marcion collection, see Peter Kirby, 'Marcion's Shorter Readings of Paul,' http://peterkirby.com/marcions-shorter-readings-of-paul.html.

[36]David Trobisch, *Paul's Letter Collection: Tracing the Origins* (Quiet Waters Publications, 2001).

[37]"Justin Martyr was born around AD 100 at Flavia Neapolis (today Nablus) in Samaria into a pagan family, and defined himself as a Gentile. His grandfather, Bacchius, had a Greek name, while his father, Priscus, bore a Latin name, which has led to speculations that his ancestors may have settled in Neapolis soon after its establishment or that they were descended from a Roman 'diplomatic' community that had been sent there. … Most of his works are lost, but two apologies and a dialogue did survive. *The First Apology*, his most well known text, passionately defends the morality of the Christian life, and provides various ethical and philosophical arguments to convince the Roman emperor, Antoninus, to abandon the persecution of the Church. Further, he also indicates, as St. Augustine would later regarding the 'true religion' that predated Christianity, that the 'seeds of Christianity' (manifestations of the Logos acting in history) actually predated Christ's incarnation. This notion allows him to claim many historical Greek philosophers (including Socrates and Plato), in whose works he was well studied, as unknowing Christians." (Wikipedia.org, 'Justin Martyr.')

Ephesians, Galatians, Philippians, Colossians, 1 and 2 Thessalonians.[38] Missing were Philemon and the Pastorals. Codices Vaticanus, Sinaiticus, Alexandrinus, and Ephraemi all had 14 letters.

It is not clear how this collection came into existence or what materials were available to a collector of Paul's writings. Also unknown is what condition the texts may have been in between the last that is heard from Paul (in his Letter to the Romans, which I will argue probably dates from 48–50 AD), and the appearance of Marcion with a collection around 110 AD or so, about 60 years later.

According to Tertullian (155–240), Marcion placed Galatians first in his collection, followed by 1 and 2 Corinthians, Romans, 1 and 2 Thessalonians, Ephesians, Colossians, Philemon, Philippians and *Laodiceans*.[39] At some point, the Marcion collection acquired prologues to the letters telling a bit about the situation of each letter, which could very well be based on accurate information now lost to us.[40] These prologues describe a pattern of disloyalty to Paul after the intrusion of the false apostles in Galatia, Corinth, Rome and Colossae. There is no indication in the prologues that Paul was successful in reclaiming his corrupted congregations. The churches that remained faithful were the Thessalonians, Philippians and Laodiceans. BeDuhn says Marcion's prologues to Paul's letters indicate Paul was in prison in Ephesus and was transported to Rome from there. (Not from Jerusalem as Acts says.)[41]

It has long been claimed that Marcion created his Gospel (*Evangelion*) by editing a Proto-Luke, and his letter collection (*Apostolikon*) by editing ten of the Pauline letters, all allegedly done in support of his theology. However, several more recent studies have demonstrated that this is not the case. It seems that whatever Marcion had, it was handed to him largely in the condition he found it.[42] By the time Tertullian was writing, Matthew, Luke and Acts already existed and that undoubtedly means that Paul's letters had already been modified.

However, what the raging controversy with Marcion suggests is that Paul and his gospel fell into disrepute early among some Christian communities, including in Rome, and had to be rehabilitated. This, of course, did not bode well for the survival of his letters intact. If it weren't for the fact that Acts had been written to make it look like everyone was on the same page and getting along famously, we could actually have doubts about the existence of Paul himself! It seems that it was only when Marcion showed up with Paul's letter collection and was so

---

[38]"Papyrus 46 (in the Gregory-Aland numbering) is one of the oldest extant New Testament manuscripts in Greek, written on papyrus, with its 'most probable date' between 175 and 225. ... P46 contains most of the Pauline epistles, though with some folios missing. It contains (in order) 'the last eight chapters of Romans; all of Hebrews; virtually all of 1–2 Corinthians; all of Ephesians, Galatians, Philippians, Colossians; and two chapters of 1 Thessalonians. All of the leaves have lost some lines at the bottom through deterioration.' ... From the page numbers on existing pages, we know that seven leaves have been lost from the beginning of the codex, which accords perfectly with the length of the missing portion of *Romans*, which they undoubtedly contained. Since the codex is formed from a stack of papyrus sheets folded in the middle, magazine-style, what is lost is the outer seven sheets, containing the first and last seven leaves of the codex. ... The provenance of the papyrus is unknown, although it was probably originally discovered in the ruins of an early Christian church or monastery. ... As with all manuscripts dated solely by palaeography, the dating of P 46 is uncertain. The first editor of parts of the papyrus, H. A. Sanders, proposed a date possibly as late as the second half of the 3rd century" though a date between 150–250 is proposed with 95% confidence. (Wikipedia.org, 'Papyrus 46.')

[39]Though BeDuhn (2013) argues that Ephesians was actually known to Marcion as *Laodiceans*, and that his collection did not contain a letter to the Ephesians.

[40]See Appendix A for the prologues.

[41]BeDuhn (2013), p. 43.

[42]BeDuhn (2013).

successful in attracting converts that the loosely affiliated bishops of various Christian groups around the Empire were galvanized to reclaim Paul as 'theirs.' But Paul's teachings were still a bit controversial, it seems. Irenaeus wrote: "Our Lord never came to save Paul alone, nor is God so limited in means that he should have but one apostle who knew the dispensation of his son."[43] That remark reveals a certain embarrassment or defensiveness.

Marcion's mission was based on his conviction that the church – that is, most Christian congregations – *had received a gospel other than Paul's* and their gospel was full of errors and misunderstandings. Marcion also thought that he had recovered and comprehended fully what Paul had originally taught by careful study of the texts; as a consequence he wished to delimit the gospel according to criteria derived exclusively from Paul's epistles.[44]

Marcion perceived Paul's insistence on the separation of the Law from the gospel of grace and faith, and from this he inferred a theological corollary: that the creator god of the Jews and the god revealed by Jesus Christ were two different gods.[45] That is, Marcion's conception was more along the line of 'gnostic' speculations about archons/demiurges as creators. And, for all we know, before editing and interpolating, Paul may very well have said something like that. Elaine Pagels certainly thinks that Paul had very Gnostic tendencies;[46] so does Robert M. Price, who writes:

> Marcion was the first Paulinist we know of. It would later be a matter of some embarrassment to the church fathers that the earliest readers and devotees of the Pauline epistles were the Marcionites and the Valentinian Gnostics. *We know of no Paulinists before these second-century Christians.* The mid-first century existence of Pauline Christianity is simply an inference, admittedly a natural one, from taking the authorship and implied dates of the Pauline epistles at face value as works representing a wing of first-century Christianity.[47]

Price has serious doubts about the existence and work of Paul and wonders if the Pauline literature isn't the product of Marcionite and Gnostic movements of the late first and early second centuries. It's a reasonable suspicion considering the fact that there appears to be no interest in Paul before Marcion. And truly, if Acts was not written until the mid-second century, as some experts propose, then even the story of Paul could possibly have been as much an invention as the Gospels. But, the fact that Paul had to be reclaimed in such a fashion, that he had to be re-modeled, so to say, even in contradiction to what he wrote in his letters, is a data point in favor of his existence and work.

Additionally, it appears strongly evident that the Gospel of Mark was based, in large part, on the letters of Paul, so they certainly existed (most of them), likely in Rome just following the end of the Jewish War. And I also think there was someone else who was equally interested in Paul and his ideas who may very well have been connected to Marcion at exactly the right time and place to have been the one who conveyed the letters to Sinope, the home of Marcion; but I will

---

[43]*Haer.* 3.13.1.

[44]R. Joseph Hoffmann, *Marcion: On the Restitution of Christianity* (Wipf and Stock, 2016), p. 102.

[45]My own assessment of the problem suggests that it was not two different 'gods' in the sense of the creator/demiurge vs. a higher god, but rather that Paul's Christ was not the same Christ followed by the Jerusalem Christians.

[46]Elaine Pagels, *The Gnostic Paul* (Trinity Press, 1992).

[47]Robert M. Price, *The Pre-Nicene New Testament* (Signature Books, 2006), p. viii.

come to that later. For the moment, what Robert M. Price has to say on the topic of Marcion is concise and broadly inclusive of the various issues:

> Marcion deemed the Jewish scriptures historically true and expected messianic prophecies to be fulfilled by a Davidic king who would restore Jewish sovereignty. But Marcion deemed all of this strictly irrelevant to the new religion of Christianity. In his view, which he claimed to have derived from Paul's epistles, Jesus Christ was the son and revealer of an alien God who had not created the world, had not given the Torah to Moses, and would not judge mankind. The Father of Jesus Christ was a God of perfect love and righteousness who would punish no one. Through Jesus, and by extension Paul, the Christian God offered humans the opportunity to be adopted as his children.
>
> ...
>
> ... So Marcion repudiated the Jewish scriptures. It wasn't that he didn't believe them, because he did. He simply felt they were the scriptures of someone else's religion and didn't overlap with Christianity as he understood it. Nor was he anti-Semitic or even anti-Judaic. For him, Judaism was true on its own terms, just not the religion of Jesus Christ or of the apostle Paul.
>
> Without the Septuagint as his scripture, Marcion felt the need to compile a new canon that would teach Christian faith and morals authoritatively. He accordingly collected the early Christian writings he felt served this purpose. These were paramountly the Pauline epistles except for the Pastorals, 1 and 2 Timothy, and Titus, because these did not exist yet, still waiting to be written in reaction to Marcion and other 'heretics' in the mid-second century. Marcion had shorter, earlier versions of the texts than ours. Likewise, he had a book he knew simply as "the gospel" corresponding to a shorter version of our Gospel of Luke. Catholic writers decades later would claim he had edited and censored the texts, cutting out material that served to link Christianity with its Jewish background. Marcion no doubt did do some editing, textual criticism as it seemed to him, but it seems that Catholic apologists did much more in the way of padding the texts with their own added material, claiming their own versions were original and should be adopted instead of the Marcionite text. Marcion called his scripture the *Apostolicon* ("Book of the Apostle").[48]

What Price has said above puts the problem in a nutshell except for one problem that I mentioned above: the Gospel of Mark. It is widely accepted as the first Gospel, and for good reason; yet, when Marcion appeared on the scene, he apparently had what many have called a 'proto-Luke' that is somewhat ill-defined despite the best efforts of scholars to extract it from the quotations of the early church fathers (no copy survives). Why did Marcion not simply use Mark, which was seemingly perfect for his purposes? S. G. F. Brandon's discussion of Mark as Roman apologetic, which I will cover much further on when we get to the end of the War, is convincing, though I think there is more to it than that: possibly even imperial propaganda, as Adam Winn proposes. My issue here is that Mark was almost certainly written in Rome following the Jewish War as apologetic propaganda for the Christian community there. It was in Mark that the Pauline Christ was superimposed on a Galilean figure and, most important of all, the figure and his theology were modeled *using the letters of Paul,* indicating that they certainly existed then and were considered – at least by the author of Mark – authoritative. It appears that Marcion's so-called 'proto-Luke' may actually have been an early redaction of Mark, which would eventually become the Gospel of Luke as we have come to know it after the addition of Luke's first chapters, and some additional editing.

As already mentioned, David Oliver Smith has demonstrated the use of Paul's letters and the Deutero-Pauline Epistle to the Hebrews in the construction of the Gospel of Mark. Additionally,

---

[48] Price (2006), pp. viii–xii.

he demonstrates that the authors of Matthew and Luke also went back to Paul's letters and expanded on Mark's text in several places using them! He has shown definitive textual evidence that the Gospels are not independent accounts of the same events, the letters of Paul certainly existed before the Gospels were written, and the first Gospel was constructed using Paul.

> [T]he writer of the Gospel of Mark used Romans and 1 Corinthians to construct the bulk of Mark 12, referring to those epistles in a chiastic format that could not have been accidental. This shows that Paul's Epistles were written prior to Mark's Gospel. That means that Paul could not have got his teachings from the Gospels. If he did not get them from the Gospels and he did not get them from an oral tradition, it is unlikely that the [other] gospel writers got Jesus' teachings from oral traditions. ... The logical conclusion is that, where they agree, the writers of the Synoptic Gospels got their teachings of Jesus from Paul's Epistles.[49]

> Six of Paul's seven 'authentic' Epistles – Romans, 1 Corinthians, 2 Corinthians, Galatians, Philippians, 1 Thessalonians and Hebrews – were used ... to construct their [fictional] stories of Jesus of Nazareth.[50]

In response to Marcion, 'Luke' (probably Polycarp [69–155 AD], according to some scholars[51]) had to re-write proto-Luke and then wrote Acts, two works that reconciled Pauline ideas with a Jewish messiah and attempted to cover over the early conflict between Paul and the Jewish Christians of Jerusalem. Matthew's extreme emphasis on the Jewishness of the Messiah and Christian beginnings was reconciled with Mark's strong anti-Jewishness by 'Luke,' which, of course, presupposes that the two former Gospels existed at the time. Matthew and Luke would have been politically troublesome in the generation that experienced the destruction of Jerusalem due to the prevailing anti-Semitism of the time and were likely written some time afterward. Mark was so blatantly constructed according to a plan, using literary sources, so obviously allegorical and ironic, that it seems certain that it was written in response to the destruction of Jerusalem and that any educated person of the time would have understood its 'secrets.' Matthew and Luke, in utilizing Mark, destroyed many elements of the rhetorical structuring, though Matthew, at least, created some of his own. Luke was a more ham-handed attempt by someone who was certainly not interested in the structural merits of Mark. So, effectively, Luke-Acts was a take-over and suppression of Paul and his messiah and thus designed to convert Christians to the

---

[49] David Oliver Smith, *Matthew, Mark, Luke, and Paul* (Resource Publications, 2011), pp. 309–10.

[50] Smith (2011), p. 312.

[51] Robert M. Price (2006), for one, makes the suggestion for the following reasons: 1) Luke-Acts is addressed to Theophilus, and Polycarp was close to Theophilus of Antioch. 2) Luke seems to be written to counter Marcionite teachings and to counter the Marcionite Gospel. 3) Acts and the Pastorals (some say that the Pastorals' author is the same as the author of Luke-Acts) seems to be an attempt at re-writing Paul's story; Paul only became significant after the appearance of Marcion. 4) Polycarp was one of the main opponents of Marcion. 5) The Pastorals, especially 2 Timothy, add aspects to Paul's life story that appear nowhere else except in the writings of Polycarp. See also: David Trobisch, 'Who Published the Christian Bible?' delivered at the January 2007 'Scripture and Skepticism' conference (Committee for the Scientific Examination of Religion); also *The First Edition of the New Testament* (Oxford University Press, 2011). Trobisch argues that the New Testament canon of 27 writings originated not in the fourth century as the result of a prolonged process of debate and custom, but rather as the work of a single editor and publisher in the late second century. Following John Knox (*Marcion and the New Testament*, 1942) and Hans von Campenhausen (*The Formation of the Christian Bible*, 1968), Trobisch argues that the New Testament was a literary response against the docetic (mythicist) Marcionite Jesus. Hans von Campenhausen had already suggested that the author of the Pastorals was Polycarp of Smyrna. Trobisch goes further to suggest Polycarp as the author of Acts and the Pastorals.

Jewish messiah. And that was the Christianity that Tertullian already knew when he went after Marcion.

What we can conclude from the above is that Paul's letters certainly existed as early as 70 AD since they were used in the construction of the Gospel of Mark just following the destruction of Jerusalem (further on this below). We lose sight of them completely for at least 60 years, until about 110 AD at the earliest, when Marcion of Sinope appears with a collection of ten letters and a Gospel that is described as proto-Luke.

Dating Paul

Despite strenuous efforts, scholars have been unable to firmly anchor Paul's letters to particular times and places using only their own internal evidence, and without falling back on Acts – an unsound proposition – to round out the picture. John Knox was the first to attempt making a chronology for Paul using *only* Paul's letters as sources, but practically all scholars then and since have resorted to using data from Acts and the Gospels to anchor their chronology. The result is that they all date Paul's 'conversion' between 31 and 34 AD – soon after the alleged crucifixion of Jesus – and Paul's last visit to Jerusalem, upon which he is about to commence in his last letter (to the Romans), 22–25 years later, in the 50s.[52]

Although Paul does mention a few things that may be linked to actual historical events or personages, he does so without tying any of these remarks to an *externally* verifiable historical date. In one place only does he mention a *historically* anchored person: King Aretas IV of Nabataea, the Arab state south and east of Judea. He says Aretas' governor in Damascus was pursuing him, and that he escaped by being lowered from the city's walls in a basket.

> In Damascus the governor under King Aretas had the city of the Damascenes guarded in order to arrest me. But I was lowered in a basket from a window in the wall and slipped through his hands. (2 Cor. 11:32-33)

It has been suggested that this tale – along with Paul's many other declared hardships – were simply rhetorical tropes of the Stoic/wise-man type common to that era.[53] However, Paul's mention of a real historical figure here does not suggest that this was merely a rhetorical ploy.[54] Also note that he gives this little vignette in the context of his sufferings as an apostle of Christ, the implication being that he was being pursued for his preaching and converting activity.

Pauline scholar Douglas Campbell analyzed the letters of Paul for chronological clues, with the interesting result that several letters whose authenticity has been widely questioned and rejected achieve rehabilitation as authentic (by Campbell), including 2 Thessalonians, in his study.[55] This

---

[52]David L. Eastman, 'Paul: An Outline of His Life,' in Mark Harding and Alanna Nobbs (eds.), *All Things to all Cultures: Paul among Jews, Greeks and Romans* (Eerdmans, 2013), p. 52.

[53]John T. Fitzgerald, *Cracks in an Earthen Vessel: An Examination of the Catalogues of Hardships in the Corinthian Correspondence* (Scholars Press, 1988).

[54]One is, of course, reminded of the spies of Joshua who were let down by rope from the city wall of Jericho (Joshua 2) by Rahab, the harlot; and David being similarly rescued from the murderous rage of King Saul by his wife Michal, who was also Saul's daughter (1 Samuel 19:11-12).

[55]He also rehabilitates Ephesians and Colossians. Most recently the Westar scholars rejected these three letters. See Arthur J. Dewey, Roy W. Hoover, Lane McGaughy and Daniel D. Schmidt, *The Authentic Letters of Paul* (Polebridge Press, 2010). See below for more discussion.

is not the space to argue his case – for that, read his book. But some comment is necessary on the issue of authenticity, because if certain chronological clues are found in fraudulent letters written decades later, they would lose their usefulness.[56] And, if there are chronological clues in an authentic letter that has been adjudged inauthentic, we have lost precious evidence. (Recall what was said above about interpolations in Paul's letters.)

Campbell suggests that 'The Man of Sin' of 2 Thessalonians – one of the letters whose authenticity is questioned – was the emperor Gaius, better known as Caligula (37–41 AD), who planned to erect a statue of himself in the Temple of Jerusalem in the year or so before he was assassinated. If that is the case, then that could give a date for the text of 2 Thessalonians as early as 40 AD.[57] So Paul could have been writing this letter as early as the time that the Alexandrian Jewish philosopher Philo was in Rome on his embassy to Emperor Gaius. Tagging 40 AD as the possible time of 2 Thessalonians helps only a little, however, because there are apparently quite a few years of Pauline activity before and after the penning of that epistle; the question is, how many years in either direction?[58]

As mentioned above, scholars who reject the authenticity of certain letters use a variety of arguments. In general, they base these on the presence of anachronisms (i.e., referencing something before it could have possibly been referenced, e.g., a reference to a person who hadn't been born yet when the text in question was supposed to have been written) and by "focusing on the [differences or contradictions in] vocabulary, phrases, social situation, Christology and ecclesial understanding of the letters," as the authors of *The Authentic Letters of Paul* put it.[59] But aside from the presence of verifiable anachronisms, all other arguments tend to be circular when applied to the letters in question; such arguments presume what they set out to answer. And, notably, most often they do not take interpolation into account (though interpolation arguments can run into the same problems, thus the mess we're in!).

For example, when it comes to issues of style, form, and the ideas presented, we would need a truly representative sample – a "universe of Pauline possibilities," as Campbell calls it – which would contain the whole range of words, ideas, and styles Paul used when writing. Only then could we judge whether certain passages or entire letters match up with it or not. We don't have such a sample. So, to say "This letter can't be written by Paul, because this other letter doesn't use these words," is begging the question. At the very least, all we can say is, "Whoever wrote this letter – Paul or someone else – used some different words." Without some other criteria for establishing which letters are authentic or not, we can't yet know whether the characteristics in question would appear in our genuine Pauline sample.

Choosing the 'authentic' sample by which to judge is largely arbitrary. If we start out not knowing what is authentic, we can't easily determine whether or not one unknown sample is authentic by comparing it to another unknown sample. We run the risk of cherry-picking data:

---

[56] See Campbell (2014), pp. 204–16, 247–53 (2 Thess.), 283–304, 321–336 (Phil., Col., Eph.), 339–85 (Titus, 1, 2 Tim.).

[57] See Campbell (2014), pp. 220–9.

[58] As Robert Price put it to me, "It may be that the threat of Caligula prompted some at the time to nominate him as the 'Son of Perdition' just like Antiochus Epiphanes earlier, but when the danger passed, he had left his stamp on the Antichrist legend. It needn't have been front-page news when 2 Thessalonians mentioned it" (personal communication). Campbell admits that placing it in 40 AD is "a rather more tentative judgment" (p. 229).

[59] Dewey et al. (2010), p. 2.

identifying arbitrary similarities between certain letters, then declaring that anything that doesn't fit must have been written by another author. But given the size of our sample, it's possible we have just eliminated authentic letters that don't happen to contain what we assumed were authentic signatures. In other words, just because we think certain things *must* be in every piece of writing from Paul, and other things simply cannot, that doesn't mean we are correct. There are other equally plausible possibilities.

For example, if one letter contains sections that are more complex on average than similar sections in other letters, we can't know whether this is because Paul never wrote above a certain level of complexity (and thus the complex letters must be forgeries), or whether this too falls into Paul's possible range of expression. Again, for that we would need a truly representative sample by which to judge. It would be like taking a sample of your emails, and excluding several as 'inauthentic' because they are too complex and use bigger words than the rest. But one sample might be emails you sent to your boss, and the other emails you sent to your eight-year-old child. In other words, the differences *are* there, but *context* accounts for them.

The best method that exists today for identifying whether a text has multiple authors is to use complex statistical computer analysis, which didn't exist at the time most style analyses of Paul were conducted, and which even today is not 100% accurate. And the latest such studies show *no obvious and meaningful variation* among the letters attributed to Paul.[60] Commenting on the latest such studies, Campbell writes: "In basic statistical terms, there is currently no evidence that these [differences in style] exceed the parameters of a normal single sample, lying so far from the mean in terms of the sample's standard deviations that another author has to be posited."[61] In short, the latest studies do not confirm previous scholars' arguments from style, and are at best inconclusive. But since we can be fairly certain that there *are* interpolations, all that can be said is that statistical analyses of style won't be much use in confirming them, disconfirming them, or finding more of them. (This may change of course, as better studies are designed and carried out.)

The best evidence for forgery is anachronism, but even that can be tricky. For years, scholars have argued that Colossians is anachronistic because it contains 'Gnostic' elements that are assumed to have existed only beginning in the second century, a hundred years after Paul. But recent discoveries and research have made that view untenable. When Paul writes of the "worship of angels" and "what he has seen, by way of initiation" (Col. 2:18), these ideas are not necessarily later Gnostic ideas. The latest research in Second Temple Judaism provides a contemporary context, in which case these passages are better translated as "worship by/like angels" and "what he has seen by way of heavenly visions" – both ideas that fit just fine in the apocalyptic, Enochian Judaism that existed in Paul's time and which obviously influenced his thinking and that of the later Gnostics.

When it comes to the so-called Pastorals, however, Campbell finds good reason to consider them later forgeries. First, the frame of events suggested by the other ten letters fits together like a puzzle, but the Pastorals either *contradict* that frame or simply *don't fit* within it. This could be because they simply come some time after the other letters, but other problems make

---

[60] " the [statistical] plots for Romans and 1 Corinthians are as widely spread in Mealand's analyses as the plots for Ephesians, while only the sample drawn from the first half of Ephesians tends to be an outlier." (Campbell, 2014, p. 288)

[61] Campbell (2014), p. 292.

that unlikely. For example, Titus is the best candidate for forgery according to the computer analyses. First Timothy contains an obvious anachronism – it quotes the Gospel of Luke and speaks of Christian 'scripture' (which Paul never otherwise mentions, because it didn't exist during his time) – and two suggestive allusions that are probably anachronistic: allusions to Marcion. Plus, Paul implausibly makes reference to charges of Timothy being "inexperienced," but by the date implied by the letter, he would've been with Paul for over a decade, perhaps two. Second Timothy has even more implausibilities: for example, geographic references that don't make sense, a close overlap of names also included in Colossians, Paul talking himself up to Timothy (who would need no such reminders, being one of Paul's closest and long-time collaborators), implausible references to sufferings otherwise *only recounted in Acts*, and a grace wish addressed in the plural.

In sum, for Campbell ten letters fit plausibly into the same 'frame' or relative chronology without contradicting each other. The Pastorals don't, and they also contain anachronisms and implausibilities of a sort not found in the other ten letters. Suggestively, by using only the letters' internal evidence Campbell identifies a collection of letters that is *identical to the first known collection of Paul's letters*: that of Marcion. On top of that, as noted previously, the Pastorals appear to be anti-Marcionite in nature, so it appears as if their author composed them in order to claim Paul for himself and his community, and to distance Paul from the Marcionites long after Paul was dead and gone.

Based on his reconstructed frame, Campbell places the authentic letters of Paul in this chronological order: 1 Thessalonians, 2 Thessalonians, Laodiceans (known as Ephesians in our NT), Colossians, Philemon, 1 Corinthians, 2 Corinthians, Galatians, Philippians, Romans. Campbell also constructs a chronology of all the events Paul mentions about his life, which he anchors using the two references to datable people mentioned above: King Aretas IV (late 36 AD) and Emperor Gaius (40 AD). The following is Campbell's Pauline timeline:

- Early/mid-34: Paul's apostolic commission or 'calling,' near Damascus

- Early 34—mid-36: Activity in Damascus and Arabia

- Late 36: Escape from Damascus; first visit to Jerusalem to meet the 'pillars' of the church (2.x years after commission)[62]

- 37–42: Activity in Syria and Cilicia; missions to Macedonia and Achaia; **1&2 Thess. written**

- Ca. 43–49: Missions to Illyricum and Galatia; many sufferings

- Late 49/early 50: The 'Antioch incident'; second visit to Jerusalem 13.x years after first visit[63]

- Mid-50: Mission to Asia; imprisonment (possibly in Apamea); **Laod., Col., Phlm. written**; founding visit to Ephesus

- Spring 51: **1 Cor. written**; 'super-apostles' visit Corinth; the 'Asian crisis'; departure from Ephesus to Macedonia

- Ca. summer 51: Travels through Macedonia; **2 Cor. written**; visit to Corinth

---

[62]Ancient sources counted years inclusively, so when Paul gives a figure of 3 years, the actual amount of time could be anywhere between 2 and a fraction and 3.

[63]See previous footnote.

- Fall 51—winter 51–52: Enemies arrive at Corinth; **Gal. written**; imprisonment and capital trial; **Phil. written**; release from prison
- Spring 52: **Rom. written**; departure (for Jerusalem)

I will propose my own chronology further on, which differs significantly from Campbell's attempt. For the moment, note that Campbell's arguments dealing with authenticity and relative chronology are meticulous, acute, and deserve a careful reading, but there are two major weaknesses. First, he is very conservative (or 'maximalist') in his use of the material in the letters: if something can't be *definitively* shown to be interpolated, he takes it to be authentic. Thus he constructs his chronology on the assumption that the letters as we have them are essentially as they were when they were written – no major interpolations and no stitching together of shorter letters to create longer ones. At the very least, by doing so he is able to show that a coherent chronology can be constructed based on the clues in those ten letters. Whether it's *true* or not is another question.

The second major weakness leaves his chronological *sequence* intact, but affects where it is 'anchored' to known history. It is his use of Josephus as his historical source and yardstick regarding King Aretas IV, which he uses to establish his second chronological hook in 36 AD. And, in fact, it was his attempt to do this that led me to do a very long study of Josephus and all related issues. I spent a considerable amount of time examining the Aretas problem and came to the conclusion that there is no way to firmly establish the date of Paul's escape from Damascus using Aretas; *we cannot firmly fix the date based on Josephus or any other text.* Paul's 'basket case' could have happened at any time between 9 BC and 40 AD, the period of the rule of Aretas. That realization unpegs Paul from a definite time window *à la* Campbell, but that is all; it doesn't tell us anything definite in a positive way. Along the way, however, I did find another, even better historical anchor that, as far as I can see, firmly places Paul's conversion in 29 AD, a rather significant date, which I will argue later.

According to the Gospels, Jesus allegedly started his career around *29 AD* (in the fifteenth year of Tiberius, according to the Gospel of Luke). The date of his alleged crucifixion is disputed: anywhere between 29 and 33 AD depending on whether his activities extended over one year or three. So if Paul began his career before or during these years, it would create a serious problem for the accepted 'Jesus timeline.' Paul would have been 'converted to Jesus' before Jesus' death! Even by Campbell's fairly standard date of Paul's commission – 34 AD – there's barely time for Jesus to be cold in his grave (or not!) and for any kind of messianic movement to form around him, much less for Paul to be persecuting said movement (assuming that he actually did in some concrete manner[64]). It's not impossible, but if the standard chronology isn't true, then our ideas about the historical processes taking place in these years may be giving us a very distorted

---

[64]Paul himself only says in 1 Cor. 15:9: "For I am the least of the apostles and do not even deserve to be called an apostle, because I persecuted the church of God." This "persecution" could mean many things. It is expanded a bit in Galatians 1:13 to: "I was excessively persecuting the church of God and was trying to destroy it," and novelized in Acts 8:3 with "But Saul began to destroy the church. Going from house to house, he dragged off both men and women and put them in prison." It is unlikely that Paul was in any position to drag people off to prison. However, given his associated claim to have been a devout Pharisee, zealous for the law, this may have been the matter of contention: Paul was criticizing and vocally condemning groups of Gentile Christians (he was, after all, addressing such in his letters), who wished to follow a modified form of Judaism which excluded the dietary laws and circumcision. This would also tie in closely with Paul's call and commission, in which his life took a 180-degree turn away from zealotry for the law to his law-free gospel. Furthermore, it also makes

picture of what actually happened. If the crucifixion as such did *not* happen, or if it happened *much earlier*, it forces us to rethink this pivotal period of Christian history.

There is another problem that is more perplexing: the timing of the governorship of Pontius Pilate, which is used to date Jesus. I will argue below that this was much *earlier* than tradition holds and that the tradition of placing Pilate in the *later* time period was fabricated and texts manipulated to support it. Placing Pilate earlier in time opens up the possibility that Paul's timeline – including his adventure in Damascus – could have happened earlier as well. An earlier date for Pilate – and thus a possible Jesus *character* too – means there is time for the development of a following of some sort, time for Paul to persecute that following (in some way, assuming he did), and time for Paul to have his conversion and commission experience, evangelize widely, write 2 Thessalonians during the reign of Caligula, and more. Further, I will suggest a new chronology for Paul that opens up some suggestive possibilities: that the career of Jesus as presented in the Gospels was largely inspired by the career of Paul (among many other influences), and that the passage in the historian Suetonius' work about Jews rioting in Rome under the influence of some 'Chrestus' *may be the earliest, authentic historical reference related to the activities of Paul.*[65]

Re-dating the governorship of Pontius Pilate has multiple and far-reaching ramifications for all of early Christian 'history.' It also frees Paul from the entanglements of the Gospels' 'Jesus of Nazareth,' whom Paul had clearly never heard of,[66] and allows us to explore possibilities for Paul – based on his own words – that no one has ever explored before, as far as I know.

---

sense of the ongoing conflict between Paul and the Jerusalem group over the requirements of circumcision and table fellowship. And all of this is assuming that the two passages in Paul's letters are not interpolations.

[65] In *Claudius* 25, Suetonius refers to the expulsion of Jews by Claudius and states: "Since the Jews constantly made disturbances at the instigation of Chrestus, he expelled them from Rome." *Lives of the Caesars* (trans. Catharine Edwards, Oxford University Press, 2001), pp. 184, 203.

[66] See Earl Doherty's excellent analysis of all the alleged references to the Gospels' 'Jesus of Nazareth' in the early Christian epistles: *The Sound of Silence*: http://www.jesuspuzzle.com/jesuspuzzle/siltop20.htm.

1. The Long, Dark Tunnel of Early Christianity

Paul's writings – those that have survived, even if heavily modified – give us the earliest and most certain window into the world of early Christianity. These letters give an overwhelming impression of a very mystical and esoteric faith and teachings about a character (human? Divine? Some of both?) named Jesus.

Well, in fact we don't really know for sure that Paul even referred to his Christ as 'Jesus.' For all we know, that could have been an editorial insertion to harmonize with later tradition. Nevertheless, Paul's Christ, as we have him in Paul's letters, appears to be independent of any particular historical personage. Again, that could be an artifact of editorial manipulation, or Paul's intention. With the state of the texts today, it's hard to say for certain. At the very least, 'Jesus' appears to be a heavenly name given to Christ upon his ascension, as we will see. The bottom line is that – regardless of these speculations – Paul's gospel is a real problem for the assertion that there was a historical Jesus *of Nazareth*.

Here it is important to keep in mind the basic premise of Judeo-Christianity: Judaism was distinguished from other religions by its claim that all history was God working out the salvation of his chosen People.[67] Gerd Theissen writes that in order to understand primitive Christianity, we have to start with Judaism:

> The grammar of the Jewish religion is a starting point. In it we find two basic axioms. On the one hand there is a negative rule of association: the one and only God may not be associated with other gods – all that goes with them is an abomination to him. On the other hand we find a positive rule of association: God is uniquely associated with his people in that he made a covenant with it and gave it the Torah in order to maintain this covenant. In abstract terms, monotheism and covenantal nomism are the two basic axioms of Judaism. ...
>
> In primitive Christianity, instead of the two Jewish basic axioms of monotheism and covenantal nomism, we find the two basic axioms of monotheism and belief in a redeemer – and here monotheism has been modified by belief in a redeemer and covenantal nomism has been extended to all human beings by belief in a universal redeemer.[68]

But Christianity actually did a lot more than that. On the one side of a great divide, nearly all religions of the time expressed themselves via ritual sacrifice of living beings. On the other side, the traditional ritual bloody sacrifices were replaced by new bloodless rites. This meant that, for Jewish Christians, the Temple lost its holiness. Primitive Christianity left behind temple, animal sacrifices, and priests, but at the same time, maintained an interpretation of their main symbol of a type of sacrifice that was already obsolete at the time: human sacrifice.

Additionally, at a certain point, Christianity, like Judaism and its tenet that the Jewish God was working out the salvation of the Jews in history, claimed that the crucial events of its origin

---

[67]In early times, the god of Israel was merely a tribal god like all other gods of the time. Only later did the Jews declare that their god was actually the creator god of the entire universe and all other gods were not really gods.

[68]Theissen (1999), p. 5.

also played out at a definite time and place in history and not in some mythical time and/or place. The Gospels and Acts are supposed to be History, with a capital H, but what they actually reveal is that some group of early Christians were urgently interested in the events from which their faith derived, and their interest does not appear to have been primarily theological.[69]

However, among the believers in the Pauline churches there appears to have been no interest at all in a life of Jesus of Nazareth.

So, the question is: how does one go from no interest in a human Jesus to the Gospel of Mark where an allegedly human Jesus is described in a quasi-historical setting, which Gospel could better be described as a highly ritualized Hellenic rhetorical structure of truly staggering literary complexity?

This brings us to consider another aspect of Paul's writings. In two of his epistles, Paul is struggling to combat the influence of opponents whom he describes as preaching "another Jesus" and "a different gospel."[70] These opponents were never named, or, if they were, the names have been excised. What is concerning is that these individuals apparently had the eminence and authority to invade Paul's mission field and challenge his authority. What seems to be apparent is that, including Paul's version, there were at least two distinct, mutually hostile gospels, i.e. interpretations of the person, nature and work of the said Jesus or, if that name was not yet used, the Christ/Messiah.

This seems to be a rather serious problem. Christianity, as we have it today, follows generally the theology of Paul attached to a Jesus of Nazareth we now know did not exist as depicted – for Paul, at least. It also appears from numerous studies that this pseudo-historical Jesus was created using Paul's teaching channeled from his Jesus and, on minor matters, from himself; and numerous literary models – a veritable smorgasbord of divine-men options and set scenes.

So, the point comes down to this: if all (or most) Christians since the Gospels were written have been inspired to faith in what Paul would have called a Satanic delusion, what effect might this have on their salvation? What effect might it have on their lives? On the world at large? I've read studies that show the damage done to the brain by believing lies and, as we all know, lies create chaos. If either or both of those are facts of our reality, and if structured information is the stuff of which our reality is made, what effect might mass belief in a lie elicit from, or impose on, our world? From my perspective, the stakes are not negligible. To borrow an obvious truism that made it into the NT, the tree is known by its fruit.

How do we find out the truth?

Several of Paul's letters agree in the representation of the control of the Christian movement having been centered at Jerusalem. Paul mentions three men as 'pillars' of the church: James, Cephas and John. (Twice in Paul's epistles, a Peter is named, but those may very well be interpolations or scribal errors.)[71] James is clearly the leader and is even distinguished from the others as 'brother of the Lord.'[72]

This set-up does not correspond with the Gospel stories at all. James is attested in the mostly fictional Acts, but in an embarrassed way. (Acts, too, uses bits from Paul's letters, Josephus, and

---

[69]S. G. F. Brandon, *The Fall of Jerusalem and the Christian Church* (Wipf and Stock, 2010), p. 2.
[70]2 Cor. 11:4; Gal. 1:6-9.
[71]Gal. 2:7, 8.
[72]Gal. 2:9. Though see footnote 20 in the Introduction.

other literature of the time to create its absurd fiction of the early Christians and most especially its highly distorted account of Paul's life and mission.)

In the Gospels, the siblings of Jesus are presented as hostile at worst, unsympathetic at best, to his mission. Peter, James and John do get a lot of action in the Gospels, but Mark, the first Gospel, presents them as un-redeemed dolts and betrayers. Matthew rehabilitates the disciples and gives Peter the starring role, not James, and Luke, later, tries to reconcile Mark and Matthew.

If the Gospel stories were true, we would have a big problem explaining how Peter was usurped by James by the time Paul came along to refer to them in his epistles. And this is not a small problem: it's a question of fact versus fiction. As noted, Mark appears to write them all off, which is at least in keeping with Paul's view that they were false apostles and he wished they would castrate themselves.[73] Matthew, Luke and Acts present a very different, idealized and mythical view.

From Paul's letters we learn that he had communities at Corinth (1 and 2 Cor.); Cenchreae (Rom. 16); Galatia (Gal. 1:8); Ephesus (1 Cor. 16:8-9); Philippi (Phil. 1:1-7); Colossae (Col. 1:1-8); Laodicea (Col. 2:1); Hierapolis (Col. 4:13); and Thessalonica (1 and 2 Thess.). The Epistle to the Romans attests to the existence of a notable Christian community in Rome, or even two, one Gentile and one Jewish, though I'll come to that further on.

The book of Acts depicts the Paul–Jerusalem conflict as amicably settled by Paul taking a collection of funds for the church from his Gentile Christians, making a third visit there, and all was just hunky dory except for some Jews wanting to kill Paul, his arrest for causing a tumult, and his eventual transfer to Rome from Jerusalem because, of course, Paul was a Roman citizen, doncha know?! All of this will come into serious question, showing that it could not possibly have been that way at all, though I won't say that the Jerusalem Christians didn't want to kill Paul. For all we know, they succeeded. But, we'll get there. The Acts fairy tale is completely contradicted by the evidence of the epistles, edited and redacted though they may be. (It seems the redaction specialists didn't get to them before they were well enough known to make some deletions and/or additions impossible. There is also the factor of 'scribal fatigue.' Working on lengthy texts that were usually in rolls, by hand, was a tedious and mind-numbing process at best.)

In nearly all of the epistles there are rumblings, allusions, or outright polemic against the Jewish teachers who demanded that Christians should be circumcised Jews first, Messianists second. In only one place does Paul refer to the alleged amicable settlement of the Jerusalem Council which supposedly took place on his second visit there, 17 years after his visionary conversion, and that short passage is, possibly, an interpolation. The fact is, not only do the extant writings of Paul give us no indication that an amicable agreement was reached (or at least honored), the very logic of Paul's emphasis on the absolute saving power of faith in Jesus Christ confirms that the charges put into the mouth of Jerusalem Christians against him were true.[74]

After the Epistle to the Romans, we hear nothing more of Paul. The author of Acts doesn't even appear to know what happened to him; the tradition of his martyrdom is much too late to be accepted as factual. And then, the puzzling lacuna in the history of early Christianity: the period immediately before, during and after the Jewish War, out of which emerged the Gospel of

---

[73]Gal. 5:12.

[74]E.g. Acts 21:21: "They have been informed that you [Paul] teach all the Jews who live among the Gentiles to turn away from Moses, telling them not to circumcise their children or live according to our customs."

Mark, which apparently floated around without much comment, though Matthew certainly used it and intended to replace it. Then, Marcion appeared with a collection of Paul's letters and a Gospel – the first New Testament.

Paul's letters are an astonishing mess – there is just no other way to put it. Second Corinthians is an almost unintelligible mosaic of fragments and many scholars think that Romans 16 is a separate letter in its own right. Further on, I will argue that Romans itself is a patchwork of at least 4 letters with some sizeable interpolated additions. Some letters of Paul referenced in the extant texts appear to be missing entirely, while the short, personal, Philemon has survived.

This deplorable state of the Pauline corpus is not consistent with Acts' presentation of the triumphant apostle to the Gentiles. It certainly does not suggest that Paul's letters were treasured mementoes of a beloved teacher except, perhaps, among certain groups. What it does suggest is that Paul's reputation was severely damaged by his opponents and, as a consequence, his letters were left to rot until, following a period of oblivion, his work was once again valued and a search was made for his writings resulting only in the poor collection we have today. And so, as S. G. F. Brandon writes:

> [W]e find ourselves ... faced with two further problems of great pertinence to a proper understanding of Christian Origins, namely those of the cause and the nature of Paul's apparent loss of reputation and his subsequent rehabilitation.[75]

Brandon points out that Paul's letters clearly attest that the 'Church' at Jerusalem was the 'mother Church,' even if Paul was completely at odds with it. Thus, it is astonishing that except for a few minor writings of almost no importance and doubtful authorship – i.e. the epistles of Peter, James, Jude and John – no important works by the leaders of this church have survived. Surely they wrote letters as Paul did, regarding matters of faith and practice? Copies of such letters should have circulated widely and should have been as likely to survive as Paul's letters – possibly more so!

So, what explains the loss of all literary documents representing and conveying the traditions and authority from the fount of Christian faith? One cannot fall back on the Gospel tale of a band of itinerant preachers who were illiterate and thus all was 'oral tradition' until some early Christian who could read and write came along. That tale is completely contradicted by the evidence. As already noted, there are enough convincing detailed studies showing how the Gospels were written and what literary sources were used – including the rehabilitated Pauline epistles – to put a complete stop to such absurd explanations.

So again, why did the writings of the obviously organized and functioning Jerusalem church NOT survive when the tattered collection of Paul's writings – Paul, who was deeply opposed to that organization – did just barely make it through the Dark Age of early Christianity? And meanwhile, the kind of Christianity we find when we encounter Tertullian is Matthean Christianity, a very different animal from Pauline Christianity even if some amalgamation has taken place thanks to the Markan bridge.

This brings us to the topic of the destruction of Jerusalem in 70 AD and the near-complete silence about this event in the Christian documents both canonical and extra-canonical. The almost studied failure of the Christian writers to exhibit any interest whatsoever in this culture-shattering event is mind-boggling; it screams 'embarrassment'! Brandon writes:

---

[75]Brandon (2010), p. 9.

But far more amazing is the fact that, except for the few remarks of Hegesippus in the second century, Christian literature contains no record of the fate of its Mother Church in this calamity. The original Jewish Church is suffered to pass away into complete oblivion until its pathetic remnants [Ebionites?] are noted with orthodox scorn some three centuries later by Epiphanius and Jerome. Thus when we recall that the Gospels and the Acts were probably all written after A.D. 70 and that they are all essentially concerned with a period of Palestinian history just anterior to the war with Rome, this silence about the catastrophe of the Jewish nation and its consequences is seen also to constitute a problem of very considerable significance for our understanding of the nature of Christianity in the first century.[76]

We note what Brandon calls the long dark tunnel: at one end we have Paul and his data about 'what was really happening'; at the other there is Mark, then a bit later, there is Matthew who is obviously antagonistic toward both Mark and Paul; then, there is Marcion and a scanty Pauline letter collection; then, and not long after, full-bore Luke-Acts with bells and whistles.

So we see that the Dark Age of early Christian history coincides with the final lead-up to the Jewish War, the War itself, and some period of aftermath. As Brandon says, we have an *a priori* case for attributing this darkness to the cataclysmic end to Jewish life as it had been known up to that time, and the concomitant near extinction of early Christianity as well.

In order to understand why the original form of Christianity emanating from Jerusalem was suppressed and replaced with a bastardized form of Pauline Christianity, it is necessary to discuss several important matters pertaining to the history of the Jews in Judea, starting with certain seminal events and moving forward until we meet Mark and his Gospel masterpiece.

Before we get started, however, let's dispense with the idea that we are even looking for someone named 'Jesus.' That said, there is that interesting passage in Philippians as follows:

> Let the same mind be in you that was in Christ Jesus, who, though he was in the form of God, did not regard equality with God as something to be exploited, but emptied himself, taking the form of a slave, being born in human likeness. And being found in human form, he humbled himself and became obedient to the point of death – *even death on a cross.* Therefore God also highly exalted him and *gave him the name that is above every name*, so that at the name of Jesus every knee should bend, in heaven and on earth and under the earth, and every tongue should confess that Jesus Christ is Lord, to the glory of God the Father.[77]

This is not the place to be diverted into a long discussion of the passage. I will only note here two things: 1) there is an allusion in the above to Christ being the 'Second Adam' – made 'in the form of God' – only he was one who did not seek to become equal with God as Adam did when he sinned by eating the fruit of the Tree of Knowledge; 2) the name 'Jesus,' which means 'savior,' was apparently given to him only *after* death.[78] That is, whatever his name was, as a

---

[76]Brandon (2010), p. 10.

[77]Phil. 2:5-11. Allusions are to Isaiah 52:13-15: "See, my servant shall prosper; he shall be exalted and lifted up, and shall be very high. Just as there were many who were astonished at him—so marred was his appearance, beyond human semblance, and his form beyond that of mortals—so he shall startle many nations; kings shall shut their mouths because of him; for that which had not been told them they shall see, and that which they had not heard they shall contemplate." And Isaiah 45:23: "By myself I have sworn, from my mouth has gone forth in righteousness a word that shall not return: 'To me every knee shall bow, every tongue shall swear.'"

[78]See P. L. Couchoud, *The Creation of Christ* (Watts & Co, London, 1939), for a discussion of how the name 'Jesus' came to be chosen as the 'secret name' of the messiah/son of man of the apocalypse of Enoch.

historical human, we do not know, and Mark must simply have taken this passage as evidence for the name of his Gospel character – thus was 'born' Jesus of Nazareth.

Two Christs

Brandon points out that the most certain thing we know about Jesus is that he was crucified as a rebel on the order of Pontius Pilate. But is that assertion even true? As we will see further on, it does appear to be true that a Jewish rebel of great significance was executed by Pontius Pilate, but his name was not 'Jesus.' The execution of this rebel was mentioned by Tacitus in his discussion of the great fire at Rome in 64 AD. Tacitus gave no name, only the title 'Christus,' as can be seen below:

> Nero fastened the guilt and inflicted the most exquisite tortures on a class hated for their abominations, called Christians by the populace. Christus, from whom the name had its origin, suffered the extreme penalty during the reign of Tiberius at the hands of one of our procurators, Pontius Pilatus, and a most mischievous superstition, thus checked for the moment, again broke out not only in Judea, the first source of the evil, but even in Rome, where all things hideous and shameful from every part of the world find their center and become popular. Accordingly, an arrest was first made of all who pleaded guilty; then, upon their information, an immense multitude was convicted, not so much of the crime of firing the city, as of hatred against mankind.[79]

We can note that Tacitus appears to have been only generally informed on the topic and did not know the actual name of Christus. The most important element in the above passage is that obviously, the "multitude" of Christians in Rome at the time were Jewish. Tacitus (*Hist.* 5.4) and other Romans had claimed before (and later) that the Jews were "haters of humanity" for the very reasons that Paul sought to do away with the Jewish Law. Circumcision was seen by Greco-Romans as an abomination, and it is likely that the "mischievous superstition" was the belief that the Messiah was going to come to destroy Rome and restore Israel's sovereignty. In short, the largest number of Christians at Rome in 64 AD were apparently *not* Pauline Christians. This fact is extremely important and we will come back to it, as well as the issue of Pilate, later on.

So far, we know that some historical individual called 'Christ' by the Jews was executed by Pontius Pilate; what we do not know is anything from Paul about him as a human. We do not know for a certainty that Paul's Jesus was executed as a rebel; in fact, the brief way he describes the impending death of his Christ leaves serious questions as to the manner of his actual death: "For I received from the Lord what I also passed on to you, that the Lord Jesus on the night when he was delivered up took a loaf of bread" (1 Cor. 11:23). The sense of the Greek translated as "delivered up" can mean 'delivered himself up,' more or less. That is, a volitional death. For example, in 1 Cor.13:3 Paul speaks of "delivering up" his own body and in Gal. 2:20 of Christ "delivering himself" for Paul.

In his most explicit statements about the death of 'Jesus,' Paul attributes it to the demonic powers that rule the lower 'heaven.'

---

[79]Tacitus, *Ann.* 15.44.

> Yet among the mature we do speak wisdom, though it is not a wisdom of this age or of the rulers of this age, who are doomed to perish. But we speak God's wisdom, secret and hidden, which God decreed before the ages for our glory. None of the rulers of this age understood this; for if they had, they would not have *crucified* the Lord of glory.[80]

Just to be clear what these "rulers of this age" are:

> For our struggle is not against enemies of blood and flesh, but against the rulers, against the authorities, against the cosmic powers of this present darkness, against the spiritual forces of evil in the heavenly places.[81]

It is apparent that Paul regarded his 'Jesus' as a divine being who incarnated as a human, with the plan that he would die in a sacrificial way and thereby save all of mankind from enslavement to demonic powers that were "rulers of the age." Paul was entirely uninterested in any idea of a messiah who was merely the savior of Israel. Brandon notes:

> That so transcendental a conception of Jesus, integrated into an esoteric soteriology unparalleled in contemporary Jewish thought, should have developed within some two decades of his crucifixion by the Romans, constitutes one of the fundamental problems of the study of Christian Origins.[82]

Well, certainly the building blocks of the idea already existed in Paul's milieu, as Richard Carrier has efficiently demonstrated.[83] There were ubiquitous dying/rising gods and apocalyptic visions of the different levels of heaven and so forth that we know about from the literature that has survived; how much more might there have been in literature that was not preserved? But Paul certainly did put it all together in a unique way. From the beginning, Paul presented Jesus to the Gentiles as a divine being whose true role transcended the Jews and historical circumstances of any earthly life.

But, as we also know from Paul, he was engaged in a struggle with the Jerusalem Christians, the Mother Church, who insisted that to be a member of their party, one had to become a Jew first with all the attendant requirements of the Jewish Law. It seems clear that Paul's interpretation of Jesus was sharply distinguished by him from the interpretation – and from the character – held by the Jewish Christians who were, essentially, the 'original Christians' following a Jewish messiah in Jerusalem; a church and its followers that disappeared almost completely after the destruction of the city in 70 AD.

A later legend claims that the Christians of Jerusalem escaped to Pella, but a critical analysis of this tradition reveals it to be little more than a pious fraud.[84] What is certain is that this church all but ceased to exist after 70 AD. Had it actually migrated, it would have continued to impose its sovereignty on Christianity.

Before the Jewish Christians of Jerusalem were obliterated in 66–73 AD, the Mother Church at Jerusalem was the unchallenged source of faith and authority. However, it appears that a few survivors in Palestine (not necessarily from Jerusalem) may have been the founders of the

---

[80]1 Cor. 2:6-8.
[81]Eph. 6:12.
[82]S. G. F. Brandon, *Jesus and the Zealots* (Charles Scribner's Sons, 1967), p. 12
[83]Carrier (2014).
[84]Cf. Brandon (2010), pp. 168–73; 176–7; 264.

Ebionites. They continued to maintain the faith of James and Peter and violently repudiated Paul.[85] The beliefs of the Ebionites, as far as can be determined, were wholly adoptionist. The Baptism and Resurrection are what determined and established the role and status of Jesus, not who he was from birth. His death had no soteriological significance. I think we can assume provisionally that this was the view of the Jerusalem church, more or less, about their messiah.

As a consequence of the destruction of Jerusalem and the resulting rise of anti-Semitic feeling throughout the Empire, the Gospel of Paul was apparently then seen as more correct, and the messiah of the Jews was metamorphosed into the divine savior of all mankind, despite the fact that Paul insisted that his Jesus was *not* the same as the Jesus of the Jerusalem church!

Early Christian Archaeology

There is another problem that I want to bring up, though I don't have any well-formulated thoughts about it as yet; it still needs to be put on the table. In G. F. Snyder's *Ante Pacem: Archaeological evidence of Church Life before Constantine*, we find some very curious evidence regarding what early Christians were actually doing:

> Jesus does not suffer or die in pre-Constantinian art. There is no cross symbol nor any equivalent. ... From 180 to 400 AD artistic analogies of self-giving, suffering, sacrifice, or incarnation are totally missing. The suffering Christ on a cross first appeared in the fifth century, and then not very convincingly.[86]

Jonathan Z. Smith writes:

> With respect to the limited corpus of early Christian symbols – the lamb, the anchor, the vase, the dove, the boat, the olive branch, the Orante,[87] the palm, the bread, the good shepherd, fish and vines and grapes – Snyder argues: "Among all the symbols ... none signifies suffering, death, or self-immolation. All stress victory, peace, and security in the face of adversity. The Jesus iconography follows the same patterns. There is no place in the third century for a crucified Christ, or a symbol of divine death."[88]

The iconography of Jesus depicts him as mainly a youthful wonder-worker and healer. Even in the case of the popular scene of Lazarus being raised from the dead:

---

[85] Hans-Joachim Schoeps, *Jewish Christianity: Factional Disputes in the Early Church* (Fortress Press, 1969).

[86] G. F. Snyder, *Ante Pacem: Archaeological Evidence of Church Life Before Constantine* (Mercer, 1985), pp. 65, 156.

[87] "*Orans*, a loanword from Medieval Latin ōrāns translated as one who is praying or pleading, also orant or orante, is a posture or bodily attitude of prayer, usually standing, with the elbows close to the sides of the body and with the hands outstretched sideways, palms up. ... The orans posture was practiced by both pagans and Jews before it was adopted by the earliest Christians. Christians may have seen the position as representing the posture of Christ on the Cross; therefore, it was the favorite of early Christians. Until the ninth century, the posture was sometimes adopted by entire congregations while celebrating the Eucharist. ... [It is thought that the Orans represented the deceased person's soul in heaven praying for those loved ones left on Earth.] ... [T]he great majority of figures are female even when engraved on the tombs of men. One of the most convincing proofs that the orans was regarded as a symbol of the soul is an ancient lead medal in the Vatican Museum showing the martyr, St. Lawrence, under torture, while his soul, in the form of a female orans, is just leaving the body." (Wikipedia.org, 'Orans.')

[88] Snyder (1985), pp. 14–26; cited by Jonathan Z. Smith, *Drudgery Divine: On the Comparison of Early Christianities and the Religions of Late Antiquity* (University of Chicago Press, 1994), p. 130.

It depicts the present reality of resurrection rather than belief in another world. ... [The early Christians] ate with the dead, talked to the dead, asked for their assistance. ... The resurrection motif supports neither a view of otherworldly immortality nor a view of end-time judgment and resurrection. The presence of the dead [within the community] was made possible through the redeeming act of the wonder-worker, Jesus. Those resurrected dead then were part of the extended Christian family.[89]

In short, what the archaeology shows is that one of the central cultic activities of the earliest Christians was a communal meal with the dead, a meal that did not recall the sacrifice of Jesus Christ. The cemetery was one of the two centers of activity. In this context, recall that Paul's most extensive discussions of resurrection of the dead – 1 Thess and 1 Cor – are both triggered by questions concerning the status of dead members.[90]

Early Christian graffiti in cemeteries concerns prayers addressed to the dead on behalf of the living. The meal, the *refrigerium*, was eaten in honor of the birthday or death day of the deceased person. The service included anointing of the headstone, antiphonal singing,[91] and dancing; wine was poured into a depression that allowed it to enter the tomb to be consumed by the dead person.

There is no sign of a more sophisticated (!) immortality, nor does resurrection, at least as revivification or resuscitation play any role.[92]

The dead remain dead, in a sphere other than the living; but there is contact, there is continuity of relationship, there is memorialization, there is presence. ... Above all ... a sense of confidence.[93]

So, that's pretty much it in a nutshell, though Snyder has an entire book with cited evidence and photographs of artifacts. Material remains are hard to shove under the rug and it really boggles the mind to try to figure out what was really going on with these groups. I have no idea what it means when taken in the context of early Patristic writings. Is it possible that there was a small coterie of Christians who were involved in the Christianity that was written about, while the large majority of followers engaged in activities that in no way reflected what that educated minority was thinking and writing? That seems difficult to conceive of, but if we look at how things are in our own day, we know that intellectual elites write and talk about many things that are of no interest to the average man on the street. Even today, many Christians (or members of other religions) go to their places of worship, perform the rituals, sing the songs, and then go home with no idea of the raging controversies in biblical studies that may actually question everything they are thinking (or not thinking) and doing in the performance of their religion. Could it be that the archaeological signs of early Christianity were something like that? Was the transition to Christianity as we know it later than we suspect? Did it take longer than we imagine?

I just don't know. It's a curious data point, but it's on the table and should be kept in mind.

[89]Snyder (1985), p. 61.
[90]Smith (1994), p. 131.
[91]"Socrates of Constantinople wrote that antiphony was introduced into Christian worship by Ignatius of Antioch (died 107) after he saw a vision of two choirs of angels. Antiphonal singing was an element of Jewish liturgy believed to have entered the monasteries of Syria and Palestine in the 4th century from the Jewish communities such as the one in Antioch." (Wikipedia.org, 'Antiphon.')
[92]Snyder (1985), p. 167.
[93]Smith (1994), p. 132.

Historical Methods

Before I get started on actually dealing with ancient texts, many of which I will quote *in extenso* for the convenience of the reader to have everything in view, I want to bring forward some essential background. This is by no means an exhaustive version of matters, but I have tried to get enough material together so that the individual who knows almost nothing about the topics will be well-enough informed to be able to make assessments on their own.

For the most part, and for a long time, biblical studies have not followed scientific historical methods, which are the techniques and guidelines that historians use to research and write histories. There are some exceptions, but generally, the mavericks are flamed and defamed by the entrenched arbiters of faith-based history.

One of the primary considerations of historical research is what is called 'source criticism,' which is to evaluate the qualities of an information source such as its validity and reliability.

> Gilbert J. Garraghan and Jean Delanglez divide source criticism into six inquiries:
>
> 1. When was the source, written or unwritten, produced (date)? 2. Where was it produced (localization)? 3. By whom was it produced (authorship)? 4. From what pre-existing material was it produced (analysis)? 5. In what original form was it produced (integrity)? 6. What is the evidential value of its contents (credibility)?
>
> The first four are known as higher criticism; the fifth, lower criticism; and, together, external criticism. The sixth and final inquiry about a source is called internal criticism. Together, this inquiry is known as source criticism.[94]

As you can probably figure out, the main goal of historical criticism is to discover the text's primitive or original meaning in its original historical context and its literal sense. The secondary goal is to establish a reconstruction of the historical situation of the author and recipients of the text. That may be accomplished by reconstructing the true nature of the events that the text describes.

When dealing with ancient texts, there are fairly standard and accepted ways of dating them. As Richard Pervo points out, the most secure external way to do this is to find an explicit declaration by or within a datable author or text that such and such a document exists. For example, in the case of the book of Acts, that evidence is provided by Irenaeus of Lyon, c. 180 AD. He cited Acts as an authoritative book. Therefore, on firm historical grounds, that should be considered the *terminus ad quem* – the latest possible date of composition. It says nothing about when the book was actually written; it could have been very recent or a long time ago. But it certainly existed in 180 AD. If you are looking for evidence *within* a document, you look for some datable piece of information within the text, and try to make sure it is integral to the text and not a later addition. The *earliest* possible date – the *terminus a quo* – can't be earlier than the *latest* datable reference in the text. For example, this book couldn't be dated earlier than 2020, because it makes references to works and events from that year.

However, that's not how biblical scholars who are also Bible believers generally operate as a tribe. They push the *terminus ad quem* back as far as the earliest possible *conjectured allusions* to the work in question which suggest that an author *may* have been familiar with it. But such

---

[94]Wikipedia.org, 'Historical method,' citing Gilbert J. Garraghan and Jean Delanglez, *A Guide to Historical Method* (Fordham University Press, 1946).

references may or may not be actual allusions. It's just as possible that the work in need of dating *took* that material *from* the earlier source. For example, in the case of Acts, the earliest possible allusion is supposedly found in the letter of Polycarp of Smyrna, c. 130–135 AD. The *real question* is whether Acts used Polycarp, or Polycarp used Acts. There's evidence that suggests Polycarp may have been the author of Acts, as has already been mentioned. Even if that is true, he could have written it either before or after his letter; the thoughts he put into the letter may have also been put into Acts before or after.

Pervo states what the principles behind such a dating operation should be:

> 1. an explicit, methodologically sophisticated intertextual [the relationship between texts] method,
> 2. economy, which privileges proposals that require fewer hypothetical sources, and 3. simplicity, where solutions that solve more problems than they create are preferable.[95]

More often than not, that's not how it works in biblical studies. NT scholars seem to make the rules up as needed, creatively, in pursuing allusions to the Gospels in Paul where there are none, and all because they desperately need the Gospel Jesus to have existed *before* Paul. When evidence contradicts a theory, science requires the discarding of the theory. Time and again, biblical scholars have been shown to discard or twist the evidence so as to preserve their pre-conceived assumptions or confessional bias.

Regarding Josephus and the author of Luke-Acts, Pervo shows definitively (in my opinion) that Acts used Josephus as a source of inspiration. He notes:

> One must decide either that Luke had access to another Jewish historian who nonetheless shared the biases and views of Josephus or deem it highly probable that Luke had access to at least some of his writings. The question does not involve certain cribbed phrases but a *range of shared incidents, views, interests, and techniques.* Again, Luke does not use Josephus as we would. One of the difficulties of this hypothesis is that it removes from the board one author often utilized in comparisons with Luke, since, if Josephus served as one source and a model, he can no longer constitute a parallel.[96]

In other words, you can't declare that Luke-Acts is true because Josephus confirms some aspect of it, because the author *used Josephus* as one of his inspirational sources. Biblical scholars, as a rule, appear to be woefully uneducated in terms of ancient practices and methods of mimesis. It's as if they assume automatically that because this or that author claimed to be inspired by Jesus of Nazareth, he was therefore a 'good Christian' and could not possibly invent, falsify, or lie outright. The truth appears to be quite different. The following table shows an example of the use of literary mimesis in Acts based on the work of Dennis MacDonald[97]:

---

[95]Richard I. Pervo, 'Acts in Ephesus (and Environs) c. 115,' *Forum* Third Series 4:2 (2015), pp. 126–7.
[96]Pervo (2015), p. 127.
[97]Dennis Ronald MacDonald, *Does the New Testament Imitate Homer? Four Cases from the Acts of the Apostles* (New Haven: Yale University Press, 2003). See also: MacDonald, *The Homeric Epics and the Gospel of Mark* (New Haven: Yale University Press, 2000); and Bruce Louden, *Homer's* Odyssey *and the Near East* (New York: Cambridge University Press, 2011).

Odyssey 10–12	Acts 20:5-12
Odysseus and his crew left Troy and sailed back to Achaea.	Paul and his crew arrive at Troas en route to Jerusalem from Achaea.
The account is narrated in the first-person plural.	The account is narrated in the first-person plural.
After a sojourn, Odysseus and his crew ate a meal.	After a sojourn, Paul and the believers there ate a meal.
Disaster came at night.	Disaster came at midnight.
The crew slept in Circe's "darkened halls."	"There were many lamps in the room upstairs where they were meeting."
The narrator switches to the third person.	The narrator switches to the third person.
"There was a man, Elpenor, the youngest …"	"A young man named Eutychus, who was sitting in the window."
Elpenor fell into "sweet sleep."	Eutychus fell into a "deep sleep."
"[He] fell down from the roof. His neck / broke from the spine, and his soul went down to the house of Hades."	"He fell to the ground three floors below and was picked up dead. But Paul went down … and said, 'Do not be alarmed, for his soul is in him.'"
Associates fetched the body, dead.	Associates took up the body, alive.
Elpenor was not buried until dawn.	Eutychus was not raised alive until dawn.

In addition to imitating the Septuagint and Homer's *Odyssey*, MacDonald proposes that Mark's Gospel and Luke-Acts used the following literary models: Homer's *Iliad*, several Homeric Hymns, Euripides' *Bacchae* and *Madness of Heracles*, and dialogues by Plato and Xenophon about Socrates.

In respect of provenance, or the location at which a document was written, Pervo remarks with some humor:

> Previously it was noted that commentators rarely give the question of provenance an entire paragraph. One must now also consider the questions of narrator and viewpoint. Although Dante's *Inferno* is set in Hell and reveals a great deal of local knowledge, critics do not presume that it was written there.[98]

In short, Acts, the author of which was most likely also the author/redactor of the Gospel of Luke, is a relatively late production: Pervo conservatively dates it to ca. 115 AD; David Trobisch dates it to the middle of the second century, which is probably correct.[99] That is, Acts was finalized not more than a few decades before it is mentioned by Irenaeus.

---

[98]Pervo (2015), pp. 128–9.

[99]Everett Ferguson, *Church History: From Christ to Pre-Reformation* (Zondervan, 2005), p. 80. "The date of Polycarp's death is in dispute. Eusebius dates it to the reign of Marcus Aurelius, c. 166–167. However, a post-Eusebian addition to the *Martyrdom of Polycarp* dates his death to Saturday, February 23, in the proconsulship of Lucius Statius Quadratus [which works out to be 155 or 156]. These earlier dates better fit the *tradition* of his association with Ignatius and John the Evangelist." (Wikipedia.org, 'Polycarp.') However, the addition to the *Martyrdom cannot be considered reliable* on only its own merits. In addition, some have proposed a date in 177. The Eusebian date would fit well enough with Trobisch's suggestion that the canon was collected, edited, and some parts written, in mid-second century.

Early 'Christian' Documents

One of the problems of biblical scholarship and biblical understanding among the laity is that the books of the Bible aren't arranged in chronological order. If early Christian texts were arranged in the proper order without exclusion of the so-called extra-canonical works, it would be possible for people to read them without the late and prejudicially complete story of Matthew in first place, followed by the earliest of the Gospels, Mark, which comes off looking like a poor Cliff-notes copy made by someone in a hurry. If the Pauline letters were placed where they should be, first, it would be easy to see how the idea of a Son of God savior was first bruited by Paul, and then how other writings developed this idea, adding to it and expanding it as time went by. And if Paul's letters were preceded by the book of Enoch and other apocalypses,[100] it would be easy to see where some of his ideas came from.

In any event, if we understand at the outset that *the letters of Paul are primary evidence*, while later texts – including the Gospels – are secondary or worse, then we have good reason to notice that Paul himself never mentions Pilate. In the epistles, *the name Pilate only occurs*

---

[100] E.g., Daniel, 2 Baruch, 2 Esdras, 4 Ezra, etc. The Book of Enoch (ascribed to the great-grandfather of Noah) is one such apocalyptic text, its oldest sections probably dating back to 300–200 BC and its latest to around 100 BC. Its peculiar themes include: "the fallen angels, who came on the earth to unite with human women [and are considered responsible for the spread of evil and impurity on the earth]; the absence in 1 Enoch of formal parallels to the specific laws and commandments found in the Mosaic Torah and of references to issues like Shabbat observance or the rite of circumcision...; the concept of 'End of Days' as the time of final judgment that takes the place of promised earthly rewards; the rejection of the Second Temple's sacrifices considered impure...; the presentation of heaven ... not in terms of the Jerusalem temple and its priests, but modelling God and his angels on an ancient near eastern or Hellenistic court, with its king and courtiers; a solar calendar in opposition to the lunar calendar used in the Second Temple...; an interest in the angelic world that involves life after death." The text was known to both Jews and Christians in the first century (Barnabas apparently considered it scripture and Tertullian said Jews rejected it because it contained prophecies about Christ): "This book was also quoted by some 1st and 2nd century authors as in the Testaments of the Twelve Patriarchs. Authors of the New Testament were also familiar with some content of the story. A short section of 1 Enoch (1:9) is cited in the New Testament Epistle of Jude, Jude 1:14–15, and is attributed there to 'Enoch the Seventh from Adam' (1 En 60:8), although this section of 1 Enoch is a midrash on Deuteronomy 33:2. Several copies of the earlier sections of 1 Enoch were preserved among the Dead Sea Scrolls. ... There is little doubt that 1 Enoch was influential in molding New Testament doctrines about the Messiah, the Son of Man, the messianic kingdom, demonology, the resurrection, and eschatology. ... It is possible that the earlier sections of 1 Enoch had direct textual and content influence on many Biblical apocrypha, such as Jubilees, 2 Baruch, 2 Esdras, Apocalypse of Abraham and 2 Enoch, though even in these cases, the connection is typically more branches of a common trunk than direct development." The early Church Fathers quoted it extensively, both positively and negatively, e.g. Justin Martyr, Minucius Felix, Irenaeus, Origen, Cyprian, Hippolytus, Commodianus, Lactantius and Cassian. (Wikipedia.org, 'Book of Enoch.') For relevant scholarship, see Margaret Barker, *An Extraordinary Gathering of Angels* (MQ Publications, 2004) and *The Lost Prophet* (Sheffield Phoenix Press, 1998); Gabriele Boccaccini, *Beyond the Essene Hypothesis* (Eerdmans, 1998), *Enoch and the Messiah Son of Man* (Eerdmans, 2007), *Enoch and Qumran Origins* (Eerdmans, 2005), *The Origins of Enochic Judaism* (Zamorani, 2002), *Roots of Rabbinic Judaism* (Eerdmans, 2002); John Joseph Collins, *The Apocalyptic Imagination* (Eerdmans, 2016); Philip R. Davies, *Scribes and Schools* (SPCK, 1998); David R. Jackson, *Enochic Judaism* (Continuum, 2004); Florentino Garcia Martinez and Eibert J. C. Tigchelaar (Eds.), *The Dead Sea Scrolls: Study Edition* (Brill/Eerdmans, 1997); George W. E. Nickelsburg, *1 Enoch 1: A Commentary* (Fortress: 2001), *Jewish Literature Between the Bible and the Mishnah* (Fortress Press, 2005), with James C. VanderKam, *1 Enoch 2: A Commentary* (Fortress: 2011); James C. VanderKam, *Enoch: A Man for All Generations* (University of South Carolina, 1995), *Enoch and the Growth of an Apocalyptic Tradition* (Catholic Biblical Association of America, 1984), with Peter Flint, *Meaning of the Dead Sea Scrolls* (T&T Clark, 2005).

in 1 Timothy 6:13, widely acknowledged as being inauthentic and written in the second century (possibly by Polycarp).

If Paul was converted only a few years after the execution of Jesus, then he certainly must have lived during the time of Pilate, but he makes absolutely no reference to Pilate at all, nor betrayal by arch-fiend Judas Iscariot, nor denial by Peter; all things one would have expected him to bring up in his own defense.

How can this be? Pilate and his doings were so obnoxious that even Philo in Egypt, one of Paul's near contemporaries, wrote about him! At the same time, Philo makes no reference to the crucifixion of a messianic claimant under Pilate in his *surviving* works, though he does mention extrajudicial executions in large numbers committed by Pilate. If he wrote of such an event in his lost works, it doesn't survive and we have no reference to it.

This evidence, in part, is used by the so-called Jesus mythicists to argue that the original conceptions of Jesus Christ were mythological, not historical, in nature. I want to briefly review some of their ideas and show how this concept, while true, has tended to obscure the fact that there was, indeed, a 'real Jesus' – or several of them, in fact. They're the characters who were utilized to 'flesh out' the earlier myth of Jesus of Nazareth created by the author of Mark based on Paul's Son of God and a Palestinian teacher with messianic claims who was, in fact, executed, and probably by Pilate.

The late Alvar Ellegård, Swedish linguist and Dean of the Faculty of Arts at the University of Gothenburg, wrote *A Statistical Method for Determining Authorship* in 1962, which he later applied to early Christian texts in order to try to situate them in a historical context and chronology. His methodology has been superseded in the intervening decades, so his results are only approximations, but his work was a good effort to apply scientific historical methods to the problems of Christian historiography. His book, *Jesus: One Hundred Years Before Christ*, is well worth reading if only for the excellent example he sets of how to attempt to perform a genuinely scholarly and scientific study of 'scripture' without prejudice or privileging of texts, even if his solution to the Jesus question is not entirely satisfactory.[101] Ellegård was inspired to some considerable extent by the works of G. A. Wells.[102] He writes:

> I am certainly not original in holding that the gospel Jesus is largely fictional. The philosophers of the Enlightenment took naturally to that view, and it received strong support from the German theologian David F. Strauss, whose *Leben Jesu* (Strauss 1835) created a sensation throughout Europe. In our own century, prominent propounders of the thesis are Arthur Drews (Drews 1910–11), P. L. Couchoud (Couchoud 1926) and G. A. Wells (Wells 1971, 1975, 1982). None of these three is a theologian. Drews was a professor of philosophy, Couchoud a doctor of medicine turned Bible scholar, and Wells is a professor of German specializing in the *history of ideas*. Of the three, Wells

---

[101] Naturally, the apologetics community went on the attack. One of the most entertaining things I read in criticism of his book was this: "Alvar Ellegård offers a compilation [sic] of questionable, unsupported speculations that are tied together into a single thesis, that Jesus (as the title inferred [sic]) was not of the first century AD." One may note the word 'compilation' – well, anybody can make a spelling error – but it is followed by the erroneous use of the term 'inferred' when 'implied' would have been correct. Sad to say, there are biblical scholars whose hermeneutics and epistemology aren't any more elegant than the above example of literary skill.

[102] See *The Jesus of the Early Christians* (Pemberton, 1971); *Did Jesus Exist?* (Prometheus Books, 1987); *The Jesus Myth* (Open Court Publishing, 1998); *Can We Trust the New Testament? Thoughts on the Reliability of Early Christian Testimony* (Open Court, 2003); *Cutting Jesus Down to Size: What Higher Criticism Has Achieved and Where It Leaves Christianity* (Open Court, 2009).

is by far the most conscientious scholar, with a thorough grasp of the present-day state of the art among the theologians.[103]

Citing Burton Mack, Ellegård notes that the biblical scholar/theologian community has pretty much ignored this type of work, especially that of Wells. It's not a surprise that Wells's work has been subjected to rather vehement criticism from biblical scholars, some of whom accuse him of 'anti-religious' intentions.[104] One of their main criticisms is that Wells was working outside his own field of expertise; that is, he was not a 'New Testament expert.' That argument is patently absurd when one considers that funding for becoming a 'New Testament scholar' generally comes from religious institutions and requires belief; those New Testament scholars who, in the course of their studies, lose their faith, often pay a high price professionally and personally. It seems to me that being a 'New Testament scholar' with confessional belief in the New Testament should exclude one from being a New Testament scholar! If you *believe* in what you are studying, you've already lost any claim to scientific objectivity, so please don't pretend to it.[105]

However, there is actually a growing list of scholars – a number of them of the biblically trained variety – who are coming to similar conclusions and leaving the faith: Michael D. Goulder,[106] Thomas L. Brodie,[107] Gerd Lüdemann,[108] Robert Price,[109] etc. But what is equally interesting is the number of non-theologian scholars who have recently turned their attention and expertise

---

[103]Alvar Ellegård, 'Theologians As Historians', Scandia.hist.lu.se (2008), p. 170.

[104]It always surprises me to note that many biblical scholars frequently accuse other scholars – some of them also biblical specialists – of 'anti-religious' intentions in their work. It's a strange form of conspiracy theory which posits that a desire for, and search for, truth is somehow blasphemous. Canadian social psychologists Bob Altemeyer and Bruce Hunsberger, in their book *Amazing Conversions*, studied the phenomenon and determined that it was the inculcation of the religious attitude that there *is* truth, and that it should be diligently sought, that disposes deeply honest people to turn that inquiry on their own beliefs. Bob Altemeyer and Bruce Hunsberger, *Amazing Conversions: Why Some Turn to Faith & Others Abandon Religion* (Prometheus Books, 1997).

[105]Philip R. Davies, *Whose Bible Is It Anyway?* (Sheffield Academic Press, 1995).

[106]See *Type and History in Acts* (SPCK, 1964); *Luke: A New Paradigm* (Sheffield Academic Press, 1989); *St. Paul versus St. Peter: A Tale of Two Missions* (Westminster John Knox Press, 1995); *Paul and the Competing Mission in Corinth* (Hendrickson, 1998); *Five Stones and a Sling: Memoirs of a Biblical Scholar* (Sheffield Phoenix Press, 2009).

[107]See *The Crucial Bridge* (Michael Glazier, 2000); *Genesis As Dialogue: A Literary, Historical, and Theological Commentary* (Oxford University Press, 2001); *The Birthing of the New Testament: The Intertextual Development of the New Testament Writings* (Sheffield Phoenix Press, 2006); *Beyond the Quest for the Historical Jesus: Memoir of a Discovery* (Sheffield Phoenix Press, 2012); and his volume edited with Dennis R. MacDonald and Stanley E. Porter, *The Intertextuality of the Epistles: Explorations of Theory and Practice* (Sheffield Phoenix Press, 2006).

[108]See *Paul, Apostle to the Gentiles: Studies in Chronology* (Fortress Press, 1984); *What Really Happened to Jesus: A Historical Approach to the Resurrection* (Westminster John Knox Press, 1996); *The Great Deception: And What Jesus Really Said and Did* (Prometheus Books, 1999); *Paul: The Founder of Christianity* (Prometheus Books, 2002); *The Acts of the Apostles: What Really Happened in the Earliest Days of the Church* (Prometheus Books, 2005); *The Earliest Christian Text: 1 Thessalonians* (Polebridge Press, 2013); with Frank Schleritt and Martina Janssen, *Jesus After 2000 Years: What He Really Said and Did* (Prometheus Books, 2001).

[109]Among Price's prolific output, see *Deconstructing Jesus* (Prometheus Books, 2000); *The Incredible Shrinking Son of Man: How Reliable is the Gospel Tradition?* (Prometheus Books, 2003); *The Pre-Nicene New Testament: Fifty-four Formative Texts* (Signature Books, 2006); *Jesus is Dead* (American Atheist Press, 2007); *The Case Against The Case For Christ: A New Testament Scholar Refutes the Reverend Lee Strobel* (American Atheist Press, 2011); *The Christ-Myth Theory and Its Problems* (American Atheist Press, 2011); *Killing History: Jesus in the No-Spin Zone* (Prometheus Books, 2014).

to this issue, popularly called the 'Jesus Myth Theory,' which postulates that Jesus of Nazareth never existed or, if he did, had nothing to do with the founding of Christianity, a statement which is certainly true enough as it stands.

The problems surrounding the alleged historicity of Jesus of Nazareth are so egregious that even among the believing scholars, there is no agreement. They may agree that Jesus was baptized by John the Baptist and crucified at the order of Pontius Pilate, but that is about all. Some of them go so far as to say that there may be a number of plausible Jesuses – revolutionary, sage, holy man, healer – but there is no certainty about which one of them was the historical Jesus. This line of thinking began in the eighteenth century with the works of Constantin François Chasseboeuf de Volney and Charles-François Dupuis, who argued "that Christianity was an amalgamation of various ancient mythologies and that Jesus was a totally mythical character."[110]

One of my own favorites is German scholar Bruno Bauer,[111] who argued that Jesus did not exist at all. He was the first to present the threefold argument, still in use:

- The Gospels were written many decades or even a century after Jesus' estimated year of death, by individuals who likely never met Jesus, and then were edited or forged over the centuries by unknown scribes with their own agendas.

- There are no surviving historical records about Jesus of Nazareth from any non-Jewish author until the second century, and Jesus left no writings or other archaeological evidence.

- Certain Gospel stories are similar to those of dying-and-rising gods, demigods (sons of gods), solar deities, saviors or other divine men such as Horus, Mithra(s), Prometheus, Dionysus, Osiris, Buddha, and Krishna, as well as Christ-like historical figures like Apollonius of Tyana.[112]

Bauer initially left open the question of whether an historical Jesus existed at all. Later, in *A Critique of the Gospels and a History of their Origin* (1850–1851), he argued that Jesus had not existed, and in 1877's *Christ and the Caesars* "he suggested that Christianity was a synthesis of the Stoicism of Seneca the Younger and of the Jewish theology of Philo as developed by pro-Roman Jews such as Josephus. Bauer's work was heavily criticized at the time; in 1839 he was removed from his position at the University of Bonn."[113] Interestingly, this can still be your fate if you are a biblical scholar whose studies bring you to the conclusion that there is little – if any – truth in the Bible, either Old Testament or New.

Following Bauer, there were quite a number of eminent scholars joining the fray (for such it certainly was!); there were a few embarrassments such as the shamanistic cult idea of John Allegro[114] and assorted Jesus conspiracies that keep coming out, all of which make the fatal

---

[110]Wikipedia.org, 'Christ myth theory,' citing Constantin-François Volney, *The Ruins, or, Meditation on the Revolutions of Empires and the Law of Nature* (Davis, 1796); Charles François Dupuis, *The Origin of All Religious Worship* (Kessinger, 2007, first published 1794).

[111]See *Christianity Exposed: A Recollection of the Eighteenth Century and a Contribution to the Crisis of the Nineteenth Century* (Edwin Mellen Press, 2002 [1843]); *Christ and the Caesars: The Origin of Christianity from the Mythology of Rome and Greece* (Xlibris, 2015 [1877]).

[112]Wikipedia.org, 'Christ myth theory.'

[113]Wikipedia.org, 'Bruno Bauer.'

[114]See *The Sacred Mushroom & the Cross Fertility Cults and the Origins of Judaism and Christianity* (Doubleday, 1970) and *The Dead Sea Scrolls and the Christian Myth* (Prometheus, 1992).

mistake of thinking that the Gospels and Acts have anything to do with history and generally base their theories on interpretations of same.[115] When we finally get to G. A. Wells, we find that his work has been acknowledged at least by a couple of eminent theologians: British theologian Kenneth Grayston[116] advised Christians to acknowledge the difficulties raised by Wells, and New Testament scholar Graham Stanton[117] said that Wells presented the most thoroughgoing and sophisticated arguments for the Christ myth theory. Burton Mack has also called attention to Wells's work.[118]

Thomas L. Thompson's book *The Messiah Myth: The Near Eastern Roots of Jesus and David*,[119] "argues that the biblical accounts of both King David and Jesus of Nazareth are ... mythical in nature and based on Mesopotamian, Egyptian, Babylonian, *and Greek and Roman literature*." He does not draw a final conclusion as to whether Jesus was real or not, and in a 2012 online article[120] he strongly rejects Bart Ehrman's misrepresentation of his views and the label 'mythicist.'[121]

Speaking of Ehrman, he claims that the view that Jesus existed is held by "virtually every expert on the planet." Despite this claim, he is forced to acknowledge that there are "a couple of bona fide scholars" who support the Christ myth theory.[122] For Ehrman, a "bona fide scholar" is only one trained in New Testament studies like himself, though one has to observe that he is trained in text criticism, which is much like a glorified copy-editor. It's a crucial step in examining an ancient text, but it is only the beginning of a long process, and his claims ultimately come off as sounding rather hysterical. It is utterly astonishing to read his claim that the four Gospels are four independent testimonies to the existence of Jesus when it is clear that Mark used Paul's letters, Matthew used Mark, Luke used Mark and Matthew, and John certainly used Mark and other sources as well. There is nothing independent about these testimonies since all of them were copying the original Mark, and his Gospel was a patchwork of literary bits and pieces from the OT and Homer and other sources. There was no 'story of Jesus' for Mark to report; he had to make one up from scratch.

---

[115]The problem with all these reconstructions is that they begin from the premise that something historical can be derived or decoded from the Gospels and Acts. Doing that can produce about any reconstruction or story or mystery, or whatever you like. Barbara Thiering and her pesher method is an extreme case in point. I began from the premise that *nothing* historical could be derived from the Gospels and Acts. The only way they can be used is if there is something that *is* historical – derived or inferred from actual historical texts – echoed there.

[116]*Methodist Recorder*, 16 Nov. 1971.

[117]Graham Stanton, *The Gospels and Jesus* (Oxford University Press, 2002 [1989]), p. 143.

[118]Wells is easy to read so I highly recommend his works. As for Mack, see *A Myth of Innocence: Mark and Christian Origins* (Fortress Press, 1988); *Patterns of Persuasion in the Gospels* (Polebridge Press, 1989); *The Christian Myth: Origins, Logic, and Legacy* (Continuum, 2001).

[119]Basic Books, 2005.

[120]'Is This Not the Carpenter's Son? A Response to Bart Ehrman,' *The Bible and Interpretation* website (2012). Available at http://www.bibleinterp.com/articles/tho368005.shtml.

[121]Wikipedia.org, 'Christ myth theory.'

[122]Ehrman, in *Did Jesus Exist?* (2012), expends a lot of energy discussing bona fides, mainly his own, and railing against anyone who is not 'qualified' by being a certified, card-carrying, NT scholar *ever* opining as to whether Jesus of Nazareth, as depicted in the Gospels, existed in history. Ehrman's touting of his status as a real, Ph.D. scholar is particularly interesting considering the fact that he violates every rule of historiographical methodology ever agreed upon by those professing to do scientific history.

Another of my favorites is Dominican Tom Brodie. After years of academic work, he concluded that Jesus is mythical, publishing *Beyond the Quest for the Historical Jesus: Memoir of a Discovery* in 2012. The book caused controversy when Brodie "endorsed the Christ myth theory that Jesus of Nazareth was not a historical figure, a belief he says he has held since the 1970s."[123] In 2013, the Dominican Order tried to muzzle Brodie, but it seems they finally came to some agreement: Brodie stays in retirement, more or less, and they leave him alone. They can't control his books since they were not published by the church. Michael Goulder (another favorite) and Brodie were among the earlier scholars noticing that the Gospels were heavily influenced by the Old Testament in both structure and stories. Intertextuality has since become an active field.[124] Michael Goulder did the unthinkable when he pointed out that Paul obviously wasn't in very friendly relations with the Jerusalem church, and he gets my hero award for that![125]

One of the most active new kids on the Mythical Jesus block is Richard Carrier, who holds a doctorate in ancient history from Columbia University and certainly knows what he is doing, methodologically speaking. He wrote a deservedly rough review of Bart Ehrman's book *Did Jesus Exist* in 2012, and the debate has been pretty hot on the internet ever since.[126]

Earl Doherty's encyclopedic writings on the topic should be mentioned here as well. His view is that "no historical Jesus worthy of the name existed, that Christianity began with a belief in a spiritual, mythical figure, that the Gospels are essentially allegory and fiction, and that no single identifiable person lay at the root of the Galilean preaching tradition."[127] He further notes that

> ... none of the major Christian apologists *before 180 AD*, except for Justin and Aristides of Athens, included an account of a historical Jesus in their defenses of Christianity. ... Doherty further argues that Theophilus of Antioch (c. 163–182), Athenagoras of Athens (c. 133–190), Tatian the Assyrian (c. 120–180), and Marcus Minucius Felix (writing around 150–270) offer no indication that they believed in a historical figure crucified and resurrected, and that *the name Jesus* does not appear in any of them.[128]

One of the most prolific writers on the topic is New Testament scholar[129] and former Baptist preacher Robert Price, who was a fellow of the Jesus Seminar, a group of writers and scholars who study the historicity of Jesus, and a member of the Jesus Project. He, too, thinks that Christianity is a synthesis of Egyptian, Jewish and Greek myths and questions the existence of a living man behind the myths. Price points out:

> What one Jesus reconstruction leaves aside, the next one takes up and makes its cornerstone. Jesus simply wears too many hats in the Gospels – exorcist, healer, king, prophet, sage, rabbi, demigod, and so on. The Jesus Christ of the New Testament is a *composite figure* ... The historical Jesus

---

[123]Wikipedia.org, 'Thomas L. Brodie.'

[124]See Brodie (2006); Dennis MacDonald (ed.), *Mimesis and Intertextuality in Antiquity and Christianity* (Trinity Press International 2001); Tom Dykstra, *Mark Canonizer of Paul: A New Look at Intertextuality in Mark's Gospel* (OCABS Press, 2012).

[125]Michael Goulder, *St. Paul versus St. Peter: A Tale of Two Missions* (London: SCM Press, 1994).

[126]See Carrier (2014) and *Proving History: Bayes's Theorem and the Quest for the Historical Jesus* (Prometheus, 2012).

[127]Earl Doherty, *Jesus: Neither God Nor Man – The Case for a Mythical Jesus* (Age of Reason, 2009), pp. vii–viii.

[128]Wikipedia.org, 'Earl Doherty,' citing Earl Doherty, 'The Jesus Puzzle,' *Journal of Higher Criticism* 4:2 (1997).

[129]I only emphasize this point because of Ehrman's rather revolting arguments about those who are not, in his estimation, qualified to offer an opinion on the topic.

(if there was one) might well have been a messianic king, or a progressive Pharisee, or a Galilean shaman, or a magus, or a Hellenistic sage. But he cannot very well have been all of them at the same time.[130]

What he is saying is certainly correct, but the problem is that so many people are taking liberties with the texts and inferring from them things that were never implied; thus, some of the confusion. He writes at the conclusion of his 2000 book *Deconstructing Jesus*: "There may have been a real figure there, but there is simply no longer any way of being sure."[131] He also states:

> I am not trying to say that there was a single origin of the Christian savior Jesus Christ, and that origin is pure myth; rather, I am saying that there may indeed have been such a myth, and that if so, it eventually flowed together with other Jesus images, some one of which may have been based on a historical Jesus the Nazorean.[132]

I think Price is correct as far as he goes, and I also think we can identify which main images of various historical figures came together to create the outline of Jesus of Nazareth and even how and approximately when; but to do so, we must avoid using the Gospels or Acts as *historical* sources.

Earliest Concepts of Jesus

Coming back now to Ellegård, while I don't think his *identification* of the Jesus figure as the Qumran community's 'Teacher of Righteousness' is warranted, his linguistic methods applied to the texts of early Christianity provide precious clues to the earliest concept(s) of Jesus. He begins his study with the writings of Paul, which are, again, as most NT scholars admit, the earliest unquestionably Christian (as we understand Christianity) writings.[133] As Ellegård points out, based on the accepted Christian chronology, Paul must have been about the same age as Jesus of Nazareth, so his silence on the life and works of this alleged messiah is quite remarkable. Ellegård tells us that his examination of the texts (though he wasn't accounting for interpolations in Paul) strongly suggests the following:

> Paul's message to his audiences in the Jewish Diaspora was that his and his colleagues' visions proved, first, that Jesus had risen from the dead, second, that he was the Messiah, and third, that the Last Judgement was imminent, at which Jesus, as the Messiah, would save the faithful from death and destruction.
>
> Messianic ideas were rife among the Jews throughout the centuries around the beginning of our era, so Paul's and the others' preaching found willing listeners. But who was Jesus? Paul says very little about him. Evidently his audiences could identify him immediately, since they asked no

---

[130]Price (2000), pp. 15–16.

[131]Price (2000), p. 250.

[132]Price (2000), p. 250.

[133]For an opposing view, see Robert Price, *The Amazing Colossal Apostle* (Signature Books, 2012), and the 'Dutch Radicals.' Price thinks the epistles are late pseudepigrapha but do attest an earlier variety of Christianity that knew of no historical Jesus. (Personal communication with the author, 2015.) Further on in this work, we may have discovered a clue that Paul was, indeed, very real and historical, *pace* Price.

questions.[134] Moreover, as the main message was that Jesus would soon return and save those who believed that he was the Messiah, the human, earthly Jesus was of little consequence to them.

Paul's only experience of Jesus was clearly through his ecstatic visions. To judge from his writings (1 Cor 15) he assumed that *his fellow apostles had had experiences of the same kind.* He certainly does not feel inferior to them on that score. But if none of the apostles had ever seen Jesus, the natural conclusion is that Jesus cannot have been contemporary with any of them. This, together with the fact that Jesus was taken for granted in all the Pauline congregations throughout the Diaspora, leads to the further conclusion that *he was a well-established figure among them,* and presumably one whose activity had been living in their memories for a long time.

Paul had seen Jesus after he had been raised to the heavens, which proved that he had in this sense risen from the dead. But neither Paul nor anybody else said anything about when Jesus' death and resurrection had taken place. It was not an essential question.[135] The chief concern of Paul and his congregations was the imminence of the Day of Judgement. Hence the one thing necessary was to arrange one's life in such a way as to be saved on that momentous day, which was assumed certainly to arrive within the lifetime of those who heard Paul.[136]

But as years and decades passed without the expected catastrophe, it is understandable that many people turned their attention to other aspects of the teaching of Paul and his fellow apostles. We may assume that Jesus was known as a revered teacher. But what exactly had he taught? How had he taught it? To whom? When? What kind of a person was he?

If those who began to ask these questions towards the end of the first century turned to the writings of Paul and his contemporaries, they found little in the way of answers. They had to construct a life of Jesus largely on their own. This is how the Gospels arose ...[137]

Ellegård makes the same mistake so many make: he assumed that there was some historical skeleton in the Gospels and Acts; there may be seeds, but there is no skeleton. In fact, it strikes me that the Parable of the Mustard Seed is a pretty good metaphor for the growth of the myth of Jesus!

In any event, Ellegård lists six texts that he believes were produced by Christian communities in the first century in addition to the letters of Paul: the *Pastor of Hermas*, the *Didache*, the *First Letter of Clement*, the *Letter of Barnabas*, the *Letter to the Hebrews*, and the *Revelation* of John. The major portion of the latter, he believes, was written right around the time of the destruction of Jerusalem, probably just prior to it, and was intended to give encouragement to the rebels to hold out for the coming of their messiah. Ellegård points out that, of course, these texts have been subjected to later editing and additions, but in general, *on linguistic grounds*, they can be situated *earlier than the Gospels.* He gives close and detailed arguments for why he dates these texts as early as he does, which I will only mention briefly here.

None of the early texts that Ellegård has identified ever use the term 'Christian'; followers are always referred to as the Elect, the Saints, the Church of God – all terms that also happen to be found in the Qumran texts, the 'Dead Sea Scrolls.' Also, they have almost nothing to say about an

---

[134]This, in itself, is curious since Paul was addressing a largely Gentile audience. Who might have been so well known to Gentiles, and honored by them, that they could be easily persuaded to 'go over' to a messianic conception of this individual?

[135]Again, this was obviously something that was known and understood about the figure Paul was preaching as an eschatological savior; *known to Gentile audiences!*

[136]Troels Engberg-Pedersen comes much closer to describing Paul's motivations in *Paul and the Stoics* (Westminster John Knox Press, 2000). Paul's chief concern was for his congregations to "make their faith active through love." The future eschatological scenario was intimately tied to this, but certainly not *more* important.

[137]Ellegård (2008), pp. 169–70.

earthly Jesus or his teaching or theology. Instead they focus on a death and resurrection, though none of them give an indication of this having occurred in a temporal context. None of them ever claim to have seen or heard an earthly Jesus, nor do they claim to know of anybody who ever did. It seems that their sources were 'revelations' that they had from interpreting passages from the Hebrew Scriptures and other literature, such as *Enoch* and various prophetic works. In contrast to Paul, who addressed mainly Gentiles, the other six documents listed by Ellegård apparently address a Jewish Diaspora audience. It is also worth noting that their arguments are consistently based on the Septuagint (LXX) version of the Hebrew Scriptures.

Among other clues, the points above lead Ellegård to argue that the early Christian communities began as Essene-type gatherings – ecclesia – all around the Empire, a conclusion also reached by Catholic scholars Étienne Nodet and Justin Taylor, as we'll see below. That, of course, may connect them in some way to the Qumran community near the Dead Sea. We can get a good idea of how the Qumran sect people were thinking and acting based on their texts: it was all (more or less) about evicting and/or destroying the hated Romans and extracting messages from the scriptures by unusual exegetical methods called 'Pesher.'[138]

Essenes, Gnostics, and Qumran

At this point, it will be useful to lay out what has been said about the Essenes by writers of antiquity. Rather than paraphrase, we will give the passages in full for the reader's convenience. First is Philo's (c. 25 BC – c. 50 AD) *first* account:

> Moreover *Palestine and Syria* too are not barren of exemplary wisdom and virtue, which countries no slight portion of that most populous nation of the Jews inhabits. There is a portion of those people called Essenes, in number something more than four thousand in my opinion, *who derive their name from their piety*, though not according to any accurate form of the Grecian dialect, because they are above all men devoted to the service of God, not sacrificing living animals, but studying rather to preserve their own minds in a state of holiness and purity. These men, in the first place, *live in villages, avoiding all cities* on account of the habitual lawlessness of those who inhabit them, well knowing that such a moral disease is contracted from associations with wicked men, just as a real disease might be from an impure atmosphere, and that this would stamp an incurable evil on their souls.
>
> Of these men, some cultivating the earth, and others devoting themselves to those arts which are the result of peace, benefit both themselves and all those who come in contact with them, not storing up treasures of silver and of gold, nor acquiring vast sections of the earth out of a desire for ample revenues, but providing all things which are requisite for the natural purposes of life; for they alone of almost all men having been originally poor and destitute, and that too rather from their own habits and ways of life than from any real deficiency of good fortune, are nevertheless accounted very rich, judging contentment and frugality to be great abundance, as in truth they are.
>
> Among those men you will find no makers of arrows, or javelins, or swords, or helmets, or breastplates, or shields; no makers of arms or of military engines; no one, in short, attending to any employment whatever connected with war, or even to any of those occupations even in peace which are easily perverted to wicked purposes; for they are utterly ignorant of all traffic, and of all commercial dealings, and of all navigation, but they repudiate and keep aloof from everything

---

[138] *Pesher* is the Jewish practice of providing 'interpretive commentary' on the Bible, based on the notion that there are two levels to the text: the literal and the concealed, discernable only by experts.

which can possibly afford any inducement to covetousness; and there is not a single slave among them, but they are all free, aiding one another with a reciprocal interchange of good offices; and they condemn masters, not only as unjust, inasmuch as they corrupt the very principle of equality, but likewise as impious, because they destroy the ordinances of nature, which generated them all equally, and brought them up like a mother, as if they were all legitimate brethren, not in name only, but in reality and truth. But in their view this natural relationship of all men to one another has been thrown into disorder by designing covetousness, continually wishing to surpass others in good fortune, and which has therefore engendered alienation instead of affection, and hatred instead of friendship; and leaving the logical part of philosophy, as in no respect necessary for the acquisition of virtue, to the word-catchers, and the natural part, as being too sublime for human nature to master, to those who love to converse about high objects (except indeed so far as such a study takes in the contemplation of the existence of God and of the creation of the universe), they devote all their attention to the moral part of philosophy, using as instructors the laws of their country which it would have been impossible for the human mind to devise without divine inspiration.

Now these laws they are taught at other times, indeed, but most especially on the seventh day, for the seventh day is accounted sacred, on which they abstain from all other employments, and *frequent the sacred places which are called synagogues*, and there they sit according to their age in classes, the younger sitting under the elder, and listening with eager attention in becoming order. Then one, indeed, takes up the holy volume and reads it, and another of the men of the greatest experience comes forward and explains what is not very intelligible, for a great many precepts are delivered in enigmatical modes of expression, and allegorically, as the old fashion was; and thus the people are taught piety, and holiness, and justice, and economy, and the science of regulating the state, and the knowledge of such things as are naturally good, or bad, or indifferent,[139] and to choose what is right and to avoid what is wrong, using a threefold variety of definitions, and rules, and criteria, namely, the love of God, and the love of virtue, and the love of mankind. Accordingly, the sacred volumes present an infinite number of instances of the disposition devoted to the love of God, and of a continued and uninterrupted purity throughout the whole of life, of a careful avoidance of oaths and of falsehood, and of a *strict adherence to the principle of looking on the Deity as the cause of everything which is good and of nothing which is evil.* They also furnish us with many proofs of a love of virtue, such as abstinence from all covetousness of money, from ambition, from indulgence in pleasures, temperance, endurance, and also moderation, simplicity, good temper, the absence of pride, obedience to the laws, steadiness, and everything of that kind; and, lastly, they bring forward as proofs of the love of mankind, goodwill, equality beyond all power of description, and fellowship, about which it is not unreasonable to say a few words.

In the first place, then, there is no one who has a house so absolutely his own private property, that it does not in some sense also belong to every one: for besides that they *all dwell together in companies*, the house is open to all those of the same notions, who come to them from other quarters; then there is one magazine among them all; their expenses are all in common; their garments belong to them all in common; their food is common, since they all eat in messes; for there is no other people among which you can find a common use of the same house, a common adoption of one mode of living, and a common use of the same table more thoroughly established in fact than among this tribe: and is not this very natural? For whatever they, after having been working during the day, receive for their wages, that they do not retain as their own, but bring it into the common stock, and give any advantage that is to be derived from it to all who desire to avail themselves of it; and those who are sick are not neglected because they are unable to contribute to the common stock, inasmuch as the tribe have in their public stock a means of supplying their necessities and aiding their weakness, so that from their ample means they support them liberally and abundantly;

---

[139]This is a distinction derived from Stoic philosophy. The astute reader may notice much of the Stoics imbued into this passage.

and they cherish respect for their elders, and honour them and care for them, just as parents are honoured and cared for by their lawful children: being supported by them in all abundance both by their personal exertions, and by innumerable contrivances.

Such diligent practises of virtue does philosophy, unconnected with any superfluous care of examining into Greek names render men, proposing to them as necessary exercises to train them towards its attainment, all praiseworthy actions by which a freedom, which can never be enslaved, is firmly established. And a proof of this is that, though at different times a great number of chiefs of every variety of disposition and character, have occupied their country, some of whom have endeavoured to surpass even ferocious wild beasts in cruelty, leaving no sort of inhumanity unpractised, and have never ceased to murder their subjects in whole troops, and have even torn them to pieces while living, like cooks cutting them limb from limb, till they themselves, being overtaken by the vengeance of divine justice, have at last experienced the same miseries in their turn: others again having converted their barbarous frenzy into another kind of wickedness, practising an ineffable degree of savageness, talking with the people quietly, but through the hypocrisy of a more gentle voice, betraying the ferocity of their real disposition, fawning upon their victims like treacherous dogs, and becoming the causes of irremediable miseries to them, have left in all their cities monuments of their impiety, and hatred of all mankind, in the never to be forgotten miseries endured by those whom they oppressed: and yet *no one, not even of those immoderately cruel tyrants, nor of the more treacherous and hypocritical oppressors was ever able to bring any real accusation against the multitude of those called Essenes or Holy.*[140] But everyone being subdued by the virtue of these men, looked up to them as free by nature, and not subject to the frown of any human being, and have celebrated their manner of messing together, and their fellowship with one another beyond all description in respect of its mutual good faith, which is an ample proof of a perfect and very happy life.[141]

Philo's second account:

But our lawgiver [Moses] trained an innumerable body of his pupils to partake in those things, who are called Essenes, being, as I imagine, honoured with this appellation because of their exceeding holiness. And *they dwell in many cities of Judaea, and in many villages, and in great and populous communities.* And this sect of them is not an hereditary or family connexion; for family ties are not spoken of with reference to acts voluntarily performed; but it is adopted because of their admiration for virtue and love of gentleness and humanity. At all events, there are no children among the Essenes, no, nor any youths or persons only just entering upon manhood; since the dispositions of all such persons are unstable and liable to change, from the imperfections incident to their age, but they are all full-grown men, and even already declining towards old age, such as are no longer carried away by the impetuosity of their bodily passions, and are not under the influence of the appetites, but such as enjoy a genuine freedom, the only true and real liberty. And a proof of this is to be found in their life of perfect freedom; no one among them ventures at all to acquire any property whatever of his own, neither house, nor slave, nor farm, nor flocks and herds, nor any thing of any sort which can be looked upon as the fountain or provision of riches; but they bring them together into the middle as a common stock, and enjoy one common general benefit from it all.

And they all dwell in the same place, *making clubs, and societies, and combinations, and unions with one another*, and doing everything throughout their whole lives with reference to the general advantage; but the different members of this body have different employments in which they occupy themselves, and labour without hesitation and without cessation, making no mention of either cold,

---

[140]The Greek is *essaion e hosion*, as if *essaion* was only a variety of the word *hosion*, 'holy.'
[141]Philo, *Quod Omnis Probus Liber* 12.75—13.91, C. D. Yonge translation.

or heat, or any changes of weather or temperature as an excuse for desisting from their tasks. But before the sun rises they betake themselves to their daily work, and they do not quit it till some time after it has set, when they return home rejoicing no less than those who have been exercising themselves in gymnastic contests; for they imagine that whatever they devote themselves to as a practice is a sort of gymnastic exercise of more advantage to life, and more pleasant both to soul and body, and of more enduring benefit and equability, than mere athletic labours, inasmuch as such toil does not cease to be practised with delight when the age of vigour of body is passed; for there are some of them who are devoted to the practice of agriculture, being skilful in such things as pertain to the sowing and cultivation of lands; others again are shepherds, or cowherds, and experienced in the management of every kind of animal; some are cunning in what relates to swarms of bees; others again are artisans and handicraftsmen, in order to guard against suffering from the want of anything of which there is at times an actual need; and these men omit and delay nothing, which is requisite for the innocent supply of the necessaries of life. Accordingly, each of these men, who differ so widely in their respective employments, when they have received their wages give them up to one person who is appointed as the universal steward and general manager; and he, when he has received the money, immediately goes and purchases what is necessary and furnishes them with food in abundance, and all other things of which the life of mankind stands in need.

And those who live together and eat at the same table are day after day contented with the same things, being lovers of frugality and moderation, and averse to all sumptuousness and extravagance as a disease of both mind and body. And not only are their tables in common but also their dress; for in the winter there are thick cloaks found, and in the summer light cheap mantles, so that whoever wants one is at liberty without restraint to go and take whichever kind he chooses; since what belongs to one belongs to all, and on the other hand whatever belongs to the whole body belongs to each individual. And again, if any one of them is sick he is cured from the common resources, being attended to by the general care and anxiety of the whole body. Accordingly the old men, even if they happen to be childless, as if they were not only the fathers of many children but were even also particularly happy in an affectionate offspring, are accustomed to end their lives in a most happy and prosperous and carefully attended old age, being looked upon by such a number of people as worthy of so much honour and provident regard that they think themselves bound to care for them even more from inclination than from any tie of natural affection.

Again, perceiving with more than ordinary acuteness and accuracy, what is alone or at least above all other things calculated to dissolve such associations, they repudiate marriage; and at the same time they practise continence in an eminent degree; *for no one of the Essenes ever marries a wife*, because woman is a selfish creature and one addicted to jealousy in an immoderate degree, and terribly calculated to agitate and overturn the natural inclinations of a man, and to mislead him by her continual tricks; for as she is always studying deceitful speeches and all other kinds of hypocrisy, like an actress on the stage, when she is alluring the eyes and ears of her husband, she proceeds to cajole his predominant mind after the servants have been deceived. And again, if there are children she becomes full of pride and all kinds of license in her speech, and all the obscure sayings which she previously meditated in irony in a disguised manner she now begins to utter with audacious confidence; and becoming utterly shameless she proceeds to acts of violence, and does numbers of actions of which every one is hostile to such associations; for the man who is bound under the influence of the charms of a woman, or of children, by the necessary ties of nature, being overwhelmed by the impulses of affection, is no longer the same person towards others, but is entirely changed, having, without being aware of it, become a slave instead of a free man.[142] This now is the enviable system of life of these Essenes, so that not only private individuals but *even*

---

[142]Philo was obviously expressing the common view of women at the time. Paul, however, did not hold such views. See Engberg-Pedersen (2000).

mighty kings, admiring the men, venerate their sect, and increase their dignity and majesty in a still higher degree by their approbation and by the honours which they confer on them.[143]

Josephus' account from *Wars* demonstrates many correspondences with Philo's account, which has a very Stoic flavor. However, there are elements in this account that correspond more closely to what we now know of the sect responsible for the Dead Sea Scrolls, which are absent in Philo. Here is Josephus' first account:

> For there are three philosophical sects among the Jews. The followers of the first of whom are the Pharisees; of the second the Sadducces; and the third sect, who pretends to a severer discipline, and called Essenes. These last are *Jews by birth,* and seem to have a greater affection for one another than the other sects have.[144] These Essenes reject pleasures as an evil, but esteem continence, and the conquest over our passions, to be virtue. They neglect wedlock, but choose out other persons' children, while they are pliable, and fit for learning; and esteem them to be of their kindred, and form them according to their own manners. They do not absolutely deny the fitness of marriage, and the succession of mankind thereby continued; but they guard against the lascivious behavior of women, and are persuaded that none of them preserve their fidelity to one man.
>
> These men are despisers of riches, and so very communicative as raises our admiration.[145] Nor is there anyone to be found among them who hath more than another; for it is a law among them, that those who come to them must let what they have be common to the whole order, – insomuch, that among them all there is no appearance of poverty or excess of riches, but everyone's possessions are intermingled with every other's possessions: and so there is, as it were, one patrimony among all the brethren.[146] They think that oil is a defilement; and if any one of them be anointed without his own approbation, it is wiped off his body; for they think to be sweaty is a good thing, as they do also to be clothed in white garments. They also have stewards appointed to take care of their common affairs, who every one of them have no separate business for any, but what is for the use of them all.
>
> They have no certain city but *many of them dwell in every city*; and if any of their sect come from other places, what they have lies open for them, just as if it were their own; and they go into such as they never knew before, as if they had been ever so long acquainted with them. For which reason they carry nothing with them when they travel into remote parts, though still *they take their weapons with them*, for fear of thieves. Accordingly there is, *in every city where they live*, one appointed particularly to take care of strangers, and to provide garments and other necessaries for them. But the habit and management of their bodies is such as children use who are in fear of their masters. Nor do they allow of the change of garments, or of shoes, till they be first entirely torn to pieces or worn out by time. Nor do they either buy or sell anything to one another; but every one of them gives what he hath to him that wanteth it, and receives from him again in lieu of it what may be convenient for himself; and although there be no requital made, they are fully allowed to take what they want of whomsoever they please.
>
> And as for their piety towards God, it is very extraordinary; for before sunrising they speak not a word about profane matters, but put up certain prayers which they have received from their forefathers, as if they made a supplication for its rising.[147] After this every one of them are sent away by their curators, to exercise some of those arts wherein they are skilled, in which they labor

---

[143]Philo, in Eusebius, *P.E.* 8.11.1–18, C. D. Yonge translation.

[144]This reminds one of Paul's injunctions to love one another.

[145]One wonders what Josephus meant by the word 'communicative'? That they were teachers or preachers?

[146]Here, one is reminded of the arrangement described in the book of *Acts*; perhaps Josephus was the inspiration for that as well? Note that Philo also discussed the communistic lifestyle.

[147]This reminds one of Pliny's description of the rites of the Christians in his 110 AD letter to Trajan.

with great diligence till the fifth hour. After which they assemble themselves together again into one place; and when they have clothed themselves in white veils, they then bathe their bodies in cold water. And after this purification is over, they every one meet together in an apartment of their own, into which it is not permitted to any of another sect to enter; while they go, after a pure manner, into the dining room, as into a certain holy temple, and quietly set themselves down; upon which the baker lays them loaves in order; the cook also brings a single plate of one sort of food, and sets it before every one of them; but a priest says grace before meat; and it is unlawful for any one to taste of the food before grace be said. The same priest, when he hath dined, says grace again after meat; and when they begin, and when they end, they praise God, as he that bestows their food upon them; after which they lay aside their [white] garments, and betake themselves to their labors again till the evening; then they return home to supper, after the same manner; and if there be any strangers there, they sit down with them. Nor is there ever any clamor or disturbance to pollute their house, but they give everyone leave to speak in their turn; which silence thus kept in their house, appears to foreigners like some tremendous mystery; the cause of which is that perpetual sobriety they exercise, and the same settled measure of meat and drink that is allotted to them, and that such as is abundantly sufficient for them.

And truly, as for other things, they do nothing but according to the injunctions of their curators; only these two things are done among them at everyone's own free will, which are, to assist those that want it, and to show mercy; for they are permitted of their own accord to afford succor to such as deserve it, when they stand in need of it, and to bestow food on those that are in distress; but they cannot give any thing to their kindred without the curators. They dispense their anger after a just manner, and restrain their passion. They are eminent for fidelity, and are the ministers of peace; whatsoever they say also is firmer than an oath; but swearing is avoided by them, and they esteem it worse than perjury; for they say, that he who cannot be believed without [swearing by] God, is already condemned. They also take great pains in studying the writings of the ancients, and choose out of them what is most for the advantage of their soul and body; and they inquire after such *roots and medicinal stones* as may cure their distempers.

But now, if anyone hath a mind to come over to their sect, he is not immediately admitted, but he is prescribed the same method of living which they use, for a year, while he continues excluded; and they give him a small hatchet, and the fore-mentioned girdle, and the white garment. And when he hath given evidence, during that time, that he can observe their continence, he approaches nearer to their way of living, and is made partaker of the waters of purification; yet is he not even now admitted to live with them; for after this demonstration of his fortitude, his temper is tried two more years, and if he appear to be worthy, they then admit him into their society. And before he is allowed to touch their common food, he is obliged to take tremendous oaths; that, in the first place, he will exercise piety towards God; and then, that he will observe justice towards men; and that he will do no harm to any one, either of his own accord, or by the command of others; that he will always hate the wicked, and be assistant to the righteous; that he will *ever show fidelity to all men, and especially to those in authority*, because no one obtains the government without God's assistance;[148] and that if he be in authority, he will at no time whatever abuse his authority, nor endeavor to outshine his subjects, either in his garments, or any other finery; that he will be perpetually a lover of truth, and propose to himself to reprove those that tell lies; that he will keep his hands clear from theft, and his soul from unlawful gains; and that he will neither conceal anything from those of his own sect, nor discover any of their doctrines to others, no, not though anyone should compel him so to do at the hazard of his life. Moreover, he swears to communicate their doctrines to no one any otherwise than as he received them himself; *that he will abstain from*

---

[148]Compare with Paul in Rom. 13:1: "Let every person be subject to the governing authorities; for there is no authority except from God, and those authorities that exist have been instituted by God."

robbery,[149] and will equally preserve the books belonging to their sect, and the means of the angels [or messengers].[150] These are the oaths by which they secure their proselytes to themselves.

But for those that are caught in any heinous sins, they cast them out of their society; and he who is thus separated from them, does often die after a miserable manner; for as is bound by the oath he hath taken, and by the customs he hath been engaged in, he is not at liberty to partake of that food that he meets with elsewhere,[151] but is forced to eat grass, and to famish his body with hunger till he perish; for which reason they receive many of them again when they are at their last gasp, out of compassion to them, as thinking the miseries they have endured till they come to the very brink of death, to be a sufficient punishment for the sins they had been guilty of.

But in the judgments they exercise they are most accurate and just; nor do they pass sentence by the votes of a court that is fewer than a hundred. And as to what is once determined by that number, it is unalterable. What they most of all honor, after God himself, is the name of their legislator [Moses]; whom, if anyone blaspheme, he is punished capitally. They also think it a good thing to obey their elders, and the major part. Accordingly, if ten of them be sitting together no one of them will speak while the other nine are against it. They also avoid spitting in the midst of them, or on the right side. Moreover, they are stricter than any other of the Jews in resting from their labors on the seventh day; for they not only get their food ready the day before, that they may not be obliged to kindle a fire on that day, but they will not remove any vessel out of its place, nor go to stool thereon. Nay, on the other days they dig a small pit, a foot deep, with a paddle (which kind of hatchet is given them when they are first admitted among them); and covering themselves round with their garment, *that they may not affront the divine rays of light,*[152] they ease themselves into that pit, after which they put the earth that was dug out again into the pit; and even this they do only in the more lonely places, which they choose out for this purpose; and although this easement of the body be natural, yet it is a rule with them to wash themselves after it, as if it were a defilement to them.

Now after the time of their preparatory trial is over, they are parted into four classes; and so far are the juniors inferior to the seniors, that if the seniors should be touched by the juniors, they must wash themselves, as if they had intermixed themselves with the company of a foreigner. They are long-lived also; insomuch that many of them live above a hundred years, by means of the simplicity of their diet; nay, as I think, by means of the regular course of life they observe also. They condemn the miseries of life, and are above pain, by the generosity of their mind. And as for death, if it will be for their glory, they esteem it better than living always; and indeed *our war with the Romans gave abundant evidence what great souls they had in their trials,* wherein, although they were tortured and distorted, burnt and torn to pieces, and went through all kinds of instruments of torment, that they might be forced either to blaspheme their legislator, or to eat what was forbidden them, yet could they not be made to do either of them, no, nor once to flatter their tormentors, or to shed a tear; but they smiled in their very pains, and laughed those to scorn who inflicted the torments upon them, and *resigned up their souls with great alacrity,* as expecting to receive them again.[153]

For their doctrine is this: – That bodies are corruptible, and that the matter they are made of is not permanent; but that the souls are immortal, and continue forever; and that they come out of the most subtle air, and are united to their bodies as in prisons, into which they are drawn by a certain natural enticement; but that when they are set free from the bonds of the flesh, they then, as

---

[149]Which of course implies that 'robbery' (Josephus' code for rebellion) was a powerful attractor.

[150]Lists and attributes of angels as derived from Enochian apocalyptic works and ideas.

[151]This finds correspondence in Paul's condemnation of a sinning member of the Corinthian church. 1 Cor. 5:1-13 and 1 Corinthians 5:2-5: "you are to deliver this man to Satan for the destruction of the flesh, that his spirit may be saved in the day of the Lord Jesus."

[152]A Zoroastrian-Enochian idea which will be discussed in full in a future volume.

[153]Does this passage attest that the Essenes Josephus knew were indeed rebels against Rome?

released from a long bondage, rejoice and mount upward. And this is like the opinion of the Greeks, that good souls have their habitations beyond the ocean, in a region that is neither oppressed with storms of rain, or snow, or with intense heat, but that this place is such as is refreshed by the gentle breathing of a west wind, that is perpetually blowing from the ocean; while they allot to bad souls a dark and tempestuous den, full of never-ceasing punishments. And indeed the Greeks seem to me to have followed the same notion, when they allot the islands of the blessed to their brave men, whom they call heroes and demigods; and to the souls of the wicked, the region of the ungodly, in Hades, where their fables relate that certain persons, such as Sisyphus, and Tantalus, and Ixion, and Tityus, are punished; which is built on this first supposition, that souls are immortal; and thence are those exhortations to virtue, and exhortations from wickedness collected; whereby good men are bettered in the conduct of their life, by the hope they have of reward after their death, and whereby the vehement inclinations of bad men to vice are restrained, by the fear and expectation they are in, that although they should lie concealed in this life, they should suffer immortal punishment after their death. These are the divine doctrines of the Essenes about the soul, which lay an unavoidable bait for such as have once had a taste of their philosophy.

There also those among them who *undertake to foretell things to come, by reading the holy books*, and using several sorts of purifications, and being perpetually conversant in the discourses of the prophets; and it is but seldom that they miss in their predictions.

Moreover, there is *another order of Essenes*, who agree with the rest as to their way of living, and customs, and laws, but differ from them in the point of marriage, as thinking that by not marrying they cut off the principal part of the human life, which is the prospect of succession; nay rather, that if all men should be of the same opinion, the whole race of mankind would fail. However, they try their spouses for three years; and if they find that they have their natural purgations thrice, as trials that they are likely to be fruitful, they then actually marry them. But they do not use to accompany with their wives when they are with child, as a demonstration that they do not marry out of regard to pleasure, but for the sake of posterity. Now the women go into the baths with some of their garments on, as the men do with somewhat girded about them. And these are the customs of this order of Essenes.[154]

Josephus' account seems to be more detailed than Philo's, as well as contradictory on a number of points. For example, Philo says that none of the Essenes live in cities while Josephus describes them as commonly living in cities. Aside from what is footnoted above, a couple of things stand out as particularly odd. In describing the actions and behavior of the Essenes, Josephus notes with some particular care the following: 1) they carry nothing with them when they travel into remote parts, though still they take their weapons with them, for fear of thieves; 2) he will ever show fidelity to all men, and especially to those in authority; 3) that he will abstain from robbery.   If one assumes that Josephus is combining a description of the Essenes with his personal knowledge of the Qumran sectarians who clearly had the destruction of Rome in mind (along with all other illegitimate Gentile rule), it is as though, here, he is providing exculpatory justifications for a certain class of rebels who were involved in the war against Rome. 1) Did some of the 'Essenes' happen to be caught carrying weapons? Oh, that was different; they were only protecting themselves from thieves and robbers. 2) You thought that the Essenes were anti-Roman? Well, you were wrong; they habitually honored those in authority. 3) Final proof is that they swore to abstain from robbery, 'robbers' being a common term used by Josephus to describe revolutionaries.[155] Finally, he describes at the end the horrible tortures that Essenes were put

---

[154] *Wars* 2.8.2–13 (119–61).

[155] Josephus' defense of the Essenes matches that of Philo in this regard. Gmirkin (personal communication, unpublished research), citing Philo's defense of the Jewish community in *Flaccus* and *Gaius*, argues that

through by the Romans, which would indicate that they were definitely suspected of complicity in rebellion if not actively engaged in the war. The passage that begins with "indeed our war with the Romans gave abundant evidence what great souls they had in their trials" seems to be the object of Josephus' apologetic here. It also smacks a bit of being inspired by 2 Maccabees.

By the time he writes *Antiquities*, Josephus seems to be somewhat less interested in glorifying the Essenes and even uses Philo's number in estimating the population, though in *Wars* he had described many of them as being tortured and killed by the Romans in the war:

> But the sect of the Essenes affirms that fate governs all things, and that nothing befalls men but what is according to its determination.[156] ... These men live the same kind of life as do those whom the Greeks call Pythagoreans ...[157]

> The doctrine of the Essenes is this: That all things are best ascribed to God. They teach the immortality of souls, and esteem that the rewards of righteousness are to be earnestly striven for; and when they send what they have dedicated to God into the temple, they do not offer sacrifices, because they have more pure lustrations of their own; on which account they are excluded from the common court of the temple, but offer their sacrifices themselves; yet is their course of life better than that of other men; and they entirely addict themselves to husbandry. It also deserves our admiration, how much they exceed all other men that addict themselves to virtue, and this in righteousness; and indeed to such a degree, that as it hath never appeared among any other man, neither Greeks nor barbarians, no, not for a little time, so hath it endured a long while among them. This is demonstrated by that institution of theirs which will not suffer anything to hinder them from having all things in common; so that a rich man enjoys no more of his own wealth than he who hath nothing at all. There are about *four thousand men that live in this way*, and neither marry wives, nor are desirous to keep servants; as thinking the latter tempts men to be unjust, and the former gives the handle to domestic quarrels; but as they live by themselves, they minister one to another. They also appoint certain stewards to receive the incomes of their revenues, and of the fruits of the ground; such as are good men and priests, who are to get their corn and their food ready for them. They none of them differ from others of the Essenes in their way of living, but do the most resemble those Dacae who are called Polistae [dwellers in cities].[158]

The bridge between the accounts of Josephus and Philo and the Dead Sea community seems to be Pliny the Elder (23–79 AD) who, in his *Natural History*, identified the Qumran area as Essene:

> To the west [of the Dead Sea] the Essenes have put the necessary distance between themselves and the insalubrious shore. They are a people unique of its kind and admirable beyond all others in the whole world; without women and renouncing love entirely, without money and having for company only palm trees. Owing to the throng of newcomers, this people is daily reborn in equal number; indeed, those whom, wearied by the fluctuations of fortune, life leads to adopt their customs, stream in in great numbers. Thus, unbelievable though this may seem, *for thousands of centuries*[159] a people

---

"Philo's two tendentious essays on the uber-peaceful Essenes and Therapeutae were intended to defend them (as representatives of Egyptian Judaism) against accusations that the Jews were instigators of the troubles in Alexandria in 38 CE."

[156] *Ant.* 13.5.9 (172).

[157] *Ant.* 15.10.4 (371).

[158] *Ant.* 18.1.5 (18–9).

[159] One suspects that Pliny was influenced by Philo's claim that the origin of the Essenes was with Moses.

has existed which is eternal yet into which no one is born: so fruitful for them is the repentance which others feel for their past lives![160]

Pliny was apparently taken in by some of the myths.[161]

Along with Ellegård, Étienne Nodet and Justin Taylor find the similarities between the early Christian movement and the Essenes convincing.[162] But they approach it from the opposite direction: the later Christian writings like the Gospels and Acts. They write that one

> ... cannot help but be struck by the points of resemblance with the first Christian community, as described in Acts 2:42 f.: network of town communities, sharing of goods, brotherhood, charity, breaking of bread, even a severe justice (cf. Acts. 5:1 f.). To these could be added the personal status of women, not mentioned by Josephus, but defined in 1 QSa 1:9-10. ...
>
> The central elements of Christianity in their entirety, including the eucharist, the cross and the system of excommunication, are directly derived from Jewish 'sects' of the most traditional type, claiming to represent the renewal of the true Covenant, **especially in Galilee.**[163]

Well, if the author of Acts was using Josephus, he could easily have been creating a mythical 'Christian community' based on the Essene model. On the other hand, perhaps he had some knowledge from another source that there was some connection?

Gabriele Boccaccini suggests that a convincing etymology for the name Essene has not been found, but that the term applies to a larger group within Palestine that also included the Qumran community.[164] According to Josephus, the Essenes had settled "not in one city" but "in large numbers in every town." Philo speaks of "more than four thousand" *Essaioi* living in "Palestine and Syria," and John Collins, conflating Philo and Josephus writes, "in many cities of Judaea and in many villages and grouped in *great societies of many members.*"[165]

The Church Father Epiphanius of Salamis (writing in the late fourth century AD) seems to make a distinction between two main groups within the Essenes, which he designates the Ossaeans and the Nazareans. Epiphanius describes each group as follows:

> The Nazarean – they were Jews by nationality – originally from Gileaditis, Bashanitis and the Transjordan ... They acknowledged Moses and believed that he had received laws – not this law, however, but some other. And so, they were Jews who kept all the Jewish observances, but they would not offer sacrifice or eat meat. They considered it unlawful to eat meat or make sacrifices

---

[160]Pliny, *Historia Naturalis* 5.17 or 29 (in other editions 5.(15).73), from Géza Vermès, Martin Goodman (eds.), *The Essenes: According to the Classical Sources* (JSOT Press, 1989).

[161]"The connection between the Dead Sea and the Essenes was also made by Synesius (c.400 C.E.) citing Dio Chrysostom (c.100 C.E.): the Essenes were 'a whole happy city by the Dead Water in the interior of Palestine, [a city] lying somewhere close by Sodom' (Synesius, *Dion* 3.2)." Joan E. Taylor, 'Philo of Alexandria on the Essenes: A Case Study on the Use of Classical Sources in Discussions of the Qumran-Essene Hypothesis,' *The Studia Philonica Annual* 19 (2007), p. 1. See also Steven D. Fraade, 'History (?) In The Damascus Document,' *Dead Sea Discoveries* 25 (2018).

[162]See Carrier (2014), p. 176, n. 50 for more references.

[163]Étienne Nodet and Justin Taylor, *The Origins of Christianity: An Exploration* (Liturgical Press, 1998), pp. 87, 437.

[164]Gabriele Boccaccini, *Beyond the Essene Hypothesis: The Parting of the Ways Between Qumran and Enochic Judaism* (Eerdmans, 1998), p. 47.

[165]John J. Collins's recent work, *Beyond the Qumran Community* (Eerdmans, 2009), supports Ellegård, Nodet and Taylor's conclusions, with discussion of such communities scattered around the empire.

with it. They claim that these Books are fictions, and that none of these customs were instituted by the fathers. This was the difference between the Nazarean and the others ...

After this Nazarean sect in turn comes another closely connected with them, called the Ossaeans. These are Jews like the former ... [they] originally came from Nabataea, Ituraea, Moabitis and Arielis, the lands beyond the basin of what sacred scripture called the Salt Sea ... Though it is different from the other six of these seven sects, it causes schism only by *forbidding the books of Moses* like the Nazarean.[166]

The relationship between the community of Qumran and the Essenes has been disputed:

Norman Golb[167] argues that ... the amount of documents is too extensive and includes many different writing styles and calligraphies; the ruins seem to have been a fortress, used as a military base for a very long period of time – including the 1st century – so they could not have been inhabited by the Essenes; and the large graveyard excavated in 1870, just 50 metres east of the Qumran ruins, was made of over 1200 tombs that included many women and children – Pliny clearly wrote that the Essenes who lived near the Dead Sea "had not one woman, had renounced all pleasure ... and no one was born in their race". ... Other scholars refute these arguments – particularly since Josephus describes some Essenes as allowing marriage. Another issue is the relationship between the *Essaioi* and Philo's *Therapeutae* and *Therapeutrides*. He regarded the *Therapeutae* as a contemplative branch of the *Essaioi* who, he said, pursued an active life. (Philo, *De Vita Contemplativa* 1.1.)[168]

Schürer accepts the identification between the Therapeutae and Essenes as probable (the early Church historian Eusebius even identified them as 'proto-Christians').[169] And modern scholars like Boccaccini[170] and VanderKam[171] continue to insist on the Essene–Qumran relationship. Some scholars have rejected the connection, pointing instead to the Sadducees, or even the straightforward choice of calling them what they called themselves in the scrolls: the *Yahad* ('Unity').[172] Each camp has good reasons for rejecting the other options, since no ancient source provides a description that matches *exactly* with the characteristics described in the scrolls.

However, the Essene hypothesis does have the advantage of being the closest fit. I think Nodet and Taylor are correct when they point out that the clearly defined categories Josephus gives *do not describe reality*. Nodet and Taylor do an excellent job teasing out what can be discerned about the varieties of first-century Judaism from the Dead Sea Scrolls, Josephus, and the Talmud. They describe a loose network of Essene-like brotherhoods in rural Galilee, with their roots in returnees from exile in Babylon. These brotherhoods shared much in common with the Pharisees, and were probably indistinguishable from them until the Pharisees became the

---

[166]Epiphanius, *Panarion* 1:18, 19, quoted by Wikipedia.org, 'Essenes.'

[167]Norman Golb, *Who Wrote the Dead Sea Scrolls?: The Search for the Secret of Qumran* (Simon & Schuster, 1996).

[168]Wikipedia.org, 'Essenes.'

[169]Schürer (vol. II, 1979), pp. 591–7.

[170]See Boccaccini (1998).

[171]James C. VanderKam, *The Jewish Apocalyptic Heritage in Early Christianity*, edited with William Adler (Fortress Press, 1996); *Enoch: A Man for All Generations* (University of South Carolina Press, 2008); *1 Enoch: The Hermeneia Translation*, with George Nickelsburg (Fortress Press, 2012); *Jubilees: The Hermeneia Translation* (Fortress Press, 2020).

[172]Glen J. Fairen, *As Below, So Above: Apocalypticism, Gnosticism and the Scribes of Qumran and Nag Hammadi* (Gorgias Press, 2013), pp. 52–67.

mainstream, majority 'party' after the war. They were probably also the groups out of which came the founders of later rabbinic Judaism.

Such brotherhoods were elitist, only accepting Jewish proselytes, and had two defining ritual practices that separated themselves from both Gentiles *and* ordinary Jews: baptism, which marked the total purification and official rite of passage into the community, and the 'purity,' a weekly communal meal. They were also apocalyptic and messianic, seeing themselves as the true Israel, the faithful remnant in contrast to the corrupt and lost majority. It's possible that, like the Sadducees, they too laid claim to the title of 'Sons of Zadok' or 'Zadokites,' as references in the Dead Sea Scrolls suggest. While Josephus distinguishes between the 'Torah-only' Sadducees and the 'written-Torah-plus-oral-law' Pharisees, the actual distinctions between groups and self-identifications may have been much more permeable.[173]

So, the Essenes were probably a fairly diverse group, ranging from contemplative to militant in ideology, and extending probably throughout the Empire. And, in addition, I think we must consider Essene-*like* groups – copycats – that admitted Gentiles or may have actually been composed of mainly or exclusively Gentiles.

The Teacher of Righteousness

Ellegård argues that what was known of the person named as 'Jesus' in the Easter visions was related to traditions about the Teacher of Righteousness who figures in the Dead Sea Scrolls, the earliest of which are thought to have been written ca. 100 BC. This individual was known as a revered founder and leader of the cult, but not the Messiah or a supernatural being. The Teacher of Righteousness was someone to whom God had made known all the mysteries of the prophets, and who had been severely persecuted. In view of this, Wells discusses Talmudic references that point to a Jesus who was killed by the Jews in Lud (Lydda) by stoning,[174] and not by the Romans in Jerusalem by crucifixion. In the Gemara, the body of commentaries on the Jewish codification of law called the Mishnah, Jesus was said to have been persecuted by King Alexander Jannaeus (103–76 BC):[175]

> The Gemara sums up Jesus' activities by saying (Sanh. 43a) that he 'practised magic and deceived and led astray Israel'. This man who learned magic in Egypt and scratched charms on his flesh has little resemblance to the gospel Jesus. ... The passage goes on to explain the incident, 'When king Jannaeus put the Rabbis to death, Rabbi Joshua b. Perahiah fled to Alexandria but later ... came back ...' (Sotah, 47a and Sanh. 107b). The persecution of the Pharisees under Jannaeus is well attested. Löw [1858] thought that the Jesus of the Talmud fled into Egypt during this persecution, learned magic there, and later founded the Essene sect, which he says, is named after him. ...
>
> In sum, if the early Christians were not followers of the gospel Jesus but Jews who believed that the Messiah, named Jesus, had come and would return, and who were otherwise orthodox, keeping the law and attending the temple, then the silence of the rabbinical literature about Jesus

---

[173]Nodet and Taylor (1998).

[174]Sanhedrin (43a): "Jesus was hanged on Passover Eve. Forty days previously the herald had cried, 'He is being led out for stoning, because he has practiced sorcery and led Israel astray and enticed them into apostasy. Whosoever has anything to say in his defense, let him come and declare it.' As nothing was brought forward in his defense, he was hanged on Passover Eve." That is to say, his dead body was hanged on a gibbet after stoning.

[175]Sanhedrin (107b), cited in Wells (1971), p. 200.

and about Christians up to the end of the first century, when the decisive break occurred, is quite intelligible; whereas if there was a historical Jesus who had the career ascribed to him in the gospels, it is not.[176]

This idea is particularly interesting in view of Birger Pearson's work *Gnosticism, Judaism, and Egyptian Christianity*. Pearson adduces new support of Moritz Friedlander's[177] idea that gnosticism is a *pre*-Christian phenomenon originating in anti-Law Jewish circles in Alexandria. That is, gnosticism arose among Jews who were exposed to Middle Platonism, but also were influenced by the events of their times, i.e. the political facts on the ground, and the evident failure of the promises of their god:[178]

> This hermeneutical principle can be described as one of revolt. In the Gnostic reinterpretation the God of Israel, the God of history and creation, is demonized; the Creator and his creation are considered to be the product of a tragic fall within the divine realm; and humanity is seen to be a part of the transcendent God imprisoned by hostile powers in an alien environment. Inasmuch as the Gnostic synthesis reflects the use and reinterpretation of Jewish scripture and tradition, it is apparent that the Gnostic phenomenon itself originates in a Jewish environment as *an expression of alienation from ('orthodox') Judaism.*[179]

Glen Fairen is even clearer on this, pointing out the close similarities not only between the Qumran and Nag Hammadi texts, but also between these 'Judeo-Christian' texts and the surrounding literature of Ancient Near and Middle East (for example, the Greek *Asclepius*, Egyptian *Potter's Oracle*, and Persian *Zand-I Vohuman Yasn* apocalypses).[180] So-called gnosticism only developed the apocalyptic themes further, using their own internal, Jewish logic. Fairen's definitions make it crystal clear:

> *Apocalypticism(s):* Ancient Near and Middle Eastern, scribally written protest literature which focuses on the loss of native kingship and expresses a phantasmagoric rectification thereof, particularly in terms of cosmic symbolism syncretistically redeployed from Ancient Near and Middle Eastern cosmologies.

> *Gnosticism(s):* An analogous expression of Ancient Near and Middle Eastern apocalypticism where, under the domination of a hegemonic foreign power, there is a belief in the inability, or lack of desire, of the titular national god to instigate an apocalyptic resolution. Hence, gnosticism – as an expression of the inherent tension within an ontological system that postulates a good deity with a corrupt world – recasts notions of 'as above, so below' so that where once the wrong king would be replaced by the right god, it now is reconfigured so that the wrong king must reflect the wrong or illegitimate god in heaven.[181]

---

[176] Wells (1971), p. 202.

[177] Austrian theologian; born in Bur Szt. Georgen, Hungary, 1842. See http://www.jewishencyclopedia.com/artic les/6381-friedlander-moritz.

[178] The failure of the independent Jewish kingdom of the Maccabees which lasted about 100 years and was brought to an end by Pompey in 63 BC.

[179] Birger A. Pearson, *Gnosticism, Judaism, and Egyptian Christianity* (Fortress Press, 2006), pp. 37–8.

[180] While 'apocalyptic' is usually considered an exclusively Jewish genre, it is not, as these texts show. They all share the following thematic characteristics: prophecy after the event (retrojecting the current political situation into past prophecies), a nostalgic view of the nation (e.g., Israel, Egypt), the nation compromised by impiety and/or foreign invaders, societal collapse, followed by cosmic calamities and a divine re-ordering (usually through a messianic agent of God).

[181] Fairen (2013), pp. 139, 151–2.

In other words, they are *political* texts, as much as they are religious, reflecting the idea that when a god's true representative is in power, all is good. The chaos of foreign rule, in contrast, necessitates a divine re-ordering, where god's rule is brought back. This was the outlook of the Jewish rebels in Josephus' *Wars*. Later on the 'gnostics' concluded that it wasn't just foreign rule – it must be that the *wrong gods* were in charge; understandable, after centuries of foreign rule, and two failed rebellions that resulted in national catastrophe.

There are a number of striking parallels between some of the Nag Hammadi texts and the texts of Qumran. This suggests strongly that similar speculations were under way both in Alexandria and in Palestine, and one wonders where they began? Is the Talmud correct that the origins were in Palestine in the time of Alexander Jannaeus? Or later, when Pompey destroyed the nationalist dreams of the Jews by taking Judea under Roman control?[182] Or was it simply a constant, receiving fresh inspiration with each new, corrupt foreign ruler?

The Hellenistically inspired exegetical activities[183] of the two groups advanced in different ways: for the Gnostics, Yahweh/Jehovah became a demon of sorts, a demiurgic creator similar to Zoroastrianism's Ahriman; and for the Qumran community, one only needed to apply more and better Pesher-izing to get the right combination and understand what was going on and how God and his messiah would set things right. This is interesting in view of the fact that the Gnosticizers tended to reject the Old Testament (even if they based their myths on it), while later Christian orthodoxy – like the sectarians at Qumran – retained the Old Testament in rejection of the gnostics and later Marcionites, while rejecting its theology in favor of Christ. There were certainly a lot of ideas fermenting and many combinations; nothing was simple.

In any event, the Dead Sea Scrolls show that the memory of their founder was treasured a long time after his death. Ellegård proposes that visions of this teacher – long dead – convinced members of the Qumran community and other groups of Essenes throughout the Empire that he was preparing to return to Earth along with the Hosts of Heaven, for the last judgment.

Overall, the descriptions of the Essenes written by Philo of Alexandria around 20 AD, and later by Josephus, suggest that they were a much more open and innovative group than what the Dead Sea Scrolls say about the xenophobic Qumran community. Perhaps that was because the Qumran group was closer to the scene of the political action and had become radicalized into Zealotry.

What Did Paul Know?

If the earliest surviving Christian documents were addressed to Diaspora communities, and if many of these communities were Essenes or Essene-type groups, some of which may have included – or been entirely composed of – Gentiles, then we can probably assume that these groups were

---

[182]It is interesting to note that this was the time that brought forth Antiochus of Ascalon beginning the phase of Greek philosophy known as Middle Platonism. Antiochus "was a pupil of Philo of Larissa at the Academy, but he diverged from the academic skepticism of Philo and his predecessors. He was a teacher of Cicero, and the first of a new breed of eclectics among the Platonists; he endeavoured to bring the doctrines of the Stoics and the Peripatetics into Platonism, and stated, in opposition to Philo, that the mind could distinguish true from false. ... [H]e had a school at Alexandria as well as in Syria, where he seems to have died." Looking into Middle Platonism reveals a rich field of comparative study for emerging Christianity. See e.g., John M. Dillon, *The Middle Platonists* (Cornell University Press, 1996).

[183]Exegesis is the critical explanation or interpretation of a piece of text.

the groups addressed by Paul. What Paul was intent on communicating to these communities was the Jesus now revealed to him as a supernatural figure, a heavenly judge, and his salvific work was exemplified as 'Christ on a cross.' This is a bit of a problem. The idea of crucifixion on its own –as Paul presents it, though the Gospels add flogging – doesn't mesh with the emphasis on blood. Discussing the Book of Revelation, Wells notes:

> ... the Jews believed in the efficacy of the shedding of blood as a means of placating God. According to Leviticus, 'the blood on the altar makes atonement for sins because it is being given for life that has been forfeited through sin. The blood is valid for atonement only when it is poured out on the altar in death'.[184] And the idea that the blood of the sacrificed animal conveys new life is found in the worship of Attis ... In this cult, a bull and a ram were sacrificed on a grille under which the initiate stood, and he was reborn as the blood rained down upon him.[185] When the Apocalypse pictures Jesus as a slaughtered lamb who redeemed the elect with his blood, a sacrificial death on the altar is indicated. ... [M]any manuscripts say that the elect are 'washed' from their sins by his blood. This implies the shedding of *streams of blood* as in sacrifice on the altar. This image of the slaughtered lamb whose blood was poured out would not be a very apposite way of referring figuratively to death by *crucifixion, which is relatively bloodless*, but could be better applied to someone who had been beheaded or *torn to pieces with knives.*[186]

> "For Jews demand signs and Greeks desire wisdom, but *we proclaim Christ crucified*, a stumbling block to Jews and foolishness to Gentiles, but to those who are the called, *both Jews and Greeks*, Christ the power of God and the wisdom of God. ... When I came to you, brothers, I did not come proclaiming the *mystery* of God to you in lofty words or wisdom. For I decided to know nothing among you except Jesus Christ, and him crucified."[187]

With these words, Paul makes clear the decisive importance he attributes to the image of Christ on a cross. Recalling the Jesus who was stoned at Lydda, and only afterwards hung on a cross, we find that this is the prescribed method derived from Deut. 21:23, which further states that the accursed body ought not to be left hanging overnight so as not to desecrate the land. It is suggested that this is probably where Paul got the idea that the ignominy of the death of Jesus freed Christians from the Law. Wells writes:

> The argument he gives to show that [the Law] is unnecessary is that a crucified Jesus contradicts the law of Deut. 21.23 that a man whose dead body is hanged upon a tree is accursed of God. Paul quotes this passage and comments: 'Christ brought us freedom from the curse of the law by becoming for our sake an accursed thing' (Gal. iii.13). The argument is: the law says that the man crucified is accursed. Jesus was crucified but could not be accursed. Therefore a case has occurred for which the law is not valid. But as it must be either valid absolutely or invalid absolutely, it is by this one case rendered wholly invalid.[188]

---

[184]Rev. G. T. Manley, *The New Bible Handbook* (London, 1960), p. 140, cited by Wells (1971), p. 282.

[185]H. Hepding, *Attis, seine Mythen und sein Kult* (Giessen, 1903), pp. 65ff., cited by Wells (1971), p. 282.

[186]Wells (1971), p. 282.

[187]1 Cor. 1:22–4, 2:1–2. At the end of this letter, commenting on Christ's resurrection or ascension, an event associated with the cross, Paul says: "If Christ has not been raised, then our preaching is in vain and your faith is in vain ... and you are still in your sins" (1 Cor. 15:14–7).

[188]Albert Schweitzer, *The Mysticism of Paul the Apostle*, translated by W. Montgomery (London, 1931), p. 72, cited by Wells (1971), p. 298.

Of course, the above says nothing about how a human Jesus may have died, as it is clear elsewhere that the 'crucifixion' of Christ was thought to have taken place in another realm and possibly reflected on Earth in some way that did involve the shedding of large amounts of blood. That the blood of a perfectly righteous man can atone for others, and that excess suffering especially can 'pay' for the sins others have committed, and is of service to others, goes back at least to the *Wisdom of Sirach* and the books of Maccabees. Wells thought that while it was possible for Jews to think of their messiah as *suffering* to atone for the sins of the world, they did not hold the idea that the Messiah might *die as a bloody, atoning sacrifice*. This probably isn't entirely true. At least some Jews may have made this connection.[189] One of the Dead Sea Scrolls manuscripts of Isaiah 53 says the suffering servant will be 'anointed' by God, i.e. 'Christed,' then "pierced through for our transgressions," rather than just 'bruised' or 'wounded' as in the canonical Isaiah. Paul either got that part of his Christology by thinking along similar lines, or directly from such groups. Commenting on how the idea of the suffering servant became associated with the Messiah, Wells writes:

> All that was necessary was that this idea [i.e. that excess suffering for the sins of others is of service to others] should be applied to the Messiah. This application was natural enough, since the Messiah was believed to be a powerful and virtuous being, and the idea that suffering gives power and is associated with virtue is almost universal. The Indian Brahmins, for instance, practiced self-inflicted suffering in the hope of attaining supernatural power, and many virtuous men or saints are reported to have endured great suffering. The idea may have arisen from the supposed connection between sin and punishment. Suffering is held to atone for wickedness, and excess of suffering is therefore like the opening of a credit account.[190]

It is fairly easy to suggest that Paul adopted the idea of the dying and resurrecting gods of the pagans,[191] but I don't think it is quite that simple. Wells proposes, based on Frazer, that when the dying and resurrecting agriculture gods were transferred to city life, the objects of their revivification became human beings themselves and the resurrection of the god was thought to ensure that of his devotees. That is, *those who associated with a particular god, and supported that deity by devotion, would also achieve a new life* after the death of the body. All around the Empire there were public and private cults focused around such promises. It was essentially an expansion of the patronage[192] system into cosmology.

---

[189]Carrier (2014), pp. 73–81 (citing Talmud and Dead Sea Scroll references), 91 (n. 62).

[190]Wells (1971), p. 228.

[191]Aside from the standard ones usually cited (Osiris, Dionysus, Mithras, Ishtar, etc.), Carrier (2014) brings attention to another dying-and-rising god whose story closely parallels that of the Gospels' Jesus: the Roman national hero Romulus. He lists over 20 parallels, including (adapted from pp. 56–8, 227): son of god, born of a virgin, attempt on his life as a baby, becomes a shepherd, hailed as king, killed by the elite, death accompanied by prodigies and darkness, missing corpse, new and shining immortal body, post-resurrection meeting with a follower, pre-ascension speech from a high place, instruction to future followers, taken up into a cloud, explicit eyewitness testimony, fleeing witnesses (including a 'Mark,' 'Luke,' and 'Gaius'), post-resurrection worship and cult, among others. As Carrier puts it: "It certainly seems as if Mark is fashioning Jesus into the new Romulus ... The Christian conception of Jesus' death and resurrection appears to have been significantly influenced by the Roman conception of Romulus's death and resurrection" (pp. 57, 228).

[192]Erich S. Gruen, 'Patrocinium and clientela,' in *The Hellenistic World and the Coming of Rome* (University of California Press, 1986), vol. 1: "Patronage (*clientela*) was the distinctive relationship in ancient Roman society between the *patronus* (plural *patroni*, 'patron') and their *cliens* (plural *clientes*, 'client'). The relationship

It is suggested that in those times of gross and outrageous vice and inequity on the part of the social elites, a popular reaction developed in the form of rapid growth and promulgation of religious groups – ecclesia – in which an ethically pure life was a condition of membership. Mysteries were multiplied, and initiates were submitted to ceremonies, rites, mystical reenactments of the death and resurrection of the god, confession of sins, sacrifices, and so on. The most consistent elements shared across these organizations were baptism, sacrifice, and a common meal that represented not just communion with other initiates, but with the god as well. But even then, the most important element in Paul is missing: the idea that believers *share* in the god's death, experience it *with* him, and are in some way actually crucified and reborn *while living*. That too was something unprecedented in the 'apocalyptic' milieu of the time.

Indeed the early Christian communities of the Diaspora had much in common with such ecclesia, but it should be noted, the 'church' in Jerusalem may have been something quite different. What Paul created and taught appears to have been very much at odds with that group, who seem to have been indistinguishable in their views from other Jewish apocalyptic/messianic groups. As Wells writes:

> Paul wrote of a Jesus of whom no traditions were current save that he was the Messiah descended from David,[193] was crucified, and that his resurrection promised his worshippers immortality. Nothing was known of his doctrines or of when he lived. Thus there is nothing in the earliest Christian documents which would have appeared unacceptable to a citizen of the Middle East at the time,

was hierarchical, but obligations were mutual. The *patronus* was the protector, sponsor, and benefactor of the client; the technical term for this protection was *patrocinium*. Benefits a patron might confer include legal representation in court, loans of money, influencing business deals or marriages, and supporting a client's candidacy for political office or a priesthood. In return, the clients were expected to offer their services to their patron as needed. A freedman became the client of his former master. A patronage relationship might also exist between a general and their soldiers, a founder and colonists, and a conqueror and a dependent foreign community. The pressures to uphold one's obligations were primarily moral, founded on the *mos maiorum*, 'ancestral custom,' and the qualities of *fides* ('trust, reliability') on the part of the patron and the *pietas* ('dutiful devotion') demonstrated by the client. The regulation of the patronage relationship was believed by the Greek historians Dionysius and Plutarch to be one of the early concerns of Romulus; hence the relationship dated to the very founding of Rome. In the earliest periods, patricians would have served as patrons; both *patricius*, 'patrician,' and *patronus* are related to the Latin word *pater*, 'father'. The client and patron were not allowed to sue or to bear witness against each other, and had to abstain from any injury to each other. In early times, the client accompanied the patron in war, being in this respect similar to the vassal of the Middle Ages. The client had to ransom the patron if the patron was taken prisoner, and to vote for the patron if the patron was a candidate for an office. The client was regarded as a minor member of their patron's *gens* ('clan'), entitled to assist in its religious services, and bound to contribute to the cost of them. The client was subject to the jurisdiction and discipline of the *gens*, and was entitled to burial in its common sepulchre. According to Niebuhr, if the client died without an heir, the patron inherited their property."

[193] Assuming that this reference from Rom. 1 to Jesus being 'made' from the 'sperm/seed' of David is not an interpolation. Fact is, in pre-Christian context, 'Son of David' as qualification to be messiah is markedly infrequent. See only: *Psalms of Solomon* 17:21. Mark 12:35-37a: Rejection of the appellation 'Son of David' as the Christ/Messiah is the obvious intention of Jesus here where he cites psalm 110:1. That is, Jesus indicates that the Christ cannot be the son of David. See: 10:47; 11:10; Mt 1:1-17; Lk 3:23-38. Jesus, in Mark, points to Divine sonship, NOT the consummation of the hope for a coming King or revolutionary. The view that the Christ is the Son of David is attributed to the scribes who have just been excoriated. This suggests to me that the claim made in Romans (and it is clear that Mark was using Paul), if intended literally, did NOT contain this statement and it was added only later. And even if authentic, it would not necessarily imply anything about the earthly descent of Jesus or have any revolutionary connotations. On this passage, see the discussion below under the heading 'Son of David?' in Chapter 7.

when the idea of the dying Saviour was very widespread. ... Murray has observed that 'the parts of Christian doctrine which a Levantine pagan of the first century would deny are chiefly the [later] historical statements. Like Paul before his conversion, he would be ready enough to discuss the doctrine of a Hebrew Messiah or a Hellenistic "Saviour", but would refuse to believe that this supernatural being had just arrived on earth in the person of a certain Jew or Nazarene.' Since it is the historical statements that are lacking in the earliest Christian traditions, it really looks as if Christianity began without them, as one of the many dying-god sects of the time which grew in popularity because of the extent to which it was able to assimilate other myths and rituals.[194]

As Nodet and Taylor point out, after analyzing all the evidence:

> The simplest conclusion is that up till then [the federation of Jewish brotherhoods initiated by Gamaliel II after 90 AD], the successors of James [and James himself] were *hardly distinguishable from the proto-rabinical groups*, whom we classed before in the general category of Essenes. This category certainly contained many currents, some of them more or less Messianic [i.e. political/religious activists and nationalists].[195]

Paul recognized that his version of Christianity was NOT that of the Jerusalem Christians. He tells us that his gospel was repudiated and his authority as an apostle was rejected by them. The fact that Paul believed that God had chosen him to preach to the Gentiles means that he believed God's intervention in this way was an act initiating something that had not hitherto existed. Therefore, the distinction that Paul makes between his gospel and that of the Jerusalem Christians must have much greater significance than the mere fact that Paul was preaching to the Gentiles and Peter to the Jews. The nature of Paul's gospel shows how un-Jewish it was and how much it depended on Greco-Roman religious concepts.

The great irony is that it is largely Paul's gospel that has survived, though 'brought down to Earth' and historicized, while the gospel of the Jerusalem Christians can only be inferred from Paul's references to it. The triumph of Paul's version – or at least the triumph of the bastardization of Paul's gospel – is due entirely to the war between the Jews and Rome and the total destruction of Jerusalem and the earliest Christians headquartered there.

Obviously, at the times the Gospels were written, there still existed documents of early Christian activity which were later destroyed and/or abandoned to decay. A shrewd and rational assessment of the historical situation, as far as it can be recovered, might permit – even assist – some recovery of actual historical information from the Gospels and Acts. This recovery can only be limited because the complete absence of earlier documents attests to the fact of a total revision of history by the authors of the Gospels and Acts, and thus their motivations are strongly in question and *their writings must be interrogated as hostile witnesses*. Brandon writes:

> The fact ... that Jesus included a Zealot among his disciples, and the fact that he is never recorded to have condemned the Zealots or their principles, constitute evidence of great importance. ... For the silence here about the Zealots [a most active group, historically speaking] must be matched with the explicit condemnation pronounced by Jesus on the Pharisees and Sadducees, and even by implication on the Herodians.[196]

---

[194]Wells (1971), pp. 237–8, citing G. Murray, *Stoic, Christian and Humanist* (London, 1950), p. 76.
[195]Nodet and Taylor (1998), p. 236.
[196]Brandon (1967), p. 200.

There is a similarly curious silence about the Qumran sectarians. It could not have been due to ignorance. The silence of the NT documents about Qumran is damning. Whatever may have been the relations of the primitive Christian movement with the Qumran community, the complete absence of any reference to them in the Christian documents that survived attests to the fact that these documents – the Gospels and Acts – provide only a revisionist, redacted, or completely fake history of the origins of Christianity.

If it is true that the Qumran sectarians and the Zealots were one and the same, the silence of the Gospels and Acts is doubly damning.

The Two Jesuses

Both Wells and Ellegård (and more recently Doherty and Carrier) point out, with example after example, that the earliest Christian documents show no knowledge of the 'Jesus of Nazareth' figure, as we saw above with the letters of Paul. With this in mind, Wells argues:

> [When] we arrange extant early Christian documents into a chronological series, we find that ... Jesus figures simply as a supernatural personage whom God had sent in human form into the world to redeem it and who was crucified there in unspecified circumstances. These early writers are so vague in what they say about his life that they may well have believed only that he had been crucified in obscure circumstances long ago.[197] I show that such a view is likely to have been suggested to them by the Jewish wisdom literature they knew well and by traditions they must have known concerning actual crucifixions of living men in Palestine one and two centuries before their time. And I argue that they were in fact probably wrong in believing this much of him.[198]

In his book *Can We Trust the New Testament*, Wells somewhat modifies his initial ideas as presented in *The Jesus Legend* (1996) and *The Jesus Myth* (1999):

> In my first books on Jesus, I argued that the gospel Jesus is an entirely mythical expansion of the Jesus of the early epistles. ... I no longer maintain this position. *The weakness of my earlier position was pressed upon me by J. D. G. Dunn, who objected that we really cannot plausibly assume that such a complex of traditions as we have in the gospels and their sources could have developed within such a short time from the early epistles without a historical basis* (Dunn, [*The Evidence for Jesus,*] 1985, p. 29). My present standpoint is: this complex is not all post-Pauline ... and if I am right, against Doherty and Price – it is not all mythical. The essential point, as I see it, is that the Q material, whether or not it suffices as evidence of Jesus's historicity, refers to a personage who is *not to be identified with the dying and rising Christ of the early epistles.*[199]

Notice that the argument used is that "such a complex of traditions ... developed within such a short time." That may not, in fact, be the case; there may be more involved than meets the eye, and Paul and Jesus may have a very different timeline once we deal with Pontius Pilate further on. Also, despite the fact that the 'Q Hypothesis' has come under serious (and reasonable) attack in recent years, it still seems that Wells is on to something when he insists that a supernatural messiah figure (Paul's Jesus) was overlaid on a real person in Palestine in the first centuries BC and/or AD.

---

[197]Or, as Carrier argues, in the heavens.
[198]G. A. Wells, *The Historical Evidence for Jesus* (Prometheus, 1988), pp. 217–18.
[199]G. A. Wells, *Can We Trust the New Testament?* (Open Court, 2003), pp. 49–50.

In the Gospels, the two Jesus figures – the human preacher of Q and the supernatural personage of the early epistles who sojourned briefly on Earth as a man and then, rejected, returned to heaven – *have been fused into one.* The Galilean preacher of Q has been given a salvific death and resurrection, and these have been set not in an unspecified past (as in the early epistles), but in a historical context consonant with the date of the Galilean preaching.[200]

As we'll see, the human figure probably wasn't 'the Galilean preacher of Q,' but he *was* from Galilee.

---

[200]Wells (2003), p. 43.

2. Paul's Literary Environment

Ancient Myths

At the heart of Christianity is the belief in a coming consummation of existence when the forces of good will prevail over the forces of evil, and human agents of pain, misery and suffering will be physically annihilated or otherwise nullified. The elect, the good people, will then live a happy, suffering-free life on a transformed Earth, purified of darkness and negative elements. This ideology has been quite powerful down through the centuries leading to all sorts of millenarian movements, end-of-the-world predictions, and so on. Yet, it seems, that this idea was not always prevalent in all places.

This idea was not new. Comparative mythologist Michael Witzel, in his enormous *The Origins of the World's Mythologies*,[201] argues that it stretches back tens of thousands of years into humanity's prehistory, part of what he calls the 'Laurasian' branch of world mythology. Witzel's work is ambitious and controversial. In the absence of written records, he uses multiple other lines of evidence to determine the mythic elements that must have originated prehistory before making their way down to us. He does so primarily through an in-depth use of comparative mythology (using similar principles as comparative linguistics), which can identify geographical similarities and differences between sets of myths, specifically in their overall storyline. He supports this approach with evidence from linguistics, anthropology, archeology and genetics, all of which use a similar methodology of cladistics/common ancestry.[202]

For example, if two widely separated cultures relate a series of myths that not only have similar mythemes, but also a similar overall storyline, Witzel argues that they must have shared a common origin. By looking at the anthropological/archeological record of when those two cultures would have branched off from a common ancestor/geographical location, supported by DNA haplogroup research, he then tests his theory and derives a date for the proposed branching. This process reveals three overall groupings of myths, which he names after the prehistoric supercontinents: Laurasia (Europe and Asia), Gondwana (Africa, Australia, etc.), and Pangea (the original unified landmass). He argues for a shared Pangean set of myths, out of which branched the roughly northern/southern branches of Laurasia and Gondwana. The latter two are compared here:

---

[201]Michael Witzel, *The Origins of the World's Mythologies* (Oxford University Press, 2013).

[202]Ray Norris of Western Sydney University also argues that we can trace back myths deep into prehistory. For example, while many cultures refer to the Pleiades as 'seven sisters,' only six stars are visible in the constellation. But 100,000 years ago, the seventh (Pleione) was visible. Myths of the 'lost Pleiad' are shared from Australia and Africa to Europe and the Americas. See https://theconversation.com/the-worlds-oldest-story-astronomers-say-global-myths-about-seven-sisters-stars-may-reach-back-100-000-years-151568.

Laurasian	Gondwana
Creation from nothing, chaos, etc. Father Heaven and Mother Earth created.	In the beginning, heaven, Earth, sea, already exist.
Father Heaven and Mother Earth engender two generations of gods/demi-gods (Titans, Olympians).	A High God lives in heaven, or on Earth, or ascends to heaven from Earth later.
Four or five generations (Ages) during which Heaven is 'pushed up' and the Sun is released.	There is a series of lower gods, children of the high god, tricksters and heroes of one sort or another.
Cosmic combat; current gods defeat/kill predecessors: killing the dragon, use of sacred drink.	The primordial period ends by some evil deed committed by son of god or humans.
Humans come on the stage and are the somatic descendants (in some way) of some god or other (Sun most popular).	Humans are created from trees or clay or rock. Totem ancestors may descend directly from the gods.
Humans show hubris and are punished by a great flood.	Humans act haughtily or make mistakes and are punished by a great flood and then re-emerge in various ways (sometimes new creations).
Trickster deities bring culture; humans spread; emergence of 'nobles' or half-human/half-gods.	
Local history begins.	
Final destruction of the world.	
A new Heaven and Earth of some sort emerge in some way.	

Gondwana myths lack certain elements of the Laurasian myths listed above. They have no true 'creation' stories, such as emergence out of nothing or out of chaos; the Earth already exists, has always existed, will always exist. They lack a continuous story line from creation to destruction. There is a distant 'high god' who doesn't pay much attention to what people do; he moves to heaven and sends a son to create humans. Humans are bad in some way, destroyed by a flood. This high god may have trickster-like descendants who become totem deities. But, since most of the peoples with the Gondwana myth structures did not develop urban-type civilizations, such trickster deities obviously didn't bring 'culture.' What appears to me to be the most striking difference is the fact that both heaven and Earth are preexistent; nobody created space and time, the universe, etc. With very few exceptions, the question about this is never asked!

The even older Pan-Gaean myths include mainly:

- The emergence of humans from trees or clay or from underground or caves.

- There is a reservoir or well of souls.

- The emergence of death. The first humans did not die, but the breaking of some rule led to humans being subjected to death. The list of possible causes/errors is long and varied. Basically, it is the search for the origin of death and whom to blame for it.

- Trickster deities/demiurge-type culture heroes.

- There are souls and an afterlife or reincarnation. These ideas apparently go back to the very oldest strata.

- No eschatology.

The birth of the Laurasian mythology, which, unlike the Gondwana mythology, includes myths about the destruction of the world, is dated to c. 70KYA. Whatever happened at that point in time, it must have been impressive and traumatic and gave some groups of people the idea that the world might very well be destroyed. They created a myth about the destruction of the world because they experienced it – almost.[203] And, since it wasn't complete and total destruction, the 'end' was then projected into the future. It would take us too far afield to engage with this topic. I can only suggest that the reader read Witzel's book and then go directly to Mary Settegast's two volumes: *Plato, Prehistorian*, and *When Zarathustra Spoke: The Reformation of Neolithic Culture and Religion*.[204] Her work is actually the bridge between Witzel and Zoroaster, to whom we now turn. Zoroastrianism influenced Jewish thinking during the 'exile,' resulting in such texts as the books of Enoch and other apocalyptic writings, which in turn ended up influencing the early Christians.

Discussing Zoroaster, Witzel points out that he telescoped the idea of the renewal of time and society at the new year into the life of the individual: one had to make the individual choice between right/truthful action and evil, right action restoring the universal order. Witzel sees this as an 'optimistic' feature of Laurasian myth: the possibility of renewal within mini-cycles.

Zarathustra

In his book *Cosmos, Chaos and the World to Come*, Norman Cohn undertook to explore the question of where the idea of the end of the world and its renewal came from. He locates the

---

[203]This date just happens to coincide with the proposed cataclysmic eruption of Toba which science journalist Ann Gibbons proposed caused a population bottleneck. Work by geologist Michael R. Rampino, volcanologist Stephen Self, and anthropologist Stanley H. Ambrose supports her suggestion. (See Wikipedia.org, 'Toba catastrophe theory.') Even more interesting is the fact that the Toba eruption does not seem to have affected Africa and certain areas in India, though it was clearly cataclysmic in other places. That alone would provide a foundation for different mythological structures. In some places, the world ended; in others, it did not.

[204]Mary Settegast, *Plato, Prehistorian* (Lindisfarne Press, 2000) and *When Zarathustra Spoke: The Reformation of Neolithic Culture and Religion* (Mazda Pub, 2005). See also R. C. Zaehner, *The Dawn and Twilight of Zoroastrianism* (Phoenix, 2003); Michael Stausberg, Yuhan Sohrab-Dinshaw Vevaina, with Anna Tessman (Eds.), *The Wiley Blackwell Companion to Zoroastrianism* (Wiley-Blackwell, 2015); Mary Boyce, *Zoroastrians* (Routledge, 2001) and *A History of Zoroastrianism*, 3 Vols. (Brill, 1975–1991). Also Pierre Lescaudron, *Earth Changes and the Human Cosmic Connection* (Red Pill Press, 2014); Martin Sweatman, *Prehistory Decoded* (Troubador, 2018); Victor Clube and Bill Napier, *The Cosmic Serpent* (Universe, 1982) and *The Cosmic Winter* (Blackwell, 1990); Richard Firestone, Allen West, and Simon Warwick-Smith, *The Cycle of Cosmic Catastrophes* (Bear & Co., 2006); James Lawrence Powell, *Deadly Voyager: The Ancient Comet Strike that Changed Earth and Human History* (Bowker, 2020).

origin of this idea among the Iranians, specifically the Iranian prophet, Zarathustra. He suggests the area of Zarathustra's origin to be somewhere south of the Ural Mountains in what is now northern Kazakhstan. The biography of Zarathustra/Zoroaster is not important at this point, but in order to understand exactly what Zoroaster did, it is important to know just a bit about what preceded him. Norman Cohn writes:

> Cosmos, in the sense of all-embracing, all-pervading order, was taken for granted in the Ancient Near East: everything in heaven and earth, in nature and in society, had been established and set in order by the gods and was still watched over by the gods. ... There were chaotic forces, restless and threatening. ... If some gods were benign, others were not – and some gods could be now benign, now destructive. ... Nevertheless, the ordered world was imagined as essentially unchanging. ... At the heart of every Near Eastern world-view was a sense of immutability.[205]

Egyptians did not believe that the world had been created out of nothing: material of some kind had been there always. They imagined the original creation as a shaping of that formless material into an ordered world. There were many versions of how that happened and Cohn describes a few of them. This 'religious' worldview was also a political ideology and the theologians who created and elaborated it were functioning as today's political propagandists do. Enemy forces – foreigners – were always perceived as forces of chaos, and it was the job of pharaoh, with his allies, the gods, to combat these forces and bring order. And, whether true or not, the king was always depicted as victorious. The propaganda worked well: Egyptian society was conservative and stable for a very, very long time.

The Egyptians did not like novelty; their ideal was periodic regeneration of what had existed before. They imagined time as stretching endlessly into the future with repeated regenerations and rejuvenation. This idea extended into their beliefs about the afterlife. In the Old Kingdom, the dead pharaoh ascended to the sky and joined the stars/gods. Peasants, however, expected no more than an indefinite extension of the hard life they had lived on Earth. It was around the time of the First Intermediate Period that immortality was democratized and eventually extended to people at all levels of society. Not only did they look forward to everlasting life, it was an improved life over what they had on Earth. By the Middle Kingdom, every Egyptian was eligible for the blessed afterlife. The wealthy constructed elaborate tombs equipped with servants and all they would need in the netherworld. But most important of all were magic spells. These spells were designed to enable the deceased to emerge from the tomb and to evade the various traps that might lie on the way to the next world. And, of course, in order to qualify, one must have worshipped Osiris and have lived one's life in accord with *ma'at*, the concept of truth, balance, order, harmony, morality and justice.

It was believed that at death, a person was tried usually by Osiris himself, and some 42 assistants, counsels for the prosecution and defense, and a court clerk. The heart of the deceased was weighed against a feather. Many tombs include self-exculpatory confessions designed to convince the god that the deceased had lived his life in accord with divine order. Interestingly, the deceased does not tell about the good he has done, but only about the evil he has avoided.

The righteous dead experienced the rejuvenating power of the primordial ocean and re-entered the ordered world renewed and immortal; but transgressors against *ma'at* underwent a 'second death' that meant, in some versions, annihilation, and in others eternal torment.

---

[205]Norman Cohn, *Cosmos, Chaos and the World to Come* (New Haven: Yale University Press, 1993), p. 3

Nothing about Egyptian beliefs implied any change in the carefully balanced world order vis-à-vis the tranquil realm of the dead. There was no idea that time was moving toward some great consummation when all would be transformed and evil destroyed forever.

The Mesopotamian religious system was similar in many ways to that of the Egyptians. The world came into being from an already existing primordial and boundless salt ocean. The ocean begat Earth and sky pancaked together; a god forced them apart, creating the present world. By the third millennium, the world was perceived as a state and Nippur and then Babylon was the center of the world.

The Mesopotamian pantheon of gods was concerned mainly with order. As in Egypt, the order of the world was perceived as essentially unchanging, but in Egypt that order was understood to have been determined by the 'first time'; in Mesopotamia, it was determined by heavenly prototypes – gods were invisible to the human eye, as was their realm and doings, for the most part. In Mesopotamia, a temple was a replica of a heavenly prototype, and not representing the primordial hillock of creation as in Egypt. No greater glory could be given to a king than to be commissioned by a god to rebuild a ruined temple. And it had to be rebuilt exactly as the former one, which was an exact copy of the one before, and so on back to the original temple that was built by the gods themselves before humans existed.

Mesopotamian kings were seldom deified, but they were appointed by gods. Kingship had existed in heaven and was sent down to Earth soon after the creation of mankind because humans were so stupid they needed someone to make sure they served the gods as they should. Again, we see a clever religio-political ideology.

The Proto-Indo-Iranians, living on the steppes of southern Russia, split about 2,000 BC, or earlier, into the Indo-Aryans and the Iranians. Whole tribes migrated south and each of them was ruled by a *raja*, or king, who was primarily a war leader. Victory in war showed that a king was in harmony with the gods and cosmic order.

Our main source of information about the Indo-Aryans is the *Rig Veda*. 'Veda' means knowledge of superhuman powers that are active in the world and of the ways to influence them. That knowledge was believed to have existed in the world forever and then, long ago, it was 'seen' by sages in states of visionary ecstasy; they had insights into the hidden origins and interconnections of things visible in the world. These insights gave them magical techniques and rules for collaborating with higher powers. The *Rig Veda* was, then, the one repository of eternal truth. The hymns collected in the *Rig Veda* served the tribes as a whole, but mainly catered to the intellectual elite and ensured their continuing dominance.

The worldview of the *Rig Veda* knows nothing of the ideas that came to dominate India later; things such as vast cycles of time, individuals reincarnating thousands of times, and so forth. The Vedic Indians took it for granted that the ordered cosmos would not change; it was always imperfect and constantly threatened by the forces of chaos, but it would nevertheless survive indefinitely. At the same time, they also thought that the cosmos had not always existed, but had been established at a certain moment in the past.

The Indo-Aryan cosmos existed and continued thanks to the principle of *rita*. *Rita* was, more or less, the order of nature, 'how things were done correctly,' similar to the Egyptian *ma'at*. Speech that was in accord with *rita* was truthful speech. Offenses against *rita* were murder, cursing, deceit, drunkenness, anger, gambling, cheating, etc. Each person had a particular function in society according to *rita*, and one was expected to devote oneself to fulfilling that place and its tasks. The god that was mainly concerned with the maintenance of *rita* was Varuna. Varuna was not a warrior god; he was remote and imperturbable and dwelt in the great ocean that surrounded the cosmos and from which the cosmos had emerged. Varuna enveloped all things. He watched over the cosmos and *rita* from a distance. It was thanks to his power that heaven and Earth stood firm and immovable; his will was the source of all law and morality. Varuna had spies everywhere and any offence against *rita* was punished.

Mitra was Varuna's close associate and was associated with fire. Varuna was static, Mitra was active. The word *mitra* meant 'contract' and represented the uniting of people in friendship and peace. The prototype was the great cosmic contract that reconciled opposites. Human life and the processes of nature were both subject to the same order, *rita*, and thus, to the personification of the contract as a principle.

Indra was the only god to rival Varuna in majesty and power. He is shown as being like Varuna, or assisting Varuna as the protector of *rita*. But he was a warrior god, which Varuna was not. In Vedic India, victory in war was a supreme affirmation of the divinely appointed order.

There are several accounts of how the god Indra mastered primordial chaos and brought the world into being. About a quarter of the hymns of the *Rig Veda* are dedicated to Indra. Originally Indra personified the brute power of Nature, especially the atmosphere. He was a Storm God, wielder of thunderbolts and bringer of rain. But he was also the divine warrior, a giant with mighty arms and hands, voracious mouth and prodigious appetite. He traveled in a golden chariot drawn by two dun-colored horses and his thousand-toothed thunderbolts never missed their mark.

The Indo-Aryan tribes had developed a warrior ethos, every able-bodied male was expected to bear arms, and the king was, above all, a warlord. As their tireless champion, Indra captured hostile towns and wiped out the inhabitants and gave their horses, cattle and goods to his own people. He was felt to be physically present in a battle and, together with his fair-skinned companions, would slay the dark men. Indra was also known as 'he with a thousand testicles,' meaning that he was possessed of boundless creative energy and vitality, which he always exercised for the benefit of human beings.

As in many other mythologies, as they developed over time, the cosmogonic tale of Indra tells us that he was the youngest of the gods, called into being as a result of a war between good and evil – Adityas and Danavas. The details need not detain us except to note that the Indra myth is very much like the combat myths of other peoples. The parallels between Egyptian and Babylonian myths are striking: the gods are helpless in the face of a monstrous power, but then a storm god appears, younger, more courageous and cleverer than the other gods. The young god tackles the monster, defeats and slays it, and in recognition of his achievements, he is exalted over all (or nearly all) of the other gods. A similar myth was part of Scandinavian heritage; in one form or another, the myth flourished over vast areas of the ancient world. The important point was that, again, the cosmic law, *rita*, was established and the other gods were set to work again in their proper stations. The takeaway was that the cosmos has always been threatened by chaos, and yet it always survives and always will. No end of the world is depicted, though the god's war against the forces of chaos can never end.

The gods and humans of Vedic India depended on soma to strengthen and restore them. The myths say it was a plant that was full of sap and grew in mountainous regions. What plant this was has been endlessly debated. Zoroastrian priests still use a plant they call *hom*, which is a species of ephedra. But one of the more plausible suggestions, according to Cohn, is that the ancient plant was actually *Pergamum harmala*, or wild rue. Soma was a powerful stimulant said to enhance thinking, give inspiration, promote strength and courage, increase sexual potency, and heal sickness. (All these stories indicate why people are so anxious to figure out what plant this was!) Soma was represented as a god and the soma sacrifice took on cosmic dimensions. It came to be seen as the power that ensured the continuation of the cyclical processes on which all life depended.

Like Soma, Agni, or fire, was both a phenomenon and a god. Cohn notes that fire was worshipped as devoutly by the Vedic Indians as by the proto-Indo-Iranians, so it must have been a god long before the splitting of the tribes. Agni was an intimate god, at home in the domestic hearth, protector of the family. In the sacrifice ritual, Agni was central. It was Agni who invited the gods to the meal and 'passed' the food to them, so to say, in the process of burning; as the fire consumed the offerings, so did the gods consume them.

As in Egypt, for the Indo-Aryans, the cow had much more than economic value; the cow symbolized everything that was good and precious. The goddess Usas was called a cow and the rays of light at dawn were called a herd of cows. The dawn was the start of the sacrificial ritual on which the survival of the ordered world depended. The gods depended on the sacrifices made by humans because, by themselves, they would not have had the strength to sustain the world and strengthen *rita*; without sacrifices, they would not be immortal. Heaven and Earth were totally dependent on one another, and what enabled the whole to continue was *rita* and what strengthened rita was sacrifice.

The god Rudra stood apart; he was the god of uncultivated land, the wilderness, and the frightening aspects of nature. He was at home with wild animals and serpents and was the patron of thieves and robbers; he brought sickness and death to humans and cattle. He was a god of the boundaries, so to say, not wholly belonging to the ordered world, but not alien either.

Demons, on the other hand, were forever striving to overthrow the gods and had to weaken *rita* to do so. There was no limit to their nefarious activities. They prowled the land, brought sickness and death, entered into their victims and ate them up from the inside. Sorcerers could employ demons and could, themselves, become a sort of demon; whole categories of humans could be regarded as demonic, as was the case with the Dasas, the dark-skinned people who occupied northern India when the Indo-Aryans arrived.

The Rig Veda gives no comprehensive account of the netherworld; we only learn that beneath the Earth there is an abyss, a bottomless pit of total and everlasting darkness. Human beings who have set themselves against *rita* go there; they are slain by the guardians of *rita*, Soma and Agni, and cast out of the ordered world. However, in the original proto-Indo-Iranian system, everyone who died went to the gloomy, eternal darkness of the netherworld. In Vedic times, this was still the fate of the common people. In contrast, the privileged elite could look forward to a happy afterlife similar to that which awaited the fortunate members of Egyptian society. The elite dead continued their lives in heaven and with Yama, the first man who was the first to die. He now reigned in heaven, a place of radiant light, harmony and joy. They were fed with milk and honey and soma. They were freed of every bodily defect, made love, and the sound of sweet music and singing was everywhere. And, there were 'wish cows' which supplied whatever was wished for. This life would last forever, free from the harassment of the agents of chaos. But the world would not end.

Meanwhile, the Iranians who had split off from the Indo-Aryans, at some point, received the revelation of Zarathustra. His teaching was a totally new perception of time and the prospects for mankind. He saw all of existence as the realization of a grand, divine plan, and this plan would achieve an ultimate fulfillment, a glorious consummation when all would be made perfect once again and forever.

Zarathustra was a priest of an even older religion – the Laurasian myths outlined above probably giving a fair idea of what that religion consisted. At some point, Zarathustra had visions in which he saw and heard the great god Ahura Mazda – Lord Wisdom – surrounded by six other radiant figures and from that moment, he believed himself to be the divinely ordained prophet of a revised religion.[206]

During the first thousand years or so of its existence, the Zoroastrian faith established itself over large areas of northeastern and eastern Iran. It later penetrated into western Iran and by the seventh century BC, the hereditary priests of western Iran, the magi, were converted. The royal dynasty of the Achaemenians comprised many Zoroastrians, including, most likely, Cyrus the Great (c. 549 BC). It became the official religion of all Iran and remained so even after the conquest of Alexander the Great.

Zoroastrianism survived because of the ethical standards contained in its teachings, and the impact of the religion was, and still is, enormous, though this is not often realized. Zoroastrianism had great influence on the Jews of the exile and their own theological speculations, which they brought back with them after Cyrus the Great became their 'savior.'[207]

Zoroastrianism possesses sacred scriptures: the Avesta. Scholarly opinion is that, despite accretions and modification, the Avesta still contains much material that embodies the original teachings of Zoroaster and even some material that was preserved by him from an even more distant past. Naturally, one would expect this to be similar to the worldview of the Vedic society, and such is the case.

In the Indo-Iranian world, *rita* changed to *asha*, but the meaning remained the same. The pantheon of gods was similar also except that the Avesta diverges from the *Rig Veda* in its treatment of the great gods who brought the ordered world into being. Indra is mentioned only briefly, and *as a demon*. The god who dominates the Avestan view is Ahura Mazda, and it is not clear that the Vedic priests even had any knowledge of him! However, Zoroaster gave Ahura Mazda a position that was more exalted than that occupied by any other deity in the ancient world.

According to the ancient Indo-Iranian doctrine, in the beginning there had been only one of everything: one plant, one animal, one man; and, according to Zoroaster, only one god, uncreated, the first cause of everything in the universe that is good. However, though Ahura Mazda was the only divine being, there existed also a *principle* that was the negation of *asha*, a principle of falsehood and distortion, a force of disorder that was constantly at work in the world. They called it *druj*, or 'falseness,' 'the lie.' Zoroaster developed this idea into the mighty antagonist of Ahura Mazda: Angra Mainyu, the spirit of destruction and active evil.

The central revelation of Zoroaster was expressed in the Gathas: "Truly there are two primal spirits, twins renowned to be in conflict. In thought and word, in act they are two: the better and the bad ..." (*Yasna* 30.3). Going further, he said: "Neither our thoughts nor teachings nor

---

[206]Again I suggest reading Mary Settegast's book *When Zarathustra Spoke*.

[207]It is likely that monotheism did not exist in Palestine until after the Persian conquest.

wills, neither our choices nor words nor acts, nor our inner selves nor our souls agree" (*Yasna* 45.2).[208]

Apparently, in Zoroaster's thought, these twin spirits were embodiments of the forces that maintained the cosmos vs. the forces that sought to destroy it. In the beginning, when they came into being, they, too, had to make a choice between the two principles. Ahura Mazda – because it was his nature to be moral – chose to support *asha*, and Angra Mainyu – because it was his nature to be perverse – chose *druj*. In these choices began the struggle that constitutes the past, present, and future of the world. Jacques Duchesne-Guillemin writes:

> The moral dualism expressed in the opposition Asha–Druj (truth–falsehood) goes back at least to Indo-Iranian times, for the Veda knows it too, as *ṛita-druh*, although the contrast is not as sharply defined as in the Avesta. Between these two principles, the Twin Spirits made an ominous choice, the Bounteous One becoming in thoughts, words, and deeds a partisan of Asha, *ashavan*, while the other became *dregvant*, partisan of the Druj. After them it was the *daevas'* turn; they all chose wrongly. Ever since, the *daevas* have tried to corrupt man's choice also.
>
> To the army of the *ashavans*, headed by the Bounteous Spirit, was counterposed the host of the *dregvants*, under the Destructive Spirit, Angra Mainyu. Each combatant faced his exact counterpart: the Good Mind opposing the Bad Mind and Aramaiti being countered by Taromaiti.
>
> In this battle, the whole material universe is, through the entities, potentially enrolled, the Bounteous Spirit being the patron of man, Asha of fire, the Good Mind of the Ox, the Dominion of the metals, Aramaiti of the earth, Integrity and Immortality of the waters and plants. Moreover, since the entities are at once divine and human (because both the spiritual and material qualities of man partake of divine), everyone faithful to the wise Ahura can commune with him.[209]

Zoroaster's reinterpretation of the traditional view of things as depicted (we suppose) in the Vedic version, where the divinely appointed order was static – constantly disturbed, but always settling down with a few tweaks here and there – had profound implications.

> In the cosmogony as expounded in the *Bundahishn*, Ormazd (Ahura Mazdā) and Ahriman are separated by the void. They seem to have existed from all eternity, when Ahriman's invidious attack initiates the whole process of creation. The question of their origin is ignored, but it was implied, ever since Ormazd had taken the place of his Bounteous Spirit in the struggle against the Destructive Spirit. Since Ahura Mazdā could no longer be the father of the two adversaries, the question of their origin was inevitable.
>
> A solution was provided by Zurvanism; it is Zurvān (Time) who is the father of Ormazd and Ahriman. But this solution upset the very essence of Mazdaism and was therefore condemned as heretical. Zurvanism was widely accepted, however, perhaps even prevalent, in Sāsānian times. Traces of it are found in Mazdean orthodoxy, some features of which cannot otherwise be explained.
>
> In Mazdean orthodoxy, when Ormazd created the material world, he first produced from Infinite Light a form of fire, out of which all things were to be born. This form of fire is "bright, white, round, and visible from afar." Gayōmart, the Primal Man, was also conceived as spherical, in the image of the sky. Mānushchihr writes that "Ormazd, the lord of all things, produced from Infinite Light a form of fire whose name was that of Ormazd and whose light was that of fire." This phrase can be accounted for only as a clumsy adaptation of a Zurvanite text that must have said, in effect, that Zurvān created Ormazd.

---

[208]Gathas, cited by Cohn (1993), p. 82.
[209]Jacques Duchesne-Guillemin, 'Zoroastrianism,' *Encyclopedia Britannica*, 2020.

The Mazdean quaternity can hardly be explained except as an adaptation of the Zurvanite one. The latter is attested in several texts citing, besides Zurvān, three other names given as those of separate gods but that must be hypostases (essences) of the first one, also called in Manichaeism the god with four faces. Among the various forms under which the Zurvanite quaternity manifested itself, the one associating Zurvān with Light, Power, and Wisdom seems to be the origin of the Mazdean quaternity. Ormazd, in the Bundahishn, has three other names, namely Time, Space, and Religion. To obtain this quaternity, it was sufficient to replace Zurvān by Time, Light by Space, Wisdom by Religion, and Power by Ormazd and to put the latter at the end of the series.

In order to vanquish Ahriman, Ormazd created the world as a battlefield. He knew that this fight would be limited in time—it would last 9,000 years—and he offered Ahriman a pact to that effect. After they had created their respective material creations, Ahriman's first attack was defeated by Ormazd with the help of the Ahuna Vairya prayer (the most sacred Zoroastrian prayer), and he lay prostrate for another period of 3,000 years, the second in a total of four. He was then stirred up by the prostitute (Primal Woman) and went back to the attack, this time in the material universe. He killed the Primal Bull, whose marrow gave birth to the plants and whose semen was collected and purified in the moon, whence it would produce the useful animals. Ahriman then killed Gayōmart, the Primal Man, whose body produced the metals and whose semen was preserved and purified in the sun. A part of it would produce the rhubarb from which the first human couple would be born.

The first human couple were perverted by Ahriman, and it is only with the advent of Zoroaster, after 3,000 years, that Ahriman's supremacy came to an end. Ormazd and Ahriman then fight on equal terms until Ormazd, at the end of the last 3,000 years, finally will triumph.[210]

For Zoroaster, nothing was static; it was constant war. Moreover, war that would ultimately end with the victory of Ahura Mazda. The perception of time changed: it was now only moving forward and moving toward a consummation, an end. In the end, Angra Mainyu will be destroyed, chaos will be overcome, and *asha* will prevail totally and everywhere.

As a result of the aggressor's attack, man is mortal. But he does not die altogether. There are five immortal parts in him: *ahu* ('life'), *daēnā* ('religion'), *baodah* ('knowledge'), *urvan* ('soul'), and *fravashi* ('preexistent souls'). The latter term seems literally to mean 'preeminent hero.' The conception that caused this term to be applied to the 'manes' (spirits) or *pitarah* of Iran is that of *a defensive, protective power that continues to emanate from a chief even after death*. This originally aristocratic notion seems to have been vulgarized in the same way as, in Greece, any dead person came to be considered a hero, or, in Egypt, an Osiris. Zoroaster ignored the *fravashi*, but he was familiar with the *daēnā*. The latter term meant 'religion' in both its objective and subjective senses.

Indian and Iranian beliefs in the afterlife have many features in common, probably dating back to the Indo-Iranian period: a feminine encounter, a bridge with dogs watching it, a heavenly journey. In the ancient Indian texts, the Upaniṣads, the soul is welcomed in heaven by 500 *apsaras* (cloud maidens). In Iran the soul meets his own religion (*daēnā*) in the form of a beautiful damsel if he has lived justly; otherwise, he meets a hideous hag.

Either before this encounter or after, according to the various texts, the soul must cross a bridge. This, with the young girl and the gods, is attested in India in the Yajurveda and the Upaniṣads. In the Gāthās it is called the Bridge of the Requiter. It leads the good souls to paradise, but the bad ones fall into hell.

The soul has also to undergo a judgment; it appears before Mithra and his two companions, Sraosha and Rashnu. Finally it ascends through successive stages representing respectively his good thoughts (the stars), good words (the moon), and good deeds (the sun) to the paradise (of infinite

---

[210]Duchesne-Guillemin (2020).

lights). In the Veda it is said only that the sojourn of the good deed is beyond the path of the sun. In paradise the soul is led by Vohu Manah, the Good Mind, to the golden throne of Ormazd.

Hell also has, symmetrically, four levels. And there is, for the souls whose good actions exactly balance their evil ones, an intermediate place.[211]

The details of the myths from which these elements were derived need not detain us; what is important is the impact of Zoroastrianism. Norman Cohn writes:

> The impact of Zoroastrianism ... though not generally recognized ... has been, and still is, immense. For some centuries before Christ Zoroaster's basic teachings were widely disseminated. ... [T]hey had much influence amongst Jews, and even more amongst the early Christians – and so, in the long run, upon the world-view of what was to become European civilisation.[212]
>
> At the heart of Zoroaster's teaching is a sense of cosmic war: a conviction that a mighty spiritual power intent on maintaining and furthering life in an ordered world is locked in struggle with a spiritual power, scarcely less mighty, intent on destroying life and reducing the ordered world to chaos.[213]

Cohn thinks that this idea was a novel version of the ancient combat myth "thoroughly intellectualized and spiritualized." Cohn notes:

> What Ahura Mazda does goes far beyond anything known to the traditional myth. The war that he fights is a spiritual war, and its aim is not simply to ensure the fertility of the land and the military victory of his people, it is not even the mere maintenance of the ordered world. It is to remove every form of disorder from the world, wholly and forever; to bring about a state in which cosmos will no longer be threatened by chaos. So in the end Angra Mainyu/Ahriman is annihilated once and for all, along with all his host of demons and all his human allies. In place of repeated but incomplete victories we are promised a final and total one.
>
> Zoroaster, it is suggested, was inspired by the ancient and potent combat myth to create a different and even more potent combat myth. And his creation survives to this day: the very core of Zoroastrianism has always been a combat myth – indeed, even the divine warrior himself is there, in the form of the future savior ... But the traditional myth, as it was known to the Ancient Near East before Zoroaster, has been transformed into an apocalyptic faith.
>
> ... Zoroastrian teachings retained their capacity, in certain circumstances, to inspire dissenting individuals or groups to look forward with confidence to the day when the established order would be abolished, the existing authorities exterminated, and they themselves vindicated and exalted. When Zoroastrian eschatology was assimilated and adapted by non-Zoroastrians, this happened ... on a grandiose scale.[214]

Zoroaster used to invoke saviours who, like the dawns of new days, would come to the world. He hoped himself to be one of them. **After his death, the belief in coming saviours developed**. Zarathushtra was expected to return, if not personally, at least in the form of his three sons who would be born, at intervals of a thousand years, from his semen. The last of these saviours, Astvatereta, or justice incarnate, was also simply called the Saviour (Saoshyans).

Only in the Pahlavi books is this theme systematically developed. It is dominated by the idea of **a final return to the initial state of things**. The first human couple had at first fed on water,

---

[211]Duchesne-Guillemin (2020).
[212]Cohn (1993), p. 79.
[213]Cohn (1993), p. 105.
[214]Cohn (1993), pp. 114–15.

then on plants, on milk, and at last on meat. The people in the last millennia will, at the advent of the three successive saviours, abstain in the reverse order from meat, milk, and plants to keep finally only water. The primeval combatants also have their counterparts at the end of time. The dragon that was killed in order to liberate the imprisoned waters will appear again at the resurrection to be killed by another hero. In the last great struggle, the host of good and the host of evil will vie with each other, and each soldier of Ormazd will defeat and kill his own special adversary. This will restore the state of peace that had prevailed initially. The wicked will then submit to an ordeal of molten metal and fire. Fire and Airyaman will cause the metals of the mountains to melt and to flow down as a river of fire. The whole of resuscitated mankind must traverse it; it will burn only the wicked, whereas to the just it will be as sweet as warm milk. The suffering of the wicked will last only three days, however, after which all mankind will enjoy much happiness. On the flattened earth (for the metal will fill in all the valleys), men and women, henceforth shadowless since they are sinless, will taste the bliss of family life. Hell will be sealed forever, and Ahriman will be either powerless or annihilated.[215]

So the idea of the end of the world, a final consummation, and the coming of a Savior was original to Zarathustra, who apparently learned of this in his visions or ecstatic experiences.

Yahweh

Contrary to what many people think, the Hebrew Bible, AKA the Old Testament, was collected, edited, and even largely written, very late – between 600 and 100 BC. In the OT, Yahwism is presented as a unified, stable worldview. That was not actually the case. The Yahwism of the Jerusalem monarchy was similar to the beliefs found in Ugarit. Originally El was the supreme god and his son, in the Ba'al cycle, was 'Yaw.' Deuteronomy 32:8 tells how when El Elyon, i.e. El the Most High, parceled out the nations between his sons, Yahweh received Israel as his portion. In other words, Yahweh was equivalent to the Canaanite Ba'al and Babylonian Marduk. The traces of these facts are there in the OT, which is surprising in so severely edited a work. But then, they didn't have modern text-manipulation technology; working with a scroll is much more complicated!

Yahweh, like Ba'al and Marduk, was eventually exalted to a higher position and came to be identified with El. Yahweh became the universal creator god and, in Psalm 82, he is depicted as presiding over an assembly of lesser gods and holding judgment. He wasn't happy with them because they failed to uphold justice, defend the poor and downtrodden, and sided with the oppressors; therefore, even though they were sons of El, they had to die.

When Jerusalem became the royal capital, a politically motivated oracle proclaimed that Yahweh would live there. Before this time, Yahweh had cult places all over Canaan, and Jerusalem actually had none. But, Yahweh, like the Judean kings, was enthroned in Jerusalem and ruled from Mount Zion as Ba'al ruled from Mount Zaphon. Mount Zion came to be seen as the center of the ordered world. The temple was built on a great rock that was imagined as the fixed point around which the world had been created. Beneath the rock, it was said, were subterranean waters, forces of chaos that threatened to flood the world. These waters were represented in the temple by a great bronze basin supported on twelve bronze bulls. Like any other Mesopotamian temple, the temple in Jerusalem united heaven and Earth and the sacrifices performed in the

---

[215]Duchesne-Guillemin (2020).

temple were to nourish the god. All of this is to say that Yahwism wasn't much different from the worldview and practices of the Canaanites, Mesopotamians, or even Egyptians: the cosmos was always liable to be disturbed by the forces of chaos.

What Israelites expected when they died was the common fate of all, rich and poor, good or evil: to go down to Sheol, 'the pit,' never to return. Some sort of lethargic existence continued there and the dead could be partly succored by offerings of food and drink, but still, there was no future and the only thing that would survive a man was his 'name' and reputation. Cohn writes:

> On the evidence of both the Bible and archaeology, polytheism must have been widespread at every level of Israelite society, from peasant hut to royal palace and to the Temple itself. Of course, all were agreed that Yahweh was the patron god of Israel, and a mighty god, and a god to be devoutly worshipped – only, many held that other gods could and should be worshipped as well. ... All this was normal. ... What was exceptional was the denunciation of polytheism by a whole series of prophets, their insistence that Israelites should worship Yahweh alone. ... [T]his demand of Yahweh's was to have prodigious consequences. It was out of the tradition of 'Yahweh alone' that monotheism developed, and it is from that tradition that Judaism and, through Judaism, Christianity and Islam are descended.[216]

The Yahweh-only movement probably began among Judean exiles in Babylon and Assyria. Cohn notes that it can be understood as a response to a condition of permanent insecurity and oppression. Destruction, capture and exile were experienced as a collapse of the ordered world (the same phenomena that led to apocalypticism and gnosticism, as we saw above). Not only had Judah ceased to exist and their king had been brought blinded and in chains to die in captivity, the conquerors were flourishing! The deportees found Babylon to be a vastly more developed and sophisticated society so, apparently, this land had superior gods. It would be only natural for a minority of foreign origin to become even more devoted to whatever is peculiarly its own. What if the patron god of Israel and Judea was punishing his people for failing to give him exclusive devotion? This enabled them to understand their suffering and much, much more! Yahweh was such a great god that he could even control the kings of Babylon and Assyria and use them to chastise his people! No matter what disaster befell them, it was only more evidence of the power of Yahweh! As Cohn notes:

> Constantly repeated divine punishment inflicted, quite explicitly, for constantly recurring national apostasy – such an interpretation of political events and of the course of history is without parallel in any other culture in the ancient world.[217]

I would suggest that such an interpretation is evidence of a pathological state similar to what we now call 'Stockholm Syndrome.'

In any event, this interpretation of their misfortunes is what some intellectuals in exile came up with and propagandized to their fellow exiles. It was further elaborated into a more-or-less coherent theology. These were the Deuteronomists, according to Cohn. It is in the book of Deuteronomy that the concept of election is made most explicit: "for you are a people holy to Yahweh your God; Yahweh your God chose you to be a people for his possession, out of all

---

[216]Cohn (1993), p. 141.
[217]Cohn (1993), p. 143.

nations on the face of the Earth. ... It was because Yahweh loves you." It was also around this time, or shortly after, that the notion of the covenant was developed and promulgated.

Yahweh called the Israelites his 'kingdom of priests' (you have to be really special to deserve that much suffering!), and stipulations such as circumcision and Sabbath observance were designed for such a people. Many of the Jewish laws were taken directly from laws applied only to priests in the ancient Near East; all this became obligatory for all the Jewish people. The Law became of central importance and obedience to the Law bestowed on individual Jews benefits comparable to those which Zoroastrians received from their own complicated religious code. Now, ordinary people could help their god to sustain the divine order! The story of being enslaved and oppressed and then liberated became the centerpiece of the ideology. That was a masterstroke of propaganda. Such a story would hardly have any appeal to the wealthy elite; it appeals strictly to the downtrodden, oppressed, widows and orphans and is, in its own way, a radical transformation of the cosmic combat to the earthly, human stage. Yahweh's operation in history became more constant, purposeful, and consistent than anything that had ever been attributed to any other god.

The book of Ezekiel was devoted to explaining the conquest of Judah as a just retribution for polytheistic worship. But Ezekiel said yet more: he assured the people that the present crisis of exile would be the final crisis! The exiled Israelites would become the true Israel and Yahweh would bring them back to Judah where the temple would be rebuilt and they would resume worship the right way! And it would be an ingathering not only of exiles from Babylon, but of all the dispersed Israelites, including those descended from the deportees of the Northern Kingdom. The long-vanished kingdom would arise again, united (and it was imagined that it had previously been united), and the center would be Jerusalem. Yahweh is transformed from a Storm God to a thoroughly benevolent patron.

Of course, the people of the land, the bulk of the population of Israel and Judah, were to have no part in this reconstitution; Ezekiel and his disciples held nothing but contempt for the peasants in the homeland! Extermination was to be the fate of all those who refused to adhere to the new program.

There was another alleged prophet in exile: Second Isaiah, author of the greater part of chapters 40–55 of the book of Isaiah. His prophecies appear to belong to the period 547–538, during which time the Medo-Persian king Cyrus II built the greatest empire ever known to that time. Isaiah needed to find how Yahweh and his people fit into these colossal events. The answer he came up with was that all of the upheavals were the work of Yahweh and the purpose was the total salvation of his adherents! And those adherents were, of course, only to be found among the exiles. What's more, Cyrus wasn't just a mere instrument of Yahweh; *he was the savior* of the Israelites. Yahweh called on him personally: "I have called you by name and given you your title, though you have not known me. ... You shall be my shepherd, to carry out all my purpose, so that Jerusalem may be rebuilt and the foundations of the temple may be laid." Cyrus was to capture Babylon and set the Israelite exiles free to return to their homeland.

But there is something more about Second Isaiah: aside from Zoroaster, Second Isaiah is the first monotheist of Israel; even those who had insisted on Yahweh-alone worship had accepted the existence of other gods.[218] Second Isaiah denies any reality to the gods of the heathen nations

---

[218]Micah 4:5: "All the peoples may walk, each in the name of its god, but we will walk in the name of Yahweh, our God for ever and ever."

and asserts that Yahweh was the creator of the cosmos and the supreme and only god. "My hand laid the foundation of the Earth, and my right hand spread out the heavens. When I call to them, they stand forth together." Cohn says that the implications are clear: the destruction of the kingdoms of Israel and Judah were the victory of chaos over cosmos and only a god who had originally created order could sort this mess out.

Second Isaiah declared that the love which Yahweh had for his chosen people was so great that he, by an act as amazing as his first creation of the world, would transform the status of the Israelites in a new world. The overthrow of Babylon would be an affirmation of right order in the world since Babylon represented all the heathen nations that had ever oppressed Israel; it embodied the forces of chaos. Cyrus was going to do the deed and demonstrate Yahweh's power: "I will make your oppressors eat their own flesh, and they shall be drunk with their own blood as with wine. Then all flesh shall know that I am Yahweh your Savior."

The return to Palestine is foretold in terms intended to recall the exodus from Egypt. Yahweh was going to turn the desert – another symbol of chaos – into a green and fertile place. A highway would run from Babylon to Jerusalem and the land would be flattened to make travel easy. The exiles were to march along this highway in triumph and would be welcomed by wild beasts and birds, the mountains would sing, and trees were going to clap their hands. Yahweh, of course, would return with the exiles to his home in Jerusalem. There would be a great ingathering of all the Israelites from all lands, the population would multiply and would enjoy blessings and happiness greater than anything known before, and this would last forever.

In short, Second Isaiah saw the end of the Babylonian exile as the beginning of a new age in which Yahweh would be sovereign over all the world with the exalted position of his people unchallenged forever. All nations that oppose Israel are to be destroyed by Yahweh. The only ones permitted to live will be those that agree to serve Israel. Cohn notes:

> Nowhere does Second Isaiah advocate proselytism, not once does he recommend that Israelites should travel the world, calling the heathen to conversion. The 'mission' of the chosen people is simply to demonstrate to the whole world, by the way it is rescued from a position of total impotence and deep humiliation, the unique power of Yahweh ...
>
> Again and again the prophet tells how the nations will watch, dazzled, dumbfounded, Yahweh's deliverance and exaltation of the people of Israel. Some will even become slaves of the Israelites, marching behind them in chains, bowing down in supplication ... Mankind as a whole is of little interest to the prophet ... What Yahweh will do for Israel – that matters; and only that.[219]

But that isn't what happened. Cohn and others think that the fourth of the 'Servant Songs' in Second Isaiah is about the unknown prophet himself, who may have been scourged and killed either by the Babylonian authorities or by deportees, disillusioned when Cyrus failed to carry out the destruction of Babylon and nobody had to eat their own flesh or drink their own blood.

Not only did the nations not stream into Jerusalem, the descendants of the Israelites deported by the Assyrians didn't come back, and the majority of the deportees to Babylon elected to remain there. So, far from becoming the center of the cosmos, Judah remained a tiny sub-province in a gigantic empire. The population was impoverished, trying to scrape a living from a land that had been repeatedly devastated by war and taxation. Meanwhile, many prophets continued to

---

[219]Cohn (1993), p. 156.

foretell the glorious consummation. Themes established by Ezekiel and Second Isaiah recur again
and again and are developed. Past and present are the age of sin, but a new age is coming.

> There is no suggestion that the [age of sin] could possibly merge into the [new age] by gradual
> improvement: the change can only be brought about by the direct intervention of Yahweh, and it
> will be total. Yahweh himself speaks of a new creation: 'For behold, I create new heavens and a new
> earth. Former things shall no more be remembered nor shall they be called to mind. Rejoice and be
> filled with delight, you boundless realms which I create ...' It is a prophecy not of a destruction of
> the universe but of a radical transformation of the world: the present order of the world, imperfect
> and precarious as it is, is to be suddenly replaced by a perfect and indestructible order.
>
> ... In the 'night-visions' ascribed to Zechariah Yahweh even announces that the rebuilt Jerusalem
> will need no walls, as he himself will be as a wall of fire surrounding it on all sides, as well as a glory
> in its midst. ...
>
> An addition to Isaiah describes how bodily life too will be transformed. Death in infancy or
> youth will be unknown: it will be an exceptional misfortune to die before the age of a hundred.
> Even the gravest infirmities will be cured: 'Then shall blind men's eyes be opened, the ears of the
> deaf unstopped. Then shall the lame leap like a deer, and the tongue of the dumb shout aloud.' ...
> The notion of a transcendental savior in human form, so important in Zoroastrianism and so central
> to Christianity, is totally unknown to the Hebrew Bible. ... Yahweh is the real ruler over the coming
> age of bliss.[220]

And, of course, the future bliss is reserved only for Yahweh's followers.

> Israel's enemies are Yahweh's enemies, and the vengeance that Yahweh will take upon such people
> will be ruthless. The lightest punishment is servitude ... a far worse fate awaits the nations that
> have oppressed or fought against Yahweh's people. While the stars are darkened in the heavens and
> the fruits of the earth are blasted, these people are given over to slaughter and destruction: 'Their
> slain shall be cast out, and the stench of their corpses shall rise, and the mountains shall flow with
> their blood.' Edom – a traditional enemy of Judah, and moreover one which had taken advantage
> of Judah's weakness in the years following the Babylonian conquest – will be fearfully chastised:
> 'For Yahweh has a day of vengeance, a year of recompense for the cause of Zion. And the streams
> of Edom shall be turned into pitch, and her soil into brimstone; and her land shall become burning
> pitch. Night and day it shall not be quenched; its smoke shall go up for ever. From generation to
> generation it shall lie waste; none shall pass through it for ever.'
>
> Yahweh's involvement is indicated with the utmost vividness: he is imagined in his ancient guise
> of the divine warrior, marching victoriously cross-county, and more terrible than ever – trampling
> Edom and suchlike nations in his fury, so that his garments are drenched in blood. And this fulfils
> his intention for the world: just as the coming age represents the consummation of history, so the
> casting down of the heathen represents the final triumph of cosmos over chaos. ...
>
> Polytheism declined, and so did the tradition of prophecy. But what had been said could not
> be unsaid. Thanks to its incorporation into the Bible, what the exilic and post-exilic prophets had
> foretold was to have vast influence, and not only amongst Jews. Confronted with the destruction
> of temple, nation and monarchy, Ezekiel and Second Isaiah and their followers had found a highly
> effective response. Shaken by events that seemed to call in question the very existence of an ordered
> world, wrestling with a sense of utter disorientation and frustration, they had produced imaginings
> of a glorious future, to be enjoyed by an elite, that were to remain a living force centuries after the
> situation which originally inspired them had lost all actuality.[221]

---

[220]Cohn (1993), pp. 158–59.
[221]Cohn (1993), pp. 161–62.

Two centuries after the Persians overthrew the Babylonians, the Persians were overthrown by Alexander the Great. Thus began the Hellenistic period in the eastern Mediterranean world. Greek colonists spread everywhere and Greek culture and ideas began to dominate. In the third century Palestine – that part of it which was called Judea – was under the rule of one of the spin-off dynasties of Alexander: the Ptolemies, based in Egypt. At the beginning of the second century, it came under the rule of the Seleucids, based in Syria. It was during this period that the earliest Jewish apocalypses were written.

For a long time, scholars have taken the prophetic writings of the OT at face value, assuming that such ideas belonged to the time in which they were said to have been promulgated – the tack taken by Cohn above. However, in more recent times, even this has come under scrutiny, and thereby, brought it into serious question. It is now thought by a number of scholars that the OT was actually put together, and much of it written, around 270 BC in Alexandria under the historiographical influence of the Greeks, which is not to say that there were not some more ancient writings of the Jews incorporated.[222] Such a situation would better explain the events chronicled in the books of Maccabees, at which time the Torah and the various rules of Judaism do not appear to have been widely known or followed in Judea. But the 'Yahweh First and Only' ideology was there, among some groups in the background, and was the trigger for a furious and bloody revolt against Antiochus Epiphanes, King of Syria (which included Judea).

Antiochus Epiphanes had already stolen the cultic ornaments and gold decorations of the temple in Jerusalem. In 167 BC, he was humiliated by the Romans and turned his rage on the Jews. He responded to a rebellion in Jerusalem by profaning the altar of Yahweh with pig's blood, replaced the altar with one of the Olympian Zeus, and installed a replica of the statue of Zeus in the sanctuary. He installed Greek gods in the villages, and synagogues were burned along with the sacred scrolls. Circumcision and other practices of the Jewish cult were banned under penalty of death. Yahweh's fanatics were galvanized and the Maccabean revolt ended with the independence of Judea for the first time since their last king was taken in chains to Babylon. The Temple was ritually cleansed and Jonathan Maccabee was installed as high priest.

The literary apocalypses that were produced during the century or so before the time of the revolt contained things that were definitely foreign to the OT as we know it today. These apocalypses purported to unveil to humans secrets of the heavenly realms, but they mostly focused on Earthly events past, present, and future. One of the main revelations was that what happens on Earth reflects what happens in heaven. This idea is, essentially, what is known today as the 'Hermetic Maxim,' i.e. 'as above, so below,' and it definitely would find a place in early Christianity.

Apocalypses are usually pseudonymous and retrojected into the past. They claim to be authored by holy men of ancient times and followed a general archaizing tendency of the times when people wrote texts in an old-fashioned style. It would be like someone of our time writing a text in the style of Shakespeare, or even Chaucer, in an effort to convince readers that it really was written back in those times. The authors of these texts wanted their works to be accepted as true, divine inspiration and one of the ruses they used was to claim that when the revelations

---

[222]Russell Gmirkin, *Berossus and Genesis, Manetho and Exodus* (Bloomsbury, 2006) and *Plato and the Creation of the Hebrew Bible* (Routledge, 2016); Philippe Wajdenbaum, *Argonauts of the Desert: Structural Analysis of the Hebrew Bible* (Routledge, 2014).

had originally been made, God had stipulated that they were to be kept secret until the time was right for them to be published. Cohn writes:

> The apocalyptists certainly did their utmost to make their books look genuine – for instance, they took care never to mention by name any individual who lived after the time of the supposed authors. *There is no mistaking the element of conscious contrivance, of deliberate pretense.* Nevertheless – when one reads these works, it seems clear that their authors regarded them as in some sense genuine. More: these men seem to have thought of their writings not only as supplementing biblical prophecy but as surpassing it, and of themselves not merely as successors of, but as superior to, the prophets. Behind the pronouncements of the prophets, they imply, lay a hidden meaning, which was understood only imperfectly by the prophets themselves. Only to a few sages had God revealed that meaning fully – and only now, with the unsealing of the writings of those sages, would the true import of biblical prophecy be made plain.
>
> ... The symbolic language is traditional, in fact it is largely derived from ancient myths; unlike biblical prophecy, apocalyptic is a learned genre, and the smell of midnight oil pervades it. Yet when every qualification is made, it seems inconceivable that without some real, compelling visions the apocalypses would ever have been written down at all.
>
> The revelations that the apocalyptist received from God were very different from the revelations received by the biblical prophets. There is no suggestion in the apocalypses that human beings can, by their obedience or disobedience, affect the shape of things to come. The future is already determined, in fact its course is already inscribed in a heavenly book. And its outcome will be different from anything foretold in classical prophecy. There will be a final judgment. There will be an afterlife when human beings, including the resurrected dead, will receive their just rewards and punishments. And if some human beings will be transformed into angels, some angels will be condemned to everlasting torment.
>
> ... To the prophets, God had spoken directly – but since their time God had become more remote ... When he communicated with the apocalyptist it was almost invariably through an intermediary, an angel. Though angels are not unknown in the Hebrew Bible, it is only in the apocalypses that they become major actors.[223]

In the book of Daniel, a second-century apocalypse, the author writes:

> I was standing on the bank of the great river (that is, the Tigris), I looked up and saw a man clothed in linen, with a belt of gold from Uphaz around his waist. His body was like beryl, his face like lightning, his eyes like flaming torches, his arms and legs like the gleam of burnished bronze, and the sound of his words like the roar of a multitude. I, Daniel, alone saw the vision; the people who were with me did not see the vision, though a great trembling fell upon them, and they fled and hid themselves. ...
>
> He said to me, "Daniel, greatly beloved, pay attention to the words that I am going to speak to you. Stand on your feet, for I have now been sent to you." ... He said to me, "Do not fear, Daniel, for from the first day that you set your mind to gain understanding and to humble yourself before your God, your words have been heard, and I have come because of your words. But the prince of the kingdom of Persia opposed me twenty-one days. So Michael, one of the chief princes, came to help me, and I left him there with the prince of the kingdom of Persia, and have come to help you understand what is to happen to your people at the end of days. For there is a further vision for those days." (Daniel 10:4-14)

In Daniel's dream of the four beasts, we know these are the four great empires which succeeded one another: Babylon, Media and Persia, Alexander, and the last, most hideous of all, the King

---

[223]Cohn (1993), pp. 164–65.

of Syria. Its ten horns are ten successive kings, and then the eleventh little horn, Antiochus Epiphanes, the 'Manifestation of God' (as he declared himself to be), the great blasphemer. Then, there are thrones ready for judgment and the Ancient of Days, i.e. God, takes his seat. Antiochus is slain, but the other beasts are kept alive to engage in the last battle that Ezekiel foretold. And then, Israel is enthroned: a human figure comes rather than another monstrous beast, the Son of Man. Daniel sees a dream-figure like a man, just as the foregoing figures were like beasts. The new empire which this Son of Man symbolizes differs from the beast empires because *the Son of Man represents the empire of the saints, the elect Jews.*

That is to say, the Son of Man is a symbol just like the Lion, Bear and Panther were symbols of empires. But others made the error of thinking that this was a celestial man beside God, and once that mistake was made, the whole messiah industry was off and running.

The date of the writing of Daniel is evident, as Couchoud points out: the death of Antiochus Epiphanes (164 BC) is the last event foretold. The purpose of establishing some verisimilitude was to lead up to the plan: the victory of Judas Maccabee is not just the freeing of the Jews and the reestablishing of a national government, it is a cosmic revolution in which the living will be clothed in glory and the dead shall be resurrected. This prophecy is a complete break with the traditional Israelite notion of death: Sheol, 'the pit,' 'land of oblivion,' which was the destiny of all, rich and poor, righteous or unrighteous.

Now that we have a good grasp on a large part of the Jewish socio-cultural and literary environment that preceded Paul and Christianity, it's time to turn to the more immediate literary environment.

The Ascension of Isaiah

The author of the *Epistle of Barnabas* (ca. 70–132 AD) wrote: "I know that the Lord journeyed with me on the way of righteousness, ... considering this therefore, that, if it shall be my care to communicate to you some portion of *that which I received*, it shall turn to my reward for having ministered to such spirits," after which he begins his communication of what he 'received.' That is to say, what 'Barnabas' is doing is completely in line with the 'inspirational' activities promoted amongst Pauline churches as described in 1 Corinthians. That, taken together with what we have learned about apocalypses, helps to explain Paul's understanding of higher realms and their denizens. Wells gives some thought to this problem and I will quote him at length here because his explication is concise and I couldn't paraphrase it better:

> In the Jewish literature of the period we find a highly developed angelology. The writer of the book of Daniel (c. 165 BC) was the first by whom angels were individualized and endowed with names and titles, and later apocalyptic literature assumed a heavenly hierarchy of stupendous proportions. In *Enoch* seven classes of angels are distinguished – the cherubim, seraphim, ofanim, the angels of power, the principalities, the Elect One (the Messiah) and the elementary powers of the earth.[224] Josephus tells us, concerning the Essene oath, that the sectary undertook to preserve, without alteration, 'the names of the angels', and the Qumran scrolls refer to them at every turn, calling them also 'holy ones', 'spirits', 'gods' (*elim*), 'honourable ones', 'sons of Heaven'. The members of the Covenant lived in the company of the celestial spirits all the time, and believed that angels, both

---

[224]More recent studies on apocalypticism suggest that the Enochian literature was prior to Daniel.

good and evil, would join in the final eschatological war between themselves and all the heathen nations.

These angels of Jewish imagination are often represented as occupying different levels in the universe. In the Slavonic *Enoch* the universe consists of a number of tiers; the abyss, then the prison of the dead, then the earth, then the firmament peopled by Satan and cruel invisible princes, then seven heavens. In the centre of each heaven is a 'throne' around which throng principalities, dominions and powers. Above them all is God, surrounded by the celestial beings called his powers, his throne, his spirit, his wisdom, his glory, his name. ...

The terms 'throne', 'principalities', 'powers' and 'dominions' are used to designate celestial beings in the *Testaments of the Patriarchs* (e.g. *Test. Levi* III) and also, as Christian commentators admit ... in the following passages from the NT epistles: ... Coloss. i.16, ... Ephes. i.21, ... Rom. viii.38, ... I Pet. iii.22.

It is clear that Paul not only believes in these angels, but also in the multi-layered universe ... For he tells of a Christian who was 'caught up into the third heaven' and also 'into paradise and heard words so secret that human lips may not repeat them' (II Cor. xii, 2–5, NEB). The continuation shows that this man was Paul himself.

It seems that certain Jews (not orthodox ones, but so-called Gnostics) not only owned the existence of angels but also worshipped them as divine beings. According to the *NBC* (p. 1044) the basis of Gnosticism is the doctrine that matter is evil, so that in creation, God cannot come into direct contact with it. 'It is necessary, therefore, to posit a number of emanations of deity, a number of spiritual beings germinating, as it were, the first from God, the second from the first and so on until they sink lower and lower and make contact with matter possible. Only thus could God have created the universe and at the same time maintained His holiness inviolate. It follows, then, that these graded beings are in control of the material universe in which man has to live. He must enlist their support.' The sum total of emanations of the godhead is denoted by the Greek word *pleroma*, and these Jewish Gnostics worshipped the *pleroma*.

This is the intellectual background against which the Pauline letters were written, and Colossians (ii, 8, 18) seems specifically to combat this doctrine that angelic agencies are necessary to salvation. Paul shows what their true place is, and asserts that one single privileged being, called Jesus the Messiah, absorbs the *pleroma* in himself, that he is the first after God, or with God, among all the celestial beings. ...

Couchoud remarks that in the passage from Colossians we have the most primitive idea of Jesus – that of a being who absorbed the *pleroma* in himself. He also notes that clearly, in Paul's view, the death of Jesus redeemed creatures in the heavens as well as on earth. ...

From Phil. ii, 5–11 we learn that Jesus is a divine figure who came down into the material world to suffer an ignominious death. Then he re-ascended and received a mystic name as powerful as the name of God. Couchoud regards this story of the descent and re-ascension of the divine being as the key to Paul's conception of Jesus and he remarks that we are fortunate enough to possess an ancient Jewish apocalypse which gives the story in greater detail, and so fills out the picture which is merely sketched by Paul. He is referring to the so-called *Ascension of Isaiah*.[225]

Carrier, too, gives the *Ascension of Isaiah* an important place in the literature.[226] Its 'as above, so below' cosmology is typical for the time. The author sees heavenly objects and beings as having 'copies' of some sort on Earth: "In this worldview everything on Earth was thought to be a mere imperfect copy of their truer forms in heaven, which were not abstract Platonic forms but actual

---

[225]Wells (1971), pp. 288–91, citing P. L. Couchoud, *The Enigma of Jesus* (London, 1924), p. 122, and *Le mystère de Jésus* (Paris, 1926).
[226]Carrier (2014), pp. 36–48, 540–45.

physical objects in outer space."[227] And its Jesus is thoroughly cosmic: Jesus descends through the heavens, progressively taking on the form of each as a disguise, so that when he reaches the lowest spiritual level, he is unrecognized as the preexistent son of God. Satan and the demons crucify him (in the heavens, and a reflection of this event occurs on Earth in some manner), he rises after the standard three days, and stays around for one and a half years in order to appear to humans in visions.

As Carrier points out, this is essentially the same story as the *Descent of Inanna*, the Sumerian goddess of love ("characteristic repetitions, seven-stage descent and disrobing, crucifixion by demons, and resurrection," resurrection secured by divine food and water of life).[228] Inanna was popular among Jews, and it looks as if someone took her story and wrapped it in contemporary Jewish elements. Most intriguingly, it is possible that Paul directly paraphrases the *Ascension* in 1 Corinthians, where he says:

> God's plan of Christ's death-defeating sacrifice was a 'secret' kept 'hidden' (1 Cor. 2:7) and only recently known by 'revelation' (1 Cor. 2:10), such that 'none of the rulers of this world knew; for had they known it, they would not have crucified the Lord of Glory' (1 Cor. 2:8). This looks like a direct paraphrase of an early version of the *Ascension of Isaiah*, wherein Jesus is also the 'Lord of Glory', his descent and divine plan is also 'hidden' and the 'rulers of this world' are indeed the ones who crucify him, in ignorance of that hidden plan (see the *Ascension of Isaiah* 9.15; 9.32; 10.12, 15). It even has an angel predict his resurrection on the third day (9.16), and the Latin/Slavonic contains a verse (in 11.34) that Paul actually cites *as scripture*, in the very same place (1 Cor. 2:9).[229]

Another curious verse in *Ascension* (9.1) has to do with Jesus' name: the Lord Christ "will be called 'Jesus' on Earth, but his name you cannot hear until you have ascended out of your body." In other words, Jesus is *not* his heavenly name, which is presumably a mystery, nor is it his earthly name, having been given to him after his death and resurrection to the heavenly spheres. So much for a guy named 'Jesus' in Nazareth.

After describing the *Ascension of Isaiah* in some detail, Wells then explains what is happening with the *Epistle of Barnabas*:

> According to Dibelius ... the motive of the author of this whole story is to explain to those who believed in a celestial redeemer, called Christ, how it could happen that this figure was able to reach the earth without opposition; why it was that the angels of the various heavens let their worst enemy redeem man without resisting his passage.
>
> What relevance has all this to Paul's idea of Jesus? Couchoud, and Dibelius some years before him..., answer that Paul seems to have had a revelation very similar to that here ascribed to Isaiah. In I Cor. ii, 9, he tells that God has revealed marvelous things to him – things, he adds, which pertain to our salvation, to God's gift to us (verse 12). ... The purpose of this descent and re-ascent is given in the passage from Colossians. By the *blood of his cross* he laid the basis for reconciling all things in heaven and earth to the Father; by his death and resurrection he broke the power of those angels who opposed God, and also *put an end to man's dependence on angels, good or bad.* Man can now commune with God via Jesus, without other intermediaries. Thus Paul declares that we need no longer be slaves to the elemental spirits of the universe (Gal. iv, 3–5); that no spirits need now separate us from the love of God (Rom viii, 38–9); and that the 'rulers of this world' are

---

[227]Carrier (2014), p. 194. This is actually a Zoroastrian idea at its origins.
[228]Carrier (2014), p. 46.
[229]Carrier (2014), pp. 47–8.

declining to their end (I Cor. ii, 6). The reference is to Satan and his angels, and in this passage from Corinthians Paul is thus saying that *it is these wicked creatures who crucified 'the Lord of Glory', not knowing who he was.* Couchoud compares this with the *Ascension of Isaiah*, ix. 14: 'And the god of that world will stretch forth his hand against the Son, and they will crucify him on a tree, and will slay him, not knowing who he is.' They do not know his identity because at every stage in his journey down he was transformed into the likeness of the creatures at that level. Just as this work goes on to tell how he rose from the dead and punished them by confronting them in his true form, so too Paul describes (Coloss. ii, 15) how they were tricked and vanquished: 'Having put off from himself the principalities and the powers, he made a show of them openly, triumphing over them in it'. The NEB says he 'made a spectacle of the cosmic powers and authorities, *and led them as captives in his triumphal procession'. ...*

Paul distinguishes as stages in the winding-up of the universe: first Christ's resurrection, then the resurrection of the dead at his second coming, and finally his destruction of the angels; he will 'abolish every kind of dominion, authority and power'. Then he will abdicate or 'deliver up the kingdom to God the Father', and the celestial harmony will be complete (I Cor. xv, 51 f.).

The later development of Christianity can be understood as an attempt to explain the repeated failure of the final judgment to materialize. ... [A]s Dibelius puts it, 'the centre of gravity of Christian expectations shifted from the future into the ... past' ... And as attention became more concentrated on Jesus' sojourn on earth, biographical details would begin to be invented, and traditions initiated which eventually became fixed in the gospels. Apocalypses and apocalyptic visions would be ousted by biographies. ... Further biographic details could be furnished by interpreting some of the prophecies which referred to a supernatural redeemer in such a way as to make them apply to a human messiah. ...

It was, then, disappointment in Jesus' failure to come in his glory to judge and end the world that led believers to concentrate their attention on what had already been achieved by his first coming, and in this way to invent traditions about the details of his stay on earth. ... Mt. [Matthew] tells how, at the death of Jesus, an earthquake occurred, rocks and graves were split open, and the saints occupying them were resurrected. ... [C]atastrophes such as Mt. depicts were what the Jews expected would occur at the second coming. Mt.'s story was, then, invented in order to show that Christians need not be disappointed at the failure of the second coming to occur, since the phenomena associated with it had, at any rate in part, been manifested at the first coming. Disappointment is being rectified in that the frustrated hopes of a future denouement are replaced by faith and belief in one that had already occurred in a definite historical situation.[230]

As to the process by which the biography of Jesus of Nazareth was gradually developed, Paul himself described how it was done in 1 Corinthians 14:26: "To sum up, my friends: when you meet for worship, each of you contributes a hymn, some instruction, a revelation, an ecstatic utterance, or the interpretation of such an utterance." That is exactly what the author of Barnabas says he did: "I know that the Lord journeyed with me on the way of righteousness. ... considering this therefore, that, if it shall be my care to communicate to you some portion of that which I received, it shall turn to my reward." As Wells points out:

Paul, obsessed with fears about the powers of the angels in the firmament, found consolation in his visions, which informed him that the redeemer had come down to earth in order to trick and put to shame these beings; and that he had tricked them by suffering an ignominious death at their hands.[231]

---

[230]Wells (1971), pp. 294–5.
[231]Wells (1971), p. 316.

But the Messiah did not come and destroy the evils of the world. Instead, the Romans destroyed Jerusalem and the Temple, and the march of elite dominance, slavery, oppression of the poor, and myriad manifestations of social inequity and insecurity continued. Nothing got better and a lot of people died in the destruction caused by the drive to absolute power. The same kinds of fears and obsessions that led to the longing for a messiah would have grown up around the failure of the predicted Messianic arrival and would then have led those who believed that they were involved in a mystic union with Christ to produce solutions to this problem in their prophetic and ecstatic utterances. Faith in the redeemer is what mattered and what would bring personal salvation since, obviously, the world wasn't being saved or transformed; at least, *not yet*.

Already the groundwork had been laid for prophecy to become the purview of an ecclesiastical elite. The *Didache* says in chapter 13:

> Every genuine prophet who wants to live among you is worthy of support. So also, every true teacher is, like a workman, entitled to his support. Every first fruit, therefore, of the products of vintage and harvest, of cattle and of sheep, should be given as first fruits to the prophets, for they are your high priests. But if you have no prophet, give it all to the poor. If you bake bread, take the first loaf and give it according to the commandment. If you open a new jar of wine or of oil, take the first fruit and give it to the prophets. If you acquire money or cloth or any other possession, set aside a portion first, as it may seem good to you, and give according to the commandment.

It was in the context of competing claims of self-described 'genuine prophets' that controversies raged during the development of Christianity, and from what we have seen thus far, it wasn't truth and righteousness that prevailed in the end: it was power of persuasion, rhetoric, drama, and playing on the fears of humans adrift in a violent and terrifying reality. In the end, orthodoxy expressed itself as raw power. "By their fruits, you shall know them."

James, Peter, John and Jude

The Epistle of James is something of an oddity. The author is obviously writing later than Paul, and he writes with the apparent intention of directly *contradicting* Paul's theology, but he cites the Old Testament as his witness and never refers to the Gospels or to Jesus as an authority (or as his brother!). The author teaches, "swear not, neither by the heaven nor by the Earth, nor by any other oath: but let your yea be yea, and your nay, nay: that ye fall not under the judgment."[232] This saying was put into Jesus' mouth in Matthew 5:34, 37, though James never mentions Jesus as the author of it. When he mentions "the Lord," there is no indication that he means Jesus. He writes that healing of the sick can be effected by "the elders," an official body, as opposed to Paul's doctrine that the power to heal could belong to any believer who had that "gift of the spirit." Either this is evidence of the development of an ecclesiastical organization, or it derives from *the already existing organization* of the Qumran community, or one like it, such as an Essene ecclesia in the Diaspora. The Epistle of James is mainly concerned with one thing: the imminent coming of a supernatural being. It shows no awareness of the destruction of Jerusalem, so it possibly dates somewhere between 50–70 AD, or earlier. As we will see further on, it would have to have been written before 47 AD to have been authored by James, the pillar of Jerusalem mentioned by Paul.

---
[232] James 5:12.

The so-called First Epistle of Peter likewise gives no information whatsoever about any life or times of a *man* called Jesus, whose companion he was supposed to have been. He mentions the sprinkling of the blood of Jesus and the legend of the descent to the underworld, and talks about the ancient prophets who foretold "the sufferings of Christ and the glories that should follow them" and that these prophecies had nothing to do with the times in which they were given, but rather applied to the times of the author and his audience, a completely apocalyptic viewpoint. As Wells points out, that is simply not true. All of the ancient prophets apparently did expect their prophecies to apply to their own time unless they are clearly *vaticinium ex eventu*, which is probably the case most often. Nevertheless, it is only by torturing the text that the authors of the NT managed to derive a 'Life of Jesus' out of the OT. Peter does mention Jesus as an example of endurance of suffering, but rather than relating it to recent life events that he ought to have witnessed himself, and for which he could have given powerful testimony if he had, he instead utilizes the descriptions from Isaiah 53: the 'Suffering Servant'! Peter has apparently augmented Paul's theology with a bit of Isaiah. At the end of Peter, the author describes himself as an elder and a "witness of Christ's suffering"; however, the Greek term used means "those who give testimony," *not an eyewitness.*

Regarding the First Epistle of John, Wells writes:

> The traditional assumption that I John was written by the author of the fourth gospel is not very plausible, since the second coming of Christ is still spoken of in I John ii.28 as a visible occurrence in time, whereas in the fourth gospel all trace of this eschatology has disappeared and the second advent means the coming of the Holy Spirit into the hearts of believers. ...
>
> The author of this epistle, and also the author of II John, complain of 'many deceivers' who deny that Jesus 'has come in the flesh'. How could anybody have denied this if his activities, as recorded in the gospels, had formed the basis of the cult? And if these canonical writers had known about his earthly life, why did they not meet the denial by giving some of the details, e.g. by alluding to his earthly parentage?[233]

There may have been very good reasons why details were not provided in these letters. If they are, in fact, connected to the sectarians behind the Dead Sea Scrolls, and supposing (as it seems) that the sectarians of the Qumran community were 'evangelizing war with the Romans,' they would not have been explicit in any writings.

Ellegård takes issue with the assumption of pseudepigraphy in discussing the letters of James, 1 Peter and Jude. He points out that biblical scholars assume this because they have a belief in the historicity of the Gospels; if the authors of these letters were who they say they are, they would have known details of the earthly life of Jesus, having been his companions in life; therefore, they conclude, the letters must be forgeries. Further, since his companions are described as rude fishermen or laborers, how could they write such fine Greek? Since scholars do not question that one, fundamental assumption – that Christianity had its origin in Jesus of Nazareth as depicted in the Gospels, an assumption that rests on the Gospels being historical – they are blocked entirely from the consideration that *these letters just might be written by exactly who they say they are written by.* Imagine that! It really is a stunning idea. Ellegård proposes:

---

[233]Wells (1971), pp. 155–6.

We have in fact every reason to believe that at least the leading members of the Jerusalem Church of God, whose 'pillars' Paul had met, *were able to write excellent Greek.*[234] ... And as, according to my hypothesis, Christianity developed out of Essene Diaspora communities, we have no reason whatever to expect our first-century AD writers to know very much about the life of their main founder and prophet, long since dead. ... Jewishness permeates the whole letter of James ... A clear Essene trait in James occurs in 1:17, where God is called 'the Father of lights', an expression not found, as far as I can see, elsewhere in the Bible, but well in line with the symbolism of light employed by Essenes, Gnostics, and Christians.[235]

Ellegård shows that the First Epistle of Peter is also written by a Jew to Diaspora Jews and gives no evidence of having actually known an earthly Jesus, speaking in consistently theological language. Ellegård points out a very interesting factor in this letter: it appears that it was written to lapsed but now repentant Jews. In 1 Peter 4:3, Peter says: "the time past of our life may suffice us to have wrought the will of the Gentiles, when we walked in lasciviousness, lusts, excess of wine, revellings, banquetings, and abominable idolatries." Ellegård takes the expression "wrought the will of the Gentiles" to represent the pressures that Diaspora Jews might be under surrounded by Gentiles. However, it is also possible, taking the history of Paul vs. Peter into account, as described by Paul in Galatians 2:11-16, that it could be a reference to the time that Peter was under the sway of Paul and enjoyed table-fellowship with Gentiles until James pulled him up short, boxed his ears, and made him understand that just eating with 'those people' was equivalent to being connected to all their other evil ways. So, when Peter says 'we,' maybe he means exactly that? And if so, that would date this writing to before 47 AD too, as will be discussed further on.

Moving to Jude, Ellegård points out that the author introduces himself as the brother of James. If the author is referring to James, the pillar of the Jerusalem ecclesia, the same one that tradition considers to be the brother of an earthly Jesus, then Jude would also be the brother of Jesus, so why doesn't he say so? Even if the author was not Jude, or the author of James was not really James of Jerusalem – the 'brother of the lord,' as Paul says – and both letters were written by a pseudonymous author, that author apparently didn't know any tradition about Jesus having brothers or he would have capitalized on it. And if the authors are really James of Jerusalem and his brother Jude, they also did not know of a Jesus of Nazareth who was their brother according to later tradition. Or, again, we may be encountering the need for secrecy because of subversive anti-Roman or otherwise subversive activities.

Ellegård believes all three of these letters to belong to the first century, before the destruction of Jerusalem, though there isn't much to go on in respect of dating. Jude complains in rather vehement language that *infiltrators have crept into their group* and the chief characteristic seems to be sexual immorality, homosexuality being hinted at. Perhaps this is metaphoric and refers to Gnostic or Pauline ideas?

In conclusion, Ellegård notes that even though these four letters are commonplace, not very long or even theologically deep, early communities obviously kept them for some reason and that reason might be the general awareness that they actually were written by important members

---

[234]Another nail in the coffin burying Josephus' claims to being a member of the Jerusalem educated elite: he wrote very bad Greek!

[235]Ellegård (1999), pp. 143–4. Note too James' opposition to oaths, which we also saw in Philo and Josephus' descriptions of the Essenes.

of the early church in Jerusalem. If that doesn't get the heart rate going, then one is dead to historical implications.

Letter to the Hebrews

The Letter to the Hebrews is a particularly interesting problem. From very early times, it was attributed to Paul, but Eusebius notes that some expressed doubts about this.[236] In his second remark on the topic, Eusebius mentions Caius, "a most learned man" who "silences the rashness and daring of his opponents in composing new books, [and] makes mention of only thirteen epistles, not reckoning that to the Hebrews with the rest; as there are, even to this day, *some of the Romans* who do not consider it to be the work of the apostles."[237] Eusebius was probably just repeating the opinion of Jerome, who says that Caius denied the Epistle to the Hebrews to be Paul's.[238]

The list of 'canonical works' contained in the Muratorian fragment[239] does not include Hebrews. (It also excludes James, Peter and 3 John.) The anonymous author of the fragment also notes that "Another [epistle] is current with the Alexandrians, forged in the name of Paul, for the sake of promoting the heresy of Marcion, and many other things."[240] This describes the Letter to the Hebrews rather well, though it could not have been forged in the time of Marcion, because we know that Hebrews was utilized in the composition of the Gospel of Mark.

Hebrews is divided into six sections, including an introduction that announces the superiority of the New Covenant over the Old, which subsequent sections go on to prove using references to Old Testament texts, comparing 'the Son' to the angel-mediators of the Old Covenant, Moses and Joshua, and Christ's high-priesthood after the order of Melchizedek to that of the Levites after the order of Aaron. For the author of Hebrews, Christ is a divine being. He uses the priestly analogy to solve any objection to that divinity, for example, death, which is a human experience.

Those to whom the author of Hebrews is writing either have begun to doubt the proclamation of the Messiah *or are just now being introduced to the teaching*. They probably believed that the Messiah prophesied in the Hebrew Scriptures was to come as a militant king and destroy the enemies of his people, and Hebrews is designed to shift their understanding. The argument achieves this by proposing that the Hebrew Scriptures also foretold that the Messiah would be a priest and this proposed Messiah, Jesus, came to fulfill this role, as a sacrificial offering to God, to atone for sins. His role of a king is yet to come, and so those who follow him should be patient and not be surprised that they suffer for now. (They had apparently stopped assembling together, possibly due to some sort of persecution or great disruption such as the destruction of Jerusalem and their hopes along with it.)

---

[236] Eusebius, *H.E.* 3.3.5.

[237] Eusebius, *H.E.* 6.20.3.

[238] *De Vir. Illus. Voc. Caius.*

[239] The Muratorian fragment is a Latin manuscript translated from Greek, long thought to be the earliest list of canonical Christian books. However, while early scholars dated it to ca. 170 AD, it's now thought to be closer to the fourth century. In other words, it doesn't give a very solid idea of the early Christian canon.

[240] Moses Stuart, Rensselaer David Chanceford Robbins, Mark Mewman, *A Commentary on the Epistle to the Hebrews*, Vol. I (Codman Press, 1827), p. 123.

To sum up, the author claims to have received the message of salvation from the personal disciples of the Lord. The author knows the letters of Paul and makes no distinction between Jew and Gentile in terms of potential salvation. Wells points out that the apparent purpose of the letter – to demonstrate that Jesus, as son of God, is superior to the angels – presupposes that *there were others who thought of Jesus as supernatural, but not divine.* The author also manages to make Jesus both a royal and a priestly messiah by arguing that the Davidic messiah has been accepted into an even older and more superior priesthood than that of the Levites, modeled on the priest-king Melchizedek. It sets before the Jew the claims of Christianity – to bring the Jew to the full realization of the relation of Judaism to Christianity, to make clear that Christ has fulfilled those temporary and provisional institutions, and has thus abolished them. Nevertheless, Jesus doesn't have an earthly biography here, either. The litany of faith never mentions any person or event having to do with the Gospel Jesus; again, nothing but the Old Testament is trotted out for review. That doesn't mean that the original of this letter might not have said more, but if it did, then such passages have been removed and that would suggest that they did not support the 'Jesus of Nazareth' story. But that's just speculation on an argument from silence and not worth much.

New Testament and Second Temple Judaism scholar Eric Mason argues that the conceptual background of the priestly Christology of the Epistle to the Hebrews closely parallels presentations of the messianic priest and Melchizedek in the Qumran scrolls.[241] We have already noted the relationship between the ideas of the Gnostics and those of Qumran. This is interesting in view of what sectarian ideas Paul might have opposed and then later been converted to uphold, though obviously with his own spin that wasn't quite what the James people were promoting. Though the writing of Hebrews is elegant and polished, unlike the Pauline epistles, it is clear that *Paul's ideas are being expanded and expounded*, and many scholars now believe that the author was one of Paul's pupils or associates.

Adolf von Harnack, A. J. Gordon, Gilbert Bilezikian, and others argue that the author of Hebrews *was a woman*, and that this is why there is no firm evidence as to authorship – authorship was deleted either to conceal the fact that it *was* a woman, or to protect the letter itself from suppression, or both.[242] Harnack thinks the letter was written in Rome to the inner circle of Paul's students and cites chapter 13 to show the author was a "high standing and apostolic teacher of equal rank with Timothy." But the author's name would not have been erased if Luke, Clemens, Barnabas, or Apollos had written it. Donald Guthrie, in 1983, suggested Priscilla[243] as the author.[244] A. J. Gordon wrote: "It is evident that the Holy Spirit made this woman Priscilla a *teacher of teachers.*" Bilezikian remarks on "the conspiracy of anonymity in the ancient church,"

---

[241] Eric F. Mason, *You Are a Priest Forever: Second Temple Jewish Messianism and the Priestly Christology of the Epistle to the Hebrews* (Brill, 2008).

[242] See Adolf von Harnack, 'Probabilia uber die Addresse und den Verfasser des Habraerbriefes,' *Zeitschrift fur die Neutestamentliche Wissenschaft und die Kunde der aelteren Kirche* (E. Preuschen, Berlin: Forschungen und Fortschritte, 1900), 1:16–41; A. J. Gordon, 'The Ministry of Women,' *World Missionary Review* 7 (December 1894): 910–921; Gilbert Bilezikian, *Beyond Sex Roles: What the Bible Says about a Woman's Place in Church and Family* (Baker Academic, 1985 1st & 2nd Editions; 2006 3rd Edition).

[243] Priscilla and Aquila were a first-century Christian missionary married couple; Paul was generous in his recognition and acknowledgment of his indebtedness to them (Rom. 16:3-4).

[244] Donald Guthrie, *The Letter to the Hebrews* (Tyndale New Testament Commentaries, Grand Rapids, Mich.: Eerdmans, 1983, reprinted 1999), p. 21.

and notes: "The lack of any firm data concerning the identity of the author in the extant writings of the church suggests a *deliberate blackout* more than a case of collective loss of memory."

As to its date, Hebrews uses tabernacle terminology,[245] and assumes that the sacrifices in the Temple are still taking place daily, suggesting it was written prior to the destruction of the Temple in 70 AD, so many scholars date it around 63–64 AD. This relatively late dating (as close to the time of the war as possible) is due, once again, to the necessity to lace the Pauline timeline with that of Jesus who was "crucified under Pontius Pilate," allegedly after the fifteenth year of Tiberius Caesar. In all of these early documents reviewed thus far, we have heard not a whisper of this allegation against Pilate.

Clement of Rome

Before heading out for Rome, Paul penned a letter to the *already existing ecclesia* there. For those who have created the Jesus chronology based on the Galilean allegedly crucified under Pilate, this is a problem. Paul addresses his letter to "all God's beloved in Rome, who are called to be saints ... because your faith is proclaimed in all the world." I will include my own breakdown of Romans in the appendices, so I will only cover it briefly here.

There are many curious things in this Epistle to the Romans, but the most obvious and generally inexplicable is the fact that *there existed an apparently long-standing Roman church*! This is the point that Ellegård argues: that the Roman, Corinthian, and possibly other churches, go back to pre–Jesus of Nazareth times and began as Essene-type communities which were known as 'Churches of God,' and the members as 'saints.'

The date of the *First Letter of Clement*, whom Eusebius says was the first bishop of Rome, is much disputed, but most modern scholars date him to post-destruction of Jerusalem, i.e. ca. 95 AD or later. Ellegård argues that Clement was written *before* the destruction of Jerusalem and, like all other texts from this time, knew nothing of the Gospels' Jesus of Nazareth. There are a couple of places where it appears that Clement is quoting Matthew or Mark, but it is more than likely that those are interpolations. Clement shows knowledge of the Letter to the Hebrews, as well as Paul's Letters to the Corinthians and Romans, but no knowledge of the Gospels' Jesus. However, placing the letter before 70 AD is less certain; it appears to *me* that it is post-war. Regardless, as Ellegård notes, once our suspicions on the accuracy of Eusebius' dating have been aroused, we are better able to see the text as it is, and decipher what it may tell us.[246]

Among the numerous things that Ellegård notes about this text is the fact that Clement refers to the 'Church of God' as both individual communities as well as a totality of communities spread around the Empire which kept in touch with one another via letters and 'apostles.' Most interestingly, he refers to the organization as being like the *hierarchy of an army*. He stresses the importance of obeying the elders, and we know that Qumran-like communities had a council of twelve elders and three priests. Apparently, the reason for the letter is the fact that some elders

---

[245]The focus on the tabernacle may suggest a Samaritan source, as it was it played on important role in Samaritan tradition as the only legitimate sanctuary in Israel's history. Thanks to Russell Gmirkin for bringing this to my attention (personal communication).

[246]One must keep in mind that the veracity of Eusebius – or, put another way, the accuracy – has been brought into serious question by the work of Walter Bauer. Read Ellegård for a more thorough critique of Eusebius and dating based on his claims.

in Corinth were being ousted by the community and Clement insists that this ought not to be done. Ellegård writes:

> In *1 Clement* 5 we read, in a section devoted to the dire effects of 'jealousy': 'Let us take the noble examples of our own generation.' The examples given are first of all Peter and Paul, whose deaths as martyrs are referred to in surprisingly veiled language. ...
>
> The opening phrase of the letter reads: 'The disasters and calamities that have suddenly and *repeatedly* struck us, have delayed us in turning to your affairs.' The writer obviously refers to very recent happenings. ... Further, in *1 Clement* 6, after mention of Peter and Paul, there is again a reference to 'our own generation', declaring that 'an immense crowd of the elect ones' have suffered 'terrible and monstrous outrages'. In both cases, the description fits excellently the Neronian persecution of Christians in connection with the great fire of Rome in 64.[247]

I would suggest that Clement was written after the Jewish War because in 7.4 he writes: "Jealousy and strife overturned great cities and uprooted great nations" and his language above could refer to the destruction of the Jerusalem church. On the dating of *1 Clement*, Ellegård finds support in the *Pastor* of Hermas. While the previously mentioned Muratorian fragment is often used to date the *Pastor*, Ellegård is not much impressed with it, and re-dates *Pastor* closer to the time of *1 Clement*.

> ... in Vision 2-4-3 an angel tells Hermas: 'make two copies [of what I say to you], one for Clement, and one for Grapte. And Clement will send it to the other cities – *that is his job*' [Ellegård's italics].

> The idea that the Clement mentioned here is Clemens Romanus has been discussed widely but rejected, chiefly, it seems, on the ground that it is contradicted by the Muratori dating ... But ... the Clement mentioned in Hermas forms a perfect fit for the author of *1 Clement*. Not only do they have the same name, they also seem to play the same role in their community. ... Keep in mind that it is Eusebius, writing in the fourth century, and referring to late second century witnesses, who says Clement was bishop of Rome. ... Paul mentions both a Hermas and a Clement as contemporaries in his letters.[248]

Clement describes the Corinthian church as "very firm and ancient" (47:6) and the Roman church is described as being *equally old*, since the messengers are described as having been members *from their youth to old age* (63:3), which echoes Paul's language in addressing this group. Clement is either using this language 'freely,'[249] or he is being literal. If the latter, all of this would be impossible according to the view that Christianity was launched by a Palestinian Jesus crucified by Pontius Pilate around 30 AD. Paul's activity is referred to in 47:2 as *"the beginning of the evangelization,"* which is a rather extraordinary statement that may turn out to be a very important clue. It tells us that there was something very special in the work of Paul, the spreading of his particular spin on the Messiah message to communities that were already established at the time he was converted. So it seems that these communities had existed for some time, but their understanding of who and what they were was very different prior to Paul; they

---

[247]Ellegård (1999), pp. 39–40.

[248]Ellegård (1999), pp. 40–1. Paul sends greetings to Hermas (among others) in Rome, in Rom. 16:14. Clement is referred to as one of Paul's co-workers (along with Euodia and Syntyche) in Phil. 4:3.

[249]I am grateful to Richard Pervo (personal communication) for reminding me that the language of antiquity could be used quite loosely. Just look at Acts!

were possibly not even on a messianic or apocalyptic trajectory. It was Paul and other apostles who began to teach about a messiah, though obviously Paul had very different ideas about how this was supposed to work from those belonging to the Jerusalem ecclesia who evangelized death and destruction to Rome.

As noted, what is striking is that *1 Clement* does not mention the 'time of Jesus' death' or 'the time of Jesus' but rather *dates things from the time of the beginning of Paul's apostolic mission.* Ellegård writes:

> The Jewishness of Clement's communities is beyond doubt. In the address, they are described as 'living as strangers' in Rome and Corinth, respectively. ... Throughout the letter, Clement refers to Old Testament examples. ... Jesus as Christ is the guarantee of salvation and of life after death. His passion and his death are indeed brought out ... they are described in terms of the suffering servant of Isaiah 53 and Psalm 22, introduced by the words 'The Lord Jesus Christ says', after which follow direct quotations from Isaiah 53:1–12 and Psalm 22:7–9 ...
>
> Crucifixion is never mentioned which is surely remarkable, in view of Paul's intense involvement in the mystique of the cross, a mystique that he quite likely originated. Clement never goes beyond bare mentions of the 'blood' of Christ, without any concrete elaboration whatever.
>
> Clement tells us nothing about Jesus' life, his disciples, his baptism by John, his betrayal by Judas, his trial and the manner of his death. His resurrection is represented as a fact, not as an event. ... There is no hint as to when and where it occurred. ... Clement sometimes calls Jesus 'High Priest', thus emphasizing the connection with ancient Jewish history, and also ... with the Qumran Essenes. Finally, when Clement in 5.1 turns from 'ancient examples from the OT' of the consequences of 'jealousy', and talks of 'our own generation', he mentions Peter and Paul – whose deaths he refers to as *recent* events – but does not mention Jesus ...[250]

Before anything else, let me just point out that it is not necessarily so that Clement's epistle was addressed to Diaspora Jews as Ellegård claims. Considering what we have examined regarding Essene-type communities, various ecclesia around the Empire, the affinity of many Gentiles for the Jewish religion, they could very well have been Gentiles largely or entirely. 'Living as strangers' in Rome, or anywhere else would describe the self-perception of any Essene-like group, Jewish, Christian or otherwise; the Epistle to the Hebrews describes Christians as strangers on this Earth looking to go 'home.'

In trying to come to some conclusion about these matters, I've read a good bit of the radical criticism of various letters that has come out of the German and Dutch schools. Since the letters of Clement and Ignatius are the earliest witnesses to the letters and activity of Paul, this is important. Complaints about *1 Clement* have been based on the hints of Gnosticism, which are thought to be a later development, but which are clearly very early, as Philo himself gives evidence. Pearson (and others) connects the Antiochene, Alexandrian, and Qumran movements together, and Ellegård connects them with Essene ecclesia around the Empire. Philo, Josephus and Pliny all testify to this latter element. So why is it so generally discounted?

One critic, Volkmar, complains that *1 Clement* "doesn't get to the point right away." I find it rather astounding that modern standards of rhetoric are being imposed on an ancient writer and used as a reason to discount the text. The criticism that a much later development, the inculcation of apostolic authority, is the main purpose of the letter, dissolves when it is understood that we are dealing with Essene-like communities with an established hierarchy long in existence.

---

[250]Ellegård (1999), pp. 42–3.

The additional criticism is that there does not seem to be any conflict between Jews and Gentiles; that is easily explained by pointing out that Paul's style of gospel was undoubtedly more at home in the Diaspora, and it was only because he sought, for reasons of his own that I will discuss further on, to try to bring the Jerusalem sectarians into accord with his vision of unifying Jews and Gentiles under the same god that he came into conflicts with them.

It seems that apostles from the Jerusalem sect were going out to evangelize along the line of über-Judaism – promoting their coming Revelation-Revolution – while Paul was doing the opposite – promoting his Revelation-Resolution. It just depended on which apostle was more convincing, as Paul's conflicts, evident in his letters, reveal. If we can take as fact some of the personal data dropped in the Letter to the Romans, it may be that connections also had a lot to do with the way the wind blew in any given ecclesia. So, that's the first thing: I think Ellegård has made a reasonable case for many of his points and, what's more, it will be seen to fit with further matters yet to be put on the table.

Second, Clement's reference to the recent deaths of Peter and Paul are couched in rather vague terms, which could be the way he wrote it or could be because a plainer statement was edited later. *First Clement* 5:2 says rather specifically: "Because of jealousy and envy the greatest and most upright pillars were persecuted, and they struggled in the contest even to death."[251] If we recall that Paul referred to Cephas, James and John as the 'pillars' in Jerusalem, I don't think it is stepping too far out on a limb to say that this sentence may very well refer to the deaths of those individuals. (We may also find those deaths actually recorded in a non-biblical source further on.)

So, having made a statement about the *pillars*, the author then moves on to *apostles*, and here he names Peter first of all. The way this is presented is as if Peter is *not* one of the pillars, which might mean that *Cephas and Peter were not one and the same person*.[252] Clement writes:

> There is Peter, who because of unjust jealousy bore up under hardships not just once or twice, but many times; and having thus borne his witness he went to the place of glory that he deserved.

The question we might wish to ask here is: was it Peter who was unjustly jealous, leading to his many hardships (a metaphor for torture?), or was he a target of unjust jealousy in others? What seems clear is that the 'bearing of hardships' was the bearing witness. Whichever it was, it very much sounds like Peter came to an ignominious end, because Clement is very brief in writing about him.

The next case is Paul:

> Because of jealousy and strife Paul pointed the way to the prize for endurance. Seven times he bore chains; he was sent into exile and stoned; he served as a herald in both the East and the West; and he received the noble reputation for his faith. He taught righteousness to the whole world, and came to the limits of the West, bearing his witness before the rulers. And so he was set free from this world and transported up to the holy place, having become the greatest example of endurance.

---

[251] From here on I use the more recent Loeb edition of *First Clement* translated by Bart Ehrman, p. 43.

[252] Paul usually uses the name 'Cephas' ('rock' in Aramaic) in his letters. He only uses 'Peter' twice, in Gal. 2:7–8: "On the contrary, they saw that I had been entrusted with the task of preaching the gospel to the Gentiles, just as Peter had been to the Jews. For God, who was at work in the ministry of Peter as an apostle to the Jews, was also at work in my ministry as an apostle to the Gentiles." He never refers to Cephas in the same context, as apostle to the Jews. In fact, in the very next sentence (Gal. 2:9) he calls "James, *Cephas* and John" the *pillars*.

Notice first of all that the jealousy in relation to Paul is not called 'unjust' as it was in the case of Peter. Does that suggest that the jealousy mentioned in relation to Peter was his own and is what led to his hardships? And here, regarding Paul, the jealousy and strife are said to have pointed the way to the prize for endurance! That suggests that Paul was the one enduring the jealousy and strife. There are any number of ways to 'read' this passage. One thing this passage seems to convey is that, after many trials, Paul's life turned around completely, he possibly evangelized and converted some 'rulers' and died an old and honored man. He may have done this in Spain, which was the Empire's 'farthest bounds of the West.' Carrier agrees on this latter point:

> The fact that this contradicts all later legend (which has Paul executed by Nero in Rome) suggests, first, that that was indeed only a later legend and, second, that Paul did in fact die in Spain – as otherwise there would be no reason for Clement to make this up … [But even if Clement was extrapolating based on Romans], Paul's martyrdom at Rome is proved to be a myth (that tale not existing yet, or it being known at Clement's time that in fact Paul was martyred in Spain).[253]

So who was Clement? Twenty-five years after the destruction of Jerusalem, 95 AD, a man named Titus Flavius Clemens was consul in Rome. Domitian executed him the year after. Syncellus, writing in the ninth century, was the first to call him a Christian, and the earlier accounts of his death suggest Syncellus may have been correct. First there is Suetonius, writing in the early second century:

> [Domitian] unexpectedly killed his own cousin Flavius Clemens, [a man] of most contemptible laziness, on a very feeble suspicion, shortly after the end of his consulship.[254]

Dio, writing a century later, adds more detail possibly from another source:

> In the same year Domitian executed among many others, also Flavius Clemens, although he was a cousin and his wife was Flavia Domitilla, a relative of Domitian. Both were *accused of godlessness*, a crime on account of which also many others, who were *inclined to Jewish practices*, were condemned. Some lost their lives, others at least their fortunes. Domitilla was only exiled to Pandateria.[255]

Since it was well known at the time that followers of Christus were following a Jewish sect, we can probably assume that Christianity is meant here.

Another century after Dio, Eusebius, most likely quoting a Roman history by Bruttius that hasn't survived, writes:

> Flavia Domitilla, a daughter of the sister of Flavius Clemens, a Roman consul at that time, was exiled to the island of *Pontia* because of *her Christian faith*. Many others were exiled too in that year.[256]

---

[253]Carrier (2014), pp. 309–10.

[254]Suetonius, *Domitian* 15.1, in Peter Lampe, *From Paul to Valentinus: Christians at Rome in the First Two Centuries* (Fortress Press, 2003), p. 198–9.

[255]Dio 67.14.1f., in Lampe (2003), p. 198.

[256]Eusebius, *Ecc. Hist.* 3.18.4, in Lampe (2003), p. 199.

Eusebius here confuses things. Domitilla was Clemens' *wife* and *Domitian's* niece. And she was exiled to Pandateria, which was a common place of exile, not Pontia. Oddly, Eusebius (and/or Bruttius) calls Domitilla a Christian, but not Clemens, whereas Dio accuses them both of the same crime.

The only other early account is from Philostratus, who probably wrote around the time of Dio in the early third century. He makes Domitilla the *sister* of Domitian, and adds the details that Domitian also ordered her execution, and her slave made an unsuccessful attempt to save her:

> And now the gods were about to cast down Domitian from his presidency of mankind. For it happened that he had just slain [Flavius] Clemens, a man of consular rank, to whom he had lately given his own *sister* [Flavia Domitilla] in marriage; and he issued a command about the third or fourth day after the murder, that she also should follow her husband and join him. Thereupon Stephanus, a freed man of the lady, he who was signified by the form of the late portent, whether because the latest victim's fate rankled in his mind, or the fate of all others, made an attempt upon the tyrant's life worthy of comparison with the feats of the champions of Athenian liberty.[257]

In any event, note that Dio says the couple was accused of *godlessness* and which he links *to Jewish practices.* At the time, this charge of atheism would have referred to the refusal to worship the emperor (Domitian in this case) as god. Early Pagan and Christian sources both refer to Christians as 'Jewish' (Suetonius, Lucian, Acts, *Acts of Peter*, *Ps. Clem.*), and Christians are repeatedly accused of atheism (attested in the writings of Justin, Tatian, Minucius Felix, Athenagoras, Tertullian, Celsus, Porphyry, Lucian). Roman Christians in particular were called "superstitious."[258] On the other hand, there's no known charge of atheism against *ordinary* Jews in any sources.[259] Based on this evidence, it seems likely that Domitilla *was* a Christian, and that "Dio changed the Christianity of Domitilla to an 'inclination of Jewish customs'."[260] Or that he changed nothing since Christians were known to be following a messiah, a term which originated in Jewish ideology.

As for Clemens, Lampe doesn't think he was a Christian, preferring to think that he was executed on suspicion of Domitian that Clemens was planning to have one of his sons (whom Domitian had chosen as successors) take the throne ahead of schedule. But the two are not mutually exclusive, and it seems just as likely that Dio was being truthful by saying they both faced the same accusation.[261]

---

[257]Philostratus, *Life of Apollonius* 8.25.

[258]Tac. *Ann.* 15.44; Seutonius, *Claudius* 25.3; Suetonius, *Nero* 16.2; Pliny, *Epistle* 10.96.8.

[259]Lampe (2003), p. 202.

[260]Lampe (2003), p. 203. Archaeological support for this comes from one of the earliest Christian catacombs, the "Domitilla," burial place of "St. Flavia Domitilla," the property of which had belonged to the Flavians. It also contains the first Christian use of the fish-and-anchor symbol, which had previously been used by Titus. See James S. Valliant and Warren Fahy, *Creating Christ: How Roman Emperors Invented Christianity* (Crossroad Press, 2018), p. 169. Thanks to Russell Gmirkin for directing me to this source.

[261]According to Valliant and Fahy (2018), p. 165, "the Church of St. Clement of Rome, built during the 5th Century, once contained an inscription dedicating it to 'Flavius Clemens, martyr,' according to a 1725 report by Cardinal Annibal Albani that has survived." Valliant and Fahy (pp. 161–173) argue that Domitian appears to have been targeting a wider group of Jewish Christians, which included Clemens, his wife Domitilla, Clemens' maternal uncle Arrecinus Clemens, and Nero's secretary Epaphroditus (see chapter 8). The timing coincides "with Pliny the Younger's claim that Christianity was in vogue around 20 years prior to his letter to Trajan – that is, in the very middle of the Flavian era when Clemens must have been flourishing" (p. 163).

Was this Clemens the same Clemens Romanus (Clement of Rome), the 'first bishop' of Rome and author of *1 Clement*? The same Clement mentioned by Hermas as being in charge of Christian correspondence for the Roman church? The same one mentioned by Paul as his fellow-worker?

For the last question to be true, Clemens would need to have been born prior to 30 AD in order to be an associate of Paul by the late 40s. His cousins Titus and Domitian were born in 39 and 51 AD, respectively, and his uncle Vespasian was born in 9 AD, but Flavius Clemens appears to have been a child in the 60s during Vespasian's attack on Rome, so no cigar for Paul's Clement.

As for the other Clements, I considered the idea for a while, but ultimately rejected it as being unlikely. However, there is one idea that solves a number of problems here: that the Clement of the letter could be a clerical freedman of Flavius Clemens. An ex-slave usually adopted the *praenomen* and *nomen* of his or her former master while retaining his or her slave name as a *cognomen*. Thus, Cicero's educated slave, Tiro, when he was freed, became Marcus Tullius Tiro; and Zosimus, the slave of Marcus Aurelius Cotta Maximus, when he was freed, became Marcus Aurelius Zosimus. The Claudian Civil Service set a precedent whereby freedmen could be used as civil servants in the Roman bureaucracy. During the early Empire, freedmen held key positions in the government and it wouldn't be inconceivable for a trained bureaucrat in the imperial family to have undertaken to utilize his particular skills on behalf of the ecclesia to which he belonged. If it is the case, it may be that Paul's connection with Clement was his entrée into the world of the elite, thus providing for his "noble reputation for his faith … bearing his witness before the rulers."[262]

Of course, "bearing his witness before the rulers" could be a euphemism for being martyred, so that cannot be entirely excluded.

Finally, it should be noted that the name 'Clement' is never mentioned in the epistle itself, so its attribution to any Clement at all is still questionable.[263]

Didache

The *Didache* or *The Teaching of the Twelve Apostles* is a brief, anonymous pastoral manual, dated by most scholars to the mid to late first century; Ellegård dates it to before the destruction of Jerusalem. The first line is: "Teaching of the Lord to the Gentiles (or Nations) by the Twelve Apostles."[264] More than any other early Christian book, it shows how Jewish-Christians saw themselves and adapted their Judaism for Gentiles. The text has three main sections dealing with ethics, rituals and Church organization, while the contents can be divided into four parts, which most scholars agree were combined from separate sources by a later redactor: the *Two*

---

[262]Since Flavius Clement was probably too young when Paul was active, Valliant and Fahy (2018) propose an interesting solution: that Paul's Clement was a freedman of Flavius Clement's *uncle*, Arrecinus Clemens, whose family "had been associated with the Praetorian Guard since at least the reign of Caligula" (p. 168). And according to the Jewish Encyclopedia, Flavius Clemens' father, Flavius Sabinus, "led during his last years a life that may be called Jewish or Christian." ('Flavia Domitilla,' JewishEncyclopedia.com.)

[263]Though as Valliant and Fahy (2018), pp. 171–172, point out, the letter cites pagan imagery and uses Roman imagery to make some arguments.

[264]I tend to think that the core of the Didache might be prior to the destruction of Jerusalem, but the claim that it was according to the "twelve apostles" puts it after the war, in my opinion. I think that Mark was the creator of the 12 apostles and he was writing after the war. Garrow (see next footnote) argues for several layers of composition, one of which predates Paul.

Ways, the Way of Life and the Way of Death (chapters 1–6); a ritual dealing with baptism, fasting, and Communion (chapters 7–10); the ministry and how to deal with traveling prophets (chapters 11–15). The final section (chapter 16) is a brief apocalypse: the community is presented as "awaiting the kingdom from the Father."

The closest parallels in the use of the Two Ways doctrine is found among the Dead Sea Scrolls community at Qumran. The community included a Two Ways teaching in its founding Charter, *The Community Rule.* The *Didache* makes no mention of Jesus' resurrection, other than a prayer of thanks for "immortality, which Thou hast made known unto us through Thy Son Jesus" in the eucharist; it does make specific reference to the resurrection of the dead just prior to the Lord's coming.

Significant similarities between the *Didache* and the Gospel of Matthew have been found; both writings share words, phrases, and motifs. The old view that the *Didache* used Matthew is being abandoned; rather, Matthew used an early version of the *Didache*, which was 'Christianized' in later times, to some extent.[265]

As noted by the *Didache*'s subtitle, the text was intended to instruct Gentiles who wished to join the ecclesia. What is evident from the *Didache* is that the Diaspora communities were not as exclusivist and xenophobic as the Jerusalem ecclesia run by the three 'pillars,' as described by Paul and which is also reflected in the Dead Sea Scrolls regarding the Qumran sectarians. There appears to have been a universalist tendency among some of these groups which probably inclined them more to Paul's unifying theology, at least until the political situation intensified, at which point, things seem to have changed, as we will see further on.

So, where are we in our account? It appears that for about a hundred years, people were finding faith in a Jesus about whom no one knew any details, or perhaps everyone knew who he was/had been in life, and thus it never had to be explained, and yet, we must remember that Tacitus did give an account of the early Christians, including the one detail that locks him into a definite historical timeline: Pontius Pilate.

Tacitus on Pilate

The earliest non-biblical mention of Pilate in relation to Christians is from Cornelius Tacitus (ca. 56–120 AD). The context of the passage is the Great Fire of Rome that burned a huge portion of the city in 64 AD during the reign of Nero. The key part of the passage reads as follows:

> Therefore, to dispel the rumor [that he personally ordered the fire], Nero supplied defendants and inflicted the choicest punishments on those, resented for their outrages, whom the public called Chrestiani. (The source of the name was Christus, on whom, during the command of Tiberius, reprisal had been inflicted by the procurator Pontius Pilatus; and, though the baleful superstition had been stifled for the moment, there was now another outbreak, not only across Judaea, the origin of the malignancy, but also across the City, where everything frightful or shameful, of whatever provenance, converges and is celebrated.)

---

[265]Alan Garrow, *The Gospel of Matthew's Dependence on the* Didache (Bloomsbury Academic, 2013).

The first to be seized were those who confessed, then, on their information, a mighty number was convicted, not so much on the charge of the conflagration as for their hatred of the human race.[266]

In 1902 Georg Andresen first noticed the odd appearance of the first 'i' in 'Christianos' in the earliest extant, eleventh-century copy of the *Annals* in Florence, suggesting that the text had been altered, and an 'e' had originally been in the text. The alteration was later conclusively shown with ultra-violet examination. According to Robert Van Voorst, it is unlikely that Tacitus himself referred to Christians as 'Chrestianos,' i.e. 'good, kind, useful, pleasant ones,' given that he also referred to them as "hated for their shameful acts," and many other sources indicate that early followers of Jesus used the term Chrestians by the second century.[267]

For example, while 'of Christ' is spelled Χριστοῦ (*Christou*) in Greek, an early Marcionite church in the Syrian village of Lebaba (Deir Ali) near Damascus contains an inscription with the words Ἰησοῦ Χρηστοῦ (*Iesou Chrestou*), dated to 318 AD, making it older than any existing Catholic inscriptions.[268] The Codex Sinaiticus (dated to 330–360 AD) is the earliest manuscript evidence for Acts 11:26 and 26:28, two instances of the word 'Christian' in the New Testament (in addition to 1 Peter 4:16). In all three appearances of this word, the Sinaiticus scribe spells the word 'Chrestian.' There are numerous other examples from manuscripts, inscriptions, and writings of the early Fathers of the Church.[269]

Pilate's rank while he was governor of Judea appeared in a Latin inscription on the Pilate Stone,[270] which called him a prefect, while this Tacitean passage calls him a procurator. Josephus refers to Pilate with the generic Greek term ἡγεμών, *hēgemōn*, or governor. Tacitus records that Claudius was the ruler who gave procurators governing power after Herod Agrippa I's death in AD 44, when Judea reverted to direct Roman rule.[271] Much has been made of the fact that

[266]Tacitus, *Ann.*, 15.44.2–4. Carrier (2014) argues that the line mentioning Pilate is a later interpolation, and that the text originally just referred to the same followers of Chrestus mentioned by Suetonius (see reference on p. 344). That's possible, but it's at least possible that some Christians had made the connection between Jesus or Chrestus and Pilate at this time. Either way, Tacitus wrote in 116 AD, so it's long after the fact and still just hearsay.

[267]Robert E. Van Voorst, *Jesus Outside the New Testament: An Introduction to the Ancient Evidence* (Eerdmans, 2000), pp. 33–5, 44–8. In the Greek of the time, both *christos* and *chrestos* were pronounced the same. (Thanks to Richard I. Pervo for pointing this out to me.) This may suggest that outsiders simply confused the two words. However, the lack of attestation to *Christian* references, and the presence of *Chrestian* ones (see below), in the earliest historical record may suggest that they got it right.

[268]William Smith and Henry Wace, *A Dictionary of Christian Biography, Literature, Sects and Doctrines*, vol. III (John Murray, 1882), p. 819.

[269]See this website for more evidence (including 13 early manuscript references, 11 inscriptions/graffiti, and references by Church Fathers Justin Martyr, Clement, Tertullian and Lactantius): http://mountainman.com.au/essenes/christians christians.htm. Nodet and Taylor (1998, p. 304) argue that Chrestiani was the name given to Jewish messianic agitators, primarily in Antioch, during the Caligula crisis in the late 30s AD.

[270]"The Pilate stone is a damaged block (82 cm x 65 cm) of carved limestone with a partially intact inscription attributed to, and mentioning, Pontius Pilate ... It was discovered at the archaeological site of Caesarea Maritima in 1961. ... It is likely that Pontius Pilate made his base at Caesarea Maritima – the site where the stone was discovered, since that city had replaced Jerusalem as the administrative capital and military headquarters of the region in AD 6 [See: *A History of the Jewish People*, H. H. Ben-Sasson editor, 1976, p. 247.], Pilate probably travelled to Jerusalem, the central city of the province's Jewish population, only when necessary. The Pilate stone is currently located at the Israel Museum in Jerusalem." (Wikipedia.org, 'Pilate stone.')

[271]Tacitus, *Histories* 5.9.8.

Tacitus mislabeled Pilate, but, as some scholars note, it was more common at the time of his writing, half a century after Pilate. It was an easy mistake to make. Most modern scholars consider the passage to be authentic and I don't see any reason to doubt it myself, considering all the material that has been covered thus far regarding Essene-type ecclesia throughout the Empire and taking into account the possible historical background to *1 Clement*. I will also add the crucial caveat: *the testimony of Tacitus does not in any way specify the dates that Pilate was in Judea*, only that it was under Tiberius. But this will be discussed in some detail below.

The Epistle of Barnabas

The *Epistle of Barnabas* represents a significant sea change in the universalist/unifying approach. Like *1 Clement*, it is a theological treatise and not properly a letter. It is cited near the end of the second century but was obviously in circulation well before. In 16:3-4, the *Epistle* reads:

> Furthermore he says again, 'Behold, those who tore down this temple will themselves build it.' *It is happening.* For because of their fighting it was torn down *by the enemies.* And now the very servants of the enemies will themselves rebuild it.

This passage indicates that Barnabas was composed after the destruction of the Second Temple in 70 AD. J. C. Treat writes:

> Since Barnabas 16:3 refers to the destruction of the temple, Barnabas must be written after 70 C.E. It must be written before its first undisputable use in Clement of Alexandria, ca. 190. Since 16:4 expects the temple to be rebuilt, it was most likely written before Hadrian built a Roman temple on the site ca. 135. Attempts to use 4:4–5 and 16:1–5 to specify the time of origin more exactly have not won wide agreement. It is important to remember that traditions of varying ages have been incorporated into this work.[272]

Considering the general tone of the text, one wonders about this alleged 'hope' for the rebuilding of the Temple in Jerusalem. It seems more likely to me that the text is laying blame on the rebels for the destruction of the temple and then implying that the Jews themselves, having become slaves/servants of the Romans, would be required to rebuild it, possibly as something else, i.e. Hadrian's Roman temple. Saying that "it is happening now" appears to me to pretty firmly put this text at the time Hadrian was building, i.e. ca. 135 AD. Such an interpretation appears to be quite in line with the polemic of *Barnabas* directed against Judaism in general.

> The writer's name is Barnabas, but scarcely any scholars now ascribe it to the illustrious friend and companion of St. Paul. External and internal evidence here come into direct collision. The ancient writers who refer to this Epistle unanimously attribute it to Barnabas the Levite, of Cyprus, who held such an honourable place in the infant Church. Clement of Alexandria does so again and again (*Strom.*, ii. 6, ii. 7, etc.). Origen describes it as "a Catholic Epistle" (*Cont. Cels.*, i. 63), and seems to rank it among the Sacred Scriptures (*Comm. in Rom.*, i. 24). Other statements have been quoted from *the fathers*, to show that they *held this to be an authentic production of the apostolic Barnabas*; and certainly no other name is ever hinted at in Christian antiquity as that of the writer. But notwithstanding this, *the internal evidence is now generally regarded as conclusive against this opinion.*[273]

---

[272] Jay Curry Treat, 'Barnabas, Epistle of,' *The Anchor Bible Dictionary*, Vol. 1 (Doubleday, 1992), pp. 613–4.

[273] *Ante-Nicene Fathers*, Vol. 1, 'Introductory Note to the Epistle of Barnabas,' available online at https://www.ccel.org/ccel/schaff/anf01.vi.i.html.

Let me just note here that the last sentence of the above statement about the *Epistle of Barnabas* ought to be recalled whenever any weight is given to the claims and attributions of the early church fathers.

Returning to the text itself, the author argues that the Christians are the only true covenant people, and that the Jewish people had never actually been in a covenant with God. His polemics against Judaizing Christians, separating the Gentile Christians from observant Jews, reflect the increase of anti-Jewish sentiment that spread through the Empire following the Jewish War and the concomitant necessity for spiritual messianists to separate themselves from rebel messianists. This is clear from the very first line: "I bid you greeting, sons and daughters, in the name of the Lord that loved us, *in peace,*" followed shortly by: "there are three ordinances of the Lord; the hope of life, which is the beginning and end of our faith; and righteousness, which is the beginning and end of judgment; love shown in gladness and exultation, the testimony of works of righteousness" (1:6). He specifically says 'we are in danger, so let's tighten up our ship' in the following: "Seeing then that the days are evil, and that the Active One himself has the authority, we ought to give heed to ourselves and to seek out the ordinances of the Lord" (2:1), i.e. the ordinances just mentioned.

Barnabas declares that the covenant promises belong only to the Christians (4:6–8). Circumcision and the entire Jewish sacrificial and ceremonial system are due to misunderstanding. Jewish scriptures, rightly understood, contain no such injunctions (chapters 9–10). In places, the author comes across as Paul-on-steroids reinterpreting the Torah:

> ... the prohibition on eating pork is not to be taken literally, but rather forbids the people to live like swine; the prohibition on eating rabbit means that the people are not to behave in a promiscuous manner; the prohibition on eating weasel is actually a prohibition of oral sex, based on the belief that weasels copulate via the mouth.[274]

The bottom line is that the author aims at proving that Jewish understanding of the Torah is completely incorrect and can now be considered superseded, since in the author's view the Jewish scriptures foreshadowed a peaceful Jesus and Christianity when rightly interpreted. In a sense, he is justifying the takeover of the Jewish scriptures by the Christians. The author quotes from the Old Testament and Apocrypha. He also appears to quote from the New Testament Gospels twice. The two passages are as follows:

> 4:14: Moreover understand this also, my brothers. When ye see that after so many signs and wonders wrought in Israel, even then they were abandoned, let us give heed, lest haply we be found, as the scripture saith, *many are called but few are chosen.*

> 5:9: And when He chose His own apostles who were to proclaim His Gospel, who that He might show that *He came not to call the righteous but sinners* were sinners above every sin, then He manifested Himself to be the Son of God.[275]

The saying "Many are called, but few are chosen" is found in Matthew 20:16 and 22:14 but not in any of the other Gospels. The saying that Jesus came to call sinners and not the righteous

---

[274]Wikipedia.org, 'Epistle of Barnabas.'

[275]Translated by J. B. Lightfoot, available online at: http://www.earlychristianwritings.com/text/barnabas-light foot.html.

is found in Mark 2:17 and Matthew 9:13, but not in Luke or John. The general agreement of Barnabas with the salvation history of the Gospels, and the inclusion of the above references, strongly suggest that he knew at least Matthew, if not Mark. Notice that the author also quotes material that is similar to *4 Esdras* (12:1) and *1 Enoch* (4:3; 16:5). The closing Two Ways section (chapters 18–21) is from the *Didache*, which the author presents as "another gnosis and teaching" (18.1).

But notice that there is no mention of Pilate executing Jesus even though it is certain that Mark, Matthew and probably an early form of Luke were written by this time. One has to wonder about this omission considering the next item to cover, Ignatius of Antioch.

Ignatius on the Warpath

Ignatius of Antioch is perhaps the first *Christian* author to mention Pilate outside the Gospels. Ignatius and his letters constitute a whole problem unto themselves. According to Christian legend, he was the third 'bishop' of Antioch, a student of John the apostle, and he penned a series of letters before his martyrdom, which is dated between 108 and 140 AD! Indeed, that is a wide window and immediately raises one's suspicions. The surviving letter collection is framed within Ignatius' final days: they are addressed to various churches around the Empire (in Asia Minor, Italy, Syria) as he *visits other churches on his way to Rome to be executed*!

But modern scholars have brought most of these details into question. While seven letters are judged 'authentic,' the collection grew over the centuries with numerous forged letters and editorial additions. But even the seven letters contain oddities.[276] While they present themselves as individual letters addressed to individual churches, each letter builds on information in the previous one, suggesting they were designed to be read as a single work. They also contain details that wouldn't have been included if they were written for the stated recipients. For example, they specify that the cities addressed are "in Asia," as if the churches there needed to be told that. Such details are clearly for non-Asian readers.

The context also seems fictitious: it's implausible that Ignatius was free to travel the Empire, write letters and visit churches, while being escorted to Rome under guard. It is very similar to Acts' fiction of Paul doing the same thing on his way to Rome after his arrest in Judea. The letters also suggest some knowledge of Valentinian (a Christian gnostic from the same period) and perhaps Marcion.

These data suggest the letters may have been composed later than previously thought (perhaps 130–135 AD or later), which might mean, of course, that they were not written by anyone named Ignatius and were possibly entirely fictitious. Like the Pastoral Epistles (the three letters forged in Paul's name around the same time), Ignatius' letters may have been composed after his death as a way to create retrospective legitimacy for a *later* power struggle against 'heresy.' And that is assuming that Ignatius is not entirely fictional himself.

A possible suspect for the author is the bishop of Smyrna, Polycarp, who we have discussed briefly in a previous section as being the likely collector, editor, and sometime author of parts of the NT around the middle of the second century. So it is curious that we have another legendary

---

[276]Hermann Detering, '1 Clement and the Ignatiana in Dutch Radical Criticism,' available online at: http://web. archive.org/web/20160318050638/http://www.radikalkritik.de/Clem_eng.pdf.

martyr and 'disciple of John,' to whom Ignatius allegedly wrote one of his seven letters. Only one of Polycarp's works survives, a letter to the Philippians. Polycarp had a role in collecting and publishing Ignatius' letters[277] and was anti-Marcionite, anti-Valentinian, and an alleged associate of Ignatius.[278] If Ignatius' letters were forged, Polycarp fits the bill as their author (or at least, their 'creative' redactor).

As noted previously, biblical scholar David Trobisch has argued that Polycarp also collected, edited and published the original edition of the New Testament, more or less in the form in which it survives today, somewhere between 155–168 AD. Other writings composed around the same time were brought together in this 'first edition,' including the Pastorals and Luke-Acts, which are also anti-Marcionite in nature.[279] They also, like Ignatius, write of false teachings in and around Ephesus.[280] *All these texts appear in the same period and have similar agendas*: to retroactively reconcile Paul and Peter, combat various 'heresies,' and bring the fledgling church into harmony and under the power of a central authority, i.e. Polycarp and his designees.[281]

Whatever is finally decided about Ignatius, we still find there an explicit connection between an alleged Jesus and Pontius Pilate, suggesting that he knew at least Mark and Matthew: "You must be completely convinced of the birth, the passion and the resurrection which happened under the governorship of Pontius Pilate."[282]

We also find the first witness to the alleged parents of Jesus – God and Mary – outside of the Gospels, so he certainly knew Matthew:

> ... Jesus Christ, who came from David's seed, who was *truly* born from Mary, who ate and drank, and was *truly* persecuted under Pilate, *truly* crucified, and who died, seen by the inhabitants of the heavens, the earth, and the underworld, who has also been *truly* raised from the dead ... For if he has only seemingly suffered ... why am I in chains ... Is it for nothing that I deliver myself to death? In that case I am lying against God.[283]

> Some people say, "if I do not find it in the ancient records, I do not believe in the gospel." And when I said, "It is written", they said, "That is just the question." For me, *the ancient records are Jesus Christ*, the inviolable ancient records are his cross, his death, and his resurrection and the faith which comes from him ... For the most beloved Prophets have announced him, but the gospel is the completion of immortality.[284]

The "ancient records" mentioned were likely the prophecies of the Old Testament. On the other hand, they may be possibly the same records that we find missing today: historical documentation

---

[277] *Phil.* 13.1; *Mart. Poly.* 10.1.

[278] See David Trobisch, 'Who Published the New Testament?', *Free Inquiry* 28.1 (2007/2008), pp. 30–33, and *The First Edition of the New Testament* (Oxford University Press, 2011).

[279] Judith M. Lieu, *Marcion and the Making of a Heretic: God and Scripture in the Second Century* (Cambridge University Press, 2015), pp. 293–4.

[280] Acts 20; 1 Tim. 1, 4, 6; *Ign. Eph.* 7–9, 16–7.

[281] The issue of heresy is anachronistic at that time, as Pervo and others point out. There was not yet any sort of established orthodoxy against which to claim heretical views; there were only 'factions'. Along these lines, the Westar Institute, including Richard Carrier, argue that the term 'Gnosticism' is out of date and devoid of meaning – there was no identifiable 'Gnostic' group – no 'Orthodoxy' and 'heresy' – only competing factions, all of whom could be called Gnostic in one sense or another.

[282] *Magnesians* 11:1, quoted in Ellegård (1999), p. 207.

[283] *Trallians* 9–10, quoted in Ellegård (1999), pp. 207–8.

[284] *Philadelphians* 8:2—9:2, quoted in Ellegård (1999), p. 208.

proving the existence of Jesus and his execution by Pontius Pilate. But the only records Ignatius can turn to for proof are the "most beloved Prophets" – the Hebrew Scriptures.

Ignatius comes off sounding like a schoolboy whose classmate has told him there is no Santa Claus: "Yes there is! He lives at the North Pole, his wife is Mrs. Claus, and he has eight reindeer and tons of elves helping him!" He writes that *true* Christians are:

> ... fully persuaded ... that he [our Lord] *really was* descended from David 'according to the flesh', and the Son of God according to the will and power of God; that he *really was* born of a virgin, and baptized by John ... nailed up [to the cross] under Pontius Pilate and the Tetrarch Herod on our behalf, in the flesh. ...
>
> For I know that even after his resurrection [Jesus] was in the flesh, and *I believe that he is so now.* When, for instance, he came to those who were with Peter, he said to them, 'Lay hold, handle me, and see that I am no bodiless demon.' And immediately they touched him, and believed, being convinced both by his flesh and by the spirit. And this is why they thought nothing of dying, and were found to be about death. After his resurrection he even ate and drank with them, as one of flesh, although spiritually he was united to the Father.[285]

One curious thing about this passage is Ignatius' insistence on the idea that Jesus was in the flesh even 'now.' This reveals two aspects of his agenda: to defend against 'false' Christians who believed that Jesus was not a flesh-and-blood man, and to provide a rationale for martyrdom. As Richard Carrier writes:

> Ignatius cannot abide the view ... that our bodies of flesh will be discarded and replaced with entirely new bodies of cosmically superior material. Willingness to die, and thus the glory of martyrdom, only makes sense to him if we will live again in the flesh ... Thus Docetism [the belief that Christ wasn't flesh-and-blood], if true, would destroy everything Ignatius *needed* to be true.[286]

Ignatius is the source of the first known mention of Mary, the virgin birth, *and Jesus' baptism by John the Baptist* outside the Gospels. He offers no evidence whatsoever other than 'the Prophets' of the Old Testament, messianic interpretations of which were used as inspiration for writing Mark and Matthew. He clearly knows the stories of Matthew at least, but he does not refer to these texts at all for some reason. Richard Pervo writes:

> The "wolves" (actually feral dogs; [*Ephesians*] 7.1) are out there, but Ignatius says that they have not gained a foothold. In 9.1 he intimates that the representatives of evil teaching are itinerant. ... Nothing specific about the nature and contents of the opposed teaching emerges. Elsewhere the good bishop attacks Judaizers and docetists, probably two different groups. Nowhere does Ignatius address teachings that are particularly characteristic of Marcion. ...
>
> Ignatius, who views himself as did Polycarp and the Pastor as a leader in the mold and tradition of Paul, identifies his readers as, with him, "fellow initiates of Paul"...[287]

Never mind that Ignatius' concept of the resurrection body totally contradicted what Paul had said: that "flesh and blood cannot inherit the Kingdom of God!" Indeed it seems that the war Ignatius was fighting was simply for dominance, control, and to exclude those pesky itinerant

---

[285] *Smyrnaeans* 1, 3, quoted by Carrier (2014), p. 318.

[286] Carrier (2014), p. 319.

[287] Pervo (2015), pp. 146, 147.

prophets traveling about, attracting followers and the resulting benefits. Such 'prophets' could too easily be in touch with a supernatural messiah and had no need of a historical Jesus for their livelihood – exactly as Paul had been. Pervo writes:

> The eventual system of bishop, presbyter, and deacon is strongly recommended by Ignatius. In the churches he addressed, the authority of a single bishop was apparently accepted. The images Ignatius employs to illustrate the roles of each order reveal that presbyters have been imposed upon a deacon-bishop structure. He likens the bishop to God or God's grace (*Magn.* 6.1; 2.1) or commandment (*Trall.* 13.2), to the father (*Magn.* 3.1; *Trall.* 3.1; *Smyrn.* 8.1), to the lord (*Eph.* 6.1), or to Jesus Christ (*Trall.* 2.1). The ... "presbytery council" is compared to the apostles (*Magn.* 6.1; *Trall.* 2.2; 3.1; *Phld.* 5.1; *Smyrn.* 8.1), and the law of Jesus Christ (*Magn.* 6.1; *Trall.* 3.1), and a divine commandment (*Smyrn.* 8.1). Deacons are routinely compared to Christ. The odd group is the presbyters, always characterized as a body, compared to a body, the apostles, and to the function of judgment and rule.
>
> The pattern of bishop/deacon is associated with the *Didache*, which lacks the word presbyter. This may reflect church organization in the region of Antioch before Ignatius. It is also Pauline (Phil 1:1).[288]

Ignatius (or someone writing in his name) appears to have been laying the groundwork for the absolute authority of the disciples of Jesus written about in Mark and Matthew at a time when those texts were not yet taken as authoritative, or at least were not understood literally. He was fighting a battle against an enemy and *he needed to firmly establish his control over his flock via the apostolic succession, which had to come from a physically existent Jesus.* In the end, it might be said that this was the ultimate reason for insisting that the story of Jesus – most likely written as a theological allegory – was factual: to have a physical power structure from which early church leaders could draw their ineluctable authority to slap down rival prophets. Jesus to the apostles to the bishops consecrated by apostles.

Even though he is adamant that Jesus came "in the flesh," Ignatius also includes a surprising detail:

> Now the virginity of Mary was hidden from the Prince of this World, as was also her offspring, and the death of the Lord; *three mysteries of renown, which were wrought in silence by God.* How, then, was he manifested to the world? *A star shone forth in heaven above all the other stars, the light of which was inexpressible, while its novelty struck men with astonishment.* And all the rest of the stars, with the sun and moon, formed a chorus to this star, and its light was exceedingly great above them all. And there was agitation felt as to whence this new spectacle came, so unlike everything else above. Hence every kind of magic was destroyed, and every bond of wickedness disappeared, ignorance was removed, and the old kingdom abolished, when God appeared in human form [or, "in a way perceptible to humans" – the Greek is ambiguous] for the renewal of eternal life.[289]

This is incompatible with the Gospel accounts, where Jesus was known to the world and 'Satan,' as was his death. Ignatius says rather clearly that the birth, life and death of Jesus were "mysteries of renown, which were wrought in silence." He then says that the only evidence given to the world was that "a star shone forth in heaven" which caused "agitation." Bizarrely, in this, Ignatius shows no familiarity with Matthew's or Luke's birth stories for Jesus (Bethlehem, the

---

[288]Pervo (2015), p. 139.
[289]*Ephesians* 19, quoted in Carrier (2014), p. 320.

star in the East, the magi, shepherds, etc.); rather *he associates this remarkable celestial event with the resurrection, after Jesus' death,* when he defeats the forces of darkness. Carrier observes:

> Ignatius appears to be saying this is how Jesus manifested to the world: not as a Galilean preacher but as a bright light in heaven. ... This 'gospel' that Ignatius is describing has the very birth and death of Jesus being hidden from the world and revealed only in the bright light demonstrating his triumph ... and that was the event that granted men eternal life.[290]

This account makes it almost certain that Ignatius was *not* familiar with the Gospels – *as* we know them today. As to when this was happening, Pervo notes:

> Recent scholarship tends to move Ignatius' martyrdom forward from the Trajanic date proposed, without substantive support, by Eusebius (*H.E.* 3.22; 3.34–36) to the second quarter of the century, perhaps 130–135. At the time of his letters, the churches of Asia with which he communicates have accepted, with varying degrees of consensus and enthusiasm, the idea that each will have a single leader, the bishop.[291]

In addition to the fact that what we see here is the first intimation of a *historical* 'Life of Jesus' in the making, outside of the allegories of the Gospels, we also have here the idea that *the earliest testimony to the connection between Pilate and Jesus wasn't very clear as to what, exactly, that connection was.* A big question about the letters of Ignatius should be: how much may be actually authentic and how much has been added? The same problem of interpolations occurs. The passage cited above, about the unknown nature of the life of Jesus, tends to make one think that at least this was written before Matthew created his birth story with the star followed by the Magi. But other passages indicate a later time of composition, for example, the mention of Pilate. Of course, the author could have gotten that from Mark.

Notice very particularly that in the above claims of Ignatius, Pilate is in no way *implicated personally* in the actual events but is simply mentioned as a marker of a period of time, and this marker could easily have been picked up by a reading of Josephus (or Philo or Mark). If Ignatius had known more, or had a text to refer to, it seems almost certain he would have declared its authority. We notice in particular that he was obviously not aware of what Tacitus had said, that "Chrestus ... suffered the extreme penalty *at the hands of* ... Pontius Pilate." The implication is that the details and timeline of the mythical Jesus becoming a historical figure were in the process of being worked out independently of historical facts at the time of Ignatius; they needed a real, flesh-and-blood guy on their team to validate their claimed God-given authority and, for all we know, it was Ignatius (and/or Polycarp) himself who masterminded the process. What is also clear is that the Chrestus who suffered at the hands of Pilate referenced by Tacitus was probably not the same Jesus that Ignatius and Polycarp were in the process of creating (or who was depicted allegorically already in Mark). On this process, Wells writes:

> Sanday has observed that 'we know that types and prophecies were eagerly sought out by the early Christians, and were soon collected into a kind of common stock from which every one drew at his

---

[290]Carrier (2014), p. 321.

[291]Pervo (2015), p. 146. See also Pervo's *Making of Paul: Constructions of the Apostle in Early Christianity* (Fortress Press, 2010), *The Mystery of Acts: Unraveling Its Story* (Polebridge Press, 2008) and *Dating Acts: Between the Evangelists and the Apologists* (Polebridge Press, 2006).

pleasure.'[292] And we have already had evidence that the early Christians possessed manuals of OT quotations, on which they drew for teaching purposes. Collections of Messianic passages from the OT would stimulate believers to invent incidents in the life of Jesus which fulfilled the supposed predictions.

All this evidence does not exclude the possibility that there was a preacher who was tried and executed and that his career formed the basis of the existing narratives. ... Sectarians meeting in the second century for some common purpose, e.g. to advocate purer living, would cast about for traditions on which to base their precepts. They would, perhaps, fasten on one particular man of the past who had led a pure life, and being semi-literate, they would not check details, but father all sorts of deeds on him, perhaps many of them performed by other men with whom they had confused him.[293]

One additional note before we leave Ignatius: he appears to be the first known Christian writer to argue in favor of Christianity's replacement of the Sabbath with the Sunday as 'The Lord's Day':

> Be not seduced by strange doctrines nor by antiquated fables, which are profitless. For if even unto this day we live after the manner of Judaism, we avow that we have not received grace ... If then those who had walked in ancient practices attained unto newness of hope, **no longer observing Sabbaths** but fashioning their lives after the Lord's day, on which our life also arose through Him and through His death which some men deny ... how shall we be able to live apart from Him? ... **It is monstrous to talk of Jesus Christ and to practise Judaism.** For Christianity did not believe in Judaism, but Judaism in Christianity.[294]

By now, we have a general overview of how the early Christian traditions developed. For a century, 'Lord Jesus Christ' was conceived as a supernatural being. Mark wrote a highly allegorical Gospel (which will be discussed in detail further on), which was countered by another likely allegorical gospel, Matthew. Only with Ignatius and Polycarp do we begin to see this figure take on the characteristics of a truly historical (claimed) flesh-and-blood man. But even at this point, the relationship of these references to the Gospels is shaky and even contradictory, likely due to many layers of editing.

The Gospel of Mark, which strongly appears to have been written not long after the destruction of Jerusalem with apologetic/propagandistic purposes in mind, pretty clearly imposes a variation of Paul's Christ Son of God on a Palestinian teacher/wonder-worker who is anti–Jewish Law, pro-Roman, and depicts the disciples as unredeemed dolts. With only a few variations, it is Pauline theology in metaphor, and Pontius Pilate is right there being bullied by the Jews into executing the Messiah. It is clearly the template on which the other Gospels were modeled, using major portions of it in their own construction. So why wasn't it mentioned? If it was written that early – and S. G. F. Brandon's arguments for it are good as will be shown further on – where was it all this time?

The first Christian publications we know of were those of Marcion, which included Paul's ten letters and a short, 'early version' (or prototype) of Luke. And since Luke itself is an edited version of Mark (with some original material added – the so-called 'Q' material), Marcion's Gospel

---

[292]W. Sanday, *The Gospels in the Second Century* (London, 1876), p. 272.
[293]Wells (1971), p. 111.
[294]*Magnesians* 8:1, 9:1-2, 10:3, Lightfoot translation.

would be just as easily or better understood as the first redaction or remix of Mark's original, which was later expanded even further to give us Matthew and Luke. But then, we have to ask where Marcion got his Gospel in the first place? And if Mark was written for various reasons in Rome as early as 73 AD, and the Pauline letters were available there also, what happened to them from that time until Marcion? Why was it that Marcion, from Sinope – so far away from Rome – came along with copies and all of a sudden everyone was a 'Pauline Christian' and 'initiates of Paul'? Why was Ignatius depicted as modeling his behavior on Paul (as depicted in Acts) while proclaiming things that were the exact opposite of what Paul taught?

David Trobisch may be correct in crediting Polycarp with publishing (and perhaps editing and writing portions of) the first edition of the New Testament ca. 155–168 AD, in reaction to Marcion's Gospel. It is possible – even likely – that early versions of the Gospels were used, but the only one for which we have any textual evidence is an early version of Luke (used by Marcion), and perhaps an early, Jewish-Christian version of Matthew, both shorter than the versions included in the NT. Both Luke and Matthew undoubtedly used Mark, so it was the first one composed, probably in Rome according to Nodet and Taylor and others, but we see no sign of it from early days. Why? John shows knowledge of all three synoptics, so it was the last written. Acts was composed by the same person who 'expanded' Marcion's version of 'Luke' (i.e. first redaction of Mark). But even if we accept early versions of Luke and Matthew, there's no solid evidence to suggest either of them were composed prior to the 130s AD, while the internal evidence for the early composition of Mark appears to be good.[295]

In our analysis of these texts, we have also noticed some striking images and themes: a) Revelation's focus on the image of Christ's blood, suggesting a violent, bloody death, b) the image of Ignatius' star as a manifestation of Jesus, c) Paul's image of Christ leading his demonic captives in a triumph, d) the *Ascension of Isaiah*'s odd remark on Jesus' secret name, and e) the thoroughly Hellenistic/Roman image of the dying and rising god.

So, now we must turn to the attempt to trace the origins of the Jerusalem church, Jewish Christianity, and their messiah, the historical 'Jesus' who was executed by Pontius Pilate. There will be several parts to this examination of the evidence, which I will try to present as chronologically as possible, though many of the subjects are topical and must follow a thread through time before backing up and picking up another thread to follow. And, before we get into the actual history, the texts and commentary, I want to introduce our historian.

---

[295]There is early evidence that the copy of Mark's Gospel that first became known and copied was already damaged; witness the opening and ending with several unusual variants: Mark 1:41, angry or compassionate? Both Matthew and Luke only had the damaged/shorter form which was the basis of the possibly oldest Western text tradition (Latin), while *an early Greek copy* survived with little or no damage and became the basis for the majority of readings. If one operates on the assumption that Luke only knew Marcion's Gospel, then many double and triple agreements must be due to later additions in all three, i.e. after Polycarp, at least. The added endings of Mark were apparently created before Matthew/Luke/John/Acts were written, but the abrupt end must have been what was in Marcion's Gospel, redacted from Mark at a still earlier time. Or, a stripped-down version of the longer ending was present in Marcion's Gospel, with minor parallels in both Matthew and Luke. This longer ending in Marcion's Gospel was added to Mark at a later time. Carrier notes the fact that Mark's post-resurrection section being so truncated is highly suggestive of a controversial ending that may have been removed entirely and is now lost to us.

3. Josephus as Historian

Titus Flavius Josephus, circa 37–100 AD, was a Jewish/Roman historian whose most well-known work is *The Wars of the Jews*, published in the late 70s AD, which covered the events in Judea that led to the Jewish war against Rome and the destruction of Jerusalem. The work is essentially a somewhat spin-doctored history of the rebellion and shows his dual loyalties at the time of writing. Josephus glosses over both the atrocities committed by the Romans – thus putting his new Roman masters of the Flavian dynasty in a good light – and the seditious Jewish rebellion, placing the blame for what was a fairly widespread insurrection on a rag-tag bunch of hooligans and exonerating 'mainstream' Jews. But Josephus – a self-described aristocratic priest[296] – himself was a part of the rebellion until his ultimate betrayal of his compatriots and his defection to the Romans. At the same time, he presents the Judean ruling class as honorable, the Jewish fighters as courageous, and the outcome not as a Roman victory, but the work of God (the *Jewish* god).

According to the standard interpretation, the necessity of a propagandistic account of the Jewish War with Rome should be apparent. Roman political philosophy and policy attempted to seek equilibrium and peaceful coexistence as far as possible. The most important thing to the Romans was tax money. Dead people cannot pay taxes. Rebels are even worse, because they are alive and not paying their taxes. Palestine was to Rome a small part of a larger area of the world that was a source of wealth to the elite. A troublesome little province was the last thing they wanted. In the aftermath of the war, what they needed was a convincing narrative to keep the aristocratic Diaspora Jews quiet about Rome practically having to wipe out their people due to a pesky rebellion. This narrative would have to be sufficiently Judaized to be acceptable, and all explanations would need to be couched in language that appealed to the Diaspora.[297] That would include many references to the Law, to God, and blaming everything on innovators and rebels – the 'lone gunmen' of the time.

Whether or not that was Josephus' intention, it would have had the same effect. Josephus consistently presents the rebellion as the work of a bunch of extremists, not as a rebellion by practically the whole 'Jewish nation.' In other words, he essentially wrote the official policy for Jewish leaders at the time: "Rome is a friend and ally. Judaism is the oldest and greatest tradition." Both sides (the Roman and Jewish elites) would benefit. Thus, even if Josephus wasn't writing Roman propaganda for mass distribution in Judea (which seems unlikely and

---

[296]I actually have some doubts about Josephus' claims about himself. One of the clues that caught my eye was his very bad Greek. Aristocrats in Judea generally were quite Hellenized and spoke Greek fluently.

[297]Steve Mason, *Josephus, Judea, and Christian Origins: Methods and Categories* (Hendrickson, 2009), pp. 45–67, argues that Josephus wrote his works for a *Roman* audience that consisted of close friends among the Roman elite. Given that the Jewish King Agrippa II was one of his intended readers, I think it would be more accurate to say that he wrote for his aristocratic friends in general, Roman and Jewish if one takes that perspective. I think that it is far more likely that Josephus was actually seeking to re-create Judaism. He did fervently believe in his god being the creator of the Universe and all mankind and he was probably seeking to unify Jews and Romans, while holding onto an exclusivity for the Jews.

impractical, given the 'publishing industry' at the time), it was essentially safe Jewish propaganda that also benefited the Roman *status quo*. And it conveniently positioned Josephus himself as the representative of the new, reorganized Jewish ruling class. (Josephus was a legend in his own mind.)

The Roman imperial family at the time, the Flavians (Vespasian and his heirs), must have found Josephus useful; he was sufficiently morally flexible to betray his colleagues and even his entire people, he was well-enough educated, and he knew who was who in Palestine. They probably cared little for his self-promoting propaganda, found in copious digressions throughout everything he penned. At best it was in and of itself amusing to the Roman elite, who perhaps saw Josephus as both useful and entertaining, with his thrilling tales of derring-do in the rough and barbaric life of a frontier people like the Jews of Palestine. And Josephus clearly understood that his comfortable life depended on maintaining his story to the bitter end. But it did benefit the Flavians to have their 'war' commemorated – they didn't have much else to boast about.

Despite problems of editorial redaction and transmission of the text, *The Wars of the Jews* is probably more reliable in some ways than his later work, *Antiquities*. Of course, the imperial support this work received strongly suggests that many representations were skewed in favor of the Flavians, Josephus' patrons, inflating what was essentially a minor colonial suppression of a freedom movement into a 'major war.' At the same time, Josephus was hiding or disguising many of his own doings, effectively writing Jewish, Josephan, and imperial apology simultaneously; the end result is a so-called history that must be handled very carefully. The most reliable reports would be those items that were generally known to the Greek-speaking and reading public, but one must keep in mind that even those can be 'spun' (just look at the news today!). And Josephus was definitely spinning and blowing smoke everywhere while still trying to establish himself in the eyes of his readers as a credible historian.

Shaye Cohen summarizes Josephus' essential claims in his first work as follows (many or all of which are probably false):

1. Not all Jews revolted, only small bands of mad fanatics.

2. The revolutionaries have no connection with any of the 'official' representatives of Judaism (the high-priests, Agrippa, and the three philosophies).

3. The revolutionary leaders, especially John of Gischala, were evil tyrants.

4. Josephus in Galilee was an ideal general, ingenious, popular, self-controlled, lucky, and an enemy of John of Gischala.

5. The aristocrats, the masses, and Agrippa strenuously opposed the war.

6. From the defeat of Cestius until the rise of the Zealots the war was directed by aristocrats who were noble figures and had nothing to do with the beginning of the revolt.[298]

---

[298]Shaye J. D. Cohen, *Josephus in Galilee and Rome* (Brill, 2002 [1979]), pp. 240–1. "[Cestius] Gallus was legate of Syria from 63 or 65. He marched into Judea with a force of over 30,000 men in September 66 in an attempt to restore order at the outset of the Great Jewish Revolt. Gallus' army comprised *Legio XII Fulminata*, detachments from the three other legions based in Syria, six cohorts of auxiliary infantry and four alae of cavalry. These regular troops were supported by 14,000 allies provided by Agrippa II and other client rulers. Gallus succeeded in conquering Beit She'arim in the Lower Galilee, and sent detachments to occupy Galilee and the Judean coast. He then turned inland to subdue Jerusalem. After suffering losses amongst his baggage train and rearguard, Gallus reached Mount Scopus and penetrated the outer city, but was apparently unable to

Josephus' second work, *The Antiquities of the Jews*, published in the mid 90s, is even more problematical: personal and Jewish apologetics on steroids. Historian Harold Attridge calls it "propagandistic history," which included a loose paraphrase of the Hebrew Scriptures with the aim of presenting Jewish history as "relevant, comprehensible and attractive in a new environment."[299] Along with his work *Against Apion*, one of Josephus' motives in writing was to defend against the idea that Judaism was a corrupt derivative version of Egyptian religion, thus his focus on the *antiquity* of the Jews.[300]

By the time he wrote *Antiquities*, Josephus' claims in *Wars* had somewhat changed. Again, Shaye Cohen's summary is useful for highlighting what biases to watch out for:

1. The Pharisees always were powerful and influential. Related to this depiction are the following:

   a) The Samaritans are scoundrels who have always caused trouble for the real Jews.

   b) Various figures are condemned as untraditional (Herod, Archelaus, Judas the Galilean, the Tiberians, Tiberius Julius Alexander, Drusilla, Agrippa II), [while] one (Agrippa I) is praised for his religiosity.

   c) High-priests are denounced.

2. The Jews as a whole participated in the revolt but were compelled by necessity; the responsibility lies with the revolutionaries, the procurators, the high-priests, Agrippa II, Nero, Sebastene troops, and [the *Life*] adds, the neighboring pagan cities.

3. Agrippa I was a loyal Jew and a good king but his children, notably Agrippa II and Berenice, violated the traditional laws.[301]

Josephus has toned down his pro-Roman propaganda and replaced it with more of a Judean nationalist flavor. He has also become more favorable to the Pharisees, probably because by that time they were emerging as leaders on the Jewish scene, and Josephus was positioning himself to be in their favor. By contrast, he now goes after the priests, even though he was favorable towards them in *Wars*. He also tones down his admiration for the Essenes, which is curious. So while he is more open about the Jews' role in the rebellion, he is still writing with several agendas.

So what was the real story? In his recent and massive book on the subject, Steve Mason argues that the Jewish War had little to do with "longterm antagonism" with Rome, intolerable conditions, or "innate national-religious conflict," which have been largely unchallenged assumptions among historians.[302] He argues that the War resulted from "the combination of deep regional

---

take The Temple Mount. After a siege of nine days, Gallus decided to fall back to the coast. During Gallus's withdrawal his column was ambushed near Beth Horon, suffering very heavy losses. He succeeded in escaping to Antipatris with the loss of about 6,000 men and a lot of armaments. Judea was now almost entirely lost to Roman control and the exultant rebels were able to engage the entire population in their folly." (Wipedia.org, 'Cestius Gallus.') That is the standard version. However, see Mason (2016) for a detailed analysis and very different view of the actions of Cestius Gallus as written by Josephus. Clearly, Josephus is not telling us the whole story.

[299] Harold W. Attridge, *The Interpretation of Biblical History in the Antiquitates Judicae of Flavius Josephus* (Scholars Press: Missoula, Montana, 1976), p. 181.

[300] Steve Mason, *Josephus and the New Testament* (second edition, Baker Academic, 2003), p. 11. As for the reliability of the work: "Recent studies of his paraphrase of the OT have shown that he carefully worked over the biblical story to serve his larger purposes" (p. 30).

[301] Cohen (2002), p. 237.

[302] Steve Mason, *A History of the Jewish War: A.D. 66–74* (Cambridge University Press, 2016), pp. 200, 201.

resentments, the new failure of Roman officials to protect Judaeans, and the underlying assumption of what we now call 'realist' assumptions about the interactions of nations," and the things
that usually start wars: "injury, threats of more injury, perceived helplessness, the closure of
avenues of redress, and ultimately the concern for survival."[303] Per Mason's reading, the situation
only came to a head after generations of uniquely close relations with Rome, late in Nero's reign.
As evidence, he points to the lack of any obvious or sustained anti-Roman sentiment or activity
related by Josephus, and observes that the initial fighting on the part of the Judeans was against
non-Judeans in neighboring cities and towns, as well as against the auxiliary garrison, composed
mostly of Samarians. Only after a series of escalations did the Roman troops become a target
during the war.

Mason's reading is plausible, and makes good sense of the texts. However, he adds:

> In this reconstruction I am not ignoring occasional literary expressions of anti-Roman sentiment,
> nor ruling out the possibility of long-running social, economic, or religious grievance, which some
> Judaeans (with some Samarians or Gadarans) might have blamed ultimately on Rome. All of that
> seems likely in some measure. ... But evidence of sustained or militant anti-Romanism of a kind
> that could generate the Judaean War is exceedingly hard to find ...[304]

In other words, hardcore nationalism and anti-Roman sentiment in all likelihood did exist (and
Josephus may have had motive to downplay them, too). Mason simply argues they did not cause
the war, and even the conflicts in the preceding decades had more to do with inter-ethnic strife
than resistance to Rome.

I argue that tracking the hints of a Judean sovereignty movement has the advantage of providing
a plausible soil in which the original Judean Christianity can be found, i.e. 'Judea-first' ethnic-
nationalist messianists. Even if they did not directly cause the war, they would have welcomed
it as fitting into God's plan. It is easy to imagine how a breakdown of the existing Roman order
would lead to a rise in anti-Roman sentiment, though in the end only a small group of militants
held out in Jerusalem, the vast majority of other localities choosing not to fight.[305]

As for his autobiography, *The Life of Josephus*, which serves as a self-congratulatory conclusion
to *Antiquities*, it is closer to auto-hagiography, though it may include valuable clues and insights,
and a reasonable sequence of events even if heavily spin-doctored. At the end of *Antiquities*,
where he introduces his *Life*, he has the chutzpah to say he is one of only two or three Jews
to have mastered the "national traditions." As Josephus scholar Steve Mason puts it, the *Life*,
"even on the most charitable reading, smacks of opportunism and routine deception."[306]

One of Josephus' goals in writing was apparently to counter what was being told by his political
rival Justus of Tiberias, of whom we know next to nothing save that *his version of events
places Josephus smack in the middle of all the ills of Galilee*, and at the center of the rebellion.
Considering the questionable nature of almost every piece of biographical data Josephus reveals,
Justus was probably on the right track; Josephus had to defend his image and justify his shameless
behavior in the face of public exposure. On the *Life of Josephus'* influences, Mason writes:
"Josephus offers an autobiography that has many parallels with the social prejudices of Cicero, the

---

[303]Mason (2016), pp. 208, 584.
[304]Mason (2016), pp. 278–79.
[305]Mason (2016), p. 588.
[306]Mason (2003), p. 140.

military exploits and virtues of [Julius] Caesar, and the stratagems of his Roman contemporary Frontinus."[307]

Coming after his thoroughly Roman-inspired treatise on the Jewish constitution, i.e., *Antiquities*, Josephus turns to a discussion of his own character in his *Life*, written on the model of the ideal aristocratic Roman public figure: a patron genuinely concerned for his clients' welfare, constantly hounded by jealous, power-hungry enemies. It says something about the size of his ego that he offers his own life "as the final exhibit in his presentation of the Judean constitution."[308] As Mason puts it:

> Almost every single paragraph in the *Life* ... confirms with no hint of subtlety either his virtues or his opponents' vices. This is clearest in such summary statements as these:
>
> > "I used to take them along in the trial of cases, and I used to render verdicts in accord with their opinion, being determined not to pervert justice through haste, and to remain pure of any material profit in these matters. I was now living my thirtieth year or so. At that age, even if one puts aside illicit yearnings, especially in a position of great authority it is hard to escape the accusations that come from envy. But I preserved every woman unmolested, and disdained all gifts as unnecessary; I did not even accept the tithes, which were due to me as a priest, from those who brought them." (*Life* 79-80)
>
> Since these moral lessons are clear, whereas the history is thoroughly obfuscated, we should conclude that Josephus' intention has little to do with history and everything to do with his character.[309]

He ends his *Life* with these words: "And this is the account of the actions of my *whole* life; and let others judge of my character by them as they please."[310] We have, and it's not very flattering; additionally, for a 'whole life' story, it's odd that it mainly discusses his role in the war with Rome. As for Josephus' reliability as a historian, like many ancient writers, he took liberties:

> ... the *Life* is filled with apparently gratuitous contradictions of the *War*. It seems rather that Josephus expects the same trusting audience that he had for the *Antiquities*, who are prepared to accept what he says without careful investigation.[311]

After opening his *Life* by claiming to have royal and priestly blood, like a good Jewish/Roman aristocrat, he tells his readers they can verify it for themselves in the priestly registers. He neglects to mention that these documents were long-since destroyed when the Temple was burnt to the ground over two decades earlier. Mason comments: "One might easily infer that he does not expect readers with much knowledge of things Judean, who could be critical of his logical leaps."[312]

Not only is he inconsistent and self-contradictory when it comes to details like names, dates, numbers, places, and sequences of events, but he also plays fast and loose with his 'historical characters.' Commenting on the instances where Josephus counters charges from his enemies

---

[307]Steve Mason, *Life of Josephus: Translation and Commentary* (Brill, 2001), pp. xx–xi.

[308]Mason (2001), p. xlviii.

[309]Mason (2001), pp. xlvii–xlviii.

[310]*Life* 76 (430). All references to Josephus' *Life* come from Mason's translation.

[311]Mason (2001), p. xxix.

[312]Mason (2001), p. xx.

that he was a tyrant,[313] Mason argues that 'knowing these to be stock charges against political figures, *he crafts them* for his opponents, just as he creates plausible speeches even for opponents in the *War*, to create a plausible narrative.'[314] Or was he simply protesting too much, as when he insists that he didn't 'betray his country'?[315] Maybe it was both.

Other scholars are more blunt with their criticism. Robert Eisler calls him "the conceited historian," a "vain braggart," a "swindler," a liar, a cheat and a war profiteer;[316] Josephus was "well acquainted with the great art of flattering those who might be useful to him," shameless (he took part in 'questioning' Jewish captives), "most anxious to whitewash himself," "insincere and unreliable," "a client and parasite of the Emperor."[317] Shaye Cohen points out: "Recent writers have generally not appreciated this factor [Josephus' vanity] sufficiently."[318]

The general tone of Josephus' autobiography is that of a man incapable of performing his duties to any consistent degree while demonstrating his total inability to accept responsibility for his failures.[319] He doesn't even come close to comparing with the great men of history he thought he was emulating. Based on his own descriptions, he commanded no loyalty among his men or subjects; they were constantly trying to kill him, to betray him, or to get him removed from office. According to Josephus, all his misfortunes are due to the calumnies and seditions of agitators and innovators who were just too stupid or too evil to see what a fantastically wonderful leader he really was; which is to say he was not, as none among those subjected to him ever seems to have perceived this greatness he constantly attempted to project. The duping delight[320] he exhibits when recounting the clever way he persuaded his companions to kill themselves so that he could escape is utterly repellant. And what is more astonishing is that he apparently has no insight whatsoever into how he would be perceived by readers of this cheap imitation of Roman autobiography. It's one thing if someone else writes praise of an individual, but quite another to write it of oneself; even the ancient Romans knew that. (Well, except for Cicero, but he was another narcissist.)

At the beginning of his *Life*, Josephus presents himself as a precocious child and his three years of study with the Pharisees, Sadducees, and Essenes:

---

[313]*Life* 50 (260), 58 (302).

[314]Mason (2001), p. xxix.

[315]*Life* 26 (129), 27 (132), 28 (140).

[316]Robert Eisler, *The Messiah Jesus and John the Baptist* (Dial Press, 1931), pp. 29, 187, 196, 184, 25.

[317]Eisler (1931), pp. 24, 26, 27, 28, 29.

[318]Cohen (2002), p. 230.

[319]Reading Josephus, I'm continually reminded of the studies of the authoritarian personality by Bob Altemeyer, University of Manitoba, or the more recent ideas of David Dunning and Justin Kruger of Cornell University: "The Dunning-Kruger effect is a cognitive bias wherein relatively unskilled individuals suffer from illusory superiority, mistakenly assessing their ability to be much higher than is accurate. Dunning and Kruger attributed this bias to a metacognitive inability of the unskilled to recognize their own ineptitude and evaluate their own ability accurately. In other words, 'If you're incompetent, you can't know you're incompetent. ... [T]he skills you need to *produce* a right answer are exactly the skills you need to *recognize* what a right answer is.'" (Wikipedia.org, 'Dunning–Kruger Effect.')

[320]'Duping delight' is a neologism coined by Paul Ekman in his book *Telling Lies* (1992) to describe the tendency of some criminal offenders when they manage to get away with a crime or a lie – it gives them pleasure. It is apparently a common feature of the psychopath.

When still a boy, really, about fourteen years old, I used to be praised by everyone because [I was] book-loving: the chief priests and principal men of the city would often meet to understand the legal matters more precisely with my assistance.

When I was about sixteen years old, I chose to gain expertise in the philosophical schools among us. There are three of these: the first, Pharisees; the second, Sadducees; and the third, Essenes, as we have often said. In this way I intended to choose the best [school] – if I might examine them all. So I toughened myself and, after considerable effort, passed through the three of them. Yet I did not regard even the resulting expertise sufficient for me. When I discovered that a certain man by the name of Bannus made his life in the desert, I became his devotee: wearing clothes [made] from trees, scavenging food that grew by itself, and washing frequently for purification – with frigid water, day and night! When I had lived with him three years and so satisfied my longing, I returned to the city [in my nineteenth year].[321]

If we are to trust Josephus' account of his childhood, he was something akin to a religious Doogie Hauser, M.D. While that makes good fare for television, and fiction in general, it flies in the face of human psychology. It wouldn't matter how smart he was; no self-respecting High Priest would kowtow to a 14-year-old kid. Such things are common tropes in fiction, and a bit of embellishment is to be expected, but "the high priests and principal men of the city" visiting a teenager *frequently* in order to "understand legal matters more precisely" is simply intellectually insulting to the reader. And, I believe it was so even for the audience of the time unless, of course, they really weren't expecting truth but merely entertainment. That, too, is a possibility, in which case one might wish to re-evaluate estimates regarding the intended audience and thus, the historical value of the narrative.

To whatever degree he investigated the Pharisees or Sadducees, it can't have been thorough, as he claims to have spent all of his three years with Bannus, whom he doesn't properly place as belonging to any of the three groups. I suppose this would be equivalent to having a job applicant claim to have pursued a certain degree at university and simultaneously admitting he spent the same span of time as a roadie for The Grateful Dead. Even if we admit to a possible translation error – perhaps he didn't spend those 3 years with *him* but with *them* – Josephus keeps it all fairly ambiguous and non-committal, the mark of any good con man then and now.[322]

But one thing I would like to draw your attention to regarding the above text: Josephus says that he studied in the *three* 'Philosophical Schools' of Judaism, but did not find that he had acquired enough 'expertise.' So then he discovered 'Bannus,' a clear John-the-Baptist type character, and what he says amounts to him admitting that he studied a 'Fourth Philosophy.' The meaning of this will soon become apparent.

Josephus of course is making use of common social and heroic tropes, in line with Roman expectations of a highbrow aristocrat writing an exciting text. That would be fine, if it was fiction and understood that way – as it possibly was at the time. We don't mind if the *Odyssey* presents tropes – that's to be expected. But when a historian fills his autobiography with them, we have to wonder where the truth lies. And the biggest problem is that modern Bible scholars often take Josephus at his word, while the people of his own time possibly did not.

---

[321] *Life* 2 (9–12).

[322] Of course I realize that I am evaluating Josephus – a man who lived 2000 years ago – by modern standards, but please notice that our modern ideas, often derided by such as Derrida, are *sometimes* applicable. Customs and ideas may change with time, but human nature hasn't. And I've read plenty of ancient literature to know that Josephus' work does stand out as very different.

At 26 years of age (63 AD), Josephus allegedly traveled to Rome on a diplomatic mission, to secure the release of some priests imprisoned by the procurator of Judea, Felix:[323]

> I reached Rome after having faced many dangers at sea. For when our ship was flooded in the middle of the Adriatic, we – being about 600 in number – had to swim through the entire night. And when by the provision of God a Cyrenian ship appeared before us around daybreak, I and some others – about eighty altogether – overtook the rest and were taken on board. After we had come safely to Dicaearcheia, which the Italians call Puteoli, through a friendship I met Aliturus: this man was a mime-actor, especially dear to Nero's thoughts and a Judean by ancestry. Through him I became known to Poppaea, the wife of Caesar [Nero], and then very quickly arranged things, appealing to her to free the priests. Having succeeded, with enormous gifts from Poppaea in addition to this benefit, I returned home.[324]

Quelle surprise – a shipwreck! And then a close encounter with the beautiful Poppaea, empress of Rome![325] Josephus doesn't disappoint.[326] The only heroic trope he doesn't seem to make use of is the 'abduction by pirates,' but perhaps that one had gone out of style by his day. One thing that does strike me as curious is that there was some reason for Nero to imprison a group of Jewish priests in 63, and then, after they were released, in the following year, the great fire of Rome occurred which was subsequently blamed on Christians, according to Tacitus. Also interesting is that Tacitus tells us about the year 63 AD in Rome: Poppaea gave birth to a child while residing in Antium, and four months later, the child died.[327] Make of that what you will.

Later in his *Life*, Josephus fights a battle against the royal troops of King Agrippa II about which he writes:

> After I made a sudden sharp turn with my force, I went to face the royal troops and put them to flight. And the action that day would have worked just right for me had not some spirit gotten in the way. For the horse on which I had done the fighting fell in muddy terrain and deposited me with it on the ground. I suffered a fracture of the bones in the flat part of my hand and was brought into a village called Cepharnocus. When those who heard these things also became anxious, in case I had suffered something more serious, they abandoned further pursuit [of the enemy] and turned back in great concern about me. So after sending for physicians and receiving care, and staying behind that day because I had caught a fever, on the physicians' advice I was conducted to Tarichea during the night.[328]

What bravery! He even makes a point of saying that the physician directed him to a town 10 kilometers from the battle. Oh, he had a doctor's note, did he? The story reads more

---

[323]"Felix was the younger brother of the Greek freedman Marcus Antonius Pallas. Pallas served as a secretary of the treasury during the reign of the Emperor Claudius. Felix was a Greek freedman either of Claudius, according to which theory Josephus (*Ant.* 20.7) calls him Claudius Felix, or for Claudius's mother Antonia Minor, a daughter of Triumvir Mark Antony and Octavia Minor and niece of Emperor Augustus. According to Tacitus, Pallas and Felix descended from the Greek Kings of Arcadia. Felix became the procurator by the petition of his brother. [Tacitus, *Annals*, 12. 54, *Histories* 5. 9; Suetonius, *Claudius*, 28.]" (Wikipedia.org, 'Antonius Felix.')

[324]*Life* 3 (14–6).

[325]Tacitus and Suetonius portray Poppaea as an ambitious and ruthless schemer. Josephus paints a different picture. He calls Poppaea a worshiper of the Jewish God who urged Nero to show compassion to the Jewish people.

[326]Neither does Paul: "Three times I was beaten with rods, once I was pelted with stones, three times I was shipwrecked, I spent a night and a day in the open sea" (2 Cor. 11:25).

[327]*Ann.* 15.23.

[328]*Life* 72 (402–4).

like an excuse for deserting the battlefield, which might have been one of the claims made by Justus of Tiberias to which Josephus was responding with this explanation. The fact that his troops "abandoned further pursuit" doesn't really suggest concern for Josephus, but rather a disinclination to be doing what he ordered them to do. Nevertheless, right here we see that Josephus was definitely a rebel leader, one of those brigands, innovators, tyrants that he so detests when talking about the revolt against Rome.

He was also a traitor to his nation. Once captured, Josephus proclaimed general Vespasian to be the Messiah based on the star prophecy in Numbers 24:17: "A star shall come out of Jacob; a scepter will rise out of Israel. He will crush the foreheads of Moab, the skulls of all the people of Sheth." He then went around to the various rebel fortresses and Jerusalem itself trying to persuade the Jewish rebels to surrender. Josephus wrote about this as follows:

> ... what did most elevate them [the Jews] in undertaking this war [against the Romans], was an ambiguous oracle that was also found in their sacred writings, how, "about that time, one from their country should become governor of the habitable earth." The Jews took this prediction to belong to themselves in particular and many of the wise men were thereby deceived in their [interpretation]. Now this oracle certainly denoted the government of Vespasian, who was appointed emperor [while] in Judea.[329]

Mason sums Josephus up:

> When ... Josephus portrays himself as a precocious intellect and youthful devotee of philosophy, a priest serving in the temple, a wise statesman and governor, a judge, a champion swimmer and wrestler, an expert builder, a brave and resourceful general, and finally an industrious writer of history and autobiography, he is only embodying the aristocrat's role in the world.[330]

Mason is right: Josephus was writing in a way that was more or less normal at the time. But he fails at every turn *even by ancient standards*. In trying to present himself as part of the aristocratic crowd, he uses the only plausible events from his life that he can, but it falls flat. His claimed ancestry is dubious at best. And his military career as a rebel 'general'? Eisler sums that up nicely:

> ... he himself ... did not have the faintest notion of the elements of strategy, in spite of his assertions to the contrary. He even has to admit that he did not manage to arm his troops adequately and that he did not have the time to drill his men, important facts which explain the easy victory of the Roman troops, inferior in numbers though they were to the army of patriots. The final paragraph [of *Wars* 2.20.8 (584)] is clearly intended to parry the accusation that he merely plundered the country with this armed rabble.[331]

Josephus is a consummate liar and a con man. He is a shameless self-promoter, but is so deluded and lacking in insight that he routinely indicts himself for sadism, cowardice, and incompetence. He is quite possibly the most unsuccessful administrator to have ever held political office. He is an indiscreet braggart, and ultimately he is a traitor to his people and their government. Not

---

[329] *Wars* 6.5.4 (312–13).
[330] Mason (2001), p. xxv.
[331] Eisler (1931), pp. 186–7.

only is he a traitor, he manages to brag about the favors and wealth given to him by the Roman Emperors as a reward for going 'Benedict Arnold' and defecting to the enemy.

Can we trust a man who plays so fast and loose with his own involvement with the history of the time? Shall we hang any critical point of history on someone who tells such puerile and pointless lies?

Only very, very carefully.

Every claim he makes should be checked, when possible, with the accounts of other, more reliable historians, and with the archaeological record. As Shaye Cohen, points out, when Josephus is using another text as a source,

> Details are added, omitted, or changed, not always with reason. Although his fondness for the dramatic, pathetic, erotic, and the exaggerated, is evident throughout, as a rule Josephus remains fairly close to his original. Even when he modifies the source to suit a certain aim he still reproduces the essence of the story. Most important, he does not engage in the free invention of episodes. Of course his imagination is at work to enliven the narrative but, unlike other authors, he has not invented sagas for Biblical heroes. We may assume that he has not invented sagas for Alexander Jannaeus, Herod, or – himself.[332]

No, he hasn't invented, but he sure spins and blows a lot of smoke over things. So when those other sources aren't available for cross-checking, we should be skeptical to the maximum extent allowed by historical methodology. We have to filter out his ego, whatever is self-serving, his apologetics, try to find what he is unlikely to have falsified because it would have been too easily detected, and even then use reason to determine if he is likely to have added a lot of distorting spin.

Now, to be fair, Steve Mason is pretty much the current living expert on Josephus, and as both a critic and defender, you could say his view is more nuanced. I most often agree with him, but I still find Josephus to be a repellent character. Mason, however, presents him as taking up a dual task in his historical writing: "to remove the ground from Roman bragging and anti-Judean slander while living in postwar Rome was a literary challenge if ever there was one." And while Mason often gives Josephus the benefit of the doubt, and sometimes takes events and descriptions as factual which I think are fictional, he is still aware that Josephus wrote for a reason. He had an agenda, which can be difficult to disentangle from his narratives.

> Whereas the conventional view envisions the *Jewish War* as Roman propaganda and *Antiquities* as Jewish apologetic, we should instead conclude that the *Jewish War* is already a bold effort to defend the Jews. *Antiquities* and *Contra Apion* more forthrightly advocates Judaism for interested gentiles. Thus we no longer need to drive a sharp wedge between Josephus's two major works. There is no reason to believe that his motives and perspective changed between the *Jewish War* and *Antiquities*.
> ...
> When Josephus walked the streets of Rome in the summer of 75 C.E., newly at work on his *Jewish War* and living in the very seat of anti-Judean resentment, his mind must have turned to the malicious accounts that connected the bloody revolt with the Judean character. He wrote to absolve surviving Judeans from war guilt by blaming the revolt on a very few reckless and un-Jewish rebel leaders who had been duly punished. He wanted to show that the Judeans had in fact been longtime allies of the Romans and exemplary world citizens. These Judeans recognized that the

---

[332]Cohen (2002), p. 233.

kingdoms of the world rose and fell under the control of their God, and so the current fortune of the Romans should not be resisted. He accordingly rejected the notion that the Roman gods had won a victory, for in his view it was the all-seeing Judean God who used Rome for his purposes. Even the Roman Titus acknowledged God's aid. Josephus could not have known that this bold literary effort would appear to later generations as a work of betrayal.[333]

I've read plenty of ancient texts of the type and yes, Josephus is generally following the usual Greco-Roman model; but I still think that the people of his time would have seen through him and found him to be as short in virtue as I do. Much of what Josephus writes in his published history reminds me of the *secret* things Cicero wrote in his letters that were never meant to be made public and which, once they were published, savaged his reputation.[334]

Moving on, let me say that I am amazed that I have yet to encounter a serious discussion of the obvious parallels between a number of Gospel pericopes and incidents in the *Life* of Josephus. The most striking is his claim to have been so precocious as to discourse with doctors of the law at the age of fourteen. Naturally, when Jesus did it, he was even younger: twelve. Like the Gospels of Luke and Matthew, Josephus' *Life* begins with his illustrious ancestry – a standard feature of ancient biography. His career focuses on Galilee, moving to Jerusalem, with a stop in Capernaum, just like Jesus in the Gospels. He recounts a shipwreck similar to that described in Acts,[335] and a scene where he addresses a crowd that is startling in its similarity when compared to the 'Sermon on the Mount/Plain.' Overall, and in general, bits of the *Life of Flavius Josephus* can be found in the mythical life of Jesus of Nazareth at several points in Matthew and Luke.

Additionally, we also see that Josephus had experiences that echo in the life of Paul as depicted in Acts (which cannot be considered history). For example, Josephus had his own 'Damascus conversion' of sorts, as mentioned above. He went from rebel rouser to Roman collaborator, shifting his allegiances to those he was warring against faster than you can bat an eye. So many tangled threads and so little possibility of making any sense of it all. Yet, we continue.

A rational scientific historical approach would recognize influence flowing from Josephus and Paul *toward* the later Gospels and Acts, but that isn't what happens in theologically driven biblical studies. Biblical scholars who are also 'believers' tend to give the stories told in the Gospels and Acts a privileged position, the assumption being that they are histories and not myths, fables or historical fiction. And the authors were Christians, doncha know? And would not ever, ever tell a fib or fabricate a history! However, if the Gospel writers and the author of Acts obviously utilized Josephus and Paul to compose their alleged histories – along with other

---

[333]Steve Mason, 'Will the Real Josephus Please Stand Up?' *Biblical Archaeology Review* 23:5 (1997). See also Mason (2016).

[334]Jérôme Carcopino, *Cicero: The Secrets of His Correspondence,* two volumes, translated by E. O. Lorimer (Yale University Press, 1951).

[335]Mason (2003), p. 292, see also pp. 251ff., argues from several lines of evidence that Luke used Josephus, including a litany of significant characters and events present in both works: "Agrippa's death after his robes shone; the extramarital affairs of both Felix and Agrippa II; the harshness of the Sadducees toward Christianity; the census under Quirinius as a watershed event in Palestine; Judas the Galilean as an arch rebel at the time of the census; Judas, Theudas, and the unnamed 'Egyptian' as three rebels in the Jerusalem area worthy of special mention among a host of others; Theudas and Judas in the same piece of narrative; the Egyptian, the desert, and the *sicarii* in close proximity; Judaism as a philosophical system; the Pharisees and Sadducees as philosophical schools; and the Pharisees as the most precise of the schools. We know of no other work that even remotely approximated Josephus's presentation on such a wide range of issues."

texts and techniques[336] – we find ourselves already on a double layer of shifting sand. We must take great care to *try* to crosscheck anything we accept as factual when we use Josephus as our historical source, realizing that many editorial efforts would have been made to bring the texts into some sort of harmony, and that the later church had such hegemony, it was easy for them to create a fake history for themselves. We must consider interpolation and editing an *a priori* assumption, and we must interrogate texts as hostile witnesses.

This realization leads us to reject *any* use of Acts or the Gospels as historical checks. Pervo makes this evident in his analysis of the speech put into the mouth of the Jewish Pharisee Gamaliel in Acts. Gamaliel mentions Judas and Theudas, two Jewish rebels discussed by Josephus in *Antiquities*. The author of *Acts* was rather careless in his use of Josephus, who mentions Theudas first, and Judas second. While the author of Acts *also* mentions them in this order, he does so in such a way as to imply that they acted in that *chronological* order, but it is clear in Josephus that Judas came first historically and was brought up as a digression after the mention of Theudas. This reversed order was carried over into Acts and reveals the novelizing tendencies – and one of the sources – of its author. Further studies by Michael D. Goulder, Thomas L. Brodie and D. R. MacDonald reveal other sources used in the composition of the Gospels and Acts.[337] It seems that creating a religious 'history' was quite an industry in the second century and the writers were using anything and everything at hand to do it. All of this makes a good, critical examination of the Pauline texts even more crucial for the understanding of the origins of Christianity as we know it; they remain the most authentic historical documents about early Christianity that we possess.

And so, having said all of that, let's turn to Josephus and see what we can find.

History by Josephus

In the Gospel of Matthew, Jesus was born a few years before Herod the Great died in 4 BC. In Luke, Jesus' birth coincided with the census of 6 AD. Instead of trying to reconcile the irreconcilable, perhaps a better question would be: is there any particular reason those dates were chosen? Is there something about either of these dates that is significant to the life of any historical person of Judea? And if so, what are the implications?

We have to go a bit further back in time to attempt to discover the threads that run and interweave together down to the time of the destruction of Jerusalem, and we find them as a side issue mentioned by Josephus in his discussion of the feud between the sons of Alexander Jannaeus: Hyrcanus II and Aristobulus.[338]

---

[336]See Tolbert (1989) for a discussion of the well-known and effectively utilized techniques of rhetoric found in the Gospel of Mark.

[337]Goulder (1995); Brodie (2006); and MacDonald's 2-volume *New Testament and Greek Literature* (2014).

[338]Jannaeus, the second Hasmonean king, ruled from 103 to 76 BC. "A son of John Hyrcanus, he inherited the throne from his brother Aristobulus I, and married his brother's widow, Queen Salome Alexandra. From his conquests to expand the kingdom to a bloody civil war, Alexander's reign has been generalised as cruel and oppressive with never-ending conflict. ... The kingdom of Alexander Jannaeus was the largest and strongest known Jewish State outside of biblical sources, having conquered most of Palestine's Mediterranean coastline and regions surrounding the Jordan River." (Wikipedia.org, 'Alexander Jannaeus.') Hyrcanus II was the eldest son of Jannaeus and Alexandra Salome. "After the death of Alexander in 76 BCE, his widow succeeded to the rule of Judea and installed her elder son Hyrcanus as High Priest. Alexander had numerous conflicts with the

All of the details are not relevant but one: this is where we first meet Antipater, the father of Herod the Great.

Antipater is described by Josephus as a rich Idumean[339] who was a friend of Hyrcanus. Josephus tells us that Nicolaus of Damascus, the friend and historian of Herod, claimed that Antipater was "of the stock of the principal Jews who came out of Babylon into Judea." But then Josephus says that this claim was just to gratify Herod and was not true. Whether we should believe Nicholas or Josephus is hard to determine. In any event, King Alexander had made Antipater a general of Idumea and he was later the ally of Hyrcanus, not Aristobulus II.

Upon the death of their mother, Queen Alexandra, despite the fact that she had named Hyrcanus as her successor, Aristobulus II took over the kingdom by force and things were back and forth between the brothers until Pompey arrived in 63 BC to settle things. Judea was made a province of Rome and the ever-rebellious Aristobulus[340] was imprisoned in Rome.

Back in Palestine, Antipater married an Idumean heiress named Cypros and had four sons and one daughter: Phasael, Herod, Joseph, Pheroras and Salome. In 49 BC, when Julius Caesar took Rome in the Civil War, he released Aristobulus II, gave him two legions, and intended to send him to pacify Syria. Pompey's followers, however, poisoned Aristobulus to prevent an ally of Caesar from taking control of the region. It is not entirely clear from Josephus' account exactly what Antipater was doing for all these years, but he managed to stay wealthy and influential and always on the right side, whichever way the winds of change would blow. Josephus tells us that after Pompey was dead, "Antipater, *who managed the Jewish affairs*, became very useful to Caesar," and "when Caesar, after some time, had finished that war and was sailed away for Syria, he honored Antipater greatly, and confirmed Hyrcanus in the high priesthood; and bestowed on Antipater the privilege of a Citizen of Rome." Then: "Now when Caesar had settled the affairs of Syria, he sailed away; and as soon as Antipater had conducted Caesar out of Syria, he returned to Judea. He then immediately raised up the wall which had been thrown down by Pompey."[341] Antipater made his eldest son, Phasaelus, governor of Jerusalem and gave Galilee to his second son, Herod.

Now, according to Josephus, there was a band of brigands, or robbers, whose leader was one Hezekiah.[342] Herod went after them and killed Hezekiah and many of his followers. According

---

Pharisees. However Hyrcanus was supported by the Pharisees, especially later in his tenure. When Salome died in 67 BCE, she named Hyrcanus as her successor and as ruler of Judea as well, but soon he and his younger brother, Aristobulus II, dissented over the right to the throne." (Wikipedia.org, 'Hyrcanus II.')

[339] The region south of Judea. "Judas Maccabeus conquered their territory for a time around 163 BC. They were again subdued by John Hyrcanus (c. 125 BC), who forcibly converted them, among others, to Judaism, and incorporated them into the Jewish nation. Josephus, when referring to Upper Idumaea, speaks of towns and villages immediately to the south and south-west of Jerusalem ..." (Wikipedia.org, 'Edom.')

[340] "Aristobulus shared his late father's views on religion and politics. He courted the nobles and military party by constituting himself the patron of the Sadducees and bringing their cause before the queen. The many fortresses which the queen placed at the disposal of the Sadducees, ostensibly for their defense against the Pharisees, constituted in reality one of the preparatory moves of Aristobulus for the usurpation of the government. ... Taken prisoner, Aristobulus was released by Julius Caesar in 49 BC in order to turn Judea against Pompey. He was on his way to Judaea with his son Alexander, when 'he was taken off by poison given him by those of Pompey's party'. His son Alexander was beheaded by the Roman commander Scipio at Antioch. His son Antigonus led a rebellion against Rome, with help from the Parthians, and became king and high priest in 40 BCE, but was defeated and killed by the Romans in 37 BCE." (Wikipedia.org, 'Aristobulus II.')

[341] *Ant.* 14.9.1.

[342] *Ant.* 14.9.2.

to the tale, the robbers had been preying on Syria, which was governed by Sextus Caesar, cousin of Julius Caesar, and thanks to Herod's action freeing him from a troublesome bandit, Sextus and Herod became friends.

The story about the killing of a common bandit, as Josephus would have it, led to unusual consequences. We are told that some of the Jewish elite complained to Hyrcanus about Herod killing Hezekiah without trial and demanded that Herod be tried for murder. Supposedly, Herod was warned to flee by Hyrcanus. He fled to Sextus Caesar and was there put in command of a troop of soldiers. After this, Josephus narrates the account of the murder of Sextus Caesar by his troops and then leaps ahead to the assassination of Julius Caesar. It was all drama, drama, drama; but what attracts our attention is the fact that such a fuss was made about the chasing down of a band of robbers, the very term that Josephus used repeatedly for rebels against Rome.

We now jump to chapter 17 of *Antiquities*, at which time things were so complicated and confused I don't think I can make this super-short, so bear with me here.

The Death of Herod and the Golden Eagle on the Temple

In his *Antiquities*, Josephus tells the story of the 'Golden Eagle Temple Cleansing' by two characters named Judas and Matthias – an act undertaken allegedly just prior to the death of Herod the Great. It has many echoes of another Temple story: that of Pilate's 'shields' which we will come to further on, so keep it in mind.[343] Here is Josephus' account of how it came about, quoted *in extenso* for the delight and edification (and convenience) of the reader:

> But Herod now fell into a distemper, and made his will, and bequeathed his kingdom to [Antipas], his youngest son; and this out of that hatred to Archelaus and Philip, which the calumnies of Antipater [their brother] had raised against them. He also bequeathed a thousand talents to Caesar [Augustus], and five hundred to Julia, [Augustus]'s wife, to [Augustus]'s children, and friends and freed-men. He also distributed among his sons and their sons his money, his revenues, and his lands. He also made Salome his sister very rich, because she had continued faithful to him in all his circumstances, and was never so rash as to do him any harm; and as he despaired of recovering, for he was about the seventieth year of his age, he grew fierce, and indulged the bitterest anger upon all occasions; the cause whereof was this, that he thought himself despised, and that the nation was pleased with his misfortunes; besides which, he resented a sedition which some of the lower sort of men excited against him, the occasion of which was as follows.
>
> There was one Judas, the son of Saripheus, and Matthias, the son of Margalothus, two of the most eloquent men among the Jews, and the most celebrated interpreters of the Jewish laws, and men well beloved by the people, because of their education of their youth; for all those that were studious of virtue frequented their lectures every day. These men, when they found that the king's distemper was incurable, excited the young men that they would pull down all those works which the king had erected contrary to the law of their fathers, and thereby obtain the rewards which the law will confer on them for such actions of piety; for that it was truly on account of Herod's rashness in making such things as the law had forbidden, that his other misfortunes, and this distemper also, which was so unusual among mankind, and with which he was now afflicted, came upon him; for Herod had caused such things to be made which were contrary to the law, of which he was accused by Judas and Matthias; for the king had erected over the great gate of the temple

---

[343]Not to forget an even later parallel: Jesus cleansing the Temple in the Gospel story. One strongly suspects that it has been displaced back in time by either Josephus or an editor because of its similarity to the Pilate event.

a large golden eagle, of great value, and had dedicated it to the temple. Now the law forbids those that propose to live according to it, to erect images or representations of any living creature. So these wise men persuaded [their scholars] to pull down the golden eagle; alleging, that although they should incur any danger, which might bring them to their deaths, the virtue of the action now proposed to them would appear much more advantageous to them than the pleasures of life; since they would die for the preservation and observation of the law of their fathers; since they would also acquire an everlasting fame and commendation; since they would be both commended by the present generation, and leave an example of life that would never be forgotten to posterity; since that common calamity of dying cannot be avoided by our living so as to escape any such dangers; that therefore it is a right thing for those who are in love with a virtuous conduct, to wait for that fatal hour by such behavior as may carry them out of the world with praise and honor; and that this will alleviate death to a great degree, thus to come at it by the performance of brave actions, which bring us into danger of it; and at the same time to leave that reputation behind them to their children, and to all their relations, whether they be men or women, which will be of great advantage to them afterward.

And with such discourses as this did these men excite the young men to this action; and a report being come to them that the king was dead, this was an addition to the wise men's persuasions; so, in the very middle of the day, they got upon the place, they pulled down the eagle, and cut it into pieces with axes, while a great number of the people were in the temple. And now the king's captain, upon hearing what the undertaking was, and supposing it was a thing of a higher nature than it proved to be, came up thither, having a great band of soldiers with him, such as was sufficient to put a stop to the multitude of those who pulled down what was dedicated to God; so he fell upon them unexpectedly, and as they were upon this bold attempt, in a foolish presumption rather than a cautious circumspection, as is usual with the multitude, and while they were in disorder, and incautious of what was for their advantage; so **he caught no fewer than forty of the young men, who had the courage to stay behind when the rest ran away, together with the authors of this bold attempt, Judas and Matthias**, who thought it an ignominious thing to retire upon his approach, and led them to the king. And when they were come to the king, and he asked them if they had been so bold as to pull down what he had dedicated to God, "Yes, [said they,] what was contrived we contrived, and what hath been performed we performed it, and that with such a virtuous courage as becomes men; for we have given our assistance to those things which were dedicated to the majesty of God, and we have provided for what we have learned by hearing the law; and it ought not to be wondered at, if we esteem those laws which Moses had suggested to him, and were taught him by God, and which he wrote and left behind him, more worthy of observation than thy commands. Accordingly we will undergo death, and all sorts of punishments which thou canst inflict upon us, with pleasure, since we are conscious to ourselves that we shall die, not for any unrighteous actions, but for our love to religion." And thus they all said, and their courage was still equal to their profession, and equal to that with which they readily set about this undertaking. And when the king had ordered them to be bound, he sent them to Jericho ...

But the people, on account of Herod's barbarous temper, and for fear he should be so cruel and to inflict punishment on them, said what was done was done without their approbation, and that it seemed to them that the actors might well be punished for what they had done. But as for Herod, he dealt more mildly with others [of the assembly] but he deprived Matthias of the high priesthood, as in part an occasion of this action, and made Joazar, who was Matthias's wife's brother, high priest in his stead. Now it happened, that during the time of the high priesthood of this Matthias, there was another person made high priest for a single day, that very day which the Jews observed as a fast. The occasion was this: This Matthias the high priest, on the night before that day when the fast was to be celebrated, seemed, in a dream, to have conversation with his wife; and because he could not officiate himself on that account, Joseph, the son of Ellemus, his kinsman, assisted him in that sacred office.[344] **But Herod deprived this Matthias of the high priesthood, and burnt the other Matthias, who had raised the sedition, with his companions, alive. And that very night there was an eclipse of the moon.**[345]

Notice the odd digression about Matthias the rebel and Matthias the high priest being two different individuals, one of whom was brother of a Joazar. Keep that name in mind as it will appear again under unusual circumstances.

Also, take note of the eclipse: theologians have placed the alleged birth of Jesus before the spring of 4 BC because of this reference to an eclipse, shortly following which, Herod the Great died before Passover. Jesus has to be born before Herod died or there's no 'Wise Men from the East' and 'Slaughter of the Innocents.' However, by selecting the eclipse of 13 March 4 BC as the chronological hook, they force a whole lot of events into a period of *just 29 days*. It is well nigh impossible for all the events mentioned by Josephus (not to mention the claims of the Gospels and theologians) to have transpired in that short window.

There are two other possible candidates for the right eclipse that would have been visible in Palestine: 15 September 5 BC (10:30 pm), which could then preserve the 4 BC death of Herod, or 10 January 1 BC. The first provides seven months in which all the things Josephus describes could have happened, with Herod dying on time. The second gives a little over three months of time before Herod dies in April. Either would work. However, if the latter is correct, then Herod the Great's death has to be moved forward to 1 BC. I personally favor the 5 BC event because there was a lot that was supposed to happen in the timeframe.

Following the executions of Matthias and his followers, the following things are recorded by Josephus as happening in the life of Herod:

1) On that night, an eclipse.

2) Josephus informs us that Herod's condition worsened the morning after the eclipse. He had already been ill for several months and the people attributed this accelerated decline to the execution of the righteous teachers.

3) Herod then tried "one remedy after another" and after these efforts, each of which must have taken some days or weeks, was advised by his physicians to go take mineral baths. He traveled 25 miles to the resort, tried the baths for a time before deciding that they were doing no good, and then went back to Jericho.

4) Back at home, Herod, knowing his death was getting closer, plotted his revenge on the Jews, who he felt did not love or appreciate him after all he had done for them:

> He commanded that all the principal men of the entire Jewish nation, wheresoever they lived, should be called to him. Accordingly, they were a great number that came, because the whole nation was called, and all men heard of this call, and death was the penalty of such as should despise the epistles that were sent to call them. And now the king was in a wild rage against them all, the innocent as well as those that had afforded ground for accusations; and when they were come, he ordered them to be all shut up in the hippodrome, and sent for his sister Salome, and her husband Alexas, and spake thus to them: "I shall die in a little time, so great are my pains; which death ought to be cheerfully borne, and to be welcomed by all men; but what principally troubles me is

---

[344]Luke, in his faked genealogy of Jesus, tells us that Jesus' father was 'Joseph, son of Heli.'

[345]*Ant.* 17.6.1–4 (146–67). Note that by the end of this account, Josephus only mentions Matthias as having been executed along with his followers.

this, that I shall die without being lamented, and without such mourning as men usually expect at a king's death."

For that he was not unacquainted with the temper of the Jews, that his death would be a thing very desirable, and exceedingly acceptable to them, because during his lifetime they were ready to revolt from him, and to abuse the donations he had dedicated to God that it therefore was their business to resolve to afford him some alleviation of his great sorrows on this occasion; for that if they do not refuse him their consent in what he desires, he shall have a great mourning at his funeral, and such as never had any king before him; for then the whole nation would mourn from their very soul, which otherwise would be done in sport and mockery only.

He desired therefore, that as soon as they see he hath given up the ghost, they shall place soldiers round the hippodrome, while they do not know that he is dead; and that they shall not declare his death to the multitude till this is done, but that they shall give orders to have those that are in custody shot with their darts; and that this slaughter of them all will cause that he shall not miss to rejoice on a double account; that as he is dying, they will make him secure that his will shall be executed in what he charges them to do; and that he shall have the honor of a memorable mourning at his funeral. So he deplored his condition, with tears in his eyes, and begged them by the kindness due from them, as of his kindred, and by the faith they owed to God, and begged of them that they would not hinder him of this honorable mourning at his funeral. So they promised him not to transgress his commands.

Now anyone may easily discover the temper of this man's mind, which not only took pleasure in doing what he had done formerly against his relations, out of the love of life, but by those commands of his which savored of no humanity; since he took care, when he was departing out of this life, that the whole nation should be put into mourning, and indeed made desolate of their dearest kindred, when *he gave order that one out of every family should be slain*, although they had done nothing that was unjust, or that was against him, nor were they accused of any other crimes ...[346]

Recall the story of the Massacre of the Innocents in the New Testament in which Herod orders the execution of all male children two years old and under in the vicinity of Bethlehem. This story is found only in Matthew 2:16-18, and Josephus does not mention any such event in either *Wars* or *Antiquities* despite writing about Herod in many unflattering ways. The majority of Herod biographers, and probably a majority of biblical scholars, consider the event to be mythical. The story in Matthew is clearly modeled on Exodus 1:22, Pharaoh's attempt to kill Israelite males, an effort that Moses survived by being hauled out of the river by an Egyptian princess who adopted him. However, in the above tale, we certainly find elements of the Massacre of the Innocents. Herod clearly planned to raise a hue and cry of mourning as soon as he was dead by a massacre of innocent citizens. Additionally, notice also the execution of 40 or so students of Matthias and Judas, a true massacre of innocents, assuming it even happened.

By any measure of time, considering travel times in those days and Herod's condition, we are well past the allotted 29 days between the March eclipse and the Passover. But there is more.

5) While this was happening, Herod's ambassadors to Augustus returned with letters from the emperor, giving Herod permission to kill or banish his son Antipater. This news 'elevated' his spirits:

... but as his pains were become very great, he was now ready to faint for want of somewhat to eat; so he called for an apple and a knife; for it was his custom formerly to pare the apple himself, and soon afterwards to cut it, and eat it. When he had got the knife, he looked about, and had a mind

---

[346] *Ant.* 17.6.5–6 (174–81).

to stab himself with it; and he [would have] done it, had not his first cousin, Achiabus, prevented him, and held his hand, and cried out loudly. Whereupon a woeful lamentation echoed through the palace, and a great tumult was made, as if the king were dead.

Upon which Antipater, who verily believed his father was deceased, grew bold in his discourse, as hoping to be immediately and entirely released from his bonds, and to take the kingdom into his hands without any more ado; so he discoursed with the jailer about letting him go, and in that case promised him great things, both now and hereafter, as if that were the only thing now in question. But the jailer did not only refuse to do what Antipater would have him, but informed the king of his intentions, and how many solicitations he had had from him [of that nature]. Hereupon Herod, who had formerly no affection nor good-will towards his son to restrain him, when he heard what the jailer said, he cried out, and beat his head, although he was at death's door, and raised himself upon his elbow, and sent for some of his guards, and commanded them to kill Antipater without any further delay, and to do it presently, and to bury him in an ignoble manner at Hyrcania.[347]

It seems reasonable that the above activities would have required a few days' time. But we have just a little way to go before Herod is dead.

6) Herod changed his will. This apparently took a few days to get written up and signed:

> And now Herod altered his testament upon the alteration of his mind; for he appointed Antipas, to whom he had before left the kingdom, to be tetrarch of Galilee and Perea, and granted the kingdom to Archelaus. He also gave Gaulonitis, and Trachonitis, and Paneas to Philip, who was his son, … by the name of a tetrarchy; and bequeathed Jamnia, and Ashdod, and Phasaelis to Salome his sister, with five hundred thousand [drachmae] of silver that was coined. He also made provision for all the rest of his kindred, by giving them sums of money and annual revenues, and so left them all in a wealthy condition. He bequeathed also to Caesar [Augustus] ten millions [of drachmae] of coined money, besides both vessels of gold and silver, and garments exceeding costly, to Julia, [Augustus]'s wife; and to certain others, five millions. **When he had done these things, he died, the fifth day after he had caused Antipater to be slain; having reigned, since he had procured Antigonus to be slain, thirty-four years; but since he had been declared king by the Romans, thirty-seven.**[348]

7) After Herod's death, a grand funeral was planned and carried out. It probably took some time to organize this. Josephus tells us that the whole army was represented in the funeral, and it would have taken a number of days to summon and assemble them. Then followed a slow procession of the funeral cortege, probably traveling about a mile a day, 25 miles in total, to reach the destination where Herod was to be buried. The public mourning period was 30 days, so Herod would just have been tucked in for eternity by the time this period was over.

8) After Herod's death, Archelaus gave an audience to the people, made changes in the army, gave out promotions, liberated prisoners (Herod's sister and her husband had not followed through on his order to execute the dignitaries – they had been set free upon his death), and sat in judgment on lawsuits. He did all these things "and many other things" *before the beginning of Passover.*

Thus, I think it is safe to conclude that the partial eclipse of 13 March 4 BC was *not* the eclipse mentioned in Josephus. There is absolutely no way possible that all of these events could have occurred between that March eclipse and the beginning of Passover 29 days later. If there is any

---

[347] *Ant.* 17.7.1 (182–7).
[348] *Ant.* 17.8.1 (188–91).

value to the mention of the eclipse, it must have been the one of 5 BC, which doesn't alter the timeline all that much, though it could have been the eclipse of 1 AD, which would give three months for all of the above to take place. I think three months is a bit short, but it is possible.

In any event, Herod has just been buried after a long funeral procession and a squabble over his will begins.

The fact that Herod had previously said he would leave the *kingdom* of Judea to Antipas, but then changed his mind and gave it to Archelaus, while tossing Antipas only Galilee and Perea, would have set up a serious conflict between the two brothers. Not only was it necessary for Augustus to confirm the terms of the will of Herod the Great; there was also going to be a legal contest about who got the kingdom. Josephus says nothing in particular about Antipas and Philip needing to have their inheritance confirmed, just Archelaus, because if confirmed, he would be a king. According to Josephus, before Archelaus could depart for his 'confirmation,' things took an ugly turn thanks to the deaths of the two revered teachers, Judas and Matthias, whom he had just previously described as *"two of the most eloquent men among the Jews, and the most celebrated interpreters of the Jewish laws, and men well beloved by the people, because of their education of their youth."* Now that the two are dead, their followers start to cause problems for Archelaus:

> At this time also it was that some of the Jews got together out of a desire of innovation [i.e. rebellion]. **They lamented Matthias**,[349] and those that were slain with him by Herod, who had not any respect paid them by a funeral mourning, out of the fear men were in of that man; they were **those who had been condemned for pulling down the golden eagle**. The people made a great clamor and lamentation hereupon, and cast out some reproaches against the king also, as if that tended to alleviate the miseries of the deceased. The people assembled together, and desired of Archelaus, that, in way of revenge on their account, he would inflict punishment on those who had been honored by Herod; and that, in the first and principal place, he would deprive that high priest whom Herod had made, and would choose one more agreeable to the law, and of greater purity, to officiate as high priest. This was granted by Archelaus, although he was mightily offended at their importunity, because he proposed to himself to go to Rome immediately to look after [Augustus]'s determination about him. However, **he sent the general of his forces to use persuasions, and to tell them that the death which was inflicted on their friends was according to the law ...**
>
> So when the king had suggested these things, and instructed his general in what he was to say, he sent him away to the people; but they made a clamor, and would not give him leave to speak, and put him in danger of his life ... they had more concern to have all their own wills performed than to yield obedience to their governors; thinking it to be a thing insufferable, that, while Herod was alive, **they should lose those that were most dear to them**, and that when he was dead, they **could not get the actors to be punished. So they went on with their designs after a violent manner ...**
>
> Now, upon the approach of that feast of unleavened bread, which the law of their fathers had appointed for the Jews at this time, which feast is called the Passover and is a memorial of their deliverance out of Egypt, when they offer sacrifices with great alacrity; and when they are required to slay more sacrifices in number than at any other festival; and when an innumerable multitude came thither out of the country, nay, from beyond its limits also, in order to worship God, **the seditious lamented Judas and Matthias**,[350] those teachers of the laws, and

---

[349]Odd that he mentions Matthias only and not Judas.

[350]Here, Judas is included, so one wonders why he forgets to include him from time to time.

kept together in the temple ... And as Archelaus was afraid ... he sent a regiment of armed men, and with them a captain of a thousand, **to suppress the violent efforts of the seditious** before the whole multitude should be infected with the like madness ... But those that were **seditious on account of those teachers of the law**, irritated the people by the noise and clamors they used to encourage the people in their designs; so they made an assault upon the soldiers, and came up to them, and stoned the greatest part of them, although some of them ran away wounded, and their captain among them; and when they had thus done, they returned to the sacrifices which were already in their hands.

Now Archelaus thought there was no way to preserve the entire government but by cutting off those who made this attempt upon it; so **he sent out the whole army upon them,** and sent the horsemen to prevent those that had their tents without the temple from assisting those that were within the temple, and to kill such as ran away from the footmen when they thought themselves out of danger; which horsemen **slew three thousand men**, while the rest went to the neighboring mountains.[351]

Obviously, Archelaus was not off to a good start. But, supposedly, immediately following this massacre, he headed out for Rome. *However*, before he could even get on a ship Josephus reports the following:

... Sabinus, [Augustus]'s steward for Syrian affairs, as he was making haste into Judea to preserve Herod's effects, met with Archelaus at Caesarea; but Varus [president of Syria] came at that time, and restrained him from meddling with them, for he was there as sent for by Archelaus, by the means of Ptolemy. And Sabinus, out of regard to Varus, did neither seize upon any of the castles that were among the Jews, nor did he seal up the treasures in them, but permitted Archelaus to have them, until [Augustus] should declare his resolution about them; so that, upon this his promise, he tarried still at Caesarea. But after Archelaus was sailed for Rome, and Varus was removed to Antioch, **Sabinus went to Jerusalem, and seized on the king's palace.** He also sent for the keepers of the garrisons, and for all those that had the charge of Herod's effects, and declared publicly that he should require them to give an account of what they had; and he disposed of the castles in the manner he pleased ...[352]

The Varus in the story is Publius Quinctilius Varus. Varus was a member of a patrician family that had fallen on hard times. Things began to look up for them when Varus became consul in 13 BC. He was governor of the province of Africa from 8 to 7 BC and he hit the jackpot when he was appointed governor of Syria. Velleius Paterculus said that Varus entered the rich province as a poor man, and left a poor province as a rich man.[353] *He was known for his harshness and high taxation.* Josephus, who is blowing smoke over the rapaciousness of the Roman rulers, tries to present Varus as lenient. However, according to a film documentary presentation of that period, the authors of which I haven't been able to track down, at the time of Varus, Roman pottery disappears almost entirely from the archaeological record.[354] Coins have been found which suggest that Varus was governor of Syria in the 25th, 26th, and 27th years after the Battle of Actium (2 September 31 BC), i.e. **7/6 to 4 BC,**[355] which would confirm Herod's death at

---

[351] *Ant.* 17.9.1–3 (206–18).

[352] *Ant.* 17.9.3 (221–3).

[353] *Vell.* 2.117.2.

[354] *66 A.D. – The Last Revolt*, History Channel.

[355] Martin (1996) presents some evidence that he was reassigned to the province in 2 BC following a two-year governorship of Sentius Saturninus. Gerard Gertoux, 'Dating the two Censuses of P. Sulpicius Quirinius,'

the earlier date rather than the later one. (Later, Varus became infamous for losing three entire legions in the Battle of the Teutoburg Forest, where he committed suicide, but that's another story.)

Meanwhile, as already mentioned, Archelaus, Antipas, and the whole Herodian circus have gone to Rome and Josephus takes some time lovingly describing the alleged debate before Augustus as to who was going to get what, borrowing (supposedly) heavily from the work of Nicolaus of Damascus, Herod the Great's friend and chronicler. Obviously, since Nicolaus' work was available at the time Josephus was writing, he didn't have a lot of wiggle room, but we will soon see how creative he could be with the materials he had to work with.

As Josephus would have it, Archelaus' alleged massacre of 3,000 rebels apparently didn't dampen the ardor of the innovators, as he called them, because he relates two additional revolts: one put down by Varus after Archelaus left for Rome, and another provoked by Sabinus after Varus left for Antioch.

Since Nicolaus of Damascus had also sailed with the Herodian party, Josephus is free to invent things in his absence. The opening line of the following refers to the debate over the inheritance going on in Rome:

> But before these things could be brought to a settlement, Malthace, Archelaus's mother, fell into a distemper, and died of it; and **letters came from Varus, the president of Syria, which informed [Augustus] of the revolt of the Jews; for after Archelaus was sailed, the whole nation was in a tumult.** So Varus, since he was there himself, brought the authors of the disturbance to punishment; and when he had restrained them for the most part from **this sedition, which was a great one**, he took his journey to Antioch, leaving one legion of his army at Jerusalem to keep the Jews quiet, who were now very fond of innovation. Yet did not this at all avail to put an end to their sedition; for after Varus was gone away, Sabinus, [Augustus]'s procurator, staid behind, and greatly distressed the Jews, relying on the forces that were left there that they would by their multitude protect him; for he made use of them, and armed them as his guards, thereby so oppressing the Jews, and giving them so great disturbance, that at length they rebelled; for he used force in seizing the citadels, and zealously pressed on the search after the king's money, in order to seize upon it by force, on account of his love of gain and his extraordinary covetousness.[356]

Reading the two passages cited above, Josephus appears to have given two versions of the same story with slight adjustments as to who was where and doing what. It sounds to me as if Josephus is trying to 'spread the blame' to obscure what was really going on.[357] Notice that *Sabinus* is the bad guy. Notice also that it seems that the revolt occurred *after* Archelaus left. It could take weeks for letters to be sent to Rome and it had certainly taken some time for the Archelaus party to get there, so time is passing here. Josephus continues:

> But on the approach of Pentecost [i.e. 50 days after Passover], which is a festival of ours, so called from the days of our forefathers, a great many ten thousands of men got together; nor did they come only to celebrate the festival, but out of their indignation at the madness of Sabinus, and at the

---

argues that Quirinius was governor during this time, and that he was reassigned later, during the census of 6 AD.

[356] *Ant.* 17.10.1 (250–3).

[357] This is part of his overall pattern in *Antiquities*, which, as Cohen (2002) observes, "redistributes the guilt [for the rebellion and war in the 60s] equitably between Jews and Romans, and more broadly within each group," p. 237.

injuries he offered them. **A great number there was of Galileans, and Idumeans**, and many men from Jericho, and others who had passed over the river Jordan, and inhabited those parts. This whole multitude joined themselves to all the rest, and were more zealous than the others in making an assault on Sabinus, in order to be avenged on him; so they parted themselves into three bands, and encamped themselves in the places following: – some of them seized on the hippodrome and of the other two bands, one pitched themselves from the northern part of the temple to the southern, on the east quarter; but the third band held the western part of the city, where the king's palace was. Their work tended entirely **to besiege the Romans**, and to enclose them on all sides.

Now Sabinus was afraid of these men's number, and of their resolution, who had little regard to their lives, but were very desirous not to be overcome, while they thought it a point of puissance to overcome their enemies; so he sent immediately a letter to Varus, and, as he used to do, was very pressing with him, and entreated him to come quickly to his assistance, because the forces he had left were in imminent danger, and would probably, in no long time, be seized upon, and cut to pieces; while he did himself get up to the highest tower of the fortress …

So Sabinus gave thence a signal to the Romans to fall upon the Jews, although he did not himself venture so much as to come down … a terrible battle ensued; wherein, though it is true the Romans beat their adversaries, yet were not the Jews daunted in their resolutions, even when they had the sight of that terrible slaughter that was made of them; but they went round about, and got upon those cloisters which encompassed the outer court of the temple, where a great fight was still continued, and they cast stones at the Romans, partly with their hands, and partly with slings, as being much used to those exercises.[358]

Now, it is not unusual that the Jews were slinging stones at the Romans, but remember this from the rebellion against Archelaus that allegedly happened at the time of Passover, 50 days earlier: "so they made an assault upon [Archelaus'] soldiers, and came up to them, and stoned the greatest part of them, although some of them ran away wounded, and their captain among them; and when they had thus done, they returned to the sacrifices which were already in their hands." Notice also that in the case of Archelaus, the Jews were agitating about their dear departed teachers of the law, Judas and Matthias, and the setting was Passover. Here, they are agitating about the 'madness of Sabinus' and the festival is Pentecost. Just what is really going on here with these two stories of mini-rebellions that read like doublets? According to Josephus, things got so bad that the temple was at least partly destroyed!

And this sort of fight lasted a great while, till at last the Romans, who were greatly distressed by what was done, **set fire to the cloisters** so privately that those that were gotten upon them did not perceive it. This fire being fed by a great deal of combustible matter, caught hold immediately on the roof of the cloisters; so the wood, which was full of pitch and wax, and whose gold was laid on it with wax, yielded to the flame presently, and those vast works, which were of the highest value and esteem, were destroyed utterly, while those that were on the roof unexpectedly perished at the same time; for as the roof tumbled down, some of these men tumbled down with it, and others of them were killed by their enemies who encompassed them.

There was a great number more, who, out of despair of saving their lives, and out of astonishment at the misery that surrounded them, did either cast themselves into the fire, or threw themselves upon their swords, and so got out of their misery. But as to those that retired behind the same way by which they ascended, and thereby escaped, they were all killed by the Romans, as being unarmed men, and their courage failing them; their wild fury being now not able to help them, because they were destitute of armor, insomuch that of those that went up to the top of the roof,

---

[358] *Ant.* 17.10.1–2 (250–9).

not one escaped. **The Romans also rushed through the fire, where it gave them room so to do, and seized on that treasure where the sacred money was reposited**; a great part of which was stolen by the soldiers, and Sabinus got openly four hundred talents.[359]

So, according to Josephus, Sabinus found himself under siege and the Jewish army of Archelaus (formerly Herod's army), which was supposed to be supporting the Romans, apparently defected to the rebels. However, 3,000 troops under "Rufus and Gratus" sided with the Romans. It is at this point that Josephus reports:

> Now at this time **there were ten thousand other disorders in Judea**, which were like tumults, because a great number put themselves into a **warlike posture**, either out of hopes of gain to themselves, or out of enmity to the Jews.[360]

He lists and describes a whole crew of messianic contenders and their activities, which we will set aside for the moment and later come back to. The main point is that Varus received the message from Sabinus and headed out for the war zone. Here we encounter Aretas, keeping in mind that this is the same Aretas who later on is named by Paul in his Basket Adventure in Damascus:

> As soon as Varus was once informed of the state of Judea by Sabinus's writing to him, he was afraid for the legion he had left there; so he took the two other legions, [for there were three legions in all belonging to Syria,] and four troops of horsemen, with the several auxiliary forces which either the kings or certain of the tetrarchs afforded him, and made what haste he could to assist those that were then besieged in Judea. He also gave order that all that were sent out for this expedition, should make haste to Ptolemais. The citizens of Berytus also gave him fifteen hundred auxiliaries as he passed through their city. **Aretas also, the king of Arabia Petrea, out of his hatred to Herod, and in order to purchase the favor of the Romans, sent him no small assistance**, besides their footmen and horsemen; and when he had now collected all his forces together, he committed part of them to his son, and to a friend of his, and **sent them upon an expedition into Galilee, which lies in the neighborhood of Ptolemais; who made an attack upon the enemy, and put them to flight, and took Sepphoris, and made its inhabitants slaves, and burnt the city.**[361]
>
> But Varus himself pursued his **march for Samaria with his whole army**; yet did not he meddle with the city of that name [i.e. Sebaste], because it had not at all joined with the seditious; but pitched his camp at a certain village that belonged to Ptolemy, whose name was Arus, which *the Arabians burnt, out of their hatred to Herod*, and out of the enmity they bore to his friends; whence they marched to another village, whose name was Sampho, which the Arabians plundered and burnt, although it was a fortified and a strong place; and all along this march nothing escaped them, but all places were full of fire and of slaughter.[362]

One wonders whether this early 'invasion' by Aretas, at the invitation of the Romans, might have provided the inspiration for Josephus' version of the later border skirmish involving Antipas,

---

[359] *Ant.* 17.10.2 (260–4).

[360] *Ant.* 17.10.4 (269).

[361] Archaeology has failed to verify traces of this alleged conflagration: Eric M. Meyers, 'Sepphoris on the Eve of the Great Revolt (67-68 C.E.): Archaeology and Josephus,' in *Galilee Through the Centuries: Confluence of Cultures* (Eisenbrauns, 1999), pp. 109ff.

[362] Ant. 17.10.9 (286–90).

Aretas, and Vitellius that supposedly followed on immediately after the death of John the Baptist, as will be recounted further on? In any event, keep it in mind. Continuing to read about the events of this war, we realize that it was quite a rebellion, though Josephus has put the responsibility for starting it first on Archelaus and then on Sabinus:

> Emmaus was also burnt by Varus's order, after its inhabitants had deserted it, that he might avenge those that had there been destroyed. From thence **he now marched to Jerusalem**; whereupon those Jews whose camp lay there, and who had besieged the Roman legion, not bearing the coming of this army, left the siege imperfect: but as to the Jerusalem Jews, when Varus reproached them bitterly for what had been done, they cleared themselves of the accusation, and alleged that the conflux of the people was occasioned by the feast; that the war was not made with their approbation, but by the rashness of the strangers, while they were on the side of the Romans, and besieged together with them, rather than having any inclination to besiege them. **There also came beforehand to meet Varus**, Joseph, the cousin-german of king Herod, as also **Gratus and Rufus**, who brought their soldiers along with them, together with those Romans who had been besieged; but **Sabinus did not come into Varus's presence, but stole out of the city privately, and went to the seaside.**[363]

Remember Gratus and Rufus. And, what a handy way to get rid of Sabinus and send him off into obscurity with the loot!

> Upon this, Varus sent a part of his army into the country, to seek out those that had been **the authors of the revolt**; and when they were discovered, he punished some of them that were most guilty, and some he dismissed: now **the number of those that were crucified on this account were two thousand.** After which he disbanded his army, which he found no way useful to him in the affairs he came about; for they behaved themselves very disorderly, and disobeyed his orders, and what Varus desired them to do, and this out of regard to that gain which they made by the mischief they did.
>
> As for himself, when he was informed that ten thousand Jews had gotten together, he made haste to catch them; but they did not proceed so far as to fight him, but, by the advice of Achiabus,[364] they came together, and delivered themselves up to him: hereupon **Varus forgave the crime of revolting to the multitude, but sent their several commanders to Caesar [Augustus]**, many of whom [Augustus] dismissed; but for **the several relations of Herod who had been among these men in this war, they were the only persons whom he punished**, who, without the least regard to justice, fought against their own kindred.[365]

So, we now hear that several of Herod's relatives were involved in the rebellion; no names given, but highly suggestive. And then, we notice something rather puzzling, or so it seems to me. In *Wars*, Josephus says:

> With Archelaus back in Rome, another legal case was being put together against **Judeans who had gone out as emissaries before the rebellion, with Varus' indulgence,** with a view to the self-government [under Roman governorship] of their nation. There were fifty of them present, but over 8,000 of the Judeans in Rome were standing by in support.[366]

[363]*Ant.* 17.10.9 (291–4).
[364]First cousin of Herod, the one who had prevented him from killing himself during his final illness.
[365]*Ant.* 17.10.10 (295–8).
[366]*Wars* 2.6.1 (80), Mason translation.

Apparently, there were many Judeans who didn't want the sons of Herod put in charge.

According to Josephus, Nicolaus of Damascus defended Archelaus, following which a Jewish embassy arrived pleading for a Roman governor, at which point Nicolaus pleads on behalf of the Herodian kingship. These speeches are interesting but will not detain us now. What is relevant here is that following the speeches of Antipater and Nicolaus (on behalf of Archelaus),

> ... letters came from Varus, the president of Syria, which informed [Augustus] of the revolt of the Jews; for after Archelaus was sailed, the whole nation was in a tumult. So Varus, since he was there himself, brought the authors of the disturbance to punishment ...

As already described above, allegedly there was *already* a revolt in progress just before Archelaus left, which Josephus put down to "seditious persons" lamenting Judas and Matthias, and another immediately after, this one due to the nastiness of the Roman procurator Sabinus. A possible window for the ambassadors' initial departure is the time when Josephus says Varus was with Archelaus in Caesarea in order to prevent Sabinus' meddling – between the two revolts – after which Archelaus sailed for Rome and Varus headed for Antioch. But given the *present* revolt, apparently in response to the Romans, why would the Jews still want a Roman governor? Josephus doesn't give any clarity on the matter. In any event, this was the alleged result:

> So then, after hearing each of them Caesar [Augustus] dissolved the council and, after a few days, gave half of the kingdom to Archelaus: he titled him ethnarch but also promised that he would make him king if he should show himself worthy. The remaining half he divided into two tetrarchies[367] and gave to the other two sons of Herod, the one to Philip and the other to Antipas (the other contending against Archelaus for the kingship). Under the latter were both Perea and Galilee, with revenue of two hundred talents, while Batanea, Trachonitis, Auranitis, and certain parts of the estate of Zenon around Panias, having revenue of a hundred talents, had been assigned under Philip. Archelaus' ethnarchy included Idumea, all Judea, and Samaria, which was relieved of a quarter of its taxes out of respect for not having revolted with the others. As subject cities he received Strato's Tower, Sebaste, Ioppa, and [Jerusalem]. The Greek cities Gaza, Gadara, and Hippos [Augustus] cut off from the kingdom and attached to Syria. Revenue from the region given to Archelaus was 400 talents.[368]
>
> And Salome, in addition to what the king bequeathed in his will, was declared mistress of both Jamnia and Azotus [Ahsdod] as well as Phasaelis, and [Augustus] granted her also the royal [holdings] in Ascalon.[369] Now, sixty talents in revenue were being collected from all these, and he set her estate under the toparchy of Archelaus. Each of Herod's other offspring acquired what had been bequeathed in the wills ...[370]

Obviously some of the mud slung at Archelaus stuck and Augustus didn't feel inclined to confirm his father's will or Archelaus' claims. In any event, all of the above is a whole lot of goings-on in Judea while Archelaus and the gang were dancing attendance on Augustus. Notice, particularly, Archelaus was *not* really put in charge of things as one might be given to believe, but that in fact, the kingdom *was* put under the ultimate oversight of the Syrian provincial governor, whoever that might be (Varus at that moment).

---

[367]This is odd since a tetrarchy, by definition, is "any form of government where power is divided among four individuals." Why does Josephus say "two"?

[368]Curious that just above we read that Sabinus openly got 400 talents before he slunk off to the seashore.

[369]Perhaps this is the explanation for the term 'tetrarchy' – Salome was the fourth party.

[370]*Wars* 2.6.3 (93–9), Mason translation.

The Ethnarchy of Archelaus

Now, let's look at Josephus' two versions of the ethnarchy of Archelaus. Keep in mind that the version in *Wars* is the one most likely to stick *closest* to the facts, though certainly Josephus felt free to innovate:

Wars 2.7.3–4 (111–6)	*Antiquities* 17.13.1–4 (339–52)
And now Archelaus took possession of his ethnarchy, and used not the Jews only, but the Samaritans also, barbarously; and this out of his resentment of their old quarrels with him. Whereupon they both of them sent ambassadors against him to [Augustus]; and in the ninth year of his government he was banished to Vienna, a city of Gaul, and his effects were put into [Augustus]'s treasury.	When Archelaus was entered on his ethnarchy, and was come into Judea, he accused Joazar, the son of Boethus, of assisting the seditious, and took away the high priesthood from him, and put Eleazar his brother in his place. He also magnificently rebuilt the royal palace that had been at Jericho, and he diverted half the water with which the village of Neara used to be watered, and drew off that water into the plain, to water those palm trees which he had there planted: he also built a village, and put his own name upon it, and called it Archelaus. Moreover, he transgressed the law of our fathers and married Glaphyra, the daughter of Archelaus, who had been the wife of his brother Alexander, which Alexander had three children by her, while it was a thing detestable among the Jews to marry the brother's wife. Nor did this Eleazar abide long in the high priesthood, Jesus, the son of Sie, being put in his room while he was still living.
	But in the tenth year of Archelaus's government, both his brethren, and the principal men of Judea and Samaria, not being able to bear his barbarous and tyrannical usage of them, accused him before [Augustus], and that especially because they knew he had broken the commands of [Augustus], which obliged him to behave himself with moderation among them. Whereupon [Augustus], when he heard it, was very angry, and called for Archelaus's steward, who took care of his affairs at Rome, and whose name was Archelaus also; and thinking it beneath him to write to Archelaus, he bid him sail away as soon as possible, and bring him to us: so the man made haste in his voyage, and when he came into Judea, he found Archelaus feasting with his friends; so he told him what [Augustus] had sent him about, and hastened him away. And when he was come [to Rome], [Augustus], upon hearing what certain accusers of his had to say, and what reply he could make, both banished him, and appointed Vienna, a city of Gaul, to be the place of his habitation, and took his money away from him.

But the report goes, that before he was sent for by [Augustus], he seemed to see nine ears of corn, full and large, but devoured by oxen. When, therefore, he had sent for the diviners, and some of the Chaldeans, and inquired of them what they thought it portended; and when one of them had one interpretation, and another had another, Simon, one of the sect of Essenes, said that he thought the ears of corn denoted years, and the oxen denoted a mutation of things, because by their ploughing they made an alteration of the country. That therefore he should reign as many years as there were ears of corn; and after he had passed through various alterations of fortune, should die. Now five days after Archelaus had heard this interpretation he was called to his trial.

I cannot also but think it worthy to be recorded what dream Glaphyra, the daughter of Archelaus, king of Cappadocia, had, who had at first been wife to Alexander, who was the brother of Archelaus, concerning whom we have been discoursing. This Alexander was the son of Herod the king, by whom he was put to death, as we have already related. This Glaphyra was married, after his death, to Juba, king of Libya; and, after his death, was returned home, and lived a widow with her father. Then it was that Archelaus, the ethnarch, saw her, and fell so deeply in love with her, that he divorced Mariamne, who was then his wife, and married her. When, therefore, she was come into Judea, and had been there for a little while, she thought she saw Alexander stand by her, and that he said to her; "Thy marriage with the king of Libya might have been sufficient for thee; but thou wast not contented with him, but art returned again to my family, to a third husband; and him, thou impudent woman, hast thou chosen for thine husband, who is my brother."

Now, before Archelaus was gone up to Rome upon this message, he related this dream to his friends: That he saw ears of corn, in number ten, full of wheat, perfectly ripe, which ears, as it seemed to him, were devoured by oxen. And when he was awake and gotten up, because the vision appeared to be of great importance to him, he sent for the diviners, whose study was employed about dreams. And while some were of one opinion, and some of another, [for all their interpretations did not agree,] Simon, a man of the sect of the Essenes, desired leave to speak his mind freely, and said that the vision denoted a change in the affairs of Archelaus, and that not for the better; that oxen, because that animal takes uneasy pains in his labors, denoted afflictions, and indeed denoted, further, a change of affairs, because that land which is ploughed by oxen cannot remain in its former state; and that the ears of corn being ten, determined the like number of years, because an ear of corn grows in one year; and that the time of Archelaus's government was over. And thus did this man expound the dream. Now on the fifth day after this dream came first to Archelaus, the other Archelaus, that was sent to Judea by [Augustus] to call him away, came hither also.

The like accident befell Glaphyra his wife, who was the daughter of king Archelaus, who, as I said before, was married, while she was a virgin, to Alexander, the son of Herod, and brother of Archelaus; but since it fell out so that Alexander was slain by his father, she was married to Juba, the king of Libya; and when he was dead, and she lived in widowhood in Cappadocia with her father, Archelaus divorced his former wife Mariamne, and married her, so great was his affection for this Glaphyra; who, during her marriage to him, saw the following dream: She thought she saw Alexander standing by her, at which she rejoiced, and embraced him with great affection; but that he complained to her, and said, O Glaphyra! thou provest that saying to be true, which assures us that women are not to be trusted. Didst not thou pledge thy faith to me? and wast not thou married to me when thou wast a virgin? and had we not children between us? Yet hast thou forgotten the affection I bare to thee, out of a desire of a second husband.

| "However, I shall not overlook the injury thou hast offered me; I shall [soon] have thee again, whether thou wilt or no." Now Glaphyra hardly survived the narration of this dream of hers two days. | Nor hast thou been satisfied with that injury thou didst me, but thou hast been so bold as to procure thee a third husband to lie by thee, and in an indecent and imprudent manner hast entered into my house, and hast been married to Archelaus, thy husband and my brother. However, I will not forget thy former kind affection for me, but will set thee free from every such reproachful action, and cause thee to be mine again, as thou once wast. When she had related this to her female companions, in a few days' time she departed this life. |

First of all, we notice that the tale is much simpler in the *Wars* version. Here we find the explanation for the embassy of Jews and Samaritans going to Rome to plead for the deposition of Archelaus and the appointment of a Roman governor and none of the protracted hearing in front of Augustus for the determination of Herod's will.

It's not hard to see the model of the dream of the Egyptian pharaoh interpreted by Joseph in Genesis 41 as the basis of the dream sequence. As you can see, the version in *Antiquities* is somewhat elaborated with many details and flourishes, most interesting being the inclusion of the bit about **the high priest aiding the rebellion** (that's what the passage about Matthias seemed to imply, too!). The number of years is increased (by only one, so we won't quibble over it but assume that *Wars* is the correct version), the threatening tone of the Glaphyra story in *Wars* is softened in *Antiquities*, etc. The building projects are added, as well as the bringing of water from a distant source to water palm trees.

As for Archelaus himself, he is only mentioned briefly in other sources. Strabo, writing in the early 20s AD, seems to refer to him without giving his name: "However, [Herod the Great's] sons were not successful, but became involved in accusations; and *one of them spent the rest of his life in exile*, having taken up his abode among the Allobrogian Gauls, whereas the others, by much obsequiousness, but with difficulty, found leave to return home, with a tetrarchy assigned to each."[371] Vienna was the capital of the Allobroges. The chronology is not clear; it sounds as if Archelaus was banished *before* his brothers, Antipas and Philip, entered their tetrarchies, implying Archelaus never got his cut of the pie.

Dio, writing close to 200 years later, also refers to him, dating his banishment to 6 AD: "Herod of Palestine, who was *accused by his brothers* of some wrongdoing or other, was banished beyond the Alps and a portion of the domain was confiscated to the state."[372] *Dio mentions Josephus,* so he probably had access to his works and was relying on him. Perhaps Judea came under Roman control when Josephus says (and Dio implies), in 6 AD.[373] But the whole period is murky. Perhaps Dio just used Josephus' mangled history and Strabo is closer to the mark: Judea was put under Roman control shortly after Herod's death, when Archelaus was denied his kingship.

---

[371]Strabo 16.2.46 (765).

[372]Dio 55.27.6.

[373]Mason (2016), p. 240, points out that technically, Judea was not made a Roman province. It was technically an ethnic region of Syria, and the equestrian procurator of Judea (headquartered at Caesarea) was subservient to the Roman legate governing the province of Syria.

What seems to me is that Josephus has conflated at least two insurrections, one that occurred just after the death of Herod, and another that occurred in 6 AD. Let's continue to see if we can find clues.

Musical Rebels

As Josephus tells us in the above account from *Antiquities*, Archelaus undertakes magnificent building projects, including diverting "half the water with which the village of Neara used to be watered" and drawing off that water into the plain "to water those *palm trees* which he had there planted."[374] Next we have Archelaus marrying his brother's widow and having a dream interpreted by Simon the Essene, *five days*[375] after which 'the other Archelaus' finds him and hauls him off to Augustus and exile. Glaphyra then has a dream and dies "a few days" later. This was allegedly in the tenth (or ninth) year of Archelaus' government, which would be about 6 AD. Archelaus is then exiled to Gaul.

There is something odd about Josephus' tale of Archelaus. In *Wars*, he tells much the same story about the trip to Rome, the legal arguments about who gets what from the will of Herod the Great, the decision made, etc. So, since this is in *Wars*, I think we can assume that it is the more reliable of the two. But then, when we come to the Varus War that apparently had gotten underway in Archelaus' absence, we find a number of interesting items.

We are told that the revolt has begun while Archelaus and the family are in Rome for some sort of trial before Augustus, who learns of it from letters of Varus. The following description of the war appears *as though it is part of the report of Varus*. Apparently Herod's army, which had devolved onto Archelaus, deserted to the rebel side. However, here we again meet Rufus and Gratus, captains of the men of Sebaste mentioned previously in the extract from *Antiquities* and, finally, we connect back to the bandit, Ezekias, whom he previously named Hezekiah!

> Now the majority of the royal troops deserted and joined up with them [the Judeans]. The contingent most fit for war, however, 3,000 Sebastenes, added themselves to the Romans. **Rufus and Gratus** were over them, the latter having the [royal] infantry under him, Rufus the cavalry, though on account of their strength and savvy each of these men [alone] was a deciding factor in war, even without a force at their command.[376]

> Now during all this, things were also being stirred up throughout the countryside from many quarters, and the opportunity induced large numbers to [seek] sovereignty. For example, in Idumea 2,000 of those who had once been soldiers under Herod united in arms and **fought strenuously against the royalists** [i.e. supporters of Archelaus]. **Among the latter Achiab, the king's cousin**, was giving battle from the most fortified positions, evading the entanglement of the plains.
>   And **at Sepphoris of Galilee Judas, son of Ezekias** (the chief bandit who in another time overran the countryside and was subdued by King Herod), united a rabble of considerable size and broke open the royal armories; having armed his group, he made attempts on those who were jealously vying for sovereign power.[377]

---

[374] *Ant.* 17.13.1 (340).

[375] It was five days after executing his son that Herod died. Later in *Antiquities*, Josephus tells the story of the bird omen seen by Antipas, who only lived five days after seeing it. *Ant.* 18.6.7 (200).

[376] *Wars* 2.3.4 (52), Mason translation.

[377] *Wars* 2.4.1 (55–6), Mason translation.

This Judas of Sepphoris must certainly be 'Judas, son of Sepphoris/Saripheus,' the greatly esteemed teacher of the law who, in *Antiquities*, was allegedly burned at the time of an eclipse just before the death of Herod![378] In fact, earlier in *Wars*, when the story of Judas and Matthias is told, we read:

> There also now happened to him, among his other calamities, a certain popular sedition. There were two men of learning in the city [Jerusalem,] who were thought the most skillful in the laws of their country, and were on that account had in very great esteem all over the nation; they were, the one **Judas, the son of Sepphoris**, and the other **Matthias, the son of Margalus**. There was a great concourse of the young men to these men when they expounded the laws, and there got together every day a kind of an army of such as were growing up to be men.[379]

Even though the story of the golden eagle is the same, and situated in the time of Herod, it *now* appears that the Judas of that event was *not* burnt alive along with his pal, Matthias. In *Wars* 1.33.2, we have "Judas, son of Sepphoris" (a city) and then in *Wars* 2.4.1 we are a bit puzzled to find Judas of Sepphoris called the son of "the chief bandit Ezekias" who, according to *Antiquities* 14.9.2 (159–60), had been executed by Herod *forty-five years earlier*. If Judas was an infant at the time of Ezekias/ Hezekiah's death, he would still be a bit old for starting and leading a revolt. I think that the most reasonable explanation is that we can probably assume that there was a generation between the two. There may have been a Judas who was burned alive, assuming that the event actually happened then, and he was the father of Judas of Sepphoris, the new rebel, since 'son' could equally be used for a grandson. This also suggests that Josephus is blowing some smoke over the antecedents of Judas, the rebel at the time of Varus' war.

Josephus gives another description of the Varus war in Book 17 of *Antiquities*, which also lays the blame on Judas and gives it a rather different spin from the story about the mourners of Judas and Matthias agitating against Archelaus, though again he makes this Judas a son of Ezekias:

> There was also **Judas, the son of that Ezekias** who had been head of the robbers; which Ezekias was a very strong man, and had with great difficulty been **caught by Herod. This Judas**, having gotten together a multitude of men of a profligate character about **Sepphoris in Galilee**, made an assault upon the palace [there,] and seized upon all the weapons that were laid up in it, and with them armed every one of those that were with him, and carried away what money was left there; and he **became terrible to all men, by tearing and rending those that came near him**; and all this in order to raise himself, and out of **an ambitious desire of the royal dignity**;[380] and he hoped to obtain that as the reward not of his virtuous skill in war, but of his extravagance in doing injuries.[381]

It is interesting to see this Judas having kingly ambitions considering the fact that the Gospels tell us that 'Jesus of Nazareth' was accused of having kingly ambitions and was crucified as 'King

---

[378]Mason (2016), p. 246, n. 171, thinks these are two different Judases, but I think the inclusion of Sepphoris in the description of both is a tad too coincidental for that.

[379] *Wars* 1.33.2 (648–49).

[380]Although Judas had 'an ambitious desire of the royal dignity,' there are no indications in this story that his aspirations were *messianic* in nature. We can also note that nowhere in this or any other account of Judas, other than the 'Golden Eagle Temple Cleansing' incident which is placed first, does Josephus tell us what happened to Judas.

[381] *Ant.* 17.10.5 (271–2).

of the Jews.' One wonders, of course, if Ezekias was a descendant of David, thus giving him and his offspring ideas about their rights to kingship? Was this what made them 'robbers' in the eyes of Herod and later, Josephus? We will see a 'son' of Judas of Sepphoris/Galilee, Menahem, was acclaimed as a king later on, and did a similar robbing-an-armory deed in respect of Masada many years further on at the time of the great war against Rome.

Continuing with *Wars*, Josephus describes another royal contender who is described in strangely similar terms to the above Judas:

> In **Perea** a certain one of the royal slaves, **Simon**, relying on **bodily physique and size**, although he **wrapped the diadem on himself, going around with the bandits** he had gathered he burned down the royal [properties] at Hierichous [Jericho] and many other villas of the rich, easily procuring plunder for himself out of the fire. And he would have been the first to incinerate every decent house had not **Gratus**, the commander of the royal infantry, taken along Trachonite archers and the best fighting unit of the Sebastenes and gone out to meet the man. As a consequence, large numbers of the Pereans were destroyed in the fighting. **As for Simon himself: while he was trying to retreat by way of a steep ravine, Gratus intercepted him; as he tried to escape, [Gratus] struck his neck from the side and lopped off [his head].**[382]

This "Simon, one of the servants to the king" who then becomes involved with bandits pings 'Simon the Essene' who interpreted the dream of Archelaus, particularly when one considers what has been discovered about him in recent years. As it happens, this Simon of Perea is the subject of discussion in Israel Knohl's book *Messiahs and Resurrection in the Gabriel Revelation*.

> 'Gabriel's Revelation', also called 'Hazon Gabriel' or the Jeselsohn Stone, is a three-foot-tall stone tablet with 87 lines of Hebrew text written in ink, containing a collection of short prophecies written in the first person and dated to the *late 1st century BC*. The unprovenanced tablet was *found near the Dead Sea* some time around the year 2000 and has been associated with the same community that created the Dead Sea Scrolls. Because the manner of death of the individual is described in the text, and rather closely matches that of Josephus' description of the death of Simon of Perea, Knohl argues that the text shows Simon's death to be "an essential part of the redemptive process. The blood of the slain messiah paves the way for the final salvation."[383]

Just to give the reader an idea of the various locations, notice that Perea is right next to Qumran, where the Dead Sea Scrolls were found. (See figure 1.)

Knohl's work – though it is still speculative – suggests there was more to this rebellion than Josephus lets on, since he is so busy obfuscating who was who and connected to who else and why. With that in mind, let's look at the next 'messianic king' that Josephus mentions emerging at that time following the death of Herod:

> And then **a certain shepherd** dared to lay claim to kingship! Athrongeus he was called. **Strength of body and a soul that held death in contempt** commended this hope to him – and besides these, **four brothers like him**. To each of these fellows he hitched an armed century, and used them just like generals and satraps for the raids, while **he himself – exactly like a king** – handled the more "august affairs." In fact, at the time, although he was **wrapping a diadem on himself,**

---

[382] *Wars* 2.4.2 (57–9), Mason translation.
[383] Wikipedia.org, 'Gabriel's Revelation.' See Israel Knohl, *Messiahs and Resurrection in 'The Gabriel Revelation'* (Continuum, 2009). Recall the importance of blood in Revelation, mentioned in the previous chapter.

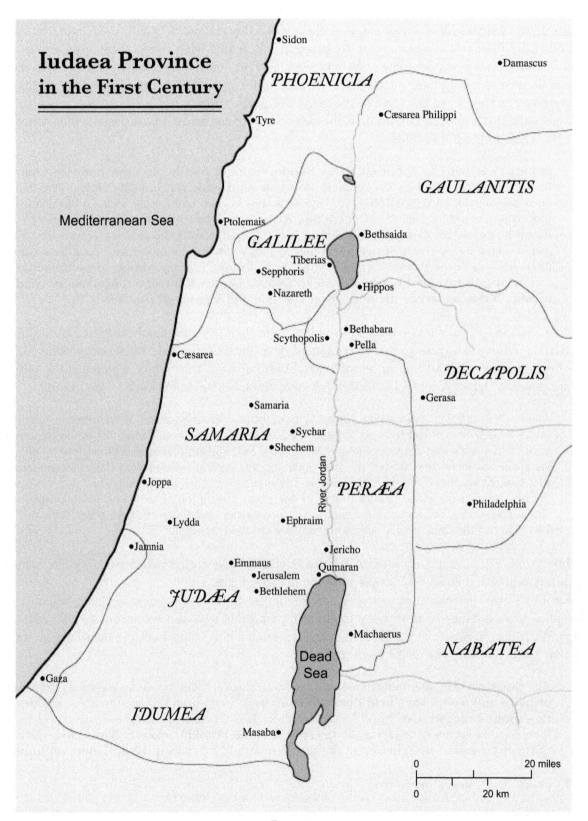

Figure 1.

he continued for a long while afterwards raiding the countryside with his brothers. Killing Romans as well as royalists was their main goal, though none of the Judeans would escape if he were to come into their hands carrying anything valuable. Once, they even dared to surround a Roman century in column near Emmaus; these men were bringing over grain and weapons to the legion. They actually shot down with spears their [the Romans'] centurion Areius and forty of his finest men, though when the remainder were in danger of suffering the same, **Gratus** came to their aid with the Sebastenes and they escaped. When they had performed many such deeds against both locals and foreigners for the entire war, after a while three of them were apprehended – the oldest by Archelaus, the next two having fallen of **Gratus** and Ptolemy – whereas the fourth surrendered to Archelaus on a pledge. Although this was indeed the final outcome that was waiting for them, at that time they filled all Judea with a bandit-style war.[384]

So, Gratus took down Simon of Perea, the servant of King Herod, and *also* brought down at least two of the brothers of "a certain shepherd" named Athrongeus, if not the man himself. The version in *Antiquities* is more elaborate, but says basically the same things; there is a slight change in the spelling of the name: Athronges. About this fellow's name, we are told:

> Rapoport has explained the name 'Athronges' by the Hebraized Persian word 'orange,' or 'melon'…, and identified it with Ben Baṭiaḥ, "Son of the Cucumber" (that is, like a cucumber), the popular hero, the size of whose fist has become proverbial in ancient rabbinical literature (*Kelim* xvii. 12; *Tosef.*, *Kelim, B. M.* vii. 2); the form of his hand having, as Rapoport thinks, given rise to both terms. At a later time, legend identified him with the leader of the insurrection, Abba Sakkara, the nephew of Johanan ben Zakkai.[385]

Josephus doesn't associate this Athronges/Athrongeus with any particular location. We notice his four brothers, two of whom were dispatched by Gratus – *as was Simon of Perea*. Both Simon of Perea and this Athronges are described in oddly similar terms: "Simon, relying on bodily physique and size" and "Athrongeus he was called. Strength of body and a soul that held death in contempt." We also notice, particularly, that Archelaus brought two of these brothers to heel, and apparently *let one of them go*. Could this hint at something more about Archelaus' relationship with at least some of the rebels? Most curiously, again, Josephus makes no specific mention of the fate of the ringleader, Athronges.

As we note in the above table about the rule of Archelaus, after almost no real details of his 'reign,' we are told in both *Wars* and *Antiquities* that complaints were made against him by both Samaritans and Jews and he was banished, though later historians said the complaints were made by his brothers. After his banishment:

> The territory of Archelaus having been marked off for a province, Coponius, a procurator from the equestrian order among the Romans, was sent. He had received from [Augustus] an authority that went as far as putting [people] to death. **In his [term] a certain Galilean man by the name of Ioudas [Judas] incited the locals to rebellion, lambasting them if they were going to put up with paying tribute to Romans and tolerate mortal masters after God. This man was a sophist of his own peculiar school, which had nothing in common with the others.**[386]

---

[384] *Wars* 2.4.3 (60–5), Mason translation. Cf. *Ant.* 17.10.7 (278–84).

[385] Richard Gottheil, Kaufmann Kohler, 'Athronges,' *Jewish Encyclopedia*: https://www.jewishencyclopedia.com/articles/2088-athronges.

[386] *Wars* 2.8.1 (117–8), Mason translation.

There must be some truth to the resurrection, because Judas is back again! This is Josephus' description of the 'Fourth Philosophy' of Judas the Galilean:

> ... for Judas and Sadduc, who excited a fourth philosophic sect among us, and had a great many followers therein, filled our civil government with tumults at present, and laid the foundations of our future miseries, by **this system of philosophy, which we were before unacquainted withal**, concerning which I will discourse a little, and this the rather because the infection which spread thence among the younger sort, who were zealous for it, brought the public to destruction. ... **of the fourth sect of Jewish philosophy, Judas the Galilean was the author**. These men agree in all other things with the Pharisaic notions; but they have an inviolable attachment to liberty, and say that **God is to be their only Ruler and Lord**. They also do not value dying any kinds of death, nor indeed do they heed the deaths of their relations and friends, nor can any such fear make them call any man lord. And since this immovable resolution of theirs is well known to a great many, I shall speak no further about that matter; nor am I afraid that anything I have said of them should be disbelieved, but rather fear, that what I have said is beneath the resolution they show when they undergo pain.[387]

The remark about these Zealots being contemptuous of death and *relatives* reminds one of the example set by Jesus in the Gospel of Mark, where he declares that his family are only those who do the will of God. Though certainly, there is another meaning intended in the Gospel, still, the similarity of the sentiment is interesting.

Notice what Josephus had written about Athronges/Athrongeus: "his soul, which despised death." Was he a member of the same group? We should also recall the descriptions of the teachings given by Matthias and Judas to the young men who were tasked with the Golden Eagle rebellion, that it was a good thing to die in the service of their god. Judas the Galilean certainly seems to be the son of Judas the great teacher of the Golden Eagle rebellion who was the son of the 'robber' Ezekias/Hezekiah, and is possibly connected to Simon of Perea, who may be the same person as Athronges/Athrongeus, whose two brothers were killed by Gratus.

This whole Archelaus period is furiously vague and suggestive of things that are being covered up and deliberately obfuscated.[388] He is accused by Josephus of being brutal to the point that the people complain about him. But did they complain at the beginning or at the end? There is nothing particular about his alleged brutality that is not also ascribed to Varus and others. In fact, there are a whole lot more details about what the Romans were doing without punishment,

---

[387]*Ant.* 18.1.1, 6 (9–10, 23–5). There are similarities here to Josephus' description of the Essenes, too. Mason (2016) adds some possible nuance to the situation: "Judas and Saddok's rejection of not only *foreign* domination but any rule other than divine seems directed against those Judaeans who would cooperate with the annexation and census, not against the Romans (18.4-10, 23/25)" (p. 247), and: "If divine sovereignty or theocracy *had* been their goal, Judas and Saddok should have been delighted with the monarch's removal and the arrival of priestly-collegial governance" (p. 253). So he argues that they weren't anti-Roman per se. More at issue was "Jerusalem's dramatic loss of status" caused by annexation into Syria: "The possibility that Judas and Saddok would recognize no mortal ruler is a problem first because the popular unrest preceded their involvement. Second, such a platform would explain neither the previous five centuries nor the timing here" (pp. 248-49). However, it's easy to see how, despite the initial cause of the unrest, Judas himself still could have been anti-Roman, and the annexation would have inspired such resentment among the monarchists.

[388]Nodet and Taylor (1998), pp. 294–5, n. 30, write: "There are good reasons for thinking that ... the attachment of these events [i.e. the rebellion of Judas at the beginning of Archelaus' reign in Judea] to Quirinius and the imperial census is only an artificial device in order to cover over a long period of disturbances and Roman repressions."

so why was Archelaus exiled? Is Dio correct that he was exiled *immediately* due to the accusations of his brothers in Rome, and if so, what accusations did his brothers bring up against him? We'll probably never know.

There is something even more interesting about this whole period. In his *Histories*, Tacitus tells us:

> On Herod's death, one Simon, without waiting for the approbation of the Emperor, *usurped the title of king.* He was punished by Quintilius Varus then governor of Syria, and the nation, with its liberties curtailed, was divided into *three* provinces under the sons of Herod.[389]

Apparently, Simon of Perea was considerably more important than Josephus lets on, important enough to be known about in Rome. According to Tacitus, it was Simon who took the title of king without the permission of Augustus, not Archelaus. Was this Simon also represented in Josephus' tale by the seemingly mythical 'Sabinus'? How long did he prevail as king? How long did it take for Varus to 'punish' him? We read that he was killed by Gratus and there is the Jeselsohn Stone/Gabriel Revelation to back it up. Tacitus says nothing about a literal tetrarchy, but rather says that the nation was divided into three provinces under the sons of Herod. He makes no mention of the exile of Archelaus then or later. Was Archelaus-the-evil invented to some degree by Josephus to take the heat off the Jews as a rebellious people? Why is Josephus so deliberately confusing about the events of this period? What is he covering up? Who was this Simon, really, and was he connected to Judas the Galilean in some way? Is it this connection that Josephus is attempting to cover up? In fact, what is Josephus' own connection to Judas and his family? What is obvious is that all of these individuals were rebels against Rome and would later be described as Zealots.

Zealots were vehemently against Roman rule in Judea because they were driven by the idea that only their god could be king. They were determined to end Gentile rule over the Jewish people. The word comes from zealous, i.e. 'zealous for the law,' the law being either the letter, as for the Sadducees, or the oral law, as for the Pharisees. It is Josephus himself who says and suggests throughout the texts of *Wars* and *Antiquities* that all the troubles of the Jews can be traced back to the founder of this Zealot ideology: Judas the Galilean.

> Since Josephus is almost our sole informant of these events and their consequences, it is necessary to examine carefully both what he tells us about them and how he tells us of them. ... On analysis, his attitude is seen to be curiously ambivalent: the logic of events, as well as the needs of self-justification, caused him to regard the Zealots as dangerous fanatics and to denigrate them as 'brigands'; yet, as a Jew, he could not fail to appreciate that such men had given themselves wholeheartedly to preserve the sovereignty of Yahweh over Israel.[390]

It could be said that a rural Jewish priest from Modi'in, Mattathias the Hasmonean, father of Judas Maccabeus, Eleazar Avaran, Simon Thassi, John Gaddi, and Jonathan Apphus, was the original, founding Zealot and *Josephus claims descent from this family.* Josephus was much more deeply involved with the Zealots than he was willing to admit. That is why he created a new category for their ideology, the 'Fourth Philosophy,' and distances himself from them by hiding

---

[389]Tacitus, *The History*, 5.9–10; translation by A. J. Church and W. J. Brodribb, edited by Moses Hadas (Modern Library, 1942), p. 663.

[390]Brandon (1967), pp. 30, 36.

and confusing connections. He may even have used the Maccabees as models for some of his stories with only loose grains of historical fact sprinkled here and there.

At every opportunity he refers to the rebels as brigands, robbers, bandits, thieves, pirates, and worse. They are blamed for everything, and most especially, for leading others astray. If you believe Josephus, all the Jews would be wonderful, law-abiding Roman citizens were it not for that bad apple, Judas the Galilean. That is because Judas' 'sons' continued the family tradition on the model of the Maccabees. His descendant Eleazar led the Zealot stand at Masada.[391] In fact, it could be said that Judas' revolt against the Romans is somewhat equivalent to the Maccabean resistance, with Judas as the main inspiration and hero. The fact that Josephus looks back to the origins of Judas seventy years later is an indication that this man, Judas the Galilean, occupied a lot of space in Josephus' mind.

So far the most telling aspect of the period following Herod the Great's death, as we have it from Josephus, is the multitude of rebellions and rebel leaders, the confusion, and the scale of Roman repression. Even though Josephus does his best to paint it over, it still comes through in the odd slip, as when he says of Judas and his followers: "All sorts of misfortunes also sprang from these men, and the nation was infected with this doctrine to an incredible degree; one violent war came upon us after another."[392]

After going through the events in Judea surrounding the death of Herod, we can note that in 5/4 BC an event occurred involving a Judas son of Saripheus/Sepphoris that was probably instrumental in the early formation of the Zealots. And then, in 6 AD, Judea was placed under direct Roman rule and Judas the Galilean, probably son of the great teacher of 5/4 BC, played a role in that rebellion. Josephus says it is the same Judas the Galilean who was the founder of the 'Fourth Philosophy' that Josephus doesn't even dare to give its proper name. In other words, **both dates selected for the birth of Jesus** by two evangelists, who may very well have had some knowledge of the origins of Jerusalem Christianity, **were of great significance to the Zealots** whose movement was founded by Judas the Galilean, and who were, undoubtedly, 'Christian,' i.e. Messianists.

Josephus' account of the 5/4 BC to 6 AD events is not very forthcoming. The reaction of the Jews to the census was hostile but, according to Josephus, they were pacified by the priest Joazar.[393] After telling us this, Josephus begins to write about Judas of Galilee and his Pharisee pal Saddok who caused a revolt. But instead of telling us about the revolt, he diverts to a discussion on the teachings and aims of these rebels and how the movement that they started led ultimately to the destruction of the Jewish state, capital city, and temple. One almost gets the impression that some part of the story has been deleted.

---

[391]Even in his dramatic tale of Masada, Josephus was novelizing. See: Nachman Ben-Yehuda, *The Masada Myth: Collective Memory and Mythmaking In Israel* (University of Wisconsin Press, 1995). Also, by the same author: *Sacrificing Truth: Archaeology and the Myth of Masada* (Humanity Books, 2002).

[392]*Ant.* 18.1.1 (6–7).

[393]*Ant.* 17.3.

Josephus and the Aretas–Antipas Problem

Now I want to take up the Aretas problem mentioned at the beginning, because this will include a lot of background to the time of Paul and the early Jerusalem church. You just never know what you are going to find when you start pulling on threads!

As noted above, Campbell has pegged Paul to a timeline based on that brief mention of the King of Natabaea, Aretas IV, in Paul's Second Letter to the Corinthians. So here, I will look at the Aretas mystery in detail, showing why we cannot rely on it as a solid chronological anchor for Paul's life, and may even have reason to doubt the historicity of the war between Aretas and Antipas used to support Campbell's argument. To do this will also require a discussion of the Artabanus mystery, which runs in the background of the tale told by Josephus. It appears to me that, once again, Josephus conflated events separated by many years, and we cannot take his description of events at face value.

King Aretas IV of Nabataea was a historical person; there are coins and inscriptions proving his existence. He is also the best-documented Nabataean ruler; 80% of surviving Nabataean coins were minted during his reign, which lasted from roughly 9 BC to 40 AD. The title that appears for this whole half a century is 'Lover of His People.' This was a bold choice: most client kings of Rome used titles such as 'Lover of Caesar' or 'Lover of Rome.' Nabataean art, architecture, pottery and script all developed during his reign. His merchants were active across the Empire, and his administration and military were thoroughly Hellenized and Romanized;[394] Rome apparently was on good terms with him and was appreciative of his trade network, and there is no indication in other histories that this ever changed.

While he didn't merit a personal mention of his name by the Roman historian, Tacitus did make a reference to 'the Arabs' that most likely included Aretas, as well as to a feast given by the king of the Arabs/Nabataeans, who was certainly Aretas. The main literary source for Aretas' life is Josephus, who tells us that he was the most powerful neighbor of Judea. Things were apparently loose enough that he could take part in political affairs by virtue of the fact that there was intermarriage between his house and the Herodian house ruling Judea.

Josephus relates three main events involving Aretas: how he became king,[395] his involvement in the Roman governor Varus' war against the Jews after Herod the Great's death,[396] and a war against Antipas many years later.[397] He tells us that Aretas was *not* on particularly good terms with Rome and it was only with great hesitation that Augustus recognized him as king and didn't send the army to depose him. But that appears to be Josephus' spin if we consider what is noted above in Tacitus. It is also a peculiar refraction of the events that Josephus recounts in relation to the succession of Archelaus, who had difficulties being recognized as ruler by Augustus. What Josephus apparently couldn't deny was that Aretas was acknowledged by Augustus and took part in the expedition of Varus *against the Jews* around 4 BC, putting his considerable army at the disposal of the Roman general. In Roman terms, that would definitely win friends and influence people. Like Herod the Great, the archaeology suggests Aretas was a successful and prosperous client king or friend of Rome, contrary to what Josephus wrote.

---

[394]David F. Graf, 'Aretas,' *Anchor Bible Dictionary,* Vol. I (Doubleday, 1992), p. 375.
[395]*Ant.* 16.9.4 (294–9).
[396]*Ant.* 17.10.9 (287).
[397]*Ant.* 18.5.1 (109–25).

The only other written source for Aretas by name is the reference by Paul in 2 Corinthians 11:32–3: "In Damascus, the governor [ethnarch] under King Aretas guarded the city of Damascus in order to seize me, but I was let down in a basket through a window in the wall, and escaped from his hands." Campbell avers that this could only have taken place during a brief window when Aretas *might* have been ruler of Damascus as a result of a little war between him and Herod Antipas, the tetrarch of Galilee and Perea (which shared a border with Nabataea). Campbell summarizes his argument:

1. We know that at some point Aretas IV controlled Damascus (a city bordering, if not in, the region of the Decapolis) through a governor (called an 'ethnarch').

2. This is also quite consistent with Nabataean political aims.

3. This is unattested, however, and largely impossible during the reign of Philip over the Decapolis, that is, up to 34 C.E.

4. This is also unattested, and highly unlikely, during the reign of Agrippa, which extended from 37 C.E. past the death of Aretas himself.

5. We know, moreover, that in late 36 C.E. Aretas launched a successful military strike against Antipas, ruler of Galilee.

6. This strike *seems* to have involved the Decapolis, as a telltale comment by Josephus concerning Gamala suggests; a region currently only under *indirect* Roman control.

7. This was a particularly well-calculated strike on Aretas's part because the Syrian governor was involved at the time in securing the eastern frontier against the Parthian threat by stabilizing its network of client kingdoms, pursuing this aim in a highly conciliatory fashion, and he was also bitterly aggrieved with Antipas. Hence, far from exciting Roman hostility, this action probably anticipated meeting with Vitellius's approval, and indeed seems initially to have done so.

8. It is therefore most likely that Aretas's control over Damascus coincided with his successful defeat of Antipas and *probable* annexation of the Decapolis region as a whole.[398]

I don't have any issue with points 1 and 2, but the rest are highly questionable since reliance is placed on Josephus for his certitude. To show why, we need to understand more about Damascus before and after Paul's time, the politics of the time, and what we really know and don't know based on our sources.

Who Ruled Damascus?

We know that Aretas died in 39 or 40 AD, based on coins and inscriptions from the time. He came into power around 9 BC. We also know that a previous king of Nabataea, Aretas III, had ruled Damascus from 84–72 BC (coins attest to his control for these years), at which point Armenia took it over, occupying the city for approximately 2 years, after which it "maintained a precarious independent presence"[399] until the Roman general Pompey occupied the city in 64/63 BC.

Coins minted in Damascus depict the Roman emperors Augustus, Tiberius (up to 34 AD), and Nero (starting in 62/63 AD), implying Roman interaction of some sort, but we don't know

[398]Douglas A. Campbell, 'An Anchor for Pauline Chronology: Paul's Flight from 'The Ethnarch of King Aretas' (2 Corinthians 11:32–33),' *Journal for Biblical Literature* 121:2 (2002), pp. 297–8.
[399]Ross Burns, *Damascus: A History* (Routledge, 2005), p. 44.

definitively who was directly ruling the city during those times. The period with no numismatic evidence (34–63 AD, almost 30 years!) is curious; it could indicate a change in rule or simply that no new coins were minted there in those years. On the other hand, a change in rule would almost certainly result in a commemorative minting, so the most likely explanation is that no new coins were minted in this period or none have been found. Either that, or there is something seriously wrong with archaeological dating and the timeline!

Explicit mention of rule over Damascus doesn't enter the historical record again until 106 AD, when it came under Roman control as a city of the province of Syria, *suggesting that it was not under direct Roman rule previously*. Interestingly, Rome *took over Nabataea at the same time*, which became the Roman province of Arabia.

Let's look at the map on page 134 again. There *are* historical references to the region south of Damascus: the Decapolis, located between Syria in the north and Nabataea to the south. To the east was impassable desert, so travel and trade were focused along the 'King's Highway,' running north from Nabataea, through the Decapolis, to Damascus. The Decapolis cities were a group of semi-autonomous city-states nominally under Roman *protection* since Pompey's reorganization of Syria, and in some way administered by the Syrian governor. Like Damascus, it is not so clear who directly controlled them at various times.

Pliny and Ptolemy both include Damascus as one of the Decapolis cities.[400] However, Pliny notes that when he was writing in the 70s AD there was confusion as to which cities exactly made up the 'Ten Cities' – different writers gave different lists. Eusebius doesn't include Damascus in his list, nor does Josephus himself.[401] So it's hard to even know Damascus's status in the Decapolis at the time in question with any certainty.

Josephus makes several references to Damascus in *Wars*,[402] in the last of which Herod the Great is described as bestowing benefits on *foreign* cities, that is, cities not under his rule:

> And when he had built so much, he showed the greatness of his soul to no small number of *foreign cities*.[403] He built palaces for exercise at Tripoli, *and Damascus*, and Ptolemais; he built a wall about Byblus, as also large rooms, and cloisters, and temples, and market-places at Berytus and Tyre, with theatres at Sidon and *Damascus*. ... Moreover, he dedicated groves and meadows to some people; nay, not a few cities there were who had lands of his donation, *as if they were parts of his own kingdom*.[404]

Further, according to Josephus, two cities of the Decapolis, Gadara and Hippos, were annexed to Herod the Great's territory by Augustus,[405] then handed over to Syria after Herod's death in 4 BC.[406] At the same time, the region between Damascus and the rest of the Decapolis cities was given to Herod's son, Philip, which he ruled until his death in 33/34 AD (recall no new coins from 34 to 63). These regions – Trachonitis, Batanea, Auranitis, and Gaulanitis – had been

---

[400] Pliny, *NH* 5.74; Ptolemy, *Georg.* 5.14.

[401] Mason (2001), p. 139, n. 1399.

[402] *Wars* 1.4.8 (103); 1.5.3 (115); 1.6.2 (127); 1.12.1 (236); 1.18.4–5; 1.20.3–4 (362); from Eleazar's speech at Masada in 7.8.7 (368).

[403] Notice how favorably Herod is depicted in *Wars* whereas he becomes quite the villain in *Antiquities*.

[404] *Wars* 1.21.11 (422–3).

[405] *Wars* 1.20.3 (396).

[406] *Wars* 2.6.3 (96).

gifted originally to Herod by Augustus around 23 BC.[407] They passed on to Agrippa I in 37 AD, after the death of Tiberius.[408]

There are two items of interest to note about this shuffling around of territories. First, indeed two cities of the Decapolis were apparently given to Syria, but the region separating them from their alleged 'brother' Damascus was given to Philip, then Agrippa I. So *they were ruled at a distance*, with territories separating them from their ruling province (kind of like how the United States includes Alaska, which borders Canada, but not any of the contiguous states). If Damascus was under the rule of Nabataea, a similar situation would apply: the rule of a city separated from its ruler's contiguous territory. However, Campbell uses this geographical separation as a reason *against* the idea that Nabataea could have ruled Damascus. But as Campbell himself observes, "the imperial allocation of territory was not always that convenient or even rational,"[409] and this is a case in point. Even Gaza, far to the southwest, was apparently put under Syrian control, with regions between under the rule of various other persons at different times. So it seems to have been a rule rather than an exception.

So when Campbell says in points 3 and 4 that Nabataean control of Damascus was impossible before 34 AD (when Philip ruled the Decapolis region) and after 37 AD (when Agrippa I ruled it), he doesn't have any real evidence, nor is the line of force of the available evidence in his favor. Assuming Aretas did control Damascus in 36–37 AD, Campbell concedes that "[Emperor] Gaius [Caligula] might conceivably have left Aretas in possession of Damascus alone [when Agrippa I acquired the Decapolis region], but we have no evidence for this."[410] We have no evidence for Campbell's suggestion either, just a *possible* window of opportunity provided by a dubious story from Josephus that contains no explicit mention of Damascus. It could very well be that Aretas controlled Damascus even while other cities of the Decapolis were ruled by others, and *the scanty evidence appears to point in that direction.*

But let's assume Campbell is correct that Damascus wasn't ruled by Aretas before Philip's death in 33/34 and after 37 AD, when Agrippa I was given control of the territories by Emperor Gaius. The next governor of Syria, L. Vitellius, didn't arrive until 35 AD following the death of the previous governor in 33 AD and his own consulship in Rome in 34 AD.[411] Josephus tells us that the Decapolis region was *governed in trust* by Syria during this time. As Campbell notes, "It is therefore quite plausible that the actual administration of the area was undertaken locally *by trusted client kings*."[412] Could Damascus have been a part of this arrangement? If Aretas was *not* ruler of Damascus before or after, could *this* provide a possible window of temporary rule for Aretas, i.e. 33–35 AD?

Campbell observes, "Aretas IV is never directly attested to elsewhere as being in charge of Damascus." Similarly, "it is as difficult to find a period when the region around Damascus was controlled by the Nabataean king as it is to find one when he controlled the actual city."[413] This

---

[407]*Wars* 1.8.5 (168); 2.6.3 (95); *Ant.* 18.4.6 (106).
[408]*Wars* 2.11.5 (215); *Ant.* 19.5.1 (274).
[409]Campbell (2002), p. 287.
[410]Campbell, (2002), p. 299, n. 45
[411]Tacitus, *Ann.* 6.27.
[412]Campbell (2002), p. 290.
[413]Campbell (2002), p. 282.

is true, but it is also true that there doesn't seem to be any direct, explicit reference to anyone *else* ruling Damascus for the period in question, either.

Given the significant Nabataean demographics of the Decapolis region (including Damascus), Damascus *previously* having been ruled by Nabataea, its importance and attractiveness to Nabataea in terms of trade, and the need of Rome to have the city managed by a competent person and to keep the citizens happy so that the trade network would continue to generate revenues, it would make sense to posit some strong Nabataean influence or control over the city.

What Is an Ethnarch?

This is the title Paul refers to in 2 Corinthians. Josephus uses the word some 22 times to refer to a Jewish official. So do the books of Maccabees (3 times) and Nicolaus of Damascus, once (fragment 136: "He gave Archelaus the title of ethnarch, and promised that if he proved himself worthy, he would soon make him king. He appointed the other brothers, Philippus and Antipas, to be tetrarchs"). Aside from these, the word is only used 7 other times in pre-second century sources. And the exact form or function of the title is anything but clear.

So, for example, we have Strabo: "The Romans, as far as they were able, corrected, as I have said, many abuses, and established an orderly government, by appointing vice-governors, nomarchs, and ethnarchs, *whose business it was to superintend affairs of minor importance.*"[414]

According to Josephus, Strabo called the leader of the Jewish community in Alexandria "ethnarch,"[415] but Philo, an Alexandrian himself, called him "genarch."[416] Elsewhere, Philo (and others) refers to an ethnarch in generic terms as *simply the founder or leader of a tribe or nation.*[417] That's it. Some have suggested the ethnarch mentioned by Paul was only the leader of the Nabataean community in Damascus, a 'trade consul' of sorts, similar to the Jewish ethnarch in Alexandria. (Nabataea had trade colonies in other Decapolis cities, e.g. Gerasa, and Damascus probably had a Nabataean quarter.)[418] Campbell rejects this idea because the degree of influence and power of the ethnarch mentioned by Paul implies total control over the security apparatus of the city, not merely control over one section of the city. But can we really make that assumption?

As Campbell says elsewhere in his paper, "one cannot rule out the possibility of large bribes."[419] We simply don't know enough about the local context to reconstruct what happened with any degree of certainty. Who's to say that, by saying "Ethnarch of Damascus under Aretas," Paul wasn't saying something of the equivalent of what could be said about certain leaders today, e.g. a reference to Ukraine's Poroshenko as "President of Ukraine under Obama," thus implying a known but officially unacknowledged power relationship? Could Aretas have 'bought' the ethnarch of Damascus? Or could a local chieftain of the Nabataean community have 'bought' the higher-ups in order to sniff out Paul for whatever reason?

[414]Strabo 17.1.13.
[415]*Ant.* 14.7.2 (117).
[416]Philo, *Flacc.* 74.
[417]*OGI* 616.2; Lucian, *Macrobii* 17 ("Asander, who, after being ethnarch, was proclaimed king of Bosporus by the divine Augustus ..."); Philo, *Quis rer. div. her.* 56 ("leader of a nation").
[418]Rainer Riesner, *Paul's Early Period: Chronology, Mission Strategy, Theology* (Eerdmans, 1998), p. 86.
[419]Campbell (2002), p. 296.

I think Campbell is wrong. What Paul says could easily be referring to something like the Jewish ethnarch of Alexandria, only in Damascus. This Jewish community leader, with the support of Aretas, went after Paul because of his preaching. To whom he was preaching, or what he was preaching, we can leave aside for the moment.

Altogether, these uncertainties – the social and political status of Damascus, the exact function or role of an 'ethnarch,' the nature of relations between Syria and Nabataea, the status of the Decapolis – don't help Campbell's theory. Even *if* the war between Aretas and Antipas took place, there is still no evidence that a takeover of Damascus took place, which is unlikely due to the lack of coinage. At the most it provides a plausible window of opportunity, but only *if* it happened, and only if Aretas wasn't *already* controlling the city. Using the same evidence Campbell uses from Josephus, one could simply argue that Aretas already controlled Damascus and waged a war with Antipas to acquire more of the Decapolis cities. But did that war even happen? Or, if it happened, did it actually happen *as Josephus described it*?

Aretas, Antipas and John the Baptist

In order to attempt to conjecture what happened, we need to take a closer look at what else was going on at the time in question. According to the Gospels of Mark (6:17-19), Matthew (14:3-5) and Luke (3:18-20), John the Baptist opposed the proposed marriage of Herod Antipas and Herodias, which resulted in John's execution.

In contrast, Josephus says that John the Baptist was executed because he was acquiring too much political clout among the masses; further he says that the masses of people thought that it was because of the execution of John that God brought punishment on Antipas by making him lose his war with Aretas, which apparently began over a territorial dispute.

First of all, recall that Herod Antipas was recognized by Augustus in 4 or 3 BC as 'tetrarch' ruler of Galilee and Perea. He was probably born around 20 BC or so. In Josephus, the marriage between Antipas and Herodias occurred just prior to the 35/36 AD war between Aretas and Antipas, so Antipas would have been about 56 years old. After the marriage, but before the war, John was supposedly executed. And remember, any involvement of Lucius Vitellius the elder could not have happened until his arrival in the region after his consulship in 34.

By Paul's own account, his escape from Damascus occurred two to three years after his 'call,' which, according to the standard chronology, means 37–38 AD at the latest (i.e. two to three years before Aretas' death). This creates a serious problem for the traditional chronology of Jesus based on the Gospels, which usually places Jesus' ministry beginning around 30 AD, and John's death shortly after that – and certainly before the crucifixion of Jesus. If that was the Gospel writers' intention, and they used Josephus, they did so carelessly or in ignorance.[420] *For John to oppose the marriage, he would have to be alive in at least in 35 AD.*[421] Both claims – that of the NT and that of Josephus – cannot be correct.[422] If Josephus is right, Jesus' ministry would then

---

[420]If Mark was written before Josephus published, and the three passages about John the Baptist are not interpolations (I don't think they are), then obviously, Mark, at least, could not have used Josephus.

[421]Eisler (1931), pp. 288–94, argues that John's death occurred in 35 AD, based on readings of Josephus.

[422]This gets into issues with the Jesus chronology, the subject of the next chapter. However, the problem may not be fatal. Nikos Kokkinos has argued (on the assumption that the Gospels and Josephus *can* be synthesized) for a 36 AD date of the crucifixion. See Kokkinos, 'Crucifixion in A.D. 36: The Keystone for Dating the Birth of Jesus,' in *Chronos, Kairos, Christos: Nativity and Chronological Studies Presented to Jack Finegan*

have to be dated later than 36/37 AD, creating a potentially impossible chronological conflict *vis à vis* Paul. How could Jesus begin his ministry that late, be executed as much as three years later, and then have Paul in a Damascus ruled by Aretas when Aretas died in 40 AD?

The story in Josephus informs us that the daughter of Aretas was married to Herod Antipas, one of the heirs of Herod the Great. At some point, she discovered that Antipas was planning on divorcing her in order to marry his brother's wife, Herodias. Herodias was (at the time of this plan) married to Herod II, the son of Herod the Great and Mariamne II, the daughter of Simon Boethus whom Herod had made high priest in order to raise his status. Herodias was the daughter of Aristobulus IV, Herod the Great's son whom he executed in 7 BC. So, Herod II was the half uncle of Herodias. Herod II was actually Herod the Great's eldest surviving son but because his mother had knowledge of a poison plot against Herod the Great, and he failed to stop it, he was excluded from the will of Herod the Great and apparently lived in Rome as a private citizen. The family tree in Figure 2 should help to sort this mess out a bit.

In the next chapter of *Antiquities*, Josephus explicitly mentions that Herodias "divorced herself from her husband, Herod II (who lived in Rome), while he was alive."

> Herodias ... was married to Herod, the son of Herod the Great, who was born of Mariamne, the daughter of Simon the high priest, who had a daughter, Salome; after whose birth Herodias took upon her to confound the laws of our country, and divorced herself from her husband while he was alive, and was married to Herod, her husband's brother by the father's side, he was tetrarch of Galilee; but her daughter Salome was married to Philip, the son of Herod, and tetrarch of Trachonitis; and as he died childless ...[423]

Right away we have a problem. Josephus says that Herodias was married to Herod II and their daughter, Salome, married Philip. But the Gospel of Mark says that Herodias herself was married to 'Philip.' This has led some NT scholars to propose that Herod II was actually also called Philip. Nikos Kokkinos, in his book *The Herodian Dynasty*, argues that it was Josephus who got it wrong: that Herodias was married to Philip, not Herod II, and that Antipas pursued the marriage with Herodias after Philip's death in 33/34 AD in order to acquire his territories. At this point, there are those who think the story of John the Baptist was interpolated into Mark, which might mean that it was invented later, utilizing Josephus as inspiration. That's quite possible. It is also possible that the author of Mark knew about John the Baptist without the intermediary of Josephus. Since so much of the Gospels and Acts are proven fiction via other analyses, I think we should stick with Josephus on the story of John the Baptist.

(Eisenbrauns 1989), pp. 133–64. This date was also earlier supported by Kirsopp Lake and Hugh Schonfield. (Thanks to Russell Gmirkin for pointing out this reference to me. See his forthcoming paper, 'The Arrest-Crucifixion Week of 36 CE.') According to this interpretation, John the Baptist would have begun his own career in 29 AD (Luke 3:1-2), baptized Jesus some years later, then was executed perhaps in 35 or 36 AD, followed by Jesus himself in 36 AD. If Kokkinos is correct, all this would prove is that the Gospel writers utilized Josephus as the source for their timeline, nesting Jesus' life in the events Josephus relates. But as we'll see, that doesn't solve the problems of how that chronology meshes with Paul's. It's also telling that in the earliest version of Luke's Gospel (Marcion's version) it wasn't John who began his ministry in 29 AD, but *Jesus himself*. So it looks as if the redactor of Luke changed it so that John began his ministry in 29 AD, thus allowing for a crucifixion in 36 AD.

[423] *Ant.* 18.5.4 (136).

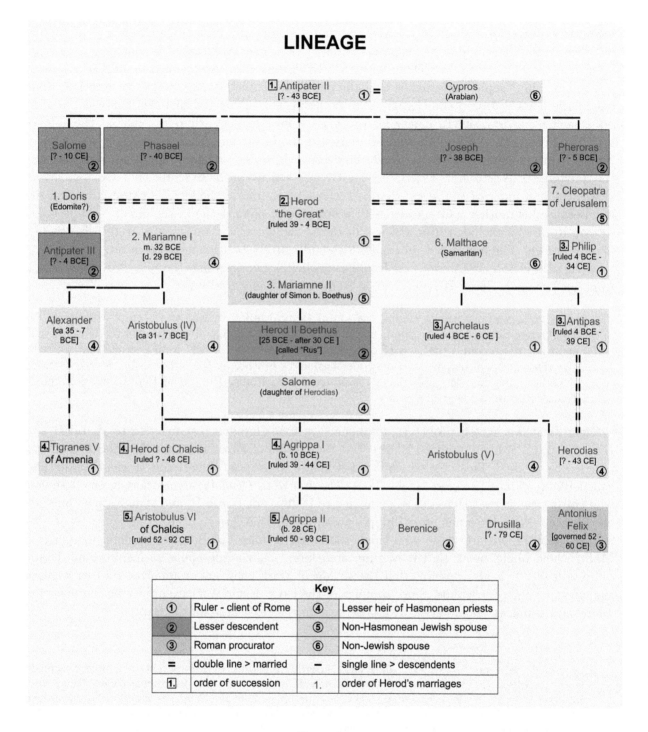

Figure 2.

So, let's pull on the thread a little and take a look at the story of Philip by Josephus:

About this time it was that Philip, Herod [Antipas]'s brother, departed this life, in the twentieth year of the reign of Tiberius [i.e. late 33 to 34 AD], after he had been tetrarch of Trachonitis and Gaulanitis, and of the nation of the Bataneans also, **thirty-seven years** [i.e. since 4/3 BC]. He had showed himself a person of moderation and quietness in the conduct of his life and government; he constantly lived in that country which was subject to him; ... He died at Julias; and when he was carried to that monument which he had already erected for himself beforehand, he was buried with great pomp. His principality Tiberius took, [for he left no sons behind him,] and added it to the province of Syria, but gave order that the tributes which arose from it should be collected, and laid up in his tetrarchy.[424]

This Philip was Philip the Tetrarch, the son of Herod the Great and Cleopatra of Jerusalem, who was one of his several wives. Philip was a half-brother of Herod Antipas and Herod Archelaus (whose mother was Herod's previous wife, Malthace), and of Herod II (mother: Mariamne II). Philip was married to his own niece, Salome, the daughter of Herod II and Herodias. This Salome – though she is not named[425] – is infamous for demanding and receiving the head of John the Baptist in the NT. However, according to both Mark and Matthew, 'Philip' was her father, not her husband.[426] Note that Josephus made no connection between Salome and John the Baptist.

If Kokkinos is correct in taking the value of the Gospels over Josephus here – a foolhardy proposition at best, an absurdity at worst – then Philip, the husband that Herodias wanted to divorce, would have died in 33/34 AD as described above, *before the proposed marriage of Herodias with Antipas*, which obviously would have eliminated the need for her to divorce him!

It is more probable that the Gospels are wrong, and perhaps the later Gospels of Matthew and Luke rely on Josephus. As Steve Mason puts it, "the standard hypothesis that Mark was in error is easy to accept, both because of numerous errors in Mark and because Matthew and Luke, which use Mark and frequently correct it, either hedge or omit the connection between Herodias and Philip (some MSS of Matt 14:3; Luke 3:20)."[427]

In any event, the *alleged* problems that arose between Aretas and Herod Antipas occurred around this time (i.e. between Philip's death in 33/34 AD and Aretas' in 40 AD). According to Campbell, the resulting mini-war between them would have resulted in Aretas' *temporary* rule over Damascus. That means that Campbell has to constrain his dating of Paul's story about being let down in a basket to escape the governor of King Aretas to that period. Placing Paul's flight from Damascus in late 36 AD would mean that Paul's call to be an apostle happened somewhere between late 33 AD and mid 34 AD. If the alleged crucifixion occurred somewhere in 29–33 AD, that would leave a period of anywhere from *less than a year* to perhaps five years for these events: visions of the risen Jesus, growth of the Jerusalem church, Paul's alleged persecution of said church, etc. Five years might be doable, but less than a year is way too tight. Also, as we've seen above, Aretas was more likely to have been in control of Damascus for the entire period, which leaves us with no chronological peg for Paul.[428]

---

[424] *Ant.* 18.4.6 (106–8).

[425] Some Greek manuscripts name her as Herodias.

[426] Mark 6:21-29; Matthew 14:6-11.

[427] Steve Mason, *Judean War 2: Translation and Commentary* (Brill, 2008), p. 155. As we'll see further on, there is strong evidence that much of Mark's narrative of John's death is interpolated.

[428] And if Kokkinos is correct in dating the Gospels' crucifixion to 36 AD, the problem is even worse, leaving two years at most before Paul's call, since the latest possible date of his call is in 38, two years before Aretas' death. This pushes Paul out of the window provided by Campbell completely, and with no basket to catch him!

Now, let's look at the story that *follows* the above passage about the modest, fair and quiet Philip, half-brother of Antipas, which we will see is the tale of Herod, Herodias and the *casus belli* between Aretas and Antipas. Notice that it begins with "about this time," referring back to the previous story about the death of Philip, i.e. the twentieth year of the reign of Tiberius, late 33 to 34 AD:

> About this time Aretas (the king of Arabia Petrea) and Herod [Antipas] had a quarrel on the account following: Herod the tetrarch had married the daughter of Aretas, and had lived with her a great while; but when he was once at Rome, he lodged with Herod [II], who was his brother indeed, but not by the same mother; for this Herod was the son of the high priest Simon's [Boethus] daughter [Mariamne II].
>
> However, he fell in love with Herodias, this last Herod's wife, who was the daughter of Aristobulus their brother [d. 7 BC], and the sister of Agrippa the Great.[429] This man ventured to talk to her about a marriage between them; which address when she admitted, an agreement was made for her to change her habitation, and come to him as soon as he should return from Rome; one article of this marriage also was this, that he should divorce Aretas's daughter.
>
> So Antipas, when he had made this agreement, sailed to Rome; but when he had done there the business he went about, and was returned again, his wife having discovered the agreement he had made with Herodias, and having learned it before he had notice of her knowledge of the whole design, she desired him to send her to Machaerus, which is a place in the borders of the dominions of Aretas and Herod,[430] without informing him of any of her intentions.
>
> Accordingly Herod sent her thither, as thinking his wife had not perceived anything; now she had sent a good while before to Machaerus, which was subject to her father and so all things necessary for her journey were made ready for her by the general of Aretas's army; and by that means she soon came into Arabia, under the conduct of the several generals, who carried her from one to another successively; and she soon came to her father, and told him of Herod's intentions.[431]

Note that Josephus seems to say that Machaerus was "subject to her father," i.e. Aretas. Elsewhere, he says that the fortress was passed to Herod Antipas on the death of Herod the Great (in 4 BC), and then passed to Agrippa I after Antipas' deposition and banishment in 39 AD, until 44 AD, at which point it came under Roman control. Josephus' other references to it include:

- *Wars* 1.8.2 (162): *"Machaerus, that lay upon the mountains of Arabia."*

---

[429] In short, the two Herods were both in love with their niece who carried the blood of the Hasmoneans through her father. Add to that the marriage of Philip to his niece, Salome, and one has a strange multiplication of uncle-niece marriages similar to that of Claudius and his niece Agrippina, who was one of the few remaining descendants of Augustus. It's often curious how the lives and affairs of the Herodians reflect the lives and affairs of the Julio-Claudian imperial family. Is it going too far to suggest that Josephus may have used the latter as a model? Or, perhaps, it was simply the way things were happening at the time.

[430] Check the map provided above. "Machaerus is a fortified hilltop palace located in Jordan fifteen miles (24 km) southeast of the mouth of the Jordan river on the eastern side of the Dead Sea. ... The ruins remain in remarkably untouched condition to this day. Archaeology reveals ... ruins of the Herodian palace, including rooms, a large courtyard, and an elaborate bath, with fragments of the floor mosaic still remaining [as well as an aqueduct]. ... Pottery found in the area extends from late Hellenistic to Roman periods and confirms the two main periods of occupation, namely, Hasmonean (90 BC–57 BC) and Herodian (30 BC–AD 72), with a brief reoccupation soon after AD 72 and then nothing further – so complete and systematic was the destruction visited upon the site by the Romans." (Wikipedia.org, 'Machaerus.')

[431] *Ant.* 18.5.1 (109–12).

- 1.16.6 (317), where, apparently, Machaerus is the name of one of the generals of the Romans under Ventidius Bassus, a protégé of Julius Caesar who later followed Antony.[432]

- 3.3.3 (46–7): "Now the length of Perea is from Machaerus to Pella, and its breadth from Philadelphia to Jordan; its northern parts are bounded by Pella, as we have already said, as well as its Western with Jordan; the land of Moab is its southern border, and its eastern limits reach to Arabia, and Silbonitis, and besides to Philadelphene and Gerasa." This places Machaerus *within* the southern borders of Perea (bordering Aretas' Nabataea to the south and east).

- 7.6.2 (172), where it is noted that *"it lay so near to Arabia."*

The point is, it is unlikely that Machaerus was subject to Aretas unless he had laid claim to it suddenly and this was the cause of the dispute. However, Josephus says that a border dispute in a different region, at the very northern tip of the Decapolis, was the true cause of the alleged set-to, as may be discerned in the next sentence:

> So Aretas made this the first occasion of his enmity between him and Herod, who had also some quarrel with him about their limits at the country of Gamalitis. So they raised armies on both sides, and prepared for war, and sent their generals to fight instead of themselves; and when they had joined battle, all Herod's army was destroyed by the treachery of some fugitives, who, though they were of the *tetrarchy of Philip*, joined with Aretas's army. So Herod wrote about these affairs to Tiberius, who being very angry at the attempt made by Aretas, wrote to Vitellius to make war upon him, and either to take him alive, and bring him to him in bonds, or to kill him, and send him his head. This was the charge that Tiberius gave to the president of Syria.

Notice that Philip *appears to be alive in the above paragraph*, so that would date the affair to before 34 AD when Vitellius was still serving as consul at Rome. Also, this Vitellius, 'president of Syria' during the reign of Tiberius, is rather problematic, as we will discover further on. It is curious that the penultimate sentence of the above passage contains "send him his head," considering all the ink (and paint) that has been spilled over the head of John the Baptist, who *immediately enters*, stage left:

> Now some of the Jews thought that the destruction of Herod's army came from God, and that very justly, as a punishment of what he did against John, that was called the Baptist: for Herod slew him, who was a good man, and commanded the Jews to exercise virtue, both as to righteousness towards one another, and piety towards God, and so to come to baptism; for that the washing [with water] would be acceptable to him, if they made use of it, not in order to the putting away [or the remission] of some sins [only], but for the purification of the body; supposing still that the soul was thoroughly purified beforehand by righteousness.
>
> Now when [many] others came in crowds about him, for they were very greatly moved [or pleased] by hearing his words, Herod, who feared lest the great influence John had over the people might put it into his power and inclination to raise a rebellion (for they seemed ready to do anything he should advise), thought it best, by putting him to death, to prevent any mischief he might cause, and not bring himself into difficulties, by sparing a man who might make him repent of it when it would be too late. Accordingly he was sent a prisoner, out of Herod's suspicious temper, **to Machaerus,**

---

[432]Plutarch, *Antony* 32–34.

the castle I before mentioned, and was there put to death. Now the Jews had an opinion that the destruction of this army was sent as a punishment upon Herod, and a mark of God's displeasure to him.[433]

Very odd. First we have the daughter of Aretas fleeing to the fortress of Machaerus, which was seemingly under the control of *her father*, then we have a flashback to John the Baptist being sent there for execution because the fortress belongs to *Antipas*. We have a demand to "send him his head" from Tiberius directed to Vitellius about Aretas (who would have been still in Rome if this was in 34, before Philip died), followed immediately by the appearance of John the Baptist. John gets executed, but it isn't said how. This is a very funny business. Keep in mind that we are supposed to be in the year 35/36 AD, which is impossible for the standard Jesus of Nazareth timeline, not to mention the problems of Philip and Vitellius.

Some scholars have suggested that the story of John the Baptist is an interpolation by a Christian scribe who screwed up badly by placing this story in the wrong time context. They argue that the text reads intelligibly if the John the Baptist passage is removed.

I would like to draw attention to this: "Now some of the Jews thought that the destruction of Herod's army came from God," and compare it to the last sentence of the last paragraph above: "Now the Jews had an opinion that the destruction of this army was sent as a punishment upon Herod, and a mark of God's displeasure to him." This is a clear *inclusio* and draws our attention to the passage thus bracketed. Now, if we exclude the Baptist text, we have the following:

> So Herod wrote about these affairs to Tiberius, who being very angry at the attempt made by Aretas, wrote to Vitellius to make war upon him, and either to take him alive, and bring him to him in bonds, or to kill him, and send him his head. This was the charge that Tiberius gave to the president of Syria. [Baptist diversion]
> So Vitellius prepared to make war with Aretas ...

Obviously, an inclusio *does not have to set off an interpolation*. I've done plenty of writing, and when I diverge off the main topic I generally write something to bring the reader's attention back to the main topic when I return to it. The problem is that there are many, many passages in Josephus like this, where he goes off to the side and discusses something that relates peripherally (or not at all!) and then gets back on track by drawing the reader's attention to the fact that he is doing so. Also, I've read Josephus cover to cover a few times and the language and style is entirely Josephan.

Another reason given to support the idea that the passage is an interpolation is the apparent error that Josephus makes when saying that Machaerus first belonged to Antipas and then to Aretas. Here is the passage again:

> Accordingly Herod sent her thither, as thinking his wife had not perceived anything; now she had sent a good while before to Machaerus, which was *subject to her father* and so all things necessary for her journey were made ready for her by the general of Aretas's army; and by that means she soon came into Arabia, under the conduct of the several generals, who carried her from one to another successively; and she soon came to her father, and told him of Herod's intentions.[434]

---

[433] *Ant.* 18.5.1–2 (113–9).
[434] *Ant.* 18.5.1 (109–12).

I did some research on this problem and found an article by Peter Kirby[435] that goes through all the reasons given by scholars that the passage is interpolated, and convincingly argues for authenticity of the passage. Regarding the Machaerus problem, Kirby writes:

> This consideration would actually be probative, if what Josephus had written before had implied that the castle of Macherus did not belong to Herod. That is not, however, what the Greek manuscripts state; it is found only later in the printed editions.
>
> F. F. Bruce, Andrew Criddle, and a previous post of mine on *A Conjectural Corruption of Josephus* reference what is actually found in the manuscripts of Josephus here: not "to Machaerus, which was at that time subject to her father" ... but rather "to Machaerus and to him who was subject to her father" ... More than a century ago, S. Sollertinsky made similar observations regarding this passage ('The Death of St. John the Baptist' in *The Journal of Theological Studies*, vol. 1, pp. 514-515):
>
>> "But Ewald ... has shown that the word ['was subject'] refers not to Macherus but to the officer who met the daughter of Aretas there. Indeed Volkmar might have asked himself why the daughter of Aretas should request Herod's permission to go to Machaerus, instead of to her father, if the fortress belonged to him: or how, in asking permission, she should conceal her intention of going to her father. The whole proceeding only becomes intelligible if it is the idea of an honourable retreat which Josephus means to ascribe to her."
>
> This should be regarded as the reading of Josephus, so the argument that the John the Baptist passage contradicts an earlier statement of Josephus regarding Macherus does not hold up.[436]

Another objection to the passage is the claim that Josephus would never have claimed that Herod would have been punished by God for his unjust treatment of John the Baptist. But actually, that is not what Josephus says. He noted that it was "some of the Jews" who thought that.[437] A few paragraphs later we see what Josephus actually thought about the whole affair: "And thus did God punish Herodias for her envy at her brother, and Herod also for giving ear to the vain discourses of a woman."[438]

Another charge made against the authenticity of the passage is that Josephus never mentions it in *Wars*. There are quite a few things that Josephus did not mention in *Wars* that he wrote about in *Antiquities*. As already discussed, Josephus was so busy exculpating himself, the Romans and the rank and file of Jews (to some extent) and loading all the blame for the war on a scapegoat, Judas the Galilean, the Zealots, robbers, brigands, etc., that he didn't dare to cover some topics as he would have liked to, considering his own previous affiliations. Only later, in *Antiquities*, did he apparently feel comfortable enough to ease up the iron control he had held over his tongue and pen when writing *Wars*. Keep in mind, at the time it was truly a life or death problem. I suspect that the story of John the Baptist was just such a tale that he felt might have been dangerous to his chosen political stance with the first volume, but was of little significance almost 20 years later (93/94 AD).

But there is actually something about this passage that is a bit more problematical: Josephus makes no mention of this little war between Aretas and Antipas in *Wars*, nor does he even mention

---

[435]Kirby is an agnostic. See: http://peterkirby.com/my-story.html.
[436]http://peterkirby.com/john-the-baptist-authentic.html.
[437]*Ant.* 18.5.2.
[438]*Ant.* 18.7.2.

Lucius Vitellius, the governor of Syria, though he makes numerous references to Vitellius the son and temporary emperor.

So, is this simply a story made up by Josephus to smear Aretas, King of the Nabataeans, and Herod Antipas? Since Vitellius has been implicated in the affair by Josephus, I think we need to pull on that thread.

Lucius Vitellius

Most of the information that is regularly repeated about Vitellius, mentioned above, actually *comes from Josephus* and therefore, in my opinion, must be scrutinized carefully.

Both Tacitus (*Ann.* 6.28) and Dio Cassius (58.24.1) confirm that, in the 20th year of Tiberius, 34 AD, the consuls were Lucius Vitellius and Fabius Persicus.[439] In the *following* year, *35 AD*, Dio records the Parthian King Artabanus' putsch for power in the East, which was resisted by local chieftains who sent to Tiberius to ask for a king from among their hostages at Rome to replace Artabanus.[440] Tiberius sent Tiridates to take the throne, asking Mithridates of Iberia to invade Armenia, thus drawing Artabanus to leave Parthia in order to assist his son in Armenia.

Tacitus, too, notes that, *in 35 AD*, Tiberius put L. Vitellius in charge of sorting out the Artabanus/Tiridates/Mithridates business, as *Vitellius was governor of Syria,* his proconsular assignment/reward.[441] We can assume that Vitellius headed out for his post in spring of 35, and the events took place in 35–36 AD. However, of any upset with the Arabs or Aretas, *the witnesses external to Josephus make no mention* and one can hardly imagine Tiberius being concerned with a border dispute between Aretas and Herod Antipas while the Parthians were on the warpath.

Regarding the Arabs, there is one tiny remark in Tacitus in the context of the above mission to deal with Artabanus we may make note of:

> Yet the withdrawal [of Tiridates, the Roman candidate, to Mesopotamia] had every appearance of flight; and, a start having been made by the race of the Arabs, the others left for their homes or for the camp of Artabanus, until Tiridates' own return to Syria with a few men provided a general redemption from the disgrace of desertion.[442]

Now, these Arabs are not *necessarily* Nabataean. Strabo points out that aside from the Arabs there, others occupied parts of Mesopotamia: the Scenitae (tent-dwellers), for example.[443] So it could be a reference to them. But on the chance that it refers to Nabataeans, it suggests that in the years 35, 36 AD, while Vitellius was governor of Syria, they were involved *on the side of the Romans in the action against Artabanus.* Tacitus, after all, may be talking about *forces sent by King Aretas to support the Romans' intention to install Tiridates.* While Josephus claims that the Aretas–Antipas war took place after the Artabanus situation was resolved, the possibility that the Arabs were just previously fighting on the side of the Romans makes it unlikely for them to have then dallied about with Antipas over a border dispute or a daughter scorned on

---

[439]Tiberius' reign was counted from August 19, 14 AD. So, for example, Tacitus could refer to the start of the year 23 AD as occurring in the "ninth year of Tiberius" (*Ann.* 4.1). So also Pliny the Elder (*NH* 33.8) and Philo (*Leg.* 21).

[440]Dio 58.26.

[441]Tacitus, *Ann.* 6.31–7. All citations of his *Annales* refer to A. J. Woodman's translation (Hackett, 2004).

[442]Tacitus, *Ann.* 6.44.5.

[443]Strabo 16.3.1 (765). Thanks to Russell Gmirkin for pointing this reference out to me.

the receiving end of Roman military might. If so, we can only conclude that, for some reason, Josephus is novelizing here. Compare the Tacitean statement about the presence of the Arab forces with the Romans in *Parthia* above with Josephus' historical fiction below:

> So Vitellius prepared to make war with Aretas, having with him two legions of armed men; he also took with him all those of light armature, and of the horsemen which belonged to them, and were drawn out of those kingdoms which were under the Romans, and made haste for Petra, and came to Ptolemais. But as he was marching very busily, and leading his army through Judea, the principal men met him, and desired that he would not thus march through their land; for that the laws of their country would not permit them to overlook those images which were brought into it, of which there were a great many in their ensigns; so he was persuaded by what they said, and changed that resolution of his which he had before taken in this matter. Whereupon he ordered the army to march along the great plain, while he himself, with Herod [Antipas] the tetrarch and his friends, went up to Jerusalem to offer sacrifice to God, an ancient festival of the Jews being then just approaching; and when he had been there, and been honorably entertained by the multitude of the Jews, he made a stay there for three days, within which time he deprived Jonathan of the high priesthood, and gave it to his brother Theophilus. But when on the fourth day letters came to him, which informed him of the death of Tiberius [March 16, 37 AD],he obliged the multitude to take an oath of fidelity to Caius [Caligula]; he also recalled his army, and made them every one go home, and take their winter quarters there, since, upon the devolution of the empire upon Caius, he had not the like authority of making this war which he had before.
>
> It was also reported, that when Aretas heard of the coming of Vitellius to fight him, he said, upon his consulting the diviners, that it was impossible that this army of Vitellius's could enter Petra; for that one of the rulers would die, either he that gave orders for the war, or he that was marching at the other's desire, in order to be subservient to his will, or else he against whom this army is prepared. So Vitellius truly retired to Antioch; but Agrippa, the son of Aristobulus, went up to Rome, a year before the death of Tiberius, in order to treat of some affairs with the emperor, if he might be permitted so to do.[444]

I think anyone with two firing neurons can see what a load of nonsense the text above actually is, especially if it was developed from the bare facts of the war between Tiridates and Artabanus to which the Arabs contributed troops in support of Rome. One can hardly imagine Vitellius acceding to the request to send his troops around by another way because the fastidious Jews couldn't bear to look on the Roman standards, since Roman standards were everywhere in Judea, excepting only within the city of Jerusalem. Notice also how glibly Josephus gets him off the hook about a war that probably never happened: he was no longer authorized, so he sent his soldiers into winter quarters. What is actually astounding is that any sensible individual has ever taken this tale seriously. As for the rest of the story, Josephus is the most astonishingly unapologetic embellisher and novelizer, so it is entirely in keeping for him to have spun the above tale just so he could put the Jews and their customs in a good light.[445]

I think we must decline to accept this story of Vitellius being sent to take the head of Aretas as factual, and thus it offers us no possibility of utilizing it to date the time the Apostle Paul was let

---

[444] *Ant.* 18.5.3 (120–6).

[445] Just as he did with Alexander the Great, fabricating a visit to Jerusalem that never happened (and couldn't have) in which he visits the Temple, offers up a sacrifice to the Jewish god, and reads from the book of Daniel. This after having Alexander fall upon his face before the Ineffable Name on the High Priest's headdress and say, "This man ... I beheld in a dream when I was in Macedon; and I know that his God will give me victory over my foes." See Victor Tcherikover, *Hellenistic Civilization and the Jews* (Hendrickson, 1999 [1959]), pp. 43–5.

down in a basket from the walls of Damascus while fleeing from the agents of King Aretas, who Douglas Campbell assumes only had a narrow window of rulership there while being in conflict with Antipas.

As Campbell writes in his paper on the dating of Paul's escape from Damascus, "One avenue for undermining this explanation [i.e. dating Paul's escape to a possible temporary takeover of Damascus by Aretas during the alleged war with Antipas] is to criticize [Josephus'] veracity."[446] And: "So unless Josephus' account is a tissue of fabrications (but nevertheless neatly stitched together...), he ought to be followed."[447]

Well, yes. We must criticize Josephus' veracity and point out that a lot of his 'history' recounted in *Antiquities* is a 'tissue of lies,' including – most likely – this incident that persuades Campbell that Josephus "ought to be followed."

There's one final problem with Campbell's theory. According to Josephus, the reason Aretas is able to defeat Antipas is because the governor of Syria, Vitellius, delays bringing his aid to Antipas, aid he was instructed by Tiberius to provide; but then Tiberius died in 37 AD, so Vitellius was off the hook, never mind that he had actually been sent to deal with Artabanus. Elsewhere, Josephus provides the 'character motivation' for Vitellius' actions: *that Vitellius successfully negotiated an agreement with the Parthian leader Artabanus, with the help of Antipas, in 36 AD.* But Antipas then upstaged Vitellius by reporting the success to Tiberius first.[448] This is supposed to explain why Vitellius was so reluctant to come to Antipas' aid when Aretas attacked: he held a grudge. So, it is here where the Artabanus issue comes to the fore and it cannot be avoided if we hope to make sense of the whole mess.

The Artabanus Mystery

The question we need to answer is this: did these negotiations described by Josephus actually take place as described, and if so, when? Douglas Campbell writes about the alleged attack of Aretas on Antipas:

> ... the date of the successful attack by Aretas on Antipas and his territories opens the chronological window, so to speak, within which Paul's escape from Damascus can be anchored. Several considerations allow us to date the invasion, and the opening of the window with reasonable precision to the year 36 CE. ...
>
> In the same year as the invasion, Vitellius had presided over a great diplomatic triumph – a successful negotiation of peace with the dreaded Parthian Empire currently gathering in strength under the leadership of the formidable Artabanus. Antipas had played a minor role in these negotiations, having been charged with managing and financing them. However, he had also taken the liberty of writing to the imperial court with a glowing account of their success prior to Vitellius's own report being written and dispatched, and had thereby upstaged Vitellius at the moment of his greatest political triumph (*Jewish Antiquities* 18.96–105).[449]

Campbell offers a footnote to the above text as follows:

---

[446] Campbell (2002), p. 287, n. 26.
[447] Campbell (2002), p. 293, n. 42.
[448] *Ant.* 18.4.5 (104–5).
[449] Campbell (2002), p. 184–85.

This important negotiation is also noted by Tacitus, *Ann.* 2.58 (although the year is far too early – 18 CE); Suetonius, *Gaius Caligula* 14.3 and *Vitellius* 2.4 (who locates the negotiation slightly more accurately during the reign of Gaius); and Cassius Dio 59.27.3–4 (who also locates it during the reign of Gaius). Josephus is certainly correct, however, in placing it where he does, in 36 CE the last year of Tiberius's reign. His intertwined chronologies of Pilate, Vitellius, and Antipas only make sense here, and yet here they make perfect sense.[450]

I can only shake my head in wonder at the will to believe nonsense. Let's take a look at Josephus' version of the Artabanus story which persuades Campbell that Tacitus is all mixed up:

Moreover, Tiberius sent a letter to Vitellius, and commanded him to make a league of friendship with Artabanus, the king of Parthia; for while he was his enemy, he terrified him, because he had taken Armenia away from him, lest he should proceed further, and told him he should not otherwise trust him than upon his giving him hostages, and especially his son Artabanus. Upon Tiberius's writing thus to Vitellius, by the offer of great presents of money, he persuaded both the king of Iberia and the king of Albania to make no delay, but to fight against Artabanus; and although they would not do it themselves, yet did they give the Scythians a passage through their country, and opened the Caspian gates to them, and brought them upon Artabanus.

So Armenia was again taken from the Parthians, and the country of Parthia was filled with war, and the principal of their men were slain, and all things were in disorder among them: the king's son also himself fell in these wars, together with many ten thousands of his army. Vitellius had also sent such great sums of money to Artabanus's father's kinsmen and friends that he had almost procured him to be slain by the means of those bribes which they had taken. And when Artabanus perceived that the plot laid against him was not to be avoided, because it was laid by the principal men, and those a great many in number, and that it would certainly take effect,—when he had estimated the number of those that were truly faithful to him, as also of those who were already corrupted, but were deceitful in the kindness they professed to him, and were likely, upon trial, to go over to his enemies, he [Artabanus] made his escape to the upper provinces, where he afterwards raised a great army out of the Dahae and Sacre, and fought with his enemies, and retained his principality.

When Tiberius had heard of these things, he desired to have a league of friendship made between him and Artabanus; and when, upon this invitation, he received the proposal kindly, Artabanus and Vitellius went to Euphrates, and as a bridge was laid over the river, they each of them came with their guards about them, and met one another on the midst of the bridge. And when they had agreed upon the terms of peace Herod [Antipas], the tetrarch[451] erected a rich tent on the midst of the passage, and made them a feast there. Artabanus also, not long afterward, sent his son Darius as an hostage, with many presents, among which there was a man seven cubits tall, a Jew he was by birth, and his name was Eleazar, who, for his tallness, was called a giant.

After which Vitellius went to Antioch, and Artabanus to Babylon; but Herod [Antipas] being desirous to give Caesar [Tiberius] the first information that they had obtained hostages, sent posts with letters, wherein he had accurately described all the particulars, and had left nothing for the consular Vitellius to inform him of. But when Vitellius's letters were sent, and [Tiberius] had let him know that he was acquainted with the affairs already, because Herod had given him an account of them before, Vitellius was very much troubled at it; and supposing that he had been thereby a greater sufferer than he really was, he kept up a secret anger upon this occasion, till he could be revenged on him, which he was after Caius had taken the government.[452]

---

[450]Campbell (2002), p. 185, n. 58.
[451]This is the Herod Antipas who was married to the daughter of Aretas and was, allegedly, plotting to ditch her and marry Herodias, the wife of Herod II.
[452]*Ant.* 18.4.4–5 (96).

Aside from the implausibility of Josephus having access to the thoughts of Vitellius, we note that the "secret anger" seems to reflect Josephus' character more than that of Vitellius. It is completely juvenile, though it is not impossible that it screens and/or misinterprets a historical reality.

Suetonius mentions Artabanus in his biography of Tiberius as follows:

> ... he was even attacked by Artabanus, king of the Parthians, who charged him in a letter with the murder of his kindred, with other bloody deeds, and with shameless and dissolute living, counselling him to gratify the intense and just hatred of the citizens as soon as possible by a voluntary death.[453]

There was no love lost between Artabanus and the Roman Emperor, so the idea of Tiberius wanting to make a pact with the guy who has just told him to off himself is absurd. Then, in his biography of Gaius Caligula, Suetonius writes:

> To this unbounded love of his [Caligula's] citizens was added marked devotion from foreigners. **Artabanus, for example, king of the Parthians, who was always outspoken in his hatred and contempt for Tiberius, voluntarily sought Caligula's** friendship and came to a conference with the consular governor; then crossing the Euphrates, he paid homage to the Roman eagles and standards and to the statues of the Caesars.[454]

Yet Josephus tells us that Tiberius instructed Vitellius to make peace with Artabanus! For some reason, between the time of Artabanus' advice that Tiberius should kill himself, and the accession of Caligula, something had changed; obviously, it wasn't the office of emperor, but who occupied that office. The same event was mentioned by Suetonius in his biography of Emperor Vitellius (the son of our Vitellius):

> Lucius [Vitellius] attained the consulate and then was made governor of Syria, where with supreme diplomacy having not only induced Artabanus, king of the Parthians, to hold a conference with him, but even to do obeisance to the standards of the legion.[455]

Suetonius firmly dates this meeting between Artabanus and Vitellius to the reign of *Gaius Caligula*. We notice also that Vitellius is credited with "supreme diplomacy." But we have already noted that Campbell is determined to give Josephus priority of accuracy and says about Suetonius that he "locates the negotiation *slightly* more accurately during the reign of Gaius [Caligula]." Suetonius hints at other dealings with Artabanus in the excerpt from the biography of Caligula, so we have to look a bit harder to find what it might be. In his account of the death of Germanicus (Tiberius' heir) – in 19 AD! – we find:

> Yet far greater and stronger tokens of regard were shown at the time of his [Germanicus'] death and immediately afterwards. On the day when he passed away the temples were stoned and the altars of the gods thrown down, while some flung their household gods into the street and cast out their newly born children. Even barbarian peoples, so they say, who were engaged in war with us or with one another, unanimously consented to a truce, as if all in common had suffered a domestic tragedy. It is said that some princes put off their beards and had their wives' heads shaved, as a

---

[453]Suetonius, *Tiberius* 66.
[454]Suetonius, *Caligula* 14.3.
[455]Suetonius, *Vitellius* 2.4.

token of the deepest mourning; that even the king of kings suspended his exercise at hunting and the banquets with his grandees, which among the Parthians is a sign of public mourning.[456]

So, it seems that at the time Germanicus died, 19 AD, the king of the Parthians was a lover of the Romans, but for some reason, after the death of Germanicus, a whole lot of enmity had grown up between the two heads of state. Notice that in his letter to Tiberius, Artabanus, king of the Parthians, charged him with the "murder of his kindred." And the student of Roman history knows well that Tiberius was widely believed to have masterminded the death of his heir, Germanicus. It seems obvious that this was why Artabanus came to hate Tiberius and suggested that he should do everyone a favor by putting a period to his existence.[457]

Dio Cassius mentions these events in retrospect during his account of the events of 40 AD, but does not date them explicitly:

> The case of Lucius Vitellius is in point. This man was neither of low birth nor lacking in intelligence, but, on the contrary, had made a name for himself by his governorship of Syria. For, in addition to his other brilliant achievements during his term of office, he forestalled Artabanus, who was planning an attack on that province also, since he had suffered no punishment for his invasion of Armenia. He terrified the Parthian by coming upon him suddenly when he was already close to the Euphrates, and then induced him to come to a conference, compelled him to sacrifice to the images of Augustus and **Gaius [Caligula]**, and made a peace with him that was advantageous to the Romans, even securing his sons as hostages. This Vitellius, now, was summoned by Gaius to be put to death. The complaint against him was the same as the Parthians had against their king when they expelled him; for jealousy made him the object of hatred, and fear the object of plots. Gaius, of course, hated all who were stronger than himself, and he was suspicious of all who were successful, feeling sure that they would attack him. Yet Vitellius managed to save his life.[458]

Again we are told that Vitellius achieved a diplomatic coup and *it wasn't in the time of Tiberius* – **it was in the reign of Gaius!** Despite the testimony of these less contentious historians, Campbell notes that Dio "also locates it during the reign of Gaius" and then goes on to make the completely astonishing claim: "Josephus is certainly correct, however, in placing it where he does, in 36 AD, the last year of Tiberius's reign. His intertwined chronologies of Pilate, Vitellius, and Antipas only make sense here, and yet here they make perfect sense." Just jaw-dropping.

Regarding Campbell's footnote, where he says initially, "This important negotiation is also noted by Tacitus, *Ann.* 2.58 (although the year is far too early – 18 AD)," I have to point out that this is completely disingenuous, assuming that Campbell has read *all* of Tacitus. With the data bits we have collected thus far, it is clear that this mystery will only be solved if we widen our investigation a bit. We need to go back to the beginning.

Tacitus gives a rather detailed account of the Artabanus saga *starting in 16 AD*, when legates from the Parthian chiefs came to Rome to fetch Vonones (the eldest son of the by now long-deceased Parthian king Phraates), who had been sent to Augustus as hostage to be brought up in the imperial court. Apparently, once he got to Parthia, the people there decided they didn't

---

[456]Suetonius, *Caligula* 5.

[457]The king of the Parthians is also mentioned in the *Life of Nero*, but in a context that is not really relevant to our topic. Just note that Nero was, apparently, a great favorite among the Parthians too, according to Suetonius.

[458]Dio 59.27.2–4.

like him because his ways were too Romanized. This is where Artabanus first enters the picture, *twenty years before Vitellius was sent to bring him to heel.* He was of Parthian royal blood also, as was the rejected Vonones, but Artabanus had grown up among the Dahae, probably a Scythian tribe. He took control of the kingdom, and the former Roman hostage and king elect, Vonones, and his band fled to Armenia, which was a hotbed of rebellion and unrest. They were kingless at that moment, so Vonones the refugee was put on the throne as king of Armenia.

Shortly thereafter, Artabanus started saber rattling against Vonones and the Armenians didn't want to support a war, so Vonones was taken into protective custody by the governor of Syria, Q. Caecilius Metellus Creticus Silanus (cos. 7 AD). Tacitus says that it was this disruption out in the East that Tiberius used as an excuse to take Germanicus away from his faithful legions and install him in new provinces where he was not so well known.[459]

In the following year, 17 AD, Tiberius removed Creticus Silanus from Syria "because he was connected to Germanicus by marriage," and installed Gnaeus Calpurnius Piso (cos. 7 BC), described as "temperamentally violent and a stranger to compliance," as legate to Germanicus and governor of Syria. Though both he and Germanicus were of equal rank, Germanicus had greater authority. Tacitus suggests that Piso was appointed to act as a check on Germanicus, and that he was given secret instructions by Tiberius to thwart and control him.[460] We don't know if that is true; nevertheless, that is what Piso actually *did* and it seems unlikely that he would have done so under the circumstances if he had not felt confidence that Tiberius would support him. Piso and Germanicus finally met at Cyrrhus, the winter camp of the Tenth Legion. They hated each other. And this is where we also find our Aretas mentioned, though not by name:

> After this, Piso was rarely on [Germanicus] Caesar's tribunal and, on the few occasions when he sat by him, was glowering and openly dissenting. And during a party **at the residence of the Nabataeans' king, when golden crowns of considerable weight were offered to [Germanicus] and Agrippina**, and lighter ones to Piso and the rest, his [Piso's] voice was heard saying that the banquet was being given for the son of the Roman princeps, not that of the Parthian king; and at the same time he flung away his crown ...
>
> During these events, **legates came from the king of the Parthians, Artabanus.** He had sent them to recall the treaty of friendship, and he desired the pledges to be renewed, he said, and as **a concession to Germanicus' honor he would advance to the bank of the Euphrates;** meanwhile he was asking that Vonones should not be kept in Syria nor use messengers from nearby to draw the aristocrats of the various races into discord. To this Germanicus replied handsomely concerning the alliance of Romans and Parthians, and with decorum and modesty concerning the arrival of the king and his courting of himself. Vonones was removed to Pompeiopolis, a maritime city in Cilicia: this was not only a concession to the plea of Artabanus, but an insult for Piso, by whom he [Vonones] was extremely favored on account of the very many duties and gifts with which he had bound Plancina [Piso's wife] to himself.[461]

In the above account, it seems obvious that there was mutual respect between Germanicus and Artabanus and it was Germanicus who acted diplomatically toward the Parthian king, engaging his friendship and acceding to his request. We also notice that **the two met at the**

---

[459]Tacitus, *Ann.* 2.1—5.2.
[460]Tacitus, *Ann.* 2.43.2.
[461]Tacitus, *Ann.* 2.57.3—58.2.

Euphrates river in 18 AD for the renewal of pledges. (This is echoed in Dio's account of the later meeting between Vitellius and Artabanus during the reign of Gaius. Suetonius and Dio both mention such talks, but don't specify that they took place on the Euphrates, though Dio mentions that Vitellius surprised Artabanus close to the river.) This apparent friendship between Germanicus and Artabanus might explain why Artabanus conceived so great a hatred for Tiberius after the death of Germanicus. It was widely thought that Tiberius was implicated in the poisoning of his nephew/adopted son and we have already read how the 'king of kings' mourned the death of his friend.

In the summer of 19 AD, Germanicus traveled to Egypt for a Nile cruise. While he was absent, things started going south back in the Syrian area thanks to the maneuvers of Piso.

> During the same period Vonones, whose removal to Cilicia I have recalled, after bribing his guards tried to flee to the Armenians and thence to ... his kinsman, the king of the Scythians. ... So it was on the bank of the river that he was bound by Vibius Fronto, prefect of the cavalry; then Remmius, a senior soldier who had been assigned to the king's guard previously, transfixed him with a sword as if in anger. ... As for Germanicus, on retiring from Egypt he realized that everything which he had ordered in the cases of the legions and cities had been annulled or changed to the opposite. Hence weighty insults for Piso ... Next Piso decided to leave Syria ... but was detained by Germanicus' adverse health ...[462]

We will skip the death of Germanicus later in 19 AD for the moment and jump forward to 35 AD where Artabanus appears again in the *Annals* of Tacitus as a retrospective digression, disingenuously omitted by Campbell:

> With C. Cestius and M. Servilius as consuls [35 AD], Parthian nobles came to the City without the knowledge of King Artabanus. (**His dread of Germanicus meant that he had been loyal to the Romans** and fair toward his own; but *later* he adopted haughtiness toward us and savagery toward his compatriots, relying on the successful wars which he had waged against surrounding nations, **despising Tiberius'** old age as defenseless, and being greedy for Armenia, where on the decease of King Artaxias he installed Arsaces, the eldest of his own children; and as an additional insult sending men to demand back the treasure left by Vonones in Syria and Cilicia. At the same time he resorted to foolish boasting and to threats, bragging of the old boundaries of the Persians and Macedonians and that he would invade the lands once possessed by Cyrus and later by Alexander.)[463]

This is about 17 years after the initial Tacitean discussion of Artabanus and his treaty with Germanicus at the Euphrates River, which did actually take place in 18 AD. There is some reflection in this description here of what Suetonius recorded about the hate mail Artabanus allegedly sent to Tiberius: "despising Tiberius' old age as defenseless." Tacitus does mention the respect that Artabanus had for Germanicus, but ascribes it to fear of the latter's military prowess, not his diplomatic skills. In any event, at this point, the Parthian nobles came (yet again) to ask for a king to replace Artabanus; they wanted another of the sons of Phraates, who was also named Phraates. This son (who probably learned from the mistakes of Vonones) was able to shed his Roman ways, but he died from disease in Syria before he was put on the Parthian

---

[462]Tacitus, *Ann.* 2.68–69.
[463]Tacitus, *Ann.* 6.31.

throne. In other words, what was going on here was meddling by Tiberius in the affairs of the Parthians, not seeking a rapprochement as Josephus writes in his account.

Tiberius, not to be denied his power of picking kings (and certainly aiming to aggravate Artabanus), selected Tiridates, Phraates IV's grandson, sent him out east, and ordered Vitellius to be in charge of the preparations to eliminate the recalcitrant Artabanus and put the new king on the throne. There was a lot of to-ing and fro-ing of a warlike nature, which Tacitus describes in some detail, and far more reliably than Josephus, and then Artabanus was rejected by his own people, becoming a fugitive. It is at this point that Vitellius has the famous meeting at the banks of the river and the offering of sacrifices to seal the deal.

> But, with Artabanus a fugitive and the minds of his compatriots turning toward a new king, Vitellius urged Tiridates to capitalize on his preparations and led the hard core of his legions and allies to the bank of the Euphrates. During their sacrifices – since the one was offering the *suovetaurilia*[464] in the Roman manner, the other had decorated a horse for placating the stream – locals announced that without any violent rain the Euphrates was rising of its own accord to an inordinate level and at the same time was coiling circles of white spray in the shape of a diadem – an augury of a favorable crossing. ...
>
> When a bridge had been made of ships and the army sent across, the first to arrive in the camp with many thousands of cavalry was Ornospades, at one time an exile and a not inglorious adjutant of Tiberius when he was finishing off the Dalmatian war, and for that reason presented with Roman citizenship; ... Vitellius, deeming that a show of Roman arms had been adequate, warned Tiridates and his chief: the former should remember Phraates his grandfather and his foster-father Caesar and the fine qualities in each of them; the latter should observe compliance toward their king, respect toward ourselves, and each his own honor and loyalty. *Thereupon he retired with his legions to Syria.*
>
> These achievements of *two seasons* I linked together to provide some mental respite from domestic afflictions.[465]

And so, we are at the end of the year 36 AD – two seasons' events being recounted in Tacitus *exactly in the time period where Josephus has Vitellius in Judea involved in an 'Aretas saga,'* which shows clearly that Campbell was not correct in saying that Tacitus only wrote about Artabanus in the wrong time frame; the Artabanus saga went on for years and years! In the above account, again, there is a big meeting and sacrifice at the river, but not a single mention of Herod Antipas and his influence on the negotiations that Josephus described with such delight.

It seems to me that Tacitus' detailed account is far more credible. We can note that there are certain elements that appear in both Josephus' account and Tacitus, though the usual spin-doctoring appears in the former. Josephus says Tiberius was afraid and that is why he sent Vitellius to make peace, while Tacitus says that Artabanus thought he could take advantage of an old man and Vitellius went to give him his comeuppance and depose him. Now, which does the knowledgeable reader think is most likely? The main difference is that the account of the second meeting of Romans and Parthians at the river, the sacrifices, and *who was involved* has changed. And of course, Josephus has a Jewish hero on the scene for good measure instead of the mention of the Dalmatian hero, Ornospades.[466]

---

[464]This sacrifice comprised a boar, a ram, and a bull. (Original footnote to the text by Woodman.)

[465]Tacitus, *Ann.* 6.37.1—38.1.

[466]One gets a crazy vertiginous sensation that Josephus' account of these events relies on Tacitus, even though we know that Tacitus published some years after Josephus. Perhaps they relied on similar sources, which Josephus proceeded to mangle.

We find confirmation in Philo that Vitellius did, indeed, go to Jerusalem *after* his successful conclusion of the Artabanus adventure *in 37 AD*: "*When Gaius assumed the imperial power* we were the first people in all Syria to congratulate him, Vitellius *at that time* being in our city, from whom you [Petronius] received the government as his successor."[467]

Tacitus also mentions a *third* encounter with the Parthians of a similar sort dated to 49 AD.[468] In this later Vitellius affair, during the reign of Claudius, we find a mention of the king of the Arabs, *Acbarus*, who apparently was on good-enough terms with Rome to provide support, though Tacitus does suggest that the Arabs were fickle in coming through on their military commitments and at the first possibility would withdraw and head for home, *recalling the actions of the (unspecified) Arabs at the time of the 35/36 AD interaction.*

To recap: Tacitus places negotiations between *Germanicus* and Artabanus on the banks of the Euphrates early in the reign of Tiberius (18 AD). Josephus, Suetonius and Dio don't mention this earlier Artabanus appearance, only the later one involving Vitellius. Josephus novelizes the events that occurred late in the reign of Tiberius (36 AD), and Suetonius discusses the similar event that occurred in the reign of Caligula (39 AD). Tacitus *also* discusses Vitellius' later actions in Syria and against Artabanus in some detail. However, his narrative ends with Artabanus a fugitive, no grand negotiations, though there was a great meeting with *Tiridates* and sacrifice at the river, the boats forming a bridge over which the army crossed, and a significant portent.

These are obviously separate events: the early truce between Germanicus and Artabanus, then a later one while Vitellius was still governor of Syria and *involving Tiridates*. Perhaps the earlier truce (18 AD) was later attributed to Vitellius in some sort of conflation of the different, but slightly similar, contexts. Josephus was novelizing freely and in full apologetic mode, including Antipas (whom he characterizes as being on very friendly terms with Tiberius) as a key player in the negotiations, thus also providing character motivation to his Vitellius *vis-à-vis* his refusal to help Antipas. In response to Campbell's absurd claim – "His intertwined chronologies of Pilate, Vitellius, and Antipas only make sense here, and yet here they make perfect sense" – let me just say it only 'works' because Josephus *makes* it work and *needs* it to work in order to satisfy his narrative demands! To get there, he had to borrow elements of events that happened earlier (18 AD) *and* later (after 39 AD) involving Artabanus, when the event of 36 AD actually involved Tiridates.

We notice also from Tacitus that in the time of Tiberius, Germanicus attended "a party at the residence of the Nabataeans' king," i.e. Aretas. *Later*, a king of the Arabs showed up in an allied context with Vitellius, so the overall tenor is that it is unlikely that the Romans were sent to get the head of Aretas. It's almost certain that Tacitus would have mentioned something like that with all the details he gives. The fact that Roman–Nabataean relations were so friendly at the time of Germanicus, and then, after Tiberius, during the reign of Caligula, would suggest that they remained so until (and after) the death of Aretas who, we must remember, in 36 AD was quite an old man. With such amicable relations, it is altogether likely that Damascus was, indeed, ruled by Aretas *throughout that time*. Campbell is wrong.

To sum up, when it comes to Josephus, it's best not to trust him as far as you can throw him. To quote Steve Mason again:

---

[467]Philo, *Legatio* 32 (231–2).
[468]Tacitus, *Ann.* 12.12 ff.

It is no less misguided to draw facts from Josephus than it would be to approach the screen at a showing of *Gladiator* and hope to reach out and touch a real character. ... His work may be relied upon to fulfill its own aims, but not as a window to real events.[469]

The same goes for Luke and Acts, and possibly Matthew, *which used Josephus as a source. If we want to determine the real conditions of early Christianity, we need to stick to the primary sources.*

On the subject of Paul's timeline, we now know that Campbell's anchor is no such thing. In a sense, we've been cast adrift. There is no evidence that Aretas *only gained control of Damascus in 36 AD for a brief moment in time; nor is there any evidence that he didn't control it in some way for his entire reign.* So we will leave Damascus in the hands of Aretas between 9 BC and 40 AD and free Paul from that cramped time window of the alleged conflict between Aretas and Herod Antipas over Herodias or a border dispute or both. The context Josephus provides for events of 36 AD regarding Antipas, Aretas, Vitellius, and Artabanus are clearly derived from the 18 AD event involving Germanicus and Artabanus, and the 39 AD event involving Gaius and Artabanus, when the event in 36 AD involved Vitellius and Tiridates.

So, we have caught Josephus red-handed: he has embellished at best, fabricated at worst. What we do know about various events of the times from more reliable historians, contrasted with his apologetic nonsense, inclines one to dismiss the breathlessly gossipy soap-opera elements of his 'history,' *in this case.*

But there is still the problem of John the Baptist, whose story was tucked up so nicely in Josephus' tale of Vitellius and Artabanus. The story of John the Baptist in the Gospels is a clear anachronism. For all we know, the event actually did take place in 35/36 AD, which would certainly leave John out of the Jesus story as presented in the Gospels.[470] If it was made up by Josephus, that's equally problematical for the Gospels. Like so many mysteries of history, we may never know.

And with that, we can move on to our next mystery: Pontius Pilate and the early Christians.

---

[469]Mason (2009), pp. 40, 42.

[470]The messianic leader named Theudas by Josephus (A. J. 20.97-99), writes Lena Einhorn, "shares distinct characteristics with John the Baptist: Like John, Theudas gathered his followers by the river Jordan, and, like John, he was arrested by the authorities, and they 'cut off his head, and carried it to Jerusalem'. Curiously, although the names of dignitaries may differ, comparing the New Testament accounts with Josephus' accounts of the mid-40s to early 50s in several respects appears to be more productive than a comparison with his accounts of the 30s." Einhorn, 'Jesus and the "Egyptian Prophet,"' Society of Biblical Literature Annual Meeting, Chicago, Nov 17-20, 2012.

4. Pilate and the Testimonium Flavianum

We need to keep in mind as we go forward that, in the texts we have, the earliest mention of Pilate *in relation to a crucified Jesus* was actually in Mark's passion narrative, assuming that Mark was written more or less as we have it, shortly after the Jewish War following the triumph of Vespasian and Titus in 71 AD. The next mention is that of Josephus in his *Wars*, published about 75 AD, though there is only a contentious mention of the execution of Jesus; and then, the Roman historian Tacitus, in his *Annales*, published about 117 AD, specifically mentions Pilate in relation to the execution of 'Christus.' Of the early Christian documents we have, there are none that mention Pilate or even a historical Jesus until Ignatius of Antioch, whose letters may have been written or redacted by Polycarp in the mid-second century. I am not including the Gospel of Matthew here as a witness since Matthew (and later, Luke) absorbed and re-oriented Mark rather than writing an original text that can be considered a witness.

Pontius Pilate is the *chronological* hook for the entire Christian creation of Jesus of Nazareth. It has always been assumed that his presence in the Gospels is proof of their historicity. Further, the chronology has been tied to the statement in the Gospel of Luke that John the Baptist began his ministry in "the fifteenth year of Tiberius Caesar" (Luke 3:1). If Jesus began his ministry very shortly after, and was then tried and executed under Pontius Pilate, Pilate must have been governor at that time, so the logic goes. According to a remark in Josephus, he ended his term with the death of Tiberius, which we know occurred in 37 AD. Another remark in Josephus says Pilate was there for ten years, so it is simple! Count backwards from 37 AD and you have Pilate coming to Judea in 26/27 AD, and that gives you the window for the activities of Jesus, which began in or soon after the fifteenth year of Tiberius, i.e. 29 AD. It all fits so beautifully![471] Unfortunately, there are big problems with these conclusions.

The crucifixion of Jesus under the governorship of Pontius Pilate is considered a historical fact by almost universal consent. Bible scholar Bart Ehrman states that the crucifixion of Jesus on the orders of Pontius Pilate is the most certain fact about him.[472] John Dominic Crossan says that the crucifixion of Jesus is as certain as any historical fact can be.[473] Scholars may agree on the historicity of the crucifixion, but they differ considerably on the reasons and even the exact date, not to mention how historical the Gospels are in respect of whether or not Jesus really knew he was going to be crucified. Discussing this crucifixion of a Jesus under Pontius Pilate is a huge industry.

---

[471] Of course, there's the nagging problem of whether the Gospels can agree on whether that ministry was one year or three and whether Jesus was crucified in 29, 30, 32, 33 or 36 AD; not to mention that pesky John the Baptist not sticking to the schedule and dying in 35/36 when he's supposed to die in the very early days of Jesus' ministry, and before Jesus! Then there is the problem of the almost immediate conversion of Paul, who supposedly was a persecutor of the early 'church,' which hardly had time to form or grow or spread, and how to fit his chronology in with the chronology of Jesus and Pilate. It's really a mess and a large amount of ink has been spilled on it.

[472] Bart D. Ehrman, *A Brief Introduction to the New Testament* (2nd ed.; Oxford University Press, 2008), p. 136.

[473] John Dominic Crossan, *Jesus: A Revolutionary Biography* (HarperOne, 1995), p. 145.

One of the most historically egregious things that biblical scholars do is to derive hypothetical earlier texts from later ones, and then treat these imaginary documents as if they were real sources. Proper procedure would be to begin with possible sources that are proven to have existed before the Gospels. To construct a hypothetical 'early oral tradition' based on later texts, or worse, a mythical 'Q document,' is just simply circular reasoning. I think that many scholars engage in this kind of faulty reasoning because they just cannot accept that there is nothing 'behind' Paul that supports the Jesus of the Gospels and Acts.[474]

Another point: for a trained *scholar* to come right out and say that the existence of a Jewish wonder worker called Jesus, as depicted in the Gospels, for whose historical reality there is not a shred of evidence, is a more plausible *hypothesis* than a mythical cult figure created by human needs out of the heroic elements of various individuals following a well-understood mythicization process, just boggles the mind.

From a strictly methodological point of view, biblical scholarship – as a rule – does not meet the minimum norms of historical study. Indeed, there exists a non-zero possibility that a Jesus of Nazareth was real and lived and died at the place and time given in the Gospels, but serious and careful examination of the evidence does not give the statement even a minimum *probability*. That, of course, does not mean that there was not somebody – or several somebodies – in the general vicinity of the place and time doing something significant and whose lives and deeds were conflated following the standard mythicization process.

Part of this myth-creation process included selecting an appropriate time and place for the setting of the mythical life of the cult figure. It seems to me that the time of Pontius Pilate in Judea was selected for very important reasons regarding one element of the composite character, as we will see; that is, that Pilate actually did execute a significant personage exactly as reported by Tacitus, though without date or details. We have that from Tacitus and I don't think it was a later interpolation.

What I have discovered is that a close and careful study of Josephus suggests Pontius Pilate was *not* the governor of Judea from 27 to 37 AD, nor was he even there for ten years. I will argue that the text of Josephus indicates clearly that Pilate was sent to Judea upon the accession of Tiberius in 14/15 AD, and that he was there for only around five years – being censured at the time that Germanicus was sent to straighten out the affairs of the Syrian province as we have already discussed above, and recalled in disgrace shortly after. Later Christian redactors/copyists of the Josephan text noticed the problem – a conflict of chronologies – and sought to adjust things by adding governors to the reign of Augustus and a couple of very small but well-placed text adjustments regarding the chronology, which forced the already confused Josephan text into at least partial congruence with the Christian timeline.

There are actually more problems with the Josephan text than just the chronology of Pilate: as noted, Josephus was very busy confabulating and writing what he thought was good copy for Roman/Jewish apologetic purposes. He wrote *Wars* not only to justify his Flavian masters and scare the bejeebies out of anybody else who might think about rebelling against Rome, but also to depict the Jews themselves as victims of ideologues and demagogues, whom he refers to regularly as robbers, brigands, tyrants, pirates, and so forth. What he is busy trying to cover up

---

[474]I'm not saying that there is nothing behind Paul at all, just that there is nothing behind Paul that supports the Jesus story as told in the Gospels and Acts. It seems to all begin with Mark.

is the fact that *he was one of them*, only the strength of his convictions was less than skin deep. Historian E. Mary Smallwood writes:

> [Josephus] was conceited, not only about his own learning but also about the opinions held of him as commander both by the Galileans and by the Romans; he was guilty of shocking duplicity at Jotapata, saving himself by sacrifice of his companions; he was too naive to see how he stood condemned out of his own mouth for his conduct, and yet no words were too harsh when he was blackening his opponents; and after landing, however involuntarily, in the Roman camp, he turned his captivity to his own advantage, and benefited for the rest of his days from his change of side.[475]

It reminds me of lines from Walter Scott's *Marmion*: "Oh, what a tangled web we weave when first we practice to deceive." Josephus was a deceiver and dissembler from the beginning. Anyone with a reasonable life experience will instantly recognize the hallmarks of a con artist. It wasn't that he was too naïve to see that he made himself look bad; it was because he suffered from the same cognitive deficits and lack of insight attributed to several types of personality disorder. Nevertheless, on the other side, he was constrained by a reading public to use historical facts and events as the skeleton on which he fleshed out his apologetics, and it is this that makes him useful, as long as controls are in place to deal with his deceptions and confabulations. We've already had a sample of the process I advocate in the discussion of the Aretas, John the Baptist and Artabanus mysteries. As we have already seen in that debacle, we must acknowledge that, since nobody else really knew what was going on in Palestine/Judea, Josephus was able to maneuver his characters without disturbing the real history too much. He borrowed Vitellius briefly to have him make a foray that came to nothing for ridiculous reasons, all the while making much of the relations between Rome and Palestine in his effort to normalize Jews and Judaism in the face of the terrific anti-Judaism that arose after the Jewish War. There is a wide and deep field for study of these issues and it is long past time that the Josephus text was interrogated competently.

So, to get started on this thread, we need to go back to the time of Archelaus, the son of Herod the Great, who went off to Rome to try to get a kingdom from Augustus, but ended up only an ethnarch (if that). Meanwhile, there was a major rebellion against Rome that Josephus later tried to cover up, and we were introduced to the clan of Judas the Galilean.

The period following the exile of Archelaus is covered *very* briefly in Josephus' *Wars*. Above, we saw that "Coponius, one of the equestrian order among the Romans, was sent as a procurator" and allegedly immediately faced the rebellion against taxation led by Judas the Galilean in 6 AD. Apparently, while that was going on:

> With the ethnarchy of Archelaus having passed over into a province, the remaining [brothers], Philip and Herod called Antipas, continued administering their own tetrarchies. When Salome [sister of Herod the Great] expired, she bequeathed to Julia, the wife of the August One, her own toparchy, as well as both Jamneia and the palm-groves in Phasaelis. And when the Roman imperium passed over to Tiberius the son of Julia, after the death of Augustus (who had been leader of the republic for 57 years plus 6 months and 2 days), both Herod and Philip continued still in their tetrarchies. The latter founded a city – Caesarea – at Panias by the sources of the Jordan, and in lower Gaulanitis, Julias, whereas in Galilee Herod [built] Tiberias and, in Perea, the eponymous Julias.

---

[475] *Josephus, Flavius: The Jewish War*, translated by G. A. Williamson, introduction by E. Mary Smallwood (Penguin, 1981), p. 24.

> When he had been sent to Judea as procurator by Tiberius, Pilatus introduced into [Jerusalem] – by night, concealed – the images of Caesar, which are called 'standards.'[476]

It is obvious that Josephus intends us to understand that, following Coponius, who had been sent by Augustus, *Pilate is the next procurator*. From at least 6 AD until the death of Augustus in 14, a period of 8 years, Coponius was procurator until he was replaced by Pilate upon the accession of Tiberius. That would put Pilate in Judea in 14/15 AD.

However, things are more complex in *Antiquities*. At the point when Archelaus was exiled, we are introduced to 'Cyrenius,' who is *not mentioned* at this point in *Wars*:

> So Archelaus's country was laid to the province of Syria [in 6 AD]; and Cyrenius, one that had been consul, was sent by Caesar [Augustus] to take account of people's effects in Syria, and to sell the house of Archelaus.[477]

Josephus expands on this further on:

> Now Cyrenius, a Roman senator, and one who had gone through other magistracies, and had passed through them till he had been consul, and one who, on other accounts, was of great dignity, came at this time into Syria, *with a few others*, being sent by [Augustus] to be a judge of that nation, and to take an account of their substance. Coponius also, a man of the equestrian order, was sent together with him, to have the supreme power over the Jews. Moreover, Cyrenius came himself into Judea, which was now added to the province of Syria, to take an account of their substance, and to dispose of Archelaus's money; but the Jews, although at the beginning they took the report of a taxation heinously, yet did they leave off any further opposition to it, *by the persuasion of Joazar, who was the son of Boethus*, and high priest; so they, being over-persuaded by Joazar's words, gave an account of their estates, without any dispute about it ...[478]

'Cyrenius' is Publius Sulpicius Quirinius. Some background: he was born about 51 BC. According to the historian Florus, Quirinius defeated a tribe of desert raiders from Cyrenaica possibly while governor of Crete and Cyrene around 14 BC. From 12 to 1 BC, he was campaigning against the Homanades, a tribe in the mountains of Galatia and Cilicia. From 5 to 3 BC he was probably legate of Galatia. About 1 AD, Quirinius was appointed tutor to Augustus' grandson, Gaius Caesar, until the latter died from wounds suffered on campaign in the East.

So it appears that after the banishment of Herod Archelaus in 6 AD, when Judea was put under direct Roman administration, with Coponius appointed as prefect, that a special job was given to Quirinius: he was appointed Legate of Syria, with instructions to carry out a census for taxation purposes.

Josephus tells us that open revolt was prevented by the efforts of the high priest Joazar, son of Boethus. Remember Boethus? Father of Mariamne II, wife of Herod the Great and mother of Herod II? Joazar would be uncle to Herod II. And yet, at the same time, according to Josephus, this census set off the revolt of Judas of Galilee and the formation of the party that would later come to be known as the Zealots!

---

[476] *Wars* 2.9.1–2 (167–9), Mason translation.
[477] *Ant.* 17.13.5 (354).
[478] *Ant.* 18.1.1 (1–3).

Quirinius served as governor of Syria with authority over Judea until 12 AD, when he returned to Rome and became a close associate of Tiberius.[479] The earliest known mention of his name is in an inscription from 12 BC discovered in Antioch Pisidia known as *Res Gestae Divi Augusti* (The Deeds of the Divine Augustus), which states: "A great crowd of people came together from all over Italy to my election, ... when Publius Sulpicius (Quirinius) and Gaius Valgius were consuls."[480]

Coins issued by Quirinius as governor of Syria, bearing the date "the 36th year of Caesar [Augustus]" (5/6 AD counted from the Battle of Actium) confirmed his position there. The census that he conducted in Syria has been confirmed by the text in a tombstone near Venice, Italy, of a Roman officer who served under him, stating among others: "By order of the same Quirinius I took a census of the city of Apamea."[481]

Quirinius, a relatively old man by Roman standards, was replaced by Creticus Silanus[482] in 11/12 AD at the latest, and one would assume that Coponius was also replaced at this time, except that Josephus apparently has him still there when Pilate arrives. Silanus and Coponius were allegedly still there in 14 AD when Augustus died and Tiberius succeeded him. As we will see, Silanus wasn't called back to Rome until 17 AD, but Coponius, having been there a number of years, was relieved and Pilate replaced him, as Josephus says: "when the Roman imperium passed over to Tiberius ... both Herod and Philip continued still in their tetrarchies. When he had been sent to Judea as procurator by Tiberius, Pilatus introduced into [Jerusalem] ... the images of Caesar."[483] This passage may have been passed over by the redactors simply because of its ambiguity.

However it sorts out, the passage puts Pilate in Judea in 14/15 AD. Even if he did remain for 10 years, which I doubt as you will see, he would have been gone in 25 AD, long before Jesus was supposed to have been crucified.

The Sons of Judas: Pillars of the Church?

Pulling on the thread of Quirinius, in *Wars* we find only two references to him, *both of which mention Judas the Galilean*. So, I'm going to go ahead and follow this thread here even though it brings in elements of the later chronology. The first one is in retrospect, because it is talking about the descendant of Judas who led the resistance at Masada:

> At this time [66 AD] a certain Manaem, son of Ioudas – the one called the Galilean, a most formidable sophist who had berated the Judeans *back in the time of Quirinius* because they were subjecting themselves to the Romans after God – took his acquaintances and withdrew to Masada. There, after he broke open the armory of King Herod and fully armed the different bandits as well

[479]https://www.livius.org/articles/person/quirinius-p-sulpicius/.
[480]Actually, the accepted list of consuls gives M. Valerius Messalla Appianus as co-consul to Quirinius in 12 BC, but notes that he died in March after serving only three months, so was replaced by C. Valgius Rufus from March to 29 August, and then replaced again by C. Caninius Rebilus who also died in office.
[481]E-10 The Tombstone of Quintus Aemilius Secundus; *Inscriptiones Latinae Selectae* 2683, dated shortly after 14 CE.
[482]Coins attest to his presence there from 11 to 17 AD, when he was replaced by Piso. See Tacitus, *Ann.* 2.4.3, Schürer (vol. I, 1973), p. 358.
[483]*Wars* 2.9.1–2 (167–9).

as the commoners, making use of these spear-bearers he returned to [Jerusalem] quite like a king ...[484]

We learn from this that Judas the Galilean was active during the years that Quirinius was governor of Syria, i.e. 6 to 11/12 AD. Since Josephus regularly refers to Judas the Galilean as the initiator of the revolt against the tax census of Cyrenius/Quirinius, it is clear that this is the same person as the following, though I want you to notice that he has given him another disguise here, in addition to 'son of Sariphaeus' or 'of Sepphoris':

> ... yet was there one Judas, a Gaulonite, of a city whose name was Gamala, who, taking with him Sadduc, a Pharisee,[485] became zealous to draw them to a revolt, who both said that this taxation was no better than an introduction to slavery, and exhorted the nation to assert their liberty ... They also said that God would not otherwise be assisting to them, than upon their joining with one another in such councils as might be successful, and for their own advantage; and this especially, if they would set about great exploits, and not grow weary in executing the same; so men received what they said with pleasure, and this bold attempt proceeded to a great height. All sorts of misfortunes also sprang from these men, and **the nation was infected with this doctrine to an incredible degree**; one violent war came upon us after another ... [F]or Judas and Sadduc, who excited a fourth philosophic sect among us, and had a great many followers therein, filled our civil government with tumults at present, and laid the foundations of our future miseries, by this system of philosophy, which we were before unacquainted withal, concerning which I will discourse a little, and this the rather because the infection which spread thence among the younger sort, who were zealous for it, brought the public to destruction.[486]

I think it is long past time for scholarly attention to be given to this 'Fourth Philosophy' that Josephus mentions several times, and to consider that this was, in fact, the original 'Christianity' of the Jerusalem messianists. We have already discussed the various uprisings in the period following the death of Herod the Great, including one Simon of Perea who was slain by Gratus and whose death resulted in a textual commemoration found near Qumran, now known as the Jeselsohn Stone. This Simon made such a splash that he was even mentioned by name by Tacitus.

Israel Knohl, an expert in Talmudic and biblical language at Jerusalem's Hebrew University, translated line 80 of the inscription as, "In three days, live, I Gabriel com[mand] yo[u]." He interpreted this as a command from the angel Gabriel to rise from the dead within three days, and understood the recipient of this command to be Simon, the Jewish rebel who was killed by the Romans in 4 BCE. Knohl asserted that the finding "calls for a complete reassessment of all previous scholarship on the subject of messianism, Jewish and Christian alike."[487]

Indeed. I've speculated on a possible relationship between Simon of Perea and Judas the Galilean, who appears to be descended from the 'robber' leader Ezekias/Hezekiah, who was

---

[484] *Wars* 2.17.8 (433–4), Mason translation.

[485] "Sadduc, a Pharisee" is something of a contradiction in terms and therefore curious.

[486] *Ant.* 18.1.1 (4–10).

[487] Israel Knohl (2008a), '"By Three Days, Live": Messiahs, Resurrection, and Ascent to Heaven in Hazon Gabriel,' *The Journal of Religion* 88 (2): 147–158; Knohl, 'The Gabriel Revelation and the Birth of Christianity,' in Lawrence H. Schiffman, Adolfo D. Roitman, Shani Tzoref (eds), 'The Dead Sea Scrolls and Contemporary Culture: Proceedings of the International Conference held at the Israel Museum, Jerusalem' (July 6–8, 2008) (Brill, 2008b), pp. 435–76; Knohl (2009), *Messiahs and Resurrection in 'The Gabriel Revelation'* (Bloomsbury, 2009). The translation of the entire text can be read here: https://web.archive.org/web/20180201192931/www.hartman.org.il/SHINews_View.asp?Article_Id=162.

chased down and murdered by Herod the Great when he was a young man. I've also noted that Josephus refers to all rebels against the rule of Rome as robbers and bandits. He made several remarks about the 'kingly pretensions' of such rebels, and I speculated about whether this indicated Davidic descent of some of them.

Now, at the time of the war, we have met Manaem (Manahem, Menahem), a 'son' of Judas the Galilean who is rampaging around in 66 AD, 60 years later![488] In *Antiquities* two other sons of Judas are mentioned:

> Then came Tiberius Alexander as successor to Fadus; ... the sons of Judas of Galilee were now slain; I mean of that Judas who caused the people to revolt, when Cyrenius came to take an account of the estates of the Jews, as we have showed in a foregoing book. The names of those sons were James and Simon, whom Alexander commanded to be crucified ...[489]

Tiberius Alexander was procurator of Judea under Claudius, from 46 to 48 AD. That puts him there in the period of Paul.

Now, the question I would like to ask is: how does Acts 12:2, the story about James, the brother of John, being executed, and Simon-Peter seized, relate to this item in Josephus? Were these individuals, James and Simon, executed by Tiberius Alexander, the same two 'pillars' of the Jerusalem ecclesia, James and Cephas (Simon-Peter)? We can note that Simon is renamed Peter in the synoptic Gospels (Mk 3:16; Mt 4:18; Lk 5:8, 6:14), and only in *John* does the writer say 'Cephas' (Jn 1:42). In Paul's letters, Cephas is always used in reference to the pillars, and a Peter is mentioned only twice in Gal 2:7, 8. As discussed above, it appears that there may have been two people: Cephas the pillar, and Peter the apostle, whose other name was said to be Simon in the Gospels.

So, the question is: were these sons of Judas the Galilean who were executed by Tiberius Alexander actually James and Simon AKA Cephas, the 'rock' of the Gospels? And was Peter someone else entirely, as suggested by the text of *1 Clement* and Paul's letters? This is the conclusion reached by Jay Raskin, who writes:

> One can easily suppose that the leadership of the Galilean based Judaic-Christian movement revolved around one family. In reconstructing their history, the Gospel writers of the second century placed their own apostolic structure into the narrative.[490]

He also notes the striking parallels:

> Both groups claim origination in Galilee around the time of the census of Quirinius, and they both had leaders named Simon and James in Jerusalem in the 40s. They both had large followings ... Both have leaders crucified by the Romans. Most significantly, Josephus does not mention the Simon and James leadership of the Christian movement and early Christian sources do not mention the revolutionary movement of Josephus' Simon and James.[491]

---

[488] But keep in mind Nodet and Taylor's suggestion that this usage of 'son' may just indicate a line of succession (1998, pp. 139–40).

[489] *Ant.* 20.5.2 (100–2). Since Judas had a 'son' named Simon, one wonders if he had a 'brother' named Simon also? Recall Athronges with his four brothers, one of whom was killed by Gratus – and 'king' Simon of Perea, also cut down by Gratus. Were they the same person?

[490] Jay Raskin, 'A Discovery, the Crucified, Simon, Zealots, and Essenes,' *Journal of Higher Criticism* 9:1 (2002), pp. 113–14.

[491] Raskin (2002).

So I think we may have found here a time peg for Paul: the deaths of two of the 'pillars' of church in 46/47 AD and that will have important implications for the dating of Paul's letters, assuming I am correct. And, all the historical evidence suggests that to be the case.

Recall that *1 Clement* does not mention the 'time of Jesus' death' or 'the time of Jesus' but rather *dates things from the time of the beginning of Paul's apostolic mission,* and we know that there was a second meeting in Jerusalem 15 to 17 years after Paul's commission vision. Cephas and James appear in 1 Corinthians and Galatians 2, but always in reference to past events and never in a sense that confirms or implies that they were still living while Paul was writing. The events that stirred up the Galatians appear to have followed Paul's second trip to Jerusalem, and the confrontation at Antioch with Cephas and the emissaries from James.

Acts depicts the execution of James and the arrest of Peter as having been ordered by Herod, but that is extremely unlikely. I'll go into this a bit more thoroughly in the proper chronological spot. Here I will only say further that if these two are the James and Simon/Cephas that Paul met in Jerusalem, that means *his second visit had to have been before these executions, in ca. 47 AD* – possibly just before. This would mean that Paul's first visit to Jerusalem was 14 years earlier ca. 33/34 AD, which would put his conversion and call in 29/30, *the 15*[th] *year of Tiberius!*[492] It is definitely intriguing how the dates just happen to work out coming at the problem from just this chronological hook. It also tells us that the governor of Aretas would have been in Damascus in 33/34, as attested by Paul. One cannot help but notice that Paul was being pursued by the governor of Aretas at about the same time that John the Baptist was executed; what was the connection? Recall that Josephus said that John was executed at Machaerus, which was also the place where the daughter of Aretas fled to when her husband, Herod Antipas, was planning to divorce her, and from which she was transferred to Nabataea.

Coming back on topic: the next reference to Cyrenius/Quirinius in *Wars* is just prior to the siege of Masada in 73 AD, conducted by Lucius Flavius Silva and the Roman *Legion X Fretensis*:

> When Bassus was dead in Judea, Flavius Silva succeeded him as procurator there; who, when he saw that all the rest of the country was subdued in this war, and that there was but one only stronghold that was still in rebellion, he got all his army together that lay in different places, and made an expedition against it. This fortress was called Masada. It was one *Eleazar, a potent man, and the commander of these Sicarii,* that had seized upon it. He was *a descendant from that Judas* who had persuaded an abundance of the Jews, as we have formerly related, not to submit to the taxation *when Cyrenius was sent* into Judea to make one ...[493]

Above, we had a "Manaem, *son of Ioudas*," who withdrew to Masada in 66 and now, in 73, we have an Eleazar also descended from Judas at Masada. 'Descendant' probably means grandson. One of the sons of the sons of Judas executed 25 years earlier during the reign of Tiberius Alexander? One might wish to note that Tiberius Alexander was second in command to Titus during the Siege of Jerusalem. If he could come back 25 years later, it's altogether possible that this Eleazar was a brother of James and Simon, who were executed ca. 47 AD. Also note that Eleazar is just another form of the name *Lazarus!*

---

[492]More precisely, somewhere in the range of 29 to 32 AD, with higher probability given to the earlier dates. If James and Simon were executed in 46 AD, the earliest possible year is 29 AD (29+3+14=46). If they were executed in 47 AD, the latest possible year is 32 AD (32+2.x+13.x=47). As mentioned above, Paul's reference to 'three' a 'fourteen' years may be inclusive, e.g., 2.5 years and 13.2 years.

[493] *Wars* 7.8.1 (252–4).

Going back again, after the death of Herod, there was a 'War of Varus,' possibly triggered by the actions of Archelaus and Sabinus, or Simon of Perea, who may have been an Essene. Then we have Judas the Galilean, who seems to be the same Judas of Sepphoris, the great expounder of the law who encouraged the Golden Eagle rebellion that led to, allegedly, the execution of a group of young Jews and possibly *one* of their teachers, Matthias, whom we don't find showing up again as we do Judas, unless there was a Judas the great teacher and a son, Judas, who created the 'Fourth Philosophy'; basically, Judas and his sons and sons of sons winding all through the works of Josephus like 'the thread of Ariadne.' In regard to Matthias, we wonder about a Pharisee named Sadduc (Zadok, Sadducee) connected so closely to Judas, and Josephus' own possible connections, considering his father was a Matthias too. What is curious is the way Josephus attempts to disguise these individuals, and to scatter their activities throughout the timeline, changing their names in a rather devious way.

Josephus tells us a lot more about Quirinius than he ever told us about Varus and Sabinus, and that seems odd. But then, we do have more background on Quirinius in Tacitus than on Varus,[494] which may suggest that there was more in the Roman records to which both may have had access. Josephus notes that, despite the fact that Coponius had the authority, "Cyrenius came himself into Judea." So, it plays again along the same model that was set by Varus and Sabinus after the death of Herod the Great (with Varus as governor and Sabinus as procurator).

The period is very mysterious because, during that time, Archelaus allegedly was involved in the capture of one of the Athronges gang – and then let him go. Was this Athronges just a folk name for the Simon of Perea who wanted to be king, or perhaps for Judas of Sepphoris/Galilee, the warrior, who then shows up again as "Judas, a Gaulonite, of a city whose name was Gamala,"[495] creating the same problems for Cyrenius/Quirinius that he had created during the Varus War, or was he just a novelistic creation? With all the talk of these giant rebels, one is reminded of the following from the Artabanus saga:

> Artabanus and Vitellius went to Euphrates, and as a bridge was laid over the river, they each of them came with their guards about them, and met one another on the midst of the bridge. And when they had agreed upon the terms of peace Herod, the tetrarch erected a rich tent on the midst of the passage, and made them a feast there. Artabanus also, not long afterward, sent his son Darius as a hostage, with many presents, among which there was *a man seven cubits tall, a Jew he was by birth, and his name was Eleazar, who, for his tallness, was called a giant.*[496]

If Josephus was trying to prevent us from knowing who was who in order to cover his own tracks and connections, he's done a pretty good job. Nevertheless, we've found several interesting things just pulling on the thread of Quirinius.

The High Priest Shell Game

Getting back to the time of Pilate, another of the mysterious aspects of this period is what was going on with the high priests. As we saw in the previous section, *Joazar, son of Boethus*, was made high priest to replace the Matthias who was allegedly *deposed* at the time of the Golden

---

[494]Another of those moments when one perceives the correspondences between Tacitus and Josephus.
[495]Gamala overlooks the Sea of Galilee and Sepphoris is also nearby.
[496]*Ant.* 18.4.4–5 (96).

Eagle incident. Then, we encounter him again with the appearance of Quirinius, as the high priest who persuaded the people to submit to the census. Also, recall that the people petitioned Archelaus at the very beginning of his ethnarchy to give them back an acceptable high priest, and Josephus said he did so. Let's review the details, because something is going on here.

Herod replaced the high priest Matthias with Joazar, Matthias' *brother-in-law*. After describing Matthias' holiness, Josephus says that during his tenure as high priest, Joseph son of Ellemus had officiated for a single fasting day because Matthias had *dreamed* that he had intercourse with his wife, which disqualified him for the day. Then he comes back to the immediate concern, which is the burning of the Golden Eagle rebellion rabbis and their followers:

> But Herod deprived *this* Matthias of the high priesthood, and burnt the *other* Matthias, who had raised the sedition, with his companions, alive. And that very night there was an eclipse of the moon.[497]

One gets the impression that Josephus 'protests too much' when he declares that there are two Matthiases. The whole narrative makes more sense without that detail: the high priest Matthias leads a rebellion, gets arrested along with his supporters, burned alive, and replaced. Later, the people lament Matthias and petition Archelaus to get rid of the high priest who was put in Matthias' place. It appears that, by adding that 'other Matthias,' Josephus obscures the *priestly leadership* of the Golden Eagle revolt.

> The people assembled together, and desired of Archelaus, that ... he would deprive that high priest *whom Herod had made*, and would choose one more agreeable to the law, and of greater purity, to officiate as high priest. This was granted by Archelaus ...[498]

That means that the people wanted a Zealous high priest and, seemingly, Archelaus granted their wish. Then, after all the messing around in Rome and the war of Varus, Archelaus returned:

> When Archelaus was entered on his ethnarchy, and was come into Judea, he accused Joazar, the son of Boethus, of *assisting the seditious*, and took away the high priesthood from him, and put Eleazar his brother in his place.[499]

If you're lost and confused so far, that's understandable! Remember, Joazar was the brother-in-law of Herod II and he was being accused by Herod II's half-brother, Archelaus. So, we have Matthias, who may actually have been the same Matthias who was one of the leaders of the Golden Eagle rebellion, being deprived of the priesthood, and Joazar – Matthias' brother-in-law – installed by Herod the Great, who was also his brother-in-law. Then, soon after Herod's death, Archelaus replaces Joazar with some unnamed high priest demanded by the people; and then, after Archelaus returns from Rome and enters his ethnarchy, we learn that *Joazar* was high priest during the rebellion all along and is *now* being replaced with an Eleazar, who is the brother of Joazar, whose connections we have just noted. One feels just a bit vertiginous with all these high priests under the shells being moved about.

---

[497] *Ant.* 17.6.4 (164–7).
[498] *Ant.* 17.9.1 (207–8).
[499] *Ant.* 17.13.1 (339).

Nor did this Eleazar abide long in the high priesthood, Jesus, the son of Sie, being put in his place while he was still living.[500]

Apparently, when a high priest was appointed, custom had it that he normally stayed in the office until he died. Josephus tells us regarding Herod the Great's first act of this kind:

> So king Herod immediately took the high priesthood away from Ananelus ... He was one of the stock of the high priests and had been of old a particular friend of Herod; and when he was first made king, he conferred that dignity upon him, and now put him out of it again, in order to quiet the troubles in his family, though *what he did was plainly unlawful, for at no other time [of old] was anyone that had once been in that dignity deprived of it.* It was Antiochus Epiphanes who first broke that law, and deprived Jesus, and made his brother Onias high priest in his stead. Aristobulus was the second that did so, and took that dignity from his brother [Hyrcanus]; and this Herod was the third, who took that high office away [from Ananelus], and gave it to this young man, Aristobulus, in his stead.[501]

Either Josephus (or a redactor) is playing fast and loose with his high priests, or something strange was going on at the time to necessitate such rapid changes in the high priesthood. Perhaps Matthias provides a clue in that direction: some of the priests were just as rebellious as the rest of them![502]

But later still, as noted, we encounter Joazar again in the story of Quirinius in 6 AD, only this time instead of fomenting rebellion as he was said to have done under Varus, he is credited with *quelling* it.[503]

> Now Cyrenius ... came at this time into Syria ... but the Jews, although at the beginning they took the report of a taxation heinously, yet did they leave off any further opposition to it, *by the persuasion of Joazar, who was the son of Boethus,* and high priest; so they, being over-persuaded by Joazar's words, gave an account of their estates, without any dispute about it ...[504]

If Judas the Galilean is agitating for resistance against taxation, and Joazar is encouraging submission to it, they are obviously at odds with each other. Further on:

> When Cyrenius had now disposed of Archelaus's money, and when the taxings were come to a conclusion, which were made in the *thirty-seventh year* of [Augustus]'s victory over Antony at Actium [i.e. 6–7 AD, 37 years after 2 September 31 BC], *he deprived Joazar of the high priesthood, which dignity had been conferred on him by the multitude,* and he appointed Ananus the son of Seth while Herod [Antipas] and Philip had each of them received their own tetrarchy, and settled the affairs thereof.[505]

Now wait a minute! Who ever said that Joazar was appointed by the people?! Our list of priests looks like this:

---

[500] *Ant.* 17.13.1 (341).

[501] *Ant.* 15.3.1 (39–41).

[502] By the time Josephus wrote *Antiquities* and his *Life*, he had aligned more with the Pharisees and was more willing to acknowledge the priests' complicity in the rebellion and war of the late 60s. See Cohen (2002).

[503] *Ant.* 18.1.1 (3).

[504] *Ant.* 18.1.1 (1–3).

[505] *Ant.* 18.2.1 (26).

- Matthias at the time of the Golden Eagle rebellion

- Joazar son of Boethus, appointed by Herod to replace Matthias

- *Unnamed mystery priest* appointed by Archelaus on the demand of the people

- Joazar son of Boethus, accused by Archelaus of assisting the sedition/war

- Eleazar (brother of Joazar), appointed by Archelaus to replace Joazar

- Jesus son of Sie replaced Eleazar "while he was still living"

And now we learn that Joazar, the high priest in office at the time of the arrival of Quirinius, was supposed to have been *selected by the multitude*, which must mean he is the 'mystery priest' appointed by Archelaus on the demand of the people, only he was already high priest because he had been appointed by Herod! We note that Joazar was accused by Archelaus of participation in the rebellion but then was credited with quelling the rebellion; we also know that Josephus lays the blame of the rebellion at the time of Quirinius squarely on Judas the Galilean.

This Joazar, son of Boethus, seems to be important since he keeps popping up, so we might want to pull on that thread just a little.

The Boethusians were a Jewish sect closely related to the Sadducees. These two sects denied the immortality of the soul and resurrection and their followers were mainly the wealthy elite. The Boethusians are believed to have been associated with members of the high-priestly family of Boethus. Boethus, who was from Alexandria, was made a high priest about 25 or 24 BC by Herod the Great, in order to raise his social rank so that his marriage with Boethus's daughter, Mariamne (II), might not be regarded as a marriage with a person thought to be unsuitable or of a lower social position. The family of Boethus produced the following high priests (mostly derived from Josephus):

- Simon, son of Boethus, or Boethus himself (24–5 BC)[506]

- Joazar, son of Boethus (4 BC and before 6 AD)[507]

- Eleazar, son of Boethus (4–3 BC)[8][508]

- Simon Cantheras, son of Boethus (41–42 AD)[509]

- Elioneus, son of Simon Cantheras (43–44 AD)[510]

- Joshua (Jesus), son of Gamaliel (64 AD)[511]

Apparently, the last member of the family on the list was executed 'as a traitor to his country' by the rebels during the war against Rome in 68 AD.[512] So, it seems all the more likely that

---

[506] *Ant.* 15.9.3; 19.6.2.

[507] *Ant.* 18.1.1.

[508] *Ant.* 17.13.1; independently attested in the Mandaean Sidra d-Yahia.

[509] *Ant.* 19.6.2.

[510] *Ant.* 19.8.1.

[511] https://www.jewishencyclopedia.com/articles/8912-joshua-jesus-ben-gamla.

[512] *Wars* 4.5.2.

the Joazar in view at present was, indeed, pro-Roman and in the role of quelling the rebellion, rather than inciting rebellion as accused by Archelaus. If Archelaus was accusing him thus, it is possible that Archelaus was part of the rebellion and that might explain his exile. It wasn't that he was a brutal ruler – nearly all the rulers of the time were brutal and that wasn't something to get exiled for generally – it was because he was against Judea being annexed into the Roman province of Syria and thus being put under Rome's direct rule.[513] That would also explain why he let Athronges or one of his brothers go after capture of that gang which had kingly aspirations. But, in the end, all we can really determine about Josephus' treatment of Archelaus is that he is, for some reason, deliberately attempting to confuse things.

The Mystery of Quirinius

Note that in the quotation above from Book 18 of *Antiquities*, Josephus tells us the tax census of Quirinius occurred **37 years** after Octavian/Augustus' victory over Mark Antony at Actium on September 2, 31 BC, i.e. 6/7 AD. The number 37 appears in three significant contexts in the works of Josephus, *all relating to texts with very confused chronologies*. In addition to this case, we find in Book 17 that Josephus notes that Herod died **37 years** after he was declared king by the Romans. This is associated with the tale of Judas and Matthias and the Golden Eagle temple cleansing and the odd mention of an eclipse.[514] Shortly after the bit about the census in Book 18 quoted above, Josephus also writes about the death of Philip, who he notes had been tetrarch for **37 years**. This is associated with the alleged problems that arose between Aretas and Herod Antipas (i.e. between Philip's death in 33/34 AD and Aretas' in 40 AD), and that tale is the platform for the inclusion of the John the Baptist story.[515]

Of course, Josephus uses many numbers throughout his works, some more than once. But to find the only three uses of this particular number within such a relatively short block of text, each dealing with matters of obviously confused chronology, strikes me as curious. All three events are *very important to Christian chronology*. And note the verbal similarities surrounding two of the events in question:

- After 37 years (since Antony made Herod king), Sabinus disposes Herod the Great's money

- After 37 years (since Antony lost to Octavian), Quirinius disposes of Herod Archelaus' money

Taken with the oddities reviewed thus far, along with others to come, these numbers are just too coincidental to blithely assume that there is no prestidigitation going on here. What to make of it? I'll be frank: I don't know. But a few thoughts do occur to me.

---

[513]Mason (2016) provides an interesting interpretation in line with my own. He speculates that the high priest Joazar led the faction that wanted to be integrated into Syria and have direct Roman rule (i.e. the high priest and elites, but not the common people), and that Archelaus removed Joazar for "associating with the anti-monarchical elite" (p. 251). Josephus only mentions unrest in Judea, Archelaus' territory, not that of his brothers, suggesting that the motivation for the rebellion during his time was directly related to these geopolitical moves: "The large Judaean populations in their tetrarchies were not subject to annexation [to Syria] and had no mentioned role in these protests of A.D. 6" (p. 247).

[514]*Ant.* 17.8.1 (191).

[515]*Ant.* 18.4.6 (106).

The doublet factor suggests to me that a fake history for the period of Herod's death and the reign of Archelaus has been created. The relevant years, 6 BC–4 AD, are missing in Dio, who records regular censuses every five years or so. Dio does mention a census in 4 AD when C. Sentius Saturninus was consul, but he explicitly says that this census was limited to Italy, "for [Augustus] did not compel the poorer citizens or those living outside out of Italy to be listed, fearing that if they were disturbed, they would become rebellious."[516] So why would he change his policy in an undoubted rebel hotspot? We do know a few things about Quirinius. Tacitus briefly recaps his career when his death is mentioned, but *never mentions his appointment as governor of Syria.*[517] However, his presence there is attested by the inscription mentioned previously, the *Titulus Venetus*, which describes the career of a knight, Aemilius Secundus, and *explicitly mentions a census* 'outside of Italy' that appears to contradict Dio's statement:

> Q[uintus] Aemilius Secundus s[on] of Q[uintus], of the tribe Palatina, who served in the camps of the divine Aug[ustus] under **P. Sulpicius Quirinius, legate of Caesar in Syria**, decorated with honorary distinctions, prefect of the 1st cohort Aug[usta], prefect of the cohort II Classica. Besides, **by order of Quirinius I made the census of 117 thousand citizens of Apamea.** Besides, sent on mission by Quirinius, against the Itureans, I took their citadel on Mount Lebanon. And prior military service, (I was) Prefect of the workers, detached by two co[nsul]s at the 'aerarium [The State Treasury]. And in the colony, quaestor, aedile twice, duumvir twice, pontiff.[518]

Apamea is certainly in the Roman Syrian province, as is Mount Lebanon. Unfortunately, it is difficult to date when these events took place. Nevertheless, there was some sort of census under Quirinius, and probably in 6 AD.

As the oddities add up, it seems more and more likely that Archelaus may never have ruled his ethnarchy at all. Perhaps Augustus ruled against him when he was in Rome, based on the testimony of his brothers and the Jewish embassy, and sent him into exile there and then? That's how Strabo makes it sound. Recall: "However, [Herod the Great's] sons were not successful, but became involved in accusations; and one of them spent the rest of his life in exile ... whereas *the others, by much obsequiousness, but with difficulty, **found leave to return home, with a tetrarchy assigned to each.***"[519]

It sounds as if Archelaus was banished before his brothers, Antipas and Philip, entered their tetrarchies, implying Archelaus never got his cut of the pie. That may mean that the doings of Archelaus are either entirely made up, or are actually the activities of someone else displaced in time, either by Josephus or by a redactor. Perhaps someone else can do a close examination of the texts and sort this out. One thing that does occur to me is this: perhaps the rejection of Archelaus' claims to part of his father's territory meant that his part was given over to the Syrian governor to rule almost immediately after the death of Herod the Great. And then, at that time, Quirinius came to do his census, triggering the rebellion of Judas the Galilean, part of which rebellion against Rome included the Golden Eagle incident, possibly around 1 BC. But that is just a speculative suggestion for further examination.

---

[516]Dio 55.13.4.

[517]Tacitus, *Ann.* 2.30.4; 3.22.1; 3.48.1.

[518]*CIL* III 6687, *ILS* 2683, quoted in Gertoux, 'Dating the two Censuses.'

[519]Strabo 16.2.46 (765).

Coponius and the Samaritans

Returning for a moment to Josephus' account of the post-Varus period leading up to Pilate, Coponius allegedly became prefect of Judea after it was annexed to Rome in 6 AD (though we suspect he came with Quirinius in 1 BC). Just like Sabinus and Archelaus, Coponius has a set-to with the Jews during a feast-festival, and again it is attributed to the Samaritans (recall that Samaritan issues brought the downfall of Archelaus, according to Josephus – they will play a part in the fall of Pilate too).

> As Coponius, who we told you was sent along with Cyrenius [Quirinius], was exercising his office of procurator, and governing Judea, the following accidents happened. As the Jews were celebrating the feast of unleavened bread, which we call the Passover, it was customary for the priests to open the temple-gates just after midnight. When, therefore, those gates were first opened, some of the Samaritans came privately into Jerusalem, and *threw about dead men's bodies* [NB: the actual Greek says *bones*], in the cloisters; on which account the Jews afterward excluded them out of the temple, which they had not used to do at such festivals; and on other accounts also they watched the temple more carefully than they had formerly done. A little after which accident *Coponius returned to Rome, and Marcus Ambivius came to be his successor* in that government; under whom Salome, the sister of king Herod died and left to Julia, [Augustus' wife,] Jamnia, all its toparchy, and Phasaelis in the plain, and Archelais, where is a great plantation of palm trees, and their fruit is excellent in its kind. *After him [Ambivius] came Annius Rufus, under whom died [Augustus]* ...[520]

Just a minute here. Recall the passage from *Wars* quoted above:

> With the ethnarchy of Archelaus having passed over into a province, the remaining [brothers], Philip and Herod called Antipas, continued administering their own tetrarchies. When Salome [sister of Herod the Great] expired, she bequeathed to Julia, the wife of the August One, her own toparchy, as well as both Jamneia and the palm-groves in Phasaelis. And when the Roman imperium passed over to Tiberius the son of Julia, after the death of Augustus (who had been leader of the republic for 57 years plus 6 months and 2 days), both Herod and Philip continued still in their tetrarchies. ... When he had been sent to Judea as procurator by Tiberius, Pilatus introduced into [Jerusalem] – by night, concealed – the images of Caesar, which are called 'standards'.[521]

As discussed previously, *Wars* says that "Coponius, one of the equestrian order among the Romans, was sent as a procurator" and allegedly immediately faced the rebellion against taxation led by Judas the Galilean in 6 AD. The passage above is the follow-up, which strongly suggests that Coponius was procurator until Pilate came at the time of the accession of Tiberius. Now, all of a sudden we have "A little after which accident Coponius returned to Rome, and Marcus Ambivius came to be his successor"!?[522]

Also, why did he specifically mention Salome's plantation of palm trees? Is that the same plantation that Archelaus was supposed to have brought water to? In *Wars*, Josephus says Salome's palm groves – gifted to Julia upon her death – were in Phasaelis. But in *Antiquities*

---

[520] *Ant.* 18.2.2 (29–32).
[521] *Wars* 2.9.1–2 (167–9), Mason translation.
[522] Interestingly, while the names 'Marcus Ambivius' and 'Annius Rufus' don't ping with anything, in 16 AD, suffect consul of Rome from July to December was C. Vibius Rufus. Somebody was having a bit of fun with the name game.

he says they were *in Archelais*, the city founded by Archelaus around the time he planted palm trees in Neara by Jericho. When did Salome acquire Archelaus' city? Josephus never says. What is interesting is that the stories of Sabinus following the death of Herod in 5/4 BC, and then Coponius following the exile of Archelaus in 6 AD, include verbal and event similarities between each other and the events under Pilate later.

Gratus and Rufus, and Musical Priests

Looking now at our procurators/governors with authority in Judea, at this point we have the following list from *Antiquities*:

- Varus (with Sabinus) – 4 BC to ?

- Archelaus – until 6 AD? (A shadow, either 9 or 10 years, or not at all?)

- Coponius (with Quirinius) – 6 to 9 AD – 3 years? (Or 1 to 9, 6 years? Or 6 to 14 AD?)

- Marcus Ambivius/Ambivulus – 9 to 12 AD – 3 years?

- Annius Rufus – 12 to 15 AD – 3 years?

- Death of Augustus – 14 AD

Then we come to Valerius Gratus, who is said to have served from 15 to 26 AD (!), to be replaced by Pilate. Of course, this opposes what Josephus says in *Wars*, where Marcus Ambivius, Annius Rufus and Valerius Gratus are not even mentioned, as opposed to this from *Antiquities*: "[Tiberius] sent Valerius **Gratus** to be procurator of Judea, and to succeed Annius **Rufus**."[523]

I feel a Miss Marple moment coming on. Where have we seen the names Gratus and Rufus *juxtaposed* before? Remember back during the rebellion against Sabinus that was quelled by Varus, helped by Aretas et al.? Recall that many of the Herodian army went over to the rebels, but with a couple of notable exceptions: "The contingent most fit for war, however, 3,000 Sebastenes, added themselves to the Romans. **Rufus and Gratus were over them.**"[524]

Gratus had a number of adventures in *Wars*, including chasing down and killing Simon of Perea, the self-declared king of the Jews, which, as noted, may be the event that was recorded in the 'Gabriel Revelation' on the Jeselsohn Stone. He also liquidated one of Athronges' brothers.

Josephus' account in *Antiquities* of the Judean governorship of the highly questionable Gratus, who followed the equally highly questionable Annius Rufus, should be read in its entirety (I have added the numbering of the replacement high priests):

> After him [Marcus Ambivius] came Annius Rufus, under whom died Caesar [Augustus], the second emperor of the Romans,[525] the duration of whose reign was fifty-seven years, besides six months and two days [of which time Antonius ruled together with him fourteen years; but the duration of his life was seventy-seven years]; upon whose death [14 AD] Tiberius Nero, his wife Julia's son, succeeded. He was now the third emperor; and he sent Valerius Gratus to be procurator of Judea, and to succeed Annius Rufus. This man deprived **Ananus** of the high priesthood, and appointed [1] **Ismael**, the son of Phabi ... He also deprived him in a little time, and ordained [2] **Eleazar**,

---

[523] *Ant.* 18.2.2 (33).

[524] *Wars* 2.3.4 (52), Mason translation.

[525] Obviously counting Julius Caesar as emperor.

the son of Ananus, who had been a high priest before, to be high priest; which office when he had held for a year, Gratus deprived him of it, and gave the high priesthood to [3] **Simon**, the son of Camithus; and when he had possessed that dignity no longer than a year, [4] **Joseph Caiaphas** was made his successor. When Gratus had done those things, he went back to Rome, **after he had waited in Judea eleven years**, when Pontius Pilate came as his successor.[526]

According to this, Valerius Gratus, not Pontius Pilate, was sent as soon as Tiberius became emperor and, at some point – we don't know when – started playing a fast and furious game of musical high priests, *just as we saw in the years after Herod the Great's death vis à vis Archelaus*. He appointed four in what seems to be rapid succession and then, apparently, was satisfied with his choice and did nothing else that Josephus considered worth recording other than the most interesting comment that he was in Judea for eleven years.

Even assuming that the list of governors of Judea is not a complete fabrication, it would only require a change in the number of years to alter the chronology; further, it is strange that of all the governors of Judea, only Gratus and Pilate have their number of years mentioned! Josephus also tells us that the proconsul Vitellius deposed the high priest Caiaphas sometime around the Artabanus affair already discussed (and which we will come back to). Nevertheless, if Gratus was sent out in 14 AD and was there eleven years, we would have Pilate showing up in 25 (in time to have him there in the fifteenth year of Tiberius, when John the Baptist and Jesus allegedly come onto the scene). And that, I think, was the point of an obvious editorial manipulation.

Let's recap our new list of high priests, including the previous list from Archelaus, and with associated ruler/governor:

4 BC	Herod	Matthias at the time of the Golden Eagle rebellion
4 BC		Joazar son of Boethus, appointed by Herod to replace Matthias
4 BC	Varus (with Sabinus) – 4 BC to ?; Archelaus (or Simon of Perea) – either 9 or 10 years or not at all	*Unnamed mystery priest* appointed by Archelaus on the demand of the people
3 BC?	Archelaus	**Joazar son of Boethus**, accused by Archelaus of assisting the sedition/war
3 BC?	Archelaus	Eleazar (brother of Joazar), appointed by Archelaus to replace Joazar
2 BC?	Archelaus	Jesus son of Sie replaced Eleazar "while he was still living"
1 AD?	Archelaus	**Joazar, son of Boethus**, brother of Eleazar – deposed 6 AD
6–9 AD	Archelaus deposed and exiled; Coponius (with Quirinius) – 6 to 9 AD	Ananus, son of Seth – 6 to 15 AD
9–12 AD	*Coponius returned to Rome, and Marcus Ambivius came to be his successor*	Ananus

---

[526] *Ant.* 18.2.2 (34–35).

12–14 AD	After him [Marcus Ambivius] came Annius Rufus, under whom died Caesar [Augustus] **14 AD**	Ananus
15 AD	Tiberius sent either Pilate (*Wars*) or Valerius Gratus to be procurator of Judea, and to succeed Annius Rufus (*Ant.*)	Gratus deprived **Ananus** of the high priesthood, and appointed **Ismael**, the son of Phabi
16 AD	Pilate or Gratus	Gratus also deprived him in a little time, and ordained **Eleazar**, the son of Ananus ... for a year
17 AD	Pilate or Gratus	Gratus gave the high priesthood to **Simon**, the son of Camithus ... no longer than a year
18 AD	Pilate or Gratus	**Joseph Caiaphas** was made his successor.
26 AD	When Gratus had done those things, he went back to Rome, **after he had waited in Judea eleven years**, when Pontius Pilate came as his successor	Caiaphas
(big jump)		
37 AD	Vitellius	Caiaphas deposed by Vitellius

The way the text is written suggests that Gratus began changing high priests soon after arriving, and left as soon as he had installed Caiaphas, except for the inclusion of the words: *after he had waited in Judea eleven years*. How long each served is impossible to know. In this chronology, it seems that Caiaphas was appointed in approximately AD 18, if Gratus appointed him within, say, five years of his alleged arrival and after he had gone quickly (as indicated) through a selection of unsatisfactory high priests. The way the text reads, Caiaphas was then removed from office by Vitellius in 37 AD, meaning he held the high priesthood for 19 years or so. (Caiaphas was the high priest who is said in the Gospels to have organized the plot to kill Jesus, being Jesus' major antagonist.[527])

Apparently, neither the alleged Marcus Ambivius nor the putative Annius Rufus saw fit to change the high priests. Or if they did, Josephus makes no remark about it, despite the fact that he's constantly tabulating – or making up – the high priests. So, in addition to a whole new raft of governors in Judea supposedly sent by Augustus, in *Antiquities* Josephus tells us that the *first* governor sent by Tiberius was a Valerius Gratus, who was there for eleven years! All of this is very problematical, especially if we recall how it is presented in *Wars*, where there is no account of the revolving-door governors and priests and it is more or less a matter of fact that *when the transfer of the Empire was made on the death of Augustus, a new procurator was sent out by Tiberius: Pontius Pilate.* William Thomas Arnold quotes Roman sources suggesting that neither Augustus nor Tiberius were in the habit of giving their governors short terms:

---

[527]One cannot help but note the similarity of the name Caiaphas to Cephas. Cephas is Hellenized Aramaic for 'rock,' which is also one of the proposed etymologies for Caiaphas (*kefa/kepa*).

Dio makes Maecenas give the advice to Augustus not to let any legate of his rule a province less than three years or more than five for so they would stay long enough to know their province thoroughly, not long enough to become dangerous. And this was perhaps the generally observed rule. ... But the exceptions are very numerous. Galba governed Spain for eight years, Sabinus was in Moesia for seven, and we find C. Silius legate in Gaul AD 14, and still in Gaul ten years afterwards. Sometimes these appointments lasted even for life: *Tiberius in particular was famous for keeping his governors long at their posts.*[528]

But this observation quoted above, that Tiberius was famous for keeping his governors long at their posts, cites Josephus as evidence for the claim. The contrary facts appear to be that Tiberius almost slavishly emulated Augustus in his rule regarding legates and governors.

In a speech to the senate in 25 Tiberius remarked of his predecessor: "I treat all his actions and words as if they had the force of law." The early years of his principate offer many examples of his devotion to Augustan precedent in major questions of policy *as well as in trivial details of routine administration.*[529]

That means that, especially at the beginning of his reign, it would have been totally out of character and unlikely that he would install Valerius Gratus for 11 years. Methodologically, I think we should stick with what Josephus says in *Wars,* his more reliable volume (which isn't saying much!). That is to say, Tiberius probably sent Pilate immediately upon his accession to power and the normal term of his office would have been about five years at most, advice followed most often by Augustus and Tiberius. Once Pilate had been named as the 'bad guy' *vis à vis* Jesus Christ,[530] someone noticed that the chronology was wrong and 'corrected' Josephus. To make their change less noticeable, they added other changes too so as to muddy the waters, pulling names out of the air because they had recently read them in the text or had heard them elsewhere, possibly mispronounced. And so, Rufus and Gratus, the cowboy captains of Herod's troops became governors of Judea in a redactor's dream world of mangling the name of C. Vibius Rufus, suffect consul for 16 AD.[531]

The real timeline was probably something like this:

[528]Dio 23; Tac. *Ann.* 16.17, 1.80, 6.27; *Hist.* 2.65, 97; Suet. *Tib.* 63. See: William Thomas Arnold, *The Roman System of Provincial Administration to the Accession of Constantine the Great* (Forgotten Books, 2013 [1879]).

[529]Robin Seager, *Tiberius* (Wiley-Blackwell, 2005), p. 147. See also: Gregorio Maranon, *Tiberius: The Resentful Caesar* (Duell, Sloan and Pearce, 1956).

[530]And he was certainly that, as we will see, just not in any 'Jesus of Nazareth' timeline constructed by second-century mythmakers.

[531]And possibly even the name of Lucius Verginius Rufus (cos. 63, 69, 97), who was quite well known, having been offered the position of emperor by his army in 67 and 69, though he refused. Instead, he retired to his estate at Alsium on the coast of Etruria northwest of Rome. There he studied, composed poems, and had a literary salon. "After the murder of Emperor Domitian, Marcus Cocceius Nerva was elected emperor by the senate. Nerva chose as his co-consul for 97 the elderly Verginius Rufus, who was enticed out of retirement. However, when Verginius Rufus was to hold a speech, he dropped a book he was carrying, and while bending down to pick it up, slipped and broke his hip. He died not long afterward at the age of 82 and was given a state funeral. At the public burial with which he was honored, the historian Tacitus (then consul) delivered the funeral oration. Pliny the Younger, his neighbor and ward, has recorded the lines which Verginius had ordered to be engraved upon his tomb: *Hic situs est Rufus, pulso qui Vindice quondam Imperium asseruit non sibi sed patriae* ('Here lies Rufus, who after defeating Vindex, did not take power, but gave it to the fatherland')." (Wikipedia.org, 'Lucius Verginius Rufus.')

- Death of Herod, 4 BC

- Usurpation of kingship by Simon of Perea, 4/3 BC

- Varus and Sabinus, War of Varus, 4–1 BC

- Quirinius and Coponius, 1 BC to 11 AD (probably served sequentially, not together)

- Silanus and Coponius, 11–14/15 AD

- Silanus and Pilate, 15–17 AD

- Piso and Pilate, 17–19 AD

- ? – Stay tuned!

Who Was Pilate?

One of the troubling aspects about Pilate is that he was an obscure, equestrian-class official with a small military unit under his command, ruling over a very minor part of the Roman Empire. An inscription with his name and title on it was discovered at Caesarea Maritima in 1961, so he certainly existed. It doesn't refer to anything datable except the emperor Tiberius, who reigned 22 years.[532] Yet, thanks to the Gospels and Pilate's few hours of alleged interaction with Jesus, Christians have chanted every Sunday for the last 1,500 years or so that Jesus Christ "suffered under Pontius Pilate." I think we have a gross misunderstanding due either to Josephus' tendency to novelize, or to the devious hand of a redactor, and the fraudulent claims of Ignatius and Polycarp, to thank for that falsehood. Only, perhaps it is not entirely false? More on that later.

Philo is extremely negative about Pilate, and he lived in Alexandria, far away from the 'scene of the crime.' Josephus, on the other hand, is less condemnatory, though his descriptions of Pilate's actions are also quite negative; moreover, he was born after Pilate's heyday. This creates a big problem when we consider the Gospels' representation of Pilate as the 'Diet Coke of evil: just one calorie!' Poor Pilate is not allowed to let Jesus go because the bad Jews made him do it! That is patently ridiculous, as reasonable familiarity with Roman history will show. The Roman governor was able to release anyone he wanted in order to implement his decision about their guilt or innocence. Furthermore, the Pilate described by Philo and Josephus would not have brooked any interference from the Jews. The whole story in the Gospels is just absurd; entirely improbable historically speaking.

Philo on Pilate

In a surviving fragment of his work, *On Providence*, Philo of Alexandria comments that he was at the "city of Syria, on the sea shore, Ascalon by name ... I was there, at the time when I was on my journey towards the temple of my native land for the purpose of offering up prayers and sacrifices therein." So he was certainly familiar with Judea and Jerusalem. In only two of his

---

[532]There are also several coins alleged to have been minted by Pilate from the late 20s/early 30s AD. However, the coins *do not include Pilate's name*. The only reason they are associated with Pilate is because they include the years they were minted, and that association is simply based on the assumption that Pilate ruled during those years. They could have been minted by anyone who was prefect of Judea at the time.

treatises does Philo write about current events in the political/social sphere. Both of the texts are polemics against individuals that include details of the events for which Philo is castigating them.

The first text is *In Flaccum* (Against Flaccus), and its subject is the attack by Greek citizens of Alexandria on the Jews of that city carried out in 38 AD. There were riots, Jews were killed, their property stolen or destroyed, synagogues burned or desecrated, and so on. Jews constituted about a third of the population of Alexandria at the time, and were the largest Diaspora Jewish population in the Empire.

The second text is *Legatio ad Gaium* (The Embassy to Gaius), which describes the fallout of the Flaccus-inspired riots of 38. The text only devotes the last few pages to the actual embassy to make appeal to the emperor, consisting mostly of lengthy invective against Gaius AKA Caligula (spring 37 to his assassination in January 41 AD). The whole story is interesting and provides a unique possibility of comparing Philo to Josephus. Here I mostly follow Mary Smallwood's 'Philo and Josephus as Historians of the Same Events' for a general outline of the events, though with added thoughts.[533]

Philo begins by recounting three political murders committed early in Gaius' reign, then moves on to discuss Gaius' demand for divine honors while still living; he then goes on to retell the Alexandrian riot story. However, regarding the latter, Philo fudges a bit. By dating Gaius' demand for divine honors to his first regnal year, Philo is able to depict the Greek attack on the Alexandrian synagogues as compliance with the emperor's demand for worship; thus he can fully blame Gaius when, formerly, it was Flaccus who bore the burden.

Then comes the description of the embassy to the emperor, of which Philo himself was a member, and this segues into the emperor's demand that the Temple in Jerusalem shall be made into a shrine for the worship of himself.

Josephus also gives an account of the mad plans of Gaius to install his cult statue in the temple at Jerusalem. His mention of the riots is cursory since he only needs it for his chronology leading to the events in Palestine. Josephus doesn't even mention the Alexandrian riots in *Wars*, and in *Antiquities* he devotes about a page to that affair. As to the embassy of Philo, Josephus says only: "After an outbreak of civil strife in Alexandria between the Jewish residents and the Greeks, three delegates were chosen by each side and appeared before Gaius." Philo, on the other hand, who might be expected to know, says that the number of delegates for each side was five.

Josephus conveys the impression that the whole issue was the Jews' refusal to worship the emperor. It is only when Josephus quotes Claudius' edict, issued after his accession, that one realizes that the riots were actually about civic rights and the resentment felt by the Greeks against the Jews because of their 'protected status.'

The Alexandrian Jews had the right of residence in the city and were part of a *politeuma*, which was a quasi-autonomous civic organization, a formal corporation of aliens with the right of domicile and independent control over their own affairs. They had their own 'city council,' assembly, law courts, records office, and so on.[534]

---

[533]E. Mary Smallwood, 'Philo and Josephus as Historians of the Same Events,' in *Josephus, Judaism and Christianity*, eds. Louis H. Feldman and Gohei Hata (Detroit: Wayne State University Press, 1987).

[534]Very likely the same situation existed in Damascus so that the 'ethnarch' who went after Paul was the head of the Jewish community there.

In the 30s AD, there was a sizeable minority of Alexandrian Jews who were agitating for admission to Greek/Roman citizenship and were ready to compromise their religion for the sake of social prestige and honors that were open only to citizens (such as Tiberius Alexander's father). Some Jews were, apparently, acquiring citizenship by possibly illegal means and this was vigorously opposed by belligerent parties of Greeks. These Greeks of Alexandria also opposed Roman rule in general and were hostile toward Flaccus, the Roman governor who was targeted for the fact that the Jews had been favored and protected by Rome ever since Julius Caesar had guaranteed their religious liberty by legislation. The Greeks felt keenly that it would be unfair for the Jews to have their special protections *and* the privileges of citizenship, heretofore open only to non-Jews because, of course, being a citizen meant participating in the city cults; Jews wanted to be citizens without that necessity imposed on them.

After the accession of Gaius, the Greek nationalists either converted Flaccus to their views, or he sought to appease them. In the summer of 38 AD, Agrippa I, the friend of Nero and newly minted King of the Jews, passed through Alexandria en route to Palestine. The Greeks created a parody parade starring the City Idiot named 'Cabbage' dressed up to play the part of the Jewish king. This was a deliberate insult to the Jews, and Flaccus neither condemned nor punished it. This further emboldened the Greeks to riot, evict Jews from their homes and massacre them, burning and looting their houses and businesses and desecrating and destroying synagogues. Smallwood notes that Josephus' few words on the event appear to be a sure indication that he did not read Philo.

Things went from bad to worse. The Greek nationalists forced Flaccus to issue an edict declaring the Jews 'aliens' and without right of legal domicile other than in the original quarter of the city which had been allocated to them at the time of its founding. Josephus never mentions the burning issue of civic status which underlay the initial outbreak, showing that he was little informed on the problems.

By October 38, the situation had moderated somewhat, but the Jews were in a precarious position, unsure of their civic status and religious rights. The embassies were organized and sent a year later in 39.

In Philo's account, Isidorus is the head of the Greek embassy, while Josephus says it was Apion, his later target in his work *Against Apion*.

The embassy arrived in Rome in the spring of 40 AD and had a brief initial hearing with Gaius after which they were left to cool their heels. The second hearing was delayed and eventually took place just a few months before Gaius was assassinated. The accounts of both Josephus and Philo end with the emperor giving no decision and terminating the interview rudely.

According to Josephus, the news of the assassination of Gaius reached Alexandria in the spring of 41 and triggered an attack on the Greeks by the Jews, but this was suppressed by Flaccus' successor. In March, unaware of the renewed violence in Alexandria, the new emperor, Claudius, issued his edict restoring to the Jews the rights they had before the riots of 38, specifically that of religious liberty. End of story for Josephus.

However, 6 months later, Claudius wrote a letter/edict to Alexandria giving a more fully considered response. This letter confirmed the Jews' *existing* rights, both civic and religious, but refused to open any avenues to Greek citizenship to them. This letter survived by chance and put a period to a whole lot of historical speculation.

Both Josephus and Philo wrote about Gaius' attack on the temple in Jerusalem with wide divergences in both chronology and detail. For Josephus, the story was a central element to his theme of Roman mis-rule in Judea, so he wrote about it in both *Wars* and *Antiquities*, with only a few minor differences between his two accounts.

Regarding the differences between the accounts of Philo and Josephus, Philo's account is preferable both because he was a contemporary to the events and had contacts in Palestine and Rome, and because his account lacks the supernatural and mythical elements with which Josephus embellishes his tale.

During the winter of 39/40, the Jews of Jamnia destroyed an altar built by Greeks there to honor Gaius. The emperor heard about it in the spring of 40. So, it seems to have been at that very time that Gaius decided to punish the Jews' insult to his person by having a statue of himself installed in the temple at Jerusalem. It was probably also the reason he was rude to the embassy from Alexandria and dismissed them to await his pleasure. Josephus claims that Gaius was simply annoyed by the Jewish embassy from Alexandria. In any event, the preparations to install the statue were well underway in the summer of 40 while Philo and the embassy were right there in Rome trying to sort out the citizenship issues.

The project to have the statue made and installed was put into the hands of Publius Petronius, the legate of Syria, who was told to take two legions with him to ensure that the Jews didn't resist the action and thwart his intentions. Philo must have had intelligence from somewhere because he alone writes about the next episode: Petronius knew that the entire Eastern Diaspora might come to the aid of the Jews in Palestine and there would be more opposition than even Gaius had estimated. So, Petronius stalled for time. He summoned the Jewish leaders and tried to get them to use their influence in order to persuade the Jews to accept the sacrilege quietly. Horrified right down to their toes, it was not a surprise that they flatly refused.

Philo says that Petronius marched his legions "south" and Josephus says "to Ptolemais," which was just north of Galilee. Galilee, of course, was newly under the rule of Agrippa I, who had been parodied in Alexandria by the Cabbage King. By this time, news of the planned sacrilege had spread through the population and masses of Jews assembled to demonstrate against the intentions of the emperor. Petronius realized that this resistance could easily turn into armed insurrection.

At this point, Philo says that the Jews asked Petronius if they could send an embassy to plead their case before Gaius, but Petronius refused. Josephus adds the complementary information that Petronius left his troops in Ptolemais and went to the capital of Galilee, Tiberias. There he faced more demonstrations. The Jewish leaders there begged Petronius to write to Gaius on their behalf.

Philo agrees with Josephus that it was the earnestness of the Jews' appeal that moved Petronius to agree to write to the emperor even at risk of his own head. Philo connects this to the only demonstration he knew about: the one at Ptolemais. One wonders, of course, if the visit to Tiberias in Galilee reported by Josephus was an embellishment or a fact of significance that Philo was reticent to mention, as we will see.

In Philo's version of the letter to Gaius, Petronius apologized for the delay in getting the statue installed, blaming it on the slow artists. Then he explained that the Jews, as a whole, were so distressed that they refused to work in the fields and he feared they might even go to the lengths of destroying the crops ready to be harvested so as to bring on food shortages, thus inconveniencing the emperor who planned a trip along the coast later in the year.

Josephus, in his version, says that the fields were not being sown, which would put the demonstrations in the autumn rather than Philo's harvesting April–June date. Since sailing was generally confined to the period between mid-March and mid-November, Gaius' projected voyage could be set for late spring/early summer but not late autumn, so Philo's dating should be preferred.

Both Josephus and Philo agree that Gaius was less than pleased by the letter from Petronius; Josephus' version was high drama, Philo not so much. Josephus tells us that Gaius was so furious that a mere legate would dare to offer advice to a god that he accused Petronius of taking bribes from the Jews and wrote back ordering him to commit suicide. Philo credited Gaius with a modicum of self-control and said that Gaius curbed his temper because he realized that an imperial legate with command over four or more legions was a dangerous person to make an enemy. Thus Gaius wrote to Petronius to proceed with all speed as soon as he got this letter, since the crops would be harvested by then anyway.

The letter from Gaius to Petronius must have arrived around August, but no action was taken to install the statue. Philo does not give any explanation for this, but in any event, in the meantime, Agrippa I, in Rome, had persuaded the emperor to give up the plan. Another letter was sent to Petronius telling him to cancel the whole project.

Philo and Josephus agree that Agrippa saved the day, but they disagree on how. Philo says that Agrippa came to visit Gaius, his friend, almost immediately after Gaius had received and answered Petronius' letter and before his ire had cooled. Philo also says that Agrippa was completely ignorant of the scheme of Gaius to install a statue of himself in the Temple at Jerusalem. I find that hard to believe. Agrippa would have had to be in complete isolation somewhere that news did not travel to be unaware of this situation. This is what causes me to think that there was something to Josephus' claim about Petronius leaving his troops at Ptolemais while he went off to Galilee. Perhaps he went to consult with Agrippa? Perhaps they arranged a plan between themselves that Petronius would write the letter and Agrippa would arrive very quickly after, feigning ignorance and just a keen desire to see his friend, the emperor. It would have been important to prevent any appearance of collusion or conspiracy. As I see it, the coincidental arrival of Agrippa means that he must have left his kingdom at about the same time the letter from Petronius did; perhaps on the same ship?

In any event, one day in September, according to Philo, Agrippa arrived to visit and noticed that his friend, Gaius, appeared to be agitated and upset. He casually asked what was troubling him? When Gaius told him about his plans to put his statue in the temple at Jerusalem, and how obstinate the Jews were being about it, Agrippa immediately and dramatically collapsed to the floor in a state of shock from which he could not be roused.

Most scholars think that Agrippa must have had a stroke, but I rather think that it was a dramatic pretense that had been cooked up between Petronius and Agrippa. I think that Agrippa was feigning illness in order to shock and scare his longtime friend. And, indeed, Gaius was very concerned for the life of his friend for a period of time; this put him in the right frame of mind to grant a request.

This interpretation of Agrippa's collapse would better explain why Petronius apparently took no action *even after receiving the second letter* from the emperor telling him to proceed immediately: he expected something about the situation to change and that was because he and Agrippa had formed a plan.

It took some time for Agrippa to begin to show signs that he would recover, and Gaius was extremely anxious about his life. Upon his recovery, Agrippa wrote a long letter of argument with citations of precedent, begging him to follow the examples of Augustus and Tiberius with regard to their tolerance and favor toward the Jews. Apparently, Philo was in on the plot and helped to draft this memorandum, as many scholars suspect.

Gaius was not happy to give up his plan but wished to avoid being the cause of death to his friend, so he sent a third letter to Petronius telling him to abandon the plan entirely. He added that the Jews must reciprocate and tolerate any future attempts of Gentiles to introduce the imperial cult outside of Jerusalem.

Josephus, in his version of the story, says that Agrippa was "staying in Rome" throughout the whole sequence of events, and he knows nothing about the high drama of Agrippa's shocked collapse and illness. He tells us in a highly novelized story that Agrippa invited Gaius to a sumptuous banquet and the emperor, wishing to further honor his friend for his support during the last year of Tiberius' reign, asked him what he would like in the way of further benefices, expecting to be asked for an expansion of his territory. He was then surprised when Agrippa only asked that he should abandon his statue-in-the-temple scheme. Gaius granted the request because he admired Agrippa's lack of personal greed and because he had made the offer in front of witnesses. According to Josephus, Gaius' letter to Petronius had a vicious twist: the scheme was to be abandoned *only if* the statue had not already been erected; if it had, it was to stay.

Again, to reiterate, Philo was there at the time; Josephus was writing over three decades later. Smallwood concludes that "it is abundantly clear that Josephus did not know Philo's account."[535]

As noted, some scholars see the hand of Philo in the drafting of the memorandum presented to Gaius, which would also explain why he had a copy of it to include in his treatise, and if that is the case, it is a very precious document. Philo's text of the memorandum includes an interesting flashback to the time of Tiberius, the grandfather of Caligula, about persecutions of the Jews:

> ... at that time *things in Italy were thrown into a great deal of confusion* when Sejanus was preparing to make his attempt against our nation; for he [Tiberius] knew immediately after his [Sejanus'] death that the accusations which had been brought against the Jews who were dwelling in Rome were false calumnies, inventions of Sejanus, who was desirous to destroy our nation ... And he sent commands to all the governors of provinces in every country to comfort those of our nation in their respective cities, as *the punishment intended to be inflicted was not meant to be inflicted upon all, but only on the guilty; and they were but few.* And he ordered them to change none of the existing customs, but to look upon them as pledges, since the men were peaceful in their dispositions and natural characters, and their laws trained them and disposed them to quiet and stability.[536]

Philo appears to be saying that Sejanus,[537] the right-hand man of Tiberius until his fall, was responsible for a persecution of the Jews in Italy and elsewhere, and this was only revealed after

---

[535]Smallwood (1987), pp. 124–25.

[536]Philo, *On the Embassy to Gaius* (Caligula) 24.159–161.

[537]"Lucius Aelius Sejanus, or Seianus (June 3, 20 BC – October 18, AD 31), commonly known as Sejanus, was a soldier, friend and confidant of the Roman Emperor Tiberius. An equestrian by birth, Sejanus rose to power as

the death of Sejanus. Probably, this persecution began with the expulsion of Jews from Rome in 19 AD, which will play a big part in this discussion further on. Sejanus was executed in 31 AD and, apparently, at this point in time, Philo suggests that Tiberius sent edicts around to counter some of those that had been made by his former second-in-command.[538] The wording is not entirely clear, so it may have been a plot of Sejanus' that was later than 19 AD, or it may be that Tiberius countered the orders at the time, before he learned that Sejanus' accusations were not true. In any event, it seems like it fits an event of 19 AD that we will cover shortly, and that it concerned mainly Rome, so it is curious that it also led to Tiberius sending orders to all the governors of provinces. There must have been tumults in the Empire about which we know nothing thanks to the loss and destruction of records and histories.

Further on in the text, Philo includes another flashback to the time of Tiberius that obviously came from his own memories, because Herod Agrippa was too young to have remembered such things:

> What again did your other grandfather, Tiberius Caesar, do? ... during the three and twenty years that he was emperor, he preserved the form of worship in the temple as it had been handed down from the earliest times, without abrogating or altering the slightest particular of it.
>
> Moreover, I have it in my power to relate one act of ambition on his part ... *Pilate was one of the emperor's lieutenants, having been appointed governor of Judaea.* He, not more with the object of doing honour to Tiberius than with that of vexing the multitude, dedicated some *gilt shields in the palace of Herod,* in the holy city; which had no form nor any other forbidden thing represented on them except some necessary inscription, which mentioned these two facts, the name of the person who had placed them there, and the person in whose honour they were so placed there.
>
> But when the multitude heard what had been done, and when the circumstance became notorious, then the people, putting forward the *four sons* of the king, who were in no respect inferior to the kings themselves, in fortune or in rank, and his other descendants, and those magistrates who were among them at the time, entreated him to alter and to rectify the innovation which he had committed in respect of the shields; and not to make any alteration in their national customs, which had hitherto been preserved without any interruption, without being in the least degree changed by any king or emperor.
>
> But when he steadfastly refused this petition (for he was a man of a very inflexible disposition, and very merciless as well as very obstinate), they cried out: 'Do not cause a sedition; do not make war upon us; do not destroy the peace which exists. The honour of the emperor is not identical with dishonour to the ancient laws; let it not be to you a pretence for heaping insult on our nation. Tiberius is not desirous that any of our laws or customs shall be destroyed. And if you yourself say that he is, show us either some command from him, or some letter; or something of the kind, that we, who have been sent to you as ambassadors, may cease to trouble you, and may address our supplications to your master.'
>
> But this last sentence exasperated him in the greatest possible degree, as he feared lest they might in reality go on an embassy to the emperor, and might impeach him with respect to other particulars of his government, in respect of his corruption, and his acts of insolence, and his rapine, and his habit of insulting people, and his cruelty, and *his continual murders of people untried and uncondemned,* and his never ending, and gratuitous, and most grievous inhumanity.

---

prefect of the Roman imperial bodyguard, known as the Praetorian Guard, of which he was commander from AD 14 until his death in AD 31." (Wikipedia.org, 'Sejanus.')

[538] Details concerning Sejanus' fall are provided by Cassius Dio. Exactly that portion of Tacitus is missing in all surviving manuscripts.

Therefore, being exceedingly angry, and being at all times *a man of most ferocious passions*, he was in great perplexity, neither venturing to take down what he had once set up, nor wishing to do anything which could be acceptable to his subjects, and at the same time being sufficiently acquainted with the firmness of Tiberius on these points. And *those who were in power in our nation*, seeing this, and perceiving that he was inclined to change his mind as to what he had done, but that he was not willing to be thought to do so, wrote a most supplicatory letter to Tiberius. And he, when he had read it, *what did he say of Pilate, and what threats did he utter against him!*

But it is beside our purpose at present to relate to you *how very angry he was*, although he was not very liable to sudden anger; since the facts speak for themselves. Immediately, without putting anything off till the next day, *he wrote a letter, reproaching and reviling him in the most bitter manner for his act of unprecedented audacity and wickedness*, and commanding him immediately to take down the shields and to convey them away from the metropolis of Judaea to Caesarea, on the sea which had been named Caesarea Augusta, after his grandfather, in order that they might be set up in the temple of Augustus. And accordingly, they were set up in that edifice. And in this way he provided for two matters: both for the honour due to the emperor, and for the preservation of the ancient customs of the city.

Now the things set up on that occasion were shields, on which there was no representation of any living thing whatever engraved. But no, the thing [now] proposed to be erected [by Caligula] is a colossal statue. Moreover, *then* the erection was in the dwelling-house of the governor [palace of Herod]; but they say, that which is *now* contemplated is to be in the inmost part of the temple, in the very holy of holies itself ...[539]

In this account we see a Pilate who would never back down if he had either condemned or released a prisoner. The entire Gospel story of Pilate being such a fair guy and washing his hands is just ridiculous in the light of this historical data to which we can give some weight.

It is in no way possible to date the events in this little digression about Pilate in the letter of Agrippa to Caligula, but it is quite clear that there was an extremely unpleasant exchange between Tiberius and Pilate, and that Pilate came to heel and did as he was told, moving the shields to Caesarea, and that this is the probable reason for the existence of the 'Pilate Stone' in that location. Nor is there any indication at all that Tiberius died before Pilate got his just deserts. In fact, the way the account is written, it seems as though Pilate may have been in Judea only a few years at the time of his brilliant idea of how to annoy the Jews.

Josephus on Pilate

According to Philo, Pilate was a nasty piece of work. Josephus agrees more or less, but tends to try to humanize him. The following are two parallel passages about Pilate and the brouhaha about the ensigns, from Josephus:

Wars 2.9.2–4 (169–77)	*Antiquities* 18.3.1–2 (55–62)
Now Pilate, who was sent as procurator into Judea by Tiberius, sent by night those images of Caesar that are called ensigns into Jerusalem.	But now Pilate, the procurator of Judea, removed the army from Caesarea to Jerusalem, to take their winter quarters there, in order to abolish the Jewish laws. So he introduced Caesar's effigies, which were upon the ensigns, and brought them into the city;

---

[539]Philo, *Embassy* 37.298—39.306.

This excited a very great tumult among the Jews when it was day; for those that were near them were astonished at the sight of them, as indications that their laws were trodden under foot; for those laws do not permit any sort of image to be brought into the city. Nay, besides the indignation which the citizens had themselves at this procedure, a vast number of people came running out of the country. These came zealously to Pilate to Caesarea, and besought him to carry those ensigns out of Jerusalem, and to preserve them their ancient laws inviolable; but upon Pilate's denial of their request, they fell down prostrate upon the ground, and continued immovable in that posture for five days and as many nights. On the next day Pilate sat upon his tribunal, in the open market-place, and called to him the multitude, as desirous to give them an answer; and then gave a signal to the soldiers, that they should all by agreement at once encompass the Jews with their weapons; so the band of soldiers stood round about the Jews in three ranks. The Jews were under the utmost consternation at that unexpected sight. Pilate also said to them that they should be cut in pieces, unless they would admit of Caesar's images, and gave intimation to the soldiers to draw their naked swords. Hereupon the Jews, as it were at one signal, fell down in vast numbers together, and exposed their necks bare, and cried out that they were sooner ready to be slain, than that their law should be transgressed. Hereupon Pilate was greatly surprised at their prodigious superstition, and gave order that the ensigns should be presently carried out of Jerusalem.

After this he raised another disturbance, by expending that sacred treasure which is called Corban upon aqueducts, whereby he brought water from the distance of four hundred furlongs. At this the multitude had indignation; and when Pilate was come to Jerusalem, they came about his tribunal, and made a clamor at it. Now when he was apprized aforehand of this disturbance, he mixed his own soldiers in their armor with the multitude, and ordered them to conceal themselves under the habits of private men, and not indeed to use their swords, but with their staves to beat those that made the clamor.

whereas our law forbids us the very making of images; on which account the former procurators were wont to make their entry into the city with such ensigns as had not those ornaments. Pilate was the first who brought those images to Jerusalem, and set them up there; which was done without the knowledge of the people, because it was done in the night time; but as soon as they knew it, they came in multitudes to Caesarea, and interceded with Pilate many days that he would remove the images; and when he would not grant their requests, because it would tend to the injury of [Tiberius], while yet they persevered in their request, on the sixth day he ordered his soldiers to have their weapons privately, while he came and sat upon his judgment-seat, which seat was so prepared in the open place of the city, that it concealed the army that lay ready to oppress them; and when the Jews petitioned him again, he gave a signal to the soldiers to encompass them routed, and threatened that their punishment should be no less than immediate death, unless they would leave off disturbing him, and go their ways home. But they threw themselves upon the ground, and laid their necks bare, and said they would take their death very willingly, rather than the wisdom of their laws should be transgressed; upon which Pilate was deeply affected with their firm resolution to keep their laws inviolable, and presently commanded the images to be carried back from Jerusalem to Caesarea.

But Pilate undertook to bring a current of water to Jerusalem, and did it with the sacred money, and derived the origin of the stream from the distance of two hundred furlongs. However, the Jews were not pleased with what had been done about this water; and many ten thousands of the people got together, and made a clamor against him, and insisted that he should leave off that design. Some of them also used reproaches, and abused the man, as crowds of such people usually do.

He then gave the signal from his tribunal [to do as he had bidden them]. Now the Jews were so sadly beaten, that many of them perished by the stripes they received, and many of them perished as trodden to death by themselves; by which means the multitude was astonished at the calamity of those that were slain, and held their peace.

So he habited a great number of his soldiers in their habit, who carried daggers under their garments, and sent them to a place where they might surround them. So he bid the Jews himself go away; but they boldly casting reproaches upon him, he gave the soldiers that signal which had been beforehand agreed on; who laid upon them much greater blows than Pilate had commanded them, and equally punished those that were tumultuous, and those that were not; nor did they spare them in the least: and since the people were unarmed, and were caught by men prepared for what they were about, there were a great number of them slain by this means, and others of them ran away wounded. And thus an end was put to this sedition.

We see Josephus' tendency to glorify Jewish devotion to their religion, as well as a softening of Pilate's attitude: he was "deeply affected" by their firm resolution; after all, who could possibly resist such a demonstration? No mention of the Judean princes and magistrates being the ones appealing to Pilate, or his fear that they would communicate with the emperor, or of Tiberius stepping in and correcting his behavior. According to Josephus, it was purely the remarkable display of devotion to their laws exhibited by the common Jews that turned the situation around.

It is at this point in the narrative that the famous *Testimonium Flavianum* (TF) appears along with two apparently absurd stories about women named Paulina and Fulvia respectively. We are going to skip them here and come to them right after we cover the final important event of Pilate's career.

It was only later, according to Josephus, after Pilate attacked a crowd of Samaritans, that *the Samaritans sent a delegation to Vitellius*. Vitellius then sent a Marcellus to replace Pilate and ordered Pilate to Rome. We haven't been previously introduced to Vitellius in Josephus' text – he just sort of appears out of nowhere – but this is the third time the Samaritans make such an appearance. First, in relation to Archelaus' downfall:

> But in the tenth year of Archelaus's government, both his brethren, and **the principal men of Judea and Samaria**, not being able to bear his barbarous and tyrannical usage of them, **accused him before [Augustus]** ...[540]

Then during Coponius' term as prefect:

> As the Jews were celebrating the feast of unleavened bread, which we call the Passover, it was customary for the priests to open the temple-gates just after midnight. When, therefore, those gates were first opened, some of the **Samaritans came privately into Jerusalem, and *threw about dead men's bodies*, in the cloisters**; on which account the Jews afterward excluded them out of the temple, which they had not used to do at such festivals; and on other accounts also they watched the temple more carefully than they had formerly done. **A little after which accident *Coponius returned to Rome* ...**[541]

---

[540] *Ant.* 17.13.1–4 (339–52).
[541] *Ant.* 18.2.2 (29–32).

And now, as the last act in the Pilate drama, after skipping here the TF and the Paulina/Fulvia stories which were about Jews being expelled from Rome, we have one of the 'brigands' and rabble-rousing messianic types:

> But the nation of the Samaritans did not escape without tumults. The man who excited them to it was one who thought lying a thing of little consequence, and who contrived every thing so that the multitude might be pleased; so he bid them to get together upon Mount Gerizim, which is by them looked upon as the most holy of all mountains, and assured them, that when they were come thither, he would show them those sacred vessels which were laid under that place, because Moses put them there.
>
> So they came thither armed, and thought the discourse of the man probable; and as they abode at a certain village, which was called Tirathaba, they got the rest together to them, and desired to go up the mountain in a great multitude together; but Pilate prevented their going up, by seizing upon the roads with a great band of horsemen and foot-men, who fell upon those that were gotten together in the village; and when it came to an action, some of them they slew, and others of them they put to flight, and took a great many alive, the principal of which, and also the most potent of those that fled away, Pilate ordered to be slain.
>
> But when this tumult was appeased, **the Samaritan senate sent an embassy to Vitellius, a man that had been consul, and who was now president of Syria**, and accused Pilate of the murder of those that were killed; for that they did not go to Tirathaba in order to revolt from the Romans, but to escape the violence of Pilate. So **Vitellius sent Marcellus, a friend of his, to take care of the affairs of Judea**, and ordered Pilate to go to Rome, to answer before the emperor to the accusations of the Jews. **So Pilate, *when he had tarried ten years in Judea*, made haste to Rome**, and this in obedience to the orders of Vitellius, which he durst not contradict; but **before he could get to Rome Tiberius was dead.**[542]

Notice that just as the Samaritans cause problems three times *immediately before someone is exiled, returns to Rome, or is sent for discipline*, there are three references to money being taken from the Temple treasure house to construct aqueducts to bring water.

After Josephus finishes off Pilate by bringing in Vitellius, he launches upon a glorious account of how friendly Vitellius was with the Jews, immediately followed by the Vitellius/Artabanus story, recounted earlier, that we already know is a complete cock-up of the history and refers, in fact, to an event that occurred in 18 AD. While the presence of Vitellius at this point in the narrative would seem to indicate that Pilate *was* in Judea until the mid 30s AD, there is another explanation that we will get to after we look at this fascinating bit of text that just may tell us something:

> But Vitellius came into Judea, and went up to Jerusalem; it was at the time of that festival which is called the Passover. **Vitellius was there magnificently received**, and **released the inhabitants of Jerusalem from all the taxes** upon the fruits that were bought and sold, and **gave them leave to have the care of the high priest's vestments, ...*this he did as an act of kindness, to oblige the nation to him. Besides which, he also deprived Joseph, who was also called Caiaphas, of the high priesthood,*** and appointed Jonathan the son of Ananus, the former high priest, to succeed him. After which, he took his journey back to Antioch.
>
> Moreover, **Tiberius sent a letter to Vitellius**, and commanded him to make a league of friendship with Artabanus, the king of Parthia; for while he was his enemy, he terrified him, because

---

[542] *Ant.* 18.4.1–2.

he had taken Armenia away from him, lest he should proceed further, and told him he should no otherwise trust him than upon his giving him hostages, and especially his son Artabanus.[543]

We find ourselves now back with Vitellius and Artabanus. We also notice a curious thing. At the end of the chunk of text above about the Samaritan–Pilate affair, we read:

> So **Vitellius sent Marcellus, a friend of his, to take care of the affairs of Judea**, and **ordered Pilate to go to Rome**, to answer before the emperor to the accusations of the Jews. So Pilate, when he had tarried ten years in Judea, made haste to Rome, and this in obedience to the orders of Vitellius, which he durst not contradict; but **before he could get to Rome Tiberius was dead.**

And then, at the beginning of the very next paragraph after Pilate is dispatched, there is this:

> But Vitellius came into Judea, and went up to Jerusalem; it was at the time of that festival which is called the Passover ... After which, he took his journey back to Antioch. Moreover, **Tiberius sent a letter** to Vitellius, and commanded him to make a league of friendship with Artabanus ...

And then a few paragraphs further on:

> *About this time* it was that Philip, Herod's brother, departed this life, **in the twentieth year of the reign of Tiberius**, after he had been tetrarch of Trachonitis and Gaulanitis, and of the nation of the Bataneans also, **thirty-seven years.**

It's pretty obvious that the rumors of Tiberius' death at the time of the departure of Pilate have been greatly exaggerated!

The Friends of Germanicus: Prosopography Lite

> Prosopographical research has the goal of learning about patterns of relationships and activities through the study of collective biography. The collection of data underlies the creation of a prosopography, the objective is to understand patterns and relationships by analysing the data.[544]

~~~

The main events of Pilate's career are described in Josephus' *Antiquities* 18.3.1–2, followed by the *Testimonium Flavianum* at 18.3.3 and the tales of Paulina and Fulvia at 18.3.4–5, which we will discuss in due course. When Josephus' history continues in the next chapter, 18.4.1–2, Pilate gets finished off with his Samaritan Debacle and then, in 18.4.3, we make a sudden leap to the Vitellius and Artabanus story, which then leads into the Antipas-Aretas conflict we have already discussed at length and caught Josephus prestidigitating with red hands! Why is this so problematical? Well, notice that the *first* mention of Pilate is at *Ant.* 18.2.2 (35), at the very end of the paragraph: "When Gratus had done those things, he went back to Rome, after he had waited in Judea eleven years, when Pontius Pilate came as his successor."

---

[543] *Ant.* 18.4.3–4.
[544] Wikipedia.org, 'Prosopography.'

Now, as we noted above, even though Josephus says Tiberius sent him to be procurator of Judea in 18.2.2 (33), this Gratus is highly suspect, and by even a reasonable count of years we shouldn't be anywhere near 27 AD. Our skepticism is supported *just one paragraph later*, at 18.2.4 (39), when Josephus states, "*About this time* died Phraates, king of the Parthians," followed by an account about Vonones.[545]   But Phraates had died in 2 BC, and Tacitus also covers the Vonones events in *Annales* 2.2ff., *dated to 16 AD*, just two years after the death of Augustus. Josephus notes further on in the same chapter (18.2.4 [52]) that Silanus was president of Syria. Tacitus, too, notes that Q. Caecilius Metellus Creticus Silanus was governor of Syria (*Ann.* 2.4.3) *from 12 to 17 AD*. So other than the confused and contradictory accounts of the governors of Judea, we are tracking well with Pilate having been sent at the time Tiberius took over, as was strongly implied in *Wars*.

The next event reported by Josephus (*Ant.* 18.2.5) is the death of Antiochus, king of Commagene. *This occurred in 17 AD*. At this point, Josephus notes that the Roman Senate decreed that Germanicus should be sent to settle the affairs of the East. Tacitus, too, notes this (*Ann.* 2.42.5), along with the following:

> At around the same time, on the decease of Antiochus and Philopator (the kings respectively of the Commageni and Cilicians), there was disruption in their nations, the majority desiring Roman, others royal, command. *And the provinces of Syria and Judaea, exhausted by their burdens, begged a diminution of taxation.* ... [T]he tremors in the East could not be settled except by the wisdom of Germanicus ... then by a decree of the fathers Germanicus was entrusted with the provinces ... with a greater command than that entrusted to those who held them by lot or on dispatch from the princeps.[546]
>
> But Tiberius had removed from Syria Creticus Silanus, who was connected with Germanicus by marriage ... and placed in charge Cn. Piso, temperamentally violent and a stranger to compliance, his defiance implanted in him by his father Piso (who in the civil war helped the resurgence of the party in Africa with the keenest of service against Caesar and then, after following Brutus and Cassius, was allowed to return ...[547]

Then, at the very end of *Antiquities* 18.2, there is a brief remark about the death of Germanicus due to being poisoned by Piso.

> At this time died Antiochus, the king of Commagene [17 AD] ... So the senate made a decree that Germanicus should be sent to settle the affairs of the east, fortune hereby taking a proper opportunity for depriving him of his life; for when he had been in the east, and settled all affairs there, his life was taken away by the poison which Piso gave him, as has been related elsewhere.[548]

---

[545]Vonones I was an Arsacid prince, who ruled as King of Kings of Parthian Empire from 8 to 12, and then subsequently as king of Armenia from 12 to 18. He was the eldest son of Phraates IV (r. 37–2 BC) and was sent to Rome as a hostage in 10/9 BC in order to prevent conflict over the succession of Phraates IV's youngest son, Phraataces.

[546]Tacitus' wording means that in whatever province Germanicus should enter, he would have greater power than the person who was governing the province as a proconsul. Then, Tacitus follows this by pointing out that Piso was "temperamentally violent and a stranger to compliance," hinting then that he was taught by his father to hate anyone of the family of Caesar. In short, Tacitus is saying that Tiberius is setting Germanicus up to have problems.

[547]Tacitus, *Ann.* 2.43.2.

[548]*Ant.* 18.2.5 (53).

When Josephus *returns* to the subject of Pilate, it is *immediately following this remark about the death of Germanicus*. After a digression on other matters (the building projects of the Herodians and the Artabanus business, which tracks with Tacitus' discussion of the Vonones/Artabanus saga of 16, 17 and 18 AD, which was why Germanicus was sent out to the East to begin with), he now comes back to Pilate, who was apparently left dangling while he finished off Germanicus. Thus, the resumption of the Pilate story is actually referring to a time *before* the death of Germanicus. In sum, **all these events cluster around the years 16 to 19 AD**.

> But now Pilate, the procurator of Judea, removed the army from Caesarea to Jerusalem to take their winter quarters there, in order to abolish the Jewish laws. So he introduced Caesar's effigies, which were upon the ensigns, and brought them into the city ...[549]

Taken as it is written, without the artificial divisions and removing the authorial asides, it would say: "At this time died Antiochus, the king of Commagene [17 AD] ... So the senate made a decree that Germanicus should be sent to settle the affairs of the east ... But now Pilate, the procurator of Judea, removed the army from Caesarea to Jerusalem."

If we recall Philo's discussion of Pilate and the affair of the *golden shields*, we can notice that the *princes and magistrates were the ones who confronted Pilate*. Based on how Philo described Pilate, as well as what Josephus included in his account, the whole scenario belongs to the period 18/19 AD. What is odd in *Wars* is how the topic then jumps to Agrippa in Rome – "in the meantime" – supposedly at the time that Tiberius is practically on his deathbed (36 AD). *Quelle surprise!* The passage tells that Agrippa went to see Tiberius to accuse Herod Antipas. Apparently, Tiberius didn't think the accusation was serious, so Herod Agrippa stayed in Rome to start cozying up to Caligula. This resulted in Herod Agrippa being indiscreet and getting himself tossed into prison by Tiberius. This happened, as Josephus says, six months before the death of Tiberius, i.e. 36 AD. (Tiberius died on 16 March 37.) In other words, there is **a big skip in the historical record**, this time in *Wars*.[550] *Antiquities* also mentions Agrippa going to Rome at the tail end of the Vitellius/Artabanus saga:

> So Vitellius truly retired to Antioch; but Agrippa, the son of Aristobulus, went up to Rome, a year before the death of Tiberius, in order to treat of some affairs with the emperor, if he might be permitted so to do.[551]

The only problem with the above tale is that Agrippa did not make the accusations against Herod Antipas *until 39 AD*,[552] and he brought the accusation to *Caligula*, at which point, by either chronology, Pilate was certainly not in Judea.[553] *Caligula* exiled Antipas to Gaul – just like Augustus did to Archelaus! – and he was apparently accompanied by the seductress Herodias.

All I can say is that the redactor who cut chunks out of these texts, and inserted what he thought were clever interpolations, was an idiot. And I don't know of anyone else who has ever noticed this before.

---

[549] *Ant.* 18.3.1 (55).

[550] *Wars* 2.9.5 (178–80).

[551] *Ant.* 18.5.3 (120–6).

[552] Tessa Rajak, 'Iulius Agrippa (1) I, Marcus,' in Simon Hornblower, *Oxford Classical Dictionary* (Oxford University Press, 1996).

[553] *Ant.* 18.7.2. Also see Charles Peter Mason, 'Agrippa, Herodes I,' in William Smith, *Dictionary of Greek and Roman Biography and Mythology* 1 (Little, Brown and Company, 1867), pp. 77–78.

In any event, after his discussion of the effigies that arrived with Pilate, Josephus mentions the Corban/water issue that also was noted in *Wars*. (In *Wars*, it was 400 furlongs; in *Antiquities*, it's 200. But who's counting?) It was allegedly this use of Temple funds that caused the next upset and led to Pilate planting his soldiers in the crowd with staves with which to beat the Jews. The *Testimonium Flavianum* follows immediately, and the two tales about the *expulsion of the Jews* and Egyptians follow that, so despite the prestidigitation of the text, we are certainly still in the temporal environment of 19 AD!

When we pick up the historical narrative in Judea again, i.e. with Pilate, we have yet another disruption due to Samaritans.[554] (As had apparently also happened under Coponius.)[555] Pilate apparently killed a number of them and the Samaritans complained to *Vitellius*, who is now, suddenly, governor of Syria when just before, as noted, it was *Silanus followed by Piso*. Vitellius pulls rank on Pilate, sends 'Marcellus' to handle Judea, and orders Pilate to Rome. But Josephus (or a redactor) then tells us that *Tiberius was dead before Pilate could get there!*

In other words, the record skips again with that absolutely astonishing leap from 19 to 36/37 AD! So how the heck did that happen?

We are told by Josephus that the Samaritans sent an embassy to Vitellius, who is suddenly 'president of Syria,' and that Vitellius sent a Marcellus – about whom nothing is known – to take care of Judea and ordered Pilate to Rome to answer the accusations of the Jews.

> So Pilate, when he had waited ten years in Judea, hurried to Rome, and this in obedience to *the orders of Vitellius*, which he dared not contradict; but before he could get to Rome, Tiberius was dead.[556]

Recall that twice now we have been told specific numbers of years for the governors of Judea: Gratus (11 years) and Pilate (10 years). And somehow we have skipped from Silanus (17 AD) to Vitellius (36 AD), some 18/19 years. Plus, we have jumped from one Artabanus story (18 AD) to another (36 AD).

Let's take up the problem of this sudden appearance of Vitellius, who had such a fun part to play in the Antipas–Aretas story and who was surely in Judea *later*: in 36/37 AD.

There are several Vitelliuses in Tacitus, but only two would have qualified for proconsular duties: 1) L. Vitellius, consul 34, 43, and 47 AD, who is our Vitellius of *later* 36/37 AD adventures; and 2) Aulus Vitellius, consul in 48 AD, who became emperor for eight months in 69 AD; he is too late to consider. But, as I continued to search, I found a P. Vitellius who was a 'friend of Germanicus.' We find him in Germany in *Annales* 1.70; in 2.6 he heads off to do *a census* of the Galliae; in 2.74, we find the most interesting mention. It is immediately following the death of Germanicus, and it *takes place in Syria*:

> There was next a debate between the legates and other senators who were present as to who should be placed in charge of Syria. And, after only modest exertions from the others, for a long time the

---

[554]*Ant.* 18.4.1 (85). Mason (2016), pp. 232–34, argues that the Samarian animosity towards Judeans was a holdover from the Hasmonean and Herodian expansions and subsequent domination of the region, which included the destruction of the Samarian temple on Mount Gerizim. These expansions left Judean minorities in many of the cities of Syria. Contributing to the inter-ethnic strife was the fact that the auxiliary forces stationed at Caesarea were recruited largely from Samaria. But Mason is assuming that anything about this story is historically accurate.

[555]Compare *Ant.* 18.2.2 (30–1). The implied year is somewhere in 6–9 AD.

[556]*Ant.* 18.4.2.

issue was between Vibius Marsus and Cn. Sentius. Then Marsus yielded to the seniority and keener contention of Sentius;[557] and he, for his part dispatched to the City [Rome] a woman infamous for poisonings in the province and particularly dear to Plancina, by name of Martina, *in response to demands from* **Vitellius and Veranius** and the rest, *who were drawing up charges and accusations* as if against persons already cited as defendants.[558]

So, that means that **P. Vitellius was with Germanicus in Syria at the time he died**. *This* Vitellius was drawing up charges and accusations, and appears to have been 'in charge,' and thus, there is a simple explanation for why Pilate was said to have been sent back to Rome by Vitellius: because he was! It just wasn't the same Vitellius who was in Judea in 37 AD.

The fact that this Vitellius was with Germanicus in Syria is detailed later in Tacitus, when Piso is being arraigned back in Rome for poisoning Germanicus:

> On the next day Fulcinius Trio arraigned Piso before the consuls. Yet **Vitellius and Veranius and the other of Germanicus' companions** maintained that there was no role for Trio; nor were they accusers themselves, they said, but *as informants and witnesses of events they would deliver Germanicus' instructions.*[559]

Next:

> Then Fulcinius embarked on past irrelevancies, namely the fact that Piso's tenure of Spain had been marked by corruption and greed [Piso had been legate there in 9/10 AD] ... After this, Servaeus and **Veranius and Vitellius** with like enthusiasm (and with much eloquence on Vitellius' part) cast the charge that in his hatred for Germanicus and his enthusiasm for revolution *Piso, by licensing maltreatment of the allies*, had corrupted the common soldiers to such a degree that the basest of them called him "parent of the legions." Conversely, they said he had been savage to all the best men, especially to the companions and friends of Germanicus. Finally, he had annihilated the man himself by curses and poison: hence the rituals and abominable offerings by himself and Plancina, his claiming the state by arms, and – to ensure his appearance as the accused – his defeat in the line of battle.[560]

One cannot help but think that Piso, governor of Syria from 17 to 19 AD, may have been behind the abominable treatment of the Jews attributed to Pilate, because he licensed "maltreatment of the allies." This is followed by another brief mention (3.17), and then:

> A few days after Caesar [Tiberius] initiated the senate's granting of priesthoods to **Vitellius and Veranius and Servaeus**. ... That was the end to the avenging, though Germanicus' death was bandied about in various rumors not only among those men who lived then but also in following times. So is it the case that all the greatest matters are ambiguous, inasmuch as some people hold any form of hearsay as confirmed, others turn truth into its converse, and each swells among posterity.[561]

---

[557] A. J. Woodman, in his translation of *The Annals*, notes in a footnote: "Epigraphic evidence shows that the appointment of Cn. Sentius Saturninus (suffect consul AD 4) was confirmed by Tiberius ..."

[558] Tacitus, *Ann.* 2.74.

[559] Tacitus, *Ann.* 3.9–10.

[560] Tacitus, *Ann.* 3.13.

[561] Tacitus, *Ann.* 3.19.

Vitellius later committed suicide under indictment for something *in 31 AD*, following the fall of Sejanus.[562] Tacitus' narrative is missing the end of 29, all of 30, and most of 31 AD. That period is, of course, the very period in which Jesus is said to have been crucified in Judea under Pontius Pilate, and might have included some pertinent information that contradicted such a claim. So, we don't know what Vitellius was being charged with – possibly revolutionary actions against Tiberius? Being in cahoots with Sejanus? Being a friend of Germanicus? P. Vitellius' wife, Acutia, was also arraigned on some charge in 37 AD.

Now, also consider that this 'Marcellus', supposed to have been sent to order Pilate to Rome and take over Judea, may have been **Vibius *Marsus*,** mentioned by Tacitus above. We've seen how often Josephus garbles names (or deliberately obfuscates them), and this may be such a case. Gaius Vibius Marsus was also sent to summon Gnaeus Calpurnius Piso to Rome to stand his trial. His name occurs again seven years later in 26 AD, in the debates of the Senate; and just before the death of Tiberius in 37 he narrowly escaped his own death, being accused as one of the accomplices of the notorious Albucilla.[563] In 47 we find him governor of Syria.[564] The name of 'Gaius Vibius Marsus,' proconsul, also appears on several coins of Utica in Africa, struck in the reign of Tiberius.[565]

As to the official governor of Syria named Vitellius, as we already know from our discussions above, he was there in 35–37 AD. And, we should notice particularly, in all of the above, that Cn. Sentius Saturninus took over as governor of Syria/Judea immediately after the death of Germanicus. This was certainly never mentioned by Josephus in the text we now have.

In addition to the governor of Syria, Sentius Saturninus, who interacted with Germanicus' friends Vitellius and Veranius after his death, there was a Gaius Sentius Saturninus who was Roman consul in 19 BC. Around 14/13 BC, Sentius Saturninus was appointed the proconsular governor of Africa. From 9 to 7 BC he served as *Legatus Augusti pro praetore* (or imperial governor) of the Roman province of Syria. It was his second son Gnaeus – our Saturninus of 19 AD – who replaced Gnaeus Calpurnius Piso as governor of Syria and compelled him to return to Rome to stand trial for the murder of Germanicus.

So, we have found a Vitellius, a Marsus/Marcellus, and now a Saturninus turn up around Germanicus, two of which are names of important characters that show up in Josephus' narrative. Now let's take a look at a few other characters we've encountered so far in Josephus' tale: Valerius Gratus, Silanus and Sabinus.

---

[562]This was the Sejanus mentioned by Philo as being responsible for the persecution of the Jews in Italy.

[563]"Albucilla was the wife of Satrius Secundus, and was infamous for having had many lovers. In 37 AD, she was accused of treason, or impiety, against the emperor (Latin: *impietatis in principem*) along with Gnaeus Domitius Ahenobarbus, Vibius Marsus, and Lucius Arruntius. As a result she was imprisoned by command of the senate ..." (Wikipedia.org, 'Albucilla.') Her husband, Satrius Secundus, "was a dependent of Sejanus. He accused Aulus Cremutius Cordus, the historian, of having eulogized Brutus and spoken of Cassius as the last of the Romans, which was considered an offence under the *lex maiestas*, and the senate ordered the burning of his writings in 25 AD. He afterwards betrayed his master, and gave information to Tiberius of the conspiracy which Sejanus had formed against him. Josephus relates that Antonia informed Tiberius of the conspiracy of Sejanus. It has been conjectured that Secundus, unwilling or unable to have an interview with the emperor, had acquainted Antonia with the plot." (Wikipedia.org, 'Satrius Secundus.')

[564]Tacitus, *Ann.* 6. 47; 2.74, 79; 4.47, 48; 9.10.

[565]Joseph Hilarius Eckhel, vol. iv, pp. 147, 148, cited in 'Gaius Vibius Marsus,' Wikipedia.org.

According to the 'biblically' understood history, Valerius Gratus was the Roman Prefect of Judea under Tiberius from 15 to 26 AD. He succeeded Annius Rufus and was replaced by Pontius Pilate. Here is the list derived from *Antiquities* again (with the 'official' chronology):

- Varus and Sabinus: 7 to 4 BC

- Archelaus (ethnarch of Judea): 4 BC to 6 AD

- Coponius: 6 to 9 AD?

- Marcus Ambivius/Ambivulus: 9 to 12 AD?

- Annius Rufus: 12 to 14 AD?

- (Death of Augustus: 14 AD)

- Valerius Gratus: 15 to 26 AD

- Pilate: 27 to 37 AD

Josephus mentions Syrian governors Cyrenius (Quirinius) who arrived with Coponius, Silanus who served from 12 to 17 AD, Piso who replaced him (though he doesn't say he was governor), but there is no mention of Cn. Sentius Saturninus, who we know took over as governor of Syria/Judea immediately after the death of Germanicus in 19 AD. That, alone, puts a spanner in Josephus' list. But let's look at the others and see if there are any clues.

We know who Varus is: Publius Quinctilius Varus is certainly attested, but Syme dates him based on the biblical dates that have been imposed on Josephus, so that information is useless.

There are a few problems with identifying Coponius. The Coponii were a plebeian family, prominent at Rome during the first century BC. The most famous was Gaius Coponius, praetor in 49 BC and a partisan of Pompey. He was proscribed by the triumvirs in 43, subsequently pardoned, and ended up a respected member of the Senate. Relying, again, on Josephus, Syme says: "When Judaea was annexed (AD 6), Coponius, a Roman knight of a respectable family from Tibur, became its first governor."[566] We find that a Marcus, Gaius, and Titus Coponius are mentioned by Cicero.[567] But while there is actually no specific mention of this Coponius on the Roman records side, since we find him in Josephus' *Wars*, we have some small confidence that he was there (remember, Josephus had a particular target audience for *Wars* and was less likely to fudge about things they could know about themselves).

Syme points out that in the last years of Augustus, 4 to 14 AD, some new names show up, indicating the advancement of *novi homines* ('new men' whose families hadn't previously been in the aristocracy), most of them military. The two Poppaei came from an obscure community in Picenum. "The most striking example of continuous service is afforded by the *novus homo* from Picenum, C. Poppaeus Sabinus (cos. AD 9). During 25 years this man had charge of Moesia, for most of the time with the provinces of Macedonia and Achaia as well."[568] This could possibly be Josephus' Sabinus of Varus war fame. He was pretty busy elsewhere for most of his career, but he could have been the legate to Varus before he was made consul in 9 AD.

We don't find any 'Marcus Ambivius' or anything similar, though I wonder if that was a deliberate garbling of the name Gaius Vibius Marsus?

---

[566] Ronald Syme, *The Roman Revolution* (Oxford, 1939), p. 476.

[567] *De Oratore* 1.39, 2.32; *Brutus* 52; *Pro Balbo* 53; *Pro Caelio* 24.

[568] Syme (1939), pp. 362, 396.

There are hundreds of coins minted in Judea that scholars have traditionally tied to the various prefects, including Coponius, Ambivius and Rufus. However, the only identifying marks on the coins are numbers indicating years in the Roman calendar; the images are neutral images like palm trees or wheat, and the only names present (if at all) are the emperor's. In other words, there is actually nothing on the coins to indicate the prefect or procurator's name! It is simply assumed, based on the biblically imposed timeline of *Antiquities* and its little collection of names that cannot otherwise be attested, that the coins were struck under this or that procurator. In fact, scholars are catching on that the picture is not so simple:

> The issue of the absolute dates of the governorships of those representing Roman rule in Judea at this time is the subject of continuing debate. Because there is in fact little agreement among historians about the chronology of many of these governorships, in 2007 the journal *Israel Numismatic Research* took the editorial position whereby governors' names are no longer employed in describing these coins.[569]

There is no Annius Rufus either. There is an L. Tarius Rufus (suffect consul in 16 BC), who was another *novus homo*, but he is obviously too old to show up in Judea at the time indicated.

Can we find Valerius Gratus in Tacitus? No, though we do find a number of other Valeriuses. (It is unlikely, with that name, that this alleged prefect of Judea would have been an equestrian, so it is also therefore unlikely he was a prefect, which was an equestrian position.) Nevertheless, the first Valerius that would have been eligible in the time period in question (i.e. 15–26 AD, according to the *Antiquities* chronology) would have been Marcus Valerius Messalla Messalinus, who was consul in 3 BC. We learn about him that, at the death of Augustus, during a debate in the Senate afterward, "Messala Valerius added that the oath in Tiberius' name should be renewed annually."[570] This Valerius was the son of the famous orator M. Valerius Messalla Corvinus. He (the son) shows up again – surprise, surprise – *around the death of Germanicus*! When Tiberius is dealing with the 'vengeance' for the death of Germanicus, Tacitus writes: "Valerius Messalinus proposed that a golden statue should be set up in the temple of Mars the Avenger."[571] Tiberius demurred. There isn't much else of interest. *There is no indication that he was ever in Syria or Judea.*

There is another M. Valerius, consul in 20 AD (five or six years too late) and, apparently, the son of Marcus Valerius Messalla Messalinus, consul in 3 BC. There is another candidate: Marcus Valerius Messalla Volesus who was consul in 5 AD and had been proconsul of Asia in 11/12 AD. But, as noted, with his rank, he would never have been a prefect of Judea. Anyway, it looks like Valerius Gratus is a bust. We have to remember that many of these names that get tossed around about Judea by Josephus are thought to have been there *only* because he said so.

Now on to Silanus, governor of Syria, whom Josephus mentions just before his introduction of Pilate. We already know that this is Q. Caecilius Metellus Creticus Silanus, who was consul in 7 AD, and governor of Syria from 13 to 17 AD.[572] Quite by accident, searching for the name 'Silanus' we find something else of interest: there was a C. Appius Junius Silanus who was consul in 28 AD:

---

[569] Donald T. Ariel, Review of David M. Jacobson, Nikos Kokkinos (eds), 'Judaea and Rome in Coins, 65 BCE–135 CE,' *Numismatic Chronicle* 174 (2014), p. 388.
[570] Tacitus, *Ann.* 1.8.4.
[571] Tacitus, *Ann.* 3.18.2.
[572] Tacitus, *Ann.* 2.4.3, 2.43.2.

With Junius Silanus and with Silius Nerva as consuls, a foul beginning to the year was made with the dragging to prison of the illustrious Roman equestrian Titius Sabinus *owing to his friendship with Germanicus.*[573]

Now, isn't it interesting that there is a *Sabinus* hanging out with Germanicus too, recalling that there was an alleged Sabinus causing problems by going after Herod the Great's estate when Archelaus headed off for Rome? Apparently, Silanus' prosecution was delayed, and we find him again in 32 AD, along with another Sabinus!

> ... Annius Pollio and Appius Silanus[574] along with Scaurus Mamercus and Sabinus Calvisius were arraigned for treason ...[575]

The name 'Annius Pollio' catches the eye. Was that where Josephus – or the redactor – got the idea for 'Annius Rufus'? I'm just struck by the names 'Rufus and Gratus' appearing in juxtaposition as governors after they appeared several other times in Josephus' text as army captains in the rebellion. I don't think Josephus made up additional procurators of Judea; I think a Christian editor did – one who saw the chronological problems of Pontius Pilate's term of office being way too early to fit the Jesus timeline. It seems that it was done by someone who didn't understand the Roman nomenclature or social/political ranking, or who thought he could get away with such name games and mangling. Well, he did get away with it, didn't he?

Coming back to Titius Sabinus, the friend of Germanicus, Tacitus writes of the year 24 AD:

> With Cornelius Cethegus and Visellius Varro as consuls ... [Tiberius] was being hounded by Sejanus, who repeatedly censured the fact that the community was split as in a civil war: there were, he said, people calling themselves members of "Agrippina's faction" [widow of Germanicus] ... It was for this reason that *he attacked C. Silius and Titius Sabinus. Ruinous to each of them was their friendship with Germanicus,* but to Silius was also the fact that, as controller of a mighty army for seven years and, after winning the triumphal insignia in Germany, as victor in the Sacrovirian war, he was likely to fall with a heavier crash ... Silius' wife was Sosia Galla, resented by the princeps *on account of her affection for Agrippina.* The decision was made to seize them both, deferring Sabinus for a time ...[576]

In short, this is perhaps either the same alleged person who was the 'agent of Augustus' after Herod's death, or his son. But if it was the son, it is odd that Tacitus does not mention the family connection, because he is usually very diligent about reciting pedigrees or connections.

In other words, it looks like Josephus – or a redactor – again has used the name of one of Germanicus' friends/staff/entourage to take some position or other in his rewriting of the tale of the Sorrows of Judea AKA *Antiquities.* The bottom line is, however, we are having a hard time lining any of these real people and events up with the novelized version by Josephus, or, actually, lining up Josephus' inventions with the facts. While some of the characters are attested in Tacitus (e.g., Creticus Silanus, governor of Syria), we can't find the alleged governors of Judea whom Josephus (or a redactor) adds into his *Antiquities*: Marcus Ambivius/Ambivulus, Annius

---

[573]Tacitus, *Ann.* 4.68.1.

[574]This Silanus was, apparently, murdered by Claudius' freedman, Narcissus, in 42 AD, which one deduces from a passing reference at *Ann.* 11.29.1.

[575]Tacitus, *Ann.* 6.9.3.

[576]Tacitus, *Ann.* 4.17–19.

Rufus, or Valerius Gratus; it seems that they never existed except in the imagination and only for the purpose of being placeholders. We noticed how in *Wars*, Josephus goes from the end of the ethnarchy of Archelaus to the death of Augustus and the sending of Pilate, to the end of Tiberius' reign in just a few paragraphs. One gets the distinct impression that something is missing. And even if we determine that Pilate was there from the death of Augustus to the death of Germanicus, we are still in the dark about what was happening during those years of the leap from 19 to 36 AD that are unaccounted for by Josephus or anyone else. That's one of the perils of history: there are some things we will just never know. But again, we do know that Cn. Sentius Saturninus took over as governor of Syria/Judea immediately after the death of Germanicus, and that this is not mentioned by Josephus. The timeline of governors is tarnished irreparably, I would suggest.

So now it appears that, in Josephus' *Antiquities*, all the externally attested events before, during, and after the account of Pilate's career and the *Testimonium Flavianum* take place in the years 16 to 19 AD, from the events surrounding Vonones (16 AD), and the deaths of Antiochus (17 AD) and Germanicus (19 AD), to the mention of Silanus (17 AD) and Artabanus (18 AD), and the references to the expulsion of Jewish and Egyptian cultists from Rome (19 AD) in the tales associated with the TF. The narrative then jumps forward 17/18 years or so into the future, utilizing Vitellius (two different men with the same name) as the hook, intermingling the characters and time periods in the process. The only other real exceptions are the short, unverifiable accounts of the other Judean prefects, which stick out like sore thumbs.

While the names of the Judean prefects do not show up in any other sources or archaeological remains, curiously, the names of several associates of Germanicus show up in these problematic chapters. Recall from the Artabanus saga that Germanicus was heir to the Roman emperor and had been sent to reorganize the Asian provinces in 18 AD, where he came into conflict with the Syrian governor Piso and negotiated with the Parthian king Artabanus; 18 years later, Artabanus makes another appearance in relation to the Syrian governor of that time, L. Vitellius.

But there was a Vitellius as temporary acting governor at the time of the death of Germanicus: P. Vitellius, who was with Germanicus in Syria and who energetically drew up accusations and ordered suspects to be sent to Rome in the wake of Germanicus' death. He also shows up in Josephus, ordering Pilate back to Rome to face Tiberius and ordering Piso to Rome to face trial for murder. Either Josephus has bridged the events of 18 AD to those of 36 AD, whether intentionally or not, using a cast of characters common to both – Tiberius, Vitellius (albeit, two different Vitelliuses), and Artabanus – or a redactor has deleted a huge portion of text and tried to tie things together from two different periods by the handy expedient of conflating individuals with the same or similar names.

Now, notice again, in the above passage from *Wars*, there is no mention of prior prefects or procurators of Judea other than Coponius back in chapter 8 (117), the mention of whom precedes the discussion of the four philosophies, as in *Antiquities*. I would argue that all of these things taken together strongly indicate that Tiberius sent Pilate to Judea immediately upon his taking over the government, i.e. in 14/15 AD. And, as Philo wrote, his governorship was a disaster and Tiberius was the one who had to order him to remove the golden shields – not standards with images, as Josephus writes – to Caesarea.[577]

---

[577]Mason (2016), p. 265, seems to accept that "apparently" these are two different episodes. I think it's much more likely that Josephus simply got the details wrong.

The 'Pilate Stone' confirms that Pilate was there as prefect. Tacitus' mention of Pilate's name is of little help chronologically because it is later hearsay.[578] Philo's discussion of Pilate really sheds no light on the chronology either, because it is retrospective and undatable. Plus, Josephus thinks that army standards were involved while Philo says gilded shields with inscriptions. The most famous Roman infantry standard was the eagle. So we have a sort of hybrid: golden eagles by way of golden shields and Roman standards. Just as Josephus – or a redactor – has conflated events of 18/36 AD, he appears to have done something similar with the events around the time of the death of Herod, mixing elements of various events in different periods. It does, seriously, appear to be the work of a redactor, because the main areas in the history that are so hopelessly muddled are *just those periods that are significant to the Jesus timeline* and which include the mysterious number 37. Was this a signal to some people 'in the know'?

It appears to me to be possible that the 'Golden Eagle Temple Cleansing,' followed by the execution of Judas the Galilean, *actually belongs to the time of Pilate*, and the reason for the massive rebellion following the death of Herod was simply *that the high priest Matthias had fomented a rebellion and Simon of Perea declared himself king.* That's just speculation. The most important point for our purpose is the evidence I have presented here that Pontius Pilate was in Judea more than a decade earlier than scholars and theologians have assumed and Josephus' list of prefects/governors has broken down completely under scrutiny. So, again, I'll present my updated list:

- Death of Herod, 5/4 BC
- Usurpation of kingship by Simon of Perea, 4/3 BC
- Varus and Sabinus, War of Varus, 3–1 BC
- Quirinius and Coponius, 1 BC – 11 AD – possibly sequential
- Silanus and Coponius, 11 AD – 14/15 AD
- Silanus and Pilate, 15 AD – 17 AD
- Piso and Pilate, 17 AD – 19 AD
- Marcellus (temporary), Gnaeus Sentius Saturninus, 19 AD – ?

Recap and Summary

I have already suggested that greater reliance might be placed on Josephus' first book, *Wars*, than his later *Antiquities*, mainly because it was an imperially sponsored project designed to be read by a Greco-Roman audience, many of whom knew full well the major events of the time and thus would not be easily bamboozled. There, we notice that Josephus does not fiddle with the Roman side of things, though he does appear to feel free to invent things on the Jewish side. In *Wars*, it is as plain as it can possibly be that Pontius Pilate was Tiberius' man and was sent to Judea upon Tiberius' accession to power.

Philo's digression about Pilate in his *Embassy to Gaius* doesn't help with the dating issue, but it helps to know Pilate better and the impression is certainly that it was further in the past from the time of the recitation than just five to ten years (i.e. from 39/40 AD back to 30–36). The

---

[578]Tacitus, *Ann.* 15.44.3. See 'Tacitus on Pilate' in Chapter 2.

tone of Philo's passage makes more sense if he is reminding the emperor Caligula of things that happened twenty years ago (or more) when he was very young. Philo would have been extremely unlikely to presume to instruct the emperor about things he could perfectly well have recalled on his own.

Then, there is the text about Pilate's doings itself surrounded with text that references events of 16 to 19 AD with Pilate situated right in the middle; and then the bizarre skip ahead 18 years.

All of these elements, taken together, argue for the fact that Pilate was in Judea much earlier than biblical 'history' suggests – or allows – and that he also left much earlier and in disgrace at the time of the death of Germanicus, not Tiberius.

It's hard to figure out why the reign of Archelaus is such a mess. One gets the impression that Josephus really knew nothing about it and, since his behavior was similar to that reported of Pilate, simply gave him some bits of Pilate's history and said less about Pilate for reasons of political discretion. Interestingly, Eusebius, quoting early apocryphal accounts, stated that Pilate suffered misfortune in the reign of Caligula (37–41 AD), *was exiled to Gaul* and eventually killed himself there in Vienna.[579] Archelaus too, was said to have been exiled to Vienna, as were Antipas and Herodias later still.

Nevertheless, the looping stories, doublets, and triplets, argue for the fact that Josephus – or a redactor – was mixing up and/or making up a lot of his material between the death of Herod the Great and his own times. The story of the Golden Eagle rebellion alleged to have occurred during the reign of Herod may very well be a backward displacement of Pilate's 'golden shields' affair with a multiple purpose: it slanders Herod the Great, makes Pilate less obnoxious, and muddles the events of the life of Judas the Galilean, Josephus' *bête noir*.

The deaths of Judas and Matthias after the Golden Eagle event were said to have been the trigger for the rebellion that caused Archelaus to kill 3,000 Jews at Passover, but I have doubts about several aspects of that affair. First, with his craving for the approval of the Jews, would Herod the Great really have been likely to have decorated his masterpiece, the Jewish temple, with a golden eagle? I don't think so. However, it seems rather certain that Varus' war took place. So what really triggered it? For the period in question, all that Tacitus has to say is that some character named Simon declared himself king and was put to death by Varus. Then, 'all was quiet' under Tiberius.

Tacitus' brief statement in the *Histories* that 'all was quiet' is contradicted by his notice of the unexplained expulsion of Jews in 19 AD, and possibly by his reference in the *Annals* to the execution of 'Christus' by Pilate under Tiberius.[580] Put together with the facts uncovered here about the actual time Pilate was sent back to Rome, and that this was concomitant with the murder of Germanicus by Piso, which took place in 19 AD, the impression is strong that the expulsion of Jews from Rome in 19 AD must be associated. As his account of the second 'Chrestian outbreak' during Nero shows, it led to unrest in Jewish enclaves around the Empire. News traveled faster than we might think. Zealot messianism was probably all over the place in the Empire; Rome had a large Jewish population, Judas was a popular figure, so it makes sense. So that 'all quiet' notice, in light of what he says elsewhere about the expulsion of Jews, pretty

---

[579] *Historia Ecclesiae* 2:7.

[580] *Ann.* 15.44.2–3. But keep in mind that this may be an interpolation. When Tacitus says there was now "another" outbreak of the "Chrestian" superstition, he may be implying that the first was the same one described by Suetonius, i.e. in Rome in 49 AD.

much smacks of a cover-up. 'Nothing to see here, move on!' It looks like whoever worked over Josephus also worked over Tacitus, with the intention of covering up anything written about the execution of Judas that contradicted the 'Jesus of Nazareth' narrative.

Many of the very same years that are missing from Tacitus' *Annals* are also missing from Josephus in that jump from 19 AD to 35/36 AD. That in itself is damning. And it comes after a similarly 'dark' period: from the ethnarchy of Archelaus to the death of Augustus. Carrier has a whole section on relevant works and specific sections of works that are missing or destroyed, including Hippolytus' two volumes on mystery religions, Tacitus' accounts for 29–31 AD, Dio's accounts for 6–2 BC and 29–37 AD, three books of Philo on his embassy to Caligula (where he discusses two key periods relating to persecutions of Jews, under Pilate and Sejanus), among other lost works.[581] Anybody who says this was not a conspiracy to hide the truth has no firing neurons.

Based on what we do have in that short paragraph from Tacitus' *Histories*, however, it looks like Herod died, Simon declared himself king, and Varus came in to put down the insurrection. Or perhaps Simon declared himself king *because* of the rapacity of Varus and his legates, and Josephus was busy rewriting history for his new masters. Maybe Archelaus was innocent, lived a boring life, and died naturally after being betrayed by his brothers. Or, perhaps he was involved in supporting the rebels, as is suggested by his releasing the brother of Athronges, a possible cover for Judas the Galilean, and it was for this kind of activity that he was banished to Vienna.

I propose that Tiberius sent Pilate – possibly at the urging of Sejanus, who according to Philo was responsible for the persecution of Italian Jews, probably in 19 AD – to replace Coponius upon his accession, and Pilate immediately set about doing all the things that Philo described him as doing:

> He feared least they might in reality go on an embassy to the emperor, and might impeach him with respect to other particulars of his government, in respect of his corruption, and his acts of insolence, and his rapine, and his habit of insulting people, and his cruelty, and his continual murders of people untried and uncondemned, and his never ending, and gratuitous, and most grievous inhumanity.

By the time Pilate sent the shields into Jerusalem, he had been there about 3 or 4 years. Maybe there is a seed of history in the tale: he sent the army to Jerusalem for the winter in late 18 AD and hung the golden shields. At that point, Judas the Galilean and his followers effected the 'Golden Eagle Temple Cleansing,' though it had nothing to do with the temple but rather destroying the private property of Pilate. This was followed by military action on the part of Pilate and his troops, and ultimately, the capture and execution of Judas. Incidentally, there was a partial eclipse of the moon on the night of 10 January 19 AD, so if we must connect the death of Judas to an eclipse as is suggested in the tale of the death of Herod, there is one to hand. Following this there were uprisings that resulted in an attack on the people at Passover with the killing of many individuals in the Temple precincts.

In the meantime, the Jews had appealed to Tiberius and he ordered Pilate to remove the shields to Caesarea. At this point, Germanicus returned from his tour of Egypt to find that the governor of Syria, Piso, had controverted his arrangements, and things were a mess in Judea thanks to Pilate. So he ordered Pilate to appear before him (perhaps via his associates Vitellius

---

[581]Carrier (2014), pp. 301–5.

and Veranius) but died shortly thereafter in Antioch, probably poisoned, before Pilate could get there. The crimes of Pilate faded into the background in the uproar over the death of Germanicus. It was widely thought throughout the Empire that Piso poisoned him under orders from Tiberius, but Piso committed suicide before he could be tried. Tacitus opined that Tiberius may have had him murdered before he could implicate the emperor in Germanicus' death. More likely, it was Sejanus who was behind it all with the intention of turning public opinion against Tiberius. The death of Germanicus destroyed the regard of the people for Tiberius and created a climate of fear in Rome.

Tertullian, the Christian law expert from Carthage in North Africa, wrote that Jesus was born while Gaius Sentius Saturninus was Legate of Roman Syria, i.e. between 9–7 BC. Could it be that he confused one Saturninus with another? Perhaps the *Jewish messianism that later became identified as Christianity was born in 19 AD under the influence of the psychological/emotional trauma of the death of Judas the Galilean, compounded by the Empire-wide mourning for the savior Germanicus, exactly when* Gnaeus *Sentius Saturninus was* governor *of Syria?*

The result of this examination of the problems with the history of Josephus regarding Pilate is profound: removing Pilate from Judea at the time *alleged* for the crucifixion of a 'Jesus of Nazareth' entirely destroys the timeline of the Jesus 'history.'

It also means that billions of people, for century after century, have been reciting a lie every Sunday when they declare their belief in the Apostles' Creed. The truth is much different.

The Apostles' Creed
I believe in God, the Father almighty,
creator of heaven and Earth.
I believe in Jesus Christ, his only Son, our Lord.
He was conceived by the power of the Holy Spirit
and born of the virgin Mary.
He suffered under Pontius Pilate,
was crucified, died, and was buried.
He descended to the dead.
On the third day he rose again.
He ascended into heaven,
and is seated at the right hand of the Father.
He will come again to judge the living and the dead.
I believe in the Holy Spirit,
the holy catholic Church,
the communion of the saints,
the forgiveness of sins,
the resurrection of the body,
and the life everlasting. Amen.

The Testimonium Flavianum

It is time to talk about the so-called *Testimonium Flavianum* (TF), Josephus' alleged mention of Jesus Christ, which comes immediately after his description of the Pilate sedition, in which he says the problem was solved because Pilate was awed by either the Jews' superstitions or their courage – and not because Tiberius came down on him and ordered him to make things right – and just before the Samaritan debacle that Josephus claims resulted in Pilate being 'sent down,' so to say, and which may very well have been a cover story for the Golden Eagle Temple Cleansing event that was displaced back into the time of Herod the Great. There's been enough ink spilled on this one to float an aircraft carrier and, frankly, if people can't see how completely it disrupts the text – as it is – and how totally out of character it is for Josephus, in any version, I just don't know what to say.

I'm going to do a recap so that when we actually come to the TF, the reader will be well oriented. I realize that all these things can be a bit confusing to someone who isn't fully familiar with the history, but just bear with me: it will make sense!

The TF seems to be an out-of-place interruption in the tale of Pilate in Book 18 of *Antiquities*. In 18.2.2 we read the account of the multiple governors of Judea: Marcus Ambivius, then Annius Rufus "under whom died Caesar [Augustus] ... upon whose death Tiberius Nero ... succeeded. He sent Valerius Gratus ... he tarried in Judea 11 years, when Pontius Pilate came as his successor," etc.

The above, as I said, is contradicted by *Wars*: "But when the Roman empire was translated to Tiberius, the son of Julia, upon the death of Augustus ... both Herod and Philip continued in their tetrarchies ... Now Pilate, who was sent as procurator into Judea by Tiberius, sent by night those images of Caesar that are called ensigns into Jerusalem. This excited a very great tumult among the Jews ..."[582]

Wars 2.9.3 is about Pilate setting his soldiers among the Jews, threatening to cut them to pieces if they do not accept the standards. They all fall down and say they are willing to die, which so impresses Pilate that he rescinds the order. In 2.9.4, Pilate takes the money from the temple to pay for building projects, which excites a tumult and many Jews are killed by Pilate's soldiers. Then, in 2.9.5, we read: "In the meantime Agrippa, the son of that Aristobulus who had been slain by his father Herod, came to Tiberius to accuse Herod the tetrarch ..." As we already know, this event actually happened between Agrippa and Gaius in 39. The Agrippa story is followed by the account of Gaius wanting to put a statue of himself in the Temple, which, as we know from other sources, occurred in 39/40.

In short, the same big skip occurs in *Wars*.

In *Ant.* 18.2.2, Pontius Pilate comes as successor to Gratus. Then 18.2.3 begins: "And about this time Herod the tetrarch who was in great favor with Tiberius, built a city of the same name ... he built it in the best part of Galilee. ... Strangers came and inhabited this city; a great number of the inhabitants were Galileans also; and many were necessitated by Herod to come ... and were by force compelled to be its inhabitants ... He also admitted poor people ..." Then 18.2.4: "About this time died Phraates, king of the Parthians, by the treachery of Phraataces his son ..." Then follows a long description of the events, including accusing the son of incest with his mother, who had been a concubine gift from no less than Julius Caesar![583] All of this was background to the problems then currently brewing in those regions in 16 AD, including a succession dispute, covered by Tacitus in *Annales* 2.2ff. In the Josephus passage, there is a mention of the problems of Artabanus that led to the meeting between him and Germanicus, but the story is very muddy and unclear. What is notable is that Josephus says, "About this time died Phraates," when that

---

[582] *Wars* 2.9.1–2.
[583] Another point in favor of the early date of these events, since Julius Caesar was assassinated in 44 BC.

certainly did not happen then – it happened in 2 BC! If Josephus understood that himself, he sure did not make it clear to his readers, or the redactor muddled things.

In 18.2.5, Josephus states, "at this time died Antiochus, the king of Commagene," which resulted in interactions with Rome regarding the succession. It is here that Josephus notes that Germanicus was sent to settle the affairs of the East. This certainly happened in 17 AD, as previously noted. Josephus then says: "So the senate made a decree, that Germanicus should be sent to settle the affairs of the east, fortune hereby taking a proper opportunity for depriving him of his life; for when he had been in the east, and settled all affairs there, his life was taken away by poison, which Piso gave him, as hath been related elsewhere." As it happens, that account "related elsewhere" is nowhere to be found in the versions of Josephus we have today.

Thus, we see that Josephus started off talking about Pilate in 18.2.2, then digressed to other events that were *contemporary*! This was not unusual for Josephus at all, as we have already seen in the discussion of John the Baptist. He often started on a topic and then went in a circle around related events, or events of the same time, and then came back and picked up where he left off, just as he does here.

In chapter 3.1, Josephus comes back to Pilate: "But now Pilate, the procurator of Judea, removed the army from Caesarea to Jerusalem, to take their winter quarters there, in order to abolish the Jewish laws. So he introduced Caesar's effigies, which were upon the ensigns and brought them into the city ..." A big demonstration of Jews went to Caesarea to plead with Pilate to remove the images; he refused for days, Josephus says, and on the sixth, he had his soldiers surround them and threatened them with death if they did not leave off disturbing him. The same scenario that was depicted in *Wars* now plays out; Pilate relents because he is impressed by the piety of the Jews, the standards were removed, and everyone went home.

In 18.3.2, we read the similar account of Pilate taking money from the temple to build an aqueduct, as we saw in *Wars* 2.9.4. However, in *Wars* he writes about Pilate sending his men disguised in civilian clothes to beat the rioters with staves; in *Antiquities* they are carrying daggers. Staves? Daggers? What's the difference? The story is much the same except for that small detail.

So, Josephus has given us an account of two consecutive tumults. It is at this point that the TF intrudes in a way that is strangely reminiscent of the case of John the Baptist in the midst of the warring of Antipas, Aretas and Vitellius of later times:

> Now, there was about this time Jesus, a wise man, if it be lawful to call him a man, for he was a doer of wonderful works – a teacher of such men as receive the truth with pleasure. He drew over to him both many of the Jews, and many of the Gentiles. He was [the] Christ; and when Pilate, at the suggestion of the principal men amongst us, had condemned him to the cross, those that loved him at the first did not forsake him, for he appeared to them alive again the third day, as the divine prophets had foretold these and ten thousand other wonderful things concerning him; and the tribe of Christians, so named from him, are not extinct at this day.[584]

The earliest witness to this passage is Eusebius, the fourth-century Bishop of Caesarea. However, in two different places, Origen states that Josephus acknowledged the righteousness of James, but did not believe Jesus was the Christ. He makes these observations when referring specifically to the passage about James found in Book 20 of *Antiquities*. Obviously, if the passage

---

[584] *Ant.* 18.3.3 (63–4).

Eusebius saw (or wrote?) was in the copy available to the third-century Origen, he would not have said such a thing. The conclusion seems to be that Origen read something that definitely repudiated that Jesus was the Messiah or named someone else as the messiah accepted by the Jews.

Problematically, Origen said that Josephus explained the overthrow of the Jews as God's revenge for the murder of the Righteous James. However, the passage on the death of James in extant copies *says no such thing*! Some argue that Origen was confused by Hegesippus, but that is unlikely.

Cutting to the chase, it seems clear that Origen had a version of Josephus that either included a very uncomplimentary account of Jesus and a very favorable one of James, or no account of Jesus at all, being rather an account of someone else, and only the reference to James as the brother of Jesus. Thus, between Origen and Eusebius, someone implemented the changes, and seems to have done so on a fairly large scale.

Further consideration leads to the idea that even Origen's copy had already been modified, for it appears to be *a priori* improbable that Josephus would have even momentarily entertained the idea that the death of James led to the divine destruction of Jerusalem. A corollary to that is that there must have been a set of earlier interpolations that were then 'adjusted' by a second editor, and the first ones were inserted before Origen got his copy. In the first set, not much was done to the passage found at 18.3.3, other than possibly to change the name to 'Jesus' and to connect James to Jesus by similarly just changing the name of his brother and writing the line about his death leading to the destruction of Jerusalem. This editor would most likely have been a Jewish Christian, not a follower of Paul, because of the favor shown to James, as we will discuss below.

Going further, we can speculate that the passage which excited this editor originally included an *explicit repudiation of the messianic claims* of someone else – someone whose claims were depicted as dangerous. We can read Josephus' own opinion of messiahship in *Wars* 6.5.4, where he states clearly that the Jews were led on to their suicidal resistance by their belief in an ambiguous oracle which foretold that a man from Palestine would become ruler of the world. The Jews interpreted this prophecy as meaning that a Jewish messiah would defeat the Romans and become ruler of the world. According to Josephus, "many of their wise men were deceived" therein, while Josephus saw clearly that the oracle referred to Vespasian, who was declared emperor on Jewish soil.

Subsequent Christian scribes found such a passage to be a scandalous comparison between the legal righteousness of James and the faith-based grace of Christ and changed it. They also changed the TF from what may have been close to the original, with only a name change, to something like what we see today.

Redactors and amenders were often influenced – consciously or not – by the text they were altering, and words from the original would slip through or be deliberately utilized by them in the pious belief that they were at least preserving something of the original. In the case of the TF about Jesus, we can note that the Greek word used for 'teacher/rabbi' is the same one used by Josephus to describe Judas the Galilean.[585]

---

[585]Cf. Brandon (1967), p. 363, for details.

S. G. F. Brandon thinks that the statement in the extant text that Pilate executed Jesus "on the indictment of our chief men" may be the preservation of a straightforward legal term. I don't agree. I think that putting the blame on the Jews was a Markan invention for apologetic/propaganda reasons, as I will discuss further on.

Now, here is the crux of the matter, the elephant in the living room: since there is the extraordinary fact that Josephus mentions Judas the Galilean or his relatives throughout his history from the time of Herod until the end of the war, the fact that there is no account of Judas' death is an equally extraordinary omission. Thus, I think we can conclude with some high degree of probability that the 'Jesus passage' in Josephus was the point at which he originally narrated something very much like the Golden Eagle Temple Cleansing episode, but with reference to Pilate's standards rather than the eagle. The text probably included terms describing Judas as a messianic pretender with revolutionary aims and followers, and that the 'tribe of Christians' – now well known in Rome – had indeed originated in Judea under the leadership of Judas the Galilean, with whom Pilate had dealt summarily. If Josephus actually used the term 'tribe of Christians' (which is doubtful), that would have put every Christian in the Empire in danger, considering how Josephus presented Judas. It would have needed excision post haste.

That Judas the Galilean was regarded as the Messiah before his death is almost logically required by the numerous mentions of his career as depicted by Josephus. To have inspired such a following that was recalled by Josephus on numerous occasions throughout his writings shows that he was a very significant figure at that time.

If Judas was regarded as the Messiah-king by his followers, his execution must surely have put a damper on such a belief. His failure should have cancelled his claim. Lack of success of the other messianic claimants of the time usually ended their careers. A further note must be taken of the fact that it was certainly no embarrassment or shame to die at the hands of the despised Romans and to join the venerated company of honored martyrs for the faith. Yet certainly one would think that the death of Judas would have so demoralized his followers that the movement would have broken up and dispersed.

But that isn't what happened. What Judas had that other messianic claimants probably did not was an extended family of replacements to the claim of Messiah. It seems that the claim must have been based on some sort of lineage, considering that we are told about his forebear, Hezekiah the brigand, who was killed by the young Herod in the time of Julius Caesar, an incident that barely merits mentioning except for the clamor raised by the Jews for some reason, which makes us suspect that there was more to the story than we presently know. At the time, the concept of being resurrected in the heavenly spheres, at least, to perform a service for the nation, was not unknown, apparently, as we have seen in the examination of the Jeselsohn Stone and apocalyptic literature.

So, it is understandable that the family and followers of Judas acquired the belief that he would return to fulfill his messianic role, no doubt accompanied by 12 legions of angelic warriors. That this group was able to convince others of this extraordinary 'superstition' only testifies to the common currency of such ideas in Judea at the time.

What is important to understand is that the people did not believe that Judas had resurrected in his body on Earth. Although the intensity of the visionary experience had by many of his followers may have eventually inspired a belief in a brief appearance in his pre-mortem body, there was clearly no claim made that he continued to live on Earth.

There then followed the problem of explaining the tragic turn of events, and traces of the solutions created can be found here and there in the Gospels, such as Mark's three passion predictions at 8:27-33, 9:31, and 10:33-34.

So the claim was made that the suffering and death of the Messiah was no barrier to him fulfilling his destined role to destroy the Romans and restore Israel: it had actually been foretold in the scriptures. And the return was certainly imminent, because the Roman yoke was becoming more unbearable every day. To prepare and wait for that day became the duty of his followers under his son James, with the able assistance of his other descendants, three more of whose names we know from Josephus: Simon, Manahem/Menahem and Eleazar.

Once the scriptural proofs had been found and elucidated by the Jewish Christians, the fact of the death itself could be further interpreted as Judas dying a martyr for the sins of Israel. He had come to save his people but they had failed to respond in sufficient numbers to support God's action. Yet, they would have one last chance. Yahweh would fulfill the promise of redemption by sending Judas back with power and glory and angels, and lots of dead, evil Romans would be the result. But, only if Israel was repentant and prepared, as John the Baptist claimed.

The above, in short, appears to be the gospel of the Jerusalem church. This interpretation, this formulation, of messianic redemption was in radical opposition to the universal gospel of Paul. The gospel of the Jerusalem church had no place for Gentiles; in fact, the end which that gospel had in view was the overthrow of Rome and widespread punishment of the Gentile nations by death, destruction and subjugation.

We need to keep constantly in mind that Josephus himself, by his own admission, *was a member of the rebel priesthood that initiated the Great Rebellion* and he had what could be said to be a 'life or death' interest in modifying anything that might create a consistently understandable history about what was going on in Judea from the time of the death of Herod the Great until the destruction of Jerusalem. Do not forget this: messianic claimants were 'robbers, thieves, brigands, tyrants,' and every other derogatory term Josephus could come up with; he did that for his own protection.

We also need to keep in mind that there are no manuscripts of Josephus that can be dated before the eleventh century. It seems obvious that, since all surviving manuscripts have been preserved by monastic scribes who hand-copied them, there are many deliberate and accidental modifications. Thus, even though there is no doubt among scholars that most (but not all) of the later copies of *Antiquities* contained references to Jesus, James, and John the Baptist,[586] it cannot be proven that these passages were original to Josephus. However, we can assume that he narrated the death of Judas the Galilean, and we know that is not there in our present copies!

Historian Robert Eisler exerted a great deal of energy to reconstruct the TF using a Slavonic version of Josephus' *Wars,* which apparently included the TF as an interpolation, which is odd, as this passage is generally found only in *Antiquities.* A tenth-century Arabic translation of the TF was discovered in 1971 in a work by Agapius of Hierapolis, and a version is also found in twelfth-century Syriac by Michael the Syrian.

Also, we have to keep in mind that during the first two centuries when the passage is claimed to have existed, not a single Christian commentator or apologist *ever* referred to it. If Josephus had said anything about a true messiah, every one of the overly prolific writers such as Justin

---

[586] An ancient Table of Contents of the 18th book of *Antiquities* omits any reference to the passage about Jesus, as does the Josephus codex of Photius.

(mid-second century), Irenaeus and Theophilus of Antioch (late second century), Tertullian and Clement of Alexandria (turn of third century), Origen and Hippolytus (early third century), Cyprian (mid-third century), Lactantius and Arnobius (late third century) would have been all over it. And if Josephus had written something hostile about someone named 'Jesus,' you can bet they would have been flaming and rebutting him over that, too. Keep in mind that Origen cited Josephus eleven times in different works. We know that Origen had read *Antiquities* because in *Contra Celsum* (1.47) he summarizes what Josephus said about John the Baptist in *Antiquities* 18.5.2. However, he notes that Josephus did not recognize Jesus as 'the Christ' *when mentioning him*. That suggests that the name had been changed to 'Jesus' by that time, or that some other earlier form of the TF existed at that point. Frank Zindler, by way of Earl Doherty, mentions another interesting reference:

> Frank Zindler has called attention to another Christian commentator who, though versed in Josephus' writings and employing them in his homilies, nevertheless makes no reference to any version of the Testimonium: St. John Chrysostom, who wrote late in the 4th century. In *Homily* 76, he subscribes to the by now well-established Christian view that Jerusalem was destroyed because of the crucifixion of Jesus. He appeals to Josephus as evidence that the destruction was indeed horrific, something that could only be explained by a deed as monstrous as deicide. Also, he says, there can be no truth to the fantasy that Josephus was actually a Christian believer, "For he was both a Jew, and a determined Jew, very zealous." Yet there is no discussion of any Josephan testimony to Jesus himself by Chrysostom, and certainly not to the question of what the historian might have had to say about Jesus' messianic or 'more than human' status. Other homilies by Chrysostom contain other appeals to Josephus, but none to the Testimonium. Most striking is *Homily* 13. Here he says that Josephus imputes the destructive war to the murder of John the Baptist. Nowhere in the extant texts of Josephus is such an imputation to be found, one which also stands in contradiction to statements by Origen and Eusebius that Josephus regarded the destruction of Jerusalem as punishment by God for the murder of James the Just—an allegation, too, which cannot be found in surviving texts. (Josephus actually implies at one point that the destruction of the war was due to the Zealots' murder of the former High Priest Ananus.)[587]

John Chrysostom may have been confused by the Antipas–Aretas war section, which includes the passage about John the Baptist in which Josephus says that *the people* believed that Antipas lost because of his execution of John. Josephus did write: "Now some of the Jews thought that the destruction of Herod's army came from God, and that very justly, as a punishment of what he did against John, that was called the Baptist ..."[588] But that has nothing to do with the war of the Jews against the Romans; this last quote relates to the hokey war between Herod Antipas and Aretas that Josephus may have made up. Is this remark what Chrysostom is referring to in *Homily* 13?[589] Or is this just another example of a redactor putting something in at the wrong place and making another layer of mess for later historians? Making that kind of mistake, assuming the text was not in a state of great flux, doesn't say much for the acuity of Chrysostom.

[587]Earl Doherty, 'Supplementary Articles No. 16: Josephus On the Rocks,' http://www.jesuspuzzle.com/jesuspuzzle/supp16.htm.

[588]*Ant.* 18.5.1 (113).

[589]Notice that here we have a piece of evidence – late though it is – that places 'John the Baptist' at the time of the war against Rome. I have wondered if Josephus' 'John the Baptist' is actually a composite character, combining aspects of other characters (Josephus' rival John of Gischala, his teacher 'Bannus') and placed in a convenient location of his narrative. Perhaps someone just creatively moved the text around, and my speculations aren't so crazy after all?

Obviously, the process of arguing over whether or not Josephus wrote something about Jesus could go on forever. I would just like to repeat emphatically that it is unlikely that Josephus would ever have written anything even remotely like the various reconstructions of the TF I have read for the simple reason that no messianic claimant ever, under any circumstances, gets good press from Josephus. He never even references the messianic promises of a restored Davidic kingdom. And that is for a very good reason: Josephus is busy as a beaver exculpating the Jews as a whole, and himself in particular, from any seditious inclinations, and all of the blame for the Great Rebellion is repeatedly and consistently put entirely on the shoulders of the messianic types that Josephus contemptuously refers to as robbers, tyrants, charlatans, bandits, and worse – mainly, Judas the Galilean and the movement he created.

So, the possibility that Josephus wrote anything like *"there was a wise man named Jesus ... a worker of glorious deeds ... thought to be the Christ ... his disciples continued to love him ... reported that he appeared alive after three days ... prophets of God spoke about him,"* etc., is vanishingly remote; pigs are more likely to fly with their tails backward. Even if such a person had made an appearance, Josephus would have *never* written anything like that, because messianic claimants were authors of sedition. It's absurd for any *intelligent* scholar who has read Josephus, who knows Roman history and the social and political conditions of the time, to even propose a reconstruction that is even just 'neutral.'[590] It boggles the mind.[591] What part of what was going on in Judea that led to the destruction of Jerusalem and the deaths of maybe a million people, or more, do they not understand? What part of Josephus' intent to preserve his own life do they not fathom?

Judas of Nazareth: The Dog That Didn't Bark

None of what became the Jesus of Nazareth story as it exists today is easily comprehended if you don't have a good grasp of the history of the time. Even with such knowledge, you are handicapped because the Christian scribes who took charge of literature for centuries made sure that their story was as consistent as they could make it. When studying the story today, you simply see elements of it here and there that you can then find scattered through time and space in other sources (if you are diligent and lucky), and when each of them is picked out and lifted

---

[590] Fernando Bermejo-Rubio argues that if the text is "basically Josephus's but with some Christian interpolations," then the original "must have been at least implicitly negative": "Nonetheless, since there are good reasons to think that Josephus must have been basically well informed about Jesus' identity, if he viewed him as a kind of seditionist, this could be used as further evidence for the hypothesis of the Galilean somehow connected to the anti-Roman resistance ideology, in the wake of the Fourth Philosophy." Bermejo-Rubio, 'Was the Hypothetical Vorlage of the *Testimonium Flavianum* a "Neutral" Text? Challenging the Common Wisdom on *Antiquitates Judaicae* 18.63–64.' *Journal for the Study of Judaism* 45 (2014), pp. 326, 364.

[591] Ken Olson writes that "many of the usual reasons given to support the authenticity of the text are weak or reversible. ... The confidence that many scholars place in the Testimonium or its reconstructed core text is misplaced." Olson, 'A Eusebian Reading of the Testimonium Flavianum,' in Aaron Johnson and Jeremy Schott (Eds.), *Eusebius of Caesarea: Traditions and Innovations* (Center for Hellenic Studies, Harvard University Press, 2013), p. 111. See also Gary J. Goldberg, 'The coincidences of the Emmaus Narrative of Luke and the Testimonium of Josephus,' *The Journal of the Study of the Pseudipigrapha* 13 (1995), 59-77; and Lester Grabbe, 'Jesus Who is Called the Christ: References to Jesus Outside Christian Sources,' in Thomas S. Verenna, Thomas L. Thompson, *"Is This Not The Carpenter?": The Question of The Historicity of the Figure of Jesus* (2013), pp. 61–67. For the most concise and up-to-date treatment of the sources, see Carrier (2014), pp. 332–42.

from the period where they are at home, you see that they have been fitted together like puzzle pieces creating a story written much *later*, and that this story was then claimed to be history.[592]

One of the more sensible ideas to come along in recent years is that of Daniel T. Unterbrink in his book *Judas of Nazareth*.[593] He points out the obvious: Jesus was a literary construct replacing Judas the Galilean.[594] More specifically, Jesus of Nazareth is a *composite* character that is only partly a modification of Judas the Galilean, whose life and deeds are 'infused with Paul's new gospel' and stripped of Judas' revolutionary tendencies.

> The synoptic gospels succeed in placing Paul's gospel back in time. It is not history, but sheer invention, shaping Jesus from the image of Paul. No wonder some see continuity between Jesus and Paul, but they are looking at the relationship from the wrong perspective. ...[595]
>
> Acts' sloppy history and obvious dependence on Josephus have been widely ignored by scholars. Very few realize that the dates and events in Acts cannot be trusted. In fact, Acts' history is polemical revisionism. In every other historical study the ancient historian would be given more credence than a religious text. But in the study of Christianity, Christian history (the gospels and Acts), is accepted as true, even if contradicted by contemporary historians (chiefly Josephus). ... [T]he scholarly community places greater emphasis on the gospels and Acts than on Josephus and the Roman historians.[596]

Unterbrink's point is that there *was* a historical 'messiah' who preached the kingdom of heaven to the Jews – and *only* to the Jews: Judas the Galilean. The Christian Jesus of Mark is *partly* based on this character, a hero to the Jews of the time, who would be spinning in his grave at how he has been represented.

> Jesus of Nazareth is fictional[597] ... [T]his Jesus is a rewrite of a real individual, Judas the Galilean, infused with the theology and life experiences of Paul. ... Judas the Galilean is not fictional! If Judas the Galilean lived, then so did his brothers and sons. Combined, they formed the Fourth

---

[592]See the footnotes in Chapter 1 for sources.

[593]Daniel T. Unterbrink, *Judas of Nazareth: How the Greatest Teacher of First Century Israel Was Replaced by a Literary Creation* (Bear & Co., 2014).

[594]The connection was also pointed out by Nodet and Taylor (1998): "There is some parallel between Jesus and Judas the Galilean, who was conceived in Galilee, then came to Judaea where he flourished, and laid claim to the Temple" (p. 157). Elaine Hilsenrath also made a rather interesting attempt at figuring out who the 'real Jesus' might have been in her book *Jesus The Nazorean* (BookSurge Publishing, 2009). While she can see the strong similarities and parallels between the Jesus of the Gospels and Judas the Galilean, she doesn't understand that the Gospels and Acts were written using the letters of Paul and Josephus, mainly, and that Josephus himself deliberately distorted history for his own purposes; you can't use a text as confirmation if that text was used as a source for the text you are analyzing! Hyam Maccoby has also entered the fray with his *Judas Iscariot and the Myth of Jewish Evil* (Free Press, 1992), *The Mythmaker: Paul and the Invention of Christianity* (HarperCollins, 1998) and *Jesus the Pharisee* (SCM Press, 2003).

[595]Nodet and Taylor agree with Unterbrink on this, pointing out how the original Jewish 'Christian' movement was essentially a fairly 'mainstream' Jewish sect. Paul's mission to the Gentiles was then retrojected back and associated with 'Jesus of Nazareth' in Gospels like Mark, and figures like Peter in Acts.

[596]Unterbrink (2014), pp. 241–2.

[597]Nazareth is apparently fictional also. See René Salm, *The Myth of Nazareth* (American Atheist Press, 2008) and *NazarethGate: Quack Archeology, Holy Hoaxes, and the Invented Town of Jesus* (American Atheist Press, 2015). His exhaustive study and critique of what has passed for archaeological excavations of Jesus' hometown make it absolutely certain that the place now called Nazareth was not inhabited from around 712 BC until sometime after 70 AD.

Philosophy, a movement that scholars and mythicists have overlooked in their search for the real 'Jesus.'[598]

Indeed. It is so obvious that the fact that it has been ignored by biblical scholars is astonishing. What is also quite obvious is that Josephus *needed* to denigrate those he formerly consorted with, and the Gospels needed to make sure their Jesus was free of any taint of revolutionary fervor. And even there they couldn't erase all the traces, as Nodet and Taylor show.[599]

The *Testimonium Flavianum* is, in fact, 'the dog that didn't bark.'[600] Josephus repeatedly refers to Judas the Galilean in various guises throughout his works, but *never mentions his death*. That is so obvious, it sticks out like a sore thumb. Josephus is so interested in this personage that every time he mentions a descendant, he recites the pedigree – even if pejoratively. The life and legacy of Judas the Galilean is the thread of Ariadne that leads one out of the labyrinth of Josephus. The question that Unterbrink asks – which is the obvious question to ask – is this:

> Was the spurious Jesus passage a replacement for Judas's death by crucifixion? The death of Judas by crucifixion should not be seriously doubted. Judas fights against Rome, actions punishable by crucifixion. In addition, two of Judas's sons, James and Simon, are crucified a generation later (46–48 CE).[601]

Unterbrink's attention to the texts allows him to adduce a lot of evidence that is compelling, and among the matters that he takes up are the dates of the birth and death of the alleged Jesus of Nazareth (according to the Gospels) and how these are *clues* that lead directly to Judas the Galilean. Then, using a convoluted (but interesting) set of texts and reasoning, he concludes that Judas was executed in 19 AD. I am arguing the same point, though I am coming at it from a very different angle – that Pilate was sent back to Rome in 19 AD. Nevertheless, this independent convergence on 19 AD is significant.

The bottom line is that a minor rebellion (including the cleansing of the Temple), the capture, and the execution, of Judas the Galilean are most probably what occupied the space where the anemic *Testimonium Flavianum* now stands. The text describing the beginning of this rebellion has been displaced to the time of the death of Herod. All the other stories about Judas the Galilean beginning with the arrival of Quirinius are mostly true (even if spin-doctored), and the story of the capture of the founder of the Fourth Philosophy and his death is close to the truth: *he wasn't crucified, he was burned alive, and it was done by Pilate, not Herod.* Also, the young men, the students of Judas and Matthias who were also killed, possibly led to Philo's remark about Pilate: "his cruelty, and *his continual murders of people untried and uncondemned,* and his never ending, and gratuitous, and most grievous, inhumanity."

The several stories about messianic claimants after the death of Herod were derived from the legends of Simon of Perea, who was known even in Rome, and merited a prophetic/magical

---

[598]Unterbrink (2014), p. 256.

[599]Nodet and Taylor (1998).

[600]In his story, *Silver Blaze*, Sir Arthur Conan Doyle chronicles the mystery of the kidnapping of a prize racehorse. Sherlock Holmes concludes "the midnight visitor was someone the dog knew well," ultimately leading to the determination that the horse's trainer was the guilty party. Gregory (Scotland Yard detective): "Is there any other point to which you would wish to draw my attention?" Holmes: "To the curious incident of the dog in the night-time." Gregory: "The dog did nothing in the night-time." Holmes: "That was the curious incident."

[601]Unterbrink (2014), p. 269.

inscription by sectarians in the desert who expected his return with God and the angels to destroy the Romans. There may certainly have been a number of such claimants, but it seems that Simon was chief among them at that time. He may very well have been related to Judas the Galilean also; for all we know, he was a son of the brigand Hezekiah/Ezekias, who was killed by Herod in the time of Julius Caesar, and father or uncle to Judas the Galilean who had a son named Simon.

The Samaritan connection is due to the fact that Judas was from Galilee[602] and Galilean Judaism had strong affinities with the Judaism of the Samaritans, which Josephus was at pains to denigrate in favor of his new target of wannabe-ism: Rabbinic/Pharisaic Judaism.

Josephus and Paul?

Now that we have dealt with the *Testimonium Flavianum*, I want to discuss the two texts that immediately follow it. As we saw above, the TF is the sore thumb that sticks out, 'the dog that didn't bark,' which absolutely does not fit the context in which it appears, and this is a red flag that perhaps something else was in that spot in the text, which was effaced and/or covered up. The tales that follow appear at first glance to be bizarre, but when examined carefully, they seem to have been included for the direct purpose of conveying the truth about Christianity from the point of view of Josephus. That is, I will argue that Josephus was in dialogue with Christianity.

Briefly: at the end of Josephus' story of the sedition caused by Pilate bringing the army ensigns into Jerusalem, we read:

> ... since the people were unarmed, and were caught by men prepared for what they were about, there were a great number of them slain by this means, and others of them ran away wounded. And thus an end was put to this sedition.

Then follows the TF, which was probably a version of the Golden Eagle Temple Cleansing. I think that the original did include something like the ending line: "and the tribe of Christians, so named from him, is not extinct at this day." It may have said "tribe of his followers" or something like that. Obviously, associating Christians with the terrifying founder of a sect that brought on the destruction of Judea, Jerusalem, and the temple, was highly contentious and most definitely dangerous to all Christians in the Empire, even including the followers of Paul. That, of course, stimulates the question: did Josephus know of Paul? Considering the time Josephus was writing, and the company he kept, it would be surprising if Josephus wasn't at least aware of him.

We may find a very suggestive answer in the two texts that followed the TF.

Keep in mind as you read the two tales that they likely follow an account of the death of the 'demagogue' Judas the Galilean who led so many Jews astray with his 'Fourth Philosophy.' The execution of a beloved teacher of the Law, as Judas was described, would have inspired something of a revolt, and that was probably described in the scattered stories of Jews being massacred in Samaria or around the Temple. And such an event would have been quickly communicated to Jews in Rome and could have caused unrest there too, which is reported by Tacitus for the year 19 AD. With that in mind, let's look at the first story that immediately follows the TF, noting

---

[602]For details on Galilee, see Nodet and Taylor, *The Historical Jesus? Necessity and Limits of an Inquiry* (T&T Clark, 2008).

the opening line which tells us that whatever was previous to this was a "sad calamity" to the Jews, which certainly would have been the case if the previous tale was about the execution of the young people who were students of Judas the Galilean – a veritable 'massacre of the innocents,' so to say, along with the added massacre of 3,000:

About the same time also **another sad calamity put the Jews into disorder**, and certain shameful practices happened about **the temple of Isis** that was **at Rome**. I will now first take notice of the wicked attempt about the temple of Isis, and will then give an account of the Jewish affairs.

There was at Rome a woman whose name was **Paulina**; one who, on account of the dignity of her ancestors, and by the regular conduct of a virtuous life, had a great reputation: she was also very rich; and although she was of a beautiful countenance, and in that flower of her age wherein women are the most gay, yet did she lead a life of great modesty. **She was married to Saturninus**, one that was every way answerable to her in an excellent character.

Decius Mundus fell in love with this woman, who was a man very high in the equestrian order; and as she was of too great dignity to be caught by presents, and had already rejected them, though they had been sent in great abundance, he was still more inflamed with love to her, insomuch that he promised to give her two hundred thousand Attic drachmae for one night's lodging; and when this would not prevail upon her, and he was not able to bear this misfortune in his amours, he thought it the best way to famish himself to death for want of food, on account of Paulina's sad refusal; and he determined with himself to die after such a manner, and he went on with his purpose accordingly.

Now Mundus had a freedwoman, who had been made free by his father, whose name was Ide, one skillful in all sorts of mischief. This woman was very much grieved at the young man's resolution to kill himself, [for he did not conceal his intentions to destroy himself from others,] and came to him, and encouraged him by her discourse, and made him to hope, by some promises she gave him, that he might obtain a night's lodging with Paulina; and when he joyfully hearkened to her entreaty, she said she wanted no more than fifty thousand drachmae for the entrapping of the woman.

So when she had encouraged the young man, and gotten as much money as she required, she did not take the same methods as had been taken before, because she perceived that the woman was by no means to be tempted by money; but as she knew that she was very much given to the worship of the goddess Isis, she devised the following stratagem: She went to some of Isis's priests, and upon the strongest assurances [of concealment], she persuaded them by words, but chiefly by the offer of money, of twenty-five thousand drachmae in hand, and as much more when the thing had taken effect; and told them the passion of the young man, and persuaded them to use all means possible to beguile the woman. So they were drawn in to promise so to do, by that large sum of gold they were to have.

Accordingly, the oldest of them went immediately to Paulina; and upon his admittance, he desired to speak with her by herself. When that was granted him, he told her that he was sent by the god Anubis, who was fallen in love with her, and enjoined her to come to him. Upon this she took the message very kindly, and valued herself greatly upon this condescension of Anubis, and told her husband that she had a message sent her, and was to sup and lie with Anubis; so he agreed to her acceptance of the offer, as fully satisfied with the chastity of his wife.

Accordingly, she went to the temple, and after she had supped there, and it was the hour to go to sleep, the priest shut the doors of the temple, when, in the holy part of it, the lights were also put out. Then did Mundus leap out, [for he was hidden therein,] and did not fail of enjoying her, who was at his service all the night long, as supposing he was the god; and when he was gone away, which was before those priests who knew nothing of this stratagem were stirring, Paulina came early to her husband, and told him how the god Anubis had appeared to her. Among her friends, also, she declared how great a value she put upon this favor, who partly disbelieved the thing, when they reflected on its nature, and partly were amazed at it, as having no pretense for not believing it, when they considered the modesty and the dignity of the person.

But now, **on the third day** after what had been done, **Mundus met Paulina**, and said, "Nay, Paulina, thou hast saved me two hundred thousand drachmae, which sum thou mightest have added to thy own family; yet hast thou not failed to be at my service in the manner I invited thee. As for the reproaches thou hast laid upon Mundus, **I value not the business of names; but I rejoice in the pleasure I reaped by what I did, while I took to myself the name of Anubis.**" When he had said this, he went his way.

But now she began to come to the sense of the grossness of what she had done, and rent her garments, and told her husband of the horrid nature of this wicked contrivance, and prayed him not to neglect to assist her in this case. So he discovered the fact to the emperor; whereupon Tiberius inquired into the matter thoroughly by examining the priests about it, and **ordered them to be crucified**, as well as Ide, who was the occasion of their perdition, and who had contrived the whole matter, which was so injurious to the woman. He also demolished the temple of Isis, and gave order that her statue should be thrown into the river Tiber; while he only banished Mundus, but did no more to him, because he supposed that what crime he had committed was done out of the passion of love. And these were the circumstances which concerned the temple of Isis, and the injuries occasioned by her priests. **I now return to the relation of** *what happened about this time* **to the Jews at Rome, as I formerly told you I would.**[603]

Now, certainly, upon reading the above story one might think that it was something that really happened at Rome – aren't we thankful that Josephus has preserved it for us, even if we suspect that he may have embellished only a little? However, if we try to find it by cross-checking with other historians, we have no luck, because, of course, we think we are in the time of Pilate – 27 to 37 AD, according to the *accepted* chronology – and that is where we might be inclined to look. However, this little story is actually more of a problem than just that, because it is so similar in dynamics to an account of a legal case that can be found in Tacitus:

About the same time **Octavius Sagitta**, a tribune of the people, who was enamoured to frenzy of **Pontia**, a married woman, bribed her by most costly presents into an intrigue and then into abandoning her husband. He had offered her marriage and had won her consent. But as soon as she was free, **she devised delays**, pretended that her father's wishes were against it, and having secured the prospect of a richer husband, she repudiated her promises.

Octavius, on the other hand, now remonstrated, now threatened; his good name, he protested, was lost, his means exhausted, and as for his life, which was all that was left to him, he surrendered it to her mercy.

When she spurned him, **he asked the solace of one night**, with which to soothe his passion, that he might set bounds to it for the future. A night was fixed, and Pontia **intrusted the charge of her chamber to a female slave** acquainted with her secret. Octavius attended by one freedman entered with a dagger concealed under his dress. Then, as usual in lovers' quarrels, there were chidings, entreaties, reproaches, excuses, and some period of the darkness was given up to passion; then, when seemingly about to go, and she was fearing nothing, he stabbed her with the steel, and having wounded and scared away the slave girl who was hurrying to her, rushed out of the chamber.

Next day the murder was notorious, and there was no question as to the murderer, for it was proved that he had passed some time with her. The freedman, however, declared the deed was his, that he had, in fact, avenged his patron's wrongs. He had made some impression by the nobleness

---

[603] *Ant.* 18.3.4–5 (65–80).

of his example, when the slave girl recovered and revealed the truth. Octavius, when he ceased to be tribune, was prosecuted before the consuls by the father of the murdered woman, and was condemned by the sentence of the Senate under "the law concerning assassins."[604]

Many of the elements of the story concocted by Josephus are there in Tacitus' report of an actual legal case: a high-ranking man in love with a married woman, who offers her many gifts but is rejected, then conspires to obtain one single night of illicit lovemaking, causing a scandal. Of course, we can see that these elements have been creatively utilized, including the striking names Paulina, Saturninus and Mundus.

In Tacitus, the event he recounted *occurred in 58 AD*. One *could* say that the story must have been something of a big scandal and perhaps stuck in Josephus' mind to be pulled out, decomposed and reworked in his own way for his own purposes. After all, Josephus was allegedly in Rome when he was 26 – between 63 and 64 AD – so he certainly could have heard about the case at a distance in his early twenties. That is a reasonable explanation, *except for one odd little detail*. When reading the Tacitus text, one can't help but notice that just a couple of paragraphs above the tragic murder story, there is an account of other affairs that *includes the name "Saturninus,"*[605] the same name as that given to the husband of Paulina in Josephus' tale. That might suggest that the story had been obtained from a written work – perhaps an annalistic account? – and the eye of the author had fallen upon, and registered, the name 'Saturninus,' which was then utilized twice, as will be seen.

Or, it might reflect the fact that Josephus knew that Saturninus had been made governor of Judea following the death of Germanicus when Pilate was sent back and Piso was summoned to appear in Rome to be tried for murder.

Either solution is interesting in its own way.

Here is another possibility: if that little slip is evidence that the author of the passage had read Tacitus, that means it could not have been Josephus himself, because Tacitus' work was published a number of years after *Antiquities*. More than that, the "law concerning assassins" mentioned by Tacitus must have been the *Lex Titia* (43 BC), which legalized the second triumvirate and gave *Octavian*, Mark Antony and Lepidus full powers to defeat the assassins of Julius Caesar.[606] What is interesting is the use of the name *Octavius* Sagitta in this story that ends with "the law concerning assassins." Also, one wonders about the possible relationship of a woman named 'Pontia' and a man named 'Pontius Pilate,' considering the way Romans named their children. Strange coincidences?[607] In any event, the passage appears to be loaded with literary allusions and deserves some serious study.

---

[604]Tacitus, *Ann.* 13.44.

[605]Tacitus, *Ann.* 13.43.2.

[606]"The passing of the Lex Titia marked the *de jure* end of the Roman Republic, though in practice it had already been almost completely subverted by the contending parties in the civil war that was then beginning. The law, ostensibly only a temporary measure, was renewed in 38 BC, but quarrels between Octavian and Antony after the downfall of Lepidus in 36 BC prevented the law from being further extended, leading to the expiration of the Lex Titia in 33 BC and the ensuing Final War of the Roman Republic." (World Heritage Encyclopedia, 'Lex Titia.')

[607]Interestingly, one of Caesar's assassins was named Lucius Pontius Aquila, a tribune of the plebs who refused to stand during one of Caesar's triumphs and later served under Caesar's betrayer, Decimus Junius Brutus Albinus.

Possibly relevant to the story, the early Church Father Irenaeus protested vehemently against the rumor that Christianity was simply a re-working of the Egyptian rites. He wouldn't have been making this protest if it were not something that was widely thought. The relationship between early Christianity and Isis worship seems to have been connected to the activities of the second-century Christian 'gnostic' theologian Valentinus (ca. 100–160), and he was probably the object of Irenaeus' ire. Now, interestingly, many of the ideas of Valentinus are curiously reminiscent of Paul. (Many early gnostics were followers of Paul, and Valentinus allegedly claimed to have derived his ideas from a disciple of Paul.[608]) This is especially the case in Paul's Letter to the Ephesians, which many scholars are pleased to exclude from the Pauline canon as non-authentic but which Douglas Campbell insists *is* authentic and perhaps the clearest statement extant of what Paul taught.[609] On that point, I think Campbell may be right.

According to Clement, "they say that Valentinus was a hearer of Theudas, and Theudas, in turn, a disciple of Paul."[610] The Valentinians insisted that their unwritten source was the secret teachings of Paul, teachings delivered only in person and never written down by him. Irenaeus struck out against the Valentinians by utilizing the Epistles to Timothy and Titus, widely recognized nowadays as definitely not Pauline. That is to say, someone had to write them to counter the idea that Paul had secret teachings. However, there are plenty of strange and mysterious remarks in the Pauline epistles that support the idea that Paul had a lot more going on than what we have in his preserved writings. Was whoever wrote this text implying that Paul was hoodwinked by a Gentile cult? That he was as debased as a woman who engaged in illicit sex as a result of a conspiracy? Is Josephus in dialogue with Paul here?

Now, let's look at Josephus' next tale, since it appears that they are a pair and go together. It concerns Jews defrauding a Roman noblewoman named Fulvia, who is also married to a Saturninus, which only raises the eyebrows even higher. Notice that this follows directly on from the end of the Paulina story where it says: "I now return to the relation of what happened about this time to the Jews at Rome, as I told you I would":

> There was a man who was **a Jew**, but **had been driven away from his own country by an accusation laid against him for transgressing their laws**, and by the fear he was under punishment for the same; but in all respects a wicked man. He, then living at Rome, **professed to instruct men in the wisdom of the laws of Moses**. He procured also three other men, entirely of the same character with himself, to be his partners. These men persuaded Fulvia, a woman of great dignity, and one that had embraced the Jewish religion, **to send purple and gold to the temple at Jerusalem**; and when they had gotten them, they employed them for their own uses, and spent the money themselves, on which account it was that they at first required it of her. Whereupon Tiberius, who had been informed of the thing by Saturninus, the husband of Fulvia, who desired inquiry might be made about it, ordered all the Jews to be banished out of Rome; at which time the consuls listed four thousand men out of them, and sent them to the

---

[608]Pagels (1992) analyzes Paul's letters in terms of Valentinian gnosticism, showing how the letters were read by second-century gnostics and how they could be considered 'proto-gnostic' in nature. In other words, the gnostics may have gotten a lot of their ideas from Paul, or Paul at least may have influenced the ideas the gnostics later developed, based on their interpretations of his ideas.

[609]In addition to Romans. Both letters are in the unique position of having been addressed to congregations that had not previously met Paul personally. For all his other letters, we can infer that he did not feel the need to spell things out so clearly that he had presumably already taught in person. Romans and Ephesians were different: he had to formulate his gospel clearly for those whom he had yet to address in person.

[610]Clement of Alexandria, *Stromata*, cited by Pagels (1972), p. 1.

island Sardinia; but punished a greater number of them, who were unwilling to become soldiers, on account of keeping the laws of their forefathers. Thus were these Jews banished out of the city by **the wickedness of four men.**[611]

Fulvia was, of course, the name of the wife of three of the most influential *Populares* of the late Republic: Publius Clodius Pulcher, Gaius Scribonius Curio, and Mark Antony. All three of her husbands were tribunes and *supporters of Julius Caesar*, which points us back to the *Lex Titia* and the name of the husband of Pontia, Octavius, in the legal case cited by Tacitus; additionally, the fact that Decius Mundus was said, in the tale of the Isis cult, to have been *a tribune*. All very odd indeed.

I want to look at this story with Paul in mind since we have been triggered to do so by the name 'Paulina.'

> There was a man who was a Jew, but had been driven away from his own country by an accusation laid against him for transgressing their laws …

This is the slur directed at Paul in Acts. When Paul visits the pillars in Jerusalem, the author has James say to Paul: "They have been told about you that you teach all the Jews living among the Gentiles to forsake Moses, and that you tell them not to circumcise their children or observe the customs."[612] This may be part of what is being conveyed in the story of Fulvia and the Jews who defrauded her.

> … and by the fear he was under of punishment for the same; but in all respects a wicked man.

In Acts, another accusation slung at Paul was that he was "a pestilence, and a stirrer-up of strife throughout the world."[613] (One wonders, of course, where the author of Acts got that? I'd say he spent some time reading Josephus …)

> He, then living at Rome, professed to instruct men in the wisdom of the laws of Moses.

It wouldn't be the laws of Moses *per se* if he was accused of *transgressing* the laws. If Paul made it to Rome after writing Romans, he would have preached *his version* of Judaism, as apostle to the Gentiles ('fulfillment of the Law through freedom *from* the Law'). And by all appearances, what Paul taught was *not* your standard Judaism. It was definitely influenced in important ways by Jewish scriptures, but it was centered on Christ and the Cross.

---

[611] *Ant.* 18.3.5 (81–4).
[612] Acts 21:21.
[613] Acts 24:5. I don't think Robert Eisenman is correct in concluding that the Dead Sea Scrolls' "spouter of lies" is in reference to Paul (he also sees the "wicked priest" as Ananus). While the connections are interesting (Paul does appear to be responding to critics calling him a liar, and he did set up churches preaching the Mosaic Law was unnecessary), the carbon-14 dating doesn't support Eisenman's theories – the Scrolls are too early – and it must have been only a few years before the second meeting in Jerusalem when it became known that Paul was preaching a significantly different messiah: one of peace and unification rather than the avenger who was going to flay and burn the Romans. See Robert Eisenman, *James the Brother of Jesus: The Key to Unlocking the Secrets of Early Christianity and the Dead Sea Scrolls* (Penguin, 1997) and *The New Testament Code: The Cup of the Lord, the Damascus Covenant, and the Blood of Christ* (Penguin, 2006). Thanks to David Oliver Smith and Russell Gmirkin for directing my attention to some of the above points (personal communication).

He procured also three other men, entirely of the same character with himself, to be his partners.

This could be a reference to Paul and his fellow helpers (e.g., Timothy, Titus, Tertius, etc.), but I leave it open since it is all speculation anyway.

These men persuaded Fulvia, a woman of great dignity, and one that had embraced the Jewish religion, to send purple and gold to the temple at Jerusalem ...

Purple and gold are the colors of a king: a messiah? Later legends about Paul (such as those recorded in *Acts of Paul*) depict him as a home-wrecker of sorts, persuading wives to leave their husbands and follow him. For example, the Iconians "complain that Paul beguiled their wives."[614] Additionally, the direct mention of Fulvia could be pointing to the idea that Paul was taking in women of rank. Hard to say. But one does have to try to imagine what was common knowledge to people back then, or even hidden knowledge to specific persons and groups, and what they might write for the 'initiated.'

... and when they had gotten them, they employed them for their own uses, and spent the money themselves, on which account it was that they at first required it of her.

Again, this is an accusation made against Paul that he refers to in his letters: that he was defrauding members of his churches.[615]

Whereupon Tiberius, who had been informed of the thing by Saturninus, the husband of Fulvia, who desired inquiry might be made about it, ordered all the Jews to be banished out of Rome; at which time the consuls listed **four thousand** men out of them, and sent them to the island **Sardinia** ... Thus were these Jews banished out of the city by the wickedness of four men.[616]

There is another way to look at the story, too: that it was an allegory of Judas the Galilean and the three pillars of Jerusalem, James, Cephas and John. The gold and purple might indicate that they claimed royal Davidic ancestry. The perversion of the law could refer to the 'Fourth Philosophy,' and the misuse of the funds could represent the collecting of monies to fund the revolution against Rome. The name of Fulvia is so unusual and specific to the wife of the supporters of Caesar, including Mark Anthony, that it seems to be suggesting that one should look in that direction for something.

On the face of it, set in the 19 AD temporal context, this appears to be about the expulsion of Jews recorded by Tacitus (below). But it is one of a pair with a bizarre story that seems to

---

[614]MacDonald (1983), p. 35; see also pp. 28, 36.

[615]2 Corinthians 12:14-8: "Here I am, ready to come to you this third time. And I will not be a burden, because I do not want what is yours but you; for children ought not to lay up for their parents, but parents for their children. I will most gladly spend and be spent for you. If I love you more, am I to be loved less? Let it be assumed that I did not burden you. Nevertheless (you say) since I was crafty, I took you in by deceit. Did I take advantage of you through any of those whom I sent to you? I urged Titus to go, and sent the brother with him. Titus did not take advantage of you, did he? Did we not conduct ourselves with the same spirit? Did we not take the same steps?" As Campbell (2014), p. 150, writes, regarding the collection for Jerusalem: "It seems to have given rise to accusations of fraud – specifically, that although nobly (or arrogantly) eschewing direct personal support from the Corinthians, he nevertheless intended to abscond with this even larger sum that he was raising ostensibly for the Christian community in Jerusalem."

[616]*Ant.* 18.3.5 (81–4).

be about Paul and his version of Christianity. Could the two stories, taken with the missing text where the TF now stands, be telling us, in a roundabout way, about a possible origin event for Christianity – the execution of Judas the Galilean – following which there was unrest among the Jews of Rome, followed by expulsion; that these events were later responsible for two different versions of Christianity: one that was similar to the Egyptian religion, and another that was a distortion of the Jewish religion? Note that it was the priests of the Egyptian religion who were crucified.

Perhaps Josephus was simply trying to indicate what he thought of Christianity in the two versions most familiar to him, that of Paul and that of the Jewish Christians of Jerusalem, followers of Judas the Galilean? It's all very mysterious and I'm just speculating; hopefully other researchers can get more out of it.

These two stories, following just after the *Testimonium Flavianum*, pose a number of interesting problems. Taken together at face value, they reflect a Roman rejection of Egyptian *and* Jewish worship. Tacitus records the banishing of the religions of the Jews and Egyptians *in the reign of Tiberius, 19 AD*, as follows:

> Measures were also taken for exterminating the solemnities of the **Jews and Egyptians**; and by decree of Senate **four thousand** descendants of franchised slaves, all **defiled with that superstition**, but of proper strength and age, were to be transported **to Sardinia**; to restrain the Sardinian robbers; and if, through the malignity of the climate, they perished, despicable would be the loss: the rest were doomed to depart Italy, unless by a stated day they renounced their profane rites.[617]

This bit of text is something of a problem considering the glowing review that Philo (in his *Embassy to Gaius*) gave Tiberius in regard to his consideration of the Jews. We've already noted that persons who adhered to that variation of Judaism that later became known as Christianity were accused of a 'vile superstition' which probably meant the expectation of the coming of a messiah who would destroy Rome. In the text of Tacitus above, we notice that he also mentions 'profane rites.' The only rites that Jews performed in public were at the Temple in Jerusalem; their synagogue meetings were readings, prayers and meals. So, unless there is something we don't know about Diaspora Jewish practices, I don't know where Tacitus came up with the idea of 'profane rites' unless he is simply referring to circumcision. We don't know what early Christians did in the way of rites, except for a vague account by Pliny the Younger from some time later about singing hymns, eating meals, and greeting the sun.[618] So are we really seeing here a notice that there were Christians that early, in 19 AD? That is, followers of Judas the Galilean? I think so.

Notice that several essential particulars match between Tacitus and Josephus: the number four thousand is present in both accounts about the expulsion, as well as Sardinia being the destination, so it is certain that both are talking about the same event. In Tacitus, it is noted that the four thousand are "descendants of franchised slaves, all *defiled with that superstition*,"

[617]Tacitus, *Ann.* 2.85.4.

[618]In his letter, Pliny mentions the Christians' "depraved, excessive superstition." This was likely in reference to continued eschatological beliefs in the early 100s. Pliny mentions that some had "stopped being Christians" as much as 25 years before he wrote, i.e., in 87 AD. Trajan's reply mentions that anyone who can prove they are no longer a Christian will not be in danger, and that proof consists in "worshiping our gods," so part of the "depravity" Pliny mentions was probably a denial of the Roman gods. Pliny, *Letters* 10.96–97, https://faculty.georgetown.edu/jod/texts/pliny.html.

which suggests that they were Jews who were messianists; that is, it was not the same Judaism that Tiberius was known to acknowledge and at least tacitly approve. Josephus' text, on the other hand, is about Romans being converted to Judaism, but *a perverted form of it* being taught by con artists. So, something is definitely being said in these two texts that is not apparent on the surface. They aren't just gossip.

Additionally, we have to ask: what are these stories doing right there in the midst of the governorship of Pontius Pilate, which, according to Christian chronology, was supposed to extend from 27 to 37 AD? These two events allegedly precede a banishing of Jewish and Egyptian rites from Rome as well as the exiling of many Jews (or pseudo-Jews) from Rome by Tiberius, something that occurred in 19 AD almost without question. So why does Josephus begin the TF with, "Now there was about this time ...", and the following stories with, "About the same time also another sad calamity ..."? The TF is clearly placed in the context of the 19 AD event. If it is redacted or a replacement text – it is still in the context of 19 AD. If there was nothing there at all and the previous section about Pilate's attack on the Jews flowed right into the Paulina and Fulvia stories, it is *still* in the context of 19 AD! Whoever inserted the TF thought that was the right place for it because Pilate was there. It was probably only later that the chronological difficulties were realized and a lot of patching and deleting was done to bring things more into line: additional governors and years were added before Pilate, a whole chunk was deleted to connect two different men named Vitellius, and the rest is fraudulent history.

What does seem clear to me is that whatever stood in that TF spot originally – assuming something did – must have been something that was a "sad calamity" that "put the Jews into disorder," because that is what the lead-in of the next paragraph refers to. Of course, the TF could be removed without any disruption in the flow at all, so it's not *necessary* to assume that something else stood there. There was already a previous sad calamity involving Pilate. However, since the two tales that follow the TF, as far as I can see, have no purpose in the local context of Pilate and his doings, it might be conjectured that they may originally have been intended to convey some message about whatever stood originally in the TF spot, some connection between the different events. Because, certainly, they taste and feel like Josephan, novelized textual excursions.

Recall Josephus' confused account of the events following the death of Herod, which he associated with the deaths of Judas and Matthias and their pupils, while Archelaus was in Rome pleading his case before Augustus:

> But now came another accusation from the Jews against Archelaus at Rome, which he was to answer to. It was made by those ambassadors who, **before the revolt**, had come, by Varus's permission, to plead for the liberty of their country; those that came were fifty in number, but there were more than **eight thousand of the Jews at Rome who supported them** ...[619]

In rather lurid terms, these ambassadors pleaded to have their country joined to Syria and to be given a Roman governor. They wanted no part of Archelaus. What we note here is the "eight thousand of the Jews at Rome." We also noticed the congruence of the second text following the TF, about the expulsion of four thousand Jews from Rome, with the account from Tacitus. What is the relationship between the eight thousand Jews at Rome in the time of Augustus, and the

---

[619] *Wars* 2.6.1 (80).

four thousand in the time of Tiberius who Tacitus says were "descendants of franchised slaves, all *defiled with that superstition*"? It doesn't seem that the same *types* of Jews are intended.

If the three stories – the TF, Paulina and Fulvia – are connected in some way, how might a calamity in Judea impact events at Rome? The execution of a popular Judean messianic figure could have prompted such a reaction in the Diaspora. So what is the text implying, if anything? I think the two tales of Paulina and Fulvia, which are told in the context of the time of Pilate and his probable execution of Judas the Galilean in 19 AD, may have been intended to convey something about the two messianic movements – that of Paul and that of the rebellious, nationalist Jews.

The placement of the texts, and the details they contain, suggest to me that they are intended to associate the two groups in some way. Or, for a more radical proposition: that they are intended to indicate that the two were combined in the time of Josephus in order to create Christianity as we know it. In the first story, the author may have been indicating Pauline messianism, and in the second, the Jewish Christians' version, which was more of a 'traditional' type of religious-political, messianic nationalism, even if Josephus considered the four men to be the equivalent of robbers. It may be that three of the men defrauding Fulvia in the second story represent the 'three pillars of Jerusalem.'

After returning again and again to these texts, I can't shake the suspicion that the text of Tacitus has been involved in the composition of the stories, which if true would imply that this is the work of a later redactor, not Josephus himself. The references to Egyptian and Jewish worship *together*, and 4,000 Jews being sent to exile in Sardinia, can also be been found in Tacitus. Also, while the stories are seemingly typical Josephus scandal mongering and religious propaganda, the fact that one of them is modeled on a legal case written up by Tacitus certainly gives one pause. Yes, Josephus could have read about it in the Roman archives to which he may have had access at one point in the writing of his history of the Jewish War, but the adjacency of the name 'Saturninus' in Tacitus' text and its use twice (in both Josephan stories) suggests either a coded message, or simply that someone had Tacitus text open before them. However, against this, if the section did in fact originally contain a discussion of the death of Judas the Galilean, it may have also referenced the death of Germanicus and Sentius Saturninus becoming the new governor of Judea at that time.[620] But I can see no reason for the deletion of a text about the death of Germanicus unless it included matters that would expose the story of Jesus of Nazareth as a fraud (or some other embarrassment).

Either Josephus made those stories up to cover up something or to send a coded message, or someone else, writing later, did so. And since the general trend of the stories is such as to indicate Pauline Christianity as we understand it coming down through Paul's letters themselves, it seems quite possible that this is what those stories are talking about: the origins of something that the author couldn't or didn't want to address directly – but which the author wished to slander in the process.

If one takes the two tales set adjacent to each other and thinks about them, a few items stand out. The first tale, modeled on the 58 AD event recorded by Tacitus, is about a Roman woman taken in by an individual who is pretending to be a god of the Egyptian cult of Isis. The second tale is about a Roman woman taken in by a 'temple cult' of Judaism, so to say.

---

[620]Tacitus relates how Sentius confronted Piso in Cilicia. After Piso gave up the stronghold, Sentius didn't make any concessions except to provide him ships and safe passage to Rome (*Ann.* 2.81.3).

As for the Anubis impersonator *Decius Mundus*, the Decians were a famous plebeian family who gained fame for two of their family sacrificing themselves for their country in war in order to secure victory. Publius Decius Mus sacrificed himself in battle through the ritual *devotio* in the fourth century BC. (A later Publius Decius was a colleague of Mark Antony, the third husband of Fulvia of the second tale.) Mundus means 'world' in Latin – 'world sacrifice' by a Roman?

Notice it is *Paulina* who is cast as being taken in by the Egyptian worship, while it is *Fulvia* who is cast as taken in by the Jews. Are these two elements important? Is Josephus (or the redactor) telling us that *Pauline Christianity* was taken in by Egyptian rites/mysteries, and that it was members of the upper classes, including the imperial family, that were bamboozled?

In the Paulina story, note that "Tiberius inquired into the matter thoroughly by examining the priests about it, and ordered them to be crucified, as well as Ide."[621] Later, Decius was exiled.

It seems to me that if the Jerusalem ecclesia was associated in some way with the sectarians at Qumran, and those sectarians were associated with the Dead Sea Scrolls, then that was the ideological inspiration for the rebellion against Rome: expulsion of the foreign occupiers, return to self-rule. Since we have Josephus' testimony about his own involvement in that rebellion – embellished though it may be – *he would have to have known about Paul and his unifying messiah.* Based on Josephus' spirited defense of Judaism, and his own peculiar interpretations of God's will working through the Romans in relation to the Jews, his affiliation with Essene-type communities might be assumed to be rather likely – at least early in the game (especially considering his association with his teacher 'Bannus'). That, too, would have put him into contact with circles that knew, or knew of, Paul. His whole attitude about messianism almost has to be read in reverse, and perhaps this little story, if it is Josephan, may be either a deliberate coded message, or a fanciful tale in which his subconscious gives him away. Either that or it is an interpolation, as suggested at various times in this chapter. I leave it to others to work that out, if possible.

At this point, I want to include a brief account of some of the family relations that may be involved here.

Robbers, Pirates, Brigands and Tyrants

We have established with a very high degree of probability that the *Testimonium Flavianum* is given in a 19 AD context. It appears that Pilate came to Judea in 14 or 15 AD and was 'sent down' in 19 AD, possibly because of the "maltreatment of the allies" encouraged by Piso, the alleged murderer of Germanicus. We have also examined the possibility that Judas the Galilean was executed under Pontius Pilate in 19 AD, and that this was described in a text that occupied the place of the TF. Since we are missing an account of the death of Judas the Galilean,[622] I think that Unterbrink is correct: it belongs there, where we currently find the TF. I have speculated that it takes the form of the account of the Golden Eagle Temple Cleansing found in Josephus'

---

[621]Remember Ide, I'll come back to her further on.

[622]Except, of course, for the account of the Golden Eagle event in the time of Herod, which is contradicted by later accounts of Judas' activities.

text in association with the time of the death of Herod the Great, where it was put either by Josephus himself, or a later redactor.[623]

Josephus refers to the nationalist messianists as robbers, pirates, brigands, tyrants, etc., leading people to rebel against Rome and get themselves killed and Jerusalem destroyed. Yet, Josephus has a lot to hide. According to his autobiography, he tried joining the Essenes/Zealots/Zadokites himself when he was young and hung out with a John-the-Baptist type named Bannus, who may be reflected in the character of John the Baptist.[624] When the Romans demonstrated that they were going to win the war (or perhaps before), Josephus completely turned and became convinced that the Jewish god was on the side of the Romans because the Jews had been so wicked in rebelling. Further, he was convinced that the Roman emperor was the messiah who was to come out of Judea and rule the world. Or, of course, he could have just claimed these things because it was convenient to do so.

Josephus tries to make a clear distinction between the 'mainstream' Jewish sects and the 'Fourth Philosophy' of Judas the Galilean, whom he blames most heartily for the revolt (in which he, himself, willingly participated, though he gives lip-service to being a pacifist) and the ultimate destruction of Jerusalem and possibly a million Jews. But as noted numerous times, Josephus was busily dissembling and covering his own backside while more or less trying to clean up the image of the Jews as a whole and the Essenes and Pharisees in particular, not to forget his Flavian masters.

Josephus was evidently familiar with the Essenes and their ideas, and our knowledge of this group (or at least one variation of it) has been greatly enhanced by the discovery of the hidden texts at Qumran. When one reads these texts, it seems that the community at Qumran was rather close in ideology to Josephus' Judas the Galilean and his Fourth Philosophy. In addition, even Josephus can't hide the connections between Judas' movement with both the Pharisees and the Essenes. For example, they shared the Essenes' attitude to death (*Ant.* 18.1.6; *Wars* 2.8.10), all participated in the war and various rebellions (which Josephus attempts to downplay), and Judas' original partner in crime, Sadduc, was allegedly a Pharisee. He even explicitly states their beliefs were indistinguishable from the Pharisees'. However, Josephus attempted to discredit the Galileans as either brigands or forced converts and downplay their 'pharisaic' credentials.[625]

Josephus more or less succeeds in keeping the Essenes clean of any revolutionary taint by simply separating out the revolutionary messianism and apocalypticism and assigning it to a 'Fourth Philosophy,' which I think he just made up as a category to hold the violent elements of the various Jewish sects of the time, including mainly the Zealots. Nodet and Taylor go so far

---

[623]It's hard to say for sure which. Josephus may have had a motive for displacing Judas' actions in time. A Christian redactor certainly would have too. As we have learned from bits and pieces reported by early Christian writers, the Josephan text they had was significantly different in some respects from the one we have now, at least in relation to those parts claimed by Christian apologists, like the TF. And as I discussed in the last chapter, the areas most important for early Christian chronology – aside from Pilate – are those three areas of the text marked by the number 37.

[624]It is likely that anyone preaching purification of the Jews at the time of John the Baptist was connected in some way to the Zealot party formed by Judas the Galilean. We noted that John the Baptist was executed at about the same time that Paul was being pursued by the governor of Damascus. Something was going on that is lost to us.

[625]Along similar lines, Russell Gmirkin sees Judas' Fourth Philosophy as "the radical political branch of the Pharisees/rabbis, which Josephus took pains to hide for apologetic reasons" (personal communication, March 2021).

as to essentially equate the Essenes and the Pharisees of this period, categorizing the 'Fourth Philosophy' messianists as a revolutionary subset, centered in rural Galilee.[626] If you read some of the Dead Sea Scrolls, you can feel their brotherhood's incandescent hatred for the Romans and all they represented. (And it wasn't just the Romans; it was all enemies, foreign and domestic.) For example, here are some excerpts from the 'War of Sons of Light against the Sons of Darkness' scroll:

> On the day when the Kittim [i.e. Romans] fall there shall be a battle and a tremendous slaughter before the God of Israel, for He has appointed a day for Himself from of old for a war of annihilation against the Sons of Darkness. ... On the trumpets of the slain they shall inscribe, "The Hand of God's Might in Battle to Strike All Treacherous Men Dead." On the trumpets of ambush they shall inscribe, "The Mysteries of God to Destroy Wickedness." On the trumpets of pursuit they shall inscribe, "God's Smiting of All the Sons of Darkness." (His anger will not return until they are completely destroyed.) ...
>
> On the blade of the javelins they shall inscribe, "The Lightning Flash of a Spear for the Power of God." Upon the weapons of the second group they shall inscribe, "Bloody Missiles to Bring down Those Slain by God's Anger." Upon the javelins of the third group they shall inscribe, "A Sword Flash Devouring the Wicked Who Are Slain by God's Judgment." ... they shall defile their hands with the corpses of the Kittim in striking them down ... *All of these [shock troops] will take up the pursuit [of the fleeing enemy] in order to exterminate the enemy in the battle of God in an eternal annihilation.* ... When the slain are falling, the priests shall keep sounding the trumpets from a distance, but they shall not come among the corpses so as to pollute themselves with their unclean blood, for they are holy men, and shall not defile the oil of their anointing as priests with the blood of a worthless nation.[627]

John J. Collins comments:

> ... the Community Rule is pacifistic only up to a point: 'I will not grapple with the men of perdition *until the day of revenge.*' ... It is well known that the settlement at Qumran was destroyed by military assault during the revolt against Rome, and was apparently defended ... While it is impossible to prove who the defenders were, the simplest hypothesis is that they were the same people who had inhabited the site for a century and a half. While the war anticipated in the War Rule has many fantastic qualities, it also shows some knowledge of realistic military tactics. *The preparation of such an elaborate War Rule strongly suggests that the community was prepared to implement it,* if the members believed that the appointed time had arrived. That time may very well have arrived in the war against Rome.[628]

Further, one finds that the sect referred to its members as 'saints' and 'the elect' and its totality as the true 'Church of God' and 'The Way,' all terms that show up in early so-called Christian literature, even Paul's writings. That leads to the proposition that the so-called early Jerusalem church was nothing more than the support/recruiting arm of an Essene/Zadokite/Zealot group fomenting rebellion against Rome. That leads to the idea that what they were doing in their so-called evangelizing was gathering recruits, supporters, and funds to conduct their eventual war of liberation, and using messianic hopes to promote it and maintain the spirits and loyalty

---

[626]Nodet and Taylor (1998).

[627]William R. Farmer, *Maccabees, Zealots, and Josephus: An Inquiry into Jewish Nationalism in the Greco-Roman Period* (Greenwood Press, 1956), pp. 163–7.

[628]John J. Collins, *Apocalypticism in the Dead Sea Scrolls* (Routledge, 1997), p. 108.

of the revolutionaries. Based on the historical evidence, that is the sum and substance of the early Jerusalem Christianity. It was certainly messianic and cultic, but not at all in the way the later Christian mythmakers and apologists imagined.

If that is the case, Paul was undoubtedly familiar with the Essene groups, at least in terms of the chapters scattered around the Empire to which Philo, Josephus, and Pliny give witness. When Paul went to Jerusalem, the men he met were probably the leaders of the coming rebellion: the three 'pillars,' James, Cephas/Simon, and John.[629]

However, the church *as understood by the later mythmakers* also has a foundation in historical elements. It seems that Paul had very different ideas about what a messiah should be. In this context, we can gain an understanding of the conflict between Paul and the 'Jerusalem James Gang.' The three pillars were intent on provoking a war and Paul was intent on preventing one. They preached two radically different messiahs, as is clear from Paul's writings, and it seems unlikely that their different Christs were based on the same human individual, assuming Paul had any human individual in mind at all.

We now have a general idea that there were several Jewish messiah figures who were exactly that – *Jewish* messiah-types of Jews, for Jews, and by Jews – and who expected to wipe out the Romans and a lot of other peoples. So far we've encountered Simon of Perea, the 'king of the Jews' slain by Gratus and commemorated on the Jeselsohn Stone; Athronges and his brothers; and Judas the Galilean, who appears to have been the most important and influential, because Josephus devotes an extraordinary amount of text to him and members of his family throughout *Wars* and *Antiquities*. Maccoby[630] and Hilsenrath[631] both highlight the fact that elements of these figures made their way into both the Gospels and Acts, which tells us that the authors of these texts may very well have been aware of what they were doing to some degree. Maccoby and Hilsenrath are convinced that the Jewish messiah was all there was and Paul just perverted it, so they go on to cast Paul in the role of betrayer and mythmaker. As we will see, there was much more to Paul and his gospel than that.

As those early Christian authors searched Jewish texts – including Josephus – for clues to create their Jesus of Nazareth, they found a number of characters whose actions were incorporated into the tale, including several with the name 'Jesus,' the saddest being Jesus son of Ananus, whom Josephus identifies as a plebeian and a husbandman and who

> ... began on a sudden to cry aloud, "A voice from the east, a voice from the west, a voice from the four winds, a voice against Jerusalem and the holy house, a voice against the bridegrooms and the brides, and a voice against this whole people!" This was his cry, as he went about by day and by night, in all the lanes of the city. However, certain of the most eminent among the populace had great indignation at this dire cry of his, and took up the man, and gave him a great number of severe stripes; yet did not he either say anything for himself, or anything peculiar to those that chastised him, but still went on with the same words which he cried before. Hereupon our rulers, supposing, as the case proved to be, that this was a sort of divine fury in the man, **brought him to the Roman procurator, where he was whipped till his bones were laid bare; yet he did not make any supplication for himself, nor shed any tears, but turning his voice to**

[629]Galatians 2:9: "... and when James and Cephas and John, who were acknowledged pillars, recognized the grace that had been given to me, they gave to Barnabas and me the right hand of fellowship, agreeing that we should go to the Gentiles and they to the circumcised."
[630]Maccoby (1998).
[631]Hilsenrath (2009).

the most lamentable tone possible, at every stroke of the whip his answer was, "Woe, woe to Jerusalem!" And when Albinus (for he was then our procurator) asked him, Who he was? and whence he came? and why he uttered such words? **he made no manner of reply** to what he said, but still did not leave off his melancholy ditty, till **Albinus took him to be a madman, and dismissed him.**[632]

One is strongly reminded of the scourging of Jesus and his refusal to reply to questions, as well as the tale of Pilate dismissing him after finding no fault in him.

Carrier, too, points out that there are actually several 'Jesus Christs' in Josephus. 'The Samaritan' who promised to reveal lost relics on Mount Gerizim; Theudas who told his followers he would part the Jordan River; 'the Egyptian' who promised to topple the walls of Jerusalem, and a nameless 'impostor' who promised salvation to those who would follow him to the wilderness.[633] All these promises echo the story of Joshua, who "inaugurated the nation of Israel by crossing the Jordan and congregating at Gerizim ... [he] also miraculously parted the Jordan upon beginning his conquest of Israel [and felled] the walls of Jericho."[634] Joshua in Greek is of course Jesus (*Iesous*). So Josephus was quite obviously and perhaps even deliberately comparing the original conqueror of Israel, Joshua, to messianic pretenders in order to slander the name 'Jesus.' Carrier comments:

> [Josephus] does not explicitly call them messiahs – he probably wanted to avoid reminding his Gentile audience that this was the product of Jewish ideology, and instead claimed that it was the product of fringe criminals and ruffians ... But the descriptions he provides belie the truth of the matter. ... their messianic basis remains unmistakable.[635]

As Carrier points out, these stories may simply be Josephan fictions. But they show that at least some Jews were tying the figures of Joshua and the Messiah together. If they were historical figures, however, they "might have even been *trying* to get themselves killed, so as to fulfill the prophecy of Dan. 9.26 and thereby usher in the end of the world as promised in Daniel 12."[636]

What are the chances of a real Jew named Joshua ('God saves,' i.e. 'savior') becoming the savior? More likely is that the name was a symbolic one: the new Joshua, messiah – 'anointed savior.'[637] According to Paul, God "gave him [Jesus] the name that is above every name," i.e. Jesus Christ Lord, but only after his ascension to heaven.[638] That leads to the question: what was his name *before*? For the Jews – or many of them, it was probably Judas the Galilean. But it appears that this was not the case for Paul; his messiah remains a mystery.

In any event, with a comprehensive knowledge of the historical texts of the period, and most especially the texts of Josephus, it becomes glaringly obvious that the Gospel writers – at least Mark and Matthew – had certain knowledge of Judas the Galilean as a messiah figure, and

---

[632] *Wars* 6.5.3 (300–5). It's odd that Josephus appears to restrict his mention of individuals with the name 'Jesus' in his *Antiquities* while there are several of them in *Wars*. One suspects that the above individual was neither a plebeian nor the son of Ananus, a husbandman.

[633] *Ant.* 18 (85–7), 20 (97–8, 169–71, 188).

[634] Carrier (2014), pp. 69–70.

[635] Carrier (2014), pp. 68–9.

[636] Carrier (2014), p. 71, italics in original.

[637] In the first century, about one out of every 26 Jewish males was named Joshua. See Carrier (2014), pp. 31, 239.

[638] Recall the *Ascension of Isaiah*, where Jesus is given a *secret* name. See Chapter 2.

were deliberately and consciously writing their texts with his historical reality in mind, but creating a fictional character and heavily overlaying it with the Pauline Christ, who was an altogether different figure. Taken at face value, it constitutes deliberate fraud and I don't think this realization can be avoided when all the pieces and context of the times are considered. The Gospels were rhetorical works consciously designed to be religious propaganda.[639] But again, when one understands the history of the time to as great an extent as possible, even that becomes understandable, as will be seen.

Founding of the Zealots = Founding of Christianity?

So, to recap a bit: from Josephus we derive the facts that indicate two dates very important to the founding of the Zealot movement: in 5/4 BC Simon of Perea declared himself messianic king but was slain in the desert by Gratus. And then, the census ordered by Augustus in 6 AD when a minor rebellion was instigated by Judas the Galilean, possibly son of Simon of Perea and/or grandson of Hezekiah/Ezekias. And, most interestingly, both events are associated with the mythologized births of Jesus of Nazareth in two different Gospels. Surely, this is no coincidence.

Jews were raised and nurtured on the ideal of the absolute sovereignty of God – the kingdom of God on Earth – and the longing for the realization of this dream was passionately expressed in apocalyptic literature. Yahweh was to be Israel's only king with a righteous high priest as his viceroy on Earth. This theocratic ideal was implied in the demands of the insurgents of 4 BC, as reported by Josephus (who was relying on the history of Nicolaus of Damascus), and was more clearly laid out in the exhortations of Judas and Saddok in 6 AD. The thread of apocalyptic expectation is tightly woven into Josephus' history, beginning with the death of Herod and growing ever more prominent as time and events moved inexorably toward the Jewish War beginning in 66 AD.

I don't think anyone could blame the Jews for their war against Rome. Though living under empire was an accepted fact for many ethnic groups,[640] that didn't make it easy. And in the lead-up to the war, Judea lost its historical support from the emperor (Nero), who rejected their bid for control of Caesarea and canceled their existing rights in the city. As Mason put it, "His emphatic refusal dramatically increased the Judaeans' peril and energized their enemies."[641] The Roman procurators' main job was to collect taxes and goods and send them to Rome; most of them saw such appointments as ways to increase their own wealth as well. Florus was particularly bad, and his plunder and violence led to a series of reprisals and escalations, ultimately leading to all-out war. The only problem was, revolting against Rome was a losing proposition. This heartbreaking reality was dealt with by creating and propagating false hopes based on the ancient biblical tales of their God fighting their wars for them as well as the success of the Maccabees against the Seleucids. Many cooler heads realized this, and one of them may have been the Apostle Paul.

---

[639]See Tolbert (1989).

[640]As Mason (2016), p. 230, writes: "The subject peoples needed only to reconcile the situation with their own dignity, and Rome suggested that their leaders view themselves as Rome's *friends*, if it would make them feel better." Subject peoples actively tried to avoid war, and get the best deal possible, including regional supremacy if possible, which Judea achieved for some time prior to the war.

[641]Mason (2016), p. 275.

5. Paul's Mission

I would ask the reader to refer back to my statement in the Foreword: "any cosmology that is sufficiently explanatory of the phenomena we observe in our universe has deeper dynamics and implications"; cosmology is definitely part of apocalyptic and Pauline literature. In my research on Paul, my eyes were constantly scanning for any evidence that his cosmology might have any resemblance to more modern formulations in terms of physics and mathematics. I was trying to determine if Paul was a true apocalyptic mystic or a con artist, because that, of course, would influence my interpretation of the few data points left to us. And that interpretation would also have a bearing on how to formulate a rational, plausible, historical reconstruction. I read several books that purported to analyze Paul psychologically, and that led me off into a year-long study of evolutionary psychology. That then led to another year of studying genetics and evolution, which led, eventually, to the topic of Intelligent Design, and I became convinced that there was much to be said for Intelligent Design by way of Information Theory. Having said that, I must also say that Intelligent Design in no way suggests that one must be a Creationist or even a religious believer; I'm not. It just means another layer of reality to try to study by inference. As far as I can see, nothing could be more fascinating.

Getting back to Paul, I needed to figure out if I thought Paul was sincere or a con-man as so many have suggested. When reconstructing history, one has to accept certain propositions and then run the experiment to see how many problems are solved and questions answered. It is clear that there were many ideas and concepts common at the time that may have influenced Paul's thinking. However, that is not necessarily evidence of fraud; rather, that is evidence of common ground with other mystics whose insights may, in fact, reflect a ubiquitous, interpenetrating, hyperdimensional information field.

It can be said that Paul did not invent much, but what he did was to apply all the material he had to an overarching messiah for all humanity with the aim of unifying human beings rather than using gods as a support for inter-ethnic hatred, war, death, and destruction. That fact alone weighed heavily on the scales in favor of Paul being sincere and truly driven to evangelize his messiah to all people, Jews and Gentiles alike. Of course, the cynical response to that is that Paul was an agent for the Empire engaged in suppressing rebellion. That it might be beneficial to the Empire is true enough on the face of it, but there was more to what Paul was saying than that and I will get into it in some depth here because I think it is important for the historical reconstruction.

And so I will proceed with the assumption that Paul was truly sincere and dedicated to his mission, and that his visions and insights were not just fraudulent claims; whether they were true reflections of some other reality cannot be determined here, though I will speculate a bit in that direction.

We cannot accept Paul's two remarks[642] stating that he had initially persecuted the 'Church,' and then came over to join them, as truly Pauline. Based on his own insistence that his conversion was not due to the Jewish Christians of Jerusalem, but rather due solely to God, together with the evidence that Paul knew how profoundly different his gospel was from the original disciples of Judas the Galilean, clearly indicate his repudiation of the gospel of the Jerusalem church and makes it unlikely that he was converted to their beliefs. That alone leads me to conclude that the passages are clearly interpolations.

J. C. O'Neill notes:

> His case rested solely on the commission from God. … Paul had asked the Galatians ironically in verse 10 whether he should now try to please men, and he is not likely, a few sentences later, to quote the men he had pleased.

> The interpolation is anachronistic because it regards Judaism as an entity distinct from Christianity. … [T]his interpolation speaks in the terms to be found in the Apostolic Fathers of the second century, when Judaism had become a foreign entity (Ignatius *Magn.* 8.1; 10.3; *Philad.* 6.1).[643]

Paul was obviously aware of the Jerusalem ecclesia's conception of the Messiah, but just as obviously, he wasn't much impressed by it, or them. He tells the Corinthians that they appear to be easily taken in by "a Jesus other than the Jesus we preached," and in the next breath he refers to those 'super-apostles' whom he then goes on to excoriate as:

> … false apostles, deceitful workers, masquerading as apostles of Christ. And no wonder, for Satan himself masquerades as an angel of light. It is not surprising, then, if his servants also masquerade as servants of righteousness. Their end will be what their actions deserve.[644]

Yes, Paul actually called the Jerusalem Christians servants of Satan. It becomes even more evident that this is who he is talking about:

> Are they Hebrews? So am I. Are they Israelites? So am I. Are they Abraham's descendants? So am I.[645]

No, Paul's Son of God was not Judas the Galilean or any other Jewish figure, despite the fact that later redactors have tried to make it appear that they were one and the same.

In Galatians he announces clearly, "Paul, an apostle – sent not from men nor by a man, but by Jesus Christ and God the Father," and then accuses his readers:

> I am astonished that you are so quickly deserting the one who called you to live in the grace of Christ and are turning to a different gospel – which is really no gospel at all. Evidently some people are throwing you into confusion and are trying to pervert the gospel of Christ. But even if we or an angel from heaven should preach a gospel other than the one we preached to you, let them be under God's curse![646]

---

[642]Gal. 1:13, 14, 22-4.

[643]J. C. O'Neill, *The Recovery of Paul's Letter to the Galatians* (London: SPCK, London, 1972), pp. 24–25.

[644]2 Cor. 11:13-15.

[645]2 Cor. 11:22.

[646]Gal. 1:6-8.

He continues:

> I want you to know, brothers and sisters, that *the gospel I preached is not of human origin.* I did not receive it from any man, nor was I taught it; rather, I received it by revelation from Jesus Christ.

Further on, when talking about his second trip to Jerusalem, he mentions the leaders of the Jerusalem ecclesia specifically, making the side comment:

> As for those who were held in high esteem – whatever they were makes no difference to me; God does not show favoritism – they added nothing to my message.[647]

His opponents finally come into focus and he names them:

> When Cephas came to Antioch, I opposed him to his face, because he stood condemned. For before certain men came from James, he used to eat with the Gentiles. But when they arrived, he began to draw back and separate himself from the Gentiles because he was afraid of those who belonged to the circumcision group.[648]

I don't think it's unreasonable to suggest that these statements, along with Paul's repeated focus on crucifixion, indicate that the pillars' gospel did *not* include any focus on crucifixion. If it did, their interpretation of it couldn't have had much in common with Paul's, because he repeatedly contrasts the two, and highlights their differences. For instance, the image of a crucified-rebel could have been a symbol for their suffering-servant messiah, but the cross clearly meant something much *more* to Paul.[649]

Based on the way this group spied on Paul, hounded him, interfered with his work and his groups, and the way he responded to them, it is obvious that *Paul was not preaching the same Christ* and the Jerusalem group was becoming more and more hostile about it. It seems fairly clear, from what we know so far, that Paul could not have been ignorant of Judas the Galilean and his Fourth Philosophy, or that he – and/or possibly other dead rebel leaders – was most likely the messianic figure preached or revered by the Jerusalem ecclesia. But *this is obviously not the messiah who inspired Paul.* The real 'Jewish Jesus' was of *absolutely no interest to Paul.* That, in and of itself, is an astonishing thing. But that realization leaves us free to speculate about exactly what it was that drove Paul, because it is clear he wasn't myth-making or running a con job; he was utterly devoted to his mission, body and soul. And since Paul is, ultimately, the author of the main Christian theology and Christology, we should very much want to discover what he saw, what he was thinking, what he experienced.

We have already discussed Wells's take on Paul's theology in our discussion of the early documents of Christianity. As he points out, the highly developed angelology of Jewish literature of the time clearly influenced Paul, who not only believed in the angels, including Satan and the demons, but also the multi-layered universe. This was part of the intellectual environment of the Zoroastrians, the Enochians, and the Middle Platonists, who apparently influenced the development of Gnosticism – and Paul.[650] Paul was engaged in a battle against these obviously

---

[647]Gal. 1:11-12.

[648]Gal. 2:11-12.

[649]Keep in mind also that Simon of Perea was killed by having his head struck off and Judas the Galilean was said to have been burned alive.

[650]Dillon (1996).

terrifying forces, and his vision was one where a single, awesome being could stand against this series of worlds lower than God himself, and act as the defender and redeemer of humanity.

> From Phil. ii, 5–11 we learn that Jesus is a divine figure who came down into the material world to suffer an ignominious death. Then he reascended and received a mystic name as powerful as the name of God. Couchoud regards this story of the descent and re-ascension of the divine being as the key to Paul's conception of Jesus and he remarks that we are fortunate enough to possess an ancient Jewish apocalypse which gives the story in greater detail, and so fills out the picture which is merely sketched by Paul. He is referring to the so-called *Ascension of Isaiah* ...[651]

As Wells notes, Paul seems to have had a revelation similar to that of the author of the *Ascension of Isaiah*. Jesus "made a spectacle of the cosmic powers and authorities, and led them as captives *in his triumphal procession*."[652]

Paul and Isaiah

Despite the fact that it was never intended as a universalist declaration,[653] we find what was driving Paul in the book of Isaiah. Messiah simply means 'anointed' and could apply to priests, kings, and prophets. Interestingly, in Isaiah we find the only non-Jew in the OT who was identified as a messiah, or anointed one of Yahweh. Isaiah tells us that Yahweh spoke "to his messiah, to Cyrus, whom I [Yahweh] took by his right hand to subdue nations before him."[654] It seems clear that, to the author of this text, 'Yahweh's anointed' is something more than a title; it is a theological construct expressing that this individual is appointed and protected by God, the God of the Jews, for a special role in relation to him and them.[655] Josephus appears to have understood the term in a similar way, because he was easily able to switch sides and announce that Vespasian was the Messiah. Did Paul do something similar?

Paul describes his call to be an apostle in Gal. 1:15-7, where he says:

> But when God, who had *set me apart before I was born and called me through his grace*, was pleased to reveal his Son to me, so that I might proclaim him among the Gentiles, I did not confer with any human being, nor did I go up to Jerusalem to those who were already apostles before me, but I went away at once into Arabia, and afterward I returned to Damascus.

Rainer Riesner points out the clear relationship between the formulation of this passage and Isaiah 49:1: "*Listen to me, you islands; hear this, you distant nations: Before I was born the Lord called me; from my mother's womb he has spoken my name.*" Riesner also highlights the numerous places where Paul identifies with the Deutero-Isaianic Servant of God and appears to have planned his mission based on this text. He notes:

---

[651]Wells (1971), pp. 288–91.

[652]Col. 2:15.

[653]Discussed above. See Cohn (1993).

[654]Isa. 45:1.

[655]This was undoubtedly a self-interested approach since local priests of other religious persuasions often hailed a powerful ruler with the titles and theologies of their own kings/religions as a diplomatic maneuver. But Paul was not analyzing the text from this point of view; he was going all-out exegetical and trying to derive meaning that applied to him and his situation and the world around him.

... the most unequivocal statements of hope concerning the Gentile world appear in the second part of the book of Isaiah (Isa. 45:20–2; 51:4f.; 56:1–8) specifically in connection with the figure of the Servant of God (Isa. 42:1, 3f, 6; 49:1, 6, 22). The promise in Isa. 9:1 belongs to a particular geographic context that was not a matter of indifference to part of Jewish and Christian expectation: "In the former time he [God] brought into contempt the land of Zebulun and the land of Naphtali, but in the coming time he will make glorious the way of the sea, the land beyond the Jordan, Galilee of the nations. The people who walked in darkness have seen a great light; those who lived in a land of deep darkness – on them light has shined." (Isa. 8:23–9)[656]

In Josephus, we learn that the territory of Naphtali extended to Damascus (*Ant.* 5.1.22 [86]), and texts from Qumran reveal a sharp interest in this region (1Qap-Gen 21:28–22:10). Essene groups settled in Damascus apparently because they thought that the messianic age would begin there. Based on the evidence adduced by Riesner, it seems clear that the Essenic/Enochian/Zoroastrian type of messianic thinking affected Paul. It has been thought that he came to understand his own revelation as the beginning of the ingathering of the Gentiles, but the situation may be a bit more complex than that.

The theological frame of the Damascus revelation in 2 Cor. 4:6 appears to exhibit similarities in language to the Essene-like *Testament of Levi*, which tells us:

> And his star shall arise in heaven as of a king, lighting up the light of knowledge as the sun the day; and he shall be magnified in the world. He shall shine forth as the sun on the earth, and shall remove all darkness from under heaven ... And in his priesthood the Gentiles shall be multiplied in knowledge upon the earth, and enlightened through the grace of the Lord.[657]

Shades of Ignatius, for whom the ascended Christ appeared in the heavens as a star! Parallels can also be drawn to the fictional transfiguration of Jesus, said to have occurred in the area around Mount Hermon, where Jesus radiates light.

In short, it looks like Paul saw himself as a sort of earthly pre-messiah, an anointed prophet chosen before he was born, the Servant of God, whose task was to proclaim the revealed Son to the Gentiles and *begin the fulfillment of the prophecies of Isaiah*. It's almost as though Paul saw himself as a John the Baptist type. Riesner also proposes that Paul's itinerary was governed by Isaiah 66:18-21:

> "And I, because of what they have planned and done, am about to come and gather the people of all nations and languages, and they will come and see my glory."

---

[656]Riesner (1998), p. 237.

[657]*Test. Patri. Levi* 8:3, 9. "The work is divided into twelve books, each purporting to be the last exhortations of one of the twelve titular patriarchs. In each, the patriarch first narrates his own life, focusing on his strengths, virtues, or his sins, using biographical material from both the Hebrew Bible and Jewish tradition. Next he exhorts his listeners to emulate the one and to avoid the other. Most of the books conclude with prophetic visions. ... Presently, scholarly opinions are still divided as to whether it is an originally Jewish document that has been retouched by Christians, or a Christian document written originally in Greek but based on some earlier Semitic-language material. ... [Robert] Charles called attention to the frequent use of the Testaments of the Twelve Patriarchs by Paul: I Thess. ii. 16 is a quotation of *Test. Patr., Levi*, 6:10-11; Rom. 12:19 is taken from *Gad*, 6:10; Rom. 12:21 is taken from *Benjamin*, 4:3; II Cor. 7:10 is a quote from *Gad*, 5:7; Ephes. 5:6 taken from *Naphtali*, 3:1." (Wikipedia.org, 'Testaments of the Twelve Patriarchs.') See: *The Old Testament Pseudepigrapha*, Volume 1.

"I will set a sign among them, and I will send some of those who survive to the nations – to Tarshish, to the Libyans and Lydians (famous as archers), to Tubal and Greece, and to the distant islands that have not heard of my fame or seen my glory. They will proclaim my glory among the nations. And they will bring all your people, from all the nations, to my holy mountain in Jerusalem as an offering to the Lord – on horses, in chariots and wagons, and on mules and camels," says the Lord. "They will bring them, as the Israelites bring their grain offerings, to the temple of the Lord in ceremonially clean vessels. And I will select some of them also to be priests and Levites," says the Lord.

Paul may have thought that he was living this plan for the Gentiles. Traces of Paul's exegesis of Isaiah can be detected in Rom. 15:16-24. Riesner writes:

But his redemptive-historical identification as "the servant of circumcision on behalf of the truth of God in order that he might confirm the promises given to the patriarchs" (Rom. 15:8) demonstrates that without an origin rooted in the ancient Jewish people of God, neither is there any hope for the Gentiles (Rom. 15:8–13). Paul cites Isa. 11:10: "The root of Jesse shall come, *the one who rises to rule the Gentiles*; in him the Gentiles shall hope" (Rom. 15:12).[658]

The 'root' terminology (*sheresh* in Hebrew) may be confusing, because 'root,' generally, means 'source' or 'origin,' which would mean that Jesse, as biological ancestor, would be the root of Jesus. The simple explanation is that here the writer uses the word to describe something that grows out of something else: Jesus grew out from Jesse; he is an extension, a descendent, of Jesse. That is, the tree was cut down, but the root survived and a shoot emerged from it. However, Paul has another idea also: Jesse may have come first, but Paul's eternal Christ *is Jesse's root* and the root of *all humanity*. Paul stated this in Colossians 1:15-17:

He [Jesus] is the image of the invisible God, the firstborn of all creation. For by him all things were created, in heaven and on earth, visible and invisible, whether thrones or dominions or rulers or authorities—all things were created through him and for him. And he is before all things, and in him all things hold together.

One can only conjecture why Jesse's name is used instead of David in Isaiah. There must have been something special about him that has been lost to us in the editing of the OT, and we only know that he was David's father. Back to Riesner:

The reign of the Christ over the nations will begin when "by the word and deed" of Paul he "wins obedience from the Gentiles" (Rom. 15:18). Just as Christ became "a servant for circumcision" (Rom. 15:8) in order to put into effect for the Gentiles the promises to the patriarchs (Rom. 15:9), so also does Paul now understand himself "because of the grace given me by God to be a minister of Christ Jesus to the Gentiles in the *priestly* service of the gospel of God, so that the offering of the Gentiles may be acceptable" ... (Rom. 15:15f)[659]

Note that Paul has taken on a priestly role even though he is not of the lineage of Levi. Clearly Paul intended that the entire temple system was made obsolete by Jesus.

---

[658]Riesner (1998), p. 246.
[659]Riesner (1998), pp. 246–47.

In Isa. 66:19, proclamation of God's glory among the "nations ... that have not heard of my fame" is the condition for the diaspora Jews being "brought as an offering ... to the holy mountain Jerusalem" (Isa. 66:20). From this perspective, it would not be surprising for Paul to consider it his commission first to win the "full number of the Gentiles" (Rom. 11:25) – a number predetermined by God – to a certain extent as an offering, by "fulfilling the gospel of Christ" (Rom. 15:19) through his geographically expansive proclamation. That was his task; he is silent here concerning the obligation of others to engage in a vigorous mission to the Jews ...[660]

Looking closely at Isa. 66:19a, "I will set a sign among them, and I will send some of those *who survive* to the nations," we notice two things: the 'setting of a sign' – Christ on the Cross – and human agents being obliged to respond to this sign appropriately. And here is where we come up against a conundrum. Going strictly by the instructions in Isaiah, Paul should have evangelized Judaism in its purest form, but that's not what he did. Judas the Galilean, who was promoting a purified Judaism, or any of the other Jewish-type messiahs, clearly meant nothing to Paul. To him, they were 'another Christ' and 'a different gospel' preached by "false apostles, deceitful workers, masquerading as apostles of Christ." For Paul, the Jewish law and temple service was no longer of any value because of Christ on the Cross. Wells thinks that this was because Paul had a vision of a *criminal* on a cross, revealed to him as the Son of God. So he had to change his mind about things and thus came to his ideas about the negating of the Jewish law. Wells's take on it bears reviewing:

> The argument [Paul] gives to show that [the Law] is unnecessary is that a crucified Jesus contradicts the law of Deut. 21.23 that a man whose dead body is hanged upon a tree is accursed of God. Paul quotes this passage and comments: 'Christ brought us freedom from the curse of the law by becoming for our sake an accursed thing' (Gal. iii.13). The argument is: the law says that the man crucified is accursed. Jesus was crucified but could not be accursed. Therefore a case has occurred for which the law is not valid. But as it must be either valid absolutely or invalid absolutely, it is by this one case rendered wholly invalid.[661]

I think Wells was going in the right direction, though I don't think that Paul had a vision of a *criminal* on a cross. As Carrier writes, Paul's cross of Jesus "sounds like a cosmically potent object, and not just some everyday pole or crossbeam manufactured by the Romans and used repeatedly for the executing of countless others besides Jesus."[662] In 1 Corinthians 15, if the passage is authentic, Paul indicates that others had visions of Christ before he did. If so, theirs would have been of the future warrior-king coming to liberate Judea with an army of angels, not 'Christ on a Cross.'

We've already seen how all the early Christian writers based their messiah on scripture, and the same goes for the Essenes at Qumran, and even Josephus with his 'Joshua'-type frauds. Even Philo wrote about a pre-existent firstborn son of God, whom he identified as the Logos, the image of God, and the true high priest in heaven, based on his interpretation of Zech. 6:12. The name of this figure? "Jesus Rising."[663] In fact, any Jewish scholar of the law could have made the connections between a limited number of texts and come up with something very close to the core 'Christian' myth:

[660]Riesner (1998), p. 247.
[661]Wells (1971), p. 298. This isn't quite the whole picture, however, as Engberg-Pedersen (2000) shows.
[662]Carrier (2014), p. 564.
[663]See Carrier (2014), p. 200.

[Such a person] would have before him, in a simple pesher of Jewish scripture, a celestial being [a:] named Jesus Christ Rising, [b:] a high priest of God, [c:] in opposition to Satan, [d:] who is wrongly executed even though innocent, [e:] and dies [f:] to atone for all sins, [g:] is buried and subsequently 'raised', [h:] exalted to the highest station in heaven, [i:] appointed king with supreme heavenly power by God, [j:] and who will then build God's house (the church).[664]

It wouldn't be surprising if many Jewish messianic groups adopted variations on this theme, including the Jerusalem Christians. Paul in all likelihood appropriated a form of this 'messiah myth,' including the name ('anointed-savior-and-lord/Lord Jesus Christ') and the scripture that 'revealed' him. Paul was very aware of just these connections in scripture, and during his vision they all coalesced around a figure that he saw as the earthly manifestation of this cosmic exemplar.

Something profoundly moved Paul to envision a man on a cross *as a sign*: "I will set a sign among them," not an "accursed" thing, but rather *a symbol of triumph:* "he made a spectacle of the cosmic powers and authorities, and led them as captives *in his triumphal procession*." How did Paul get from an image of abject failure to one of cosmic triumph?

Consider again that Paul's guide, Deutero-Isaiah, referred to the king of Persia as the Lord's anointed, a messiah. The entire passage reads:

> This is what **the Lord says to his anointed, to Cyrus, whose right hand I take hold of** to subdue nations before him and to strip kings of their armor, to open doors before him so that gates will not be shut: I will go before you and will level the mountains; I will break down gates of bronze and cut through bars of iron. I will give you hidden treasures, riches stored in secret places, so that you may know that **I am the Lord, the God of Israel, who summons you by name.** For the sake of Jacob my servant, of Israel my chosen, **I summon you by name and bestow on you a title of honor, though you do not acknowledge me.** I am the Lord, and there is no other; apart from me there is no God. I will strengthen you, though you have not acknowledged me, so that from the rising of the sun to the place of its setting people may know there is none besides me. I am the Lord, and there is no other. ...
>
> Woe to those who quarrel with their Maker, those who are nothing but potsherds among the potsherds on the ground. Does the clay say to the potter, 'What are you making?' Does your work say, 'The potter has no hands'? Woe to the one who says to a father, 'What have you begotten?' or to a mother, 'What have you brought to birth?'
>
> This is what the Lord says – the Holy One of Israel, and its Maker: Concerning things to come, **do you question me about my children**, or give me orders about the work of my hands? It is I who made the earth and created mankind on it. My own hands stretched out the heavens; I marshaled their starry hosts. **I will raise up Cyrus in my righteousness: I will make all his ways straight.** He will rebuild my city and set my exiles free, but not for a price or reward, says the Lord Almighty. ...
>
> Gather together and come; **assemble, you fugitives from the nations.** Ignorant are those who carry about idols of wood, who pray to gods that cannot save. Declare what is to be, present it – let them take counsel together. **Who foretold this long ago, who declared it from the distant past? Was it not I, the Lord?** And there is no God apart from me, a righteous God and a Savior; there is none but me.

---

[664]Carrier (2014), p. 83. The sources for these motifs are as follows. Wisdom of Solomon's "righteous man, son of God who dies a shameful death": e, g, i. Isaiah 52–3's "suffering-and-dying servant": d, e, f. Daniel 9's "messenger": e, f. Zechariah 3, 6's "Jesus called Rising": a, b, c, f, h, i, j. 11Q13's "messiah": e, f. See Carrier (2014), pp. 78–83.

Turn to me and be saved, all you ends of the earth; for I am God, and there is no other. By myself I have sworn, my mouth has uttered in all integrity a word that will not be revoked: **Before me every knee will bow; by me every tongue will swear.** They will say of me, "In the Lord alone are deliverance and strength." All who have raged against him will come to him and be put to shame.[665]

Cyrus is called God's anointed; he was designed and qualified for his great service by God himself, and we see God condemning those who criticize the fact that he has chosen a non-Jew to do his work: "Does the clay say to the potter, 'What are you making?'" We find this echoed in Romans 9:20-1:

> But who are you, a human being, to talk back to God? "Shall what is formed say to the one who formed it, 'Why did you make me like this?'" Does not the potter have the right to make out of the same lump of clay some pottery for special purposes and some for common use?

Isaiah makes it clear that the true God (from Isaiah's and Paul's perspective) was *unknown to Cyrus and yet God foreknew him*, called him by name. Philip R. Davies writes:

> Daniel, although tempered by the experience of oppressive (non-Persian) rule, retains in its older narratives (chapters 1–6) the idea of Yhwh the lord of history *assigning government of the entire world to non-Judean kings*, who in turn "inherit" his "kingdom" (2:37, 4:34ff.; 5:30).
>
> The idea of a universal world order decreed by Yhwh is even retrojected into the Neo-Babylonian period; Jeremiah 27–29 represents Nebuchadnezzar as allotted the world empire of Yhwh, and in the closing verses of 2 Kings, Evil-Merodach (Amel-Marduk) frees Jehoiachin from confinement and sits him at the "king's table" (25:29–30). Most commentators have detected here a hint of hope for the future of a Davidic dynasty; but it is equally likely that the hint is of *the incorporation of the Davidic monarchy into the new world-empire*: Evil-Merodach is here *the inheritor of the "Davidic covenant."* Indeed, Jer. 25:9, 27:6 and 43:10 refer to Nebuchadnezzar as Yhwh's "servant" (the other two "servants" in Jeremiah being Jacob and David).[666] But this perspective of a series of world rulers under the patronage of Yhwh probably has its root in the favourable attitude of Judeans, and especially Jerusalemites, to the Persians who restored their city. From this (and not from the experience of deportation) came *a Yahwistic ideology of world-empire, in which the Judean national god ensures the well-being and triumph of his own nation by means of benevolent world empires which he controls.*[667]

If Jews could see Gentile kings as messiahs (Cyrus, Vespasian) and the agents of God's world-empire (Nebuchadnezzar, Evil-Merodach) and even inheritors of the Davidic covenant, then Paul's Christ may very well have been based on a very different historical person, assuming he was based on a real person at all.

Paul tells us that after his conversion experience, he went off to Arabia for an unspecified period of time before *returning* to Damascus. It's probably correct to assume that the conversion experience occurred in Damascus, which we can date to around 29 AD by the reference in Josephus to the execution of the sons of Judas the Galilean, James and Simon, most likely the 'pillars' of the Jerusalem church. Evidently, Paul needed to work out what had happened to him

---

[665]Isaiah 45.

[666]Also recall Paul's statement in Rom. 15:8 about Jesus being "servant to the circumcised."

[667]Philip R. Davies, *On the Origins of Judaism* (Equinox, 2011), pp. 94–5.

on his own – or with some group about which we know nothing – and in the process it seems that Hellenistic concepts were more meaningful than his traditional Judaism.

We don't know how or why his attention became concentrated on the image of a cross. For all we know, there was a cross-like object present at the time of his initial vision and it was associated with death. In any event, Paul was transported into a visionary world that is well described in many studies on shamanic practices.[668] What Paul saw, it seems, was the whole of fallen mankind in subjection to demonic powers that ruled the universe from some sphere of heaven lower than where the immortal God resides. Somehow Cross + Death + Messiah was revealed to him as the potential salvation for all of humanity by the descent and incarnation of a divine being, a 'son of God,' who was hidden, or somehow occluded during his descent, as Ishtar was, in order to deceive the demonic powers into exceeding their rights by manipulating events leading to his death. That he knew he was going to be killed was patent, because he was described as "obedient unto death." Thus Paul's 'Jesus' was the savior of all mankind from their fallen state and probably demonic powers, or at least all who accepted him as patron, and not just a Jewish Messiah who was coming to save only the Jews from their oppressors.

Paul states that the meaning of the death of Christ was "that one died for all, therefore all died," so that the living should no longer live unto themselves but unto him who had died in their behalf. No clearer exposition of the ancient patronage system could be found.

The logic of Paul's vision was inexorable: it deprived the Jews of their status as 'the elect,' since all humanity, one way or another, was fallen and under the rule of the demonic powers. There are suggestions even that the Jews were more dominated by these powers by virtue of their delusional belief in the power of their laws to save them.

The idea of the spirit-given origin of his gospel is fervently maintained by Paul in several passages of his writings. Any suggestion that some part of his knowledge might have been derived from the Jerusalem Christians is just as fervently repudiated.

In 2 Cor. 5:12-19, Paul says he is going to provide his converts with defenses on his behalf so that they will have the means to oppose certain men who boast about outer appearances and not about the inner essential reality. Then he adds remarks that appear to reveal what is behind his words: he says that even if he is out of his mind, this state is only evidence of a mind oriented towards God, whilst toward his converts, he maintains a normal state of mind. This strongly indicates that his opponents accused him of being out of his mind, that his spiritual revelations were evidence of his lack of mental soundness. This idea made it into Mark's Gospel where Jesus is accused by his family of being out of his mind.

However, one has to ask how a group of individuals who believed their messiah was going to come with 12 legions of angels to physically destroy the Romans could accuse Paul of being of unsound mind for proclaiming a universal, unifying, spiritual principle in the guise of a Divine Man who only operated through the hearts and minds of his adherents?

And what, pray tell, was Paul doing mixing up with the Jerusalem Christians at all? He knew that his was a different Jesus! He knew that his was a different gospel! He acknowledged this to his converts! Paul's references in 2 Corinthians to "another Jesus" and "another spirit" show that a more profound issue was involved here than simply an easier way for Gentiles to get in the door without having to submit to obnoxious customs and vile rituals of self-mutilation.

---

[668]See, e.g., Colleen Shantz, *Paul in Ecstasy* (New York: Cambridge University Press, 2009).

Problematic Paul

In the early days of the modern approach to biblical studies, Baruch Spinoza wrote: "The universal rule, then, in interpreting Scripture is to accept nothing as an authoritative Scriptural statement which we do not perceive very clearly when we examine it in the light of its history."[669] Around the same time, John Locke wrote about Paul:

> The Light of the Gospel he had received from the Fountain and Father of Light himself, who, I concluded, had not furnished him in this extraordinary Manner, if all this plentiful Stock Learning and Illumination had been in danger to have been lost, or proved useless, in a jumbled and confused Head; nor have laid up such a Store of Admirable and useful Knowledge in a Man, who, for want of Method and Order, Clearness of Conception, or Pertinency in Discourse, could not draw it out into Use with the greatest Advantages of Force and Coherence.[670]

Locke believed that Paul was "a coherent, argumentative, pertinent Writer; and Care, I think, should be taken, in expounding of him, to show that he is so."

However, this view comes up against considerable difficulties when trying to reconcile one part of Paul's writing to another; and Paul to Acts and the Gospels. Trying to figure out Paul's theology is hampered by issues addressed in the Introduction: interpolations in Paul's letters. There is no need to repeat all that here, but what I do want to note is that, for a long time, the conflict between the letters of Paul and the stories in the Gospels and Acts was solved to the detriment of Paul's original thought by numerous anonymous redactors and editors. The belief was that the Gospels and Acts were 'history' and Paul's letters were distorted or entirely fraudulent. This attitude prevails even to the present day, with the invention of all sorts of traditions and prior sayings collections or miracle stories collections that are said to lie behind Paul and the Gospel of Mark. Well, as we've seen, it is certain that there was a LOT going on in the historical background; it just wasn't what the NT scholars would like to accept as the beginnings of Christianity.

In 1792, Edward Evanson[671] denied the authenticity of a number of Paul's epistles because they just didn't 'fit' with the story in Acts and certainly did not support the Gospel accounts of the life of Jesus. He rejected Romans, Ephesians, Colossians, and the Pastorals and Hebrews. He also rejected most of the books of the NT as forgeries and only accepted the Gospel of Luke as authentic (!).

At the beginning of the nineteenth century, Ferdinand Christian Baur cast doubt on the reliability of Acts.[672] However, he considered only four epistles authentic: Galatians, 1 and 2 Corinthians, and Romans.

---

[669]Baruch Spinoza, *A Theological-Political Treatise* (1670), chapter VII.

[670]Locke (1632–1704) 'An Essay for the Understanding of St Paul's Epistles, by Consulting St Paul Himself, in Paraphrase and Notes on the Epistles of St Paul to the Galatians, I & II Corinthians, Romans, and Ephesians.'

[671]Edward Evanson, *The Dissonance of the four generally received Evangelists* (1792). There are 15 editions published between 1790 and 2016 in English.

[672]Ferdinand Christian Baur, *Paul, the apostle of Jesus Christ, his life and work, his Epistles and his Doctrine*, translated by Eduard Zeller (London: Williams and Norgate, 1845).

Bruno Bauer,[673] in 1850, attacked the conclusions of F. C. Baur. He was later convinced by Weisse that Mark was used by Matthew and Luke, and was, itself, a product of the church's imagination. He also concluded that Acts was the expression of the triumph of Judaism over the revolutionary movement of Paulinism. It appears he was probably correct.

> Bauer became the first author to systematically argue that Jesus did not exist. Beginning in 1841, in his *Criticism of the Gospel History of the Synoptics*, Bauer argued that the Biblical Jesus was primarily a literary figure. However, he left open the question of whether a historical Jesus existed at all until his 1851 work, *Criticism of the Gospels and History of their Origin*, and then in 1877 proposed his theory for the true origin of Jesus in *Christ and the Caesars*. ... Bauer wrote, "Everything that the historical Christ is, everything that is said of Him, everything that is known of Him, belongs to the world of imagination, that is, of the imagination of the Christian community, and therefore has nothing to do with any man who belongs to the real world."[674] ... In *Christ and the Caesars* (1877) he suggested that Christianity was a synthesis of the Stoicism of Seneca the Younger and of the Jewish theology of Philo, as developed by pro-Roman Jews such as Josephus.[675]

Only a few years after Bruno Bauer's book was published, Christian Hermann Weisse attacked Bauer's conclusions. (Weisse was the scholar who had first proposed the now generally accepted two-document hypothesis,[676] which was accepted by Bauer, and which was one of the reasons he considered the Gospels frauds.) Weisse concluded that 1 Corinthians was a completely authentic example of Paul's writings, 2 Corinthians had been compiled from three different letters of Paul; Romans and Philippians are also compilations in which the original letters have been interwoven with interpolations which, in some places, almost destroy the style completely; an interpolator has worked on Galatians and Colossians.

The above is just to give a general background of the controversies that have been raised over Paul and which continue to this day, though a group of scholars did get together some years back and, by something like a voting process, decided which of Paul's letters they accepted as authentic, and even which parts of those letters. I've reviewed their work at some length and don't find it convincing *when the historical background is taken into account*.[677]

Moving on, J. C. O'Neill took up the task of showing how Galatians has been both glossed and interpolated because, as Bruno Bauer demonstrated, it is full of obscurities, contradictions, improbable remarks and non-sequiturs. Weisse's conclusion was that, "Nobody but Paul could have written Galatians, yet the Galatians we possess is not entirely Paul's."[678] O'Neill further notes:

---

[673] *Christianity Exposed: A Recollection of the 18th Century and a Contribution to the Crisis of the 19th Century* (1843, ed. Paul Trejo, 2002); see also: *Kritik der paulinischen Briefe* ("Critique of Paul's epistles") (Berlin, 1850–1851); and *Christus und die Cäsaren. Der Ursprung des Christenthums aus dem römischen Griechenthum* (1877, 2d ed. 1879), transl. Frank E. Schacht, *Christ and the Caesars: The Origin of Christianity from Romanized Greek Culture* (Charleston House, 1998).

[674] Bruno Bauer, *Kritik der evangelischen Geschichte der Synoptiker* (O. Wigand, 1842), p. 308.

[675] Wikipedia.org, 'Bruno Bauer.'

[676] The two-source hypothesis is an explanation for the synoptic problem, the pattern of similarities and differences between the three Gospels of Matthew, Mark, and Luke. It posits that the Gospel of Matthew and the Gospel of Luke were based on the Gospel of Mark and a hypothetical sayings collection from the Christian oral tradition, called 'Q.'

[677] Dewey et al. (2010).

[678] O'Neill (1972) p. 8.

It is often almost impossible to recover a clear train of argument from a paragraph, the reason being that it is made up of, perhaps, one pregnant sentence from Paul, a meditation on that sentence by a theologian who wished to apply an argument directed to the Galatian situation of the 50s to the life of all Christians fifty years later, plus a gloss on one word by a scribe interested in clearing up an exegetical puzzle. ... We must, at all costs, discover what Paul himself wrote, and we must discover as precisely as we can, the history of the text of his epistles, from the time they were received by those he first addressed until the time when they were gathered together, in a more or less fixed form, into the Christian canon.[679]

In his conclusions, O'Neill writes:

If the choice lies between supposing that Paul was confused and contradictory and supposing that his text has been commented upon and enlarged, I have no hesitation in choosing the second ... The aim is to hear Paul, for he is *an apostle, not from men, but through Jesus Christ, and through God the Father who raised Jesus Christ from the dead.*[680]

Paul's Theology

In this section, I am diverting from strictly historical matters into the realm of theology and speculation. I debated a considerable time over whether to severely edit this material down to bare essentials, or whether I should exclude it entirely. I decided, finally, to edit it and publish the whole text in a separate volume, since it goes off into highly esoteric matters. I am retaining enough to help the reader to better understand the allegorical nature of the Gospel of Mark, which will be discussed further on in this text. It is in understanding what Mark was doing with Paul's teachings that we finally come to realize exactly how the Jesus myth, which was never intended to be taken as historical, was created, and why.

Paul writes: "It was the good pleasure of God ... to reveal his son in me, that I might preach him among the Gentiles."[681] As S. G. F. Brandon notes:

When carefully considered as a statement of fact, the words really constitute a tremendous, indeed a preposterous, claim for any man to make, and more especially a man of Paul's antecedents. They mean literally that in the person of Paul God had revealed his Son to the end that Paul might "evangelize" him among the Gentiles.[682]

Paul's words mean, pretty clearly, that the revelation he had received was a completely new understanding that was hitherto unknown to the church such as it was – or even the world, for that matter. And yet, many of Paul's ideas appear to find echoes in other literature to which he certainly had access, from Zoroaster, Plato, the Stoics, Philo, various apocalyptic works (*Enoch, Ascension of Isaiah,* etc.) and on to Qumran. The sectarian documents from Qumran make clear that *they* expected a priestly messiah at the end of days, the 'messiah of Aaron,' as well as two additional eschatological figures: a quasi-messianic prophet and a lay, presumably royal, messiah.[683] Jewish traditions about the figure of Enoch have been noted as analogs of the Christ

---

[679]O'Neill (1972) pp. 11–12.

[680]O'Neill (1972), p. 86.

[681]Gal. 1:15-16.

[682]Brandon (2010), p. 59.

[683]Joseph L. Angel, *Otherworldly and Eschatological Priesthood in the Dead Sea Scrolls* (Leiden: Brill, 2010).

of the New Testament. However, we cannot forget the military function of this figure: that he was to return with legions of angels to defeat the Gentiles of all nations (especially the Romans), and elevate Israel to its proper place as ruler and judge (a priestly nation) over all the world.

Paul, on the other hand, laid extraordinary stress on the *death* of Jesus alone, understood as an apocalyptic event *in and of itself*, the turning point of the ages; a new age in which Jews and Gentiles would be on an equal footing before God. He wasn't preaching a Christ who had been a teacher of a new way of living, as he is depicted in the Gospels – teaching a new way of living was *Paul's* job and his own innovation. In contrast, Paul's Christ lived a life about which he says nothing except in one reference to approaching death, and as far as we know, Christ did nothing else Paul would note other than to die. I've read many exegetical efforts that seek to prove that Paul was alluding to something Jesus said or did, but they are methodologically faulty since Paul clearly and unequivocally states that his gospel was not from others, but had been directly revealed to him. As to using the Gospels to find proof that Paul knew about a real Jesus, it is far more likely, even most probable, that words and actions of Paul were used as the model for the literary Jesus, as we will see in the discussion of Mark, further on.

In Gal. 6:14, the cross of Jesus is the means for the crucifixion of the old world; Jesus' subsequent resurrection to the higher realms, *not ever on Earth*, confirms this eschatological change, but does not supersede it.[684] As J. Christiaan Beker puts it, "The cross ... is itself both the judgment of the world, and the victory over the world."[685]

Paul acknowledges that his proclamation of Christ on the cross is scandalous and against good sense because it calls on humans to see God's power in a scene of the starkest human weakness, degradation and death.[686] The polemics in Paul's letters against opposing theologies suggest strongly that Paul's cross-centered version was quite controversial and brought him into disrepute. In Philippians 3:18, he refers to "enemies of the cross of Christ," and, upon analysis, these turn out to be most probably the Jerusalem Christians, the supposed followers of 'Jesus of Nazareth' as the Gospels would have it.

There are quite a number of books that discuss Paul's 'mental health,' so to say, including one with the intriguing title *Paul in Ecstasy* by Colleen Shantz, who concludes:

> The preceding chapters have presented evidence for the widespread and enduring fact of ecstatic religious experience as a meaningful part of the lives of individuals and a contributing factor in the health and growth (as well as some of the conflicts) of their communities. Such positive effects derive in part from the fact that the neurological mechanisms that permit ecstatic experience also provide access to rich ways of knowing that are otherwise often veiled from consciousness. ... It really is a means of coming to know as well as the source of some of the content of what is known.
> ...
> Much hermeneutical theory is blind to a large proportion of human perception because it construes "reality as verbally constituted" and ignores the "perceptive, affective, and intellectual experience" of the majority of people, whose primary interface "with the world is not verbal."[687] ...
> ... [I]t would seem that the assemblies were not founded solely on the basis of preaching but took hold in part because of ecstatic phenomena understood to be directed by the spirit of God. Often

---

[684] Joel Marcus, 'Mark – Interpreter of Paul,' in *Mark and Paul: Comparative Essays Part II*, edited by Eve-Marie Becker, Troels Engberg-Pedersen (De Gruyter, 2014).

[685] Beker, *Paul the Apostle* (2000), p. 201, cited in Marcus, 'Mark.'

[686] Gal. 5:11.

[687] Terry Eagleton, *After Theory* (New York: Basic Books, 2003), p. 60, cited by Shantz.

Paul reminds the recipients of some extraordinary corporate manifestation that accompanied their reception of his message (e.g., 2 Cor 12:12; Gal 3:1-3; 1 Thess 1:5) and the surviving correspondence with Corinth suggests that such manifestations were central to the continued participation of some of the members, although troublesome to the community as a whole. ...

... [T]he body knows more than the conscious mind reveals. Likewise, early Christianity knew more than the texts reveal. ... The text, like the conscious mind, is kept in the dark about much of the comprehension of the body. ... In the end, the fact that a biblical text can still sometimes speak the truth about that wider world of knowing – even in spite of its ostensible ignorance of the facts – is a delight and a mystery.[688]

In Paul's time, the terms and imagery used were quite physical in nature: the Stoic pneuma was the 'stuff' of stars, and the levels of the heavens were literally levels of outer space occupied by the planets and stars, to which one could ascend in visions. When Paul talks about 'spiritual' things, he is speaking quite literally about that airy element, but today we might call it 'pure consciousness.' In terms of modern physics, one might speak of a realm of consciousness or field of information. When considering the idea of a multidimensional and multilayered universe, we might even think that the ancient idea of 'levels' wasn't so primitive after all; realities/realms may actually be nested, literally, some with paraphysical qualities while others are purely non-physical.[689] I'm suggesting that the neurological circuits described by Shantz may very well be capable of perceiving other realities in actuality. Perhaps this is what the ancients were doing, and they simply used the primitive cosmological concepts at their disposal to attempt to describe it.

Paul's Theodicy: Sin and the Fall

A close reading of Paul reveals that perhaps his primary concern was the same thing that has occupied the minds of great thinkers and ordinary persons alike throughout the ages: How can a good god permit the manifestation of evil in a world over which he has complete knowledge and control? What is the nature of evil? Why does it exist? And what can be done about it?

Of the hundreds of books about Paul I've read through the years, two stand out as truly extraordinary insights into the mind of the apostle: *Paul and the Stoics* by Troels Engberg-Pedersen[690] and *Paul's Necessary Sin* by Timothy Ashworth.[691] If a person could only read one, I would suggest Ashworth because he explains many of the same things as E-P but in language that is easier for the lay reader to understand. Ashworth really brings Paul to life.[692] What

---

[688]Shantz (2009), pp. 204–11.

[689]In considering the general theory of relativity, science usually utilizes a four-dimensional space-time continuum. In classical general relativity, the metrical properties of the continuum are intrinsic to the continuum, but a fifth dimension in which our normally sensed space-time is embedded can also be used to account for the curvature and properties of physical space. In the space-time continuum, one can say that all parts of the four-dimensional world exist simultaneously, in the sense of a mathematical formalism, and this would naturally lead to a complete collapse of the philosophical ideas of causality. However, many scientists who work with these ideas do not think that this continuum is 'real' in a physical sense, such that physical entities could move back and forth at will in and out of time as easily as changing direction in three-dimensional space. We, on the other hand, think that it is not only possible, but also extremely likely based upon research.

[690]Westminster John Knox Press, 2000.

[691]Routledge, 2016.

[692]Notably, Ashworth's insights followed his own transcendental experience.

follows is an exposition of Paul's thought inspired largely by Ashworth's book but with *Paul and the Stoics* in mind also.

Paul's theology wasn't academic. It was inspired by his direct experience of inner transformation. When properly analyzed, as Ashworth does, with awareness of the factor of interpolation and redaction, his ideas all fit together, mutually supporting each other in a tapestry of images, insights, metaphors, arguments, and the inspired interpretation of scripture. His radically new perception of himself put everything else into perspective, and it's what holds his ideas together.

Ashworth's analysis focuses on consistent translation of key words and phrases in Paul's letters, revealing a handful of basic ideas: a) faith and law as alternative and mutually exclusive ways of knowing God's will, the former being known directly, from within, and the latter experienced only externally and serving a temporary function for humanity; b) sin as the universal state of humanity, a collective childhood in which we have become enslaved, made blind and from which all need to be liberated; c) the liberation itself, in which we enter adulthood, reconciling spirit and flesh, restoring our function as the 'image of God,' making God incarnate in ourselves, and seeing the sin of our 'childhood' as a painful but necessary stage in gaining the knowledge of good and evil; and d) the faith demonstrated by Jesus to die for others, and his victory over death symbolized by the cross, and one's participation in that faith and suffering, establishing the new way of relating to the divine. Central to all is the nature of the transformation itself: the new way of being is accompanied by a new way of SEEing the self, others, the world, God, and our true role in relation to all of them; what amounts to *seeing the unseen*, the spiritual reality, as at least as real as the physical reality, if not more so.

Without the transformation described by Paul, one cannot see the 'invisible things of God.' For Paul, the most important of these are God's eternal qualities, his righteousness, faithfulness, and dominion. What comes out uniquely in Paul is that these features aren't exclusively manifested by God or unilaterally imposed on his creation. Nor are they imbued in a single figure, like a divine king. Rather, these qualities are open and accessible to all of humanity, at least in potential. In fact, it is precisely within and through humanity that these qualities of God are made manifest. They are the means by which God acts in the world. And the transformation process experienced by Paul, and into which he initiated his own students, was the means by which this manifestation came about, made possible by the crucifixion in some mysterious way. One's eyes are opened to what was previously hidden: spiritual truth. One is then empowered by confident knowledge of the spiritual reality to become what they now see: 'righteous,' 'faithful,' and 'sovereign,' with true will, conscience, and right action.

The accounts in Genesis of creation and the Garden of Eden are central to Paul's conception of the nature of God, humanity, our present state, and our ideal relationship with each other and with God. In Genesis, mankind is created in the 'image of God,' male and female, with dominion or sovereignty over creation. This is humanity's true form and purpose: to embody and participate in God's creative and loving dominion in the midst of physical creation. Whereas God is a unity – One – humanity becomes a multiplicity of individuals, which can nevertheless unite, as 'one flesh,' represented in Genesis as the first man and first woman. In this pre-Fall state, they know no sin, enjoy a direct connection with God, and live together in harmony: naked and separate, and yet unashamed and in harmony. This is the creation God saw on the sixth day, "and, behold, it was very good."

But this state was not to last. The creation of 'the flesh' – individuals in their own physical bodies, with their own sense of self, yet somehow still sharing God's unlimited nature – may have been good, but it led to sin and death. With the unlimited thirst for knowledge came the necessity of limitation. Just as a child wishes to explore, discover, and learn, but does not have the parent's awareness of the dangers of the world, so humanity cannot perceive the full meaning and significance – and the wrongness – of their actions, some of which will lead to the destruction of self and others. Without a certain level of experience, some things are beyond our capacity to see and understand. So just as a parent places a limit on the child's expansive exploration of the world with rules and restrictions – to protect it from its own ignorance, willfulness, and the presence of dangers of all sorts – God does the same thing with humanity. For Paul, this was 'the Law.'

However, this creates an impossible situation. By their very nature as unlimited beings, children willfully resist the prohibitions placed upon them by their parents – their natural desire for knowledge is thwarted. The child must assert itself against its parents, if it is to be true to its nature. Also, the prohibition only serves to provoke desire for the thing prohibited, and given the opportunity, the child will disobey its parents' rule. The prohibition thus serves two necessary but contradictory purposes: to protect the child from harm, and to provoke the desire for the very things prohibited. In order to survive, the child needs limitations, but in order to truly learn and thus know – in other words, to see things from the parents' vantage, with the benefit of their age, experience, and knowledge – rebellion and self-assertion are both required and inevitable. As Ashworth puts it:

> Humankind aligned with what God requires with no choice in the matter is not free. Humankind aligned with what God requires, knowing the serious consequences of action, any action, knowing the reality of good and evil, is in a position of freedom.[693]

Children must learn, and they must learn for themselves. They must disobey in order to know. Likewise humanity: it is only through opposition to God that humanity can come to understand its true state, that is, the nature of sin. This is what the story of the Fall in Genesis portrays to Paul.

In Eden, God singles out one tree as forbidden, the tree of knowledge of good and evil, eating the fruit of which will lead to death. The serpent tempts Eve to eat its fruit, promising that she will not die, but will be like God, knowing good and evil. Like all good lies, it contains some truth. Eve sees that the tree is "to be desired to make one wise," and eats, giving some to Adam as well. Their eyes are indeed open, but they see their nakedness and become fearful and ashamed. They hide from God. Adam blames Eve for his disobedience, and she blames the serpent for deceiving her. In return for their disobedience, God drives them out of the garden, cutting off their access to the tree of life. Thus, whereas before the Fall humanity lived as a diversity-in-unity, in right relationship with God, after the disobedience of the Fall comes isolation and division. Humanity was left mortal, disconnected from their source and true purpose, and with enmity to each other.

Only through this opposition does humanity come to understand the true nature of sin, that is, through painful and hard-won experience. Part of the serpent's promise came true: our eyes were opened, and we came to know the nature of good and evil. But we became mortal, corruptible,

---

[693] Ashworth (2016), p. 226.

identified with our own separate, fleshly existence. And with the corruptibility of our bodies came the corruptibility of our minds: blind to the higher realities, our higher purpose, and imprisoned in our own selfishness, self-importance, and self-centeredness, unable to see the true nature of our present existence. So now our perceptions of reality are dulled, our aim and purpose infirm and half-forgotten. Worst of all, we cannot even see the wrongness of our present state and how it shapes all our lives due to the infirmity of our minds, let alone conceive of an alternative way of being. We are truly in a state of slavery, imprisonment, condemnation.

Through the prohibitions of the law – as experienced externally – we come to know all the 'bad' things we can potentially do. We can engage in all sorts of debauchery, exploit our fellow humans, experience all sorts of pleasures at the expense of others and our own higher potentials. So the law – a yardstick that measures our behavior externally – leads to sin; that is, we learn to know that we are sinning when we fall short of the yardstick. So it is through sinning that we come to understand sin as sin – to see that it is not the best path to take in life. It leads to death and it cuts us off from the expansive, creative force of the cosmos. Ashworth writes:

> Paul considered there to be a radical split in each person: 'For I rejoice in the law of God according to the inner man, but I see another law in my members fighting against the law of my reason and taking me captive in the law of sin existing in my members' (Rom 7:22f). The 'law of God' is operative in the 'inner man' or 'reason' and the 'law of sin' is imperative in 'the flesh' or 'members'. Good and evil could not be known more intimately because they operate in conflict in each human being. This is 'the knowledge of good and evil' promised by God as a consequence of that assertion of will against God in taking from the tree. God's word to Adam and Eve has proved true. This is the situation which evokes the human cry of anguish: 'O wretched man that I am! Who will deliver me from the body of this death?' (Rom 7:24). This is the cry of the unlimited creature hemmed in my limitation. ...
>
> What is necessary is to acknowledge the scale of Paul's conception: he is concerned with nothing less than the Genesis picture of humankind being made in God's image and likeness. The radical conclusion that he has faced is that being in God's image has to include the knowledge of good and evil. So Paul has come to view the God-given law as instrumental in bringing about a radical split in each human being leading to an infirmity of purpose: even though what is good is known, what is evil continues to be done. This, in the terms of the Genesis account, is the knowledge of good and evil which comes as a consequence of disobeying God. Further, Paul does not avoid the fact that this disobedience is inevitable. Just as the disobedience of the child towards the supervision of the parent is inevitable, so is the disobedience of humankind towards God.[694]

Just as God singles out the tree of knowledge of good and evil as forbidden, which only provokes desire for its fruit, the Law singles out certain thoughts and actions as forbidden, which has the effect of eliciting a desire for those things. As Paul put it in Romans 7:

> But I had not known sin, except through law; for I had not known desire except the law said, 'You shall not desire'. For the sin, receiving a foothold through the commandment, worked in me every desire; for without law sin is dead. For I once lived without the law, but when the commandment came, the sin came to life and I died, and the commandment which was to be life was found to be death to me. [Ashworth's translation][695]

---

[694] Ashworth (2016), pp. 97–98.
[695] Ashworth (2016), p. 92.

So we see the curse of the knowledge of good and evil: to be stuck in that place where one part of us knows we are doing something wrong, but where we do not have the power to DO any different. Our social programming, our neural circuits, have been aligned in certain ways, and breaking through those set patterns requires, first of all, to know something different exists, a different way by which we can align our behavior and lives, to *see the unseen*:

> ... the state of being trapped in a struggle between good and evil which Paul is expressing in Romans 7:7-25 is precisely the 'condemnation' spoken of at the beginning of Romans 8. The selfishness that is the consequence of being 'identified with the flesh' is precisely the 'plight' of humankind. The limited perception that inevitably arises from a self-centered point of view makes it impossible to even see, yet alone to live, the liberated and completely unselfish life of the Spirit.[696]

The same themes and images from Genesis – flesh and law leading to sin and death – are central to Paul's thought, where they are set in opposition to spirit, freedom, right action and eternal life, respectively. While Genesis 1 establishes God's ultimate purpose for man (as the image of God, exercising his creative dominion), Genesis 3 explains our present state of entropy and disconnection, and why liberation is necessary. Paul describes the state of humanity after the Fall in these terms in Romans 1, "claiming to be wise, they became fools and exchanged the glory of the immortal God for an imitation" (echoing Eve's desire for wisdom), and coming to worship the things created, including "the image of a mortal human being," rather than their creator, the immortal God. Humanity "exchanged the truth about God for a lie," as Adam and Eve exchanged their connection with God for the serpent's deception. The Fall's loss of sexual innocence is also reflected: "For this reason God gave them up to degrading passions," as well as its divisive isolation and enmity: "God gave them up to a debased mind and to things that should not be done. They were filled with every kind of wickedness, evil, covetousness, malice." Identification with the flesh gives rise to interpersonal friction and conflict where there should be peace and harmony.

In Paul's thought, 'the flesh' can be understood as directly opposed to the Spirit of God, that is, as the moving force in each individual or any striving against God.[697] Whenever there is conflict between people, you can take that as clear evidence that the persons involved are being motivated by 'the flesh.'[698]

While Paul doesn't *always* use 'flesh' with negative connotations,[699] he generally uses it to indicate something morally destructive, while he uses the term 'body' neutrally. So, it seems that Paul uses the term 'flesh' much the way we use the term 'materialism,' though often he is more specific. 'The flesh,' like 'the body,' is mortal, material, of this world, and Paul says "flesh and blood cannot inherit the kingdom of God."[700] And just as 'flesh and blood' is always mortal and corruptible by nature, so is human understanding that is 'according to the flesh.' So Paul sees 'flesh' in three ways: individuality, selfish assertion, and mortality. To 'set the mind on the flesh' is to set up 'our individual differences' as the locus of selfish assertion over and against others and God.

Ashworth sums up Paul's view of the Fall as follows:

---

[696]Ashworth (2016), p. 99.

[697]See Rom. 8:7f.

[698]See 1 Cor. 3:1-4.

[699]See 2 Cor. 7:5, Phil. 1:20, 22, 24; Rom. 8:13.

[700]1 Cor. 15:50.

In Paul's account of the fall, the loss of the appropriate response to God, which Paul says is to honour and give thanks to God, worship and serve God, is tied together with a coarsening of human consciousness – 'they became futile in their thinking, and their senseless minds were darkened' – and a descent into idolatry. The implication of this is important for understanding Paul. The assertion of futile human thinking is tightly linked with the loss of the ability to perceive the invisible things of God. The 'futile thinking' and 'darkened mind' is bound up with a situation in which God is not glorified and thanked and, as a further consequence, is no longer 'known'. Once, according to Paul, the perception of the invisible things of God is lost, all that can be perceived is that which is created. The fall, according to Paul, is a change in perception, a loss of the perception of the divine connected with the assertion of futile human thought and a darkening of the heart. The consequence of this is that *humankind can only see clearly the physical and comes to be identified with the physical stuff of human existence. This is 'the lie'.* Having been created to be the image of the Creator in the world of what is created, doing the creative work of the Creator, humankind ends up blind to the invisible things of God and identifying existence with what is created – physical, visible and mortal. And, very importantly, *'the invisible things of God' includes that 'image of God' in humankind itself.*[701]

Note that this slavery is not perceived by those still in chains (Plato's cave analogy comes to mind). For Paul, believers must learn consciously to separate the 'I' (which wills good) and the 'it' (which does evil), and through daily effort to build the strength of this I – to make the divine will our own. The wish to be real must be stronger in us than the wish to be mechanical, and for the 'body' to have its way. Until then, we're not just blind to higher realities, we're blind to ourselves.

For Paul, sin takes the role of Eden's serpent. Just as the serpent deceives Eve, we are deceived by sin. It is the Lie: humanity's willful arrogance and fundamental self-centeredness, rooted in our understanding of ourselves as separate, physical beings, which in turn colors all our thoughts and feelings, and from which flows all wrongdoing. God gave the Law, for humanity's own protection, knowing sin would and must arise.

Paul likens the process of liberation to the transition between childhood and adulthood: while as a child we had to live under the law of our parents (the Jewish people following the Mosaic Law, Pagans following their codes) to keep us safe and prevent us from walking off the path, at some stage we have to grow up and 'create our own laws' as adults (living by faith). And to be able to do so, we need to intimately know the consequences of our doings (to know good and evil). In that regard, the 'original sin' was a necessary stage to adulthood, to emancipate us from the slavery of the Law that was imposed on us from 'outside.'

The Law – in the sense of any and all social and religious rules and practices – is essential in order for sin to arise, to become known, and knowledge of sin is necessary in order to grow and thereby come to truly know the good, as a contrast to the evil we experience and engage in. Sin causes the original, divine 'I' to die. So when we say 'I,' it is our lower nature speaking, the sin in us, aspects of our own self-serving nature. There is thus a radical split within each person, between one's 'inner self,' their higher reason or real 'I' by which they know good, and the outer 'flesh' and its members by which they know evil. According to Ashworth:

> ... It is presumably the 'inner man/person' who looks 'at the things which are not seen' – the things that are eternal. It is important to note what follows from this: in Paul's thinking, the dividing

---

[701] Ashworth (2016), p. 157. Ashworth's italics.

line between seen and unseen, temporal and eternal, corruptible and incorruptible is drawn within each human being.

    ... Once the false identification of existence with the flesh which humankind has fallen into and which is characterized by folly and a darkened understanding is at an end then there is, in humankind, a conscious integration of that which creates – 'the inner person' – and that which is created; that which is created – 'the outward person'/'the flesh' – is no longer served; existence can now be identified with the Spirit which is eternal and which, while bringing about diversity, is always itself one with God ...[702]

Humanity is Adam, born not under original sin, but original death or mortality, of which sins are just the symptoms. For the real 'I' to re-emerge, we must be reconciled with God and with each other. We need to experience a disintegration of our current, false self-identity to re-establish our original form and purpose as the image of God.

But the story of the Fall makes clear that our pre-Fall state also wasn't complete. We cannot truly share in God's dominion over creation, glorifying him and giving thanks, while we are still children. In order to truly function as the image of God, we *need* knowledge of good and evil. So the Fall was necessary. It was part of God's grand design for creation. The purpose of creation is to provide a school where we can gain that knowledge, and our collective Fall is an integral part of that learning process. To reverse it is to rediscover our original purpose, *enriched by the knowledge we have gained*, thus coming into our promised inheritance as fully fledged and vetted children of God, inheritors of the kingdom.

In short: Paul's solution to the problem of theodicy was that the 'fall from pure goodness' was all a divine plan from the very beginning. His answer is as interesting as it is astonishing in its subtlety: we need free will in order to learn. If all knowledge were just automatically implanted in us, it wouldn't be *knowledge*; it wouldn't have any weight. What happens when you 'create' beings with free will – portions of the divine will, sparks of the divine being, unlimited in nature? It is inevitable that they will choose for themselves. They will rebel against the divine order, to greater or lesser degrees. They will have to *learn* for themselves. Hence they *had* to revolt against God at some stage to become fully emancipated and free. So the 'original sin' was *necessary* for humans (thus the title of Ashworth's book). And, as noted, the 'original sin' consisted of losing sight of the creator, replacing that with 'what is created' (material things), and denying the reality of spirit, i.e. pure consciousness and information, 'God's will.'

Important for our later discussion, Paul's statement in Gal. 1:4-5, 8-9 provides the crucial clue that *all of humanity* – not just the Pagans – were slave to the gravitational, entropic force of the material universe, which compelled the human being, via his habitation of flesh, to be in a constant state of sin due mainly to egocentric covetousness. Paul saw something in a vision that caused his own false self-identity to disintegrate, and that is at the heart of the change he has been through and which he hopes to assist others to experience as well. For Paul, it was the death of Jesus that was both the catalyst for his own transformation and what enabled his understanding of its universal significance.

    Therefore, just as sin came into the world through one man, and death came through sin, and so death spread to all because all have sinned ... And the free gift is not like the effect of the one man's sin. For the judgment following one trespass brought condemnation, but the free gift following many

---

[702] Ashworth (2016), pp. 97, 159, 168.

trespasses brings [right action]. ... Therefore just as one man's trespass led to condemnation for all, so *one man's act of righteousness* leads to justification and life for all. For just as by the one man's disobedience the many were made sinners, so by the one man's obedience the many will be made righteous.[703]

Paul contrasts the continuous state of 'imprisonment' in a life dominated by the flesh and materialism as opposed to 'doing what is right' according to the Spirit. He is saying that those who live by the Spirit are empowered to act rightly in a way that is not possible under the domination of flesh/materialism. This fundamental state affects and informs all human actions; even if you do right actions, if you are still fundamentally identified with fleshly existence, your right action is still 'sin' according to Paul. With this understanding of sin, one can then understand what Paul meant when he said that Jesus "knew no sin" (2 Cor. 5:21): in Jesus, there was no assertion against God in anything he did; there was no selfishness. When Jesus acted, *he acted in the same way God himself would have acted* in whatever situation he found himself, even if that meant acting against his own flesh/material existence.

Law, Faith and Liberation

For Paul, as noted above, the role of the Law was that of a child-minder: to provide "protective restraint of the wandering child," as Ashworth puts it. It exists in the form of Moses' tablets, the written word, and the teaching of priests and rabbis. But true adults don't need the Law. For them, the external word of the parent has become their own inner word – the voice of conscience, written on their hearts. When that happens, the purpose of the Law as a guide to behavior is fulfilled. If the behavior comes naturally, from within, the Law is no longer necessary. Since actions of love do no wrong to another, love is what fulfills the Law.

As a devout Jew, this was a radical departure for Paul, and would have put him at odds with fellow Jews, like James. Seeing the Law in this way, he essentially placed it on a level with all other religious laws. Before the coming of faith, all were under law. Both Jew and Gentile have equal status – equally low, that is. Neither is privileged. Both are enslaved to mortality and the flesh. The Jews may have the Torah, but the Gentiles also have access to God's will as revealed through the created world and in their own hearts. But neither can do anything about it because *they cannot see the unseen reality.*

As for faith, Ashworth discusses the issue of 'faith in Jesus' versus 'faith of Jesus,' pointing out that there are translation problems here. He writes:

> Most modern translations replace the phrase rendered 'by the faith of Jesus Christ' ... with the phrase 'through' or 'by faith in Jesus Christ'. This is a significant difference. ... The translation 'faith *of* Jesus Christ' leads to a different interpretation. It means that those who come to faith can be understood as entering into the way of life of Jesus, sharing ... his 'state/manner of existing'. This is an extraordinarily bold claim for the life of faith and it is this issue that has arguably distorted the plain sense in the Greek which would most straightforwardly be translated 'faith *of* Jesus' rather than 'faith *in* Jesus.' Clearly if Jesus is the one 'who knew no sin' then he is separated from all the rest who 'have sinned and fall short of the glory of God.' (Rom 3:23); if living by faith is solely associated with continuing sin then it is not something that describes the way Jesus lived. However an alternative understanding has already been offered: the life of faith can be conceived of, in Paul's

---
[703]Rom. 5:12-19.

understanding, as the way of liberation, crossing over the line between God and that which falls short of his glory. To live by faith is to begin living the same kind of life that Jesus lived, free from sin with all actions directly guided by God.[704]

How does this 'faith' come about, and how is it related to 'spirit'? One aspect of faith is its receptivity and responsiveness to the spirit (Greek *pneuma*, breath). The spirit or breath of God (which is also the spirit of Christ) is heard within. Paul calls this "faith's heard thing," the direct prophetic word of truth, or divine inspiration. As with the prophets of old, God speaks through mortals. But unlike those prophets, crying in the wilderness and rejected by their own people, the coming of faith opens up the channel *for everyone*. All now have the ability to know the will of God by receiving the prophetic word, which provides direction for behavior, but also the power to see it through. God speaks in and through the faithful, providing "immediate illumination on questions of behavior," in Ashworth's words. In other words, true conscience. The "obedience of faith" of which Paul speaks can then be understood as a deep, responsive hearing: one hears, one knows it to be true for oneself, and one acts on that knowledge. Faith is the obedient, faithful response to the prophetic word – divine inspiration, spirit, *pneuma*.

This too was a radical innovation. Not only has Paul relegated the Law to the status of a babysitter, he has eliminated the need for exclusive prophetic and priestly classes, and the need for temples as the only places in which to experience the presence of God. Every one of the faithful has the potential to hear God's word within their own temple – the body – which the spirit of God enters via the heart. Faith is the obedient response to a 'first installment' of spirit deposited in the heart, the seat of conscience. Paul's letters reveal a few ways in which this transfer of spirit may take place: directly from Paul himself via his words as he shares his gospel and through his letters (both of which are examples of Paul sharing the prophetic word as he receives it from above), and most importantly, through baptism, in which the person baptized participates willingly and consciously in the death and resurrection of Christ. Just as Christ's resurrection was effected by the transformative power of spirit giving him new life, the spirit similarly raises the baptized into new life following the figurative crucifixion of the old self.

In Genesis, God breathes into Adam's nostrils, making him a "living soul." For Paul, Christ – 'the last Adam' – becomes an "alive-making spirit" able to imbue new spiritual life into others in a similar manner as when God breathed life into Adam. It is Christ's spirit which gives life to that which is 'dead' and mortal. It has the power to reverse the Fall and end the hostility between humans and with God. It gives the power to do, which the law cannot provide – the power of God that works in and through the individual. All animated by the same spirit – sharing the same mind – the community of the faithful retain their separate individuality and identities, but are united. True diversity and unity are restored, without the isolation and enmity of the Fall. The activity of the spirit has the effect of destroying the rigid identification with the self – the sin, the lie – as each member sees their intrinsic connection to God and to each other, resulting in a new way of living and relating. This is the 'body of Christ' – one unified, corporate being composed of a variety of members, each with their own individual talents, skills, and roles, coordinated by the same divine guidance.

Paul uses a number of phrases and images to describe these different levels of transformed being. For example, with the reception of spirit the baptized become "sons and daughters of

---

[704]Ashworth (2016), pp. 178–79.

God," heirs, like Christ. But heirs still have to grow up before receiving their inheritance, which is the full reception of the spirit. Until that time, they live by faith (with a partial infusion of spirit), after which they will live by spirit (completely). The thread linking the state of infancy to the future perfection is love – the subject of Paul's most famous piece of writing in 1 Corinthians 13 – the gift of the spirit that functions as a bridge to the future life when all of humanity will come of age and inherit the dominion or kingdom of God, that is, live the life of the spirit.

And just as the spiritual transformation is taking place in the faithful, the power of spirit is also working towards a universal, total transformation of the whole cosmos. This is the great change of which Paul speaks, and to which the faithful are to look towards with hope, not some earthly throne.

Just as there are degrees of spirit, there are corresponding degrees of faith, or faithfulness. The Genesis story of Abraham[705] is central to Paul's thought, as mentioned above. Already a childless old man, he is promised by God to be the father of many *nations*. Then, after his wife Sarah miraculously gives birth to a son, Isaac, God instructs Abraham to sacrifice him as a test. Unlike Adam, who disobeys God's word, Abraham displays the degree of his faith by following through, at which point God intervenes to stop him. Abraham is faithful and obedient, despite the apparent contradiction. While the tale is grim, the message is that *appearances can be deceiving*, and right decisions often require a leap of faith in the absence of full knowledge, or despite seemingly contradictory evidence.

Intimately tied to faithfulness is the word commonly translated as 'justification' or 'righteousness': *dikaiosunē*. This Pauline idea – 'justification by faith' – has been interpreted in several ways, for example, the notion that by simply believing *in* Jesus, one can continue to be a sinner and yet have one's status changed from 'lost' to 'saved' in God's account books. This is not what Paul was describing. The meaning carried by the word is closer to this: 'a state or manner of existing which subsists in a way of doing what is right.' You can't be 'righteous' and yet continue to be a 'sinner.' What Paul means by 'justification by faith' is that *only faith can lead to this state of being in which right action is possible.* It can't be done by Law. One can only become righteous by living a life guided by prophetic inner word, via spirit. And it is not *instantly* given:

> Therefore, my beloved, just as you have always obeyed me, not only in my presence, but much more now in my absence, *work out your own salvation with fear and trembling*; for it is God who is at work in you, enabling you both to will and to work for his good pleasure. Do all things without murmuring and arguing, so that you may be blameless and innocent, children of God without blemish in the midst of a crooked and perverse generation, in which you shine like stars in the world. It is by your holding fast to the word of life that I can boast on the day of Christ that I did not run in vain or labor in vain. (Phil. 2:12-16)

The righteousness that faith brings involves an empowering liberation from the state of sin, the ability to see the unseen, and it necessarily results in right action. It is a state of being in which one both knows and does what is right – the real 'I' of Conscience that emerges once the false 'I' of the flesh has been killed in oneself by repeated acts of seeing and doing what is right. It involves a change in self-perception in which the wrongness of the habitual state of death or sin is exposed – seeing oneself in a new light. Righteousness, salvation, absolution – whatever

---

[705] It's irrelevant that the story of Abraham is almost identical to a Vedic story of Manu; the theme was re-worked for a specific purpose. (Meillet, Antoine, *Memoires de la Society de Linguistique de Paris*, XXII, 1992.)

you call it – is the product of an inner transformation, not based on any exclusive social or religious status symbols, like circumcision, birth, race, worldly accomplishments, etc. All those things are now seen to be worthless, and the real, fundamental problem is clearly seen for what it is: the selfishness and sin caused by blind identification with the flesh, the material world, experienced as fundamentally constraining: a prison, slavery, a state of deadness and mortality. The transfer from the state of condemnation to that of absolution must involve a death of the old self. Selfish assertion – sin – *must be crucified in order for righteousness to take its place.* In this new state of faith, living in alignment with God's will is now possible, as the locus of God's righteousness; *God's way of acting in the world is through individual mortals.* For Paul, Christ is the embodiment of God's image/wisdom/righteousness. His action is one with God's action. And by sharing in Christ's spirit, this also applies to the faithful.

How does this look on the practical level? Paul presents himself and his fellow apostles as exemplars of righteousness, 'adults in Christ,' masters of real wisdom who have already experienced the death of their own self-interest (the sin in them). Already reconciled with God, they have seen and participated in Christ's death and new life in visionary experience, and have responded faithfully to the calling that comes with such an experience, a mission that will require sacrifice and suffering: to act as ambassadors for Christ, acting and speaking in his place, embodying his will in performing their ministry of reconciliation. Possessing the faith and spirit of Christ, and therefore speaking the same word, they are equally willing to suffer. And, most importantly for understanding what this actually entails, they are invested with the authority to challenge others, to exercise the divine power within them to oppose any fleshly human assertion – in themselves and in others. Paul writes:

> Indeed, we live in the flesh, but we do not wage war according to the flesh; for the weapons of our warfare are not fleshly, but they have divine power to destroy strongholds. We destroy arguments and every proud obstacle raised up against the knowledge of God, and we take every thought captive to obey Christ.[706]

Paul's ministry was completely oriented to peace, though his work was anything but peaceful once the Jerusalem Christians got wind of what he was doing. The ministry of reconciliation certainly involved a kind of warfare that was necessary to bring people to the new perception of sin and the recognition that they were sinners in a way of which they had not previously been aware. Naturally, that would bring strong resistance and conflict, even as it does today.

Absolution may bring liberation and peace, but it is not a peaceful process. Ordinarily people only see the symptoms of their state, i.e., various sins, not the state itself which leads to them. But having this state exposed can naturally lead to conflict, not to mention suffering on both sides of the exchange. It involves bringing people to a new perception of their own deeply rooted flaws, weaknesses, and errors. Most people resist this kind of challenge to their self-image and will calm themselves with excuses, rationalizations, lies, and illusions to maintain it. Self-knowledge is difficult, and seeing oneself as one truly is, is painful. Facilitating this process in others is holding up a 'mirror' to another, providing them with a reflection that reveals what is wrong with them.

---

[706]2 Cor. 10:4-5.

The Crucifixion

The Ark of the Covenant was the instrument through which the people interacted with God via Moses. God was apparently so awesome that he terrified the people, so communication had to take place through the mediation of a chosen individual. The blood of the sacrifice was to be sprinkled *on the mercy-seat*, which was the mode of communication from the people *to* God, their means of expressing their knowledge of their sins and their asking for forgiveness.[707] This understanding is important in order to perceive how Paul regarded the death of Jesus. Jesus wasn't a sin offering per se, although the idea of sacrifice and atoning blood is involved. The important thing is the mercy-seat as the location of God's communication; whereas the *hilasterion* is the place of communication between God and one chosen individual, the faith of Jesus in going obediently to death somehow transformed him, upon his ascension to the higher spheres, *into the mercy-seat itself*. The soul of Jesus somehow became the locus of communication between God and humankind and the everlasting atonement for absolution of sins.

Central to Paul's theology and his understanding of how this comes about is the nature of Christ's crucifixion and resurrection. Ashworth writes:

> [W]hen Paul speaks of the death of Christ as a death 'for' or, better, 'in place of' all, this is a further indication of how radical is the nature of what has gone wrong in humankind. From within the closed circle of sin, death, law and flesh that Paul so vividly describes in Romans 7 there is no escape; the actions of humankind are always veiled with selfishness. Paul's words imply that it is only the death of humankind and a new creation that is adequate to transform this situation. But somehow through the death of Christ, Paul claims that the situation is saved and a new beginning comes about without the destruction of the old. How can this be?[708]

According to Ashworth, the clue is to be found in 2 Corinthians 5:19-21:

> So if anyone is in Christ, there is a new creation: everything old has passed away; see, everything has become new! All this is from God, who reconciled us to himself through Christ, and has given us the ministry of reconciliation; that is, in Christ, God was reconciling the world to himself, not counting their trespasses against them, and entrusting the message of reconciliation to us. So we are ambassadors for Christ, since God is making his appeal through us; we entreat you on behalf of Christ, be reconciled to God. For our sake he made him to be sin who knew no sin, so that in him we might become the righteousness of God.

The idea is that Christ, as the 'one who knew no sin,' i.e. the one in whom there was no identification of existence with the flesh and therefore no assertion against God, was 'made to be sin in place of us'; his body of flesh came to be wholly identified with essential assertion against God, the fundamental sin of all humankind, in the same way an ambassador is completely identified with the ruler or state he represents; and thus, he died as the representative of all humanity. This was a death in the place of all; the consequences are as if all have died. It was the sin in the flesh that had to die, and the sin in the flesh is the identification with the separate and mortal flesh. Jesus mastered himself, mastered his fear because he could see the unseen, and went obediently to his death knowing exactly what he was doing.

---

[707]Obviously, there is a lot more to the history of blood sacrifice than this, but here, we are dealing with how Paul is using the text to underwrite certain concepts.
[708]Ashworth (2016), p. 219.

Recall that, for Paul, the death of Jesus was of apocalyptic significance. It was at the moment he died that his divine sonship was revealed to the archons. And Paul repeatedly asserts that **it is in weakness that the power of God is revealed**. How can this be? Quite simply: it was because accepting suffering and death in obedience to God was a demonstration of *the power of God over the flesh*; Jesus accepted death by his faith in the unseen; he was not identified with his flesh or the material separation of the self from God. And so, God's way of doing what is right was made manifest: here is a creature who acted as God in the face of all material evidence to the contrary of his choice. The allegorical depiction of this in the Gospel of Mark makes this plain, as will be seen further on.

But regarding humanity, so complete had been the identification with separate fleshly existence that it even blinds the individual to their own state and colors all their actions. Ashworth writes:

> Working from within this identification with what is created there is no way out. Human life without sin is inconceivable; sin will only end with the destruction of humankind. What Paul does is present Jesus as one who is sent from outside this circle of selfishness whose death is essential to bringing about a shift in human perception such that this new creation can happen. This shift in perception is so powerful according to Paul that it enables humankind to consistently do what is right but now in full knowledge of good and evil – now truly the image of God.[709]

The significance of Christ's death is that it provides the power to break the identification. Paul says Christ died in our place. So like a non-local chain reaction, in some real sense all died with Christ. At the very least the process was started in those hearing the gospel, and becoming aware of another way of being. As Paul puts it, Jesus' one right action made possible right action for all. He established the model to follow, and the event provided the necessary energy or power to break through the ingrained power of sin, a state from which one cannot free oneself – outside help is required. As a result, one can see what is wrong for the first time, can see the unseen because Christ did and acted on it, and God's righteousness can truly manifest in the world, via the liberated and completely unselfish life of the Spirit.

Paul presents his own flesh as weak – though the spirit is strong in him. As mentioned above, Paul presents the spirit as entering the physical body, coating its mortality with immortality, blending and reconciling the physical and spiritual worlds, thus establishing a clear connection between the lower and the higher. In Ashworth's words, "In the flesh of humankind, God the creator has been truly united with the creation."[710] For Paul, the body itself is the locus of transformation, the true temple. (This was also a radical departure from Judaism for Paul, who essentially relegated the Jewish Temple to obsolescence decades before its destruction at the hands of the Romans.)

Paul believed that what he experienced was available to all, and his ministry of 'God's word' was designed to bring this about. He was not speaking about a collection of stories about some historical individual named Jesus; his was a message of speaking words from God which had the intent of revealing what was wrong with the world and what needed to be done about it to make it right. And when he was exposing what is wrong with the condition of humankind, he was acting as an ambassador on behalf of God through Christ within. Paul's faith was in the living

---

[709]Ashworth (2016), p. 220.
[710]Ashworth (2016), p. 230.

word of God, not in a previous, external word, given by an individual who walked about teaching clever aphorisms or doing miracles.

Paul claimed that he and others had gone through a death to self so that the spiritual life could be made manifest.

> The flesh – 'that which is created' – is no longer worshipped and served; it is no longer the source of motivation. It is 'the life of Jesus' that is now at work in him. This is precisely what Paul says of himself:
>
> 'I have been crucified with Christ; and it is no longer I who live, but it is Christ who lives in me. And the life I now live in the flesh I live by the faith of the Son of God, who loved me and gave himself for me.' (Gal 2:19f, incorporating alternative translation [of Ashworth])[711]

Paul experienced the crucifixion (death) and resurrection (new life) in a visionary state. Thus, for him it was primarily a metaphysical, spiritual event in which he participated. It was a catalyst for his own transformation – his own crucifixion – and also the means to understand its universal significance. As a catalyst, it is essential in bringing about the shift in perception that reverses the Fall with focus on the 'new life' aspect of the experience.

> The death of Jesus only discloses the righteousness of God to the extent to which those who witness it do so in the light of an experience of the continuing life of Jesus, the 'alive-making Spirit'. As they encounter that 'alive-making Spirit' which fully illuminates their hearts revealing what was wrong as well as the way to act rightly, they are themselves transformed and become ministers of the same transformation for others: they become 'the righteousness of God', God's way of acting rightly, God's dominion, and speakers of God's revealing and reconciling word as Jesus was.[712]

This, for Paul, is the new covenant. Summed up, the old covenant was this: follow the Law, receive your inheritance, which is the possession of land. Turn away from the law, and you will lose that land, be cursed and die. Jesus follows the will of God to die *under one of those curses*. By becoming sin and dying, the death of sin both erases the need for the law and fulfills it, by bringing about its true purpose: right action. The accursed Jesus is revealed to be a blessing by seeing the unseen. And the inheritance is no longer land – a fleshly/material possession – but a new relationship with God and others, a new way of seeing, a new channel of communication and connection, and a release from sin and law. It cannot be effected from within on one's own, because the nature of the identification with the material world is so deep and ingrained.

The bottom line of Paul's thinking appears to be a radical shift in human consciousness and a new way of seeing things: accepting spiritual realities as real, more real than material realities.

> Paul writes out of a conviction based in experience that what has happened to him and others is a real and effective liberation, once for all, for good. ... His central affirmations about the righteousness of God confirm it: the righteousness of God is disclosed in the faith of Jesus, specifically in how he goes to his death. ... It is from and only from this radical experience of liberation that the law is seen to be no longer needed. The law is God's gift to bring humankind safely to this destination. Once the living word is established, the need for the written word falls away.[713]

---

[711] Ashworth (2016), p. 222.

[712] Ashworth (2016), p. 225.

[713] Ashworth (2016), p. 225.

This is the adulthood of humankind we have discovered in Paul's thought. And it is also the life of faith. Faith as listening to words from God, entering a place of communication with the divine. … Once human life trapped in sin is truly seen in all its emptiness and horror, a way opens which is literally inconceivable before the change takes place. Being trapped in sin involves a blindness which has to shift; a veil has to be lifted. Only the gift of revelation can do this. The consequence of this seeing is true liberation into the glory for which humankind was created. Living in that glory, constantly and without struggle, awake to the Spirit, knowing the cost of selfishness, there is true freedom … with nothing to be gained from getting lost once again in darkness.[714]

In summary, the 'new creation' is not a change in the outside world, but an inner transformation, a break with the old way of being human, the false identification with the mortal flesh/material world. As the individual makes the connection with true conscience, the inner Spirit, growing in their ability to see, they become the means by which others may also encounter the same liberation; they cannot help but expose what is wrong in the world and in others, becoming ministers of reconciliation. In this way, humankind can freely do what is right, and become conscious instruments of God's love in creation.

The change involves both a steady development – growth in knowledge and understanding – as well as a dramatic transition at 'adulthood,' at which point everything is seen differently.

When I was a child, I spoke like a child, I thought like a child, I reasoned like a child; when I became an adult, I put an end to childish ways. For now we see in a mirror, dimly, but then we will see face to face. Now I know only in part; then I will know fully, even as I have been fully known. And now faith, hope, and love abide, these three; and the greatest of these is love.[715]

Sacrifice and Paul's Christ

I've said a number of times through this text that I do not think that Paul's Jesus was the same Jesus as the Messiah of the Jerusalem Christians, James, John, Cephas, etc. To me, considering all the historical background I've collected thus far, this fact is glaringly obvious. But I do think that Paul had a certain human being in mind, one who actually lived and died in a special way so as to draw to himself the ideas explicated by Paul.

The human identity of Paul's 'son of God' is actually a great mystery, because there are clearly no correspondences between his conception of Jesus, and the life, work and death of Judas the Galilean or any of the other Jewish messiahs. Paul conceived of this divine being as pre-existent, as the image of God, like Adam, and in a position to grasp at equality with God, as Adam attempted to do, but refusing to do so, as an obedient son.[716] He is designated as both Lord and Christ[717] and the appellation 'Lord' seems to be of crucial significance, having been conferred on Christ at his triumphal exaltation after his incarnated life.[718] The title 'Christ' is a theological concept that originated in Jewish messianic beliefs, but Paul uses it in strange ways. He equates it with a spiritual rock that followed the Israelites in the desert[719] and with Moses' description

---

[714]Ashworth (2016), p. 226.

[715]1 Cor. 13:11-13.

[716]Phil. 2:6; Gal. 4:4; 2 Cor. 4:4.

[717]Phil. 2:11; Rom. 14:9; 1 Cor. 8:5-6.

[718]Phil. 2:5-11.

[719]1 Cor. 10:4: "and all drank the same spiritual drink. For they drank from the spiritual rock that followed them, and the rock was Christ." The remark "and the rock was Christ" could as well be a later gloss.

of God's word in Deuteronomy. Below is a comparison of a passage from Romans that echoes Deuteronomy.[720]

Rom 10:6-7	Deut 30:11-14
But the righteousness that comes from faith says, "Do not say in your heart, 'Who will ascend into heaven?'" (that is, to bring Christ down) "or 'Who will descend into the abyss?'" (that is, to bring Christ up from the dead). But what does it say? "The word is near you, on your lips and in your heart" (that is, the word of faith that we proclaim); because if you confess with your lips that Jesus is Lord and believe in your heart that God raised him from the dead, you will be saved.	Surely, this commandment that I am commanding you today is not too hard for you, nor is it too far away. It is not in heaven, that you should say, "Who will go up to heaven for us, and get it for us so that we may hear it and observe it?" Neither is it beyond the sea, that you should say, "Who will cross to the other side of the sea for us, and get it for us so that we may hear it and observe it?" No, the word is very near to you; it is in your mouth and in your heart for you to observe.

Despite these allusions, Paul evinces little interest in the incarnate paragon. That may be due to the fact that the identity of his human Christ was 1) so well known that it didn't need to be mentioned; or 2) an initiatory secret revealed only to selected initiates.

In his writings that remain to us, two facts only are of *apparent* interest to Paul: that his Christ died in a special, obedient way, and that he was resurrected to heaven in order to initiate the new reality, the kingdom of God. Full stop.[721] For Paul, the death of his Christ was the most significant event of his human incarnation. This death was salvific for all persons who would subsequently claim patronage of Christ. Despite Ashworth's bold efforts, the exact mode of this redemption is still not entirely clear.

Paul and the Cross

Paul begins with the highest Christology imaginable: the incarnation into a human body of a divine being, THE son of God, with a plan. The Jewish idea of a 'son of god,' on the other hand, applied to either angels (divine beings who never incarnated as human) or 'adopted' human 'sons' such as kings, priests, and prophets. Brandon remarks on this as follows:

> The soteriological interpretation of the death of Jesus, with the concomitant assertion of its universal validity in this respect, is essentially connected with Paul's evaluation of the person of Jesus; but again we are faced with the problem of the origin of such an idea. That Paul did not derive it from a Jewish *milieu* seems to be certain, for ... no passage has been found in the relevant Jewish literature which contains or makes reference to the idea of an incarnated savior of mankind who redeems by virtue of his own sacrificial death.[722]

Though Brandon was operating from the idea that Paul had merely re-evaluated the meaning of the death of the Jewish messianic claimant, which he did not connect to Judas the Galilean, a Zealot rebel against Rome, he certainly notices that this idea has many problems. He goes on to say:

---

[720]Again, assuming that this is not an interpolation. Romans chapters 9 through 11 are highly problematical.
[721]I will discuss the nature of the crucifixion itself in the next section.
[722]Brandon (2010), p. 68.

[I]n the synoptic writings and in Acts there is evidence that the Jewish Christians saw in the Passion and Death of Jesus the fulfillment of Isaiah's prophecy of the Suffering Servant of God. But this interpretation of Jesus curiously finds no place in Paul's theology, which fact has reasonably been thought to mean that the Apostle had some special reason for refraining from its use.[723]

Indeed, savior gods who rescue their initiates from some dreaded fate *were* familiar in the religious thought of the Greco-Roman world, as was the idea of *devotio*, or one man sacrificing himself for his fellows. There was certainly a widespread hunger for assurances of individual immortality with a number of varied cults which promised ritual assimilation to the god and thus, survival after death. Paul was undoubtedly familiar with such and this likely had an influence on his experiences and thinking.

Everything taken together, it seems to me highly unlikely that Paul had simply re-evaluated the death of the messiah who was preached by the Zealot Christians in Jerusalem. Yet, that brings us back to the all-important question: what was Paul doing in his association with the Jewish Christians he apparently opposed, not *before* being converted, but only afterward, by teaching so un-Jewish an interpretation of Christianity?

We have a pretty good idea that being executed by the Romans was no shame or embarrassment to the Jews of the time; martyrs were glorified. So why does Paul write in 1 Corinthians 1:22-23: "Seeing that Jews ask for signs, and Greeks seek after wisdom: but we preach Christ crucified; unto Jews a stumbling block, and unto Gentiles foolishness." In Galatians, Paul engages in a rabbinical argument for the abandonment of the Law:

For all who rely on the works of the law are under a curse; for it is written, "Cursed is everyone who does not observe and obey all the things written in the book of the law." Now it is evident that no one is justified before God by the law; for "The one who is righteous will live by faith." But the law does not rest on faith; on the contrary, "Whoever does the works of the law will live by them." Christ redeemed us from the curse of the law by becoming a curse for us – for it is written, "Cursed is everyone who hangs on a tree" – in order that in Christ Jesus the blessing of Abraham might come to the Gentiles, so that we might receive the promise of the Spirit through faith.[724]

The sense of the argument is that he is using his Christ on a cross as a refutation of the Jewish Christians' messiah. That is to say, it strongly suggests that *their* messiah was not crucified.

Brandon thinks that this may reveal Paul's earlier rejection of Jewish Christianity, that he was scandalized by the elevation and exaltation of a Zealot rebel to the position of messiah and that somehow this objection was overcome by Paul's reflective re-evaluation of the death of the Jewish messianic claimant.

It seems like a plausible argument: Paul's vision converted the death of a rebel Zealot to that of the universal savior for all mankind. But given everything else we know, I think we can see that no, it's not plausible. It seems impossible that Paul could have thought that a rebel leader whose main goal in life had been to drive the Romans out of his homeland, killing as many of them as was necessary to do so, and thereby restoring a theocracy wherein Jews ruled over the Nations of Gentiles, converting them (by force if necessary) to Judaism, could have been the universal savior of mankind whose true aim had been to defeat the forces of darkness and their

---

[723]Brandon (2010), p. 68.
[724]Gal. 3:10-14.

energetic economic sanctions on humanity. Even imagining that such an incarnation and life had all been a ruse on the part of the divine being to trick the archons of the age into crucifying him doesn't fly. No manipulation by archons was necessary to get Judas the Galilean killed. He was in no way 'without sin' by anyone's standards – Jewish or Roman – and he was certainly not innocent of some of the charges brought against him, as depicted in the Gospels; his death was not a shocking betrayal or extra-judicial murder.

No, as I have noted previously, it rather seems that Paul, confronted with the image of a cross, saw something else: a truly shocking murder of a benevolent, innocent man, a man of love and mercy, who was, indeed, 'set up' by the archons to be murdered in a particularly vile and heinous way, whose blood was spilled copiously, and whose death, by virtue of the fact that he was a son of God, had value for all of humanity; and for this man, the cross – ordinarily a sign of defeat – signified victory, triumph over the forces of darkness; and thus, the cross of exaltation was placed at the forefront of Paul's gospel.

It appears that, to Paul, the cross actually represents the *triumph* over death (this will be more significant when we look at the Gospel of Mark). Paul's most explicit statement was that the death of his Christ was accomplished by demonic powers and was a 'mystery':

> But we speak God's wisdom, secret and hidden, which God decreed before the ages for our glory. None of the rulers of this age understood this; for if they had, they would not have crucified the Lord of glory. But, as it is written, "What no eye has seen, nor ear heard, nor the human heart conceived, what God has prepared for those who love him" – these things God has revealed to us through the Spirit; for the Spirit searches everything, even the depths of God.[725]

So far in this text I have made numerous references to the 'cross' (*stauros*) and 'crucifixion' (*stauroo*). But before we go any further it is time to clear up some misconceptions. Just as the Gospels' account of the 'life of Jesus' has influenced Christians and scholars to read that account back into the early Christian documents such as the letters of Paul, the account of the crucifixion in the Gospels and later Christian iconography has similarly influenced our understanding of crucifixion in the first century AD and prior. As a result, we think of crucifixion as a method of execution where the victim is often first flogged, then nailed or tied to a cross-shaped object to die a slow death. But as Gunnar Samuelsson has shown, the pre-Christian sources are not so detailed.

After an exhaustive analysis of all the ancient references to crucifixion in Greek, Latin and Hebrew, Samuelsson concludes that prior to the New Testament, the best definitions we can come up with for the words associated with crucifixion are the following: the Greek verb *stauroo* simply meant "to suspend someone (*dead or alive*) ... on a pole (or similar structure)"[726] and the noun *stauros* simply meant the pole or wooden frame on which the body (dead or alive) was suspended. There's no reason to think it was often cross-shaped. Outside the NT, the Greek word most often used to describe 'crucifixion' is *anastauroun*. About this word he writes:

> [*Anastauroun*] is commonly used in connection with suspension of corpses, whole or in parts, and impaling. The verb is used in some texts for executionary, ante-mortem, suspensions. ... However

---

[725]1 Cor. 2:7-10.

[726]Gunnar Samuelsson, *Crucifixion in Antiquity: An Inquiry into the Background and Significance of the New Testament Terminology of Crucifixion* (Mohr Siebeck, 2011), p. 283.

the majority of the texts containing [*anastauroun*] and referring to human suspensions are undefined when it comes to nature of the suspension.[727]

The only thing to be concluded for certain regarding Paul's use of the word for Jesus' crucifixion is that his death somehow involved the suspension of his body (dead or alive) on some type of wooden frame. Based on Samuelsson's work I would argue that despite Paul's frequent references to and emphasis on the 'cross' and 'crucifixion,' we cannot say with certainty that Paul's Jesus actually even *died* from crucifixion. In fact, his reference to the Deuteronomy curse against suspended corpses may even suggest just that. And while scourging did precede some executions by crucifixion, the references to blood in the early Christian sources seem to imply a bloodier mode of death, perhaps prior to 'crucifixion' or suspension.

So why did the *stauros* become the *cross*, specifically, if there was no historical crucifixion of 'Jesus of Nazareth' to base it on? When we consider that Jesus "made a spectacle of the cosmic powers and authorities, and led them as captives *in his triumphal procession,*"[728] and the idea of the cross as a 'potent object,' one is reminded of the Roman *tropaeum*, a pole with a crossbeam on which spoils from a military campaign were displayed in the Roman triumphal procession to the accompaniment of music, *clouds of incense*, and the strewing of flowers. At the end of the parade, the captured items would be dedicated to the gods.[729] Like the *stauros*, it could take the shape of a pole or tree, but its most iconic form is the cross shape, used to display the armor of the defeated foe. I don't think it's a coincidence that the early Christians chose this form to represent the *stauros*.

We will come back to this later.

Paul and the Zealots

So what was Paul doing hanging out with the Jewish Christians since they were so fundamentally opposed to each other? Was he pretending to be a Jewish Christian with a special 'mission to the Gentiles' so as to have a platform from which to work, all the while developing and teaching the *concepts* of his universal Christ, in secret at first, and later, more boldly and out in the open? That does appear to be the logical solution. Paul wrote:

> If I proclaim the gospel, this gives me no ground for boasting, for an obligation is laid on me, and woe to me if I do not proclaim the gospel! For if I do this of my own will, I have a reward; but if not of my own will, I am entrusted with a commission. ... For though I am free with respect to all, I have made myself a slave to all, so that I might win more of them. **To the Jews I became as a Jew, in order to win Jews.** To those under the law I became as one under the law (though I myself am not under the law) so that I might win those under the law. To those outside the law I became as one outside the law (though I am not free from God's law but am under Christ's law) so that I might win those outside the law. To the weak I became weak, so that I might win the weak.

---

[727]Samuelsson (2011), p. 144.

[728]Col. 2:15.

[729]"The symbolism of the *tropaeum* became so well known that in later eras, Romans began to simply display images of them upon sculpted reliefs ... to leave a permanent trace of the victory in question rather than the temporary monument of the *tropaeum* itself." (Wikipedia.org, 'Tropaion.')

> I have become all things to all people, that I might by all means save some. I do it all for the sake of the gospel, so that I may share in its blessings.[730]

Imagine the burden he carried in his mind and heart. His teaching, as it has been transmitted to us, places an absolute emphasis on accepting the atoning death of Jesus – *a psychic energetic process* – as the only essential qualification for membership in the Christian corporate body, and all national and cultural differences are reduced to nothing: "there cannot be Greek and Jew, circumcision and uncircumcision, barbarian, Scythian, bondman, freeman: but Christ is all, and in all."[731] Paul's gospel totally negated the Jewish claim to be the 'chosen people.' Considering the stakes, it is likely that he did whatever he had to in order to spread the gospel given to him in a vision. And, based on the analysis above in the section on Paul's theology, it was a pretty horrific vision with dreadful implications if humanity did not learn the truth.

On the other side, the Jewish Christians thought of their messianic beliefs and hopes as just a more intense expression of their nationalistic Judaism; they worshiped at the temple and were 'zealous for the Law.' The Jews' unique status with God was, for them, so fervent a belief that they organized themselves to kill those who violated the Law, even including fellow Jews. There is some evidence in the epistles that Paul initially strove to be considered 'one of them' because it suited his mission needs and evangelistic purposes to do so; he "became a Jew to win Jews." But word about his actual teachings was bound to get out, and it did.

To the Jewish Christians, Paul's teachings outraged their deepest convictions. And definitely, based on what is known about the Zealots, this was not a group of which one would wish to run afoul! That the death of their master, Judas the Galilean, at the hands of the hated Romans, their future messiah who was coming with legions of angels, should be displaced by the incarnation of a divine being whose death had a universal saving value even for the hated Gentiles, who deserved the perdition God should bring on them, was just simply blasphemy and apostasy and deserving of death. Paul was most certainly a marked man once the word got out about what he was really teaching. In Galatians, Paul writes about his opponents:

> But my friends, why am I still being persecuted if I am still preaching circumcision? In that case the offense of the cross has been removed. I wish those who unsettle you would castrate themselves![732]

Notice in the above that Paul says, "if I am *still* preaching circumcision." That suggests that, at one time, he was preaching circumcision but that he had a change of heart and mind, and it was this change that caused him to be persecuted.

> It is those who want to make a good showing in the flesh that try to compel you to be circumcised – only that they may not be persecuted for the cross of Christ. Even the circumcised do not themselves obey the law, but they want you to be circumcised so that they may boast about your flesh. May I never boast of anything except the cross of our Lord Jesus Christ, by which the world has been crucified to me, and I to the world. For neither circumcision nor uncircumcision is anything; but a new creation is everything![733]

---

[730] 1 Cor. 9:16-23.
[731] 1 Cor. 12:13; Gal. 3:28; 5:6.
[732] Gal. 5:11-12.
[733] Gal. 6:12-15.

The Jewish Christians were demanding that the Gentile converts be circumcised and thus fully converted to Judaism. The reason that Paul gives is that they feared being "persecuted for the cross of Christ." Since circumcision was not likely to save Jews from persecution by the Roman authorities at that time, the action envisioned can only have a Jewish reference. The congregations were being taken over by apostles who wished to prove their loyalty to the Zealot movement and to bring more support to same. And, most likely, there was a threatening element from the Zealots, who were likely manifesting as Sicarii by about this time,[734] according to Josephus; these were not idle threats.

The book of Acts gives the impression that the early Christians in Jerusalem were totally insulated from the surrounding social and political turmoil of the years leading up to the revolt. Acts paints a picture of a Church that was in good standing with the general population, including that some Pharisees were converts and 'zealous for the law.' This lovely, peaceful picture is completely out of synch with the reality on the ground at the time. It is disturbed by only two violent incidents in Acts, which contain features that attest to their dislocation from their proper chronology and context.

In Acts chapters 6 and 7 and the first few lines of 8, the character 'Stephen' was created by the Lukan author as a pro-Gentile Christian before Paul was converted. You really have to read the whole tale to get the implications of it, keeping in mind all the while that this is supposed to be about the Gentile-hating Zealots who were planning mayhem against the Romans, many of whom were Sicarii who went about murdering people if they heard they had violated the Law of Moses. Below I give some excerpts and a few comments:

> Now during those days, when the disciples were increasing in number, the Hellenists complained against the Hebrews because their widows were being neglected in the daily distribution of food. And the twelve called together the whole community of the disciples and said, "It is not right that we should neglect the word of God in order to wait on tables. Therefore, friends, select from among yourselves seven men of good standing, full of the Spirit and of wisdom, whom we may appoint to this task, while we, for our part, will devote ourselves to prayer and to serving the word."[735]

We are expected to believe that a Hellenizing group *among the Zealots* were clamoring for welfare, and that the disciples – Zealots all – had become waiters? The likelihood of there being Hellenists among the Zealot followers of Judas the Galilean is ridiculous. These were the guys the Maccabees railed against during the early second century BC and the reason for their fundamentalist revolution. There is, however, an echo of Paul's dispute with Peter at Antioch over table fellowship with Gentiles, which Acts otherwise never mentions. Notice that the Hellenizing members are being selected to "wait on tables" while the hardcore Jewish members are just going to pray and "serve the word."

> What they said pleased the whole community, and they chose Stephen, a man full of faith and the Holy Spirit, together with Philip, Prochorus, Nicanor, Timon, Parmenas, and Nicolaus, a proselyte of Antioch. They had these men stand before the apostles, who prayed and laid their hands on them.[736]

---

[734]The Sicarii were not a specific group per se, but rather described those who killed using a specific method: by concealing curved daggers in their robes. See Mason (2016), pp. 255–57.

[735]Acts 6:1-4.

[736]Acts 6:5-6.

For the author of this text, the only way one could be anything at all in the church organization was if the 'power' had been passed via one of the apostles, i.e. disciples of Jesus of Nazareth. That is clearly implied here and is thus part of the effort to close down the church hierarchy against 'heretics.' Note also that a possible nod is given to the Antioch incident between Paul and Peter by the mention of Nicolaus of Antioch.

> The word of God continued to spread; the number of the disciples increased greatly in Jerusalem, and a great many of the priests became obedient to the faith.[737]

That was certainly true enough. Josephus says that many of the lower-order priests joined the Zealots and he describes the Fourth Philosophy of Judas the Galilean as being almost identical to that of the Pharisees.

> Stephen, full of grace and power, did great wonders and signs among the people. Then some of those who belonged to the synagogue of the Freedmen (as it was called), Cyrenians, Alexandrians, and others of those from Cilicia and Asia, stood up and argued with Stephen. But they could not withstand the wisdom and the Spirit with which he spoke. Then they secretly instigated some men to say, "We have heard him speak blasphemous words against Moses and God." They stirred up the people as well as the elders and the scribes; then they suddenly confronted him, seized him, and brought him before the council. They set up false witnesses who said, "This man never stops saying things against this holy place and the law; for we have heard him say that this Jesus of Nazareth will destroy this place and will change the customs that Moses handed on to us."[738]

The above passage sure sounds like it could have been a description of the experiences of Paul in Antioch, as well as being echoed in the accusations against Jesus as depicted in Mark. This makes sense, considering Acts' goal of rehabilitating Paul, whitewashing the Christians' Zealot roots, and creating harmony between the Zealot and Pauline factions where there had been none. It seems almost certain that Paul's letters, Mark and Josephus were used as inspiration to infuse Acts with verisimilitude, all the while the author pretends not to know Paul's letters at all. But in this tale, Stephen is a stand-in for Paul.

> And all who sat in the council looked intently at him, and they saw that his face was like the face of an angel. Then the high priest asked him, "Are these things so?" And Stephen replied: "Brothers and fathers, listen to me. The God of glory appeared to our ancestor Abraham ..."[739]

After a long speech on the history of the Jews, which I will omit mostly, we finally come to this:

> "But it was Solomon who built a house for him. Yet the Most High does not dwell in houses made with human hands; as the prophet says, 'Heaven is my throne, and the earth is my footstool. What kind of house will you build for me, says the Lord, or what is the place of my rest? Did not my hand make all these things?'"
>
> "You stiff-necked people, uncircumcised in heart and ears, you are forever opposing the Holy Spirit, just as your ancestors used to do. Which of the prophets did your ancestors not persecute? **They killed those who foretold the coming of the Righteous One, and now you have become his betrayers and murderers.** You are the ones that received *the law as ordained by angels*, and yet you have not kept it."[740]

---

[737] Acts 6:7.

[738] Acts 6:8-14.

[739] Acts 6:15–7:2a.

[740] Acts 7:47-53.

Oh boy, now he's done it! He not only eliminates any need for the temple and sacrifice (as Paul did), he also accuses the Jews of killing Jesus! Well, we know that didn't come from Paul.[741] But do note how it is cast in Pauline language.

> When they heard these things, they became enraged and ground their teeth at Stephen. But filled with the Holy Spirit, he gazed into heaven and saw the glory of God and Jesus standing at the right hand of God. "Look," he said, "I see the heavens opened and the Son of Man standing at the right hand of God!" But they covered their ears, and with a loud shout all rushed together against him. Then they dragged him out of the city and began to stone him; and the witnesses laid their coats at the feet of a young man named Saul. While they were stoning Stephen, he prayed, "Lord Jesus, receive my spirit." Then he knelt down and cried out in a loud voice, "Lord, do not hold this sin against them." When he had said this, he died.[742]

What an ending! The author has introduced Saul/Paul in a context borrowed from the crucifixion of Jesus and has put words into Stephen's mouth straight from Jesus in Luke's Gospel.[743] And then, the grand finale:

> And Saul approved of their killing him. That day a severe persecution began against the church in Jerusalem, and **all except the apostles were scattered** throughout the countryside of Judea and Samaria. Devout men buried Stephen and made loud lamentation over him. But Saul was ravaging the church by entering house after house; dragging off both men and women, he committed them to prison. Now those who were scattered went from place to place, proclaiming the word.[744]

Just bizarre. Stephen, a Hellenistic Jew, makes a polemical speech against the Jews, and then the Lukan author says that a persecution against the Jerusalem church arose as a consequence of the tumult caused by the stoning of Stephen. The end result was that the church was scattered throughout Judea and Samaria. *Except*, of course, the apostles were exempted from this persecution! Meanwhile, Paul is supposed to be lurking in the background, hovering over a pile of garments in a scene reminiscent of the soldiers casting lots for Jesus' clothing. And, immediately following this, the movement was dispersed while the leaders continued on unmolested? And then, Paul is rabidly dragging people out of their homes and throwing them into prison?! That is so historically implausible as to stagger the mind. One hopes that the intended audience of Acts was not expected to believe any of this was history, but rather would read it as the novel it is. What is utterly jaw dropping is that any trained scholar of modern times takes any of it seriously.

In Galatians 1:13, Paul states that he "persecuted the church of God, and made havoc of it." Then in Philippians 3:6 he says the same thing very briefly: "as touching zeal, I persecuted the church." I think these are clear interpolations, set up to be statements of a convert about his past and designed to draw a contrast between his former zeal for Judaism and his present opposition to it. But, as we know, Paul was *still* very much opposed to the 'church of God' as represented by the Jewish Christians – at least at the time he was writing these letters. At the same time,

---

[741]Carrier (2014), pp. 566–69 – no fan of most interpolation theories – ably shows that 1 Thess. 2:15-16 ("[the Jews] both killed the Lord Jesus and the prophets, and drove out us, and please not God, and are contrary to all men") should be seen as an interpolation.

[742]Acts 7:54-60.

[743]Luke 23:34.

[744]Acts 8:1-4.

Paul states that as long as three years after his conversion, he was still unknown by face to the churches of Judea: that is, he had never been among them! So, obviously, Paul could not have been a persecutor of any Christians in Judea.

A further consideration is a remark he makes in the closing of Romans 16:7: "Greet Andronicus and Junia, my relatives who were in prison with me; they are prominent among the apostles, and they were in Christ before I was." What are we to make of that? Paul had relatives who were Christians before him? And those relatives were "prominent among the apostles"? Among which apostles were they prominent? The ones that persecuted Paul? The ones that Paul was opposed to? Whatever kind of Christians they were, they were in prison with Paul and we suspect that Paul was arrested probably under suspicion of being a rebel Zealot, when he was actually preaching an opposing doctrine. Were these relatives also followers of the opposing doctrine of Paul and thus opposed to the Jewish Christians in Jerusalem? We come back to the same question: among what apostles were they prominent?

I can think of a couple of solutions, neither of which is entirely satisfactory: 1) It is an interpolation. But how much is interpolated – the whole chapter or just the odd statement describing his relatives? 2) His relatives were Zealot supporters and after his conversion, he converted them to his version of the gospel. But then, he says that they *are* prominent among the apostles, not they *were*. That leads to: 3) Paul is talking about apostles of the very different Christ he preaches. Thus, there were others before him; he is not the first, though he may have put his own particular spin on things. That, of course, leads back to the question: *who* was this other Christ? By the end of this volume, after laying out all the clues, I will suggest my own solution, though it will require an entire book of its own to bring the evidence together.

Just to be thorough, I want to go a bit deeper into the problem of Paul the persecutor of the church. There *are* some interesting elements in Josephus that were probably utilized by the author of Acts in his efforts to infuse his composition with verisimilitude. They involve a fellow named Costobarus and his brother Saul, followed by a Simon son of Saul. We have to go back in time to pick up the thread we are going to pull.

According to Josephus, in c. 37 BC, Mark Antony appointed Herod the Great as Tetrarch of Judea, and Herod appointed Costobarus as Governor of Idumea and Gaza.[745] Soon afterwards, c. 34 BC, Herod gave his sister Salome in marriage to Costobarus. Not long after, Costobarus got on the wrong side of Herod. Supposedly, Salome issued a writ of divorce (which a woman was not permitted to do under Jewish law), c. 27–25 BC. Salome then informed Herod that *Costobarus was getting ready to flee the country in the company of Herod's own brother Pheroras*, who was out of favor because of his romantic attachment to a slave. Even worse, Costobarus had been hiding some of Herod's enemies for years. These were the 'Sons of Baba,' a politically powerful family that led the resistance against Herod at the time of the siege of Jerusalem in 37 BC. Costobarus and the Sons of Baba were, apparently, arrested and executed by Herod c. 25 BC, and that should be the end of that. However, Josephus also tells us that Salome and Costobarus had a son.[746]

Now let's look at a short passage from *Wars* discussing the early days of the Jewish insurrection. Here, three descendants of Herod – the second Costobarus, Saul and Antipas – called on Agrippa

---

[745] *Ant.* 15.7.9–10 (254–61).

[746] *Ant.* 16.7.6 (227).

II to send help to fight the rebels. What followed was the Battle of Beth-horon (25 November 66 AD) in which the Jews defeated the Roman general Cestius:

> After the calamity of Cestius, many of the eminent Judeans began, as if from a sinking ship, to swim away from the city. At any rate, Costobar[us] and Saul, brothers, with Philip son of Iacimus – this was the camp prefect of Agrippa the king – fled from the city and went off to Cestius. ... Cestius dispatched *Saul's group* up to Achaea, to Nero, so that they might explain their own constraint and also direct responsibility for the war at Florus. For he [Cestius] hoped that his [Nero's] fury against that man would ameliorate his own risks.[747]

In the first case, Salome's husband Costobarus is planning to *flee* with the *brother* of Herod the Great. In the second instance, another Costobarus is going to *flee* with his *brother* and a friend. Florus was the Roman procurator of Judea from 64 to 66 AD, so this Saul probably has nothing to do with the Apostle Paul. Paul is referred to as 'Saul' *only in Acts*; Paul himself never indicates or suggests that his real name was Saul. In view of Paul's own statements about his activities and whereabouts at various points, the further parts of the above passage are interesting:

> In the meantime, **the people of Damascus**, when they were informed of the destruction of the Romans, set about the slaughter of those Jews that were among them; and as they had them already cooped up together in the place of public exercises, which they had done out of the suspicion they had of them, they thought they should meet with no difficulty in the attempt; **yet did they distrust their own wives, which were almost all of them addicted to the Jewish religion**; on which account it was that their greatest concern was, how they might conceal these things from them; so they came upon the Jews, and cut their throats, as being in a narrow place, in number ten thousand, and all of them unarmed, and this in one hour's time, without anybody to disturb them.[748]

It's curious that Paul's alleged statements about persecuting the 'church' were turned into a rather violent sort of activity by the author of Acts, who drew on Josephus. And several researchers, including Robert Eisenman, have read into the story about Costobarus and Saul that this was the Apostle Paul, and that he was a Herodian; never mind the late date and implausibility, and forget the fact that none of this is even remotely hinted at in the epistles. However, the dynamics of the story might indicate something of the reason why Paul was persecuted in Damascus at a much earlier time: the wives of the Damascenes were quite taken with the Jewish religion. Perhaps that was also true in Paul's time and his teachings didn't go over so well with their husbands!? Probably any messianic group was considered to be *a group fomenting rebellion against Rome*. The ethnarch of Aretas was having none of that revolutionary stuff going on in his city!

There is a further passage in *Wars* that may have given ideas and shape to the author of Acts in his novelization of the reconciliation of the Pauline and Petrine camps and activities.[749] It refers to an individual named Simon, a son of one Saul. I would suggest that these names and the activity of the character Simon are what attracted the attention of the author of Acts

---

[747] *Wars* 2.20.1 (556–8), Mason translation.

[748] *Wars* 2.20.2 (559–61).

[749] Acts is primarily concerned with showing the harmony between the two important early Christian figures: Paul and Peter. However, this agenda overrides concern with the facts, presenting a whitewashed version of both Paul and Peter, almost totally at odds with the data available in Paul's letters. See Goulder (1995) and Pervo (2006).

– he thought he might make use of the dynamic in his portrayal of Paul in his former life as an antagonist toward the Jerusalem Christian Zealots.[750] This Simon ben Saul was a "man of reputation among the Jews," who, for some reason or another, was *at war with his own people* (Jews):

> This man [Simon] was distinguished from the rest by the strength of his body,[751] and the **boldness of his conduct**, although he abused them both to the mischieving of his countrymen; for **he came every day and slew a great many of the Jews of Scythopolis, and he frequently put them to flight**, and became himself alone the cause of his army's conquering. But a just punishment overtook him for the murders he had committed upon those of the same nation with him; for when the people of Scythopolis threw their darts at them in the grove, he drew his sword, but did not attack any of the enemy; for he saw that he could do nothing against such a multitude; but he cried out after a very moving manner, and said, "O you people of Scythopolis, I deservedly suffer for what I have done with relation to you, when I gave you such security of my fidelity to you, by slaying so many of those that were related to me. Wherefore we very justly experience the perfidiousness of foreigners, while we acted after a most wicked manner against our own nation. I will therefore die, polluted wretch as I am, by mine own hands; for it is not fit I should die by the hand of our enemies; and let the same action be to me both a punishment for my great crimes, and a testimony of my courage to my commendation, that so no one of our enemies may have it to brag of, that he it was that slew me, and no one may insult upon me as I fall." Now when he had said this, he looked round about him upon his family with eyes of commiseration and of rage [that family consisted of a wife and children, and his aged parents]; so, in the first place, he caught his father by his grey hairs, and ran his sword through him, and after him he did the same to his mother, who willingly received it; and after them he did the like to his wife and children, every one almost offering themselves to his sword, as desirous to prevent being slain by their enemies; so when he had gone over all his family, he stood upon their bodies to be seen by all, and stretching out his right hand, that his action might be observed by all, he sheathed his entire sword into his own bowels. This young man was to be pitied, on account of the strength of his body and the courage of his soul; but since he had assured foreigners of his fidelity [against his own countrymen], he suffered deservedly.[752]

Elements of this Simon surely could have been used for novelistic inspiration about Paul in Acts retrojected into his 'anti-church' past.[753]

Now, let's come back to the problem with Acts and the episodes which betray that all was not sweetness and light: six chapters after the Stephen episode, "Herod the king" pops in and "killed James, the brother of John with the sword; and when he saw that it pleased the Jews, he proceeded to arrest Peter also."[754]

NT scholars tend to identify this Herod as Herod Agrippa I, who had received additional lands after the accession of Claudius in 41 BC. Completely ignored by such scholars is the fact that Josephus recounts that Tiberius Alexander in c. 47 executed the sons of Judas the Galilean, who

---

[750]While Acts focuses on Peter within the Jerusalem church, Paul's letters strongly imply that James was the church's main leader.

[751]Just like Simon of Perea and Athronges before him!

[752]*Wars* 2.18.4 (469–76).

[753]I partially agree with Unterbrink (2014), p. 241, on this point: "Paul of Tarsus [as represented in Acts] is also a composite character, with the life and deeds of the Herodian Saul and Josephus himself rewritten in order to hide Saul's true identity."

[754]Acts 12:1-3.

just happen to have been named James and Simon (recalling that Peter was Simon before being given his nickname 'Rocky'). Also ignored is the fact that the Jews were not allowed to execute anyone without the permission of the Romans. Even Herod the Great sought the permission of Augustus to execute his son.

Such a raft of nonsense as we find in Acts could only have been written by someone separated from the events by a great span of time, someone who had powerful motivations to conceal the facts. Certain details of the story give further reason to question what is going on here: Peter allegedly makes a miraculous escape from prison and then, POOF!, just disappears from the story entirely with only the remark, "Then he departed and went to another place."[755] That's it. End of Peter in Acts.

Overall, with its depiction of the early church of Jerusalem being all friendly and full of miracles, Acts gives no real hint that the Jewish Christians, as Zealots, were continuously, actively under threat by the Jewish and Roman officials. In only these two instances – Stephen's stoning debacle and the execution of James and arrest of Peter – does Acts acknowledge that things weren't all sweetness and light, but the author does his best to scatter the evidence in the text, minimize it, or cover it up entirely with fake story ideas borrowed from the literature of the time, mainly Josephus.

Paul's epistles testify that he made two visits to Jerusalem, widely separated in time, and those two visits suggest that, in some way, there was some stability of the organization in that period and that Paul may have been trying to subvert it. But apparently, at some point, things changed and the Zealots were hunted. According to the most rational timeline for Paul that can be established based on clues within the epistles themselves, compared with the actual history of the time as can be extracted from Josephus with some care, and disregarding Acts' timeline and itinerary for Paul entirely as being not just fictitious, but deliberately so, we find that the stability of the early Jewish church was seriously threatened almost immediately after Paul's second visit and that this was undoubtedly the event that caused the 'scattering' that was attributed to the activities (and suggested time) of Stephen, who stood in for Paul. Paul mentions in 1 Cor. 1:16 that he baptized the household of Stephanas and that they were the first converts in Achaia, so that is likely where the Lukan author got the inspiration to create his character, Stephen, and set him up as a pseudo-Paul, oh so cleverly using him to introduce Saul/Paul![756]

It is far more likely that the actual events behind Acts 6–8 and 12 were the actions of Tiberius Alexander in c. 47 AD, and were considerably later than Acts would have us think. This leads us to assume that Paul's second visit to Jerusalem occurred no later than the year when James and Simon were executed by Tiberius Alexander, that is, 46/47 AD.[757] We can calculate backward 14 years to his first visit to Jerusalem in 32 AD, and 3 years prior to that would be his conversion, i.e. 29 AD.

So, let's put together a tentative Pauline timeline now:

- 29 AD: Paul's conversion. Goes into desert.

- 32 AD: Escape from Damascus and Aretas. 1st trip to Jerusalem for 15 days, 3 yrs after conversion.

---

[755]Acts 12:17b.

[756]Genius? Well, not so much. Anybody who can read, has a reasonably good memory, and a few firing neurons, could figure that one out. No cigar, Polycarp!

[757]I give further arguments and evidence for these dates below in the section 'Paul's Timeline.'

- 40 AD: 2 Thess. written; dated by Gaius and his statue project. (Suggested by Campbell.)

- 43 AD: Paul dates his vision/conversion as "14 years ago" in 2 Cor. 12:2; this dates at least part of the Corinthian correspondence prior to the rift with Jerusalem

- 46 AD: 2nd visit to Jerusalem, 14 yrs after 1st. The Antioch incident follows shortly after: compare to the story of Stephen.

- c. 47 AD: Execution of James and Simon by Tiberius Alexander.

- 48 AD: Apostles/Zealots scatter and go underground. Paul probably also arrested not long after this, accused of being an associate of Zealots and sent to Rome. Galatians, Philippians, Colossians, Romans written.

It is of some interest that when this method is followed, Paul's conversion date (46-17 = 29 AD) just happens to be the "fifteenth year of Tiberius Caesar," the famous opening line of the third chapter of the Gospel of Luke, thought by many experts to have been the original beginning of 'proto-Luke,' which was derived from Mark in some form and which may suggest that such a date originally belonged to Mark.

Of course, it is a big problem for the Gospels to have Paul converted just as the mythical Jesus began his ministry, by at least one estimate. But knowing that the real Jewish messiah was Judas the Galilean and that he was executed in 19 AD, we do not need to be detained by that; there is something far more important implied by the timeline.

The first thing we should note, taking the times into account, and considering all the evidence about the two Christianities adduced thus far, is that it is very likely that Galatians 2 does not provide the complete picture of the conflict between Paul and the Jewish Christians. But something of what really did happen is suggested by this remark: "But because of false brethren secretly brought in to spy on our freedom ...",[758] which is echoed in the tale of Stephen: "Then they secretly instigated some men to say, 'We have heard him speak blasphemous words against Moses and God.' They stirred up the people as well as the elders and the scribes."

With two of the 'pillars' dead, and the Zealots scattered and gone underground due to the persecutions of Tiberius Alexander, and with Paul himself soon to be thrown into prison, probably on suspicion of being 'one of them,' i.e. a Zealot Christian rebel, I highly doubt there was a third visit to Jerusalem, and probably no 'collection for the poor' that allegedly led to the idea in the first place. As I argue below, anything in Paul's epistles about these two items are most probably later editorial additions written in an attempt to smooth over the complete rift between Paul and the Jerusalem Christians. How else was the author of Acts to show that Paul supported the Jerusalem church? Why, have him take up a collection for them!

Considering the historical evidence and the few brief notices in Paul attesting to a serious conflict, I think we can take it as given that his letters were subjected to serious and heavy modification when they were taken out of mothballs years later and Marcion appeared with his own collection. The absence of any Christian tradition of notable persecutions suffered during the terrible years preceding the Jewish War and, further, the failure to commemorate the martyrdom of James and Simon (Peter? Cephas?) confirms that the picture of early Christian life in Jerusalem portrayed in Acts is almost a complete fraud, and that Paul's epistles have been heavily redacted.

---

[758]Gal. 2:1-10

As far as we know, from the time of his arrest, Paul was effectively removed from pastoral and missionary activity. The author of Acts either did not know what happened to him, or chose to conceal what he did know, but he certainly hints at the ruin of Paul's efforts in a farewell speech he puts into Paul's mouth in Acts 20:18-35. It's interesting to speculate that this might actually have been from a real letter of Paul that was not independently preserved, though certainly the mention of going to 'Jerusalem' is wrong; he was actually going to Rome, according to the prologue of the Marcion collection. It could also very easily have been composed using elements from his known letters (and that is most likely; it just amuses me here to speculate). Anyway, here's the speech, and I've only changed 'Jerusalem' to 'Rome':

> When [the elders of the church at Ephesus] came to him, he said to them: "You yourselves know how I lived among you the entire time from the first day that I set foot in Asia, serving the Lord with all humility and with tears, enduring the trials that came to me through the plots of the Jews. I did not shrink from doing anything helpful, proclaiming the message to you and teaching you publicly and from house to house, as I testified to both Jews and Greeks about repentance toward God and faith toward our Lord Jesus. And now, as a captive to the Spirit, I am on my way to Rome, not knowing what will happen to me there, except that the Holy Spirit testifies to me in every city that imprisonment and persecutions are waiting for me. But I do not count my life of any value to myself, if only I may finish my course and the ministry that I received from the Lord Jesus, to testify to the good news of God's grace."
>
> "And now I know that none of you, among whom I have gone about proclaiming the kingdom, will ever see my face again. Therefore I declare to you this day that I am not responsible for the blood of any of you, for I did not shrink from declaring to you the whole purpose of God. Keep watch over yourselves and over all the flock, of which the Holy Spirit has made you overseers, to shepherd the church of God that he obtained with the blood of his own Son. I know that after I have gone, savage wolves will come in among you, not sparing the flock. Some even from your own group will come distorting the truth in order to entice the disciples to follow them. Therefore be alert, remembering that for three years I did not cease night or day to warn everyone with tears. And now I commend you to God and to the message of his grace, a message that is able to build you up and to give you the inheritance among all who are sanctified. I coveted no one's silver or gold or clothing. You know for yourselves that I worked with my own hands to support myself and my companions. In all this I have given you an example that by such work we must support the weak, remembering the words of the Lord Jesus, for he himself said, 'It is more blessed to give than to receive'."

The 'savage wolves' which entered in among them were undoubtedly the emissaries of the Jewish Zealot Christians, who intensified their propaganda when Paul was no longer there to defend his flocks. As previously noted,[759] the Christians of Rome at the time of the great fire were obviously Jewish Christians, indistinguishable from Jews in general except for their 'vile superstition' about the coming of a messiah with 12 legions of angels who was going to destroy the Romans and install the Kingdom of the Jewish God with the Jews as judges, juries and executioners. Undoubtedly, there were communities of Pauline Christians that managed to resist the 'wolves,' but I don't think they were the majority at that time. Recall the Christian archaeology: there was no evidence of a cross as a major symbol for a very long time. Paul and his Christ on the cross were certainly eclipsed.

---

[759] See 'Two Christs' in Chapter 1.

Paul in Rome

Francis Watson's book, *Paul, Judaism and the Gentiles: A Sociological Approach*, examines the legacy of Lutheranism in Pauline studies. He contends that the Lutheran interpretation that sees 'works of the law' as a hold-all term for merit theology is "seriously flawed."[760] Instead, Watson seeks a solution that respects the socio-historical context of Paul's writings. In other words, he tries to figure out the facts on the ground around Paul in order to understand what was going on and what was triggering Paul to write and do as he did. Unfortunately, like nearly every other scholar in the field, he simply does not take the full historical context into account. Nor does he take into account interpolations, glosses and redaction as thoroughly as might be wished. Nevertheless, he provides some interesting perspectives suggesting that something divisive was going on. As a consequence, some of what he has written is very helpful in understanding the differences between Paul and the Jerusalem Christians.

As noted, Watson criticizes Luther's interpretation of 'works' (human effort to earn salvation).[761] Watson uses his sociological approach to see Pauline Christianity as the transformation of a Jewish reform movement into a sect, supported by an ideology that legitimates separation. Some of what Watson says about Paul's theology comes very close to that of Ashworth, discussed above, but more importantly, Watson discusses the 'separating' elements which are what interest us here.

In regards to the writing of the Epistle to the Romans, Watson quotes Ferdinand Christian Baur, who wrote: "it is unthinkable that the apostle, without definite circumstances present in the Roman congregation ... should have felt himself obliged to write a letter with such a content to this congregation."[762] Baur thought that the Roman church was composed mainly of Jewish Christians who denied the legitimacy of Paul's apostleship and that Paul, hearing of tensions there between the Jewish majority and a Gentile minority, wrote a defense of Christian universalism against Jewish particularism.

Baur was wrong about this because, at the time Romans was written, Paul was most certainly persona non grata among Jewish Christians, as is revealed in Galatians. If the prologue to Romans in Marcion's letter collection is true, Paul was transferred from prison in Ephesus to Rome, giving him a definite motivation to write to a congregation there in hopes of having allies when he arrived. This understanding helps one to read Romans in a different way and to discern that there is obviously more than one letter combined there: one written to a Gentile group he was hoping would receive him, and another one written to Jewish Christians in Rome in hopes of converting them to his gospel, possibly sent to them *after* he had arrived. Recall the previous discussion where it was noted that Christian Hermann Weisse had concluded that Romans was a compilation in which the original letter was so interwoven with interpolations that it almost destroyed the style completely.

W. Wiefel (in 'The Jewish Community in Ancient Rome and the Origins of Roman Christianity') suggests that the alleged expulsion of Jews from Rome by Claudius brought the first

---

[760]Francis Watson, *Paul, Judaism and the Gentiles: A Sociological Approach* (Eerdmans, 2007), p. 27
[761]Watson recommends following the path of Ferdinand Christian Baur and certain other scholars of that ilk, such as W. D. Davies, K. Stendahl, E. P. Sanders, H. Räisänen, G. Howard, M. Barth, J. D. G. Dunn, N. T. Wright, and U. Wilckens, all of whom recognized the problem of Jewish particularism in relation to the circumstances of Paul's writings.
[762]Cited by Watson (2007), p. 163.

Roman congregation to an end. After that, there were only Gentile house churches and the letter addresses tensions between this now Gentile Christian majority and returning Jewish Christians. Wiefel proposes that the intent was to help the Gentile Christian majority to live together with the Jewish Christians in a society marked by hostility toward Jews.[763]

So Wiefel thought Paul was writing to mainly Gentile Christians, but with words to some Jewish Christians as well. It never occurs to him that a letter to Gentile Christians was interwoven with a separate letter to Jewish Christians to make what we now call the Epistle to the Romans, as Weisse suggested. Also, taking a more historically oriented dating into account, based on external events and clues within the texts of Paul that we have established here, it appears to the present writers that the expulsion from Rome of Jews must have occurred *after* Paul arrived there from prison in Ephesus. Further, so-called 'Christians' in Rome were perceived as simply Jews with a particular "vile superstition" in mind, i.e. messianism.

Continuing with Watson's review of the various positions taken by Pauline scholars, J. Jervell (in 'The Letter to Jerusalem'), on the other hand, writes: "The letter itself clearly states that its *raison d'être* does not stem from the situation of the Roman congregation, but is to be found in Paul himself at the time of writing."

> Jervell sees Romans 1:18–11:36 as "the defense Paul plans to give before the church in Jerusalem." Here, "Paul is absorbed by what he is going to say in Jerusalem," and he writes as he does because he wishes to ask the Roman congregation for its solidarity, support, and intercession. ... "Paul wants to represent the whole Gentile world in Jerusalem, including the West." ... "Paul needs the congregation just as much as they need him."[764]

This idea could be considered reasonable if one could take Acts as historically accurate (it isn't even close) or the Epistle to the Romans at face value (one can't). The actual situation appears to be that the *second* meeting in Jerusalem took place c. 46/47 AD; the upset between Paul, Cephas and Barnabas in Antioch took place just after that meeting; James and Simon/Cephas were soon after executed by Tiberius Alexander in c. 47 AD; the Jerusalem church was 'scattered'; the Galatian congregation was subjected to a takeover by Zealot Christians not long after that; Paul was then arrested and put in prison in Ephesus (possibly accused of being associated with the recently executed James and Simon, sons of Judas the Galilean, all rebels). If all this is true, then I find it patently absurd to think that Paul was just going along, making a collection to take to Jerusalem, and actually planning to go there! If so, the parts of Romans – and other epistles – that refer to the collection and an upcoming trip to Jerusalem must be forgeries.

In any event, Watson attempts to incorporate these different views noted above into his own argument: that Romans presupposes a particular social situation within the Roman church and that the contents of the theological discussions of Romans 1–11 are determined by the letter's intended function within that highly contentious social situation. He gives no thought to the simmering social and political tensions all over the Empire, nor does he ever make a connection between the Zealots and the Jerusalem Christians.

In any event, the problem with connecting the composition of Romans to any expulsion of Jews from Rome is twofold: 1) There were two expulsions in the first century: one in 19 AD (at the time of the execution of Judas the Galilean and the tumult this caused); and the second in 49.

---

[763]Watson (2007), pp. 164–65.
[764]Watson (2007), p. 165.

Acts is written to cover up the truth about early Christianity, not to document it, and displaces this event, saying it was the reason Paul met Prisca and Aquila (as they had made their way to Corinth from Rome). However, Prisca and Aquila are mentioned in 1 Cor. 16:19, which seems to have been written *before* the second meeting in Jerusalem in 46/47 because Barnabas is also mentioned favorably in the same letter, but he and Paul had apparently split up just after the second meeting, when there was the confrontation with Cephas in Antioch. Paul mentions that Barnabas was 'led astray' at that time, and the implication seems to have been that it was for good, though that is not certain.

It is far more likely that Paul was sent to Rome from prison in Ephesus as already noted, not very long after the arrests and executions of James and Simon, and that the tumult in 49/50 in Rome was caused by both the executions of the latter two, and the presence/influence of Paul himself. I say this is possible, but it seems to me almost certain that there would have been unrest among Jews throughout the Empire in response to the executions of the sons of Judas the Galilean. Keep in mind that this man and his doings, and those of his kin, dominated the mind of Josephus, and are the thread running throughout *Antiquities of the Jews* that leads right to the end, the resistance at the famous fortress of Masada.

Suetonius writes in his *Life of Claudius* about an expulsion of Jews from Rome during the reign of that emperor. He gives no date but says, basically, they were expelled because of disturbances instigated by 'Chrestus.' Watson writes that "it is probable that 'Chrestus' is to be identified with 'Christus'; the substitution occurred because 'Chrestus' was a popular personal name. According to Tertullian,[765] opponents of Christianity habitually mispronounced 'Christianus' as 'Chrestianus'." While it is actually *unlikely* that Suetonius would make such an error (he makes a separate reference to Christians, spelled correctly, as Watson admits), Watson still brings out some important observations, including that the disorders mentioned likely occurred "*within* the Roman Jewish community." But whoever Chrestus was, he was more likely agitating on behalf of the *Zealot* cause, not Christianity as Watson and practically all other scholars imagine it to have been:

> [T]he compressed phrase *impulsore Chresto* is *not incompatible with an awareness of the Judean origin of the disturbances in the Roman Jewish communities.* ... "the *deadly superstition* broke out again, not only in Judea, the origin of this evil, but even in Rome" (*Ann.* 15.44). If, for Tacitus, "Christus" is the originator of an evil that began in Judea but spread to Rome, then the same may be true of Suetonius's "Chrestus," the *impulsor* of disturbances in the Roman Jewish community ... [B]y the time of the fire in 64 [AD], the name "Christiani" identifies a specific group of people, hated for their shameful practices ... and for their [*hatred of humanity*] (Tacitus, *Ann.* 15.44).[766]

"Shameful practices and hatred of humanity." That just happens to be exactly how Paul – and most Greco-Romans – saw Judaism, particularly the Judaism of the messianists. Both events mentioned by Suetonius – the 49 AD 'Chrestus' riots and the punishment of 'Christians' during Nero – are likely to have referred to Zealots.[767]

---

[765] *Apol.* 3.5.

[766] Watson (2007), pp. 168–69.

[767] "Any 'Christians' causing trouble in Rome or elsewhere at those early dates must have advocated the strictly observant form of messianic Judaism that sparked their rebellion against Rome and their conflict with Paul in the New Testament." Valliant and Fahy (2018), p. 176.

Considering the events of Paul's second trip to Jerusalem, and subsequently in Antioch and then Galatia, we have to conclude that Paul's *main* letter to the Romans was written to Gentile converts to a gospel other than the gospel preached by the Zealot Christians of Jerusalem and believed by many practicing Jews throughout the Empire, i.e. that Judas the Galilean was going to come back from heaven with 12 legions of angels and stomp the Romans into the dust, after which the Jews would rule the world. That ideology would certainly qualify as a 'deadly superstition' that included 'hatred of humanity' (which is how Tacitus elsewhere refers to Jews, in *Hist.* 5.5). Thus, that Paul was *not* writing primarily to Jewish Christians is far more likely considering his experiences with the Jewish Christians in Asia to that point in time, as documented in Galatians, and his total opposition to their ideology.

Now, the Book of Acts is clearly involved in covering up the facts while still trying to pepper the story with historical seeds for the sake of verisimilitude.[768] Nearly the whole book is one story after another about Paul preaching in synagogues to Jews. Knowing Paul's own self-declared mission, from the beginning, to the Gentiles, plus his recent experiences with the Jewish Christians in Galatia, we can discard this nonsense as pure apologetic fiction. Acts 18:2 says that Paul, on his arrival in Corinth, "found a Jew named Aquila, a native of Pontus, who had recently come from Italy with his wife Priscilla, because Claudius had ordered all Jews to leave Rome." The Lukan author (probably Polycarp) doesn't say why Claudius issued such an edict (or how it would be possible to expel *all* the Jews of the city, who probably numbered 10,000 or more). Watson asks:

> When, at Ephesus, Paul encounters people who are already Christians, they are clearly identified as "disciples" (Acts 19:1). Yet neither does Luke claim that Aquila and Priscilla were converted by Paul; it is simply taken for granted that they are Christians (Acts 18:18, 26). Is there a connection between Luke's failure either to give a reason for the expulsion or to mention that Aquila and Priscilla were already Christians when they met Paul? *Is it the arrival of Christianity in Rome that is at both points concealed* (cf. 28:15)? Luke's strangely emphatic reference to "all the Jews" would be compatible with such a hypothesis: Luke knows that Christians were implicated in the events that led to the expulsion from Rome but does not wish to acknowledge this.[769]

Watson is certainly dancing around the crux of the matter here. He may be right that there was a reason to cover up what happened in Rome, but not for the reason he thinks. If it was simply a matter of Jews causing trouble for Christians in Rome, and the Jews being blamed and punished for it by the Romans, 'Luke' probably would have mentioned it, but he doesn't.[770] But Luke *is* concerned with covering up the early equivalence between 'Jewish Christianity' and Zealotry, which he and all other later Christian writers whitewashed out of existence after the Jewish War.

The reference to Acts 28:15 is interesting too. It is part of the 'we' text in Acts, claimed to be a travel diary kept by a companion of Paul (allegedly Luke). The story at this point is about Paul being sent to Rome *from Jerusalem*, where he had almost been killed by the Jews (stoning of Stephen? Paul *does* say he was stoned more than once). After several previous adventures,

---

[768] That this was consciously being done, there can be no doubt.

[769] Watson (2007), p. 170.

[770] Acts frequently presents Jews causing trouble for Christians, and the Romans taking the Christians' side, e.g. letting Jason go in 17:7, driving off the Jews harassing Paul in Corinth in 18:16, and coming to favorable conclusions about Christians in 23:6, 24:14-21, 26:23, 28:20.

the text says about Paul's arrival in Italy, starting at verse 11 and going right through to the end of Acts:

> Three months later we set sail on a ship that had wintered at the island [of Malta], an Alexandrian ship with the Twin Brothers as its figurehead. We put in at Syracuse and stayed there for three days; then we weighed anchor and came to Rhegium. After one day there a south wind sprang up, and on the second day we came to Puteoli. *There we found believers* and were invited to stay with them for seven days. And so we came to Rome. *The believers from there*, when they heard of us, came as far as the Forum of Appius and Three Taverns to meet us. On seeing them, Paul thanked God and took courage. When we came into Rome, Paul was allowed to live by himself, with the soldier who was guarding him.
>
> Three days later he called together the local leaders of the Jews. When they had assembled, he said to them, "Brothers, though I had done nothing against our people or the customs of our ancestors, yet I was arrested in Jerusalem and handed over to the Romans. When they had examined me, the Romans wanted to release me, because there was no reason for the death penalty in my case. But *when the Jews objected*, I was compelled to appeal to the emperor – even though I had no charge to bring against my nation. For this reason therefore I have asked to see you and speak with you, since it is for the sake of the hope of Israel that I am bound with this chain."
>
> They replied, "We have received no letters from Judea about you, and none of the brothers coming here has reported or spoken anything evil about you. But we would like to hear from you what you think, for with regard to this sect we know that everywhere it is spoken against." After they had set a day to meet with him, they came to him at his lodgings in great numbers. From morning until evening he explained the matter to them, testifying to the kingdom of God and trying to convince them about Jesus both from the law of Moses and from the prophets. Some were convinced by what he had said, while others refused to believe. So they disagreed with each other; and as they were leaving, Paul made one further statement: "The Holy Spirit was right in saying to your ancestors through the prophet Isaiah, 'Go to this people and say, You will indeed listen, but never understand, and you will indeed look, but never perceive. For this people's heart has grown dull, and their ears are hard of hearing, and they have shut their eyes; so that they might not look with their eyes, and listen with their ears, and understand with their heart and turn – and I would heal them.' Let it be known to you then that this salvation of God has been sent to the Gentiles; they will listen."
>
> He lived there two whole years at his own expense and welcomed all who came to him, proclaiming the kingdom of God and teaching about the Lord Jesus Christ with all boldness and without hindrance.[771]

I'm not going to completely discount this tale, because, as noted, there are seeds of historical data peppered through the text and the Lukan author may have had access to texts that were left to rot, or deliberately destroyed, or cut up to be used any way they chose. The point is, the above text may very well describe some of the events and conditions Paul met when he arrived in Rome as possibly recorded by a companion.

Notice in particular this response from his Jewish interlocutors in the scene above:

> We have received no letters from Judea about you, and none of the brothers coming here has reported or spoken anything evil about you. But we would like to hear from you what you think, for *with regard to this sect we know that everywhere it is spoken against.*

---

[771] Acts 28:11-31.

Well, butter wouldn't melt in their mouths! The Lukan author is trying to make it look like the Jews in Rome were not messianists and that there were just Christians (all one happy family) vs. Jews and unsaved Gentiles. And Paul was living in his own house with just a guard? What happened to him? The whole story, even if using some historical data (and that is an assumption!), is a complete farce. Nevertheless, what the text strongly suggests is that Paul was met by groups of Gentile Christians, and then *later* had meetings with Jews. When the Epistle to the Romans is correctly separated, it can be seen that there is one letter to Gentiles, the original letter, and another letter to Jews (messianic or not), plus interpolations and fragments of a letter *to* Ephesus, which makes it clear that Paul was sent to Rome from prison there.

Getting back to the expulsion of Jews from Rome, Dio Cassius reports that Claudius banned the Jews from assembly at the beginning of his reign in 41 AD. This was most likely due to a build-up of tensions related to the plan of Caligula, his predecessor, to erect his own statue in the Jewish temple at Jerusalem, which has already been discussed. Yet, as noted above, in his biography of Claudius, Suetonius refers to an *expulsion* of Jews: "Since the Jews constantly made disturbances at the instigation of Chrestus, he expelled them from Rome."[772]

Let's look at Suetonius' remark more closely. The Latin original of this statement can be understood in one of two ways: either Claudius expelled the Jews from Rome because there was a tumult, or he only expelled those Jews that were causing the disorder. The latter is more probable, as a mass expulsion of Jews at the time is highly improbable.[773] The expulsion event Suetonius refers to is difficult to date precisely, because he wrote topically, not chronologically. But, we can say it is after 41 and before 54 AD (the duration of Claudius' reign). Cassius Dio's reference in his *Roman History* says:

> As for the Jews, who had again increased so greatly that by reason of their multitude it would have been hard without raising a tumult to bar them from the city, **he did not drive them out**, but ordered them, while continuing their traditional mode of life, not to hold meetings.[774]

This is dated to the year 41/42 AD. However, Dio does not mention any Chrestus or exiling of Jews. In fact, he mentions no reason for the action at all though it could be related to the very recent agitation of Jews due to the actions of Caligula. The fifth-century Christian writer Paulus Orosius makes a possible reference to the event, citing two sources:

> Josephus reports, 'In his ninth year the Jews were expelled by Claudius from the city.' But Suetonius, who speaks as follows, influences me more: 'Claudius expelled from Rome the Jews constantly rioting at the instigation of Christ [*Christo*, or rather X].' As far as whether he had commanded that the *Jews rioting against Christ* [*Christum*] be restrained and checked or also had wanted the Christians, as persons of a cognate religion, to be expelled, it is not at all to be discerned.[775]

We recognize the citation from Suetonius, but the quote from Josephus is not present in the extant texts. It is that which gives the date of 49 AD, the "ninth year of Claudius." There is a

---

[772]Suetonius, *Claudius* 25. Obviously, a lot of ink has been expended on this remark! But, since it is highly unlikely that a hypothetical Christian interpolator would have called Jesus 'Chrestus,' placed him in Rome in 49 AD, or called him a 'troublemaker,' the overwhelming majority of scholars conclude that the passage is genuine.
[773]See Richard Pervo, *Acts: A Commentary* (Fortress Press, 2008), pp. 446–47.
[774]Dio 60.6.6–7.
[775]Orosius, *History* 7.6.15–16, quoted by Wikipedia.org, 'Claudius' expulsion of Jews from Rome.'

lot of arguing back and forth over this, but we can note that, even if we have eschewed Acts as a historical source, it dates the expulsion with reference to the proconsul of Achaia, Gallio (Acts 18:12). Lucius Junius Gallio Annaeanus was a Roman senator and the son of the rhetorician Seneca the Elder and the elder brother of Seneca the Younger.[776] An inscription found at Delphi preserves a letter from Claudius concerning Gallio, dated during the 26th acclamation of Claudius, sometime between January 51 and August 52; he was referred to by Claudius as "my friend and proconsul." Acts says that Paul met Aquila and Priscilla in Corinth, who had "recently" come from Italy, *after Claudius ordered all Jews to leave Rome*. It isn't any more specific than that, so the author could have intended them to have left Rome in 49 AD, then Italy any time after that and before 51 AD. But of course, we have no reason to trust Acts for historical accuracy, and Paul's letters suggest he probably knew Prisca and Aquila well before the second Jerusalem meeting that took place before the execution of James and Simon in 47 AD.

All this suggests it is unlikely that the Apostle Paul had any dealings with Gallio between 51 and 52 AD. Gallio was probably borrowed by the Lukan author to give historical verisimilitude to the novelized version of early Christian history. However, knowing already that the author of Acts was using Josephus as a source, it is possible that the Josephan reference mentioned by Orosius existed, and was utilized by the author of Acts, but is now missing from Josephus, having been redacted or simply dropped during copying.

The differences between the event as reported by Dio and Suetonius lead some scholars to conclude that they are *two separate events* of different natures. It seems likely that this is the case. In 41 AD, Rome's new emperor, Claudius, responded to an embassy from the Alexandrians in response to the violence there between the Jewish and Greek population. This violence had its origin around 38 AD, in the last years of the reign of Caligula, and has already been discussed at length. Claudius' edict to the Alexandrians (41 AD) happens to have been preserved. In it, we find the following:

> Tiberius ... to the City of the Alexandrians, greetings.
>
> Tiberius Claudius Barbillus [et al.], having delivered to me the decree, discoursed at length concerning the city, directing my attention to your goodwill towards us, which, from long ago, you may be sure, had been stored up to your advantage in my memory; for you are by nature reverent towards the Augusti, as I know from many proofs, and in particular have taken a warm interest in my house, warmly reciprocated, of which fact (to mention the last instance, passing over the others) the supreme witness is my brother Germanicus addressing you in words more clearly stamped as his own.
>
> Wherefore, I gladly accepted the honors given to me by you, though I have no weakness for such things. [List of various honors accepted.] But I deprecate the appointment of a high priest to me and the building of temples, for I do not wish to be offensive to my contemporaries, and my opinion is that temples and such forms of honor have by all ages been granted as a prerogative to the gods alone.
>
> Concerning the requests which you have been anxious to obtain from me, I decide as follows. ... As for the question, which party was responsible for the riots and feud (or rather, if the truth be

[776]"Not long after the death of his brother, Seneca, Gallio (according to Tacitus, *Ann.* 15.73) was attacked in the Senate by Salienus Clemens, who accused him of being a 'parricide and public enemy', though the Senate unanimously appealed to Salienus not to profit 'from public misfortunes to satisfy a private animosity'. He did not survive this reprieve long. When his second brother, Annaeus Mela, opened his veins after being accused of involvement in a conspiracy (Tacitus, *Ann.* 16.17), Gallio seems to have committed suicide, perhaps under instruction in 65 AD, at the age of 64." (Wikipedia.org, 'Lucius Junius Gallio Annaeanus.')

told, the war) with the Jews, although in confrontation with their opponents your ambassadors, and particularly Dionysios the son of Theon, contended with great zeal, nevertheless I was unwilling to make a strict inquiry, though guarding within me a store of immutable indignation against whichever party renews the conflict. And I tell you once and for all that unless you put a stop to this ruinous and obstinate enmity against each other, I shall be driven to show what a benevolent Prince can be when turned to righteous indignation. Wherefore, once again **I conjure you that, on the one hand, the Alexandrians show themselves forebearing and kindly towards the Jews** who for many years have dwelt in the same city, and **dishonor none of the rites observed by them in the worship of their god, but allow them to observe their customs as in the time of the Deified Augustus, which customs I also, after hearing both sides, have sanctioned;** and on the other hand, **I explicitly order the Jews not to agitate for more privileges than they formerly possessed, and not in the future to send out a separate embassy as though they lived in a separate city (a thing unprecedented), and not to force their way into gymnasiarchic or cosmetic games, while enjoying their own privileges and sharing a great abundance of advantages in a city not their own, and not to bring in or admit Jews who come down the river from Egypt or from Syria, a proceeding which will compel me to conceive serious suspicions.** Otherwise I will by all means take vengeance on them as **fomenters of which is a general plague infecting the whole world.** If, desisting from these courses, you consent to live with mutual forebearance and kindliness, I on my side will exercise a solicitude of very long standing for the city, as one which is bound to us by traditional friendship. I bear witness to my friend Barbillus of the solicitude which he has always shown for you in my presence and of the extreme zeal with which he has now advocated your cause; and likewise to my friend Tiberius Claudius Archibius.

Farewell.[777]

Claudius' edict is fairly even-handed, assuring certain rights to the Jews in Alexandria but forbidding them from crossing certain lines in the future, e.g. in agitating for full citizenship if they choose to remain religious Jews, or *recruiting Jews from other regions to help renew their struggle* against the Alexandrians or foment rebellion. Notice the particular terms of that statement:

> ... not to bring in or admit Jews who come down the river from Egypt or from Syria, a proceeding which will compel me to conceive serious suspicions. Otherwise I will by all means take vengeance on them as *fomenters of which is* a general plague infecting the whole world.

Apparently, persons coming "down the river from Egypt" and from Syria, were fomenters – agitators of rebellion – and Claudius states that it is a "general plague infecting the whole world." That would certainly describe the Zealots and their messianism within the Diaspora, and we can note that the 'Christians' of that time were written about in the same terms, particularly if they were Jewish Christians.

Josephus includes a text in *Antiquities* that purports to reproduce two edicts of Claudius, one addressed to the Alexandrians and the other addressing Jews throughout the Empire, issued at the request of Agrippa I and Herod of Chalcis (sons of Aristobulus IV and grandsons of Herod the Great).[778] While he twists the facts in order to make it appear as if the Jews were full citizens of Alexandria, which Claudius' edict contradicts, the second edict appears to ring true

[777] A. S. Hunt and G. C. Edgar (eds.) *Select Papyri* II (Loeb Classical Library, 1934), pp. 78–89.
[778] *Ant.* 19.5.2–3 (278–91).

in certain respects when viewed next to the letter just quoted above. In it, he grants the same privileges enjoyed by Alexandria's Jews to Jewish communities in all towns of Roman right (i.e. colonies and cities within and without Italy).[779] So it seems likely that the problem of fomenting rebellion was, indeed, an Empire-wide issue at the time.

Additionally, after the assassination of Caligula in 41 AD, Agrippa I was involved in the struggle over the accession between Claudius, the Praetorian Guard, and the Senate. Cassius Dio simply writes that Agrippa I cooperated with Claudius in seeking rule. Josephus gives us two versions. In *Wars*, Agrippa I is presented as only a messenger to a confident and energetic Claudius, which is likely the truest version. But in *Antiquities*, Agrippa I plays a central and crucial role, i.e. Josephus is embellishing wildly, as usual. In any event, Claudius was thankful to Agrippa I for support and gave him Judea and Samaria to rule as king, among other honors. Agrippa I died soon after, in 43 AD.[780] The biblical description of Agrippa I as a cruel, heartless king who persecuted the Jerusalem church, having James son of Zebedee killed and imprisoning Peter,[781] stands in contrast with Josephus' account of a kindly man (if we can believe him). We have already noted that it was Tiberius Alexander who executed the sons of Judas the Galilean in c. 47 AD, which was likely the historical seed for the execution and imprisoning of James and Simon/Peter in Acts.[782] Had Agrippa I been the guilty party, the death of James would have had to have taken place before the death of Agrippa I in autumn of 43 AD.

The result of this short survey indicates that there are strong reasons to reject the idea that Claudius expelled Jews from Rome in 41 AD. It just doesn't make sense in the context of what is said about Claudius, the reality of the edict, and the fact that he was supported by Herod Agrippa I.[783]So, I think we can say that *Claudius was actually being conciliatory toward the Jews in 41 AD*, and the expulsion from Rome did not occur until 49 AD. That leaves open the possibility that the riot in Rome was caused *by Paul's appearance and promulgation of an 'anti-Judaism' gospel, and the Jewish rebel reaction against it*. All of these clues indicate the widespread nature of the Zealot messianic movement and its simmering, volatile undercurrent throughout the Empire.

Philo, writing specifically about the Roman Jewish community, said that Augustus was well aware of the sizeable Jewish population of ex-slaves on the farther bank of the Tiber who met together in their houses of prayer each Sabbath and sent money for sacrifices to the Temple

---

[779]See H. Stuart Jones, 'Claudius and the Jewish Question at Alexandria,' *Society for the Promotion of Roman Studies* 16:1 (1926).

[780]See *Ant.* 19.8.2—19.9.2 (343–361). Daniel R. Schwartz, in *Agrippa I: The Last King of Judaea* (Mohr Siebeck, 1990), pp. 108–10, argues that Agrippa I died in in the period between Sept./Oct. 43 and Jan./Feb. 44, favoring September/October 43 AD, in the third year of Agrippa I's rule under Claudius. He bases this on evidence from numismatics (coins), Josephus, and the times of the games at Caesarea Maritima.

[781]Acts 12.

[782]Mason (2016), p. 253, argues that the death of Agrippa I and the executions of Simon and James may be connected: "The date raises the possibility that they were involved in the turmoil following Agrippa's death and the renewed shift of power from Jerusalem to Caesarea. ... If they became involved in confrontations with Samarian auxiliary soldiers, Tiberius Alexander would have had little choice but to punish them." In other words, they were supporters of a monarchy, a sovereign Judea in a position of primacy in the region. The death of Agrippa once again shifted the power center from Jerusalem to Caesarea.

[783]Agrippa I (along with his son and Herod of Chalcis) was brought up at Rome with the imperial princes and, as Jones (1926) notes, would have had powerful friends at court. Antonia, the younger daughter of Mark Antony and Octavia Minor (Augustus' sister), was at the center of this coterie.

in Jerusalem.[784] Such individuals would be highly attracted to a messianic form of Judaism that promised them a chance to destroy their oppressors and rule over them. Thus it seems extremely likely that there was a Roman-Jewish messianic community at least since the time of the execution of Judas the Galilean, probably about 19 AD as I have previously argued. It also seems evident that this community was under constant tension and easily stirred up to unrest.

Interestingly, Hengel suggests that the disorders in Roman Jewish communities could be due to 'Hellenists' preaching a law-free gospel.[785] Watson thinks that the preaching of Jesus as the Messiah was controversial enough. Hengel may be right, at least when Paul arrived in Rome, probably in 49 AD, and Watson is surely wrong. There was nothing controversial to Jews about a messiah; it was the going thing at the time, many of them popping up all over the place according to Josephus, the messiah of the Jewish Christians at Jerusalem, Judas the Galilean, being the most persistent, having been transformed from an earthly Torah teacher and rebellion leader to a heavenly war leader after his execution. Josephus even suggests (though we have reason to doubt his accuracy) that the entire Jewish War came about because of the widespread belief in the coming of the messiah to help wipe out the Romans![786] As I have said before and repeat: Judas the Galilean was most likely the Jewish messiah; he was executed in 19 AD, which caused an uproar in Rome and elsewhere in the Jewish Diaspora; his sons, James and Simon (and John), were the pillars of the Jerusalem church of 'Christians,' i.e. messianists and Zealots; they turned against Paul when they learned he was preaching a law-free gospel and a universal savior for all mankind, not just the Jews, and not one who was going to destroy Rome; and James and Simon were executed by Tiberius Alexander in c. 47 AD.

Paul's Timeline

Based on everything so far collected, here's my more comprehensive construction of Paul's time-line.

29 AD – Conversion in the 15th year of Tiberius, i.e. "The Beginning of the Gospel of Jesus Christ," as Mark has it. (Ten years after the execution of Judas). This date is achieved by connecting James and Simon/Cephas/Peter to James and Simon, sons of Judas the Galilean, who were executed c. 47 AD. They were apparently still alive when Paul made his second visit to Jerusalem (see below), but were possibly dead when Paul referred to them in Galatians:

> Now of those esteemed to be something [i.e. the pillars], *whatsoever they were formerly* makes no difference to me. God does not accept the person of a man—for the esteemed added nothing to me. But on the contrary, ... having recognized the grace having been given to me, James and Cephas and John, those esteemed to be pillars, gave to me and Barnabas the right hands of fellowship, that we should go to the Gentiles ... (Gal. 2:6-9)[787]

---

[784]Philo, *Leg.* 155-56.

[785]Hengel, *Acts and the Early History of Christianity*, pp. 107–8, cited by Watson (2007), p. 173.

[786]But see Mason (2016) for why this is a simplistic explanation. It's likely the Zealots just piggybacked on a conflict that would have and did start regardless of their beliefs.

[787]Borean Literal Bible translation. Some translations make it seem as if the second reference to the pillars is written in the past tense: "James and Cephas and John, who *were* acknowledged pillars." However, the Greek is more ambiguous. The Greek word for 'acknowledged' or 'esteemed' (*dokuontes*) is an active present participle, i.e. 'seeming to be.' By itself it doesn't suggest anything in the past, just that the pillars are 'reputed' to be

Notice particularly this: "whatsoever they were formerly." Regarding his conversion experience, Paul wrote:

> But when God, who had set me apart before I was born and called me through his grace, was pleased to reveal his Son to me, so that I might proclaim him among the Gentiles, I did not confer with any human being, nor did I go up to Jerusalem to those who were already apostles before me, but I went away at once into Arabia, and afterwards I returned to Damascus. (Gal. 1:15-17)

32 AD – Escape from Damascus, first visit to Jerusalem, visits Cephas (not Peter?). Estimated by backdating from execution of James and Simon.

> In Damascus, the governor under King Aretas guarded the city of Damascus in order to seize me, but I was let down in a basket through a window in the wall, and escaped from his hands. (2 Cor. 11:32-33)

> Then after three years I did go up to Jerusalem to visit Cephas and stayed with him fifteen days; but I did not see any other apostle except James the Lord's brother. (Gal. 1:18-19)

> Then I went into the regions of Syria and Cilicia, and I was still unknown by sight to the churches of Judea that are in Christ. (Gal. 1:21-23)

40 AD – 2 Thessalonians written, alluding to Caligula and his plans to erect statue in Temple in the Man of Sin passage.

43 AD – Writing of at least some of the Corinthian correspondence. Dated by vision "14 years ago" = conversion experience. (This is speculative, but I think likely.)

> I know a person in Christ who fourteen years ago was caught up to the third heaven – whether in the body or out of the body I do not know; God knows. And I know that such a person – whether in the body or out of the body I do not know; God knows – was caught up into Paradise and heard things that are not to be told, that no mortal is permitted to repeat. (2 Cor. 12:2)

This would mean that some if not all of the Corinthian issues occurred *before* the second visit to Jerusalem if this letter is dated to 14 years after conversion, and the second visit occurred 14 years after the first visit, which was three years after conversion. 1 Corinthians, written from Ephesus, mentions Cephas in a friendly way; Barnabas is with Paul (1 Cor. 9:6); the main focus is orderly conduct and the danger of reversion to idolatry. But then, at the end:

> Now concerning the collection for the saints: you should follow the directions I gave to the churches of Galatia. On the first day of every week, each of you is to put aside and save whatever extra you earn, so that collections need not be taken when I come. And when I arrive, I will send any whom you approve with letters to take your gift to Jerusalem. (1 Cor. 16:1-3)

'something' – whether or not they're dead. (E.g., Both JFK and Putin can be reputed to be good presidents, though one is dead and the other is alive.) However, the literal translation of the parenthesis ("whatsoever they were formerly") *does suggest a past tense*, though it is still somewhat ambiguous. It can be read in two ways. Either the pillars are still alive, but were only 'formerly' esteemed to be something (which is interesting on its own, suggesting a possible loss of status), or they are dead and were esteemed to be something when alive. If anything speaks in favor of the latter interpretation it is that Paul makes no unambiguous statements about them in the present to imply they are still alive, as he does with individuals like Barnabas, Timothy, Prisca, Aquila, etc. Nevertheless, with the evidence that James and Simon were executed in 47, but present at the time of Paul's second trip to Jerusalem, I think the weight goes slightly to the side of this being a reference to the fact that they were dead.

It seems to me that the topics of 1 Corinthians as a whole do not mesh well with chapter 16 at all. But things get even stranger with 2 Cor. In this letter, chapters 10–13, there are opponents who are Jewish Christians, but apparently not from Jerusalem. Paul speaks about false apostles and Watson argues that this group of attackers is Apollos and his companions. Nothing is said about the problem of circumcision or submitting to the law.

2 Cor. 8:1-21	2 Cor. 9:1-14
We want you to know, brothers and sisters, about the grace of God that has been granted to **the churches of Macedonia; for during a severe ordeal of affliction, their abundant joy and their extreme poverty have overflowed in a wealth of generosity on their part.** For, as I can testify, **they voluntarily gave according to their means**, and even beyond their means, begging us earnestly for the privilege of sharing in this ministry to the saints – and this, not merely as we expected; they gave themselves first to the Lord and, by the will of God, to us, so that we might urge Titus that, as he had already made a beginning, so he should also complete this generous undertaking among you. Now as you excel in everything – in faith, in speech, in knowledge, in utmost eagerness, and in our love for you – so we want you to excel also in this generous undertaking.	Now it is not necessary for me to write you about the ministry to the saints, for I know your eagerness, which is the subject of **my boasting about you to the people of Macedonia, saying that Achaia has been ready since last year; and your zeal has stirred up most of them. But I am sending the brothers** in order that our boasting about you may not prove to have been empty in this case, so that you may be ready, as I said you would be; otherwise, if some Macedonians come with me and find that you are not ready, we would be humiliated – to say nothing of you – in this undertaking. **So I thought it necessary to urge the brothers to go on ahead to you, and arrange in advance for this bountiful gift that you have promised, so that it may be ready as a voluntary gift and not as an extortion.**
I do not say this as a command, but I am testing the genuineness of your love against the earnestness of others. For you know the generous act of our Lord Jesus Christ, that though he was rich, yet for your sakes he became poor, so that by his poverty you might become rich. And in this matter I am giving my advice: **it is appropriate for you who began last year not only to do something but even to desire to do something – now finish doing it**, so that your eagerness may be matched by completing it according to your means.	The point is this: the one who sows sparingly will also reap sparingly, and the one who sows bountifully will also reap bountifully. Each of you must give as you have made up your mind, not reluctantly or under compulsion, for God loves a cheerful giver. And God is able to provide you with every blessing in abundance, so that by always having enough of everything, you may share abundantly in every good work. As it is written, "He scatters abroad, he gives to the poor; his righteousness endures forever."
For if the eagerness is there, the gift is acceptable according to what one has – not according to what one does not have. I do not mean that there should be relief for others and pressure on you, but **it is a question of a fair balance between your present abundance and their need**, so that their abundance may be for your need, in order that there may be a fair balance.	He who supplies seed to the sower and bread for food will supply and multiply your seed for sowing and increase the harvest of your righteousness. You will be enriched in every way for your great generosity, which will produce thanksgiving to God through us; for the rendering of this ministry not only supplies the needs of the saints but also overflows with many thanksgivings to God.

288

As it is written, "The one who had much did not have too much, and the one who had little did not have too little." But thanks be to God who put in the heart of **Titus** the same eagerness for you that I myself have. For he not only accepted our appeal, but **since he is more eager than ever, he is going to you of his own accord. With him we are sending the brother who is famous among all the churches for his proclaiming the good news**; and not only that, but he has also been appointed by the churches to travel with us while we are administering this generous undertaking for the glory of the Lord himself and to show our goodwill. We intend that no one should blame us about this generous gift that we are administering, for we intend to do what is right not only in the Lord's sight but also in the sight of others.

Through the testing of this ministry you glorify God by your obedience to the confession of the gospel of Christ and by the generosity of your sharing with them and with all others, while they long for you and pray for you because of the surpassing grace of God that he has given you. Thanks be to God for his indescribable gift!

The above two chapters from 2 Corinthians contradict each other and cannot possibly belong to the same letter. How can Paul have told the Macedonians that the Corinthians collection has been ready since the previous year when he has just told them to finish what they started? His comments about Macedonia in the two chapters are also bizarre when juxtaposed. Further, we know that he has not yet been to Jerusalem for the second meeting, so no collection has been organized.

In 2 Cor. 1–9, we see a different letter, but still puzzling if it is supposed to be a follow-up to the letter that is said to consist of chapters 10–13; however, it does not appear that way to me at all. It seems that what Paul is referring to is the condemnation of an individual from within their congregation and not any 'opponents' as a group.

> We do not want you to be unaware, brothers and sisters, of the affliction we experienced in Asia; for we were so utterly, unbearably crushed that we despaired of life itself. Indeed, we felt that we had received the sentence of death so that we would rely not on ourselves but on God who raises the dead. He who rescued us from so deadly a peril will continue to rescue us; on him we have set our hope that he will rescue us again, as you also join in helping us by your prayers, so that many will give thanks on our behalf for the blessing granted us through the prayers of many. (2 Cor. 1:8-10)

> Since I was sure of this, I wanted to come to you first, so that you might have a double favor; I wanted to visit you on my way to Macedonia, and to come back to you from Macedonia and have you send me on to Judea. (2 Cor. 1:15-16)

> So I made up my mind not to make you another painful visit. For if I cause you pain, who is there to make me glad but the one whom I have pained? And I wrote as I did, so that when I came, I might not suffer pain from those who should have made me rejoice; for I am confident about all of you, that my joy would be the joy of all of you. **For I wrote you out of much distress and anguish of heart and with many tears**, not to cause you pain, but to let you know the abundant love that I have for you. **But if anyone has caused pain, he has caused it not to me, but to some extent – not to exaggerate it – to all of you. This punishment by the majority is**

enough for such a person; so now instead you should forgive and console him, so that he may not be overwhelmed by excessive sorrow. So I urge you to reaffirm your love for him. I wrote for this reason: to test you and to know whether you are obedient in everything. Anyone whom you forgive, I also forgive. What I have forgiven, if I have forgiven anything, has been for your sake in the presence of Christ. And we do this so that we may not be outwitted by Satan; for we are not ignorant of his designs. When I came to Troas to proclaim the good news of Christ, a door was opened for me in the Lord; but my mind could not rest because I did not find my brother Titus there. So I said farewell to them and went on to Macedonia. (2 Cor. 2:1-13)

We are putting no obstacle in anyone's way, so that no fault may be found with our ministry, but as servants of God we have commended ourselves in every way: through great endurance, in afflictions, hardships, calamities, beatings, imprisonments, riots, labors, sleepless nights, hunger; by purity, knowledge, patience, kindness, holiness of spirit, genuine love, truthful speech, and the power of God; with the weapons of righteousness for the right hand and for the left; in honor and dishonor, in ill repute and good repute. **We are treated as impostors, and yet are true; as unknown, and yet are well known**; as dying, and see – we are alive; **as punished, and yet not killed**; as sorrowful, yet always rejoicing; as poor, yet making many rich; as having nothing, and yet possessing everything. We have spoken frankly to you Corinthians; our heart is wide open to you. (2 Cor. 6:3-11)

Make room in your hearts for us; we have wronged no one, we have corrupted no one, we have taken advantage of no one. I do not say this to condemn you, for I said before that you are in our hearts, to die together and to live together. I often boast about you; I have great pride in you; I am filled with consolation; I am overjoyed in all our affliction. **For even when we came into Macedonia, our bodies had no rest, but we were afflicted in every way – disputes without and fears within.** But God, who consoles the downcast, consoled us by the arrival of Titus, and not only by his coming, but also by the consolation with which he was consoled about you, as he told us of your longing, your mourning, your zeal for me, so that I rejoiced still more. **For even if I made you sorry with my letter**, I do not regret it (though I did regret it, for I see that I grieved you with that letter, though only briefly). Now I rejoice, not because you were grieved, but because **your grief led to repentance**; for you felt a godly grief, so that you were not harmed in any way by us. So although I wrote to you, it was not **on account of the one who did the wrong, nor on account of the one who was wronged**, but in order that your zeal for us might be made known to you before God. (2 Cor. 7:2-12)

Clearly, the above letter refers to a previous letter of reproof of a particular individual. Was this the case of incest that was referred to in 1 Cor where a man was living with his father's wife and the Corinthians were told to expel him from their community?

It is actually reported that there is sexual immorality among you, and of a kind that is not found even among pagans; for a man is living with his father's wife. And you are arrogant! Should you not rather have mourned, so that he who has done this would have been removed from among you? For though absent in body, I am present in spirit; and as if present I have already pronounced judgment in the name of the Lord Jesus on the man who has done such a thing. When you are assembled, and my spirit is present with the power of our Lord Jesus, you are to hand this man over to Satan for the destruction of the flesh, so that his spirit may be saved in the day of the Lord. (1 Cor. 5:1-5)

So, there is clearly a letter still missing, and it also seems highly likely that redactional efforts are much of the cause of the confusing sequences. It appears to be quite possible that the 'collection' chapters were tacked onto letters where they did not belong at all, that the reference was inserted about going to Judea simply to confirm the idea that Paul was totally 'in' with the Jerusalem church so as to harmonize with Acts. Are the collection chapters and references even original to Paul, or have they been 'cooked up' to make it look like things were all hunky dory, even after the bust up in Antioch following the second Jerusalem visit?

If correct, this would date the writing of 2 Cor. 1-9, which was one letter, distinct from 2 Cor. 10-13, and would also give some idea of the itinerary of Paul at that time. That is, most or all of 1 and 2 Corinthians, and a third letter, must have been written between 43 and 46. But why then does he speak of the collection in 1 Cor. 16:1-2, where he also references the directions he gave to the churches in Galatia where the very negative events were to happen, which assuredly occurred *after* the second visit, at which time the alleged collection was supposedly initiated? If this is not from another letter written to the Corinthians after the events in question, then surely we are seeing here evidence of interpolation geared at harmonizing the letters with Acts' fake history and itinerary.

46 AD – 14 years after first visit, second visit to Jerusalem. Hand of fellowship, collection.

> Then after fourteen years I went up again to Jerusalem with Barnabas, taking Titus along with me. I went up in response to a revelation. Then I laid before them (though only in a private meeting with the acknowledged leaders) the gospel that I proclaim among the Gentiles, in order to make sure that I was not running, or had not run, in vain. But even Titus, who was with me, was not compelled to be circumcised, though he was a Greek. But because of false believers secretly brought in, who slipped in to spy on the freedom we have in Christ Jesus, so that they might enslave us – we did not submit to them even for a moment, so that the truth of the gospel might always remain with you. And from those who were supposed to be acknowledged leaders (what they actually were makes no difference to me; God shows no partiality) – those leaders contributed nothing to me. On the contrary, when they saw that I had been entrusted with the gospel for the uncircumcised, just as Peter had been entrusted with the gospel for the circumcised (for he who worked through Peter making him an apostle to the circumcised also worked through me in sending me to the Gentiles), and when James and Cephas and John, who were acknowledged pillars, recognized the grace that had been given to me, they gave to Barnabas and me the right hand of fellowship, agreeing that we should go to the Gentiles and they to the circumcised. They asked only one thing, that we remember the poor, which was actually what I was eager to do.
>
> But when Cephas came to Antioch, I opposed him to his face, because he stood self-condemned; for until certain people came from James, he used to eat with the Gentiles. But after they came, he drew back and kept himself separate for fear of the circumcision faction. And the other Jews joined him in this hypocrisy, so that even Barnabas was led astray by their hypocrisy. But when I saw that they were not acting consistently with the truth of the gospel, I said to Cephas before them all, "If you, though a Jew, live like a Gentile and not like a Jew, how can you compel the Gentiles to live like Jews?"(Gal. 2:1-14)

Keep in mind that the Qumran people referred to themselves as 'the poor,' and they were certainly connected to the Zealots in some way and were expecting the arrival of their messiah to eradicate the Romans.

The above is written as though Cephas came to Antioch very shortly after the second Jerusalem meeting and was getting on like a house afire with Paul and the gang until people came from James, and spoiled the party. It is what happened next that suggests that there is some connection between this event and the story about Stephen in Acts. That story, too, was about table fellowship in a sense. And the character, Stephen, sounds remarkably like Paul. In the story of Stephen, the Jews stone him to death – something unlikely to happen under Roman rule. Paul tells us:

> Are they [ministering] servants of Christ (the Messiah)? I am talking like one beside himself, [but] I am more, with far more extensive and abundant labors, with far more imprisonments, [beaten] with countless stripes, and frequently [at the point of] death. Five times I received from [the hands of] the Jews forty [lashes all] but one; Three times I have been beaten with rods; **once I was stoned**. Three times I have been aboard a ship wrecked at sea; a [whole] night and a day I have spent [adrift] on the deep; Many times on journeys, [exposed to] perils from rivers, perils from bandits, perils from [my own] nation, perils from the Gentiles, perils in the city, perils in the desert places, perils in the sea, perils from those posing as believers [but destitute of Christian knowledge and piety]; In toil and hardship, watching often [through sleepless nights], in hunger and thirst, frequently driven to fasting by want, in cold and exposure and lack of clothing.[788]

Perhaps it wasn't Saul/Paul standing around guarding garments, but rather being at the center of a controversy that raged out of control resulting in the arrests of James and Simon/Cephas later at Jerusalem?

47 AD – James and Simon, sons of Judas the Galilean and identified here as James and Simon/Peter of the Jerusalem church, executed by Tiberius Alexander. The apostles/Zealots scatter and go underground?

If they were both executed in this year, there are powerful reasons for the later church to alter documents to cover up this fact and completely remove the history of the early church from that of the Zealots and rebels against Rome. If Cephas (the pillar) and Peter (apostle to the Jews) are different persons, then perhaps the former was still in Antioch, escaped execution and took over the leadership of the Zealots. It may have been John, the third pillar, who took over the leadership at this point. These points require more study. There is a great deal of uncertainty, but what is certain is that there is a great deal we do not know because it has been deliberately covered up.

I have wondered quite a bit whether this John might have been John of Gischala, who was a leader of the Jewish revolt. The way Josephus writes about him makes it altogether likely that he was part and parcel of that same group referred to as 'robbers, pirates and brigands,' i.e. messianists. When Titus called on the people of Gischala to surrender, John apparently prevailed on him to wait until tomorrow because it was the Sabbath. During the night, John escaped to Jerusalem. Josephus writes disparagingly of him:

> John ... went about among all the people, and persuaded them to go to war, *by the hopes he gave them*. He affirmed that the affairs of the Romans were in a weak condition, and extolled his own power. He also jested upon the ignorance of the unskillful, as if those Romans, although they should take to themselves wings, could never fly over the wall of Jerusalem, who found such great difficulties in taking the villages of Galilee, and had broken their engines of war against their walls. These harangues of John's corrupted a great part of the young men, and puffed them up for the war. (*Wars* 4.126–28)

John played a major role in the Zealot siege of the Temple, following which he set himself up as ruler of Jerusalem. He was challenged by Simon Bar Giora in 69, and both of them were challenged by a third faction led by Eleazar ben Simon.

---

[788] 2 Corinthians 11:23-27.

Eleazar ben Simon was a Zealot, and we've already established that some Zealots were also Sicarii; the distinctions appear to have been rather permeable depending on Josephus' mood. Both adhered to a radical anti-Roman (or pro-Judea) policy and eradication of the moderate temple aristocracy from Jerusalem. It was the attitude and actions of the Zealots that prevented any peaceful agreement with Rome to avoid the death and destruction of Jerusalem in 70 AD. "Although the Jewish defeat at Jerusalem cannot be entirely attributed to Eleazar ben Simon, his inability to establish unity with John of Gischala and Simon bar Giora resulted in a bitter civil war that weakened the Jewish resistance against Rome."[789]

In any event, John of Gischala was finally captured by Titus during the Siege of Jerusalem. He was sentenced to life imprisonment, taken to Rome, and paraded in chains in the triumph of Vespasian and Titus (*Wars* 7).

Late 47, early 48 AD – Galatia crisis. Galatians written. While Paul refers to James, Cephas and John and their status as pillars in relation only to past events, and we hypothesize that James and Simon (Peter?) were executed, there is no notice of the death of John. Perhaps he 'scattered and went underground' to Gischala and was no longer a pillar in Jerusalem.

So it seems likely that, after the reprisals against the Zealots/Christians by Tiberius Alexander, two things must have happened. First, representatives from the Jerusalem church scattered, probably traveling around to all the various churches to drum up more support, including Paul's congregations, thereby creating the situation that caused Paul to write Galatians. Second, the authorities were also after the Zealots, so Paul may have been caught in the net. That would explain why he was in prison when he wrote Philippians, which has strong echoes of the Galatians agitation, and Paul is strongly warning his community to *not* get involved with those people!

49 AD – Paul made it as far as Ephesus before he was arrested. It may be that he was not arrested for his association with James and Simon, but rather that he was arrested because of his own activities. In any event, at this point, Paul wrote Romans because he knew he was being sent there.

Paul and the Jewish Christians

It is interesting to note that Paul identifies the Galatian agitators as Christian Jews, yet his theological argument is directed purely against Judaism, which suggests that the line between plain Jews[790] and Jewish Christians was almost non-existent and that the gospel of the Jerusalem Christians was more widely accepted among Jews than is usually thought by theologians who have not studied the historical and sociological context. Paul does not, apparently, regard the distinction between Christian and non-Christian Judaism as significant.

The Jewish elite initially resisted messianism because they were concerned about their standing with Rome, the source of their wealth and power. But Roman brutality eventually turned almost all Jews against Rome, and when the rebellion actually began, even the elite came over, hoping to retain their status in the event the rebellion succeeded. So, basically, it can be said that the Jews did accept the Jerusalem Christians' gospel of Judas the Galilean as Messiah, but their

---

[789]Wikipedia.org, 'Eleazar ben Simon.'

[790]I use the term 'Jews' loosely in this text with the proviso that Judaism was not a single, monolithic religion and 'Jews' was not yet a term used as I have done in this text for the sake of simplicity.

messiah never showed up! Thus, Paul was vindicated later. If Paul had been preaching the same messiah, he would have gone into oblivion along with the Jerusalem church.

Watson states that it is because of his experiences of Jewish rejection of the gospel and the Gentile openness to it that Paul reflected on the law of Moses in a polemic way – the law being the foundational document for the Jews and the gospel. Watson says that the Jews rejected the claim that the Messiah had come in the person of Jesus of Nazareth. However, as noted above, the real history shows that, in fact, the vast majority of Jews actually did accept the preaching of the Jerusalem Christians that the Messiah (identified as Judas the Galilean) was going to return with legions of angels – witness the hopeless revolt against Rome.[791]

Thus, if Paul experienced early rejection by Jews, it had to be because he was preaching more than a different gospel, but a different messiah altogether. Only after 70 AD was Jesus of Nazareth created by amalgamating Paul's Jesus with a stripped-down version of Judas the Galilean. It was Paul's 'Jesus' who was rejected by the Jewish Christians.

The following, from Watson, should be read while holding in view the previous discussion of Ashworth's interpretation of Paul; here further aspects are accounted for and fit quite well:

The theological argument of Galatians is characterized by its frequent use of antitheses, especially the fundamental antithesis between "faith" and "works" that has played such an important part in Western theology since the Reformation. According to the Reformation tradition, this antithesis portrays two possible human responses to God. The way of "works" is the way of morality and/or religious observance, in which one tries to please God and earn salvation by scrupulous obedience to God's commandments. The way of "faith" is the way of submission to God's grace, which comes to us as a sheer gift, quite apart from all moral attainment. ...

... [K]ey points in this theology are not there in Paul at all. For Paul, the expression "works (of law)" refers not to morality in general but to the practice of the law within the Jewish community; and the expression "faith (of Jesus Christ)" refers not to a willingness to receive God's grace as a free gift and to renounce reliance on one's own achievements, but to the Christian confession of Jesus as the Messiah and the social reorientation that this entails (Gal. 2:16). ... The antithesis between faith and works does not express a general theoretical opposition between two incompatible views of the divine-human relationship. Rather, it articulates the Pauline conviction that the church should be separate and distinct from the Jewish community. ...

The faith/works antithesis thus has only a limited function. ... [F]or Paul, faith includes within itself a commitment to Christian norms of behavior. From a sociological perspective, "faith" represents a radical social reorientation. It entails a breach with characteristic norms and beliefs of one's previous social environment, and the adoption of new norms and beliefs within a new social environment. The transition from the old to the new takes place in baptism. For Paul, faith is inconceivable without, for example, the abandonment of participation in idolatry (1 Thess. 1:9) or the practice of "love," i.e., commitment to the new community and its members (Gal. 5:6). It is not simply that these things *follow* from faith, so that one could theoretically distinguish them from faith. On the contrary, faith *is* the abandonment of old norms and beliefs and the adoption of new ones. ...

Faith for Paul is thus essentially active – an action enabled by the kerygma [proclamation]. There is no question of an antithesis between a passive reception of the gift of salvation followed by secondary active consequences. Paul can therefore state quite consistently that certain prohibited

---

[791] Keeping in mind Mason's analysis that it was not strictly a 'revolt against Rome' by the majority of Jews; at least, not at the beginning. Radical elements created a situation that required a response and the Zealot types apparently attached their cause to the situation, turning it into full-blown revolt in several areas.

forms of conduct prevent people from entering the kingdom of God (Gal. 5:21), and warn: "Do not be deceived; God is not mocked, for whatsoever a person sows, that he will also reap. For one who sows the flesh will from the flesh reap corruption; but one who sows to the spirit will from the spirit reap eternal life." (Gal 6:7-8) Paul is not contradicting himself when he makes salvation dependent here on one's behavior and elsewhere on the faith generated by God's saving act in Christ, for Christian conduct is integral to faith. The faith/works antithesis is not an antithesis between faith and morality-in-general but an antithesis between life as a Christian, with its distinctive beliefs and practices, and life as an observant Jew.[792]

Paul does not separate faith from ethics. Nor does he separate works from the context of the divine covenant with Israel. And this leads me to conclude that Paul's Christ couldn't have been founded on a nationalist Zealot. If there was a real person behind the myth, he must have been someone else. Because certainly, the whole concept of the Zealot gospel was that Jews had to become righteous *as* Jews in order to prepare the way for the coming of the Messiah/Son of Man with his legions of angels to destroy Rome and restore the Jews' autonomy, or even domination over all the nations.

For Paul, faith stands for the reorientation in its totality – a reorientation grounded in a prior divine action that is recognized by the individual and accepted as true. 'Faith' and 'works' stand as synecdoches for mutually exclusive cosmic schemes and human responses to same. Paul never meant faith as it was interpreted by the Reformation; you can't just 'believe in Jesus' and be 'saved.'[793]

Some have said that Paul opposed 'works' as external religious rites, sacramentalism, etc., in general. But that cannot be the case, because he instituted his own sacraments: the Eucharist and baptism. Thus it can be seen that Paul opposed circumcision because it represented entry and continuing membership in the Jewish religious community.

> Divine grace operates rather differently in the two "patterns of religion," and the divergent views correspond to the fact that membership of the Jewish community is dependent primarily on birth, whereas membership of a Pauline community is dependent on conversion. Any religious group that declares the necessity of conversion is likely to emphasize the distinction between the old life and the new. The old life is characterized by sin, ignorance, and death, and against this dark background the nature of the new life as a miraculous divine gift will shine out all the more brightly. Romans 5:12–6:23 is perhaps the clearest Pauline exposition of this viewpoint, which might also be illustrated from the Qumran *Hodayoth* ... Such groups take a *dynamic* view of God's grace, in contrast to the more *static* view of grace in groups where membership is determined by birth and upbringing. But this is by no means the same as the alleged Pauline contrast between salvation as a pure gift and salvation as human achievement. Even if, in some passages, Paul does stress the idea of the miraculous divine gift, in others he stresses the human activity through which the gift is appropriated. The first group of passages has the function of reinforcing the community's belief that it originates in a supreme act of creative and gracious divine agency. The second group of passages has the function of reinforcing the norms of conduct that give the group its identity. ...
>
> It is therefore correct to say, as E. P. Sanders does, that Paul opposes Judaism not because of any inherent errors such as "self-righteousness" or "legalism", but simply *because it is not Christianity.* ... The opposition of faith and works is contingent rather than necessary, concrete rather than abstract.[794]

---

[792]Watson (2007), pp. 121–23. Watson's italics.

[793]For a more comprehensive discussion of faith vs. works, see the appendix on Romans.

[794]Watson (2007), p. 126. Watson's italics.

All of the above strongly implies – even demands – that Paul was not preaching the Jewish messiah, Judas the Galilean as Jesus, but a very different Jesus anchored to a different historical personage. The reorientation to a new life is enabled by Paul's gospel message that there IS a savior for all humanity.

Faith, though undeniably a human action, is fundamentally oriented toward the divine action that it acknowledges.[795]

> Paul here [in Gal. 5:2-12] grounds his insistence on the incompatibility of allegiance to Christ with membership of the Jewish community not on further theological argumentation, but on his own apostolic authority: the two things are incompatible because he says they are. Once again, it is clear that Pauline antithesis *asserts* the separation of the church from the synagogue, but does not *explain* theologically why such a separation is necessary. Theological arguments for the church's distinct existence occur not in Paul's antitheses per se but in his reinterpretations of scriptural traditions.
>
> ... The [Galatian] agitators appear to have claimed that the promises of salvation were originally bestowed on Abraham and his seed and that the seed or children of Abraham are those who are circumcised and law observant. ... Thus their understanding of Christ is set in the framework of the Jewish community as a whole. For them, although no longer for Paul, Jesus is still a thoroughly and exclusively *Jewish* messiah.[796]

That is, Judas the Galilean as Jesus, who is coming post haste to destroy the Romans and establish the rule of the Jews over all nations. "If you want to get in on the ground floor as a world ruler and judge, get your circumcision now!"

Paul (in Galatians 3) reinterprets the scriptures, the question being 'who is the seed of Abraham?'

> Well then, does God supply you with the Spirit and work miracles among you by your doing the works of the law, or by your believing what you heard? Just as Abraham "believed God, and it was reckoned to him as righteousness," so, you see, those who believe they are the descendants of Abraham. And the scripture, foreseeing that God would justify the Gentiles by faith, declared the gospel beforehand to Abraham, saying, "All the Gentiles shall be blessed in you." For this reason, those who believe are blessed with Abraham who believed. For all who rely on the works of the law are under a curse; for it is written, "Cursed is everyone who does not observe and obey all the things written in the book of the law."[797]

Paul states that Abraham's 'seed' refers not to the Jewish people, but to those who are 'in Christ.' That is, Paul, in one stroke of the pen, disinherits the Jews. Scripture is reinterpreted to show that Gentile believers share in the 'blessing of Abraham' while the Jews are under a curse because they received the Law hundreds of years after Abraham, which *basically nullified their previous promise when they accepted the 'new rules.'* Not only that, but the law consists of two parts, blessings and curses, and the entire subsequent history of Israel stands under the shadow of the curse.

Paul argues that the law has nothing to do with the promise to Abraham because it was impossible for the divine will to change or be altered by the introduction of new stipulations

---

[795]Watson (2007), p. 129. See also: Engberg-Pedersen (2000).
[796]Watson (2007), p. 131. Watson's italics.
[797]Gal. 3:5-10.

(Gal. 3:15-18). Again, Paul's arguments are grounded in scripture: 1) the contrast between what was said to Abraham and what was said at Sinai (Deut. 27:26); 2) the unconditional promise to Abraham is said by Paul not to be related to the salvation of Jews, but an unconditional salvation tied to the coming of Christ, the true seed of Abraham (Gen. 22:18: "and by your offspring [seed] shall all the nations of the earth gain blessing for themselves, because you have obeyed my voice").

Paul additionally states that the law was a temporary phase that has to give way in order for the unconditional promise of salvation to be realized for all. Paul certainly concedes the law is the possession of the Jews, but he grounds the necessary separation of his church from the Jews in the fact that those who live under the law inevitably fall under its curses.

Watson states that Paul's radical reinterpretation of the traditional views of Abraham is solely designed to justify the separation of the Pauline congregations from the Jewish community. As we have seen from Ashworth, it was likely way more than that, but certainly Watson is correct about the sociological manifestations.

Regarding Paul's opponents in Galatia: it is clear that they are Christians and that their church exists wholly *within* the larger community of Jews. For them, Jerusalem is the place of the pillars of the church and the Jewish people as a whole. It is clear that Paul was arguing against a form of Christianity (the Jerusalem Jewish Christians) that was founded on continuous participation in the community of Jews, and that he was seeking to reform Judaism by evangelizing his version of the Messiah. Paul's critique of this group is focused on the incompatibility between Paul's Jesus and the Jesus of the Jerusalem Christians; the two forms of Christianity were clearly two entirely different conceptions.

In Galatians, Paul repeatedly asserts that circumcision and the law are utterly opposed to the cross of Christ. In Phil. 3:18-19, he says, "For many, of whom I have often told you and now tell you even with tears, live as enemies of the cross of Christ." Further, Paul's repeated assertions that the Jewish Christians' antagonism to the 'cross of Christ' (Gal. 2:21; 3:1; 5:11; 6:12-14; Phil. 3:18) was part and parcel of their gospel suggests either: 1) their Jesus died on a cross but his death was given no soteriological value; 2) their Jesus did not die at all and their entire gospel was based on a promise that a sky-man would come and restore Israel by destroying the Romans; 3) their Jesus died some other way than on a cross, as Josephus says about Judas the Galilean (i.e. burned alive); or 4) the Jerusalem Christians found Paul's gospel of the cross highly offensive for some other reason that the texts can no longer reveal due to redaction.

Watson sees Philippians as having been written from prison in Ephesus, prompted by the Galatian crisis and its aftermath, and he is undoubtedly correct. Was the Galatian crisis part of a multi-pronged attack against Paul and his work that resulted in his being imprisoned? Watson suggests that Philippians was written to warn the congregation of what had happened and that they, too, might be visited by such agitators. In other words, there is not an actual 'situation' there yet, but the Jerusalem Christians could arrive at any moment!

In Philippians, Paul refers to his opponents as 'dogs,' a pejorative Jewish term for Gentiles. Watson suggests that he is reversing the application: he, and his communities, are the 'new circumcision of the heart,' and the Jewish Christians headed up by the Jerusalem church are the 'dogs.'

Paul not only calls the Jerusalem Christians 'dogs,' he says that they have "minds set on earthly things" (Phil. 3:19), in contrast to Pauline communities where "citizenship is in heaven" (v. 20).

He excoriates them by saying, "Their god is in their belly, and they glory in their shame, with minds set on earthly things." Watson points out that 'shame' used in this context is a euphemism for genitals and that the 'god in their belly' remark is a similar euphemism, alluding to phallic cults that practiced various forms of genital mutilation and castration. In Gal. 5:11, Paul links circumcision with castration and forms of mutilation practiced by pagans, and here in Philippians, he is identifying circumcision with phallic worship. In other words, Paul is coming right out into open warfare against the Jerusalem Christians and saying that circumcision, signifying male membership in the Jewish community, is nothing other than castration, mutilation, and phallic worship! In short, Paul was really, really angry and had descended to downright dirty rhetoric. But, considering his opponents, the Zealots, and what was at stake, who can blame him? At the same time, who can blame the Jews for hating the Roman occupation? Everyone was between a rock and a hard place.

In any event, by means of these polemic attacks on Jewish Christianity, Paul is reinforcing Gentile stereotypes about Jews and circumcision that were common throughout the Empire at the time. He was working to create an unbridgeable gulf between the Jerusalem Christians and his own congregations. Watson writes: "He is probably referring to the [same] people who caused the Galatian crisis. Just as he had warned the Galatians during his first visit to beware of such people (Gal. 1:9), so he here indicates that he had repeatedly warned the Philippians of the possibility of their arrival."[798] And then, Paul repeats a liturgical hymn that was extremely unlikely to have had Zealot Christian origins, all things considered:

> Let the same mind be in you that was in Christ Jesus, who, though he was in the form of God, did not regard equality with God as something to be exploited, but emptied himself, taking the form of a slave, being born in human likeness. And being found in human form, he humbled himself and became obedient to the point of death – even death on a cross. Therefore God also highly exalted him and gave him the name that is above every name, so that at the name of Jesus every knee should bend, in heaven and on earth and under the earth, and every tongue should confess that Jesus Christ is Lord, to the glory of God the Father.[799]

Now, in chapter 45 of Isaiah, the chapter where God speaks to his anointed, Cyrus the Persian, it says:

> "I call you by your name, I surname you, though you do not know me. ... Does the clay say to him who fashions it, 'What are you making?' or 'Your work has no handles.' ... Will you question me about my children, or command me concerning the work of my hands? ... Turn to me and be saved all the ends of the Earth. For I am God, and there is no other. By myself I have sworn, from my mouth has gone forth in righteousness a word that shall not return: To me every knee shall bow, every tongue shall swear."[800]

Verbal and conceptual echoes of the Isaiah passage quoted above are found in several places in Paul's writing and, as noted before, Isaiah was important to Paul. It appears now that *there is a concentration of Isaianic thought in the liturgical passage from Philippians* quoted above, which

---

[798]Watson (2007), p. 146.
[799]Phil. 2:5-11.
[800]Isa. 45:4, 9, 11, 22-23.

gives the strong impression that Paul used just this material from Isaiah as justification for his 'Jesus' for a specific reason.[801]

Paul's liturgical text has strong echoes of the *Descent of Ishtar*, as well as incorporating ideas of the New Adam who did not yield to temptation and sin. What the passage also makes clear is that Paul's Christ was not originally named Jesus/Joshua as a man, but something else altogether. The name 'Jesus/Joshua,' or 'savior,' was given to him only after his death and return to heaven. It also seems clear that Paul's idea of resurrection probably did not include bodily resurrection at all.

Philippians 3:2-11 is designed to show that Jewish Christianity and Paul's Christianity are mutually exclusive. In Philippians, Paul emphasizes that his own life as a righteous Jew was worthless. Watson points out that this is not a contrast between two mutually exclusive principles (active achievement/works vs. passive submission/grace), but between two different communities. It strongly suggests two different conceptions of Christ, at the very least, and most likely, two different anchoring historical personages.

In Phil. 2:12, Paul writes: "Work your own salvation with fear and trembling" and then goes on to say (v. 13), "God is at work in you." That is, to Paul, concurrent human and divine work are both necessary to bring about salvation. Paul would have never countenanced the idea that faith alone saves. For Paul, faith means believing in his Christ and what that Christ stands for, which is the adoption of a new way of life exemplified by that Christ, and the social reorientation that such a change entails. Faith oriented toward Christ is not renunciation of self-work and personal spiritual achievement. Both are still required.

Righteousness and Paul

In Jewish usage, the righteous are those who are approved by God. There are very few of them and they are always sharply contrasted against a multitude of the unrighteous. This is because there are so many laws to keep, and righteousness is determined by how many of them a person can keep, how consistently, and well. Obviously, it is a real burden that no one can carry. In this system, divine agency is present only in the form of the gifts of the covenant and the law, the means by which God, long ago, established the *possibility* of righteousness for a community whose membership is dependent on birth. The emphasis is on human praxis, the response of obedience to a static situation.

Paul had a dynamic view of righteousness. Divine agency is powerfully present and operative in the life of the person who has accepted that possibility as real via the exemplary agent of Christ. In this dynamic interaction, the person who strives to conform to the norms of the Christian life is brought from the darkness of their former life into the experience of salvation. Thus, in Paul's statement, "the righteousness from God that depends on faith," righteousness is not human conduct, but the reaching down of divine grace to draw up and transform the person's life in the process of transformation from sin, darkness and death to salvation, light and

---

[801]See passages such as 42:1, 5-8; 45:1-25; 51:2-6) referring to Cyrus. It seems certain that Paul saw particular passages in Isaiah as applying to himself, such as Isaiah 49:1-6; 52:7, 13-15; 53:1-12, and so on. The 'Suffering Servant' chapter of Isaiah (Isa. 53) has long been assumed to be one of the models for the crucifixion of Jesus of Nazareth (i.e. the mythical Jesus), but based on many remarks made by Paul, it might be said that he took this as his own template and never applied it to his Christ Triumphant.

life. Active righteousness from God is concurrent with the active human participation of faith, i.e. accepting the exemplar of Christ and conforming to the Christian norms. Paul is emphatic about this process:

> Not that I have already attained or am already perfected, but I press on to lay hold of that for which Christ laid hold of me. My brothers and sisters, I do not consider that I have already laid hold of it. But one thing I do: forgetting what lies behind, and straining towards what lies ahead, I press on to the finishing line, for the prize of God's upward call in Christ Jesus.[802]

Faith is strenuous activity and isn't just 'believing.' The role of divine agency as the complement to human agency is far more emphatically asserted in Paul's Christianity, thus its total incompatibility with Judaism.

---

[802]Phil. 3:12-14. According to Engberg-Pedersen (2000), Paul is referring to the 'call' of God via Christ, which pulls up the believer toward Him – in this case Paul. This is achieved via the *pneuma* or spirit, a portion of which has entered into the bodies of the community of believers, and which will come in its full power at the *parousia* to transform their bodies into pneumatic/spiritual/heavenly bodies.

6. Ante-Bellum

Getting back to the history, Tiberius Alexander was succeeded by Ventidius Cumanus (48–52 AD) as procurator of Judea,[803] who, like Pilate and others before and after, was soon embroiled with various acts of Jewish resistance to Rome. An explosive atmosphere prevailed, and Jewish–Roman relations continued to deteriorate. According to Josephus, during the Passover festival, one of the Roman soldiers on duty on the roof of the Temple porch made an obscene gesture to the Jews assembled to worship below. Josephus actually describes the soldier as 'mooning' the Jews. The Jews then began to stone the soldiers, Cumanus sent in reinforcements, and apparently there was a massive slaughter. In *Wars* (2.12.1), Josephus says ten thousand; in *Antiquities* (20.5.3), he says twenty thousand. I suspect both figures to be highly exaggerated.

Not long after, an imperial servant was attacked and robbed. In *Wars*, Josephus blamed it on "brigands," but in *Antiquities*, it is "those disposed to revolt" who operated as brigands. By now, these words should be familiar. The Roman reaction was typical: the procurator sent troops to pillage the neighboring villages and arrest the leading inhabitants, holding them responsible for not preventing the attack. During this operation, a Roman soldier desecrated and burned a copy of the Torah. This immediately caused a widespread tumult and demands that the perpetrator be punished. The situation apparently became so menacing that Cumanus sacrificed the soldier and ordered his execution to appease the Jews.

Another incident under Cumanus: some Galileans traveling to Jerusalem were attacked and killed by the inhabitants of a Samaritan village. The Galileans appealed to Cumanus for justice, but he took no action. Josephus said he was paid off by the Samaritans.[804] At this point, the Galileans called on the Judean Jews to take arms on their behalf. The Jews called on one Eleazar, son of Deinaios, a brigand, who had a camp in the mountains. It's difficult to sort out when you have to keep in mind that Josephus is always embellishing or hiding things, but the gist of it is that the Zealots are revealed here as persons with experience in conducting guerrilla warfare against the Romans, and under Eleazar, the Jewish rebels attacked and massacred the inhabitants of a number of Samaritan villages.

Cumanus was now galvanized to action and went after the rebels, killing and capturing many, but the Zealots withdrew to their strongholds. Then Josephus adds a comment that from this time on, the whole of Judea became full of 'brigands.' That is, everyone was going over to the Zealots.

The Samaritan leaders appealed to the legate of Syria, Quadratus,[805] who came to investigate the situation in 52 AD. He ended up crucifying the prisoners taken by Cumanus, executed other

---

[803] A disagreement between Josephus and Tacitus makes it unclear whether his authority was over some or all of the region.

[804] See Mason (2016) for a more detailed and nuanced discussion of the problems between the Samaritans and Judeans.

[805] "Gaius Ummidius Durmius Quadratus ... was the first member of the Ummidii to reach the office of consul in his family, or a *homo novus*. Quadratus [was] Roman governor of Syria from ca. 50 until his death [ca. 60 AD]." (Wikipedia.org, 'Gaius Ummidius Durmius Quadratus.')

revolutionaries, and sent the high priests (Jonathan and Ananias) and the commander of the Temple (Ananus) in chains to Rome.[806]   Other Jewish and Samaritan leaders, together with Cumanus and a tribune named Celer, were also ordered before the emperor. Agrippa intervened and the Jews got a favorable decision: Cumanus was sent into exile and Celer was sent back to Judea to be publicly executed. After this, Felix succeeded to Cumanus' position, according to Josephus.

The situation above is actually not so simple, because Tacitus' version of the story (*Ann.* 12:45–54) cannot be reconciled with that of Josephus. According to the former, Felix and Cumanus were procurators *at the same time*, the one in Samaria and the other in Galilee. According to Tacitus, Quadratus himself sat in judgment upon Cumanus, and he expressly states that Quadratus was superior to the procurator in authority.

In any event, the stories go on and on leading up to the revolt, and ever-present are the 'brigands' or Zealots, the members of the early Jerusalem messianic church. Brandon notes:

> They probably called themselves, or were known to their compatriots as, *Kannā'im* or Zealots; some of them were actually led by descendants of Judas [the Galilean]. Josephus' concentration of attention on the steadily deteriorating relations of the Jews and their Roman masters does, indeed, give the impression that the conflict between the two *dominated the whole of Jewish life in Palestine*. But *there is no obvious reason for thinking that this impression does not correspond to the real situation*; for to the natural resentment of any subject people towards the unjust government of their foreign masters, there must be added the profound devotion of the Jews to their peculiar religion which logically envisaged Israel as a theocracy. From the standpoint of our own particular subject here, *this evidence of a fundamental detestation of the Romans on the part of the Jews must mean that the Jewish Christians would have shared in it, unless there is clear proof to the contrary.* The silence of Acts ... cannot be interpreted as proof of this kind. Indeed, all that we do know of the Jewish Christians during this period suggests that they would inevitably have been involved in such clashes with the Romans ...
>
> This conclusion must also be valid for the remaining years before the outbreak of the fatal revolt in A.D. 66. ... It began with the appointment of Antonius Felix (A.D. 52–60). ... According to Josephus, the whole land was now full of 'brigands' and 'impostors', who deceived the people. The association of these two categories is significant: it means, translating Josephus' tendentious terminology, that *the Zealots were connected with men who were reputed to be 'wonder workers'.* The nature of the wonders or miracles which these men claimed to work is evident ... from some examples cited by Josephus ... they were *signs portending divine intervention* ... Felix ... succeeded in capturing Eleazar, whom he sent to Rome, and he crucified many of his Zealot followers and the ordinary folk, who had supported them.[807]

After Felix, the new procurator of Judea was Porcius Festus, who was there probably around 59 to 62 AD, though the exact dates are not known. There was a change of coinage pointing to 59, so that may be as close as we get. Josephus writes:

---

[806]Recall that in his *Life*, Josephus claimed that, at 26 years of age (63 AD), he traveled to Rome on a diplomatic mission, to secure the release of some priests imprisoned by the procurator of Judea, Felix. It would appear that priests were very active as rebels.

[807]Brandon (1967), pp. 107–9. Mason (2016) takes a more prosaic view of the events that led to the war; surely, the truth must be somewhere in the middle?

Now it was that Festus succeeded Felix as procurator, and made it his business to correct those that made disturbances in the country. So he caught the greatest part of the robbers, and destroyed a great many of them.[808]

So much for what *Wars* does *not* say about the topic at hand: the death of Festus followed by the interregnum during which 'James the brother of Jesus' was executed. In *Wars*, Josephus just heads straight on to Albinus and his many crimes against the Jews. Of course, that's assuming that parts of *Wars* have not been redacted, which is highly unlikely; the evidence for redaction is too great.

According to Acts, it was around this time that Paul had gone to Jerusalem on his *third* visit, was arrested there and had his final hearing before Festus, who sent him to Rome. We now know that this was probably fiction, so can disregard it. In any event, around 62 AD, Festus died and Lucceius Albinus was sent to replace him. In between the time of the death of Festus and the arrival of Albinus, the high priest Ananus ben Ananus convened the Jewish Sanhedrin to try "James the brother of Jesus." *Antiquities* 20.9.1 says:

> And now [Nero], upon hearing the death of Festus, sent Albinus into Judea, as procurator; but the king deprived Joseph of the high priesthood, and bestowed the succession to that dignity on the son of Ananus, who was also himself called Ananus. ... But this younger Ananus ... was a bold man in his temper, and very insolent; he was also of the sect of the Sadducees, who are very rigid in judging offenders, above all the rest of the Jews, as we have already observed; when therefore, Ananus was of this disposition, he thought he had now a proper opportunity [to exercise his authority]. Festus was now dead, and Albinus was but upon the road; so he assembled the Sanhedrin of judges, and brought before them **the brother of Jesus, who was called Christ, whose name was James**, and some others [or some of his companions]; and when he had formed an accusation against them as breakers of the law, he delivered them to be stoned; but as for those who seemed the most equitable of the citizens, and such as were the most uneasy at the breach of the laws, they disliked what was done; they also sent to the king [Agrippa], desiring him to send to Ananus that he should act so no more, for that what he had already done was not to be justified; nay, some of them went also to meet Albinus, as he was upon his journey from Alexandria, and informed him that it was not lawful for Ananus to assemble a sanhedrin without his consent; whereupon Albinus complied with what they said, and wrote in anger to Ananus, and threatened that he would bring him to punishment for what he had done; on which king Agrippa took the high priesthood from him, when he had ruled but three months, **and made Jesus, the son of Damneus, high priest**.

Just like the other *Testimonia Flaviana*, this one has had a lot of ink spilled over it. What is significant about the above passage is the part where Josephus says that the "most equitable of the citizens" were so angered that they actually went to meet Albinus to tell him what had been done behind his back, so to say. It is thought that a Christian scribe would not have inserted "who was called the Christ" without adding more details, and the passage is otherwise so Josephan in character that it is thought to be authentic.

Obviously, that conclusion creates a lot of problems, since we know that Josephus considered messianic claimants – christs (though he never uses the word) – to be little more than brigands and deceivers. Also, recall that the name 'Jesus' was given to the messiah only upon the death of whoever he was, so we certainly are not looking for someone named Jesus in real life. Another

---

[808] *Wars* 2.14.1.

problem is that apparently eminent citizens were unanimous in their condemnation of the act and so strongly moved about it that they took hostile action against Ananus. So how can this be?

Origen, who cited Josephus numerous times in around 248 AD, gave an account of the death of James which said that one of the main causes of the destruction of Jerusalem was the murder of James. There is certainly nothing like that in our current texts. However, what Eusebius reported may indicate that he had a similar version.

Eusebius cited Hegesippus, who wrote:

> ... the more sensible even of the Jews were of the opinion that this (James' death) was the cause of the siege of Jerusalem, which happened to them immediately after his martyrdom for no other reason than their daring act against him. Josephus, at least, has not hesitated to testify this in his writings, where he says, 'These things happened to the Jews to avenge James the Just, who was a brother of Jesus, that is called the Christ. For the Jews slew him, although he was a most just man'.[809]

In describing James's alleged ascetic lifestyle, Eusebius, quoting Hegesippus again, wrote:

> James, the Lord's brother, succeeds to the government of the Church, in conjunction with the apostles. He has been universally called the Just, from the days of the Lord down to the present time. For many bore the name of James; but this one was holy from his mother's womb. He drank no wine or other intoxicating liquor, nor did he eat flesh; no razor came upon his head; he did not anoint himself with oil, nor make use of the bath. He alone was permitted to enter the holy place: for he did not wear any woollen garment, but fine linen only. He alone, I say, was wont to go into the temple: and he used to be found kneeling on his knees, begging forgiveness for the people-so that the skin of his knees became horny like that of a camel's, by reason of his constantly bending the knee in adoration to God, and begging forgiveness for the people.[810]

According to Hegesippus, the scribes and Pharisees came to James for help in putting down Christian beliefs.

> They came, therefore, in a body to James, and said: "We entreat thee, restrain the people: for they have gone astray in their opinions about Jesus, as if he were the Christ. We entreat thee to persuade all who have come hither for the day of the passover, concerning Jesus. For we all listen to thy persuasion; since we, as well as all the people, bear thee testimony that thou art just, and showest partiality to none. Do thou, therefore, persuade the people not to entertain erroneous opinions concerning Jesus: for all the people, and we also, listen to thy persuasion. Take thy stand, then, upon the summit of the temple, that from that elevated spot thou mayest be clearly seen, and thy words may be plainly audible to all the people. For, in order to attend the passover, all the tribes have congregated hither, and some of the Gentiles also." To the scribes' and Pharisees' dismay, James boldly testified that "Christ himself sitteth in heaven, at the right hand of the Great Power, and shall come on the clouds of heaven". The scribes and pharisees then said to themselves, "We have not done well in procuring this testimony to Jesus. But let us go up and throw him down, that they may be afraid, and not believe him." ...
>
>   So they [the scribes and Pharisees] went up and threw down the just man ... [and] began to stone him: for he was not killed by the fall; but he turned, and kneeled down, and said: "I beseech thee, Lord God our Father, forgive them; for they know not what they do."

---

[809] *Historia Ecclesiae* 2.23.
[810] *Historia Ecclesiae* 2.23.

And, while they were there, stoning him to death, one of the priests, the sons of Rechab, the son of Rechabim, to whom testimony is borne by Jeremiah the prophet, began to cry aloud, saying: "Cease, what do ye? The just man is praying for us." But one among them, one of the fullers, took the staff with which he was accustomed to wring out the garments he dyed, and hurled it at the head of the just man.

And so he suffered martyrdom; and they buried him on the spot, and the pillar erected to his memory still remains, close by the temple. This man was a true witness to both Jews and Greeks that Jesus is the Christ. And shortly after Vespasian besieged Judaea, taking them captive.[811]

That's an amazing and quite imaginative story. However, I think we find the creative inspiration for it right there in Josephus, dated just a bit later than the arrival of Albinus:

But the rage of the Idumeans [allies of the Zealots] was not satiated by these slaughters; but they now betook themselves to the city, and plundered every house, and slew every one they met; and for the other multitude, they esteemed it needless to go on with killing them, but they sought for the high priests, and the generality went with the greatest zeal against them; and as soon as they caught them they slew them, and then standing upon their dead bodies, in way of jest, upbraided Ananus with his kindness to the people, and *Jesus* [the oldest of the high priests] *with his speech made to them from the wall.*

Nay, they proceeded to that degree of impiety, as to cast away their dead bodies without burial, although the Jews used to take so much care of the burial of men, that they took down those that were condemned and crucified, and buried them before the going down of the sun. **I should not be wrong in saying that** *the capture of the city began with the death of Ananus*; and **that the overthrow of the walls and** *the downfall of the Jewish state dated from the day on which the Jews beheld their high priest, the captain of their salvation, butchered in the heart of Jerusalem.*

A man on every ground revered and of the highest integrity, Ananus, with all the distinction of his birth, his rank and the honours to which he had attained, had delighted to treat the very humblest as his equals. Unique in his love of liberty and an enthusiast for democracy, he on all occasions put the public welfare above his private interests. To maintain peace was his supreme object.[812]

Note that the name of the high priest is Ananus, the same as the name of the high priest alleged to have illegally executed James, the brother of Jesus. Notice also, Jesus, the eldest high priest who, earlier in the text of Josephus, *stood on the tower over the temple and gave a speech* obviously made up by Josephus, but a fine speech nonetheless! You can almost hear the whirring gears in the fertile mind of the creator of the fictional story of James.

So no, indeed, Josephus never attributed the destruction of Jerusalem to the death of any person named James, and I think the "who was called Christ" part of the James passage is an interpolation, perhaps carried on from a Christian scribal annotation. The simplest explanation for the passage in question is that Ananus executed a guy named James, brother of Jesus *son of Damneus.* After Ananus was removed from office, he was replaced with the deceased James' brother, Jesus.[813] As we already suspect, James brother of Judas had already been executed in 47 AD. But, as to the later stories about James, I think they were fictional creations out of the

---

[811] Hegesippus, *Commentaries on the Acts of the Church*, 'Concerning the Martyrdom of James, the Brother of the Lord,' Book 5, http://www.earlychristianwritings.com/text/hegesippus.html.

[812] *Wars* 4.5.2.

[813] See Carrier (2014), pp. 337–42.

fertile mind of a person who read the passages about Jesus and Ananus, high priests in Josephus, and used them to inspire his own creation for a 'brother' of Jesus "who was called Christ" because he had read in one of Paul's epistles about James, "The Lord's Brother." (As to whether there were two Jameses, one a brother of Judas the Galilean, and another James who was his son, I think it is quite possible, even likely.)

The Jewish War in Seven Paragraphs

In the year 66, Florus, the last Roman procurator, on orders from Nero, stole vast quantities of silver from the Temple (perhaps more than usual for a Roman procurator). The outraged Jewish masses rioted and wiped out the small Roman garrison stationed in Jerusalem. Judeans living in Caesarea were also massacred. Cestius Gallus, the Roman ruler in neighboring Syria, sent in a larger force of soldiers, burning Judean villages along the way. But the Jewish insurgents attacked them as well.[814]

It was very unfortunate that the Jews defeated Cestius, because it gave them a false sense of invincibility; they felt that God was protecting Jerusalem and the Temple and thus their cause would succeed. Many more Jews came over to the side of the Zealots and their messianic claims, including many of the upper elite classes. It can be said that the Jews did *not* reject or kill *their* messiah; in fact, they believed in him so fervently that they made war against the Romans in expectation of his arrival and were nearly entirely destroyed in the process; the Messiah never came with 12 legions of angels.

When the Romans finally returned seeking vengeance for Cestius, as the Jews knew they would, they had 60,000 heavily armed and highly professional troops. Vespasian entered Palestine at the north and worked his way south laying waste to everything in his path that offered resistance (many surrendered, wanting no part in the war). He launched his first attack against the Jewish state's most radicalized area, Galilee. The Romans vanquished the Galilee, and an estimated 100,000 Jews were killed or sold into slavery.

The Zealot Christian refugees who escaped the Galilean massacres (including John of Gischala) fled to Jerusalem. There, they killed anyone in the Jewish leadership who was not as radical as they. Thus, all the more moderate Jewish leaders who headed the Jewish government at the revolt's beginning in 66 were dead by 68 – and not one died at the hands of a Roman; all were killed by fellow Jews.

The scene was now set for the revolt's final catastrophe. Outside Jerusalem, Roman troops prepared to besiege the city; inside the city, the Jews were engaged in a suicidal civil war. In later generations, the rabbis declared that the revolt's failure, and the Temple's destruction, was due not to Roman military superiority but to hatred among the Jews (*Yoma* 9b). While the Romans would have won the war in any case, the Jewish civil war both hastened their victory and immensely increased the casualties. One horrendous example: in expectation of a Roman siege, Jerusalem's Jews had stockpiled a supply of dry food that could have fed the city for many years. But one of the warring Zealot factions burned the entire supply, apparently hoping that destroying this 'security blanket' would compel everyone to participate in the revolt, which would

---

[814]What follows is a mostly standard retelling of the major events of the war. For a nuanced account that challenges much of it, see Mason (2016).

hasten the coming of the Messiah. The starvation resulting from this mad act caused suffering as great as any the Romans inflicted.

We do know that some eminent Jews opposed the revolt, most notably Rabbi Yochanan ben Zakkai. Since the Zealot leaders ordered the execution of anyone advocating surrender to Rome, Rabbi Yochanan arranged for his disciples to smuggle him out of Jerusalem, disguised as a corpse. Once safe, he personally surrendered to the Roman general Vespasian, who later granted him concessions that allowed Jewish communal life to regroup and continue after the war.

During the summer of 70, the Romans breached the walls of Jerusalem and initiated an orgy of violence and destruction that has seldom been equaled in the history of ancient warfare. Shortly thereafter, they destroyed Herod's magnificent Temple. This was the final and most devastating Roman blow against Judea. And, as noted above, Josephus wrote:

> I should not be wrong in saying that the capture of the city began with the death of Ananus; and that the overthrow of the walls and the downfall of the Jewish state dated from the day on which the Jews beheld their high priest, the captain of their salvation, butchered in the heart of Jerusalem.[815]

Tacitus Fragment 2

Above I've discussed the well-known reference to 'Christians' (or, more properly, 'Chrestians') in Tacitus (*Ann.* 15.44), where Nero blamed them for the fire and it was noted that, based on his description, they were definitely not Pauline Christians. There is also something known as Tacitus' Fragment 2, which is now widely considered to be a part of the lost portion of Tacitus' fifth book of his *Histories*. This fragment was preserved/cited by the Christian historian Sulpicius Severus in his *Chronica* (2.30.6–7) (c. 400–403 AD). It seems to confirm that *Christiani* was the Latin name for a group of major participants in the Jewish War against Rome and that Titus deliberately destroyed the Temple to cripple Judaism and eliminate the base of operations of this group because they were dangerous rebels. The relevant portion reads as follows:

> It is reported that Titus first deliberated, by summoning a council of war, as to whether to destroy a Temple of such workmanship. For it seemed proper to some that a consecrated Temple, distinguished above all that is human, should not be destroyed, as it would serve as a witness to Roman moderation; whereas its destruction would represent a perpetual brand of cruelty.
>
> But others, on the contrary, disagreed – including Titus himself. They argued that the destruction of the Temple was a number one priority *in order to destroy completely the religion of the Jews and the Christiani.* For although these religions are conflicting, they nevertheless developed from the same origins. The Christiani arose from the Jews: with the root removed, the branch is easily killed.

The scholars are still arguing over this text (and have been for a long time), but it looks more and more as though it is going to be accepted as authentically Tacitean. It's a pretty damning statement about early Jewish Christianity, confirming that they were little more than messianic rebels.

So, as just noted, apocalyptic expectations were rife. Paul's letters and the Gospels derived from them, in part, reveal abundant evidence of the conviction that the then present world

---

[815] *Wars* 4.5.2.

order was going to end, to be replaced by the 'Kingdom of God.' But there appears to be a big difference between how the Zealot messianists expected this to transpire, and its result, and how the Apostle Paul saw it manifesting and its meaning for all humanity. Again, these very sharp differences are such that it becomes impossible to think that they were even about the same messianic figure.

Sicarii, Zealots, Christians by Any Other Name

In both of his accounts, *Wars* and *Antiquities*, Josephus blames the war against Rome on the pernicious influences of robbers, pirates, Sicarii, Zealots, brigands, and so on. In his account of the events leading up to the war, Josephus tells us about a certain Manahem:

> In the meantime, one Manahem, the son of Judas, that was called the Galilean, (who was a very cunning sophister, and had formerly reproached the Jews under Cyrenius, that after God they were subject to the Romans,) took some of the men of note with him, and retired to Masada, where he broke open king Herod's armory, and gave arms not only to his own people, but to other robbers also. These he made use of for a guard, and *returned in the state of a king to Jerusalem;* he became the leader of the sedition.[816]

The term "cunning sophister" has also been translated as "redoubtable doctor of the law." And notice that Manahem "returned in the state of a king." Just what was it about the family of Judas the Galilean, and was he related to Simon of Perea who declared himself king after Herod was dead? By what right – excluding, of course, Josephus' ridiculous explanation that he was just a greedy brigand or some such words – did they have such lofty aspirations and acclamations?

In describing the last stand at Masada of the Sicarii, we learn that their leader was Eleazer, also a descendant of Judas the Galilean:

> When Bassus was dead in Judea, Flavius Silva succeeded him as procurator there; who, when he saw that all the rest of the country was subdued in this war, and that there was but one only stronghold that was still in rebellion, he got all his army together that lay in different places, and made an expedition against it. This fortress was called Masada. It was one *Eleazar, a potent man, and the commander of these Sicarii,* that had seized upon it. He was *a descendant from that Judas* who had persuaded an abundance of the Jews, as we have formerly related, not to submit to the taxation *when Cyrenius was sent* into Judea to make one ...[817]

Above, we had a "Manaem, *son of Ioudas*," who withdrew to Masada in 66, and now, in 73, we have an Eleazar also descended from Judas. (As noted previously, "descendant" probably means grandson in this case.)

Even though Josephus chose to blame Judas and his influence for the disasters that befell the Jews, it is most peculiar that he never writes about him in a *personally* hostile or condemnatory way. He refers to him as 'learned,' 'teacher,' and a word that can be translated as 'terrible,' 'strange,' 'powerful.' Brandon writes:

---

[816] *Wars* 2.17.8.
[817] *Wars* 7.8.1 (252–4).

... Judas obviously conceived of Israel as a theocracy [Kingdom of God], and he was prepared to face the practical consequences of that conception, namely, to refuse to recognize and support the alien power that had possessed itself of Judaea, the holy land of Yahweh. Moreover, as a teacher of his people, he felt obliged to make clear to them the religious significance of their act, if they paid tribute to Rome. ... Such a description of Judas and his teaching, brief though it is, is sufficient to show that the party or movement which he founded was essentially religious in inspiration and purpose.[818]

The influence of Judas the Galilean must have been formidable, since Josephus looks back at him some seventy years later and designates him as a significant political figure who influenced events right down to Josephus' own day.

Despite the fact that he describes Judas the Galilean and his 'Fourth Philosophy,' he still fails to name the group. Only at the end of *Wars* does he call Eleazer, the leader of the resistance at Masada, one of the *Sicarii*, and informs us that he was a descendant of Judas. He had earlier described the Sicarii as beginning during the procuratorship of Felix (52–60 AD). In that passage he described a new kind of brigand who killed their victims in public by stabbing them with short daggers concealed in their robes. The first to be killed in this way was the high priest Jonathan.

There is an echo of the Sicarii in Acts 21:37-38: the Roman captain of the Antonia garrison mistakes Paul for a certain Egyptian messianic pretender who had led 4,000 Sicarii out into the wilderness at about that time.[819] And we cannot forget that two of the mythical Jesus' disciples are named 'Simon the Zealot' and 'Judas the Sicarii.' Maybe they weren't mythical persons, though they were placed in a mythical story. The ultimate irony of the Gospel of Mark may have been that he named the betrayer of Paul's Christ after the authentic Jewish Christian messiah.

The fact that Josephus refers to the followers of Judas via his descendant, Eleazer, as Sicarii, tells us that he considered them 'brigands,' so we should always be alert to this concealing mechanism whenever we encounter such terms in his writings. And that, of course, reminds us of Herod and his murder of Hezekiah/Ezekias, the alleged leader of a band of robbers making things difficult for Sextus Caesar. How much more was there to that story that we will never know? If he was the father (or grandfather) of Judas the Galilean who was hailed as a celebrated rabbi, Hezekiah is unlikely to have been an illiterate bandit. We are also curious about Simon of Perea, said by Josephus to be a 'servant of Herod,' who made himself king and created such a stir that even Tacitus commented on it. Simon was "going about with the bandits." So again, who was this Simon really, and how might he have been connected to Judas the Galilean? Since there is such a span of time between Hezekiah the bandit and Judas the Galilean, said to be his son, is it possible that Judas was actually the grandson of Hezekiah and son of Simon who was

---

[818]Brandon (1967), p. 32.

[819]Mason (2002), p. 292 (see also pp. 251ff.), argues from several lines of evidence that Luke used Josephus, including a litany of significant characters and events present in both works: "Agrippa's death after his robes shone; the extramarital affairs of both Felix and Agrippa II; the harshness of the Sadducees toward Christianity; the census under Quirinius as a watershed event in Palestine; Judas the Galilean as an arch rebel at the time of the census; Judas, Theudas, and the unnamed 'Egyptian' as three rebels in the Jerusalem area worthy of special mention among a host of others; Theudas and Judas in the same piece of narrative; the Egyptian, the desert, and the sicarii in close proximity; Judaism as a philosophical system; the Pharisees and Sadducees as philosophical schools; and the Pharisees as the most precise of the schools. We know of no other work that even remotely approximated Josephus's presentation on such a wide range of issues."

slain in the desert not long after the death of Herod? Did everyone in this family think they were entitled to kingship?

Certainly, throughout this time – the 60 to 70 years leading up to the war against Rome – there were many groups of real brigands, which always spring up like mushrooms after a rain in times of political turmoil. It is also evident that this term and related words were Josephus' favored designations for any group that resisted the established order. And yet, it is still evident from Josephus' record that Judas the Galilean stood out from all of them and founded and inspired a resistance movement against the Roman occupation based on the most intensely Jewish of ideals; its members saw it as their duty to God to act with violence against both the Romans and those Jews who cooperated with them. They were also ready to sacrifice their own lives for their beliefs.

However, it should also be obvious that those persons concerned with peace and just getting on with life would not have any appreciation for suicidal idealism or violent actions that threatened security. The upper classes, the aristocracy, members of the Herodian family and their numerous dependents, would also find such fanatical idealism threatening. Thus we can understand why Josephus was so critical of the 'brigands.' By using such terms he was able to sidestep calling them by the name they used to refer to themselves: Zealots, and the name that others used to refer to them: messianists, or Christians.

Josephus does use the name – he could not have avoided doing so – but he does so without explicitly connecting it to the followers of Judas the Galilean. His first mention of them comes in *Wars* 2.22.1:

> In Hierosolyma [Jerusalem], Ananus the high priest and also those of the powerful [men] who were not wise concerning the Romans were readying the wall and many of the war engines. Throughout the entire city, while arrows and full armor were being forged, the mass of the youth were in regular exercises, and everything was full of clamor. The despondency of the reasonable [fold] was terrible: many could see in advance, and loudly bewailed, the calamities that were about to occur. Divine omens were full of foreboding among the lovers of peace, but among those who had kindled the war they were being improvised at their pleasure, and the condition of the city before the Romans' attacking was that of [a place] about to be completely destroyed. Ananus nonetheless had the intention of bending the insurgents and **the recklessness of the so-called Zealots** to the more advantageous course, as he gradually sidelined the preparations for war; but he succumbed to the violence. In what follows we shall detail the sort of end that befell him.[820]

And then, in 7.8.1, he gives a summary of the various rebel factions. After his introduction of Flavius Silva and Eleazar, already quoted above, Josephus continues:

> ... for then it was that the Sicarii got together against those that were willing to submit to the Romans, and treated them in all respects as if they had been their enemies, both by plundering them of what they had, by driving away their cattle, and by setting fire to their houses; for they said that they differed not at all from foreigners, by betraying, in so cowardly a manner, that freedom which Jews thought worthy to be contended for to the utmost, and by owning that they preferred slavery under the Romans before such a contention. Now this was in reality no better than a pretense and a cloak for the barbarity which was made use of by them, and to color over their own avarice, which they afterwards made evident by their own actions; for those that were

---

[820]Mason translation, pp. 417–18.

partners with them in their rebellion joined also with them in the war against the Romans, and went further lengths with them in their impudent undertakings against them; and when they were again convicted of dissembling in such their pretenses, they still more abused those that justly reproached them for their wickedness. And indeed that was a time most fertile in all manner of wicked practices, insomuch that no kind of evil deeds were then left undone; nor could any one so much as devise any bad thing that was new, so deeply were they all infected, and strove with one another in their single capacity, and in their communities, who should run the greatest lengths in impiety towards God, and in unjust actions towards their neighbors; the men of power oppressing the multitude, and the multitude earnestly laboring to destroy the men of power. The one part were desirous of tyrannizing over others, and the rest of offering violence to others, and of plundering such as were richer than themselves. They were the Sicarii who first began these transgressions, and first became barbarous towards those allied to them, and left no words of reproach unsaid, and no works of perdition untried, in order to destroy those whom their contrivances affected.

Yet did **John [of Gischala]** demonstrate by his actions that these Sicarii were more moderate than he was himself, for he not only slew all such as gave him good counsel to do what was right, but treated them worst of all, as the most bitter enemies that he had among all the Citizens; nay, he filled his entire country with ten thousand instances of wickedness, such as a man who was already hardened sufficiently in his impiety towards God would naturally do; *for the food was unlawful that was set upon his table, and he rejected those purifications that the law of his country had ordained*; so that it was no longer a wonder if he, who was so mad in his impiety towards God, did not observe any rules of gentleness and common affection towards men.

Again, therefore, what mischief was there which **Simon the son of Gioras** did not do? Or what kind of abuses did he abstain from as to those very free-men who had set him up for a tyrant? What friendship or kindred were there that did not make him more bold in his daily murders? For they looked upon the doing of mischief to strangers only as a work beneath their courage, but thought their barbarity towards their nearest relations would be a glorious demonstration thereof. The Idumeans also strove with these men who should be guilty of the greatest madness! For they [all], vile wretches as they were, cut the throats of the high priests, that so no part of a religious regard to God might be preserved; they thence proceeded to destroy utterly the least remains of a political government, and introduced the most complete scene of iniquity in all instances that were practicable; **under which scene that sort of people that were called zealots grew up,** and who indeed corresponded to the name; for they imitated every wicked work; nor, if their memory suggested any evil thing that had formerly been done, did they avoid zealously to pursue the same; and **although they gave themselves that name from their zeal for what was good, yet did it agree to them only by way of irony,** on account of those they had unjustly treated by their wild and brutish disposition, or as thinking the greatest mischiefs to be the greatest good.

Accordingly, they all met with such ends as God deservedly brought upon them in way of punishment; for all such miseries have been sent upon them as man's nature is capable of undergoing, till the utmost period of their lives, and till death came upon them in various ways of torment; yet might one say justly that they suffered less than they had done, because it was impossible they could be punished according to their deserving. But to make a lamentation according to the deserts of those who fell under these men's barbarity, this is not a proper place for it. I therefore now return again to the remaining part of the present narration.

Note the rebel leader John of Gischala and how he was described as abandoning the laws of Judaism both in regards to food and purifications. Since John of the Jerusalem pillars was no doubt a Zealot, they were probably not the same person – unless something had changed or Josephus was just slinging slander. A remark by Origen cited by the church father Jerome said that the Apostle Paul actually came from Gischala in Upper Galilee.[821] Was this John a convert of Paul's? Or a deadly enemy? Louis Feldman writes:

> As for the impiety of which Josephus accused (John of Gischala), it stems to some extent from the fact that John, like many others, gave a favorable interpretation to the Scriptural prophecies, whereas Josephus saw them as foretelling the ruin of Jerusalem.[822]

Notice also that Josephus seems to say that it was at the time of the census in 6 AD that the *"Sicarii got together."*[823]

It's really almost impossible to recite the history of the Jews' war against Rome in any simple way, because it was just a mess of rivalries and conflicting interests that had been simmering for many years. Josephus' sarcasm about the Sicarii and Zealots above shows how deeply they agitated him and how desperately he needed to denigrate them and *their claim to righteousness.* Josephus was regarded by his own people as a traitor, a turncoat, a coward, and even the record of the war he was writing was being done as a servant and sycophant of the Romans who had crushed his people and destroyed the temple of their god. Yes, as Brandon says, the name 'Zealot' was a claim that was justified and Josephus had to denigrate it.

Josephus' apologetic concerns are, of course, suspect, especially relating to his own conduct during the war. He apparently clashed with the Zealots, who suspected him of being not fully committed to resistance against Rome.[824] They were correct; he went over to the Romans. In his writings he appears to have had two main themes to propound. First, to excuse his people to his Gentile readers, whose natural antipathy to the Jews had been amplified to an extreme degree by their ferocious behavior during the war. To this end, he depicted them as the hapless dupes of evil fanatics who played upon their superstitious fears, thus leading them to their doom. Second, to excuse his Roman masters from responsibility for the destruction of the Temple and the general brutal conduct they exhibited toward the Jews for over 60 years leading up to the war.

Despite the fact that Josephus loaded blame on the Zealots (by whatever name he was calling them at any given point in his text), he still comes across as curiously ambivalent about the founder and leader of the sect and other members of that fanatical family. He frequently praises his fellow Jews to the skies for their willingness to die rather than transgress their laws, so he certainly could not have failed to admire those who actually did give their lives for their belief that only Yahweh might be sovereign over Israel. And yet, his logical assessment of their chances of succeeding combined with his own drive for self-preservation demanded that he describe them as madmen, bandits, brigands and deceivers of the masses.

When he was writing *Wars*, Josephus had a difficult and dangerous task before him. Passions excited by the conflict were still inflamed and angry, and Jews were the targets of much blame and opprobrium. Over fifteen years later, when he wrote *Antiquities*, the political situation had

---

[821] Jerome, *In epist. ad Philem.* 23, *De viris inlustr.* 5.

[822] Feldman and Hata (eds.), *Josephus, the Bible, and History* (Wayne State University Press, 1989), p. 234

[823] Mason (2016), p. 255, argues that this is just a misreading of an ambiguous text, and that after a digression, he merely returns to speaking of the lead-up to the war. If so, that would only imply that the cloaked-dagger method of assassination only sprung up at that time. It does not imply that violent or revolutionary elements didn't exist beforehand.

[824] *Life* 363.

moved on and Josephus himself could look at things with a bit more detachment. Still, one has to remember that he is often covering up as much as he reveals.

In any event, the facts are that the Jerusalem church depicted in the letters of Paul, which are the earliest Christian documents, was eclipsed in that long dark tunnel of obscurity before the appearance of Marcion. But, in the meantime, there was the Gospel of Mark, clearly a product of a Pauline Christian. And to that I now turn.

7. Paul and The Gospel of Mark

> Within any text are embedded a myriad of conscious and unconscious relationships to historical and contemporary events, people, and other texts that are likewise connected historically and contemporaneously.[825]

The Gospel of Mark is a puzzling mystery. On the one hand, it is a literary Rubik's Cube written by a rhetorician of obviously great ability, but on the other hand, it is composed in the language of the common people. It is a composition utilizing mimesis[826] and intertextuality,[827] woven in a dizzying ring composition utilizing chiasmus[828] and antimetabole,[829] with nests nested within nests within nests. The more I study it, and the works of a number of Markan scholars, the more I shake my head in amazement. Michael Turton writes about Mark's Gospel:

> There's something about the Gospel of Mark. Matthew instructs, Luke pleases, John drones, but Mark? Mark obsesses. People dive into Mark and emerge for air, months later, not certain what happened to them, and wondering who strangers living in their house are. You know you've been reading Mark too long when you look at the description of the Gerasene Demoniac in chains, and wonder if it might not be a sly parody of Paul in chains in Ephesus …
>
> After many months of interacting with the Gospel of Mark, all I can say is that its writer was one of the great literary geniuses of history. He makes nothing plain and demands that the reader do the hard work of going back to the documents he has sourced to refract what he has written through what the reader discovers in his sources. He invites broad interpretation, and eludes easy pigeon-holing. He has a tricksy sense of humor that laughs at the reader, loves irony and can't get enough of it. His work is carefully composed and structured, yet elucidating the structures is often difficult. He toys with you: the writer of Mark is the masked lady who invites you to follow her out

---

[825]Eve-Marie Becker, *Mark and Matthew II*, edited by Eve-Marie Becker and Anders Runesson (Tübingen: Mohr Siebeck, 2013), from the introduction.

[826]"Mimesis, or imitation (imitatio), was a widely used rhetorical tool in antiquity … Mimesis criticism looks to identify intertextual relationships between two texts that go beyond simple echoes, allusions, citations, or redactions. The effects of imitation are usually manifested in the later text by means of distinct characterization, motifs, and/or plot structure. … From the late first century BCE/early first century AD, Dionysius of Halicarnassus represents a change from the Aristotelian rhetorical notion of mimesis, from imitation of nature to imitation of literature. His most important work in this respect, *On Mimesis…*, survives only in fragments. Apparently, most of this work concerned the proper selection of literary models." (Wikipedia.org, 'Mimesis criticism.')

[827]"Intertextuality is the shaping of a text's meaning by another text. It is the interconnection between similar or related works of literature that reflect and influence an audience's interpretation of the text. Intertextuality is the relation between texts that are inflicted by means of quotations and allusion. Intertextual figures include: allusion, quotation, calque, plagiarism, translation, pastiche and parody." (Wikipedia.org, 'Intertextuality.')

[828]"Chiasmus is a rhetorical device in which two or more clauses are balanced against each other by the reversal of their structures in order to produce an artistic effect." (Literarydevices.net, 'Chiasmus.') For example: "Never let a Fool Kiss You or a Kiss Fool You."

[829]"An antimetabole is the repetition of words in consecutive clauses, but in an inverted or transposed order. For example: 'You forget what you want to remember, and you remember what you want to forget.'" (Literarydevices.net, 'Chiasmus.')

of Carnival in Venice down back alleys to a secret rendezvous, only to deliver you into the hands of kidnappers ...[830]

The text of the Gospel of Mark is not impressive on its face. The Greek often appears awkward and was smoothed out by later writers who used Mark as a source text. Events occur without apparent reason, in fulfillment of a design not clearly expressed in the text. Characters pop into existence for a verse or two, then fade away. Many Markan locations do not appear to have existed at the time the Gospel was written, and the travels of Jesus in Mark sometimes seem to run counter to common sense. All this is [exacerbated] by the numerous emendations made to the text by scribes who tried to alter what they perceived as Markan errors and misunderstandings. The writer of Mark manages to combine ambiguity, plainness, dynamism, inevitability, pathos, and irony in a way that has spawned numerous scholarly interpretations of his Gospel, none of which have managed to attract a very large following.

   Despite this, the brief Gospel of Mark, just 16 short chapters accounting for 25 or so pages in English, is perhaps the single greatest piece of literature ever written. The other canonical gospel writers all incorporated the Gospel of Mark into their own works, giving it tremendous influence over the subsequent history of the West, and later, of the world. In our own era the Jesus of Mark appears in many writings, from science fiction novels like *The Stars My Destination* to literary works like *Slaughterhouse-5*. Over the last two centuries, as scholars began to recognize the importance of the Gospel of Mark to the development of the Christian canon, scholarly interest in the Gospel has grown exponentially. Exegetes have come to realize the brilliance and complexity of its composition while at the same time puzzling over the many enigmas it poses.[831]

Many past studies of Matthew and Luke reveal that they most definitely used Mark; Mark was first. Matthew was apparently aware of the rhetorical structures of the text; he sometimes utilizes similar forms in his modifications, making a new chiasmus, other times he breaks them deliberately because he apparently didn't like what was being said, and sometimes he creates his own entirely new structures. It is in examining how he has handled the text in these ways that one can be certain that he was using Mark, more or less as we have it, and not the other way around. Luke is more ham-handed even if he writes more elegantly. He breaks Mark's structures with abandon and only rarely does he create new or otherwise complex rhetorical structures, though he certainly adds new, creative story material.

When a person first reads Mark, it is usually after reading Matthew, and the impression is that Mark is just a quick and dirty synopsis of Matthew made on the fly. That impression is very, very misleading. As I said, Mark is a literary Rubik's Cube, and it was first. Nevertheless, many Christians will still insist that Matthew was first because they have been programmed to believe this by its placement in the New Testament, and by their belief that Matthew was actually written by a disciple of Jesus of Nazareth. Just to give an idea of that kind of argumentation, consider the following from one online Christian blog:

Modern Biblical scholarship seems to be overwhelmingly in the position that the first gospel to be written was Mark. The primary reason for this claim is that they believe Matthew used Mark as a basis. This, in effect, is saying that a direct apostle of Christ used a non-apostles' writing on which to base his own narrative. ...
   Proponents of the Markian theory also overwhelmingly overlap with those claiming a source Q gospel that was in circulation before the writing of any gospel. This suggests that the writers of

---

[830]http://www.michaelturton.com/Mark/GMark_myintro.html.
[831]https://www.michaelturton.com/Mark/GMark_intro.html.

the Gospels were not first or second hand witnesses but basing their writings on a mysterious list of sayings, one never mentioned by anyone in antiquity. Additionally, those advocating Markan priority tend to push back [sic] dating of most books of the Bible until after the destruction of the temple at Jerusalem, because they cannot imagine a world in which Jesus could allude to this before the fact. This is despite Josephus naming an entirely different Jesus who did just that (*Wars of the Jews, book 6*).

The primary reason people believe Mark predates Matthew is because they want to claim the longer versions of stories are fabrications or embellishment. They want to show a progressive evolution and expansion of the narrative of Christ and wish to discredit the Bible. For example, atheist Early Christian scholar Bart Ehrman, while never positing a defense for Markan priority, tends to insert this point as an indisputable fact when trying to make points against the inherency [sic] of the Bible (see *Misquoting Jesus*). It is unfortunate that many Christians follow suit with these people for the sake of making themselves appear more scholarly.[832]

The above effort is a prime example of how a little knowledge can be a dangerous thing. Notice that the writer does not appear to have a firm grasp of even basic concepts such as which direction time flows, or the difference between 'inherent' and 'inerrant.' Little clues like that can tell a lot about a person's mental landscape. It is amusing, however, to note that he accuses Bart Ehrman of being an atheist! While this individual may be rather uneducated, there are others who are very well educated and hold similar views. They all seem to think that analysis of the Bible texts is an effort to 'discredit' the Bible. In *Whose Bible Is It Anyway?*, Philip R. Davies wrote:

> Assuming a historical identity to something that was properly a literary construct is simply bad method.
>
> ... Scholars who earn PhDs and write devotional books may well convey the impression that competence in scholarship delivers authority in pastoral matters and questions of Christian belief. But it is a mischievous impression. As a general principle, scholarship does not make a better religious believer, nor religious belief a better scholar. ... The purpose of 'bible study' is religious understanding of scripture ... such study may occasionally draw on academic methods or resources.
>
> ... Academic study, for which I reserve the term 'biblical studies', by contrast is interested in how and why biblical literature came to be written, in the constraints and nuances of the original languages, the history of transmission of text and canon. It is by contrast uninvolved in questions of authority or inspiration.
>
> ... So even though both 'scripture' and 'biblical studies' appear to an outsider to be examining the same thing, namely a book with the name 'Bible' on its cover, in fact they are not. A discipline is not the same thing as a subject area like 'bible' – or else astronomy and astrology would be the same discipline, as would alchemy and chemistry. A discipline is defined by methodology, by aims, practices and presuppositions.[833]

Quite a number of experts in biblical studies, by Davies's definition, began with 'bible study.' Michael Goulder was determined to follow the text wherever it led, even if it took him to conclusions that upset everything he ever thought he knew and believed.[834] Goulder was rather unique in that he was an expert in both Old and New Testaments, knew Hebrew and Greek,

---

[832]Christopher Fisher: https://realityisnotoptional.com/2012/01/10/matthew-was-the-first-gospel-written/.

[833]Philip R. Davies, *Whose Bible Is It Anyway?* (Sheffield Press, 1995), pp. 11, 20–22.

[834]Goulder's academic honesty and humility are almost legendary; he paid a great price for his relentless desire for the truth. His memoir *Five Stones and a Sling* is highly recommended.

and was best known for his work on the 'synoptic problem' and his contribution to the Farrer-Goulder hypothesis which postulates Markan priority and dispenses with Q. That is, Matthew knew and used Mark and other sources, and his own creativity, and Luke knew and used both Mark and Matthew, other sources, and his own creativity. Goulder thought that the evangelists were highly creative, and he was certainly correct! He also wrote about the conflict between Paul and the Jerusalem Christians,[835] reviving some of the ideas of Ferdinand Christian Baur. One excellent follow-up to Goulder's work in recent years is Tom Dykstra's *Mark, Canonizer of Paul*,[836] which, like Goulder's *St Paul versus St Peter*, is an easy read for the layperson. Both are highly recommended.

Gerd Lüdemann, former Chair in New Testament Studies in the Theological Faculty of the University of Göttingen, published *The Great Deception: And What Jesus Really Said and Did* in 1999,

> ...in which he argued that only about five per cent of the sayings attributed to Jesus are genuine, and that the historical evidence does not support the claims of traditional Christianity. Lüdemann stated that his studies convinced him that his previous Christian faith, based as it was on biblical studies, had become impossible: "the person of Jesus himself becomes insufficient as a foundation of faith once most of the New Testament statements about him have proved to be later interpretations by the community."[837] The Confederation of Protestant Churches in Lower Saxony called for his dismissal from the Chair of New Testament Studies. Although the call for his dismissal was rejected by the state government of Lower Saxony, the members of the faculty, under pressure from the Church, complained to the University President that Professor Lüdemann had "fundamentally put in question the intrinsic soundness of Protestant theology at the University." As a result, a search for a new Chair of New Testament Studies was instituted, and Lüdemann was "assigned to the field of 'History and Literature of Early Christianity'."[838] His research funding was cut. All his courses were thereafter "explicitly identified as 'outside of the programs of study required for the training of future ministers of the Church'." Lüdemann complained that "most of my colleagues have long since left the principles of the Church behind them yet still seek to attach themselves to this tradition by symbolic interpretation and by other interpretative skills."[839]

Dominican priest Thomas Brodie wrote *The Birthing of the New Testament*,[840] focusing on how Luke-Acts used the Elijah-Elisha narrative in constructing many of its pericopes. His early conclusion, based on this type of research, which reveals that the Gospels are not history but made up out of bits and pieces of other stories, was that Jesus of Nazareth was a mythical construct.[841] In the cited volume, he assumed that 'Proto-Luke' was the original Gospel and that Mark was a "thorough adaptation." However, what actually becomes clear when reading

---

[835]Goulder (1995, 1989, 1964), also *Midrash and Lection in Matthew* (SPCK, 1974), *The Evangelists' Calendar: A Lectionary Explanation of the Development of Scripture* (SPCK, 1978). Mark Goodacre has compiled a comprehensive bibliography of Goulder's work, available here: http://www.markgoodacre.org/goulderbiblio.pdf.

[836]Dykstra (2012).

[837]Gerd Lüdemann, 'The Decline of Academic Theology at Göttingen,' *Religion* (2002) 32, pp. 87–94

[838]'Statement of the Dean in regard to the Academic position to be Held by Professor Dr Gerd Lüdemann,' *Religion* (2002) 32, pp. 141–42.

[839]Lüdemann (2002), cited in Wikipedia.org, 'Gerd Lüdemann.'

[840]Brodie (2006).

[841]Brodie (2012).

Brodie's discussion of Mark and Proto-Luke is that proto-Luke appears to be a Cliff Notes version of Mark. I think that Brodie has since revised his views to accord with Markan priority.

In any event, Brodie points out that Luke-Acts has affinities not only with ancient historiography and biography, but also with ancient novels. He notes that, in the case of 'scripture,' when the text gets difficult to explain, NT scholars tend to appeal to some unknown quantity such as 'oral tradition' or some document that must be 'lost' (such as 'Q'). Being unknown quantities, such imagined 'sources' can be utilized to solve any problem by a wave of the hand. Very bad method.

One of Brodie's students, Adam Winn, has written *Mark and the Elijah-Elisha Narrative*, the purpose of which was to build on Brodie's initial work, especially with the view to determining how Mark used the Elijah-Elisha narrative. The conclusion is that, yes, indeed, the Elijah-Elisha correspondence exists in Mark, along with a whole lot of other literary connections! The great thing about this small book is that they begin the study by showing the relationship between Virgil's *Aeneid* and Homer's works so that you get a really good idea of what you are looking for, how many transformations are achieved from one text to another, and how to establish some basic criteria for determining literary allusions.

Even earlier, in 1992, Jerry Camery-Hoggatt published *Irony in Mark's Gospel*, which showed that the text was just littered with dramatic and verbal ironies, right down to the crucifixion scene. He demonstrated conclusively that the ironies were intentional and most definitely part of Mark's compositional strategy. He also showed how these effects were often produced by chiastic structures and other rhetorical devices. Once you have it pointed out to you, you can never not see it again, and many of the set-ups for the ironic twist are shockingly clever. It is clear that the author intended for his audience to 'get it' when such lines were delivered.

Elizabeth S. Malbon has written a fascinating literary analysis, *Mark's Jesus*, in an effort to figure out the theological agenda of the author, how the author presents the main character, how the character sees himself, and how others see him. Yeah, it's complicated, but some excellent points are made providing a lot of food for thought.

One book that lays out the complexity of the Markan structure is Mary Ann Tolbert's *Sowing the Gospel*. Her diagrams reveal much of how it was done. The whole darn thing was one gigantic, complicated set of interrelated structural set pieces. It is one of her structural diagrams you will see in the appendices. But surpassing even Tolbert's work in this department is David Oliver Smith's *Unlocking the Puzzle*, which builds upon Turton's online work quoted earlier.

Dennis R. MacDonald published *Mythologizing Jesus*, showing the use of Homeric themes in Mark and Luke. He diagrams things also, and I will include a sample in the appendices.

A very recent book, *Deciphering the Gospels* by R. G. Price, brings some really interesting data to the table. He makes the claim that his work "proved Jesus never existed." Well, *quelle surprise*! We already know that the Jesus of the Gospels never existed *as depicted*, but Paul certainly had a Jesus of some sort, and the Jewish Christians had a messiah who led them to their doom, Judas the Galilean and his family, so one should not get carried away and forget nuances! R. G. Price has a table of allusions that are furiously interesting, so I'll include that in the appendices also with some expansion.

Finally, for this short list of texts, there is David O. Smith's *Matthew, Mark, Luke and Paul*, which is, as far as I can see, undeniable evidence that the author of Mark used the epistles of Paul. He has diagrams too, and I'll include a sample in the appendices. Even though his book is a bit tedious in his setting out of the examples, diagrams, text comparisons and so forth, it is still almost essential reading for anyone who wishes to go deeper and be convinced that Mark's Gospel could not in any way be a story of a single historical person; it borrows too heavily from other literature in its construction for that to be the case. Many scholars have long been aware of the use of Paul's epistles in the Gospels, but this study takes it pretty much to the limit and shows what Mark was doing, and what Matthew and Luke were doing as well. All three of them had access to copies of at least some of Paul's epistles and were freely using them in creating their stories of what Jesus said and did. The obvious inference to be drawn from that is that there was no 'oral tradition'; there was only Judas the Galilean and his band of Zealous rebels, and Paul's epistles; no Q, no oral history.

To recap: the Gospel of Mark is built as a very complexly structured text. Mark utilizes rhetorical structures to deliver some profoundly ironic messages that are rather stunning in their implications. The structures incorporate material from the Old Testament such as the Elisha-Elijah narrative, as well as material and themes from Homer and more. Matthew and Luke, in my opinion, also use Josephus. There are many allusions that can lead the sharp reader to other texts, and which may very well be designed to convey the 'hidden meaning' of the simpler Markan text; in this way, messages could be delivered to 'those who have eyes to see and ears to hear.' And finally, there is powerful evidence that the letters of Paul were used in building some of the structures, leaving hard evidence that the author knew the Pauline corpus.

Now, if thinking about that doesn't just boggle your mind, I don't know what to say! It boggles my mind. Just looking at the few books I've listed above, knowing what is in them, the evidence they produce for the various angles of the prismatic Mark, fills me with awe at whoever did that. Sure, the Old Testament and loads of other ancient texts are complicated in many of the same ways – even Shakespeare liked to play around with such things – but this one little text, which more or less 'founded' the myth of Jesus of Nazareth, has it all, from start to finish! It was most definitely not a simple history of a guy in Palestine who wandered around doing miracles and getting himself killed; it was definitely not based on any kind of 'oral histories' or 'sayings Gospels' or 'Q' or other such nonsense. It is a well and deliberately constructed *prose metaphor* that was probably never intended to be taken as history by any *educated* persons at the time it was written. But most certainly, as a *rhetorical product designed to persuade*, it must have been written as propaganda for the poorly educated and illiterate who would only know it by hearing it read to them. And it was written in the language of the common man by a master rhetorician who knew what he was doing and had an agenda. So we would very much like to know more about it.

What follows are insights gleaned from the latest scholarly forays into the question of Paul's relation to Mark, featuring articles written by a number of scholars on both sides of the fence.

The Genre and Readers of Mark

In *Ancient Audiences and Expectations*, John Marincola[842] pointed out that Roman historiography is quite similar to what we find in the Gospel writings. That is, in contrast to Greek

---

[842] John Marincola, 'Ancient Audiences and Expectations,' in *The Cambridge Companion to the Roman Historians*, edited by A. Feldherr (Cambridge University Press, 2009), pp. 11–23, cited by Eve-Marie Becker in 'Earliest Christian *literary activity*: Investigating Authors, Genres and Audiences,' in Becker *et al.* (2014), p. 100.

historiography, we do not find explicit references to the groups of audience that are addressed. Therefore, the scholar is obliged to infer the audience from certain signals inherent to the text itself. This can sometimes be done by identifying genre. That is, the subject of the literary work will correspond to the audience, i.e. its social location.

Taking that as a given, it appears that the audience of Mark is mainly Christ believers that are "neither locally nor temporally connected directly to the story told in the gospel narrative," as Eve-Marie Becker puts it. Mark apparently intended his account "to be either a founding story or to deliver exceptional insights into Jesus' mission." Additionally, Mark is written in Koine, the language of the "dominant power."[843]

What is a bit unusual here is the fact that the vast number of text manuscripts documenting the spread of Matthew's Gospel is not matched by Mark's text. The history of the transmission of Mark seems to be less successful.

Since the Gospel of Mark was a new genre, it could not, therefore, be written in response to readers' expectations. That raises, of course, the question as to whether Mark was a known or unknown author at the time the Gospel was written. Becker states: "It could be that Mark – in contrast to Paul – was not able to reveal his name, since he was not established nor legitimized as a literary author."[844]

Since Mark can't rely on 'generic expectations,' he needs to affiliate his book to some other literature in a different way. He does this in two ways: he refers to Isaiah (Mark 1:2), thus affiliating his work with Israelite prophecy, and then he uses the term *evangelion* (gospel), the keyword of Paul's mission and teaching, thereby affiliating himself with Paul. The question then arises: was Mark addressing an audience that was specifically acquainted with Paul's teachings, and was his literary effort intended to give a deeper understanding of Paul's gospel proclamation? In Mark's Gospel, the term evangelion was transferred from Paul's missionary preaching to Jesus' Galilean ministry. Also, in the act of writing the text, the term evangelion was made to describe the narrative itself.

As Becker points out, "the Pauline letters and the Markan gospel share a topic: the engagement of the evangelion." The letters are authoritative writings "based on Paul's ongoing interactions with certain communities." The Markan gospel is a literary narration with an "informative purpose and proclamatory message."[845] Most scholars, still looking for a tradition about 'Jesus of Nazareth,' think that there are passages in Paul that refer to this tradition, but only because there are echoes of Paul's writings in the Gospels, beginning with Mark.

See the following comparisons between Paul, on the left, and Mark, right:

1 Cor. 11:23 For I received from the Lord Himself that which I passed on to you [it was given to me personally], that the Lord Jesus on the night when He was treacherously delivered up and while His betrayal was in progress took bread,	**Mk. 14:22** And while they were eating, He took a loaf [of bread], praised God and gave thanks and asked Him to bless it to their use. [Then] He broke [it] and gave to them and said, Take. Eat. This is My body.

[843]Becker (2014), pp. 100–1.
[844]Becker (2014), pp. 101–2.
[845]Becker (2014), p. 103.

1 Cor. 11:24 And when He had given thanks, He broke [it] and said, Take, eat. This is My body, which is broken for you. Do this to call Me [affectionately] to remembrance.

1 Cor. 11:25 Similarly when supper was ended, He took the cup also, saying, This cup is the new covenant [ratified and established] in My blood. Do this, as often as you drink [it], to call Me [affectionately] to remembrance.

1 Cor. 11:26 For every time you eat this bread and drink this cup, you are representing and signifying and proclaiming the fact of the Lord's death until He comes [again].

1 Cor. 7:10 But to the married people I give charge – not I but the Lord – that the wife is not to separate from her husband.

2 Cor. 3:7 Now if the dispensation of death engraved in letters on stone [the ministration of the Law], was inaugurated with such glory and splendor that the Israelites were not able to look steadily at the face of Moses because of its brilliance, [a glory] that was to fade and pass away, [Exod. 34:29-35.]

2 Cor. 3:8 Why should not the dispensation of the Spirit [this spiritual ministry whose task it is to cause men to obtain and be governed by the Holy Spirit] be attended with much greater and more splendid glory?

2 Cor. 3:10 Indeed, in view of this fact, what once had splendor [the glory of the Law in the face of Moses] has come to have no splendor at all, because of the overwhelming glory that exceeds and excels it [the glory of the Gospel in the face of Jesus Christ].

2 Cor. 3:16 But whenever a person turns [in repentance] to the Lord, the veil is stripped off and taken away.

2 Cor. 3:18 And all of us, as with unveiled face, [because we] continued to behold [in the Word of God] as in a mirror the glory of the Lord, are constantly being transfigured into His very own image in ever increasing splendor and from one degree of glory to another; [for this comes] from the Lord [Who is] the Spirit.

Mk. 14:23 He also took a cup [of the juice of grapes], and when He had given thanks, He gave [it] to them, and they all drank of it.

Mk. 14:24 And He said to them, This is My blood [which ratifies] the new covenant, [the blood] which is being poured out for (on account of) many. [Exod. 24:8.]

Mk. 14:25 Solemnly and surely I tell you, I shall not again drink of the fruit of the vine till that day when I drink it of a new and a higher quality in God's kingdom.

Mk. 10:11-12 And He said to them, Whoever dismisses (repudiates and divorces) his wife and marries another commits adultery against her; And if a woman dismisses (repudiates and divorces) her husband and marries another, she commits adultery.

Mk. 9:2 Six days after this, Jesus took with Him Peter and James and John and led them up on a high mountain apart by themselves. And He was transfigured before them and became resplendent with divine brightness.

Mk. 9:3 And His garments became glistening, intensely white, as no fuller (cloth dresser, launderer) on Earth could bleach them.

Mk. 9:4 And Elijah appeared [there] to them, accompanied by Moses, and they were holding [a protracted] conversation with Jesus.

Mk. 9:5 And Peter took up the conversation, saying, Master, it is good and suitable and beautiful for us to be here. Let us make three booths (tents) – one for You and one for Moses and one for Elijah.

Mk. 9:6 For he did not [really] know what to say, for they were in a violent fright (aghast with dread).

Mk. 9:7 And a cloud threw a shadow upon them, and a voice came out of the cloud, saying, This is My Son, the [most dearworthy] Beloved One. Be constantly listening to and obeying Him!

Mk. 9:8 And looking around, they suddenly no longer saw anyone with them except Jesus only.

Becker suggests that:

> While Mark narrates an explicit story based on pre-Markan traditions, Paul only alludes to it and, thus, he presupposes that his readers know what this story is actually about and which protagonists

he has in mind. While Paul's readers seem to be familiar with all circumstances related to the delivery and possibly also to divergent interpretations of this story, Mark obviously addresses an audience which he intends to sustain with solid narrative material.[846]

That is certainly one way to read it, but it is based on the assumption that the story in Mark, on which the other Gospels are based, was about a historical Jesus of Nazareth. It appears to me that this Jesus is a literary creation of Mark's, and he used Paul for his theological underpinning and even many of his story themes. He also provably used the OT and Homeric epics in the construction of his Gospel. There is not a shred of evidence anywhere that there was a Jesus of Nazareth as a historical person nor any traditions or 'Q' material relating to him. What is historical is that there was a Zealot founder named Judas the Galilean who was executed and was expected to return by his Zealot family and followers, bringing legions of angels to destroy the Romans. On the other side, there was Paul with his universal Christ/Son of God, who came to Earth to give his life for humanity and do away with divisions, war and so forth.

When and Where Was the Gospel of Mark Written?

Most NT scholars who accept the priority of Mark still try to make it as early as possible, holding to the idea that it was written between 66–70 AD, that is, during the time of the Jewish War. This allows them to tie Mark to a possible 'eyewitness' of the 'life of Jesus of Nazareth,' though most of them have discarded the idea that there is any truth to the claim of the Church Fathers that the author was 'John Mark,' who was an alleged companion of the apostle Peter.

Early testimony and Patristic tradition place the writing of Mark's Gospel in Rome in the mid-to-late 60s AD. John Chrysostom claimed that Mark was written in Egypt (*Homily on Matthew* 1.7). This was surely due to his misinterpretation of Eusebius' comments in *H.E.* 2.16. Clement of Alexandria (Eusebius' *H.E.* 6.14.5-6), Irenaeus (*Adv. Haer.* 3.1.1), and the Anti-Marcionite prologue attest to the Gospel's composition in Rome or the regions around Italy.[847] Several pieces of internal evidence point toward a Roman provenance of the Gospel.

First of all, there are 18 occurrences of Latinisms in the New Testament and 10 of them are in Mark. Several of the Latinisms are unattested in any Greek texts prior to the first century, a portion of which appear uniquely within Mark or sources that have clearly used Mark.

The Anti-Marcionite prologue and Irenaeus both attribute the date of composition to after Peter's death ca. 65 AD.[848] Clement of Alexandria suggests that the Gospel was written within Peter's lifetime. Modern scholars claim to set these claims aside and to focus on whether the Gospel was written in the years before the Jewish War and the destruction of the Temple (August 70 AD), or after. Several have pointed out that the Parable of the Tenants and the Little Apocalypse of chapter 13 argue for a post-70 AD date. Michael Theophilos states that this is not convincing since "there were other prophetic figures who are recorded as prophesying the ruin of the temple during a time of peace," giving Jesus ben Ananias, reported by Josephus to have

---

[846]Becker (2014), pp. 104–5.

[847]Helmut Koester, *Ancient Christian Gospels: Their History and Development* (London: SCM, 1990), cited in Michael P. Theophilos, 'The Roman Connection: Paul and Mark,' in Wischmeyer *et al.* (2014), p. 50.

[848]Which again suggests that Peter and Cephas were two different people.

prophesied in 62 AD (*War* 6.300.309), as his example.[849] Well, that's just jaw-dropping. Allow me to quote Steve Mason on the subject:

> To set up a compelling backdrop for the destruction, Josephus paints a picture of the former glory of Jerusalem and its magnificent Temple. About three million Jews, who had traveled to Jerusalem for the pilgrimage festival of Passover, were trapped in the city when the Roman siege began, Josephus says; famine struck and, in combination with the rebels' plundering, led to starvation and even cannibalism. Omens foreshadowed the destruction of the Temple: the massive eastern gates opened by themselves, a sacrificial cow gave birth to a lamb, terrifying scenes were observed in the heavens and mysterious voices were heard announcing the divine departure from the Temple. These omens of destruction were confirmed by the peculiar figure of Jesus, son of Ananias, who patrolled the streets of Jerusalem day and night for more than seven years, pronouncing doom on the city in Jeremianic verse. Finally, after overcoming the city walls, the Romans entered the Temple and set fire to it – unwittingly accomplishing the purging ordained by the Judean God. This action was taken against the express will of Titus, who even tried to extinguish the fire.
>
> Thus Josephus has elaborately proven his thesis: most Judeans were drawn into the war reluctantly, by the arrogant and un-Jewish behavior of a few tyrants; the fall of Jerusalem was their punishment for sins against God's holy sanctuary.[850]

If Theophilos doesn't grok ancient literary rhetorical techniques, I just don't know what to say.

As far as I can see, S. G. F. Brandon's take on when and why Mark was written comes closest to nailing it, though there are still some problems to solve. He proposes that it was written *after* 70 AD as a *reaction* to the destruction of Jerusalem, the Jewish Temple, and the Jerusalem Christian church there – the Zealots – and that it was written as apology expressly to distance Christians from the Zealots and all the bad press that had gone before in respect of Christianity. He gives three pieces of evidence for this conclusion: 1) the rejection of the Davidic messiah; 2) the tax pericope; 3) the torn curtain in the temple.

As we know, there is no evidence of a narrative of the life of Jesus or any other messianic figure outside of Josephus that was *written* and circulated among the early churches prior to Mark. The very fact that both Matthew and Luke adopt, adapt and expand on Mark points at the definitive conclusion that Mark was the only prototype. The non-Markan material they add to their Gospels were most likely just literary pieces that they wanted or needed to make their own theological points, though it is possible that they knew some traditions about Judas the Galilean as Messiah that they included as well. In any event, as Brandon says, we are justified in regarding the Gospel of Mark, a 'biography of a human Jesus,' as an innovation in Christian faith and practice. And that leads to the question: what caused this 'unprecedented and highly pregnant departure'?

Such departures from the way things have been done rarely happen if there is not some pressing need in reference to the environment, some specific need in the life of the church which produced the consciousness of a need for the composition of a biography of Jesus. However, as we have seen, a biography of Judas the Galilean would definitely not have been politically wise at the time. Something was needed to replace him both for the congregations and for outsiders who might feel some hostility towards the group that had caused so much death and destruction because of

---

[849]Theophilos (2014), p. 52.
[850]Steve Mason, 'Will the Real Josephus Please Stand Up?' *Biblical Archaeology Review* 23:5 (1997).

their stubborn clinging to a 'vile superstition' about the coming of a messiah with 12 legions of angels to destroy the Romans. As things stood after the war, that clearly didn't work out well for them.

In 71 AD popular interest in Jewish affairs was rampant as a result of the news of the destruction of Jerusalem and the Temple, plus the magnificent triumphal display made by Vespasian and Titus in that year through the streets of Rome.[851] Josephus gives an account of it that is rather long, so I will only include an excerpt. Keep in mind, this is a victory parade, festival, banquet, celebration, all rolled into one, with games, free food, and beer and wine for all.

> Now it is impossible to describe the multitude of the shows as they deserve, and the magnificence of them all; such indeed as a man could not easily think of as performed, either by the labor of workmen, or the variety of riches, or the rarities of nature; for almost all such curiosities as the most happy men ever get by piece-meal were here one heaped on another, and those both admirable and costly in their nature; and all brought together on that day demonstrated the vastness of the dominions of the Romans; for there was here to be seen a mighty quantity of silver, and gold, and ivory, contrived into all sorts of things, and did not appear as carried along in pompous show only, but, as a man may say, running along like a river.
>
> Some parts were composed of **the rarest purple hangings, and so carried along**; and others accurately represented to the life what was embroidered by the arts of the Babylonians. ...
>
> But what afforded the greatest surprise of all was the structure of the pageants [parade floats] that were borne along; for indeed he that met them could not but be afraid that the bearers would not be able firmly enough to support them, such was their magnitude; for many of them were so made, that they were on three or even four stories, one above another. ... many resemblances of the war, and those in several ways, and variety of contrivances, affording a most lively portraiture of itself. For there was to be seen a happy country laid waste, and entire squadrons of enemies slain; while some of them ran away, and some were carried into captivity; with walls of great altitude and magnitude overthrown and ruined by machines; with the strongest fortifications taken, and the walls of most populous cities upon the tops of hills seized on, and an army pouring itself within the walls; as also every place full of slaughter, and supplications of the enemies, when they were no longer able to lift up their hands in way of opposition. **Fire also sent upon temples was here represented**, and houses overthrown, and falling upon their owners: rivers also, after they came out of a large and melancholy desert, ran down, not into a land cultivated, nor as drink for men, or for cattle, but through a land still on fire upon every side; for the Jews related that such a thing they had undergone during this war.
>
> Now the workmanship of these representations was so magnificent and lively in the construction of the things, that it exhibited what had been done to such as did not see it, as if they had been there really present. On the top of every one of these pageants was placed the commander of the city that was taken, and the manner wherein he was taken. Moreover, there followed those pageants a great number of ships; and for the other spoils, they were carried in great plenty. But for those that were **taken in the temple of Jerusalem, they made the greatest figure of them all**; that is, the golden table, of the weight of many talents; the candlestick also, that was made of gold, though its construction were now changed from that which we made use of; for its middle shaft was fixed upon a basis, and the small branches were produced out of it to a great length, having the likeness of a trident in their position, and had every one a socket made of brass for a lamp at the tops of them. These lamps were in number seven, and represented the dignity of the number seven among the Jews; and the last of all the spoils, was carried the Law of the Jews. ...

---

[851] Mason (2016) makes the case that the Flavians really over-emphasized their defeat of the Jews and the destruction of Jerusalem as a political maneuver.

After which Vespasian marched in the first place, and Titus followed him; Domitian also rode along with them, and made a glorious appearance, and rode on a horse that was worthy of admiration.[852]

I have put in bold above the veiled reference to the display of the Veil of the Temple carried in the triumph. In an earlier passage, Josephus described it:

[B]efore these doors there was a veil of equal largeness with the doors. It was a Babylonian curtain, embroidered with blue, and fine linen, and scarlet, and purple, and of a contexture that was truly wonderful. Nor was this mixture of colors without its mystical interpretation, but was a kind of image of the universe; for by the scarlet there seemed to be enigmatically signified fire, by the fine flax the earth, by the blue the air, and by the purple the sea; two of them having their colors the foundation of this resemblance; but the fine flax and the purple have their own origin for that foundation, the earth producing the one, and the sea the other. This curtain had also embroidered upon it all that was mystical in the heavens, excepting that of the [twelve] signs, representing living creatures.[853]

Coins were issued commemorating the event inscribed *IVDAEA CAPTA*, the humiliated figure of Judea shown as a woman seated beneath a palm tree. It this way, the whole war with the fanatical atrocities of the Jews was made dramatically real to all the people in Rome. Naturally, this inflamed already existing anti-Semitism, and Jewish Christians, long known as just a sect of Judaism with a 'vile superstition' at the center, became the main targets of abuse.

For the Christians in Rome, as well as Christians who were visiting Rome at the time, this display was no doubt distressing and even terrifying. They were all fully aware that their religion had originated in Judea, that their messiah had been executed as a rebel against Rome, that he had been resurrected into heaven as the messiah who was supposed to come and save the Jews and crush the Romans. Despite the fact that a large number of Jews, both in Judea and the Diaspora, had been supportive of this conception, their messiah had failed again.

Obviously, knowing this could be both personally embarrassing, and dangerous. They understood that they would be viewed with suspicion as persons disposed to sedition.

Along came Mark to save the day.

Utilizing all the rhetorical derring-do that I have already described above, the Gospel of Mark does a number of useful things for the shocked and disoriented Christian churches. First of all, Mark lets us know that the Jewish religious leaders were bitter and determined enemies of the peaceful Jesus. They constantly thwart and oppose him and finally plan and accomplish his death, being blind to his divine nature and mission of peace and unification.

Sounds like Paul? Yes, indeed. Paul, who was driven out of town like a scapegoat, whose congregations were taken over by mad, bad messianists, whose letters were left in a box somewhere to rot, is all of a sudden seen to have been right all along.

Paul's views on the Jewish law versus grace are also on full display. Mark tells us that one cannot preserve the old garment of Judaism by new patches, nor conserve the new wine of Christianity in the old wineskins of Judaism. The Sabbath and ritual cleanliness are also done away with in short order.

---

[852] *Wars* 7.5.5.
[853] *Wars* 5.5.4.

Mark gets in a really good one on behalf of Paul in the story of the "scribes which came down from Jerusalem" (Mk. 3:22) and who accused Jesus as being possessed by a demon from whom he got his miraculous powers. Not only is this turned back on the Jewish authorities, but blasphemy against the Holy Spirit, or God's great mysterious work, is named as the "unforgivable sin," as we will discuss more fully below.

The Parable of the Wicked Husbandmen (Mk. 12:1-9), which is an encapsulated history of the Jews, ends with: "What therefore will the lord of the vineyard do? He will come and destroy the husbandmen, and will give the vineyard unto others." This is an obvious reference to the Jewish War.

Some scholars have argued in the past that if Mark was written soon after the war, he would have made more explicit references to it. This idea does not take into account the historical reality, what Mark's purposes were, that the consequences of the war were what needed to be dealt with, and his apparent lack of consciousness and explicit references to the war itself are evidence that he was writing an account that was retrojected into the past, creating a Jesus who did not promote war and mayhem. Mark wasn't stupid; he knew that if his story was to be believable propaganda, it had to appear to have been written before the war, at least to the less educated who didn't understand Mark's story as an allegory and the more subtle literary allusions. Thus, references to the war were couched as prophecies with a bit of disingenuous uncertainty added as a nice touch. The fact that the war is thus so studiously avoided is further evidence of this position.

The story of the tribute money is an extremely important little bit of text that comes next (Mk. 12:13-17) and makes the point even stronger. Payment of tribute was the obligation of all peoples subjected to the Empire; only the Jews had rebelled against it back in 6 AD *at the instigation of Judas the Galilean.* The issue of paying tax to Rome was constantly in the background in the lead-up to the war, and though it may not have been claimed as the reason for revolt, it was one of the primary motivators of the Zealots, and the Zealots were the prime ideological supporters of rebellion (even if they didn't inspire the war).[854] That Mark even raised the issue of the payment of tax by Jews implies that it was an issue at the time he was writing. The incident is short, almost throw-away, has no special spiritual implications, and yet Mark includes it. The answer that is put in Jesus' mouth is what would be expected from a loyal subject of the Romans: the obligation of the Jews to pay taxes to Rome. It also definitely distances this Jesus from Judas the Galilean, the rebel against the taxation of Quirinius!

But there is actually more. Mark is demonstrating here that the Jewish *authorities* attempted to compromise Jesus on the subject of paying taxes, and Jesus gave the right answer as a good subject of Rome – though, of course, that answer (among others) is loaded with irony.

> Then they sent to him some Pharisees and some Herodians to trap him in what he said. And they came and said to him, "Teacher, we know that you are sincere, and show deference to no one; for you do not regard people with partiality, but teach the way of God in accordance with truth. Is it lawful to pay taxes to the emperor, or not? Should we pay them, or should we not?" But knowing their hypocrisy, he said to them, "Why are you putting me to the test? Bring me a denarius and let me see it." And they brought one. Then he said to them, "Whose head is this, and whose title?"

---

[854]See Mason (2016).

They answered, "Caesar's." Jesus said to them, "Pay to Caesar the things that are Caesar's, and to God the things that are God's." And they were utterly amazed at him.[855]

The pericope is built around the question of the right of the Jews to rebel against their Roman overlords. The messianic element was widely known as a potent factor in the development of extreme Jewish nationalism leading to the war. One can see here a reaction to some situation in which the Christians were in danger of being associated in popular thought with the rebellious Jews, an association that Mark is here attributing to Jewish malice. The Jewish leaders, the official representatives of Jewish life, are represented repeatedly as the constant opponents of Jesus, who repeatedly condemns them.

And, from what has been written above, we know exactly when it was likely that the issue of the Jewish payment of tax to Rome would have been a topic of such vital concern to the Roman Christians that it needed to be established that they were not persons who refused to pay taxes, nor had their messiah advised against doing so.

In Mk. 12:35-37 Jesus denies the scribal doctrine of the Davidic descent of the Messiah. This is strange because of the regular ascription of Davidic descent to Jesus in Matthew and Luke. Most people miss the main issue, which is that Mark definitely says that the Davidic descent doctrine was that of the *Jewish scribes*. His clear purpose here is to refute a teaching that he represents as coming from official Jewish sources. There are other issues with this passage that we will return to further on.

When you take into account that the original Christian community at Rome was pre-Pauline, and likely in close in sympathy with the Jerusalem church, it follows that they, indeed, believed in the Davidic descent of the Messiah, an overtly political statement connected to apocalyptic ideas and nationalistic aspirations. So, Mark, writing for this community, firmly refutes that doctrine, ascribing it to the 'scribes of the Jews.' Brandon shows that the term 'scribes' was well known to the Roman Christians as a designation for the *local* rabbis, the official teachers of the Jews. So, when Mark used the term, it had a double meaning. His disavowal of the association of Jesus with Jewish Davidic sonship was employed to dissociate the Christian interpretation of Jesus from any connection with the distinctive Jewish interpretation. This action was clearly important to Mark and it demonstrates that his purpose was to repudiate Jesus' connection with any sort of nationalistic aspirations and rebellions.

The significance of the rejection of the Davidic title, and the account of the tax money incident, are extremely important issues for evaluating the timing of the writing of Mark, because it clearly had contemporary significance.

Any common reader of the time (or listener to a reading of the text) would understand not only that Jesus was independent of Judaism in his teaching and deeds, but that he was definitively repudiated by the official representatives of Judaism. Thus, Mark isolated Jesus from the religion, messianism and national interest of the Jews.

Further representations in Mark show that the Jewish people, too, were hard-hearted and obdurate, even including the disciples. Jesus comes right out and plainly says that a prophet has no honor in his own country. The depiction of Jesus at odds with his own family was designed to isolate him from the kin of Judas the Galilean, who had ruled the Zealots and the Jerusalem church. There is the bizarre statement that his relatives, having heard of his evangelizing activity,

---

[855]Mark 12:13-17.

came "to lay hold on him: for they said, He is beside himself (out of his mind)" (Mk. 3:31-35). Later, after the Beelzebul episode, his family is depicted as visiting, apparently in order to take him into custody and restrain him! At that point, he disavows his family and says that only those who do the will of God are his kin.

Such demeaning depictions of the relatives of Jesus are strange, but can be understood as a necessary distancing of Jesus from the Zealots. Thus, it can be concluded that the author was writing at a time when belittling the status and reputation of the actual family of the messiah preached by the Jerusalem church was expedient and would not result in any risks to the propagator of such an idea, since they were all dead.

Mark's treatment of the apostles was also aimed at detaching Jesus from his fellow countrymen. They are represented as weak, vacillating, thick-headed dolts who can't be trusted to watch for even a single hour, and who quarrel among themselves over childish matters of precedence; and, of course, the big one: one of them betrays Jesus to the authorities. Peter, the best of them, denies him when the going gets tough. At the end, they all desert Jesus, with no indication of return or redemption. With what must have been ironic audacity, Mark even names the betrayer *Judas*.

The whole picture presented by Mark is that of a faith misunderstood and persecuted by the Jews from the beginning.

The account of the trial of Jesus is plainly meant to create the impression that the Romans recognized Jesus' innocence and Pilate's hand was forced by the Jewish leaders who were bent on his destruction. At the end, the Markan thesis of Jewish responsibility for the death of Jesus reaches its ironic end when the Roman centurion, in contradistinction to the Jews, is depicted as recognizing the divine nature of Jesus. And, at that very moment, something extraordinary happens in Mark's account:

> Then Jesus gave a loud cry and breathed his last. And the curtain of the temple was torn in two, from top to bottom. Now when the centurion, who stood facing him, saw that *in this way* he breathed his last, he said, "Truly this man was God's Son!"[856]

Mark is clearly proclaiming that the sacrificial death of the Son of God brought an end to the Temple cult of sacrifice, that the last breath of Jesus tore the temple veil. But, as Brandon notes, for this short statement to have any meaning for his readers, they would have to be familiar with the fact that the Temple had such a curtain and must have known something of its significance – Mark does not explain it to them as he does other Jewish customs and practices. We know from the Josephan passage about the Roman triumph of Vespasian and Titus that the curtain of the temple was included along with the other spoils from Jerusalem. And from the way Josephus described how everything was displayed and explained in tableaux on passing parade floats, undoubtedly the temple curtain was similarly explained. In fact, it is even a bit curious that Josephus separates it from the rest of the temple spoils as he does in the passage, and passes over it so quickly. Either Josephus was embarrassed about this, or something has been edited and rearranged by a later redactor.

What seems to be most probable is that the temple curtain was, indeed, explained to the people and was an object of awe and wonder. And equally probably, Jewish Christians understood that

---

[856]Mark 15:37-39.

the presence of the object in the procession meant the catastrophic end of a cult that was the exclusive privilege of Jews and which gave them their sense of superiority over other people. And, to at least some Roman Christians, the evidence of the end of the Jewish religious cult was nothing other than confirmation of what the Apostle Paul had taught: "Christ redeemed us from the curse of the Torah ..." The death of Paul's Christ had made the Law obsolete years before and thereby anticipated what the Romans had finished.

The total extermination of the Mother Church of Jerusalem, after they had all demonstrated their adherence to the Jewish messiah who never showed up, must have confronted the Christians – Gentile and Jewish alike – with a terrible dilemma that was not only ideological; it was dangerous to life and limb to be a Christian at that time.

So someone wrote Mark to solve the problem.

Brandon notes that Mark was inspired by the theology of Paul, but he wonders whether this inspiration was due to loyalty preserved during the period of Paul's eclipse or whether it was due simply to the realization by somebody that Paul must have been the one with the 'right' gospel after all. The sudden annihilation of the Jerusalem church and the catastrophic overthrow of Judaism must have caused many of Paul's former converts and adherents to recall the great principle of Christian freedom from Judaistic control for which the apostle to the Gentiles had so passionately fought. They must have seen the disaster that had overwhelmed Israel as divine confirmation of Paul's gospel.

And so, therefore, it seems rather certain that Mark was written in Rome, soon after the triumph of Vespasian and Titus in 71 AD. Michael Turton notes:

> The reality is that today no one can say who wrote the Gospel of Mark. Not even the writer's gender is known, though traditionally it is ascribed to a man. However, John D. Crossan[857] has pointed out that verse 14:9: "And truly, I say to you, wherever the gospel is preached in the whole world, what she has done will be told in memory of her" may well be a slyly ironic reference to the author herself. Additionally, a number of exegetes have felt that the mysterious young man of Mark 14:51-52 is actually the author of Mark. Whatever the case, given the low taste for high irony of the writer of Mark, it is perhaps fitting that the writer of one of the great pieces of world literature has gone anonymously into history.[858]

Mark as Allegory

Recent biblical scholarship supports nineteenth-century German theologian Gustav Volkmar's theory that the Gospel of Mark was narrative or allegory intended to place *Pauline* Christianity at the center of 'the new, true religion.' Anne Vig Skoven[859] explains how Volkmar reached his then-contentious position on Mark:

---

[857] John D. Crossan, *The Historical Jesus: The Life of a Mediterranean Jewish Peasant* (New York: HarperCollins, 1991), p. 416.

[858] https://www.michaelturton.com/Mark/GMark_intro.html.

[859] Anne Vig Skoven was a guitarist for all-female Danish rock band Miss B Haven in the 1980s and 90s. She left the music scene in 1995 to enroll in the Faculty of Theology at the University of Copenhagen, becoming an award-winning theologian and parish priest. Tragically, she died of lung cancer at just 52 years of age in 2013, shortly before her work in this volume was published, posthumously.

Unlike exegetes of the patristic tradition and also unlike most of the 20th century scholarship, biblical scholars of the 19th century were not put off by the idea that Paulinism was to be found in the Gospel of Mark. The founder of the so-called Tübingen School, Ferdinand Christian Baur (1792–1860), for instance, regarded the Gospel of Mark as a synthesis of Petrine and Pauline traditions. Baur argued that Mark was based on Matthew and Luke and composed in the 2nd century. According to the Tübingen School, the Gospel of John was the final synthesis of the antitheses between Jewish Christian orthodoxy and the Pauline spirit – and Mark was one step on that way.

In 1857, the German exegete Gustav Hermann Joseph Philipp Volkmar (1809–93) characterized the Gospel of Mark as a Pauline gospel. Although Mark's story was concerned with Jesus' life and death, it was also, so Volkmar argued, permeated by Pauline theology. ...

... According to Volkmar, Mark's only sources were: the Old Testament writings, four Pauline letters (Romans, Galatians, 1 and 2 Corinthians), the oral tradition of early Christian communities – and, surprisingly, Revelation. ...

Volkmar argues that Mark was written in the seventies, that is, a hundred years earlier than the Tübingen School presumed. ... Volkmar thought that the author of Mark was a Hebrew-thinking, Greek-speaking Jew, who had spent some time in Galilee and Jerusalem, and who was acquainted with the Pauline gospel as well as with early oral traditions. ...

Volkmar saw the Gospel of Mark as a didactic poem based on historical events. ... Mark's Gospel had a distinctly *doctrinal* character which, from the very beginning, was polemically directed against Revelation. ... Volkmar believed Mark to have been carefully composed ...

According to Volkmar, Mark's primary purpose was not to write a historical biography about Jesus, but to give an exposition of the true Christ ... Consequently, Mark made every effort for his gospel *not* to be considered a biography of Jesus. ... The true protagonist of the gospel is not Jesus, but the risen Christ. Also, when traditional material is included, the gospel narratives remain symbolic representations of Pauline theology. ... But above all, the Gospel of Mark is a didactic narrative, which presents (the true) Pauline Christianity in a new genre ...

Volkmar argued that Hebrew parallelisms shaped the structure of the gospel on every level. On the macro-level, Mark was divided into two major sections, 1:14–8:26 and 8:27–16:20. Both of these sections could be divided into four subsections, etc.

[T]his Paulinized version of Christ is connected to Judaism only in the respect that he emerged *from* it. The greatest person within Judaism was John the Baptist ... Volkmar takes John's baptism of Jesus only to show that Christianity is rooted in Judaism. ...

... Mark demonstrates how Jesus transcends Judaism in his authoritative teachings and also through the universal scope of his ministry, which is not directed to the Jewish world alone, but also to the Gentiles. ... Mark 4 addresses the greatest obstacle to Jesus' legitimacy, namely the continuing *sarkan* [fleshly] non-understanding which characterized the Jewish Christian majority. (4:1–3:4) ...

The first person in Mark's Gospel to realize that Jesus is the Christ is Peter, but the first *historical* person to understand what this meant was the apostle to the Gentiles. Paul understood *how* Jesus was the Christ – namely, through his suffering ... These are the two focal points in Paul's Christology: crucifixion and glorification. Although Jesus rebukes Peter for his lack of understanding of the Son of Man's inexorable fate (8:31-33), his confession leads to the transfiguration, which shows Jesus Christ in his – otherwise hidden – glory (9:2-13).

Through Jesus' instruction of his disciples on the way to Jerusalem, the reader is taught what proper discipleship and true faith imply: confidence in God's power (9:14-29) ... [T]he reader ... must realize that the *true* law consists of higher, eternal ... commandments (10:2-12), the fulfilment of which presupposes the attitudes of true faith (10:13-16), true love (10:17-27) and true hope (10:28-31). On his way to his own suffering, Jesus makes it clear to his disciples that all apocalyptically inspired ambitions of ruling must be abandoned in favor of serving and (potential) suffering (10:35-45).[860]

Vig Skoven concludes that, with this understanding, "the Gospel of Mark cannot be regarded as a Jesus biography." Mark's Gospel, she says, "is to be seen as an odyssey in which the reader travels with Jesus," via the Apostle Paul and the risen Christ. The Markan Jesus is a literary character who is based on several literary and historical figures. When speaking of Christ, the author of Mark often has Paul in mind. "Mark has projected Paul and his Gentile mission – as we know it from Paul's letters ... – back into Jesus' life," a procedure Vig Skoven refers to as "an allegorical rewriting of Paul."[861] Volkmar also finds Pauline theological concepts expressed in the Markan Jesus' words and deeds.

An example of the allegorical nature of Mark is the healing of the paralyzed man in 2:1-12, understood as a symbolic representation of fallen mankind. Vig Skoven notes that, in Volkmar's interpretation of the story, he adds an ethnic element since the predicament "is especially characteristic of the Gentile world." "After the healing of the (sinfully) paralyzed man," the sinner tax collector Levi is called to follow Jesus, following which Jesus eats at Levi's house along with "many tax collectors and sinners" (2:13-17).[862] This meal is a scandal to the Pharisaic scribes. Since it is unlikely that Pharisaic scribes would have been present in table fellowship with Gentiles, that is the clue that this is an analog of the episode in Antioch which Paul described in his letter to the Galatians (2:11-14).

> The disciples who are called first in Mark include the pillars mentioned in Gal 2:9 (Peter and John). Levi, who is called next, fills in the place of the Gentile Christians at Antioch (Gal 1:12). The third party, the Pharisaic scribes from Mark, play the same part at the common meal as "those from James" in Antioch in Gal 2:12. "Those from James", who have a Pharisaic orthodox interpretation of the Law, may very well have posed the same question to [Cephas], Barnabas and the other Jews as the scribes do in Mark: Are we to eat with sinners? Volkmar concludes that both texts deal with an *inner* Christian conflict between Jews and Gentiles, with Paul and Mark on the one side and James and the author of Revelation on the other.
>
> ... Compared to the conflict between the Jewish Christians from James and Paul, Mark's achievement was ... to breathe the Pauline Christ-spirit into the Markan Jesus' words. ... Paul's description of the Antioch episode in Galatians makes Volkmar wonder whether [Cephas] was at all present at the meal(s) to which Mark's narrative refers, and whether he ever understood the Pauline scope of Jesus' words about the righteous and sinners. Obviously James and the author of Revelation did not.[863]

To be clear, Volkmar "never employed the term allegory himself; he argued for a *parabolic* reading of the gospel," listing ten features in Mark that legitimized his interpretation, including the symbolism of the cursing of the fig tree (Mk. 11:12-14).[864] Vig Skoven further points out that, despite early opposition to Volkmar, aspects of his reading of Mark anticipated modern scholarship, the most important being the hypothesis of Markan priority and the approach to

---

[860] Anne Vig Skoven: 'Mark as Allegorical Rewriting of Paul: Gustav Volkmar's Understanding of the Gospel of Mark,' in Becker *et al.* (2014), pp. 13–21. Vig Skoven's italics.

[861] Vig Skoven (2014), p. 21.

[862] Vig Skoven (2014), p. 22.

[863] Vig Skoven (2014), pp. 23–4.

[864] Vig Skoven (2014), p. 25.

the Gospel as a piece of *literature* and the evangelist as an author, as opposed to a chronicler describing literal historical events.

Volkmar was opposed by Martin Werner in *Der Einfluss paulinischer Theologie im Markusevangelium*, published in 1923. Werner saw Volkmar's work as a dangerous development in the mythical Jesus trend. Werner's monograph is devoted to showing that there are differences between Paul's theology and that of Mark, often on matters of fine detail. Werner's conclusions in that respect do not follow. After all, Luke considers himself a Paulinist but there are so many differences there that it is clear that Luke didn't understand Paul at all. It has been noted by scholars that there are differences between the accepted and rejected Pauline letters, yet if someone else wrote Colossians and Ephesians, they either believed they were following Paul, or intended for others to think that when they signed his name. Of course, in the case of the letters, the problem of redaction, glossing, etc., must be taken into account. Werner insisted on a literal reading of the gospel which he thought was more Petrine than Pauline, rendering his work little more than apologetic aimed at protecting the idea of a historical Jesus.

The Use of Mark

Mogens Müller notes the long slog it has taken to reach this understanding of the Gospel of Mark as allegory:

> [T]he New Testament literature has come into existence to fulfil the needs of the Christian congregations. Thus these writings were primarily meant for internal use. If this is obvious enough in the case of Paul's letters, it has been more difficult to realise with respect to the Gospel of Mark – and the later gospels. It has taken some pain to reach the view that also the gospels were primarily written to answer the needs of the congregations.[865]

Müller explains that Paul's letters were "written in concrete situations" to address specific problems related to living in obedience to the will of God. For Paul, freedom from the material law, and obedience to the spiritual rule of God, was the turning point for the Christian. His story of the life of Jesus is short and to the point in Philippians 2:6-11: Jesus renounces his divinity to become human, and the only thing Paul cares to tell us about that human life is that Jesus was obedient – even unto death – and which obedience was rewarded.

The few times that Paul mentions "words of Jesus" (one assumes), they are "words of the Lord," and "it is always in the context of admonition." "Only once ... does Paul tell about an event in the human life of Jesus, namely the institution of the Lord's Supper" (1 Cor 11:23-25).[866] If there were ever any other clues about Paul's Jesus in his writings, they have long since disappeared thanks to redactors or loss of texts. That, in itself, is most curious.

Thus it is, Müller notes, when Paul talks about "what is basic in Christianity," as far as we know, it is only ever about "the new conduct of life" based on the model of obedience of Jesus.[867] Even though he tosses out the whole Jewish legislation concerning ritual things and what makes one a Jew, when he writes about the new behavior of the Christian, it mostly consists of basic

---

[865]Mogens Müller: 'In the Beginning was the Congregation: In Search of a *Tertium Comparationis* between Paul and Mark,' in Becker *et al.* (2014), p. 108.

[866]Müller (2014), p. 109.

[867]Müller (2014), p. 109.

tenets of Jewish law! Paul's writings suggest that the earliest Christian communities considered themselves the fulfillment of the prophecy of Jeremiah:

> Behold, days are coming, quoth the Lord, and I will make a new covenant with the house of Israel and the house of Juda. It will not be like the covenant that I made with their fathers in the day when I took them by their hand to bring them out of the land of Egypt, because they did not abide in my covenant, and I was unconcerned for them, quoth the Lord, because this is the covenant that I will make with the house of Israel after those days, quoth the Lord. Giving I will give my laws in their mind, and I will write them on their hearts, and I will become a god to them, and they shall become a people to me. And they shall not teach, each his fellow citizen and each his brother, saying, "Know the Lord," because they shall all know me, from their small even to their great, because I will be gracious regarding their injustices, and remember their sins no more.[868]

Müller writes that, in the book of Ezekiel, "the concept of the new covenant ... is expanded with the feature that God at that time will also offer his people a new heart and a new spirit":

> And I will give you a new heart, and a new spirit I will give in you, and I will remove the stone heart from your flesh and give you a heart of flesh. And I will give my spirit in you, and will act so that you walk in my statutes and keep my judgments and perform them.[869]

This covenant theology is probably the presupposition of Paul's whole thinking about the new life. In 2 Corinthians 3[:3] it becomes explicit. In this chapter Paul speaks of the Corinthians as a letter from Christ, delivered by the apostle, "written not with ink but with the Spirit of the living God, not on tablets of stone but on tablets of human hearts."[870]

Paul's gospel teaching was to facilitate the new life which he expected his congregations to realize. Paul, of course, did not intend to produce 'scripture,' as he was addressing problems in various situations. The author of Mark, however, "took the step of writing anonymously and ... for all [Christian] congregations." For Mark, the term 'gospel' means the whole series of events which he describes and has the same content as it has for Paul: the sum of the meaning of the life of Jesus. That is, Jesus Christ IS the gospel.[871]

By the transformation of a Pauline vertical Christology concerned with the heavenly authority of Christ into a horizontal story, the author behind the Gospel of Mark seemingly wanted to "narrativise" this very authority. However, by moving away in this manner from the more charismatic sort of authority, he opened the door for a more traditional authority that insisted upon offering the true and therefore correct 'Jesus tradition'. ... Troels Engberg-Pedersen is inclined to understand the Gospel of Mark as a narrativisation of concepts which in one way or the other are central in the letters of Paul as well. This demands a reading of the Gospel of Mark as a narrative construction. Once this is done, it is quite remarkable to notice the amount of meaning which is indisputably present in the text, but which is only seen once one allows oneself to read it in this way.[872]

The inner meanings of the Gospel of Mark can only be perceived if it is understood that Mark was composed as an allegory.

---

[868]Jeremiah 38:31-34, LXX, cited by Müller, p. 110.
[869]Ezekiel 36:26-27, cited by Müller, p. 111.
[870]Müller (2014), p. 111.
[871]Müller (2014), p. 114.
[872]Müller (2014), pp. 114–15.

... Mark was *written* the way Philo *interpreted* the biblical narratives about the lives and journeys of Abraham and Moses ... by means of allegorical *composition* Mark continued the aim and strategy of Paul's allegorical *interpretation* of scripture, the law and the Jewish ethnic identity markers in the construction of a Christ-believing identity *vis-à-vis* non-Christ-believing, law-abiding Jews.[873]

Müller thinks it is likely that Mark was not only later received as scripture, but that it was intended to be so when it was written. That the Gospel of Mark was written to be read in worship services was proposed by Michael Goulder in his lectionary hypothesis.[874] The oldest reference to written Gospels is in Justin Martyr's *Apology*, where he tells about "the memoirs of the apostles" being read alongside "the writings of the prophets" at Christian gatherings (1.67). Just prior to this, he had identified them as "gospels" (1.66). In Justin's *Dialogue with Trypho*, he mentions four gospels (*Dial.* 103:8).

Müller concludes:

[The Gospel of Mark] is a story meant for devotional reading to reveal the divine to hearers/readers who constitute a "community of interpretation" by participating in the new covenant and possessing the spirit. Martin Dibelius' definition of the Gospel of Mark "as a book of secret epiphanies", is still valid. ...

Maybe the use of the Gospel of Mark for devotional reading in Christian congregations also offers the clue to the writing of the later gospels. Since it was primarily a *theological* narrativisation of the gospel of Jesus Christ, representatives of other theological positions found it necessary to rewrite the story of the earthly Jesus as they received it from their predecessor or predecessors. A comparison of the four New Testament gospels reveal an astonishing freedom to construct and reconstruct the Jesus tradition in order to promote the authors' special understanding of the gospel. In turn, such freedom must be attributed to the author of the first gospel.[875]

In short, no oral tradition, no Q.

Mark: Interpreter of Paul

The title of Joel Marcus's contribution is a play on Papias' famous description of Mark as the interpreter of Peter,[876] which, Marcus notes, Rudolf Pesch has suggested, "like the pseudonymous ascription of 1 Peter to Peter, is an attempt to reconcile the Pauline and Petrine wings of the church by attributing to Peter a work that highlights Pauline theology."

Marcus further notes that Volkmar's *Die Religion Jesu* (1857) "claimed that Mark was an allegory in which Jesus stood for Paul, the family of Jesus stood for the Law-observant Jerusalem church led by James, and the Pharisees stood for Paul's Pharisaic Christian opponents."[877] William Wrede said of Volkmar:

---

[873]Henrik Tronier, 'Philonic Allegory in Mark,' cited by Müller, pp. 115–16.

[874]Michael Goulder, *Midrash and Lection in Matthew* (London: SPCK, 1974) and *The Evangelists' Calendar* (London: Spck, 1978), pp. 241–306.

[875]Müller (2014), pp. 116–17.

[876]Eusebius, *Church History* 3.39.15.

[877]Joel Marcus, 'Mark – Interpreter of Paul,' in Becker *et al.* (2014), p. 29.

The sum total of what is false and impossible in his work is great in things both great and small ... [Yet] without a doubt Volkmar's book is the most perceptive and shrewd, and to my mind altogether the most important, that we possess on Mark.[878]

Recent scholarship has come back around to the idea that Mark is a Pauline gospel, which, Marcus writes, "has led to the re-emergence of Ferdinand Christian Baur's thesis that Paul was a polemical theologian, and that his opinions about subjects such as the Law and the theology of the cross were not consensus positions, but embattled outposts" at the edge of Jerusalem Christianity. That is, Paul was "a lonely and contentious figure," and thus it is remarkable that, on nearly every point, Mark agrees with him. Thus, Mark too is a polemical writer who was against the Jerusalem church.[879]

Marcus points out that both Mark and Paul "make the term [evangelion] a central aspect of their theology (e.g. Mark 1:1; Gal 1:6-9; Rom 1:16-17). Both stress the significance of Jesus' crucifixion as the apocalyptic turning point of the ages," with a resurrection to Heaven, not Earth. "Both highlight Jesus' victory over demonic powers and see his advent as the prophesied dawn of the age of divine blessing ... Both portray Jesus as a new Adam." But where Adam was tempted and failed, Jesus was tempted and succeeded.

> [I]t is commonly recognized that [Mark's] temptation narrative has background in the Adam story ... But it is not only the temptation narrative but also the entire sequence of which it is part, 1:9-15, that has Adamic background. ... The Markan transfiguration narrative also has Adamic features; in contrast to Matthew and Luke ... it is Jesus' *clothes* rather than his face that shines. This motif of radiant clothing corresponds to a widespread emphasis in early Judaism and Christianity on Adam's "garments of glory"; see e.g. *Targum Yerusalmi* on Gen 3:7, 21; *Gen. Rab.* 18:56; 20:12; *Pirqe R. El* 14: but cf. already Ezek 28:13.[880]

Further similarities highlighted by Marcus include the fact that both Paul and Mark emphasize the importance of the faith *of* Jesus and faith in God, depicting this faith as "a new mode of seeing," while others are condemned for their blindness (Mark 4:10-12; Rom. 11:7-10; 1 Cor. 2:6-16). "Both Mark and Paul have negative things to say about Peter and about members of Jesus' family (Mark 3:20-21, 31-35; 8:31-33; Galatians 2). Both assert that Jesus came not for the righteous but for ungodly sinners (Mark 2:17; Rom 4:15; 5:18-19)." Finally, both Mark and Paul see an "apocalyptic change in the Law that ... included an abrogation of the OT food laws."[881]

One of the main differences that Werner and his followers saw between Paul and Mark was the fact that Paul said almost nothing about the 'life of Jesus,' while Mark gives detailed accounts of many incidents. However, once one realizes that these 'detailed accounts of incidents in the life of Jesus' are all borrowed from the OT, from the Pauline letters, from Homeric epics and other literature of the time, it becomes obvious that Mark was simply writing a story to teach Pauline theology: the Gospel of Mark *really is* an allegory. Paul's theology was controversial, as we already know, so Mark was embedding it in a story with many clues to the reader/listener that it was what it was: an allegory.

---

[878]William Wrede, *The Messianic Secret* (1901), cited by Marcus, p. 29, n. 2.
[879]Marcus (2014), p. 30.
[880]Marcus (2014), p. 31.
[881]Marcus (2014), p. 32.

Marcus compares the theology of the cross in Paul and Mark to demonstrate that they are identical. He writes:

> Both Paul and Mark lay *extraordinary* stress on the death of Jesus. This theme dominates Paul's Christological affirmations. Similarly, Mark's whole narrative, at least from 2:20 and 3:6 on, points toward the crucifixion scene that is its climax. ... In both Paul and Mark the death of Jesus on the cross is understood as an apocalyptic event, the turning point of the ages ... [882]

Marcus then goes on to note the apocalyptic metaphors in 1 Cor. 1-2: "this age," "in a mystery," "that which has been hidden," and "revealed." The allegory for this is the cosmic darkness and rending of the Temple curtain in Mark 15. In Gal. 6:14, "the cross of Jesus is also the means for the crucifixion of the old world," and in Mark 15:33 there are echoes of Amos 8:9, "in which the sun will go down at noon 'on that day' of God's judgment." Jesus' resurrection to heaven confirms the eschatological change, "but does not supersede it."[883] There is nothing in Paul or Mark about a physical resurrection on Earth. The original ending of Mark does not describe a resurrection appearance because, for him, "The cross ... is itself both the judgment of the world, and the victory over the world."[884] Mark's narrative is climaxed when a human being recognizes his divine sonship at the moment of his death (Mk. 15:39) and, startlingly, it is a Roman soldier.

> [B]oth Paul and Mark ... use the perfect passive participle [of the Greek word translated as 'crucified'] to remind their readers that the Risen Jesus continues to be the Crucified One ...[885]

> ... but we proclaim Christ crucified ... (1 Cor. 1:23)

> But he said to them, "Do not be alarmed; you are looking for Jesus of Nazareth, who was crucified. He has been raised; he is not here." (Mark 16:6)

Marcus writes that both Paul and Mark "acknowledge that the proclamation of a crucified Messiah is scandalous and contrary-to-sense because it calls on human beings to see God's eschatological power, life, and glory displayed in a scene of the starkest human weakness, degradation, and death."[886] In a deliberate provocation, Paul emphasizes that Jesus was hung on a cross, and thus, according to the Law, was cursed and unclean (Gal. 3:13; Deut. 21:23) and, therefore, outside the Divine Covenant with Israel. Marcus concludes that when Mark has the Temple curtain rip apart at the moment of Jesus' death, he symbolizes "the end of the central institution of Judaism (15:38)."[887]

I concur with Marcus that Paul's polemics in his letters strongly suggest that his "cross-centered theology was controversial," especially to the Jerusalem Christians, and many remarks in his letters let us know that his gospel brought him into disrepute. In Gal. 5:11, he tells us that the cross is scandalous and in Phil 3:18 he refers to "enemies of the cross."

---

[882] Marcus (2014), p. 36.
[883] Marcus, (2014), p. 36.
[884] Beker, *Paul* (2000), p. 201, cited by Marcus, p. 37.
[885] Marcus (2014), p. 37.
[886] Marcus (2014), p. 37.
[887] Marcus (2014), p. 38.

The other evangelists do, of course, regard the crucifixion as the turning point of the ages; Matthew emphasizes it by adding an earthquake and a series of resurrections to his crucifixion scene. (Matt. 27:51-53). But in none of the other Gospels is the revelation of Jesus' divine sonship to human beings withheld until the exact moment of his death (remember, Peter didn't really get it). Additionally, the other Gospels avoid the total focus on the crucifixion alone by adding resurrection appearances. Marcus notes that Luke also "strikes from Mark 16:6 the perfect passive participle [of the Greek word translated as 'crucified,'] which suggests the continuing relevance of Jesus' crucifixion."[888]

Both Matthew and Luke soften "the Markan emphasis on the weakness and abandonment experienced by Jesus in the Passion Narrative." Neither of them could understand that, for Paul, the fact that Jesus went to his death with absolute faith, even in the face of total, utter abandonment, was the point: that was the demonstration of God's power.

Marcus observes that, in the Gethsemane scene, "Luke eliminates Jesus' depression" while Matthew retains it but changes Mark's graphic Greek word translated as "he became depressed," to the "less colorful word" for "he became sad." Yet both retain the fact that Jesus was overwhelmed at the threat of his coming death and falls to the ground. Luke, by contrast, presents a far more modulated scenario where Jesus doesn't throw himself down, but kneels in a dignified way.[889] Further, he is succored by angels who keep his spirits up.

When comparing the passages below, both in the NRSV and the Greek/ English interlinear translation, I noticed that NRSV tended to harmonize the translations, making them almost the same. What is below is from the Amplified translation (Zondervan), which comes closer to the original Greek wherein you can see the distinct differences.

Mar 14:33-36 And He took with Him Peter and James and John, and began to be struck with terror and amazement and deeply troubled and depressed. And He said to them, **My soul is exceedingly sad (overwhelmed with grief) so that it almost kills Me!** Remain here and keep awake and be watching.	**Mat 26:37-39** And taking with Him Peter and the two sons of Zebedee, He began to show grief and distress of mind and was deeply depressed. Then He said to them, **My soul is very sad and deeply grieved, so that I am almost dying of sorrow.** Stay here and keep awake and keep watch with Me.	**Luk 22:40-44** And when He came to the place, He said to them, Pray that you may not [at all] enter into temptation. And He withdrew from them about a stone's throw and knelt down and prayed, Saying, Father, if You are willing, remove this cup from Me; yet not My will, but [always] Yours be done.
And going a little farther, He fell on the ground and kept praying that if it were possible the [fatal] hour might pass from Him. And He was saying, Abba, [which means] Father, everything is possible for You. Take away this cup from Me; yet not what I will, but what You [will].	And going a little farther, He threw Himself upon the ground on His face and prayed saying, My Father, if it is possible, let this cup pass away from Me; nevertheless, not what I will [not what I desire], but as You will and desire.	And there appeared to Him an angel from heaven, strengthening Him in spirit. And being in an agony [of mind], He prayed [all the] more earnestly and intently, and His sweat became like great clots of blood dropping down upon the ground.

Marcus writes:

[888]Marcus (2014), p. 40.
[889]Marcus (2014), p. 40.

Matthew is less radical in his retouching of Mark, but he still qualifies Mark's *theologia crucis* somewhat. In the scene of Jesus' arrest, for example, he introduces a saying in which Jesus stresses that he could if he wanted to, even at this moment, escape arrest by appealing for heavenly intervention (Matt 26:53-54). Although he retains the cry of dereliction [at the moment of death], there is more of an element of control in his version of Jesus' decease than there is in Mark's ... [890]

Again I use the Zondervan Amplified translation to compare the texts:

Mar 15:37 And Jesus uttered a loud cry, and breathed out His life.	**Mat 27:50** And Jesus cried again with a loud voice and gave up His spirit.	**Luk 23:46** And Jesus, crying out with a loud voice, said, Father, into Your hands I commit My spirit! And with these words, He expired.

John's Jesus is in control all the way through the passion. He doesn't even give up the ghost until "all has been accomplished," including the "I thirst" routine, which was to "fulfill the scripture" (John 19:28-30). In short, John's Jesus is certainly nothing like Mark's or Paul's Jesus, who "took the form of a slave" (Phil. 2:8), i.e. was totally human.

Marcus's conclusion is that Mark's Jesus is, indeed, Paul's Jesus, including "Paul's peculiar emphasis on the cross as the instrument for the revelation of the apocalyptic power of God in a devastated landscape of human weakness and death."[891]

Werner has argued that Paul's 'Kardinaldogma' is that Jesus' death represented his triumph over the demonic powers that were responsible for crucifying him (1 Cor. 2:8). Marcus points out that there is no trace of this idea in Mark, since Mark's story places the responsibility for his crucifixion on human enemies.[892] However, that difference is not so clear. Mark's portrayal of the human opposition to Jesus is simply an extension of the cosmic opposition, which is portrayed in the temptation narrative and the exorcisms, where demons are operative through human beings. Marcus notes:

> This intertwined demonic/human opposition culminates in Jesus' crucifixion. Mark probably means his readers to understand that the Jewish leaders' conspiracy to liquidate Jesus (3:6; 11:18) reflects the demons' fear that he will liquidate *them* (1:24); the [Greek verb translated as "to destroy"] is used in both cases and resurfaces in the description of a demon's intention to destroy a human being in 9:22. Various features of the Markan passion narrative imply that the climax of this reciprocal hostility is Jesus' death. Mark portrays the latter as a scene of cosmic darkness (15:33), and darkness suggests demonic powers elsewhere in the NT (e.g. Eph 6:12) and in Jewish sources ... Mark himself, moreover, links an apocalyptic darkening of the sun with the disturbance of cosmic (demonic?) powers in 13:24-25. And at the climax of the Passion Narrative Mark uses exactly the same phrase to describe Jesus' death-scream (... 15:34, 37) as he has employed previously to describe the screams of demoniacs who are in the process of being exorcised (1:26; 5:7), thereby suggesting that Jesus' death is equivalent to an exorcism.[893]

In short, for Mark, as for Paul, Jesus' death is a defeat of the demonic forces, a vicarious sacrifice for the sins of humanity, the beginning of a new age, all accomplished in a scene of

---

[890]Marcus (2014), p. 41.

[891]Marcus (2014), p. 41.

[892]Marcus (2014), pp. 42–3.

[893]Marcus (2014), p. 43. In 1:26 the demon cries with a loud voice as it comes out of the demoniac; cf. 9:26.

weakness, suffering and death, the significance of which is only apparent to those who have learned to see and think in a radically new manner. As Marcus concludes: "Not everyone agreed with Paul that the Law was passé for Christians – but Mark did."[894]

Mark and the Pauline Mission

In 1997, John Painter "suggested that Mark is an expression of the Pauline mission, rather than a Petrine Gospel as claimed by Papias." Further, "that Mark is shaped by and provides a basis for the Pauline Law-free mission."[895] In contradiction to this thesis, in his 2004 book *The Date of Mark's Gospel*,[896] James G. Crossley sets out to prove that the commonly accepted date of Mark (c. 70 AD) is not convincing (to him, at least), and that the Gospel should be dated well before Paul.

> Around 320 AD, Eusebius (*H.E.* 6.25.3) refers to Origen (c. 185–251 AD) in his commentary on Matthew, defending the canon of the church. This rare use of ['canon'] describes Origen's defence of the four-Gospel canon. Origen was building on the clear defence of the four Gospels by Irenaeus (*Adv. Haer.* 3.11.8). [897]

For the identification of the author of each Gospel, we cannot get further back than this. Whether the testimony of Papias to Mark and Matthew is related to the titles, or is of comparable age and value, is debatable.

Painter writes, "When it comes to dating the Gospels, the evidence is no better. Clement of Alexandria thought that the Gospels with genealogies were earlier than those without ... (Eusebius *H.E.* 6.14.4b-7)" Augustine thought that Mark was dependent on both Matthew and Luke, in agreement with Clement. "The dominant view of experts today is that Mark was first and was used by both Matthew and Luke" (and probably John). "Austin Farrer challenged the Q hypothesis in his revolutionary essay of 1955, 'On dispensing with Q.'"[898]

In any event, with no real hard evidence to prove anything, "Crossley argues for a date for Mark between the mid-thirties and mid-forties"! He claims that it lacks any signs of Paul's Law-free position, and this is his main evidence that Mark was earlier than Paul. The motivation for this maneuver is that he wishes "to exclude a reading of Mark 7:19b as evidence of Pauline influence." He focuses on Mark's use of Jewish legal material, arguing that Mark's Jesus breaks no biblical law and the Torah is not challenged. He regards Mark's presentation of Jesus as Law observant to be pre-Pauline and this, then, provides evidence for its early date.[899] (Yeah, I know, it's circular, but there you have it!) Here is the text in question from Mark 7:

---

[894]Marcus (2014), p. 44.

[895]John Painter, *Mark's Gospel* (1997), cited by Painter, 'Mark and the Pauline Mission,' in *Paul and Mark: Comparative Essays Part I*, edited by Oda Wischmeyer, David C. Sim, Ian J. Elmer (Berlin/Boston: De Gruyter, 2014), p. 527.

[896]James G. Crossley, *The Date of Mark's Gospel: Insight from the Law in Earliest Christianity* (London: T&T Clark International, 2004).

[897]Painter (2014), p. 528, n. 6.

[898]Painter (2014), p. 528.

[899]Painter (2014), p. 529.

1 Now when the Pharisees and some of the scribes who had come from Jerusalem gathered around him, 2 they noticed that some of his disciples were eating with defiled hands, that is, without washing them. 3 (For the Pharisees, and all the Jews, do not eat unless they thoroughly wash their hands, thus observing the tradition of the elders; 4 and they do not eat anything from the market unless they wash it; and there are also many other traditions that they observe, the washing of cups, pots, and bronze kettles.) 5 So the Pharisees and the scribes asked him, "Why do your disciples not live according to the tradition of the elders, but eat with defiled hands?"

6 He said to them, "Isaiah prophesied rightly about you hypocrites, as it is written, 'This people honors me with their lips, but their hearts are far from me; 7 in vain do they worship me, teaching human precepts as doctrines.' 8 You abandon the commandment of God and hold to human tradition." 9 Then he said to them, "You have a fine way of rejecting the commandment of God in order to keep your tradition! 10 For Moses said, 'Honor your father and your mother'; and, 'Whoever speaks evil of father or mother must surely die.' 11 But you say that if anyone tells father or mother, 'Whatever support you might have had from me is Corban' (that is, an offering to God) – 12 then you no longer permit doing anything for a father or mother, 13 thus making void the word of God through your tradition that you have handed on. And you do many things like this."

14 Then he called the crowd again and said to them, "Listen to me, all of you, and understand: 15 there is nothing outside a person that by going in can defile, but the things that come out are what defile." 16 If any man has ears to hear, let him be listening.

17 When he had left the crowd and entered the house, his disciples asked him about the parable. 18 He said to them, "Then do you also fail to understand? Do you not see that whatever goes into a person from outside cannot defile, 19 since it enters, not the heart but the stomach, and goes out into the sewer?" (Thus he declared all foods clean.) 20 And he said, "It is what comes out of a person that defiles. 21 For it is from within, from the human heart, that evil intentions come: fornication, theft, murder, 22 adultery, avarice, wickedness, deceit, licentiousness, envy, slander, pride, folly. 23 All these evil things come from within, and they defile a person."

Painter responds to Crossley's claims:

> In the quest to find a Law observant Marcan Jesus, he allows the expectation to become an assumption that leads him to overlook the implications of the parabolic saying of Mark 7:15 and to an unacceptable reading of Mark 7:19b: "making all foods clean." Thus, for him, "all foods" means, in this context, only all "permitted food." ... He is wrong to limit Mark's editorial conclusion to this meaning, and unjustified in arguing that Matt 15:20b correctly interprets Mark 7:19b. Rather, it seems, Matthew has recognized that Mark 7:19b is an unacceptable (to him) Marcan editorial comment, and replaces Marcan editorial with words attributed to Jesus: "but to eat with unwashed hands does not defile a person" (Matt 15:20b). Matthew's conclusion fits the context, whereas the Marcan conclusion opens up a new issue that is nevertheless implied by Jesus' parabolic saying in Mark 7:15, and his explanation in 7:18-19a, 20-23)[900]

Bizarrely, "Crossley argues that Mark's words ... only took on an unacceptable meaning for Matthew in light of the later (subsequent to Mark) Pauline influence." That is, he claims that Mark 7:19b is only saying that such foods were not made unclean by unwashed hands, which is what Matthew says; he defends Matthew's reading of Mark, not as a correction, but that Matthew got Mark right! The problem is that this reading takes no account of Mark 7:15, 18-19a, 20-23. That is, Crossley, in his blindness, misses the whole point of the passage, the radical nature of Jesus' parabolic response to his critics: "there is nothing outside a person that by going

---

[900]Painter (2014), p. 530.

in can defile, but the things that come out are what defile." Crossley has completely lost the spiritual import of the text. He is, effectively, thinking exactly like the "scribes from Jerusalem"! Painter destroys Crossley's argument, quoted here *in extenso*:

> The Marcan form of the parable does not specify the part of the person anything enters and exits. Given the discussion is about eating food, Matthew's clarification, naming the mouth as the point of entry and exit might seem obvious (Matt 15:11). As it turns out in the explanation, he was wrong. In Mark, only in Jesus' explanation does it become clear that what goes in is *into the belly* while what defiles comes *out of the heart* ...
>
> Matthew seeks to soften and limit possible implications by leaving out the [italicized] words above and adding some interpretative changes; "It is not what goes into the *mouth* that defiles a person but what comes out of the *mouth* defiles a person" (Matt 15:11). The potential stark crudeness of the parable in Mark 7:15 was unacceptable to Matthew. In Mark the parabolic saying is capable of meaning; "it is not food going into a person that defiles, but human excreta coming out defiles a person." In Jesus' explanation in Mark what goes into the belly goes out as human excreta into the latrine. Hence the wording of the parable in Mark is open to this meaning. That this is not the meaning only becomes clear in the explanation of the parable, clarified by "what comes out of the heart." In Matthew, the parable already excludes this crude possibility by changing the wording to say; "it is not what goes into the *mouth* but what comes out of the *mouth* that defiles" (Matt 15:11). This is a step in the direction of Jesus' explanation in Mark. But while the common use of mouth for what goes in and out excludes any possible reference to human excreta, the mouth is hardly the source of "fornication, theft, murder, adultery, wickedness, deceit, licentiousness, envy, pride, folly," for which the Marcan use of heart is entirely appropriate. ...
>
> In Mark, the implications of Jesus' parabolic saying (Mk. 7:15) are spelt out in his response (Mk. 7:18-23) to the request of the disciples for clarification (Mk. 7:17). The issue with which Matthew struggles, the abolition of the food laws, is inherent in Jesus' parabolic saying and explanation, not only the blatant statement of Mark's conclusion. As Jesus explains to the disciples; "nothing from outside entering into a person is able to defile him, because it does not enter into his heart but into the belly, and goes out into the latrine" (Mk. 7:18-19a). The Marcan Jesus identifies the human heart as the source of defilement and evil (Mk. 7:20-23) and in this he is followed, though less clearly, by Matthew (15:18-20a), who concludes; "These [what comes out of the mouth proceeding from the heart] are what defile a person, but to eat with unwashed hands does not defile" (Mk. 15:20).
>
> ... Mark's conclusion reflects the perspective of Paul's Law-free gospel. Matthew's modifications of Mark 7:1-23 struggle to neutralize this perspective but his conclusion limits the implications of Jesus' parable and explanation to the hand-washing incident.[901]

Obviously, Crossley wanted to see Mark as a true account of the mission of Jesus, prior to Paul, and thus, that Paul was just continuing with the Jesus tradition. His case depends on a very early date for Mark and certainly doesn't address the many other facts that have been adduced about Mark, particularly in reference to the literary sources from which the pericopes were drawn.

Further, if the Pauline mission was just a continuation of the mission of Jesus, the opposition of the Jerusalem church toward Paul becomes inexplicable. Painter points out that the seeming acceptance of Peter's report by the Jerusalem church in Acts 1:1-18 makes the incidents at Antioch reported by Paul in Gal. 2:11-14 totally out of synch. He then asks: "Does this cast some doubt on the credibility of the Acts account...?" Well, yes. However, such an eminent

[901]Painter (2014), pp. 530–32. Painter's italics.

scholar as Heikki Räisänen notes: "A broad consensus among NT scholars that this [Mark 7:15] belongs to the bedrock of those *ipissima verba*, the authenticity of which is hardly open to serious doubt."[902]

Frankly, considering all the evidence compiled in this volume thus far, which is certainly available to the eminent scholars, I can only shake my head in amazement. The saying of Mark 7:15 is quite dissimilar from Judaism, clearly promoted by the Jerusalem church, but hardly dissimilar from Paul. It is blazingly clear that Mark depends on Paul. And it is clear that Matthew has modified Mark back to a more 'Jewish' interpretation. It is obvious that both of them were putting words in Jesus' mouth quite freely and with no compunction. That, of course, leads one to think that both were quite aware that the figure of 'Jesus of Nazareth' was a mythical creation and they were simply using allegory to promote their own versions of Christian theology. At one point, Painter asks the obvious question:

> How, in a very short time, did a predominantly Gentile church emerge from a distinctively Jewish movement? This has long been a matter of contention between scholars of early Christianity. The most likely answer is complex, and includes the following lines of evidence and argument. The success of the Pauline Law-free mission to the nations is one side of this. Another involves the destruction of the Jewish leadership of the Jerusalem church.[903]

He then goes on to cite the problem of the death of James, 'the Lord's brother,' accepting the date of 62 AD, and then, after the destruction of Jerusalem, the alleged reconstitution of the Jerusalem church under "Symeon, the cousin of Jesus and James," according to Eusebius (*H.E.* 3.11), and that the influence of the Jerusalem church ended with the second Jewish revolt of 135 AD, again, following Eusebius (*H.E.* 4.5). As has already been discussed, all of this is complete fabrication. What is true is that the Law-free church grew apace following the destruction of Jerusalem; some elements of the Pauline gospel fell away from prominence, but the Law-free aspect largely prevailed. As Painter writes: "No significant Jewish church remained to balance or restrain the drive of burgeoning Gentile Christianity."[904]

We are left with the very strong suspicion that, despite the fact that it seems almost certain that Paul's Christ was not Jewish, *it was Mark who created the Jewish Jesus*, and for several reasons. First of all, the whole messianic idea was Jewish, and the movement began in Palestine; second, Paul himself was Jewish and the character of Jesus was partly modeled on Paul; third, the God Paul was promoting as the creator of the Universe, all and everything, and the father of the pre-existent messiah (no matter his incarnational nationality), was the Jewish god, Yahweh/Jehovah; finally, there were many Jewish Christians all around the Empire and it only made sense to Mark to try to unite Jewish and Gentile Christians into the same faith, that of Paul, to which Mark clearly was strongly attached. This approach further attached the allegedly ancient and venerable Jewish scriptures to the new religion giving it the cachet of antiquity.

Mark (nor Matthew, for that matter) never intended for any educated person to believe that the Jesus of Nazareth he created was a fully historical person. The audience he wrote for knew the story of Paul, very likely knew the story of Judas the Galilean, knew what had happened to

---

[902]Heikki Räisänen, 'Jesus and the Food Laws: Reflections on Mk 7:15,' in *Jesus, Paul and Torah: Collected Essays* (Sheffield: JSOT Press, 1992), 127–48.

[903]Painter (2014), p. 537.

[904]Painter (2014), p. 538.

the Jerusalem church of Zealots, and were, themselves, by virtue of this association, in somewhat of a parlous situation; tarnished by association, as it were. What was needed was a story that conveyed the truth of Paul's messiah and got the Christians who had been misled by the Jerusalem church out of hot water. Mark's Gospel, written in the common language of the time, but displaying incomparable brilliance in its construction, was just the ticket. Mark retained the perspective of the messianic movement of the Jews while moving strongly in the direction of Paul's Law-free mission, but in such a way as to lessen the shock to any Jewish Christian believers. Issues that would have been of concern to Jewish believers are dealt with creatively, such as Sabbath observance and purity issues. Painter notes:

> It is notable that the first of Jesus' mighty works according to Mark occurred in a synagogue in Capernaum on a Sabbath where Jesus drove out an *unclean* spirit from a man (1:23-27). Then there is the *cleansing* of a leper (1:40-45), and the case of the woman with an issue of blood who touched Jesus to be made whole (5:24b-34) before the two issues involved in 7:1-30. These are followed immediately by the first of two healings, found only in Mark, in which Jesus uses spittle to heal. The first of these occurred in the Gentile region of the Decapolis where Jesus healed a deaf and dumb man by putting his fingers into the man's ears, spat and touched his tongue (7:31-37). In the second, Jesus spat on the eyes of a blind man in Bethsaida and laid his hands on his eyes twice before he saw clearly (8:22-26). This use of bodily fluids was irregular, revealing Jesus pushing at the boundaries of the purity laws. Mark seems to stress these issues, which are treated in more detail in the two incidents in 7:1-30. Mark 7:1-30 is in a part of Mark with no Lucan parallel.[905]

It appears that one of the primary reasons Mark was written was with the idea to bring the Jewish Christians around to Paul's theology and to dissociate Gentile Christians from any taint of Jewish Zealotry that might have been implied by their adherence to the Jewish God.

Traditions in Conflict

Theodore J. Weeden writes:

> The only way to interpret the Gospel as the author intended it is to read his work with the analytical eyes of a first century reader. That means in some way assuming the conceptual and analytical stance of a reader in the first century, a solution that is easier stated than implemented.[906]

The difficulty should not stop us from trying. The first thing one needs to do is have a good grasp of the history and social conditions of the time, including awareness of the principles and procedures of reading and literary analysis that the first-century reader had. Greek and Roman education of the time focused on a very pedantic study of the great literary works of the past: the epic poets such as Homer, and the tragedians such as Euripides, Aeschylus and Sophocles. Also respected were Herodotus, Xenophon, Hellanicus and Thucydides. The effort was aimed at learning everything possible, down to the minutest details, about the works of these literary giants. Once the content of a work had become very familiar to the student by hearing it described, and then reading it, attention turned to interpretation.

---

[905]Painter (2014), p. 550.
[906]Theodore J. Weeden, *Mark, Traditions in Conflict* (Philadelphia: Fortress Press, 1971), p. 11.

In terms of interpretation of a work, characterization was of particular interest. There was a preoccupation with knowing all there was to know about the characters so as to be able to make a judgment illustrating some moral principle based on their thoughts and behavior. Thus, heroes of ancient works served as models of behavior or examples of virtue or vice. In Roman education, the authors studied were more often Roman rather than Greek, but the methodology was the same. The bottom line is, though, that the education of that time sought to understand the purpose of a work and the mind of the writer and all the characters through the events, actions and words portrayed. And then, of course, having been trained this way, students who grew up to be authors would then write their works the way the ancients did. They wrote history not so much to provide accurate information, but to guide the reader to a moralistic interpretation. Livy (59 BC–17 AD) wrote in the preface to his monumental work on the history of Rome, *Ab Urbe Condita*:

> The subjects to which I would ask each of my readers to devote his earnest attention are these – the life and morals of the community; the men and the qualities by which through domestic policy and foreign war dominion was won and extended. Then as the standard of morality gradually lowers, let him follow the decay of the national character, observing how at first it slowly sinks, then slips downward more and more rapidly, and finally begins to plunge into headlong ruin, until he reaches these days, in which we can bear neither our diseases nor their remedies.
>
> There is this exceptionally beneficial and fruitful advantage to be derived from the study of the past, that you see, set in the clear light of historical truth, examples of every possible type. From these you may select for yourself and your country what to imitate, and also what, as being mischievous in its inception and disastrous in its issues, you are to avoid.[907]

Livy does not add much in the way of commentary since, as he notes in his preface, he provides interpretations indirectly by how he depicts and highlights traits and actions of his characters within the historical situation. And of course, because he has an agenda, he often takes liberties with historical characters and sets aside historical accuracy.

Thus we may imagine the mindset of the first-century reader of Mark's Gospel. This interpretative stance was fixed by his culture regardless of his level of education. He or she would have looked at the Gospel as something written in the style of a Greek drama combined with a popular 'Life of So-and-so' of the time. He would have naturally understood that the characters' portrayal, the events depicted, and the points of focus deliver a message that is 'between the lines and characters.'

The author of Mark displays no great literary finesse in terms of his language, but he undoubtedly followed the literary perspectives and techniques of other authors of his time. In the Gospel of Mark, the author tells his readers a great deal by the way he portrays his characters and the events in which they participate. The reader would have likewise reflected on the attitudes, speeches and behavior of the characters in order to understand the message of the author. And the author would have intended and assumed such an approach on the part of his readers.

There was, of course, an additional field of information from which the first readers of Mark would have drawn elements for their understanding: the historical and social situation in which they lived, as well as other information that they would have possessed, obtained orally or from other literary works that are now lost to us. We can have a generally good idea of the historical

---

[907]Translated by Rev. Canon Roberts (1905).

time thanks to the few works along that line that have survived, such as Josephus, Tacitus and a few others, but regarding early Christianity, all we really have in the way of documents are the letters of Paul; but, as far as we can tell, Paul's letters were the main earliest Christian documents.

Taking our lead from the literary methods of the time, let's consider the main characters in Mark's drama: Jesus, the disciples, the religious authorities (as a group), the ever-present crowds of people. These characters are present from the beginning to the end. Other key characters who play significant but minimal roles are John the Baptist, Pilate and the Galilean women.

It doesn't take a genius to realize that the religious authorities are the villains of the piece; that is, the Pharisees, scribes, and high priests. (The Herodians, civil authorities that were closely associated with the high priests according to Josephus, play a small role.) With almost rhythmic regularity and increasing intensity, the conflict between Jesus and the authorities is flashed before the eyes of the reader with crescendos at 3:6; 8:31; 9:31; 10:33; 11:18; 12:12, and finally culminating in the execution of Jesus by the nefarious plots and designs of the Jewish authorities (Mk. 15:1-39).

Since we know from Josephus that all of these groups were often at odds with each other and did not form any kind of cohesive 'authorities' grouping, we have to wonder what this depiction conveys. We also know about Judas the Galilean and his 'Fourth Philosophy' – close to the Pharisaic view of things, but rather more strict, seemingly closer to the Dead Sea Scrolls sectarians than anything else – and that this group morphed into the Zealots, who, along with a large group of lower-level priests, incited the rebellion against Rome. Once the rebellion was enjoined, all the other groups joined it. So, it could be said that the only time the 'authorities' were ever acting even somewhat together was during the war against Rome. And that is stretching things, because we also know from Josephus that even in the midst of war against an invading force, the Jewish groups continued to fight against each other. So finding the authorities in general all acting together and aligned against Jesus in Mark's Gospel is an oddity that needs an explanation. The only social/historical situation that would fit would be the period right after the war, when a programmatic assault on the Jewish religious establishment would have been a defensive and apologetic maneuver for early Christians not wanting to be painted with the same brush with which the rebels against Rome were blackened.

The second group of characters is the amorphous mass of people that emerges again and again throughout the Gospel: the crowds. This 'character' flocks to Jesus with eagerness, responds to his healing powers with joy, and listens to his teachings enthusiastically again and again in the text. They often crowd Jesus, but not in a negative way; it just highlights his popularity with them. The crowds of people who apparently love Jesus are starkly contrasted against the Jewish authorities. Until, of course, the end, when the chief priests stir up the crowds to have them demand Jesus' crucifixion (Mk. 15:8-15). Of course, we know that the whole Pilate episode *vis-à-vis* the crowds and Jesus is a load of hogwash, considering what we know of Pilate and his relationship with Jewish crowds from Josephus and Philo. But remember, this isn't history; it's a literary work designed to convey a message.

Second only to Jesus, the disciples occupy much of Mark's attention. The authorities and crowds are depicted rather two dimensionally, while the disciples are drawn rather more sharply and in more detail, several of them standing out even more than the others. It is unlikely that there was ever such a thing as 'the Twelve'; more likely it was an invention of Mark's to symbolize Jewish Christianity with twelve disciples as there were twelve tribes of Israel. The ones that concern Mark the most are Peter, James and John – exactly the same group named by Paul in his epistles. Mark has given the others names, and perhaps those names were actually names of Jewish Christian brothers and were known to the first readers of Mark's Gospel, but we can't know that for sure. We do know that after Mark, Matthew and Luke took up the names, changing a few, and treating the disciples very differently from how Mark treated them, yet following Mark up to 90% of the time in their subsequent Gospels. This fact advocates strongly for the idea that, before Mark, no such 'life story' of a Jesus of Nazareth was even known.

The characterization of the disciples is almost confusing. First, Jesus calls them and they respond and follow him. They are apparently receivers of special revelation (4:10ff., 34; 9:30-31; 13:1ff) and his confidants (14:32). At times they appear to be his closest friends and trusted companions, and then at other times, because of their inability to see and understand, one would be forgiven for thinking that they belonged with the religious authorities as enemies of Jesus (4:13; 6:51-52; 8:14-21; 9:32). Weeden writes:

> Though the disciples are the carefully picked confidants of Jesus, heroes of the early church, authorities for authentic Christology and discipleship, ironically they emerge in the Markan drama with extremely poor performances both in terms of their perspicacity about Jesus' teaching and ministry and in terms of their loyalty to him.[908]

This depiction of the disciples, long thought to be historical, has long puzzled scholars. Some, back in the nineteenth and twentieth centuries, argued that Mark was an objective historian recounting the reminiscences of Peter (thanks to the lying testimony of Papias), who was more or less confessing what dolts he and the gang were and how silly they acted back when they were newbies, but thank goodness they learned better! Other exculpatory views have been developed, but they need not detain us here since whatever unfavorable picture of the disciples Mark produced, the effort has been to prove that there was no attempt on Mark's part to bring opprobrium down on their heads. It was believed that Mark's readers must have known about the glorified and highly esteemed post-resurrection images that had been painted by Matthew and Luke, because, of course, they too were writing 'history.' (Never mind that Matthew's inventions were at least a decade or more after Mark, and mostly used Mark; and Luke's even later, possibly a generation or more.) The whole point of such interpretations was to preserve the honor of the disciples no matter how disgracefully they acted in Mark's Gospel. Weeden writes:

> What all these scholars have refused to consider is the possibility that these Markan episodes in which the disciples are placed in such an unfavorable light may be more than just the result of the passing on of a tradition of the consequence of the development of a theological motif to set off the greatness of the Christ-event. They have failed to consider seriously the possibility that the evangelist might be attacking the disciples intentionally, for whatever reason. ... I am convinced ... that a careful analysis of Mark's presentation of the disciples supports the contention that Mark is engaged in a polemic against the disciples ...[909]

Weeden develops his reading of the disciples' relationship to Jesus in Mark's Gospel and proposes a three-stage development. At Stage 1, there is *unperceptiveness*. This is in the first half

---

[908]Weeden (1971), p. 24.
[909]Weeden (1971), pp. 25–6.

of the Gospel (Mk. 1:16-8:26), characterized by the disciples' inability to perceive who Jesus is. Despite all his healings, exorcisms, nature miracles, and teachings, they just do not get it! Even when they become involved in producing miracles after their commissioning (Mk. 3:15–6:7), they still don't get it. And what is worse, as you read through the text, you notice that their unbelievable lack of perception actually increases and hardens in spite of the fact that they enjoy a special and privileged relationship with Jesus that is open to no one else. Their inability to recognize Jesus' miraculous power is just mind-boggling. Meanwhile, those less close to Jesus seem to recognize his power instantly. For example, the woman with the hemorrhage in Mk. 5:25ff; she recognizes the power in Jesus that is so great that she knows if she just touches his garment she will be healed. But the disciples, who have been with him through repeated miracles, are unaware of this power (Mk. 5:30-31) and respond without comprehension to Jesus' declaration that someone has touched him to be healed. Crowds flock to Jesus to be healed because they recognize something in him; they recognize his miraculous powers. But in contrast to this, the disciples are bewildered. How, they ask, is Jesus going to feed four thousand people in the desert (Mk. 8:4), even though he has just previously fed five thousand by miraculous multiplication? And then, immediately after that, the disciples worry about how they are going to subsist on one loaf of bread, never mind that he has just recently fed about nine thousand people with just a few loaves of bread and a couple of fish! In short, for some strange, inexplicable reason, while crowds swarm to Jesus for miracles, the disciples are just oblivious.

What makes the Markan view stand out so sharply is the later treatment that Matthew and Luke give it. Keep in mind that they both used 90% or more of Mark's text, since they obviously didn't have any other story or traditions to tell. But in practically every instance in which the disciples are pictured as obtuse, obdurate, or inept, Matthew either omits or alters the Markan passages in question. He is very concerned to show that there is no question of the disciples being out of harmony with Jesus. In Mark 4:13, where the disciples are depicted as incapable of understanding the parable of the sower, Matthew deletes the uncomplimentary insinuation. In fact, Matthew re-writes the scene. In Mark 4:38-41 where the disciples fail to recognize in Jesus the supernatural help which could save them from the raging sea, the Matthean parallel has the disciples cry to Jesus for help (Mk. 8:25). In Mark 6:47-52, when the disciples can't understand Jesus' mastery of the storm, and Mark says "their hearts were hardened," Matthew turns the scene into a confessional expression of recognition and worship. Take a look:

Mark 6:47-52	Matt 14:23b-33
When evening came, the boat was out on the sea, and he was alone on the land. When he saw that they were straining at the oars against an adverse wind, he came towards them early in the morning, walking on the sea. He intended to pass them by. But when they saw him walking on the sea, they thought it was a ghost and cried out; for they all saw him and were terrified. But immediately he spoke to them and said, "Take heart, it is I; do not be afraid."	When evening came, he was there alone, but by this time the boat, battered by the waves, was far from the land, for the wind was against them. And early in the morning he came walking toward them on the sea. But when the disciples saw him walking on the sea, they were terrified, saying, "It is a ghost!" And they cried out in fear. But immediately Jesus spoke to them and said, "Take heart, it is I; do not be afraid."

| Then he got into the boat with them and the wind ceased. And they were utterly astounded, for they did not understand about the loaves, but their hearts were hardened. | Peter answered him, "Lord, if it is you, command me to come to you on the water." He said, "Come." So Peter got out of the boat, started walking on the water, and came toward Jesus. But when he noticed the strong wind, he became frightened, and beginning to sink, he cried out, "Lord, save me!" |
| | Jesus immediately reached out his hand and caught him, saying to him, "You of little faith, why did you doubt?" When they got into the boat, the wind ceased. And those in the boat worshiped him, saying, "Truly you are the Son of God." |

And on and on it goes, with only a few minor instances where Matthew does not delete or completely re-write Mark (in scenes where the disciples are depicted as dolts). Notice what Matthew has done: he hasn't just deleted text or altered a word or two, he's added entirely new material. And since we know that the whole walking-on-water scene is just an allegorical tale that Mark made up, possibly based on some other literary text of his time, we can be sure that Matthew isn't adding some traditional material about the life of a historical Jesus of Nazareth – he's just making stuff up. And the same is true of Luke, who used Mark and Matthew, Josephus and Paul's letters, and probably other sources for his own modifications, when he wasn't freely making stuff up. Luke's re-writing of Mark removed the hints of discord between Jesus and the disciples and damaging insinuations about the disciples' capacity for discernment. In fact, there is a large section of Mark that Luke omits entirely: 6:45–8:26. And, like Matthew, Luke presents the disciples as venerated individuals.

Since Paul's letters are the earliest Christian documents, and Mark comes next in chronology – and they have a great deal of agreement between them – those who are seeking any facts at all about earliest Christianity should look there and then, full stop. If they look at Matthew and Mark at all in any comparative study, they should keep in mind that what they are seeing is the growth of a myth predicated on an allegorical representation of Paul's theology. To actually think that Matthew and Luke were drawing on any kind of 'authentic traditions' about a historical Jesus is almost absurd. I'm not closing the door entirely on the possibility that there were traditions of the work and teachings of Judas the Galilean that were passed down somewhere or other, but the history of the time argues more for the complete destruction of the Jerusalem Christian Zealots. The only traditions that might have continued would have been those already held at other locations around the Empire; and those traditions would have definitely been dangerous to hold or promote after the destruction of Jerusalem and its temple in 70 AD, and for some time after that.

Getting back to Weeden's three-stage polemic against the disciples, Stage 2, following unperceptiveness, is *misconception*. This stage is inaugurated at Mk. 8:27 with the episode at Caesarea Philippi. Here, a sudden change takes place in Mark's depiction of the disciples' capacity for discernment. At this point, Peter is shown as apparently getting it and blurting out that Jesus is the Messiah. But then, Jesus begins to teach them what that actually means: suffering and death. Peter is repulsed by this and rebukes Jesus! It is evident that the disciples do not have the same understanding of what a messiah is and should do as Jesus. The next scene is the

Transfiguration, where God Almighty speaks from heaven, says that Jesus is his son and tells the disciples to *listen* to him, the obvious implication being that they should listen to him about his role as Messiah. But despite being given direction by God himself, the disciples continue to misunderstand and refuse to accept a suffering messiah.

From this point on, the disciples and Jesus are locked in an ongoing conflict over the characteristics of an authentic messiah and proper discipleship. Each time Jesus tries to explain it to them, they rebuke him, react in fear and lack of understanding, or indicate their misunderstanding by seeking a type of discipleship which stands in diametric opposition to the type of discipleship Jesus teaches (9:33-35; 10:23-31, 35-45). This conflict widens into a general conflict and could be seen as leading to the defection and betrayal by Judas. The plot to kill Jesus gets off the ground at Mk. 14:1. Then, there is the insertion of the story of the anointing of Jesus by the woman with the alabaster jar at Bethany (Mk. 14:3-9). In the story of the anointing, it is implied that the disciples are present and that some of them were angry about the waste of money on the ointment. This is apparently a build-up of the conflict between Jesus and the disciples and drives Judas to his betrayal at Mk. 14:10-11.

Again, Matthew and Luke delete and/or tone down any unfavorable Markan comments about the disciples, or depictions of the conflict. Matthew can be seen to consciously re-word the Markan material to enhance the image of the disciples. In Luke, however, we find that he follows Mark more closely, but with a twist: he relieves the disciples of any responsibility for their actions by declaring that it is God's plan for them to fail to understand the meaning or purpose of the passion until after the resurrection (Luke 9:45)! Luke even invents a story that causes Jesus to rebuke James (Lk. 9:51-56). It seems that Luke is attempting to 'harmonize' Mark and Matthew, giving and taking a little from each perspective, but in general, creating material that pronounces blessings on the disciples.

Finally, we come to stage three of Mark's polemic against the disciples: *rejection*. It is with Judas' decision to conspire with the high priests that this phase begins. The simmering conflict erupts into full-scale rejection and abandonment on the part of all the disciples, not just Judas. Despite the disciples' assurances that they support Jesus, they become indifferent and unconcerned when put to the test. At the most critical point in his life, when Jesus is pondering his upcoming death in the Garden of Gethsemane, Peter, James and John remain completely oblivious of his suffering (Mk. 14:32-42). Jesus implores them more than once to support him, but they fall into sleep. Just after this, Jesus is betrayed by Judas and, with his arrest, all the disciples abandon him, though Peter sticks around from a distance for just a bit longer. But then, he too leaves the stage after completely renouncing Jesus and his suffering. I'm sure Mark's audience would have thought this was at least as good as a Greek tragedy, because it has all the hallmarks of one.

Interestingly, Matthew does not alter the passion narrative very much. Keep in mind he was writing probably a decade or two later when the Empire's anger at the Jews had diminished and it was not so dangerous to speak or write of a Jewish messiah. Yet, Matthew does not 'correct' the rejection of Jesus by his disciples. Why? Was it because he knew of no real different tradition about the execution of a messiah and felt uncomfortable meddling with the one Mark had produced out of his imagination? Or, perhaps he did know and felt it expedient to keep silent.

Luke, on the other hand, did not stay his hand from modifying even the passion narrative to ensure that the disciples were seen in a better light. Again, he trots out 'the devil made them do it' excuse so that Judas and Peter are not really responsible for their betrayal and rejection of Jesus. Luke also makes the disciples more empathetic toward Jesus and his upcoming suffering and death. At the last supper, the disciples are singled out by Jesus as those who will stand by him and will continue to do so, instead of those who will reject and abandon him. The three occasions of Jesus returning to find the disciples sleeping while he agonizes in the Garden of Gethsemane have been reduced to only a single instance, and he adds the touch that they only fell asleep because of the emotional stress they are experiencing with Jesus! Luke also exonerates the disciples from abandoning Jesus at his arrest. With the exception of the devil-haunted Judas, and Peter's momentary lapse from which he recovers, the disciples are true models of loyal behavior under very trying circumstances.

Weeden thought that the denigration of the disciples was due to Markan bias, noting:

> While the tradition before Mark may have cited periods when Jesus' closest associates turned their backs on him, nowhere is there evidence that they were so completely recalcitrant as Mark would have us believe.
>
> Paul certainly paints no such picture. It is an extremely curious phenomenon that Paul, with the exception of the betrayal (1 Cor 11:23), never refers to the pre-Easter apostasy of the disciples. An argument from silence is never conclusive. Yet such information about the disciples' dissonant relationship with and rejection of Jesus would have been formidable ammunition for Paul at Antioch (Gal 2:11ff) and elsewhere in his contention that his own apostolic credentials and *kerygma* were no less authentic or commendatory than those of Peter and others who had been with Jesus during his public ministry. If the disciples' response to Jesus was anywhere nearly as poor as Mark paints it, it is hard to understand how Paul could have restrained himself from drawing upon it for appropriate polemical or apologetic purposes.[910]

What Weeden and others did not and do not take into account is the obvious fact that Mark was writing a story that allegorically presented Paul's theology and its opposition to, and difference from, that of the Jewish Christian Zealots of Jerusalem. There never was a Jesus of Nazareth as depicted by Mark; he was a composite character mainly based on Paul himself, the Jewish messianic/apocalyptic concepts, with parts of dying and rising gods of myth tossed in, and some bits of the real history of Judas the Galilean and his family/followers added in for verisimilitude. There was no 'Q' source; there was just the creative imagination of Mark, fed by the scriptures and then-current literary models and procedures.

Let's look at something else Weeden wrote:

> The crowning evidence for attributing the programmatic, denigrated picture of the disciples in Mark to the evangelist himself lies in his treatment of, or rather his failure to treat, the disciples after the denial of Peter. Following Peter's denial the disciples do not reappear again in the narrative. They cannot be found at the cross (15:22-41). They do not share in the burial (15:42-47). They are not present at the empty tomb (16:1-8). Yet the tradition of the early church was that the witnesses of these kerygmatic events were the disciples. By the time of Luke this was certainly an accepted fact ... A cardinal attestation of the budding Christian faith, according to the creed of 1 Corinthians 15:3-5, was that the Twelve had witnessed the resurrection. ... What is even more

---

[910]Weeden (1971), p. 42.

startling, following their total renunciation of Jesus, not only are the disciples conspicuously absent from all subsequent events – even the kerygmatic event upon which any claim for apostleship must be based: the resurrection – but there is no indication by Mark that the disciples were rehabilitated, that apostolicity *was* conferred upon them after their apostasy, as the other evangelists clearly record (Matt 28:16-20; Luke 24:36-49; John 20:19-23).

I take such a position with regard to Mark convinced by the evidence that Mark intentionally ended his Gospel at 16:8, and thereby intended his reader to take the full implications of 16:8b seriously.[911]

Here, I would again remind the reader of two salient facts: 1) the letters of Paul are the earliest Christian documents we have and Mark is second – Paul and Mark agree in that Mark is a narrative expression of Paul's theology and experiences; 2) the other evangelists based their stories, with modifications, on Mark, so there does not appear to have been a 'Jesus of Nazareth' tradition prior to Mark. Therefore, it is reasonable to suggest that, except for well-known Jewish Christian Zealots who appear in disguise in Mark (Peter, James, John), the other disciples are very likely fictional and meant to represent Jewish Christianity (followers of Judas the Galilean), by being numbered twelve, an allusion to the twelve tribes of Israel. Further, Mark, having once created the characters for his narrative allegory of Paul's theology, had let the genie out of the bottle and processes of mythicization and historicization rapidly went into action. The tradition of the early church that the disciples were witnesses of the kerygmatic events was a myth too.

Matthew didn't know any real traditions about 'Jesus of Nazareth,' but he knew about a more Jewish form of Christianity to which he belonged, and he probably did have some traditions about Peter, James, John and the Zealots, which influenced the way he viewed what Mark had written. He may not have realized that it was fiction, he just knew that there was disagreement between Jewish Christianity and Pauline Gentile Christianity, and so he corrected accordingly. On the other hand, Matthew may very well have known that Mark's Gospel was fiction meant to teach the theology of Paul in narrative form, and he deliberately and consciously modified it to teach the theology of a more Jewish Christianity. What weighs on the side of that view is his addition of the birth narrative, which he certainly knew was mythical. This view also makes Matthew a cynical propagandist – though his piety made him do it. He intended for his Gospel to replace Mark completely, and it is probably the Gospel of Matthew that caused Mark to fade to the background at this point (perhaps the mid-80s or 90s AD onward). Mark was still venerated and there was awareness that his text was old and the earliest, but it was now thought to be 'incomplete,' because didn't Matthew clear up so many things? Still, since the two Gospels were so alike, thanks to Matthew following Mark so closely, it was thought that we now have 'two witnesses'; and the rumors and stories multiplied like mushrooms after rain, including many tales of this or that disciple and their adventures and martyrdoms. When Marcion appeared on the scene with his gospel of the alien god, pushing Paul's theology to extremes, something had to be done; thus, Luke and Acts.

Now, as to the creed of 1 Corinthians 15:3-5, which is considered by many scholars to be a very early statement of belief, just notice that it begins with, "For I delivered to you as of first importance what I also received ..." Then he tells of the appearances of Jesus to "Cephas, then to the twelve. Then he appeared to more than five hundred brothers and sisters at one time,

---

[911]Weeden (1971), pp. 44–45.

most of whom are still alive, though some have died. Then he appeared to James, then to all the apostles. Last of all, as to one untimely born, he appeared also to me" (1Cor. 15:5b-8).

Contrast this to Paul's vehement insistence in Galatians, when under attack by the Jewish Christians of Jerusalem:

> For I want you to know, brothers and sisters, that the gospel that was proclaimed by me is not of human origin; for I did not receive it from a human source, nor was I taught it, but I received it through a revelation of Jesus Christ.[912]

> And from those who were supposed to be acknowledged leaders (what they actually were makes no difference to me; God shows no partiality) – those leaders contributed nothing to me.[913]

So the likelihood that Paul would actually write that he had received something of "first importance" – which includes a list of 'sightings' of Jesus, which could only have come from the Jerusalem church – is so unlikely as to be laughable. That anybody can't see that this is a later interpolation is beyond my ken, though the fact that the events listed here bear little or no resemblance to any later 'resurrection appearance' legends raises its own questions. The 'twelve' see Jesus, not the eleven (i.e. minus Judas); Cephas isn't included among the twelve; James doesn't seem to be an apostle (a possible reading of Gal. 1:19 suggests the same thing); there is no other tradition about the 'five hundred; and the twelve are *distinguished from* the apostles. It seems to me that the stories of 'Jesus sightings' began to grow only after Mark wrote his Gospel. What appears to actually be one of the earliest creedal statements makes no such mentions (Phil. 2:6-11).

Weeden writes:

> Mark is assiduously involved in a vendetta against the disciples. He is intent on totally discrediting them. He paints them as obtuse, obdurate, recalcitrant men who at first are unperceptive of Jesus' messiahship, then oppose its style and character, and finally totally reject it. As the *coup de grace*, Mark closes his Gospel without rehabilitating the disciples.[914]

Weeden, despite his promising beginning, was taken in by the tale and later 'traditions' and did not understand what Mark was actually doing and how important it was at the time he did it.

The Strange Family of Jesus and his Strange Disciples

Ferdinand Christian Baur was the first scholar to make a major statement about the fact that the early Christian movement was divided into two major factions in bitter conflict with each other. Others came along and restated the theory: one group of Jewish Christians argued that all followers of Jesus, both Jew and Gentile, should observe the Mosaic Law in its entirety; the second group, composed of Hellenists (and later, Paul), claimed that the Torah was obsolete in view of the Christ event. This was obviously a somewhat primitive statement of the problem,

---

[912]Gal 1:11-12.
[913]Gal 2:6.
[914]Weeden (1971), pp. 50–51.

but it at least got the issue on the table. Unsurprisingly, Baur was severely criticized; after all, hadn't all issues been solved amicably as Acts portrays?

Many scholars of recent times may agree with Baur in general, but there are disagreements over different points, mainly about the direct involvement of the Jerusalem church led by the family and disciples of Jesus in opposition to Paul. Ian J. Elmer,[915] Michael D. Goulder,[916] J. Louis Martyn,[917] and James D. G. Dunn[918] all joined the fray.

David C. Sim[919] points out that the dispute between the two major strands of the Christian tradition was carried down to the next generation of texts. Some of these continued the Pauline battle against Torah, examples being the Pastoral Epistles, Colossians, parts of the epistles of Ignatius of Antioch, etc. On the other side, the Law-observant and anti-Pauline tradition is represented by the Gospel of Matthew, the Epistle of James, and others.

Mark is clearly in the Pauline camp. In creating his story of 'Jesus of Nazareth,' imposing Pauline theology on a loose reflection of Judas the Galilean and his band of Zealots, Mark took advantage of the opportunity to refer both to the family of this 'Jesus' as well as his followers in very negative terms. How else could he co-opt the Jewish Jesus to Pauline purposes and thereby induce the Jewish Christians to change camps and join with Paul?

As S. G. F. Brandon noted, we have no documents of the Jerusalem church, though Ellegård thinks that the Epistle of James may actually have been written by James, the pillar of the Jerusalem church. Sim notes that 1 Cor. 15:3-8 – authentic or not – suggests that Paul was never included in an early list of resurrection witnesses that may have been compiled by the Jerusalem church. Sim writes:

> This tradition attests that Christ died for our sins in accordance with the Scriptures, that he was buried and then raised in accordance with the Scriptures, and it then lists in order those who received personal appearances from the risen Christ. The resurrected Jesus appeared first to Cephas and then to the twelve (disciples). He next appeared to a group of more than five hundred, then to his brother James, and then he appeared to all the apostles.[920]

I'll repeat the text here for ease of reference:

> For I handed on to you as of first importance what I in turn had received: that Christ died for our sins in accordance with the scriptures, and that he was buried, and that he was raised on the third day in accordance with the scriptures, and that he appeared to Cephas, then to the twelve. Then he appeared to more than five hundred brothers and sisters at one time, most of whom are still alive, though some have died. Then he appeared to James, then to all the apostles. Last of all, as to one untimely born, he appeared also to me. For I am the least of the apostles, unfit to be called an apostle, because I persecuted the church of God.[921]

[915]Ian J. Elmer, *Paul, Jerusalem and the Judaisers: The Galatian Crisis in its Broadest Historical Context* (Tubingen: Mohr Siebeck, 2009).

[916]Michael D. Goulder, *A Tale of Two Missions* (London: SCM, 1994); and *Paul and the Competing Mission in Corinth* (Peabody, Mass: Hendrickson, 2001).

[917]J. Louis Martyn, *Theological Issues in the Letters of Paul* (Edinburgh: T&T Clark, 1997) and *Galatians: A New Translation with Introduction and Commentary* (New York, N.Y.: Doubleday, 1997).

[918]James D. G. Dunn, *Christianity in the Making, vol. 2, Beginning from Jerusalem* (Grand Rapids, Mich: Eerdmans, 2009).

[919]David C. Sim, 'The Family of Jesus and the Disciples of Jesus in Paul and Mark: Taking Sides in the Early Church's Factional Dispute,' in Wischmeyer *et al.* (2014).

[920]Sim (2014a), p. 75.

[921]1 Cor. 15:3-9.

As I pointed out in the previous section, I think that this bit of text is mostly bogus and an early interpolation. I've given reasons already for why the story of Paul's persecution of church before his conversion is most likely an effort of the Lukan author or someone of his ilk to reconcile the two factions, even if his efforts didn't quite cover all the cracks in the story. The text reads just as well if not better if you completely remove the witnesses section; then you have this:

> Now I would remind you, brothers and sisters, of the good news that I proclaimed to you, which you in turn received, in which also you stand, through which also you are being saved, if you hold firmly to the message that I proclaimed to you – unless you have come to believe in vain. For I handed on to you as of first importance what I in turn had received: that Christ died for our sins in accordance with the scriptures, and that he was buried, and that he was raised on the third day in accordance with the scriptures ... so we proclaim and so you have come to believe. Now if Christ is proclaimed as raised from the dead, how can some of you say there is no resurrection of the dead?[922]

At the same time, as an interpolation, the resurrection appearances listed are strange, as mentioned previously. They are at odds with the other accounts of resurrection appearances in the Gospels. Indeed, "last" and "least" appear to have been picked up in Mark, as in "the last will be first," but that only suggests that there was a text that was possibly about resurrection appearances which has been so mangled we may never recover it. It very well may be an interpolation that reveals to us what the Jerusalem church may have thought of Paul *in their own words*. I agree that the resurrection appearance list and the attached creedal formula may represent a very early tradition of the Jewish Christians, but I don't think Paul was citing it; it was interpolated later. The fact that it includes the statement about Paul persecuting church is firm evidence, in my opinion, that it is not Pauline.

Paul's relationship with the Jerusalem church comes into focus in the Epistle to the Galatians. Certain people had approached the Pauline communities and were, according to Paul, preaching another gospel than the one he preached. This gospel demanded that followers of Jesus must also observe the Jewish Law in every respect. In his response, Paul focuses on circumcision and Jewish holy days, and it becomes apparent in his arguments that the intruders preached Abraham as the prototypical Gentile who was converted to Judaism and circumcised, and all in his household likewise. Paul re-interprets the Abraham story to focus on faith alone and even goes so far as to claim that one's salvation might be imperiled by circumcision because that was a reliance on 'the flesh.'

Apparently, the intruders claimed that Paul was not a legitimate apostle, that he came under the authority of the Jerusalem church and was answerable to it. And they must have been telling a story about the Jerusalem council that Paul attended which suggested that Paul had broken his agreement by continuing to preach a Law-free gospel. Paul's responses to these three charges were given in the first part of the letter. In the following, I have placed in [*bracketed italics*] what I think are interpolations that were intended to bring the story more into line with the account of Acts:

> I want you to know, brothers and sisters, that the gospel that was proclaimed by me is not of human origin; for I did not receive it from a human source, nor was I taught it, but I received it through a

---
[922] 1 Cor. 15:1-4, 11b-12. Verses 5-11a are unattested in Marcion, which supports the possibility that they are not original to the letter. See BeDuhn (2013), p. 240.

revelation of Jesus Christ. You have heard, no doubt, of my earlier life in Judaism. *[I was violently persecuting the church of God and was trying to destroy it.]* I advanced in Judaism beyond many among my people of the same age, for I was far more zealous for the traditions of my ancestors. But when God, who had set me apart before I was born and called me through his grace, was pleased to reveal his Son to me, so that I might proclaim him among the Gentiles, I did not confer with any human being, nor did I go up to Jerusalem to those who were already apostles before me, but I went away at once into Arabia, and afterwards I returned to Damascus. Then after three years I did go up to Jerusalem to visit Cephas and stayed with him fifteen days; but I did not see any other apostle except James the Lord's brother. In what I am writing to you, before God, I do not lie! Then I went into the regions of Syria and Cilicia, and I was still unknown by sight to the churches of Judea that are in Christ. *[They only heard it said, "The one who formerly was persecuting us is now proclaiming the faith he once tried to destroy." And they glorified God because of me.]*

Then after fourteen years I went up again to Jerusalem with Barnabas, taking Titus along with me. I went up in response to a revelation. *[Then I laid before them (though only in a private meeting with the acknowledged leaders) the gospel that I proclaim among the Gentiles, in order to make sure that I was not running, or had not run, in vain. But even Titus, who was with me, was not compelled to be circumcised, though he was a Greek.]* But because of false believers secretly brought in, who slipped in to spy on the freedom we have in Christ Jesus, so that they might enslave us – we did not submit to them even for a moment, so that the truth of the gospel might always remain with you. And from those who were supposed to be acknowledged leaders (what they actually were makes no difference to me; God shows no partiality) – those leaders contributed nothing to me. On the contrary, when they saw that I had been entrusted with the gospel for the uncircumcised, just as Peter had been entrusted with the gospel for the circumcised (for he who worked through Peter making him an apostle to the circumcised also worked through me in sending me to the Gentiles), and when James and Cephas and John, who were acknowledged pillars,[923] recognized the grace that had been given to me, they gave to Barnabas and me the right hand of fellowship, agreeing that we should go to the Gentiles and they to the circumcised. *[They asked only one thing, that we remember the poor, which was actually what I was eager to do.]*

But when Cephas came to Antioch, I opposed him to his face, because he stood self-condemned; for until certain people came from James, he used to eat with the Gentiles. But after they came, he drew back and kept himself separate for fear of the circumcision faction. And the other Jews joined him in this hypocrisy, so that even Barnabas was led astray by their hypocrisy.

But when I saw that they were not acting consistently with the truth of the gospel, I said to Cephas before them all, "If you, though a Jew, live like a Gentile and not like a Jew, how can you compel the Gentiles to live like Jews? We ourselves are Jews by birth and not Gentile sinners; yet we know that a person is justified not by the works of the law but through faith in Jesus Christ. And we have come to believe in Christ Jesus, so that we might be justified by faith in Christ, and not by doing the works of the law, because no one will be justified by the works of the law. But if, in our effort to be justified in Christ, we ourselves have been found to be sinners, is Christ then a servant of sin? Certainly not! But if I build up again the very things that I once tore down, then I demonstrate that I am a transgressor. For through the law I died to the law, so that I might live to God. I have been crucified with Christ; and it is no longer I who live, but it is Christ who lives in me. And the life I now live in the flesh I live by faith in the Son of God, who loved me and gave himself for me. I do not nullify the grace of God; for if justification comes through the law, then Christ died for nothing."[924]

---

[923]NB: Immediately after mentioning *Peter* as an apostle, Paul names James, *Cephas*, and John as pillars. Was he reverting to a nickname, or definitely referring to two different people?

[924]Gal. 1:11–2:21.

Now, the above is a rather sustained discussion on Paul's part, of what things were like in the very earliest days of Christianity and it sure is peculiar. It's pretty clear that the Jerusalem Christians were behind the invaders of Paul's congregation in Galatia. When he recounts his conversion/mission history above, Paul says that he did not immediately go to Jerusalem after his conversion, suggesting that there *was some* connection between his experience and the Jerusalem church. After three years he did finally go to Jerusalem, which is something of an admission that his mission was connected to theirs, or at least that he was using their mission as a cover for his own. There he met with Cephas and James but he doesn't tell us what was discussed. Sim notes that:

> [I]t is safe to assume that they did not talk about the Law-free mission to the Gentiles that Paul earlier in the letter said had been revealed to him. The reason for this conclusion is that Paul says that it was only when he visited Jerusalem the next time did he set out the gospel he preached to the Gentiles (2:2). The implication is that this matter had not been raised previously with Peter and James.[925]

So, basically, for 17 years, Paul was preaching a gospel that was NOT the same as that preached by the Jerusalem church!

Alvar Ellegård's idea of Essene-*like* communities scattered throughout the Empire seems to fit best when one considers the reference to Cephas eating with Gentiles at Antioch. They may or may not have been messianists, though it appears that, at some point, radical followers of Judas the Galilean began to co-opt those groups and began promoting Judas as the militant messiah; while, at the same time, Paul came along and began promoting *his* messiah of love and reconciliation. In his claimed rebuke to Cephas, I've extended the quote to include more than most scholars allow, since everything I've included appears to go with what Paul might have claimed to have said to Cephas, especially all the "we" statements. He was talking to Cephas, who was another Jew like himself. Still, what he claimed to have said and what actually may have been said could be quite different; Paul was using the opportunity to make a rhetorical point.

Finally, in addition to what I have suggested was interpolated – remarks about Paul's prior persecution of church – we have no idea what may have been expurgated entirely. What we have in the above text is possibly a good approximation of what happened, but we suspect that the situation was a lot more fraught with tension than the words themselves state, since it was likely that shortly after this event at Antioch, and before the invasion of the Galatian congregation, James and Simon (Cephas/Peter?) were executed by Tiberius Alexander (c. 47 AD). Everything went south shortly after, and Paul himself ended up in prison, most likely in Ephesus, from where he was sent to Rome.

In any event, in his further response to the situation at Galatia, Paul states that the intruders have "bewitched" the Galatians and that they preach a contrary gospel which perverts the gospel of Christ. He then curses the intruders:

> I am astonished that you are so quickly deserting the one who called you in the grace of Christ and are turning to a different gospel – not that there is another gospel, but there are some who are

---

[925]Sim (2014a), p. 80. Obviously, Sim believes that Cephas and Peter are one and the same. I don't think it is so certain.

confusing you and want to pervert the gospel of Christ. But even if we or an angel from heaven should proclaim to you a gospel contrary to what we proclaimed to you, let that one be accursed! As we have said before, so now I repeat, if anyone proclaims to you a gospel contrary to what you received, let that one be accursed![926]

Noticing that Paul restates the curse immediately gives me the uneasy feeling that there is something missing between the first curse and the second that has been expurgated, which would suggest that it might have told us something extremely important. Paul is obviously enraged beyond reason and vents his anger against these Jewish Christians with some flair, even going so far as to wish they would castrate themselves (Gal. 5:12). The Jerusalem leadership is targeted as well. Sim thinks that this indicates that there were close relations between them and Paul, and this may be true. But clearly, something happened to break up the happy family after so many years. What could it be? Is it possible that it had something to do with this?

But because of false believers secretly brought in, who slipped in to spy on the freedom we have in Christ Jesus, so that they might enslave us ...[927]

Is it possible that Paul had been *secretly* preaching his Law-free gospel of love and reconciliation, piggy-backing on the organizational structure of the militant messianists, and had gotten away with it for a long time – 17 years – until someone got suspicious and began to spy on him and his communities? And now, he is insisting that his gospel is the true one and that of the Jerusalem Christians is not?

One thing that is interesting is this:

It is those who want to make a good showing in the flesh that try to compel you to be circumcised – only that they may not be persecuted for the cross of Christ. Even the circumcised do not themselves obey the law, but they want you to be circumcised so that they may boast about your flesh. May I never boast of anything except the cross of our Lord Jesus Christ, by which the world has been crucified to me, and I to the world. For neither circumcision nor uncircumcision is anything; but a new creation is everything![928]

Now, why would Jewish Christians promote circumcision so as not to be "persecuted for the Cross of Christ"? Who is doing the persecution? Were the Zealots on the warpath as Josephus has described them, running rampant and killing people who were not obeying the Law? That is certainly what seems to have been happening in the real historical background, and perhaps this is an allusion to that in Paul's writing.

Sim states that there are serious difficulties in accepting Paul's account of the Jerusalem council where he privately met with James, Cephas and John to set out the substance of his gospel. Paul says that "false brothers" came in and one assumes that they gave opposing testimony about Paul and his teaching. The result of the meeting, according to the text, was that Paul won the day and agreed to collect money for 'the poor.' As I've noted elsewhere, this was a term for sectarian messianists, and, if this is not an interpolation, one suspects that this agreement was also a cover for collecting resources for rebellion against Rome. That may, in fact, have been

---

[926]Gal. 1:6-9.
[927]Gal. 2:4.
[928]Gal. 6:12-15.

part of the reason Paul was later arrested and put in prison. The agreement may not be an interpolation, but a true record of what Paul agreed to do in exchange for not being targeted by the Jerusalem Christians.

That being said, however, the fact that the issue came up again at Antioch makes one seriously doubt the terms that were agreed upon, according to Paul, at Jerusalem, and so we see here another small interpolation. Paul says that when Cephas came to Antioch, he was happy enough to hang out with Gentiles until men came from James in Jerusalem and put an end to that sort of thing. Things broke out into the open at this point and Paul says he publicly accused Cephas of hypocrisy. Did the men coming from James in Jerusalem have anything to do with the fact that one suspects that it was almost exactly at this time that James and Simon (Cephas/Peter?), sons of Judas the Galilean were executed by Tiberius Alexander? Did Paul come out against Cephas in public so as to dissociate himself from the Jerusalem Christians? Sim notes:

> In short what James and then Peter attempted to do in Antioch, to introduce circumcision and the whole Torah to the Gentile community there, was precisely what Paul's opponents in Galatia were doing. We have to infer from this evidence that these Christian Jewish missionaries who came to Galatia came at the behest of James in Jerusalem. ... James' strategy of intervention by way of envoys was well-known to Paul.[929]

But we already think that James and Simon (Cephas/Peter?) are dead by this time, as Galatians never refers to them in the present tense ("what they were formerly makes no difference to me").

In his allegory of Sarah and Hagar in Gal. 4:21-31, "Hagar represents the Sinai covenant and is the mother who bears children for slavery, and she corresponds to the present Jerusalem. This enslaved Jerusalem is then contrasted with the free [spiritual] Jerusalem [of Sarah, the mother of Paul's Law-free Christians]." And, just as the son of the slave, Hagar, persecuted the son of the free woman, Sarah, so now do those who are of the flesh persecute those born according to the spirit. Thus Paul is saying that the Jerusalem Christians enslave people by forcing them to circumcision and following Torah. He makes the explicit point that the relationship between him and the Jerusalem church is one of persecution. From this, Sim infers that Paul was referring to a pattern of interference, that James had done this sort of thing more than once. In short, Paul's relationship to the Jerusalem church was one of bitter conflict.[930] So the idea that there was rapprochement and the agreement to take a collection seems to be strongly contraindicated.

The evidence that exists in later writings, most especially the Gospel of Matthew, supports the idea that this conflict continued; the Jewish Christians, the Zealots, continued to persecute Paul and his churches and Law-free Gospel right up to the rebellion against Rome, at which point the tables were turned and Paul was seen to have been right all along. The Jewish messiah never came, Rome destroyed Jerusalem, and everyone would have been better off to have followed Paul.

Sim, and others, think that the 'collection' that is mentioned in several of Paul's letters actually took place. I would suggest that it did not, that those passages were based on Paul's alleged mention that he had agreed to collect money for 'the poor,' and were interpolated into several letters, including at least one that was written even before the Jerusalem meeting took place (1 and 2 Corinthians). One interesting item in this regard is that Luke, who devotes a lot of space

[929]Sim (2014a), p. 81.
[930]Sim (2014a), p. 82.

to Paul's alleged final visit to Jerusalem, never mentions anything about the collection. Since it is almost certain that Luke was using Paul's letters, though pretending to be ignorant of them, *it appears that the copies he had did not have the passages about the collection.* Pervo argues that Luke had a reason not to include the collection story (though he assumes it to be true).[931] Sim notes, however, the little notice that was put into Paul's mouth in Acts 24:17, when he was defending himself before the governor, Felix: "Now after some years I came to bring alms to my nation and to offer sacrifices." I think Hell would have frozen over before Paul would have gone to Jerusalem to offer sacrifices, considering all he had to say about the Law being superseded by the cross of Christ.

Sim, too, thinks that Mark was written in the years immediately following the deaths of Paul, Peter and James in the early 60s.[932] I am quite convinced by a number of arguments that Mark was written probably around 73 AD, or shortly after the triumphal parade of Titus and Vespasian in which the torn curtain of the Temple was displayed, which inspired Mark's drama about the splitting of the curtain at the moment of Christ's death. I am also convinced that James and Simon, the sons of Judas the Galilean who were executed in 47 AD, were the very same James and Simon (Cephas/Peter) of Jerusalem pillars fame in Paul's epistles. Thus, they were dead a good 16 years before Sim suggests. It also appears that Paul himself may have survived until after the destruction of Jerusalem and the Temple if part of Romans 9–11 can be attributed to him, written in response to the destruction of Jews and the Temple in 70 AD. If not, of course, then that idea falls and we are left with a total blank about what happened to Paul.

Sim thinks that it was the death of Paul that inspired the writing of Mark, that something was needed to fill the gap created by the loss of their teacher. He suggests that it is in such a context that we should expect Mark to discredit the major opponents of Paul, i.e. the family and disciples of Jesus who "formed the power bloc in the Jerusalem church."[933] I would suggest, considering the ferocity of the Zealots and their networks, that it would be extremely unlikely for Mark to write such a portrait of those individuals if they were still living, which they were not after 70 AD.

Indeed, Mark's portraits of the disciples (especially James and Peter) and the family are positively negative! Yet, for some reason, Mark keeps them separate. He writes about James, John and Simon-Peter as though they were unrelated to the Jesus he constructs for his narrative. At the same time, he constructs a devastating portrait of the family of Jesus. I would suggest that the reason for this was that Mark was constructing a mythical Jesus based loosely on Paul himself, and he wished to encourage former followers of Judas the Galilean and his Zealots to turn to the truth of Paul's teachings; therefore he dissociated his Jesus of Nazareth from his family so that his audience would know, clearly, that this Jesus of power and miracles, the Son of God, was most assuredly not Judas the Galilean whose sons took over the leadership of his party and became the 'pillars' of the Jerusalem church.

---

[931]Pervo (2008), p. 48. He argues that Paul's alleged fears about reception of the collection in Rom. 15:25-33, "followed by Luke's avoidance of the issue, suggests that the leaders at Jerusalem rejected the Collection." However, consistent with the interpolation hypothesis, most of these passages mentioning the collection aren't attested in Marcion's letter collection, except the initial promise in Gal. 2:10. Then again, as BeDuhn points out, the passages aren't identified as actually omitted, and none of that material was relevant to Marcion's detractors, so the evidence could go either way. BeDuhn (2013), pp. 289, 304–5.
[932]Sim (2014a), p. 85.
[933]Sim (2014a), p. 85.

Judas the Galilean was widely known among the Jews, as we have seen from our survey of Josephus. He was most likely to have been the messianic figure of the Jewish Christians, the Zealots, most of whom died in the rebellion against Rome. The execution of his sons, James and Simon, by Tiberius Alexander around 47 AD was most likely the historical reality behind the silly tale told in the Book of Acts about the execution of James by 'King Herod' and the arrest and miraculous release of Peter, following which Peter disappears entirely from the story.

After 70 AD, when the Zealots were all dead (or nearly, since a descendant of Judas the Galilean was still holed up at Masada), when their messiah had failed to arrive on schedule, when it seemed clear that Yahweh had deserted them and gone over to the side of the Romans, the stock of the Jewish Christians was destroyed and Mark stepped in to provide a story of a unified messiah for Jewish and Gentile Christians. While many Jewish Christian followers of Judas the Galilean and his sons, the pillars of Jerusalem church fame, might have been somewhat offended by Mark's portrayal of Jesus' disciples, it appears that it was done for serious apologetic reasons: to distance Christians from Judas and his revolutionary ilk and offspring. Mark was written at a time when anti-Jewish sentiment was rife due to the hardships the Roman people suffered as a consequence of the war with the Jews. You could say that, in a sense, Mark was 'sanitizing' Judas by imposing Paul's theological Christ on a similar Jewish figure. You could say that it was an effort to rewrite the history of Christianity, distancing Christians from any slightest odor of affiliation to "those rebellious Jews who thought their messiah was going to come and destroy Rome." Not only was the newly minted Jesus not, in any way, in cahoots with a family of Zealots, he was also ill-served by a gaggle of thick-headed disciples who got everything wrong and abandoned him at the end, with no redemption.

But all of this was being put together in full view of an audience that knew the facts, more or less. They knew who Judas was, they knew who his sons were, they knew what they had stood for and what they had done. At the same time, they knew who Paul was and what he stood for and how desperately he had sought to bring people over to his Son of God who came to suffer and die for their sins and initiate a new Millennium. So naturally, they also understood that this Jesus of Nazareth that Mark had created was an allegory, devoid of any historical reality, and that the stories and sayings were designed to convey the teachings of Paul in narrative form.

The Gospel of Mark has two passages that refer to the relatives of Jesus in very harsh terms. The references are immediately preceded by Jesus' selection of the twelve, which is intended to make it clear that they are separate from his actual family. Here is the text:

> He went up the mountain and called to him those whom he wanted, and they came to him. And he appointed twelve, whom he also named apostles, to be with him, and to be sent out to proclaim the message, and to have authority to cast out demons.
>
> So he appointed the twelve: Simon (to whom he gave the name Peter); James son of Zebedee and John the brother of James (to whom he gave the name Boanerges, that is, Sons of Thunder); and Andrew, and Philip, and Bartholomew, and Matthew, and Thomas, and James son of Alphaeus, and Thaddaeus, and Simon the Cananaean, and Judas Iscariot, who betrayed him.
>
> Then **he went home**; and the crowd came together again, so that they could not even eat. **When his family heard it, they went out to restrain him**, for people were saying, "He has gone out of his mind."
>
> And the scribes who came down from Jerusalem said, "He has Beelzebul, and by the ruler of the demons he casts out demons." And he called them to him, and spoke to them in parables, "How can Satan cast out Satan? If a kingdom is divided against itself, that kingdom cannot stand. And

if a house is divided against itself, that house will not be able to stand. And if Satan has risen up against himself and is divided, he cannot stand, but his end has come. But no one can enter a strong man's house and plunder his property without first tying up the strong man; then indeed the house can be plundered. Truly I tell you, people will be forgiven for their sins and whatever blasphemies they utter; but whoever blasphemes against the Holy Spirit can never have forgiveness, but is guilty of an eternal sin" – for they had said, "He has an unclean spirit."

Then his mother and his brothers came; and standing outside, they sent to him and called him. A crowd was sitting around him; and they said to him, "Your mother and your brothers and sisters are outside, asking for you." And he replied, "Who are my mother and my brothers?" And looking at those who sat around him, he said, "Here are my mother and my brothers! Whoever does the will of God is my brother and sister and mother."[934]

In 3:19b, we read: "Then he went home." In 3:21 we read: "When his family heard it, they went out to restrain him, for people were saying, 'He has gone out of his mind'." Sim writes:

> ... 3:19-35 is a typical "Marcan sandwich;" it begins with the family of Jesus and concludes with his mother and brothers, which points to the same identity for both groups. That the relatives of Jesus believe him to be possessed by a demon is evident ... The material that follows immediately after, the Beelzebul controversy ... also concerns possession, and this strengthens the case that v. 21 also refers to this theme. ... The evangelist wanted his readers to understand that the family of Jesus believed he was possessed by a demon, and so they attempted to seize him to conceal him from public view.[935]

The Beelzebul controversy is contained within the 'sandwich' that begins with the first appearance of Jesus' family, and ends with their attempt to seize him. Thus, it contains enormous implications *about* his family. Note that this dispute was between Jesus and scribes who had come from Jerusalem. They accused him of being able to cast out demons. Jesus responds to this quite cleverly, concluding that a "divided household" cannot stand, *a direct reference to his family.* And then he says something extremely important: he points out that no one can enter a strong man's house and steal his goods without first binding him. The implication is clear: it is Jesus' power over Beelzebul, the prince of demons, that enables him to exorcise his demonic minions. Sim writes:

> Having made this point and defended himself against these charges, Jesus next spells out the consequences for those who made the accusations (vv. 28-30). All sins and blasphemies can be forgiven with the sole exception of blasphemies against the Holy Spirit; this is an eternal sin for which there can be no forgiveness. Mark concludes this short section with the authorial comment "for they said he has an unclean spirit." From the perspective of the evangelist, any charge that Jesus is possessed by a demonic entity amounts to blasphemy against the Holy Spirit. Mark had made the point at the baptism of Jesus by John the Baptist that Jesus was in fact filled with or even possessed by the Spirit which descended from heaven upon him (1:9-11). To accuse Jesus of demon-possession rather than possession by the Holy Spirit therefore entails blasphemy against the latter.[936]

Sim then goes on to point out that the question now presents itself: "Just who, according to Mark, has committed this single sin for which there is no forgiveness?" The first part of the

---

[934]Mark 3:13-35.
[935]Sim (2014a), pp. 86–87.
[936]Sim (2014a), pp. 87–88.

answer is clear: the scribes from Jerusalem. But it is also clear that Jesus' relatives, too, had accused him of being possessed by a demon. That Mark intends his readers to understand this is confirmed by the final pericope of this text where Jesus' family come and stand outside calling for him. Jesus' answer – "Who are my mother and my brothers?" – is a clear rejection of his family, because they, too, have committed the unforgivable sin.

Later we encounter a reference to Jesus' family again:

> He left that place and came to his hometown, and his disciples followed him. On the sabbath he began to teach in the synagogue, and many who heard him were astounded. They said, "Where did this man get all this? What is this wisdom that has been given to him? What deeds of power are being done by his hands! Is not this the carpenter, the son of Mary and **brother of James and Joses and Judas and Simon**, and are not his sisters here with us?" And they took offense at him. Then Jesus said to them, "Prophets are not without honor, except in their hometown, and among their own kin, and in their own house." And he could do no deed of power there, except that he laid his hands on a few sick people and cured them. And he was amazed at their unbelief. Then he went about among the villages teaching.[937]

Here we notice that his brothers are named, including James, Judas and Simon. The people of Nazareth take offense that someone who is so familiar to them could speak and act with authority, while Jesus' criticism, "Prophets are not without honor, except in their hometown, and among their own kin, and in their own house," is clearly intended to include his own family in the charge. Sim writes:

> The brothers of Jesus who played leading roles in the early Jerusalem Church, have committed blasphemy and are guilty of a sin for which there can be no redemption or atonement. This means that their guilt remains during the period of the church, and it applies in particular to James, the brother of Jesus, who led the Jerusalem church in its dispute with Paul. The evangelist makes it very clear that the siblings of Jesus, and James in particular, had no right to lead the primitive movement ... People who are guilty of this crime stand condemned forever ... In historical terms, this is an outright and vitriolic attack upon James.[938]

Now, consider the fact that Paul was certainly unhappy with James and the pillars in Jerusalem, but he never accused James of being guilty of an eternally damning sin. Mark, however, taking up Paul's cause, was downright vicious toward the kin of his Jesus character. I would say that this further supports the view that this fulfilled an extremely important apologetic purpose during perilous times for early Christian followers of Paul, but especially for those who had followed James. It was necessary to condemn and discredit James and the rest of the Jerusalem Christian Zealots completely; survival depended on it.

When considering the disciples of Jesus as portrayed by Mark, we can note that, at the beginning, they are not depicted negatively at all. They are called, they follow, they are sent out to preach and perform exorcisms and healings. Their special position is highlighted when Jesus tells them that they are being given the secrets of the kingdom of God (4:10-13, 35). However, as the story progresses, negative indications increase dramatically. Sim gives a list:

---

[937] Mark 6:1-6.
[938] Sim (2014a), p. 89.

In the episode of the stilling of the storm, they demonstrate a distinct lack of faith (4:35-51), and their lack of faith and prayer affects their ability to cast out an evil spirit (9-18-19, 28-29). They are criticized by Jesus for keeping the children away from him (10:13-16) and for complaining about a non-disciple performing exorcisms in his name (9:38-41). Perhaps the most serious failing of the disciples in the Gospel of Mark is their failure to understand the teaching of Jesus and the nature of his mission. This runs right through the Marcan story. The disciples ask Jesus about his parables (4:10) and Jesus questions whether they will ever understand the parables he teaches (4:13). They also fail to comprehend the significance of the two miraculous feedings (6:51-52). More importantly, the disciples never understand the suffering nature of Jesus' messianic mission, despite Jesus' constant teaching on this issue.[939] The passion predictions make this point with the utmost clarity. At Caesarea Philippi Peter correctly identifies Jesus as the messiah (10:29). Jesus then teaches the disciples that his messianic mission involves suffering, being killed and then being raised from the dead (v. 31). Peter refuses to accept this and rebukes Jesus (v. 32), and Jesus responds by associating Peter with Satan: "Get behind me Satan. For you are not on the side of God, but of men" (v. 33). ... In the second passion prediction in 9:31-32, Jesus again teaches the disciples that he must suffer, die and be raised, but again they did not understand and were afraid to ask him about it. The disciples in fact condemn themselves all the more by discussing who was the greatest among them while Jesus was instructing them on his ultimate fate (9:33-37). Jesus explains for the third time the necessity of his suffering, death and resurrection, but his teaching only evokes a response by James and John that they be placed either side of him when he enters his glory (10:35-45). A further passage of interest in this regard is 9:9-10. In this episode, Jesus comes down the mountain after the transfiguration accompanied by Peter, James and John, and instructs them to tell no-one what they witnessed until the Son of Man has been raised from the dead. They keep the matter to themselves but question what was meant by the resurrection from the dead. These texts in particular are extremely damning of the disciples, especially those two who formed part of the later Jerusalem church's triumvirate.[940]

Finally, we can't forget Jesus' prediction that one of his disciples will betray him (14:17-21), that Peter will deny him three times (14:29-31), and that the rest of the disciples will desert him (14:27-28). And then, to add insult to injury, in the Garden of Gethsemane, Peter, James and John – the Jerusalem triumvirate – sleep while Jesus agonizes over his imminent death (14:32-42). Judas then betrays him (14:10-11, 43-49), all the disciples flee when he is arrested (14:50), Peter denies him three times (14:66-72), and these shameful events pretty much conclude the activities of the disciples in the Gospel of Mark.

For centuries, scholars have interpreted Mark's portrayal of the pusillanimous and dull-witted disciples as either a foil for Mark to introduce teachings of Jesus, or Mark encouraging his readers to identify with the disciples' failings in order to gain courage to repent and transform. The main problem with these explanations, as Sim notes, is that these were real people familiar to Mark's readers/hearers; well, at least some of them were – namely Peter, James and John. And again I suggest strongly that this was done to distance the Jesus character of Mark's creation, the embodiment of Paul's Christ, from the Jerusalem church, its pillars and their revolutionary, anti-Gentile ideology.

---

[939]David Oliver Smith also argues that the disciples are presented as believing Jesus will be the messiah warlord king, thus explaining their lack of comprehension when he doesn't live up to their expectations. See Smith (2016), pp. 180, 183–86.

[940]Sim (2014a), pp. 91–92.

At the end of the Gospel of Mark, certain women who followed Jesus come onstage: Mary Magdalene, Mary the mother of James the younger and Joses, Salome, and other women who witness the crucifixion (15:40-41). The three women named are also the ones who discover the empty tomb where an angel tells them of his resurrection. The angel gives them a message that mentions Peter, telling them to instruct the disciples that Jesus will be in Galilee, but then, the women flee the tomb and tell no one (16:8). There is no indication that such a meeting ever took place; the opposite is implied. In other words, Peter never got the memo. The disciples are never rehabilitated by Mark. As Mary Ann Tolbert shows, the disciples are examples of the 'rocky ground' in the Parable of the Sower: "Because there is a little earth covering the rock, the seed springs up immediately in rocky ground, but since the rock blocks the growth of roots, when the sun comes up the plant quickly withers."[941] They "accept at first, endure for a time, and then fall away when opposition threatens."[942]

In the other Gospels, which used Mark as their main model and inspiration, the disciples are rehabilitated, forgiven for their failings, and prepared for their future work. Even the Gospel of Mark had an ending added later to make it conform to the new view of things in Matthew and Luke. However, as Sim notes, at the end of Mark's Gospel, the disciples "stand condemned as cowards, deniers and as ones who never grasped the nature of Jesus' mission on the significance of his resurrection."[943] For Mark, it was only Paul who was visited by the risen Christ and who understood and appreciated fully the significance of Jesus' death and resurrection.[944]

Undoubtedly, Mark's readers/hearers knew what he was doing and why. Mark gave them a reason to continue as Christians because Paul had been proven right and the Jerusalem Christians had been wrong to oppose and persecute him. Now, they were all dead, their dreams had died in the fires of Jerusalem and if the faith was to continue, it needed a new foundation: voila! Jesus of Nazareth.

Here it is useful to note that the conflation of John Mark from the book of Acts with 'Mark,' the alleged author of the second Gospel, is iffy at best. Adela Yarbro Collins points out that "the book of Acts presents a fairly negative portrait of Mark as a backslider or reluctant missionary to the Gentiles. Since the author of Acts also wrote the Gospel according to Luke, it could be that this critical portrait was intended to undercut the authority of the second Gospel."[945]

Markan Epistemology

In 1984, Joel Marcus wrote an article[946] discussing Markan epistemology that began with the strange passage in Mark in which Jesus explains that he speaks in parables so that "those outside" will not understand, *lest they be converted*.

---

[941]Tolbert (1996), p. 154.

[942]Tolbert (1996), p. 192.

[943]Sim (2014a), p. 94.

[944]One cannot help but wonder if the ending of the Gospel, the notice that Jesus would be in Galilee, might not refer to Paul himself, considering the notice cited earlier in this text that Paul actually was from Galilee, not Tarsus.

[945]Adela Yarbro Collins, *Mark: A Commentary* (Minneapolis, Minn.: Fortress Press, 2007), p. 5, cited in Elizabeth V. Dowling, '"Do this in Remembrance": Last Supper Traditions in Paul and Mark,' in Wischmeyer *et al.* *(2014)*, p. 225.

[946]Joel Marcus, 'Mark 4:10-12 and Marcan Epistemology,' in *Journal of Biblical Literature* 103:4 (1984), pp. 557-74.

When he was alone, those who were around him along with the twelve asked him about the parables. And he said to them, "To you has been given the secret of the kingdom of God, but for those outside, everything comes in parables; in order that 'they may indeed look, but not perceive, and may indeed listen, but not understand; so that they may not turn again and be forgiven.'"[947]

Marcus notes that this passage is very significant for understanding Mark's epistemology and the function of the Gospel as a whole as expressing an apocalyptic viewpoint. That is, the knowledge conveyed by the Gospel is an unveiling. The Greek word *apokalypsis* means, literally, 'unveiling' and refers to the revelation of heavenly events, which provide the key for understanding earthly events. Marcus' example here is Dan. 10:20-21, where the archangel Gabriel speaks to the seer Daniel:

> Then he said, "Do you know why I have come to you? Now I must return to fight against the prince of Persia, and when I am through with him, the prince of Greece will come. But I am to tell you what is inscribed in the book of truth. There is no one with me who contends against these princes except Michael, your prince."

In other words, wars on Earth are reflections of wars in the heavenly spheres in some sense and the fall of Persia and Greece will be due to the archangel Gabriel's conquest of the patron angels of those two states. The understanding of earthly events by way of a revelation to a seer is a form of epistemology, a way of knowing that may, indeed, be true, but cannot be proven.[948]

Edmund Gettier, in a 1963 paper entitled 'Is Justified True Belief Knowledge?', called into question the concept of knowledge as justified true belief. Gettier argued that there are situations in which one's belief may be justified and true, yet fail to count as knowledge. As in the diagram, a true proposition can be believed by an individual (region overlapping both truths and beliefs) but still not fall within the 'knowledge' category (central circle).

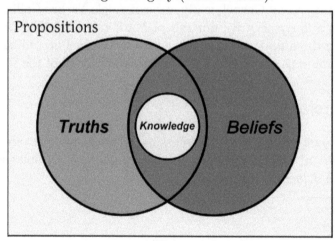

Figure 3.

---

[947]Mark 4:10-13.

[948]One wonders, of course, if a beginning to the study of hyperdimensional realities, implied by the consequences of Intelligent Design (not to mention other factors, including paranormal phenomena), might consist of inferences drawn from observations of our reality?

In Mark 10:42, Jesus refers to *hoi dokountes archein tōn ethnōn,* "Those who are *thought* to rule over the Gentiles," and this appears to be a clear link between Mark's apocalyptic viewpoint and epistemology when you link this back to Daniel 10:20-21 above. Both Matthew and Luke altered this to "rulers of the Gentiles" and the NRSV translation also reflects this sort of correction. The Amplified Zondervan translation shows how awkward the translations are and how they may be distorting the intended meaning:

> But Jesus called them to [Him] and said to them, You know that those who are recognized as governing and are supposed to rule[949] the Gentiles (the nations) lord it over them [ruling with absolute power, holding them in subjection], and their great men exercise authority and dominion over them.

Marcus writes about the awkwardness of this bit of text and the alterations made by Matthew and Luke:

> These elucidations are, in a way, correct; Mark did have in mind pagan kings and rulers when he wrote "those who are thought to rule over the Gentiles." But his exact phraseology is not without significance. Those who are commonly thought to be rulers are not, for the apocalyptic viewpoint, the real rulers of this world. Behind them stand the real rulers, God and Satan, each with a host of servants. Therefore, the common view is wrong, since it does not penetrate to the stage upon which the real rulers are acting; those who maintain this viewpoint do not know; they only opine, being blind to the apocalyptic drama that is unfolding for those with eyes to see it.[950]

In Mark, true knowledge is a gift of God. The truth of the identity of Jesus – the Son of God – is not knowledge that can be understood with the ordinary human way of thinking. God knows it, for sure (1:11; 9:7). Also, such knowledge is available to the demons (and Satan), who have it by virtue of being part of the unseen world (1:24, 34; 3:11; 5:7; 9:20). Satan and his minions know that these truths are hidden from human beings who do not know the truth about God, Satan, or even their own condition. Here, one can refer back to Paul's theology of the First and Second Adam, as explicated by Ashworth: that when humanity fell from the Edenic state, their bodies and minds became mortal and corruptible, blind to higher realities, and incapable of perceiving this reality or finding their own way out. For human beings to know truths that are hidden from them, an act of God is necessary; knowing is connected with the kingdom of God.

Jesus, of course, has this knowing, this ability to see the unseen reality. His perceptions are beyond those of ordinary human beings. He knows the unspoken thoughts of others (2:8; 9:33ff); he sees the heavens open at his baptism and hears God speak to him and tell him that he is pleased, apparently because his son has embarked upon his earthly mission (Mk. 1:10-11). So, God and Jesus, and Satan and his demons, know truths that are hidden from human beings.

In Mark 4:11-12 and 4:33-34, we see a distinction between two groups of people: the disciples and 'those outside.' The latter are those who 'look and do not perceive, listen but do not understand.' Throughout the Gospel, the disciples are witnesses of miracles and recipients of private teachings, the knowledge of which is kept from outsiders.

---

[949]Notably, this phrase, "those who are thought to rule," uses the same word Paul uses to describe the pillars, as "those thought [esteemed] to be something" in Gal. 1.

[950]Marcus (1984), p. 558.

As Marcus notes, the theme of secrets revealed only to insiders or initiates is found in many religious traditions before, during and after the NT era. It was commonplace in Jewish apocalyptic literature, among the sectarians at Qumran, in Gnostic and Hermetic literature, etc. Marcus cites numerous examples that need not detain us here, though he does bring up an interesting comparison that is worth considering: in Gnostic epistemology, the revelatory moment is at creation, and revelation in the present only means recovering what was lost, that original revelation. In apocalyptic literature, the real revelation only comes at the eschaton, the end times; until then, the knowledge of even the elect can only be imperfect. This latter view is characteristic of both Pauline theology and Markan epistemology. So, that is one thing that separates Paul from the gnostics.

Marcus explains that three of the Greek words in Mk. 4:11-12 (*dedotai, ginetai, aphethē*) are circumlocutions for divine activity. That is, it is God who is behind the ability of an individual to see or hear, or failure thereof. This, of course, reminds one of 2 Thess. 2:9-12, where we read:

> The coming of the lawless one is apparent in the working of Satan, who uses all power, signs, lying wonders, and every kind of wicked deception for those who are perishing, because they refused to love the truth and so be saved. For this reason *God sends them a powerful delusion, leading them to believe what is false*, so that all who have not believed the truth but took pleasure in unrighteousness will be condemned.

In the Qumran literature and other apocalyptic writings, the same condition prevails: God is behind the person's ability to see and hear or not see and not hear. In *Enoch* 41:8 the Lord made a separation between the light and the darkness, and "divided the spirits of men." Other examples from Qumran literature tell us that God established the destinies of human beings before ever they were (1QH 1:19-20) and He made known his Holy Spirit to the Israelites while "those whom he hated he led astray" (CD 2:13). God has accomplished this division by the mediation of two spirits, the Spirit of Truth and the Spirit of Falsehood, which were his creations. There is the Prince or Angel of Light and the Prince or Angel of Darkness (1QS 3:18-21). The ways of the Spirit of Falsehood include "blindness of eye and dullness of ear, stiffness of neck and heaviness of heart" (1QS 4:11). Note that these attributes are similar to those ascribed to "the ones outside" in Mark 4:12. And, despite all the insider teachings he has received, when Peter rejects the idea of a suffering and dying messiah, Mark's Jesus tells him, "Get behind me, Satan! For you are setting your mind not on divine things but on human things" (Mk. 8:33).

In other words, Jesus was saying that Peter was under the control of the Prince of Darkness. How to reconcile that with the fact that Mark tells us that the disciples were "given the secret of the kingdom of God"? It seems that they were only partly aware, much like the scribe in Mk. 12:34: "When Jesus saw that he answered wisely, he said to him, 'You are not far from the kingdom of God.'" In fact, that particular scribe may have been closer than Peter! But Peter, and the other disciples, unlike the demons who had a supernatural view, and the centurion at the cross, did not recognize Jesus fully during his lifetime, according to Mark.

There are many exhortations to 'hear' and to 'see' in Mark and the Dead Sea Scrolls, but it appears that behind this is the idea that free will to choose one's destiny is somewhat limited. In Mark 4:9, 23, not all are exhorted to hear, but only 'those with ears to hear.' That is, only those who are of the fertile soil as described in the Parable of the Sower; those to whom God has given ears to hear, can hear. Hearing and seeing is not something that anyone can just decide to do; you have to be specially equipped with organs of spiritual hearing and sight.

"Let anyone with ears to hear listen!" And he said to them, "Pay attention to what you hear; the measure you give will be the measure you get, and still more will be given you. For to those who have, more will be given; and from those who have nothing, even what they have will be taken away."[951]

Marcus writes regarding the above text:

> With regard to Mark 4:24, "take heed what you hear," it should be noticed that this warning is framed by "Let anyone with ears to hear listen!" and "For to those who have, more will be given; and from those who have nothing, even what they have will be taken away," both of which imply that "hearing" is not something that one can simply decide to do. Thus, both in Mark and at Qumran, the clearsightedness of the members of the covenant community and the blindness of those outside that community are connected with a divine appointment that works itself out through the mediation of God's spirit and that of his enemy.[952]

In other words, the battle is taking place within the human being very much as Paul described it as between spirit and flesh. But apparently, some individuals actually *belong* to the dark side. In 2 Thessalonians, such are described as those who "refused to love the truth" and "took pleasure in unrighteousness." Romans 1:32 says: "Although they know God's righteous decree that those who do such things deserve death, they not only continue to do these very things but also approve of those who practice them." 1QS 5:11-12 describes the wicked as follows: "They have neither inquired nor sought after Him concerning His laws, that they might know the hidden things in which they have secretly gone astray, and matters revealed they have treated with insolence." In Mark, of course, the "hidden things" are not secrets of the law/Torah, but rather the identity of Jesus and its full implications and "the mystery of the kingdom of God."

Marcus writes that part of the "mystery of the kingdom of God" is exactly the fact that there is a division of humanity into the blind and the illuminated, "a division which God, for unfathomable reasons of his own, both wills and calls into being."[953] He cites Enoch again, the revelations of which include the fact that the kingdom is divided between the holy and the sinners. Part of the mystery is that the righteous will be rewarded, but the sinners will perish, in accordance with God's design.

As just noted, it appears, as Marcus lays out the evidence, that the identity of Jesus is only a part of the mystery of Mark; the major mystery is the 'kingdom of God.' In Mark 4:11, Jesus tells his disciples that to them the mystery of the kingdom has been given (*dedotai*, perfect passive). However, the secret of who Jesus is has not yet been given and only begins to emerge gradually within the story world of Mark, with Peter's confession that Jesus is the Messiah (8:29), even if Peter's idea of what the Messiah should be and do is not known by him. And, in fact, the whole truth is not known by any human being until the centurion at the cross sees that Jesus is the Son of God (15:39).

Regarding the mystery of the kingdom of God, Marcus writes:

> On the face of it, the perfect passive *dedotai* should limit the "mystery" of 4:11 to something that has already put in an appearance in the Gospel. As J. L. Martyn has suggested, the disciples'

[951] Mark 4:23-25.
[952] Marcus (1984), pp. 563–64.
[953] Marcus (1984), p. 564.

question in 4:10 provides a key to what that "something" is. They ask Jesus about the parables, and his answer in vv 11-12 is related to that question. Jesus answers, "To you the mystery of the kingdom of God has been given" – in parables should be supplied.[954]

In a footnote, Marcus supplies a paraphrase of Mark 4:11-12 as follows:

To you disciples the mystery of the kingdom of God has been given in parables, but for those outside, the reason that everything is in parables is so that they may indeed see but not perceive, etc.

And then, in 4:21, Mark writes:

He said to them, "Is a lamp brought in to be put under the bushel basket, or under the bed, and not on the lampstand? For there is nothing hidden, except to be disclosed; nor is anything secret, except to come to light. Let anyone with ears to hear listen!"

In other words, it's all right out in the open, only not everyone can see or hear or understand, because some have the spiritual faculties and some do not. Jesus' parables are "a two-edged sword: to his disciples they reveal 'the mystery of the kingdom of God', but to those outside they are weapons of blinding."[955]

And, of course, the parables referenced are those that have already appeared in the Gospel up to this point. The first parable – or set of parables – was in response to the accusation by the scribes from Jerusalem that Jesus was possessed by a demon and was thereby able to cast out demons. Jesus' response was as follows:

And he called them to him, and spoke to them in parables, "How can Satan cast out Satan? If a kingdom is divided against itself, that kingdom cannot stand. And if a house is divided against itself, that house will not be able to stand. And if Satan has risen up against himself and is divided, he cannot stand, but his end has come. But no one can enter a strong man's house and plunder his property without first tying up the strong man; then indeed the house can be plundered. Truly I tell you, people will be forgiven for their sins and whatever blasphemies they utter; but whoever blasphemes against the Holy Spirit can never have forgiveness, but is guilty of an eternal sin" – for they had said, "He has an unclean spirit."[956]

The next major parable before Mk. 4:11 is the Parable of the Sower, with Jesus' explanation following:

"Listen! A sower went out to sow. And as he sowed, some seed fell on the path, and the birds came and ate it up. Other seed fell on rocky ground, where it did not have much soil, and it sprang up quickly, since it had no depth of soil. And when the sun rose, it was scorched; and since it had no root, it withered away. Other seed fell among thorns, and the thorns grew up and choked it, and it yielded no grain. Other seed fell into good soil and brought forth grain, growing up and increasing and yielding thirty and sixty and a hundredfold." And he said, "Let anyone with ears to hear listen!"

When he was alone, those who were around him along with the twelve asked him about the parables. And he said to them, "To you has been given the secret of the kingdom of God, but for those outside, everything comes in parables; in order that 'they may indeed look, but not perceive,

---

[954]Marcus (1984), p. 565.
[955]Marcus (1984), p. 566.
[956]Mark 3:23-30.

and may indeed listen, but not understand; so that they may not turn again and be forgiven'." And he said to them, "Do you not understand this parable? Then how will you understand all the parables?

The sower sows the word. These are the ones on the path where the word is sown: when they hear, Satan immediately comes and takes away the word that is sown in them. And these are the ones sown on rocky ground: when they hear the word, they immediately receive it with joy. But they have no root, and endure only for a while; then, when trouble or persecution arises on account of the word, immediately they fall away. And others are those sown among the thorns: these are the ones who hear the word, but the cares of the world, and the lure of wealth, and the desire for other things come in and choke the word, and it yields nothing. And these are the ones sown on the good soil: they hear the word and accept it and bear fruit, thirty and sixty and a hundredfold."[957]

Obviously, the different types of soil are *different types of human beings*; the good soil can receive the word, have their eyes and ears opened, and learn to see, hear and understand. The other types of soil, hardened path, rocky ground, among thorny overgrowth, apparently have no chance of acquiring perceptions of higher realities. What is more, there is no suggestion at all that one can alter the sort of soil one is. One assumes that it is 'God's will' that there are so many different types of human beings. But what is said in v. 12 is that God's will works itself out in opposition to Satan, who is an explicit actor in leading humans astray. Cares of the world (tribulations), the lure of wealth, desire for things, etc. are the agents of Satan.

So, Marcus concludes that a big part of the mystery of the kingdom of God is the mystery of God's will: he causes some to bear fruit while he hardens others by the mediation of Satan and Satan's agents. That, taken together with the Parable of Satan casting out Satan and the Strong Man, finished off by the declaration that there is an 'unforgiveable sin,' establish the following: 1) there are two kingdoms, that of God and that of Satan, which are in deadly opposition to each other; 2) Jesus has come to rout Satan, 'plunder his house' and retrieve those who have spiritual organs of seeing and hearing; 3) in spite of the fact that Jesus has come to do this, Satan can still impede the kingdom of God in some ways and one must guard against those wiles if one is capable. Marcus calls this "the collision of the kingdoms":

The "mystery of the kingdom of God" thus has to do with God's strange design of bringing his kingdom in Jesus Christ, yet unleashing the forces of darkness to blind human beings so that they oppose that kingdom.[958]

Again, one is reminded of 2 Thess. 2:9-12. Apparently, the "collision of the kingdoms," this war in the hearts and minds of human beings, will continue until the time of the full disclosure of God's secrets will occur in an age to come. That means that, until that time, the secrets of God are, at best, imperfectly understood. One is, of course, reminded of Paul saying:

For we know only in part, and we prophesy only in part; but when the complete comes, the partial will come to an end. When I was a child, I spoke like a child, I thought like a child, I reasoned like a child; when I became an adult, I put an end to childish ways. For now we see in a mirror, dimly, but then we will see face to face. Now I know only in part; then I will know fully, even as I have been fully known. [959]

---

[957] Mark 4:1-20.
[958] Marcus (1984), p. 567.
[959] 1 Cor. 13:9-12.

Even though the perfection of knowledge is not possible until the 'end of the age' (or graduation to a higher sphere of existence), for the present, knowledge is imparted to each person with spiritual organs that have been opened, "according to the spirit of each" and "according to the rule of the age" (1QS 9:18). Thus, the disciples were able to comprehend something, but didn't have the full picture. The drama of Jesus' disciples in Mark reveals that even the children of righteousness can have their minds darkened by the Angel of Darkness. Qumran texts emphasize the problem of incomprehension within the community, that even those who start on a good way can be led astray. Satan is seen to be actively at work even among the elect.

The motif of incomprehension among the disciples continues throughout Mark's Gospel. The disciples themselves are described and spoken of as those who have eyes but do not see, have ears, but do not hear, and act quite often like 'those outside.' In Mark 6:52 and 8:17, the disciples are accused of having hard hearts. This is the same charge leveled at Jesus' opponents in 3:5. Yes, they do understand something, but not enough, and not the most important things, as the Gospel shows again and again. Their seeing is like that of the partially-healed blind man in 8:24 who sees men, but as trees, walking. This pericope is significantly placed by Mark between two instances of the disciples' misunderstanding (8:14-21 and 8:31-33), Marcus writes about the disciples as depicted in the passion narrative:

> In 13:32-37, Jesus has warned his disciples three times to keep awake. Remaining awake, however, is precisely what the disciples cannot do in Gethsemane; in 14:37-38 Jesus twice uses the same verb he had used in 13:35, 37, *grēgorein* ("stay awake") to describe what the disciples are not able to do. In 14:40 he comes to the disciples a second time and finds them sleeping, "for their eyes were heavy and they did not know what to answer him." The "not knowing" of the disciples echoes other passages in Mark where the disciples do not know, for example, 4:13 and 10:38, but in particular it is almost exactly parallel to the notice about Peter at the transfiguration in 9:6, "he did not know what to answer." The verbal similarity suggests that Jesus' glory, which is revealed at the transfiguration, is linked with his suffering, which begins at Gethsemane, but that neither his glory nor the significance of his suffering is comprehended by the disciples.
>
> The climax of the motif of the incomprehension of the disciples is found in Peter's denials of Jesus. In 14:68 Peter says to the slave girl who identifies him as a follower of Jesus, "I neither know nor understand what you are saying," and in 14:71 he proclaims to the bystanders, "I do not know this man about whom you are speaking." Thus, in the denials, he twice says *ouk oida* ("I do not know") and once *oute epistamai* ("I do not understand"), thereby driving home the blindness which the denials represent. From these examples it is clear that in Mark, as at Qumran, members of the elect group as well as "those outside" are, in the penultimate age before the "renewal," subject to the blinding onslaughts of the forces of darkness.[960]

Now, apparently, according to Mark, the turn of the ages, the beginning of the period in which the secrets of God's kingdom can begin to be revealed, is accomplished with the death of Jesus. The great secret of the gospel which Mark announces at the beginning, Jesus' identity as Son of God, had to be kept under wraps during his ministry as depicted in the story world of Mark, but must then be preached to all the nations, as is declared in the Olivet Discourse (13:10).

The cross is the climax of revelations vs. incomprehension; it was, effectively, the point at which the two kingdoms collided. Of the two events – death and resurrection – it is death on the cross that receives the greatest emphasis in Mark, which has often been called 'a passion

---

[960]Marcus (1984), pp. 569–70.

narrative with a long introduction.' Nevertheless, resurrection is mentioned as part of the plan in every one of Jesus' passion predictions and is mentioned alone after the Transfiguration; the disciples are told to "tell no one about what they had seen, until after the Son of Man had *risen from the dead*" (Mk. 9:9b).

Peter, after Jesus' arrest, has become one who, by his own admission, neither knows nor understands. The mockery of Jesus on the cross reveals clearly that those 'outside' could not see:

> Those who passed by derided him, shaking their heads and saying, "Aha! You who would destroy the temple and build it in three days, save yourself, and come down from the cross!" In the same way the chief priests, along with the scribes, were also mocking him among themselves and saying, "He saved others; he cannot save himself. Let the Messiah, the King of Israel, come down from the cross now, so that we may see and believe." Those who were crucified with him also taunted him.[961]

Their mockery reveals that what they were seeing was the physical reality but not the spiritual one. But there, at the cross, was someone who did see: a Roman centurion. He perceives the truth and speaks it, the first human being in the entire Gospel who realizes the full dignity and import of what Jesus was doing; and bizarrely, it was a Roman soldier. Marcus writes:

> The moment of light for the centurion and for the redeemed humanity whom he represents, however, is a moment of darkness for Jesus. "My God, my God, why have you forsaken me?" Jesus himself seems to have become here an "outsider"; he has been thrown out of the vineyard, as 12:8 had foretold. The sentence of 4:11-12 has now fallen on Jesus himself; the cosmic darkness that previously enveloped not only the crowds but also the disciples has now cast its shadow on him. The cry of dereliction, in conjunction with the words of the centurion, implies that Jesus takes the place of humanity in the darkness of the old age, under the power of Satan; and because he does that, humanity lives in the light of the new age. Jesus gives his life as "a ransom for many." (10:45)[962]

But does that mean that the period in which Satan is able to blind the elect has come to an end, that the period during which God's mysteries must be concealed has ended, as Marcus proposes? If one refers back to the farewell prophecies of the Olivet Discourse, it appears to be not so simple. Even after Jesus is gone, false Christs and false prophets will come and do signs and wonders and only by the grace of God will the elect escape being taken in, though their discernment will be tested to the limit. The elect can escape deception only if they are watchful; otherwise, they will be like Peter, James and John in the Garden of Gethsemane, falling asleep and under the power of Satan.

Mark and his community, as described by Brandon, were living in difficult times following the destruction of Jerusalem and its temple. There was undoubtedly some persecution, though probably not institutionalized except in the case of Jews. But anyone who had been connected at all with a messianic movement that led to the rebellion of the Jews against Rome was seriously tarnished. Mark had his chance to bring Paul's Christ to the fore, to utilize Paul's theology to create a Jesus to reassure the Christians that the external reality was not necessarily the spiritual reality: there was much more going on in the heavenly spheres, and they needed to hold the faith. The secrets of Jesus' true identity and the kingdom of God, taught by Paul, are now the open proclamation of the Markan community. As Marcus writes:

---

[961] Mark 15:29-32.
[962] Marcus (1984), pp. 571–72.

> For Mark ... the very darkest moment of the Gospel ... actually marks the turn of the ages. ... In the middle of that darkness, light breaks forth; the centurion sees, and the Gospel ends with the rising of the sun, the empty tomb (its door thrown open!), the splendid messenger, the amazing message. True, the women run away terrified and tell the message to no one. Yet even this last act of human disobedience, this last shadow of cosmic darkness, cannot defeat God's purpose, for Mark has transmitted the tale that the women kept to themselves. Somehow, the news has leaked out; it could not remain hidden.[963]

And how did the 'news leak out'? Well, of course, all was revealed to Paul, and from Paul to Mark. That appears to me to be the obvious implication of the narrative set-up of the end of Mark's Gospel: that Paul was the ultimate source for the revelations about Christ that Mark wrote his Gospel to portray in allegory.

Son of David?

Jan Dochhorn[964] writes about what he calls "a collection of polemical apophthegmata in Mark 2:23-28":

> One Sabbath He was going along beside the fields of standing grain, and as they made their way, His disciples began to pick off the grains (Deut. 23:25). And the Pharisees said to Him, Look! Why are they doing what is not permitted or lawful on the Sabbath? And He said to them, Have you never [even] read what David did when he was in need and was hungry, he and those who were accompanying him? How he went into the house of God when Abiathar was the high priest, and ate the sacred loaves set forth [before God], which it is not permitted or lawful for any but the priests to eat, and [how he] also gave [them] to those who were with him (I Sam. 21:1-6; II Sam. 8:17)? And Jesus said to them, The Sabbath was made on account and for the sake of man, not man for the Sabbath (Exod. 23:12; Deut. 5:14). So the Son of Man is Lord even of the Sabbath.

He notes, "I consider that Mark 2:1-3:6 has roots in an older written collection of polemical apophthegmata ... and I assume that this collection originally included the four pericopae written down in Mark 2."[965] The four pericopae are: Jesus heals the paralytic claiming the right to forgive sins; Jesus calls Levi, he came for sinners; the question about fasting with the "bridegroom" answer; and Jesus is Lord of the Sabbath. In chapter 3 is a fifth pericope: the man with a withered hand cured on the Sabbath.

Dochhorn justifies his claim by pointing out that the four pericopae are related to each other by strong links making them a composition of specific cohesion, including the fact that the first and the last pericope both end in statements concerning the authority of the Son of Man (Mark 2:10 and Mark 2:28); they form a complete circle. Additionally, the circular composition dealing with the authority of the Son of Man harmonizes with another compositional device, which is that each apophthegma is marked by statements made by Jesus concerning his role: the Son of Man who can forgive sins (2:10); a doctor who heals the sick (2:16); one who has come to call sinners (2:17); the bridegroom whose wedding guests cannot fast (2:19-20); and Lord of the

[963]Marcus (1984), p. 574.
[964]Jan Dochhorn, 'Man and the Son of Man in Mark 2:27-28,' in Becker et al. (2014).
[965]Dochhorn (2014), p. 148.

Sabbath (2:28).[966] In short, the author believes that there was a Jesus of Nazareth as described in the text he is analyzing, and that this Jesus defended his own and his disciples' religious practice against the objections of the scribes and Pharisees; that is to say, a Jesus of Nazareth who was teaching that the Law was 'breakable.'

Considering what we now know from all the discussion in this text, we know pretty well that Judas the Galilean, the most likely messiah of the Jewish/Jerusalem Christians, was extremely unlikely to have ever said or promoted such an idea in any context. Thus, what actually comes about by reading this analysis is the conviction that there was no prior written source; Mark was composing freely, and he was a brilliant composer.

Now, it is true that there are some aspects of Mark 2:1-28 that differ from the Gospel of Mark as a whole. For one thing, the importance of fasting is relativized in contradistinction to the notice that fasting is sometimes necessary when exorcising demons (Mark 9:29). I would suggest that the context is important, the general rule being that the guests do not fast when the bridegroom is present, but an exorcism is not a bridal feast. Other factors mentioned by Dochhorn are that only in this small section is Jesus referred to as doctor, bridegroom, one who can forgive sins, violate the law (Lord of the Sabbath), and so on. Considering that Mark is not a lengthy text, and that each part of it is clearly carefully planned and constructed to convey a particular theological point, I don't think it is relevant that titles and functions that appear in one place do not appear in another; the author has moved on to different points, different purposes.

Next item is Dochhorn's discussion of the 'Picking Grain on the Sabbath' episode quoted above. Dochhorn notes about this pericope:

> The narration seems to imply that the Pharisees *see* the disciples plucking ears of corn. Perhaps the narrator even presupposes that the Pharisees are in the field. This would, if it were the case, indicate that the narrative introduction of this apophthegma has been composed by someone who was not really well informed about the rules pertaining to walking around on the Sabbath.[967]

I would further suggest that this is evidence that free composition was being used to make a point, i.e. the apophthegma, composed by Mark, and was not in any way intended to be taken as a historical event.

In the above pericope, Jesus begins his response with a biblical story based on 1 Samuel 21:2-7.

> David said to the priest Ahimelech, "The king has charged me with a matter, and said to me, 'No one must know anything of the matter about which I send you, and with which I have charged you.' I have made an appointment with the young men for such and such a place. Now then, what have you at hand? Give me five loaves of bread, or whatever is here." The priest answered David, "I have no ordinary bread at hand, only holy bread – provided that the young men have kept themselves from women." David answered the priest, "Indeed women have been kept from us as always when I go on an expedition; the vessels of the young men are holy even when it is a common journey; how much more today will their vessels be holy?" So the priest gave him the holy bread; for there was no bread there except the bread of the Presence, which is removed from before the LORD, to be replaced by hot bread on the day it is taken away.

---

[966]Dochhorn (2014), p. 149.
[967]Dochhorn (2014), p. 152. Dochhorn's italics.

The obvious point is not that David did anything on the Sabbath, but that he broke the law reserving the loaves of presence for the priests. What was important for the priest in the story was that David and his men should be undefiled by relations with women if they were going to eat the holy bread. Mark was wrong when he named the priest Abiathar; it was actually Achimelekh, the son of Abiathar. The 'house of God' in the story was a temple in Nob, not in Jerusalem, and the motive for David was that he and his men were hungry, though this is not explicitly stated in 1 Samuel. The intended parallel was that Jesus and his disciples corresponded to David and his companions, and David and Jesus both take the initiative, Jesus invoking his power as "Lord of the Sabbath" to allow his disciples to pluck ears of corn. In order to argue for his Sabbath ruling, Jesus refers to the order of creation, that is, man was created before the Sabbath was instituted. The Son of Man is the one who represents the superiority of man to the Sabbath because of the order of creation. As Dochhorn puts it:

> The Son of Man is "the man", the exemplary man who realizes what mankind generally has or is. We can also use a more biblical term: the Son of Man is the New Adam ...
>
> Tradition-critical evidence corroborates an Adamic interpretation of Mark 2:27-28. Indeed, in many texts – especially in Pauline literature or literature associated with Paul – one may detect elements that seem better understandable if read with the notion that Christ is the exemplary man, who realizes the principal (original) cosmic superiority of man. ...
>
> Features pointing to an Adamic Christology may also be found in a text written by Paul himself: 1 Cor 15:23-28. This passage depicts how God after Christ's resurrection subordinates everything to Christ (excluding himself). This scenario is mainly built upon two biblical texts, Ps 109:1-2 and – again – Ps 8. Especially the notion that everything will be put under Christ's feet (1 Cor 15:27) points to Psalm 8 (cf. Ps 8:7). ... Paul was probably aware of the anthropological implications of this Psalm. This is indicated by the fact that the whole unit is preceded by an Adam-Christ typology (1 Cor 15:22). Apparently for him, Christ was the New Adam ...
>
> ... [T]he temptation of Jesus by Satan in Mark 1:13 ... points to contemporary concepts about Adam as they are developed in the Vita Adae et Evae: 1. ... it is primarily the Devil who misleads (first Eve and then) Adam to eat from the forbidden tree ... 2. The animals accompanying Jesus in the desert fit the harmony between Adam and the animals [in Eden] ... 3. The angels serving Jesus possibly remind the reader of Adam's superiority to the angels ... We have, as a consequence, good reason to assume that Mark 1:13 presents Jesus as the New Adam. With a certain degree of probability we can also assume that this New Adam Christology is connected to the Son of Man Christology as attested in other parts of the Gospel of Mark. ... [T]he temptation of Jesus, the New Adam, by Satan in Mark 1:13 is strongly linked to the temptation of Jesus, the Son of Man, by the Satan Peter in Mark 8:31-33. ...
>
> According to Hebrews 1:1–2:9, Christ's superiority to the angels has consequences for Christians as well: they no longer belong to the Torah which is promulgated by angels (Hebr 2:2), but to Christ (Hebr 2:3). Here, being associated with the "New Adam" obviously constitutes a distance from the Torah.[968]

Now, what is common to all the parallels to Mark 2:27-28 is the fact that Psalm 8 plays an important role. This is especially true for 1 Cor. 15:23 and Heb. 1:1–2:9. This Psalm was used to support a Son of Man Christology which interpreted the Son of Man as the New Adam:

> O Lord, our Lord, how admirable is your name in all the earth, because your magnificence was raised beyond the heavens. Out of mouths of infants and nurslings you furnished praise for yourself,

---

[968]Dochhorn (2014), pp. 160–64.

for the sake of your enemies, to put down enemy and avenger, because I will observe the heavens, works of your fingers – moon and stars – things you alone founded. What is man that you are mindful of him, or son of man that you attend to him: You diminished him a little in comparison with angels; with glory and honor you crowned him. And you set him over the works of your hands; you subjected all under his feet, sheep and cattle, all together, and further the beasts of the plain, the birds of the air and the fish of the sea – the things that pass through paths of seas. O Lord, our Lord, how admirable is your name in all the earth![969]

In the above Psalm, you see 'man' and 'son of man' side by side, exactly as it appears in Mark 2:27-28: man (humankind) and Son of Man. Further, the use of Psalm 8 for the same purpose is attested in 1 Cor. 15:23 and in Hebrews 1:1–2:9, a Pauline-affiliated text.

Dochhorn points out that reference to the order of creation can also be found in Mark 10:2-9, where Jesus indicates Genesis 1:27 and 2:24 in order to refute the possibility of divorce allowed by Moses. This is obviously aimed at neutralizing the Torah itself.

And some Pharisees came up, and, in order to test Him and try to find a weakness in Him, asked, Is it lawful for a man to dismiss and repudiate and divorce his wife? He answered them, What did Moses command you? They replied, Moses allowed a man to write a bill of divorce and to put her away (Deut. 24:1-4). But Jesus said to them, Because of your hardness of heart [your condition of insensibility to the call of God] he wrote you this precept in your Law. But from the beginning of creation God made them male and female (Gen. 1:27; 5:2). For this reason a man shall leave [behind] his father and his mother and be joined to his wife and cleave closely to her permanently, and the two shall become one flesh, so that they are no longer two, but one flesh (Gen. 2:24). What therefore God has united (joined together), let not man separate or divide.

This is a Pauline perspective (1 Cor. 7:10-16) and unlikely to be part of some mythical collection of pre-Pauline apophthegmata.

The concluding statement of the pericope, "the Son of Man is Lord even of the Sabbath," suggests that the Son of Man is already known as Lord of *something else*, which can only refer back to Mark 2:1-12, dealing with the power of the Son of Man to forgive sins. It is stated there, in Mk. 2:7, that the power to forgive sins is *the right of God alone*. (Keep in mind that Mark is putting words into the mouths of all the characters for his own narrative purposes!) Thus, when Jesus declared he had the right to forgive sins, he was putting himself in the position of God. And so, Mark 2:28 should be read in that context; the Lord of the Sabbath is the one who possesses the Secret Name which brings us again to the Philippians hymn:

Let the same mind be in you that was in Christ Jesus, who, though he was in the form of God, did not regard equality with God as something to be exploited, but emptied himself, taking the form of a slave, being born in human likeness. And being found in human form, he humbled himself and became obedient to the point of death – even death on a cross. Therefore God also highly exalted him and gave him the name that is above every name, so that at the name of Jesus every knee should bend, in heaven and on earth and under the earth, and every tongue should confess that Jesus Christ is Lord, to the glory of God the Father.[970]

In this way, as Dochhorn states, Mark 2:23-28 concludes with the strongest and highest Christology imaginable, thus concluding a circular construction that includes other Christological

---

[969] Psalm 8, LXX.
[970] Phil. 2:5-11.

claims. However, Dochhorn then falls down by again trying to attribute this high Christology to some 'pre-Markan' and 'pre-Pauline' source! As we have pointed out again and again in the above text, it was Paul who formulated the Christology that was such an offense to the Jerusalem Christians and, as far as I can see, it doesn't go any further back than Paul. So even the Philippians hymn must be Pauline, or composed by a member of Paul's congregations, or, perhaps written about someone other than the messiah of the Jerusalem Christians, i.e. Paul's unknown Christ on the cross.

The designation 'Lord' probably refers back to Psalm 110:1 (109:1 in the LXX), which is a stand-in for both the Tetragrammaton and the royal messianic or Christological title, thus ascribing to the Messiah the name and position of God. In 1 Cor. 8:6, the phrase "one Lord Jesus Christ" parallels the phrase "one God, the Father," derived from the Shema Israel,[971] which Paul has applied to Jesus Christ.

This leads to the further matter of Jesus as the 'son of David.' Mark's Jesus implies that it is not an appropriate designation for the Son of God:

> While Jesus was teaching in the temple, he said, "How can the scribes say that the Messiah is the son of David? David himself, by the Holy Spirit, declared, 'The Lord said to my Lord, 'Sit at my right hand, until I put your enemies under your feet.'" [Ps. 110:1] David himself calls him Lord; so how can he be his son?" And the large crowd was listening to him with delight.[972]

This passage formulates a Christological claim to the position of God in relation to David (in the psalm quoted, it is God who is addressed as 'Lord,' not Jesus). Dochhorn points out that the Davidic Christology was prior to Paul, and this is most likely correct based on Jewish writings and the common currency of the idea in the times preceding the Jewish War. The only hint that Paul ever gives is in Romans 1:3-4:

> ... the gospel concerning his Son, who was descended from David according to the flesh and was declared to be Son of God with power according to the spirit of holiness by resurrection from the dead, Jesus Christ our Lord ...

There are problems with this bit of text. Here we seemingly find the Davidic Christology (flesh) overlaid by the Christological title 'Son of God' (spirit). Taken as it is written, this almost describes an *adoptionist* Christology; that is, that Jesus was adopted as the Son of God at his baptism, resurrection, or ascension. If read in this way, it produces rather extreme tension with many things Paul says elsewhere, not least his emphasis on the Philippians hymn quoted above. It is not consistent with Paul's Christology.

Brendan Byrne writes that Romans 1:3:

> ... overwrites the more primitive Christology of the creedal formula [of Philippian hymn 2:6-11]. The latter associates Christ's divine sonship with the moment of his resurrection, whereas in Paul's eyes Jesus is uniquely God's Son (cf. 5:10; 8:3, 29, 32 [...]), not simply from the time of his resurrection but during his earthly obedience and possibly even as 'pre-existent' ...[973]

---

[971] "Hear, O Israel: the LORD our God, the LORD is one." (Deut. 6:4)

[972] Mark 12:35-37.

[973] Quoted by Gitte Buch-Hansen, 'The Politics of Beginnings – Cosmology, Christology and Covenant: Gospel Openings Reconsidered in the Light of Paul's Pneumatology,' in Becker *et al.* (2014), p. 216.

Note below Byrne's scriptural citations for his claim:

Rom. 5:9-10 Therefore, since we are now justified (acquitted, made righteous, and brought into right relationship with God) by Christ's blood, how much more [certain is it that] we shall be saved by Him from the indignation and wrath of God. For if while we were enemies we were reconciled to God through the death of His Son, it is much more [certain], now that we are reconciled, that we shall be saved (daily delivered from sin's dominion) through His [resurrection] life.

Rom. 8:3 For God has done what the Law could not do, being weakened by the flesh. Sending His own Son in the guise of sinful flesh and as an offering for sin, [God] condemned sin in the flesh [subdued, overcame, deprived it of its power over all who accept that sacrifice] [Lev. 7:37].

Rom. 8:29 For those whom He foreknew, He also destined from the beginning to be molded into the image of His Son [and share inwardly His likeness], that He might become the firstborn among many brethren.

Rom. 8:32 He who did not withhold or spare [even] His own Son but gave Him up for us all, will He not also with Him freely and graciously give us all [other] things?

So Paul's Christology is pretty much the highest and yet, we have to contend with v. 3 of Romans 1 where suddenly, Jesus only becomes Son of God at his resurrection. In his commentary on Romans, James D. G. Dunn sees no tension in this and states that "Paul would certainly see the earlier formula as congruent with his own Christology." He suggests a 'two-stage Christology':

For those aware that the royal Messiah was also called God's Son [...] the phrase "in power" would be a natural qualification: Jesus did not become God's Son at the resurrection; but he entered upon a still higher rank of sonship at resurrection. [...] That being said, it remains significant that these early formulations and Paul saw in the resurrection of Jesus a "becoming" of Jesus in status and role, not simply a ratification of a status and role already enjoyed on earth or from the beginning of time.[974]

Gitte Buch-Hansen makes the claim that Dunn's idea can be confirmed by Paul's cosmology and that Mark's 'messianic secret' theme can be viewed as the evangelist's narrative version of the two-stage Christology; that is, something happened at Jesus' baptism, but more was to happen of even greater import, i.e. the atoning death of cosmic significance, and the demons knew it.

It is said by many experts that the hymnal passages in the Epistles to Philippians and Colossians represent the earliest Christian traditions preserved in the New Testament. These passages depict a high Christology of Christ's heavenly preexistence as the firstborn son of God in the heavenly spheres. They are usually assumed to represent Paul's Christology too, since he apparently used them and there is no reason to think that the Philippians passage was interpolated. The texts again, for ease of reference:

Let this same attitude and purpose and [humble] mind be in you which was in Christ Jesus: Who, although being essentially one with God and in the form of God [possessing the fullness of the attributes which make God God], did not think this equality with God was a thing to be eagerly grasped or retained, But stripped Himself [of all privileges and rightful dignity], so as to assume

---

[974]Quoted by Buch-Hansen (2014), p. 217.

the guise of a servant (slave), in that He became like men and was born a human being. And after He had appeared in human form, He abased and humbled Himself [still further] and carried His obedience to the extreme of death, even the death of the cross! Therefore God has highly exalted Him and has freely bestowed on Him the name that is above every name, That in (at) the name of Jesus every knee should (must) bow, in heaven and on earth and under the earth, And every tongue confess and acknowledge that Jesus Christ is Lord, to the glory of God the Father.[975]

He is the exact likeness of the unseen God [the visible representation of the invisible]; He is the Firstborn of all creation. For it was in Him that all things were created, in heaven and on earth, things seen and things unseen, whether thrones, dominions, rulers, or authorities; all things were created and exist through Him [by His service, intervention] and in and for Him. And He Himself existed before all things, and in Him all things consist (cohere, are held together).[976]

But, Dunn and Buch-Hansen are right in that there are two *phases* to Paul's account of Jesus, but they get the details wrong. In Paul, his 'earthly' life is distinguished from his post-resurrection 'spiritual' life in that his true identity was *hidden* from the archons. Paul's Jesus wasn't baptized; *believers* were baptized in order to participate in Christ's crucifixion and resurrection. But Buch-Hansen conflates Paul and Mark's perspectives, and thinks that since Paul didn't bother to give any biographical details about Jesus, the job was left to Mark, who tells us that Jesus *received* the title 'Son of God' at his *baptism*, that is, stage one of the two-stage Christology.

In those days Jesus came from Nazareth of Galilee and was baptized by John in the Jordan. And when He came up out of the water, at once he [John] saw the heavens torn open and the [Holy] Spirit like a dove coming down [to enter] into Him. And there came a voice out from within heaven, You are My Beloved Son; in You I am well pleased. [Ps. 2:7; Isa. 42:1.][977]

That raises the problem of why Paul, in Romans (as interpreted), and Mark would feature a two-stage Christology in the face of the claimed primitive Christology of the Philippians and Colossians hymns, and other statements by Paul elsewhere? And then why did Matthew and Luke change it back up again – to correct Mark – with their extended birth narratives of a divine son fathered, literally, by God? Since Mark obviously portrays Pauline ideas, it's not difficult to see that Jesus' baptism is modeled on how Paul understood baptism as the reception of spirit, which brings about "your adoption to sonship," accompanied by the cry, "Abba! Father!" (Rom. 8:15, also Gal. 4:6).[978] The sequence is the same: baptism, reception of pneuma, sonship. As for Romans 1:4, it can simply be read as following Paul's two-phase secret/revealed mystery of Jesus: at his resurrection he was "declared son of God in power," *revealing* his true identity.

Now, it seems clear to me, making inferences from the evidence of both Josephus and Paul, that the Lord of the Jerusalem Christians may very well have been the 'royal Davidic messiah' and had therefore received the royal 'son' title via adoption, perhaps even during his lifetime. We saw a number of hints of this in our review of what Josephus had to say about the many messianic claimants, that they sought royal dignities. On the other side, it is also pretty clear that Paul's messiah was the eternal son from the beginning of time, but that he was *first recognized (in the*

---

[975]Phil. 2:5-11.
[976]Col. 1:15-17.
[977]Mark 1:9-11.
[978]See Engberg-Pedersen (2010), pp. 53, 68–9.

heavenly realms) as such only at the resurrection to heaven, and not before. That's the whole theme of his 'mystery of the ages,' that God had a plan to redeem humanity already in place, but it had to be carried out in secret so the forces of evil wouldn't get in there and mess things up (one supposes).[979]

Paul's messiah was clearly something – and someone – altogether different, as we have seen repeatedly throughout this text; his messiah was so different that he even spoke of 'another Christ' and 'another gospel.' He castigated the Jerusalem Christians for being the 'enemies of Christ' or 'enemies of the cross.' So I want to state as strongly as possible here that I do not think that Paul ever conceived of his messiah as "descended from David according to the flesh." The verse itself is not attested in Marcion, so may well have been interpolated.

But there's one more problem. Despite being used by modern scholars and believers to support the idea that Paul thought Jesus was descended from David, that's not what the text actually says. Richard Carrier points out that the Greek says Jesus was "*manufactured* from David's sperm," not 'descended' or 'born' like a normal human being. When Paul describes physical descent, he uses the word *gennao*. Here, however, Paul uses the word *ginomai*, which he elsewhere uses to describe how God created Adam in Paradise (i.e. in the third heaven), and how God will make the future bodies of the resurrection. He never uses it to refer to physical conception and birth. Additionally, 'sperm' could be and *was* used allegorically in Jewish texts. Irenaeus even documents "celestial 'seeds' impregnating the celestial 'wombs' of celestial 'women'." Divine beings could even be 'buried' in the heavens, as Adam was in the *Revelation of Moses*.[980] And we've already seen how Paul can use the word seed/sperm allegorically.[981] After all, he says that anyone who comes to believe in Christ will become the 'seed' of Abraham, and that believers are 'children' of Sarah (the 'free woman' of Gal. 4:31). So if a Gentile convert can be 'the seed of Abraham,' there's no reason Jesus cannot similarly be 'the seed of David,' regardless of his actual physical descent.

In fact, the term used in Mark ('son of David') as qualification to be messiah is markedly infrequent in a pre-Christian context (see *Psalms of Solomon* 17:21). If, as I've already suggested, Judas the Galilean traced back his descent to David, this may have been a title claimed by him and his supporters. Mark's rejection of the title suggests that it must have been in use. But the fact that the Zealots had certain ideas about what the Davidic messiah would be does not necessarily imply that Paul himself would reject all Davidic allusions or connections in response. As we've already seen, in Romans 15 he presents Jesus as the root of Jesse (David's father), and the Epistle to the Hebrews, which we argued was Pauline in nature, contains Davidic references. Also recall the point raised by Davies in the discussion on Cyrus as messiah: Jews could see Gentile kings as messiahs, agents of God's world-empire, "and even inheritors of the David covenant."

Paul is also no stranger to referencing Davidic psalms and imagery. For example, Ephesians 4:8 quotes Psalm 68:18: "When he ascended on high, he took many captives, and gave gifts to

---

[979]See 1 Cor. 2:8, where Paul says that the "rulers of this age ... crucified the Lord of glory." As discussed already, these rulers are something like demonic archons, not human rulers, though human rulers could be manipulated and controlled by demons.

[980]Zoroastrianism (from which comes the original concept of the Messiah) includes the belief that after his death Zarathustra's sperm was kept in a lake, from which the future messiah's body would be formed. See Boyce (2001), pp. 42, 86.

[981]Carrier (2014), pp. 575–82, 196. See Gal. 3:29.

his people." And he alludes to the Davidic royalty psalms 8 and 110 in 1 Cor. 15:25-27 "as prophecies of Christ's enthronement at the right hand of God and ultimate authority over all creation."[982] But as usual with his use of scripture, Paul does not interpret it as other Jews do – he does so in the light of his universal savior, not through the lens of a nationalist revolutionary.

If I am right about Romans largely consisting of two main letters – one to Gentile and another to Jewish Christians – this line may even be culled from Paul's greeting to the Jewish Christians. As Paul said, "To the Jews I became like a Jew, to win the Jews." So *if* authentic, all it would suggest is that Paul had in mind the prophecy from 2 Samuel 7:12-14 (LXX): "And it shall come to pass when thy days shall have been fulfilled, and thou shalt sleep with thy fathers, that *I will raise up thy seed* after thee, even thine own issue, and *I will establish his kingdom.*" Since the Davidic line was broken, the only way for that prophecy to be fulfilled would be for God to somehow make the future messiah from David's seed. And we have no reason to think Paul was not speaking allegorically, as he had about Abraham.

Of course, none of this proves that the passage is authentic, and the data from Marcion suggests it may indeed be an interpolation. It just goes to show that either way, there is no reason to read it in a way that implies anything about Jesus' actual lineage, or Paul's thoughts on the nature of the Davidic covenant. If it is interpolated, it must have been early, since a later interpolator wouldn't have used the word 'made/manufactured' (in fact, various scribal copyists later changed the word to read 'descended,' seemingly to avoid its awkwardness). For all we know, this could be how the early Jewish Christians thought of their messiah, strange as it may be. But either way – interpolated or not – it still offers no support for the idea that Paul conceived of Jesus as being a descendant of David or having any connotations hinting towards an earthly kingdom of Davidic domination of the nations.

So, just as Romans 1:3 provides no reason to think that Paul thought of Jesus as the 'son of David,' Mark 12:35-37 pretty firmly rejects this Davidic messiah title as applicable to Mark's Jesus; and this, despite the fact that the blind Bartimaeus addresses him as such and in the very next pericope, the triumphal entry into Jerusalem, again, Jesus is acclaimed as descended from David. "Blessed is the coming kingdom of our ancestor David!"

There is another very powerful reason to assert that Mark used his character, Jesus, to reject the Davidic messiah role: it would have been extremely dangerous not to have done so in Rome just after the Jewish War had ended. Nothing would more surely bring down the wrath of Vespasian and Titus on the Christians than to intimate that their Christ had been the Davidic kingly messiah. And, in fact, that is exactly what Paul was against and what Mark is clearly against as well.

It might help to keep in mind the context of the discussion. Following his second entry into Jerusalem, Jesus curses the fig tree which represents the Temple and Judaism, then cleanses the temple violently, following which the lesson of the withered fig tree is expounded in terms of throwing "this mountain," i.e. Mount Zion where the temple stood, into the sea. Next, Jesus answers the challenges to his authority by referring to John the Baptist. Then comes the 'Parable of the Tenants,' which clearly refers to the Jews, specifically to the stone that was rejected (Jesus) becoming the cornerstone of a new, eschatological temple of the spirit. Following this, the episode about paying taxes to Caesar, and then the discussion of resurrection followed by 'The Great

---

[982]Hays (1989), p. 84.

Commandment.' Finally, he gets to 'Whose Son is the Christ,' at which point, having pretty much done away with Judaism, the Law of Moses, the Temple, the absolute authority of God as opposed to the Jewish scribes and Pharisees, and the juxtaposition of the 'stone that was rejected' with the command to render to Caesar what is Caesar's, and to God what is God's, he then makes it clear that he is no descendant of David, and that the idea of the Davidic messiah, who was to come with legions of angels to destroy the Romans and establish the rule of the Jews over all the nations, is not what he is about – contrary to the disciples' wishes and expectations.

Dochhorn notes that Mark not only subordinates the Davidic Christology, he even abrogates it, thereby radicalizing the God Christology (pre-existent Son of God). Therefore, it was not Davidic Christology being echoed in the story of the disciples picking corn on the Sabbath, but rather *a replacement of a Davidic hope*, and in this way he has also responded to Bartimaeus and those acclaiming him during the triumphal entry into Jerusalem. Everything that followed was an answer to those claims.

Just like Paul, Mark includes Davidic/messiah imagery in addition to the three mentions of the name or title, such as the allusions to Zech. 9 in Mark 11 and 14, and Psalms 8 and 110, both Davidic royal hymns (and which Paul also references). But also as with Paul, the Gospel makes clear that these allusions are not a claiming of a lineage or promise to David in the literal sense that the Zealots or disciples would think. They are a re-purposing of the whole idea of what the Messiah really is and the nature of his rule (i.e. the kingdom of God). This shows up in the cagey 'non-denial denial' he gives when asked about being the son of David. He doesn't simply deny it by saying, "No, I cannot trace my lineage back to David, so the claim is ridiculous." Instead he quotes scripture and says David wouldn't call his son 'Lord.' It seems more a way of saying, "No I'm not, but yes I am," as in: yes I'm the fulfillment of the Davidic expectations for an eternal king, but I'm not some fleshly son or descendant from David, and I'm no Zealot messiah-king. Basically it is the same sort of answer he gave Peter: "You are setting your mind not on divine things but on human things," i.e. royal lineage and earthly rule. The real messiah-king is not a human king descended from David's line but the heavenly king/agent of God's dominion. It's a similar dynamic that shows up in several forms: yes, Jesus is the Messiah, but not in the way the disciples think. No, he's not God, but in a way he is. No, it's false to say he'll destroy the temple, but in fact, he will. No he's not a king, but he's the king of kings. Yes, he's the fulfillment of the Davidic (and Danielic) promise, but he isn't of the lineage of David and won't be Israel's warrior-messiah.

While I have found much of value in Dochhorn's paper, I can't agree with him that "Mark and Paul share Christological ideas because they are witnesses to Early Christian theology,"[983] i.e. relying on the existence of a historical 'Jesus of Nazareth.' No, indeed. The 'theology,' if it can be called such, of the Jerusalem Christians who expected a martial messiah, likely Judas the Galilean, was not the theology of Paul, which we do find clearly stamped on and interwoven through the Gospel of Mark. And in Paul we find that the theology was a consequence of his visionary experience(s) combined with his critical exegesis of the Hebrew Scriptures: "Nothing beyond what is written" (1 Cor. 4:6).

Michael Peppard reads Mark's story about Jesus' baptism in the context of the practice of Roman adoption, and in particular, the adoption of Octavian by Julius Caesar. According

---

[983]Dochhorn (2014), p. 168.

to Suetonius, Caesar's choice of Octavian as his son and successor was accompanied by the appearance of a dove. He then suggests that the Markan readers would have understood this as a divine adoption modeled on Roman imperial adoptions. "If readers of Mark consider the resonance of the concept of adoption in the Roman ideology of Mark's era, it does not appear to be a 'low' Christology at all."[984] Considering adoption as 'low Christology' is the application of modern, foreign standards to the ancient ideas and material.

> When one investigates father-son relationships in the Roman family, one finds a strong emphasis on inheritance and transmission of power. Despite the appearance of smooth patrilineal transitions, Roman familial and political succession exhibited a tension between meritocratic and dynastic ideologies. However, the Romans had a technique at their disposal—the adoption of adult men—that enabled the different ideologies of succession to coexist for hundreds of years. To read a list of powerful Roman men is necessarily to read a list of adopted Roman men: Scipio Africanus the Younger, Caesar Augustus, Tiberius, Germanicus, Gaius Caligula, Nero, Pliny the Younger, Trajan, Hadrian, Antoninus Pius, Marcus Aurelius, Lucius Verus, and Constantius I, to name only the most famous. ...
>
> In the Roman worldview, sonship did not primarily point *backward* to begetting, but *forward* to inheritance, often through the medium of adoption. For emperors, this observation is especially crucial, since these "fathers" of the Empire had no small trouble propagating their family lines through natural begetting. These divine fathers usually had to adopt their divine sons. Therefore, the transmission of power from a powerful father to a powerful son necessitates an understanding of the competing family ideologies of natural ("begotten") sons and adopted ("made") sons. My research further shows that scholarship on divine sonship has been hampered by mistaken assumptions about adopted sons. Far from being second-class family members, they were pivotal and often favored. The adoption of adult males helped to stabilize or expand ruling families and formed a key part of imperial ideology.[985]

Indeed, what would the Christian hearer/reader of Mark have thought about the baptismal scenario at the beginning of Mark's Gospel? What did they know as part of their socio-cultural experience that would have informed them on how to understand this text? Somehow, I don't think that they were necessarily thinking about the 'adoption' issue primarily, though they would have had the idea of being adopted as a child of God.

First, let's consider John the Baptist. Recall that John the Baptist, according to Josephus, was executed about the same time that a Lucius Vitellius became governor of Syria. We've already sorted out the fact that it was a different Vitellius who was in Syria at the time of Pontius Pilate (and the death of Germanicus), and that this present Vitellius, who was consul (with Paullus Fabius Persicus) in 34, was the one who came to the Syrian province in 35/36 (at least a year after his consulship). As has already been noted, this creates a serious problem for the traditional chronology of Jesus based on the Gospels, which usually places Jesus' ministry beginning around 30 AD, and John's death shortly after and certainly before the crucifixion of Jesus in 31 or 33 AD (depending on which Gospel you are reading). If the Gospel writers used Josephus, they did so carelessly or in ignorance. *For John to oppose the marriage, he would have to be alive in 35/36 AD.* Jesus' ministry would then have to be dated later than 35 AD, creating a potentially

---

[984]Michael Peppard, 'The Eagle and the Dove: Roman Imperial Sonship and the Baptism of Jesus (Mark 1:9-11),' *NTS* 56 (2010), pp. 441, cited by Buch-Hansen (2014), p. 218.

[985]Michael Peppard, 'Powerful Sons Were Adopted Sons: A Roman Imperial Perspective' (2012), https://bibleint erp.arizona.edu/articles/pep368014.

impossible chronological conflict. How could Jesus begin his ministry that late, be executed as many as three years later, and then have Paul in a Damascus ruled by Aretas when Aretas died in 40 AD?

Yet, Mark has Jesus baptized by John the Baptist and then, later, includes the story about John's execution as an extended background digression about King Herod hearing of the miracles of Jesus and thinking that Jesus was John raised from the dead.[986]

Well, after reading the very confusing story of the family relationships and doings of the Herodians as we did earlier in this book, along with Josephus' last remark about it after having included the tale of John the Baptist, i.e. "And thus did God punish Herodias for her envy at her brother, and Herod also for giving ear to the vain discourses of a woman," one can almost see the work of a very sloppy redactor on display here. Not only that, but this redactor knew and used Josephus.

However, we already know for other reasons that Mark was written well before Josephus published *Wars*, in which we do not find the tale of John, and *Antiquities* was published about 20 years after Mark was written. But that does not mean the story of John the Baptist baptizing Jesus was not originally a part of Mark. I've thought about this problem a lot. The presence of John the Baptist is actually essential to move the plot along; he is there at the beginning, there in the middle, and then he is there again in a dramatic scene that triggers the Parable of the Tenants and clearly talks about John.[987]

So, indeed, the presence of John the Baptist is integral to this tightly woven text. Yet nearly everything in the 'background story' of John the Baptist and his execution is wrong, as we've already learned. What's more, it appears to be confirmed by Josephus, even if in a mangled way. So, it seems to me that the only conclusion to be drawn from this is that much of the story of John the Baptist that we find in the sixth chapter of Mark has been interpolated, most especially, the ridiculous tale of the daughter of Herodias demanding his head on a platter.

David Oliver Smith argues the same for structural and linguistic reasons. He speculates that the original pericope just said something like the following and the rest was interpolated:

> But Herod when he heard about it, said, 'John, whom I beheaded, is risen'. For Herod himself sent out men who laid hold of John, and locked him in prison on account of Herodias, the wife of his brother Philip because he had married her. And immediately the king sent an executioner and commanded him to bring his head. And he went and beheaded him in the prison. And hearing about it, his disciples came and took his body. And they laid it in a tomb.[988]

But Smith believes that Josephus *was* a source for Mark, and thus includes verse 17 and its mention of Herodias and Philip. But there is no other reason to think those verses were present. They do not match any larger chiastic structures in the Gospel, or contain any of Mark's special triplet words, and Mark was written *before* Josephus. For these reasons, I think the original text was probably even shorter, and read something like this: "But when Herod heard [of it], he said, [This very] John, whom I beheaded, has been raised [from the dead]. For [this] Herod himself had sent and seized John and bound him in prison," followed by a short description of his execution

---

[986]Mark 6:14-29.
[987]Mark 11:27-33.
[988]Smith (2016), pp. 125–27. Of course, there is still the problem of Philip having died in 34 AD, and the fact that Herodias was not married to Philip.

and perhaps something like explanation given in Mk. 11:32, "for [he] was afraid of [him], because everybody considered and held John actually to be a prophet."[989]

Consider the following comparison:

King Herod heard of it, for [Jesus'] name had become well known. He and they [of his court] said, John the Baptist has been raised from the dead ... [But] others kept saying, It is Elijah! And others said, It is a prophet, like one of the prophets [of old]. (Mark 6:14a-15)	And Jesus went on with His disciples to the villages of Caesarea Philippi; and on the way He asked His disciples, Who do people say that I am? And they answered [Him], John the Baptist; and others [say], Elijah; but others, one of the prophets. (Mark 8:27-28)

Clearly the redactor has borrowed a bit from Mark 8:27-28 to construct Mark 6:15, which then leads into the story of the dancing stepdaughter and the head on the platter. If that is removed, the flow of the text still works very well, and even is improved without the lengthy, uncharacteristic editorial digression.

Nevertheless, as I said, the story of John the Baptist is still integral to Mark. Certainly the hearers/readers of Mark, the very first Gospel, knew something about him. John's agency, place and time are not explained at all, so that he seems to be known by the intended audience. They also undoubtedly knew that the messiah of the Jews had been dead for a long time, and had long been expected to return to smash Rome, but had failed to show up. Mark's group were also very likely adherents of Paul; that is, Mark writes from an 'internal perspective' to a Pauline Christ-believing readership. Thus, I think the inclusion of John the Baptist was a *signal* to the audience regarding how they were to understand the entire text, a very broad wink, if you will.

So, imagine yourself as one of these hearers of the Gospel of Mark. You know Paul and his history, you know about the Jerusalem Christians and what happened to them and their messiah; and this story – the Gospel of Mark – begins to be read to you or you are reading it yourself. What do you understand from it?

Paul said that "the *beginning* of the gospel" was his proclamation of Christ (Phil 4:15). So, the first audience of Mark would already *know* that the real beginning of the gospel was something that happened to Paul. Recall that even Clement thought so: that *the gospel began with Paul.* To illustrate what I'm getting at here, let's look at two passages side by side:

But when He, Who had chosen and set me apart before I was born and had called me by His grace, saw fit and was pleased To *reveal His Son within me* so that I might proclaim Him among the Gentiles as the glad tidings (Gospel), immediately I *did not confer with flesh and blood,* nor did I go up to Jerusalem to those who were apostles before I was, but *I went away and retired into Arabia,* and afterward I came back again to Damascus. (Gal 1:15-17)	In those days Jesus came from Nazareth of Galilee and was baptized by John in the Jordan. And when He came up out of the water, at once he saw the heavens torn open and *the Spirit like a dove coming down into Him.* And *there came a voice out from within heaven,* You are My Beloved Son; in You I am well pleased. Immediately *the Spirit drove Him out into the wilderness,* and He stayed in the wilderness forty days ... (Mark 1:9-13)
Scriptural allusions: Isa. 49:1; Jer. 1:5.	Scriptural allusions: Ps. 2:7; Isa. 42:1.

[989]Whatever was there, however, it was unlikely to have been a verbatim copy of Mk. 11:32, and if Smith is right about Mark's abundant use of triplets, the word 'prophet' wouldn't have been mentioned in this pericope (at least not in the singular). Those are reserved for 1:2, 6:4, and 11:32.

The similarity is remarkable in my view. So if Mark's first audience knew Paul's story and knew who John the Baptist was, perhaps it was *Paul* who was baptized by John?

What was Paul doing in Arabia – equivalent to the 'wilderness' – and how long was he there? If we are speculatively interpreting Mark by way of Paul, can we do the reverse? Can we suppose that Paul was fasting and praying and having revelations after being baptized by John? Was that the real meaning of the opening of the heavens and the revelation of the Son of God that is announced at the beginning of Mark? Was he receiving the prophetic word of God, as Ashworth suggests?

We recall that John was the only preaching type that Josephus approved of, or at least did not accuse of trying to foment rebellion. And we recall he said that many of the Jews thought that Herod lost his little war with Aretas because Herod had executed John. If Paul had been associated with John, was that why Aretas went after him? Mark apparently thought highly of John and has his character, Jesus of Nazareth, challenge the scribes and Pharisees over John, putting them in a tight spot (Mk. 11:30-33). In that particular pericope, we are told that "everybody considered and held John actually to be a prophet." That certainly matches with what Josephus said about him.

Further, notice the opening of the third chapter of Luke, which is considered by the experts to have been the original beginning:

> In the *fifteenth year of Tiberius Caesar's reign* – when Pontius Pilate was governor of Judea, and Herod was tetrarch of Galilee, and his brother Philip tetrarch of the region of Ituraea and Trachonitis, and Lysanias tetrarch of Abilene – In the high priesthood of Annas and Caiaphas, *the Word of God* [concerning the attainment through Christ of salvation in the kingdom of God] *came to John son of Zachariah* in the wilderness (desert).

Recall the Pauline timeline that I have established based on the date of the executions of James and Simon, sons of Judas the Galilean, in 47 AD, and showing that this must have been shortly after Paul's second visit to Jerusalem. That puts Paul's conversion event at 29 AD, i.e. the fifteenth year of Tiberius Caesar. Now, some have tried to argue that the fifteenth year of Tiberius would have been 27 AD because he shared ruling responsibilities in the last two years of Augustus' life. This is done to give more time to the 'Jesus timeline' and really doesn't stand up to historical scrutiny. So, I would suggest that the beginning of the Gospel of Luke may have originally read something like this:

> In the *fifteenth year of Tiberius Caesar's reign, the Word of God* [concerning the attainment through Christ of salvation in the kingdom of God] *came to John son of Zachariah* in the wilderness (desert).[990]

And the "word of God" that came to John was actually that he baptized Paul, who received a vision and had the spirit of Christ revealed in him.

So, as I said, it seems to me that the placement of John the Baptist at the beginning of the narrative was intended as a deliberate statement that this portrait of 'Jesus of Nazareth' was really an allegory, and the figure of Jesus at the beginning, baptized by John, was a stand-in

---

[990]Marcion's version jumps straight from 3:1 to 4:31: "In the fifteenth year of Tiberius Caesar, when Pilate was governing Judea, Jesus came down to Capharnaum, a city of Galilee."

for Paul, thus the adoptionist elements of the baptism. The Markan audience would understand that Mark is not writing about a 'Jesus tradition'; he is creating it based on Paul and Paul's teachings.[991] The Jesus who was announced as the Beloved Son to Paul in the fifteenth year of Tiberius was now going to be depicted by Mark saying and doing things that would convey examples and teachings; it was a rhetorical exercise. And perhaps, originally, the Gospel of Mark included something very much like the original beginning of Luke? And perhaps there was also originally something that led Matthew and Luke both to disconnect Jesus' lineage from Judaism, because it is certain that if Jesus is not born from the physical/fleshly semen of David, but rather his mother was "overshadowed by the Holy Spirit" and thereby became pregnant, then we see a rejection of Israel as God's chosen and privileged nation. According to the birth stories of Matthew and Luke, God creates a brand new beginning, a new race and family independent of Judaism and its patriarchs. And as we've seen, Mark even has Jesus question the Davidic descent of the messiah. Here it is again in a different translation:

> And as Jesus taught in [a porch or court of] the temple, He said, How can the scribes say that the Christ is David's Son? David himself, [inspired] in the Holy Spirit, declared, The Lord said to my Lord, Sit at My right hand until I make Your enemies [a footstool] under Your feet. [Ps. 110:1.] David himself calls Him Lord; so how can it be that He is his Son? Now the great mass of the people heard [Jesus] gladly [listening to Him with delight].[992]

As mentioned before, this is a fairly legalistic way of avoiding a simple 'no.' It appears that this was in response to Jesus having been addressed as 'son of David' several times earlier in the text. Here, he rejects such address, yet he does so using a Davidic messiah/royal psalm in which David is promised a seat at the right hand of God, and whose enemies will be put under his feet – both images associated with Jesus, e.g. 1 Cor. 15:25, Mark 14:62. Even the quote from Ps. 110 arguably is presenting Jesus as the 'Davidic' messiah who will sit by God and stamp out his enemies. But it is revealed throughout the Gospel that these enemies are primarily demonic. So Jesus is at once accepting that the text *does* apply to him, but elevating himself above the identification as a simple fleshly descendant of David. Mark seems to be deflecting any negative associations with the Zealots and their Davidic messiah through this non-denial denial. He is showing that the real meaning of the messiah is much greater than the ordinary conceptions. Jesus isn't an earthly warrior king – as he is in the Davidic and Danielic expectations of the apocalyptic literature – he's a cosmic warrior king. He *is* the fulfillment of the Davidic promise of the psalms and other OT texts like 2 Samuel, but just not in the way people like the Zealots expected.

At the beginning of Mark's Gospel, the Holy Spirit tears heaven open and descends upon Jesus in the form of a dove. At the end of Mark's Gospel, Jesus screams to the heavens as he dies, and the curtain of the temple is torn from top to bottom, leading the centurion who was facing Him to declare, "Truly this man was God's son!" In other words, it was a Gentile Roman who first truly recognized the Son of God, which highlights Paul's mission to the Gentiles. The tearing of the temple curtain symbolized that God's presence there has ended – now available to all Christ-believers, just as the dove/spirit descended into Jesus through the torn sky at baptism – and Israel's time as God's chosen people is at an end.

[991] As argued also by Dykstra (2012).
[992] Mark 12:35-37.

The sun is glorious in one way, the moon is glorious in another way, and the stars are glorious in their own [distinctive] way; for one star differs from and surpasses another in its beauty and brilliance. So it is with the resurrection of the dead. [The body] that is sown is perishable and decays, but [the body] that is resurrected is imperishable (immune to decay, immortal). (Dan. 12:3) It is sown in dishonor and humiliation; it is raised in honor and glory. It is sown in infirmity and weakness; it is resurrected in strength and endued with power. It is sown a natural (physical) body; it is raised a supernatural (a spiritual) body. [As surely as] there is a physical body, there is also a spiritual body. Thus it is written, The first man Adam became a living being (an individual personality); the last Adam (Christ) became a life-giving Spirit [restoring the dead to life]. (Gen. 2:7) But it is not the spiritual life which came first, but the physical and then the spiritual. The first man [was] from out of earth, made of dust (earthly-minded); the second Man [is] the Lord from out of heaven. (Gen. 2:7) Now those who are made of the dust are like him who was first made of the dust (earthly-minded); and as is [the Man] from heaven, so also [are those] who are of heaven (heavenly-minded). And just as we have borne the image [of the man] of dust, so shall we and so let us also bear the image [of the Man] of heaven.[993]

Mark on Being a Christian

Troels Engberg-Pedersen[994] (E-P from here) is another scholar who is convinced that in constructing his text, Mark was drawing on Paul in specific and clearly identifiable ways. He notes that the failure of many other scholars to see this is due to a lack of adequate understanding of the text itself. From my perspective, the conviction that there was a historical Jesus of Nazareth *as depicted in the Gospels*, inspiring Mark, is the single greatest barrier to understanding the true Christianity revealed by Paul and narrativized by Mark. E-P points out that only if one reads Mark in the light of Pauline conceptions does it becomes possible, even easy, to achieve an adequate understanding of what it was that Mark was trying to accomplish with his narrative. He is not worried about accusations that he might read Paul back into Mark since there is certainly enough material in the Markan text that calls for – even demands – a Pauline interpretation, and I definitely agree.

Here is the text he discusses in his chapter:

Mar 8:34 And Jesus called [to Him] the throng with His disciples and said to them, If anyone intends to come after Me, let him deny himself [forget, ignore, disown, and lose sight of himself and his own interests] and take up his cross, and [joining Me as a disciple and siding with My party] follow with Me [continually, cleaving steadfastly to Me]. 35 For whoever wants to save his [higher, spiritual, eternal] life, will lose it [the lower, natural, temporal life which is lived only on earth]; and whoever gives up his life [which is lived only on earth] for My sake and the Gospel's will save it [his higher, spiritual life in the eternal kingdom of God]. 36 For what does it profit a man to gain the whole world, and forfeit his life [in the eternal kingdom of God]? 37 For what can a man give as an exchange (a compensation, a ransom, in return) for his [blessed] life [in the eternal kingdom of God]? 38 For whoever is ashamed [here and now] of Me and My words in this adulterous (unfaithful) and [preeminently] sinful generation, of him will the Son of Man also be ashamed when He comes in the glory (splendor and majesty) of His Father with the holy angels. 9:1 AND JESUS said to them,

---

[993]1 Cor. 15:41-49.
[994]Troels Engberg-Pedersen: 'Paul in Mark 8:34–9:1: Mark on what it is to be a Christian,' in Becker *et al.* (2014).

Truly and solemnly I say to you, there are some standing here who will in no way taste death before they see the kingdom of God come in [its] power. [995]

The most frequent interpretation of "If anyone intends to come after Me, let him deny himself and take up his cross, and follow with Me" is rather materialistic: Jesus was about to die and his followers must be prepared to die too. It has been assumed by most scholars that the sociological situation (*Sitz im Leben*) of the community of which Mark was a part was such that persecution was a real threat, and that this influenced the writing of this passage. Ernst Haenchen, an advocate of this view, is aware that there are no indications that any persecution was going on at the time Mark was writing, but he suggests that the fear of it was real.[996] E-P writes about this view:

> Basically, what I find wrong about the half-consensus to be found among commentators and already articulated here by Haenchen is this idea that what Mark's Jesus has primarily in mind is his followers literally taking up 'their' cross and marching towards crucifixion and the concomitant claim that one should adopt this interpretation in order to avoid 'weakening' what it said. Instead, I shall argue that the phrase is to be understood metaphorically (but no less 'strongly') and that it concerns the kind of exclusive 'directedness' away from oneself and the world towards Christ that constitutes the essence of 'conversion'. Such directedness may also imply a willingness to die for the sake of Christ, but that is not the primary meaning of the phrase as it stands here.[997]

Later interpreters have taken rather extreme positions on the meaning of v. 34, going so far as to use it to speculate that Mark was writing at the time of Nero's persecutions following the Great Fire of Rome.

Other scholars point out that Jesus is promising eschatological vindication and true life in the spirit for those who suffer condemnation and death for his sake, and that this should be understood literally. This is used to support the materialist interpretation. ('Be ready to die now, and you will be rewarded then.') As E-P notes, this dissolves the paradox of losing one's life to save it. He goes on to note:

> However, the fact that the idea of post-mortem vindication complements the [materialist] interpretation in such a straightforward manner does not, of course, determine the correctness of the [materialist interpretation] itself. For there might well be other interpretations of 8:34 that might be similarly complemented by the idea of post-mortem vindication. That would also hold if the contrast to gaining life in the future was not the event of literally dying in the present, but for instance the state of being metaphorically 'dead to the world' in the present.[998]

> What does it in fact mean to 'deny oneself'? And what is the point of doing it? Similarly, what does it mean here to 'take up one's cross'? And what is the point? The sense underlying these questions is that there is some central content to the two acts that gets lost once one sees only two alternatives here: either a means to an eschatological goal or apocalyptic victory – or masochism (or self-contempt).[999]

---

[995]Mark 8:34–9:1. Zondervan Amplified translation.
[996]Cited in Engberg-Pedersen (2014), p. 190.
[997]Engberg-Pedersen (2014), p. 191.
[998]Engberg-Pedersen (2014), p. 194.
[999]Engberg-Pedersen (2014), p. 196.

Further on, E-P gives his own interpretation, saying that the Markan text is clearly about the underlying self's 'dying to' the present world by denying the individual self. The person or 'self' should be exclusively and cognitively directed away from himself and the material world, and towards Jesus, the gospel and his words. By dying to oneself and the present world, the person, or 'underlying self' will gain life and a new self/soul, though a life that is not of this world, but of the kingdom of God.[1000] It is about the death of the underlying self to the material world, denying the individual self, and turning toward Jesus, his example, and the world to come.

This interpretation, as E-P notes, can be derived from the text itself, but it gains added light when considering Galatians 2:19-20:

> For I through the Law have myself died to the Law and all the Law's demands upon me, so that I may live to and for God. I have been crucified with Christ; it is no longer I who live, but Christ (the Messiah) lives in me; and the life I now live in the body I live by faith in (by adherence to and reliance on and complete trust in) the Son of God, Who loved me and gave Himself up for me.

... and Gal. 6:14:

> But far be it from me to glory [in anything or anyone] except in the cross of our Lord Jesus Christ (the Messiah) through Whom the world has been crucified to me, and I to the world!

In the above two passages, Paul is describing the radical effects of his own conversion and uses 'being crucified with Christ' to express what he is trying to describe. And here, we must note, there is no question but that this is metaphorical. Being converted as Paul was can certainly include being martyred, but it means so much more than that, as has been discussed extensively above in the section on Paul's theology.

E-P states that there are a number of features of the Markan text that *point to Paul being directly behind it*. He writes:

> Not only in the two quoted passages from Galatians, but also, for instance, in Phil 3:10 (in context) and Rom 6:1-14 does Paul employ the metaphor (as it clearly is) of 'dying with Christ' as the best way of spelling out the radical change of self-direction that he took to go with conversion. ... As Christ had himself literally died for human beings, so they on their side should metaphorically 'die to themselves' and instead turn their directedness towards him. [Footnote: In fact, they should also – and in the very same movement – turn their directedness towards other human beings. That this is implied in Mark comes out very clearly in Mark 10:45 in its context (10:42-45). It is a central point also in Paul ...][1001]

Moving on to vv. 35-37, E-P notes that there is a similarity in v. 36 for which there is no counterpart in any alleged earlier tradition such as the contentiously theorized 'Q' material. That is, Mark's use of the two Greek terms that are translated as 'to gain' and 'to forfeit.' "For what does it profit a man to gain the whole world, and forfeit his life?" In this verse Mark is contrasting the values of this world with that of one's soul utilizing terms of financial gain and loss in a way that is very similar to what Paul wrote in Phil. 3:7-8.

[1000]Engberg-Pedersen (2014), pp. 201–2.
[1001]Engberg-Pedersen (2014), p. 204. Also see Engberg-Pedersen (2000).

But whatever former things I had that might have been gains to me, I have come to consider as loss for Christ's sake. Yes, furthermore, I count everything as loss compared to the possession of the priceless privilege (the overwhelming preciousness, the surpassing worth, and supreme advantage) of knowing Christ Jesus my Lord and of progressively becoming more deeply and intimately acquainted with Him. For His sake I have lost everything and consider it all to be mere rubbish (refuse, dregs), in order that I may win (gain) Christ (the Anointed One) ...

After several comments on the comparisons of saving one's spiritual life in contrast to losing one's earthly life in v. 35, and how this was modified by Matthew and Luke, who may not have understood the passage when they took it over, E-P notes:

It seems difficult to get rid of the feeling that Mark is here in fact drawing directly on Paul and hence that the topic of his whole account is precisely that of Paul's own account in that particular passage: conversion. ... In light of the corresponding contrast in Phil 3:7-8, which Mark seems to draw on directly in 8:36, **it seems justified to claim that Paul *could* have written Mark 8:35!** [E-P's footnote: I am of course fully aware of the oddity of this claim. The aim is to make the reader think of the very precise character of what is said in 8:35. It is 'Pauline.']

However, once one has got so far, a striking and illuminating difference between Paul and Mark comes to light, one that we have already noted without quite giving it its due emphasis. Where Paul spoke in the first person of himself, Mark has his Jesus speak in the third person of his potential followers ... The difference is huge and highly suggestive. *What Mark has done in 8:34-37 – on the proposed reading – is to generalize what Paul had said of himself so as to make it cover all Christ followers and then to put that generalization back into the mouth of Jesus.*[1002]

In considering v. 38, "For whoever is ashamed of Me and My words in this adulterous (unfaithful) and sinful generation, of him will the Son of Man also be ashamed when He comes in the glory (splendor and majesty) of His Father with the holy angels," we find another Pauline precedent in Rom. 1:16:

For I am not ashamed of the Gospel (good news) of Christ, for it is God's power working unto salvation [for deliverance from eternal death] to everyone who believes ...

So again, it appears that what Paul had written about himself was generalized by Mark and put into the mouth of Jesus. The passages are not, therefore, about a concrete situation as envisaged by Haenchen and others, but rather are about what it is to be a Christian, the fundamental decision to turn one's life around and become oriented towards Jesus. The context is also important. This passage comes right after Jesus makes one of his death and resurrection predictions:

And He began to teach them that the Son of Man must of necessity suffer many things and be tested and disapproved and rejected by the elders and the chief priests and the scribes, and be put to death, and after three days rise again. And He said this freely (frankly, plainly, and explicitly, making it unmistakable). And Peter took Him by the hand and led Him aside and then began to rebuke Him. But turning around [His back to Peter] and seeing His disciples, He rebuked Peter, saying, Get behind Me, Satan! For you do not have a mind intent on promoting what God wills, but what pleases men [you are not on God's side, but that of men].[1003]

[1002]Engberg-Pedersen (2014), pp. 205–6. E-P's italics, my bolding.
[1003]Mark 8:31-33.

So the passage on what it means to be a Christian, to take up your cross and follow Jesus, to value the spirit life over the material life, and the rest, was exactly what we learned in the discussion of Pauline theology following Ashworth. Mark is giving the explanation for why Peter was 'Satan': he was focused on the material world. And in the real, historical events, it seems that Simon (Cephas/Peter) was, indeed, a Zealot who promoted a messiah who would come with 12 legions of angels to destroy the Romans and establish an earthly rule of the Jews. E-P writes:

> We should conclude that Mark 8:34–9:1 is not primarily about confessing Christ in a trial situation and hence being prepared to take up one's cross quite literally on one's way towards being crucified – but instead about the initial conversion, to be understood metaphorically as a death to one's worldly self and the world at large in favour of a total directedness towards Jesus. We should also conclude that this reading can be elicited from Mark's own text – but also that one is greatly helped in doing so by bringing in selected, but quite central ideas from Paul. Finally, we should conclude that these ideas are so special to Paul (since they were apparently invented by him to articulate his sense of his own conversion) that it is extremely unlikely that Mark either articulated them for himself or else found them somewhere else in early Christian tradition; instead he adopted them directly from Paul.
> ... [O]n this reading – even more than on any other – the text comes out as being exceedingly shrewdly constructed, where by calling it 'shrewd' I mean that it has real philosophical depth at the same time as it is both terse and immediately and strikingly impressive. ... I consider this text paradigmatic of Mark's Gospel as a whole ...[1004]

Even though I have severely abbreviated E-P's discussion and arguments above, I hope that the reader can see that it is a brilliant piece of exegesis and exposes to our view the extraordinary cleverness with which the Gospel of Mark is constructed.[1005] Mark wrote a narrative that generalized Paul's gospel and put it back into the mouth of a fictive 'Jesus of Nazareth.' In this way, he directly addressed his readers/hearers with Paul's gospel. The passage is at the beginning of the second half of the Gospel when Jesus is on his way to Jerusalem, instructing his disciples that what is about to happen to him has, or should have, immediate and total consequences for everyone; that they, following his example, must die to themselves. Mark makes his Jesus character say that the whole point of what happened to Jesus was death of the self for the sake of others. This is later emphasized in Mark 10:43b-45:

> ... whoever desires to be great among you must be your servant, and whoever wishes to be most important and first in rank among you must be slave of all. For even the Son of Man came not to have service rendered to Him, but to serve, and to give His life as a ransom for (instead of) many.

One should note also that this last passage was part of Jesus' answer to James and John, who wanted positions of authority; in other words, they too were focused on the material world. The passage itself is also full of Pauline language.

Finally, as E-P notes, there is a lot of theological anthropology going on in the text here: what it is to be a Christian, humanity directly connected to spirit, i.e. God.

[1004]Engberg-Pedersen (2014), p. 207.

[1005]And I can hear the true believers in the historicity of Jesus of Nazareth as depicted in the text howling with rage at this interpretation.

The Struggle for Paul

Most experts think that Paul died in the Neronian purge of Christians following the Great Fire of Rome in 64 AD. There isn't any real proof of this, just rumors and legends repeated (or created) by early church commentators. Nevertheless, Alan Cadwallader suggests that after Paul's death:

> Those who were Paul's familiar opponents were supplemented by those who scrambled over his authority and influence, divided about the direction that his legacy should follow. ... There was no univocal or unilinear succession. The reference to the growing authority of Paul's letters at the beginning of the second century in 2 Pet 3:16 ought not mask the admission in the same verse that contentions over meaning and application were equally part of the Pauline trajectory of authority formation.[1006]

Here I will give the text in question with its fuller context:

> This is now, beloved, the second letter I am writing to you; in them I am trying to arouse your sincere intention by reminding you that you should remember the words spoken in the past by the holy prophets, and the commandment of the Lord and Savior spoken through your apostles.
>
> First of all you must understand this, that in the last days scoffers will come, scoffing and indulging their own lusts and saying, "Where is the promise of his coming? For ever since our ancestors died, all things continue as they were from the beginning of creation!" They deliberately ignore this fact, that by the word of God heavens existed long ago and an earth was formed out of water and by means of water, through which the world of that time was deluged with water and perished. But by the same word the present heavens and earth have been reserved for fire, being kept until the day of judgment and destruction of the godless. But do not ignore this one fact, beloved, that with the Lord one day is like a thousand years, and a thousand years are like one day.
>
> The Lord is not slow about his promise, as some think of slowness, but is patient with you, not wanting any to perish, but all to come to repentance. But the day of the Lord will come like a thief, and then the heavens will pass away with a loud noise, and the elements will be dissolved with fire, and the earth and everything that is done on it will be disclosed. Since all these things are to be dissolved in this way, what sort of persons ought you to be in leading lives of holiness and godliness, waiting for and hastening the coming of the day of God, because of which the heavens will be set ablaze and dissolved, and the elements will melt with fire?
>
> But, in accordance with his promise, we wait for new heavens and a new earth, where righteousness is at home. Therefore, beloved, while you are waiting for these things, strive to be found by him at peace, without spot or blemish; and regard the patience of our Lord as salvation. *So also our beloved brother Paul wrote to you according to the wisdom given him, speaking of this as he does in all his letters. There are some things in them hard to understand, which the ignorant and unstable twist to their own destruction, as they do the other scriptures.* You therefore, beloved, since you are forewarned, beware that you are not carried away with the error of the lawless and lose your own stability. But grow in the grace and knowledge of our Lord and Savior Jesus Christ. To him be the glory both now and to the day of eternity. Amen.[1007]

The tradition that this letter was the work of Peter was in question in very early times, and it is a certainty that it was not. It is dependent on the letter of Jude (compare 2 Pet. 2:1-8 with Jude 4-16), and the author refers to all the letters of Paul in such a way as to suggest a

---

[1006]Alan H. Cadwallader, 'The Struggle for Paul in the Context of Empire: Mark as a Deutero-Pauline Text,' in Wischmeyer *et al.* (2014), p. 557.

[1007]2 Pet. 3:1-18.

collection that was considered 'scripture.' This condition only existed some time after Marcion and probably in reaction to Marcion. What is rather shocking about this letter is that, in order to support the claim that the author is Peter, he says:

> For we did not follow cleverly devised myths when we made known to you the power and coming of our Lord Jesus Christ, but *we had been eyewitnesses* of his majesty. For he received honor and glory from God the Father when that voice was conveyed to him by the Majestic Glory, saying, "This is my Son, my Beloved, with whom I am well pleased." *We ourselves heard this voice come from heaven, while we were with him on the holy mountain.*[1008]

That should have been a 'struck by lightning' moment if ever there was one! What happened to "strive to be found by him at peace, *without spot or blemish*"?! One would think that outright lying would be a definite "spot or blemish." But it seems that any and every sort of prevarication was acceptable in the war against Marcion, who was most likely the main target of this: "*There are some things in them hard to understand, which the ignorant and unstable twist to their own destruction, as they do the other scriptures.*" The early church fathers sure hated Marcion. But that's another topic. For the moment, let me just point out what Cadwallader wishes to convey.

His idea is that Colossians and Mark are both deutero-Pauline texts, that is, produced by the second generation of Pauline followers. He compares how the two texts treat family relationships. Colossians includes a 'household code' that is much in line with Roman imperial ideology, while Mark does not. Cadwallader writes:

> The shadow of Paul's death was a salutary warning that confrontation with the Empire was dangerous, threatening the survival of the Church. For the writer of Colossians, the inheritance of Paul was to be accommodated to those imperial realities, taking up the ubiquitous valorization of the familial household that privileged the male head and addressed the relationships that he had within the household. It did not relinquish a commitment to Christ but it modeled that commitment on the imperial template ... Paul was the authority providing the resources for this Christian commitment just as the resulting formulation was designed to narrow the "proliferation of meaning" that was equally part of the legacy of Paul. For the second evangelist, the cost of such a rapprochement with the Roman empire was too great, a betrayal of the memory of Jesus and his greatest exponent (for Mark, that is), Paul ... Accordingly Paul's references to community and his metaphorical use of familial language became, in the second gospel, the warrant for a major critique of the household code, part of the apparatus of an empire against which the early followers of Jesus (and Paul) were pitted.[1009]

What Cadwallader does not appear to consider[1010] is the idea that the 'household code' of Colossians is an interpolation, and that the letter, at least in part as we have it today, is truly Pauline. On this point, Jason D. BeDuhn writes about the version of Colossians found (reconstructed) in the *Apostolikon*, Marcion's collection of Paul's letters:

> The Apostolikon provides the earliest documented identification of this letter as a genuine composition of Paul. Many modern researchers do not accept its authenticity. ... Tertullian implies

---

[1008] 2 Pet. 1:16-18.

[1009] Cadwallader (2014), p. 582.

[1010] And many other Pauline scholars, apparently, since Colossians has been kicked out of the list of 'Authentic Letters of Paul.'

that Marcion's text lacked the phrases found in Colossians 1:15b-16, which form part of a poetic passage often referred to as the "Colossians hymn." Precisely these phrases, lacking from Marcion's text, have caused a great deal of comment and consternation in modern scholarship. Paul nowhere else refers to Christ in these terms as creator of the universe, or as the goal of end of creation, a role he elsewhere ascribes to the father (e.g., Rom 11:36; 1 Cor 8:6) ... No one, to my knowledge, has taken into consideration the evidence of the Apostolikon in a possible solution to the problem. The version of the hymn reported for Marcion's text conforms to the Christological views Paul expresses elsewhere, and from that perspective the longer version found in the catholic text has the appearance of containing interpolated phrases.[1011]

Marcion also lacks the household code section (Col. 3:18–4:1), though a version *is* found in his version of Laodiceans (i.e. Ephesians). But Paul could be a 'Gentile to Gentiles' if the situation called for it, so it's possible modern scholars read too much into the inclusion of this household code.

It seems to me that Cadwallader is attempting to 'fill the gap.' There is very little evidence for any widespread and/or sustained attention to Paul from the time he disappears after writing Romans, until Marcion showed up with a cache of his letters sometime around the early-to-middle second century. Most writers of the period between Paul and Marcion show no knowledge of him or his letters. The passage from 2 Peter above acknowledges Paul's stature (Marcion had a huge following), but refers to him as a problem. Acts tried to harmonize the two early branches of Christianity, which suggests strongly that something of the reverse of what Mark was trying to do had to be done later. Mark tried to incorporate the Jewish Christians to Paul's mission. But somehow he too faded into obscurity for quite a period while some form of Jewish Christianity *à la* Matthew held sway and sought to incorporate Pauline Christians and suppress Paul.

Only Clement of Rome explicitly cites and endorses Paul in a letter to Corinth, where Paul's name was probably known and revered. So, certainly, there were copies of Paul's letters around before Marcion, but for some reason they were not much used and I suggest that this is perhaps because Mark was a bit too successful in bringing together the Roman Christians of both Jewish and Gentile ilk; the Jewish Christians who had followed Judas the Galilean as their messiah, who was to come and destroy Rome, may have been the majority and they soon produced Matthew to replace Mark and appear to have been rather busy editing and interpolating Paul's letters.

It seems that Mark's idea to pull the Christian buns out of the Roman fire was seen as a useful maneuver and Paul's opponents found it expedient to follow along with Mark's agenda with modifications. As has been noted, the archaeology of earliest Christianity is strangely lacking any iconography that would point to Paul and his Christ on the cross.

Among all the symbols ... none signifies suffering, death, or self-immolation. All stress victory, peace, and security in the face of adversity. The Jesus iconography follows the same patterns. There is no place in the third century for a crucified Christ, or a symbol of divine death.[1012]

In short, what the archaeology shows is that one of the central cultic activities of the earliest Christians was a communal meal with the dead, a meal that did not recall the sacrifice of Jesus Christ. The cemetery was one of the two centers of activity. In this context, recall that Paul's

[1011]BeDuhn (2013) p. 225.
[1012]Snyder (1985), p. 64.

most extensive discussions of resurrection of the dead – 1 Thess and 1 Cor – are both triggered by questions concerning the status of dead members.[1013]

And then, along came Marcion. He had such a large following that his opponents decided it was probably better to co-opt Paul to their own purposes – to neutralize him. They worked hard to modify the Pauline corpus. BeDuhn writes:

> If one assumes that Marcion's collection contained the original form of Paul's letters, then the additional material found in the catholic version of the letters would be second-century non-Pauline inventions, meant to "correct" the letters in a non-Marcionite direction. Alternatively, if one assumes that Marcion had edited the letters to suit his own purposes, then it could be that his opponents retrieved pre-Marcionite copies of the letters (and even additional letters) in their original form for their own rival collection.[1014]

One thing seems apparent: there are things left in Paul's letters that I am sure the 'harmonizers' would have dearly loved to have removed, but could not for some reason. Likely, Paul's letters were at least well-enough known so that too much modification of the texts would have raised questions; but for many changes, they could, indeed, claim that they had 'found an original' that was different from Marcion's. Knowing how these propaganda games work from many other situations, both historical and modern, it could be said that the very things that Marcion's opponents accused him of doing are the things the opponents were most likely doing themselves. And we certainly have good evidence of that sort of thing in the second Epistle of Peter quoted above, including outright lying. Also, it is interesting to note that the distinctive readings of the *Apostolikon* of Marcion are also found in the Old Latin version of Paul's letters and in a set of Greek manuscripts, as well as in the Syriac textual tradition.[1015]

So, according to some very good recent research, it has been proposed that there was a common, pre-Marcionite form of Pauline texts that was current around the beginning of the second century and this group of texts, whether it formed a formal collection or not, also very likely included the Gospel of Mark, from which Marcion's 'Luke' was derived. Nevertheless, Marcion is a witness to the earlier form of the text of Paul's letters, more than half a century before the oldest existing manuscript, P^{46}.[1016] Yet, it has to be kept in mind that the letters acquired by Marcion were already edited, probably to produce a body of instruction for general use; letters were combined, probably local issues and details specific to time and place were removed; undoubtedly, quite a number of modifications had already entered the texts.[1017] It is possible that Paul's letters were originally shorter than what we now have; Romans and 1 Corinthians are most certainly composites of several letters; in some cases, the letters may have been supplemented beyond the original.

Marcion suspected that the teachings of Jesus and Paul had been enveloped by a Judaizing development in the Christian movement. What if Marcion was right? What if Paul's letters

---

[1013]Smith (1994), p. 131.

[1014]BeDuhn (2013), p. 204.

[1015]BeDuhn (2013), p. 204.

[1016]"Papyrus 46 is one of the oldest extant New Testament manuscripts in Greek, written on papyrus, with its 'most probable date' between 175 and 225. Some leaves are part of the Chester Beatty Biblical Papyri, and others are in the University of Michigan Papyrus Collection." (Wikipedia.org, 'Papyrus 46.')

[1017]See, for example, Trobisch (2001), who argues that Paul himself may have had a hand in creating one of the first such collections of edited letters for publication.

were touched up in order to incorporate his ideas and authority into a wing of the Christian movement that did not agree with some of his more radical positions, such as we see with the editorial maneuvers of Matthew in respect of Mark?

Matthew versus Paul and Mark

The Matthean evangelist used about 90% of the Gospel of Mark in the composition of his text. David O. Smith's *Matthew, Mark, Luke and Paul* exposes undeniable evidence that the author of Mark used the epistles of Paul as well. And yet, as David Sim shows, Matthew was clearly un-Pauline and represented a type of Christianity that was completely uninfluenced by Paul.[1018] Yet, he used Mark and reveals pretty clearly that he was not favorably disposed toward him either! It appears that the 'first evangelist' (in order in the NT, not in order in time), wrote his own Gospel with the intention of replacing Mark completely.

Michael D. Goulder and Thomas L. Brodie thought that Paul was an authority for Matthew. However, Sim concludes that Matthew was not just un-Pauline; he was openly anti-Pauline and his utilization of Paul was to refute, not confirm, his ideas. In this, Sim is following S. G. F. Brandon,[1019] who proposed that Matthew's Gospel critiqued Paul on several points. Brandon, a classical historian using standard historical methods in his analysis, was soundly ripped to shreds by Congregationalist minister and Professor of New Testament studies William D. Davies; for the NT crowd, that was good enough, so the topic faded into obscurity until Ulrich Luz came along in 1993. Luz claimed that *Matthew stood very close to the 'Judaisers' who opposed Paul in Galatia*, but did not think that the Gospel contained any anti-Paul polemic. He noted that Paul and Matthew apparently agreed on many points, such as the priority of Grace, the theology of works, righteousness, love as the core of the Law, and the universality of faith in Christ.[1020]

Sim states that it is only natural for Paul and Matthew to agree, since they were both Christians and "followers of Jesus of Nazareth, whom they jointly regarded as Messiah and Lord, as crucified and vindicated, as the fulfiller of the ancient prophecies, and now residing in heaven with all power and authority until his triumphant return at the judgement."[1021]

But is it really that simple? All the evidence collected thus far suggest a very different scenario: that there was no 'Jesus of Nazareth,' he was simply a creation of Mark's designed to allegorize Paul's life and theology, with Paul's Christ dimly in the background, represented by a Jewish peripatetic messianic healer loosely based on Judas the Galilean, and the whole project was intended to reconcile Gentile and Jewish Christians at a time fraught with peril because of the latter's association with the rebel Zealots who opposed Rome and brought on the destruction of Jerusalem and the temple there. So how can it be said that Matthew's Christ and Paul's Christ were one and the same person?

I would suggest that it was certainly true that Matthew belonged to another Christian tradition, the very one that opposed Paul, but that he was at least a generation after Mark. Matthew was also certainly aware of what Mark had done in writing his Gospel and generally approved of the tactic, even if he did not agree with the theology. And so, he took the project even further

[1018]David C. Sim, 'The Reception of Paul and Mark in the Gospel of Matthew,' in Wischmeyer *et al.* (2014).
[1019]Brandon (2010), pp. 234–40.
[1020]See Sim (2014b), pp. 591–92.
[1021]Sim (2014b), p. 592.

into myth by creating a birth story that began with a most interesting genealogy that began – surprise, surprise! – with Abraham, the same figure that most crucially interested Paul in his own arguments for the Gentiles being the seed of Abraham. Even more interesting are the names that appear once one gets to the end:

> Josiah the father of Jechoniah and his brothers, at the time of the deportation to Babylon. And after the deportation to Babylon: Jechoniah was the father of Salathiel, and Salathiel the father of Zerubbabel, and Zerubbabel the father of Abiud, and Abiud the father of Eliakim, and Eliakim the father of Azor, and Azor the father of Zadok, and **Zadok** the father of Achim, and Achim the father of Eliud, and Eliud the father of **Eleazar**, and **Eleazar the father of Matthan**, and **Matthan the father of Jacob**, and **Jacob the father of Joseph** ...[1022]

We recall all the smoke that Josephus was blowing around the family of Judas the Galilean, including Hezekiah/Ezekias the bandit chased down by Herod the Great when he was a young man. Then there was Matthias, who was associated with Judas the Galilean in the 'Golden Eagle Temple Cleansing' that was supposed to have occurred shortly before the death of Herod the Great, but may actually belong to the time of Pontius Pilate, 15–19 AD. And of course, the other companion of Judas called 'Sadduc,' which may actually have been Zadok. And Jacob, of course, is the same name as 'James.'[1023] Added to that is the fact that the sons of Judas the Galilean continued the family tradition on the model of the Maccabees, including Eleazar, who led the Zealot stand at Masada. One is also reminded of the names of the brothers of Jesus of Nazareth in Mark's fictive account: James, Joses, Judas and Simon.

So, my question would be: was Matthew giving an actual genealogy of Judas the Galilean, or perhaps just hinting at what he was doing by the inclusion of certain names? The bizarre thing about this is that, despite the fact that he has just given a genealogy of Joseph, the husband of Mary, Matthew then completely disconnects Jesus from this lineage by declaring that Mary became pregnant by the actions of the Holy Spirit!

Leaving speculation and getting back to Luz, he acknowledged that the major issue that separated Paul and Matthew was the role of the Torah. Considering the fact that this was the very issue that divided Paul from the Jerusalem Christians and led Paul to state that they worshipped another Christ and were enemies of the cross, I don't think it is safe to assume that Matthew was even writing about the same 'Jesus,' even if he was using Mark as his platform. As Sim notes, speaking specifically about the dispute over Torah:

> If the point of disagreement is fundamental and serious enough to both parties in a dispute, then it can easily outweigh the many other factors that they may share in common.[1024]

Indeed. And I would argue that it wasn't just an argument over Torah; it was an argument over who Christ really was, and Matthew knew the differences and sought to replace a story that was gaining ground with a different version that was at least theologically more acceptable, even if he knew that he still could not tell the truth about the messiah of the Jerusalem Christians: that he was supposed to have come with legions of angels to destroy Rome, but had failed to show

---

[1022]Matt. 1:11-16.
[1023]James is simply the English form of Iakobos, or Jacob.
[1024]Sim (2014b), p. 592.

up and the destruction of Jerusalem could be laid at the door of the Christians there, Zealots all. So I don't think it was a matter of a common commitment to the same messiah.

In a 1998 monograph,[1025] Sim argued that Matthew and Paul stood on different sides of the early Christian factional dispute and, further, that Matthew, in his Gospel, included critiques of the Law-free theology of Paul, on full display in Mark. You could say he was fighting fire with fire. In the years since, Sim has continued to work on his arguments, summarizing them as follows:

> The triad of sayings in Matt 5:17-19, whereby Jesus dispels the notion that he has abolished the Torah and affirms that every part of the Law is to be obeyed, is a clear refutation of the Pauline position that the Torah was only a temporary measure that has been brought to an end by Christ (cf. Gal 3:23-25; Rom 10:4).
>
> The eschatological scenario in Matt 7:21-23, in which Jesus condemns those who call him Lord because of their lawlessness, is a strict condemnation of Law-free Christians and recalls Pauline passages such as Rom 10:9-10 and 1 Cor 12:3. Likewise, the material created by Matthew in 13:26-43 makes the point that the Law-free Christian tradition has its origin in Satan and its members will be punished in the fires of Gehenna.
>
> The evangelist also confronts the issue of the leadership of the early Christian movement. While Mark presents the future leaders of the Jerusalem church, the disciples and the family of Jesus, in a very poor light, Matthew rehabilitates both groups. In the heavily edited material in 16:17-19, Jesus proclaims the supremacy of Peter as the head of the church *using the very language and motifs that Paul employs when referring to his own divine call and mission* (Gal 1:12-17). At the end of the Gospel the risen Christ commissions the disciples to lead and oversee both the Jewish and Gentile missions (28:16-20), which completely undercuts Paul's constant claim to have been appointed the apostle to the Gentiles (e.g. Rom 15:16; Gal 1:16).[1026]

Sim's point is to show that Matthew didn't just differ from Paul (and Mark), but that he was consciously responding to, and criticizing, particular claims and theological positions that are clearly Pauline. There are parallels and intertextual echoes between certain Pauline texts and Matthean texts. Thus, there appears to be no doubt that Paul's letters were available to the author of Matthew, and that Matthew was rather hostile toward Paul.

At the same time that Matthew was waging a covert war against Pauline ideas, he was also apparently threatened by the Judaism that was taking shape at that time. It has been noted that, after writing *Wars*, in which the Pharisees were not singled out as particularly favored, when Josephus wrote *Antiquities*, he apparently had changed his stance somewhat and his views were rather more in line with theirs. Since the Pharisees became the mainstream Jewish party after the war, it is thought that Josephus was aligning with them to gain favor among other Jews who most likely continued to view him as a traitor. We know the approximate year that Josephus published *Antiquities*, 93 AD, so I would suggest that it was around the same time that Matthew wrote.[1027] In any event, the Pharisees of emergent Rabbinic Judaism were a significant

---

[1025]David C. Sim, *The Gospel of Matthew and Christian Judaism: The History and Social setting of the Matthean Community.*(Edinburgh: T& T Clark, 1998), pp. 188–211.

[1026]Sim (2014b), p. 593.

[1027]Sim suggests that Matthew was writing some two or three decades after Mark. If Mark was written just after the destruction of Jerusalem, that would put it at 93 to 103 AD, which is about right when comparing it to Josephus' apparent reaction to the rise of Rabbinic Judaism via Pharisaism.

problem for Matthew and his community, and they receive even more polemical attention than Paul!

As Sim writes, Gerd Theissen defends the thesis that there is anti-Pauline polemic in Matthew and finds it in the five major Matthean discourses (Matt. 5:19; 10:9; 13:25; 18:6; 23:15). Eric K. Wong agrees with Theissen and they both argue independently that the Parable of the Tares and its interpretation (Matt. 13:24-30.36-43) identifies the enemy who sows weeds among the wheat as Paul.[1028] According to Wong and Theissen, in Matt. 10:9, Matthew attacks Paul's manner of conducting his mission by working to supplement his endeavors; and in 23:15, Matthew has Paul, the former Pharisee, in mind: "Woe to you, scribes and Pharisees, hypocrites! For you cross sea and land to make a single convert, and you make the new convert twice as much a child of hell as yourselves."

Well, that's pretty damning. And I don't mean for Paul, either; it is damning for the author of Matthew and for Christianity as we know it today. Sim writes:

> Ulrich Luz ... has correctly reminded us that the evangelist has written his story of Jesus on two distinct levels; one is the story of Jesus of Nazareth, while the other concerns the history of the Matthean church. Matthew shapes his narrative about Jesus to be meaningful for his intended readers and to address the issues that were most pressing to them at the end of the first century. Most scholars would agree that Matthew's depiction of the conflict between Jesus and the scribes and Pharisees tells us more about the dispute between Matthew's community and formative Judaism than about Jesus and his scribal and Pharisaic opponents. In the same way we can interpret the sayings of the Matthean Jesus about true and false Christians as much more applicable to the time of the evangelist than to the time of the historical Jesus.[1029]

Of course, the Bible-believing scholars react to this sort of normal historical analysis in a very hostile way. Some of them have even gone so far as to claim that Matthew could not possibly have had access to Paul's letters or to have even known about Paul. Such arguments simply do not stand up to scrutiny and Sim demolishes them easily. My observation would be that those individuals who make such claims obviously don't know very much about the history of the times and the widespread networks of communication that existed then. It seems certain that, by the end of the first century, Paul's letters were circulating as a distinct corpus around the Empire, and that Ignatius of Antioch and Polycarp had access to an extensive Pauline collection, though recent research suggests that Ignatius was actually later than has been previously thought (perhaps 130–135 AD or even later). The conclusion to be drawn is that Paul was highly influential in some areas and heavily criticized in others, but the claim that Matthew was ignorant of Paul "almost beggars belief and can be safely dismissed."[1030]

Thus, it appears most likely that Matthew wrote his Gospel to discredit Paul and his theology. For example, consider the following comparison:

Mark 8:27 Jesus went on with his disciples to the villages of Caesarea Philippi; and on the way he asked his disciples, "Who do people say that I am?"	Matthew 16:13 Now when Jesus came into the district of Caesarea Philippi, he asked his disciples, "Who do people say that the Son of Man is?"

[1028]See Sim (2014b), pp. 594–95.
[1029]Sim (2014b), p. 597.
[1030]Sim (2014b), p. 601.

28 And they answered him, "John the Baptist; and others, Elijah; and still others, one of the prophets."	14 And they said, "Some say John the Baptist, but others Elijah, and still others Jeremiah or one of the prophets."
29 He asked them, "But who do you say that I am?" Peter answered him, "You are the Messiah."	15 He said to them, "But who do you say that I am?" 16 Simon Peter answered, "You are the Messiah, the Son of the living God."
Gal 1:12 for I did not receive it from a human source, nor was I taught it, but I received it through a revelation of Jesus Christ.	17 And Jesus answered him, "Blessed are you, Simon son of Jonah! For flesh and blood has not revealed this to you, but my Father in heaven."
15 But when God, who had set me apart before I was born and called me through his grace, was pleased	18 "And I tell you, you are Peter, and on this rock I will build my church, and the gates of Hades will not prevail against it."
16 to reveal his Son to me, so that I might proclaim him among the Gentiles, I did not confer with any human being,	19 "I will give you the keys of the kingdom of heaven, and whatever you bind on Earth will be bound in heaven, and whatever you loose on Earth will be loosed in heaven."
Mark 8:30 And he sternly ordered them not to tell anyone about him.	20 Then he sternly ordered the disciples not to tell anyone that he was the Messiah.

Notice that all of the additional material added by Matthew has echoes in Paul's claim in italics. So, as Sim states,

> It is very likely that Matthew was in direct contact and conflict with contemporary followers of Paul (Matt 7:15-23; 24:11-12). If that was the case, then we can well imagine that in the heat of the debate these Pauline opponents would have cited certain texts from the Pauline corpus to defend the apostle … Paul's defence of his apostleship and his justification of his Law-free gospel would doubtless have been hot topics of debate, just as they were in the time of the apostle.[1031]

For those who demand that Matthew's intertextual references to Paul be verbally extensive, keep in mind that people of ancient times were not stupid; if they wanted to take down an opponent without appearing to directly engage with him, they were perfectly capable. I would suggest that Matthew left enough in his text to be recognized by his contemporaries, and the only people who don't catch the implications and, therefore, cannot draw the correct inferences are modern scholars blinded by their belief that all was sweetness and light among the early Christians.[1032]

The thesis that Mark was the first Gospel to be written and was then used by Matthew and Luke is favored by nearly all NT scholars. Many of them support the Two Document hypothesis that holds that Matthew and Luke combined Mark with a sayings source Q. The Farrer-Goulder hypothesis, on the other hand, maintains that Matthew used Mark, and that Luke used both Mark and Matthew, and all used their own creativity, thus dispensing with Q. I think that Q is a nowhere proposition, because it is purely speculative, unnecessary given the Farrer-Goulder

---

[1031]Sim (2014b), p. 603.

[1032]See also Smith (2011), pp. 242–308, who demonstrates quite conclusively how Matthew directly used Paul's letters while editing Mark at the same time.

theory, and based on a historical Jesus of Nazareth and a 'tradition' about him and his sayings when it is clear from all the foregoing analyses that no such individual existed as described in the Gospels.

Sim operates on the assumption that Matthew used Mark as his major source in terms of genre, order and content. However, Matthew wasn't happy with Mark, and that comes through in several ways. It has been noted already that Mark uses language that is "simplistic, ungrammatical, and pleonastic."[1033] Yet, it is clear from the studies of a number of scholars that the complex structure reveals a brilliant, educated mind. So, I would suggest that the language used was deliberate. It was written to be read to ordinary people, many of them illiterate, who would be able to 'get' the emphases, including the irony; at the same time, the more educated readers/hearers would also get the many literary allusions and would know that the text was, purely and simply, an allegory.

Matthew took pains to rewrite Mark in an improved literary style. He also added details to the narrative and teaching material. It seems obvious that he was aware of the structure because in some places he created his own literary structures similar to those of Mark (and much other literature of the time), while in other places, he broke Mark's structure and didn't bother to try to fix it. He also omitted whole pericopes that one assumes were offensive to him or unhelpful to his agenda. He frequently corrected what Mark wrote so as to fit another theological view; in other words, it wasn't just another 'witness to Jesus,' as guys like Bart Ehrman would have us think; it was, in modern terms, out and out plagiarism, though certainly the ancient writers did not understand it as such. As noted already, Matthew created an infancy narrative at the beginning and resurrection appearances at the end. He also apparently 'updated' his Gospel to reflect then current issues; that is, he intensified the opposition to the scribes and Pharisees, reflecting his community's problems with early Judaism.

Naturally, many NT scholars seize on the fact that Matthew used 90% of Mark as evidence that 1) the story was true and 2) Mark was an authority for Matthew. They think that Matthew treated Mark with respect and care, preserving the majority of what he wrote. They gloss over the fact of Matthew's severe treatment of Mark, his drastic omissions, additions, modifications, etc. – he wasn't trying to supplement Mark, he was trying to supplant him. And, of course, they think that Matthew shares Mark's theology and that he was just developing what Mark had started. However, when considered in the light of the deep factional conflicts in the early church, evident in Paul – who is, I should reiterate, a primary source – one has to realize that the Christian community was deeply and bitterly polarized. And, as David Sim notes, when one examines Mark and Matthew, one has to realize that these two Gospels were on different sides of the factional divide. Mark and Matthew stood in very different theological traditions.

In contrast to Mark's liberal Jesus, Matthew consistently edits the Markan sections that deal with the Law so that his narrative Jesus always preserves the Torah. The Matthean Jesus spells out clearly that all of the Mosaic Law, down to the last jot and tittle, was to be obeyed until the *Parousia*.

Mark's narrative has been called a passion narrative with an extended introduction because of the emphasis that he gives to the sacrificial death of Jesus rather than any teachings. Paul, too, emphasized the death of Jesus and made almost no reference to any teachings. Matthew

---

[1033]Sim (2014b), p. 605. Pleonastic means using more words than are needed to express a meaning, either unintentionally or for emphasis.

introduces a lot of teaching. One wonders, of course, if this was material traditional to Judas the Galilean, a great teacher and interpreter of the Torah, as Josephus has told us, or if Matthew was just making things up. (Note that anything that appears to be made up is attributed to the mythical Q or oral traditions.)

Mark depicts Jesus as having embarked on a Gentile mission which precedes and validates Paul's mission. Matthew totally rejects this and makes it clear that Jesus' mission was to the Jews alone (Matt 15:24; 10:5-6). In Matthew, the Gentile mission is commissioned by the resurrected Christ and is given into the charge of his disciples, thus completely pulling the rug out from under the feet of Paul. Mark supports Paul in the battle against the disciples and the pillars, while Matthew extensively rehabilitates them. So, despite agreeing on a few theological and Christological points, Mark and Matthew are definitely in opposition.

Sim also thinks that Matthew intended to completely replace Mark and that this was one of the reasons for reproducing ninety percent of Mark's text. He writes:

> After the publication of Matthew, Mark had very little distinctive material to offer. Why would the later evangelist want his readers to consult the earlier Gospel when his own text reproduced almost all of that source and often improved and corrected what he did retain? ... Why would he want his community to read of the healing of the blind man of Bethsaida in Mark 8:22-26 when he himself had deemed it unworthy of inclusion? Why would he be content to have his readers learn that Jesus' power was limited in Mark 6:5 when he had rewritten that text in Matt 13:58 so as not to convey that impression? Why would he desire his intended readers to learn from Mark 3:19b-21 that the family of Jesus believed he was demon-possessed after he himself deemed it to be so offensive that he ensured that it did not appear in his parallel account? Why would Matthew think it beneficial for his community to read in Mark 7:19b that Jesus declared all foods clean when he clearly opposed this view and omitted the offending statement, and elsewhere took pains to depict Jesus as a Law-observant Jew?
>
> ... Matthew saw Mark for what it really was, a narrative account of the mission of Jesus that was designed, at least in part, to support the activity and the theology of Paul. Such a depiction of Jesus, for Matthew, was utterly wrong and perhaps even dangerous, since it contradicted the theology and praxis of the Jerusalem church and it probably misrepresented the teaching and activity of the historical Jesus on some fundamental points. ... Matthew does not continue Mark's trajectory but attempts to overturn it and to replace it.[1034]

We can easily imagine what happened. Immediately after the war with the Jews, Rome's Christian population was in a very vulnerable state, both the Gentile and Jewish groups. The author of Mark wrote his Gospel based on Greco-Roman biographical models with apologetic/propagandistic purposes in mind, and he clearly imposes Paul's Christ, Son of God, on a (semi?) fictitious Palestinian teacher/wonder-worker who is anti-Jewish Law, pro-Roman, and depicts the disciples and family of this Jesus as unredeemed dolts. If one takes into account what Mark's purposes were, which have been described in detail previously, then his Gospel makes complete sense.

And, if we take into account the likely survival of groups of Jewish Christians as well, some may have reluctantly accepted the blanket of protection that Mark's Gospel offered, but others may have resisted and kept their own counsel. And from such a group, along came Matthew, probably in the next generation. Sim writes:

[1034]Sim (2014b), pp. 610–11.

Matthew was not simply un-Pauline, as many scholars suggest; he was vehemently anti-Pauline. He stood with the Jerusalem church against the Pauline tradition in the early church's factional dispute, and used his narrative about the mission of Jesus to discredit, where possible, the mission and theology of the apostle [Paul]. ... Matthew must have known a good deal about Paul, who was well known in the early church and whose influence was increasing in the late first century, and it is perhaps only to be expected that the Law-observant evangelist would use his story of Jesus to respond and critique the Law-free theology of the apostle. ... In the case of Mark, Matthew correctly identified the original Gospel as a Pauline-influenced account of Jesus' ministry.[1035]

Indeed, Matthew was hostile toward Mark, and through him, toward Paul. But Mark's Gospel was already out there, spreading in Christian circles for a generation, so he found himself between a rock and a hard place. He did what a very smart person would do in the same circumstances: he wrote a more storyful, engaging, grammatically correct Gospel, and hoped, no doubt, to so completely eclipse Mark that the latter's text would fade into obscurity and then total oblivion. And it almost worked.

Papias and Mark

The most frequently cited reason to deny any Pauline influence on the author of the second Gospel is the Patristic testimony that the author was 'John Mark,' who was a follower of both Paul and Peter. This individual was mentioned in the NT in several places:

Epaphras, my fellow prisoner in Christ Jesus, sends greetings to you, and so do Mark, Aristarchus, Demas, and Luke, my fellow workers. (Phm. 1:23-24)

Aristarchus my fellow prisoner greets you, as does Mark the cousin of Barnabas, concerning whom you have received instructions – if he comes to you, welcome him. (Col. 4:10)

Only Luke is with me. Get Mark and bring him with you, for he is useful in my ministry. (2 Tim. 4:11)

Your sister church in Babylon, chosen together with you, sends you greetings; and so does my son Mark. (1 Pet. 5:13)

When Peter came to himself and said, "Now I am sure that the Lord has sent his angel and rescued me from the hands of Herod and from all that the Jewish people were expecting." As soon as he realized this, he went to the house of Mary, the mother of John whose other name was Mark, where many had gathered and were praying. (Acts 12:11-12)

Then Paul and his companions set sail from Paphos and came to Perga in Pamphylia. John, however, left them and returned to Jerusalem ... (Acts 13:13)

Barnabas wanted to take with them John called Mark. But Paul decided not to take with them one who had deserted them in Pamphylia and had not accompanied them in the work. The disagreement became so sharp that they parted company; Barnabas took Mark with him and sailed away to Cyprus. (Acts 15:37-39)

[1035]Sim (2014b), pp. 611–12.

I would suggest that only one of the mentions of Mark is authentic: that in Philemon, which Paul apparently wrote from prison in Ephesus before being shipped to Rome. That would place Mark as a companion of Paul as late as 47/48 AD according to the timeline we have established based on historical clues. Then, there are mentions in Colossians, 2 Timothy and 1 Peter, the latter two being well-known forgeries. Colossians is more problematic; I suspect that parts of Colossians may be authentically Pauline, but that's a topic for another time. Acts is, of course, the fictionalized tale of the early church designed to reconcile the mess presented in the letters of Paul, to depict the Jerusalem church and the Pauline mission in harmony with only a few bumps along the way.

Eusebius preserved fragments in his *Historia Ecclesiastica* (3.39.15) attributed to the second-century bishop, Papias of Hierapolis (c. 70-140 AD), which are attributed to an even earlier 'presbyter' or 'elder,' that the author of the second Gospel was a follower and 'interpreter' of Peter, and that the Gospel was based on Peter's anecdotes.

> I shall not hesitate also to put into ordered form for you, along with the interpretations, everything I learned carefully in the past from the elders and noted down carefully, for the truth of which I vouch. For unlike most people I took no pleasure in those who told many different stories, but only in those who taught the truth. Nor did I take pleasure in those who reported their memory of someone else's commandments, but only in those who reported their memory of the commandments given by the Lord to the faith and proceeding from the Truth itself. And if by chance anyone who had been in attendance on the elders arrived, I made enquiries about the words of the elders – what Andrew or Peter had said, or Philip or Thomas or James or John or Matthew or any other of the Lord's disciples, and whatever Aristion and John the Elder, the Lord's disciples, were saying. For I did not think that information from the books would profit me as much as information from a living and surviving voice.[1036]

On Mark, Papias cites John the Elder:

> The Elder used to say: Mark, in his capacity as Peter's interpreter, wrote down accurately as many things as he recalled from memory – though not in an ordered form – of the things either said or done by the Lord. For he neither heard the Lord nor accompanied him, but later, as I said, Peter, who used to give his teachings in the form of *chreiai*, but had no intention of providing an ordered arrangement of the *logia* of the Lord. Consequently Mark did nothing wrong when he wrote down some individual items just as he related them from memory. For he made it his one concern not to omit anything he had heard or to falsify anything.

The excerpt regarding Matthew says only: "Therefore Matthew put the logia in an ordered arrangement in the Hebrew language, but each person interpreted them as best he could" (*H.E.* 3.39.15–16).

Eusebius concluded from the writings of Papias that he was a chiliast, understanding the Millennium as a literal period in which Christ will reign on Earth, and he chastised Papias for his literal interpretation of figurative passages, writing that Papias "appears to have been of very limited understanding," and felt that his misunderstanding misled Irenaeus and others (*Hist. Eccl.* 3.39.11–13). In short, Eusebius did not think that Papias was the brightest light bulb in the pack.

[1036]Eusebius, *H.E.* 3.39.3–4. Richard Bauckham translation, cited by Ian J. Elmer, 'Robbing Paul to Pay Peter: The Papias Notice on Mark,' p. 690, in Wischmeyer *et al.* (2014).

Irenaeus indeed quotes the fourth book of Papias for an otherwise-unknown saying of Jesus, allegedly recounted by John the Evangelist, which Eusebius doubtless has in mind when he disparages Papias' intellect:

> The Lord used to teach about those times and say: "The days will come when vines will grow, each having ten thousand shoots, and on each shoot ten thousand branches, and on each branch ten thousand twigs, and on each twig ten thousand clusters, and in each cluster ten thousand grapes, and each grape when crushed will yield twenty-five measures of wine. And when one of the saints takes hold of a cluster, another cluster will cry out, 'I am better, take me, bless the Lord through me.' Similarly a grain of wheat will produce ten thousand heads, and every head will have ten thousand grains, and every grain ten pounds of fine flour, white and clean. And the other fruits, seeds, and grass will produce in similar proportions, and all the animals feeding on these fruits produced by the soil will in turn become peaceful and harmonious toward one another, and fully subject to humankind ... These things are believable to those who believe." And when Judas the traitor did not believe and asked, "How, then, will such growth be accomplished by the Lord?", the Lord said, "Those who live until those times will see."[1037]

Parallels have often been noted between this account and Jewish texts of the period such as *2 Baruch*. Eusebius concludes his account of Papias by saying that he relates "another account about a woman who was accused of many sins before the Lord, which is found in the Gospel according to the Hebrews." Agapius of Hierapolis (tenth century) offers a fuller summary of what Papias said, calling the woman an adulteress. The parallel seems to be to the famous *Pericope Adulterae* (John 7:53–8:11), a problematic passage absent or relocated in many ancient Gospel manuscripts. A wide range of versions have come down to us, in fact. Since the passage in John is virtually unknown to the Greek patristic tradition, Eusebius has cited the only parallel he recognized, from the now-lost Gospel according to the Hebrews. The nearest agreement with 'many sins' actually occurs in the Johannine text of the Armenian codex Matenadaran 2374; this codex is also remarkable for ascribing the longer ending of Mark to 'Ariston the Elder,' a name connected with Papias.

According to a scholium attributed to Apollinaris of Laodicea, Papias also related a tale on the grotesque fate of Judas Iscariot:

> Judas did not die by hanging but lived on, having been cut down before he choked to death. Indeed, the Acts of the Apostles makes this clear: "Falling headlong he burst open in the middle and his intestines spilled out." Papias, the disciple of John, recounts this more clearly in the fourth book of the Exposition of the Sayings of the Lord, as follows: "Judas was a terrible, walking example of ungodliness in this world, his flesh so bloated that he was not able to pass through a place where a wagon passes easily, not even his bloated head by itself. For his eyelids, they say, were so swollen that he could not see the light at all, and his eyes could not be seen, even by a doctor using an optical instrument, so far had they sunk below the outer surface. His genitals appeared more loathsome and larger than anyone else's, and when he relieved himself there passed through it pus and worms from every part of his body, much to his shame. After much agony and punishment, they say, he finally died in his own place, and because of the stench the area is deserted and uninhabitable even now; in fact, to this day one cannot pass that place without holding one's nose, so great was the discharge from his body, and so far did it spread over the ground."[1038]

[1037]Irenaeus, *Adv. Haer.* 5.33.3–4, quoted on Wikipedia.org, 'Papias of Hierapolis.'
[1038]Michael W. Holmes, *The Apostolic Fathers in English* (Baker Academic, 2006), p. 316 (Fragment 18).

Two late sources (Philip of Side and George Hamartolus) cite the second book of Papias as recording that John and his brother James were killed by the Jews.[1039] According to the two sources, Papias presented this as fulfillment of the prophecy of Jesus on the martyrdom of these two brothers.

Papias relates, on the authority of the daughters of Philip, an event concerning Justus Barsabbas, who according to Acts was one of two candidates proposed to join the Twelve Apostles (Acts 1:21-26). The summary in Eusebius tells us that he "drank a deadly poison and suffered no harm" (*H.E.* 3.39.9), while Philip of Side recounts that he "drank snake venom in the name of Christ when put to the test by unbelievers and was protected from all harm."[1040] This account may be connected to a verse from the longer ending of Mark: "They will pick up snakes in their hands, and if they drink any deadly thing, it will not hurt them" (Mark 16:18).

Now that we have collected the main texts from or about Papias, and have seen quite a bit of text meddling in the process, let's come back to his claim that Mark was a follower and recorder of Peter. Ian J. Elmer asks some crucial questions:

> Is Papias' information about Mark's association with Peter trustworthy; and, if not, is it merely hagiography, or intentional misdirection?[1041]

This claim made by the presbyter via Papias and recorded by Eusebius is held as highly questionable by a majority of scholars. Elmer suggests that Papias or the presbyter extrapolated their information from 1 Peter (above). The chain of transmission is complicated and problematical and need not detain us here. Elmer concludes after laying it all out as follows:

> Regardless of how one reads the transmission history, what emerges from this exploration is the conclusion that we are dealing with a convoluted and complex chain of custody. The tradition linking Mark to Peter was read by Eusebius in Papias (or, perhaps, in a secondary source that quoted Papias), who in turn received it second-hand from some unknown person who by mere happenstance knew the presbyter John, to which both Papias and Eusebius have added their interpretations (the extent of which we can no longer determine). ... David C. Sim has suggested that Eusebius may have intentionally dated Papias early in his list of church fathers on account of Papias' millenarian beliefs so as to imply that his information was accurate – i.e. close proximity to the fountainhead guarantees the integrity of the flow of data.[1042]

Of course, the most important issue is the reliability of the claim. Papias' alleged information is implausible and even inexplicable compared with what we know about the Gospel of Mark from examining it, and from Paul – a primary source, remember – as he wrote in his letters.

Papias was alleged to have said that Mark composed his Gospel based on his reminiscences of Peter's preaching and anecdotes and that it was an anthology of disparate sayings. Since scholars have proven effectively that the Gospel of Mark is a complex and carefully constructed narrative, we can easily see that it is anything but a collection of anecdote-derived reminiscences. So, if we

---

[1039]Holmes (2006), p. 312 (Fragments 5–6).
[1040]Holmes (2006), p. 312 (Fragments 5).
[1041]Elmer (2014), p. 672.
[1042]Elmer (2014), p. 679.

are to allow Papias and his sources to be truthful, we almost have to assume that he was talking about a very different text. What Papias describes sounds more like the Gospel of Thomas.[1043]

Papias also reported that Matthew was written in the 'Hebrew dialect.' Scholars know for certain that Matthew was written in Greek and further, that it undoubtedly existed at the time of Papias and was widely known. So, if Papias said something so clearly untrue about Matthew, what does that suggest about what he said about Mark? The only conclusion is that Papias' testimony is utterly worthless.

The most glaring problem with the claim that Mark was written based on the remembrances of Peter is, of course, the fact that the Markan perspective on Peter – and the rest of the disciples – is quite negative. As we've seen, some scholars want to interpret Mark as presenting Peter as 'well meaning' but deeply flawed. However, a close reading of the Gospel puts a period to that wishful thinking. The disciples are presented in Mark as bickering about their own importance (9:33), climbing over each other to gain exalted positions (10:35-37), disdaining the meek and lowly, especially children (10:13-16). At the end of the story, Jesus is betrayed by one disciple, denied by another, and abandoned by the rest. Only the women remain to share his suffering and they are the first to learn of his resurrection and to be commissioned to proclaim it. Mark clearly had no intention of presenting a sympathetic portrait of Peter, the rest of the disciples, and even the family of Jesus.

The Gospel of Matthew, on the other hand, presents Peter as the chief disciple and the focus of special, laudatory attention. If Papias or his presbyter had said that this Gospel was a collaboration with Peter, it would have made some sense. But, as already noted, what Papias did say about Matthew was also untrue.

There is an additional problem with taking Papias' testimony as true: virtually everything else that Papias says is widely, and rightly, discounted by scholars as pious imagination and not historical fact – witness the lurid and fantastic version of the death of Judas (quoted above) attributed to Papias. Elmer writes:

> [W]hat Papias tells about Mark is probably no more accurate than what he tells us about the death of Judas or the daughters of Philip. Like those other, wildly fanciful stories, Papias' story about Mark being a follower and interpreter of Peter is little more than wishful thinking or, perhaps, willful misdirection.[1044]

Oddly, Papias never mentions Paul, which is surprising since Papias was said to be Bishop of Hierapolis, a city in the Lycos Valley that was part of the Pauline mission. This silence has led some scholars to propose that Papias was anti-Paul. Some scholars have noted a strong Jewish Christian tendency in Papias and his sources. Elmer writes:

> [T]he Biblical and extra-Biblical books with which Eusebius claims Papias was familiar are ones that we might traditionally ascribe to Christian Judaism – 1 John; 1 Peter; Matthew's Gospel; the Gospel to the Hebrews (*H.E.* 3.39.16). Missing from that list are any texts from the Pauline corpus, which

---

[1043] A number of scholars argue that the Gospel of Thomas was a source for Mark. However, Mark Goodacre has argued that the author of Thomas knew Mark, Matthew, and Luke and utilized them in a number of ways. Goodacre's arguments and detailed examples are convincing and it seems we must dispense with any idea of Thomasine priority based on some kind of 'oral tradition.' See Goodacre, *Thomas and the Gospels: The Case for Thomas's Familiarity with the Synoptics* (Eerdmans, 2012).

[1044] Elmer (2014), p. 686.

must suggest that the "books" that Papias disparaged were the letters of Paul. ... It would appear hypocritical, if not completely nonsensical, for Papias to denigrate book learning in the preface to a five-volume set of books. ... it is improbable to suppose that a Christian-Jewish writer like Papias would be referring to either the books of the Old Testament or the Christian-Jewish texts known to him. ... The only other set of "books" considered as Scripture by some Christians contemporaneous with Papias was the Pauline corpus. ... Nielsen is probably correct in suggesting that while Papias does not admit that the Pauline collection is Scripture, he may have taken unfavourable notice that other Christians did.[1045]

It appears that, for a time, the letters of Paul may have been dominating the Christian literary landscape, at least among certain groups of Christians. At the same time, there appears to have been other groups that were not affiliated to Paul, and may have been actually hostile to him and his followers in the second and third generations. So, as Elmer notes, it is against this background that we must read Papias on Mark. He writes:

Why does Papias and his source link Mark to Peter? Why not Paul? If we are right in assuming that Papias differed ideologically from the Paulinists, it is unlikely that he would have ascribed Mark to the Pauline library, especially given that he may have already considered Paul to have said far too much already. But there may be more to Papias' motives for choosing Peter in particular.

Commentators assume that Mark's reputation benefited greatly by the link to Peter. By contrast, it is often assumed that the legacy of Paul was greatly enhanced by the tradition yoking Luke/Acts to the Pauline school. Is it not possible that the same is true of Peter? Would not the ascription of Mark to Peter provide a similar increase for the Petrine school? ...

We can probably conclude that the titles of the Gospels are earlier than the Papias tradition, which give grounds for associating the Gospel with someone called Mark quite independent of the Petrine tradition. The tradition identifying this Mark with John Mark of Jerusalem is undoubtedly even later again. Nevertheless, by the time Papias was writing, Mark's Gospel was well established and had attained an assured place within the nascent Christian orthodoxy of the second century, a movement that also increasingly embraced Peter as the key figure to its underlying mythos. Like Paul, the hallmark of the apostle Peter was claimed for a variety of texts emerging during the Patristic period. But, unlike Paul, a majority of these texts were later deemed heretical with the two canonical letters, 1 and 2 Peter, being the exceptions. Contrary to what we might normally assume, the figure of Peter was the source of some controversy in the latter part of the first, and during the early decades of the second centuries. Only later was Peter styled as the archetypical disciple and chief apostle much lauded by orthodox Christianity.[1046]

Many scholars have assumed that attaching Peter to Mark was supposed to give a 'suspect Gospel' a patina of authority. But it actually appears, from Elmer's review, to have been quite the opposite: Peter was given authority by being attached to a Gospel that already was laden with gravitas for having been long known and used. The name of Luke was already co-opted to be ascribed to the third Gospel, which gave it authority. We notice in the fraudulent letter 1 Peter that Mark is described as Peter's 'son' and companion in Babylon (Rome). This piece was probably written to provide 'background material evidence' that Peter had actually been in Rome. For Papias and Eusebius, the issue is apostolic succession in service of their own interests. The decades of the late first and early second century probably saw a growing body of Pauline

[1045]Elmer (2014), p. 689.
[1046]Elmer (2014), pp. 692–93.

literature, including pseudonymous works. This situation no doubt gave much concern to Jewish Christians such as Matthew and, later, Papias. It seems that ascribing Mark to Petrine influence was a means of bolstering the invented legacy of Peter against the dominance of Pauline theology. As Elmer writes:

> All agree that the stature and authority of Mark's Gospel benefited from its association with Peter. But few consider the reverse: what did the memory and legacy of Peter gain by this association between the chief apostle and the second evangelist? Perhaps Papias wanted to provide Peter with a Gospel, so that he could join the other apostolic evangelists Matthew, John and, via the well-established association with Luke, Paul. Or, put otherwise, is Papias attempting to rob Paul to pay Peter?[1047]

This whole discussion just shows how deep and muddy the waters really are. As we have recounted previously, it appears to be more than likely that the sons of Judas the Galilean were the pillars of the Jerusalem church of Zealots, and that two of them, James and Simon, were executed by Tiberius Alexander around 47 AD shortly after Paul's second visit to Jerusalem, and that Paul, himself, may have been arrested and imprisoned in Ephesus due to his association with the Zealots. We have also noted that Acts certainly has no clue what happened to Peter: he disappears from the tale right after his miraculous escape from prison after James was executed. So it's a fair bet that it was Simon *Peter* who was executed[1048] along with James. In a very real sense, the whole discussion about Peter's authority is a discussion about a fraudulent history. But that's NT studies all the way through, for the most part.

The Cross

We can recognize an undisputed Adam-Christ typology in Paul (1 Cor. 15:20-22, 44-49; Rom. 5:12-21). There is also an implicit Adam-Christ typology in Mark as has been previously discussed. The Markan narrative is clearly an expansion of the Christian proclamation: "That Christ died for our sins in accordance with the scriptures, and that he was buried, and that he was raised on the third day in accordance with the scriptures" (1 Cor. 15:3-4). As previously discussed, this passage includes the problematic bits about post-resurrection appearances to the twelve, the apostles, the five hundred, etc., so at least a portion of this section may be interpolated. However, Romans 6:4 provides some support for these particular verses, stating that the baptized have been 'buried with him' in baptism. In the cosmology of the time, one could die and be buried, both occurring in the heavens, so it doesn't have to imply anything took place on Earth. Nevertheless, as Ole Davidsen notices:

> The kerygmatic Christ myth is not simply a set of motifs (Death and Resurrection), but a narrative structure. Here we should remind ourselves that Paul could not convert Gentiles simply by telling them that Christ had been crucified and raised. He was urged to unfold this kerygma into a narrative of a kind (answering questions like: "Christ? Whom are you talking about?"; "Which God do you

---

[1047]Elmer (2014), p. 672.

[1048]If Peter and Cephas were two persons, which seems likely, perhaps the author of Acts knew the difference and was there indicating that it was Simon who was called "Peter" and not Cephas. Of course, that leaves the fate of Cephas hanging.

have in mind?"; "What happened to whom, when, and where, and how are these events to be understood?" ... Paul's proclamation of God's [evangelion] presupposes and can only be based on such a narrative, the core of which is the general kerygma as cognitive paradigm.[1049]

In short, only a Christ narrative can reveal what his death was all about. The story of Jesus in Mark is given in the context of narratives from the Old Testament and from Greco-Roman literature. The audience would have known this; many of them would have recognized pericopes based on the Jewish scriptures, and Homeric references as well. But most of all, they would have recognized the Adam-Christ typology. The interpretation of Jesus' death was influenced by the typology.

Indeed, there is no explicit reference to Adam in Mark. However, as previously noted, there is Adam imagery behind the temptation story in Mark 1:12-13. In this story, it is the Spirit that drives Jesus into the wilderness to be tempted by Satan. Later in the story, we have a situation that contains echoes of Abraham's almost-sacrifice of his son, Isaac, i.e. Jesus' crisis in Gethsemane at Mark 14:32. He is depicted as not wanting to die, but God the Father demands obedience from him even to the point of death. Jesus' death on the cross is understood not as the taking of his life by his opponents, but as his own sovereign act of giving his life. During his trial, Jesus renounces the use of his divine competence to protect or save himself (Phil. 2:7).

While hanging on the cross, Jesus is mocked by those around him, taunting him to prove his divinity by coming down from the cross. He does not – not because he cannot, but because he is obliged not to do so in obedience. Thus, the bystanders see him as just a weak human being who can save neither himself nor others. But, in reality – in secret – he is actually performing an act that will lead to the saving of others and his own exaltation. The readers of Mark would not have missed the irony: that Jesus was actually demonstrating his power – his devotion to obedience – by remaining on the cross and suffering in the face of total abandonment and desolation.

So, of course, the question is: if this allegory was derived from Paul's teachings, who was Paul really teaching about? It is highly unlikely that Paul could have convinced others, much less himself, with just a short, stylized Adam-Christ kerygma.

In only a few places is it *thought* that Paul is citing traditional materials and, in those instances, it is debated where the tradition ends and Paul resumes. Taking a look at one of these instances, we find that it may not at all be 'tradition' in the sense of having been received from any human source:

> For *I received from the Lord Himself* that which I passed on to you [it was given to me personally], that the Lord Jesus on the night when He was treacherously delivered up and while His betrayal was in progress[1050] took bread, And when He had given thanks, He broke [it] and said, Take, eat. This is My body, which is broken for you. Do this to call Me [affectionately] to remembrance. Similarly when supper was ended, He took the cup also, saying, This cup is the new covenant [ratified and established] in My blood. Do this, as often as you drink [it], to call Me [affectionately] to remembrance. For every time you eat this bread and drink this cup, you are representing and signifying and proclaiming the fact of the Lord's death until He comes [again].[1051]

[1049] Ole Davidsen, 'Adam-Christ Typology in Paul and Mark: Reflections on a Tertium Comparationis,' in Becker *et al.* (2014). pp. 254–55.

[1050] As an example of how misleading English translations can be, here is the literal translation of this clause: "that the Lord Jesus in the night in which He was betrayed [i.e. delivered up] took bread" – no "treacherously," no "while His betrayal was in progress." The translators obviously have the Gospel accounts in mind.

[1051] 1 Cor. 11:23-26. Zondervan Amplified translation.

Jesper Nielsen points out that this bit of text is fragmentary.[1052] The narrative is only evident in traces such as "in the night when he was delivered up." That, of course, raises the question about what else may have been conveyed by the text were it complete?

The second instance of 'tradition' is from 1 Cor. 15:3-7:

> For I passed on to you first of all what I also had received, that Christ (the Messiah, the Anointed One) died for our sins in accordance with [what] the Scriptures [foretold], [Isa. 53:5-12.] That He was buried, that He arose on the third day as the Scriptures foretold, [Ps. 16:9, 10.] And [also] that He appeared to Cephas (Peter), then to the Twelve. Then later He showed Himself to more than five hundred brethren at one time, the majority of whom are still alive, but some have fallen asleep [in death]. Afterward He was seen by James, then by all the apostles (the special messengers) ...[1053]

Nielsen points out that the terminology here is untypical of Paul, thus we have to consider this text to be an interpolation, as I've already suggested in previous sections. Nevertheless, even taken on its own, it, too, is extremely fragmentary. Yet, if you add the text about the Eucharist to this fragment, you have the bare outlines of the passion narrative. But no passion narrative is ever described in Paul's writings, or if it was, it has been excised; and the only reason for excision seems to me to be that it did not match someone's idea of what it ought to say. In short, it is completely impossible from the two fragments to even guess what the real narrative may have been.

Regarding, yet again, the opening of Romans, which might be another 'tradition,' according to Nielsen, again we see that it contains untypical wording and *only here, and nowhere else*, is Jesus presented as somehow related to David, though the nature of that relation is ambiguous (either cosmic in nature or allegorical, but certainly not literal in the sense of physical descent and birth):

> From Paul, a bond servant of Jesus Christ (the Messiah) called to be an apostle, (a special messenger) set apart to [preach] the Gospel (good news) of and from God, Which He promised in advance [long ago] through His prophets in the sacred Scriptures – [The Gospel] regarding His Son, Who as to the flesh (His human nature) was descended from [literally, 'manufactured from the sperm of'] David [to fulfill the covenant promises], and [as to His divine nature] according to the Spirit of holiness was openly designated to be the Son of God with power [in a triumphant and miraculous way] by His resurrection from the dead: Jesus Christ our Lord.[1054]

The term translated as 'flesh' is the same term that Paul uses repeatedly in a pejorative sense throughout his writings, but sometimes neutrally,[1055] and even less often with positive connotations.[1056] It is also untypical of Paul to describe the resurrection as the proclamation; he usually focuses on death and the cross, though the resurrection is always implied. And this brings up another consideration: since it seems obvious that the resurrection of Christ was just

---

[1052] Jesper Tang Nielsen, 'The Cross on the Way to Mark,' in Becker *et al.* (2014), p. 277.
[1053] Zondervan Amplified translation.
[1054] Rom. 1:1-4. Zondervan Amplified translation.
[1055] As in ordinary references to human bodies, for example, Paul's physical body (2 Cor. 7:5), meeting 'in person' (Phlm. 1:16), an illness of the body (Gal. 4:13), bodies of birds and animals (1 Cor. 15:39), ethnicity as Gentiles (Eph. 2:11), etc.
[1056] For example, as something that can be cleansed of defilement (2 Cor. 7:1), as wife and husband becoming 'one flesh' (Eph. 5:31), and the place in which the life of Jesus may become manifest (2 Cor. 4:11).

as important – it is only with the resurrection that God's dominion can be brought about, and baptism apparently signified both, death and new life, two sides of the same coin – then it seems logical that *the cross itself might signify both*: death and resurrection. Lastly, as previously noted, this is something of a two-stage Christology, which may or may not be resonant with Paul's own 'two-phase' understanding of Christ.

Still another bit of text thought to be a possible 'tradition' that Paul is passing on is Galatians 4:4f.

> But when the proper time had fully come, God sent His Son, born of a woman, born subject to [the regulations of] the Law, To purchase the freedom of (to ransom, to redeem, to atone for) those who were subject to the Law, that we might be adopted and have sonship conferred upon us [and be recognized as God's sons].

Again, this is extremely fragmentary and only tells us that Christ was the Son of God who was incarnated as a human being as a precondition for the salvation he came to accomplish.

Ultimately, the only Pauline text that forms any kind of complete 'story of Jesus' is the Philippians 'hymn':

> Let this same attitude and purpose and [humble] mind be in you which was in Christ Jesus: Who, although being essentially one with God and in the form of God [possessing the fullness of the attributes which make God God], did not think this equality with God was a thing to be eagerly grasped or retained, But stripped Himself [of all privileges and rightful dignity], so as to assume the guise of a servant (slave), in that He became like men and was born a human being.
>
> And after He had appeared in human form, He abased and humbled Himself [still further] and carried His obedience to the extreme of death, even the death of the cross!
>
> Therefore [because He stooped so low] God has highly exalted Him and has freely bestowed on Him the name that is above every name, That in (at) the name of Jesus every knee should (must) bow, in heaven and on earth and under the earth, And every tongue [frankly and openly] confess and acknowledge that Jesus Christ is Lord, to the glory of God the Father.[1057]

For Nielsen and others, there are a number of reasons that this text is thought to be from a tradition before Paul. First of all, the rest of the text works quite well without this section. Second, the text contains words that Paul never uses elsewhere in the texts we currently have, though there may be much that was expurgated as we have already noted. Third, the text expresses ideas that Paul does not use elsewhere. The hymn is based on humiliation and exaltation, while Paul repeatedly references the cross. Also, the idea of Christ as Lord of the Universe does not sit comfortably with Paul (though, as argued previously, this is only the case if Ephesians and Colossians are rejected as authentic letters).

However, if Paul himself used this hymn, as we have argued, he must have thought it had an authoritative influence that would back up his ethical admonition. The effect would depend on the Philippians already being familiar with this presentation of Christ. Nielsen gives a concise analysis of this text:

> These observations all point to the traditional character of the hymn. And if it is traditional, it must have had its social setting in worship in the form of some kind of devotional expression.

[1057]Phil. 2:5-11. Zondervan Amplified translation.

The hymn contains a whole and complete narrative in a highly condensed form. The beginning is found in the description of the divine being who is legitimately equal to God (v. 6). Because of the obedience motif that follows, a commissioning can be presupposed in this phase … From this starting point the narrative middle phase consists of the divine being emptying himself when he takes on human form and subjects himself. His obedience culminates in death (v. 7-8). According to the narrative logic it is possible to see the transformation into human form as the qualifying test that he must pass in order to carry out the decisive test. The incarnation provides him with the proper competence. In human form he is able to fulfil the task he was given by being obedient unto death … His death is the culmination of the middle phase from which the narrative moves into the end. Because of … his obedient self-subjection, the divine being is vindicated by God, over-exalted and given the ultimate name of honour (v. 9). … The final verses connect this fundamental Christological narrative to the cultic situation behind the hymn by letting the community's devotion take place in the name that is attributed to the divine being as a consequence of the narrative trajectory (v. 10-11).[1058]

In short, *the Philippians hymn is the only whole narrative about Jesus that can be recovered from the earliest Christian writings*: the letters of Paul. The subject of the hymn is a divine person both at the beginning and at the end, and the focus of the text is his relationship with God. Death (by crucifixion, or was that added by Paul?) is the culmination of the divine being's human existence, but its function is not described; it is not explained why the divine being had to die or what effect that death had. In other words, "Jesus' 'vertical' relation to God and his 'horizontal' function as saviour," may not have been connected at all in the pre-Pauline tradition.[1059] This is an interesting point: did Paul provide the 'horizontal function' for an even older cultic conception?

But all of this creates something of a difficulty. Judaism had strong inhibitions about abolishing the distance between God and mankind. The one and only God of the Jews was transcendent. The idea of the incarnation of a God certainly goes beyond the limits of Judaism. In Judaism, the attributes of God can be hypostatized, such as Wisdom, which can be found in many people. Wisdom and Sophia can be states, but they do not become flesh and blood.

In the Synoptic Gospels, the idea of a real presence of God among human beings, an incarnation, is expressed by the impregnation of a human woman by God or his 'Holy Spirit.' The Jews, on the other hand, had a horror of sexual union between gods and humans; it was contrary to nature. The apocalyptic literature, with which Paul was quite familiar (Enoch), presents this miscegenation as the origin of all evil. Thus it can be seen that introducing the pagan notion of the procreation of a human being by sexual union between a god and a woman is quite extraordinary for a Jew. Gerd Theissen writes:

For Paul, the authority of Jesus is not based on the words and actions of the earthly Jesus, but on the one action of God. God sent Jesus as his only son. And God raised him from the dead in a sovereign creative act. Thus the exalted one owes his divine status wholly and exclusively to God alone. Any suspicion that a human being has made himself God is excluded. *For Paul is not interested in Jesus the human being. He does not want to know Christ 'after the flesh'.* We can probably reverse the connection: because Paul is still deeply rooted in basic monotheistic convictions, he cannot find any positive relationship to the earthly Jesus. Paul had a fear of surrounding the earthly Jesus with a divine aura, because for him there is a great distance between any human being and the one God.

[1058]Nielsen (2014), pp. 282–83.
[1059]Nielsen (2014), p. 285.

> For him Jesus' earthly existence is only his divesting himself so that he is bare humanity. Jesus' total failure in earthly life, the cross, shows that all his dignity is the work of God. If Paul worships him as a godlike being, what he worships in him has come into being exclusively through God's sovereign action and not through the great deeds or words of a human being.[1060]

Paul transforms the vertical Jesus story into a theology. He connects Jesus' death directly to the human condition – humans can participate in the death and resurrection – and he does this by connecting Jesus to Adam. Adam was disobedient and thereby introduced sin and death into the world. Christ was obedient and thereby introduced righteousness and life. Paul's *kerygma* was as much about the action of God as about the obedience of Jesus. God had effected a new creation and the Adam-Christ typology answered the questions: why are human beings sinners and how has Christ changed the situation? To this end, Paul elaborates the motif of obedience: Adam is disobedient, Christ is obedient; just as Adam's sin had consequences for all human beings, so did Christ's obedience have consequences to the benefit of humanity. Therefore, Christ's death was for the sake of the sins of all humanity. Further, the individual can be incorporated into the narrative, brought by a symbolic repetition of Christ's death, i.e. baptism. And then, the individual is expected to follow the modeled faith of Jesus. It's not faith IN Jesus, as Ashworth points out. It's faith OF Jesus that sets the example. And the example was put in a metaphor of the story of this crucifixion or death, but the metaphor represents basically the crucifixion of every person. They're crucified inside and outside because they are faced with this reality that rejects their spirituality, their more or less divine connection.

In the following text from 1 Corinthians, it is essential to Paul's argument that Christ is understood as a divine being from the beginning. Paul constructs this argument on the 'vertical' Christological structure of the Philippians hymn: Christ descends from his divine abode to take on the lowly form of sinful man, yet sins not, suffers an ignominious death and then returns to heaven. The fact that God's power and glory are revealed by the disgraceful cross is at the core of the argument. He demonstrates that what is seen to be good and fair and right by the human perspective is the very opposite as seen from the spiritual perspective. Then, human beings are divided into two groups according to their perception of the cross: they either understand it as the revelation of God's power, or they see it as a scandal. This perception also overturns earthly hierarchical judgments. What is astonishing is that Paul focuses on the cross as the fundamental part of the Jesus narrative. Of course, the resurrection to heaven is assumed, but never explicated here. And, as in Rom. 4:24, 4:25, 6:4-5, 6:9, 7:4, 8:11, 8:34, 1 Cor. 6:14, and Phil. 3:10, Paul uses 'obedience unto death' as the model for Christian behavior.

> For the story and message of the cross is sheer absurdity and folly to those who are perishing and on their way to perdition, but to us who are being saved it is the [manifestation of] the power of God. For it is written, I will baffle and render useless and destroy the learning of the learned and the philosophy of the philosophers and the cleverness of the clever and the discernment of the discerning; I will frustrate and nullify [them] and bring [them] to nothing. (Isa. 29:14) Where is the wise man (the philosopher)? Where is the scribe (the scholar)? Where is the investigator (the logician, the debater) of this present time and age? Has not God shown up the nonsense and the folly of this world's wisdom?
>
> For when the world with all its earthly wisdom failed to perceive and recognize and know God by means of its own philosophy, God in His wisdom was pleased through the foolishness of preaching

---

[1060]Theissen (1999), p. 48.

[salvation, procured by Christ and to be had through Him], to save those who believed (who clung to and trusted in and relied on Him). For while Jews [demandingly] ask for signs and miracles and Greeks pursue philosophy and wisdom, We preach Christ (the Messiah) crucified, [preaching which] to the Jews is a scandal and an offensive stumbling block [that springs a snare or trap], and to the Gentiles it is absurd and utterly unphilosophical nonsense. But to those who are called, whether Jew or Greek (Gentile), Christ [is] the Power of God and the Wisdom of God. [This is] because the foolish thing [that has its source in] God is wiser than men, and the weak thing [that springs] from God is stronger than men.

For [simply] consider your own call, brethren; not many [of you were considered to be] wise according to human estimates and standards, not many influential and powerful, not many of high and noble birth. [No] for God selected (deliberately chose) what in the world is foolish to put the wise to shame, and what the world calls weak to put the strong to shame. And God also selected (deliberately chose) what in the world is lowborn and insignificant and branded and treated with contempt, even the things that are nothing, that He might depose and bring to nothing the things that are, So that no mortal man should [have pretense for glorying and] boast in the presence of God.

But it is from Him that you have your life in Christ Jesus, Whom God made our Wisdom from God, [revealed to us a knowledge of the divine plan of salvation previously hidden, manifesting itself as] our Righteousness [thus making us upright and putting us in right standing with God], and our Consecration [making us pure and holy], and our Redemption [providing our ransom from eternal penalty for sin]. So then, as it is written, Let him who boasts and proudly rejoices and glories, boast and proudly rejoice and glory in the Lord. (Jer. 9:24)

As for myself, brethren, when I came to you, I did not come proclaiming to you the testimony and evidence or mystery and secret of God [concerning what He has done through Christ for the salvation of men] in lofty words of eloquence or human philosophy and wisdom; For I resolved to know nothing (to be acquainted with nothing, to make a display of the knowledge of nothing, and to be conscious of nothing) among you except Jesus Christ (the Messiah) and Him crucified. And I was in (passed into a state of) weakness and fear (dread) and great trembling [after I had come] among you. And my language and my message were not set forth in persuasive (enticing and plausible) words of wisdom, but they were in demonstration of the [Holy] Spirit and power [a proof by the Spirit and power of God, operating on me and stirring in the minds of my hearers the most holy emotions and thus persuading them], So that your faith might not rest in the wisdom of men (human philosophy), but in the power of God.

Yet when we are among the full-grown (spiritually mature Christians who are ripe in understanding), we do impart a [higher] wisdom (the knowledge of the divine plan previously hidden); but it is indeed not a wisdom of this present age or of this world nor of the leaders and rulers of this age, who are being brought to nothing and are doomed to pass away. But rather what we are setting forth is a wisdom of God once hidden [from the human understanding] and now revealed to us by God – [that wisdom] which God devised and decreed before the ages for our glorification [to lift us into the glory of His presence]. None of the rulers of this age or world perceived and recognized and understood this, for if they had, they would never have crucified the Lord of glory. But, on the contrary, as the Scripture says, What eye has not seen and ear has not heard and has not entered into the heart of man, [all that] God has prepared (made and keeps ready) for those who love Him [who hold Him in affectionate reverence, promptly obeying Him and gratefully recognizing the benefits He has bestowed]. (Isa. 64:4; 65:17)

Yet to us God has unveiled and revealed them by and through His Spirit, for the [Holy] Spirit searches diligently, exploring and examining everything, even sounding the profound and bottomless things of God [the divine counsels and things hidden and beyond man's scrutiny]. For what person perceives (knows and understands) what passes through a man's thoughts except the man's own spirit within him? Just so no one discerns (comes to know and comprehend) the thoughts of God except the Spirit of God.

Now we have not received the spirit [that belongs to] the world, but the [Holy] Spirit Who is from God, [given to us] that we might realize and comprehend and appreciate the gifts [of divine favor and blessing so freely and lavishly] bestowed on us by God. And we are setting these truths forth in words not taught by human wisdom but taught by the [Holy] Spirit, combining and interpreting spiritual truths with spiritual language [to those who possess the Holy Spirit]. But the natural, nonspiritual man does not accept or welcome or admit into his heart the gifts and teachings and revelations of the Spirit of God, for they are folly (meaningless nonsense) to him; and he is incapable of knowing them [of progressively recognizing, understanding, and becoming better acquainted with them] because they are spiritually discerned and estimated and appreciated. But the spiritual man tries all things [he examines, investigates, inquires into, questions, and discerns all things], yet is himself to be put on trial and judged by no one [he can read the meaning of everything, but no one can properly discern or appraise or get an insight into him]. For who has known or understood the mind (the counsels and purposes) of the Lord so as to guide and instruct Him and give Him knowledge? But we have the mind of Christ (the Messiah) and do hold the thoughts (feelings and purposes) of His heart. (Isa. 40:13.)[1061]

So again, despite the fact that the cross is central to Paul, there is also what it implies: resurrection. As Engberg-Pedersen shows, many of the quite numerous references to power and spirit throughout Paul's letters are indirect references to the resurrection.[1062] So it seems logical to suggest that the cross itself symbolized resurrection as well, just as baptism represented both death and resurrection. For Paul, the death, as an act of obedience, is central, but resurrection is either directly connected or indirectly implied with all mentions of the 'new life' that comes with the spirit. And thus, *the cross must also symbolize triumph.*

The theology of Paul is represented in Mark's *narrative.* There are no devotional statements or rhetorical arguments as there are in Paul; instead, there are stories set out in time and space with persons speaking and acting out the rhetoric. And Mark has made sure to notify the reader/hearer that this space and time is mythical. He did this at the beginning by introducing John the Baptist, who everyone must have known had nothing to do with baptizing any Jesus, and likely everything to do with Paul. He constructed his stories using bits and pieces from the Old Testament, Homer and other literature of the time. He placed the crucifixion of Jesus in the time of Pilate knowing full well that Judas the Galilean had been executed by Pilate, that he had been the Jewish messiah who was to come and destroy Rome, but failed, and that his hearers/listeners knew this as well. He deliberately overlaid Paul and his theology on the figure of Judas, the martial messiah of the Jewish Christian Zealots, and he did it with the full expectation that his readers – most of them – would know what he was doing and would approve of his way of presenting and preserving the teachings of Paul in story form. His story was a way to 'save face' for both types of Christians, and he may have hoped that the Jewish Christians, followers of Judas the Galilean, would accept it and join the Gentile Christians.

In terms of Pauline theology, at two points in the narrative, the Markan Jesus explicitly directs the reader's attention to the task he came to accomplish, i.e. to die as a means of salvation for humanity. First, in Mark 10:45: "For even the Son of Man came not to have service rendered to Him, but to serve, and to give His life as a ransom for (instead of) many." Then, in the Garden

---

[1061]1 Cor. 1:18–2:16. Amplified translation by Zondervan.

[1062]Engberg-Pedersen (2010), pp. 28, 43–4, 47, 70, 89, 151.

of Gethsemane, the conflict between his own will and his obligation plays out, making clear that death is the objective:

> Then they went to a place called Gethsemane, and He said to His disciples, Sit down here while I pray. And He took with Him Peter and James and John, and began to be struck with terror and amazement and deeply troubled and depressed. And He said to them, My soul is exceedingly sad (overwhelmed with grief) so that it almost kills Me! Remain here and keep awake and be watching. And going a little farther, He fell on the ground and kept praying that if it were possible the [fatal] hour might pass from Him. And He was saying, Abba, [which means] Father, everything is possible for You. Take away this cup from Me; yet not what I will, but what You [will]. And He came back and found them sleeping, and He said to Peter, Simon, are you asleep? Have you not the strength to keep awake and watch [with Me for] one hour? Keep awake and watch and pray [constantly], that you may not enter into temptation; the spirit indeed is willing, but the flesh is weak. He went away again and prayed, saying the same words. And again He came back and found them sleeping, for their eyes were very heavy; and they did not know what answer to give Him. And He came back a third time and said to them, Are you still sleeping and resting? It is enough [of that]! The hour has come. The Son of Man is betrayed into the hands of sinful men (men whose way or nature is to act in opposition to God). Get up, let us be going! See, My betrayer is at hand![1063]

The whole Markan narrative is focused around the question: will Jesus fulfill his obligation as the Son of God? And then, at his death, the Roman centurion announces that he was, indeed, the Son of God, making it clear that yes, his death has successfully fulfilled the task he was given by God. The symbolic empty tomb at the end implies his resurrection and ascension and the divine recognition of his mission accomplished.

The perfect narrative structure of Mark places the cross event as the decisive test in the middle. Except for the fact that Mark is telling a 'horizontal' story set in space and time, the vertical structure of Mark corresponds to the Philippians hymn. In strict accord with Paul's reconfiguring the hymn, adding the horizontal elements of the purpose of the death of Jesus, Mark attributes that same purpose in his narrative: Jesus' death on the cross initiates a new reality, a new state possible for humans who choose the Jesus option.

In the Markan narrative, the idea that the Christ should suffer an ignominious death at the hands of the Jews was a complete scandal to Peter, as we see in the first passion prediction:

> Then he began to teach them that the Son of Man must undergo great suffering, and be rejected by the elders, the chief priests, and the scribes, and be killed, and after three days rise again. He said all this quite openly. And Peter took him aside and began to rebuke him. But turning and looking at his disciples, he rebuked Peter and said, "Get behind me, Satan! For you are setting your mind not on divine things but on human things."[1064]

Mark is portraying the Jerusalem Christians, opponents of Paul, as unable to 'get it.' One is reminded of Paul writing about "false apostles ... disguising themselves as apostles of Christ ... Even Satan disguises himself as an angel of light" (2 Cor. 11:13-14). Here, Jesus rebukes Peter as 'Satan,' indicating that he was acting in the role of tempter just as Satan did to Jesus in the wilderness and as the serpent acted in Eden toward Adam. By Adam's disobedient response, he became mortal, corruptible, and identified with his own separate, fleshly existence. And this

---

[1063]Mark 14:32-42.
[1064]Mark 8:31-33.

became the state of humanity: corruptible bodies and corruptible minds, selfish and blind to higher realities and our higher purpose, incapable of seeing our wrongness, let alone to conceive of an alternative way of being. It is this alternative way of being, the original semi-physical/semi-spiritual state of being that Jesus explains to his disciples in the next paragraph:

> He called the crowd with his disciples, and said to them, "If any want to become my followers, let them deny themselves and take up their cross and follow me. For those who want to save their life will lose it, and those who lose their life for my sake, and for the sake of the gospel, will save it. For what will it profit them to gain the whole world and forfeit their life? Indeed, what can they give in return for their life? Those who are ashamed of me and of my words in this adulterous and sinful generation, of them the Son of Man will also be ashamed when he comes in the glory of his Father with the holy angels." And he said to them, "Truly I tell you, there are some standing here who will not taste death until they see that the kingdom of God has come with power."[1065]

As Troels Engberg-Pedersen notes, the Markan text is clearly about the death of the underlying self to the material world, denying the individual self, and turning toward Jesus, his example, and the world to come. Jesus is clearly giving himself and his death as a model for Christian being. The Christian needs a new state of mind, a new attitude toward life and reality; the Christian must follow the example of Christ and metaphorically (or literally!) take up their own cross, die to their old distorted understanding of the world, in order to truly be alive, not only here and now, but forever. As discussed in the section on Paul's theology, it is clear that one has to lose the life of the flesh and begin to see the unseen life of the spirit in order to gain it. "Get behind me, Satan! For you are setting your mind not on divine things but on human things."

The second passion prediction:

> They went on from there and passed through Galilee. He did not want anyone to know it; for he was teaching his disciples, saying to them, "The Son of Man is to be betrayed into human hands, and they will kill him, and three days after being killed, he will rise again." But they did not understand what he was saying and were afraid to ask him.[1066]

Again, Mark has set up a scene where he can expound on Paul's theology of the cross. At the same time, he shows that the Jerusalem Christians, followers of Judas the Galilean, were oblivious to the truth and, at this point, afraid to say anything after Peter had been called 'Satan'! Just as the first passion prediction was followed by a teaching about how to be a Christian, so is this one:

> Then they came to Capernaum; and when he was in the house he asked them, "What were you arguing about on the way?" But they were silent, for on the way they had argued with one another who was the greatest. He sat down, called the twelve, and said to them, "Whoever wants to be first must be last of all and servant of all." Then he took a little child and put it among them; and taking it in his arms, he said to them, "Whoever welcomes one such child in my name welcomes me, and whoever welcomes me welcomes not me but the one who sent me."[1067]

[1065]Mark 8:34–9:1.

[1066]Mark 9:30-32.

[1067]Mark 9:33-37.

In this teaching, children and servants represent the most powerless individuals in the hierarchy of the Empire (women had only slightly more status). Jesus here is using his upcoming shameful death, which he will embrace willingly, as the paradigm for reversing the hierarchy of values of the flesh in favor of those of the spirit. Those who serve others, those who are weak and helpless and require help, are to be placed first in the consideration of the good Christian.

The third passion prediction again is set up as a platform for teaching:

> He took the twelve aside again and began to tell them what was to happen to him, saying, "See, we are going up to Jerusalem, and the Son of Man will be handed over to the chief priests and the scribes, and they will condemn him to death; then they will hand him over to the Gentiles; they will mock him, and spit upon him, and flog him, and kill him; and after three days he will rise again."[1068]

Again, the focus is on individuals who were pillars in the Jerusalem church and simply didn't get what Paul was teaching, and opposed him with their authority. (And we know that they were likely of the family of Judas the Galilean, so 'Zebedee' is simply a disguise.[1069])

> James and John, the sons of Zebedee, came forward to him and said to him, "Teacher, we want you to do for us whatever we ask of you." And he said to them, "What is it you want me to do for you?" And they said to him, "Grant us to sit, one at your right hand and one at your left, in your glory." But Jesus said to them, "You do not know what you are asking. Are you able to drink the cup that I drink, or be baptized with the baptism that I am baptized with?" They replied, "We are able." Then Jesus said to them, "The cup that I drink you will drink; and with the baptism with which I am baptized, you will be baptized; but to sit at my right hand or at my left is not mine to grant, but it is for those for whom it has been prepared."[1070]

We know that James and Simon, the sons of Judas the Galilean, were executed by Tiberius Alexander around 47 AD, though we found no reference to the death of the pillar John in the historical sources.[1071] Yet, this passage may suggest that he met the same fate as James and Simon-Peter: "The cup that I drink you will drink; and with the baptism with which I am baptized, you will be baptized ..."

[1068] Mark 10:32b-34.

[1069] "The name given in the Gospels, Greek: [*zebedaios*], is probably a transliteration of the Hebrew name Zebadiah according to Spiros Zodhiates (The Complete Wordstudy Dictionary), or the truncated version Zabdi, says BDB Theological Dictionary, and so means Yahweh (or The Lord) Has Bestowed. Other popular interpretations of the name are: abundant (Hitchcock's Bible Names Dictionary) or my gift (Smith's Bible Dictionary)." (Wikipedia.org, 'Zebedee.')

[1070] Mark 10:35-40.

[1071] One wonders, of course, if Cephas and Peter were one and the same, though several items argue against that, and if John of Gischala was in any way related to Judas the Galilean? Of course, Josephus has smeared John of Gischala with accusations of breaking the Jewish Law in a number of ways, which one would not expect of a relative of Judas the Galilean. Was all that blowing smoke over John's identity? It would certainly be a bizarre and astonishing historical event if the son of the 'real' Jewish messianic claimant had been captured by the Romans and marched in their triumphal parade in Rome. Along this same line, one cannot help but wonder about the Apocalypse of John, recalling that Ellegård thought the main part of it was written during the siege of Jerusalem to encourage the militants. What if it was written by John of Gischala, and he was a son of Judas the Galilean? All just speculation; but we certainly know that we know very little about that period and a whole lot of textual prestidigitation was going on.

When the ten heard this, they began to be angry with James and John. So Jesus called them and said to them, "You know that among the Gentiles those whom they recognize as their rulers lord it over them, and their great ones are tyrants over them. But it is not so among you; but whoever wishes to become great among you must be your servant, and whoever wishes to be first among you must be slave of all. For the Son of Man came not to be served but to serve, and to give his life a ransom for many."[1072]

The question is explicitly one of status in a Christian context. Again, Jesus reverses the normal hierarchy, explicitly that of the Gentile rulers – the emperors – and places those who serve others at the top in the world of spirit, the Kingdom of God.[1073] Additionally, Jesus refers to the cup of the eucharist and baptism, the two rites that were important to Paul and were both references to Jesus' death and the ability of the Christian follower to participate in that death and rebirth. Nielsen writes:

> The Gospel of Mark contains an interpretation of the cross that mainly focuses on two aspects. First of all Jesus' obedience is presented as part of a narrative structure that constructs his death as the task he as Son of God has to carry out. Furthermore, in this narrative structure Jesus' death is interpreted as a ransom for many. It has a salvific character. The narrative structure combines the 'vertical' role as Son of God with the 'horizontal' function as savior. Secondly, the contexts of the passion predictions present Jesus' death as paradigmatic for the reversal of value hierarchies that is expected to be characteristic of Christians. The believers constitute a cognitive community based on an understanding of social hierarchies and value systems. A third aspect may be the ritual repetition of Jesus' death as a means of being included in the Christ event and enjoying its effect.[1074]

Mark's presentation of the theology of Paul takes the form of a narrative, which demands that the events take place in time and space. Theological structures are represented in narrative actions by persons in specific places. Nielsen proposes that the oldest pre-Pauline tradition is represented in the Philippians hymn and suggests that there were other pre-Pauline traditions about a Son of God who had died for the sins of humanity. If we are to take Romans 16:7[1075] seriously, there was certainly a Christianity of sorts in existence long before Paul that was probably not the Christianity of the Jerusalem Christians who were focused on a martial messiah who was to come and destroy the Romans. Therefore, I think it is quite possible that the Philippians hymn was pre-Pauline and referred to this other Christ. I think that the Adam-Christ connection was due to Paul and his visions and that the idea that one God-man died for sins, to reverse the failure of Adam, was Paul's original inspiration. Paul develops this idea into a complete cosmological and theological structure with his main focus on the obedient, salvific death of the pre-existent Son of God. For Paul, Christ is the model for all to follow in terms of obedience to God, which of course requires a complete change in thinking and perception. Mark's Gospel simply narrativizes Paul's theology. As Nielsen writes:

> Mark builds on and continues Paul's interpretation of the earliest traditions about Jesus' death. He constructs his narrative on the basis of Paul's interpretation of Christ's obedience as a willingness

[1072]Mark 10:41-45.

[1073]Keep in mind also the previous discussion of this passage where the 'rulers of the age,' or archons of darkness, are the controllers of rulers on earth.

[1074]Nielsen (2014), p. 293.

[1075]"Greet Andronicus and Junia, my relatives who were in prison with me; they are prominent among the apostles, and they were in Christ before I was."

to give his life for the sake of our sins. This obligation constitutes the narrative core in the Gospel of Mark.[1076]

At this point, we must fully realize that the Gospel of Mark was a story that was completely made up almost from its foundations and clearly based on Paul and his development of a theology that may have been based on an older tradition about a Son of God who came to Earth for the purpose of dying (for what?) and then, after doing so, was resurrected into heaven and glorified. As noted, this was not a Jewish idea. However, at the same time, having reviewed the historical sources, we notice that there are a few aspects of the Jesus of Nazareth story that appear to be derived from the biography of Judas the Galilean, including his associated relatives, James, Simon (and John?), who later were the pillars of the Jerusalem church.

We know that it is almost certain that Judas the Galilean was executed in 19 AD by Pontius Pilate and that Pilate was then recalled to Rome. The execution of Judas apparently caused an uproar among Jews in Rome, leading to a crackdown on their activities there. We know that John the Baptist was executed by Herod Antipas probably in 35 or 36 AD. We know that Paul's conversion probably occurred in 29 AD, the same year Luke declares John the Baptist began his ministry and, supposedly, baptized Jesus of Nazareth. Since there was no real 'Jesus of Nazareth,' and since we know that Mark's Gospel – the original Gospel on which the others were based – was written as an allegory, I think we are justified in speculating that it was Paul who was baptized by John the Baptist. But Paul never mentions John the Baptist. Of course, if John was a relative of Judas the Galilean and was executed for that reason, despite the fact that Josephus never mentions any such thing (which makes it unlikely), one would not expect Paul to mention him. On the other side, if he did mention him, then there is no doubt that such mention would have been expurgated to preserve the Jesus timeline. Finally, despite all of this, we still do not know who Paul's Christ was; we just know it wasn't Judas the Galilean or any 'Jesus of Nazareth.'

[1076]Nielsen (2014), p. 294.

8. Christ Under Caesar

As I have maintained from the beginning, in order to even attempt to solve the mystery of the origins of Christianity, one needs a complete grasp of the historical and social environment in which this phenomenon appeared. More than just learning all that is possible about the world of that time, by any and all means available, one has to *take the realities on the ground seriously.* Of course, at the point in time when studying the Bible as a historical document, and the New Testament in particular, first came to be a scholarly endeavor, the amount, type, and value of available sources, not to mention methods of analysis, was more limited than it is today. Over the past century or so, different methodological schools have applied their tools to the problem of the Gospel of Mark, each of them contributing a bit to the available data.[1077]

In the beginning of scientific analysis of the Bible as a whole, there was what is called 'source criticism,' which in the context of biblical studies is the process attempting to identify the sources (often hypothetical) used by the author of a particular text. It was related to textual criticism, which compares the variants found in different copies of manuscripts or books. But as the alleged sources were often identified based entirely on the text in question, and not any actual *existing* source material, the sources 'discovered' were more often than not purely the products of the historian's imagination, such as the Q Document thought by many to be a source for Luke and Matthew.

Early New Testament scholars assumed that the early traditions of Christianity were oral, passed on from one person to another by spoken words. Only later were these bits and pieces written down. Form criticism was developed in an attempt to discern the alleged oral traditions of units of text by classifying their genre, or form (e.g. proverb, poem, letter, etc.), and then determining the sociological setting (*Sitz im Leben*) that produced the alleged oral tradition. As such, it was most often just as speculative, if not more so, as source criticism. So it was that studies based on form criticism concluded that the Gospels were drawing on oral traditions and were, effectively, just "unsophisticated compilations of Christian traditions," as Winn puts it, that had been passed on orally; parables and aphorisms were said to be the bedrock of the tradition.[1078] Form critics didn't bother with trying to make out whether a text had an overarching plan or connected literary strategy; they were blinded to that by their assumptions about early Christianity inculcated in them by their *own* social environment and beliefs.

One form critic, Rudolf Bultmann, went a bit further than most of his contemporaries: he noted that early Christian literature seemed more concerned with faith in the Christian kerygma or proclamation than with any actual details of Jesus' life. Like the other form critics, he thought that one could identify the original 'form' of any given piece of text, thus creating a 'history' of traditions based on these speculative (and often non-existent) developments. That is, Bultmann

---

[1077]The following discussion follows and expands on the overview given by Adam Winn in *Reading Mark's Christology Under Caesar: Jesus the Messiah and Roman Imperial Ideology* (Downers Grove, Illinois: IVPAcademic, 2018).
[1078]Winn (2018), p. 8.

was interested in the 'history of the tradition,' not in any history of Jesus, because he thought that there was almost nothing to recover; it had all been obscured with myth.

Using these methods, Bultmann believed that the Gospel of Mark presented a 'divine man' Christology in which the divine man was the power of the divine coming onto and residing in a human being, thereby bestowing supernatural abilities, divine knowledge, and wisdom. As Winn writes:

> For Bultmann, Mark was a representative Gospel for Pauline Hellenistic churches, churches where the concept of the divine man was borrowed from the Hellenistic religious world and imported into Christianity.[1079]

Form criticism was followed, more or less, by redaction criticism. While source criticism tries to identify sources, redaction critics try to look at a text as a collection of such sources, with emphasis on how the author (or redactor/editor) shapes, organizes, and adds to them, trying to determine their theological or ideological goals in the process. So while they make a large assumption about the nature of the alleged sources, at least they recognize that the text's author has some creative agency, less concerned with chronology and history (though that may be present) than they are with a particular agenda.

In the previous chapters we have seen how this can be used to come to some insightful conclusions, such as about Matthew's use of Mark. Distinct characteristics of a particular author can be detected by paying attention to things like repetition of themes and images (e.g. Matthew's fulfillment of prophecies); what is retained, omitted, or changed from the earlier source (e.g. Matthew's rehabilitation of the disciples); and idiosyncratic word choices and vocabulary. By comparing Matthew to Mark one can see to what degree the original text has been changed, and how Matthew tends to change it when he does so. As you can see, this methodology opened the door a crack to the idea that there was more going on in the Gospels than just a compilation of oral traditions faithfully recorded by scribes who strung them together with no thought for any literary conventions.

Winn notes that virtually all redaction critics accepted the main thrust of Bultmann: that Mark was all about a divine man of power. On the other hand, such critics rejected the idea that the Gospel authors were mere compilers and accepted that they were creative authors themselves, intentional in the way they constructed their Gospels. And there was a problem that needed solving: if Jesus was a powerful divine man, how to explain the elements of suffering and death? True to form, they found their answer: different sources were used by the evangelist, some of which talked about the divine man of power, while others talked about the suffering messiah. Mark had simply (and somewhat haphazardly) assembled them together and thereby left some tensions in the text, raising the obvious question: "Will the real Jesus please stand up?"

As noted, redaction critics were interested in the surrounding social conditions of the author and his audience. Many concluded from their analyses that Mark's community had an unhealthy esteem for power and glory driven by the divine-man Christology, and that Mark was written to address this imbalance, to take them down a peg or two, so to say. The first half of the Gospel presents the imbalanced perspective, and the second half corrects that view. So, for the redaction critics, the suffering Messiah was the dominant image. Believe it or not, this interpretation of Mark dominated the work of redaction critics for 30 years or more.

[1079]Winn (2018), p. 9.

Both schools of thought – form and redaction – were criticized. The concept of the Hellenistic divine man proved to be vague and didn't really describe the 'power pieces' of Mark's Christology at all, nor the way he used 'Son of God.' The power pieces were actually presented quite positively by Mark and therefore could not be a view of Jesus that he was criticizing. Additionally, the maneuver of the redaction critics to separate pre-Markan material from Markan material, which allowed for the competing views of Jesus to be highlighted, was highly subjective and inconsistent. Apparently, there was a lot of disagreement about what was what, which was good evidence that nothing was clear enough to be agreed on by all and, thus, highly unlikely to be the right conclusion.

Along came narrative criticism, which focuses on the text as a literary whole and the role of the author and audience in imparting meaning. Like modern literary analysis, it studies features such as form, genre, structure, plot, characterization, and various literary techniques. The first book to take this approach to one of the Gospels was David Rhoads's *Mark as Story* in 1982. In 1983, Jack Dean Kingsbury published *The Christology of Mark's Gospel*, criticizing the redaction critics' reading of Mark. Kingsbury made no distinction between Markan and alleged pre-Markan material. He located the meaning of Mark's Christology within the Gospel itself and ignored any *Sitz im Leben*. And he paid close attention to the narrative itself, noting that the secrecy motif was prominent and played a role in understanding the Christology presented there. He also paid close attention to the different titles that Mark gave his Jesus: Messiah/Christ, Son of God, Son of David, King of the Jews, Son of Man. Kingsbury notes that Messiah/Christ, Son of David, and King of the Jews, while being correct Christological titles that can reveal things about Jesus, prove to be ultimately insufficient and point to an incomplete understanding of Jesus. Winn notes:

> As insufficient titles, they are not kept secret but are made known throughout the Gospel. In contrast to these titles is the title "Son of God," the title that Kingsbury argues is the central christological identification of Mark's Gospel. It is this title and this title alone that is the subject of the Markan secrecy motif, and Kingsbury argues that this title is kept secret in Mark until after Jesus' crucifixion, where it is proclaimed by a Roman centurion. For Kingsbury, the significance of Mark's "Son of God" secret is that Jesus' identity as "Son of God" can only be understood in terms of Jesus' suffering and death. Any understanding of Jesus as the Messiah apart from his death (understandings conveyed in Mark by the correct yet insufficient titles "Messiah/Christ," "Son of David," or "King of the Jews") is incomplete. ... For Kingsbury "Son of Man" is a technical term that points to Jesus' divine authority in the face of opposition with one significance of that term being Jesus' judgment of opposition at the parousia.[1080]

Nevertheless, while Kingsbury gave a lot of attention to the Christology of Mark, he paid very little attention to the structure and development of the Markan narrative itself. There are many narrative features that are ignored by Kingsbury which play a significant role in the construction of Mark's Christology. We will sketch the main components, lightly paraphrasing Winn's outline.

John baptizes Jesus at the beginning of Mark's Gospel, at which point, "he saw the heavens torn apart and the Spirit descending like a dove on him. And a voice came from heaven, 'you are my Son, the Beloved; with you I am well pleased'" (Mark 1:10b-11). In Mark's story world, apparently no one else saw or heard this phenomenon – only Jesus. But, of course, Mark the

---

[1080]Winn (2018), p. 12.

author, the implied narrator, and the audience know it now. What Mark means by Jesus being God's son is only revealed in the narrative. The title, Son of God, must have carried specific meanings for Mark's audience, while the other Christological titles that come into play also carried their own specific meanings. Therefore, not only does the narrative show how these titles are to be understood, the titles themselves – already loaded with meaning – tell the audience something about the narrative's meaning.

So, at the very beginning, Mark presents Jesus as the powerful Son of God. He then proceeds to narrate exactly what this power means. His first act is victory over Satan, out in the wilderness. Then there are four detailed episodes in which Jesus exorcizes a demon or demons (1:23-28; 5:1-20; 7:24-30; 9:14-29). There are other references to exorcisms without details (1:32-34, 39; 3:11-12, 20-30). So, apparently, being the powerful Son of God gives one power over demons and Satan himself.

Then, there are healings. There are nine episodes of healing (1:29-31, 40-45; 2:1-12; 3:1-6; 5:21-43; 7:31-37; 8:22-26; 10:46-52) and three references to Jesus' general healing ability (1:32-34; 3:10; 6:53-56). Being the Son of God means you also have power to heal the human condition of sickness and imbalances in the soul which often manifest as sickness.

Then there are episodes showing Jesus' power over the natural world, such as calming a raging storm at sea with only a word (4:35-41), and walking on a stormy sea and thereby calming it by his mere presence (6:45-52). The two feeding miracles also display power over the natural world (6:30-44; 8:1-10).

All through the Gospel, supernatural beings declare the powerful identity of Jesus: at the very beginning, as already noted; then God reappears for a pronouncement at the transfiguration (9:7); and on three occasions it is demons who call him the "Holy One of God" (1:24), "Son of God" (3:11), and "Son of the Most High God" (5:7).

Jesus is depicted as being extraordinarily popular, people coming from miles around to see him, speak to him, or be healed by him. Apparently, large crowds follow him wherever he goes and those he heals spread his fame widely. His words evoke amazement and proclamations by the people, and the most significant public proclamation is at the triumphal entry into Jerusalem where he is hailed as the one who "comes in the name of the Lord," which is then immediately identified with the kingdom of David (11:7-10).

Throughout the Gospel, Jesus exhibits divine knowledge, knows the thoughts of others (2:8; 3:5; 9:33-35; 12:15), and predicts future events, including his own death (8:31; 9:31; 10:33-34; 11:2-3; 13:2-9; 14:13-15, 18, 27, 30). He exercises divine prerogatives, including the right to forgive sins (2:5-10) and lordship over the Sabbath (2:28).

Finally, as an individual of power, Jesus is an authoritative teacher whose authority distinguishes his teaching from that of the scribes (1:22). Jesus' teaching is closely associated with his acts as both healer and exorcist (1:22-28; 2:1-12; 3:1-6). That is to say, it looks like his miracles were physical examples of his teaching or utilized to make a point. Then, there are strong links between Jesus' teaching and the kingdom of God (4:1-20, 26-32; 9:1; 10:13-31; 12:28-34). Mark also presents Jesus as thwarting and frustrating the Jewish religious authorities with his superior wisdom and knowledge of Israel's scriptures (2:18-22, 25; 7:1-15; 12:13-34).

So, all of the above focuses on Jesus as a figure of power probably greater than any other figure of power known at the time. Mark's audience would have understood this as an impressive catalog of abilities, proof that Jesus was the Son of God.

The suffering savior motif is mostly absent from the first half of Mark's Gospel (1–8). However, there are a few scenes that include narrative elements that foreshadow the suffering and death to come.

> Now John's disciples and the Pharisees were fasting; and people came and said to him, "Why do John's disciples and the disciples of the Pharisees fast, but your disciples do not fast?" Jesus said to them, "The wedding guests cannot fast while the bridegroom is with them, can they? As long as they have the bridegroom with them, they cannot fast. The days will come when the bridegroom is taken away from them, and then they will fast on that day."[1081]

The removal of the bridegroom is presumably an allusion to Jesus' death.

The next 'disturbance in the force' is at the end of the pericope where Jesus heals the man with the withered hand on the Sabbath. Jesus asks the observers, "Is it lawful to do good or to do harm on the Sabbath, to save life or to kill?" Then, he heals the man, after which, "The Pharisees went out and immediately conspired with the Herodians against him, how to destroy him" (Mk 3:1-6).[1082] Winn suggests that Jesus' rejection in his hometown (Mk 6:1-6) is a foreshadowing of Jesus' future rejection by the Jews.

The first explicit passion prediction comes at Caesarea Philippi.

> Jesus went on with his disciples to the villages of Caesarea Philippi; and on the way he asked his disciples, "Who do people say that I am?" And they answered him, "John the Baptist; and others, Elijah; and still others, one of the prophets." He asked them, "But who do you say that I am?" Peter answered him, "You are the Messiah." And he sternly ordered them not to tell anyone about him.
>
> Then he began to teach them that the Son of Man must undergo great suffering, and be rejected by the elders, the chief priests, and the scribes, and be killed, and after three days rise again. He said all this quite openly. And Peter took him aside and began to rebuke him. But turning and looking at his disciples, he rebuked Peter and said, "Get behind me, Satan! For you are setting your mind not on divine things but on human things."[1083]

There are two additional passion predictions at 9:31 and 10:33-34. Each prediction includes the prediction of rising after three days, and is followed by a teaching from Jesus focusing on the themes of service, humility, and suffering. As Jesus willingly sacrifices himself for others, so also must his disciples follow his example; only those with the lowness and humility of a child are able to receive the kingdom of God (Mk 10:14-15).

Mark 12 begins with the Parable of the Tenants, a clear allegory in which Jesus is identified as the son of the vineyard owner (God). The tenants seizing and killing the son is an explicit prediction of Jesus' impending arrest and execution. Winn notes that it is here that Mark ties together Jesus' identity as God's son with suffering and death. Then, in Mark 14:3-9, a woman anoints Jesus' head with oil, an act that parallels the anointing of a royal figure. Jesus then redefines the anointing as being for his burial; thus, another reference to his impending death. In both of these pericopes, Mark gives Christological import to suffering and death.

In Mark 14:18-25 – the celebration of the Passover meal – the death of Jesus as sacrifice for humanity is presented unequivocally. Immediately following the meal, Jesus is betrayed by one

---

[1081] Mark 2:18-20.

[1082] The irony of this conspiracy being instituted on the Sabbath is clear.

[1083] Mark 8:27-33.

of his inner circle (14:10-11, 35-43); agonizes over his coming death, pleading with God to remove from him the cup of suffering (14:36); is arrested by armed men (14:42-49); is abandoned by his followers (14:50); is falsely accused (14:55-59); is spat on and beaten (14:65); is denied three times by Peter (14:66-72); is flogged and mocked by Roman soldiers (15:16-20); is sentenced to crucifixion by Pontius Pilate (15:15); during his crucifixion his clothes are divided among his executioners (15:24); he is mocked by spectators (15:29-31); he is executed alongside criminals (15:27); he cries loudly from the cross expressing utter abandonment (15:34); he is mocked for his cry by bystanders (15:35-36); then, with a final loud cry, he dies; with his final utterance, the temple veil splits from top to bottom (15:38); and then, oddly, the centurion standing at the foot of the cross, seeing him die, declares, "Truly this man was God's Son!"

Mark's passion narrative is an unrelenting representation of suffering on many levels, and this suffering is announced as that of the Son of God. Winn comments:

> After outlining the Markan material that illustrates Jesus as both a figure of extreme power and a figure of suffering, it is important to comment on how these two sets of Christological pieces are arranged. ... [T]he Jesus of power dominates the first half of Mark, with only a handful of details that foreshadow Jesus' suffering. ... But at the end of Mark 8, the tenor of the narrative takes a dramatic turn in regard to the nature of its Christological material. While the powerful Jesus of the first half of Mark does not disappear entirely, he seems to take a backseat to the suffering Jesus. Thus it seems that the first eight chapters of Mark emphasize Jesus' power, while the last eight emphasize Jesus' suffering. Such an organization of Christological material should play a significant role in the assessment of Mark's Christology.[1084]

There are certainly two sets of Christological material in Mark: one presents Jesus as powerful and successful, the other as suffering and human. Yet, even in his powerful aspect, Jesus is dedicated to serving others, exorcisms, healings and teaching. It is the Markan narrator, through the voice of God at the beginning and at the Transfiguration, through the voices of demons (supernatural beings), and, through the mouth of the Centurion at the end, who proclaims Jesus as the Son of God. Jesus, on the other hand, seeks to distance himself from such identification, preferring to focus on service, sacrifice and suffering.[1085] It was in the death and suffering aspect that Jesus truly revealed his identity as the Son of God, the divine agent of God's salvation, doing only what God could do: truly human, fully identified with human weakness and yet, with the knowledge and will to understand what God wanted, and to fulfill the mission in total obedience. In other words, God's power within was revealed in Jesus' human suffering and death, chosen freely and accomplished as a service to humanity. As Winn notes, "the theological content of Mark is embedded in and inseparable from the narrative itself."[1086]

Winn, like many others, thinks that the most plausible provenance for the writing of Mark was Rome. He cites the patristic evidence and then points out that the internal evidence – many Latinisms in the text – also support this view. The conclusion is that Mark had an audience more familiar with Latin than Greek. He also notes, as others have, that the date must be in close temporal proximity to the Jewish War. Mark's presentation of the temple is decidedly negative. Jesus' symbolic judgment of the temple is sandwiched between episodes concerning a

---

[1084]Winn (2018), p. 9.

[1085]See Elizabeth Struthers Malbon, *Mark's Jesus: Characterization as Narrative Christology* (Waco, TX: Baylor University Press, 2009).

[1086]Winn (2018), p. 24.

fig tree that Jesus curses and which withers the next day (Mk 11:12-14, 20-21). There is a clear connection between the fig tree and the temple; as the cursed fig tree withered and died, so will the cursed temple. The Parable of the Tenants is about the temple and its guardians, the high priests, Pharisees, and scribes. In fact, chapters 11–12 are an entire literary unit with a distinct, negative temple motif. At the end of this comes an explicit prediction that the temple will be destroyed utterly (Mk 13:2). And that is clearly *vaticinium ex eventu*. Winn writes:

> [O]ne must ask about the rhetorical purpose of Mark's entire antitemple motif. In what way is this antitemple motif functioning for Mark's readers? Given that the Evangelist devotes two chapters to this motif, it must be of great importance and may in some way address the situation of Mark's audience. ... a related question becomes relevant concerning the ethnic makeup of Mark's audience. Scholars have long argued that Mark was written for a primarily Gentile audience. Mark 7:3-4 offers a detailed explanation of Jewish purity rituals, something one would expect in a Gospel written for Gentiles rather than Jews, who would not require such an explanation. ... Mark specifically refers to "all the Jews," a reference that seems to suggest a separation between his intended audience and those who are Jews. ...
>
> ... The amount of attention the Markan Evangelist gives to the Jewish temple surely indicates that Mark's Gentile audience is interested in it. But such an interest is strikingly absent in the New Testament. Our best window into the concerns of the early Gentile churches is no doubt the undisputed letters of Paul. But in these letters we see no interest in the Jerusalem temple. ... Paul never argues that the Jerusalem temple is corrupt and that it needs to be replaced. Nor does Paul argue that the temple has been replaced by the church. ... In light of this evidence it seems that the Jerusalem temple played no role in Paul's pastoral and missional work among Gentile churches. ... Thus all the existing evidence portrays an early Gentile Christian church that has no interest in the Jerusalem temple.
>
> I propose that the sharp contrast between the apparent lack of interest in the Jewish temple among Gentile Christians and Mark's clear interest in that same temple suggest that a significant development has taken place, something that has led otherwise uninterested Gentile Christians to care about the Jewish temple. Two obvious and related possibilities for such a development emerge: the Jewish revolt against Rome and the destruction of the Jewish temple itself. ... if the temple were still standing, the rhetorical power of such an antitemple motif is significantly weakened ...
>
> A far better option seems to be the destruction of Jerusalem itself. This destruction played a central role in the propaganda of the Flavian family and in its attempt to legitimize its power. It was featured in a massive triumph celebrating Vespasian and Titus's military accomplishments. It was also featured prominently on Roman architecture and coins. The message of this propaganda was quite clear: the Flavian family was a recipient of divine favor and that the gods who favored it, the Roman gods, were greater that the God of the Jews. Such propaganda would have almost certainly raised challenges for Gentile Christians, in particular recent converts from Roman paganism. Such Flavian propaganda would likely have led to serious questions among fledgling Christians about the legitimacy of their new faith. Perhaps a commitment to one crucified by the Roman power was indeed misguided, particularly since the God of that crucified savior had just been defeated by that same power. ...
>
> ... Like the Jewish prophets explaining the destruction of the first temple and like Jewish contemporaries explaining the destruction of the second temple, Mark claims that the Roman destruction of the temple was a result of its corruption, that it occurred according to God's purpose and was predicted by God's appointed ruler, Jesus. Through this move Mark disarmed Flavian propaganda and made Rome a pawn in the plans of Israel's God and Messiah.[1087]

[1087]Winn (2018), pp. 35–39. See also Mason's detailed study of the Jewish War.

After the death of Nero in 68 AD, the Roman Empire descended into political chaos. Nero had no heir and military leaders vied for power in civil war. Rome had four emperors in one year: Galba, a Roman governor who had rebelled against Nero was the first; he was replaced by one of his fellow conspirators, Otho, who betrayed him; Otho was opposed and defeated by the general Vitellius; Vitellius was then opposed and defeated by Vespasian, who had been serving in Galilee and Judea, putting down the Jewish revolt beginning in 66 AD.

> The Flavians, admittedly an obscure family, none of whose members had ever enjoyed high office, at last brought stable government to the Empire; they had found it drifting uneasily through a year of revolution in the course of which three successive emperors lost their lives by violence. We have no cause to be ashamed of the Flavian record, though it is generally admitted that Domitian's cruelty and greed justified his assassination.[1088]

When Vespasian assumed the purple, he had a mess on his hands. Again closely following Winn's account, Nero's irresponsible fiscal policies had left the Roman economy in shambles. But more problematical were Vespasian's ignoble origins. Having a lower-class citizen ruling over them did not sit well with the aristocratic elite families. Nevertheless, Vespasian had the backing of his legions and, while he was still suppressing revolts around the Empire, he launched another kind of war: propaganda.

A major piece of Vespasian's propaganda was his victory against the Jewish rebels and the destruction of Jerusalem and the Jewish temple. According to the ancient theology of victory, military victory could legitimate rule; victory in battle represented the gods' choice of ruler. The Roman triumphal procession was a display of the theology of Victory. In addition to an extravagant triumph, Vespasian began construction of a temple of peace to house the war booty paraded through the city of Rome. He minted coins to promote the theology of victory, and turned the temple tax that all Jews sent to Jerusalem into the *fiscus Judaicus*, which now had to be paid for the upkeep of the temple of Jupiter.[1089]

Vespasian's propaganda campaign also included stories about miraculous healings, prophecies and portents. While Vespasian was in Alexandria, prior to traveling to Rome as the new emperor, two persons were said to have been healed by him. These individuals claimed that they were sent to Vespasian to heal them by the god Serapis through dreams. The first person was blind and Vespasian applied his own spit to the man's eyes, resulting in sight being restored. The second had a withered or disfigured hand that was restored when Vespasian touched it with his foot! Having the power to heal further legitimized Vespasian's divine right to rule. Tacitus claimed that these miracles were still talked about thirty years later.

Suetonius lists eleven portents, some of which are also recorded by Tacitus and Cassius Dio.

> When Nero and Galba were both dead and Vitellius was disputing the purple with Otho, Vespasian began to remember his Imperial ambitions, which had originally been raised by the following omens. An ancient oak-tree, sacred to Mars, growing on the Flavian estate near Rome, put out a shoot for each of the three occasions when his mother was brought to bed; and these clearly had a bearing on the child's future. The first slim shoot withered quickly: and the eldest child, a girl, died within the year. The second shoot was long and healthy, promising good luck; but the third seemed more like a tree than a branch. Sabinus, the father, is said to have been greatly impressed by an inspection of

---

[1088]Suetonius, *Vesp.* 1, Robert Graves translation (1965).

[1089]Recall Brandon's interpretation of the tax pericope in Mark discussed above.

a victim's entrails, and to have congratulated his mother on having a grandson who would become Emperor. She roared with laughter and said: 'Fancy your going soft in the head before your old mother!'

Later, during Vespasian's aedileship, the Emperor Gaius Caligula, furious because Vespasian had not kept the streets clean, as was his duty, ordered some soldiers to load him with mud; they obeyed by stuffing into the fold of his senatorial gown as much as it could hold – an omen interpreted to mean that one day the soil of Italy would be neglected and trampled upon as the result of civil war, but that Vespasian would protect it and, so to speak, take it to his bosom.

Then a stray dog picked up a human hand at the cross-roads, which it brought into the room where Vespasian was breakfasting and dropped under the table; a hand being the emblem of power. On another occasion a plough-ox shook off its yoke, burst into Vespasian's dining room, scattered the servants, and fell at his feet, where it lowered its neck as if suddenly exhausted. He also found a cypress-tree lying uprooted on his grandfather's farm, though there had been no gale to account for the accident; yet by the next day it had taken root again and was greener and stronger than ever.

In Greece, Vespasian dreamed that he and his family would begin to prosper from the moment when Nero lost a tooth; and on the following day, while he was in the Imperial quarters, a dentist entered and showed him one of Nero's teeth which he had just extracted.

In Judaea, Vespasian consulted the God of Carmel and was given a promise that he would never be disappointed in what he planned or desired, however lofty his ambitions. Also, a distinguished Jewish prisoner of Vespasian's, Josephus by name, insisted that he would soon be released by the very man who had now put him in fetters, and who would then be Emperor. Reports of further omens came from Rome; Nero, it seemed, had been warned in a dream shortly before his death to take the sacred chariot of Jupiter Greatest and Best from the Capitol to the Circus, calling at Vespasian's house as he went. Soon after this, while Galba was on his way to the elections which gave him a second consulship, a statue of Julius Caesar turned of its own accord to face east; and at Betriacum, when the battle was about to begin, two eagles fought in full view of both armies, but a third appeared from the rising sun and drove off the victor.[1090]

Vespasian's most important piece of propaganda was the claim to be the long-awaited messiah of the Jews. Josephus wrote that the Jews rebelled against Rome because of misguided expectations that a world ruler would arise from among them. Considering the time in which he was writing, Suetonius could very well have read Josephus, but it is more likely that he got his information from Tacitus, who wrote about the Jewish War against Rome, including the following about Jerusalem:

Already the home of a motley concourse, [Jerusalem's] population had been swollen by the fall of the other Jewish cities, for the most determined partisan leaders escaped to the capital, and thereby added to the turmoil. There were three different leaders and three armies. The long outer perimeter of the walls was held by Simon, the central part of the city by John, and the Temple by Eleazar. John and Simon could rely on numbers and equipment, Eleazar on his strategic position. But it was upon each other that they turned the weapons of battle, ambush and fire, and great stocks of corn went up in flames. Then John sent off a party of men, ostensibly to offer sacrifice but in reality to cut Eleazar and his followers to pieces, thus gaining possession of the Temple. Hence-forward, therefore, Jerusalem was divided between two factions, until, on the approach of the Romans, fighting the foreigner healed the breach between them.

Prodigies had occurred, but their expiation by the offering of victims or solemn vows is held to be unlawful by a nation which is the slave of superstition and the enemy of true beliefs. In the sky

---

[1090]Suetonius, *Vesp.* 5.

appeared a vision of armies in conflict, of glittering armour. A sudden lightning flash from the clouds lit up the Temple. The doors of the holy place abruptly opened, a superhuman voice was heard to declare that the gods were leaving it, and in the same instant came the rushing tumult of their departure. Few people placed a sinister interpretation upon this. The majority were convinced that the ancient scriptures of their priests alluded to the present as the very time when the Orient would triumph and from Judaea would go forth men destined to rule the world. This mysterious prophecy really referred to Vespasian and Titus, but the common people, true to the selfish ambitions of mankind, thought that this mighty destiny was reserved for them, and not even their calamities opened their eyes to the truth.[1091]

Recall what Josephus said about the war and Vespasian's role:

> What did the most to induce the Jews to start this war, was an ambiguous oracle that was also found in their sacred writings, how, about that time, one from their country should become governor of the habitable earth. The Jews took this prediction to belong to themselves in particular, and many of the wise men were thereby deceived in their determination. Now this oracle certainly denoted the government of Vespasian, who was appointed emperor in Judea.[1092]

The "ambiguous oracle" was known as the Balaam prophecy: "a star shall come out of Jacob and a scepter will rise out of Israel. It shall crush the foreheads of Moab and break down all the sons of Sheth. Edom shall be dispossessed" (Num. 24:17-19).

In the view of Josephus, the Sicarii and Zealots had ruined Judea, and God had sent the Roman general to punish the Jews.

> I cannot but think that it was because God had doomed this city to destruction, as a polluted city, and was resolved to purge his sanctuary by fire, that he cut off those who clung to them with such tender affection.[1093]
>
> But these Zealots came at last to that degree of barbarity as not to bestow a burial either on those slain in the city, or on those that lay along the roads; but as if they had made an agreement to cancel both the laws of their country and the laws of nature, and, at the same time that they defiled men with their wicked action, they would pollute the Divinity itself also, they left the dead bodies to putrify under the sun.
>
> ... These men, therefore, trampled upon all the laws of man, and laughed at the Laws of God; and for the oracles of the prophets, they ridiculed them as the tricks of jugglers. Yet did these prophets foretell many things concerning virtue and vice, by the transgression of which these Zealots occasioned the fulfilling of those very prophecies belonging to their country.
>
> For there was a certain ancient oracle of those men, that the city should then be taken and the sanctuary burnt, by right of war, when a sedition should invade the Jews and their own hands should pollute the Temple of God. Now, while these Zealots did not disbelieve these predictions, they made themselves the instruments of their accomplishment.[1094]

In previous times, God had sent the Jews into exile in Egypt and Babylon; and he had used the Assyrian and Babylonian armies to punish them. This punishment was God's way to restore the true Israel. Also, to call a foreigner a messiah was nothing new: the Persian king Cyrus the Great had already been considered the Messiah, as already discussed.

[1091] Tacitus, *Histories* 5.12–13.
[1092] *War* 6.312–313.
[1093] *War* 4.5.2 (323).
[1094] *War* 4.6.3 (381–388).

Suetonius gave the same information, though he did not reference any Jewish prophecies. He may have used the same source that Tacitus used.

> There had spread over all the Orient an old and established belief, that it was fated for men coming from Judaea to rule the world. This prediction, referring to the emperor of Rome – as afterwards appeared from the event – the people of Judaea took to themselves; accordingly they revolted ...[1095]

Finally, there was a comet in late 64:

> At the close of the year, report was busy with portents heralding disaster to come – lightning-flashes in numbers never exceeded, a comet (a phenomenon to which Nero always made atonement in noble blood); two-headed embryos, human or of the other animals, thrown out in public or discovered in the sacrifices where it is the rule to kill pregnant victims. Again, in the territory of Placentia, a calf was born close to the road with the head grown to a leg; and there followed an interpretation of the soothsayers, stating that another head was being prepared for the world; but it would be neither strong nor secret, as it had been repressed in the womb, and had been brought forth at the wayside.[1096]

And apparently another comet in 66 AD, according to Josephus:

> Thus were the miserable people persuaded by these deceivers, and such as belied God himself; while they did not attend nor give credit to the signs that were so evident, and did so plainly foretell their future desolation, but, like men infatuated, without either eyes to see or minds to consider, did not regard the denunciations that God made to them.
>
> Thus there was a star resembling a sword, which stood over the city, and a comet, that continued a whole year.
>
> Thus also before the Jews' rebellion, and before those commotions which preceded the war, when the people were come in great crowds to the feast of unleavened bread, on the eighth day of the month Xanthicus, [Nisan, April, about a week before Passover] and at the ninth hour of the night, so great a light shone round the altar and the holy house, that it appeared to be bright day time; which lasted for half an hour. This light seemed to be a good sign to the unskillful, but was so interpreted by the sacred scribes, as to portend those events that followed immediately upon it. At the same festival also, a heifer, as she was led by the high priest to be sacrificed, brought forth a lamb in the midst of the temple.
>
> Moreover, the eastern gate of the inner temple, which was of brass, and vastly heavy, and had been with difficulty shut by twenty men, and rested upon a basis armed with iron, and had bolts fastened very deep into the firm floor, which was there made of one entire stone, was seen to be opened of its own accord about the sixth hour of the night. Now those that kept watch in the temple came hereupon running to the captain of the temple, and told him of it; who then came up thither, and not without great difficulty was able to shut the gate again. This also appeared to the vulgar to be a very happy prodigy, as if God did thereby open them the gate of happiness. But the men of learning understood it, that the security of their holy house was dissolved of its own accord, and that the gate was opened for the advantage of their enemies. So these publicly declared that the signal foreshowed the desolation that was coming upon them.
>
> Besides these, a few days after that feast, on the one and twentieth day of the month Artemisius, [Iyar, May or June] a certain prodigious and incredible phenomenon appeared: I suppose the account of it would seem to be a fable, were it not related by those that saw it, and were not the events that

---

[1095]Suet., *Vesp.* 4.5.
[1096]Tac., *Ann.* 15.47.

followed it of so considerable a nature as to deserve such signals; for, before sun-setting, chariots and troops of soldiers in their armor were seen running about among the clouds, and surrounding of cities.

Moreover, at that feast which we call Pentecost, as the priests were going by night into the inner [court of the temple,] as their custom was, to perform their sacred ministrations, they said that, in the first place, they felt a quaking, and heard a great noise, and after that they heard a sound as of a great multitude, saying, "Let us remove hence."

But, what is still more terrible, there was one Jesus, the son of Ananus, a plebeian and a husbandman, who, four years before the war began, and at a time when the city was in very great peace and prosperity, came to that feast whereon it is our custom for every one to make tabernacles to God in the temple [Sukkot, autumn, 62 CE], began on a sudden to cry aloud,

"A voice from the east, a voice from the west, a voice from the four winds, a voice against Jerusalem and the Holy House, a voice against the bridegrooms and the brides, and a voice against this whole people!"

This was his cry, as he went about by day and by night, in all the lanes of the city.

However, certain of the most eminent among the populace had great indignation at this dire cry of his, and took up the man, and gave him a great number of severe stripes; yet did not he either say any thing for himself, or any thing peculiar to those that chastised him, but still went on with the same words which he cried before.

Hereupon the magistrates, supposing, as the case proved to be, that this was a sort of divine fury in the man, brought him to the Roman procurator, where he was whipped till his bones were laid bare; yet he did not make any supplication for himself, nor shed any tears, but turning his voice to the most lamentable tone possible, at every stroke of the whip his answer was,

"Woe, woe to Jerusalem!"

And when Albinus (for he was then our procurator) asked him, Who he was? and whence he came? and why he uttered such words? he made no manner of reply to what he said, but still did not leave off his melancholy ditty, till Albinus took him to be a madman, and dismissed him.

Now, during all the time that passed before the war began, this man did not go near any of the citizens, nor was seen by them while he said so; but he every day uttered these lamentable words, as if it were his premeditated vow,

"Woe, woe to Jerusalem!"

Nor did he give ill words to any of those that beat him every day, nor good words to those that gave him food; but this was his reply to all men, and indeed no other than a melancholy presage of what was to come.

This cry of his was the loudest at the festivals; and he continued this ditty for seven years and five months, without growing hoarse, or being tired therewith, until the very time that he saw his presage in earnest fulfilled in our siege, when it ceased; for as he was going round upon the wall, he cried out with his utmost force,

"Woe, woe to the city again, and to the people, and to the Holy House!"

And just as he added at the last,

"Woe, woe to myself also!"

there came a stone out of one of the engines, and smote him, and killed him immediately; and as he was uttering the very same presages he gave up the ghost.[1097]

To the ancients, comets always portended momentous events, usually disasters. As G. Goldberg writes:

[1097] *Wars* 6.5.3 (288–309).

The next six signs that are described occur within days of each other, in an unspecified year ... Just before the Passover celebration three of these signs occur together, and just after it the chariots in the air appear. Fifty days after this same Passover, on Shavuot (Pentecost), the earthquake and strange sounds occur. And Jesus ben Ananias first makes his appearance at the festival of Sukkot.

One notes that Passover is a spring festival, and Sukkot an autumn one, suggesting that these all occurred within the same year, which, by the clues given (Albinus as procurator, the duration of Jesus' lamentation), would have been 62. As it happens, Josephus was most likely in Rome in that year, not in Jerusalem [according to his *Life*].

[One] cannot fail to notice the parallels in these passages with events surrounding Jesus of Nazareth. The fantastic events occurring at the Passover bring to mind those related [to the passion narrative], also at Passover, when the curtain of the Temple was split in two [and the sky went dark]. At the following Pentecost [according to Acts] the apostles have a vision of Jesus and begin to speak in tongues [accompanied by rushing sounds]. [In Josephus' text, rushing] sounds and voices are heard ...

The sad story of Jesus son of Ananias related by Josephus has a number of parallels with the New Testament, the first of which is the coincidence of a man named Jesus prophesying against the Temple. ... one wonders if the tales of the two Jesuses became intertwined by their tellers, with elements of one story creeping into the narrative of the other.[1098]

Coming back now to Vespasian and his propaganda, Winn writes:

But perhaps the most important piece of propaganda for my purposes is Vespasian's claim to be the true fulfillment of Jewish messianic prophecies and expectations. Three different Roman historians claim that Jews rebelled against Rome because of misguided expectations that a world ruler would arise from among them, expectations that find their origin in the prophecies of Jewish Scripture. All three of these historians claim that the true fulfillment of such prophecies was the political rise of Vespasian, who became ruler of the world while in the Roman East.[1099]

Winn goes on to note that there was obviously some kind of prophecy or tradition going around in Rome itself. He points out that despite the fact that some think this idea originated with Josephus, Tacitus does not seem to be dependent on Josephus, nor does Suetonius. Josephus scholars note that this block of text in Josephus appears to have been lifted directly from a different source and forced into the longer narrative. Winn believes that the idea of Vespasian being the fulfillment of prophecy originated in the propaganda of the Flavian family itself. The propaganda was cleverly crafted to do several things, according to Winn: 1) it pointed to Vespasian's military victory as divine legitimation; 2) it tied Vespasian to the prophecies from sacred texts furthering his divine legitimation; 3) it sent an ominous warning to any Jewish (or Christian?) group that might consider using its sacred scriptures as justification for rebellion.

Vespasian's propaganda would have communicated the superiority of Rome's gods over the god of Israel, thus seriously challenging the Christian belief in the god of Israel and Jesus as his chosen sovereign ruler over the world.

Now, we have mentioned numerous times that it seems clear that Paul's Christ was not the same 'Jesus' as was promoted by the Jewish Christians of Jerusalem. It has even been noted that it appears quite possible that Paul's Christ was not even Jewish, though Paul saw him as the chosen messiah of the Jewish God just as Cyrus had been. So, at this point, I think it

---

[1098]http://www.josephus.org/causeofDestruct.htm.
[1099]Winn (2018), p. 46.

needs to be seriously considered that Mark deliberately made his fictional Son of God Jewish in order to cement the claim to his being the son of the Jewish God; to strengthen the tie; to help to reconcile the differences between the Jewish Christians of Rome and the Gentile Christians there. After all, it was by way of the Jewish scriptures that Paul identified his Christ and figured out what God's plan was. Even though I have diverged strongly from Winn on this point, his comments are nevertheless helpful:

> Certainly some Roman converts to Christianity, converts who had committed themselves to a crucified world ruler who currently reigned in the heavens ... might have questioned whether they were actually on the right side. ... For potential Gentile converts to Christianity, a crucified Jewish lord and savior would have paled in comparison to the impressive resume of Vespasian. ... Such a crisis would require a strong pastoral response that undermined Flavian propaganda and made a convincing case that Jesus was God's Messiah and the true ruler of the world.
> It is from within this historical situation that I propose Mark's narrative be read ...[1100]

As the reader can see, Winn's historical situation and reading of Mark is quite similar to that of S. G. F. Brandon, as well as Joel Marcus. Brandon proposed that Mark was written as apology, while Winn is proposing that it was written as counter-propaganda. The two concepts are not actually that far apart, though Winn makes more and stronger arguments for his case. (Curiously, Brandon is never mentioned by Winn.)

Winn points out that the different Christological titles that Mark applies to Jesus, through the voices of his characters or narrator, probably were not unknown to his audience; in fact, the Markan text assumes that the reader has some knowledge of those terms. Jesus is clearly defined as the Jewish messiah at three different points: 8:29, 9:41 and 14:61-62. However, how would Mark's readers understand this title? There was a great variety of Jewish messianic thought, as we have learned from many texts, including Josephus and the Dead Sea Scrolls. What is most likely is that Mark's audience of Gentile Christians would have understood 'messiah' as Paul did: God's appointed ruler both on Earth and in heaven, as well as the new Adam. Though they would also see that for the characters of the story, the word would have more militant and 'fleshly' connotations. In other words, they would see what the disciples in the story cannot. But Mark is not content to leave it there, since 'messiah' isn't enough for him. So one suspects that by using additional titles, Mark is shaping the way his audience will understand who Christ is, at the same time redefining and enlarging the scope of the familiar titles.

Jesus is identified as God's son seven times in Mark (1:1, 11; 3:11; 5:7; 8:7; 14:61; 15:39), and two of those times are the *voice of God* affirming the fact (1:11; 9:7). Two times, demons with supernatural knowledge affirm it, and then Jesus himself affirms it in his answer to the high priest (14:61). In short, this title is at the beginning, middle, and end of the narrative. Thus, it appears to me that Mark's understanding of 'messiah,' or the understanding he wished to shape in the minds of his readers, was significantly different than the understanding of the rank and file of Jews. This is surely clear in Jesus' response to Peter after the latter identifies Jesus as messiah (8:33) and then rebukes him for declaring that the messiah Son of Man must suffer and die. Jesus replies: "Get behind me, Satan! For you are setting your mind not on divine things but on human things." Recall that the Jews expected their messiah to come and be an earthly king and, barring that, to come from heaven with legions of angels to destroy the Romans. That

---

[1100]Winn (2018), p. 48.

didn't happen, and now Mark is using his narrative to explain why: the Jews didn't understand; only Paul did.

On the other side, the title 'Son of God' had a very definite meaning in a Greco-Roman context. As Winn writes, "rulers were commonly identified as sons of gods." Augustus adopted the title because the deified Julius Caesar had adopted him as his heir. Julius Caesar himself was identified as the son of the goddess Venus, who was said to have taken his spirit out of his body before – or as – he was killed. Many successors of Augustus, like Tiberius, Germanicus and Nero, also claimed divine sonship. Thus, it seems that these elements would have come immediately to mind in Mark's audience. Perhaps they would have understood that Paul's Son of God was being affirmed as the Jewish messianic ruler and that Mark was placing him in the same category as the great rulers of the world. Winn writes:

> This type of "double coding" would have allowed the Markan Evangelist a wide range of options for how the title "Son of God" might be employed. Such a tool that would be particularly useful if realities grounded in a Jewish context were perceived to be in conflict with realities grounded in a Greco-Roman one.[1101]

Though Winn is arguing in a different direction than I am, I agree that there was double coding going on and that there were many clues in Mark as to the identity of Paul's Christ.

The Son of Man

Mark's Jesus *identifies himself* as 'Son of Man,' which is extremely interesting. The Hebrew expression 'son of man' (*ben-'adam*) appears 107 times in the Hebrew Bible as a form of address, the majority of occurrences (93 times) in the book of Ezekiel. In the book of Daniel, it is used to describe a future eschatological figure whose coming will signal the end of history and the time of God's judgment (Dan. 7:13-14). The phrase "one like a man" certainly implicates a 'human being,' but also stands for "the saints of the Most High" (Mk 7:18, 21-22) and "the people of the saints of the Most High" (Mk 7:27).

It is only in Mark that the indefinite 'son of man' is transformed into the definite 'the Son of Man.' It is said to be an awkward and ambiguous expression in Greek.

> German theologian Rudolf Bultmann sees the phrase not as one genuinely used by Jesus but as one inserted by the early Church. [The opposite opinion is expressed by] theologian C. F. D. Moule, who argues that the phrase 'the Son of Man', "so far from being a title evolved from current apocalyptic thought by the early Church and put by it into the mouth of Jesus, is among the most important symbols used by Jesus himself to describe his vocation and that of those whom he summoned to be with him."[1102]

So, the primary evidence is ambiguous and we really don't know how Mark's readers would have understood 'Son of Man' (though Winn notes that no character in Mark hails Jesus by that title aside from Jesus himself. To understand what Mark intended here, we need to look at the different uses of the phrase in the Gospel. Winn writes:

[1101]Winn (2018), p. 54.
[1102]Wikipedia.org, 'Son of man.'

The first two instances of Jesus' use of "Son of Man" come in the context of Jesus' claiming significant power (i.e. the power to forgive sins [Mk 2:10] and lordship over the Sabbath [Mk 2:28]). Thus it seems the title is closely associated with unique powers possessed by Jesus. It is noteworthy that no explanation is given to the reader of Jesus' identity as "Son of Man" or of why that identity might bring with it these unique powers. One might then conclude that either the readers are expected to already possess knowledge that will enable them to understand the significance of these claims or they are expected to look for such knowledge as they encounter the rest of the narrative.[1103]

It may be notable that the vast majority of the rest of the uses of 'Son of Man' are in the context of Jesus' approaching suffering and death, including the passion predictions (8:31; 9:31; 10:33-45), Jesus' purpose to give his life as a ransom for humanity (10:45), and his betrayal (14:21, 41). The reader is given no explanation, nor is it clear how the power to forgive sins – and over the Sabbath – are related to Jesus' suffering and death.

There are three uses of 'Son of Man' that relate Jesus to Daniel's apocalyptic Son of Man (Dan. 7:13-14), a figure to whom God grants eternal dominion over the entire Earth. Winn notes that this usage expands the 'Jewish Messiah' concept (rule over Judea) to global import (over the entire world). Since Mark did not have to explain the usage to his readers, Winn suggests that they already understood that 'Son of Man' was in some way synonymous with 'messiah.' He gives three examples that strongly support his contention. The first is when Mark follows Peter's declaration of Jesus' identity as the Messiah by saying, "Then he began to teach them that the Son of Man must undergo great suffering" (Mk 8:31). This is best understood as Jesus clarifying Peter's messianic claim. The second is in the transfiguration narrative where, after God declares that Jesus is his son, Mark narrates: "As they were coming down the mountain, he ordered them to tell no one about what they had seen, until after the Son of Man had risen from the dead" (Mk 9:9). Mark apparently sees 'Son of Man' as somehow equivalent to, or contained within, 'Son of God.' Third, during Jesus' trial before the high priest, he is asked, "Are you the Messiah, the Son of the Blessed One?" (Mk 14:61), to which Jesus replies: "I am; and 'you will see the Son of Man seated at the right hand of the Power,' and 'coming with the clouds of heaven'." Effectively, then, for Mark's audience, all of these titles were in some way equivalent. Jesus *was* the Danielic messiah, the Son of Man, but he was also *more* than that, the Son of God, which that entailed.

And yet, in Mark's text, it is only Jesus who refers to himself that way. Why? Contra Winn's suggestion that the title was remembered from some actual 'Jesus of Nazareth' tradition, I would suggest that it reflects Paul's 'Second Adam' theology – which Paul got from Enoch and Daniel – and that it was understood that way by Pauline Christians.

As we saw earlier when examining Paul's theology, the Genesis account was essential for Paul's vision of a new 'kingdom' of 'faith' and 'right action' to replace the old kingdom. Adam (and Eve) represented mankind in their original, pure form, manifesting God's creative dominion over creation. Their disobedience and resulting Fall were not a mistake, but a necessary feature of creation. Through them humanity acquires experience and knowledge in order to fully come into its true potential. Christ's purpose was to reverse the Fall – to complete the lesson plan. Whereas Adam was a 'living soul,' Christ was an 'alive-making spirit' – the 'last Adam' – to give life to what was dead, and this transformation applied to both humanity and the cosmos at large. Whereas Adam introduced sin and separation, Christ killed the power of sin in order to reestablish the connection, by dying in the place of all humanity.

[1103]Winn (2018), p. 57.

Recall that, for Paul, it was the death of Jesus that was of apocalyptic significance. It was at the moment he died that his divine sonship was revealed to the archons. And Paul repeatedly asserts that it is in weakness that the power of God is revealed. How can this be? Quite simply: it was because accepting suffering and death in obedience to God was a demonstration of the power of God *over the flesh*; Jesus accepted death by his faith in the unseen; he was not identified with his flesh or the material separation of the self from God. And so, God's way of doing what is right was made manifest: here is a creature who acted as God in the face of all material evidence to the contrary of his choice. The allegorical depiction of this is what Jesus as 'the Son of Man' in the Gospel of Mark makes plain.

Consider the fact that in the 'Similitudes of Enoch' (*1 Enoch* 37–71), Daniel 7 is used to produce "an unparalleled messianic Son of Man, *pre-existent and hidden yet ultimately revealed*, functioning as judge, vindicator of righteousness, and universal ruler," just as Paul and Mark depicted Christ. "The Enochic messianic figure is an individual representing a group (the Righteous One who represents the righteous, the Elect One representing the elect) ... Whether these messianic 'Son of Man' references are genuinely Jewish or the result of Christian interpolation is disputed."[1104]

Consider Mark's incipit: "The beginning of the good news (gospel/evangelion) of Jesus Christ, the Son of God."[1105] This title and programmatic announcement has echoes in Isaiah 40:9; 41:27; 52:7; 60:6; 61:1.

> The "one who proclaims good news" announces God's victory over the enemies of Israel (Is 41:27) and the reestablishment of God's righteous reign over Israel (Is 40:9-10; 52:7). [The fact that] the incipit is followed by a citation from Isaiah's Servant Song (Is 40:3) serves to strengthen the connection between Mark's incipit and "the one who proclaims good news." [This] conclusion is also supported by the first words spoken by the Markan Jesus, who enters Galilee saying, "The time is fulfilled, and the kingdom of God has come near; repent, and believe in the good news" (Mk 1:15). Thus, [Mark's incipit identifies] Jesus as the one who both proclaims and establishes, in his own being and death, the Isaianic good news.[1106]

At the same time, the language of the incipit is most decidedly reflective of the Roman imperial world. *Evangelion*, a Greek word, was "regularly associated with Roman emperors [and] was often used to describe their birth, political ascension, and military victories." Josephus strongly associates the word with Vespasian (*War* 4). More important, however, is the Priene Calendar Inscription which honored Augustus:

> Since Providence, which has ordered all things and is deeply interested in our life, has set in most perfect order by giving us Augustus, whom she filled with virtue that he might benefit humankind, sending him as a savior, both for us and for our descendants, that he might end war and arrange all things, and since he, Caesar, by his appearance (excelled even our anticipations), surpassing all previous benefactors, and not even leaving to posterity any hope of surpassing what he has done, and *since the birthday of the god Augustus was the beginning of the good tidings for the world* that came by reason of him.[1107]

[1104]Wikipedia.org, 'Son of Man,' citing G. Nickelsburg, 'Son of Man,' in *Anchor Bible Dictionary* 6.138.

[1105]Leaving aside textual issues discussed by Winn, I think that this is original to Mark mainly because it appears in dramatic context at the beginning, in the middle, and at the end of the Gospel. Mark is so finely structured it would 'break the set' for it to not be present. David Oliver Smith argues similarly in *Unlocking the Puzzle* (2016).

[1106]Winn (2018), p. 71.

[1107]Craig A. Evans translation, quoted by Winn (2018), p. 72.

Notably, in this inscription, Augustus is identified as a god, but that appeared to be interchangeable with 'Son of God,' as it was for his adopted father, Julius Caesar.

Therefore, undoubtedly, Mark's audience would have recognized the Roman imperial language as had been applied to Julius Caesar and nearly every emperor since him. It appears that one cannot argue for a strictly Jewish background nor a strictly Roman one. It appears that Mark has intentionally brought them together, just as Vespasian had already merged Jewish messianism with Roman reality on the ground. Winn believes that Mark intentionally mirrored Vespasian's merging of these two concepts and was, more or less, in dialog with it.

In Mark 1:11, when God announces to Jesus, "You are My Beloved Son; in You I am well pleased," there are clear echoes of both Psalm 2:7, a royal coronation psalm, and Isaiah 42:1, the latter being about Cyrus the Great: "I have put My Spirit upon Him; He will bring forth justice and right and reveal truth to the nations." And: "I am the LORD, I have called you in righteousness, I have taken you by the hand and kept you; I have given you as a covenant to the people, a light to the nations, to open the eyes that are blind, to bring out the prisoners from the dungeon, from the prison those who sit in darkness." That entire chapter of Isaiah is worth reading for themes that appear in Mark's Gospel.[1108] But the most important point is that at least some of Mark's audience very likely were aware of the scriptural allusion and it was those who had "eyes to see and ears to hear" at whom the allusions were aimed; those allusions were to *a Gentile messiah*.

Next begins Jesus' ministry of power in Galilee. Why Galilee? Was it intended to create an allusion to Judas of Galilee? One would think that a Davidic messiah would hail from Judea. But we also can recall a remark by Origen cited by the church father Jerome, which said that the Apostle Paul actually came from Gischala in Upper Galilee.[1109] If true, then Mark's audience most likely knew it too and would have made the connection, understanding that the "beginning of the Gospel" was exactly as Clement said: with Paul. They would have understood that this story of Jesus of Nazareth (a town that did not even exist at that time[1110]) was an allegory of Paul's Christ. And still, with the locale being Galilee, the less-educated Christians would be able to conflate the Jewish messiah with Paul's Christ; and I think that was intentional, just as the merging of the Isaianic allusions with Roman imperial ideology was intentional. Whoever the Markan author was, he was a very clever individual. The educated members of Mark's audience would have been aware of the many literary allusions in the rest of Mark's text and would have understood that the entire story was an allegory of Paul's Christ; of that, there is no doubt in my mind. But, again, the less educated would not.

Jesus' first miracle, the healing of the man with an unclean spirit (Mk 1:21-26) alludes to the Christ that Paul presented, whose main objective was to defeat the powers of the supernatural realm that opposes God. Then he heals Peter's mother-in-law, followed by a narrative mention of many healings and exorcisms: "And he cured many who were sick with various diseases, and cast out many demons; and he would not permit the demons to speak, because they knew him" (Mk 1:34). His popularity grew to the point that crowds pressed on him wherever he went,

---

[1108]See also Joel Marcus's *The Way of the Lord: Christological Exegesis of the Old Testament in the Gospel of Mark* (Westminster John Knox Press, 1992), which focuses on some of these themes.

[1109]Jerome, in *Epist. ad Philem.* 23, *De viris inlustr.* 5.

[1110]Salm (2008). Additionally, David Oliver Smith (2016, pp. 33–34, 63) argues that the single occurrence of 'Nazareth' in Mark 1:9 originally read 'Nazarene,' and that Jesus' hometown in Mark is actually Capernaum.

all of which is intended to demonstrate his enormous power, and then, in the pericope of the healing of the paralytic in Capernaum, the source of his power is addressed. Instead of healing the paralytic, who has been lowered through a hole in the roof, he instead says, "Your sins are forgiven." This angers the scribes sitting nearby, who questioned this act "in their hearts," since only God can forgive sins. Jesus read their thoughts and let them know that he was doing so: "Why do you raise such questions in your hearts? Which is easier, to say to the paralytic, 'Your sins are forgiven,' or to say, 'Stand up and take your mat and walk'?" (Mk 2:8b-9). The point appears to be: who can do either, since it is as difficult to heal as it is to forgive sins; only great supernatural power and authority can accomplish such things. And then he declares that he will demonstrate his ability to do the healing so that they will know that he also has the power to forgive sins. And it is here that he first refers to himself as 'Son of Man': "'But so that you may know that the Son of Man has authority on Earth to forgive sins'– he said to the paralytic – 'I say to you, stand up, take your mat and go to your home'" (Mk 2:10-11). In this maneuver, Jesus demonstrates his power to heal and forgive sins and links that power explicitly to his identity as the 'Son of Man.' Winn writes:

> The intention of Jesus' statement seems to be an explanation of the scope of the Son of Man's power on earth, power that presumably, to the surprise of Jesus' audience, includes the power to forgive sins. This statement by Jesus presumes that his audience knows what "Son of Man" he is talking about, otherwise his explanation of the scope of the Son of Man's power becomes unintelligible. Jesus' statement makes perfect sense as a statement about the scope of the divine power and authority granted to the eschatological "Son of Man" in Daniel (Dan 7:13-14), a figure that Mark presupposes both the characters in his narrative and his readers are familiar with. Thus I contend that the Markan Jesus is identifying himself as God's Messiah in this passage. Literally, the passage functions as a culmination of the series of miraculous deeds that illustrate Jesus' messianic power, but it also expands that power to include the forgiveness of sins and grounds that power in Jesus' identity as the eschatological and Danielic Son of Man.[1111]

I agree completely. I would add, however, that Daniel's Son of Man was perceived by Mark's audience as somehow associated with the Second Adam of Paul – perhaps the association was even created by Paul himself, who may have been inspired to the connection via his scriptural exegesis and/or visionary experiences.

There is yet another take on the 'Son of Man' from Thomas R. Hatina,[1112] who points out that Mark's audience may very well have understood the title as *a reference to divine judgment*, particularly in relation to the destruction of Jerusalem and the temple. I think it is probably reasonable to assume that Mark's readers/hearers had some idea of this role of 'Son of Man' as the arbiter of judgment and destruction, and, like a sub-theme, it threads its way through the Gospel of Mark, hinting that the destruction of Jerusalem and its temple was due to the Jewish Christian Zealots' rejection of the true Messiah, Paul's Christ. I will return to this below.

Winn points out that the pattern of illustrating Jesus' power by providing signs, followed by examples of how different persons, or groups, respond to those signs and interpretations of Jesus' identity, continues through Jesus' Galilean ministry. The religious leaders of the Jews consistently respond negatively while the reactions of the public and Jesus' disciples is mixed. Sometimes

---

[1111]Winn (2018), p. 76.

[1112]Thomas R. Hatina, 'The Focus of Mark 13:24-27: The Parousia, or the Destruction of the Temple?' *Bulletin for Biblical Research* 6 (1996), pp. 43–66.

the disciples are shown to be responding correctly, but more often, they show complete lack of understanding and faith. The pattern culminates in Mark 7:24–8:9 which records the exorcism of the Syrophoenician woman's daughter, the healing of a deaf-mute, and the feeding of the four thousand, all three apparently taking place in Gentile territory. This series is followed by a scene in which Jesus encounters the Pharisees, who ask for a sign, a request that Jesus denies (Mk 8:11-13). This is a highly ironic episode, considering that it follows such a series of miracles from the beginning of his ministry. One is almost aghast at the request; what was Jesus doing if not providing signs? The Markan audience may even have laughed uproariously at this cheek and its indicated lack of faith and opposition toward God.

However, even more significant is when Mark immediately notes in the next pericope that the disciples were apparently worried about the fact that they had forgotten to bring any bread when they got in the boat to sail across the lake. At this moment, Jesus cautions them to "beware of the yeast of the Pharisees and the yeast of Herod." Since he has just encountered Pharisees asking for a sign, it is clear what this "yeast" is: again, it is lack of faith in who Jesus is, and opposition toward God; seeking after a sign. And here, Jesus is concerned that this yeast has invaded his disciples.[1113] And truly, they do not seem to understand even at this point, which causes Jesus to rebuke them harshly: "Why are you talking about having no bread? Do you still not perceive or understand? Are your hearts hardened? Do you have eyes, and fail to see? Do you have ears, and fail to hear?" (Mk 8:17b-18). These words echo the earlier words (Mk 4:12) where the Markan Jesus talks about outsiders who cannot receive the secrets of the kingdom; at this point, the implication is that the disciples, too, are outsiders. He reminds them of the miracles of feeding thousands of people and having food left over, and still they do not seem to get the point. The pericope ends with no positive resolution for the disciples (Mk 8:21).

Immediately after the episode where he asks his disciples if they have eyes, but fail to see, Jesus heals a blind man. And in this case, he has to use physical means to do so: he puts spittle on the man's eye. Yet, that doesn't quite do it; it requires a second laying on of hands to effect a total cure. It has long been thought that this blind man represents the disciples, and his healing is to be contrasted to the healing of blind Bartimaeus (Mk 10:52), in which case he didn't even touch him as his faith was sufficient for a word to heal him.

Note the name: Bar Timaeus. *Timaeus* is a work by Plato (c. 360 BC) featuring a long monologue by Timaeus of Locri on the nature of reality: the physical world of change and entropy, and the eternal one which never changes. Whereas the physical world is one known only through sensation and opinion, the eternal is known via reason. There is also a remarkable saying found in this text: "As being is to becoming, so is truth to belief" (29c). Most certainly, those of Mark's audience who were educated would have gotten this allusion.

The Galilean ministry presents Jesus as a powerful healer and exorcist. The masses bring their sick to him to be healed. Most spectacular of all is Jesus' ability to even raise the dead back to life. Supernatural healings were a significant part of the Flavian propaganda about Vespasian. As noted, he healed a blind man and restored a withered or disfigured hand. The Markan Jesus

---

[1113] And note the possible allusion to 1 Corinthians 5:6-8: "Your boasting is not a good thing. Do you not know that *a little yeast leavens the whole batch of dough?* Clean out the old yeast so that you may be a new batch, as you really are unleavened. For our paschal lamb, Christ, has been sacrificed. Therefore, let us celebrate the festival, not with the old yeast, *the yeast of malice and evil*, but with the unleavened bread of sincerity and truth."

performs these same miracles, and even more significantly, he uses spittle to restore sight exactly as Vespasian did. Most certainly, Mark's audience knew the Flavian propaganda and recognized this comparison. Winn notes that the presence in Mark of two healings that directly parallel healings attributed to Vespasian must be an intentional comparison. And Jesus does so much more! This shows that Jesus is superior to Vespasian and therefore is the true messiah of the world. Additionally, the ability of Mark's Jesus to exorcise demons demonstrates his tremendous supernatural power. The fact that he can send demons packing with just words alone makes him more powerful than the known exorcists of ancient literature who had to rely on incantations and magical formulas to do anything even remotely close.

There are no known accounts of Roman emperors exorcising demons; one account of exorcism in Mark is of interest in this respect. In Mark 5:1-20, Jesus encounters a demoniac in what seems to be a Gentile area, Gerasa,[1114] and in his dialog with the man, he asks for the name of the demon. He receives the reply, "My name is Legion; for we are many" (5:9). A legion was a Roman military unit consisting of five or six thousand soldiers. Winn writes that there are many details in this pericope that suggest an intentional reference to the Roman military force. One of these details is that the Greek word used to describe the herd of pigs into which Jesus sends the demon(s) is the same word often used to describe military forces. Also, the Greek word used to describe the pigs rushing over the cliffs and into the sea is the same word commonly used to describe the charge of soldiers.[1115]

At this point, Winn goes slightly off track, stating that the Tenth Roman legion, *Legio X*, was stationed in Palestine (true), that its shields and banners carried the image of a boar (not true), and that this might somehow be related to the pigs of this pericope. In fact, *Legio X Fretensis* and *Legio X Gemina* both had *bulls* as their symbol. Indeed, some historians later came to believe that *Legio X Fretensis* adopted the wild boar as its emblem after the First Jewish Revolt because the image of a pig was raised by Hadrian at Jerusalem, where the legion was based. But Eusebius pointed out that Hadrian placed a marble idol of a domestic pig, not a boar, over Jerusalem's Bethlehem gate, for the purpose of "signifying the subjugation of the Jews to Roman authority" (Eus. *Chron.* Hadrian.19). Consequently, coins of the *Legio X Fretensis* which later showed a pig image – not the running boar used by other legions as an emblem – *refer to the city of Jerusalem*, not to the legion stationed there. When the 10th *Fretensis* later transferred to Arabia it was no longer associated with the pig symbol of Jerusalem.[1116]

What can one make of that? Hadrian's activity was later than the writing of Mark so could not have influenced it. However, looking at it another way, consider the description of the demoniac:

... a man out of the tombs with an unclean spirit met him. He lived among the tombs; and *no one could restrain him any more, even with a chain*; for he had often been restrained with shackles and chains, but the chains he wrenched apart, and the shackles he broke in pieces; and *no one had the strength to subdue him.* Night and day among the tombs and on the mountains he was always howling and bruising himself with stones. *When he saw Jesus from a distance, he ran and bowed*

[1114]One of the cities of the Roman Decapolis. Josephus mentions the city as being principally inhabited by Syrians, and also having a small Jewish community. (*Wars* 2.18.1)

[1115]There were several legions with the image of a boar on their shields: 1st Italica; 16th Gallica; 17th, 18th, 19th Gallica; 20th Valeria Victrix; 21st Rapax.

[1116]Stephen Dando-Collins, *Legions of Rome: The Definitive History of Every Imperial Roman Legion.* (London: Quercus, 2010), p. 160.

down before him; and he shouted at the top of his voice, "What have you to do with me, Jesus, Son of the Most High God? I adjure you by God, do not torment me."[1117]

We notice particularly that "no one could restrain him any more," "no one had the strength to subdue him," and then, surprisingly: "When he saw Jesus from a distance, he ran and bowed down before him." A force that cannot be restrained or subdued sounds a lot like the Roman Empire and its armies. So indeed, it appears that Winn was going in the right direction. But this demonically strong individual bowed down to Jesus, even from a distance, and recognized him: "What have you to do with me, Jesus, Son of the Most High God?" And then, Mark appears to depict the demonic strength and madness being cast out into the pigs, which possibly were intended to represent the Jewish rebels, all of whom immediately went over the cliff to destruction. Winn proposes:

> [T]he reader is invited to interpret Jesus' dramatic exorcism as a symbolic exorcism and defeat of Roman military power. Through the name "Legion," Mark intertwines the identity of supernatural demonic forces with those of Roman power ... and thus the Markan Jesus defeats both.[1118]

Winn is certainly right, as far as it goes, but in my opinion, the pigs may very well have represented the maddened Jews in revolt. However, I don't think that the pericope represents a reversal of Vespasian's military success. What it may represent is the openness of Gentiles to the gospel and the madness of Jews in rejecting Jesus.

The healing of the Gerasene demoniac is followed immediately by the pericope about Jairus, the leader of the synagogue (Jesus has crossed back over the lake), whose 12-year-old daughter was sick and dying, and the woman with an issue of blood for 12 years who touches Jesus and is healed. In the case of the woman, Jesus feels power go out of him at her touch. In the case of the little girl, he raises her from the dead, a pretty amazing display of power. The number 12 may suggest Israel, the Jews.

Then, Jesus returns home to be rejected by his family, friends and acquaintances. Mark says that "he could do no deed of power there," except for a few small healings. So power and the ability to heal link these pericopes together. The message seems to be "if you have faith, you have access to the power of Jesus." And, "No faith, no power."

In two pericopes, Mark presents Jesus as displaying power over nature. In the first, Mark 4:35-41, Jesus calms a raging storm on the lake with only words:

> And leaving the crowd behind, they took him with them in the boat, just as he was. Other boats were with him. A great windstorm arose, and the waves beat into the boat, so that the boat was already being swamped. But he was in the stern, asleep on the cushion; and they woke him up and said to him, "Teacher, do you not care that we are perishing?" He woke up and rebuked the wind, and said to the sea, "Peace! Be still!" Then the wind ceased, and there was a dead calm. He said to them, "Why are you afraid? Have you still no faith?" And they were filled with great awe and said to one another, "Who then is this, that even the wind and the sea obey him?"

The second, Mark 6:45-52, follows the feeding of the five thousand:

[1117]Mark 5:2b-7.
[1118]Winn (2018), p. 84.

Immediately he made his disciples get into the boat and go on ahead to the other side, to Bethsaida, while he dismissed the crowd. After saying farewell to them, he went up on the mountain to pray. When evening came, the boat was out on the sea, and he was alone on the land. When he saw that they were straining at the oars against an adverse wind, he came towards them early in the morning, walking on the sea. He intended to pass them by. But when they saw him walking on the sea, they thought it was a ghost and cried out; for they all saw him and were terrified. But immediately he spoke to them and said, "Take heart, it is I; do not be afraid." Then he got into the boat with them and the wind ceased. And they were utterly astounded, for they did not understand about the loaves, but their hearts were hardened.

There are other analyses of these stories that reveal various types of affinities to prior texts, including an episode in Homer; an adaptation of the Jonah narrative; comparison to Yahweh "passing by," commanding the storm, and so on. Winn points out that commanding seas and storms was a common motif in the propaganda of ancient rulers and that, in this light, Jesus' control of the wind and waves takes on a political and polemical dimension. Jesus, in fact, outdoes them all; while other rulers bring metaphorical peace to the seas, Jesus does so literally. This would be a further demonstration of Jesus' superiority to Vespasian.

The feeding miracles are, of course, supernatural provision of food, just as God provided manna to the wandering Israelites in the desert after they had fled Egypt. In 2 Kings 4:42-44, Elisha also multiplies loaves. Winn notes that few have considered how these stories fit into a Roman imperial context where the emperor is patron of the citizens of Rome and assures them of survival with provision of bread. This fact has become part of a commonplace: 'bread and circuses.' It was the duty of the emperor to ensure the grain supply to the city and to give generous gifts of it in times of need. And, as it happens, as soon as Vespasian was declared emperor, while in Alexandria, he sent grain to Rome, which was already in danger of running out of supplies due to the civil war that was raging at the time.

So, Jesus' act of giving out bread to the people, in addition to being an echo of the Eucharist, was also an emulation of the emperor's gifts of grain and bread to the Roman citizens. What's more, while emperors had to use existing commodities to alleviate scarcity, Jesus was able to create abundance from scarcity. Winn writes: "Through the presentation of this powerful Jesus, Mark deftly crafts a powerful resume for Jesus to counter the powerful resume of Vespasian and to demonstrate that Jesus is in all ways superior to this new Roman emperor."[1119]

As for the suffering side of the Jesus equation, Winn provides evidence for that being part of imperial propaganda as well. But before he does, he talks about the 'narrative hinge' of the two halves of the Gospel, Mk 8:22–10:52. Within this 'hinge' we find the three passion predictions sandwiched between two healings of blind men, as discussed above. Following the healing of the first blind man (8:22-26), there is the scene where Peter acknowledges Jesus as the Messiah:

Jesus went on with his disciples to the villages of Caesarea Philippi; and on the way he asked his disciples, "Who do people say that I am?" And they answered him, "John the Baptist; and others, Elijah; and still others, one of the prophets." He asked them, "But who do you say that I am?" Peter answered him, "You are the Messiah." And he sternly ordered them not to tell anyone about him.[1120]

[1119]Winn (2018) p. 88.
[1120]Mark 8:27-30.

One would be forgiven for thinking that at least Peter has finally gotten the memo; he says, "You are the Messiah." But it is not so simple, as the next pericope, the first passion prediction, reveals. At this point, Jesus begins to explain to them what it actually means to be 'the Messiah,' that "the Son of Man must undergo great suffering, and be rejected by the elders, the chief priests, and the scribes, and be killed, and after three days rise again" (Mk 8:31b). That, apparently, is not quite what Peter had in mind when he stated that Jesus was the Messiah. "And Peter took him aside and began to rebuke him" (Mk 8:32b). Mark doesn't tell us what he imagined Peter to say in his rebuke, but we can get some idea from what Jesus says next (Mk 8:33): "But turning and looking at his disciples, he rebuked Peter and said, 'Get behind me, Satan! For you are setting your mind not on divine things but on human things.'"

Obviously, Peter is being depicted as one who wants a human Messiah who fulfills the requirements that were well known at the time, one who is going to assemble the troops and fight the Romans. There are no allusions here to the idea of a messiah coming on the clouds with legions of angels, as some ancient texts reveal was the hope of many sectarians, so we know we are in the realm of fiction. That a physical, militaristic messiah was 'in the air' of this fictional scene is evident from what follows.

> He called the crowd with his disciples, and said to them, "If any want to become my followers, let them deny themselves and take up their cross and follow me. For those who want to save their life will lose it, and those who lose their life for my sake, and for the sake of the gospel, will save it. For what will it profit them to gain the whole world and forfeit their life? Indeed, what can they give in return for their life?"[1121]

We have already discussed the positive interpretation of the above text, that it is clearly about the death of the underlying self to the material world, denying the individual self, and turning toward Jesus, his example, and the world to come. But here, we consider the negative aspect: what it argues against. Obviously, in the narrative world, Peter and the other disciples wanted to 'save their lives' in the sense of fighting against Rome; this is not stated in the text, but seems obvious from the words put into Jesus' mouth in this teaching pericope (Mk 8:38): "Those who are ashamed of me and of my words in this adulterous and sinful generation, of them the Son of Man will also be ashamed when he comes in the glory of his Father with the holy angels."

Verse 38, as has been discussed above, leads us again to Paul: "For I am not ashamed of the Gospel (good news) of Christ, for it is God's power working unto salvation [for deliverance from eternal death] to everyone who believes" (Rom. 1:16). Clearly, someone was ashamed of Paul's gospel and probably thought it was a coward's way to avoid war with Rome. It seems that the Markan text is suggesting that this was part of what Peter had said to Jesus when rebuking. But, as Jesus had just said: "you are setting your mind not on divine things but on human things."

The teaching that follows Peter's declaration that Jesus was the Messiah (probably having in mind a military leader) makes it clear what it is to be a Christian, the fundamental decision to turn one's life around and become oriented towards Jesus. It means to take up your cross and follow Jesus, to value the spirit life over the material life, exactly what we learned in the discussion of Pauline theology following Ashworth. Mark is giving the explanation for why Peter was 'Satan': he was focused on the material world. And in the real, historical events, it seems

---

[1121]Mark 8:34-37.

that Simon-Cephas/Peter was, indeed, a Zealot who promoted a messiah who would come with 12 legions of angels to destroy the Romans and establish an earthly rule of the Jews.

Finally: "And he said to them, 'Truly I tell you, there are some standing here who will not taste death until they see that the kingdom of God has come with power'" (Mark 9:1). Considering the fact that this verse finishes off the passion prediction, it must be related back to that: "Then he began to teach them that the Son of Man must undergo great suffering, and be rejected by the elders, the chief priests, and the scribes, and be killed, and after three days rise again." It was obviously meant that the Kingdom of God coming with power was the sacrificial death of Christ. The power of Jesus' will to obedience, his death and the display of power on the cross was, effectively, the inbreaking of the Kingdom of God, and thus, the Good News. *The cross was everything.* Winn writes:

> In one sense Peter's confession is the culmination of Mark's motif of blind disciples, as finally at Caesarea Philippi the disciples correctly identify Jesus as the Messiah for the first time – in other words, they see! But as many narrative critics have demonstrated, Peter's sight (and presumably that of all Jesus' disciples) parallels the sight of the blind man, a healing that is only partial, so Peter's recognition of Jesus' identity is only partial. ...
>
> ... Peter's rebuke of Jesus for the passion prediction and Jesus' subsequent identification of Peter with Satan make it quite clear to the reader that what Peter does not see clearly is Jesus' messianic mandate to suffer and die, a mandate that is inseparable from his identity.
>
> ... Yet while the disciples are finally able to recognize Jesus as Messiah after the Galilean ministry, they consistently fail to see Jesus fully throughout Mark's central section, as they are confused by his passion predictions and persistently pursue greatness and authority over humility and service.[1122]

Next in the central section, the narrative hinge, is the Transfiguration (Mk 9:2-13). Obviously, the Transfiguration didn't produce sufficiently awesome special effects for the disciples to get it, even if Jesus is declared to be greater than all of Israel's greatest prophets and God Himself declares audibly that this is his son and the disciples should "listen to him." The Transfiguration is followed by the healing of a boy with an unclean spirit who the disciples had been unable to heal. At this point, Jesus is made to say (Mk 9:19), "You faithless generation, how much longer must I be among you? How much longer must I put up with you? Bring him to me." He exorcises the demon in a dramatic scene and then explains to the disciples that this was a really powerful demon and they should only expect to be able to deal with such via prayer, that is, calling on the help of God, *even though Jesus can do it with words.*

Then follows the second passion prediction, in which the narrator tells us the disciples did not understand, followed by the petty squabble about who was greatest. Here, Jesus sits them down and explains to them, "Whoever wants to be first must be last of all and servant of all" (Mk 9:35). He uses a child as his example: "Whoever welcomes one such child in my name welcomes me, and whoever welcomes me welcomes not me but the one who sent me" (Mk 9:37). In other words, taking care of the weak and powerless is a measure of greatness.

Next comes the petty complaint from John: "Teacher, we saw someone casting out demons in your name, and we tried to stop him, because he was not following us" (Mk 9:38). To which Jesus responds: "Do not stop him; for no one who does a deed of power in my name will be able soon afterward to speak evil of me. Whoever is not against us is for us. For truly I tell you,

---

[1122]Winn (2018), pp. 90–91.

whoever gives you a cup of water to drink because you bear the name of Christ will by no means lose the reward" (Mk 9:39).

Jesus continues to teach about temptations to sin, divorce, another teaching about little children, and then the encounter with the rich man, saying at the end: "But many who are first will be last, and the last will be first" (Mk 10:31).

Then, there is the final passion prediction.

> "See, we are going up to Jerusalem, and the Son of Man will be handed over to the chief priests and the scribes, and they will condemn him to death; then they will hand him over to the Gentiles; they will mock him, and spit upon him, and flog him, and kill him; and after three days he will rise again."[1123]

No sooner is this out of his mouth than James and John ask: "Grant us to sit, one at your right hand and one at your left, in your glory" (Mk 10:37). Since it is God who will be at Jesus' right hand, James and John are obviously envisioning being seated next to Jesus exercising earthly dominion – another failure to understand his words. And again Jesus' response is "whoever wishes to become great among you must be your servant, and whoever wishes to be first among you must be slave of all. For the Son of Man came not to be served but to serve, and to give his life a ransom for many" (Mk 10:43-45).

Finally comes the healing of blind Bartimaeus to close the section. Bartimaeus hails Jesus: "Jesus, Son of David, have mercy on me!" (Mk 10:47). Now, keep in mind that Jesus has been completely re-framing and re-defining what it means to be 'the Messiah' since the healing of the blind man at Bethsaida. He has been demolishing any and all ideas of a militant Davidic messiah, and here, a blind man is hailing him as 'son of David,' i.e. just such a messiah. In the very next scene is the triumphal entry into Jerusalem where the people acclaim, "Blessed is the coming kingdom of our ancestor David!" (Mk 10:10). And then: "Then he entered Jerusalem and went into the temple; and when he had looked around at everything, as it was already late, he went out to Bethany with the twelve" (Mk 11:11).

Such an anti-climactic ending, with no teaching or explaining of anything following the events narrated, raises serious questions in my mind regarding the text. In Matthew, the triumphal entry is said to produce turmoil in the city and is followed immediately with the scene in which Jesus drives out the moneychangers and merchants from the temple (Matt. 21:10-12). In Mark, we are expected to believe that after all that, Jesus just went into the temple, looked around, and, because it was late, headed back out of the city to spend the night? Considering the fact that blind Bartimaeus first raised the 'Son of David' theme, which was then picked up by the crowds as Jesus entered Jerusalem, and this following a series of teachings about the coming suffering and death, a complete reorientation of the concepts of what the Messiah really came to do, it appears to me that the probable missing text had to do with rejecting this idea of being descended from David and fulfilling militant messianic hopes.

Consider the fact that Mark structures his narrative from Mk 11:1–13:37 around three successive journeys by Jesus to the temple on three successive days. The outline of events looks something like this:

[1123]Mark 10:33-34.

A. First Trip to the Temple (11:1-11)

    a) Travel to the Temple: The Triumphal Entry (11:1-10)

    b) Observation of the Temple and Departure to Bethany (11:11)

B. Second Trip to the Temple (11:12-19)

    a) Travel to the Temple: Cursing of the Fig Tree (11:12-14)

    b) Cleansing of the Temple (11:15-18)

    c) Departure out of the City (11:19)

C. Third Trip to the Temple (11:20–13:37)

    a) Travel to the Temple: Dead Fig tree; prayer of faith moving mountains.

    b) Teaching in the Temple (11:27–12:44)

    c) Departure from the temple and prediction of its destruction. (13:1-2)

Notice that on days two and three – items B and C above – there are three components to the episode: going to the temple, doing something in the temple, then leaving the temple. But in episode A, there are only two items: arrival and departure. In episodes B and C, there is a significant amount of *activity* in the temple, but in episode A, there is nothing. Considering the remarkably tight structure of Mark's text, I would say that this is evidence that something has definitely been removed, and very early in the history of this text! And given the fact that chapter 12 includes the issue of Jesus' rejection of the title 'Son of David,' which both Bartimaeus and the crowds have just called him in the preceding chapters. I think it probably had something to do with that. (Since Jesus' response does not constitute an explicit denial, that might explain why the early editors felt it could be left intact.) David Oliver Smith says that Mk 11:3-11 is part of a wider chiastic structure that corresponds to Mk 10:46b–11:3 and that the structure is pretty tight, and the chiastic structure continues pretty seamlessly back from 10:46b, and forward from 11:11.[1124] That being said, I still think that the anticlimactic arrival at the temple is a sore thumb and needs another look.[1125]

Winn writes that in the second half of the Gospel, the powerful Jesus is certainly not eclipsed by a weak individual who is only persecuted, suffers and dies. He suggests that the Transfiguration and dealing with the powerful demon were placed at this point in the narrative to reassure the audience that, despite the growing emphasis on the coming suffering and death, Jesus is still powerful. Additionally, the way Mark introduces the upcoming suffering death into the narrative, as a *prediction* of Jesus himself, was a sign of significant power. So, how would Mark's audience have understood the suffering and death of Jesus?

[1124]See Smith (2016), pp. 80, 91. Mark 11:1-7 is also part of a large-scale chiastic structure tied to Mk 14:12-15 (Smith, p. 110). Smith argues that at this point in the Gospel, the author is still setting up a 'kingly messiah' red herring, which will only be finally dispelled at the scene in Gethsemane: "It is at this point that the reader realizes that Jesus will not foment a revolution but has submitted himself to God's plan" (p. 242). I argue it isn't so much a red herring for a Pauline audience as it is for the characters within the story, and for Jewish Christians hearing the Gospel for the first time.

[1125]I also think the Mk 10:46 episode is missing something important. "Then they came to Jericho. And as He was leaving Jericho …" Smith (2016, pp. 90, 100, 109) solves this, also using multiple large chiastic structures to guide his choices, by relocating Mk 7:1-23 from its current position to the place between those two references to Jericho in 10:46.

The Patron's Honor

The ancient Romans were truly a peculiar people. After a few bad experiences with tyrants, they had very early rejected monarchical rule in favor of a republic governed by a senate of patricians and elected consuls: an oligarchy. It was not a very efficient form of government, truth be told, and many abuses against the common people were perpetrated by the elite. Realizing the inefficiency of the senatorial and consular system in special situations, the Senate would often appoint a dictator, an absolute ruler, for a limited period of time. The dictator was expected to handle the emergency situation and then, when things had settled down, he was expected to retire and give up his powers: *recusatio*.

In late Republican times, this anti-monarchical history was amplified and the distaste for kingly rule exaggerated to an extreme degree because of the widespread propaganda spread by Julius Caesar's political rivals that he was seeking to become king. What Caesar was actually seeking was better treatment of the lower classes, especially retiring soldiers, via the restoration of the rule of law and older, conservative values. The conditions of retired soldiers and the lower classes had been a big issue that created crises from time to time, most notably during the time of the Gracchi brothers between 133 and 121 BC. They attempted to redistribute public land controlled by aristocrats to the urban poor and veterans, among other constitutional reforms. They were assassinated by the 'Optimates,' i.e. the conservative patricians who opposed reforms. Caesar was attempting the same types of reforms and thus became the target of propaganda designed to terrify everyone: that he was seeking to become an absolute tyrant king. Cicero contributed a great deal to this propaganda and, as a consequence, Julius Caesar, the champion of the people, was assassinated. And, unfortunately, much of the propaganda of Cicero is still believed by many who have not studied the matter carefully.

Caesar's adopted son, Octavian, having learned a harsh lesson from the assassination of his adopted father, developed a strategy of rather dramatic *recusatio*. This meant that he outwardly rejected, resisted, or protested against any honors or acts that might suggest he had absolute political power; at the same time, he actually *did have* absolute political power via various clever maneuvers. An article on UNRV.com describes Augustus' political savvy:

> "In my sixth and seventh consulships [28–27 BC], after I had extinguished civil wars, and at a time when with universal consent I was in complete control of affairs, *I transferred the republic from my power to the dominion of the senate and people of Rome* ... After this time I excelled all in influence [*auctoritas*], although I possessed no more official power [*potestas*] than others who were my colleagues in the several magistracies." (*Res Gestae Divi Augusti* 34.1-3)
>
> [In the above,] Augustus not only describes, but also justifies his unique political position. Although it is easy [in retrospect] to see through his transparent ruse, it is also easy to see how the above statement embodies the subtle political delicacy used by Rome's first emperor. His political power ... [was] achieved through his military supremacy passed off as rule by universal consent. ... after the war against Antony came to a close [at Actium], Augustus (or as he was known then, Octavian) was at the head of Rome's empire: he had, at his disposal, over five hundred thousand legionaries (many of whom defected from Antony to Octavian after Actium) as well as a recently seized Ptolemaic treasury. As Tacitus puts it, "Opposition did not exist."[1126]

[1126]'Why Was Augustus So Successful in Creating the Roman Empire?', https://www.unrv.com/fall-republic/why-was-augustus-so-successful.php.

Nor could it. To use a historical cliché, Augustus was the archetypal 'master of spin.' Neverthe-less, the sheer tact of Augustus made the transition from oligarchy to autocracy almost painless to the Republican Romans. This was not to say that senators were none the wiser, but those who complained were reduced to nothing or eliminated covertly. The article continues:

> Realizing the need to keep individuals in check, Octavian set about reforming his position; this was achieved in 27 BC through the medium of the so-called First Settlement. According to Suetonius, the build-up to the settlement happened thus:
>
> "He then actually summoned... the Senate to his house and gave them a faithful account of the military and financial state of the Empire."
>
> And then, in a great display of political tact, he resigned [*recusatio*]. Naturally the Senate im-plored Octavian to stay in office by offering him a new set of powers. With [exaggerated] reluctance, Octavian accepted [*only*] the following: Proconsular imperium (the legitimate right to command legions) in most militarized provinces – Gaul, Spain and Syria – which was to be reviewed every ten years; a continuation of his consecutive consulships, thus placing himself in a position similar to that of Pompey during 59-48 BC [against whom Julius Caesar had fought]; and he was also awarded the honorific title of Augustus, a title held by all Augustus' successors. ...
>
> [Later,] Augustus gave up the consulship and instead was awarded *tribunicia potestas* (tribuni-cian powers)[1127] for life by the senate; a position that gave him tremendous civil authority, but at the same time freed up one of the consulships [so he could be seen to be 'sharing power']. To maintain authority in all militarized provinces, Augustus was awarded *imperium maius*. This enabled him to override the imperium of any provincial governor and potentially have military authority in any province; however, Augustus only really intervened with senatorial provinces on a few occasions.
>
> With such care and effort put in this acquisition of accumulated power, it seems that Augustus had reached a state of political perfection: [he had absolute power in everything that mattered, all the while giving the impression that he was sharing power around generously;] not only would he hold these powers until his long life came to an end, but his successor would also. Thus in 23 BC, Augustus made the principate a permanent establishment; the rule of the autocrat ended only at death.

In the histories of Suetonius and Cassius Dio, and the writings of Seneca, Philo, and Tacitus, Winn writes, "Emperors who consistently practiced *recusatio* ... generally receive favorable evalu-ations, while emperors who did not always receive negative evaluations."[1128] Tiberius, Claudius and Vespasian pretty much followed the example of Augustus; Caligula, Nero and Domitian did not and were assassinated, and remembered as tyrants.

In later times, in the history of Cassius Dio (164–c. 235, grandson of Dio Chrysostom, a contemporary of Vespasian and probably employed by him in his propaganda campaign) wrote an interesting long passage about the advice given to Augustus by his friends, Agrippa and Maecenas.

[1127]"*Tribunus plebis*, rendered in English as tribune of the plebs, tribune of the people or plebeian tribune, was the first office of the Roman state that was open to the plebeians, and was throughout the history of the Republic, the most important check on the power of the Roman Senate and magistrates. ... Tribunes had the power to convene and preside over the *Concilium Plebis* (people's assembly); to summon the senate; to propose legislation; and to intervene on behalf of plebeians in legal matters; but the most significant power was to veto the actions of the consuls and other magistrates, thus protecting the interests of the plebeians as a class. The tribunes of the plebs were sacrosanct, meaning that any assault on their person was [prohibited by law]." (Wikipedia.org, 'Tribune of the plebs.')

[1128]Winn (2018), pp. 96–97.

Obviously, the speech is Dio's creation, but it reflects how people of that time understood the system of Augustus, putting a noble spin on what was clearly cynical pragmatism[1129]:

> As regards your subjects, then, you should so conduct yourself, in my opinion. So far as you yourself are concerned, permit no exceptional or prodigal distinction to be given you, through word or deed, either by the senate or by any one else. For whereas the honour which you confer upon others lends glory to them, yet nothing can be given to you that is greater than what you already possess, and, besides, no little suspicion of insincerity would attach to its giving. No subject, you see, is ever supposed to vote any such distinction to his ruler of his free will, and since all such honours as a ruler receives he must receive from himself, he not only wins no commendation for the honour but becomes a laughing-stock besides. You must therefore depend upon your good deeds to provide for you any additional splendour. And you should never permit gold or silver images of yourself to be made, for they are not only costly but also invite destruction and last only a brief time; but rather *by your benefactions fashion other images in the hearts of your people*, images which will never tarnish or perish. Neither should you ever permit the raising of a temple to you; for the expenditure of vast sums of money on such objects is sheer waste. This money would better be used for necessary objects; for wealth which is really wealth is gathered, not so much by getting largely, as by saving largely. Then, again, from temples comes no enhancement of one's glory. For *it is virtue that raises many men to the level of gods*, and no man ever became a god by popular vote. Hence, if you are upright as a man and honourable as a ruler, the whole earth will be your hallowed precinct, all cities your temples, and all men your statues, since *within their thoughts you will ever be enshrined and glorified.*[1130]

Augustus was careful to show respect to Rome's traditional institutions and values. He allowed complete freedom of speech in any matter that did not affect his actual power. When in the Senate, even if he was harassed or interrupted, he never punished or rebuked anyone – publicly, that is. In short, Augustus worked very hard to present himself as just an ordinary guy living under the law like everyone else. He dressed modestly, went about on foot, avoided public ceremonies and lived in the same unpretentious house for forty years. Tiberius followed the modest practices of Augustus and so, too, did Vespasian. Winn cites Wallace-Hadrill, who noted: "Only an emperor could regard self-degradation as magnificent."[1131]

In short, the imperial strategy of *recusatio* was recognized as an impressive demonstration of nobility and power. Roman emperors of the early principate went to great lengths to distance themselves from any whiff of monarchy, and presented themselves as servants of the state and its people. As Seneca wrote: "instead of sacrificing the state to themselves, they have *sacrificed themselves* to the state."[1132]

Now, keeping in mind that the first-century reader of Mark certainly was aware to one extent or another of all of the above, consider Mark 10:42-45:

> So Jesus called them and said to them, "You know that among the Gentiles those whom they recognize as their rulers lord it over them, and their great ones are tyrants over them. But it is not so among you; but whoever wishes to become great among you must be your servant, and whoever

---

[1129]There is also the school of thought that ancient authors put speeches into the mouths of characters with the intention of trying to influence their leaders. Of course, Augustus was long dead when Cassius Dio wrote, so it could not be him who was intended to be influenced, but perhaps rulers or officials of Dio's time and place.

[1130]Cassius Dio, *Roman History* 52.35. Loeb translation.

[1131]Winn (2018), p. 101.

[1132]Seneca, *Ben.* 4.31.2.

wishes to be first among you must be slave of all. For the Son of Man came not to be served but to serve, and to give his life a ransom for many."

This passage is part of the response to the request of James and John: "Grant us to sit, one at your right hand and one at your left, in your glory" (Mk 10:37). Jesus was speaking to the twelve. As Winn notes, presumably the Markan audience knew that James, John and others held positions of power in the early church. But how would those readers/hearers react to, "You know that among the Gentiles those whom they recognize as their rulers lord it over them, and their great ones are tyrants over them"? Except in the cases of Caligula and Nero, both of whom were assassinated for being tyrants, Roman emperors strove to be seen (at least) as servants of the state and the people. Yet it appears that Mark is contrasting the way Jesus uses authority with the way the Roman rulers use theirs. Winn concludes that this was a strategy in which Mark's readers would understand that their ideals of rejecting tyrannical abuse were shared and taught by Jesus. More than that, Winn proposes that some of Mark's readers would have been aware that the practice of *recusatio* actually masked tyrannical ambition. He notes Tacitus' critique of Augustus:

> On the other side it was argued that 'filial duty' and the critical position of the state had been used merely as a cloak: come to facts, and it was from the lust of dominion that he excited the veterans by his bounties, levied an army while yet a stripling and a subject, seduced the legions of a consul, and affected a leaning to the Pompeian side.[1133]

And so, for this, Winn notes:

> ... Mark presents Jesus as a ruler promoting their ideals over and against past and present rulers who are tyrants in sheep's clothing, rulers who include Augustus, Tiberius, and Vespasian. However, for many readers, emperors such as Augustus would have been highly esteemed, and any association between these rulers and tyranny would have been regarded as unlikely. Such readers would have recognized in Mark 10:42 a contrast not so much between Jesus and all Roman rulers but between good rulers and bad ones. That is, Jesus is instructing his disciples not to imitate the behavior of tyrants such as Caligula and Nero.[1134]

It's plausible enough, certainly, but that would presuppose that the author of Mark had a certain 'insider's view' of Roman authorities similar to that of Tacitus, or that he was possibly even more intimate with what went on in imperial circles.

As far as Jesus' instructions that those who wish to be great should be the servant of all, this was clearly not breaking news, as we have seen from the above short discussion on how Augustus set up the principate. What was unusual was to contrast being 'first' with being somehow an actual 'servant' or slave, which was a bit outside the Roman political ideal. An emperor could serve his people without being a slave. Winn proposes that Mark was stretching the boundaries: "Thus, while Roman political ideals call rulers to serve the state, Jesus calls his disciples to even greater service and humility in their capacity as servants."[1135] This idea comes from Paul in 1 Cor. 9:19: "Though I am free and belong to no one, I have made myself a slave to everyone, to win as many as possible."

[1133]Tacitus, *Ann.* 1.10, cited by Winn (2018), p. 108.

[1134]Winn (2018), pp. 108–9.

[1135]Winn (2018), p. 110.

And, of course, Jesus grounds his instruction in his own service: that of giving his very life for humanity: "For the Son of Man came not to be served but to serve, and to give his life a ransom for many." Winn notes that the language Mark uses is remarkably similar to that of Seneca: "instead of sacrificing the state to themselves, they have sacrificed themselves to the state," and they "preferred to be conquered than to conquer because in this way [they] could serve the interest of the state."

> Mark's phrase "came not to be served but to serve" and Seneca's "preferred to be conquered rather than to conquer" are structurally similar as are the meanings of the two phrases. By "conquer" Seneca does not have military victory in mind but political superiority and domination. The ideal ruler chooses not to dominate his people (conquer them) but to serve them (be conquered by them). Thus we see that both Seneca and Jesus are promoting the ideal of a ruler who serves rather than is served.
>
> Perhaps of even greater significance is the similarity between the ideal emperor's willingness to "sacrifice [himself] to the state" and Jesus' willingness to "give his life as a ransom for many," that is, sacrifice himself for the subjects of his kingdom. Seneca is obviously speaking figuratively ... There was no precedent or even expectation for the emperor to sacrifice his own life for that of the state. But again, Mark may be radicalizing Roman political ideals by taking them to their extreme but logical conclusion: a ruler who sacrifices his own power, glory, and wealth for his people is good, but a ruler who would sacrifice his very life for his people is even better.[1136]

As Winn has demonstrated, Mark sent very clear signals from the beginning that the Gospel should be read in light of Roman imperial ideology. Elements of Mark's Gospel certainly do share strong conceptual similarities. Winn also suggests that it should be read as a response to Roman imperial power. I'm not sure that I think it is so much a response as it is apology, as is suggested by Brandon; but then, the difference is only rhetorical I think. Winn even anticipates objections to his theory: Roman political ideology rejects kings and tyrants, but isn't Mark's Jesus represented as a king?

Elizabeth Struthers Malbon notes that only Jesus' opponents identify him as a king. There is Pilate: Mk 15:2, 9, 12, and Pilate's inscription at Mk 15:26. Additionally, Roman soldiers at Mk 15:18 and the chief priests and scribes at Mk 15:32. Note what I have written above about Mark's Jesus apparently rejecting totally the Davidic messianic role. It is also significant that Matthew uses the title more frequently and in a positive way, reflecting his Jewish Christian background and probable affiliation with those who saw Judas the Galilean as the Davidic messiah. Winn writes:

> [T]he astute reader knows that no trustworthy voice in the story ... has identified Jesus as [king]. ... Therefore it might be more accurate to interpret the derisive identification of Jesus as king not only as derisive but also as wrong! Thus for the author and audience, identifying Jesus as king is just one more false charge among many others ...[1137]

The irony is that Jesus really *is* a king: the king of kings. Here I will note that the same false accusations were made against Julius Caesar, who vigorously resisted such acclamation, and the propaganda spread by Cicero – that he was seeking to become a tyrant – is what led to his assassination. There are many parallels between Jesus, as presented by Mark, and Julius Caesar.

[1136]Winn (2018), pp. 110–11.
[1137]Winn (2018), p. 113.

Winn cites David F. Watson's social-scientific criticism study[1138] respecting the problem of the secrecy motif in Mark. Many scholars have thought that Jesus' identity as the Son of God, not the Messiah, was meant to be kept a secret until the crucifixion, but Watson thinks otherwise and Winn agrees. Watson demonstrates that ultimately, what is often described as a 'secrecy' motif in Mark is misleading. He proposes that the apparent secrecy motif should rather be understood in terms of the honor-shame value system of the ancient Mediterranean world. Consider the pericopes in which Jesus performs a healing and commands the recipient not to report or speak of the healing:

> A leper came to him begging him, and kneeling he said to him, "If you choose, you can make me clean." Moved with pity, Jesus stretched out his hand and touched him, and said to him, "I do choose. Be made clean!" Immediately the leprosy left him, and he was made clean. After sternly warning him he sent him away at once, saying to him, "See that you say nothing to anyone; but go, show yourself to the priest, and offer for your cleansing what Moses commanded, as a testimony to them." But he went out and began to proclaim it freely, and to spread the word, so that Jesus could no longer go into a town openly, but stayed out in the country; and people came to him from every quarter.[1139]

> When Jesus had crossed again in the boat to the other side, a great crowd gathered around him; and he was by the sea. Then one of the leaders of the synagogue named Jairus came and, when he saw him, fell at his feet and begged him repeatedly, "My little daughter is at the point of death. Come and lay your hands on her, so that she may be made well, and live." So he went with him. And a large crowd followed him and pressed in on him. ... While he was still speaking, some people came from the leader's house to say, "Your daughter is dead. Why trouble the teacher any further?" But overhearing what they said, Jesus said to the leader of the synagogue, "Do not fear, only believe." He allowed no one to follow him except Peter, James, and John, the brother of James. When they came to the house of the leader of the synagogue, he saw a commotion, people weeping and wailing loudly. When he had entered, he said to them, "Why do you make a commotion and weep? The child is not dead but sleeping." And they laughed at him. Then he put them all outside, and took the child's father and mother and those who were with him, and went in where the child was. He took her by the hand and said to her, "Talitha cum," which means, "Little girl, get up!" And immediately the girl got up and began to walk about (she was twelve years of age). At this they were overcome with amazement. He strictly ordered them that no one should know this, and told them to give her something to eat.[1140]

> When he returned from the region of Tyre, and went by way of Sidon towards the Sea of Galilee, in the region of the Decapolis. They brought to him a deaf man who had an impediment in his speech; and they begged him to lay his hand on him. He took him aside in private, away from the crowd, and put his fingers into his ears, and he spat and touched his tongue. Then looking up to heaven, he sighed and said to him, "Ephphatha," that is, "Be opened." And immediately his ears were opened, his tongue was released, and he spoke plainly. Then Jesus ordered them to tell no one; but the more he ordered them, the more zealously they proclaimed it. They were astounded beyond measure, saying, "He has done everything well; he even makes the deaf to hear and the mute to speak."[1141]

[1138] David F. Watson, *Honor Among Christians: The Cultural Key to the Messianic Secret* (Minneapolis: Fortress Press, 2010).

[1139] Mark 1:40-45.

[1140] Mark 5:21-24, 35-43.

[1141] Mark 7:31-37.

They came to Bethsaida. Some people brought a blind man to him and begged him to touch him. He took the blind man by the hand and led him out of the village; and when he had put saliva on his eyes and laid his hands on him, he asked him, "Can you see anything?" And the man looked up and said, "I can see people, but they look like trees, walking." Then Jesus laid his hands on his eyes again; and he looked intently and his sight was restored, and he saw everything clearly. Then he sent him away to his home, saying, "Do not even go into the village."[1142]

Watson says that in these pericopes, presented above, the dynamics of a client-patron relationship are present. Winn writes:

> Once Jesus has healed the sick person, the client is obligated to reciprocate by showing Jesus, the patron, honor – honor that would involve public praise of the patron. Watson argues that Jesus' actions of silencing the healed person would not have been understood as an attempt to keep the actions a secret but as resistance to "achieved" honor. ...
>
> Such an explanation runs into trouble, however, when one considers the numerous places in Mark where Jesus embraces rather than resists public honor. ...
>
> Existing primary sources make it quite clear that honor was one of the greatest and most prized virtues.[1143]

Winn then goes on to search for possible paradigms that might explain Jesus' rejection of honor in the above cases. It appears that Jesus' resistance to honor is situation-specific and sporadic. He comes back to Roman political ideology and the concept of *recusatio* as offering the only meaningful paradigm. Mark's readers would likely have understood it this way.

Winn proposes that Mark's narrative was carefully crafted to respond to Flavian propaganda and ultimately functioned to address the various crises that such propaganda created for the Roman church. Included in this was Jesus' relationship with the temple in Jerusalem. It is in chapters 11 and 12, a distinct literary unit, that the temple looms large and as very negative space. Winn notes that the triumphal entry falls flat: after such a build-up of crowds hailing Jesus as the "one who comes in the name of the Lord" and "Blessed is the coming kingdom of our ancestor David!", when Jesus arrives at the temple he looks around and goes home. However, Winn thinks that Mark is deliberately creating a scene that exposes the temple authorities as failing to recognize or receive God's messiah. That may be the case, but as I have noted above, the whole series of pericopes leading up to that text calls for a teaching session that is *not there* and thus I think that it has been redacted and must have said something quelling about the Davidic messiah.[1144]

As for the 'cleansing' of the temple, there is a growing trend to understand this as a symbolic destruction of the temple which is bracketed by the cursing of the fig tree that withers, the tree representing the temple. Jesus' actions are a prophetic act signaling the permanent end of temple operations.

> Then they came to Jerusalem. And he entered the temple and began to drive out those who were selling and those who were buying in the temple, and he overturned the tables of the money changers and the seats of those who sold doves; and he would not allow anyone to carry anything through the temple. He was teaching and saying, "Is it not written, *'My house shall be called a house*

[1142]Mark 8:22-26.
[1143]Winn (2018), pp. 121, 122, 123.
[1144]*Pace* David Oliver Smith.

of prayer for all the nations'? But you have made it a den of robbers." And when the chief priests and the scribes heard it, they kept looking for a way to kill him; for they were afraid of him, because the whole crowd was spellbound by his teaching. And when evening came, Jesus and his disciples went out of the city.[1145]

The citation fuses two OT texts together: Isaiah 56:7 and Jeremiah 7:11:

And the foreigners who join themselves to the LORD, to minister to him, to love the name of the LORD, and to be his servants, all who keep the sabbath, and do not profane it, and hold fast my covenant – these I will bring to my holy mountain, and make them joyful in my house of prayer; their burnt offerings and their sacrifices will be accepted on my altar; **for my house shall be called a house of prayer for all peoples.**[1146]

Do not trust in these deceptive words: "This is the temple of the LORD, the temple of the LORD, the temple of the LORD." For if you truly amend your ways and your doings, if you truly act justly one with another, if you do not oppress the alien, the orphan, and the widow, or shed innocent blood in this place, and if you do not go after other gods to your own hurt, then I will dwell with you in this place, in the land that I gave of old to your ancestors forever and ever. Here you are, trusting in deceptive words to no avail. Will you steal, murder, commit adultery, swear falsely, make offerings to Baal, and go after other gods that you have not known, and then come and stand before me in this house, which is called by my name, and say, "We are safe!" – only to go on doing all these abominations? **Has this house, which is called by my name, become a den of robbers in your sight?** You know, I too am watching, says the LORD. Go now to my place that was in Shiloh, where I made my name dwell at first, and see what I did to it for the wickedness of my people Israel. And now, because you have done all these things, says the LORD, and when I spoke to you persistently, you did not listen, and when I called you, you did not answer, therefore I will do to the house that is called by my name, in which you trust, and to the place that I gave to you and to your ancestors, just what I did to Shiloh.[1147]

By citing Isaiah, which was a vision of an eschatological temple, the Markan Jesus is pointing out that the then current temple was no better than the first and thus must be destroyed. Jeremiah 7 is equally damning and predicts the destruction of the temple. By sandwiching 11:15-19 within the story of the cursing of the fig tree, Mark is making it quite plain how one should interpret Jesus' actions in the temple:

On the following day, when they came from Bethany, he was hungry. Seeing in the distance a fig tree in leaf, he went to see whether perhaps he would find anything on it. When he came to it, he found nothing but leaves, for it was not the season for figs. He said to it, "May no one ever eat fruit from you again." And his disciples heard it. ...[Cleansing the temple scene is here.] ... In the morning as they passed by, they saw the fig tree withered away to its roots. Then Peter remembered and said to him, "Rabbi, look! The fig tree that you cursed has withered." Jesus answered them, "Have faith in God. Truly I tell you, if you say to this mountain, 'Be taken up and thrown into the sea,' and if you do not doubt in your heart, but believe that what you say will come to pass, it will be done for you. So I tell you, whatever you ask for in prayer, believe that you have received it, and it will be yours. Whenever you stand praying, forgive, if you have anything against anyone; so that your Father in heaven may also forgive you your trespasses."[1148]

[1145]Mark 11:15-19.
[1146]Isa. 56:6-7.
[1147]Jer. 7:4-14.
[1148]Mark 11:13-14, 20-25.

The cursing of the fig tree brackets and parallels the cursing of the temple. The fig tree was a common symbol for Israel and its temple. The Markan sandwich makes the 'cleansing' of the temple an obvious symbolic action intending destruction, not purification. Consider also that the pericope depicts Jesus as powerful and authoritative in exercising God's judgment against the leaders of Israel and their temple. That, of course, reminds one of the Son of Man theme of judgment and destruction.[1149]

In response to Peter's announcement that the fig tree had withered, Jesus says things about faith and mountains that are seemingly unrelated. But, if one considers that Jesus is talking about Mount Zion, on which the temple was situated, then it makes more sense. The reader/listener has just been reminded – via the citations from Isaiah and Jeremiah – about the eschatological temple that was to serve all mankind, and here Jesus is assuring the disciples that the prayer of faith will be accompanied by power and effectiveness. Thus, he appears to be saying that the Christian community is to become the new temple. The place where atonement once was facilitated is to be replaced by forgiveness between God and Christians, and between Christians themselves. Thus, Jesus symbolically destroyed the temple and actually destroyed its symbol, the fig tree, and then established the terms for the new, eschatological temple, located in the hearts of men.

However, there is something else, something deeply ironic there. Note that it is Peter who says, "Rabbi, look! The fig tree that you cursed has withered." And it was Simon and James, the sons of Judas the Galilean, the pillars of the Jerusalem church, who were executed by Tiberius Alexander in 47 AD, 23 years before the destruction of the temple. And it was the followers of Judas the Galilean, the Zealots, who ultimately fired the wrath of Rome to the point that they utterly destroyed Jerusalem and the temple. Certainly Mark and his audience knew this and could therefore appreciate the deep irony when Mark makes his character Jesus say: "Have faith in God. Truly I tell you, if you say to this mountain, 'Be taken up and thrown into the sea,' and if you do not doubt in your heart, but believe that what you say will come to pass, it will be done for you." It had, indeed, come to pass, though that was not what the Jewish Christian Zealots had been aiming for. One is also struck by the expression "thrown into the sea" and immediately recalls the fate of the pigs in the exorcism of the demoniac of Gerasa:

> Then Jesus asked him, "What is your name?" He replied, "My name is Legion; for we are many." He begged him earnestly not to send them out of the country. Now **there on the hillside a great herd of swine was feeding**; and the unclean spirits begged him, "Send us into the swine; let us enter them." So he gave them permission. And the unclean spirits came out and entered the swine; **and the herd, numbering about two thousand, rushed down the steep bank into the sea, and were drowned in the sea.**[1150]

Again I suggest that the pigs may very well have represented the maddened Jews in revolt, plunging into the sea as Jesus has just suggested could happen to the Temple mount.

Immediately after the lesson from the withered fig tree, the authority of Jesus is challenged by the temple authorities:

[1149]One is, of course, also reminded of the actions of Judas the Galilean in the Golden Eagle temple cleansing incident that may very well have occurred in 19 AD rather than in the time of Herod, and might have been what got him captured and executed.

[1150]Mark 5:9-13.

Again they came to Jerusalem. As he was walking in the temple, the chief priests, the scribes, and the elders came to him and said, "By what authority are you doing these things? Who gave you this authority to do them?" Jesus said to them, "I will ask you one question; answer me, and I will tell you by what authority I do these things. Did the baptism of John come from heaven, or was it of human origin? Answer me." They argued with one another, "If we say, 'From heaven,' he will say, 'Why then did you not believe him?' But shall we say, 'Of human origin'?" – they were afraid of the crowd, for all regarded John as truly a prophet. So they answered Jesus, "We do not know." And Jesus said to them, "Neither will I tell you by what authority I am doing these things."[1151]

To Mark's audience, the answer to the question asked of Jesus is obvious: the Gospel has revealed that Jesus wields the power of God Himself. But the question functions to expose the temple authorities as being in opposition to God. When Jesus questions them about the authority of John the Baptist, they are further exposed as ignorant of the very God whose temple they claim as their own. And so Jesus gives another parable:

Then he began to speak to them in parables. "A man planted a vineyard, put a fence around it, dug a pit for the wine press, and built a watchtower; then he leased it to tenants and went to another country. When the season came, he sent a slave to the tenants to collect from them his share of the produce of the vineyard. But they seized him, and beat him, and sent him away empty-handed. And again he sent another slave to them; this one they beat over the head and insulted. Then he sent another, and that one they killed. And so it was with many others; some they beat, and others they killed. He had still one other, a beloved son. Finally he sent him to them, saying, 'They will respect my son.' But those tenants said to one another, 'This is the heir; come, let us kill him, and the inheritance will be ours.' So they seized him, killed him, and threw him out of the vineyard. What then will the owner of the vineyard do? He will come and destroy the tenants and give the vineyard to others. Have you not read this scripture: 'The stone that the builders rejected has become the cornerstone; this was the Lord's doing, and it is amazing in our eyes'?" When they realized that he had told this parable against them, they wanted to arrest him, but they feared the crowd. So they left him and went away.[1152]

Unlike other parables, this one is easy to understand; even the chief priests, the scribes, and the elders understood it. The parable functions to indict the leadership of the Jews and to prophesy the destruction of Jerusalem and its temple. But, more than that, the parable echoes and alludes to Isaiah 5, which was clearly in Mark's mind when he wrote this dramatic scene:

Let me sing for my beloved my love-song concerning his vineyard: My beloved had a vineyard on a very fertile hill. He dug it and cleared it of stones, and planted it with choice vines; he built a watchtower in the midst of it, and hewed out a wine vat in it; he expected it to yield grapes, but it yielded wild grapes. And now, inhabitants of Jerusalem and people of Judah, judge between me and my vineyard. What more was there to do for my vineyard that I have not done in it? When I expected it to yield grapes, why did it yield wild grapes? And now I will tell you what I will do to my vineyard. I will remove its hedge, and it shall be devoured; I will break down its wall, and it shall be trampled down. I will make it a waste; it shall not be pruned or hoed, and it shall be overgrown with briers and thorns; I will also command the clouds that they rain no rain upon it. For the vineyard of the LORD of hosts is the house of Israel, and the people of Judah are his pleasant planting; he expected justice, but saw bloodshed; righteousness, but heard a cry![1153]

[1151]Mark 11:27-33.
[1152]Mark 12:1-12.
[1153]Isa. 5:1-7.

Ah, you who drag iniquity along with cords of falsehood, who drag sin along as with cart ropes, who say, "Let him make haste, let him speed his work that we may see it; let the plan of the Holy One of Israel hasten to fulfillment, that we may know it!" Ah, you who call evil good and good evil, who put darkness for light and light for darkness, who put bitter for sweet and sweet for bitter! Ah, you who are wise in your own eyes, and shrewd in your own sight! Ah, you who are heroes in drinking wine and valiant at mixing drink, who acquit the guilty for a bribe, and deprive the innocent of their rights!

Therefore, as the tongue of fire devours the stubble, and as dry grass sinks down in the flame, so their root will become rotten, and their blossom go up like dust; for they have rejected the instruction of the LORD of hosts, and have despised the word of the Holy One of Israel. Therefore the anger of the LORD was kindled against his people, and he stretched out his hand against them and struck them; the mountains quaked, and their corpses were like refuse in the streets. For all this his anger has not turned away, and his hand is stretched out still. He will raise a signal for a nation far away, and whistle for a people at the ends of the earth; Here they come, swiftly, speedily! None of them is weary, none stumbles, none slumbers or sleeps, not a loincloth is loose, not a sandal-thong broken; their arrows are sharp, all their bows bent, their horses' hoofs seem like flint, and their wheels like the whirlwind. Their roaring is like a lion, like young lions they roar; they growl and seize their prey, they carry it off, and no one can rescue. They will roar over it on that day, like the roaring of the sea. And if one look to the land – only darkness and distress; and the light grows dark with clouds.[1154]

Notice that the Isaiah passage describes the coming of foreigners, summoned by God himself, to deliver destruction. And then, after the tale of the destruction of the vineyard, Mark quotes Psalm 118:22-23: "He will come and destroy the tenants and give the vineyard to others. Have you not read this scripture: 'The stone that the builders rejected has become the cornerstone; this was the Lord's doing, and it is amazing in our eyes'?" The entire psalm is worth reading for insight as to Mark's meaning.

Following the Parable of the Tenants, there are three short pericopes in which Jesus is challenged with difficult questions in an effort to trap him. The first test question is about paying taxes to Caesar:

Then they sent to him some Pharisees and some Herodians to trap him in what he said. And they came and said to him, "Teacher, we know that you are sincere, and show deference to no one; for you do not regard people with partiality, but teach the way of God in accordance with truth. Is it lawful to pay taxes to Caesar [the emperor], or not? Should we pay them, or should we not?" But knowing their hypocrisy, he said to them, "Why are you putting me to the test? Bring me a denarius and let me see it." And they brought one. Then he said to them, "Whose head is this, and whose title?" They answered, "The emperor's." Jesus said to them, "Give to Caesar the things that are the Caesar's, and to God the things that are God's." And they were utterly amazed at him.[1155]

The "they" who sent the Pharisees and Herodians are identified back at Mk 11:18 as "the chief priests and the scribes," and figure as "they" several times from then forward.

[1154]Isa. 5:18-30. There are differences between Isaiah and Mark's use of the passage. In Isaiah, no fruit is borne even though the gardener did all he could. In Mark, fruit is present, but it is stolen by the wicked tenants. In Isaiah, divine judgment falls upon the fruitless vineyard. In Mark, divine judgment falls on the greedy tenants. In Isaiah, the vineyard is destroyed. In Mark, the vineyard is given to others.
[1155]Mark 12:13-17.

Recall what was said about this pericope previously when discussing the work of S. G. F. Brandon. Payment of tribute was the obligation of all peoples subjected to the Empire; only the Jews had rebelled because of it back in 6 AD, at the instigation of Judas the Galilean. That Mark even raised the issue of the payment of tax by Jews implies that it was an issue at the time he was writing. The answer that is put in Jesus' mouth is what would be expected from a loyal subject of the Romans: the obligation of the Jews to pay taxes to Rome.

But there is actually more. Mark is demonstrating here that the Jewish authorities attempted to compromise Jesus on the subject of paying taxes, and Jesus gave the right answer of a good subject of Rome, though, of course, that the answer, among others, is loaded with irony is evident.

The messianic element was widely known as a potent factor in the development of extreme Jewish nationalism leading to the war. One can see here a reaction to some situation in which the Christians were in danger of being associated in popular thought with the rebellious Jews, an association that Mark is here attributing to Jewish malice. The Jewish leaders, the official representatives of Jewish life, are represented repeatedly as the constant opponents of Jesus, who repeatedly condemns them.

And, from what has been written above, we know exactly *when* it was likely that the issue of the Jewish payment of tax to Rome would have been a topic of such vital concern to the Roman Christians, and that it needed to be established that they were not persons who refused to pay taxes, nor had their messiah advised against paying taxes. This is pure apologetic.

Next, the Sadducees ask about the resurrection, keeping in mind what Josephus said about this group, that they did not believe in any sort of resurrection and that most of the high priests (and probably scribes) belonged to this sect.

> Some Sadducees, who say there is no resurrection, came to him and asked him a question, saying, "Teacher, Moses wrote for us that if a man's brother dies, leaving a wife but no child, the man shall marry the widow and raise up children for his brother. There were seven brothers; the first married and, when he died, left no children; and the second married the widow and died, leaving no children; and the third likewise; none of the seven left children. Last of all the woman herself died. In the resurrection whose wife will she be? For the seven had married her." Jesus said to them, "Is not this the reason you are wrong, that you know neither the scriptures nor the power of God? For when they rise from the dead, they neither marry nor are given in marriage, but are like angels in heaven. And as for the dead being raised, have you not read in the book of Moses, in the story about the bush, how God said to him, 'I am the God of Abraham, the God of Isaac, and the God of Jacob'? He is God not of the dead, but of the living; you are quite wrong."[1156]

This response is purely Pauline: "flesh and blood cannot inherit the kingdom of God, nor does the perishable inherit the imperishable" (1 Cor. 15:50).

Finally, one of the scribes is sent to try to trap or embarrass Jesus by asking about the greatest commandment.

> One of the scribes came near and heard them disputing with one another, and seeing that he answered them well, he asked him, "Which commandment is the first of all?" Jesus answered, "The first is, 'Hear, O Israel: the Lord our God, the Lord is one; you shall love the Lord your God with all your heart, and with all your soul, and with all your mind, and with all your strength.' The second is this, 'You shall love your neighbor as yourself.' There is no other commandment greater

---
[1156]Mark 12:18-27.

than these." Then the scribe said to him, "You are right, Teacher; you have truly said that 'he is one, and besides him there is no other'; and 'to love him with all the heart, and with all the understanding, and with all the strength,' and 'to love one's neighbor as oneself,' – this is much more important than all whole burnt offerings and sacrifices." When Jesus saw that he answered wisely, he said to him, "You are not far from the kingdom of God." After that no one dared to ask him any question.[1157]

Now, even though Jesus has just commended the scribe for his understanding, he next launches into a curious teaching that has been touched on several times already: an argument that the Messiah is not descended from David: "David himself calls [the Messiah] Lord; so how can he be his son?" As noted, he attributes this teaching – that the Messiah must be descended from David – to the scribes. Winn writes that the fact that the scribe agrees with Jesus radically marginalizes the temple's primary function, i.e. sacrifice and atonement. I would suggest that it is highly ironic. Not only is Jesus affirming the pre-existent Son of God idea of Paul, he is disconnecting the Messiah from David and thereby any revolutionary claims to kingly authority. Again, Jesus is blaming the Jewish authorities for ideas and teachings that were known to have contributed to the revolt against Rome and writing apology for Christians.

Winn thinks that Jesus is creating a *link* between Solomon, who built the first Jewish temple, and the Messiah, and that Mark is claiming that the Messiah has Solomonic authority over the temple. I don't see that at all. Jesus is well into temple-destruction mode, so it doesn't make much sense that he would associate himself with the builder of the temple unless it was with the intention of suggesting that Jesus is the builder of the new spiritual temple. Winn also reads this as functioning to establish Jesus as the messianic 'Son of David,' but I think it is doing exactly the opposite, and for very obvious reasons considering the Roman attitude toward the Jews and Christians at the time the Gospel was written.

Now, Jesus has agreed with a scribe, and then pointed out that the scribes taught ideas that were associated with the revolt against Rome, and in the very next breath, he goes on the attack against the scribes in general.

> As he taught, he said, "Beware of the scribes, who like to walk around in long robes, and to be greeted with respect in the marketplaces, and to have the best seats in the synagogues and places of honor at banquets! They devour widows' houses and for the sake of appearance say long prayers. They will receive the greater condemnation." He sat down opposite the treasury, and watched the crowd putting money into the treasury. Many rich people put in large sums. A poor widow came and put in two small copper coins, which are worth a penny. Then he called his disciples and said to them, "Truly I tell you, this poor widow has put in more than all those who are contributing to the treasury. For all of them have contributed out of their abundance; but she out of her poverty has put in everything she had, all she had to live on."[1158]

So it seems that, even though the scribe may have agreed with Jesus, such agreement may have been little more than liking to be "greeted with respect" while "devouring widow's houses." And then, a widow handily shows up to demonstrate that giving your all, even if it is small, is more than giving lip service to a commandment while robbing the poor. The story functions to sharpen the wickedness of the scribes since those who should be taking care of widows are

---

[1157]Mark 12:28-34.
[1158]Mark 12:41-44.

robbing them instead, via the temple. And that, of course, reminds us again of Isaiah 56 and Jeremiah 7, cited above.

And so, what we have seen thus far is that Jesus entered Jerusalem only to find that its leaders – Sadducees, scribes and Pharisees – have corrupted the temple until it is a sanctuary that bears no fruit and is a den of "robbers and brigands," i.e. revolutionaries. He symbolically destroys the temple via the fig tree. This is followed by a parable that indicts the leaders (Mk 12:1-11), and which echoes Isaiah 5 and Jeremiah 7, about the destruction of the temple. At the end of the parable Jesus assures his listeners that a new cornerstone will be fixed so that righteousness can prevail (Ps. 118:22; Zech. 10:4). The remainder of this section of text is taken up with disputes with those who oppose him, the religious leaders of the Jews, ending with a vivid portrayal of a poor widow who gives all she has to the scribes who "devour widows' houses" (Mk 12:40). All of these scenes were created to incite anger and disgust in the audience toward the Jewish leaders in the temple, and the temple itself.

Winn suggests that Mk 13:1-2 are the proper ending for the above set of pericopes about Jesus' experiences in the temple:

> As he came out of the temple, one of his disciples said to him, "Look, Teacher, what large stones and what large buildings!" Then Jesus asked him, "Do you see these great buildings? Not one stone will be left here upon another; all will be thrown down."

Winn thinks that the connection between these verses and the predictions of the destruction of the temple in Mark 11 and 12 are "much stronger and more obvious" than the connections with the temple's destruction in the rest of Mark 13.[1159] Surely this is correct. These verses nicely end the whole set, which is really about the failure of the temple, the Jewish authorities, and justification for its destruction; it makes explicit what was only implicit up to that point. This bit of text also has Jesus leaving the temple for the last time.

Winn argues that Mark 13 mostly concerns the future parousia, or 'second coming.' He further points out that, in chapters 9 and 10, the reader is introduced to the idea of Jesus' coming death, but it is in chapters 11 and 12 that *why* he will be killed is explained: because of his harsh critique of the Jewish temple and its authorities. Not only does the anti-temple motif tell the reader about the corruption and subsequent destruction of the temple, symbolized by Jesus' actions there, but it makes a claim about the 'new temple' which will not be a physical building but the new eschatological community of Christ believers. Winn further establishes creditably that the Jesus of Mark 11:1–13:2 is an incredibly powerful figure, despite the fact that he is effectively forcing the Jewish authorities to execute God's will in condemning him to death, to die as a sacrifice for humanity.

The destruction of the temple was one of the centerpieces of Flavian propaganda used as evidence of Vespasian's divine legitimization. This propaganda effectively implied a challenge to the power and honor of the god of Israel – Paul's god, and the god of the Christians. By destroying the temple and defeating the Jews, the Romans had shamed the god of the Jews. There was, no doubt, a lot of mockery and derision directed at Jews and Christians alike wherever they were in the Greco-Roman world at the time. This was nothing new since it had happened before at the time of the Babylonian destruction of Jerusalem and the first temple. Isaiah 52:5 reports:

[1159]Winn (2108), p. 144.

"Their rulers howl, says the Lord, and continually, all day long, my name is despised." This was certainly a crisis for the early Christians of Mark's community. And so, according to Winn, Mark 11:1–13:2 addresses Vespasian's destruction of Jerusalem and its temple by implying that it was not the result of the power of Rome, but rather the result of Yahweh judging a corrupt temple and its greedy authorities for opposing and rejecting Jesus. Jesus has not only exposed and condemned the temple and its authorities, he has also fallen victim to it/them. And so, Rome is just the tool of Israel's god. This completely removes the power from Vespasian and transfers it to God and his Son, Jesus; Vespasian and Titus and all the Romans are just pawns in the plans of Yahweh.

It is true, as Winn points out, that this very same kind of response was articulated by Jewish prophets of old in response to the exile to Babylon. They interpreted those horrific events as Yahweh's punishment of his unfaithful people, utilizing the Babylonians as the means.[1160] And so, Winn concludes that Mark is just following the precedent of Israel's prophets. Additionally, Jews contemporary with Mark did the same thing. *Second Baruch* presents God as using foreign powers as tools and orchestrating the destruction of the temple; the *Apocalypse of Abraham* 27 attributes the Roman destruction of the temple to Yahweh himself. And, of course, we cannot forget Josephus whose explanation has been described above. For him, the destruction of Jerusalem and its temple was down to Judas the Galilean and his gang of Zealots, who drove the people mad with rebellion. Vespasian and Titus were just God's tools to punish them and those who followed them. And, in a way, that was exactly the propaganda that the Flavians wished to propagate: the God of the Jews was now in their corner, too!

And so, according to the Markan evangelist and his depiction of the anti-temple words and actions of Jesus in chapters 11 and 12, the Markan community itself is now the new eschatological temple, already inhabited by the spirit of God, and this happened long before the temple was destroyed. The new place of atonement and true house of prayer for all the nations is within the true followers of Christ, God's appointed world ruler/Son of Man, ruling from heaven. And thus, the community of believers now possesses power greater than that of the Roman legions, since it was implied that it was the faith of Christians that cast the temple mount into the sea – via the soldiers and arms of Rome, that is.

But even more important than Winn's view that the anti-temple motif was one-upmanship on the Flavian propaganda, I think that Brandon's view that it was defensive apology is also important, possibly more so. Mark's Gospel makes it clear that the Christians, too, were persecuted by those rebellious Jews who caused so much pain, suffering, death and destruction. Their messiah, far from being a rebel against Rome, was actually a supporter of Rome, because didn't he advocate paying taxes? Didn't he condemn the corrupt priests who, according to Josephus, got the whole rebellion going by refusing sacrifices for Rome?

[1160] See Isaiah 42:24-25; Lamentations 2:1; Jeremiah 25:8-9; Ezekiel 21.

The Olivet Discourse

But now we come to Hatina's interpretation of chapter 13, Mark's 'Little Apocalypse,'[1161] or Olivet Discourse, which Winn sets aside as just a prophecy of the Parousia. It seems it was much more than that, even something quite different. "When he was sitting on the Mount of Olives opposite the temple, Peter, James, John, and Andrew asked him privately, 'Tell us, when will this be, and what will be the sign that all these things are about to be accomplished?'" (Mk 13:3-4).

Mark 13 is often understood (as Winn does) as referring to two separate events: (1) the destruction of Jerusalem and the Temple, and (2) the final judgment and Parousia at the end of history. However, in opposition to the idea that there is anything there about the Parousia, Thomas Hatina writes that, in his view, Mark 13 is the genre of *parenesis*,[1162] or what is commonly called a 'farewell discourse.' That is, Jesus, aware of his coming death, is teaching his disciples *what will come after his death*, mainly the destruction of the temple! In literary terms, it is important to remember that the prophecy is attributed to Jesus who, as a character in the story, antedates the destruction of Jerusalem, that is, it is a prophecy written after the fact (*vaticinium ex eventu*). The Markan Jesus is applying the prophecies of imminent suffering and chaos *to his disciples*. The point is that the prophecies are intended to find their fulfillment in the *near future*, not the 'end times.'

Throughout the narrative in chapters 11–13 the Markan Jesus takes the role of a prophetic critic who, like the ancient prophets of Israel, announces impending judgment against a corrupt and greedy religious leadership presiding in and over the Temple. Since this section is saturated in OT imagery and allusion, we might assume that Mark's audience was familiar with traditions of Jewish prophetic criticism.

So, having set up the negative view of the temple and its leaders, and having declared that the temple will be destroyed, a parenesis at this point in the Markan narrative is due and appropriate. It follows the pattern that has run all the way through the Gospel of connected events to give a narrative example, followed by private instruction and explanation to the disciples of what is really going on. In this way, Mark 13 serves as a bridge between Jesus' public ministry and the events leading up to his crucifixion. So, without further ado, let's just look at the text.

> When he was sitting on the Mount of Olives opposite the temple, Peter, James, John, and Andrew asked him privately, "Tell us, when will this be, and what will be the sign that all these things are about to be accomplished?"
>
> Then Jesus began to say to them, "Beware that no one leads you astray. Many will come in my name and say, 'I am he!' and they will lead many astray. When you hear of wars and rumors of wars, do not be alarmed; this must take place, but the end is still to come. For nation will rise against nation, and kingdom against kingdom; there will be earthquakes in various places; there will be famines. This is but the beginning of the birth pangs."

[1161] "The common designation for Mark 13 as a 'little apocalypse' has its origin with T. Colani and W. Weiffenbach, who posited that the discourse is based on a Jewish or Christian Jewish apocalyptic tractate." Hatina (1996).

[1162] According to Hatina (1996), p. 48, "this combination of predictions and ethical admonitions closely resembles the pattern of Jewish parenetic material, such as Genesis 49, *The Assumption of Moses* and *The Testaments of the Twelve Patriarchs*. The character of parenesis is further noticed by the frequent use of imperatives and four occurrences of temporal clauses followed by imperatives. Both of these features are integral to an exhortatory or parenetic address."

"As for yourselves, beware; for they will hand you over to councils; and you will be beaten in synagogues; and you will stand before governors and kings because of me, as a testimony to them. And the good news must first be proclaimed to all nations. When they bring you to trial and hand you over, do not worry beforehand about what you are to say; but say whatever is given you at that time, for it is not you who speak, but the Holy Spirit. Brother will betray brother to death, and a father his child, and children will rise against parents and have them put to death; and you will be hated by all because of my name. But the one who endures to the end will be saved."

"But when you see the desolating sacrilege set up where it ought not to be (let the reader understand), then those in Judea must flee to the mountains; the one on the housetop must not go down or enter the house to take anything away; the one in the field must not turn back to get a coat. Woe to those who are pregnant and to those who are nursing infants in those days! Pray that it may not be in winter. For in those days there will be suffering, such as has not been from the beginning of the creation that God created until now, no, and never will be. And if the Lord had not cut short those days, no one would be saved; but for the sake of the elect, whom he chose, he has cut short those days. And if anyone says to you at that time, 'Look! Here is the Messiah!' or 'Look! There he is!' – do not believe it. False messiahs and false prophets will appear and produce signs and omens, to lead astray, if possible, the elect. **But be alert; I have already told you everything.**"

"But in those days, after that suffering, the sun will be darkened, and the moon will not give its light, and the stars will be falling from heaven, and the powers in the heavens will be shaken. Then they will see 'the Son of Man coming in clouds' with great power and glory. Then he will send out the angels, and gather his elect from the four winds, from the ends of the earth to the ends of heaven."

"From the fig tree learn its lesson: as soon as its branch becomes tender and puts forth its leaves, you know that summer is near. So also, when you see these things taking place, you know that he is near, at the very gates. Truly I tell you, this generation will not pass away until all these things have taken place. Heaven and earth will pass away, but my words will not pass away."

"But about that day or hour no one knows, neither the angels in heaven, nor the Son, but only the Father. Beware, keep alert; for you do not know when the time will come. It is like a man going on a journey, when he leaves home and puts his slaves in charge, each with his work, and commands the doorkeeper to be on the watch. Therefore, keep awake – for you do not know when the master of the house will come, in the evening, or at midnight, or at cockcrow, or at dawn, or else he may find you asleep when he comes suddenly. And what I say to you I say to all: Keep awake."[1163]

Hatina's arguments are technical for the most part, so I will just bring forward what is relevant here. He points out that the question asked by the disciples is in two parts: "Tell us, 1) when will this be, and 2) what will be the sign that all these things are about to be accomplished?" Hatina convincingly establishes that the two questions are about the same thing: *the predicted destruction of the temple.* He also shows that the answer is in two parts as well, though the second question – "what will be the sign when all these things are going to be fulfilled?" – is answered first in vv. 5-23, the last words of which are, "But be alert; I have already told you everything," bolded above. The 'when' is answered by vv. 28-37.

Winn notes that in the OT cosmic portents, such as begin part two of the discourse, were commonly found in contexts of judgment where a prophet would predict the imminent arrival of a "day of the Lord" when God would come and destroy political, religious and economic structures of a given people or nation. And in fact, Mark begins the second half with what

---

[1163]Mark 13:3-37.

appears to be a remodeling and condensing of Isaiah 13:9-16, which is a clue that Mark intended his audience to refer to the passage he echoes or alludes to:

> See, the day of the LORD comes, cruel, with wrath and fierce anger, to make the earth a desolation, and to destroy its sinners from it. **For the stars of the heavens and their constellations will not give their light; the sun will be dark at its rising, and the moon will not shed its light.** I will punish the world for its evil, and the wicked for their iniquity; I will put an end to the pride of the arrogant, and lay low the insolence of tyrants. I will make mortals more rare than fine gold, and humans than the gold of Ophir. Therefore **I will make the heavens tremble, and the earth will be shaken out of its place**, at the wrath of the LORD of hosts in the day of his fierce anger. Like a hunted gazelle, or like sheep with no one to gather them, all will turn to their own people, and all will flee to their own lands. Whoever is found will be thrust through, and whoever is caught will fall by the sword. Their infants will be dashed to pieces before their eyes; their houses will be plundered, and their wives ravished.

The historical situation in question in Isaiah was the Babylonian exile. The references to the heavenly bodies and earthquake are most likely metaphorical, but we can't entirely exclude literal cosmic portents. There were certainly a number of them attending the destruction of Jerusalem! In any event, the cosmic signs referred to the demise of a political/religious entity within a historical framework. The same cosmic portents appear in Ezekiel 32:7-8:

> When I blot you out, I will cover the heavens, and make their stars dark; I will cover the sun with a cloud, and the moon shall not give its light. All the shining lights of the heavens I will darken above you, and put darkness on your land, says the Lord God.

Joel 2:1-11:

> Blow the trumpet in Zion; sound the alarm on my holy mountain! Let all the inhabitants of the land tremble, for the day of the LORD is coming, it is near – **a day of darkness and gloom, a day of clouds and thick darkness!** Like blackness spread upon the mountains **a great and powerful army comes**; their like has never been from of old, nor will be again after them in ages to come. Fire devours in front of them, and behind them a flame burns. Before them the land is like the garden of Eden, but after them a desolate wilderness, and nothing escapes them. They have the appearance of horses, and like war-horses they charge. As with the rumbling of chariots, they leap on the tops of the mountains, like the crackling of a flame of fire devouring the stubble, like a powerful army drawn up for battle. Before them peoples are in anguish, all faces grow pale. Like warriors they charge, like soldiers they scale the wall. Each keeps to its own course, they do not swerve from their paths. They do not jostle one another, each keeps to its own track; they burst through the weapons and are not halted. They leap upon the city, they run upon the walls; they climb up into the houses, they enter through the windows like a thief. **The earth quakes before them, the heavens tremble. The sun and the moon are darkened, and the stars withdraw their shining.** The LORD utters his voice at the head of his army; how vast is his host! Numberless are those who obey his command. Truly the day of the LORD is great; terrible indeed – who can endure it? v. 31: **The sun shall be turned to darkness, and the moon to blood**, before the great and terrible day of the LORD comes.

And there is more like that. The point is that there was a sort of universal language of cosmic portents that were used to describe the destruction of a political entity within a historical context. And these 'prophecies' are all, no doubt, *ex eventu*. The darkening of celestial bodies is not equated in any of these prophecies with the end of the world but rather, they mark the shift from one age to another in terms of political dominance. Just as the ancients thought that military actions and victories reflected the will of the gods on Earth, so did they think that those same actions and victories and defeats were somehow reflected in the heavenly spheres with cosmic displays. Hatina shows that there is an abundance of literature of the time that utilizes cosmic metaphors to describe the end of political/religious entities. Even the Lukan author utilized this system of metaphors. In Acts 2:14-21, Peter associates the celestial portents with the coming of the Holy Spirit at Pentecost. The prophecy in Joel 2:28-32 concerning the eschatological age or the 'last days' when God will pour out his Spirit on every person is now considered fulfilled according to 'Luke.' Hatina writes:

> In sum, the cosmic portents in the Hebrew scriptures and in early Jewish and Christian interpreta-
> tion function metaphorically to describe an act of divine judgment against a given political and/or
> religious entity ... An aftermath of judgment is often anticipated in terms of restoration when Israel's
> god will gather his people and reign over the nations of the earth. The imagery is used in a temporal
> manner to describe a divine judgment in history and not the termination of history. In light of this
> function, the imagery in Mark 13:24-25 can be read as yet another prophecy of judgment against a
> group whose agenda is viewed as antagonistic toward Yahweh's expectations. ... But this time, it is
> Jerusalem and the Temple establishment that takes on the role of adversary.[1164]

Hatina has a further, most interesting idea about the Son of Man title as used by Mark. The text:

> "But in those days, after that suffering, the sun will be darkened, and the moon will not give its
> light, and the stars will be falling from heaven, and the powers in the heavens will be shaken. Then
> **they will see 'the Son of Man coming in clouds'** with great power and glory. Then he will
> send out the angels, and gather his elect from the four winds, from the ends of the earth to the ends
> of heaven."[1165]

The allusion is to Daniel 7:13 (and I include 14):

> "As I watched in the night visions, **I saw one like a human being coming with the clouds
> of heaven**. And he came to the Ancient One and was presented before him. To him was given
> dominion and glory and kingship, that all peoples, nations, and languages should serve him. His
> dominion is an everlasting dominion that shall not pass away, and his kingship is one that shall
> never be destroyed."

This bit of text is the one on which many make the claim that the second part of the Olivet Discourse is about the Parousia, i.e. the 'second coming' at the end of history/time. Hatina's opinion is that the "coming of the Son of Man in clouds" is *a direct reference to the destruction of the temple.* He bases this on 1) the original context of the passage in Daniel to which Mark was referring the reader; 2) the various future uses of the title 'Son of Man' throughout the text of Mark.

Regarding the first point, Hatina writes:

[1164]Hatina (1996), p. 59.
[1165]Mark 13:24-26.

In the context of Daniel the coming of "one like a Son of Man" must be read in contrast to the preceding four beasts who represent four nations hostile toward Israel. The beasts are judged in a heavenly courtroom and consequently lose their power and dominion over the earth and, most importantly, over Israel. Subsequently, a cryptic human figure or someone who appears as such is presented an eternal kingdom by the Ancient of Days. The kingdom is then given to the "saints of the Most High." Since the four beasts function in the context as symbols for kings and their kingdoms, the same symbolic reference should be extended to the figure who resembles the Son of Man. ... The contrasting symbolism evokes the idea that the people of God are true humanity while the hostile kingdoms are merely animals. ... The arrival of the Son of Man figure is expressed primarily in political fashion whereby the "coming" ... is intended to reflect a coming to God to receive power instead of a messianic descent to earth. ... The overall picture in Dan 7 is one of political transition in which the old hostile kingdoms are destroyed and replaced by a new everlasting kingdom ruled by God's people.

... Throughout Jewish apocalyptic literature *the function of the Son of Man*, like the traditional concepts of a Davidic messiah, *was to destroy the enemies of Israel's righteous* and to institute an age of unending peace. ... Despite the variety of opponents, the motif of judgment against Israel's enemies and the vindication of the righteous remains constant. Extending this motif to the reading of the Son of Man's function in Mark ... is fitting, for the narrative context which focuses on the opposition against the [Jewish leaders] by Jesus demands a similar conclusive promise of judgment and restoration. ...

... In Mark's story, Jesus as Son of Man has already been invested with power and authority from the moment of his baptism, and thus the notion of receiving a kingdom can be presupposed. For those, however, who are unaware of Jesus' identity, like his inquisitors, the matter will become clear after his death and resurrection *when he comes to judge his opponents through the destruction of their beloved Temple.*[1166]

This view does not negate the idea of the 'Second Adam,' though 'Son of Man' seems to be, as Hatina said, *a particular role involving judgment and destruction.* With that thought in mind, taking up Hatina's second point, one can look at every instance the title occurs in Mark and note that all of them belong to a scenario of conflict with the Jewish authorities. The two isolated instances in the first half of the Gospel are the dispute over Jesus' authority to forgive sins and his being 'Lord of the Sabbath' (2:10; 2:28). The title doesn't reappear again until the first passion prediction: "Then he began to teach them that the Son of Man must undergo great suffering, and be rejected by the elders, the chief priests, and the scribes, and be killed, and after three days rise again" (Mk 8:31). And then again, in reference to that prediction in what now seems to be a direct allusion to the coming destruction of Jerusalem and the temple: "Those who are ashamed of me and of my words in this adulterous and sinful generation, of them the Son of Man will also be ashamed when he comes in the glory of his Father with the holy angels" (Mk 8:38). After the Transfiguration, the title is used again in reference to Jesus' coming death and resurrection, a resurrection that will not be physical, but a glorification in heaven similar to what has just transpired on the mountain: "As they were coming down the mountain, he ordered them to tell no one about what they had seen, until after the Son of Man had risen from the dead" (Mk 9:9).

The title is used in Mk 9:12-13:

He said to them, "Elijah is indeed coming first to restore all things. How then is it written about the Son of Man, that he is to go through many sufferings and be treated with contempt? But I tell you that Elijah has come, and they did to him whatever they pleased, as it is written about him."

[1166]Hatina (1996), pp. 60–62.

Then in Mk 9:30-32:

> They went on from there and passed through Galilee. He did not want anyone to know it; for he was
> teaching his disciples, saying to them, "The Son of Man is to be betrayed into human hands, and
> they will kill him, and three days after being killed, he will rise again." But they did not understand
> what he was saying and were afraid to ask him.

And Mk 10:32-34:

> They were on the road, going up to Jerusalem, and Jesus was walking ahead of them; they were
> amazed, and those who followed were afraid. He took the twelve aside again and began to tell them
> what was to happen to him, saying, "See, we are going up to Jerusalem, and the Son of Man will
> be handed over to the chief priests and the scribes, and they will condemn him to death; then they
> will hand him over to the Gentiles; they will mock him, and spit upon him, and flog him, and kill
> him; and after three days he will rise again."

Every single use of this title, 'Son of Man,' is in the context of the opposition of the Jewish
leaders which leads to betrayal, suffering and death. In Mk 10:45: "For the Son of Man came
not to be served but to serve, and to give his life a ransom for many."

In chapter 13, the Son of Man is described as "coming in clouds with great power and glory,"
certainly a scene similar to the visitations of God when he *judged and destroyed* in the past, and
specifically in the Danielic context. At this point, the usage of 'Son of Man' changes somewhat;
it is still in the context of conflict, but now, it is a warning. At the Last Supper, it is a warning
to Judas: "For the Son of Man goes as it is written of him, but woe to that one by whom the Son
of Man is betrayed! It would have been better for that one not to have been born" (Mk 14:21).
And then, a bit later, in the Garden of Gethsemane, after Peter, James and John failed to watch
with him: "He came a third time and said to them, 'Are you still sleeping and taking your rest?
Enough! The hour has come; the Son of Man is betrayed into the hands of sinners'" (Mk 14:41).
At his trial before the Sanhedrin, it is used again as a warning:

> Some stood up and gave false testimony against him, saying, "We heard him say, 'I will destroy this
> temple that is made with hands, and in three days I will build another, not made with hands.'" But
> even on this point their testimony did not agree. Then the high priest stood up before them and
> asked Jesus, "Have you no answer? What is it that they testify against you?" But he was silent
> and did not answer. Again the high priest asked him, "Are you the Messiah, the Son of the Blessed
> One?" Jesus said, "I am; and 'you will see the Son of Man seated at the right hand of the Power,'
> and 'coming with the clouds of heaven.'"[1167]

So it seems that Mark's audience may, indeed, have understood the title 'Son of Man' in the
context of *divine judgment* on Jerusalem, as described in Daniel, and being the result of the Jews'
opposition to Jesus. Hatina writes:

> Despite the variety of opponents, the motif of judgment against Israel's enemies and the vindication
> of the righteous remains constant. Extending this motif to the reading of the Son of Man's function
> in Mark 13 is fitting, for the narrative context which focuses on the opposition against the Temple
> establishment by Jesus demands a similar conclusive promise of judgment and restoration. Moreover,

---

[1167]Mark 14:57-62.

there appears to be nothing in the narrative that would steer the implied audience to interpret the Son of Man's function in an alternate direction – that is, away from the motif found in the exegetical traditions. ...

Likewise, the coming of the Son of Man in 14:62 must be read in light of the destruction of the Temple. During the trial scene, Jesus is falsely accused of claiming that he will destroy the physical Temple and in three days build a spiritual replacement. It is difficult to know why Mark considers the accusation false ... I suspect that the scene is deliberately ironic. Unknown to the accusers, their testimony is accurate. The implied audience would have probably understood the accusation in this way after 70 CE. ... The destruction of the Temple is an integral part of the trial scene, and thus should underlie Jesus' words of judgment and vindication in 14:62.[1168]

Throughout the Olivet Discourse, the Markan Jesus addresses his disciples most often by using the second person plural. Yet, when he says, "Then they will see 'the Son of Man coming in clouds' with great power and glory," he is using the third person plural. In Mk 14:62, in his answer to the high priest, the Markan Jesus uses the same verb to refer to the future coming of the Son of Man, and the same reference to Dan. 7:13. It is a prediction of divine judgment directed against the Temple hierarchy. Thus, the temple hierarchy would see the Son of Man coming metaphorically in the literal and temporal destruction of the Temple. And it seems to be most likely, if not quite certain, that Mark's audience would have understood the allusion in chapter 13 to have been the destruction of Jerusalem and its temple.

Hatina states that the Markan author used this imagery in Mark, in the way it was used, to make the claim that Jesus was directly associated with the divine judgment on Jerusalem and the Jews. To the Roman Christians, Mark's audience, the fact that Jesus' predictions in the Olivet Discourse *had been fulfilled* in the destruction of the temple and its hierarchy was validation of Jesus as truly the vindicated Son of God. Further, the fact that the destruction had been effected by Vespasian, Titus, and the Roman army placed the Romans under the control of God, the father of Jesus.

The prediction of restoration immediately following the prophecy of judgment was standard in prophecies of this type. The criteria for being 'gathered' was usually obedience and persevering to the end in times of turmoil. Usually it was Yahweh who did the gathering; in the case of Mark 13:27, the usual translation says 'angels.' However, in other places this same Greek word is often translated as 'messengers.' In this sense, messengers could be preachers of the gospel who would gather the elect by their missionary endeavors.

There is no mention at all of a collective resurrection, which Hatina says militates against the idea that the Parousia is the topic. Since the author of Mark did mention a collective resurrection in Mk 12:18-27, it would be odd for him not to include it here if he intended the scenario to be understood as the Parousia. Thus, the idea that this was a description of the eschatological 'Rapture' must be discarded, and Hatina's argument that the Markan Jesus is talking about the destruction of Jerusalem and the temple in the "coming of the Son of Man" is the most likely solution/conclusion. All the features of the literary context support a temporal act of judgment as opposed to any End Times scenario. The genre appears to be parenesis, a farewell address, in which Jesus warns his disciples about coming afflictions, and the answer is to a two-part question about the destruction of the temple. Mark has used the OT texts to describe just another 'day of the Lord' in which God's 'visitation' is directed against the Jews and Jerusalem.

[1168]Hatina (1996), pp. 61, 62–63.

What is utterly ironic is that the Jerusalem Christians expected their messiah to come on the clouds of heaven with legions of angels to destroy the Romans, but here, Mark is saying that the true messiah did come and destroyed Jerusalem, the temple, and the Zealot supporters of revolution via the Romans. It just doesn't get any more ironic than that.

Now, we return to the first part of the Olivet Discourse: "Then Jesus began to say to them, 'Beware that no one leads you astray. Many will come in my name and say, 'I am he!' and they will lead many astray'" (Mk 13:5). This was certainly Paul's experience, as is revealed in 1 Corinthians, Galatians and Philippians. He came right out and said that there were those preaching a different Christ, and enemies of the cross, leading his congregations astray.

> When you hear of wars and rumors of wars, do not be alarmed; this must take place, but the end is still to come. For nation will rise against nation, and kingdom against kingdom; there will be earthquakes in various places; there will be famines. This is but the beginning of the birth pangs.[1169]

There were rebellions and rumors of rebellion going around, especially at the time that Caligula was pushing to have his statue erected in the temple. That history was covered in the discussion of Josephus and Paul's timeline, and I pointed out that it seems likely that 2 Thessalonians is actually an authentic Pauline letter with some interpolation, and can be dated to 40/41 AD because of the implied references to Caligula and his intentions.

Then, of course, nation did rise against nation, both in Alexandria, during the time of Caligula, and pretty much in all the years following the execution of Judas the Galilean in 19 AD until the rebellion against Rome.

Several famines occurred during the reign of Claudius (41 to 54 AD) in different parts of the Empire, but no universal famine is recorded such as Eusebius writes. According to Josephus a severe famine took place in Judea while Cuspius Fadus and Tiberius Alexander were successively procurators. Fadus was sent into Judea upon the death of Agrippa (44 AD), and Alexander was succeeded by Cumanus in 48 AD. The exact date of Alexander's accession we do not know, but it took place probably about 45 or 46 AD. Then, there was Josephus mentioning a famine in conjunction with Queen Helena of Adiabene whose son converted to Judaism:

> Her arrival was very advantageous to the people of Jerusalem; for a famine oppressed them at that time, and many people died for want of money to procure food. Queen Helena sent some of her servants to Alexandria with money to buy a great quantity of grain, and others of them to Cyprus to bring back a cargo of dried figs. They quickly returned with the provisions, which she immediately distributed to those that need. She has thus left a most excellent memorial by the beneficence which she bestowed upon our nation. And when her son Izates was informed of this famine, he sent great sums of money to the principal men in Jerusalem.[1170]

> The successor of Fadus was Tiberius Alexander ... [I]t was in that (or their) administration that the great famine occurred in Judea, during which Queen Helen bought grain from Egypt for large sums and distributed it to the needy, as I have stated above.[1171]

Among the other historians, only Dio and Tacitus mention famine at this time – in Rome. Eusebius also mentions famines in Greece and Rome during Claudius' reign.[1172] Mark is very

---

[1169]Mark 13:7-8.
[1170]*Ant* 20.2.5 (49–53).
[1171]*Ant* 20.5.2 (101).
[1172]Dio 60.11; Tacitus, *Ann.* 12.13; Eusebius, *Chron.*, year of Abr. 2070.

creatively utilizing historical events that we can only partly recover via Josephus, Tacitus, and others, and putting words into Jesus' mouth 'back in the past' for verisimilitude.

> "As for yourselves, beware; for they will hand you over to councils; and you will be beaten in synagogues; and you will stand before governors and kings because of me, as a testimony to them. And the good news must first be proclaimed to all nations. When they bring you to trial and hand you over, do not worry beforehand about what you are to say; but say whatever is given you at that time, for it is not you who speak, but the Holy Spirit. Brother will betray brother to death, and a father his child, and children will rise against parents and have them put to death; and you will be hated by all because of my name. But the one who endures to the end will be saved."[1173]

The above passage appears to me to be loaded with allusions to the mission of Paul. Paul himself told us that he had experienced countless floggings, five times punished with 40 lashes minus one, three times beaten with rods, was stoned once, shipwrecked, adrift at sea, he escaped from the governor in Damascus, etc. (2 Cor. 11:23-33). Notice this important clue: "And the good news must first be proclaimed to all nations," which was exactly what Paul set out to do. And he was certainly hated by the Jewish Christians of Jerusalem. Mark may have used Paul's experiences as a model; it may even have been the experience of his own community *vis à vis* the Jewish Christians, and then, later, after the war, when the messianists – Jewish and Gentile alike – were hated because of their association with a 'Jewish superstition' about the coming messiah, and therefore guilty by association with the rebels of Jerusalem.

> "But when you see the desolating sacrilege set up where it ought not to be (let the reader understand), then those in Judea must flee to the mountains; the one on the housetop must not go down or enter the house to take anything away; the one in the field must not turn back to get a coat. Woe to those who are pregnant and to those who are nursing infants in those days! Pray that it may not be in winter. For in those days there will be suffering, such as has not been from the beginning of the creation that God created until now, no, and never will be. And if the Lord had not cut short those days, no one would be saved; but for the sake of the elect, whom he chose, he has cut short those days."[1174]

The "abomination of desolation" or "desolating sacrilege" is an interesting topic that we don't have time to pursue in any depth. Nevertheless, the short version is that the first "abomination that desolates" was apparently the desecration of the temple by Antiochus Epiphanes, written about by Daniel (Dan. 11:31; 12:11). Of course, in Daniel, it was *vaticinium ex eventu*.

Then, in 2 Thessalonians, there is a close equivalent, "the lawless one" who "takes his seat in the temple of God, declaring himself to be God" (2 Thess. 2:3-4). Of course, that crisis was expected to end with the coming of the Messiah who was going to destroy him "with the breath of his mouth, annihilating him by the manifestation of his coming" (2 Thess. 2:8). Instead, Caligula was assassinated by officers of the Praetorian Guard led by Cassius Chaerea. But, considering all that has been said, who's to say that the author of 2 Thessalonians (I opt for Paul) did not think that the assassination was under the control of Christ just as Vespasian and Titus were later backed by Christ? (There was also a famine in Rome during the time of Caligula, allegedly brought on by some financial crisis.)[1175]

[1173]Mark 13:9-13.
[1174]Mark 13:14-20.
[1175]Suetonius, *Caligula* 38.

Now, according to Josephus, when the Romans captured Jerusalem, they carried standards into the sanctuary at the east gate and sacrificed to them. The priests were executed by Titus (*Wars* 6.316–322). It is almost certain that this was widely known and may have been depicted in one of the scenes displayed in the triumph of Vespasian and Titus. This may very well be what the Markan author is referring to and why he adds the parenthetical caveat: "let the reader understand." Mark's audience would have understood that these prophecies were a series of references to Isa. 13:10; 34:4; Dan. 7:13; Deut. 30:4; Zech. 2:6, and were pointing directly at the destruction of the Temple in 70 AD and its abomination by Titus and his soldiers.

The conclusion of all this is that Mark's anti-temple, anti-Jewish Christian motif has held true right through chapter 13, where all of those people who rejected Paul and his Messiah got their just reward. Never mind that he had to make up a character to act the role of Jesus; his audience certainly understood that it was allegory almost from start to finish.

Mark's Passion Narrative

Mark's passion narrative is unique in respect of the rest of the Gospel. Unlike the first half, where Jesus is all over the place, with episode after episode interwoven into a complex tapestry of multiple types of references and situated in numerous settings, the passion narrative takes place entirely in and around Jerusalem (though Jerusalem is hardly mentioned), and reads like a smoothly constructed story with one event leading to the next. Many, if not most, scholars think that the characteristics of this part of Mark point to the use of a pre-Markan passion story about the real, 'historical' Jesus.

But we must remember, Mark's Gospel is a literary work, a narrative with a story that has settings, plot, and characterizations. The two main plot lines that connect the story as a whole are the conflict between Jesus and the religious authorities and Jesus and his disciples. At the very beginning, the religious leaders take on the task of seeking to destroy Jesus (Mk 3:6). The religious opponents of Jesus shift from the scribes and Pharisees in the first half, to the chief priests, elders and scribes in the second half. This represents the escalation in power and position of said opposition and thus, increased danger for Jesus.

Meanwhile, the disciples display an abysmal lack of understanding in both halves of the Gospel, though the nature of their incomprehension changes from a lack of insight into Jesus' power and care for them, to a lack of insight into Jesus' destiny and the implications of the destiny for their own lives. The narrative reveals whether or not the disciples will live up to the expectations of Jesus and whether or not the religious leaders will achieve their goal of doing away with him. The passion narrative brings to culmination and resolution the two plot lines and thus is, in my opinion, Mark's literary construction, designed to do exactly what we see it doing.

In chapter 14, Judas, one of the disciples, is split off and joins the religious opponents, the chief priests. The rest of the disciples move from misunderstanding to abject failure. They have simply not been able to comprehend the importance of suffering and sacrificial service no matter how many times Jesus has tried to teach them. So, at the moment of crisis, they desert Jesus; at his arrest, all the disciples flee except Peter (Mk 14:50). Peter hangs around at a distance for a bit, but ultimately, he fails even more spectacularly by denying Jesus three times (Mk 14:54, 66-72). Although the disciples are mentioned later, they never again appear in the narrative.

The passion narrative begins with a repetition of the desire of the religious authorities to destroy Jesus (Mk 14:1-2) and the remaining narrative explains how they go about doing this. It is a deeply ironic story in which the reader/hearer sees the religious leaders help to fulfill the will of God through their own malicious acts. The irony comes out most clearly in the mocking scenes in which Jesus is ridiculed. To the corrupt temple authorities, it was utterly preposterous to consider that Jesus was, actually, a prophet (Mk 14:65), or Christ or the Son of God. Yet, to Mark's audience, all those things were true. The temple authorities were wrong about Jesus, and they did not actually destroy him because he gave his life obediently for all humanity and was raised and glorified by God. For Mark, the darkest moment in the Gospel is the crucifixion; and, at the same time, it is the moment that marks the turn of the ages, the inauguration of the Kingdom of God. In the middle of the darkness, light breaks forth in the splitting of the temple veil and the centurion sees the truth. The Gospel ends with the rising of the sun and the empty tomb guarded by a messenger who delivers the Good News. Indeed, the women run away in terror and tell no one what they saw, but even this last act of human disobedience and abandonment cannot defeat God's purpose. The news was given to Paul by divine revelation, and Paul taught Mark.

As Winn notes, Mark has brought Jesus' power and suffering together using Roman political ideology taken to an extreme. Mark's narrative amplifies Jesus' suffering with details of his shaming, humiliation and torturous death. Jesus is betrayed, abandoned by his disciples, lied about, mocked, beaten and spit on by Jewish and Roman authorities. During his crucifixion he is mocked even more cruelly and his quotation of Psalm 22 from the cross gives the impression that he has been abandoned by God himself. And yet, this is the death that he has prophesied for himself on three distinct occasions, and alluded to at other times; he predicted the betrayal by Judas, the abandonment by the disciples, and the denial by Peter, and so the passion narrative is fulfillment of Jesus' predictions in every aspect, proving his power as a prophet, and thus his divine power. According to Winn, this death is the proper outcome for the true ruler of the world: giving his life for humanity, an act of greatness not weakness.

Mark does not explicitly claim that Jesus' death fulfills scripture, but the use of Psalm 22 implies it. It is referenced at Mk 15:34 in Jesus' cry from the cross just before he dies. "My God, my God, why have you forsaken me?" Most scholars think that the citation of the psalm invokes the entirety of it, which contains unmistakable parallels between the details of the psalm and the passion narrative:

> My God, my God, why have you forsaken me? Why are you so far from helping me, from the words of my groaning? ... But I am a worm, and not human; scorned by others, and despised by the people. ... All who see me mock at me; they make mouths at me, they shake their heads; ... they open wide their mouths at me, like a ravening and roaring lion. I am poured out like water, and all my bones are out of joint; my heart is like wax; it is melted within my breast; my mouth is dried up like a potsherd, and my tongue sticks to my jaws; you lay me in the dust of death. ... a company of evildoers encircles me. My hands and feet have shriveled; I can count all my bones. They stare and gloat over me; they divide my clothes among themselves, and for my clothing they cast lots.
>
> But you, O LORD, do not be far away! O my help, **come quickly to my aid!** Deliver my soul from the sword, my life from the power of the dog! Save me from the mouth of the lion! **From the horns of the wild oxen you have rescued me.** I will tell of your name to my brothers and sisters; in the midst of the congregation I will praise you ... For he did not despise or abhor the affliction of the afflicted; **he did not hide his face from me, but heard when I cried to**

him. ... All the ends of the earth shall remember and turn to the LORD; and all the families of the nations shall worship before him. ... To him, indeed, shall all who sleep in the earth bow down; before him shall bow all who go down to the dust, and I shall live for him.

So, it seems clear that Mark intends for Jesus' death to be understood as prophetic fulfillment of Psalm 22. The psalm does not end in suffering and death, but rather in deliverance and vindication. Thus Winn says that the citing of the psalm, in invoking its entirety, looks at the suffering and the resurrection. He says further that it seems illogical to think that the crucified Jesus of Mark sees in his citation nothing but suffering and abandonment by God, considering the fact that he has already predicted that he will suffer, die, and be resurrected. And the fact that the Gospel does end in apparent resurrection makes it more likely that the citation of the psalm means more than just abandonment. Thus Winn proposes that this psalm reveals the unity of the powerful and suffering Jesus. The 'cry of dereliction' looks forward to the glory and vindication on the other side of suffering.

In addition to the clue of the psalm, the death of Jesus was accompanied by two supernatural events: the darkness that covered the land at noon and the tearing of the temple veil. Interestingly, both Plutarch and Virgil claimed that the sun hid its face at the death of Julius Caesar.[1176] Perhaps Mark was borrowing that detail as well?

Recall that the temple veil was captured by the Romans and displayed in the triumph of Vespasian and Titus. As I have noted already, some scholars have argued in the past that if Mark was written soon after the war, he would have made more explicit references to it. This idea does not take into account what Mark's purposes were, that the consequences of the war were what needed to be dealt with, and his apparent lack of consciousness and explicit references to the war are evidence that he was deliberately writing an account that was retrojected into the past. The fact that the war is thus so studiously avoided is further evidence of this position.

Winn brings up the fact that scholar T. E. Schmidt draws parallels between Mark's passion narrative and a Roman imperial triumph.[1177] The first item in this list is Mark's use of the word *praetorium* in Mark 15:16, which was where Jesus' trial was held. Many modern translations convert this word into 'governor's headquarters,' so the allusion is lost, but it is retained in the King James Version and Zondervan's Amplified Translation, among others. Schmidt proposes that there was a double reason for Mark to use this word, because it was both the identification of the physical location of the trial and would have drawn the reader's mind to the Roman imperial world.[1178] After the soldiers led Jesus into the courtyard, they "called together the whole cohort."

[1176]Plutarch, *Caesar*, 69, Thomas North translation: "Again, of signs in the element, the great comet, which seven nights together was seen very bright after Caesar's death, the eighth night after was never seen more. Also the brightness of the sun was darkened, the which all that year through rose very pale and shined not out, whereby it gave but small heat: therefore the air being very cloudy and dark, by the weakness of the heat that could not come forth, did cause the Earth to bring forth but raw and unripe fruit, which rotted before it could ripe." Virgil (http://www.perseus.tufts.edu/hopper/text?doc=urn:cts:latinLit:phi0690.phi002.perseus-eng1:1.466): "He too it was, when Caesar's light was quenched, For Rome had pity, when his bright head he veiled In iron-hued darkness, till a godless age Trembled for night eternal; at that time Howbeit Earth also, and the ocean-plains, And dogs obscene, and birds of evil bode Gave tokens."

[1177]Winn (2018), pp. 157–62.

[1178]T.E. Schmidt, 'Mark 15:16-32: The Crucifixion Narrative and the Roman Triumphal Procession,' *NTS* 41 (1995): 1–18.

A cohort was something like 600 soldiers. There would have been a lot of soldiers – at least a cohort – in a triumph.

The next item is the fact that there, in the praetorium, Jesus was clothed in purple (Mk 15:17). Since purple garments were extremely expensive and rare in the Roman world, it is highly unlikely that such a robe would actually have been placed on a criminal.[1179] However, if Mark is trying to make a point, or draw an allusion, it finds a home in the Roman imperial triumph wherein the triumphator would have been clothed in purple. Next, a crown of thorns parallels the laurel crown that the triumphator would have worn. And then, the soldiers began to mock him in negative imitation of the homage Roman soldiers paid to the triumphator at the start of the Roman triumphal procession.

> Both the combination and the very presence of these symbols is striking. The wearing of purple was outlawed for anyone below equestrian rank. The only available robe of this kind would be that of Pilate, but it is inconceivable that he would lend such a precious garment to be struck and spat upon by common soldiers. Along similarly practical lines, one wonders where in the courtyard of a palace thorns would be available to form a crown. Are we to imagine that the solders delayed their mockery while someone looked for a thorn bush nearby? The strangeness of these details, their likeness to the ceremonial garb of a triumphator, and their combination with other details of the narrative suggest a purpose rather than a coincidence.[1180]

Parallels continue with the detail of Simon of Cyrene carrying the cross (Mk 15:21).[1181] In a Roman triumph, the bull that was to be sacrificed at the end of the parade was led in the procession. Next to the bull walked an official carrying a double-bladed ax (cross shaped) that was to be used to kill the bull for the sacrifice. In Mark, Jesus replaces the sacrificial bull as Simon carries the instrument of death over his shoulder.

The place where Jesus' anti-triumph ended was Golgotha (Mk 15:22), Aramaic for 'place of the skull.' A Roman triumph ended at the temple of Jupiter, the Capitolium, a Latin word derived from the word *caput* or 'head.' At this point, Jesus is offered wine mixed with myrrh, which he refuses. This is a striking parallel to a Roman triumph as, at the end of the procession, the

---

[1179]Matthew changes the color to scarlet, the color of a Roman soldier's cloak.

[1180]Schmidt (1995), p. 7.

[1181]Cyrene, a Roman city on the coast of Libya, has links to both Jewish rebels and early Christianity. According to Dio (68.32), the Jews of Cyrene revolted in 73 AD after the revolt in Judea was considered to be suppressed. Considering what the emperor Claudius had to say in his edicts in respect of the Alexandrian troubles, it appears that messianists were based in Judea (Syria) and were widely 'evangelizing' and were considered to be a plague on the Empire. (The Cyrenes also revolted in 117 AD, during the Kitos War.) Acts 2:10 has Jews from Cyrene hearing the disciples speaking in their own language in Jerusalem on the day of Pentecost; Acts 6:9 depicts some Cyrenian Jews disputing with a disciple named Stephen; Acts 11:20 tells of Jewish Christians originally from Cyrene who (along with believers from Cyprus) first preached the Gospel to non-Jews; Acts 13:1 names Lucius of Cyrene as one of several to whom the Holy Spirit spoke, instructing them to appoint Barnabas and Saul (later Paul) for missionary service, which gives the whole fraud away. ('Cyrene, Libya,' Wikipedia.org.) These passages in Acts may have influenced the creation of the tradition of the Coptic Orthodox Church, that its founder, Mark was a native of Cyrene. (See "St. Mark the Apostle, the Founder of the Coptic Church," https://www.suscopts.org/coptic-orthodox/church/saint-mark/.) The claim is that Mark was an African native of Jewish parents and a Levite! Obviously, whoever made this nonsense up had already read Acts. Nevertheless, because of the mention in the Gospel of Mark, of Simon of Cyrene, as well as the passages in Acts which may have been a distorted reflection of some facts available to its author that are no longer extant, one wonders if Paul had some connection to Cyrene?

triumphator would be offered wine, which he would ritually refuse. Immediately after refusing the wine, the bull would be sacrificed. So, just after Jesus was offered wine, the text says, "And they crucified him" (Mk 15:24).

Indeed, it appears that Mark has created a mock Roman triumph, though Matthew obscures this by having Jesus taste the wine instead of refusing it, as the triumphator would do. And, at the end of the triumph, the triumphator would be elevated above the ground, often flanked by two men. Tiberius was between his two consuls; Claudius was between his two sons-in-law; Vespasian was between his two sons. Jesus, on the other hand, was between two 'bandits.'

Expanding on Schmidt's scenario, Winn adds that the confession of the centurion at the moment of Jesus' death might also represent the triumph, since the centurion recognized the triumph of Jesus at that moment. He writes:

> For the Markan Evangelist the confession is a true one, to be sure, as Jesus is indeed Son of God. But more importantly, Mark presents a Roman soldier offering allegiance that would normally have been reserved for the Roman emperor to Jesus – to the Roman reader, the centurion's declaration would have represented a change in allegiance.[1182]

In the confession of the centurion, the passion has turned to triumph and there is fulfillment of the Markan incipit which presents Jesus, in Roman imperial language, as the Son of God. One can't help but wonder whether the whole set of allusions to a Roman triumph, and the declaration of the centurion, wasn't a hint at the true identity of Paul's 'Jesus'? In 2 Corinthians 2:14-16, Paul writes:

> But thanks be to God, who in *Christ always leads us in triumph*, and through us spreads the fragrance of the knowledge of him everywhere. For we are the aroma of Christ to God among those who are being saved and among those who are perishing, to one a fragrance from death to death, to the other a fragrance from life to life. Who is sufficient for these things?

One is reminded that the Roman triumphal procession included music, the strewing of flowers, and *clouds of incense.*

As noted above, the passion narrative has long been thought to be older and well established among Christ believers. Many, if not most, scholars think that the characteristics of this part of Mark point to the use of a pre-Markan passion story about the real, 'historical' Jesus. But as we've seen, Paul lacks such a narrative. If one ever existed before Mark, it is lost to us.

Paula Fredriksen discusses some of the historical problems caused by Jesus' crucifixion:

> We are so habituated to knowing that Jesus was crucified that we fail to notice how awkwardly that fact fits with what else we have. If Pilate were simply doing a favor for the priests, he could have disposed of Jesus easily and without fanfare, murdering him by simpler means. (I repeat: Pilate's seriously thinking that Jesus did pose a serious revolutionary threat – the simplest implication of crucifixion – is belied by Jesus' solo death.) So too with the priests: if for whatever reason they had wanted Jesus dead, no public execution was necessary, and simpler means of achieving their end were readily available.[1183]

[1182]Winn (2018), p. 161.

[1183]Paula Fredriksen, *Gospel Chronologies, the Scene in the Temple, and the Crucifixion of Jesus* (2002), cited by Turton.

As Michael Turton has shown, the structure of the passion narrative must have been deliberately created by the Markan author (see Appendix on Mark's textual sources). Like the rest of the Gospel, it is a literary creation, not an eyewitness account.

Dio Chrysostom and Mark

In ancient times, at the best of times, the people who could compose a literary or philosophical work of any superior quality were highly educated, exceptional and rare – less that one percent of the population. This brings us to another possible influence on the passion narrative. Vernon K. Robbins[1184] noted that Dio Chrysostom's *Oration 4* presents an "alternative to traditional interpretation of the scenes" of Mark's passion narrative. There are numerous parallels with Dio's account of a Persian ritual during the Sacian feast. These similarities include: taking a condemned prisoner and treating him as a king, and then stripping and scourging him before hanging him, with his response being crying out or wailing.

I pulled on this Dio Chrysostom thread a bit and wasn't terribly impressed with the mentioned oration as a possible model for the passion narrative. It turns out *Oration 4* isn't exactly as presented and the story is told much better in Herodotus. So if it had any influence on the passion narrative, it was probably due to him rather than Chrysostom. Not only that, but the dates for that oration make it too late to have served as a model for Mark. Yet, further investigation of Dio Chrysostom revealed a few extremely interesting tidbits for our purposes here. But first, a little recap of what was going on in Rome.

The bits and pieces of evidence from Suetonius, Tacitus and Dio give the clear impression that the political atmosphere in Rome following the destruction of Jerusalem was tense and dangerous, especially for Jews and most especially for messianic Jews AKA Christians. After the year of the three emperors, many high-ranking and wealthy individuals realized that they, too, could become emperor. Meanwhile, there were still die-hard Republicans who dreamed of the restoration of the former oligarchy. Suetonius states that Vespasian's reign was *plagued by conspiracies* (*Vesp.* 25). Titus was viewed with suspicion because of his liaison with a Jewess, she being seen as a potential Cleopatra and Titus himself suspected of Neronian proclivities (*Tit.* 7.1).

David Ladouceur writes that from almost the start of his reign, Vespasian and his ally, Gaius Licinius Mucianus,[1185] faced resistance from a so-called 'philosophic opposition.'[1186] The leaders of this opposition were survivors of the Stoic types who had targeted Nero. One of the main figures was Helvidius Priscus, who married the daughter of Thrasea Paetus,[1187] who had been

---

[1184]Vernon K. Robbins, 'The Reversed Contextualization of Psalm 22 in the Markan Crucifixion,' in *The Four Gospels: Festschrift Frans Neirynck*, edited by F. Van Segbroeck (Leuven: Leuven University Press, 1992), pp. 1161–83.

[1185]An ancient Roman general, statesman and writer, "considered to have played a role behind the scenes in the elevation of Vespasian to the throne." As a witness to his literary interests, "Mucianus *collected the speeches and letters* of Romans of the older republican period, probably including a corpus of proceedings of the Senate (*res gesta senatus*). He was also the author of a memoir, chiefly dealing with the natural history and geography of the East, a text often quoted by Pliny as the source of miraculous occurrences." (Wikipedia.org, 'Mucanius.')

[1186]Ramsay MacMullen, *Enemies of the Roman Order* (Harvard University Press, 1966), pp. 1–94, cited by Ladouceur.

[1187]"Publius Clodius Thrasea Paetus (died 66 AD), Roman senator, who lived in the 1ˢᵗ century AD. Notable for his principled opposition to the emperor Nero and his interest in Stoicism, he was the husband of Arria, who

forced to commit suicide by Nero. According to Dio, Vespasian hated him because "he was a turbulent fellow who cultivated the mob and was forever praising democracy and denouncing the monarchy" (Dio, 65.12.2). Cynic-type philosophers also were part of this opposition (Dio 66.13.1).[1188]

Between 71 and 75 AD, Vespasian, at the instigation of Mucianus, banished and later executed Helvidius.[1189]

> When Vespasian sent for Helvidius Priscus and commanded him not to go into the senate, he replied, "It is in your power not to allow me to be a member of the senate, but so long as I am, I must go in." "Well, go in then," says the emperor, "but say nothing." "Do not ask my opinion, and I will be silent." "But I must ask your opinion." "And I must say what I think right." "But if you do, I shall put you to death." "When then did I tell you that I am immortal? You will do your part, and I will do mine: it is your part to kill; it is mine to die, but not in fear: yours to banish me; mine to depart without sorrow."[1190]

At the same time, Vespasian expelled Stoic and Cynic philosophers from Rome. Two of the expelled cynics, Diogenes and Heras, sneaked back into the city in order to agitate opposition to Titus's intended marriage to Berenice. Diogenes was flogged and Heras was beheaded (Dio 65.15).

It was at the same time as the conflict with philosophers that Dio Chrysostom appeared on the scene:

> He was born at Prusa (now Bursa) in the Roman province of Bithynia … He went to Rome during Vespasian's reign (69–79 AD) … He [later] became a critic of the Emperor Domitian, who banished him from Rome, Italy, and Bithynia in 82 [AD] for advising one of the Emperor's conspiring relatives. … He was a friend of Nerva, and when Domitian was murdered in 96 AD, Dio used his influence with the army stationed on the frontier in favour of Nerva. Under Emperor Nerva's reign, his exile was ended, and he was able to return home to Prusa. He adopted the surname Cocceianus in later life to honour the support given to him by the emperor, whose full name was Marcus Cocceius Nerva. [Nerva's successor Trajan held Dio in high esteem and showed him favor.] [Dio's] kindly disposition gained him many eminent friends, such as Apollonius of Tyana and Euphrates of Tyre, and his oratory was the admiration of all. [Chrysostom comes from the Greek *chrysostomos*, which literally means "golden-mouthed."] In his later life Dio had considerable status in Prusa, and there are records of him being involved in an urban renewal lawsuit about 111 [AD]. He probably died a few years later.[1191]

---

was the daughter of A. Caecina Paetus and the elder Arria, father-in-law of Helvidius Priscus, and a friend and relative by marriage of the poet Persius. Thrasea was the most prominent member of the political faction known today as the Stoic Opposition." (Wikipedia.org, 'Publius Clodius Thrasea Paetus.')

[1188] David J. Ladouceur, 'Josephus and Masada,' in *Josephus, Judaism, and Christianity*, edited by Louis H. Feldman and Gohei Hata (Tokyo: Yamamoto Shoten Publishing House, 1987), p. 99.

[1189] "Priscus was distinguished for his ardent and courageous republicanism. Although he repeatedly offended his rulers, he held several high offices. During Nero's reign he was quaestor of Achaea and tribune of the plebs (AD 56); he restored peace and order in Armenia, and gained the respect and confidence of the provincials. His declared sympathy with Brutus and Cassius occasioned his banishment in 66." (Wikipedia.org, 'Helvidius Priscus.')

[1190] Epictetus, *Discourses* 1.2.19–21, quoted in Wikipedia.org, 'Helvidius Priscus.'

[1191] Wikipedia.org, 'Dio Chrysostom.'

The orator Fronto, writing in the middle of the second century, includes Dio in a group of men "endowed with the greatest eloquence and yet no less celebrated for their wisdom than their oratory," all of them pupils of the famous Stoic, Gaius Musonius Rufus.

Musonius taught philosophy in Rome during Nero's reign. He was a companion of Nero's cousin Rubellius Plautus, who had been ordered by Nero to retire to the province of Asia where he died in 62 AD. Musonius then returned to Rome, but was exiled by Nero in 65 AD for supposed involvement in the conspiracy of Piso.[1192] He returned to Rome under Galba and was active in the turbulence of the first months of Vespasian's rule at Rome. He was a friend of Titus and was exempted when Vespasian banished philosophers from Rome in 71 AD. He was eventually banished anyway, returning only after Vespasian's death, apparently recalled by Titus.

Musonius was a Stoic and what survives of his work indicates that he wasn't so much interested in logical or theoretical inquiry, but paid more attention to practical ethics. His most famous pupil, Epictetus, frequently cites him.

It is possible that Dio met Musonius Rufus when the latter was with Rubellius Plautus in Asia, the neighboring province to Bithynia. In the *Life of Apollonius of Tyana*, written by Philostratus of Athens, he (Apollonius) was in Alexandria when Vespasian arrived there at the beginning of his campaign for the throne. Dio Chrysostom and Euphrates of Tyre were said by Philostratus to have been agents and counselors of Vespasian and held formal debates with Apollonius on the best constitution for Vespasian to establish at Rome; Euphrates urged democracy, Dio proposed that the people should be allowed to choose, and Apollonius argued for monarchy. Although Vespasian agreed with Apollonius, he retained Dio as a counselor since he was one who "gave delightful discourses, avoided quarrels, and had a beauty in his speech like the incense wafted from sanctuaries, together with an unsurpassed gift for improvisation." Vespasian was said to have reconciled Dio with his old teacher, Apollonius, and also released a pupil of Dio's from Bithynia from military service.[1193]

Though Vespasian's visit to Alexandria is an attested fact, little of this narrative is corroborated elsewhere. The constitutional debate is suspiciously similar to a famous one in Herodotus, and the *Life of Apollonius* is so full of fantasy that an incident for which it is the sole source should be accepted only cautiously. Philostratus may have made it up to make Apollonius Dio's teacher. The stimulus may have been Dio's Alexandrian oration, which shows him to be in that city and a friend of an unnamed emperor who was most likely Vespasian. There are other indications of Dio's closeness to the Flavians, and particularly to Vespasian's son, Titus. Titus was also a friend of Dio's teacher, Musonius Rufus.

Dio's connection to the Flavians may explain his 'sophistry' and attacks on philosophers. According to Synesius, Dio particularly attacked "Socrates and Zeno and their followers."[1194] If this is true, his target seems to have been that left wing of Stoicism which sympathized with

[1192] "The conspiracy of Gaius Calpurnius Piso in AD 65 was a major turning point in the reign of the Roman emperor Nero (reign 54–68). The plot reflected the growing discontent among the ruling class of the Roman state with Nero's increasingly despotic leadership ... At least 41 individuals were accused of being part of the conspiracy. Of the known 41, there were 19 Senators, 7 Equites, 11 soldiers, and 4 women." (Wikipedia.org, 'Pisonian conspiracy.')

[1193] Philostratus, *VA* 5.24 ff., esp. 27 (Vespasian, Dio, Euphrates), 32–37 (debate), 37 (characterization of Dio), 38 (reconciliation, pupil). Cited by C. P. Jones, *The Roman World of Dio Chrysostom* (Cambridge and London: Harvard University Press, 1978).

[1194] Synesius, *Ep.* 154, cited by Jones (1978).

the libertarian views of the Cynics. In Dio's day, there was a considerable distance between such Stoics as Thrasea Paetus, whose views were not incompatible with monarchy, and Paetus' son-in-law, Helvidius Priscus, who was closer to the Cynics.[1195] Musonius preached that kings should be philosophers;[1196] Euphrates exhorted Pliny to the political life; Epictetus, though he exalts Cynicism as a remote ideal, scorns the professed Cynics who do nothing but "haunt tables and gateways."[1197] So, it seems that Dio's work *Against the Philosophers* was not exactly against all philosophers, but only those who incited social unrest. According to Synesius, Dio continued his campaign against philosophers in a work entitled *To Musonius*, though it does not appear that he attacked his teacher.

Vespasian encouraged rhetoric and founded chairs in it at Rome.[1198] Philosophy, on the other hand, was very much in disfavor. With executions and floggings of philosophers, it is not surprising that Dio suppressed his philosophical interests and indulged his sophistic tendencies.

Dio's Alexandrian oration was devoted to improving the behavior of its citizens *vis à vis* the Flavian emperors. As we have seen, this was a particularly urgent issue at the time. The oration seems to insinuate that he bore a message directly from the emperor, as he compares himself to Hermes sent against his will by Zeus. Thus, the oration had a very serious purpose.

In any event, having discovered that Dio Chrysostom was certainly in Rome at the time Mark was written, that he was associated with Musonius Rufus and Epictetus, and that Vespasian was probably using him and others as propagandists and there is later evidence that Chrysostom certainly knew about the Persian ritual that was apparently rather similar to the passion narrative, even if he actually got it from Herodotus and knew of it much earlier, one cannot help but wonder if Chrysostom had any influence on the writing of Mark. Dio's *Oration 4* is cast in the form of a dialogue between Diogenes of Sinope and Alexander the Great. The stripping, scourging, hanging and the loud cry are certainly there:

> "Have you never heard about the Sacian feast held by the Persians, against whom you are now preparing to take the field?" And Alexander at once asked him what it was like, he wished to know all about the Persians. "Well, they take one of their prisoners," he explained, "who has been condemned to death, set him upon the king's throne, give him the royal apparel, and permit him to give orders, to drink and carouse, and to dally with the royal concubines during those days, and no one prevents his doing anything he pleases. But after that they strip and scourge him and then hang him. ... And so, when the fellow is freed from his chains, the chances are, if he is a fool and ignorant of the significance of the procedure, that he feels glad and congratulates himself on what is taking place; but if he understands, he probably breaks out into wailing and refuses to go along without protesting, but would rather remain in fetters just as he was."[1199]

So here we have 'substitute king ritual' as model for the passion, in contrast to Schmidt and Winn's exposition of the passion narrative as a mock Roman triumph.[1200] It seems to me that

---

[1195]Dio Chrysostom 66.12.2–3. Thrasea was accompanied by a Cynic in his last hours according to Tacitus (*Ann.* 16.32).

[1196]Note Musonius' political feud with a Stoic and a Cynic in Tacitus (*Hist* 4.10, 40; cf. *Ann.* 16.32).

[1197]Arrian, *Epictetus* 3.22, esp. sect. 80.

[1198]Suetonius, *Vespasian* 18; Dio Chrysostom 66.12.1a.

[1199]Diogenes of Sinope in Dio Chrysostom, *Oration 4*.

[1200]Philo's story of Carabbas being mocked as a king in Alexandria (*Flaccus*) may be an even stronger parallel (Gmirkin, personal communication). See, for example, https://www.patheos.com/blogs/anxiousbench/2013/06/the-mocking-of-carabbas/.

there is no reason why both rituals might not have been combined to produce the unique passion narrative for the Markan Gospel, since it appears rather compelling that the Markan passion narrative was written with the Roman triumph in mind.

Savior of the World: Jesus' True Identity?

I've noted several times that it appears to me that Paul's Christ was not the same as the messiah of the Jerusalem Christians. It also seems that whoever Paul's Christ was, he was well enough known to his congregations as to need no discussion, unless there was discussion that has been redacted. Assuming that, of course, would raise its own set of problems and questions. The only reference Paul appears to make to a historical person at all is his description of one night when Jesus was at dinner with his friends and shared the wine and bread in a symbolic remembrance ceremony, and that was the night he was 'given up' or betrayed, however it is translated. But knowing how Paul perceived the world as a shadow of spiritual realities, that didn't mean very much. We know that Paul was talking about a spiritual revelation, not necessarily a material fact in the earthly life of his Christ.

But now, as we are approaching the end of examination of early Christianity, I think we have collected enough clues to propose a candidate for the earthly man who inspired Paul's spiritual messiah. Throughout our discussion of Paul's letters and Mark's Gospel, we have noticed something that previous generations of Bible scholars haven't picked up on. While Jewish influences are taken as a given, and even Hellenistic ones are nowadays considered fair game, it has only been in recent years that scholars have begun to notice a distinctly Roman influence on early Christianity's texts and imagery. Once it is pointed out, it stares you right in the face. I think it goes even deeper than that.

We have already pointed out Paul's imagery of Christ's triumphal procession, and the similarities between the cross and a Roman *tropaeum*. Well, if one is looking for the original image of a divine man on a cross, look no further than the wax image of Julius Caesar mounted on a *tropaeum* at his funeral.

> As this wax figure would not have been visible if it had lain flat on the bier which covered the actual corpse of Caesar, Antonius ordered it hung on a cross-like *tropaeum* where, as tradition required, the insignia of victory were affixed. This created an ironic, provocative, unbearable *tropaeum*, **where the image of the victor himself was hung in the midst of the trophies of war**. The wax figure was clad in his bloody passion garment, and the *tropaeum* was constructed in such a way that it could be rotated so that everybody could clearly see the image.[1201]

We even see the same ironic reversal of valuations, where a symbol of defeat (crucifixion, display as a trophy of war) transforms into one of victory. And given the flexibility of the Greek word 'crucifixion,' it wouldn't be incorrect to say that the image of Caesar's corpse was displayed as 'crucified' on a cross.

[1201] See: Francesco Carotta, *Jesus was Caesar* (Soesterberg, The Nederlands: Uitgeverij Aspekt, 2005), Chapter 3: Crux. Cf. Nicolaus Damascenus, *Bios Kaisaros*, FGrH, ed. F. Jacoby, 26.97: "as the curtains were drawn back, the dangling arms and the wounds on his face could be seen from both sides." Cf. also Suet. *Jul.* 82: "After *all had fled* he lifelessly lay there for some time until three young slaves placed him in a litter and carried him back home with one arm hanging over the side."

Around six years ago I was reading Stefan Weinstock's *Divus Julius*, and found myself mentally noting again and again, "Just like Jesus!", when one thing or another was described in reference to the life, acts, or words of Caesar. That caused me to reflect quite a bit on historical methodology. I knew, of course, that the early Church Fathers had declared that anything that resembled Christianity before Christ came was a Satanic imitation designed to lead the credulous astray, but for modern scholars to act like that was true nowadays just baffled me. Because, indeed, here was a man whose character was so extraordinary, and events in his life so similar to the broad outline of the 'life of Jesus' as presented in the Gospels, that I couldn't imagine why I had never read anyone comparing the two. Caesar was famous for his mercy, his loyalty to his friends, his almost supernatural intellect, and more. He was accused of wanting to be a king and was betrayed, murdered, and abandoned by many he held as close friends. In fact, Caesar's betrayal by Brutus was probably the most famous heinous act of all true historical events, then and since, and undoubtedly still loomed large in the minds of first-century inhabitants of the Roman Empire. So why had no one ever thought that this just might have influenced the story of Jesus?

With the idea in mind that Julius Caesar was at the very least the model for some aspects of the life of Jesus of Nazareth, I began a years-long review of all the literature in search of any possible clues that this was true. I discovered rather soon that a few other people had a similar idea, though they were coming at it from slightly different directions, with different motivations. As far as I can tell, the first to make the connection explicit was James Anthony Froude in his 1899 biography of Caesar. These are its final words:

> Strange and startling the resemblance between the fate of the founder of the kingdom of this world [Caesar] and of the Founder of the kingdom not of this world, for which the first was a preparation. Each was denounced for making himself a king. Each was maligned as the friend of publicans and sinners; each was betrayed by those whom he had loved and cared for; each was put to death; and Caesar also was believed to have risen again and ascended into heaven and become a divine being.[1202]

Italian essayist Giovanni Papini was the next to draw on these similarities in his 1932 book *La Scala di Giacobbe*:

> We have discovered a Caesar who had inclinations and virtues entirely different from that of other Romans – a Caesar, who forgives his enemies, who gives generously to all, who was the legitimate head of the Roman religion and who imagined himself to be of divine origin and was honored as a god – a Caesar, who loved and protected the people, from which the true God would be born – a Caesar, who was betrayed by one of his closest friends and who was killed, because he, like Jesus, was accused of wanting to elevate himself to king.[1203]

After this, Papini writes about the poet Virgil: "As man could find the Incarnation of the coming Christ, in my opinion, in the greatest Roman hero [Caesar]; so was the greatest Roman poet Virgil, according to many Christians, the Prophet."

[1202] James Anthony Froude, *Julius Caesar* (D. Appleton and Co., 1899), p. 450.

[1203] Translation by Quantum Future Group, available online at https://www.cassiopaea.org/forum/threads/was-jul ius-caesar-the-real-jesus-christ.31732/page-63#post-613925.

Next came Gary Courtney's book *Et tu, Judas? Then Fall Jesus!* in 2004. Courtney argued that Caesar was a direct model for the Gospels' Jesus. Francesco Carotta's book comparing Mark with the literature on Caesar was first published in German in 1999, then in English in 2015.

At the very least, I think a solid case can be made for a purely literary influence of the accounts of Julius Caesar on the story of Jesus as depicted in Mark (and elements in Paul). But as I dug very deeply into the problem I began to think beyond literary influence, and to notice that the problems between Paul and the Jerusalem Christians might have been much deeper than anyone has imagined; that Paul may actually have had a vision *of the deified Julius* and understood that he was the true Son of God (even more than Cyrus the Great had been), had come to earth already and been murdered in a particularly bloody way, then an image of him had been raised on a *tropaeum* at his funeral – 'Christ on the cross.' Not long after, he was glorified to heaven in the form of a comet, so what could all this mean? But it was obvious that proving such an idea would be almost impossible. I have to admit that all I have found is here in this book, and it isn't a smoking gun, for sure. It is more like entering a room and smelling the gun smoke, seeing a lot of spilled blood, but no body, no murderer, no gun; most of the evidence has been removed.

And yet, there are those two truly bizarre stories in Josephus, following the so-called Testimonium Flavianum, that initially appear like nothing more than Josephan gossip. But when one takes a closer look, it is almost as though someone – Josephus or a redactor – intended them to be a coded message. All the elements of Christianity are there in metaphor, and in the first story, about Paulina and the man she fell in love with, Decius Mundus – of a family famed for self-sacrifice – we notice one truly surprising detail: the freedwoman who "contrived the whole matter" was named Ide. There we have a clue to the "Ides of March."[1204] The following story concerns Fulvia and her husband Saturninus being converted to Jewish worship. Saturninus was also the name of Paulina's husband. This makes us think that she is just another aspect of Paulina, and Fulvia leads us straight to Caesar and his funeral, where a wax image of his body was mounted on the tropaeum.

Recall what Michael Turton noted, quoted above: that the reference to the unnamed woman in Mark 14:9 being remembered long after for what she had done may be a sly reference to "the author herself." That made me think of the discussion about the author of the Epistle to the Hebrews, which I included earlier in this book, arguing the possibility that a female companion of Paul had composed the letter, perhaps Priscilla. (I am not suggesting that Priscilla wrote Mark; I'm going in a slightly different direction here.)

Those two curious tales in Josephus seem to me to be Josephan allusions to the origins of Christianity and that Josephus may very well have been in dialogue with Christianity. What is significant about Fulvia is she was married to three *populares*, supporters of Julius Caesar.

To give the reader some background on Fulvia and her life, here is a quick summary, culled from Wikipedia, with my own additions in brackets:

> Her first marriage was to Publius Clodius Pulcher, circa 62 BC. Fulvia and Clodius had two children together, a son also named Publius Clodius Pulcher and a daughter, Clodia Pulchra. As a couple they went everywhere together. ...

[1204]The name in Greek (*Ide/Ida*, which means 'wooded hill') bears a phonetic resemblance to the Greek and Latin words for Ides: *eidos* (plural *eidoi*) and *idus*. It should be added that in the story, Tiberius has Ide and the priests crucified.

In 52 BC, Clodius ran for *praetor* and political competition with a consular rival, Titus Annius Milo, escalated to violence. Milo and his gang killed Clodius on January 18 on the Appian Way, the road built by Clodius's ancestors. Fulvia first appears in the record after his death. [She stirred the anger of the mob by publicly displaying his wounded corpse and dramatically lamenting over it.] ...

[While alive, Clodius had many followers.] As Clodius' widow and mother of his children, [Fulvia] was also a symbol and reminder of him, and was able to transfer this power to her future husbands. ... Fulvia most likely married her second husband, Gaius Scribonius Curio, soon after [her mourning period] for Clodius was ended in 52–51 BC. Like Clodius, Curio was very popular with the plebeians. ... Though initially an *optimate*, Curio became a *popularis* soon after marrying Fulvia, and continued many of Clodius' popularist policies. He soon became important to Gaius Julius Caesar and Clodian supporters. In 50 BC, the year after he married Fulvia, Curio won election as a tribune.

Curio died in 49 BC during the Battle of the Bagradas in North Africa, fighting for Julius Caesar against King Juba I of Numidia. During the civil war, Fulvia was most likely in Rome or nearby, due to Caesar's troops taking over Italy. At the time, she would have had her two children by Clodius and was either pregnant with Curio's son or had delivered him.

After Curio's death in Africa, Fulvia was still an important widow in elite circles. She provided an important tie to Clodius and his *clientela*, and could offer a husband money and political organization. Also, her husband would become the stepfather of Clodius' children, further linking him to Clodian politics. [And so,] Fulvia's third and final marriage was to Mark Antony in 47 or 46 BC, a few years after Curio's death, although Cicero slanderously suggested that Fulvia and Antony had had a relationship since 58 BC. ... At the time of their marriage, Antony was an established politician. He had already been tribune in 49 BC, commanded armies under Caesar and was the Master of the Horse in 47 BC. As a couple, they were a formidable political force in Rome, and had two sons together, Marcus Antonius Antyllus and Iullus Antonius. [That is to say, they named one of their sons after Julius Caesar.] ...

After Gaius Julius Caesar was assassinated, Antony became the most powerful man in Rome. Fulvia was heavily involved in the political aftermath. After Caesar's death, the senate realized his popularity and declared that it would pass all of Caesar's planned laws. ...

Antony formed the Second Triumvirate with Octavian (the future emperor Augustus) and Marcus Aemilius Lepidus in 43 BC and began to conduct proscriptions.[1205] To solidify the political alliance, Fulvia's daughter Clodia was married to the young Octavian. ... In 42 BC, Antony and Octavian left Rome to pursue Julius Caesar's assassins, Marcus Junius Brutus and Gaius Cassius Longinus. Fulvia was left behind as the most powerful woman in Rome. ...

Shortly afterwards, the *triumvirs* distributed the provinces ... Lepidus took the west and Antony went to Egypt, where he met Cleopatra VII. Octavian returned to Rome in 41 BC to dispense land to Caesar's veterans, divorced Fulvia's daughter and accused Fulvia of aiming at supreme power. Fearing that Octavian was gaining the veterans' loyalty at the expense of Antony, Fulvia traveled constantly with her children to the new settlements in order to remind the veterans of their debt to Antony. [She] also tried to delay the land settlements until Antony returned to Rome, so that the two *triumvirs* could share the credit. With Octavian in Italy and Antony abroad, Fulvia allied with her brother-in-law Lucius Antonius and publicly endorsed Mark Antony in opposition to Octavian.

[1205]Inevitably, the head of the orator Cicero, a bitter enemy of Antony, was brought to Rome. Other sources record Antony's satisfaction, but only the much later author, Cassius Dio, adds a detail of Fulvia's response: "Antony uttered many bitter reproaches against it and then ordered it to be exposed on the rostra more prominently than the rest, in order that it might be seen in the very place where Cicero had so often been heard declaiming against him, together with his right hand, just as it had been cut off. And Fulvia took the head into her hands before it was removed, and after abusing it spitefully and spitting upon it, set it on her knees, opened the mouth, and pulled out the tongue, which she pierced with the pins that she used for her hair, at the same time uttering many brutal jests." (Dio 47.8)

These actions caused political and social unrest. In 41 BC, tensions between Octavian and Fulvia escalated to war in Italy. According to Appian, Fulvia was a central cause of the war, due to her jealousy of Antony and Cleopatra's affair in Egypt; she may have escalated the tensions between Octavian and Lucius in order to draw back Antony's attention to Italy. However, Appian also wrote that the other main causes were the selfish ambitions of the commanders and their inability to control their own soldiers.

Together with Lucius Antonius, she raised eight legions in Italy to fight for Antony's rights against Octavian, an event known as the Perusine War. The army occupied Rome for a short time, and Lucius organized his troops at Praeneste, but eventually retreated to Perusia (modern Perugia), where Octavian besieged him. Lucius waited for Antony's legions in Gaul to come to his aid. However, unaware of the war, Antony was still in the eastern provinces, and his legions were unsure of his commands and did not assist Lucius. Although during this conflict Fulvia was at Praeneste, there is evidence she helped Lucius. According to Appian, she "urged Ventidius, Asinius, and Calenus from Gaul to help Lucius, and having gathered another army, she sent it to Lucius under the command of Plancus." During the war, Octavian's soldiers at Perusia used sling bullets inscribed with insults directed at Fulvia personally and Octavian wrote a vulgar epigram directed at her in 40 BC, referring to Antony's affair with the ex-courtesan queen of Cappadocia, Glaphyra. It is recorded by Martial within one of his poems ...

[Following Lucius' surrender, Fulvia fled from Praeneste with her children, along with the commander Plancus and a guard of cavalry, to Greece, where she soon succumbed to an unknown illness and died. Plutarch (*Vit. Ant.* 30.5) simply states that Fulvia fell sick and died; Appian (*B. Civ.* 5.7.62) reports that she fell sick because Antony was angry at her and that she wasted away from her grief.] Fulvia died in Sicyon, near Corinth, Achaea. After her death, Antony and Octavian used it as an opportunity to blame their quarrelling on her. ... After Fulvia's death, Antony married Octavian's sister, Octavia Minor, to publicly demonstrate his reconciliation with Octavian. ...

Once Antony and Octavia were married, she took in and reared all of Fulvia's children. The fate of Fulvia's daughter, Clodia Pulchra, after her divorce from Octavian is unknown. Her son Marcus Antonius Antyllus was executed by Octavian in Alexandria, Egypt in 30 BC. Her youngest child, Iullus Antonius, was spared by Octavian and raised from 40 BC by Octavia Minor. Iullus married Octavia's daughter and Octavian's niece Claudia Marcella Major and they had a son, Lucius Antonius, and possibly a daughter Iulla Antonia.[1206]

Now, the problem is that Fulvia's role in history has been heavily veiled by the propaganda of her contemporaries and her portrayal in imperial sources. One thing that should be noted is that Fulvia was the first non-mythological Roman woman to appear on Roman coins.[1207] But there are a few other important things that ought to be said.

First of all, notice what Fulvia did upon the murder of her first husband, Clodius: she displayed his body publicly and demonstrated her grief in such a way as to incite the followers of Clodius to riot and use the Curia as his funeral pyre, which resulted in the destruction of the Curia Hostilia, the original senate house. The unrest in Rome caused the Senate to appoint Pompey as sole consul in order to restore order.

Second, notice that Fulvia was married to Mark Antony at the time Julius Caesar was assassinated and how similar the funeral of Caesar was to that of Clodius: the display of the wax image

---

[1206]Wikipedia.org, 'Fulvia.' See also: Jeffrey Tatum, *The Patrician Tribune: Publius Clodius Pulcher* (University of North Carolina Press, 2010), and Allison J. Weir, 'A Study of Fulvia,' Masters Thesis, Queen's University, Kingston, ON (2007).

[1207]Weir (2007), cited by Wikipedia. https://www.scribd.com/document/57621341/Allison-Weir-A-Study-of-Fulvia.

on the *tropaeum* and the resulting agitation of the mourners so that they cremated Caesar's body right there. The fire went out of control and seriously damaged the forum. The crowd then went rampaging through the city, attacking the houses of Brutus and Cassius and ultimately sparking another civil war.

Third, note that Fulvia traveled constantly around to the new settlements of soldiers who had been given land upon retirement. This was to remind the veterans of their debt to Antony. But one must suspect that there was more to this than just gaining support for Antony. At this point in time, Julius Caesar was still mourned and it would be Antony's association with Caesar that would garner the most support from the veterans. Caesar had been the first Roman – aside from the semi- if not totally mythological Romulus – to be officially deified. On 1 January 42 BC, the Senate posthumously granted him the title *Divus Iulius*. As already related previously, the comet that appeared during the games held in his honor was seen as confirmation of his divinity because he ascended into heaven. The cult set up to honor Divus Iulius was promoted by both Octavian and Mark Antony, Antony having been appointed its *flamen* (priest). So it seems to me to be rather obvious that Fulvia would be promoting the cult of *Divus Iulius* among the veterans, and especially her husband as the friend, associate, heir and priest of the divine Julius.

Finally, notice that the children of Fulvia were raised by Octavia, the sister of the emperor Augustus, adopted son of Julius Caesar, after she married Mark Antony. Antonia, known as Julia Antonia Minor, was the younger of two daughters of Mark Antony and Octavia. Later in adulthood, Antonia employed Julius Alexander Lysimachus, the ruler of the Alexandrian Jews and friend of Claudius, as her financial steward. This Julius was the older brother of the philosopher, Philo. Antonia's private secretary, Caenis, was the mistress of Vespasian. Julius Alexander had two sons; the older one, Marcus, married Herod's niece Berenice. (Remember that Herod had been put in power by Julius Caesar.) Marcus died young and Berenice became the mistress of Titus, the son of Vespasian. Julius' younger son was Tiberius Alexander, who executed the sons of Judas the Galilean and later assisted the Flavians in their war against the Jews.[1208]

Even after Jerusalem was destroyed, the messianic ferment of the time remained a threat. Such aspirations were not solely Jewish, but reflected the populative ideas and acts of Julius Caesar and those who went before him, including the Gracchi, Clodius, Curio and then, Antony, the last three of which were husbands of Fulvia, so it might be thought that some of the political ideas of populism were actually hers. Thus, Caesar's cult would have been a cult that faithfully maintained such aspirations, possibly expanded and elucidated by Caesar's veterans all over the Empire. Such a cult may very well have been supported by noble women of the Empire, including women of the imperial household. And perhaps this is what Josephus was trying to convey in his Fulvia story – only, Josephus presents a case where the noble Fulvia has been taken in by

---

[1208]Valliant and Fahy (2018), pp. 177–189, point out some further connections. Berenice's sister Drusilla was married to the Roman governor of Judea, Felix. And her brother, Agrippa II, was a friend of Titus. Valliant and Fahy argue that this group of Herodians and Jews with close connections with Rome, who due to their reputations and occupations could be considered "sinners and tax collectors," were "pro-Roman and pro-peace messianic Jews," like Paul. "Just as the rebellious messianic Jews of the 1st Century were conflated with 'Christians,' so, too, have these likely Flavian *Christians* been conflated with religious 'Jews'" (p. 189). Interestingly, the author of Acts portrays Felix, Agrippa II, and Berenice as sympathetic to Paul – as well as Gallio (brother of Stoic philosopher Seneca). Keep in mind the Stoic connection during the discussion of Epictetus and Epaphroditos below.

Jewish frauds. Was that the message? That the honoring of Julius Caesar, with whom Fulvia was associated, had been taken over by a Jewish fraud?

As Gary Courtney notes in his brilliant little book, *Et tu Judas? Then fall, Jesus!*, there should be a solid historical reason why 'Jesus' conquered the old gods. There has to have been emotion, tragedy, a truly great event to drive the spread of Christianity. The alleged trial and execution of Jesus is presented as a great injustice against a good man who was not widely known, which was later developed into 'The Jews killed God's Son.' But this really doesn't fly. Even Josephus had no sympathy for the Jewish rebels and their belief that their god would send a war leader to fight against Rome. Christianity is a great religion without a solid founding event. Caesar's death was a great founding event, but his religion was seemingly forgotten.

It is preposterous when you think about it. According to the Gospels, Jesus was a Jewish messiah with a great popular following and pretensions to be King of the Jews. This certainly may have been true of Judas the Galilean but, as we have seen, as a messiah, he failed.

On the other side we see the heartfelt and sincere honoring of Julius Caesar and an annual commemoration of the tragedy of his death by multiplied thousands of his faithful veterans who were witnesses to his greatness. Passed on to their children and grandchildren, the stories may have been modified, but still, no doubt, contained the main ideas of Caesar and certainly the profound emotions of his betrayal and death. There would have been remembrance of the release of his great soul on the third day via cremation, and the confirmation of his apotheosis by the sign of the comet during the funeral games given in July, the month of his birth. Courtney writes:

> Julius did not inherit his title as a god, he earned it and it was conferred upon him. Even his most ardent detractors cannot deny his essential greatness and magnanimity, unprecedented in strongmen in the annals of Rome, and it is almost universally conceded that this, embodied in his *Clementia*, was instrumental in bringing about his downfall. That clemency was destroyed by the circumstances and aftermath of his murder, and was never really seen again in the ancient world. What hope was there for reconciliation when the great reconciler himself had been slain by the men he had pardoned and promoted.
>
> ... the story of the death of Christ eclipsed that of Caesar's by stealing all his thunder. The figure of Jesus, standing at the crossroads of history, obscures the events that took place in Rome just prior to his time setting, and diverts our attention into Hebrew history as if the civilizations of Greece and Rome had never existed. It masks the death of Julius Caesar and the agonized death of the old order. ...
>
> In the meantime the deity Jesus Christ, just like his formulaic predecessor Attis, continues to die and resurrect every year. But a creed that grew to be as great as Christianity could not have come into being had there not been a truly remarkable man hailed as a god, treacherously betrayed and murdered right here on earth – an event so momentous as to shake the ground, wake the dead and dim the sun. That man was Julius Caesar.[1209]

I've noted already that I think that Brandon and Winn are definitely onto something in their interpretation of why the Gospel of Mark was written: as apologetic and propaganda. But we have also seen that it was never intended to be taken by an educated person as anything but an allegory. We have also seen hints here and there that the allegory carried a lot of information between the lines, so to say. So it is not taking things too far to suppose that the hidden text within the text was possibly designed to explicate Caesar as the true Son of God – a true messianic

---

[1209]Gary Courtney, *Et tu, Judas? Then Fall Jesus!* (iUniverse, 2004), pp. 159, 160–61.

secret – adopted by Paul's Jewish god, Yahweh, just as Cyrus had been.[1210] The heightened anti-Judaism after the war against the Jews was a dangerous condition for all Christians and Mark apparently intended to bring them together with a shared story that blamed the destruction of Jerusalem on the Jews, most especially those Jews that hadn't gotten with Paul's program of a suffering – yet powerful – reconciling Son of God. Mark suggests that the decision to kill Jesus was shared by the Jewish leaders and the Roman governor, Pilate. Matthew had Pilate washing his hands and the Jewish people crying out for the blood of Jesus to be on them and their descendants. Luke has Pilate declaring Jesus innocent so the blame falls on the Jewish leaders alone.

The Jerusalem Christians followed Judas the Galilean and his family, including James and Simon. Judas was a wholly Jewish messiah of the earthly, kingly, rebel sort. When he was executed, his family kept his movement alive and promised that he would return with legions of angels to destroy the Romans and put Israel in charge.

Paul's 'Jesus,' on the other hand, appears to have originally derived from the worship of Julius Caesar, the cult created and propagated all around the Empire and strongly supported by the veterans of Caesar possibly in Essene-like ecclesia. It was understood by Paul that it was Caesar and his principle of *clementia* – forgiveness and reconciliation – that was the way to heaven. It seems to me that, despite the heavy hands of editors, the line of force of Paul's letters still contains hints of these things, and that at least some of his followers had been initiated into the truth; they had eyes to see and ears to hear. And the individual who wrote Mark was certainly in on the messianic secret, the 'mystery of the ages,' and wrote the passion narrative with the intention of conveying this truth.

But I also wonder if there was an even earlier passion play written for the rites of the Caesar cult? And further, if Fulvia may have played a role in the composition of something like that?[1211] After all, she was the originator of the style of funeral that was held for Julius Caesar when she acted out of grief at the death of her husband Clodius. That Caesar's funeral was styled similarly can't be coincidence. Fulvia was there. Perhaps that is the intended understanding for the first-century Christian hearers/readers of the pericope of the woman with the alabaster jar?

Now, considering the suggestion that a woman was the author of Mark, I'm not averse to the idea at all, but I think a few things need to be considered. First of all, as a number of scholars have demonstrated, the structure of Mark is so incredibly complex that it boggles the mind to think of a single person putting that together in any restricted period of time, as might be expected for the text to act fully as apologetics and propaganda within a fairly narrow timeframe. The brilliance of it, even that it is written in the common Greek of the time, is just staggering. How could one person do that? Of course, human genius seems to know no limits, but I think that it would have taken a committee to produce it in a timely manner. And that leads back to

---

[1210] Bizarrely, Cyrus too was 'crucified.' According to Diodorus Siculus 2.44.2: "Cyrus, the king of the Persians, the most powerful in his days, made a campaign with noteworthy forces to Scythia. [But] the Queen of the Scythians slaughtered the Persian soldiers and she suspended [*anestaurose*] Cyrus who had been imprisoned." The word for 'suspended' is a variation on the Greek word for crucifixion. See Samuelsson (2011), p. 79.

[1211] Francesco Carotta (2005) has proposed the same, but I don't find his treatment convincing. He argues specifically that Mark is a direct transformation (via 'diegetic transposition') of a Latin Caesar passion play. While some of his parallels are fascinating, in the end he imagines more evidence than is actually there. Mark is such a masterfully composed text that it is highly unlikely to have resulted from such a messy process as Carotta proposes.

Dio Chrysostom and his colleagues in Rome at the time. We should also consider the idea that Paul had contacts in high places.

Consider Musonius Rufus. He was a Roman of the equestrian class, born around 20–30 AD, and as mentioned above, was exiled by Nero and returned to Rome under Galba in 68 AD. When Marcus Antonius Primus, the general of Vespasian, was marching upon Rome (69 AD), he joined the ambassadors that were sent by Vitellius to the victorious general, and going among the soldiers of the latter, preached about the blessings of peace and the dangers of war, but was soon made to stop. When the party of Vitellius gained the upper hand, Musonius was able to accuse, and obtain the conviction of, Publius Egnatius Celer, the Stoic philosopher who had condemned Barea Soranus. It was perhaps about this time that Musonius taught Epictetus, his most famous student.

We don't know if Musonius wrote anything for publication, or if they just haven't survived. Two of his students later collected his philosophical opinions. One collection of discourses includes titles such as 'That Women Too Should Study Philosophy,' and one is reminded of the ideas of Paul that women, too, could be leaders of the church.

> His philosophy, which is in many respects identical with that of his pupil, Epictetus, is marked by its strong practical tendency. The philosophy he would have everyone cultivate is not a mere matter of words, of instruction, or of the school; but one that everyone by their own reflection and practice may pursue for himself. … Musonius argued [that] because men's and women's capacity to understand virtue is the same, both should be trained in philosophy. … At the same time he is convinced of the power of philosophy over the minds of people; by it he hopes to heal all the corruption of the human mind. His philosophy consists entirely of the rules for the conduct of life; all knowledge ought to be serviceable to action. … he regards philosophy as the mental art of healing, and lays great stress on the practice of virtue, preferring practice to precept. He distinguishes two kinds of practice: the exercise of the mind in reflection and the adoption of good rules in life, and the endurance of bodily pains which affect both the soul and the body. A life lived according to nature consists in social, friendly sentiments and temper, and in contentment with what will simply alleviate the primary needs of nature. He combats all selfishness, and regards marriage not merely as becoming and natural, but as the principle of the family and state, and the preservation of the whole human race. He zealously protests against the exposure of children as an unnatural custom, and at every opportunity recommends the practice of benevolence.[1212]

Epictetus, the student of Musonius Rufus, along with Dio Chrysostom, is equally interesting. He was born about 50 AD, possibly at Hierapolis, Phrygia, and spent his youth as a slave at Rome. His master was Epaphroditos, a wealthy freedman and secretary to Nero.

> His most famous pupil, Arrian, studied under him when a young man (ca. AD 108) and claimed to have written the famous Discourses from his lecture notes. Arrian describes Epictetus as being a powerful speaker who could "induce his listener to feel just what Epictetus wanted him to feel." …
>
> Epictetus maintains that the foundation of all philosophy is self-knowledge, that is, the conviction of our ignorance and gullibility ought to be the first subject of our study. … The first and most necessary part of philosophy concerns the application of doctrine, for example, that people should not lie. … To repel evil opinions by the good is the noble contest in which humans should engage; it is not an easy task, but it promises true freedom, peace of mind, and a divine command

---

[1212]Wikipedia.org, 'Gaius Musonius Rufus.' See also: Cynthia King, *Musonius Rufus: Lectures and Sayings*, edited by William B. Irvine (CreateSpace, 2011).

over the emotions. ... The essence of divinity is goodness; we have all good that could be given to us. The deities too gave us the soul and reason, which is not measured by breadth or depth, but by knowledge and sentiments, and by which we attain to greatness, and may equal even with the deities. We should, therefore, cultivate the mind with special care. If we wish for nothing, but what God wills, we shall be truly free, and all will come to pass with us according to our desire; and we shall be as little subject to restraint as Zeus himself. Every individual is connected with the rest of the world, and the universe is fashioned for universal harmony. ... For our country or friends we ought to be ready to undergo or perform the greatest difficulties. The good person, if able to foresee the future, would peacefully and contentedly help to bring about their own sickness, maiming, and even death, knowing that this is the correct order of the universe. ... Those who go wrong we should pardon and treat with compassion, since it is from ignorance that they err, being, as it were, blind. ... Every desire degrades us, and renders us slaves of what we desire. We ought not to forget the transitory character of all external advantages, even in the midst of our enjoyment of them; but always to bear in mind that they are not our own, and that therefore, they do not properly belong to us. Thus prepared, we shall never be carried away by opinions.

... Arrian ... compiled a popular digest, entitled the *Enchiridion*, or *Handbook*. In a preface to the *Discourses* that is addressed to Lucius Gellius, Arrian states that "whatever I heard him say I used to write down, word for word, as best I could, endeavouring to preserve it as a memorial, for my own future use, of his way of thinking and the frankness of his speech." ... The final entry of the *Enchiridion* ... begins: "Upon all occasions we ought to have these maxims ready at hand":

> Conduct me, Zeus, and thou, Destiny,
> Wherever thy decree has fixed my lot.
> I follow willingly; and, did I not,
> Wicked and wretched would I follow still.
> (Diogenes Laërtius quoting Cleanthes; quoted also by Seneca, *Epistle 107.*)

> Whoe'er yields properly to Fate is deemed
> Wise among men, and knows the laws of Heaven.
> (From Euripides' *Fragments*, 965)

> Crito, if it thus pleases the gods, thus let it be.
> (From Plato's *Crito*)

> Anytus and Meletus may indeed kill me, but they cannot harm me. (From Plato's *Apology*)[1213]

In the above passages about Musonius Rufus and Epictetus, I've selected those points that are particularly in harmony with Paul's writings, the point being that it would not be hard to imagine these men inspiring the thinking of Paul and possibly even assisting in the creation of the Gospel of Mark. What tickles my brain are the names 'Rufus' and 'Epaphroditus,' since both of them appear in Paul's epistles (Rom. 16:13; Phil. 2:25; 4:18), and Rufus is mentioned in the passion narrative as the son of Simon of Cyrene (Mark 15:21). Notably, Matthew, Luke and John do not mention Rufus. Probably, the Epaphroditus Paul mentions is not the same as Nero's freedman,[1214] nor is it likely at all that the Rufus of Paul's epistles has any connection

---

[1213]Wikipedia.org, 'Epictetus.' See also Epictetus, *Discourses, Fragments, Handbook*, translated by Robin Hard (Oxford: Oxford University Press, 2014) and Brian E. Johnson, *The Role Ethics of Epictetus: Stoicism in Ordinary Life* (Lanham: Lexington Books, 2014).

[1214]However, it is not impossible. Epaphroditus was freed by either Claudius or Nero, and was probably born between 20 and 25 AD, which would have made him in his late twenties at the time Paul wrote. Probably the

to Musonius Rufus, but one never knows and the mention in Mark is more curious. It could be that Mark's audience knew who Simon of Cyrene was, and his two sons, Alexander and Rufus; on the other hand, as part of the story world, the tale could simply be told without explaining anything about this Simon except that he was "coming in from the field" and was just a passerby. Nevertheless, it is a very odd statement, all things considered, and as odd as the mention of the woman with the alabaster jar: "wherever the good news (the Gospel) is proclaimed in the entire world, what she has done will be told in memory of her." And what did she do but plan the funeral of Julius Caesar, something that might be considered an 'anointing.'

All of the above makes me wonder if a descendant of Fulvia, a Roman Christian noblewoman, was friendly with Dio Chrysostom, Musonius Rufus and Epictetus, and engaged one or all three of them, along with at least one other Christian well-versed in the Jewish scripture, to produce the Gospel of Mark? Notice that Dio Chrysostom was exiled in 82 AD by Domitian for advising one of his 'conspiring relatives.' One wonders who that could have been? Clement?

According to what Dio said himself, on the advice of the Delphic oracle, he put on the clothes of a beggar, and with nothing in his pocket but a copy of Plato's *Phaedo* and Demosthenes's oration on the *Embassy*, he lived the life of a Cynic philosopher, undertaking a journey to the countries in the north and east of the Roman Empire. He thus visited Thrace, Mysia, Scythia, and the country of the Getae. One wonders if it is possible that he took a bit more than Plato and Demosthenes with him? Could he have had a copy of Mark, which he left off in Sinope, an edited version of which later came into the hands of Marcion?

As for Fulvia being taken in by four con men (or rather, one con man and his three assistants) promoting a royal messiah, could it be any more obvious? It seems to me to be a clear message of the origins of Paul's Christ and how that worship was taken over by a conspiracy promoting a Jewish messiah. After all, what did Fulvia do but hand over the Roman purple, the symbol of rulership, to Jewish con artists.

Then, in the Gospel of Mark, we find at the very beginning that Mark's Jesus is acknowledged by God, accompanied by the sign of a dove – the symbol of Venus, the claimed ancestress of Julius Caesar. As Froude and Papini note above, both Jesus and Caesar are presented as having kingly ambitions, both are betrayed by a close friend, killed, and ascend into heaven transformed.

---

same Epaphroditus was a friend of Josephus, who dedicated several of his works to him. Philippi, to whom Paul addressed his letter, was a Roman veterans' colony, and Paul sends warm greetings to the Philippians from those "in Caesar's household" and mentions his own warm reception with the palace guard. Was Epaphroditus, Claudius' freedman and courtier to Nero, his link to "Caesar's household"? See Valliant and Fahy (2018), pp. 212–218. Valliant and Fahy believe the Epaphroditus and Clement mentioned by Paul are the historical, high-ranking Roman officials we have discussed (see chapter 2 for Clement), though I have serious difficulty seeing either of these historical figures acting as an apostle or messenger. Another possibility, as I mentioned above, is that the characters in Paul's epistles are freedman-servants with those names. I leave open the possibility that they could have actually been connected in some way to the historical characters. I also think it is as likely that their names could have been added into Paul's letters to support a later fiction or agenda. Conversely, the names could be original to Paul, and they were later conflated with the historical characters to serve an agenda. Valliant and Fahy also argue that the fish-and-anchor symbol used by some 2nd-century Christians was a continuation of its use by emperor Titus thus demonstrating that Christianity was invented by the Roman elite. However, because of the late date of the use of those symbols by early Christians, that is more than can be inferred directly from the evidence. 'Matthean' (Jewish/Pauline) Christians of the time could have simply adopted it years after its use by Titus, perhaps in their effort to co-opt and replace Pauline/Marcionite Christianity.

Caesar was the Roman high priest (*pontifex maximus*), and Jesus is presented as the figurative Jewish high priest.[1215] The passion narrative, fashioned after the Roman triumph, taken together with Paul's remark (Jesus "made a spectacle of the cosmic powers and authorities, and led them as captives *in his triumphal procession*"), adds to the overwhelming impression that this is the correct solution.

I've noted that a big part of Paul's inspiration was Isaiah's passage about Cyrus the Great, a Gentile messiah, so Julius Caesar as a candidate for Paul's messiah isn't something unthinkable. For Paul, it was the obedient death that meant everything, and it is certainly true that Caesar disregarded everything that might have saved him and went resolutely to the place of his death almost as though he knew what was coming. Here is Suetonius' account of his final days:

> Caesar had warning given him of his fate by indubitable omens. A few months before, when the colonists settled at Capua, by virtue of the Julian law, were demolishing some old sepulchres, in building country-houses, and were the more eager at the work, because they discovered certain vessels of antique workmanship, a tablet of brass was found in a tomb, in which Capys, the founder of Capua, was said to have been buried, with an inscription in the Greek language to this effect "Whenever the bones of Capys come to be discovered, a descendant of Iulus will be slain by the hands of his kinsmen, and his death revenged by fearful disasters throughout Italy." Lest any person should regard this anecdote as a fabulous or silly invention, it was circulated upon the authority of Caius Balbus, an intimate friend of Caesar's.
>
> A few days likewise before his death, he was informed that the horses, which, upon his crossing the Rubicon, he had consecrated, and turned loose to graze without a keeper, abstained entirely from eating, and shed floods of tears. The soothsayer Spurinna, observing certain ominous appearances in a sacrifice which he was offering, advised him to beware of some danger, which threatened to befall him before the ides of March were past. The day before the ides, birds of various kinds from a neighbouring grove, pursuing a wren which flew into Pompey's senate-house, with a sprig of laurel in its beak, tore it in pieces. Also, in the night on which the day of his murder dawned, he dreamt at one time that he was soaring above the clouds, and, at another, that he had joined hands with Jupiter. His wife Calpurnia fancied in her sleep that the pediment of the house was falling down, and her husband stabbed on her bosom; immediately upon which the chamber doors flew open.
>
> On account of these omens, as well as his infirm health, he was in some doubt whether he should not remain at home, and defer to some other opportunity the business which he intended to propose to the senate; but Decimus Brutus advising him not to disappoint the senators, who were numerously assembled, and waited his coming, he was prevailed upon to go, and accordingly set forward about the fifth hour. In his way, some person having thrust into his hand a paper, warning him against the plot, he mixed it with some other documents which he held in his left hand, intending to read it at leisure. Victim after victim was slain, without any favourable appearances in the entrails; but still, disregarding all omens, he entered the senate-house, laughing at Spurinna as a false prophet, because the ides of March were come, without any mischief having befallen him. To which the soothsayer replied, "They are come, indeed, but not past."
>
> When he had taken his seat, the conspirators stood round him, under colour of paying their compliments; and immediately Tillius Cimber, who had engaged to commence the assault, advancing nearer than the rest, as if he had some favour to request, Caesar made signs that he should defer his petition to some other time. Tillius immediately seized him by the toga, on both shoulders; at which Caesar crying out, "Violence is meant!" one of the Cassii wounded him a little below the throat. Caesar seized him by the arm, and ran it through with his stylo; and endeavouring to rush forward

[1215]Neil Godfrey, 'How the Gospel of Mark Portrays Jesus as High Priest,' https://vridar.org/2014/11/10/how-the-gospel-of-mark-portrays-jesus-as-high-priest/.

was stopped by another wound. Finding himself now attacked on all hands with naked poniards [small daggers], he wrapped the toga about his head, and at the same moment drew the skirt round his legs with his left hand, that he might fall more decently with the lower part of his body covered. He was stabbed with three and twenty wounds, uttering a groan only, but no cry, at the first wound; although some authors relate, that when Marcus Brutus fell upon him, he exclaimed, "What! art thou, too, one of them? Thou, my son!" The whole assembly instantly dispersing, he lay for some time after he expired, until three of his slaves laid the body on a litter, and carried it home, with one arm hanging down over the side. Among so many wounds, there was none that was mortal, in the opinion of the surgeon Antistius, except the second, which he received in the breast.[1216]

There was certainly a lot of blood spilled when Caesar died.

Nicolaus of Damascus, a major source for Josephus, wrote a *Life of Augustus* which includes an almost contemporary account of the events surrounding the assassination of Caesar. His account, which includes some interpretations that are most interesting in view of his activity as a diplomat and having an insider's view of state affairs, is worth including here. I will put in bold some of Nicolaus' more interesting comments that refer to the character of Caesar:

> At first a few men started the conspiracy, but afterwards many took part, more than are remembered to have taken part in any earlier plot against a commander. They say that there were more than eighty who had a share in it. Among those who had the most influence were: Decimus Brutus, a particular friend of Caesar, Gaius Cassius, and Marcus Brutus, second to none in the estimation of the Romans at that time. All these were formerly members of the opposite faction, and had tried to further Pompeius' interests, but when he was defeated, they came under Caesar's jurisdiction and lived quietly for the time being; but **although Caesar tried to win them over individually by kindly treatment**, they never abandoned their hope of doing him harm. **He on his part was naturally without grudge against the beaten party, because of a certain leniency of disposition**, but they, using to their own advantage **his lack of suspicion**, by seductive words and pretence of deeds treated him in such a way as to more readily escape detection in their plot. There were various reasons which affected each and all of them and impelled them to lay hands on the man. Some of them had hopes of becoming leaders themselves in his place if he were put out of the way; others were angered over what had happened to them in the war, embittered over the loss of their relatives, property, or offices of state. They concealed the fact that they were angry, and made the pretence of something more seemly, saying that they were displeased at the rule of a single man and that they were striving for a republican form of government. Different people had different reasons, all brought together by whatever pretext they happened upon.
>
> At first the ringleaders conspired; then many more joined, some of their own accord because of personal grievances, some because they had been associated with the others and wished to show plainly the good faith in their long standing friendship, and accordingly became their associates. There were some who were of neither of these types, but who had agreed because of the worth of the others, and who resented the power of one man after the long-standing republican constitution. They were very glad not to start the affair themselves, but were willing to join such company when someone else had initiated proceedings, not even hesitating to pay the penalty if need be. The reputation which had long been attached to the Brutus family was very influential in causing the uprising, for Brutus' ancestors had overthrown the kings who ruled from the time of Romulus, and they had first established republican government in Rome. **Moreover, men who had been friends of Caesar were no longer similarly well disposed toward him when they saw people who were previously his enemies saved by him and given honours equal to their**

[1216]Suet., *Jul.* 81–82.

own. In fact, even these others were not particularly well disposed toward him, for their ancient grudges took precedence over gratitude and made them forgetful of their good fortune in being saved, while, when they remembered the good things they had lost in being defeated, they were provoked. **Many also hated him because they had been saved by him although he had been irreproachable in his behaviour toward them in every respect**; but nevertheless, the very thought of receiving as a favour the benefits which as victors they would readily have enjoyed, annoyed them very much.

Then there was another class of men, namely those who had served with him, whether as officers or privates, and who did not get a share of glory. They asserted that **prisoners of war were enrolled among the veteran forces and that they received identical pay**. Accordingly, his friends were incensed at being rated as equal to those whom they themselves had taken prisoners, and indeed they were even outranked by some of them. To many, also, the fact that they benefitted at his hands, both by gifts of property and by appointments to offices, was a special source of grievance, since he alone was able to bestow such benefits, and everyone else was ignored as of no importance. When he became exalted through many notable victories (which was fair enough) and began to think himself superhuman **the common people worshipped him**, but he began to be obnoxious to the optimates and to those who were trying to obtain a share in the government. And so, every kind of man combined against him: great and small, friend and foe, military and political, every one of whom put forward his own particular pretext for the matter in hand, and as a result of his own complaints each lent a ready ear to the accusations of the others. They all confirmed each other in their conspiracy and they furnished as surety to one another the grievances which they held severally in private against him. Hence, though the number of conspirators became so great, no one dared to give information of the fact. Some say, however, that a little before his death, Caesar received a note in which warning of the plot was given, and that he was murdered with it in his hands before he had a chance to read it, and that it was found among other notes after his death.

However, all this became known subsequently. At that time some wished to gratify him by voting him one honour after another, while others treacherously included extravagant honours, and published them, so that he might become an object of envy and suspicion to all. **Caesar was of guileless disposition and was unskilled in political practices by reason of his foreign campaigns, so that he was easily taken in by these people, supposing, naturally enough, that their commendations came rather from men who admired him than from men who were plotting against him.**

To those who were in authority this measure was especially displeasing: that the people were now rendered powerless to make appointments to office, and that Caesar was given the right of bestowing [offices] upon whomsoever he pleased. An ordinance voted not long before provided this. Furthermore, all sorts of rumours were being bandied about in the crowd, some telling one story, others another. Some said that he had decided to establish a capital of the whole empire in Egypt, and that Queen Cleopatra had lain with him and borne him a son, named Cyrus [(?) Caesarion], there. This he himself refuted in his will as false. Others said that he was going to do the same thing at Troy, on account of his ancient connection with the Trojan race.

Something else, such as it was, took place which especially stirred the conspirators against him. There was a golden statue of him which had been erected on the Rostra by vote of the people. A diadem appeared on it, encircling the head, whereupon the Romans became very suspicious, supposing that it was a symbol of servitude. Two of the tribunes, Lucius and Gaius, came up and ordered one of their subordinates to climb up, take it down, and throw it away. When Caesar discovered what had happened, he convened the Senate in the temple of Concordia and arraigned the tribunes, asserting that they themselves had secretly placed the diadem on the statue, so that they might have a chance to insult him openly and thus get credit for doing a brave deed by dishonouring the statue, caring nothing either for him or for the Senate. He continued that their action was one which indicated a more serious resolution and plot: if somehow they might slander him to the people as a seeker after unconstitutional power, and thus (themselves stirring up an insurrection) to slay him. After this address, with the concurrence of the Senate he banished them. Accordingly, they went off into exile and other tribunes were appointed in their place. **Then the people clamoured that he become king** and they shouted that there should be no longer any delay in crowning him as such, for Fortune had already crowned him. But Caesar declared that although he would grant the people everything because of their good will toward him, **he would never allow this step**; and he asked their indulgence for contradicting their wishes in preserving the old form of government, saying that he preferred to hold the office of consul in accordance with the law to being king illegally.

Such was the people's talk at that time. Later, in the course of the winter, a festival was held in Rome, called Lupercalia, in which old and young men together take part in a procession, naked except for a girdle, and anointed, railing at those whom they meet and striking them with pieces of goat hide. When this festival came on Marcus Antonius was chosen director [*hegemon*]. He proceeded through the forum, as was the custom, and the rest of the throng followed him. Caesar was sitting in a golden chair on the Rostra, wearing a purple toga. At first Licinius advanced toward him carrying a laurel wreath, though inside it a diadem was plainly visible. He mounted up, pushed up by his colleagues (for the place from which Caesar was accustomed to address the assembly was high), and set the diadem down before Caesar's feet. Thereupon Caesar called Lepidus, the *magister equitum*, to ward him off, but Lepidus hesitated. In the meanwhile Cassius Longinus, one of the conspirators, pretending to be really well disposed toward Caesar so that he might the more readily escape suspicion, hurriedly removed the diadem and placed it in Caesar's lap. Publius Casca was also with him. While Caesar kept rejecting it, and among the shouts of the people, Antonius suddenly rushed up, naked and anointed, just as he was in the procession, and placed it on his head. But Caesar snatched it off, and threw it into the crowd. Those who were standing at some distance applauded this action, but those who were near at hand clamoured that he should accept it and not repel the people's favour. Various individuals held different views of the matter. Some were angry, thinking it an indication of power out of place in a democracy; others, thinking to court favour, approved; still others spread the report that Antonius had acted as he did not without Caesar's connivance. There were many who were quite willing that Caesar be made king openly. All sorts of talk began to go through the crowd. When Antonius crowned Caesar a second time, the people shouted in chorus, "Hail, King"; but Caesar still refusing the crown, ordered it to be taken to the temple of Capitoline Jupiter, saying that it was more appropriate there. Again the same people applauded as before. There is told another story, that Antonius acted thus wishing to ingratiate himself with Caesar, and at the same time was cherishing the hope of being adopted as his son. Finally, he embraced Caesar and gave the crown to some of the men standing near to place it on the head of the statue of Caesar which was near by. This they did. Of all the occurrences of that time this was not the least influential in hastening the action of the conspirators, for it proved to their very eyes the truth of the suspicions they entertained.

Not long after this, the praetor Cinna propitiated Caesar to the extent of securing a decree which allowed the exiled tribunes to return; though in accordance with the wish of the people they were not to resume their office, but to remain private citizens, yet not excluded from public affairs. Caesar did not prevent their recall, so they returned.

Caesar called the annual *comitia* (for he had the authority of a decree to do so) and appointed Vibius Pansa and Aulus Hirtius as consuls for the ensuing year; for the year after that, Decimus Brutus, one of the conspirators, and Munatius Plancus.

Directly after this, another thing happened that greatly aroused the conspirators. Caesar was having a large handsome forum laid out in Rome, and he had called together the artisans and was letting the contracts for its construction. In the meanwhile, up came a procession of Roman nobles, to confer the honours which had just been voted him by common consent. In the lead was the consul (the one who was Caesar's colleague at that time), and he carried the decree with him. In front of him were lictors, keeping the crowd back on either side. With the consul came the praetors, tribunes, quaestors, and all the other officials. Next came the Senate, in orderly formation, and then a multitude of enormous size – never so large. The dignity of the nobles was awe inspiring – they were entrusted with the rule of the whole empire, and yet looked with admiration on another as if he were still greater. Caesar was seated while they advanced and because he was conversing with men standing to one side, he did not turn his head toward the approaching procession or pay any attention to it, but continued to prosecute the business which he had on hand, until one of his friends, nearby, said, 'Look at these people coming up in front of you.' Then Caesar laid down his papers and turned around and listened to what they had come to say. Now among their number were the conspirators, who filled the others with ill-will toward him, though the others were already offended at him because of this incident.

Then those also were excited who wished to lay hands on him not to recover liberty but to destroy the entire extant system; they were looking for an opportunity to overcome one who seemed to be absolutely invincible. For, although he had participated up to this time in three hundred and two battles in both Asia and Europe, it appeared that he had never been worsted. Since, however, he frequently came out by himself and appeared before them, the hope arose that he could be taken by treachery. They tried to bring about, somehow, the dismissal of his bodyguard by flattering him when they addressed him, saying that he ought to be considered sacred in the eyes of all and be called *pater patriae* [father of the fatherland]; and by proposing decrees to that effect in the hope that he would be thus misled and actually trust to their affection, and that he would dismiss his spearmen in the belief that he was guarded by the good will of everyone. This actually came to pass, and made their task far easier.

The conspirators never met to make their plans in the open, but in secret, a few at a time in each other's houses. As was natural, many plans were proposed and set in motion by them as they considered how and when they should commit the awful deed. Some proposed to attack him while on his way through the 'Via Sacra', for he often walked there; others, at the time of the *comitia*, when he had to cross a certain bridge to hold the election of magistrates in the field before the city. They would so divide their duties by lot that some should jostle him off the bridge and the others should rush upon him and slay him. Others proposed that he be attacked when the gladiatorial shows were held (they were near at hand), for then, because of these contests no suspicion would be aroused by the sight of men armed for the deed. The majority urged that he be killed during the session of the Senate, for then he was likely to be alone. There was no admittance to non-members, and many of the senators were conspirators, and carried swords under their togas. This plan was adopted.

Fortune [Tyche] had a part in this by causing Caesar himself to set a certain day on which the members of the Senate were to assemble to consider certain motions which he wished to introduce. When the appointed day came the conspirators assembled, prepared in all respects. They met in the portico [*stoa*] of Pompeius' theatre, where they sometimes gathered. Thus the divinity showed the vanity of man's estate – how very unstable it is, and subject to the vagaries of fortune – for Caesar was brought to the house of his enemy, there to lie, a corpse, before the statue of one whom, now dead, he had defeated when he was alive. And Fate [Moira] becomes a still stronger force if indeed one acknowledges her part in these things: on that day his friends, drawing conclusions from certain auguries, tried to prevent him from going to the Senate Room [*bouleuterion*], as did also his physicians on account of vertigoes to which he was sometimes subject, and from which he was at that time suffering; and especially his wife Calpurnia, who was terrified by a dream that night. She clung to him and said that she would not let him go out on that day. But Brutus, one of the conspirators, though he was at that time thought to be one of his most intimate friends, came up to him and said, 'What do you say, Caesar? Are you going to pay any attention to a woman's dreams and foolish men's omens, a man such as you? Are you going to insult the Senate which has honoured you and which you yourself convened, by not going out? No; if you take my advice you will dismiss from your mind the dreams of these people and go, for the Senate has been in session since morning, and is awaiting you.' He was persuaded and went out.

Meanwhile the assassins were making ready, some of them stationing themselves beside his chair, others in front of it, others behind it. The augurs brought forward the victims for him to make his final sacrifice before his entry into the Senate Room. It was manifest that the omens were unfavourable. The augurs substituted one animal after another in the attempt to secure a more auspicious forecast. Finally they said that the indications from the gods were unfavourable and that there was plainly some sort of curse hiding in the victims. In disgust, Caesar turned away toward the setting sun, and the augurs interpreted this action still more unfavourably. The assassins were on hand and were pleased at all this. Caesar's friends begged that he postpone the present session on account of what the soothsayers had said; and for his part, he was just giving the order to do this, but suddenly the attendants came to summon him, saying that the Senate had a quorum. Then Caesar cast a look toward his friends. And Brutus approached him again and said, 'Come Sir, turn your back on these people's nonsense and do not postpone the business that deserves the attention of Caesar and of the great empire, but consider your own worth a favourable omen.' Thus persuading him, he at the same time took him by the hand and led him in, for the Senate-chamber was nearby. Caesar followed in silence. When he came in and the Senate saw him, the members rose out of respect to him. Those who intended to lay hands on him were all about him. The first to come to him was Tullius Cimber, whose brother Caesar had exiled, and stepping forward as though to make an urgent appeal on behalf of his brother, he seized Caesar's toga, seeming to act rather boldly for a suppliant, and thus prevented him from standing up and using his hands if he so wished. Caesar was very angry, but the men held to their purpose and all suddenly bared their daggers and rushed upon him. First Servilius Casca stabbed him on the left shoulder a little above the collar bone, at which he had aimed but missed through nervousness. Caesar sprang up to defend himself against him, and Casca called to his brother, speaking in Greek in his excitement. The latter obeyed him and drove his sword into Caesar's side. A moment before Cassius had struck him obliquely across the face. Decimus Brutus struck him through the thigh. Cassius Longinus was eager to give another stroke, but he missed and struck Marcus Brutus on the hand. Minucius, too, made a lunge at Caesar but he struck Rubrius on the thigh. It looked as if they were fighting over Caesar. He fell, under many wounds, before the statue of Pompeius, and there was not one of them but struck him as he lay lifeless, to show that each of them had had a share in the deed, until he had received thirty-five wounds, and breathed his last.[1217]

Here, I will not analyze the above texts as I am saving that for a future volume. However, I'm sure that the astute reader can draw many conclusions about Caesar's character and the events surrounding his death and how it compares to the later myth of Jesus of Nazareth without my input. I will note, however, that not only was Caesar's blood copiously spilled, it was done in the 'house of his enemy,' Pompey. And yet, the result of his death was the loss of literally everything the conspirators claimed to be seeking to preserve. If the 'as above, so below' principle is considered, it is easy to see how Caesar's death might be described in the terms Paul has used, with the earthly reality symbolizing what has taken place in the heavenly spheres.

Caesar's funeral was described by Suetonius:

At the instance of Lucius Piso, his father-in-law, his will was opened and read in Mark Antony's house. He had made it on the ides [13th] of the preceding September, at his Lavican villa, and committed it to the custody of the chief of the Vestal Virgins. Quintus Tubero informs us, that in

---

[1217] *Nicolaus of Damascus: Life of Augustus*, translated by C. M. Hall (1923). The Greek text of the fragments has been edited by F. Jacoby in *Fragmente der Griechischen Historiker* (FGrH_90).

all the wills he had signed, from the time of his first consulship to the breaking out of the civil war, Cneius Pompey was appointed his heir, and that this had been publicly notified to the army. But in his last will, he named three heirs, the grandsons of his sisters; namely, Caius Octavius for three fourths of his estate, and Lucius Pinarius and Quintus Pedius for the remaining fourth. Other heirs [in remainder] were named at the close of the will, in which he also adopted Caius Octavius, who was to assume his name, into his family; and nominated most of those who were concerned in his death among the guardians of his son, if he should have any; as well as Decimus Brutus amongst his heirs of the second order. He bequeathed to the Roman people his gardens near the Tiber, and three hundred sesterces each man.

Notice of his funeral having been solemnly proclaimed, a pile was erected in the Campus Martius, near the tomb of his daughter Julia; and before the Rostra was placed a gilded tabernacle, on the model of the temple of Venus Genitrix; within which was an ivory bed, covered with purple and cloth of gold. **At the head was a trophy [*tropaeum*, cross], with the [bloodstained] robe in which he was slain.** It being considered that the whole day would not suffice for carrying the funeral oblations in solemn procession before the corpse, directions were given for every one, without regard to order, to carry them from the city into the Campus Martius, by what way they pleased. To raise pity and indignation for his murder, in the plays acted at the funeral, a passage was sung from Pacuvius's tragedy, entitled, "The Trial for Arms:"

> That ever I, unhappy man, should save
> Wretches, who thus have brought me to the grave!

And some lines also from Attilius's tragedy of 'Electra,' to the same effect. Instead of a funeral panegyric, the consul Antony ordered a herald to proclaim to the people the decree of the senate, in which they had bestowed upon him all honours, divine and human; with the oath by which they had engaged themselves for the defence of his person; and to these he added only a few words of his own. The magistrates and others who had formerly filled the highest offices, carried the bier from the Rostra into the Forum. While some proposed that the body should be burnt in the sanctuary of the temple of Jupiter Capitolinus, and others in Pompey's senate-house; on a sudden, two men, with swords by their sides, and spears in their hands, set fire to the bier with lighted torches. The throng around immediately heaped upon it dry faggots, the tribunals and benches of the adjoining courts, and whatever else came to hand. Then the musicians and players stripped off the dresses they wore on the present occasion, taken from the wardrobe of his triumph at spectacles, rent them, and threw them into the flames. The legionaries, also, of his veteran bands, cast in their armour, which they had put on in honour of his funeral. Most of the ladies did the same by their ornaments, with the *bullae*, and mantles of their children. In this public mourning there joined a multitude of foreigners, expressing their sorrow according to the fashion of their respective countries; **but especially the Jews, who for several nights together frequented the spot where the body was burnt.**
...

They afterwards erected in the Forum a column of Numidian marble, formed of one stone nearly twenty feet high, and inscribed upon it these words, TO THE FATHER OF HIS COUNTRY. At this column they continued for a long time to offer sacrifices, make vows, and decide controversies, in which they swore by Caesar.

Some of Caesar's friends entertained a suspicion, that he neither desired nor cared to live any longer, on account of his declining health; and for that reason slighted all the omens of religion, and the warnings of his friends. Others are of opinion, that thinking himself secure in the late decree of the senate, and their oaths, he dismissed his Spanish guards who attended him with drawn swords. Others again suppose, that he chose rather to face at once the dangers which threatened him on all sides, than to be for ever on the watch against them. Some tell us that he used to say, the commonwealth was more interested in the safety of his person than himself: for that he had for some time been satiated with power and glory; but that the commonwealth, if any thing should befall him, would have no rest, and, involved in another civil war, would be in a worse state than before.

This, however, was generally admitted, that his death was in many respects such as he would have chosen. For, upon reading the account delivered by Xenophon, how Cyrus in his last illness gave instructions respecting his funeral, Caesar deprecated a lingering death, and wished that his own might be sudden and speedy. And **the day before he died, the conversation at supper, in the house of Marcus Lepidus,** turning upon what was the most eligible way of dying, **he gave his opinion in favour of a death that is sudden and unexpected.**

He died in the fifty-sixth year of his age, and was ranked amongst the Gods, not only by a formal decree, but in the belief of the vulgar. For during the first games which Augustus, his heir, consecrated to his memory, **a comet blazed for seven days** together, rising always about eleven o'clock; **and it was supposed to be the soul of Caesar, now received into heaven**: for which reason, likewise, he is represented on his statue with a star on his brow. The senate-house in which he was slain, was ordered to be shut up, and a decree made that the ides of March should be called parricidal, and the senate should never more assemble on that day.[1218]

Virgil wrote in the *Georgics* that several unusual events took place following Caesar's assassination:

Who dare say the Sun is false? He and no other warns us when dark uprising threaten, when treachery and hidden wars are gathering strength. He and no other was moved to pity Rome on the day that Caesar died, when he veiled his radiance in gloom and darkness, and a godless age feared everlasting night. Yet in this hour Earth also and the plains of Ocean, ill-boding dogs and birds that spell mischief, sent signs which heralded disaster. How oft before our eyes did Etna deluge the fields of the Cyclopes with a torrent from her burst furnaces, hurling thereon balls of fire and molten rocks. Germany heard the noise of battle sweep across the sky and, even without precedent, the Alps rocked with earthquakes. A voice boomed through the silent groves for all to hear, a deafening voice, and phantoms of unearthly pallor were seen in the falling darkness. Horror beyond words, beasts uttered human speech; rivers stood still, the earth gaped upon; in the temples ivory images wept for grief, and beads of sweat covered bronze statues. King of waterways, the Po swept forests along in the swirl of his frenzied current, carrying with him over the plain cattle and stalls alike. Nor in that same hour did sinister filaments cease to appear in ominous entrails or blood to flow from wells or our hillside towns to echo all night with the howl of wolves. Never fell more lightning from a cloudless sky; never was comet's alarming glare so often seen.[1219]

Notice, in the above passage about the funeral, this in particular: "In this public mourning there joined a multitude of foreigners, expressing their sorrow according to the fashion of their respective countries; but especially the Jews, who for several nights together frequented the spot where the body was burnt."

Four months after the assassination, a bright comet visible in daylight appeared during Caesar's funeral games, held around his birthday in July.[1220] According to Suetonius, as celebrations were getting underway, "a comet shone for seven successive days, rising about the eleventh hour,

[1218]Suet., *Jul.* 83–88.

[1219]https://www.theoi.com/Text/VirgilGeorgics1.html.

[1220]"In 1997, two scholars at the University of Illinois at Chicago – John T. Ramsey (a classicist) and A. Lewis Licht (a physicist) – published a book [*The Comet of 44 B.C. and Caesar's Funeral Games* (Atlanta, GA: Scholars Press, 1997)] comparing astronomical/astrological evidence from both Han China and Rome. Their analysis, based on historical eyewitness accounts, Chinese astronomical records, astrological literature from later antiquity and ice cores from Greenland glaciers, yielded a range of orbital parameters for the hypothetical

and was believed to be the soul of Caesar."[1221]   Ovid describes the deification of Caesar in *Metamorphoses* (8 AD):

> Then Jupiter, the Father, spoke … **"Take up Caesar's spirit from his murdered corpse, and change it into a star**, so that the deified Julius may always look down from his high temple on our Capitol and forum." He had barely finished, when **gentle Venus stood in the midst of the Senate, seen by no one, and took up the newly freed spirit of her Caesar from his body, and preventing it from vanishing into the air, carried it towards the glorious stars.** As she carried it, she felt it glow and take fire, and loosed it from her breast: it climbed higher than the moon, and drawing behind it a fiery tail, shone as a star.[1222]

Julius Caesar was greatly loved by the common people and particularly by the Jews, so it is not hard to imagine that many of them continued to pay him honors in some way in subsequent years, though certainly not as a god. Nevertheless, it's entirely possible that there was a persistent mythos about him even among the Jews, both in Palestine and in other communities around the Empire. It is more than likely that Paul grew up knowing a great deal about Julius Caesar, probably more than we know today, having to rely on the survival of scattered ancient texts. Certainly, the account of Nicolaus of Damascus, above, was quite detailed with astute comments about Caesar himself.

One of the greatest historians of Rome, Theodor Mommsen, called Caesar "the sole creative genius produced by Rome, and the last produced by the ancient world." His assessment is worth reading in full, but these excerpts are representative:

> His remarkable power of intuition revealed itself in the precision and practicability of all his arrangements, even where he gave orders without having seen with his own eyes. His memory was matchless; and it was easy for him to carry on several occupations simultaneously with equal self-possession. Although a gentleman, a man of genius, and a monarch, he had still a heart. … With the ablest and most excellent men of his time, of high and of humble rank, he maintained noble relations of mutual fidelity, with each after his kind.
>
> … he was no doubt a great orator, author, and general, but he became each of these merely because he was a consummate statesman. … If he had a preference for any one form of services rendered to the State, it was for the sciences and arts of peace rather than for those of war.
>
> The most remarkable peculiarity of his action as a statesman was its perfect harmony. In reality all the conditions for this most difficult of all human functions were united in Cæsar. … A born ruler, he governed the minds of men as the wind drives the clouds, and compelled the most heterogeneous natures to place themselves at his service … No statesman has ever compelled alliances, no general has ever collected an army out of unyielding and refractory elements, with such decision, and kept them together with such firmness, as Cæsar displayed in constraining and upholding his coalitions and his legions.
>
> He was monarch; but he never played the king. Even when absolute lord of Rome, he retained the deportment of the party leader: perfectly pliant and smooth, easy and charming in conversation, complaisant towards every one, it seemed as if he wished to be nothing but the first among his peers.

---

object. They settled on a perihelion point of 0.22 AU for the object which was apparently visible with a tail from the Chinese capital Chang'an (in late May) and as a star-like object from Rome (in late July)." (Wikipedia.org, 'Caesar's Comet.')

[1221]Suet., *Jul.* 88.

[1222]Ovid, *Metamorphoses* 15, 745–842.

He is perhaps the only one among the mighty men of the earth who in great matters and little never acted according to inclination or caprice, but always without exception according to his duty as ruler ...

Of the mightiest creative power and yet at the same time of the most penetrating judgment; no longer a youth and not yet an old man; of the highest energy of will and the highest capacity of execution; filled with republican ideals and at the same time born to be a king; a Roman in the deepest essence of his nature, and yet called to reconcile and combine in himself as well as in the outer world the Roman and the Hellenic types of culture, — Cæsar was the entire and perfect man.[1223]

In response to Thomas Jefferson saying that the three greatest men were Bacon, Newton, and Locke, Alexander Hamilton responded, "The greatest man that ever lived was Julius Cæsar."[1224]

As noted, *Caesar bled to death from his wounds*, and then, at his funeral, a wax effigy was mounted on a cross – a tropaeum – draped in the bloody toga in which he died. According to Ovid, his soul was immediately taken from his body up to the heavens where he became a star. Terrible portents accompanied his death, according to Virgil, and then, four months later, a daylight comet appeared during his funeral games. It would not be surprising at all for someone like Paul to have a vision of the risen, deified Caesar, and to believe that he was the pre-existent Son of God who, by his death, and his apparition on a cross, a *tropaeum*, was victorious over the powers of darkness and the flesh in the same way he was ever victorious in life. I'm reminded of the words of Obi-wan Kenobi in *Star Wars*: "If you strike me down I shall become more powerful than you can possibly imagine."

If Paul's Christ was Julius Cæsar, how could such a thing be covered up? Assuming my speculation to be correct, I think there are a number of answers to that question. First of all, the whole idea of the Messiah was a Jewish apocalyptic phenomenon (borrowed from Zoroastrianism via Enochian apocalypticism). Whatever else he thought, Paul would have been convinced that his messiah was the son of the Jewish God in the same way Cyrus had been. Perhaps this is why he stressed the Second Adam point as well as Abraham's example of faith as being more in line with his presentation. And it would certainly explain many other odd things about his theology and arguments, even if they were couched in what he knew best: Jewish scripture. In such a context, it would also be likely that he would present such a Christ without reference to his human life, as he, in fact, did. Paul was not concerned with things 'of the flesh' so much as their spiritual significance or heavenly 'copy.' If it was important at all, I think the knowledge of the human identity of his Christ would most likely have been an initiatory secret, considering the environment in which he lived and worked. I've even considered the idea that Paul may not have revealed the identity of his Christ to anyone except his closest associates. When Paul says, "To the Jews I became as a Jew, in order to win Jews," one can imagine that Paul may have applied a similar policy to his presentation of his Christ. As to why no trace remains of such a secret, that should be no surprise at all considering the extensive myth-making and text creation and modification that was going on.

[1223] Theodor Mommsen, 'The Character of Cæsar,' from *History of Rome* (1854–1856), translated by William Purdie Dickson, available online at https://www.bartleby.com/library/prose/3629.html.

[1224] Letter from Thomas Jefferson to Benjamin Rush, 16 January 1811, available at https://founders.archives.gov/documents/Jefferson/03-03-02-0231.

Recall that the most complete 'story of Jesus' in Paul's letters is found in the so-called Philippians hymn, widely thought to be a pre-Pauline tradition (see 'The Cross' in chapter 7). For the Philippians to accept it as authoritative, they must already have been familiar with its presentation of Christ. I propose that if the Philippians (and many others) paid honors to Divus Julius – a widespread cult throughout the Empire at the time, though it faded as Christianity blossomed – they would know without saying who 'Christ' was, the one who had received the name of 'Savior.' And since there was only one god, as far as Paul was concerned, and that god was the Jewish Yahweh, obviously Julius Caesar must have been *his* son. That would have been the main element of Paul's gospel, the thing he was most anxious to convey to all: that there was a man who had been a perfect man (as Caesar was said to be by many, though of course, not by his enemies – same for the fictional Jesus), who had the courage to be obedient unto death in order to save all of mankind who would accept his patronage, and whose death – as Paul experienced it in its heavenly copy – had cosmic significance. That's the short version.

As I said at the beginning of this book, I presented this idea to several eminent biblical scholars; they thought it was interesting but wanted to see more work. While I was working, two of them died within months of each other, which upset me greatly. I continued to plug away at the research, which constituted a veritable mountain of reading, making notes, and looking for even the tiniest clues. Now I'm done with it and I'm sad that I cannot send it to them and say, "I did all I could and it's close, but I don't think it's time for a cigar."

And that is what it is: close, but no cigar. But truly, what would one expect? The creation and elaboration of the fiction of Jesus of Nazareth was an enterprise that required the obliteration of any hint that he was anything other than the Jewish messiah, even though the real Jewish messiah had failed spectacularly. The creators and promulgators of the mythical version had centuries in which to do it and almost ideal conditions following the collapse of the Roman Empire. But *why* would they do it? Julius Caesar as messiah would have been a threat to all the emperors and certainly to Judaism itself, or so it seems to me, and most especially to the nascent Catholic Church. What was wanted was a nice, malleable savior who could be bent to do the heavy lifting in support of a church hierarchy that ultimately sought to control the world – and actually did control a large portion of it for a while.

In the end, I think it is true: Caesar was Paul's Christ, and I think the few, faint, remaining clues point to my solution as the correct one.

The Reception of Mark

The Gospel of Mark apparently achieved early success and was spread, read and used by Matthew, Luke and, eventually, even John. But this success did not last, apparently. We also must recognize that there is no strong material evidence. The only papyrus manuscript documenting Mark is P^{45}, dated to the third century. There are older and more numerous papyri of Matthew dating back to the second century. Yet, in the codices of the fourth and fifth centuries, such as Sinaiticus, Vaticanus, Alexandrinus and Bezae Cantabrigiensis, Mark is present in its entirety. (The original ending at Mark 16:8 is present in Sinaiticus and Vaticanus.)

This data tells us something: it cannot be an accident that Matthew has so many more witnesses than Mark in the second and third centuries. The fact that optional endings were appended in some manuscripts, and that there were several literary versions of Mark, tells us that the circulation of Mark was not broad enough to establish a consistent, self-reinforcing textual tradition.[1225] The number and variety of textual versions of Mark are out of proportion to the number of manuscript copies. Such variety suggests that some people were not happy with Mark, though it can also be said that Christian texts were rather fluid and subject to revision by anyone who had a different agenda than the original author. Eve-Marie Becker suggests that it was the Matthean re-writing of Mark that initiated further literary creativeness by which other texts such as apocryphal gospels appeared.[1226]

And yet, in terms of chronology, Mark was clearly first. Mark is the prototype with no forerunners and no contemporaries. "Matthew's use of Mark is illuminating much beyond the questions of literary dependency: it can reveal to us how and why the earliest gospel-writing ('Mark') was not simply copied and preserved, i.e. considered as a concise textual outline."[1227] To the contrary, it was rather more imitated, enlarged, modified, and – tentatively – substituted.

What is of great interest is that Matthew uses Mark as a literary template and restricts himself to the Markan outline; he retains the topographical and chronological order: Galilee to Jerusalem and a one-year ministry. At the same time, Matthew feels free to rearrange things and move beyond Mark, significantly enlarging the text. Matthew's technique reveals that it was his intention to replace Mark.

All of the above considered, it appears that Mark's Gospel only succeeded because it was upheld – though suppressed at the same time – by others, i.e. Matthew, Luke and John. It was seen that Mark's Gospel was a 'literary success' and Matthew moved quickly to 'get in on the ground floor.' And so did many others. The power of Mark's Gospel lay in its invention, a literary concept of Gospel-writing that was soon imitated and modified. Matthew approved of the concept, but did not approve of much of the content of Mark, which he modified. Matthew's Gospel soon overshadowed Mark because it incorporated it, and was more thorough with more comprehensive coverage.

Despite the apparent resounding success of Matthew, Becker thinks that there must have been a literary and theological reversion to Mark, the original Gospel, after Papias claimed that it was the memoirs of Peter. As Ian J. Elmer notes above, it is more likely that handing Mark's Gospel over to Peter was more in the way of glorifying Peter than validating Mark. It appears that Mark was certainly there and being read and used, and with its views of the disciples, obviously, *something* had to be done! It couldn't be declared false since Matthew had used about 90% or more of it. It could be said that the survival of Mark meant that Matthew had been hoist with his own petard. In any event, by this time, Justin, Tatian, and Irenaeus confirmed the ideal of four Gospels, and Clement of Alexandria indicated a need for securing the Markan text. And so, a search for consistency began. It was in the interests of canonization that Mark was finally saved from being totally adulterated. As David C. Sim notes, Mark almost slipped into oblivion after Matthew's efforts to replace it, and the fact that it now sits in the canon is more than a touch ironic. It is clear that Mark survived because the groups that used it – even if they were few and small – survived.

[1225]H. Gamble, *Books and Readers in the Early Church: A History of Early Christian Texts* (New Haven/London: Yale University Press, 1995), p. 126.

[1226]In *Mark and Matthew II: Comparative Readings: Reception History, Cultural Hermeneutics, and Theology*, edited by Eve-Marie Becker and Anders Runesson (Tübingen: Mohr Siebeck, 2013).

[1227]Becker (2013), p. 24.

Marcion Redux

As has already been discussed, Paul pretty much went into something of an eclipse until Marcion appeared with a collection of his letters and a Gospel which he had assembled together as the First New Testament. Marcion was known by his 'orthodox opponents' – from Polycarp of Smyrna to Eznik de Kolb – "as a thief who attempted to rob the Church of its deposit of received truth, corrupted the oracles of the Lord," as R. Joseph Hoffmann puts it, and one who "drove such a wedge between the Law and the Gospel as to make two separate Gods" (Tertullian).[1228]

Marcion saw the contrast between the Jewish law and Paul's teachings and determined that the god who gave the law could not possibly have been the god of Jesus. Marcion argued that the god of the Old Testament, the Jewish god, created the world, chose Israel to be his people, and then gave them his law. So the Old Testament god was justified in damning everyone who could not keep his law. He was a ruthlessly judicial, wrathful god, but not evil as some gnostics proposed.

Along came a superior god, the true god of the Universe, who was even higher than the Jewish god, and he sent his son into the world to pay the debt of sin for humanity – those who accepted him – in order to save them from the clutches of the wrathful Jewish god. Since the god who was the father of Jesus was not the god of the Old Testament who created the world, Jesus could not belong to this created order, or belong to the Jews in any way. Jesus came from heaven, from the true superior god and, for that reason, he could not have been an actual physical being.

The only texts Marcion accepted as true were certain letters of Paul and a Gospel that appears to be something like a stripped down Luke.[1229] Yet, since these texts contained many references to the Old Testament as an authority, Marcion was convinced that Jewish followers of Jesus changed the teachings and went back to their old Jewish ways. It was for this reason that God called Paul to be an apostle – to set things straight.

According to Marcion, this wide misinterpretation of Jesus' message had affected many Christians, including the scribes who had copied the writings of Paul and his gospel. Scribes who did not understand the truth had recopied and altered the texts, inserting false or wrong views into them.

Hoffmann's extended study of Marcion and his critics indicates that Marcion must be dated considerably earlier than the patristic descriptions would have us believe, and certainly earlier than the canonical redaction of Luke, which was undoubtedly carried out by Polycarp in reaction to Marcion. The whole doctrine of 'false apostles' and the doctrine of apostolic authority coming down from the disciples of Jesus, and the claim of the apostolic authorship of the Gospels, stems from reactions to Marcion.

> Marcion's appeal was not an appeal 'away from the traditions of men', to use the phrase which his orthodox opponents turned back on him; it was an appeal directly to man's experience of God, and to the divine mystery of revelation made known to Paul, and only to Paul. ... for Marcion Paul commands papal authority. He is the sole infallible teacher. Our knowledge of this claim makes it possible to understand how Christianity emerged from the second century with the letters of the

---

[1228]Hoffman (2016), p. xi.

[1229]Marcion is missing most of Luke's first four chapters along with several subsequent verses and periscopes. Tyson (2006), p. 87, writes: "About 12 percent of Lukan material with synoptic parallels is probably absent from Marcion's gospel. But 41–43 percent of Lukan Sondergut [i.e. unique to Luke] material is omitted."

Apostle in trust. Had it not been made, it is difficult to imagine that a Pauline renaissance, at least of the proportion which Marcion's heresy brought about, would have transpired. We have yet to recognize that Marcion, far from depriving the Church of its 'old' testament, reminded it of its debts to the Apostle who proclaimed himself a member of the Tribe of Benjamin, and preached to the gentiles a God of love ...[1230]

Based on a careful examination of the data, Hoffmann gives the following timeline for Marcion:

70 AD	Born in Sinope
110–150 AD	Active in Asia Minor
154 AD	Died

In the map below, Sinope is located on the northern coast (Sinop in modern Turkey), just above the 'U' in 'PONTUS.'

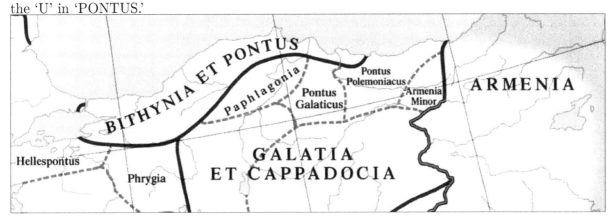

The closest to Sinope that Paul ever got, as far was we know, was Galatia, the region surrounding Ankara. During Paul and Marcion's time, Sinope was in the region then known as Pontus, part of the Roman province known as Bithynia and Pontus. Bithynia, the western half of the province, is where we find Pliny the Younger writing about Christians in about 112 AD, over 40 years after the birth of Marcion. Tertullian describes the region as barbaric and inhospitable:

> All is torpid here, everything stark. Savagery is there the only thing warm – such savagery as has provided the theater with tales of Tauric sacrifices, Colchian love-affairs, and Caucasian crucifixions. Even so, the most barbarous and melancholy thing about Pontus is that Marcion was born there, more uncouth than a Scythian, more unsettled than a Wagon-sweller, more uncivilized than a Massagete, with more effrontery than an Amazon, darker than fog, colder than winter, more brittle than ice, more treacherous that the Danube, and more precipitous than Caucasus.[1231]

Considering the fact that Tertullian wasn't born until 155 AD, nor was he an active adult until at least 20 or 30 years later, he sure is feeling hostile! But then, he was trained as a lawyer and we can recognize his rhetorical tricks. Actually, Sinope was not at all a cultural backwater. Strabo (63 BC – 24 AD), the great Greek geographer, philosopher and historian, was from Sinope, as

---

[1230]Hoffmann (2016), pp. 308–9.
[1231]This is from Hoffmann (2016), p. 1, and he notes that it appears to be based on that of Herodotus (484 BC), though it actually doesn't match what Herodotus wrote.

was the famous philosopher, Diogenes of Sinope (fl. 360 BC). There was also a sizeable Iranian diaspora there. Hoffmann thinks that Marcion may have been greatly influenced by Zoroastrian religious ideas, which we covered earlier. The Sinopeans knew the cults of Mithra, Ahura Mazda, and Yahweh.

We know nothing of Marcion's teaching career in Pontus and next-to-nothing about his activity after leaving Sinope for Rome. However, the success of Marcion's teaching is attested by the volume, distribution, and virulence of the polemics *against* him beginning with Justin in Rome (150 AD), Theophilus of Antioch (160), Dionysius and Modestus in Greece (170), Irenaeus in Lyons (176), Rhodon in Rome (180), Clement of Alexandria (200), Tertullian in Carthage (200), Commodianus in Gaul (300), Adamantius in Greece (320), Ephraem in Syria (370), Philastruius in Brescia (385), Eznik de Kolb at Bagrevand (445). As late as the mid fifth century, Theodoret, bishop of Cyrrhus in Syria, wages battle against Marcionite teachers in his diocese.

I'm not going to go into a detailed discussion of Marcionism; what interests me here is how and why Marcion showed up at some point in time in Rome with letters of Paul and a Gospel in his luggage, when, based on what Hoffmann noted, there didn't seem to be a single sign of any such items among the 'orthodox' churches at the time.

There is *only* a short version of his bio: Epiphanius wrote that Marcion was the son of a bishop in Pontus. Rhodo and Tertullian described him as a "mariner" and a "ship-master" respectively. Allegedly, some time in the late 130s AD, Marcion traveled to Rome, joined the Roman church, and made a large donation of 200,000 sesterces to the congregation there. Conflicts with the church of Rome arose and he was eventually excommunicated in 144 AD, his donation being returned to him. After his excommunication, he returned to Asia Minor, where he continued to lead his many church congregations and teach the gospel of Marcion.[1232]

When the case is examined carefully, as Hoffmann does, it appears that Marcion, *even in Rome*, knew nothing of a 'deposit of faith' delivered to the saints and preserved intact by an unbroken succession of teacher-bishops who had been authorized by the disciples of Jesus. What he does know is a muddled tradition of apostolic preaching, half-hearted acceptance of the gospel, and strong opposition to the doctrines of Paul.[1233]

Apparently, Mark's Gospel was in eclipse. Perhaps that is why what we know of the earliest extant text gives evidence that it was damaged, possibly through neglect. We are pretty certain that Mark was written in Rome for Roman Christians, to get them out of trouble, and that Mark – or a committee – used Paul and a lot of other sources in the writing. But the early patristic literature and the case of Marcion suggest strongly that few people were actually using Mark's Gospel or Paul's letters; Matthew was so much better! That means that Mark's Gospel and Paul's letters probably were both dumped in a box somewhere – except for a few communities – and left to rot; until Marcion came along and was so successful that the 'orthodox' had to work, and work fast, to validate their claims to authentic apostolic succession and, thereby, control.

In a sense, when Paul stepped forward and claimed that he alone knew the truth, and others had misunderstood or distorted who Jesus was, he took the stopper off the bottle holding the genie of confusion. After that, anyone could do it; and they did. And thus, forgery of documents became a primary weapon in this war against both outsiders and 'wrong' Christians.

[1232]BeDuhn (2013), p. 165; Adolf Harnack, *Marcion: The Gospel of the Alien God* (Wipf and Stock, 2007), pp. 17 –18; Knox (1942), p. 5.
[1233]Hoffman (2016).

And all of the above suggests that it was Matthew – whoever he was – who took Mark's allegorical Gospel and incorporated it into a Gospel that became the founding myth of Christianity. Indeed, the author(s) of Mark never intended the Gospel to be taken as history, but Matthew certainly did.

9. PaleoChristianity

The term 'paleo' means 'ancient,' 'early,' 'prehistoric,' 'primitive.' It is most often used to form compound words denoting the most ancient manifestation of a given phenomenon. Attached to the word 'Christianity,' it obviously means 'original,' 'early,' or 'first' Christianity, as formulated and practiced by the earliest, even the very first, Christians.

In this reconstruction, I've attempted to infer, from what little data is available, what that might have been. The process has been complicated by the fact that it seems, from very early on, that Christianity was already two different things. Well, more properly, Jewish messianism was undoubtedly first, but that was more a Jewish reform movement than a new revelation; it was Paul who, like Zoroaster, had a vision and radically altered messianism.

Paul thought that single persons ought to remain unmarried because the end of all things was near; he thought that he was living at the very end of time. According to Jewish thinking, the resurrection was to arrive when this age had come to an end. Paul called Jesus the 'first fruits' of the resurrection: the resurrection had started. Paul believed that he would be alive when Jesus returned; he only saw a short interim between the resurrection of Jesus and the end of time. Everyone was supposed to spend their time getting ready for the end using their individual spiritual gifts.

When writing to his churches to address problems, Paul did not address only leaders of a church and tell them how to get their people in order. There apparently were no leaders as we understand such a term today. There were only groups of individuals, each of whom had a 'gift of the spirit' to contribute to the benefit of the whole group in the short time before the end. "In Christ there is neither slave nor free, neither male nor female ..." (Gal 3:28). It was all about equality and a network of sharing.

For Paul, there was not going to be a long haul – the end was coming soon and he was working like mad to get the word out. He was emphatic that Christians who had been baptized had 'died' to the powers of the world, the demonic archons of the age; the Christians had died with Christ. But, they had not yet been raised with Christ; that would happen at the end of time when Jesus returned.

We have extensively reviewed the conflicts between the Zealot Christians and the Pauline Christians. The former, who believed in a physical messiah who was going to come and rule the world or, at the very least, straighten things out, had an obvious advantage over Paul, who taught that the resurrection was something like a spiritual event: "Flesh and blood cannot inherit the kingdom of God." He saw the resurrection at the end of time as basically a restoration of the Edenic order of things, much like Zoroaster did.

The Holy City

Before Jerusalem, Rome was the original Holy City. It was established as such in the eighth century BC by a caste of holy priests, the 'fathers,' whose primary duties were to govern according to the will of Jupiter. Every magistrate was an augur of some sort, and no business was ever conducted, even down to the time of Caesar, without 'reading the signs' – taking the 'auspices' – to determine the will of the gods. Jerusalem, on the other hand, only seems to have become a 'holy city' as a consequence of the Maccabean revolt and reforms in 167–160 BC, when Judas Maccabeus and his Judean rebels fought the Seleucid Empire of Antiochus IV.

According to the most rational biblical scholarship, the Old Testament was produced in the early third century in Alexandria and modeled largely on Greco-Roman literature, from Herodotus to Plato, even borrowing incidents and concepts from Roman History.[1234] It seems that among the ideas borrowed from the Romans was the conviction that their god was the one true god, who had endowed them with the character and right to rule over others. For the Romans, it became a reality; for the Jews, it was, *at that point*, just a dream.

Julius Caesar, like any good Roman of the time, also believed that the gods had ordained Rome to rule over the world. However, he had a very different idea of how it ought to be done, as is evident from the surviving details of his life. Caesar made it clear that he believed in equality, extending citizenship and rights to those who were conquered, that the workers and soldiers should benefit from their labors equally, and not be subjected to rapacious oligarchs with unlimited power. Caesar believed in mercy and forgiveness and, altogether, everything he represented scared the ruling oligarchs to death. And so, they killed him.

But the love of the people for Caesar would not allow them to believe that all those promises of justice, mercy and equality were gone forever. They undoubtedly immediately formed the hope that some way, somehow, soon, Caesar, in his new capacity as a god, would return and finish his work. The philosophical Jesus, shaped by Roman ideas promulgated by (of all people) Caesar's enemy Cicero,[1235] was most likely the Caesar that Paul saw. This was the Jesus that was partly shaped by Roman concepts of Caesar and by Jewish concepts of an exclusive god and an exclusive truth formulated by Paul. No doubt, many in the Greek-speaking world had already designated Julius Caesar as 'Christ.'

It seems that the worship of Caesar began spontaneously at the time of his death and continued thereafter. However, after the civil war, when Augustus didn't need Caesar as much as he needed the old elite (those he hadn't proscribed and/or killed), Caesar was pushed into the background deliberately and, as a human, was an embarrassment. However, it appears that this only gave impetus to the private worship which appears to have taken on the characteristics of a Mystery Religion. The Caesar cult expanded all over the Empire because of the great love the common people felt for him and his championship of their rights. It was especially strong in areas settled by the retired soldiers from Caesar's army. There were several major colonies, including in North Africa, Corinth, Sinope, the Narbonne area and probably Spain.

In the beginning, Augustus encouraged the worship of his adopted father/uncle because, by that, he was able to be known as the 'Son of God.' But after a time, he decided that it was better to just sort of fade it out, give it less emphasis, and concentrate on his own position as 'Son of God.' Nevertheless, for many years the Caesar cult persisted and there are archaeological finds attesting to this. There was a temple dedicated to Julius Caesar in Ephesus.

[1234]See Gmirkin (2006), Gmirkin (2016), Wajdenbaum (2014). While Wajdenbaum cites Roman parallels, Gmirkin sees those as too late to be relevant, focusing on Greek and Hellenistic parallels prior to ca. 270 BC.

[1235]See Cole (2013).

Paul may also have been convinced, as a result of a Caesar cult experience, that Caesar was the son of God – the Jewish creator god – and that this meant that God intended for all peoples to be united in one worship. He may have taught this directly as 'Christ on the cross,' the cross/*tropaeum* being the symbol both of death and triumph at one and the same time. Paul may not have seen it as necessary to identify his Christ on the cross as Caesar; on the other hand, he may not have needed to. In his preaching, he may have tapped into the network of the Caesar cults for his first converts. His letters may have been redacted to remove any such clues, which would have been small, if present at all, due to the one-sided conversational nature of letters where a lot of things are understood by both parties that are not explicitly set out in the letter.

What seems important to me is that Paul apparently did have some deep and profound visionary experiences from which he distilled his theories of another world, semi-physical and other-dimensional, which would be the new reality of the 'saved' Christian. What seems clear is that this was partly based on the Roman *clientela* system: if you align yourself with Christ, then you will be saved at the end when he returns. On the other hand, the elements of his teaching can also be found among Greek and Jewish religious ideas laying close to hand.

Since Paul was so desperately seeking to counter revolutionary activities and engage the worship of the Gentiles for the same creator god of the Jews, it may be that he used the idea of an eschatological Parousia as both carrot and stick to achieve his objective of reconciliation of humanity. He may very well have understood the true nature of this other hyperdimensional reality – and he may have surely seen the 'principalities' as energetic constructs of information – and that the Jews were almost certainly doomed if something wasn't done, and quickly.

But he failed. The end did come for Jerusalem and more than a million Jews. After which, it seems to me, he may have been the one who wrote chapters 9–11 of Romans in an excess of grief, though it was later redacted by Jewish Christians of the Matthean type.

Meanwhile, in Judea, there were potential messiahs, and one that stood out from among the rest: Judas the Galilean. Ultimately, the Jews did not reject Judas the Galilean; Rome did. Jerusalem rejected Paul's messiah. Mark wrote an allegorical Gospel to portray Christ as a son of the Jewish god rejected by the Jews, and, as a consequence, Rome eventually embraced both, though it forgot that the Messiah was its own native son: Gaius Julius Caesar.

Isaiah prophesied that the Wolf would lie down with the Lamb. The Roman Wolf certainly did submit to the Christian Lamb thanks to Constantine and, for the past 1,700 years, Rome has been, more or less, 'twice holy,' since it was claimed that it became the Christian holy city only after Jerusalem rejected her messiah. But that doesn't seem to be true at all.

Since its inception, Rome was ruled by a group of patricians who thought they had the right to despoil and rule the world. They were overthrown more completely by Caesar's death than ever could have been possible had he lived. Caesar didn't want the destruction of the Republic; he wanted to repair and reform it and leave it better than before. When Brutus and his conspirators struck their blow for 'freedom' (i.e., the rights of the oligarchs), they didn't realize that it was to be the freedom of the grave for both them and their precious oligarchic republic. Like the Judas character of the Gospels, the assassins all suffered ignoble deaths and Dante placed them in the ninth circle of Hell together – a three-faced Satan gnaws on Cassius, Brutus, and Judas in the center. Somehow Dante must have sensed – or known? – that the story about the betrayal of Jesus was actually the betrayal of Caesar.

Julius Caesar, the son of Venus, symbolized by the dove, was elevated to the status of an imperial god after his violent death at the hands of those he had loved and forgiven. The cult that surrounded him dissolved gradually as Christianity developed. The 'historical Jesus' has long been a mystery to scholars for a variety of reasons, not least of which is the failure of the Gospels to agree with not just known history, but also with each other. The traditional Gospel timeline is simply impossible. Early historians never mention Jesus.

At the same time, there is an actual historical figure missing his cult while a major religion is missing its actual historical figure. In the 1950s, German theologian Ethelbert Stauffer researched the relationship between the Roman sources and early Christianity. He showed that the Easter liturgy does not follow the Gospel but the funerary ritual of Julius Caesar and that the *Clementia Caesaris* was the pre-Christian forerunner of Christ's forgiveness.[1236]

In addition to his famous mercy – *clementia* – Caesar extended rights of citizenship and legal protection to the provinces. After Caesar's model, Christianity extended the rights of citizenship in heaven even to slaves and barbarians. Rome is – and has been since the conquest of Greece in the second century BC – the mystical Acropolis of the Earth, the supernatural *de Civitas Dei*. If such it is, it is because it was consecrated by the death and deification of Julius Caesar.

[1236]Ethelbert Stauffer, *Christ and the Caesars: Historical Sketches*, translated by Kaethe Gregor Smith and Ronald Gregor Smith (London: SCM-Press, 1955).

Appendix A: The Marcionite Prologues

The **Galatians** are Greeks. These accepted the true teaching first from the Emissary, but after his departure were tempted by false emissaries to turn to the Law and to circumcision. The Emissary recalls these people to the trust of truth, writing to them from Ephesus.

Corinthians are Achaeans. These also likewise heard the true teaching from the Emissary and were perverted by various false emissaries, some by the wordy eloquence of philosophy, others led on by the sect of the Jewish Law. The Emissary recalls these people to the true and evangelical wisdom, writing to them from Ephesus.

Romans are in the region of Italy. These were reached beforehand by false emissaries and under the name of our lord Jesus Christos had been led on to the Law and the Prophets. The Emissary recalls these people to the true and evangelical faith, writing to them from Athens [variant: from Corinth].

The **Thessalonians** are Macedonians, who having accepted the true teaching, persevered in the faith even under persecution from their own citizens; and moreover they did not accept what was said by false emissaries. The Emissary congratulates these people, writing to them from Athens.

Loadiceans are of Asia. They had been reached beforehand by false emissaries, and the Emissary himself does not come to them; but he corrects them by a letter ... writing to them from Ephesus.

Colossians, like the Laodiceans, are of Asia. They, too, had been reached beforehand by false emissaries, and the Emissary himself does not come to them; but he corrects them also by a letter. For they had heard his word from Archippus, who also accepted a service to them. So the Emissary, already in bonds, writes to them from Ephesus.

Philippians are Macedonians. These, having accepted the true teaching, persevered in the faith and they did not receive false emissaries. The Emissary congratulates these people, writing to them from prison at Rome by Epaphroditus.

To **Philemon** he composes a private letter by Onesimus his slave. He writes to him from Rome out of prison.[1237]

[1237]BeDuhn (2013), pp. 229, 233, 246, 250, 252, 255, 258, 259.

Appendix B: Analysis of The Epistle to the Romans

As discussed in the section 'Paul in Rome,' here is a closer look at Francis Watson's work on the Epistle to the Romans.[1238] Watson wants to orient the composition of the community by his reading of Romans 14:1–15:13. Others have noted that this section is a generalized re-writing of 1 Cor. 8–10. Compare below:

Rom. 14 Welcome those who are weak in faith, but not for the purpose of quarreling over opinions. Some believe in eating anything, while the weak eat only vegetables. Those who eat must not despise those who abstain, and those who abstain must not pass judgment on those who eat; for God has welcomed them. Who are you to pass judgment on servants of another? It is before their own lord that they stand or fall. And they will be upheld, for the Lord is able to make them stand. Some judge one day to be better than another, while others judge all days to be alike. Let all be fully convinced in their own minds. Those who observe the day, observe it in honor of the Lord. Also those who eat, eat in honor of the Lord, since they give thanks to God; while those who abstain, abstain in honor of the Lord and give thanks to God. We do not live to ourselves, and we do not die to ourselves. If we live, we live to the Lord, and if we die, we die to the Lord; so then, whether we live or whether we die, we are the Lord's. For to this end Christ died and lived again, so that he might be Lord of both the dead and the living. Why do you pass judgment on your brother or sister? Or you, why do you despise your brother or sister? For we will all stand before the judgment seat of God. For it is written, "As I live, says the Lord, every knee shall bow to me, and every tongue shall give praise to God." So then, each of us will be accountable to God.	**1 Cor. 8** Now concerning food sacrificed to idols: we know that "all of us possess knowledge." Knowledge puffs up, but love builds up. Anyone who claims to know something does not yet have the necessary knowledge; but anyone who loves God is known by him. Hence, as to the eating of food offered to idols, we know that "no idol in the world really exists," and that "there is no God but one." Indeed, even though there may be so-called gods in heaven or on earth – as in fact there are many gods and many lords – yet for us there is one God, the Father, from whom are all things and for whom we exist, and one Lord, Jesus Christ, through whom are all things and through whom we exist. It is not everyone, however, who has this knowledge. Since some have become so accustomed to idols until now, they still think of the food they eat as food offered to an idol; and their conscience, being weak, is defiled. "Food will not bring us close to God." We are no worse off if we do not eat, and no better off if we do. But take care that this liberty of yours does not somehow become a stumbling block to the weak. For if others see you, who possess knowledge, eating in the temple of an idol, might they not, since their conscience is weak, be encouraged to the point of eating food sacrificed to idols? So by your knowledge those weak believers for whom Christ died are destroyed. But when you thus sin against members of your family, and wound their conscience when it is weak, you sin against Christ. Therefore, if food is a cause of their falling, I will never eat meat, so that I may not cause one of them to fall.

[1238]Watson (2008).

Let us therefore no longer pass judgment on one another, but resolve instead never to put a stumbling block or hindrance in the way of another. I know and am persuaded in the Lord Jesus that nothing is unclean in itself; but it is unclean for anyone who thinks it unclean. If your brother or sister is being injured by what you eat, you are no longer walking in love. Do not let what you eat cause the ruin of one for whom Christ died. So do not let your good be spoken of as evil. For the kingdom of God is not food and drink but righteousness and peace and joy in the Holy Spirit. The one who thus serves Christ is acceptable to God and has human approval. Let us then pursue what makes for peace and for mutual upbuilding. Do not, for the sake of food, destroy the work of God. Everything is indeed clean, but it is wrong for you to make others fall by what you eat; it is good not to eat meat or drink wine or do anything that makes your brother or sister stumble. The faith that you have, have as your own conviction before God. Blessed are those who have no reason to condemn themselves because of what they approve. But those who have doubts are condemned if they eat, because they do not act from faith; for whatever does not proceed from faith is sin.

Rom. 15 We who are strong ought to put up with the failings of the weak, and not to please ourselves. Each of us must please our neighbor for the good purpose of building up the neighbor. For Christ did not please himself; but, as it is written, "The insults of those who insult you have fallen on me." For whatever was written in former days was written for our instruction, so that by steadfastness and by the encouragement of the scriptures we might have hope. May the God of steadfastness and encouragement grant you to live in harmony with one another, in accordance with Christ Jesus, so that together you may with one voice glorify the God and Father of our Lord Jesus Christ. Welcome one another, therefore, just as Christ has welcomed you, for the glory of God. For I tell you that Christ has become a servant of the circumcised on behalf of the truth of God in order that he might confirm the promises given to the patriarchs, and in order that the Gentiles might glorify God for his mercy.

1 Cor. 10:12-33 So if you think you are standing, watch out that you do not fall. No testing has overtaken you that is not common to everyone. God is faithful, and he will not let you be tested beyond your strength, but with the testing he will also provide the way out so that you may be able to endure it.

Therefore, my dear friends, flee from the worship of idols. I speak as to sensible people; judge for yourselves what I say. The cup of blessing that we bless, is it not a sharing in the blood of Christ? The bread that we break, is it not a sharing in the body of Christ? Because there is one bread, we who are many are one body, for we all partake of the one bread. Consider the people of Israel; are not those who eat the sacrifices partners in the altar? What do I imply then? That food sacrificed to idols is anything, or that an idol is anything? No, I imply that what pagans sacrifice, they sacrifice to demons and not to God. I do not want you to be partners with demons. You cannot drink the cup of the Lord and the cup of demons. You cannot partake of the table of the Lord and the table of demons. Or are we provoking the Lord to jealousy? Are we stronger than he?

"All things are lawful," but not all things are beneficial. "All things are lawful," but not all things build up. Do not seek your own advantage, but that of the other. Eat whatever is sold in the meat market without raising any question on the ground of conscience, for "the earth and its fullness are the Lord's." If an unbeliever invites you to a meal and you are disposed to go, eat whatever is set before you without raising any question on the ground of conscience. But if someone says to you, "This has been offered in sacrifice," then do not eat it, out of consideration for the one who informed you, and for the sake of conscience – I mean the other's conscience, not your own. For why should my liberty be subject to the judgment of someone else's conscience? If I partake with thankfulness, why should I be denounced because of that for which I give thanks?

So, whether you eat or drink, or whatever you do, do everything for the glory of God. Give no offense to Jews or to Greeks or to the church of God, just as I try to please everyone in everything I do, not seeking my own advantage, but that of many, so that they may be saved.

As it is written, "Therefore I will confess you among the Gentiles, and sing praises to your name"; and again he says, "Rejoice, O Gentiles, with his people"; and again, "Praise the Lord, all you Gentiles, and let all the peoples praise him"; and again Isaiah says, "The root of Jesse shall come, the one who rises to rule the Gentiles; in him the Gentiles shall hope." May the God of hope fill you with all joy and peace in believing, so that you may abound in hope by the power of the Holy Spirit.

If you were paying attention as you read, you would have noticed that the 1 Cor. chapter ten excerpt pretty much directly contradicts the chapter eight excerpt! All things considered, the passage from chapter ten about eating appears to be a later non-Pauline interpolation.

Nevertheless, it is pretty easy to see that Romans 14:1–15:13 is a complete rip-off of the Corinthians text, yet this is the text that Watson chooses to orient his 'social situation' of the community to whom the Epistle to the Romans was sent. Combining the ideas of Wiefel – who thought that the Jewish Christians had formerly been the majority, but were expelled in 49 AD, so that now Gentile Christians are the majority, though Jewish Christians are, bit by bit, drifting back to town – and Jervell's idea that Paul is planning on going to Jerusalem and wants to engender the support of the Roman combined congregation *and* write his defense for Jerusalem, Watson believes that this letter was written to a congregation that was mixed and was having a hard time getting along.

Watson's estimate of the situation is clearly wrong. Keep in mind Paul's likely situation: he's been pretty much at war with Jewish Christianity for the whole of his career (at least on an ideological level). And in the few years before writing Romans, he has been in open warfare with the James gang, beginning with the incident with Cephas/Peter at Antioch. Then, there were the executions of James and Simon/Peter/Cephas, followed by the Galatians incident. Paul has been arrested and put in prison. He is probably writing Romans from there and, in fact, makes a few small remarks that support that, even if any blatant information regarding same has been redacted so as to make the letter appear more in line with the story of Acts. At this point, Paul has written several other letters strongly condemning Jewish Christians either overtly or covertly. Now he learns that he may be transferred to Rome. Thus, indeed, he needs friends and support there. That is most obviously the reason for writing the epistle. And with that more rational estimate of the situation, reading Romans takes on a whole new significance. We have to keep in mind redaction, cover-up, and what was probably really happening. It is vanishingly unlikely that Paul would be appealing to Zealot/messianic Jews.

Watson writes: "Romans 14 is incompatible with the claim that the letter was addressed exclusively and straightforwardly to the Gentiles."[1239] True. Which means that Romans 14–15:13 was not part of the original letter. It must be set aside. He continues: "Paul's denial of a positive soteriological role to the Law is an imperative. He is calling on the Roman Gentile Church to finalize their break with Judaism."

[1239]Watson (2008), p. 178.

Denial of a positive role of the law is characteristic of only Romans 1:18–4:24, and this section is decidedly addressed to Jewish leaders and not Gentile Christians, therefore it too must be set aside as a separate text.

Watson relies on the 'greetings list' of chapter 16 of Romans to give him clues as to who was there and what the social situation was. He combines this information with the stories of Acts to find his bearings – a very shaky foundation, to seriously understate the matter!

In chapter 16, Paul allegedly sends greetings to Prisca and Aquila: "Greet Prisca and Aquila, who work with me in Christ Jesus, and who risked their necks for my life, to whom not only I give thanks, but also all the churches of the Gentiles. Greet also the church in their house" (Rom. 16:3-5). As noted in the main text, they were mentioned in 1 Cor. 16:19 as having a house church in Ephesus, and recall that the 1 Cor. correspondence was before the second Jerusalem meeting, in complete contradiction to the fiction in Acts. (This alone exposes Acts for the complete fraud it is, though it is far from the only example to do so.) Here he says they "risked their lives" for him. In Acts, Prisca and Aquila are said to be Jews, but Paul never says they are Jews and, in fact, we do not know that they are; they are more likely Gentiles. But Watson relies on them being Jews and being *in Rome*, because this passage with a load of greetings is at the end of that epistle.

Paul's next greeting is to "beloved Epaenetus, who was the first convert *in Asia* for Christ." Why would Epaenetus now be in Rome, and why would Paul be writing as though he were still "in Asia"?

Then to "Andronicus and Junia, *my relatives who were in prison with me*; they are prominent among the apostles, and they were in Christ before I was" (Rom. 16:17). This bit is interesting. The implication is that Paul was formerly in prison, but is now no longer, and here mentions the fact that some of his relatives had actually been put in prison with him. If, in fact, he had been in prison in Ephesus, then he is sending greetings to them from Rome! Further, that these relatives were Christians before he was is furiously interesting. He further says that these two were "prominent among the apostles." As far as we know, Paul considered a person to be an apostle if they had received a vision of Christ. If Paul had relatives who were Christians before him, and he was converted in 29 AD as the evidence shows, then what kind of Christians were his relatives? And if Paul was persecuting 'the church,' as he allegedly admits in 1 Cor. 15:9, what are we to make of this? Let's look at the passage:

> Now I would remind you, brothers and sisters, of the good news that I proclaimed to you, which you in turn received, in which also you stand, through which also you are being saved, if you hold firmly to the message that I proclaimed to you – unless you have come to believe in vain. *For I handed on to you as of first importance what I in turn had received*: that Christ died for our sins in accordance with the scriptures, and that he was buried, and that he was raised on the third day in accordance with the scriptures, and that he appeared to Cephas, then to the twelve. Then he appeared to more than five hundred brothers and sisters at one time, most of whom are still alive, though some have died. Then he appeared to James, then to all the apostles. Last of all, as to one untimely born, he appeared also to me. *For I am the least of the apostles, unfit to be called an apostle, because I persecuted the church of God.* But by the grace of God I am what I am, and his grace toward me has not been in vain. On the contrary, I worked harder than any of them – though

it was not I, but the grace of God that is with me. Whether then it was I or they, so we proclaim and so you have come to believe.[1240]

As discussed at numerous times in the main text (Chapter 7), there are several problems with the above passage, and many NT experts are convinced that at least part of it is a later addition. I've put in italics that Paul "handed on what I received." This is written as though he is talking about a tradition that some person taught him and which he then just handed on. He then segues to the visions of the resurrected Jesus, starting with Peter/Cephas, then "the twelve" (no indication that there should only be eleven if Judas was the betrayer), then to 500 people all at once, then to James, then to "all the apostles." Those are some pretty odd categories and a strange order of appearances, and, overall, it does indeed smack of textual prestidigitation. Does that mean that the other italicized item – the claim that Paul "persecuted" the early church – was also added by a much later editor? I think it is very possible.

The second Pauline text which makes the claim that Paul persecuted the church is Galatians 1:13 and 1:23, as follows:

> I am astonished that you are so quickly deserting the one who called you in the grace of Christ and are turning to a different gospel – not that there is another gospel, but there are some who are confusing you and want to pervert the gospel of Christ. But even if we or an angel from heaven should proclaim to you a gospel contrary to what we proclaimed to you, let that one be accursed! As we have said before, so now I repeat, if anyone proclaims to you a gospel contrary to what you received, let that one be accursed!
>
> Am I now seeking human approval, or God's approval? Or am I trying to please people? If I were still pleasing people, I would not be a servant of Christ. For I want you to know, brothers and sisters, that the gospel that was proclaimed by me is not of human origin; for I did not receive it from a human source, nor was I taught it, but I received it through a revelation of Jesus Christ. *You have heard, no doubt, of my earlier life in Judaism. I was violently persecuting the church of God and was trying to destroy it.* I advanced in Judaism beyond many among my people of the same age, for I was far more zealous for the traditions of my ancestors. But when God, who had set me apart before I was born and called me through his grace, was pleased to reveal his Son to me, so that I might proclaim him among the Gentiles, I did not confer with any human being, nor did I go up to Jerusalem to those who were already apostles before me, but I went away at once into Arabia, and afterwards I returned to Damascus. Then after three years I did go up to Jerusalem to visit Cephas and stayed with him fifteen days; but I did not see any other apostle except James the Lord's brother. In what I am writing to you, before God, I do not lie! Then I went into the regions of Syria and Cilicia, and I was still unknown by sight to the churches of Judea that are in Christ; *they only heard it said, "The one who formerly was persecuting us is now proclaiming the faith he once tried to destroy." And they glorified God because of me.*[1241]
>
> Then after fourteen years I went up again to Jerusalem with Barnabas, taking Titus along with me. I went up in response to a revelation. Then I laid before them (though only in a private meeting with the acknowledged leaders) the gospel that I proclaim among the Gentiles, in order to make sure that I was not running, or had not run, in vain.[1242]

[1240] 1 Cor. 15:1-11.

[1241] Gal. 1:6-24.

[1242] Gal. 2:1-2.

Paul is pretty adamant here that the gospel he preaches did NOT come from any human teaching. And notice, if you were to remove from the text the phrases I have put in italics, it would actually read much smoother.

Richard Pervo has argued strongly (and definitively, in my opinion) that the author of Acts used Josephus *Antiquities* and possibly *Wars* as a source for ideas to write his fairy tale of early Christianity. In Josephus, there does happen to be a character named Saul, and there are strong verbal echoes with those passages and Acts. This Simon ben Saul was a "man of reputation among the Jews," who, for some reason or another, was at war with his own people (Jews).[1243] Paul is referred to as 'Saul' only in Acts; Paul himself never indicates or suggests that his real name was Saul.

If Paul's statement that he 'persecuted the church' is authentically Pauline (which I doubt, since I think it was made up by the Lukan author as an attempt to paper over the Galatians dispute and other things Paul said against the Jerusalem Christians), then we have to wonder, based on the above bit of text, where Paul says his relatives were Christians before he was, what the heck was going on?

Back to Romans 16, skipping a few greetings that offer no clues, we come to this: "Greet those who belong to the family of Aristobulus. Greet my relative Herodion. Greet those in the Lord who belong to the family of Narcissus" (Rom. 16:10-11). Aristobulus? There was a Greek historian of that name associated with Alexander the Great and a few others of historical interest. But we won't get sidetracked on that. At the time of Paul, the name was associated with the Jewish royal family; Aristobulus, the third son of Herod of Chalcis (*Wars* 2.221), and who was the third husband of Salome, daughter of Herodias. Apparently, the emperor Claudius thought well of him (*Ant.* 20.13). In 54 AD, Nero gave him the kingdom of lesser Armenia (*Wars* 2.252, *Ant.* 20.158, Tacitus *Ann.* 13.7). So, is Paul indicating that he was friends with a lesser member of the Judean royal family?

What about Herodion? Considering naming customs of the time, the name seems to imply that he was a freedman of the Herods, that is, a member of the household of Aristobulus, the grandson of Herod the Great. This is followed by the mention of 'Narcissus.' The emperor Claudius had a freedman named Narcissus who apparently murdered a guy named Silanus in 42 AD (*Ann.* 11.29.1). If it weren't all so coincidental finding this set of names grouped together, one could just pass this by with no serious interest. But it is the grouping that grabs attention. It appears that Paul may have had some very helpful Christian-convert family and friends. That would explain why he may have been a Roman citizen (though only Acts provides that detail) and why he was sent to Rome from Ephesus and there released from prison.

Then: "Greet Rufus, chosen in the Lord; and greet his mother – a mother to me also" (Rom. 16:13). This attracts attention because of a short passage in Mark: "They compelled a passer-by, who was coming in from the country, to carry his cross; it was Simon of Cyrene, the father of Alexander and Rufus" (Rom. 15:21). Then: "Greet Asyncritus, Phlegon, Hermes, Patrobas, Hermas, and the brothers and sisters who are with them. Greet Philologus, Julia, Nereus and his sister, and Olympas, and all the saints who are with them" (Rom. 16:14-15). Julia? A relative of the Julian family?

[1243] *Wars* 2.18.4 (469–76).

All taken together, the list of names of people to whom Paul sends greetings strongly suggests that chapter 16 of the Epistle to the Romans is the ending of a different letter: one sent *from* Rome to a church or churches in Asia. Therefore, Rom. 16:1-17 must be excluded from the letter.[1244]

Going back to the beginning of the epistle, a Gentile readership is suggested by the greeting:

> Paul, a servant of Jesus Christ, called to be an apostle, set apart for the gospel of God, which he promised beforehand through his prophets in the holy scriptures, the gospel concerning his Son, *who was descended from David according to the flesh and was declared to be Son of God with power according to the spirit of holiness by resurrection from the dead,*[1245] Jesus Christ our Lord, through whom we have received grace and apostleship to bring about the obedience of faith among all the Gentiles for the sake of his name, including yourselves who are called to belong to Jesus Christ, To all God's beloved in Rome, who are called to be saints: Grace to you and peace from God our Father and the Lord Jesus Christ. First, I thank my God through Jesus Christ for all of you, because your faith is proclaimed throughout the world. For God, whom I serve with my spirit by announcing the gospel of his Son, is my witness that without ceasing I remember you always in my prayers, asking that by God's will I may somehow at last succeed in coming to you. For I am longing to see you so that I may share with you some spiritual gift to strengthen you – or rather so that we may be mutually encouraged by each other's faith, both yours and mine. I want you to know, brothers and sisters, that I have often intended to come to you (but thus far have been prevented), in order that I may reap some harvest among you as I have among the *rest of the Gentiles.* I am a debtor both to Greeks and to barbarians, both to the wise and to the foolish – hence my eagerness to proclaim the gospel to you also who are in Rome.[1246]

So far, so good. But then Paul supposedly writes something absolutely impossible considering the basic outline of his experiences up to this point in time: "For I am not ashamed of the gospel; it is the power of God for salvation to everyone who has faith, *to the Jew first and also to the Greek*" (Rom. 1:16). Paul clearly did not write the part in italics. Either it was inserted by an editor – the same one inserted similar un-Pauline remarks elsewhere in the letter (see below) – or Paul is quoting his opponents' words to use against them (also see below). The phrase will be repeated two more times at Rom. 2:9-10.

But there is another problem: Paul starts out by saying that he wants to "share some spiritual gift" and then to be "mutually encouraged." That comes across as though he is writing to someone or some group he considers 'equal,' so to say, not someone he has to evangelize, as is suggested by "reap some harvest" and then stated explicitly in the last sentence above. Obviously, if the fame of this group is proclaimed throughout the world, and Paul wishes to be "mutually encouraged," I don't think he's going to preach to these folks. Oh, I don't doubt that Paul wrote something about his reasons for coming to Rome, but I suspect that it was very different from what we see now. In relation to the above passage – "I have often intended to come to you (but thus far have been prevented), in order that I may reap some harvest among you" – there are a couple of connected passages toward the end of the letter as we have it that must be editorial activity

---

[1244]Trobisch (2001), pp. 71–73, comes to a similar conclusion, though he thinks that Romans 16 was composed as a cover letter for a collection of 4 letters (Romans, 1 & 2 Corinthians, Galatians), collected and edited by Paul to be sent to Ephesus to provide them with information on all the recent crises and thus to be prepared for what may come.

[1245]See the section 'Son of David?' in chapter 7. This verse isn't attested in Marcion's collection.

[1246]Rom. 1:1-15.

designed to bring the epistle into conformity with Acts. It's difficult sometimes to know how much to reject, and I tend to be conservative. I have reconstructed the original letter of Romans as including part of chapter 1, chapters 5, 6, 7, 8, 12, and 13 in full, and then the second half of 15 – with rejected insertions – as the general closing to that initial epistle.

Below you will see how the bit of text from the beginning – "I have often intended to come to you (but thus far have been prevented), in order that I may reap some harvest among you" – ties into the editorial additions later, which, considering the actual historical situation, we know are impossible. What I believe has been added by an editor is in bold italic, and pay particular attention to what I have underlined. Try reading the text with and then without the text to be excluded. If I am right, then the Gentile congregation in Rome is a product of Paul's own work via his own converts. The 'lacuna' indicates where I think words have been deliberately omitted, words that would tell us something about the debacle at Galatia, Paul's imprisonment, and perhaps more.

> I myself feel confident about you, my brothers and sisters, that you yourselves are full of goodness, filled with all knowledge, and able to instruct one another. ***Nevertheless on some points I have written to you rather boldly by way of reminder, because of the grace given me by God to be a minister of Christ Jesus to the Gentiles in the priestly service of the gospel of God, so that the offering of the Gentiles may be acceptable, sanctified by the Holy Spirit.*** In Christ Jesus, then, I have reason to boast of my work for God. For I will not venture to speak of anything except what Christ has accomplished through me to win obedience from the Gentiles, by word and deed, by the power of signs and wonders, by the power of the Spirit of God, so that ***from Jerusalem*** and as far around as ***Illyricum I have fully proclaimed the good news of Christ.*** Thus I make it my ambition to proclaim the good news, not where Christ has already been named, so that I do not build on someone else's foundation, but as it is written, "Those who have never been told of him shall see, and those who have never heard of him shall understand." **[LACUNA]** This is the reason that I have so often been hindered from coming to you. I appeal to you, brothers and sisters, by our Lord Jesus Christ and by the love of the Spirit, to join me in earnest prayer to God on my behalf, that I may be rescued ***from the unbelievers in Judea, and that my ministry to Jerusalem may be acceptable to the saints***, so that by God's will I may come to you with joy and be refreshed in your company. ***But now, with no further place for me in these regions,*** I desire, as I have for many years, to come to you when I go to Spain. For I do hope to see you on my journey and to be sent on by you, once I have enjoyed your company for a little while. The God of peace be with all of you. Amen.[1247]

The excluded verses in italics must be rejected entirely, since they so completely contradict what we know was going on with Paul, as we can read in his other letters written around this time. The passages about the 'collection' that were added to 2 Corinthians have already been noted: they were added to letters that were written before the second Jerusalem meeting even took place. It looks like the same redactor who worked on those letters also worked on Romans – again, in an effort to bring it into conformity with Acts, and to heck with what kind of confusion it might cause. The following should be excluded entirely:

> At present, however, I am going to Jerusalem in a ministry to the saints; for Macedonia and Achaia have been pleased to share their resources with the poor among the saints at Jerusalem. They were pleased to do this, and indeed they owe it to them; for if the Gentiles have come to share in their

[1247]Rom. 15:14-33.

spiritual blessings, they ought also to be of service to them in material things. So, when I have completed this, and have delivered to them what has been collected, I will set out by way of you to Spain; and I know that when I come to you, I will come in the fullness of the blessing of Christ.[1248]

Obviously, the redactor desperately needed to get Paul to Jerusalem so as to confirm the bogus 'everything is beautiful and we are all happy campers' scenario dreamed up by the Lukan author.

In v. 27 above, Paul allegedly writes something that the Paul we know by now would never write: "they were pleased to do this, and indeed they owe it to them; for if the Gentiles have come to share in their spiritual blessings, they ought also to be of service to them in material things." He suggests that the Achaians and Macedonians seek, by material means, to repay a spiritual debt to the Jews. This idea of Gentile indebtedness to the Jerusalem church, the James gang, etc., is utterly foreign to Paul's thinking, though it is right in line with certain verses in Romans 9–11. Notice also a dead giveaway: Paul seemingly states that he began his preaching career in Jerusalem; we know from Paul's own words that this is not true. Thus, in violent contradiction to what Paul writes in Galatians 1–2, Romans 15 presents a thoroughly Jerusalem/Acts-oriented account of his own ministry!

No, in Romans Paul is not trying to reconcile Gentile Christians with Jewish Christians, nor is he rehearsing what he is going to say on his alleged trip to Jerusalem that never happened; he is writing to a group of Gentile Christians, 'offspring' of his own converts, letting them know the trials he has suffered, that he is in prison, but will be sent to Rome and hopefully released there if he has friends and assistance. All of that was presumably removed from the text, other material – some of it Pauline for sure – was combined with that original letter, and some carefully contrived editorial additions were placed throughout the text to make link-ups. But the whole fraud doesn't really work if one reads attentively, as we are going to do with the help of Watson; even though he got the social situation all wrong, his exegetical acumen is still amazing and of great use.

After looking at the beginning and the ending of Romans, let's continue with what follows the apparently doctored introduction.

Chapters 1–4

Romans 1:18-32 has strong verbal and ideological echoes with the *Sibylline Oracles* 3:97–829.[1249] It is thought that these oracles were written in imitation of the Roman Sibylline Oracles and that they date to before the historian Alexander Polyhistor; they apparently are related to, and represent, a revival of Jewish nationalism following the Maccabean Revolt.

The oracle in question reads, in part:

> They [the Jews] are mindful of holy wedlock. Nor do they practice unholy intercourse with boys, as do the Phoenicians, Egyptians and Romans, spacious Greece and many other nations, Persians and Galatians and all Asia, transgressing the holy law of immortal God, which they transgressed. Therefore the Eternal will inflict on all people disaster and famine and woes and groans and war and pestilence and lamentable ills, because they would not honor in holiness the eternal Father of all people but honored idols made with hands, revering them.

[1248]Rom. 15:25-29.
[1249]See Collins, *Seers, Sibyls and Sages in Hellenistic Roman Judaism*, p. 18, cited by Watson (2008), p. 196.

So, basically, it is an anti-Gentile polemic that was very likely well-enough known at the time to be recognizable, but probably only to Jews, and it is developed and expanded in Romans 1:18-32:

> For the wrath of God is revealed from heaven against all ungodliness and wickedness of those who by their wickedness suppress the truth. For what can be known about God is plain to them, because God has shown it to them. Ever since the creation of the world his eternal power and divine nature, invisible though they are, have been understood and seen through the things he has made. So they are without excuse; for though they knew God, they did not honor him as God or give thanks to him, but they became futile in their thinking, and their senseless minds were darkened. Claiming to be wise, they became fools; and they exchanged the glory of the immortal God for images resembling a mortal human being or birds or four-footed animals or reptiles. Therefore God gave them up in the lusts of their hearts to impurity, to the degrading of their bodies among themselves, because they exchanged the truth about God for a lie and worshiped and served the creature rather than the Creator, who is blessed forever! Amen. For this reason God gave them up to degrading passions. Their women exchanged natural intercourse for unnatural, and in the same way also the men, giving up natural intercourse with women, were consumed with passion for one another. Men committed shameless acts with men and received in their own persons the due penalty for their error. And since they did not see fit to acknowledge God, God gave them up to a debased mind and to things that should not be done. They were filled with every kind of wickedness, evil, covetousness, malice. Full of envy, murder, strife, deceit, craftiness, they are gossips, slanderers, God-haters, insolent, haughty, boastful, inventors of evil, rebellious toward parents, foolish, faithless, heartless, ruthless. They know God's decree, that those who practice such things deserve to die – yet they not only do them but even applaud others who practice them.

This is a thoroughly Jewish critique of Gentile life. We are expected to believe that just after Paul greets the Roman Gentile Christians whose "faith is proclaimed throughout the world," the same group that he says he is longing to see so they can be "mutually encouraged by each other," he is now going to insult them by repeating a slander against Gentiles common to Jews of the time?! What is going on?

The solution appears in Rom. 2:1: "Therefore you have no excuse, whoever you are, when you judge others; for in passing judgment on another you condemn yourself, because you, the judge, are doing the very same things." Something may be missing, but it appears that Paul is going after an unknown person who appears to endorse the previous anti-Gentile passage above.[1250]

Romans 2 is addressed from the outset to a Jewish interlocutor.[1251] In vv. 1-6, Paul warns his addressee not to think that he will escape God's judgment, since he does precisely the things he condemns in others. There are strong thematic links between Rom. 2:1-5 and Rom. 2:17-25 written in second person singular, a direct attack on the leaders of Judaism:

[1250]Douglas Campbell, in *The Deliverance of God: An Apocalyptic Rereading of Justification in Paul* (Eerdmans, 2009), pp. 587–90, argues similarly, that Rom. 1:18-32 is written in the voice of Paul's opponent, and that various verses following that have Paul using that opponent's own words sarcastically (e.g. the phrase, "to the Jew first and also to the Greek") in order to refute or reinterpret them.

[1251]Watson (2008), pp. 198–99.

Rom. 2:1-5	Rom. 2:17-25
Therefore you have no excuse, whoever you are, when you judge others; for in passing judgment on another you condemn yourself, because you, the judge, are doing the very same things. You say, "We know that God's judgment on those who do such things is in accordance with truth." Do you imagine, whoever you are, that when you judge those who do such things and yet do them yourself, you will escape the judgment of God? Or do you despise the riches of his kindness and forbearance and patience? Do you not realize that God's kindness is meant to lead you to repentance? But by your hard and impenitent heart you are storing up wrath for yourself on the day of wrath, when God's righteous judgment will be revealed.	But if you call yourself a Jew and rely on the law and boast of your relation to God and know his will and determine what is best because you are instructed in the law, and if you are sure that you are a guide to the blind, a light to those who are in darkness, a corrector of the foolish, a teacher of children, having in the law the embodiment of knowledge and truth, you, then, that teach others, will you not teach yourself? While you preach against stealing, do you steal? You that forbid adultery, do you commit adultery? You that abhor idols, do you rob temples? You that boast in the law, do you dishonor God by breaking the law? For, as it is written, "The name of God is blasphemed among the Gentiles because of you." Circumcision indeed is of value if you obey the law; but if you break the law, your circumcision has become uncircumcision.

There is thematic unity between 2:6-15 and 25-29, a defense of Gentiles:

Rom. 2:6-15	Rom. 2:26-29
For he will repay according to each one's deeds: to those who by patiently doing good seek for glory and honor and immortality, he will give eternal life; while for those who are self-seeking and who obey not the truth but wickedness, there will be wrath and fury. There will be anguish and distress for everyone who does evil, the Jew and also the Greek, but glory and honor and peace for everyone who does good, the Jew and also the Greek. For God shows no partiality. All who have sinned apart from the law will also perish apart from the law, and all who have sinned under the law will be judged by the law. For it is not the hearers of the law who are righteous in God's sight, but the doers of the law who will be justified. When Gentiles, who do not possess the law, do instinctively what the law requires, these, though not having the law, are a law to themselves. They show that what the law requires is written on their hearts, to which their own conscience also bears witness; and their conflicting thoughts will accuse or perhaps excuse them	So, if those who are uncircumcised keep the requirements of the law, will not their uncircumcision be regarded as circumcision? Then those who are physically uncircumcised but keep the law will condemn you that have the written code and circumcision but break the law. For a person is not a Jew who is one outwardly, nor is true circumcision something external and physical. Rather, a person is a Jew who is one inwardly, and real circumcision is a matter of the heart – it is spiritual and not literal. Such a person receives praise not from others but from God.

Romans 2:6 alludes to Psalm 61:13 (LXX): "Once God spoke: these two things I heard: that might is God's and to you, O Lord, belongs mercy, because you will repay to each according to his works."

Romans 2, as a whole, may plausibly be read as a critique of Jewish covenantal theology based on the law and circumcision. Thus it totally rejects the traditional Jewish polemic against Gentiles reproduced in Rom. 1:18-32. With the sharpest of contrasts, the 'sacred race' ideology is totally debunked by the realities of actual conduct as seen by Paul.

Verses 1-11 appear to deal with the Jew who falsely relies on his covenant status. Verses 12-24 deal with the two components of covenant status: law and circumcision. Paul is saying that certain Jews do the same things they condemn others for, but they rely on their status as Jews to gain immunity from judgment (v. 4). Paul insists, however, that God is impartial (vv. 6-11).

This chapter appears to be an attack mainly on Jewish leaders and not the Jewish community as a whole. The Jew addressed here is "a guide to the blind, a light to those in darkness, an instructor of the foolish, a teacher of children" (vv. 19-20, echoes of which are found in the Gospel of Mark *vis à vis* Scribes and Pharisees). Paul utilizes a quote from Isaiah 52:5 (LXX): "For the name of God because of you is blasphemed among the Gentiles." The second person pronoun indicates that this is a representative figure, a group, whose conduct is collectively responsible for Gentile hostility to Jews and God.

In a curious reversal, in Romans 2 it is Paul who insists on salvation by works, and his Jewish interlocutor/addressee who insists on salvation by grace (by virtue of being a Jew) alone! It is the Jewish standpoint that is being attacked here, which only appears to espouse a salvation by works by keeping the law (vv. 26-27); that is, Paul is throwing the conceit of the Jews back in their faces for the sake of developing his argument. When Paul argues for a judgment according to one's works, he deploys the argument "to remove the soteriological difference between Jew and Gentile."[1252]

There is a complete lack of any reference to Christ's saving role in Romans 2, though he is presented as God's judge. There is also a vague reference to divinely enabled human agency in v. 15: "They [Gentiles] show that what the law requires is written on their hearts, to which their own conscience also bears witness ..."

The fact is, opposed to those who claim that Paul was only and ever about 'salvation by grace' and that that was the whole thing, he actually made a number of strong statements about salvation by works: "The one who sows to his own flesh will from the flesh reap corruption" (Gal. 6:8); "those who do such things [works of the flesh] will not inherit the kingdom of God" (Gal. 5:21); and Christians must "Work your own salvation with fear and trembling" (Phil. 2:12). In short, even with grace, salvation or condemnation will be decided at a judgment.

It is important to understand that this is not 'salvation by works' as commonly understood, i.e. salvation attained by unaided human effort. Nor is it salvation by grace in a passive sense. Watson compares Paul's argument to *Jubilees'* account of angel marriages (from Gen. 6:1-4), expanded under the influence of Enochic tradition into an account of a final universal judgment. Note that the Enochian ideas were derived from a heavy dose of Zoroastrianism modified by Babylonian themes. *Jubilees* 5:13-18 says:

[1252]Watson (2008), p. 205.

And the judgment of all is ordained and written on the heavenly tablets in righteousness – all who depart from the path that is ordained for them to walk in; and if they walk not therein, judgment is written for every creature and for every kind. And there is no exception in heaven or on earth, or in light or in darkness, or in Sheol or in the depth, or in the place of darkness; and all their judgments are ordained and written and engraved. In regard to all he will judge, the great according to his greatness, and the small according to his smallness, and each according to his way. And he is not one who will regard the person, nor accept anything at his hands, for he is a righteous judge.

And of the children of Israel it has been written and ordained: if they turn to him in righteousness, he will forgive all their transgressions and pardon all their sins. It is written and ordained that he will show mercy to all who turn from their guilt once each year.[1253]

In short, *Jubilees* proposes that Jews have a 'get-out-of-jail-free card' as long as they repent of their sins once a year on the Day of Atonement! That is to say, theoretically, a Jew would be judged only minimally, if at all, while everyone else will be judged according to the full weight of their lifetime of transgressions.

Paul radically reinterprets this, removing the soteriological advantage from the Jews, declaring God's judgment to be universally impartial: "There will be anguish and distress for everyone who does evil, the Jew and also the Greek, but glory and honor and peace for everyone who does good, the Jew and also the Greek. For God shows no partiality" (Rom. 2:9-11).

In verses 12-13, Paul states that Jews who possess the law may be condemned and Gentiles who observe the law "will be justified." The contrast is between hearers who do not do, and doers who have not heard: "They show the work of the law written on their hearts ... on the day when God judges the secrets of humans according to my gospel, through Jesus Christ" (vv. 15-16).

In verses 25-29, Paul denies that circumcision is a guarantee of salvation. In verses 28-29, he argues that being a Jew is a matter of an inward disposition of the heart, not external rites. It is therefore possible for Gentiles and Jews to do good and be saved (vv. 10, 14-15, 26-29).

What we are seeing here is Paul the Jew arguing against Jews on strictly Jewish terrain. Watson argues that the purpose of Romans 2 is to persuade Roman Jewish Christians (i.e. Zealots, according to the thesis of this book) to distance themselves from the Jewish community entirely and to recognize the reality of genuine obedience to the law of God in the heart, not the ritual law, and that this confirms the salvation of Gentiles alongside Jews.

Some of the polemic in the Gospel of Mark appears to be derived from these arguments, so surely Mark had access to this text. The question is; was it originally part of the letter Paul wrote to the Roman Gentile Christians from prison in Ephesus?

Against the background of events in Jerusalem under Tiberius Alexander, the following 'invasion of Galatia' by Jewish Zealot Christians spying on and disrupting Paul's communities, the likely fact that Paul was arrested and in prison in Ephesus under suspicion of being a Zealot himself, and the probable plan to transfer him to Rome, it would have been suicidal for Paul to write such things to Roman Jewish Christians in advance!

The interpretative problems would be easily solved by supposing that Paul wrote a different letter to the Jewish Christian community in Rome, possibly even after he had arrived in Rome and was safely ensconced among his Gentile community. There are merits to this idea. The Jewish Christian Zealots were likely the majority of Christians in Rome and it is likely that it was they who disrupted the entire mass of Jews there, leading to expulsion by Claudius. Perhaps

[1253]Cited by Watson (2008), p. 206.

it was such a letter from Paul that triggered the outrage? And perhaps it is this very same letter we are reading here, a second letter that has been incorporated into the letter to the Gentile Church at Rome, creating massive confusion.

Watson points out that all of Paul's references to 'works' and 'law written on the heart' may be alluding to Jeremiah 31:33: "But this is the covenant that I will make with the house of Israel after those days, says the LORD: I will put my law within them, and I will write it on their hearts; and I will be their God, and they shall be my people."

As noted, Christ is referred to once in this chapter, and then only as the divinely appointed judge. It has also been noted that 'doers of the law' appears to contradict what we will read in Rom. 3:20a ("For 'no human being will be justified in his sight' by deeds prescribed by the law..."). However, as already noted, it is important to understand that this is not 'salvation by works' as commonly understood, i.e. salvation attained by unaided human effort. Nor is grace, received by faith, passive. For Paul, 'faith' is a public renunciation of one way of life and the adoption of another, with Christ as both template and intercessor. To say that 'faith' earns salvation would be wrong; faith is the reaching up to Christ who has extended himself downward to meet the Christian. This is not 'salvation by works,' but rather God's prior grace working in and through the human agent who reorients his or her life along the Christian model. In Romans 2, the Law is God's law on the heart and obedience to that. This contrasts with Paul's usual use of the term 'law' to mean the Torah, which he declares is unable to save a person no matter how hard they try to fulfill its demands. Living in the Jewish community 'under the law' means, for Paul, living under the 'wrath of the law.' And that is the topic of chapter 3, which is clearly part of the same missive to Jews.

Having started with citing a common slander of the Gentiles propagated by Jews, then moving to accuse the Jews of being just as bad as Gentiles and on an equal footing before God, based on non-scriptural foundations, Paul then moves on, in chapter 3, to more refined arguments against Judaism and for universalism. Watson writes:

> Romans 3 is based on the single antithesis between "law" and "faith." In vv. 1-20 Paul argues that being a law-observant Jew is not the indispensable presupposition for salvation. ... [T]he law rightly understood places the Jew in the same position of guilt before God as the Gentile. In vv. 21-31, it is argued that the faith associated with Christ is God's means of salvation and that one of the chief characteristics of this faith is that Jews and Gentiles are treated in exactly the same way.[1254]

In Romans 3:1-8, Paul describes 'the word of God' as being what is conveyed in scripture. Verse 4 references Psalm 115 (LXX): "I believed, therefore I spoke; I was greatly humbled. I said in my astonishment, 'Every human is a liar!'" The affirmation "I believed, therefore I spoke" is cited in 2 Cor. 4:13, where Paul claims to embody in his ministry "the same spirit of faith" as is expressed in the psalm text, which continues as follows:

> What shall I return to the Lord for all that he returned to me? A cup of deliverance I will take and the name of the Lord I will call upon. Precious before the Lord is the death of his devout ones. Ah Lord, I am a slave of yours; I am a slave of yours and son of your serving girl. You broke through my bonds. To you I will sacrifice a sacrifice of praise. My vows to the Lord I will pay before all his people, in courts of the Lord's house, in your midst, oh Jerusalem.

[1254]Watson (2008), p. 218.

In this Psalm, Paul found not only the disclosure of universal human depravity ("everyone is a liar"); he also found divine grace. For Paul, it must have been shattering to realize that universal falsehood is a scriptural doctrine, especially because the Jews are convinced that they only have to confess once a year to keep their salvation account balance topped up.

In scripture, God speaks an indictment of the whole human race. The indictment follows in Rom. 3:9-20:

> What then? Are we any better off? No, not at all; for we have already charged that all, both Jews and Greeks, are under the power of sin, as it is written: "There is no one who is righteous, not even one; there is no one who has understanding, there is no one who seeks God. All have turned aside, together they have become worthless; there is no one who shows kindness, there is not even one." "Their throats are opened graves; they use their tongues to deceive." "The venom of vipers is under their lips." "Their mouths are full of cursing and bitterness." "Their feet are swift to shed blood; ruin and misery are in their paths, and the way of peace they have not known." "There is no fear of God before their eyes." Now we know that whatever the law says, it speaks to those who are under the law, so that every mouth may be silenced, and the whole world may be held accountable to God. For "no human being will be justified in his sight" by deeds prescribed by the law, for through the law comes the knowledge of sin.

This indictment is based on Psalm 13:1-3 (LXX), where Paul selectively modifies the text:

> The fool said in his heart, "There is no God." They caused corruption and were abominable in their practices; there is no one practicing kindness; there is not even one. The Lord peered down from the sky on the sons of men to see if there was any who had understanding or who sought after God. All turned away, as well they became useless; there is no one practicing kindness; there is not even one.

In Rom. 3:13-18, Paul assembles his argument from Psalms and Isaiah: Ps. 14:1-2; 53:1-2; 5:9; 140:3; 10:7; Is. 59:7; Ps. 36:1. (See also Gal 3:19-29.) Paul makes his assertion and then backs it up with scripture about the universality of sin. This tells us that Paul knows that the persons to whom he is writing are going to recognize these allusions and would consider them to be authoritative commentators on the law. So, what is being declared here by a Jew, to other Jews, via their common terrain of scripture, is the law's totally negative verdict on mankind and Jews in particular. That is, Paul is telling other Jews that he, himself, has figured out God's hidden message about humanity, the true meaning of the scriptures which are the word of God. The bottom line of it all is that there is no "optimistic reading" of the Torah.[1255] As Watson points out, Rom. 3:9-20 is articulating not a general doctrine of the human condition, but the *true meaning* of a text, i.e. the Jewish Torah! According to Paul, the text, God's word, declares universal guilt, especially of Jews!

This is addressed to Jews who know the texts, the only ones who could be expected to catch the catena of allusions. And here, in contrast to chapter 2 where 'Law' is an abstraction, a thing of the heart, the 'Law' is specifically that of the Jewish covenant. This is a devastating attack on Judaism as a whole, and Jewish communities in particular.

Paul's arguments here are complicated and tricky (and this is a very short piece of text!). As noted, he began with Psalm 115 (LXX), which declares that everyone is a liar, and then

---

[1255]Watson (2008), p. 221.

immediately refers to Psalm 50 (LXX). This psalm has been traditionally ascribed to David's remorse at his sin with Bathsheba and against her husband Uriah the Hittite. It reads:

> Have mercy on me, O God, according to your great mercy, and according to the abundance of your compassion blot out my lawless deed. Wash me thoroughly from my lawlessness and from my sin cleanse me because my lawlessness I know and my sin is ever before me. Against you alone did I sin, and what is evil before you I did, so *that you may be justified in your words and be victorious when you go to law.*

Having brought up those two scriptural references – that everyone is a liar and that God will be proved true at the judgment – Paul then asks a question based, apparently, on the following logic:

1) At the final judgment (a lawsuit as in the psalm), those who are under the Law (Jews) will be compelled to face the divine judgment based on the cited scripture, "Everyone is a liar," and

2) God is true if, and only if, the scriptures are true, to which Jews are bound by covenant.

Then, the question: if, as scripture says, our state of unrighteousness (all are liars) serves to show that God is truthful (scriptures are true), what can we conclude from this? Does God really intend to carry out the sentence that would be imposed in a legal case (judgment day)? God would not be unjust to do that as the law, the scripture says. If God did not carry out what he said (and he is truthful), "how then could God judge the world?"

However, Paul seems to imply, if human sinfulness ("every man is a liar") serves to vindicate God's assertions and prove God's truthfulness, thus giving him the 'win' in court, why isn't God satisfied with this? Why would God, who has already been justified as to his words by winning his case, still want to annihilate the sinner? Obviously, this is where, according to Paul, God's grace comes in, his mercy. Having shown that the law does not lead to righteousness, Paul argues that righteousness is attained through faith (vv. 21-30). Notice that the word 'faith' occurs eight times, closely correlated with righteousness. Faith is the mode of life oriented toward Jesus Christ and his example of love and mercy and the grace of God.

> But now, apart from law, the righteousness of God has been disclosed, and is attested by the law and the prophets, the righteousness of God through faith in Jesus Christ for all who believe. For there is no distinction, since all have sinned and fall short of the glory of God; they are now justified by his grace as a gift, through the redemption that is in Christ Jesus, whom God put forward as a sacrifice of atonement by his blood, effective through faith. He did this to show his righteousness, because in his divine forbearance he had passed over the sins previously committed; it was to prove at the present time that he himself is righteous and that he justifies the one who has faith in Jesus. Then what becomes of boasting? It is excluded. By what law? By that of works? No, but by the law of faith. For we hold that a person is justified by faith apart from works prescribed by the law. Or is God the God of Jews only? Is he not the God of Gentiles also? Yes, of Gentiles also, since God is one; and he will justify the circumcised on the ground of faith and the uncircumcised through that same faith.

For Paul, according to Watson, faith was related to social behavior and sole allegiance to Jesus Christ and the social norms this represented: universalism, love, mercy. Thus, in practice, this absolutely excluded allegiance to any other 'Lord,' such as the Jewish Law. As Ashworth shows, these are two conflicting means of knowing God's will: through direct communion, and via the mediation of an external code.

The conclusion is that we ALL stand unprotected and exposed to divine judgment, at which time the scriptural indictment of humankind – and more specifically, the Jews – will be vindicated, judged and executed, unless we call on God's mercy by faith (active) in Christ. The catena of vv. 9-20, already quoted above, leads inexorably to this conclusion. Its logic is based on scriptural references, and the conclusion of the argument is in Rom. 3:20: "For 'no human being will be justified in his sight' by deeds prescribed by the law, for through the law comes the knowledge of sin." That is, in the catena, scripture interprets scripture and definitively interprets the law of Moses as the divine indictment of human kind.[1256] Paul rejects any reading of scripture that could validate the idea that works of the law is "the way of righteousness."

> ... Paul does not reject "works of the law" because they represent an abstract principle of achievement that is incompatible with an equally abstract principle of submission to the lordship of the divine grace. He understands "works of the law" as the prescribed or proscribed practices ... of the Jewish community, the privileged inheritors of the divine election and covenant. He rejects this form of life in order to affirm another, founded on a shared allegiance to Christ ... in which Jewish and Gentile adherents are united.[1257]

These arguments are most certainly aimed at Jewish Christians for the purpose of promoting the abandonment of Judaism and the embracing of faith in Christ and the Christian lifestyle.

This, of course, brings us back to the actual social situation. The Jewish Christians of Rome were more than likely die-hard supporters of the Zealots in Jerusalem who were always agitating for freedom from the Roman yoke. They were no doubt already in a serious state of tension after receiving news of the executions of the sons of their messiah (Judas the Galilean), James and Simon, pillars of the Jerusalem church who were very much at odds with Paul. The fact that Paul may have been arrested by Romans on suspicion of having ties to the rebels/Zealots, and had been transferred to Rome and possibly/probably released due to intercession from friends, and who was now telling the Roman Jewish Christians that the Jerusalem version was all wrong, may very well have excited quite a tumult.

Therefore, the letter that begins at Romans 1:18 must be a second letter directed specifically to Jewish Christians in Rome, and written only after Paul's arrival there. The passages examined thus far are arguments about the Law, based on the Law, and rendered in true Pharisaic fashion. One can imagine the leaders of the Roman Jewish Christians literally tearing their hair and clothing in rage upon reading or hearing these claims. In short, such a letter to such people in such a time would have gone off like a bomb – and probably did.

In several places, the text says, "To the Jew first and also to the Greek" (Rom. 1:16; 2:10; etc.). I have removed the "first" since I believe that this is an editorial/redactional insertion.[1258] Note that Rom. 3:22b-23 says, to the contrary, "For there is no distinction, since all have sinned and fall short of the glory of God." In Rom. 3:29-30, Paul says God is the god of the Gentiles and Jews. Later, in Rom. 4:9-12, Paul argues that Abraham is the father of both Jewish and Gentile Christians. Therefore, the emphasis on Jewish Christians over Gentile Christians is very strikingly non-Pauline. But notice how cleverly the editorial insertion is made; with the simple addition of a single word to a phrase!

[1256]Watson (2008), p. 228.

[1257]Watson (2008), p. 230.

[1258]Or, if Campbell is correct, it is Paul quoting his opponents' words against them in order to refute them.

At the end of the argument, Paul asks another question: "Do we then overthrow the law by this faith? By no means! On the contrary, we uphold the law." Paul here reveals some of the criticisms directed against his gospel: "And why not say (as some people slander us by saying) that we say 'Let us do evil that good may come'?" His answer is "By no means! On the contrary, we uphold the law." And, of course, he means the Law of the Heart.

Paul isn't done with the Jews just yet. In Romans 4, he reinterprets scripture to show that his doctrine of justification by faith, apart from the law, even prior to the law, is confirmed in the story of Abraham. He denies the Jewish view that Abraham underwrites Jewish practices and beliefs; instead, Paul asserts that what the scripture is really saying is that the promise to Abraham meant that all people who have faith in God are justified via the promise to Abraham. Paul is attacking the most vital elements of the Jew's self-understanding, and he transforms Abraham into a symbol of unity for all mankind.

Paul opens the argument with a question that he asks on behalf of any Jew or Jewish Christian: "What then are we to say was gained by Abraham, our ancestor according to the flesh?" Chapter 4 is the answer.

> ... Abraham was initially "ungodly" (v. 5) but was reckoned as righteous (vv. 3, 5, 6) and had his sins forgiven (vv. 7, 8) by means of God's grace and the faith it evoked in him (vv. 3-5). ... [T]he transition between ungodliness and blessedness (cf. vv. 7-8) occurs through an act of forgiveness on the divine side and an act of faith on the human side. ... Abraham, then, is a model for the convert, the one who has passed from ungodliness to righteousness by a transforming event whose divine side is the forgiveness of all past sins and whose human side is simply faith in the God who acts this way ... He is not a model for the person committed to a lifetime of law observance.[1259]

To reconstruct Abraham as a model for Jewish and Gentile unity is quite a feat for Paul, but he manages to do it with skillful use of scriptures: "For what does the scripture say? 'Abraham believed God, and it was reckoned to him as righteousness'" (Rom. 4:3).

Paul's intention here is to completely reconceive Abraham as the father of Jewish and Gentile unity; the brotherhood and sisterhood of all humanity under one god with one intercessor: Jesus Christ. It is Paul's claim that since Abraham enjoyed righteousness both before and after he was circumcised, he is the symbol of both Jewish and Gentile Christians. Jews must learn to recognize that righteousness by faith is more fundamental than circumcision, thus actually prior to Abraham as the 'ideal Jew.'[1260] "Law-observant Jews are not as such the true seed of Abraham that is heir to the promise of salvation".[1261]

Thus, Paul goes from the question at the beginning of the chapter about "Abraham OUR (Jews') forefather" to "Our (all humanity's) father Abraham." In vv. 16-17, Abraham is "father of us all in fulfillment of the promise" in Gen. 17:5. "Through Paul's exegetical virtuosity, 'our forefather according to the flesh' has shifted his communal location and now points the way towards a united community of Christian Jews and Gentiles."[1262]

[1259]Watson (2008), pp. 262, 263, 265.
[1260]Watson (2008), p. 267.
[1261]Watson (2008), p. 268.
[1262]Watson (2008), p. 269.

Chapter 5

Watson notes that the 'Jew-Gentile' issue that has dominated the letter from Rom. 1:16 to the end of chapter 4 now disappears entirely and Christological statements come in cascades. In Romans 3 and 4, Paul is a Jew, a maestro of scriptural exegesis, and suddenly, now, he is an apostle of Christ, apostle to the Gentiles in fact.

The reason for this break seems obvious: there are at least two (perhaps more) letters combined to make the *Epistle to the Romans* as we have it today. One of the letters was the first and it was exclusively to a group of Gentile Christians, possibly converted by some of Paul's converts in Greece or Asia; and the other to a group of Jewish messianists, probably supporters of the Zealots and followers of the gospel of the Jerusalem church and their messiah, Judas the Galilean, who was supposed to return with twelve (or however many) legions of warrior angels to overthrow the Romans and put the Jews in control of the world.

Notice that the beginning of Romans 5 is a natural continuation of Rom. 1:12:

> For I am longing to see you so that I may share with you some spiritual gift to strengthen you – or rather so that we may be mutually encouraged by each other's faith, both yours and mine *** Since we are justified by faith, we have peace with God through our Lord Jesus Christ, through whom we have obtained access to this grace in which we stand; and we boast in our hope of sharing the glory of God. And not only that, but we also boast in our sufferings, knowing that suffering produces endurance, and endurance produces character, and character produces hope, and hope does not disappoint us, because God's love has been poured into our hearts through the Holy Spirit that has been given to us.

I put three asterisks at the beginning of chapter 5, and I think it is obvious that the juxtaposition flows quite naturally. One can easily see that there was an original letter to Gentile Christians and, later, a letter to Jewish Christians in Rome, also written by Paul (that is not in doubt in my mind), and much later, an editor patched them together with some other odd bits and pieces in an effort to conform the impression to that of Acts. The end result has been a dreadful state of confusion about what Paul was thinking, doing, writing. Watson's effort to put the letter into a social context has been extremely helpful, even if he is wrong, in my opinion, and not taking into account the historical facts. Watson himself is something of an exegetical virtuoso and his endeavor was to make all of Romans comprehensible as a totality. If it weren't for those pesky historical facts, he would have succeeded. Despite that, on each section of the letter, the most intractable texts in all of NT studies, I think, he has undoubtedly come closest to laying out what Paul was thinking and writing, theologically speaking. I think that even he might look at the letter in a different way, as I have, if the historical context was brought into sharper relief as background.

This leads us to what Paul was actually writing in that first letter to the Gentile Christians at Rome. We now know that we can set aside the text from 1:18 to 4:25 as a completely separate letter and go straight from 1:12 to chapter 5 as above. About this, Watson writes:

> There is some disagreement about the theme that binds together Romans 5:1-11. ... It is better to interpret the passage as a meditation on hope. ... Thus the various themes of the passage – justification, reconciliation, suffering, the Holy Spirit, the death of Christ – all converge on hope. Hope is the theme that binds all these subordinate topics together.[1263]

[1263]Watson (2008), pp. 270, 271.

Exactly so. Paul is in prison in Ephesus, soon to be transferred to Rome, and is writing to a group of his 'god-children' in Christ. He is hoping for mercy and to be able to continue his work; he is hoping that the Roman community will welcome him, will help him, and that all things will come out for the best; naturally, he is going to write about hope; it's part of his intention that he stated at the beginning of the letter: "that I may share with you some spiritual gift to strengthen you – or rather so that we may be mutually encouraged by each other's faith, both yours and mine." In the text of the first letter, that is what we are looking for and that is what we find if we reject 1:18 to 4:25 as part of the first letter, jump straight to chapter 5, continue through to the end of chapter 8, skip 9–11, pick up at chapter 13, and then 15:14-33 and 16:17-27 with minor redactions in the latter two sections. Once you know what the situation was, and how Paul thinks, then it seems to me to be fairly easy to see where someone else has interfered with his text. Watson writes more about the hope Paul is expressing in chapter 5:

> The focus on hope is maintained in 5:12-21, which highlights the "life" that through Christ is the object or content of hope, set against the background of the death inherited from Adam. ... Yet it is the disanalogies that bear the greatest rhetorical weight. Rather than simply reversing the effects of Adam's action, Christ's impact on "the many" far outweighs Adam's (v. 15). ... The disanalogies are not just contrasts ... they highlight the disproportionate or excess of grace, signified by repeated references to "abundance" [vv. 15, 17, 21]. Far from merely counteracting Adam's action with a saving act that restores the disrupted status quo, the divine grace enacted in Jesus Christ is characterized by prodigality, extravagance, and excess.[1264]

In Genesis 3, Adam's disobedience and desire 'to be like the gods' subject all his descendants to the curse of sin and death. (Eve is not mentioned here as she is in 2 Cor. 11:3.) Apparently following the model of the Zoroastrian myths of primal man and bull to coming savior, i.e. Saoshyant, humanity can be restored to a state of existence that was semi-heavenly – paradise – where people did not suffer or die. Thus, Adam is a 'type of the coming one,' a universal primal man, father of all humanity, therefore the Coming One must also be a universal savior. Paul's messiah is nothing like the Jewish messiah who is to come just for Israel and not the whole world (except perhaps to subject the nations to the rule of the Jews). It is thus universal salvation that is the object of Paul's hope. And no doubt he is hoping to get through his difficult situation so that he can continue to evangelize the world.

Chapters 6–7

Superabundant grace might certainly create problems, as Paul realizes. He has completely laid aside the Jewish law code as a way of life; the law discloses sin, but provides no real remedy (Rom. 3:20) and obeying the Jewish law is irrelevant to being adjudged righteous (Rom. 3:28). This tells us that Paul knows what Jews have said about his gospel and he heads them off at the pass. "What then are we to say? Should we continue in sin in order that grace may abound?" (v. 1). Paul has his Gentile reader in mind; that they need to fully understand why they live by faith, hope and grace.

Romans chapters 6 and 7 are a two-part argument about the correct basis for righteous conduct. Step one of the argument is that grace is not arbitrary but is oriented toward a sin-free future

---

[1264]Watson (2008), pp. 273–74.

state of the Christian, a state already attained by the crucified and resurrected Christ (Rom. 6:2-14).

Step two is to show that grace demands total obedience to the standards of righteousness and rejection of one's pre-Christian past life and behavior.

Gentile Christians, more even than Jews, represent the embodiment of grace, but Paul, wishing to avoid any further debacles such as occurred in Galatia, wants to make darn sure that the Roman Gentile Christians understand why Judaism and Jewish messianism are not only undesirable, but positively damning.

In chapter 6, Paul wants to persuade his addressees that their baptism represents their death to an old way of life and the creation of a new identity. Conversion is "dying to sin" (v. 14) in union with Christ's death (vv. 3-7). The convert has moved from being enslaved by sin/death (ostensibly against one's true wishes at the mental/spiritual level) to choosing obedience to Christ and righteousness. Being a slave to sin leads to death; being a slave of God leads to life. "For the wages of sin is death, but the free gift of God is eternal life in Christ" (v. 23).

Following chapter 6, in chapter 7 Paul continues to develop his argument in respect of the Law. He writes: "Do you not know, brothers and sisters – for I am speaking to those who know the law – that the law is binding on a person only during that person's lifetime?"

Watson and others assume a Jewish audience because of this remark. However, if that were the case, there would be no need to say such a thing at all. Here, it is aimed at those Gentile Christians who may have met with Jewish messianists and had been subjected to the legal demands in the same way the Galatians had been. It could also be aimed at 'God-fearers,' Gentiles who attended synagogue meetings or otherwise admired Judaism. Clearly, many Gentiles were familiar with the Old Testament. Paul intends to make very sure that the Galatian scenario never happens again and that is the raison d'être underlying the arguments of chapter 7.

The first argument is a very simple one: the law is only binding on a person during their lifetime; this is true about any law. As the saying goes, two things are certain: death and taxes. The argument then gets a little bit weird and convoluted because Paul sets up the example of a woman whose husband has died and so she is free to marry another. He then compares the convert to the one who has died (!), who can then belong to another, i.e. the still living wife in the example. It's obviously not the best example Paul ever thought up, but the point is at least partly made: Christ's death and the Christian's death-by-proxy (baptism) takes them out of the sphere of the law into a new regime.

Paul then begins to move step-by-step toward his goal. He says: "While we were living in the flesh, our sinful passions, aroused by the law, were working in our members to bear fruit for death" (Rom. 7:5).

But Paul does not mean that the law, in and of itself, is sin – rather that, in the presence of the law, known to a person, Sin, depicted by Paul as a demonic personification, excites urges against the law that are, effectively, overpowering. The apparent reason for this, derived from allusions to the OT in this text, is that humanity as a whole became entrapped in bodies of flesh which had urges that overpowered the mind/spirit that was aware of right and wrong by virtue of its connection to God (created in God's image; breath from God, etc.), and thus became helpless to do what was right even when part of the self wanted to.

The 'sin' focused on by Paul is that of 'desire,' eliminating any specific objects such as the neighbor's wife, house, money, goods, etc. This 'desire' is the effect, essentially, of being incarnated in bodies of flesh, and is a cruel fate rather than deliberate acts of rebellion. Obviously, Adam and Eve were the original rebel sinners, but the rest of us didn't have any choice in the matter.

The place of the original life, before the law (knowledge of good and evil) was Paradise, known to Paul as the third heaven. (2 Cor. 12:2-4) Paul is undoubtedly alluding to the myth of the soul's fall from an originally heavenly life into an embodied existence and applying it specifically to Jewish life under the law. "Through the commandment Sin deceived me" (Rom. 7:11). In Gen 3:13, Eve says that the serpent, using the commandment, "deceived me." That is, Sin, personified as the serpent, argued persuasively for the benefits of transgressing and it's been all downhill ever since.

Paul says "Sin ... wrought in me every kind of desire" (Rom. 7:8). This points at the sexual nature of awakening after knowing the law (eating the fruit). And then, with the 'fall,' the serpent has somehow taken up residence within human flesh. The effect of this is mortality. Being embodied in flesh means being subject to death. All this is actually very Gnostic in flavor, but it is written in such a difficult way that most people don't catch on to it.

Paul is narrating this from a first person point of view, describing in a breathless dramatization the living death that came about from the primal event (Rom. 7:7-12). Paul has adopted the persona of one under the law. Watson writes:

> [Paul's] own Jewish roots give the "fiction" its plausibility and integrity: this is no mere play-acting but a re-engagement for the sake of others with Paul's own pre-Christian identity. The speech ... is so compelling and so poignant that generations of readers have assumed that Paul must be articulating his present experience as a Christian. Yet, in its context, the passage can only be speaking of life under another regime than grace.[1265]

Paul's strategy is obviously to evoke horror in his readers/hearers – horror at the very thought of life under the law. And keep always in mind that Paul was targeting life as a Jew and Jewish communities. Paul's intentions are to save his communities from the predations of the Zealots, the Jewish messianists.

Chapter 8

Above it was said that Romans chapters 6 and 7 are a two-part argument about the correct basis for righteous conduct. Chapter 6 is the argument for grace; chapter 7 is the argument against the Jewish law; and now, chapter 8 is the argument for a life in the spirit. We just left Paul in chapter 7 saying, "Wretched man that I am! Who will rescue me from this body of death? Thanks be to God through Jesus Christ our Lord! So then, with my mind I am a slave to the law of God, but with my flesh I am a slave to the law of sin" (Rom. 7:24-25). In other words, Paul was saying that, under the Law, i.e. while a person is in Judaism, their mind may be a "slave to the law of God" but that doesn't do anything to help the fact that the body is a "slave to the law of sin." But help is on the way! Paul now says that, even in this state of duality, "There is

---

[1265]Watson (2008), p. 290.

therefore now no condemnation for those who are in Christ Jesus. For the law of the Spirit of life in Christ Jesus has set you free from the law of sin and of death" (Rom. 8:1-2). This was already anticipated in Rom. 7:6: "But now we are discharged from the law, dead to that which held us captive, so that we are slaves not under the old written code but in the new life of the Spirit."

What does this mean, exactly? The 'spirit' of Romans 8 is life, which counteracts the death that dominates life under the law. Watson writes: "Romans 7–8 elaborates the double antithesis of 2 Cor. 3:6: 'The letter kills, but the spirit gives life.'"[1266]

In chapter 8, Paul juxtaposes positive and negative uses of the term 'Law.' In Rom. 8:2 there is "the law of the Spirit of life in Christ Jesus"; "the just requirement of the law might be fulfilled in us" (Rom. 8:4); "I delight in the law of God in my inmost self" (Rom. 7:22); "the law of my mind" (Rom. 7:23); as opposed to: "the law of sin and of death" (Rom. 8:2); "the law of sin" (Rom. 7:25); so we see that "the law of sin that is in my members" is contrasted with "the law of God," a law that is weak through the flesh. It would be easy to get confused here but what Paul means, in short, is that the flesh overpowers the mind/spirit/will for most people. Watson again:

> If the "law of my mind" is the law of God, whose authority my mind acknowledges, the "the law of sin in my members" is the opposing set of imperatives whose authority is acknowledged by my body. ... The law of sin is parasitic on the law of God, which it subjects to a process of textual emendation in which prohibitions become requirements and requirements prohibitions.[1267]

In Rom. 7:21 Paul states, "So I find it to be a law that when I want to do what is good, evil lies close at hand." That is, whenever one seeks the good, one comes up against one's own evil. That is, evil is close at hand precisely as "I seek the good." Paul is saying that even willing the good has doing evil as its necessary consequence.

> The attempt to makes one's conduct conform to God's law in full recognition that what the law prescribes is holy and just and good, generates only evil: that is the desperate situation of the person who is under the law of Moses and who delights in it and acknowledges its goodness.[1268]

That is to say, the very actions taken to 'live under the law' amount to nothing more than assertion of the power of the self against God, self-aggrandizement in imagining one has succeeded in becoming righteous, and covetousness thereby for self-glory that becomes 'pious ungodliness.' Refer back to the catena in Rom. 3:9b-20 (especially 13-18):

> "Their *throats* are opened graves; they use their *tongues* to deceive." "The venom of vipers is under their *lips*." "Their *mouths* are full of cursing and bitterness." "*Their* feet are swift to shed blood; ruin and misery are in their paths, and the way of peace they have not known." "There is no fear of God before their *eyes*."

The 'law of sin' is located in my members, i.e. the sins of the throat, tongue, lips, mouth, feet, eyes, for those who seek righteousness by 'works of the law,' i.e. Judaism. Watson again:

[1266]Watson (2008), p. 291.
[1267]Watson (2008), p. 293.
[1268]Watson (2008), p. 294.

More closely related to the law of sin is "sin dwelling within me," which produces evil when I strive for the good. (vv. 7:17-20) Indeed, the "law of sin in my members" simply adds a further metaphorical layer to "sin dwelling within me," where the background is the phenomenon of demonic possession. How, though, has it come about that my very own agency has been usurped by this external power that has taken up residence within me? Pursuing the law of sin back to its source, we find ourselves back in the Garden of Eden on the fateful occasion when the prohibition that preserved access to the tree of life became the occasion of death.[1269]

Putting all this in more modern esoteric terms, we find G. I. Gurdjieff's divided self and Carlos Castaneda's 'predator's mind' to be apt translations.[1270]

What sin did once – working evil through what is good – sin still does to this day. [...] The law's effect in the realm of the flesh is uniformly disastrous. From a pragmatic point of view, Paul's argument functions as a warning to his Roman addressees to avoid further entanglement with the law of Moses and the individual and communal praxis that it sanctions.[1271]

So far then, that is Paul on "the law of sin and death." Those who are in the clutches of this demonic entrapment can only become free by connecting with "the law of the spirit of life in Christ Jesus."

A significant difference between Rom. 7:7-25 and Rom. 8 is the use of the first person singular in the former and first person plural ('we') in the latter. In chapter 7, Paul took the role of a Jew under the law, depicting himself as engaged in a failing, lethal struggle against hostile powers. In chapter 8, he leaves that role behind with relief and joins with his addressees as members of one community in Christ. The first person plural address is that of a community experiencing the first fruits of the life of the age to come. And, curiously, Law is now at the heart of that shared identity; this is Paul's 'law of love.' And within the law of love lies a whole new landscape of interactions, behaviors, duties and obligations based on giving to those who ask; a realm of mutually reciprocal service to others empowered by a network centered on Christ who provides both a template and psychic energy/intercession, to draw one up out of the mire of the flesh back into the reality of paradise.

Chapters 9–11

I am speaking the truth in Christ – I am not lying; my conscience confirms it by the Holy Spirit – I have great sorrow and unceasing anguish in my heart. For I could wish that I myself were accursed and cut off from Christ for the sake of my own people, my kindred according to the flesh.[1272]

Chapter 9 begins with a passionate declaration of anguish about the Jewish people to whom "belong the adoption, the glory, the covenants, the giving of the law, the worship, and the promises" (vv. 4-5). It is pretty clear, after all that has been examined in chapters 1 through 8, that Paul could not possibly have written verses 4-5. What also seems clear is that Romans 9–11

[1269]Watson (2008), p. 295.
[1270]See Ouspensky (2001) and Castaneda (1999).
[1271]Watson (2008), p. 296.
[1272]Rom. 9:1-3.

was written with the destruction of Jerusalem, the Temple, and probably hundreds of thousands of Jews in mind.

The text goes on to say: "It is not as though the word of God had failed" (Rom. 9:6a). Clearly, something extraordinary has occurred that would make it seem as though there was some sort of terrific failure. The disaster language continues, and I have put in bold certain expressions that support the idea that this text is post 70 AD:

For not all Israelites truly belong to Israel, and not all of Abraham's children are his true descendants; but "It is through Isaac that descendants shall be named for you." This means that it is not the children of the flesh who are the children of God, but the children of the promise are counted as descendants. For this is what the promise said, "About this time I will return and Sarah shall have a son." Nor is that all; something similar happened to Rebecca when she had conceived children by one husband, our ancestor Isaac. Even before they had been born or had done anything good or bad (so that God's purpose of election might continue, not by works but by his call) she was told, "The elder shall serve the younger." As it is written, "I have loved Jacob, but I have hated Esau."

What then are we to say? Is there injustice on God's part? By no means! For he says to Moses, "I will have mercy on whom I have mercy, and I will have compassion on whom I have compassion." So it depends not on human will or exertion, but on God who shows mercy. For the scripture says to Pharaoh, "I have raised you up for the very purpose of showing my power in you, so that my name may be proclaimed in all the earth." So then **he has mercy on whomever he chooses, and he hardens the heart of whomever he chooses.**

You will say to me then, "Why then does he still find fault? For who can resist his will?" But who indeed are you, a human being, to argue with God? Will what is molded say to the one who molds it, "Why have you made me like this?" Has the potter no right over the clay, to make out of the same lump one object for special use and another for ordinary use? What if **God, desiring to show his wrath and to make known his power, has endured with much patience the objects of wrath that are made for destruction**; and what if he has done so in order to make known the riches of his glory for the objects of mercy, which he has prepared beforehand for glory – including us whom he has called, not from the Jews only but also from the Gentiles? As indeed he says in Hosea, "Those who were not my people I will call 'my people,' and her who was not beloved I will call 'beloved.'" "And in the very place where it was said to them, 'You are not my people,' there they shall be called children of the living God." And Isaiah cries out concerning Israel, "Though the number of the children of Israel were like the sand of the sea, **only a remnant of them will be saved; for the Lord will execute his sentence on the earth quickly and decisively." And as Isaiah predicted, "If the Lord of hosts had not left survivors to us, we would have fared like Sodom and been made like Gomorrah."**

What then are we to say? Gentiles, who did not strive for righteousness, have attained it, that is, righteousness through faith; but **Israel, who did strive for the righteousness that is based on the law**, did not succeed in fulfilling that law. Why not? Because they did not strive for it on the basis of faith, but as if it were based on works. **They have stumbled over the stumbling stone**, as it is written, "See, I am laying in Zion a stone that will make people stumble, a rock that will make them fall, and whoever believes in him will not be put to shame."

Brothers and sisters, my heart's desire and prayer to God for them is that they may be saved. I can testify that **they have a zeal for God, but it is not enlightened**. For, being ignorant of the righteousness that comes from God, and seeking to establish their own, **they have not submitted to God's righteousness**. For Christ is the end of the law so that there may be righteousness for everyone who believes.

The scripture says, "No one who believes in him will be put to shame." For *there is no distinction between Jew and Greek*; the same Lord is Lord of all and is generous to all who call on him. For,

"Everyone who calls on the name of the Lord shall be saved." But how are they to call on one in whom they have not believed? And how are they to believe in one of whom they have never heard? And how are they to hear without someone to proclaim him? And how are they to proclaim him unless they are sent? As it is written, "How beautiful are the feet of those who bring good news!"

But not all have obeyed the good news; for Isaiah says, "Lord, who has believed our message?" So faith comes from what is heard, and what is heard comes through the word of Christ. But I ask, **have they not heard?** Indeed they have; for "Their voice has gone out to all the earth, and their words to the ends of the world." Again I ask, **did Israel not understand?** First Moses says, "I will make you jealous of those who are not a nation; with a foolish nation I will make you angry." Then Isaiah is so bold as to say, "I have been found by those who did not seek me; I have shown myself to those who did not ask for me." But **of Israel he says, "All day long I have held out my hands to a disobedient and contrary people."**

I ask, then, **has God rejected his people?** By no means! I myself am an Israelite, a descendant of Abraham, a member of the tribe of Benjamin. God has not rejected his people whom he foreknew. Do you not know what the scripture says of Elijah, how he pleads with God against Israel? "Lord, they have killed your prophets, they have demolished your altars; I alone am left, and they are seeking my life." But what is the divine reply to him? "I have kept for myself seven thousand who have not bowed the knee to Baal." So too **at the present time there is a remnant**, chosen by grace. But if it is by grace, it is no longer on the basis of works, otherwise grace would no longer be grace. What then? **Israel failed to obtain what it was seeking.** The elect obtained it, but the rest were hardened, as it is written, **"God gave them a sluggish spirit, eyes that would not see and ears that would not hear, down to this very day."** And David says, "Let their table become a snare and a trap, a stumbling block and **a retribution for them**; let their eyes be darkened so that they cannot see, and keep their backs forever bent."

So I ask, **have they stumbled so as to fall?** By no means! But **through their stumbling salvation has come to the Gentiles**, so as to make Israel jealous. Now if their stumbling means riches for the world, and **if their defeat means riches for Gentiles**, how much more will their full inclusion mean! Now I am speaking to you Gentiles. Inasmuch then as I am an apostle to the Gentiles, I glorify my ministry in order to make my own people jealous, and thus save some of them. For if **their rejection** is the reconciliation of the world, what will their acceptance be but life from the dead![1273]

The following verses, Rom. 11:16–29 about differences between Jews and Gentiles, the Jews being the 'holy root' and grafting in Gentiles onto the Jewish root, which echoes vv. 4-5, are certainly a non-Pauline interpolation; Paul would never have written text that glorified the Jewish lifestyle, considering all else he has written just in the conglomerate of *Romans* alone, even insisting that the Gentiles have priority in Abraham's faith. And, in fact, Rom. 11:15 continues more smoothly going directly to Rom. 11:30:

Just as you were once disobedient to God but have now received mercy because of their disobedience, so they have now been disobedient in order that, by the mercy shown to you, they too may now receive mercy. For God has imprisoned all in disobedience so that he may be merciful to all. O the depth of the riches and wisdom and knowledge of God! How unsearchable are his judgments and how inscrutable his ways! "For who has known the mind of the Lord? Or who has been his counselor?" "Or who has given a gift to him, to receive a gift in return?" For from him and through him and to him are all things. To him be the glory forever. Amen.[1274]

[1273]Rom. 9:6b–11:15.
[1274]Rom. 11:30-36.

I think the only rational conclusion that can be drawn about Romans 9–11 is that it was written in grievous reaction to the destruction of the Jews in 66–70 AD.

Was this separate letter then patched in with two other letters and some fragments to create the Epistle of Romans we have today? I think it is not only possible, but likely. Except for some minor interpolations to bring the text more in line with the agenda of Acts, the taste and feel of it is Pauline.

Chapter 12

This chapter seems to me to be the natural continuation from chapter 8, the original letter to the Gentile Christians at Rome. Observe how they connect together:

> For I am convinced that neither death, nor life, nor angels, nor rulers, nor things present, nor things to come, nor powers, nor height, nor depth, nor anything else in all creation, will be able to separate us from the love of God in Christ Jesus our Lord. *** I appeal to you therefore, brothers and sisters, by the mercies of God, to present your bodies as a living sacrifice, holy and acceptable to God, which is your spiritual worship. Do not be conformed to this world, but be transformed by the renewing of your minds, so that you may discern what is the will of God – what is good and acceptable and perfect.

Again, I have placed asterisks at the junction of 8 and 12. Recall what I wrote about chapter 8, that Paul juxtaposes positive and negative uses of the term 'law,'; "the law of sin that is in my members" is contrasted with "the law of God," a law that is weak through the flesh. In other words, the flesh overpowers the mind/spirit/will for most people. And here, chapter 12 moves directly to, "Do not be conformed to this world, but be transformed by the renewing of your minds." This is followed by typical Pauline statements that amount to the 'law of love in Christ,' and have many verbal echoes with chapters 6, 7 and 8.

Chapter 13

This chapter is a continuation of chapter 12, with 'Rules for Christian Life,' most particularly aimed at what could be considered making peace with the authorities. Additionally, Paul makes a couple of statements indicating that he felt the Parousia was imminent: "Besides this, you know what time it is, how it is now the moment for you to wake from sleep. For salvation is nearer to us now than when we became believers; the night is far gone, the day is near. Let us then lay aside the works of darkness and put on the armor of light" (vv. 11-12).

Chapter 14

This chapter has already been excluded as a generalized re-writing of 1 Cor. 8–10 and was the chapter Watson used to orient his social situation.

Chapter 15

The last lines of chapter 13 flow smoothly into Rom. 15:14. Again, I have placed an asterisk at their junction:

> Let us then lay aside the works of darkness and put on the armor of light; let us live honorably as in the day, not in reveling and drunkenness, not in debauchery and licentiousness, not in quarreling and jealousy. Instead, put on the Lord Jesus Christ, and make no provision for the flesh, to gratify its desires. *** I myself feel confident about you, my brothers and sisters, that you yourselves are full of goodness, filled with all knowledge, and able to instruct one another. Nevertheless on some points I have written to you rather boldly by way of reminder, because of the grace given me by God to be a minister of Christ Jesus to the Gentiles in the priestly service of the gospel of God, so that the offering of the Gentiles may be acceptable, sanctified by the Holy Spirit. In Christ Jesus, then, I have reason to boast of my work for God.

As mentioned previously, there are some editorial insertions in this passage that obviously attempt to bring Paul's itinerary into line with *Acts*, even in direct contradiction to what Paul says elsewhere. For example: "from Jerusalem and as far around as Illyricum I have fully proclaimed the good news of Christ." And, of course, the insertion promotes the idea that Paul is going to take a collection of money to Jerusalem before he travels to Rome. As we know, Paul is unlikely to have ever returned to Jerusalem for a third visit as Acts depicts, because the main pillars of the church there have been executed, Paul himself was arrested and put in prison, and most likely his trip to Rome was from Ephesus, not Jerusalem.

Chapter 16

As noted previously, the greetings that constitute most of chapter 16 were undoubtedly part of a letter sent from Rome to Ephesus, and probably after Paul was set free in Rome. He makes mention of Priscilla and Aquila who risked their lives for him, and that probably had something to do with his imprisonment there. Considering what has been said earlier about Clement/Clemens, the collection of names – Aristobulus, Herodion, Narcissus – makes somewhat better sense. All we can say is that not much is known about Paul's actual life and ministry, so we can only lay out the few pieces we have and try to make sense of it. One thing for sure is that Acts is not anywhere near a true account of the early Church and the activities of Paul.

However, having said that, I think that part of chapter 16 (vv. 17-20) may be part of the conclusion to the original letter to the Gentile Roman Christians:

> I urge you, brothers and sisters, to keep an eye on those who cause dissensions and offenses, in opposition to the teaching that you have learned; avoid them. For such people do not serve our Lord Christ, but their own appetites, and by smooth talk and flattery they deceive the hearts of the simple-minded. For while your obedience is known to all, so that I rejoice over you, I want you to be wise in what is good and guileless in what is evil. The God of peace will shortly crush Satan under your feet. The grace of our Lord Jesus Christ be with you.

Considering what Paul himself has been through *vis à vis* the Galatians and being put in prison, it is likely that he would include such a warning. Note again that Paul expects the Parousia soon.

And the final ending (Rom. 16:21-27):

> Timothy, my co-worker, greets you; so do Lucius and Jason and Sosipater, my relatives. I Tertius, the writer of this letter, greet you in the Lord. Gaius, who is host to me and to the whole church, greets you. Erastus, the city treasurer, and our brother Quartus, greet you. Now to God who is able to strengthen you according to my gospel and the proclamation of Jesus Christ, according to the revelation of the mystery that was kept secret for long ages but is now disclosed, and through the prophetic writings is made known to all the Gentiles, according to the command of the eternal God, to bring about the obedience of faith – to the only wise God, through Jesus Christ, to whom be the glory forever! Amen.

If this last part is actually the ending of the letter of Paul to the Roman Gentile Christians, it conveys some valuable bits of information suggesting that Paul had converts even among the bureaucrats of the Empire. Gaius was mentioned in 1 Cor. 1:14. Acts claims that Gaius was a Macedonian, but we know that Acts used bits and names from Paul's letters to create its fairytale of early Christian unity. Acts refers to "Sopater son of Pyrrhus from Beroea" in contradiction to Paul's claim above that he was a relative of Paul's (assuming he is not using 'relative/kinsman' as a way of referring to fellow Jews and not literally family members).

Conclusion

At the end of this examination, the conclusion is that Watson is correct to say that the social situation can tell us a lot about a text; the problem is that one must have in mind the real social situation, as closely as it can be determined based on all available evidence, in order to construct a reliable yardstick for what is reasonable and what is not in a given text.

Appendix C: Textual Sources of Mark

The following table is adapted from R. G. Price (2018), greatly expanded with additions from MacDonald (2015), Smith (2011, 2016), Winn (2010), Hays (1993, 2017), and others.

Pericope	Mark	References	Subject
John the Baptist prepares the way for Jesus	Mk 1:1-8	Isa 40:3; Ex 23:20-21; Mal 3:1-2; 4:4-5; 2 Kings 1:8; 1 Cor 15:9	God's judgment of Israel; identification of Elijah
John baptizes Jesus	Mk 1:9-11	1 Kings 17:2-6; Isa 11:1-3; 42:104; 63-64; Ps 2; *Od.* 1	God sends Elijah to the Jordan; identification of God's servant; God's judgment; God's son; Athena emboldens Telemachus
Satan tempts Jesus in the desert	Mk 1:12-13	1 Kings 19:4-13	Elijah in the wilderness
Jesus preaches in Galilee	Mk 1:14-15	1 Kings 19:15-18; *Od.* 1	Anointing of Jehu; Telemachus takes authority
Four fishermen follow Jesus	Mk 1:16-20	1 Kings 19:19-21; Jer 16:14-18; Gal 2; *Od.* 2	Calling of Elisha; fishes of men; Simon/Peter, James and John; Telemachus acquires a crew
Jesus teaches with great Authority	Mk 1:21-28	1 Kings 17:18, 24; *Od.* 1	Elijah as the man of God; suitors amazed at Telemachus' boldness
Jesus heals Peter's mother-in-law & many others	Mk 1:29-34	1 Kings 17:15; Isa 41:13-14; Ps 103:2-4	Woman follows Elijah; God helps Israel; God forgives and heals
Jesus preaches throughout Galilee	Mk 1:35-39	Ps 18:37	Pursuit of enemies
Jesus heals a man with leprosy	Mk 1:40-45	2 Kings 5:1-8	Elisha heals a leper
Jesus heals a paralyzed man	Mk 2:1-12	2 Kings 1:1-17; Isa 35:5-6	Ahaziah falls through ceiling, dies; healing the lame
Jesus eats with sinners at Matthew's house	Mk 2:13-17	1 Kings 19:20-21; Gal 2:15	Elisha follows Elijah; eating with sinners
Religious leaders ask Jesus about fasting	Mk 2:18-22	Jer 7, 16, 25; Josh 9:13	Bridegrooms and wineskins
Disciples pick wheat on Sabbath	Mk 2:23-28	Deut 24:1; 1 Sam 21:1-7	Fields; show bread
Jesus heals a man's hand on the Sabbath	Mk 3:1-6	1 Kings 13:4-6; Rom 9, 11	Healing the withered hand; grief and wrath
Large crowds follow Jesus	Mk 3:7-12		
Jesus selects the twelve disciples	Mk 3:13-19	Rom 8:32; 1 Cor 15:5	Jesus "handed over"; 12 apostles

Pharisees say Jesus is under Satan's power	Mk 3:20-30	2 Cor 15:13; Ps 27:10; Jer 12:6; Isa 49:24-25; Gal 5:2-6	Paul "lost his mind"; parents forsake son; the strong man; divided house
Jesus describes his true family	Mk 3:31-35	Gal 1:9-10	Fleshly status does not matter
Jesus tells the parable of the four soils	Mk 4:1-9	1 Cor 3, 15; 2 Cor 9; Gal 5; Col 1:6	Agricultural imagery; gospel bearing fruit and increasing
Jesus explains the Parable of the Four Soils	Mk 4:10-25	Rom 11:7-14; Col 1	Paul quotes Isaiah; gospel bears fruit
Jesus tells the parable of the growing Seed	Mk 4:26-29	Joel 3:13	Harvest sickle
Jesus tells the parable of the Mustard Seed	Mk 4:30-34		
Jesus calms the Storm	Mk 4:35-41	Ps 107:23-29; Jonah 1:3-16; *Od.* 10	God commands the storm; Jonah braves a storm; Odysseus sleeps while sailing
Jesus sends the Demons into a herd of Pigs	Mk 5:1-20	*Od.* 9, 10	Odysseus encounters the Cyclops; Circe turns his crew into pigs
Jesus heals a bleeding lady & raises girl from dead	Mk 5:21-43	1 Kings 17; 2 Kings 4; *Il.* 16	Elijah/Elisha healings; Glaukos prays for healing
The people of Nazareth refuse to believe	Mk 6:1-6	1 Cor 3:9-10	God as skilled builder
Jesus sends out the 12 Disciples	Mk 6:7-13	1 Cor 1, 9	Apostles sent in groups, housed by others
Herod kills John the Baptist	Mk 6:14-29	2 Kings 2	Elisha's followers fail to find Elijah's body
Jesus feeds Five Thousand	Mk 6:30-44	1 Kings 22:17; Ez 34; 2 Kings 4:38-44; Rom 11:12; *Od.* 3	Sheep without a shepherd; God as shepherd; Elisha feeds one hundred; "fullnesses" from the Jews; Telemachus feasts with "shepherd king" Nestor
Jesus walks on Water	Mk 6:45-52	Job 9:4-11; 1 Kings 19:11; Ps 77:19-20; Isa 43; *Il.* 24	God walks on sea; God "passes by"; God passes through water, identified as shepherd; Israel's rejection of God; Zeus sends Hermes to guide Priam
Jesus heals all who touch him	Mk 6:53-56		
Jesus teaches about inner purity	Mk 7:1-23	Gal 2:11-14; 3:15, 17; Rom 14:14-20; Rom 1	Eating with Gentiles; "making void" God's word; all things are clean; sin list
Jesus sends a demon out of a girl	Mk 7:24-30	1 Kings 17:8-16; Rom 1:16	Sidonian woman and her children; first to Jews, then Greeks
The crowd marvels at Jesus' healings	Mk 7:31-37		

Jesus feeds four thousand	Mk 8:1-9	2 Kings 4:38-44; 2 Cor 8:13-14; *Od.* 4	Elisha feeds one hundred; "surpluses" of Gentile followers; Spartan wedding feast
Religious leaders ask for a sign in the sky	Mk 8:10-12	1 Cor 1:22	Jews ask for signs
Jesus warns against wrong teaching	Mk 8:13-21	1 Sam 21:1-7; 1 Cor 5:8	David and the leaven; leaven of malice
Jesus restores sight to a blind man	Mk 8:22-26		
Peter says Jesus is the Messiah	Mk 8:27-30		
Jesus predicts his death the first time	Mk 8:31-9:1	Gal 1:10; 2:11-14; Phil 1:12-29; 2 Kings 2:1-4; Phil 1:20-21; 3:7-8; 2:14-15; 3:18-19	Things of God vs. of people; Paul rebukes Peter; speaking boldly; prediction, response, teaching on discipleship; to die is gain; lose all to gain Christ; crooked generation; glory and shame
Jesus is transfigured on the mountain	Mk 9:2-13	Dan 12; Gal 2:2; *Od.* 16	Shining like stars; Paul speaks to apostles in private; Odysseus is transfigured
Jesus heals a demon-possessed boy	Mk 9:14-29		
Jesus predicts his death the second time	Mk 9:30-32	2 Kings 2:5-6	Prediction, response, teaching on discipleship
The disciples argue about who would be Greatest	Mk 9:33-37	2 Kings 2:5-6; 1 Cor 15:8-9; 1 Thess 2:11-16	Prediction, response, teaching on discipleship; Paul as greatest and least apostle; Gentile followers as children
The disciples forbid another to use Jesus' name	Mk 9:38-42	Suet. *Jul* 75.1	Caesar says those who are neutral are his friends
Jesus warns against temptation	Mk 9:43-50	Isa 66:24; Rom 14:21; 1 Thess 5:13	Punishment of God's opponents; causing to stumble; be at peace
Jesus teaches about marriage and divorce	Mk 10:1-12	1 Cor 6-7	Paul quotes Genesis, gives rules for divorce for both men *and* women
Jesus blesses little children	Mk 10:13-16	1 Thess 2	Paul's approach to children/Gentiles
Jesus speaks to the Rich Young Man	Mk 10:17-31	Gal 2:15-3:29	Jew as "rich" in Law, inheritance, life, Law as insufficient
Jesus predicts his death the third time	Mk 10:32-34	1 Kings 2:9-11	Prediction, difficult request only God can grant
Jesus teaches about serving others	Mk 10:35-45	1 Kings 2:9-11; Gal 2:6-9; 1 Cor 9:19	Prediction, difficult request only God can grant; "those reputed to be" rules; serving
Jesus heals a blind beggar	Mk 10:46-52	*Od.* 11	Odysseus encounters the blind seer Tiresias

Jesus rides into Jerusalem on a donkey	Mk 11:1-11	Zech 9:9; 14:4-5; 1 Sam 10:2; 2 Kings 9:13; *Od.* 6-7	Meek savior riding an ass; Mount of Olives; seeking asses; laying of garments; Odysseus encounters Nausicaa
Jesus clears the temple again	Mk 11:12-19	Hos 9; Joel 1:6-12; Zech 14:21; Isa 56:6-8; *Od.*	The dried-up fig tree, driving out of house; nation as fig tree; den of vipers; Odysseus expels suitors from his house
Jesus says the disciples can pray for anything	Mk 11:20-25	Hos 9; Gal 4:25-27; 1 Cor 13:2	The dried-up fig tree; Mount Sinai as barren woman; faith to move mountains
Religious leaders challenge Jesus' authority	Mk 11:26-33	Gal 1:1; 2:1-14	Paul's authority to preach is not from men
Jesus tells the parable of the wicked tenants	Mk 12:1-12	2 Kings 9:14-26; Isa 5:1-7; Rom 8:31-38; Gal 3:16-18; 4:6-7; *Od.* 16	Jehu takes kingship and vineyard from Joram; Israel as vineyard; Paul quotes Ps 118; Jesus as the heir; suitors plot to steal Telemachus' inheritance
Pharisees question Jesus re: paying taxes	Mk 12:13-17	Rom 13:1-7	Pay taxes to whom they are due
Pharisees question Jesus re: resurrection	Mk 12:18-27	1 Cor 15	The question of resurrection
Pharisees question Jesus re: greatest command	Mk 12:28-34	Rom 13:8-10; Gal 5:14	The greatest commandment; Paul quotes Lev 19:18 and Deut
Religious leaders cannot answer Jesus' Question	Mk 12:35-37	1 Cor 15:24-26	Paul quotes Ps 110
Jesus warns against the Religious Leaders	Mk 12:38-40	Exod 22:22-24; Isa 10:1-4; *Od.* 16	Widows; the poor; suitors "consume my house"
A poor widow gives all she has	Mk 12:41-44	1 Kings 17:7-14; 2 Kings 4:1-7	Widow gives her last and receives blessings.
Jesus tells about the future	Mk 13:1-20	Isa 19:2; 2 Chron. 15:6; Micah 7:6; Dan 9, 11, 12; 2 Thess 2:3-10	Nation against nation; children against parents; abomination of desolation
Jesus tells about his return	Mk 13:21-31	Deut 13:1-2; 30:4; Dan 7; Zech 2:6; *Od.* 19	False prophets; gathering the elect; Son of Man; the four winds; Odysseus prophesies his own return
Jesus tells about remaining watchful	Mk 13:32-37	1 Thess 5:1-3; *Od.*	"Like a thief in the night"; Odysseus, master of the house, is coming
Religious leaders plot to kill Jesus	Mk 14:1-2	*Od.*	Suitors plan to kill Odysseus, but fear his people
A woman anoints Jesus with perfume	Mk 14:3-9	2 Kings 9; *Od.* 19	Anointing of Jehu; anointing of Odysseus, slaves object to such good treatment
Judas agrees to betray Jesus	Mk 14:10-11	Amos 2	Selling the righteous for silver

Disciples prepare for the Passover	Mk 14:12-16	1 Sam 10:1-9; *Od.* 10	Samuel's predictions for Saul fulfilled; the Laestrygonian cannibals' meal
Jesus and the disciples have the Last Supper	Mk 14:17-25	Zech 11:17; Ps 41:9; 1 Cor 5:7; 11:23-26; *Od.* 10	"Woe" to the man; betrayal by close friend; good not to have been born; Passover lamb; Last Supper; the Laestrygonian cannibals' meal
Jesus again predicts Peter's denial	Mk 14:26-31	2 Kings 2:2, 4, 6	Elisha's triple promise to Elijah
Jesus agonizes in the garden	Mk 14:32-42	1 Kings 19; Jonah 4:9; Rom 8:14-30; Gal 5:6-7; *Od.* 10	Elijah prays; Grieved to death; the Abba prayer; Odysseus agonizes over Hades
Jesus is betrayed and arrested	Mk 14:43-52	Amos 2:16; Prov 27:6; 2 Sam 20:9-10; *Od.* 10; 17-22	The naked shall flee; an enemy's kisses; Elpenor's soul goes to Hades; Melanthius the treacherous slave
Caiaphas questions Jesus	Mk 14:53-65	Gen 2:4; Ex 3:14; Deut 32:39; Ps 35:11; Dan 6:4; 7:13-14; Isa 50:6; 53:7	God's "I Am"; ruthless witnesses question me; accusers could find no corruption; Son of Man; beating of the messiah; went silent like lamb to slaughter
Peter denies knowing Jesus	Mk 14:66-72	Gal 1:8-9; 2:11; *Od.* 12	Let those proclaiming other gospel be accursed; Peter stands condemned; Eurylochus breaks his oath not to kill the cattle of Helios
Jesus stands trial before Pilate	Mk 15:1-5	Isa 53:7	He opened not his mouth
Pilate hands Jesus over to be crucified	Mk 15:6-15	Isa 53:5; Lev 16; Rom 3:24-25	His stripes; Yom Kippur sacrifice of atonement, scapegoat
Roman soldiers mock Jesus	Mk 15:16-20	Isa 50:6; Micah 5:1; 1 Cor 1:18-29; 2:6-8; 2 Cor 6:8-10; 12:9-10; Rom 1:22; Col 2:15; *Od.* 18	Beating and spitting; victory in defeat; triumphal imagery; suitors favour Irus over Odysseus
Jesus is led away to be crucified	Mk 15:21-24	Prov 31:6	Wine for those in anguish
Jesus is placed on the cross	Mk 15:25-32	Ps 22	Pierced hands and feet, cast lots for clothes
Jesus dies on the cross	Mk 15:33-41	Ps 69; Amos 8; *Il.* 22	Vinegar; sun down, ceiling of temple shall howl; the death of Hector
Jesus is laid in the tomb	Mk 15:42-47	Ps 23; 1 Cor 15:4; *Il.* 24	Funeral psalm; Christ buried; Priam requests Hector's body for burial
Jesus rises from the dead	Mk 16:1-8	2 Kings 13:20-21; Ps 24; 1 Cor 15:4; *Od.* 12	Resuscitation of Elisha; exaltation psalm; Christ raised on third day; Elpenor is buried

Three representative examples follow, demonstrating Mark's use of the Elijah-Elisha narrative from Kings, Homer's *Odyssey*, and Paul's letters.

Mark's Use of Kings

Winn (2010), pp. 106–7.

Jehu's Rebellion (2 Kings 9:14-26)	The Parable of the Wicked Tenants (Mark 12:1-12)
	Story preceded by a cleansing of Israel's temple (Mark 11:15-25)
Jehu, God's anointed king comes to take kingship from the corrupt king, Jehoram (14-16)	The vineyard owner seeks his share of the vineyard's produce from corrupt tenants (2)
Corrupt king sends a messenger to the anointed king – messenger fails (17-18)	Vineyard owner sends a messenger to corrupt tenants – messenger fails (2-3)
Corrupt king sends a messenger to the anointed king – messenger fails (19-20)	Vineyard owner sends a messenger to corrupt tenants – messenger fails (4)
	Vineyard owner sends a messenger to corrupt tenants – messenger fails (5)
Corrupt king himself goes to the anointed king (20-21)	Vineyard owner sends his own son to the corrupt tenants (6)
Corrupt king is killed by the anointed king (22-24)	Son is killed by corrupt tenants (7-8)
By removing the corrupt king, the anointed kings (the new ruler of Israel) rights the wrong of a stolen vineyard. (25-26)	Because of the death of his son, the vineyard owner destroys the corrupt tenants and places new leaders in charge of the vineyard. (9)
Story followed by cleansing Israel of Baal's temple/prophets (10:18-25)	

Mark's Use of Homer

MacDonald (2015), pp. 42–43.

Odysseus and the Cyclopes (*Od.* 9, 10)	The Gerasene Demoniac (Mark 5:1-20)
Odysseus and his crew sailed to the land of the Cyclopes [and of Circe].	Jesus and his disciples sailed to the region of the Gerasenes.
On the mountains of the Cyclopes "countless goats" grazed. [Circe turned Odysseus's comrades into swine.]	On the mountains "a large herd of swine" grazed, about two thousand of them.
Odysseus and crew went ashore.	Jesus and his disciples went ashore.
They discovered a savage, lawless giant who lived in a cave.	They discovered a savage, lawless demon-possessed man who lived among the caves.
Polyphemus usually was depicted nude.	The savage was nude.

(Circe recognized Odysseus and asked him not to harm her.) The giant asked if Odysseus had come to harm him.	The savage recognized Jesus and asked him not to harm him.
The giant asked Odysseus his name.	Jesus asked the monster his name.
Odysseus answered, "Nobody."	The savage answered, "Legion."
Odysseus subdued the giant with violence and trickery. (Circe had turned Odysseus's soldiers into swine.)	Jesus subdued the demons with a word and sent them into the swine and then into the lake.
The shepherd called out to his neighbors.	The swineherd reported to their neighbors.
The Cyclopes came to the site asking about Polyphemus's sheep and goats.	The neighbors came to the site to find out about their swine.
Odysseus and crew boarded ship.	Jesus and his disciples boarded ship.
Odysseus told the giant to broadcast that he had blinded him.	Jesus told the healed monster to broadcast what God had done for him.
The giant asked Odysseus, now on ship, to come back.	The savage asked Jesus, now on ship, if he could be with him.
Odysseus refused the request.	Jesus refused the request.
Odysseus and his crew sailed away.	Jesus and his disciples sailed away.
Odysseus awoke during a storm in the episode immediately *following* Polyphemus.	Jesus awoke during the storm and calmed the wind and sea immediately *before* the savage.

Mark's Use of Paul

Adapted from Smith (2011), pp. 36–47.

Mark	Paul	Chiastic use of sources
		(Talking to scribes)
Mk 12:10-11: "Have you not read this scripture. 'The stone that the builders rejected has become the cornerstone; this was the Lord's doing, and it is amazing in our eyes?'" (Ps 118:22-23)	Rom 8:31: "What are we to say about these things? If God is for us, who is against us?" (Ps 118:6)	A. Ps 118 to Maccabeus
Mk 12:12-17: Jesus says to render to Caesar	Rom 13:1-7: Paul says to pay your taxes	B. Rom 13:1-7
Mk 12:18-23: The Sadducees, who deny resurrection, try to trick Jesus on its nature	1 Cor 15:12-14: Paul responds to those denying the resurrection	C. 1 Cor 15:12-14
Mk 12:24-27: Jesus says the resurrection is spiritual in nature	1 Cor 15:35-51: Paul says the resurrection is spiritual in nature	C'. 1 Cor 15:35-51

Mk 12:28-34: Jesus says love is the greatest commandment	Rom 13:8-10: Paul says love is the summation of the law	B'. Rom 13:8-10
Mk 12:36: "David himself, by the Holy Spirit, declared, 'The Lord said to my Lord, 'Sit at my right hand, until I put your enemies under your feet.'" (Ps 110:1)	1 Cor 15:25: "For he must reign until he has put all his enemies under his feet." (Ps. 110:1)	A'. Ps 110 to Maccabeus (1 Cor 15:25)
		(Beware the scribes)

Chiastic Structures

The above example also demonstrates Mark's intricate use of structure, in this case by his use of sources in a chiastic structure (ABCC'B'A'). The first/last stiches (A/A') quote psalms also quoted by Paul in Romans in 1 Corinthians. The next set (B/B') uses consecutive sections of Romans 13. And the inner set (C/C') use sequential sections of 1 Corinthians 15. Smith shows that Paul also varies his use of sources within a chiastic theological structure stretching the entire length of the Gospel (OT is Old Testament, P is Paul):

| OT – P – OT | Parable Discourse – P – OT – P – Olivet Discourse | OT – P – OT |

The entirety of Mark's Gospel uses chiastic structures. Every pericope is a self-contained chiasm. In the following example (Mark 1:21-29) the stiches are labeled,[1275] with matching elements in bold:

A 1:21 And **they go into Capernaum**.

B And immediately on the Sabbath he entered **into the synagogue** and **taught**.

C 1:22 And they were **astonished** at his teaching. For he **taught** them as having **authority**, and not as the scribes.

D 1:23 And immediately in their synagogue there was a man with an **unclean spirit**.

E And he shouted, 1:24 **saying**, "What are we to you, Jesus, the Nazarene? Have you **come** to destroy us? I know who you are, they Holy One of God."

E' 1:25 And Jesus admonished him, **saying**, "Be silent and **come** out of him."

D' 1:26 And having thrown the man into convulsions the **unclean spirit** shouted with a loud voice and came out of him.

C' 1:27 And they were all **amazed**, such that they asked each other, saying, "What is this? New **teaching**? He commands with **authority**, and the unclean spirits obey him."

B' 1:28 And immediately **the news about him went out** everywhere **into all the surrounding region** of Galilee.

A' 1:29 And immediately, when they had come out of the synagogue, **they came into the house** of Simon and Andrew, with James and John.

[1275]Smith (2016), p. 21.

In addition, Smith has discovered five 'long chiastic structures' in Mark, where a long stretch of text matches up with another stretch of text further in the Gospel, forming one extensive chiasm. For example, in the opening and closing sections, elements of 1:2-38 align with 16:8 back to 14:32 (1:2 and 16:8 form the outermost A/A' stich, while 1:38 and 14:32 form the innermost T/T' stich).[1276] The prologue and epilogue also from a long *parallel* structure (1:1/15:39 to 1:15/16:8).[1277]

Smith utilizes the work of Michael Turton. The following excerpt from Turton shows the structure of the passion narrative:

- Soldiers mock Jesus as King
- compel passerby to help carry cross to Golgotha
- offer wine
- crucify him
- divide his garments
- 3rd hour
- Title on Cross: King of the Jews
- Robbers are crucified
- Passers-by mock Jesus
- priests and teachers of the law mock Jesus
- Robbers mock Jesus
- 6th-9th hour darkness
- Jesus cries that God has forsaken him
- bystanders think Jesus calls Elijah for help
- offer vinegar
- dies with great cry
- temple curtain torn
- centurion says Jesus is "Son of God"
- three women watch
- many women, from Jerusalem

As we have seen, these elements form a neat chiastic structure whose parts are internally parallel and center on an A-B-B'-A' chiasm:

- A. And they compelled a passer-by, Simon of Cyre'ne, who was coming in from the country, the father of Alexander and Rufus, to carry his cross. And they brought him to the place called Gol'gotha (which means the place of a skull).
- B. [missing verse? Or is 15:39 a back-assimilation from Matthew?]

[1276]Smith (2016), pp. 38–52.

[1277]Smith (2016), pp. 24–37. See this work for additional structural features of Mark, including his use of parallel centers, in which the inner stiches of a chiasm include a parallel structure (e.g. ABCA'B'C'), and word triplets, where Mark uses a word or phrase precisely three times throughout the Gospel, with the second instance differing in some way from the first and third (e.g. 3:11 "Son of God," 5:7 "Son of the most high God," 15:39 "Son of God"). Smith identifies 14 parallel centers and 81 triplets that follow these rules.

- C.a. And they offered him wine mingled with myrrh; but he did not take it.

- C.b. And they crucified him,

- C.c. and divided his garments among them, casting lots for them, to decide what each should take

- D. And it was the third hour, when they crucified him.

- E. And the inscription of the charge against him read, "The King of the Jews."

- F.a. And with him they crucified two robbers, one on his right and one on his left.

- F.b. And those who passed by derided him, wagging their heads, and saying, "Aha! You who would destroy the temple and build it in three days, save yourself, and come down from the cross!"

- F'.b'. So also the chief priests mocked him to one another with the scribes, saying, "He saved others; he cannot save himself. Let the Christ, the King of Israel, come down now from the cross, that we may see and believe."

- F'.a'. Those who were crucified with him also reviled him.

- E'. And when the sixth hour had come, there was darkness over the whole land until the ninth hour.

- D'. And at the ninth hour Jesus cried with a loud voice, "E'lo-i, E'lo-i, la'ma sabach-tha'ni?" which means, "My God, my God, why hast thou forsaken me?"

- C'.a'. And some of the bystanders hearing it said, "Behold, he is calling Elijah." And one ran and, filling a sponge full of vinegar, put it on a reed and gave it to him to drink, saying, "Wait, let us see whether Elijah will come to take him down."

- C'.b'. And Jesus uttered a loud cry, and breathed his last.

- C'.c'. And the curtain of the temple was torn in two, from top to bottom.

- B'. And when the centurion, who stood facing him, saw that he thus breathed his last, he said, "Truly this man was the Son of God!"

- A'. There were also women looking on from afar, among whom were Mary Mag'dalene, and Mary the mother of James the younger and of Joses, and Salo'me, who, when he was in Galilee, followed him, and ministered to him; and also many other women who came up with him to Jerusalem.

Now, the same scene in Matthew 27:31-54 copies virtually every element from Mark.

- Mocked as king

- Help from Simon to Golgotha

- vinegar

- Crucifixion

- Garments divided

- *third hour*

- **and sitting down, they were watching him there**

- Title: 'king of the Jews'

- Robber crucified

- Passers-by mock

- Chief priests/scribes mock

- Robbers insult him
- And from the sixth hour darkness came over all the land unto the ninth hour
- 'My God, my God, why didst Thou forsake me?'
- Calling Elijah
- vinegar
- Jesus dies
- veil torn
- **earth did quake, and the rocks were rent**
- **tombs were opened, and saints walk**
- Truly this was 'God's Son.'
- three women
- women *from Jerusalem*

Now we have problems. The neat chiastic structure of Mark has been torn here in several ways. 1. Matthew has no reference to the third hour. If you return to Mark 13 you will see:

> 13:35: Watch therefore – for you do not know when the master of the house will come, in the evening, or at midnight, or at cockcrow, or in the morning –

The writer of Mark has provided the timetable for the arrest, trial, denial, and trial of Jesus, setting up careful three hour intervals that are finished up in the 3-6-9 structure of the Crucifixion. This passage is not in Matthew 24-5, which parallels Mark 13. Instead, there is a whole slew of parables. In other words, in Mark 14-15 we see a carefully wrought structure that extends back through the Gospel to Mark 13; while in Matthew we have his usual dull didacticism. Why does Matthew preserve the reference to the 6th hour? In Mark it relates to a time scheme that does not exist in Matthew. Looking at the time reference, the reader is invited to consider which of these two came first.

2. The second problem is that there are two elements in Matthew that spoil the chiasm "*earth did quake, and the rocks were rent, tombs were opened, and saints walk.*" Matthew-firsters would have us argue that the writer of Mark has extracted that chiasm above from Matthew. Does that make sense? In other words, Matthew-firsters argue that Matt wrote what *would* have been a neat chiasm if Matt hadn't screwed it up by adding elements and deleting two. Then the writer of Mark came along and said to himself: "Hey! This is almost a chiasm! Now if I just add another parable to Mark 13 to signal the time, pop in the *third hour* there, delete the quake, the dawn of the dead, and VOILA! It's poetry!"

The question is clear: did Matt write an almost-chiasm adjusted by the writer of Mark, or did Matt delete and interpolate a beautiful Markan chiasm?[1278]

Dick Harfield has also done work on the structure of Mark.[1279] He argues for a grand parallel structure spanning the whole of the Gospel. The 24 parallels he identifies proceed mostly in sequence, with a few exceptions (e.g. Mark 1:1-8 parallels Mark 16:6-8, which is more typical of a chiastic structure, rather than a parallel one). For example, the baptism of Jesus in Mark 1:9 parallels the transfiguration in Mark 9:2-3. Then, the voice from heaven in Mark 1:11 parallels

---

[1278] http://www.michaelturton.com/Mark/GMark15.html.

[1279] See his paper, 'A Proposed Framework Structure of Mark's Gospel,' https://www.academia.edu/12106716/A__Proposed_Framework_Structure_of_Mark_s_Gospel.

the voice in Mark 9:7. Jesus' forty days in the wilderness (Mark 1:13) parallels Elijah and Moses (Mark 9:4-13); the people's astonishment (Mark 1:23) and amazement (Mark 9:15); Jesus casting out an unclean spirit (Mark 1:23-26) and a dumb spirit (Mark 9:17-27); and so on. The strongest of his examples seem to be the clusters of closely placed parallels. For example, chapter 1 has five that parallel another five in chapter 9; four in chapter 3 parallel four in chapter 10; five in chapter 6 parallel five in chapter 11 and the beginning of chapter 12; and five in chapter 8 parallel five in chapters 14 and 15. That leaves just five parallels that aren't as tightly grouped.

Finally, Tolbert (1989) was perhaps the first to attempt to discern Mark's full rhetorical structure. Her full diagram is reproduced below.[1280]

I. Prologue—Mark 1:1–13
    A. 1:1–3
    B. 1:4–8
    B'. 1:9–10
    A'. 1:11–13

II. DIVISION ONE—Jesus, the Sower of the Word—Mark 1:14—10:52
    A. Introduction—1:14–15
    B. 1:16—3:6
        1. 1:16–20—calls disciples
            a. 1:21–28—healing in synagogue
            b. 1:29–34—healing of Simon's mother-in-law and crowds
                [1:35–39—prayer alone]
            c. 1:40–45—healing of leper
            d. 2:1–12—healing of paralytic/controversy with scribes
        2. 2:13–14—calls disciple
            a. 2:15–17—controversy over eating with sinners
            b. 2:18–22—controversy over fasting
            c. 2:23–28—controversy over picking grain on Sabbath
            d. 3:1–6—controversy/healing on Sabbath
    C. 3:7—6:34
        1. 3:7–35
            a. 3:7–12—by sea, crowds from named towns, boat, heal
            b. 3:13–19a—calls and appoints the Twelve
            c. 3:19b–35
                1. 3:19b–30—controversy with "those near him" and Jerusalem scribes
                2. 3:31–35—rejects old family, establishes rule for new
        2. 4:1—5:43
            a. 4:1–34—parables

[1280]Tolbert (1989), pp. 311–15.

```
          ⎡ 1.  4:1-2—introduction
          │  2.  4:3-32—teaching in parables
          │       a.  vv. 3-9—parable of the Sower
          │       b.  vv. 10-23—first interpretation
          │       c.  vv. 24-32—second interpretation
          ⎣ 3.  4:33-34—close
       b.  4:35—5:43—sea crossings to "other side"
          1.  4:35-41—calming the sea storm
          2.  5:1-20—healing the demoniac
          3.  5:[21-24a] 24b-34—healing of woman with flow of
              blood
          4.  5:21-24a, 35-43—healing of Jairus's daughter
    3.  6:1-34
      ⎧ c'.  6:1-6—rejected by neighbors; family named
      ⎪ b'.  6:7-13, 30—calls and sends out the Twelve
      ⎨        [6:14-29—death of John the Baptist by Herod]
      ⎩ a'.  6:31-34—by boat to lonely place, crowds from all towns,
              teaches
```

D. 6:35—8:21
- 1. 6:35-52
  - a. 6:35-44—feeding of five thousand
  - b. 6:45-52—walking on water; disciples' hearts hardened
- 2. 6:53—7:37
  - a. 6:53-56—general healing; immediately recognized
  - b. 7:1-23—inner heart vs. outer tradition
    1. vv. 1-13—controversy with scribes over heart vs. show
    2. vv. 14-15—teaching to crowd on inner vs. outer uncleanness
    3. vv. 17-23—repetition to disciples of inner vs. outer
  - c. 7:24-30—healing of Syrophoenician woman's daughter
  - d. 7:31-37—healing of deaf mute
- 3. 8:1-21
  - a. 8:1-10—feeding of four thousand
  - b. 8:11-21
    1. vv. 11-13—Pharisees demand a sign
    2. vv. 14-21—boat trip; disciples do not understand

E. 8:22—10:52
- 1. 8:22-26—healing of a blind man
- 2. 8:27—9:29—first Passion prediction unit
  - a. 8:27-30—Peter identifies Jesus as Christ
  - b. 8:31—first Passion prediction
  - c. 8:32-33—Peter rebukes Jesus and Jesus rebukes Peter
  - d. 8:34—9:13—Jesus teaches: save life/lose life
    1. 8:34—9:1—save/lose; shame/glory
    2. 9:2-13—transfiguration
       a. vv. 2-8—on the mount: Elijah and Moses
       b. vv. 9-13—down the mount: Elijah

c. 9:14–29—healing of boy
    1. 9:14–27—healing
    2. 9:28–29—need for prayer
3. 9:30—10:31—second Passion prediction unit
    a. 9:30–31—second Passion prediction
    b. 9:32—disciples do not understand
    c. 9:33—10:31—Jesus teaches: first/last
        1. 9:33—10:16—care for the least
            a. 9:33–50—receive children
                1. vv. 33–37—receive child in Jesus' name
                2. vv. 38–41—nonfollower exorcises in Jesus' name
                3. vv. 42–50—reject causes of falling away
            b. 10:1–12—rejection of divorce
                1. vv. 1–9—response to Pharisees
                2. vv. 10–12—response to disciples
            c. 10:13–16—receive children; kingdom of God
        2. 10:17–31—reject riches/gain eternal life
            a. 10:17–22—rich man
            b. 10:23–30—riches/new family and eternal life
            c. 10:31—first/last
4. 10:32–52—third Passion prediction unit
    a. 10:32–34—third Passion prediction
    b. 10:35–40—James and John request seats of glory
    c. 10:41–45—Jesus teaches: greatest/servant
[5.] d. 10:46–52—calls and heals blind Bartimaeus, who follows him on the way

III. DIVISION TWO—Jesus, the Heir of the Vineyard—Mark 11:1—16:8
    A. Introduction—11:1–11
    B. 11:12—13:37
        1. 11:12–25—unfruitfulness and fig tree
            a. 11:12–14—failure of fig tree
            b. 11:15–19—cleansing of temple
            c. 11:20–25—fig tree and faith
        2. 11:27—12:12—Jesus' and John's authority
            a. 11:27–33—controversy over authority
            b. 12:1–12—parable of the Vineyard and the Tenants
        3. 12:13–44—tests and teachings
            a. 12:13–34—three controversies to test Jesus
                1. 12:13–17—payment of taxes
                2. 12:18–27—resurrection
                3. 12:28–34—Great Commandment
            b. 12:35–44—three teachings by Jesus
                1. 12:35–37—David's Lord
                2. 12:38–40—hypocrisy of scribes
                3. 12:41–44—widow's offering

4. 13:1–37—Apocalyptic Discourse
   a. 13:1–2—introduction—stones of temple
   b. 13:3–37—when will this be and what are signs?
      1. 13:3–4—disciples question
      2. 13:5–23—the tribulations
         a. vv. 5–8—take heed; false Christs
         b. vv. 9–20—take heed to yourselves
         c. vv. 21–23—false Christs; take heed
      3. 13:24–27—coming of the Son of man
      4. 13:28–37—parable of the Fig Tree
         a. vv. 28–32—this generation and my words will not
            pass away
         b. vv. 33–37—take heed and watch

C. 14:1—16:8
  1. 14:1–11—time reference; death plot; unnamed woman anoints Jesus for burial
    a. 14:1–2—plot against Jesus
    b. 14:3–9—unnamed woman anoints Jesus for burial
    c. 14:10–11—Judas joins plot
  2. 14:12–26a—the supper
    a. 14:12–16—prediction and preparation
    b. 14:17–21—dialogue with disciples on betrayal
    c. 14:22–26a—monologue of institution: bread, cup, hymn
  3. 14:26b–52—on the Mount of Olives
    a. 14:26b–31—dialogue with disciples on falling away
    b. 14:32–42—monologue in Gethsemane
    c. 14:43–52—betrayal, arrest, and flight
  4. 14:53–72—Jesus affirms identity; Peter denies
    a. 14:53–54—Peter follows Jesus to courtyard
    b. 14:55–65—Jesus before council: affirms identity
    c. 14:66–72—Peter's three denials in courtyard
  5. 15:1–15—Jesus before Pilate
    a. 15:1–5—Pilate questions Jesus
    b. 15:6–15—Pilate's three attempts to release Jesus fail
  6. 15:16–39—crucifixion
    a. 15:16–20—soldiers mock Jesus as king
    b. 15:21–22—compel passerby to help to Golgotha
    c. 15:23—offer him wine
    d. 15:24a—crucify him
    e. 15:24b—divide his garments
    f. 15:25–27—3d hour—King of Jews
    g. 15:29–32—ironic mocking
    f'. 15:33—6th to 9th hour—darkness
    g'. 15:34—Jesus' cry to God

        b'. 15:35—bystanders think he calls Elijah
        c'. 15:36—offer vinegar
        d'. 15:37—dies with great cry
        e'. 15:38—temple curtain torn
     a'. 15:39—centurion says Jesus is "Son of God"
7. 15:40—16:8—Epilogue
   a. 15:40-41—introduction of women followers
   b. 15:42-47—time reference; burial
      1. vv. 42-43—Joseph asks for corpse
      2. vv. 44-45—Pilate checks on death
      3. v. 46—Joseph buries corpse
      4. v. 47—women witness burial
   c. 16:1-8—time reference; women go to empty tomb to anoint
     Jesus

Bibliography

Angel, Joseph L. *Otherworldly and Eschatological Priesthood in the Dead Sea Scrolls.* Leiden: Brill, 2010.

Altemeyer, Robert. *The Authoritarians.* Cherry Hill Publishing, 2008.

Altemeyer, Bob, and Bruce Hunsberger. *Amazing Conversions: Why Some Turn to Faith & Others Abandon Religion.* Prometheus Books, 1997.

The Apostolic Fathers. 2 volumes. Edited and translated by Bart D. Ehrman. Loeb Classical Library. Cambridge, MA: Harvard University Press, 2003.

Ariel, Donald T. 'Review of David M. Jacobson, Nikos Kokkinos (eds), *Judaea and Rome in Coins, 65 BCE–135 CE.*' *Numismatic Chronicle* 174 (2014), 385-391.

Arnold, William Thomas. *The Roman System of Provincial Administration to the Accession of Constantine the Great.* Forgotten Books, 2013 (1879).

Barker, Margaret. *An Extraordinary Gathering of Angels.* MQ Publications, 2004.

—. *The Lost Prophet: The Book of Enoch and Its Influence on Christianity.* Sheffield Phoenix Press, 1998.

Bauer, Bruno. *Christ and the Caesars: The Origin of Christianity from the Mythology of Rome and Greece.* Trans. Byron Marchant and Helmut Brunar. Xlibris, 2015 (1877).

—. *Christianity Exposed: A Recollection of the Eighteenth Century and a Contribution to the Crisis of the Nineteenth Century.* Ed. Paul Trajo. Trans. Jutta Hamm and Esther Ziegler. Edwin Mellen Press, 2002 (1843).

Bauer, Walter. *Orthodoxy and Heresy in Earliest Christianity.* Sigler Press, 1996 [1971].

Baur, F.C. *Paul the Apostle of Jesus Christ. His Life and Works, His Epistles and Teachings.* 2 vols. Hendrickson, 2003 (1845).

BeDuhn, Jason D. *The First New Testament: Marcion's Scriptural Canon.* Polebridge Press, 2013.

Becker, Eve-Marie. 'Earliest Christian *literary activity*: Investigating Authors, Genres and Audiences.' In Eve-Marie Becker, Troels Engberg-Pedersen, Mogens Müller (Eds.). *Mark and Paul: Comparative Essays Part II.* Berlin/Boston: De Gruyter, 2014.

Becker, Eve-Marie, Troels Engberg-Pedersen, Mogens Müller (Eds.) *Mark and Paul: Comparative Essays Part II.* Berlin/Boston: De Gruyter, 2014.

Becker, Eve-Marie, and Anders Runesson (Eds.). *Mark and Matthew II: Comparative Readings: Reception History, Cultural Hermeneutics, and Theology.* Tübingen: Mohr Siebeck, 2013.

Behe, Michael J. *Darwin Devolves: The New Science About DNA That Challenges Evolution.* HarperOne, 2019.

—. *Darwin's Black Box: The Biochemical Challenge to Evolution.* 2nd ed. Free Press, 2006.

—. *The Edge of Evolution: The Search for the Limits of Darwinism.* Free Press, 2008.

Ben-Yehuda, Nachman. *The Masada Myth: Collective Memory and Mythmaking In Israel.* University of Wisconsin Press, 1995.

—. *Sacrificing Truth: Archaeology and the Myth of Masada.* Prometheus Books, 2002.

Berlinski, David. *The Deniable Darwin.* Discovery Institute, 2010.

Bermejo-Rubio, Fernando. 'Was the Hypothetical Vorlage of the *Testimonium Flavianum* a "Neutral" Text? Challenging the Common Wisdom on *Antiquitates Judaicae* 18.63-64.' *Journal for the Study of Judaism* 45 (2024), 326-365.

Boccaccini, Gabriele. *Beyond the Essene Hypothesis: The Parting of the Ways Between Qumran and Enochic Judaism.* Eerdmans, 1998.

— (ed.). *Enoch and the Messiah Son of Man: Revisiting the Book of Parables.* Eerdmans, 2007.

— (ed.). *Enoch and Qumran Origins: New Light on a Forgotten Connection.* Eerdmans, 2005.

— (ed.). *The Origins of Enochic Judaism.* Zamorani, 2002.

—. *Roots of Rabbinic Judaism: An Intellectual History, from Ezekiel to Daniel.* Eerdmans, 2002.

Bonamente, Giorgio. 'The Disappearance of the Name of Caesar From the Divi's Archives.' University of Macerata. No other identifiable information.

Boyce, Mary. *Zoroastrians: Their Religious Beliefs and Practices.* Routledge, 2001.

—. *A History of Zoroastrianism.* 3 vol. Brill, 1975–1991.

Brandon, S. G. F. *The Fall of Jerusalem and the Christian Church: A Study of the Effects of the Jewish Overthrow of A.D. 70 on Christianity.* Wipf and Stock, 2010 (1951).

—. *Jesus and the Zealots.* Charles Scribner's Sons, 1967.

Brodie, Thomas. *Beyond the Quest for the Historical Jesus: Memoir of a Discovery.* Sheffield Phoenix Press, 2012.

—. *The Birthing of the New Testament: The Intertextual Development of the New Testament Writings.* Sheffield Phoenix Press, 2006.

—. *The Crucial Bridge.* Michael Glazier, 2000.

—. *Genesis As Dialogue: A Literary, Historical, and Theological Commentary.* Oxford University Press, 2001.

Brodie, Thomas, Dennis R. MacDonald and Stanley E. Porter (eds.). *The Intertextuality of the Epistles: Explorations of Theory and Practice.* Sheffield Phoenix Press, 2006.

Burns, Ross. *Damascus: A History.* Routledge, 2005.

Cadwallader, Alan H. 'The Struggle for Paul in the Context of Empire: Mark as a Deutero-Pauline Text.' In *Paul and Mark: Comparative Essays Part I.* Eds: Oda Wischmeyer, David C. Sim, Ian J. Elmer (Eds.). Berlin/Boston: De Gruyter, 2014.

Camery-Hoggatt, Jerry. *Irony in Mark's Gospel: Text and Subtext.* Cambridge University Press, 1992.

Campbell, Douglas A. 'An Anchor for Pauline Chronology: Paul's Flight from 'The Ethnarch of King Aretas' (2 Corinthians 11:32–33).' *Journal for Biblical Literature* 121:2 (2002), 279-302.

—. *The Deliverance of God: An Apocalyptic Rereading of Justification in Paul.* Eerdmans, 2009.

—. *Framing Paul: An Epistolary Biography.* Eerdmans, 2014.

Carcopino, Jérôme. *Cicero: The Secrets of His Correspondence.* Two volumes. English translation by E. O. Lorimer. Yale University Press, 1951.

Carotta, Francesco. *Jesus was Caesar.* Soesterberg, The Nederlands: Uitgeverij Aspekt, 2005.

Carrier, Richard. *On the Historicity of Jesus: Why We Might Have Reason for Doubt.* Sheffield Phoenix Press, 2014.

—. *Proving History: Bayes's Theorem and the Quest for the Historical Jesus.* Prometheus, 2012.

Castaneda, Carlos. *The Active Side of Infinity.* Harper Perennial, 1999.

—. *The Fire from Within.* Washington Square Press, 1991.

Clube, Victor, and Bill Napier. *The Cosmic Serpent.* Universe, 1982

—. *The Cosmic Winter.* Blackwell, 1990.

Cohen, Shaye J. D. *Josephus in Galilee and Rome.* Brill, 2002 (1979).

Cohn, Norman. *Cosmos, Chaos and the World to Come.* New Haven: Yale University Press, 1993.

Cole, Spencer. *Cicero and the Rise of Deification at Rome.* Cambridge University Press, 2013.

Collingwood, R. G. *The Idea of History.* Oxford University Press, 1994 (1946).

Collins, John J. *The Apocalyptic Imagination: An Introduction to Jewish Apocalyptic Literature.* 3rd edition. Eerdmans, 2016 (1998).

—. *Apocalypticism in the Dead Sea Scrolls.* Routledge, 1997.

—. *Beyond the Qumran Community.* Eerdmans, 2009.

Couchoud, P. L. *The Creation of Christ.* Watts & Co., London, 1939.

Courtney, Gary. *Et tu, Judas? Then Fall Jesus!* iUniverse, 2004.

Crossan, John Dominic. *Jesus: A Revolutionary Biography.* HarperOne, 1995.

Dando-Collins, Stephen. *Legions of Rome: The Definitive History of Every Imperial Roman Legion.* London: Quercus, 2010.

Davidsen, Ole. 'Adam-Christ Typology in Paul and Mark: Reflections on a Tertium Comparationis.' In Eve-Marie Becker, Troels Engberg-Pedersen, Mogens Müller (Eds.). *Mark and Paul: Comparative Essays Part II.* Berlin/Boston: De Gruyter, 2014.

Davies, Philip R. *On the Origins of Judaism.* Equinox, 2011.

—. *Scribes and Schools: The Canonization of the Hebrew Scriptures.* SPCK, 1998.

—. *Whose Bible Is It Anyway?* Sheffield Academic Press, 1995.

Dewey, Arthur J., Roy W. Hoover, Lane McGaughy and Daniel D. Schmidt. *The Authentic Letters of Paul.* Polebridge Press, 2010.

Dillon, John M. *The Middle Platonists: 80 B.C. to A.D. 220.* Rev. ed. Cornell University Press, 1996.

Dio Cassius. *Roman History.* 9 volumes. Translated by Earnest Cary, Herbert B. Foster. Loeb Classical Library. Cambridge, MA: Harvard University Press, 1914–1927.

Doherty, Earl. *Jesus: Neither God Nor Man – The Case for a Mythical Jesus.* Age of Reason, 2009.

—. 'The Jesus Puzzle.' *Journal of Higher Criticism* 4:2 (1997).

Dykstra, Tom. *Mark Canonizer of Paul: A New Look at Intertextuality in Mark's Gospel.* OCABS Press, 2012.

Eastman, David L. 'Paul: An Outline of His Life.' In Mark Harding and Alanna Nobbs (Eds.). *All Things to all Cultures: Paul among Jews, Greeks and Romans.* Eerdmans, 2013.

Ehrman, Bart D. *A Brief Introduction to the New Testament.* 2nd ed. Oxford University Press, 2008.

—. *Did Jesus Exist? The Historical Argument for Jesus of Nazareth.* HarperOne, 2012.

Einhorn, Lena. 'Jesus and the "Egyptian Prophet."' Society of Biblical Literature Annual Meeting, Chicago, Nov 17–20, 2012.

Elmer, Ian J. 'Robbing Paul to Pay Peter: The Papias Notice on Mark.' In *Paul and Mark: Comparative Essays Part I.* Eds: Oda Wischmeyer, David C. Sim, Ian J. Elmer (Eds.). Berlin/Boston: De Gruyter, 2014.

Einstein, A., and P. Bergmann. 'On a Generalization of Kaluza's Theory of Electricity.' *Annals of Mathematics* 39:3 (July 1938), 683–701.

Eisenman, Robert. *James the Brother of Jesus: The Key to Unlocking the Secrets of Early Christianity and the Dead Sea Scrolls.* Penguin, 1997.

—. *The New Testament Code: The Cup of the Lord, the Damascus Covenant, and the Blood of Christ.* Penguin, 2006.

Eisler, Robert. *The Messiah Jesus and John the Baptist: According To Flavius Josephus' Recently Rediscovered Capture Of Jerusalem And The Other Jewish And Christian Sources.* Trans. Alexander Haggerty Krappe. Dial Press, 1931.

Ellegård, Alvar. *Jesus – One Hundred Years Before Christ: A Study In Creative Mythology.* Overlook, 1999.

—. 'Theologians as Historians.' *Scandia* 59:2 (2008), 169-204. http://journals.lub.lu.se/scandia/article/download/1078/863.

Engberg-Pedersen, Troels. *Cosmology and Self in the Apostle Paul: The Material Spirit.* Oxford University Press, 2011.

—. *Paul and the Stoics.* Westminster John Knox Press, 2000.

—. 'Paul in Mark 8:34–9:1: Mark on what it is to be a Christian.' In Eve-Marie Becker, Troels Engberg-Pedersen, Mogens Müller (Eds.). *Mark and Paul: Comparative Essays Part II.* Berlin/Boston: De Gruyter, 2014.

Eusebius. *Ecclesiastical History.* 2 volumes. Translated by Kirsopp Lake. Loeb Classical Library. Cambridge, MA: Harvard University Press, 1926–1932.

Fairen, Glen J. *As Below, So Above: Apocalypticism, Gnosticism and the Scribes of Qumran and Nag Hammadi.* Gorgias Press, 2013.

Farmer, William R. *Maccabees, Zealots, and Josephus: An Inquiry into Jewish Nationalism in the Greco-Roman Period.* 2nd ed. Praeger, 1982 (1956).

Feldman, Louis H., and Gohei Hata (eds.). *Josephus, the Bible, and History.* Wayne State University Press, 1989.

Ferguson, Everett. *Church History, Volume One: From Christ to Pre-Reformation: The Rise and Growth of the Church in Its Cultural, Intellectual, and Political Context.* Zondervan, 2005.

Firestone, Richard, Allen West, and Simon Warwick-Smith, *The Cycle of Cosmic Catastrophes.* Bear & Co., 2006.

Fraade, Steven D. 'History (?) In The Damascus Document.' *Dead Sea Discoveries* 25 (2018), 412-428.

Froude, James Anthony. *Julius Caesar.* D. Appleton and Co., 1899.

Fitzgerald, John T. *Cracks in an Earthen Vessel: An Examination of the Catalogues of Hardships in the Corinthian Correspondence.* Scholars Press, 1988.

Gaiseanu, Florin. 'Informational Model of Consciousness: From Philosophic Concepts to an Information Science of Consciousness.' *Philosophy Study* 9:4 (April 2019), 181–196, https://www.researchgate.net/publication/334207912_Informational_Model_of_Consciousness_From_Philosophic_Concepts_to_an_Information_Science_of_Consciousness.

Gamble, H. *Books and Readers in the Early Church: A History of Early Christian Texts.* New Haven/London: Yale University Press, 1995.

Garrow, Alan. *The Gospel of Matthew's Dependence on the* Didache. Bloomsbury Academic, 2013.

Gertoux, Gerard. 'Dating the two Censuses of P. Sulpicius Quirinius.' https://www.academia.edu/3184175/Dating_the_two_Censuses_of_Quirinius

Gmirkin, Russell. 'The Arrest-Crucifixion Week of 36 CE.' *Revue Biblique* (forthcoming).

—. *Berossus and Genesis, Manetho and Exodus.* Bloomsbury, 2006.

—. *Plato and the Creation of the Hebrew Bible.* Routledge, 2016.

Goldberg, Gary J. 'The coincidences of the Emmaus Narrative of Luke and the Testimonium of Josephus.' *The Journal of the Study of the Pseudipigrapha* 13 (1995), 59-77.

Goodacre, Mark. *Thomas and the Gospels: The Case for Thomas's Familiarity with the Synoptics.* Eerdmans, 2012.

Goulder, Michael D. *Five Stones and a Sling: Memoirs of a Biblical Scholar.* Sheffield Phoenix Press, 2009.

—. *Luke: A New Paradigm.* Sheffield Academic Press, 1989.

—. *Paul and the Competing Mission in Corinth.* Hendrickson, 1998.

—. *St. Paul versus St. Peter: A Tale of Two Missions.* Westminster John Knox Press, 1995.

—. *Type and History in Acts.* SPCK, 1964.

Grabbe, Lester. 'Jesus Who is Called the Christ: References to Jesus Outside Christian Sources.' In Thomas S. Verenna, Thomas L. Thompson, *'Is This Not The Carpenter?': The Question of The Historicity of the Figure of Jesus.* Routledge, 2013.

Griffin, David Ray. *God Exists But Gawd Does Not: From Evil to New Atheism to Fine-Tuning.* Process Century Press, 2016.

Gruen, Erich S. *The Hellenistic World and the Coming of Rome.* University of California Press, 1986.

Harfield, Dick. 'A Proposed Framework Structure of Mark's Gospel.' https://www.academia.edu/12106716/A_Proposed_Framework_Structure_of_Mark_s_Gospel.

Harnack, Adolf. *Marcion: The Gospel of the Alien God.* Trans. John E. Steely, Lyle D. Bierma. Wipf and Stock, 2007 (1921).

Hatina, Thomas R. 'The Focus of Mark 13:24-27: The Parousia, or the Destruction of the Temple?' *Bulletin for Biblical Research* 6 (1996), 43–66.

Hays, Richard B. *Echoes of Scripture in the Gospels.* Baylor University Press, 2017.

—. *Echoes of Scripture in the Letters of Paul.* Yale University Press, 1993 (1989).

Hilsenrath, Elaine. *Jesus, The Nazorean: An Investigation and Analysis of the Origins, Ideology, and Activities of the Community of Jews Who Followed Jesus.* BookSurge Publishing, 2009

Hoffmann, R. Joseph. *Marcion: On the Restitution of Christianity: An Essay on the Development of Radical Paulinist Theology in the Second Century.* Wipf and Stock, 2016 (1984).

Hunt, A. S., and G. C. Edgar (Eds.). *Select Papyri* II. Loeb Classical Library, 1934.

Irenaeus. *Against Heresies.* https://ccel.org/ccel/schaff/anf01/anf01.

Jackson, David R. *Enochic Judaism: Three Defining Paradigm Exemplars.* Continuum, 2004.

Jones, C. P. *The Roman World of Dio Chrysostom.* Cambridge and London: Harvard University Press, 1978.

Jones, H. Stuart. 'Claudius and the Jewish Question at Alexandria.' *Society for the Promotion of Roman Studies* 16:1 (1926).

Josephus. *The Works of Josephus: Complete and Unabridged.* New Updated Edition. Translated by William Whiston. Hendrickson, 1980.

Kastrup, Bernardo. *The Idea of the World: A Multi-Disciplinary Argument for the Mental Nature of Reality.* Iff Books, 2019.

Koester, Helmut. *Ancient Christian Gospels: Their History and Development.* London: SCM, 1990.

Knohl, Israel. *Messiahs and Resurrection in 'The Gabriel Revelation.'* Continuum, 2009.

Knox, John. *Chapters in a Life of Paul.* Ed. Douglas R. A. Hare. Mercer University Press, 1987 (1950).

—. *Marcion and the New Testament: An Essay in the Early History of the Canon.* Chicago University Press, 1942.

Kokkinos, Nikos. 'Crucifixion in A.D. 36: The Keystone for Dating the Birth of Jesus.' In Jerry Vardaman, Edwin M. Yamauchi (Eds.). *Chronos, Kairos, Christos: Nativity and Chronological Studies Presented to Jack Finegan.* Eisenbrauns, 1989.

Koortbojian, Michael. *The Divinization of Caesar and Augustus: Precedents, Consequences, Implications.* Cambridge University Press, 2013.

Ladouceur, David J. 'Josephus and Masada.' In *Josephus, Judaism, and Christianity.* Louis H. Feldman and Gohei Hata (Eds.). Tokyo: Yamamoto Shoten Publishing House, 1987.

Lampe, Peter. *From Paul to Valentinus: Christians at Rome in the First Two Centuries.* Fortress Press, 2003.

Leisola, Matti and Jonathan Witt. *Heretic: One Scientist's Journey from Darwin to Design.* Discovery Institute, 2018.

Lescaudron, Pierre. *Earth Changes and the Human Cosmic Connection.* Red Pill Press, 2014.

Lieu, Judith M. *Marcion and the Making of a Heretic: God and Scripture in the Second Century.* Cambridge University Press, 2015.

Livy. *From the Founding of the City.* Translated by Rev. Canon Roberts (1905). https://en.wikisource.org/wiki/From_the_Founding_of_the_City.

Louden, Bruce. *Homer's* Odyssey *and the Near East.* New York: Cambridge University Press, 2011.

Lüdemann, Gerd. *The Acts of the Apostles: What Really Happened in the Earliest Days of the Church.* Prometheus Books, 2005.

—. *The Earliest Christian Text: 1 Thessalonians.* Polebridge Press, 2013.

—. *The Great Deception: And What Jesus Really Said and Did.* 2nd ed. Prometheus Books, 1999.

—. *Paul, Apostle to the Gentiles: Studies in Chronology.* Fortress Press, 1984.

—. *Paul: The Founder of Christianity.* Prometheus Books, 2002.

—. *What Really Happened to Jesus: A Historical Approach to the Resurrection.* Trans. John Bowden. Westminster John Knox Press, 1996.

Lüdemann, Gerd, Frank Schleritt and Martina Janssen. *Jesus After 2000 Years: What He Really Said and Did.* Prometheus Books, 2001

Maccoby, Hyam. *Jesus the Pharisee.* SCM Press, 2003.

—. *Judas Iscariot and the Myth of Jewish Evil.* Free Press, 1992.

—. *The Mythmaker: Paul and the Invention of Christianity.* HarperCollins, 1987.

MacDonald, Dennis R. *Christianizing Homer: The Odyssey, Plato, and The Acts of Andrew.* Oxford University Press, 1994.

—. *Does the New Testament Imitate Homer? Four Cases from the Acts of the Apostles.* Yale University Press, 2003.

—. *The Gospels and Homer: Imitations of Greek Epic in Mark and Luke-Acts.* Rowman & Littlefield, 2014.

—. *The Homeric Epics and the Gospel of Mark.* Yale University Press, 2010.

—. *The Legend and the Apostle: The Battle for Paul in Story and Canon.* Westminster John Knox Press, 1983.

—. *Luke and Vergil: Imitations of Classical Greek Literature.* Rowman & Littlefield, 2014

— (Ed.). *Mimesis and Intertextuality in Antiquity and Christianity.* Bloomsbury T&T Clark, 2001.

—. *Mythologizing Jesus: From Jewish Teacher to Epic Hero.* Rowman & Littlefield, 2015.

Mack, Burton L. *The Christian Myth: Origins, Logic, and Legacy.* Continuum, 2001.

—. *A Myth of Innocence: Mark and Christian Origins.* Fortress Press, 1988.

—. *Patterns of Persuasion in the Gospels. Foundations & facets – Literary facets.* Polebridge Press, 1989.

MacMullen, Ramsay. *Enemies of the Roman Order: Treason, Unrest, and Alienation in the Empire.* Harvard University Press, 1966.

Malbon, Elizabeth Struthers. *Mark's Jesus: Characterization as Narrative Christology.* Waco, TX: Baylor University Press, 2009.

Maranon, Gregorio. *Tiberius: The Resentful Caesar.* Duell, Sloan and Pearce, 1956.

Marcus, Joel. 'Mark – Interpreter of Paul.' In Eve-Marie Becker, Troels Engberg-Pedersen, Mogens Müller (Eds.). *Mark and Paul: Comparative Essays Part II.* Berlin/Boston: De Gruyter, 2014.

—. *The Way of the Lord: Christological Exegesis of the Old Testament in the Gospel of Mark.* Westminster John Knox Press, 1992.

Martin, Ernest L. *The Star of Bethlehem: The Star That Astonished the World.* 2nd ed. Associates for Scriptural Knowledge, 1996. https://www.askelm.com/star/index.asp.

Martinez, Florentino Garcia and Eibert J.C. Tigchelaar (Eds.). *The Dead Sea Scrolls: Study Edition.* Brill/Eerdmans, 1997.

Martyn, J. Louis. *Galatians: A New Translation with Introduction and Commentary.* New York: Doubleday, 1997.

—. *Theological Issues in the Letters of Paul.* Edinburgh: T&T Clark, 1997.

Mason, Steve. *A History of the Jewish War, A.D. 66–74.* Cambridge University Press, 2016.

—. *Flavius Josephus: Translation and Commentary, Volume 1B: Judean War 2.* Brill, 2008.

—. *Flavius Josephus: Translation and Commentary, Volume 9: Life of Josephus.* Brill, 2001.

—. *Flavius Josephus on the Pharisees: A Composition-Critical Study.* Brill, 1991.

—. *Josephus and the New Testament.* 2nd ed. Baker Academic, 2002.

—. *Josephus, Judea and Christian Origins: Methods and Categories.* Baker Academic, 2009.

—. 'Will the Real Josephus Please Stand Up?' *Biblical Archaeology Review* 23:5 (1997).

Meyer, Stephen C. *Darwin's Doubt: The Explosive Origin of Animal Life and the Case for Intelligent Design.* HarperOne, 2013.

—. *Signature in the Cell: DNA and the Evidence for Intelligent Design.* HarperOne, 2009.

Mithen, Steven. *The Prehistory of the Mind.* Thames & Hudson, 1999.

Mommsen, Theodor. 'The Character of Cæsar.' From *History of Rome* (1854–1856). Translated by William Purdie Dickson. https://www.bartleby.com/library/prose/3629.html.

Müller, Mogens. 'In the Beginning was the Congregation: In Search of a *Tertium Comparationis* between Paul and Mark.' In Eve-Marie Becker, Troels Engberg-Pedersen, Mogens Müller (Eds.). *Mark and Paul: Comparative Essays Part II.* Berlin/Boston: De Gruyter, 2014.

Nagel, Thomas. *Mind & Cosmos: Why the Materialist Neo-Darwinian Conception of Nature Is Almost Certainly False.* Oxford University Press, 2012.

Nickelsburg, George W. E. *1 Enoch 1: A Commentary on the Book of 1 Enoch.* Fortress: 2001.

—. *Jewish Literature Between the Bible and the Mishnah.* 2nd ed. Minneapolis: Fortress Press, 2005.

Nickelsburg, George W. E., James C. VanderKam. *1 Enoch 2: A Commentary on the Book of 1 Enoch, Chapters 37-82*. Fortress: 2011.

Nicolaus of Damascus. *Life of Augustus*. Translated by C. M. Hall (1923). https://www.attalus.org/translate/nicolaus1.html.

Nielsen, Jesper Tang. 'The Cross on the Way to Mark.' In Eve-Marie Becker, Troels Engberg-Pedersen, Mogens Müller (Eds.). *Mark and Paul: Comparative Essays Part II*. Berlin/Boston: De Gruyter, 2014.

Nodet, Étienne, and Justin Taylor. *The Historical Jesus? Necessity and Limits of an Inquiry*. T&T Clark, 2008.

—. *The Origins of Christianity: An Exploration*. Liturgical Press, 1998.

The Old Testament Pseudepigrapha. 2 volumes. Edited by James H. Charlesworth. Hendrickson, 2010.

Olson, Ken. 'A Eusebian Reading of the Testimonium Flavianum.' In Aaron Johnson and Jeremy Schott (Eds.), *Eusebius of Caesarea: Traditions and Innovations*, Center for Hellenic Studies, Harvard University Press, 2013.

Ouspensky, P. D. *In Search of the Miraculous*. Mariner Books, 2001.

Ovid. *Metamorphoses*. Translated by A.S. Kline. https://ovid.lib.virginia.edu/trans/Metamorph15.htm.

Pagels, Elaine. *The Gnostic Paul: Gnostic Exegesis of the Pauline Letters*. Trinity Press, 1992 (1975).

Painter, John. 'Mark and the Pauline Mission.' In Oda Wischmeyer, David C. Sim, Ian J. Elmer (Eds.). *Paul and Mark: Comparative Essays Part I*. Berlin/Boston: De Gruyter, 2014.

Pearson, Birger A. *Gnosticism, Judaism, and Egyptian Christianity*. Fortress Press, 2006.

Pervo, Richard I. *Acts: A Commentary*. Ed. Harold W. Attridge. Fortress Press, 2008.

—. 'Acts in Ephesus (and Environs) c. 115.' *Forum* Third Series 4:2 (2015), 125–51.

—. *The Acts of Paul: A New Translation with Introduction and Commentary*. Cascade Books, 2014.

—. *Dating Acts: Between the Evangelists and the Apologists*. Polebridge Press, 2006).

—. *The Gospel of Luke*. Polebridge Press, 2014.

—. *The Making of Paul: Constructions of the Apostle in Early Christianity*. Fortress Press, 2010.

—. *The Mystery of Acts: Unraveling Its Story*. Polebridge Press, 2008.

—. *Profit With Delight: The Literary Genre of the Acts of the Apostles*. Fortress Press, 1987.

Philo. *The Works of Philo: Complete and Unabridged*. New Updated Edition. Translated by C. D. Yonge. Hendrickson, 1993.

Philostratus. *Apollonius of Tyana, Life of Apollonius of Tyana*. 2 volumes. Edited and translated by Christopher P. Jones. Loeb Classical Library. Cambridge, MA: Harvard University Press, 2005.

Plutarch. *Lives*. 11 volumes. Translated by Bernadotte Perrin. Loeb Classical Library. Cambridge, MA: Harvard University Press, 1914–1926.

Popper, Karl, and John C. Eccles. *The Self and Its Brain: An Argument for Interactionism*. Routledge, 1984.

Powell, James Lawrence. *Deadly Voyager: The Ancient Comet Strike that Changed Earth and Human History*. Bowker, 2020.

Price, R. G. *Deciphering the Gospels: Proves Jesus Never Existed*. Lulu, 2018.

Price, Robert M. *The Amazing Colossal Apostle*. Signature Books, 2012.

—. *The Case Against The Case For Christ: A New Testament Scholar Refutes the Reverend Lee Strobel*. American Atheist Press, 2011.

—. *The Christ-Myth Theory and Its Problems*. American Atheist Press, 2011.

—. *Deconstructing Jesus*. Prometheus Books, 2000.

—. *The Incredible Shrinking Son of Man: How Reliable is the Gospel Tradition?* Prometheus Books, 2003.

—. *Jesus is Dead*. American Atheist Press, 2007.

—. *Killing History: Jesus in the No-Spin Zone*. Prometheus Books, 2014.

—. *The Pre-Nicene New Testament: Fifty-four Formative Texts*. Signature Books, 2006.

Puig i Tàrrech, Armand, John M.G. Barclay, and Jorg Frey. *The Last Years of Paul.* Mohr Siebeck, 2015.

Raskin, Jay. 'A Discovery, the Crucified, Simon, Zealots, and Essenes.' *Journal of Higher Criticism* 9:1 (2002), 92–124.

Riesner, Rainer. *Paul's Early Period: Chronology, Mission Strategy, Theology.* Trans. Douglas W. Stott. Eerdmans, 1998.

Robinson, James M., and Helmut Koester. *Trajectories through Early Christianity.* Wipf and Stock, 2006.

Robbins, Vernon K. 'The Reversed Contextualization of Psalm 22 in the Markan Crucifixion.' In *The Four Gospels: Festschrift Frans Neirynck.* F. Van Segbroeck (Ed.). Leuven: Leuven University Press, 1992.

Salm, René. *The Myth of Nazareth: The Invented Town of Jesus.* American Atheist Press, 2008.

—. *NazarethGate: Quack Archeology, Holy Hoaxes, and the Invented Town of Jesus.* American Atheist Press, 2015.

Schmidt, T. E. 'Mark 15:16-32: The Crucifixion Narrative and the Roman Triumphal Procession'. *NTS* 41 (1995): 1–18.

Schoeps, Hans-Joachim. *Jewish Christianity: Factional Disputes in the Early Church.* Fortress Press, 1969.

Schürer, Emil. A History of the Jewish People in the Time of Jesus Christ. 5 vols. Eds. Geza Vermes and Fergus Millar and Matthew Black. T&T Clark, 1973-87.

Schwartz, Daniel R. *Agrippa I: The Last King of Judaea.* Mohr Siebeck, 1990.

Seager, Robin. *Tiberius.* Second edition. Wiley-Blackwell, 2005.

Settegast, Mary. *Plato, Prehistorian.* Lindisfarne Press, 2000.

—. *When Zarathustra Spoke: The Reformation of Neolithic Culture and Religion.* Mazda Pub, 2005.

Shantz, Colleen. *Paul in Ecstasy.* New York: Cambridge University Press, 2009.

Sheldrake, Rupert. *Morphic Resonance: The Nature of Formative Causation.* Park Street Press, 2009.

—. *Science Set Free: 10 Paths to New Discovery.* Deepak Chopra, 2013.

Sim, David C. 'The Family of Jesus and the Disciples of Jesus in Paul and Mark: Taking Sides in the Early Church's Factional Dispute.' In *Paul and Mark: Comparative Essays Part I.* Eds: Oda Wischmeyer, David C. Sim, Ian J. Elmer (Eds.). Berlin/Boston: De Gruyter, 2014a.

—. 'The Reception of Paul and Mark in the Gospel of Matthew.' In *Paul and Mark: Comparative Essays Part I.* Eds: Oda Wischmeyer, David C. Sim, Ian J. Elmer (Eds.). Berlin/Boston: De Gruyter, 2014b.

Smallwood, E. Mary. 'Philo and Josephus as Historians of the Same Events.' In Louis H. Feldman and Gohei Hata (Eds). *Josephus, Judaism and Christianity.* Detroit: Wayne State University Press, 1987.

Smith, David Oliver. *Matthew, Mark, Luke, and Paul: The Influence of the Epistles on the Synoptic Gospels.* Resource Publications, 2011.

—. *Unlocking the Puzzle: The Keys to the Christology and Structure of the Original Gospel of Mark.* Wipf and Stock, 2016.

Smith, Jonathan Z. *Drudgery Divine: On the Comparison of Early Christianities and the Religions of Late Antiquity.* University of Chicago Press, 1994.

Snyder, G. F. *Ante Pacem: Archaeological Evidence of Church Life Before Constantine.* Mercer, 1985.

Stauffer, Ethelbert. *Christ and the Caesars: Historical Sketches.* Translated by Kaethe Gregor Smith and Ronald Gregor Smith. London: SCM-Press, 1955.

Stausberg, Michael, Yuhan Sohrab-Dinshaw Vevaina, with Anna Tessman (Eds.). *The Wiley Blackwell Companion to Zoroastrianism.* Wiley-Blackwell, 2015.

Strabo. *Geography.* 8 volumes. Translated by Horace Leonard Jones. Loeb Classical Library. Cambridge, MA: Harvard University Press, 1917–1932.

Suetonius. *Lives of the Caesars.* Trans. Catharine Edwards. Oxford University Press, 2001.

Sweatman, Martin. *Prehistory Decoded*. Troubador, 2018.

Syme, Ronald. *The Roman Revolution*. Rev. ed. Oxford Paperbacks, 2002.

Tacitus. *The Annals*. Trans. A. J. Woodman. Hackett, 2004.

—. *The History*. Trans. A. J. Church and W. J. Brodribb. Ed. Moses Hadas. Modern Library, 1942.

Tatum, Jeffrey. *The Patrician Tribune: Publius Clodius Pulcher*. University of North Carolina Press, 2010.

Taylor, Joan E. 'Philo of Alexandria on the Essenes: A Case Study on the Use of Classical Sources in Discussions of the Qumran-Essene Hypothesis.' *The Studia Philonica Annual* 19 (2007), 1-28.

Tcherikover, Victor. *Hellenistic Civilization and the Jews*. Hendrickson, 1999 (1959).

Theissen, Gerd. *A Theory of Primitive Christian Religion*. London: SCM Press, 1999.

Theophilos, Michael P. 'The Roman Connection: Paul and Mark.' In *Paul and Mark: Comparative Essays Part I*. Eds: Oda Wischmeyer, David C. Sim, Ian J. Elmer (Eds.). Berlin/Boston: De Gruyter, 2014.

Thompson, Thomas L. *The Messiah Myth: The Near Eastern Roots of Jesus and David*. Basic, 2005.

Tolbert, Mary Ann. *Sowing the Gospel: Mark's World in Literary-Historical Perspective*. Fortress Press, 1989.

Trobisch, David. *The First New Testament*. Oxford University Press 2011 (2000).

—. *Paul's Letter Collection: Tracing the Origins*. Quiet Waters Publications, 2001.

—. 'Who Published the Christian Bible?' delivered at the January 2007 'Scripture and Skepticism' conference (Committee for the Scientific Examination of Religion).

—. 'Who Published the New Testament?' *Free Inquiry* 28:1 (2007/8), 30-33. https://www.trobisch.com/david/wb/media/articles/20071226%20FreeInquiry%20Who%20Publish ed%20Christian%20Bible%20BW.pdf

Jim B. Tucker, *Life Before Life: Children's Memories of Previous Lives*. St. Martin's Griffin, 2008.

—. *Return to Life: Extraordinary Cases of Children Who Remember Past Lives*. St. Martin's Griffin, 2015.

Tyson, Joseph B. *Marcion and Luke-Acts: A Defining Struggle*. University of South Carolina Press, 2006.

Unterbrink, Daniel T. *Judas of Nazareth: How the Greatest Teacher of First Century Israel Was Replaced by a Literary Creation*. Bear & Co., 2014.

Valliant, James S., and Warren Fahy. *Creating Christ: How Roman Emperors Invented Christianity*. Crossroad Press, 2018.

Van Voorst, Robert E. *Jesus Outside the New Testament: An Introduction to the Ancient Evidence*. Eerdmans, 2000.

VanderKam, James C. *Enoch: A Man for All Generations*. University of South Carolina Press, 2008.

—. *Enoch and the Growth of an Apocalyptic Tradition*. Catholic Biblical Association of America, 1984.

—. *Jubilees: The Hermeneia Translation*. Fortress Press, 2020.

VanderKam, James C., and William Adler (Eds.). *The Jewish Apocalyptic Heritage in Early Christianity*. Fortress Press, 1996.

VanderKam, James C., and Peter Flint. *Meaning of the Dead Sea Scrolls*. T&T Clark, 2005.

VanderKam, James C., and George Nickelsburg. *1 Enoch: The Hermeneia Translation*. Fortress Press, 2012.

Vermès, Géza, Martin Goodman (Eds.). *The Essenes: According to the Classical Sources*. JSOT Press, 1989.

Vig Skoven, Anne. 'Mark as Allegorical Rewriting of Paul: Gustav Volkmar's Understanding of the Gospel of Mark.' In Eve-Marie Becker, Troels Engberg-Pedersen, Mogens Müller (Eds.). *Mark and Paul: Comparative Essays Part II*. Berlin/Boston: De Gruyter, 2014.

Virgil. *Georgics*. Translated by H. Rushton Fairclough. Revised by G. P. Goold. Loeb Classical Library. Cambridge, MA: Harvard University Press, 1916.

Wajdenbaum, Philippe. *Argonauts of the Desert: Structural Analysis of the Hebrew Bible*. Routledge, 2014.

Walker, William O., Jr. *Interpolations in the Pauline Letters.* Sheffield Academic Press, 2002.

Watson, Francis. *Paul, Judaism and the Gentiles: A Sociological Approach.* Eerdmans, 2007.

Ward-Perkins, Bryan. *The Fall of Rome and the End of Civilization.* Oxford University Press, 2005.

Watson, Francis. *Paul, Judaism, and the Gentiles: Beyond the New Perspective.* Rev. exp. ed. Eerdmans, 2007.

Weeden, Theodore J. *Mark: Traditions in Conflict.* Philadelphia: Fortress Press, 1971.

Weinstock, Stefan. *Divus Julius.* Oxford University Press, 1972.

Weir, Allison J. 'A Study of Fulvia.' Masters Thesis. Queen's University, Kingston, ON, 2007.

Wells, G.A. *Can We Trust the New Testament?* Open Court, 2003.

—. *Cutting Jesus Down to Size: What Higher Criticism Has Achieved and Where It Leaves Christianity.* Open Court, 2009.

—. *Did Jesus Exist?* Prometheus Books, 1987.

—. *The Historical Evidence for Jesus.* Prometheus, 1988.

—. *The Jesus of the Early Christians.* Pemberton, 1971.

—. *The Jesus Myth.* Open Court Publishing, 1998.

—. *Can We Trust the New Testament? Thoughts on the Reliability of Early Christian Testimony.* Open Court, 2003.

Wheeler, John Archibald. *A Journey Into Gravity and Spacetime.* New York: W.H. Freeman, 1990.

Williamson, George. 'Mucianus and a Touch of the Miraculous: Pilgrimage and Tourism in Roman Asia Minor.' In Jaś Elsner and Ian Rutherford (Eds.). *Pilgrimage in Graeco-Roman and Early Christian Antiquity: Seeing the Gods.* Oxford University Press, 2006.

Winn, Adam. *Mark and the Elijah-Elisha Narrative: Considering the Practice of Greco-Roman Imitation in the Search for Markan Source Material.* Pickwick Publications, 2010.

—. *Reading Mark's Christology Under Caesar: Jesus the Messiah and Roman Imperial Ideology.* Downers Grove, Illinois: IVPAcademic, 2018.

Wischmeyer, Oda, David C. Sim, Ian J. Elmer (Eds.). *Paul and Mark: Comparative Essays Part I.* Berlin/Boston: De Gruyter, 2014.

Witzel, Michael. *The Origins of the World's Mythologies.* Oxford University Press, 2013.

Zaehner, R. C. *The Dawn and Twilight of Zoroastrianism.* Phoenix, 2003.

Scripture Citation Index

Old Testament

New Testament

Index

Etna, 503
Etruria, 181
Eucharist, 24, 294, 413, 447
Euodia, 85
Euphrates, 155–161, 171, 482–484
Euripides, 28, 344, 494
Eurylochus of Same, 553
Eusebius of Caesarea, 28, 41, 47, 82, 84, 85, 88, 89,
    99, 141, 204, 209, 212, 213, 304, 323, 335,
    340, 343, 406–410, 445, 474
Eutychus, 28
Evanson, Edward, 243
Eve, 249–252, 376, 440, 538, 540
evolution, xvi, xvii
Ewald, Heinrich, 151
Eznik of Kolb, 508, 510
Ezra, 29, 95

Fabius Persicus, 152, 384
Fadus, 169, 474
Fahy, Warren, 89, 90, 278, 490, 495
Fairen, Glen J., 47, 49
faith of Jesus, 254, 258, 260, 416, 466
fall, the, 242, 247–249, 251, 253, 255, 260, 332, 440
Farmer, William R., 228
Farrer, Austin, 318, 340, 402
Farrer–Goulder hypothesis, 318, 402
Feldman, Louis H., 183, 312, 482
Ferguson, Everett, 28
Finegan, Jack, 144
Firestone, Richard, 59
First Letter of Clement, 36, 84
Fiscus Judaicus, 432
Fisher, Christopher, 317
Fitzgerald, John T., 11
Flavia Domitilla, 88–90
Flavia Neapolis, 6
Flavian dynasty, 89, 103, 104, 164, 227, 325, 431,
    432, 437, 438, 445, 458, 465, 466, 483, 484,
    490
Flavius Clemens, 88–90
Flavius Josephus, 3, 15, 18, 27, 32, 41, 43, 45–48, 50,
    75, 81, 86, 92, 99, 103–116, 118–128,
    130–133, 135–157, 160–187, 189, 191–196,
    198–216, 218–221, 223–231, 236, 237, 239,
    241, 244, 267, 268, 270–273, 278, 281–285,
    291, 292, 296, 301–313, 317, 320, 323–326,
    329, 346, 349, 358, 361, 380, 384, 385, 387,
    399, 400, 404, 421, 423, 433–435, 437, 438,
    441, 445, 463, 466, 474–476, 482, 487, 490,
    491, 495, 497, 524
Flavius Silva, 170, 308, 310
flesh, the, xv, 43, 80, 97, 98, 249–251, 253, 254,
    257–260, 266, 289, 294, 355, 356, 358, 359,

378, 379, 381, 413, 415, 419–421, 441, 505,
    525, 530, 536, 539, 541–543, 545, 546
Florence, 92
Fourth Philosophy, 109, 136–138, 168, 171, 213, 215,
    216, 222, 227, 228, 235, 268, 309, 346
Frazer, James George, 52
Fredriksen, Paula, 480
Friedlander, Moritz, 49
Fulcinius Trio, 197
Fulvia, 191–193, 220–222, 224–226, 487–492, 495

Gabriel's Revelation, 133, 137, 168, 178
Gad [prophet], 237
Gadara, 106, 127, 141
Gaddi, John, 137
Gaius Maecenas, 181, 453
Galatia, 7, 14, 19, 166, 279, 286, 290, 292, 296, 357,
    359, 398, 509, 526, 531, 539
Galba, 181, 432, 433, 483, 493
Galilee, 9, 34, 35, 56, 84, 99, 105, 113, 124, 135–138,
    151, 165, 167–169, 173, 174, 176, 177,
    203–207, 209–211, 213–217, 222, 223,
    225–227, 229–231, 234, 235, 239, 241, 261,
    262, 264, 266–268, 272, 274, 277–279, 284,
    285, 291–293, 295, 296, 301, 302, 306,
    308–310, 319–321, 323, 324, 327, 328, 343,
    346, 349, 351, 352, 354, 357, 359–361, 375,
    381, 383, 387, 396, 398, 399, 404, 411, 418,
    420, 421, 423, 443, 444, 449, 456, 460, 463,
    466, 474, 490–492, 515, 535, 537
Gallio, 282, 490
Gamala, 140, 168, 171
Gamaliel II, 54
Gamaliel the Elder, 114, 174
Gamalitis, 149
Garden of Eden, 248, 542
Garden of Gethsemane, 338, 350, 351, 364, 372, 373,
    412, 419, 451, 472
Garraghan, Gilbert J., 26
Garrow, Alan, 90, 91
Gathas, 65
Gaul, 4, 128, 131, 181, 195, 196, 204, 453, 489, 510
Gaulanitis [Golan], 120, 168, 171
Gaza, 127, 142, 270
Gehenna, 400
Gemara, 48
Gentiles, 4, 6, 15, 19, 20, 23, 31, 36, 37, 44, 48, 50,
    51, 54, 81, 83, 86, 87, 90, 91, 94, 137, 187,
    208, 211, 214, 220, 221, 229, 230, 233,
    235–239, 241, 242, 245, 246, 254, 263,
    265–267, 276, 277, 279–281, 285, 286, 290,
    291, 293, 295–297, 304, 312, 330–332, 343,
    344, 352, 353, 355–357, 359, 361, 364, 365,
    367, 381, 382, 386, 388, 396, 398–400, 402,